ENCYCLOPEDIA OF
SPECIAL EDUCATION

ENCYCLOPEDIA OF SPECIAL EDUCATION

A REFERENCE FOR THE EDUCATION
OF THE HANDICAPPED AND OTHER
EXCEPTIONAL CHILDREN AND ADULTS

VOLUME 3

EDITORS

CECIL R. REYNOLDS, Ph.D.
Texas A&M University

LESTER MANN, Ph.D.
Hunter College,
City University of New York

A WILEY-INTERSCIENCE PUBLICATION

JOHN WILEY & SONS

NEW YORK   •   CHICHESTER   •   BRISBANE   •   TORONTO   •   SINGAPORE

Library of Congress Cataloging-in-Publication Data

Encyclopedia of special education.

    "A Wiley–Interscience publication."
    1. Handicapped children—Education—United States—
Dictionaries. 2. Exceptional children—Education—
United States—Dictionaries. 3. Handicapped—Education—
United States—Dictionaries. I. Reynolds, Cecil R.,
1952– . II. Mann, Lester.
LC4007.E53 1987   371.9′03′21   86-33975
ISBN 0471-63006-3 (Vol. 3)
ISBN 0471-82858-0 (Set)

Printed in the United States of America

10 9 8 7 6 5 4 3 2 1

PORTAGE PROJECT

The Portage project was first funded in 1969 as a model home-based program by the Bureau of Education for the Handicapped under the Handicapped Children's Early Education Program (HCEEP). In rural Portage, Wisconsin, the project's staff traveled to the homes of children to help parents learn how to work with children in a home setting (Lerner, 1985). The experimental edition of the Portage project was developed during the first 3 years of the project and was published by McGraw-Hill in 1972. The revised edition (1976) was developed by Susan Bluma, Marsha Shearer, Alma Froham, and Jean Hillard (Bailey & Worley, 1984; Bluma, et al., 1976; Thurman & Widerstrom, 1985). The project is a developmental, criterion-referenced, behavioral model that employs precision teaching to evaluate a child's developmental level and to plan an educational program for children from birth to 6 years of age. The complete guide comes in three parts: a checklist of behaviors on which to record an individual child's developmental progress; a file card listing possible methods of teaching these behaviors; and a manual of directions for use of the checklists, card files, and various methods of remediation. The assessment procedure can be administered in 20 to 40 minutes. The behavioral checklist consists of a 25-page color coded booklet that contains 580 developmentally sequenced behaviors.

Ages are listed at one-year intervals. The first 45 items are grouped under infant stimulation. Many of the items in this development area are activities that a parent or teacher performs with a child. These behaviors serve as a guide for teaching infants up to 4 months. The area of socialization evaluates the young child's interactions with other people. A systematic pattern of language development that focuses on content and the form that is used to express that content is outlined in the checklist. The self-help-category defines those behaviors that enable the child to care for himself or herself in feeding, dressing, and toileting. Cognition is the ability to remember, see, and hear differences; it is measured by what the child says or does in the assessment of this area. The motor area is primarily concerned with the coordinated movements of the large muscles of the body. For each of the 580 items, there are curriculum cards that provide teaching suggestions. These cards are in a card file and are color coded to match corresponding sections in the checklist.

For a home-based program, children are assigned to a home teacher who spends about an hour and a half a week with each child assigned. Instruction during the remainder of the week is the responsibility of the parent. Prescriptions are modified according to each child's individual progress from week to week. Three new behavior targets are identified each week, and it becomes the parents' responsibility to provide instruction on these behaviors between the home teacher's visits. The home teacher collects data before and after instruction and helps parents with

their teaching skills by modeling techniques and allowing parents to try the skills each week.

The success of the Portage model can be seen in its wide dissemination and replication. Over 30 replications across the United States have been reported. The project staff provided training and technical assistance to the replicated sites while the sites provided input regarding changes and additions. (Thurman & Widerstrom, 1981; Southworth, Burr, & Cox 1980; Bluma et al., 1976).

REFERENCES

Bailey, D., & Worley, M., (1984). *Teaching infants and preschoolers with handicaps.* Columbus, OH: Merrill.

Bluma, S., Shearer, M., Froham, A., & Hilliard J. (1976). *The Portage project: Portage guide to early education manual* (revised ed.). Portage, WI: Cooperative Educational Services Agency.

Lerner, J. (1985). *Learning disabilities: Theories, diagnosis, and educational strategies.* (4th ed.). Boston: Houghton Mifflin.

Southworth, L., Burr, R., & Cox, A. (1980) *Screening and evaluating the young child: A handbook of instruments to use from infancy to six years.* Springfield, IL: Thomas.

Thurman, K. S., & Widerstrom, H. A. (1985). *Young children with special needs: A developmental and ecological approach.* Boston: Allyn & Bacon.

FRANCES T. HARRINGTON
Radford University

HOMEBOUND INSTRUCTION
PARENT EFFECTIVENESS TRAINING
PARENTS OF THE HANDICAPPED

POSITIVE PRACTICE

Positive practice is a behavior change technique whereby a misbehaving individual is required to practice correct or appropriate behaviors repeatedly. The term positive practice is frequently used as a synonym for overcorrection, a mild punishment technique. In fact, positive practice is actually a subcomponent of overcorrection. With overcorrection, a misbehaving individual is required to overcorrect the environmental effects of his or her inappropriate act and/or repeatedly practice correct forms of relevant behavior in situations where the misbehavior commonly occurs (Foxx & Bechtel, 1982a). The first part of the overcorrection procedure outlined is commonly referred to as restitution and the latter portion of the procedure is often labeled positive practice. Foxx and Bechtel (1982a) have recommended the terms restitution and positive practice be dropped and replaced by overcorrection for purposes of conceptual clarity and communication.

The concept of positive practice has been the central feature of numerous intervention techniques such as theft reversal (Azrin & Wesolowski, 1974), cleanliness training

(Azrin & Foxx, 1971), and social apology training (Carey & Bucher, 1981). Two common misconceptions about positive practice, however, exist. The first is that positive reinforcement is part of positive practice. This is probably owed to the fact that many people associate the performance of appropriate behaviors solely with the delivery of positive reinforcers. In overcorrection, the performance of appropriate behaviors is elicited by graduated guidance (verbal and physical) from a therapist, not positive reinforcement. The second misconception is that positive practice is similar to negative practice (Dunlap, 1930), a procedure whereby an individual repeatedly practices an inappropriate behavior. Clearly, positive practice is conceptually and pragmatically antithetical to negative practice.

By design, positive practice is a consequence to be used as an aversive stimuli following the occurrence of an inappropriate behavior. Therefore, when the presentation of positive practice results in the reduction of a response in the future, it functions as a punishment procedure. The research literature documents that positive practice, or more accurately overcorrection, can produce large, fairly enduring reductions in inappropriate behavior. Overcorrection procedures have been used with several response classes of behaviors (e.g., aggressive-disruptive behaviors, self-stimulating behaviors, self-injurious behaviors, personal hygiene, social interactions), populations (e.g., mentally handicapped, behaviorally disordered, undersocialized children and adults), and settings (e.g., schools, homes, and institutions). Foxx and Bechtel (1982b) provide an extensive review of the outcomes and side effects of overcorrection, and detailed guidelines for the use of overcorrection.

REFERENCES

Azrin, N. H., & Foxx, R. M. (1971). A rapid method of toilet training the institutionalized retarded. *Journal of Applied Behavior Analysis, 4,* 89–99.

Azrin, N. H., & Wesolowski, M. D. (1974). Theft reversal: An overcorrection procedure for eliminating stealing by retarded persons. *Journal of Applied Behavior Analysis, 7,* 577–581.

Carey, R. G., & Bucher, B. (1981). Identifying the educative and suppressive effects of positive practice and restitutional overcorrection. *Journal of Applied Behavior Analysis, 14,* 71–80.

Dunlap, K. (1930). Repetition in the breaking of habits. *Scientific Monthly, 30,* 66–70.

Foxx, R. M., & Bechtel, D. R. (1982a). Overcorrection. In M. Hersen, R. M. Eisler, & P. M. Miller (Eds.), *Progress in behavior modification* (pp. 227–288). New York: Academic.

Foxx, R. M., & Bechtel, D. R. (1982b). Overcorrection: A review and analysis. In S. Axelrod & J. Apsche (Eds.), *The effects of punishment on human behavior* (pp. 133–220). New York: Academic.

STEPHEN N. ELLIOTT
Louisiana State University

APPLIED BEHAVIOR ANALYSIS
BEHAVIOR MODIFICATION
OVERCORRECTION
NEGATIVE PUNISHMENT
POSITIVE PUNISHMENT

POSITIVE REINFORCEMENT

Behavioral psychology, in particular operant conditioning theory, is based on the supposition that behavior is maintained by its consequences. A consequence that leads to an increase in the frequency of a behavior is called a reinforcer. Conversely, a consequence that results in a decrease in the frequency of a behavior is called punishment.

The principle of positive reinforcement has two parts: (1) if in a given situation a person's behavior is followed close in time by a consequence, then (2) that person is more likely to exhibit the same behavior when he or she is in a similar situation at a later time. This consequence is referred to as a positive reinforcer and is roughly synonomous with the concept of reward.

The person credited with first experimentally investigating the effects of rewards on learning is E. L. Thorndike. In 1898 he began seminal work with hungry cats who learned to escape from a cage to acquire food. After many investigations, Thorndike (1911) conceptualized the law of effect, which in part stated that if a stimulus was followed by a response and then a satisfier, the stimulus-response connection would be strengthened. Skinner (1938, 1953) followed up on Thorndike's work and chose the term positive reinforcer in place of satisfier because he felt satisfier was clumsy and not appropriate for a scientific system of behavior. With the work of Skinner and others such as Premack (1959), the principle of positive reinforcement has become the cornerstone of behavior theory and technology.

The application of positive reinforcement is deceptively simple. Two important components in the successful application of positive reinforcement are the selection of a reinforcer and the schedule for delivering the reinforcer. Some stimuli are positive reinforcers for virtually everyone. For example, food is a reinforcer for almost anyone who has not eaten in several hours; money also is generally reinforcing. It is very important, however, to understand that one can actually determine if a stimulus is reinforcing only after it has been administered contingent on the appearance of a desired behavior. In other words, a stimulus is defined as a reinforcer only by its effect on behavior. Failure to select a stimulus that is reinforcing is one of the most common errors in implementing a behavior change program.

The relationship between a behavior and its consequence is called a contingency. Contingencies can operate continuously (i.e., the consequence follows every occurrence of the target behavior) or intermittently (i.e., the consequence follows only a portion of the occurrences of the target behavior). Most contingencies operate on intermittent schedules (e.g., variable ratio, variable interval, fixed ratio, fixed interval). Each reinforcement schedule has been demonstrated to have a different effect on behavior. In general, continuous schedules are used effectively to develop a new behavior, whereas intermittent schedules are used effectively to increase and maintain a behavior already in a person's repertoire. Ratio schedules generally produce high rates of response, and interval schedules produce lower rates of response. In summary, the selection of a stimulus that is reinforcing and the schedule by which it is administered will determine the strength of the positive reinforcement.

REFERENCES

Premack, D. (1959). Toward empirical behavioral laws. I. Positive reinforcement. *Psychological Review, 66,* 219–233.

Skinner, B. F. (1938). *The behavior of organisms.* New York: Appleton-Century-Crofts.

Skinner, B. F. (1953). *Science and human behavior.* New York: Macmillan.

Thorndike, E. L. (1898). Animal intelligence: An experimental study of associative processes in animals. *Psychological Review, Monograph Supplement, 2,* 8–7, 28–31.

Thorndike, E. L. (1911). *Animal intelligence.* New York: Macmillan.

STEPHEN N. ELLIOTT
Louisiana State University

APPLIED BEHAVIOR ANALYSIS
BEHAVIOR MODIFICATION

POSTLINGUAL DEAFNESS

Postlingual deafness is a general term for profound hearing loss that occurs after the normal acquisition of language and speech. It is also called acquired or adventitious deafness. Those who sustain this type of hearing loss are referred to as deafened rather than deaf.

Postlingual deafness is differentiated from prelingual deafness. The latter interferes with the normal acquisition of language and speech, and frequently affects educational achievement to such an extent that deaf students leaving special schools at the age of 18 are often 7 or 8 years behind their hearing peers (Thomas, 1984). A postlingually deafened child has learned to speak before losing his or her hearing. The child has the memory of the sound and rhythm of speech and has acquired vocabulary and grammar normally. If the child had normal hearing, even for a short time, the outlook is improved (Webster & Elwood, 1985). The education of postlingually deaf children should

encourage creative thinking and verbal expression, and include vocabulary enrichment, aural rehabilitation, and the opportunity for speech refinement and maintenance (Northcott, 1984).

The etiology of acquired or adventitious hearing loss may be familial, noise-induced, by accident or illness, or, in the case of adults, the result of old age (presbycusis). The onset of a hearing loss is sometimes so gradual that it may go unnoticed for a long time. However, any hearing loss, whether acquired gradually or suddenly, that is extensive enough to interfere with the normal communication process creates a myriad of problems so complex that coping with the hearing world becomes difficult (Giolas, 1982). Formal speech-reading lessons are required in most instances. Sometimes individual hearing aids can supplement residual hearing to facilitate communication.

Children who lose their hearing between the ages of 3 and 12 sometimes complete their education in programs for the deaf and later become the leaders and spokespeople of the deaf community. Children who lose their hearing at ages older than 12 are more likely to remain with their former hearing friends and not join the community of deaf adults (Jacobs, 1980). Modern technological devices such as hearing aids, auditory trainers, TDDs (telecommunication devices), and television decoders that display captions, are of great assistance in the education of deaf and deafened children.

REFERENCES

Giolas, T. (1982). *Hearing-handicapped adults.* Englewood Cliffs, NJ: Prentice-Hall.

Jacobs, L. (1980). *A deaf adult speaks out.* Washington, DC: Gallaudet College Press.

Northcott, W. (1984). *Oral interpreting: Principles and practices.* Baltimore, MD: University Park Press.

Thomas, A. (1984). *Acquired hearing loss: Psychological and psychosocial implications.* Orlando, FL: Academic.

Webster, A., & Ellwood, J. (1985). *The hearing-impaired chld in the ordinary school.* Dover, NH: Croom Helm.

ROSEMARY GAFFNEY
Hunter College, City University of New York

DEAF
DEAF EDUCATION

POVERTY, RELATIONSHIP TO SPECIAL EDUCATION

Poverty alone does not cause learning and behavior problems. However, poverty is associated with a variety of environmental variables that could result in the manifestation of learning and behavior problems in children.

Mental retardation, learning disabilities, and emotional disturbances have all been linked to environmental circumstances associated with poverty. The vast majority of retarded individuals fall into the mild category, and the majority of mildly retarded children come from lower socioeconomic status families (MacMillan, 1982). Although difficult to confirm, poverty has also been linked to learning disabilities (Reid & Hresko, 1981). There is evidence that supports the lower socioeconomic environment's contribution to learning problems. Furthermore, many of these same environmental circumstances have also been linked with emotional disturbance and social maladjustment (Smith, Price, & Marsh, 1985).

Although the connection between poverty and special education is easy to establish, it is difficult to separate the many variables and determine which is the most critical to the child. This is because many of the variables are interwoven at points in the child's development. Malnutrition, poor maternal health, inadequate prenatal care, a child's poor health, and general environmental deprivation demonstrate complex interrelationships that make it difficult to isolate a single and specific causal agent. Nevertheless, all of these factors associated with poverty have been shown to have an influence on an individual's cognitive and behavioral development.

A lower socioeconomic environment harbors many potential hazards for a developing child (Robinson & Robinson, 1976). For instance, children from these environments are exposed to greater health risks, and their health care is generally inferior to that of children from higher socioeconomic families; nutritional deficiencies are more common in poor families owing to a lack of food or adequate nutritional intake; and the use of standard English in this environment is generally poorer than it is in more affluent families.

Child rearing also takes a somewhat different form in many poor families than in middle-class families. Low-income families tend to have more children and fewer adults. Discipline in lower-income families tends to rely on punishment, especially physical punishment; middle-class families tend to rely more on reasoning, isolation, and appeals to guilt. Poor families also tend to delay training their children for independence until they are able to learn rapidly, which provides few opportunities for learning how to make mistakes without disgrace.

Another negative aspect of this environment is a restricted range of sensory stimulation. Low-income families are usually associated with restricted developmental stimulation because there are fewer objects for the child to react to (Smith, Neisworth, & Hunt, 1983). This restricted range of sensory stimulation will hinder a child's interaction with physical and social environments by providing fewer behavioral cues.

An inadequate home environment that fails to interest children and promote learning is still another environmental factor associated with poverty. It is common to find less value placed on education in lower income homes. Parents existing at the poverty level may have experienced poor academic progress themselves and dropped out of school early. They may not see education as a vehicle for their child's escape from a similar situation. After all, education did not help them escape poverty. In addition, the parents may be more concerned with day-to-day survival than the perceived value of education. Consequently, when their children ask questions, they may fail to respond or regard that behavior as an interruption.

The environmental factors mentioned are not meant to be inclusive. There are many other factors associated with poverty that also influence learning and behavior. But these factors do point out that poverty is an underlying cause for many of the negative environmental variables associated with handicapping conditions. In some cases (e.g., poor maternal nutrition and health care), these factors can affect the child's development prenatally, resulting in an organic origin for the disability (e.g., damage to brain cells). In other cases, poor environmental circumstances cause children to be ill-prepared to start school. These children lack the experiences that are common to children of higher income families.

Even though these poverty factors underlie many of the negative variables associated with handicapping conditions, it must be remembered that these learning and behavior problems apply to only a small number of children. The large majority of children living in poor environments will show normal development. While these factors can cause cognitive and behavioral problems in some children, they produce no ill effects in others.

REFERENCES

MacMillan, D. L. (1982). *Mental retardation in school and society* (2nd ed.). Boston: Little, Brown.

Reid, D. K., & Hresko, W. P. (1981). *A cognitive approach to learning disabilities.* New York: McGraw-Hill.

Robinson, N. M., & Robinson, H. B. (1976). *The mentally retarded child* (2nd ed.). New York: McGraw-Hill.

Smith, R. M., Neisworth, J. T., & Hunt, F. M. (1983). *The exceptional child: A functional approach* (2nd ed.). New York: McGraw-Hill.

Smith, T. E. C., Price, B. J., & Marsh, G. E. (1985). *Mildly handicapped children and adults.* St. Paul, MN: West.

LARRY J. WHEELER
Southwest Texas State University

CULTURAL DEPRIVATION
CULTURAL FAMILIAL RETARDATION
SOCIOECONOMIC IMPACT OF DISABILITIES
SOCIOECONOMIC STATUS

POWER AND RESEARCH IN SPECIAL EDUCATION

The scientific method has evolved in such a way as to allow researchers to observe phenomena, question, formulate hypotheses, conduct experiments, and develop theories. In hypotheses testing, one compares scientific theories in the form of a statistical hypothesis (H_1) versus a null hypothesis (H_0). According to Kirk (1984), the "statistical hypothesis is a statement about one or more parameters of a population distribution that requires verification" (p. 236). An example is

$$H_1 : \mu > 80,$$

where the mean score of a population of children is hypothesized to be greater than 80 after participating in a remedial reading program. The statistical hypothesis is thus based on the researcher's deductions from the appropriate theory and on prior research. The null hypothesis involves formulating a hypothesis that is mutually exclusive of the statistical hypothesis. In other words, if the researcher believes that children's mean reading scores will be greater than 80 after participating in a reading program, a mutually exclusive hypothesis by which to test the researcher's premise is given by

$$H_0 : < 80.$$

If the null hypothesis is rejected, by default the statistical or alternative hypothesis is assumed to be true but not proven; it is retained as the most likely truth.

In hypothesis testing, rejection or nonrejection of the null hypothesis is based on probability. Incorrect decisions can occur in two ways. If the null hypothesis is rejected when it is in reality true, this is defined as a Type I error. Should the null hypothesis fail to be rejected when it is in fact false, a Type II error is said to have occurred. The following Table displays the possible decision outcomes.

Power is a basic statistical concept that should be taken into consideration in the design of any research study that samples data for inferential purposes. Rejecting the null hypothesis is dependent on whether the test statistic falls

Decision Outcomes for Hypothesis Testing

		True State	
		H_0 True	H_0 False
Decision	Fail to reject H_0	Correct acceptance	Incorrect acceptance (Type II error)
	Reject H_0	Incorrect rejection (Type I error)	Correct rejection

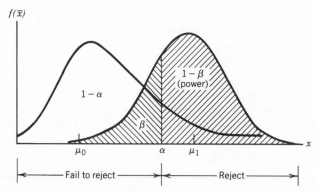

Figure 1. Relationship among power, alpha, one minus alpha, and beta.

within a specified critical region at a particular level of significance, or alpha level (α). The probability of committing a Type I error depends on the alpha level specified. The alpha level also determines the probability of correctly accepting the true null hypothesis ($1 - \alpha$). The probability of committing a Type II error is labeled β; the probability of a correct rejection is based on $1 - \beta$, or the power level. Figure 1 illustrates the relationship among the four outcomes α, $1 - \alpha$, β, and $1 - \beta$, or power. β and power are affected by (1) the size of the sample; (2) the level of significance (α); (3) the size of the difference between μ_1 and μ_0; (4) the size of the population; and (5) whether a one- or two-tailed test is used. One method of increasing the power of a statistical test is to increase the sample size. Figure 2 demonstrates this relationship in a correlational study.

Using power in an a priori fashion enables the researcher to compute the sample size necessary for testing the null hypothesis, given a level of power and alpha. Often, a researcher is faced with a restricted or small sam-

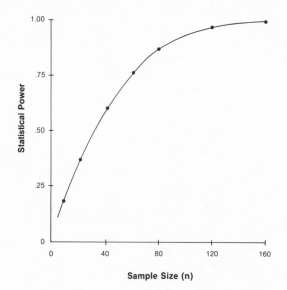

Figure 2. The relationship between sample size and statistical power for detecting a correlation of approximately .30 when p < .05.

ple size on which he or she wishes to determine the power level. Furthermore, in many research situations, as in evaluating special education programs, assessing the impact of a new teaching technique, or exploring the effectiveness of new medication compared with existing therapies, power allows the experimenter to consider, while in the planning stages, what effect size is needed to detect a significant difference. Similarly, the use of two-tailed tests, greater alpha levels, and small population standard deviations contribute to studies with more powerful results. However, it is worthy to note that the cost of committing a Type I error can be as damaging as committing a Type II error. Adopting a new diet program for the treatment of attention deficit children by falsely deciding that the diet is more effective than behavior therapies and medications is as serious as denying the new diet plan any effectiveness as a springboard for future research. Although power is of central consideration in research design and planning, its contribution must be weighted with other important statistical, methodological, and practical facets of the study.

REFERENCE

Kirk, R. E. (1984). *Elementary statistics* (2nd ed.). Monterey, CA: Brooks/Cole.

MARY LEON PEERY
Texas A&M University

RESEARCH

PRADER-WILLI SYNDROME (PWS)

First described in 1956 by Swiss physicians A. Prader, A. Labhart, and H. Willi, Prader-Willi syndrome (PWS) is a complex disorder and a rare birth defect. Common characteristics include hypotonia in early infancy, hypogonadism, short stature, and, after age 2, excessive weight gain and obesity (Cassidy, 1984). Perhaps the most outstanding characteristic of PWS is the individual's constant preoccupation with food and the compulsion to be eating all the time (Otto, Sulzbacher, & Worthington-Roberts, 1982; Pipes, 1978). This voracious craving for food finds PWS victims often exhibiting unselective and bizarre food behaviors such as eating spoiled meat, rotten vegetables, and/or cat food as well as foraging, stealing, or gorging food (Bottel, 1977; Clarren & Smith, 1977; Otto et al., 1982).

The excessive appetite of PWS victims is not the only factor contributing to their obesity. They seem to require fewer calories than the average person of comparable age to maintain weight (Nardella, Sulzbacher, & Worthington-Roberts, 1983; Neason, 1978). In order to lose weight, further reduction in caloric intake is necessary, sometimes restricting the person to a 1000-calorie or less daily diet plan (Cassidy, 1984; Nardella et al., 1983).

Characteristics of PWS individuals usually include erratic and unpredictable behavior such as stubborness, outbursts of temper, depression, and even rage (Otto et al., 1982). Personality problems, behavioral disorders, and emotional problems are frequent though not consistent findings in people with PWS (Cassidy, 1984). Many of the more aggressive behaviors escalate out of anger or desire for food.

Current research indicates that an aberration in a portion of chromosome 15 may be the cause of PWS (Nardella et al., 1983). However, PWS is not a high-risk condition and is most likely a noninherited chromosome defect (Neason, 1978). Another prevailing theory is that PWS is due to a defect within the hypothalmus and thus PWS victims never reach a sense of satiety (Clarren & Smith, 1977).

Mental retardation, particularly in the borderline to moderate range, has been considered to be an integral part of the syndrome (Cassidy, 1984; Neason, 1978). However, recent reports by Holm (1981) indicate that for many of these people, cognitive functioning is more typical of learning disabilities. That is, the child has strengths in several areas and weaknesses in others, unlike a retarded child, who tends to be developmentally delayed across skill areas. Academic weaknesses are commonly found in arithmetic, particularly in the understanding of time and the handling of money, and in writing. Reading and language commonly are mentioned as academic strengths. Holm (1981) sees the intellectual functioning of the PWS individual as a central nervous system disorder.

Because of its rarity, insufficient evidence exists on the social and emotional consequences of having PWS. However, there is no question that those afflicted with the disorder have sufficient intelligence to recognize the social stigma obesity has in our society (Cassidy, 1984). At the present time there is no known cure or treatment for PWS. The critical component of any program, however, is the constant monitoring of caloric intake. If the weight of the individual with PWS is not kept under control, death may occur at an early age from complications associated with extreme obesity.

Educational intervention for individuals with Prader-Willi syndrome should begin in early childhood with a program that assists and supports parents and children in managing eating behaviors. Food and nutrition management must be the first and foremost objective of any school program. Deliberate and calculated attempts by the teacher must be made to rid the classroom of any and all food, including pet food. Alternate reward and reinforcement systems other than food reinforcers such as candy must also be instituted. All school personnel who come in contact with the child (particularly lunchroom aides) must be made aware of the child's condition and the consequences of additional caloric intake. The child should be encouraged to stay away from food at all cost.

Physical activity designed to enhance body awareness and activities that encourage social interaction should be stressed and deliberately planned in any class with a PWS child. Academic weaknesses should be addressed as well, and particular attention should be paid to eliminating or modifying temper tantrums or extreme stubborness by using a behavior-modification approach (Cassidy, 1984). Seocndary-level students should be prepared in independent living skills such as math in daily living and vocational/occupational skills, with an emphasis on increasing the child's responsibilty for weight control. Competitive employment is rare and most adults are employed in noncompetitive structured workshops and centers. At all times, in any school or workshop program, students with PWS must be watched to prevent their consuming other people's leftovers and food items.

REFERENCES

Bottel, H. (1977, May). The eating disease. *Good Housekeeping,* 176–177.

Cassidy, S. B. (1984). Prader-Willi syndrome. *Current Problems in Pediatrics, 14*(1), 18.

Clarren, S. K., & Smith, D. W. (1977). Prader-Willi syndrome: Variable severity and recurrence risk. *American Journal of Diseases in Children, 131,* 798–800.

Hom, V. A. (1981). The diagnosis of Prader-Willi syndrome. In V. A. Holm, S. Sulzbacher, & P. L. Pipes (Eds.), *Prader-Willi syndrome.* Baltimore, MD: University Park Press.

Nardella, M. T., Sulzbacher, S. I., Worthington-Roberts, B. S. (1983). Activity levels of persons with Prader-Willi syndrome. *American Journal of Mental Deficiency, 89,* 498–505.

Neason, S. (1978). *Prader-Willi syndrome: A handbook for parents.* Longlake, MN: Prader-Willi Syndrome Association.

Otto, P. L., Sulzbacher, S. I., Worthington-Roberts, B. S. (1982). Sucrose-induced behavior changes of persons with Prader-Willi syndrome. *American Journal of Mental Deficiency. 86,* 335–341.

Pipes, P. L. (1978). Weight control. In S. Neason (Ed.), *Prader-Willi syndrome: A handbook for parents.* Longlake, MN: Prader-Willi Syndrome Association.

MARSHA H. LUPI
Hunter College, City University of New York

**CHROMOSOME ABNORMALITIES
GENETIC DISORDERS**

PRECISION TEACHING

Precision teaching, a measurement system developed by Ogden R. Lindsley at the University of Kansas in the mid-1960s (McGreevy, 1984), involves daily measurement and graphing of student performance for the purpose of formative evaluation. Frequency of behavior (the number of occurrences divided by minutes of observation) is charted on the Standard Behavior Chart, a graph designed to highlight changes in frequency. Data are evaluated daily to determine if changes in curriculum are necessary to promote learning and progress toward performance goals (or, in the language of precision teaching, aims).

There are four steps in precision teaching. First, a precisely stated behavior or pinpoint is selected. An example of a pinpoint statement is "see word/say word." Next, frequencies of correct and incorrect responses are obtained and charted on the Standard Behavior Chart. Third, curricular events are modified to change performance in the desired direction. Finally, the graph is evaluated and instructional decisions are made according to trends in the data. Of course, these final two steps are repeated as necessary until progress allows for the attainment of aims.

The Standard Behavior Chart is a semilogarthmic or equal-ratio graph. Frequency is represented along its vertical axis as Movements/minute (M/m). Equal changes in the frequency of behavior are represented by equal distances along this Y-axis. Thus, the distance between 10 and 20 M/m is identical to the distance between 50 and 100 M/m since both represent a $2\times$ (times 2) change. In fact, any $2\times$ change, regardless of where along the Y-axis it occurs, will appear as the same distance on the Standard Behavior Chart. Behaviors ranging in frequency from 1 to 1000 minutes (.001 M/m) to 1000 in 1 minute (1000 M/m) can be represented on the Standard Behavior Chart. The unit along the X or horizontal axis is actual calendar days.

Data are obtained directly through observations of student behavior. For example, word recognition could be measured each day by counting the number of words said correctly and incorrectly per minute of reading. Also, in precision teaching, data are recorded continuously. Once recording starts, behavior is monitored without interruption until the recording period stops.

One of the principal measures used in precision teaching is celeration (Pennypacker, Koenig, & Lindsley, 1972). Celerations are standard straight line measures describing the trend of graphed data. For example, an upward trend or acceleration in correct responses and a downward trend or deceleration in incorrect responses, describe a desirable pattern. Precision teaching suggests that certain teaching decisions be based on a minimum acceptable celeration toward a performance aim. In practice, if the teacher sees the student's performance drop below acceptable minimums, then decisions are made to change some aspect of the curriculum (White & Haring, 1980). The changes are evaluated to see if restoration of student progress is obtained. Various adjustments are tried until acceptable celerations and progress toward aims are achieved.

The Figure shows examples of correct (•) and incorrect (x) data points on a standard behavior chart. The lines drawn through the data represent celerations. Various

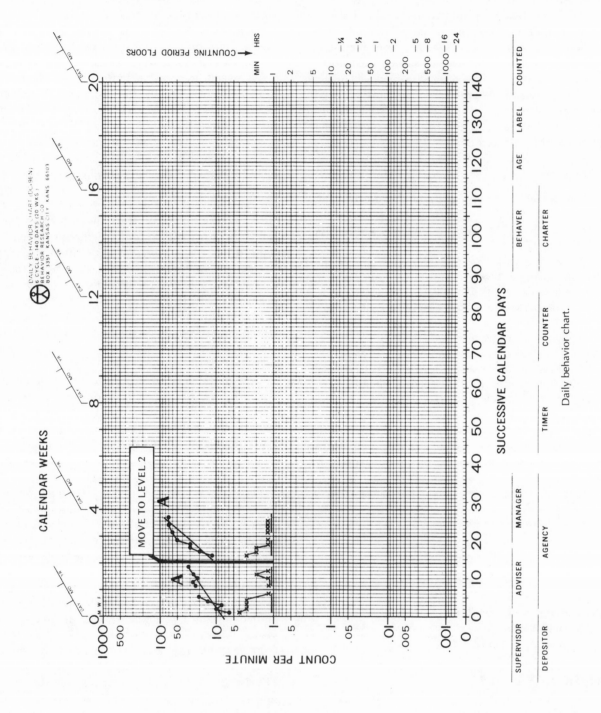

Daily behavior chart.

changes in the teaching procedures are indicated by notations on the chart. The correct data are accelerating to the previously chosen performance aim, the symbol "A" on the chart. Incorrect responses are decelerating. This pattern is a desirable one showing learning and growth in both accuracy and fluency of performance. If the data change in an undesirable manner—e.g., if frequency correct decelerates and frequency wrong accelerates—then teachers must select a program adjustment and try again (Lindsley, 1971).

Thus the process of precision teaching is an optimistic one. Once responses are precisely defined, observed, and recorded, the elements of a self-correcting instructional system are in place. Teachers may not interpret failure to maintain adequate progress toward an aim as a limitation of the student. Rather, such failure signals a limitation of the existing instructional program. Their ability to solve even the most difficult instructional problems of handicapped learners is limited only by their creativity in developing program adjustments.

The *Journal of Precision Teaching* is dedicated to dissemination of data-based information about human performance and is an excellent resource. The journal is available through Louisiana State University, Special Education, 201 Peabody Hall, Baton Rouge, Louisiana 70803.

REFERENCES

Lindsley, O. R. (1971). From Skinner to precision teaching: The child knows best. In J. B. Jordan & L. S. Robbins (Eds.), *Let's try doing something else kind of thing* (pp. 1–11). Arlington, VA: Council for Exceptional Children.

McGreevy, P. (1984). Frequency and the standard celeration chart: Necessary components of precision teaching. *Journal of Precision Teaching, 5*(2), 28–36.

Pennypacker, H. S., Koenig, C. H., & Lindsley, O. R. (1972). *Handbook of the standard behavior chart.* Kansas City, KS: Precision Media.

White, O. R., & Haring, N. G. (1980). *Exceptional children* (2nd ed.). Columbus, OH: Merrill.

MARK A. KOORLAND
PAUL T. SINDELAR
Florida State University

DIRECT INSTRUCTION
DATA-BASED INSTRUCTION
TEST-TEACH-TEST

PREHM, HERBERT J. (1937–   )

A native of Aurora, Illinois, Herbert J. Prehm received his BS (1959) in elementary education and psychology from Concordia Teacher's College, River Forest, Illinois. He re-

Herbert J. Prehm

ceived both his MS (1962) and PhD (1964) in education and psychology from the University of Wisconsin, Madison. He is currently assistant executive director of the Department of Professional Development of the Council for Exceptional Children.

Trained as an elementary school teacher, and with experience as a reading consultant for dyslexic children, Prehm was always interested in the learning problems of children. His early work was concerned with the effective teaching of mentally retarded children (Prehm, 1967; Prehm & Stinnett, 1970). Part of this interest has been evident in his work in the preparation of teachers (Hersh & Prehm, 1977) and as a professor of education for several universities for approximately 20 years.

Prehm has been a fellow of the American Association on Mental Deficiency. He has also been president of the Teacher Education Division of the Council for Exceptional Children. He has received the TED–Merril Award for Excellence in Teacher Education.

REFERENCES

Hersh, R., & Prehm, H. J. (Eds.), (1977). Issues in teacher preparation. *Teacher Education & Special Education, 1*(1) 320–349.

Prehm, H. J. (1967). Rote learning and memory in the retarded: Some implications for the teacher-learning process. *Journal of Special Education, 1*, 397–399.

Prehm, H. J., & Stinnett, R. D. (1970). Effects of learning method on learning stage in retarded and normal adolescents. *American Journal of Mental Deficiency, 75*, 319–322.

E. VALERIE HEWITT
Texas A&M University

PRELINGUAL DEAFNESS

Prelingual deafness refers to profound hearing loss sustained before language has been acquired. Age at onset of profound hearing loss is a major factor because of its implications for language development. The critical age at onset of profound hearing loss is about 2 years (Quigley & Kretschmer, 1982). Children born deaf, or deafened before the age of 2 years, are prelingually deaf. Deafness is a profound degree of hearing impairment, a bilateral loss of 90 dB or greater on the audiometric scale of − 10 to 110 dB (Quigley & Paul, 1984).

Prelingually deaf children rely on vision as their primary channel of communication and language acquisition. Since language plays such a important role in thinking and in conceptual growth (Webster & Ellwood, 1985), prelingually deaf children require special educational programs with emphasis on all the skills related to language and communication.

Prelingual deafness is more than the inability to hear sound. It is a pervasive handicap that, because of its effects on language and communication, has an impact on almost all aspects of child development.

REFERENCES

Forecki, M. C. (1985). *Speak to me*, Washington, DC: Gallaudet College Press.

Quigley, S., & Kretschmer, R. (1982). *The education of deaf children: Issues, theory and practice*. Baltimore, MD: University Park Press.

Quigley, S., & Paul, P. (1984). *Language and deafness*, San Diego, CA: College-Hill.

Webster, A., & Ellwood, J. (1985). *The hearing-impaired child in the ordinary school*. Dover, NH: Croom Helm.

ROSEMARY GAFFNEY
*Hunter College, City University
of New York*

DEAF
DEAF EDUCATION
SPEECH, ABSENCE OF

PREMACK PRINCIPLE

The original definition of reinforcement (Skinner, 1938; Spence, 1956) was circular. A stimulus could not be identified as a reinforcer until it had been tested and shown to increase the probability of a response. This left behavior modifiers with no a priori method of choosing effective reinforcers. However, Premack (1965) solved this problem of circularity by devising an independent means of determining the reinforcing power of different consequences. Premack found that under certain circumstances, an organism's own behavior can function as a reinforcer. More specifically, a less probable behavior within a person's repertoire can be strengthened by making the occurrence of a more probable behavior contingent on it.

This principle was first demonstrated in an intensive set of experiments in which Premack shifted the probability of animals drinking or running by alternately depriving them of water or activity. When drinking was made a high-probability behavior by depriving the animals of water, drinking reinforced the low-probability behavior of running. Similarly, when running was made a high-probability behavior by depriving the animals of activity, running served as a reinforcer for drinking. In both situations, low-probability behavior was increased by following it with high-probability behavior.

Moving from the animal laboratory to the applied setting is always a difficult transition. Identifying reinforcers by the Premack principle requires assessing the relative probabilities of the reinforcing behavior and the behavior to be changed by counting their rate of occurrence in a free environment. This arduous task seriously limits the usefulness of the Premack principle in applied settings. Fortunately, behavior modifiers have found it adequate to identify high-probability behaviors by asking a person about preferred activities or by casually observing the person to determine the activities from which he or she derives overt pleasure (Danaher, 1974). Once the preferred behavior is identified, the behavior modifier will allow the person to engage in that behavior only after performing the targeted low-probability or less preferred behavior. Because of this formulation, the Premack principle is sometimes referred to as "Grandma's rule" (Becker, 1971; Homme, 1971) or "you do what I want you to do before you get to do what you want to do."

Preferred activities have been frequently used in special education to reinforce or increase the rate of less preferred activities as demonstrated in the following three examples. First, in a deaf education class, Osborne (1969) allowed students to earn 5 minutes of free time, the preferred activity, for every 15 minutes they remained in their seats, the less preferred activity. Second, Hart and Risley (1968) gave economically disadvantaged children access to recreational materials contingent on the appropriate use of adjectives in spontaneous speech. Third, Kane and Gantzer (1977) showed that in a special class, academically preferred activities could be used to increase the amount of time spent in less desirable academic activities.

REFERENCES

Becker, W. C. (1971). *Parents are teachers*. Champaign, IL: Research.

Danaher, B. G. (1974). Theoretical foundations and clinical applications of the Premack principle: Review and critique. *Behavior Therapy, 5*, 307–324.

Hart, B. M., & Risley, T. R. (1968). Establishing use of descriptive adjectives in the spontaneous speech of disadvantaged preschool children. *Journal of Applied Behavior Analysis, 1*, 109–120.

Homme, L. (1971). *How to use contingency contracting in the classroom*. Champaign, IL: Research.

Kane, G., & Gantzer, S. (1977). Preferred lessons as reinforcers in a special class: An investigation of the Premack principle. *Zeitschrift fur Entwicklungspsychologie and Padagogische Psychologie, 9*, 79–89.

Osborne, J. G. (1969). Free time as a reinforcer in the management of classroom behavior. *Journal of Applied Behavior Analysis, 2*, 113–118.

Premack, D. (1965). Reinforcement theory. In D. Levine (Ed.), *Nebraska symposium on motivation*. Lincoln: University of Nebraska Press.

Skinner, B. F. (1938). *The Behavior of organisms*. New York: Appleton-Century-Crofts.

Spence, K. (1956). *Behavior theory and conditioning*. New Haven, CT: Yale University Press.

JOHN O'NEILL
*Hunter College, City University
of New York*

**BEHAVIOR MODIFICATION
OPERANT CONDITIONING
POSITIVE REINFORCEMENT**

PREMATURITY/PRETERM

Prematurity or preterm refers to the 8 to 10% of all live births born prior to completion of 37 weeks gestation, regardless of birth weight. The overall survival rate of premature infants has increased with improved perinatal care (Sills & Coen, 1984).

The exact cause of the majority of premature births is uncertain. It is hypothesized that the cause is a combination of maternal, paternal, fetal, and environmental factors. Among the maternal factors that increase the risk for prematurity are pregnancy-induced hypertension, blood dyscrasias, placenta previa, premature separation of the placenta, and an incompetent cervix. Maternal social factors related to prematurity include low socioeconomic status, cigarette smoking, age less than 16 or greater than 40, heavy physical labor, past history of previous premature births, past history of multiple abortions, lack of prenatal care, and poor nutrition. Paternal factors include genetic makeup and older age. Fetal factors related to prematurity include the presence of congenital anomalies, fetal diseases, and multiple gestation. Environmental factors include stress, falls, and pollution with heavy metals. There is often difficulty in predicting a premature birth because of other currently unknown factors that influence premature labor (Johnson, 1986).

Gestational maturity is determined by both neurological and physical characteristics (Dubowitz & Dubowitz, 1977). The premature infant's head generally appears large for its small body, and the skin appears bright pink, loose, wrinkled, and translucent. The eyes are large, abdomen distended, and genitalia not fully developed. The fingernails are thin, hair is sparse, and the body is covered with fine downy hair and a layer of sebaceous skin covering. The premature infant's arms and legs are thin and frequently lie extended on a firm surface. In the preterm infant, reflex movements are only partially developed, and breathing and crying are often spasmodic and weak (Schuster & Ashburn, 1986).

Premature infants often have physiologically immature organ systems that cause clinical problems. These clinical problems may include immature lungs, apnea, hemorrhaging into the brain, inflammatory disease of the gastrointestinal tract, poor weight gain, inability to maintain body temperature, hepatic immaturity, and infection (Avery & Taeusch, 1984).

These clinical problems may be intensively managed with intravenous fluids, medications, and technological supports such as ventilators and incubators. With technological advances, the survival rate of premature infants having clinical complications is continuously improving. Even infants born at approximately 24 to 26 weeks gestation have about a 45% survival rate. However, approximately 20% of those surviving premature infants who had a clinical complication and whose birth weight was less than 1000 grams have long-term handicapping conditions. These long-term sequelae include retrolental fibroplasia, neurologic impairment, and sudden infant death syndrome (Koops, 1980).

The long-range sequelae of prematurity are closely associated with both prenatal and postnatal complications and the disruption of the parent-infant bonding process. Many long-range effects appear to be due to the clinical complications associated with prematurity rather than the prematurity itself. There is an increased incidence of mental retardation, cerebral palsy, convulsive disorders, and learning disabilities associated with prematurity (Koops, 1980).

A potential long-range complication of prematurity secondary to oxygen treatment of lung disease in the preterm infant is retrolental fibroplasia. Retrolental fibroplasia is caused by high concentrations of oxygen necessary in treating the lung disease. The high concentration of oxygen causes retinal scarring and detachment, which results in mild to severe visual impairment. The concentration of oxygen that causes retrolental fibroplasia is unknown but increasingly sophisticated methods of monitoring oxygen concentration is decreasing the incidence of this disease (Healy, Hein, & Rubin, 1983).

Other potential long-range complications of prematurity include maladjustment of the parent-infant bond and lags in growth and development. Maladjustment of the parent-infant bond can be caused by separation, fear, guilt, or poor parenting skills. The parent-infant bond can be strengthened by encouraging and supporting early parent-infant interaction even in the intensive care unit, and by including the parents in the care of the infant (Jensen & Bobak, 1985).

Often premature infants experience a lag in growth and development, but with anticipatory guidance, stimulation, and close supervision many of the preterm infants are developmentally appropriate by the ages of 2 or 3 years. The most important factors for assisting preterm infants with developmental needs seem to be sensory stimulation and environmental enrichment given by the parents (Johnson, 1986).

REFERENCES

Avery, M. E., & Taeusch, H. W. (Eds.). (1984). *Schaffer's diseases of the newborn* (5th ed.). Philadelphia: Saunders.

Dubowitz, L. M. S., & Dubowitz, V. (1977). *Gestational age of the newborn.* Menlo Park, CA: Addison-Wesley.

Healy, A., Hein, H. A., & Rubin, I. L. (1983). Perinatal stresses. In T. D. Levine, W. B. Carey, A. C. Crocker, & R. T. Gross (Eds.), *Developmental-behavioral pediatrics* (pp. 390–403). Philadelphia: Saunders.

Jensen, M. D., & Bobak, I. M. (1985). *Maternity and gynecologic care, the nurse and the family* (3rd ed.). St. Louis: Mosby.

Johnson, S. H. (1986). *Nursing assessment and strategies for the family at risk, high-risk parenting* (2nd ed.). Philadelphia: Lippincott.

Koops, B. L. (1980). Studies on long-term outcome in newborns with birthweights under 1500 grams. *Advances in behavioral pediatrics, 1,* 1–28.

Schuster, C. S., & Ashburn, S. S. (1986). *The process of human development, a holistic life-span approach* (2nd ed.). Boston: Little, Brown.

Sills, J., & Coen, R. W. (1984). The neonate. In R. K. Creasy & R. Resnik (Eds.), *Maternal-fetal medicine, principles and practice* (pp. 1093–1111). Philadelphia: Saunders.

ELIZABETH R. BAUERSCHMIDT
University of North Carolina,
Wilmington

AMNIOCENTESIS
BABY JANE DOE
BIRTH INJURIES

PREREFERRAL INTERVENTION

Graden, Casey, and Christenson (1985) state that the goal of a prereferral intervention model "is to implement systematically intervention strategies in the regular classroom and to evaluate the effectiveness of these strategies before a student is formally referred for consideration for special education placement " (p. 378). The prereferral intervention model is intended to prevent unnecessary referrals for psychoeducational testing for purposes of determining eligibility for special education programs. The prereferral intervention model is an indirect, consultative service, and has several advantages as an alternative to the traditional process of teacher referral, psychoeducational testing, determination of eligibility, and special education placement.

First, while traditional psychoeducational testing assumes the child's problem resides in the child (e.g., a learning disability, low intelligence, or a personality disorder), the prereferral intervention model assumes that the child's problems are a result of the interaction of the child's characteristics with setting and task variables. When those setting and task variables that result in improved child performance are identified through careful observation and problem-solving efforts, modifications can be implemented in the classroom without removing the child from the regular class. Second, in the traditional testing approach, if the child is found ineligible for special education services, a great deal of resources are allocated to the child, but the child does not necessarily benefit from these resources. Third, because some testing does not use instructional data, the recommendations may not have instructional ramifications. Contributing to the problem of the relevance of recommendations is the fact that the problem for which the child is referred often does not show up in the testing situation. For example, a child who is fidgety and has trouble concentrating in the classroom may demonstrate excellent concentration in the one-on-one testing relationship. In this example, the testing results and recommendations would not address the referral problem. Fourth, when special education services are the only assistance available to children with problems, teachers will refer children whose needs could be met in the less restrictive environment of the regular classroom. If consultative help were available to the teacher, the child's needs could be served through an indirect model. Fifth, indirect services serve preventive goals. If teachers can request consultation from a school psychologist or special education teacher-consultant soon after a child's problem becomes evident, more severe problems can be avoided. In the traditional testing model, children who do not qualify tend to get referred again and again by teachers until the problems are severe enough to qualify these children for special education programs. Finally, the teacher develops new knowledge and skills in consultation that will assist in providing for the needs of other children.

Because 73% of referred children are placed in special education (Algozzine, Christenson, & Ysseldyke, 1982), referral for testing is a critical point in the referral-testing-determination-placement process. The preferral interventions model is aimed at increasing the probability that a child referred for testing has needs that cannot be met by modifications in the regular classroom. Graden et al. (1985a) delineate four steps in the preferral intervention model. These steps occur prior to a formal referral for special education testing. First, the teacher requests consultation from the school psychologist or special education teacher-consultant. This step may be a requirement or an option for the teacher. Second, the consultant and teacher engage in a problem-solving process that involves specifying the problem, generating alternative interventions, and evaluating the intervention. This step may be repeated. Third, if the interventions tried out during the first consultation are unsuccessful, the consultant and teacher collect additional observational data. The data include an analysis of antecedents and consequences of the child's behavior. These more detailed observations are used to plan interventions that are then implemented and evaluated. If these interventions are unsuccessful, the teacher and consultant refer the child to a child review team that reviews the problem and the data collected. This team may recommend additional data to collect or additional interventions, or it may formally refer the child for psychoeducational testing for purposes of determining eligibility for special education. If the child is referred for testing, the data collected in the prereferral phases are used to select an assessment strategy and to plan for the child's instructional needs.

The prereferral model is a consultative model. The consultant must possess the consultation skills necessary to engage the teacher in a collaborative, problem-solving process to create an open and trusting relationship with the consultee and to guide the teacher in a problem-solving sequence.

Although there have been many studies evaluating the effectiveness of consultation, few of these have evaluated consultation as a systematic strategy for reducing inappropriate referrals for special education testing. An exception is the case study by Graden, Casey, and Bonstrom (1985), they found that four out of six schools that implemented the prereferral model experienced a decrease in referrals for testing and special education placements. The authors suggest that the model was not successful in the other two schools because there was a lack of system support and the model was not fully implemented.

REFERENCES

Algozzine, B., Christenson, S., & Ysseldyke, J. E. (1982). Probabilities associated with the referral to placement process. *Teacher Education and Special Education, 5,* 19–23.

Graden, J., Casey, A., & Bonstrom. (1985). Implementing a prereferral intervention system: Part II. The Data. *Exceptional Children, 51,* 487–496. (a)

Graden, J., Casey, A., & Christenson, S. (1985). Implementing a prereferral intervention system: Part I. The Model. *Exceptional Children, 51,* 377–384. (b)

JAN N. HUGHES
Texas A&M University

PRESCHOOL SCREENING CONSULTATION
PREVENTION, PRIMARY

PRESCHOOL-AGE GIFTED CHILDREN

Services for gifted children below kindergarten age have received increased attention as a means of encouraging development of the child's potential, stimulating interest in learning, and providing support for parents. Several authors (Fox, 1971; Isaacs, 1963; Whitmore, 1979, 1980) have pointed to lack of support and intellectual challenge in the early years as one source of later underachievement among the gifted. Programs for young gifted children facilitate early interaction between parents and educators that can promote supportive parenting practices and parent advocacy (Karnes, Shwedel, & Linnemeyer, 1982). Early identification and parent training are particularly critical for gifted children from economically disadvantaged backgrounds.

Despite the need, few programs exist that are specifically designed for preschool 3- to 4-year-old children (Roedell, Jackson, & Robinson, 1980). Several factors account for the sparsity of such programs. First, lacking state and federal incentives for providing appropriate education to preschool-age gifted and talented children, few systematic procedures have been implemented for early identification and service delivery. Second, critics have questioned the reliability and validity of currently available measures for identifying giftedness in 3- and 4-year-old children. Third, parents of young gifted children frequently have little access to information about referral characteristics, available services, and need for advocacy in initiating services.

A review of current literature on gifted education, however, reveals growing recognition of the special needs of gifted and talented children in the early years (Karnes, 1983; Whitmore, in press). Significant topics include identification procedures, characteristics, programs, and issues.

As indicated, one of the major obstacles to large-scale development of preschool programs for the gifted has been the concern that current measures lack reliability and validity in discriminating among children who are truly precocious, children of average ability who are early developers, and children of average ability whose high performance stems from an enriched environment. Another concern has been the efficacy of such measures in identifying gifted children who are "late bloomers." However, it has recently been argued that standardized intelligence measures truly differentiate between advanced and normal development at the preschool level (Silverman, 1986), and that giftedness should be conceptualized as significantly advanced development at the time of testing rather than as potential for adult achievement. Moreover, the imperfection of currently available measures should not preclude the delivery of services to children.

Because of concerns about reliability and validity of standardized measures when employed with young children, there is general consensus that multiple sources of data, formal and informal, should be used to identify gifted preschool-age children.

Karnes and Johnson (1986) list a number of formal instruments that have been used to assess the potential and current functioning of young gifted and talented children in intellectual, perceptual-motor, social, creative, self-concept, and musical areas. Commonly used formal measures for identifying gifted preschool-age children are the Stanford-Binet and Draw-a-Man for intelligence; the Peabody Individual Achievement Test and Woodcock-Johnson Psychoeducational Battery, Part II, for achievement; and Thinking Creatively in Action and Movement (Torrance, 1981) and the Structure of Intellect Learning Ability Tests, Primary Form (Meeker, 1984) for creativity and divergent thinking.

Informal data sources include parent and community nominations, teacher checklists, and child products (Karnes & Johnson, 1986). The Seattle Child Development Preschool Comprehensive Parent Questionnaire (Roedell, Jackson, & Robinson, 1980) provides an excellent source of data based on both parent perception and parent assessment of child performance. Pediatricians, artists, religious instructors, and other community members who are familiar with the child constitute valuable referral sources. Teacher checklists (Karnes et al., 1978a, 1978b) have been developed to assess young children's performance in a variety of talent areas. Finally, collections developed by the child as well as artistic, scientific, and other creative products provide useful assessment data.

Formal and informal data collected for each child being assessed may be reviewed by an identification/selection committee composed of professionals in gifted education, diagnostic specialists, parents, and community members. While not always possible or desirable, use of identification criteria consistent with criteria used by local school districts can facilitate children's transition to programs after preschool age.

Characteristics of young gifted children are most readily observable in comparison with other children of the same age, sex, and cultural group. Cognitively, young gifted children often display advanced vocabulary and general information, early interest in books and numbers, long attention spans, persistence and creativity in solving problems, vivid imaginations, broad or intense interests, unusual memory for detail, and an intense desire to know "why."

Many young gifted children also possess social-emotional characteristics such as preference for associating with older children, capacity for intense emotions, and a high level of empathy, traits that render them vulnerable to stress. Additionally, young gifted children may become frustrated by their uneven development, e.g., when their advanced thinking but average fine-motor coordination results in products that fail to meet their goals. Kitano (1985a) found characteristics of competitiveness and perfectionism in some children attending a preschool for the

gifted. These socio-emotional vulnerabilities (Roedell, 1986) may become manifested in withdrawn, shy, aggressive, or attention-getting behaviors.

Program goals for gifted children in preschool settings derive from these children's cognitive, socio-emotional, and developmental characteristics and from the rationale underlying early identification: the need to provide challenge and stimulation. Goals include (1) developing a positive attitude toward oneself and toward learning; (2) developing positive social values and interaction skills, including prosocial attitudes, independence, responsibility, task commitment, and risk taking; (3) developing and using creative and higher level thinking skills; and (4) developing competency in basic skills (language, readiness, motor) and in general knowledge.

Many of the models employed in programs for elementary-age gifted children have been successfully applied to preschool-level programs. For example, programs at the University of Illinois, Champaign-Urbana (Karnes & Bertschi, 1978; Karnes, Shwedel, & Linnemeyer, 1982) have incorporated Structure-of-Intellect and open classroom models. The Hunter College (Camp, 1963) and New Mexico State University (Kitano & Kirby, 1986a, 1986b) programs involve children in unit-based curricula and independent projects. The Astor program (Ehrlich, 1980) focuses on the higher level skills of Bloom's (1956) taxonomy as well as on academic skills and creative investigation. Taylor's (1968) multiple talent approach and Renzulli's (1977) enrichment triad model have also been applied to programs for preschool-level gifted children.

Experience with gifted preschool-age children over the last several years raises a number of issues that must be considered in serving this population (Kitano, 1985b). Evaluation studies of individual preschool programs for the gifted (Karnes, Shwedel, & Lewis, 1983a, 1983b; Vantassel-Baska, Schuler, & Lipschutz, 1982) indicate that young gifted children make academic, social, and affective gains if given services designed to meet their needs. However, several questions pertinent to preschool programs for the gifted have yet to be answered: Should gifted children acquire skills at an early age just because they are able to? What are the long-term effects of early identification and early education for the gifted? Does early identification as gifted alter parent expectations for the child as well as the child's self-expectations? Does enriched preschool programming render later regular education experiences redundant?

Many gifted children enter preschool programs with academic skills and knowledge well above their chronological age expectancy levels. A major focus for these children might well be the encouragement of humanistic values and prosocial motivation. Some gifted children lose their previously acquired status as top achievers when they enter homogenously grouped preschools for the gifted. Further research might explore the effects of early identification and early education on self-concept. Finally, it is clear that many gifted preschool-age children acquire new knowledge and skills at a rapid rate. Without stimulation and challenge, some will find their first school experiences to be alienating. It is critical that preschools for the gifted facilitate the continuation of enrichment programs beyond the preschool level.

REFERENCES

Bloom, B. S. (1956). *Taxonomy of educational objectives, the classification of educational goals—Handbook I: Cognitive domain*. New York: McKay.

Camp, L. T. (1963). Purposeful preschool education. *Gifted Child Quarterly, 7*, 106–107.

Ehrlich, V. Z. (1980). The Astor program for gifted children. In *Educating the preschool/primary gifted and talented* (pp. 248–250). Ventura, CA: Office of the Ventura County Superintendent of Schools.

Fox, A. E. (1971). Kindergarten: Forgotten year for the gifted? *Gifted Child Quarterly, 15*, 42–48.

Isaacs, A. F. (1963). Should the gifted preschool child be taught to read? *Gifted Child Quarterly, 7*, 72–77.

Karnes, M. B. (Ed.). (1983). *The underserved: Our young gifted children*. Reston, VA: Council for Exceptional Children.

Karnes, M. B. et al. (1978a). *Preschool talent checklists manual*. Urbana, IL: Institute for Child Development and Behavior, University of Illinois.

Karnes, M. B. et al. (1978b). *Preschool talent checklists record booklet*. Urbana, IL: Institute for Child Behavior and Development, University of Illinois.

Karnes, M. B., & Bertschi, J. D. (1978). Teaching the young gifted handicapped child. *Teaching Exceptional Children, 10*(4), 114–119.

Karnes, M. B., & Johnson, L. J. (1986). Identification and assessment of the gifted/talented handicapped and nonhandicapped children in early childhood. In J. R. Whitmore (Ed.), *Intellectual giftedness in young children: Recognition and development*. New York: Haworth.

Karnes, M. B., Shwedel, A. M., & Lewis, G. F. (1983a). Long-term effects of early programming for the gifted/talented handicapped. *Journal for the Education of the Gifted, 6*(4), 266–278.

Karnes, M. B., Shwedel, A. M., & Lewis, G. F. (1983b). Short-term effects of early programming for the young gifted handicapped child. *Exceptional Children, 50*(2), 103–109.

Karnes, M. B., Shwedel, A. M., & Linnemeyer, S. A. (1982). The young gifted/talented child: Programs at the University of Illinois. *Elementary School Journal, 82*(3), 195–213.

Kitano, M. K. (1985a). Ethnography of a preschool for the gifted: What gifted young children actually do. *Gifted Child Quarterly, 29*(2), 67–71.

Kitano, M. K. (1985b). Issues and problems in establishing preschool programs for the gifted. *Roeper Review, 7*(4), 212–213.

Kitano, M. K., & Kirby, D. F. (1986a). *Gifted education: A comprehensive view*. Boston: Little, Brown.

Kitano, M. K., & Kirby, D. F. (1986b). The unit approach to curriculum planning for the gifted. *G/C/T, 9*(2), 27–31.

Meeker, M. (1984). *The structure of intellect: Its interpretation and uses*. Los Angeles: Western Psychological Services.

Renzulli, J. S. (1977). *The enrichment triad model: A guide for developing defensible programs for the gifted and talented*. Wethersfield, CT: Creative Learning.

Roedell, W. C. (1986). Socioemotional vulnerabilities of young gifted children. In J. R. Whitmore (Ed.), *Intellectual giftedness in young children: Recognition and development*. New York: Haworth.

Roedell, W. C., Jackson, N. E., & Robinson, H. B. (1980). *Gifted young children*. New York: Teachers College Press.

Silverman, L. K. (in press). What happens to the gifted girl? In C. J. Maker (Ed.), *Critical issues in gifted education*. Rockville, MD: Aspen.

Taylor, C. W. (1968). Multiple talent approach. *The Instructor, 77*(8), 27, 142, 144, 146.

Torrance, E. P. (1981). *Thinking creatively in action and movement*. Bensenville, IL: Scholastic Testing Service.

Vantassel-Baska, J., Schuler, A., & Lipschutz, J. (1982). An experimental program for gifted four year olds. *Journal for the Education of the Gifted, 5*(1), 45–55.

Whitmore, J. R. (1979). The etiology of underachievement in highly gifted young children. *Journal for the Education of the Gifted, 3*(1), 38–51.

Whitmore, J. R. (1980). *Giftedness, conflict, and underachievement*. Boston: Allyn & Bacon.

Whitmore, J. R. (Ed.). (in press). *Intellectual giftedness in young children: Recognition and development*. New York: Haworth.

MARGIE K. KITANO
New Mexico State University

GIFTED CHILDREN
GIFTED CHILDREN, MINORITIES
GIFTED CHILDREN, UNDERACHIEVEMENT

PRESCHOOL ASSESSMENT

Preschool assessment has been conceptualized as a "continuous, general-to-specific process of defining functional capabilities and establishing treatment goals" (Bagnato & Neisworth, 1981, p. 7) for children between the ages of 3 and 6 years. Broadly conceived, the process is carried out for the purpose of determining eligibility for services, obtaining information for individual program development, and evaluating program effectiveness (Neisworth et al., 1980). With these as broadly based goals, preschool assessment encompasses screening procedures, but it also involves in-depth and comprehensive analyses of developmental strengths and weaknesses, the setting of instructional goals, and the evaluation of progress made by a child within a particular intervention plan.

To accomplish these purposes effectively, preschool assessment is comprised of multidimensional processes. It involves the synthesis of developmental information from multiple measures and sources and across multiple domains that include cognitive, social, language, motor, and adaptive behavior areas. The emphasis on multidimensionality is essential at the preschool level because of the lack of reliability of global scores and assessment devices for children undergoing rapid behavioral and developmental change.

Related to the concept of multidimensionality is the ecological validity of preschool assessment procedures. To be ecologically valid, the procedures must sample behavior and developmental skills as they are exhibited in a number of different environments at multiple points in time (Paget & Nagle, 1986). This emphasis implies that (1) a preschool child's functioning is assessed in an individual examining situation, as well as in the home, and when appropriate, in the classroom environment; (2) professionals who assess preschool-age children must be knowledgeable about a variety of assessment devices and be able to apply them adaptively in various situations to answer specific referral problems; (3) a multidisciplinary perspective on referral problems is necessary, both from legal and ethical vantage points; (4) such a perspective may produce incongruence among the results, which is important to correct interpretation; and (5) a longer time frame is needed than for assessment of older children to tap variations in performance at multiple points in time (Lidz, 1983; Paget, 1985). Moreover, ecologically valid assessment at the preschool level depends as much on nontest-based assessment as on test-based assessment (Barnett, 1984). Thus the results from norm-referenced and criterion-referenced instruments are important but must be supplemented by behavioral observation and interview procedures.

Norm-referenced preschool measures typically yield developmental age and standard scores that represent the child's most stable level of skill development (Bagnato & Neisworth, 1981). A profile of strengths and weaknesses across developmental domain areas is also provided by these instruments. The standard scores are sometimes termed IQ scores (e.g., from the Wechsler Preschool and Primary Scale of Intelligence and the Stanford-Binet), but they have also been given alternative designations (e.g., the Mental Processing Index from the Kaufman Assessment Battery for Children and the General Cognitive Index from the McCarthy Scales of Children's Abilities). Regardless of the label used, the global standard scores are considered to represent a construct that is similar, yet different from, later IQ scores (McCarthy, 1972). Thus, the power of these instruments to predict later IQ and school achievement is an important practical and research issue. Given this issue, all normative comparisons made at the preschool level must be made with an understanding of the influence of behavioral variation on the scores.

Criterion-referenced measures provide the opportunity for task analysis, or the specific breakdown of skills that precede or follow the skills from norm-referenced tests. Thus criterion-referenced tests are important to the identification of partially developed and emerging skills that characterize young, rapidly developing children (Barnett, 1984). This process of task analysis also lends itself to the identification of processes and strategies used by a child to solve problems and master skills. This procedure assists in the translation of assessment results to instructional strategies. Practical guidelines for the translation of results from criterion-referenced measures to intervention strategies are provided by Bagnato & Neisworth (1981).

Balancing formal testing procedures with informal "testing the limits" procedures and "test-teach-test" approaches is also essential at the preschool level. Advocates of this approach, termed dynamic assessment (Lidz, 1983) or adaptive-process assessment (Bagnato & Neisworth, 1982), suggest a flexible yet systematic method of evaluating upper and lower limits of the child's ability to complete tasks. In particular, they stress the need to modify activities in a structured manner to compensate for a particular impairment and to allow for alternative response modes. Thus, this less formal approach combines testing and teaching as part of a single diagnostic process. Applying these procedures after the administration of tests in a standardized format provides a basis for comparing a preschool child's performance under standardized and adapted conditions.

Naturalistic observations and interview procedures comprise the cornerstone of nontest-based preschool assessment and provide information on the environmental influences that impact a preschool-age child. The Social Assessment Manual for Preschool Level (SAMPLE) (Greenwood, Todd, Walker, & Hops, 1979) is an example of a structured observation instrument that guides observation in a preschool classroom setting. The Home Observation for Measurement of the Environment (HOME) (Caldwell & Bradley, 1978) is an instrument for home observation. Additionally, there are numerous developmental checklists that structure analyses of developmental concerns from teachers and parents (Linder, 1983). Such procedures are essential in revealing adults' perceptions of a child's development, their teaching and coping strategies, belief systems, goals, and caregiving skills (Barnett, 1984).

Given the complexity of the preschool assessment process, it is clear that determining eligibility and establishing instructional objectives involve much more than the administration of a standard battery with one measure as the prime integral component. Similarly, the limitations of traditional test scores in evaluating program effectiveness have been enumerated (Keogh & Sheehan, 1981). Thus, numerous innovations are emerging; they include the Proportional Change Index (Wolery, 1983), the Intervention Efficiency Index (Bagnato & Neisworth, 1980), and adaptations of Goal Attainment Scaling (Schuster, et al., 1984).

REFERENCES

Bagnato, S. J., & Neisworth, J. T. (1980). The Intervention Efficiency Index: An approach to preschool program accountability. *Exceptional Children, 46,* 264–271.

Bagnato, S. J., & Neisworth, J. T. (1981). *Linking developmental assessment and curricula.* Rockville, MD: Aspen Systems.

Barnett, D. W. (1984). An organizational approach to preschool services: Psychological screening, assessment, and intervention. In C. Maher, R. Illback, & J. Zins (Eds.), *Organizational psychology in the schools: A handbook for practitioners* (53–82). Springfield, IL: Thomas.

Caldwell, B. W., & Bradley, R. H. (1978). *Home Observation for Measurement of the Environment.* Little Rock, AR: University of Arkansas.

Greenwood, C. R., Walker, H. M., Todd, N. M., & Hops, H. (1979). Selecting a cost-effective screening device for the assessment of preschool social withdrawal. *Journal of Applied Behavioral Analysis, 12,* 639–652.

Keogh, B., & Sheehan, R. (1981). The use of developmental test data for documenting handicapped children's progress: Problems and recommendations. *Journal of the Division for Early Childhood, 3,* 42–47.

Lidz, C. S. (1983). Dynamic assessment and the preschool child. *Journal of Psychoeducational Assessment, 1,* 59–72.

Linder, T. W. (1983). *Early childhood special education: Program development and administration.* Baltimore, MD: Brookes.

McCarthy, D. (1972). *Manual for the McCarthy Scales of Children's Abilities.* New York: Psychological Corporation.

Neisworth, J. T., Willoughby-Herb, S., Bagnato, S. J., Cartwright, C. A., & Laub, K. W. (1980). *Individualized education for preschool exceptional children.* Germantown, MD: Aspen Systems.

Page, K. D. (1985). Preschool services in the schools: Issues and implications. *Special Services in the Schools, 2,* 3–25

Paget, K. D., & Nagle, R. J. (1986). A conceptual model of preschool assessment. *School Psychology Review, 15,* 154–165 (See additional references on)

KATHLEEN D. PAGET
University of South Carolina

PRESCHOOL SCREENING
PRESCHOOL SPECIAL EDUCATION

PRESCHOOL SCREENING

Preschool screening is the evaluation of large groups of children 3 to 5 years of age with brief, low-cost procedures to identify those who may be at risk for later problems. It is based on the assumptions that early intervention should produce a significant positive effect on development, that children with developmental problems must be identified accurately as their problems are developing, and that early identification and intervention programs should be implemented without prohibitively high costs (Lichtenstein & Ireton, 1984). While also used frequently in the field of medicine, screening in special education and related fields refers to the early identification of risk factors associated with later school achievement and social adjustment. Because of the complexity of outcomes from many early childhood health problems such as otitis media (Mandell & Johnson, 1984), screening approaches that

draw from several disciplines are considered the most comprehensive (Elder & Magrab, 1980).

Historically, several movements and philosophies from various disciplines have been associated with preschool screening and have defined its methods and purposes. These movements include the early enrichment and compensatory education programs (e.g., Head Start); the Early and Periodic Screening, Diagnosis, and Treatment (EPSDT) program designed to focus on medically oriented services for children with developmental handicaps or neurological impairment; and the Education for All Handicapped Children Act (PL 94-142), which included "child find" provisions and mandated a broad range of special educational and related services for handicapped children in schools.

Preschool screening can be seen as a continuum of opportunities available any time in a child's early development. Within this larger conceptual context, procedures can be initiated before the child's birth, with the identification of mothers who possess characteristics linked with developmental or learning problems (e.g., genetic defects, maternal illness, high maternal age, exposure to drugs, toxins, and radiation, and poor maternal health or nutrition during pregnancy). Factors occurring at birth or shortly thereafter can also impact a child's later development. These include anoxia, birth injury, low birth weight, and physical or sensory defects. Because some infants with known risk factors show no early signs of disability, have mild impairments, or exhibit developmental delay falling within the boundaries of normal functioning, the establishment of registries for periodic rescreening has been suggested as a strategy for identifying and monitoring the progress of these hard-to-detect children (Lloyd, 1976).

Screening activities constitute the first stage of a longer assessment process. Other stages include readiness, diagnosis, instructional-related assessment, evaluation of the results of instruction, and program evaluation (Boehm & Sandberg, 1982). Screening is sometimes confused with readiness, which focuses on a child's preparedness to benefit from a specific academic program (Meisels, 1980). All stages of the assessment process comprise a sequence proceeding from general to specific, culminating with individualized programming and ongoing monitoring of the child's progress within the intervention program (Bagnato & Neisworth, 1981). As the first stage of this process, screening does not comprise diagnostic procedures leading to recommendations about instructional programming. Rather, it involves general decision making that differentiates children in need of further assessment. This must be done with the knowledge that most screening instruments do not meet the requirements of PL 94-142 for educational placement. When done with proper understanding of its major purpose and the limitations of screening instruments, screening can enhance a school's or district's ability to identify and serve handicapped preschoolers. If used to substitute for comprehensive individual examinations, it can lead to major errors in identification and educational programming (Reynolds & Clark, 1983).

Screening can be conceptualized as a process consisting of two components (Lichtenstein & Ireton, 1984). The first component, outreach, involves initial contact with parents, professionals, preschool centers, and community agencies to inform them about the services offered and to arrange for children to participate in the screening program. Other terms used to refer to this initial location of children are "child find" (Meisels, 1980), from the provisions of PL 94-142, and "case finding" (Barnes, 1982; Harrington, 1984). The major goals are to locate a target population and to maximize attendance at the actual screenings. To these ends, it has been recommended (Zehrback, 1975) that outreach procedures emphasize the growth-related needs of all children instead of developmental impairments. Thus strong case finding and publicity efforts are essential so that services will be rendered to all families rather than only those families who have the sophistication to find out about them. (Crocker & Cushna, 1976).

An approach designed to maximize correct identification within the target population is mass screening. This refers to a program that has the goal of screening every child in the target population. Such a program serves an entire preschool population; hence, there is little stigma associated with parents' positive response to the offer of screening services. Selective screening, a variation of mass screening, provides services to particular demographic subgroups or geographic areas that have a large number of unidentified children with special needs.

The second component of the screening process consists of the assessment of those children found eligible, the synthesis of information, and the determination of need for further assessment. Generally, the structure of this component is based on: (1) the kinds of questions that need to be answered; (2) the types and severity of handicapping conditions to be assessed; (3) the ages of the children; and (4) the psychometric properties of available instruments (Harrington, 1984; Scott & Hogan, 1982). Specifically, screening activities should answer whether the child is delayed enough in one or more domains (cognitive, sensory, motor, social/emotional, speech, language) to be considered at risk and in need of further diagnosis. If so, the screening should provide direction regarding what types of diagnostic assessments are needed to confirm or refute the screening impressions (Horowitz, 1982). The handicapping conditions should have a prevalence rate high enough to justify screening large numbers of children but not so high that every child must receive a diagnostic evaluation. Also, instruments should be chosen that have been normed on the ages of children represented in the target population and that have good reliability and validity. The precision of screening instruments is not as crucial as that of diagnostic instruments because of the general nature of the decisions made from them. A review of various

screening systems and instruments, their psychometric properties, and their usefulness is provided by Buros (1985), Harrington (1984), and Lichtenstein and Ireton (1984). Although group and individually administered instruments are reviewed in these sources, it should be realized that individual administration maximizes the validity of test results with preschool-age children (Reynolds & Clark, 1983).

With respect to the psychometric properties of screening instruments, reliability and validity are often reported in correlational terms. These correlations provide only an approximation of a measure's accuracy in assigning individuals for further assessment (Lichtenstein, 1981). Thus a more strongly recommended method of determining a screening instrument's psychometric adequacy is in terms of classificational outcomes. In this way, validity is measured by comparing the screening decision (whether or not to refer a child for further evaluation) with the child's actual status as determined by a criterion measure. This is called the hit rate method (Lichtenstein & Ireton, 1984) and provides a direct indication of the suitability of decisions from screening. The validity of an entire screening system rests on correct understanding of the problem to be identified (the base rate), the rate of referrals for further assessment (the referral rate), and the hit rate (the percentage of children identified as needing services).

Generally, screening outcomes can be organized into screening positives (children regarded as high risk and referred for further assessment) and screening negatives (children regarded as low risk and not referred). For each child screened, four results are possible, based on the accuracy of the screening decision and the child's actual performance on criterion measures during a diagnostic evaluation. A child may be found to be in need of special services and referred by the screening procedures, or a child may be found to not need additional help. Given the possibility of error in screening decisions, however, a child may be referred by the screening procedure but not need special services (a false positive or overreferral error), or not referred but be in need of services (a false negative or underreferral error). To evaluate the consequences of using a given screening system, then, it must be determined whether children are referred at the rate intended, whether the right children are referred, and whether alternative procedures might accomplish the task more successfully. Other relevant issues are the appropriateness of the criterion measures used, the possibility of bias in the screening process (Reynolds & Clark, 1983), and strategies for maximizing parent involvement.

Given the long-held recognition that parents are vitally important in meeting the educational needs of their children, they should be involved in every phase of screening (Lichtenstein & Ireton, 1984). Not only is parent involvement mandated by PL 94-142, but parents also constitute a rich source of information about specific aspects of their child's development that may be unavailable elsewhere.

A range of formal and informal techniques are available for gathering parental information. Two examples of formal techniques are the Denver Prescreening Developmental Questionnaire (PDQ) (Frankenburg, van Doornick, Liddell, & Dick, 1976) and the Home Screening Questionnaire (HSQ) (Coons, et al., 1981). The screening of environmental influences from home and classroom settings is a rapidly growing area of research and clinical attention (Adelman, 1982).

REFERENCES

Adelman, H. S. (1982). Identifying learning problems at an early age: A critical appraisal. *Journal of Clinical Child Psychology, 11,* 255–261.

Bagnato, S. J., & Neisworth, J. T. (1981). *Linking developmental assessment and curricula.* Rockville, MD: Aspen Systems.

Barnes, K. E. (1982). *Preschool screening: The measurement and prediction of children at-risk.* Springfield, IL: Thomas.

Boehm, A., & Sandberg, B. (1982). Assessment of the preschool child. In C. R. Reynolds & T. B. Gutkin (Eds.), *Handbook of school psychology* (82–120). New York: Wiley.

Buros, O. K. (Ed.). (1985). *The ninth mental measurements yearbook.* Highland Park, NJ: Gryphon.

Coons, C. E., Gay, E. C., Fandal, A. W., Ker, C., & Frankenburg, W. K. (1981). *The Home Screening Questionnaire.* Denver, CO: Ladoca.

Crocker, H. C., & Cushna, B. (1976). Ethical considerations and attitudes in the field of developmental disorders. In R. B. Johnson & P. R. Magrab (Eds.), *Developmental disorders.* Baltimore, MD: University Park Press.

Elder, J. O., & Magrab, P. R. (1980). *Coordinating services to handicapped children.* Baltimore, MD: Brookes.

Frankenburg, W. K., van Doornick, W. J., Liddell, R. N., & Dick, N. P. (1976). The Denver Prescreening Developmental Questionnaire. *Pediatrics, 57,* 744–753.

Harrington, R. (1984). Preschool screening: The school psychologist's perspective. *School Psychology Review, 13,* 363–374.

Horowitz, F. D. (1982). Methods of assessment for high risk and handicapped infants. In C. T. Ramey & P. L. Trohanis (Eds.), *Finding and educating high risk and handicapped infants.* Baltimore, MD: University Park Press.

Lichtenstein, R. (1981). Comparative validity of two preschool screening tests: Correlational and classificational approaches. *Journal of Learning Disabilities, 14,* 68–73.

Lichtenstein, R., & Ireton, H. (1984). *Preschool screening.* Orlando, FL: Grune & Stratton.

Lloyd, L. L. (1976). Discussant's comments: Language and communication aspects. In T. D. Tjossem (Ed.), *Intervention strategies for high risk infants and children* (199–212). Baltimore, MD: University Park Press.

Mandell, C. J., & Johnson, R. A. (1984). Screening for otitis media: Issues and procedural recommendations. *Journal of the Division of Early Childhood, 8,* 86–93.

Meisels, S. J. (1980). *Developmental screening in early childhood: A guide.* Washington, DC: National Association for the Education of Young Children.

Reynolds, C. R., & Clark, J. (1983). Assessment of cognitive abilities. In K. D. Paget & B. A. Bracken (Eds.), *The psychoeducational assessment of preschool children* (163–189). New York: Grune & Stratton.

Scott, G., & Hogan, A. E. (1982). Methods for the identification of high-risk and handicapped infants. In C. T. Ramey & P. L. Trohanis (Eds.), *Finding and educating high-risk and handicapped infants.* Baltimore, MD: University Park Press.

Zehrback, R. R. (1975). Determining a preschool handicapped population. *Exceptional Children, 42,* 76–83.

KATHLEEN D. PAGET
J. MICHAEL COXE
University of South Carolina

HEAD START
HEAD START FOR THE HANDICAPPED
PRESCHOOL ASSESSMENT
PRESCHOOL SPECIAL EDUCATION

PRESCHOOL SPECIAL EDUCATION

Preschool special education is the delivery of therapeutic and educational services to handicapped infants and children from birth to age 6. These services are designed to provide optimum learning experiences during the crucial early childhood developmental period for children with a wide variety of handicapping conditions. The importance of the preschool years to future success has been documented by many child development authorities, who emphasize that the first 5 or 6 years of a child's life are the periods of highest potential growth in physical, perceptual, linguistic, cognitive, and affective areas (Lerner, Mardell-Czudnowski, & Goldenberg, 1981). These early periods of development are particularly important to the handicapped child, since the earlier that these children are identified and education begun, the greater the chances of lessening the impact of the handicapping condition on the child and society. A recent report by the House Select Committee on Children, Youth, and Families (1985) stated that for every dollar invested in preschool special education programs, there is a $3 reduction in special education cost later. In addition, programs for handicapped infants can save as much as $16,078 per child in education costs over the course of a school career.

In 1968 Congress recognized the need for services and models of effective preschool special education programs, and the Handicapped Children's Early Education Assistance Programs (HCEEP; PL 90-583) was enacted. This act, sometimes known as the First Chance program, provided monies for the development and implementation of experimental projects for young handicapped children and their families. These projects developed effective programs for children, but they also were required to include parents in the activities, operate in-service training, evaluate the progress of both the children and the programs, coordinate their activities with the public schools and other agencies, and disseminate information on the projects (DeWeerd, 1977). The HCEEP continues to support new early education programs, and many of the materials and models used in programs across the country were originally developed with HCEEP support.

The Head Start movement, which began in 1964 as part of the War on Poverty and was funded by the Office of Economic Opportunity, was another reason for the growth of preschool special education programs. The goal of the Head Start program was to offer preschool children from economically deprived homes a comprehensive program to compensate for their deprivation. These programs involved medical care, nutrition, parent involvement, socialization, and educational intervention. The Head Start legislation, amended in 1972 and 1974 by PL 92-924 and PL 93-644, required all Head Start programs to include handicapped children as a minimum of 10% of their enrollment (Hayden & Gotts, 1977).

A further influence on preschool special education was the passage and implementation of PL 94-142, the Education for All Handicapped Children Act of 1975, which mandated services for all handicapped children from 3 to 5 years of age unless such a mandate conflicted with state law. This legislation provided the following two sources of funds for handicapped preschool children: state entitlement money, which depends on the number of handicapped children counted by the state in its child-find activities; and incentive grants, available to states with approved state plans that offer services for 3- to 5-year-old handicapped children (Lerner et al., 1981).

Despite all the federal support, the current commitments for early intervention vary from state to state based on combinations of mandatory and permissive legislation, rules, regulations, and practice (Swan, 1981). There are still many states that are not providing preschool special education. As of 1979, 27 states had mandated legislation for preschool special education for handicapped children from ages 3 to 5, and 10 states had legislation for children starting at birth (Hayden, 1979).

One of the important areas in preschool special education is the early identification of children with handicapping conditions. Attempts are being made to locate children who will need additional or special assistance in order to succeed in school because of physical, social, intellectual, emotional, or communications problems. The federal child-find program, which mandates states to actively seek out handicapped children, is one way to locate children who can benefit from early intervention services. Identifying children who should receive special services is a complex task because of the wide variety of needs and characteristics of the children (Lerner et al., 1981). Children with severe handicapping conditions are often identified at birth or shortly thereafter; however, many children with milder or less obvious handicaps are not so easily identified. Tjossem (1976) has presented three categories of high-risk infants. First, there are those at established risk; they have diagnosed medical disorders that are known to result in developmental delays. The early medical, social, and educational interventions used with these children are designed to help them function at the higher end of potential for those with their disorders. Second, children at biological risk have a history that suggests biological insults to their developing central nervous system. While early diagnosis is often inconclusive for these children, close monitoring and modified care are important during the developmental years. Third, children at environmental risk are those who are biologically sound, but who have early life experiences, that, without intervention, have high probability for resulting in delayed development. These early experiences could include problems with maternal and family care, health care, and opportunities for expression and stimulation. These three categories are not mutually exclusive, and when they interact, they increase the probability of abnormal development.

Being identified and placed into preschool intervention programs is a difficult process for many handicapped young children. However, for early intervention to be effective, provisions must be made for early identification and rapid entrance into community preschool special education programs (Tjossem, 1976). This identification process begins with both medical and educational screening to locate children at high risk for developmental and learning problems. Three comprehensive screening tests used in this process are the Denver Developmental Screening Test, Developmental Indicators for the Assessment of Learning, and the Developmental Screening Inventory. Once these children have been identified, the next step, a comprehensive diagnostic assessment, can be done to pinpoint a child's particular skills and deficits. The purpose of this assessment should be to prepare appropriate intervention programs. It is critical to match the assessment techniques to the needs of the individual child (Hayden & Edgar, 1977). Two criterion-referenced tests that can be used for diagnosis and program planning for many children with handicaps, in many curriculum areas, are the Brigance Diagnostic Inventory of Early Development and the Learning Accomplishment Profile Diagnostic Assessment Kit. Detailed descriptions of screening instruments and diagnostic tests can be found in Lerner et al. (1981), Fallen and McGovern (1978), Safford (1978), and Salvia and Ysseldyke (1985). This assessment of handicapped children requires the expertise of many professionals and needs to be a team effort.

Identifying, screening, and assessing handicapped preschool children are meaningless tasks unless appropriate services are then provided to them (Hobbs, 1975). Once the child has been identified and diagnostic information is complete, then an appropriate program plan and curriculum must be developed. There are many different program delivery models that can be used, as well as a wide variety of philosophical bases for the programs.

Preschool special education programs have evolved from many varied theoretical positions, ranging from a child development model to precision teaching and systematic instruction. These approaches may be used with different populations, or in different environments, but they have all been shown to be beneficial. The child development model is mainly an enrichment model that provides multiple activity centers such as often found in many regular preschool programs. This is the model that many Head Start programs follow, and it is most successful with children with mild handicapping conditions. The sensory-cognitive model is based on the work of Maria Montessori. It emphasizes materials designed for the child's developmental level; these materials are presented in a carefully constructed environment. Other programs are based on the verbal-cognitive model, which draws heavily from the developmental theory of Piaget and stresses structured teacher-child interactions. A more formal approach was proposed by Bereiter and Englemann in their verbal-didactic model; this approach attempts to raise each child to the essential level for success in first grade by frequent repetition of teacher-child responses accompanied by the principles of reinforcement (Ackerman & Moore, 1976). Severely handicapped children often benefit from highly structured systematic instruction programs that rely on detailed task analysis and behavioral theory.

Other factors to be considered include the type of handicapping condition, the age of the child, and the geographical area to be served. Some programs are noncategorical and serve children from a wide variety of handicapping conditions; the Portage Project and the Rutland Center are examples. Other programs specialize in serving children from limited categories or even subcategories of handicapping conditions. One of the best known programs of this type is the Seattle Model Preschool Center for children with Down's syndrome.

The age of the child often affects where the educational services are delivered; since it is difficult to transport infants for long distances, many of the programs for younger children are home-based, with the teacher traveling to the students. As the child becomes older, programs may be center-based, with the child attending a school program or a combination of home and school program. Another factor that affects where programs are delivered is the geographic region. Sparsely populated rural regions may not have sufficient numbers of children within a reasonable distance of a school; therefore, they may rely on more home-based services than might be found in large urban areas. Examples of home-based projects are the Portage project, the Marshalltown project, and Project SKI*HI; the Precise Early Education of Children with Handicaps (PEECH) project, the Chapel Hill project, and the Mag-

nolia Preschool are all combined home- and center-based programs. Center-based programs include the Rutland Center, the Seattle Model Preschool Center, and the UNISTAPS project. These programs were all originally supported by HCEEP funding and are representative of many programs across the United States (Karnes & Zehrbach, 1977).

The actual curriculum content in preschool special education programs varies depending on the needs of the children; however, in most cases, the programs are based on one or more of the following approaches. Some preschool special education curricula are organized around an amelioration of deficits approach, which builds the curriculum based on an assessment of a child's problems; the content areas are directed toward correcting identified deficits. Other programs use a basic skills area approach. In this, curricula are organized around skills or processes such as attention, language, sensory motor processes, social skills, perception, auditory processes, gross and fine motor skills, self-help skills, and memory. The developmental tasks approach uses sequences of normal development to derive the curricula. The content areas in this approach are broad categories of child development that are task analyzed and sequenced. Finally, the educational content approach begins with areas of academic content; it defines areas of learning on the basis of preacademic or academic content. The most often included areas are prereading, numbers, music, art, dance, play, storytelling, social studies, and nature. In many cases these various approaches are combined to develop appropriate educational programs (Wood & Hurley, 1977).

A crucial component to any preschool special education program is parent involvement. As stated by Shearer & Shearer (1977), there are several reasons to involve parents in their child's education. The parents are the consumers and often want to participate in the education of their children. When parents are taught how to teach their children, they can help transfer what is being learned in school to the home environment. These teaching skills can also be used in new situations, and with the handicapped child's siblings, making the parents better teachers of all their children. Research has shown that significant gains made by children are often lost when the school programs end. A key factor in preventing this is the effective involvement of parents. In addition, if parents are knowledgeable about their child's program, they can be advocates for the services that the child needs; this skill can be used all through the child's life.

Recent research studies have demonstrated the effectiveness of preschool special education programs for handicapped young children. Karnes et al. (1981) presented a review of many studies that examined the efficacy of preschool special education. While there are some methodological questions about early studies by Skeels and Dye, the research, in general, has shown that early stimulation and preschool attendance make a significant difference in the rate of growth of children, and that these gains are maintained over time. In addition, it has been shown that diverse curriculum models can be equally effective in promoting school success if high standards of quality are maintained (Schweinhart & Weikart, 1981).

A longitudinal study of the Perry Preschool Program (Schweinhart & Weikart, 1981) has provided a strong argument for preschool special education programs. This study followed 123 children from age three through the school years. It found that those children who attended preschool had consistently higher school achievement, higher motivation, fewer placements in special education programs, and less delinquent behavior. An economic benefit-cost effectiveness analysis of the Perry Preschool Program was conducted; it found that there was a 248% return on the original investment when savings from lowered costs for education, benefits from increases in projected earnings, and value of mothers' time released when the child attended preschool were considered.

There are many reports of successful preschool special education programs. While many of these programs differ greatly in the populations they serve, their theoretical bases, and their curriculum content, their effectiveness has been demonstrated. It is essential that these benefits be recognized, and that programs for all handicapped preschool children be supported.

REFERENCES

Ackerman, P., & Moore, M. (1976). Delivery of educational services to preschool handicapped children. In T. Tjossem (Ed.), *Intervention strategies for high risk infants and young children* (pp. 669–689). Baltimore, MD: University Park Press.

DeWeerd, J. (1977). Introduction. In J. Jordan, A. Hayden, M. Karnes, & M. Wood (Eds.), *Early childhood education for exceptional children* (pp. 2–7). Reston, VA: Council for Exceptional Children.

Fallen, N., & McGovern, J. (1978). *Young children with special needs.* Columbus, OH: Merrill.

Hayden, A. (1979). Handicapped children, birth to age three. *Exceptional Children, 45,* 510–517.

Hayden, A., & Edgar, E. (1977). Identification, screening, and assessment. In J. Jordan, A. Hayden, M. Karnes, & M. Wood (Eds.), *Early childhood education for exceptional children* (pp. 66–93). Reston, VA: Council for Exceptional Children.

Hayden, A., & Gotts, E. (1977). Multiple staffing patterns. In J. Jordan, A. Hayden, M. Karnes, & M. Wood (Eds.), *Early childhood education for exceptional children* (pp. 236–253). Reston, VA: Council for Exceptional Children.

Hobbs, N. (1975). *The futures of children.* San Francisco: Jossey-Bass.

Karnes, M., Schwedel, A., Lewis, G., & Esry, D. (1981). Impact of early programming for the handicapped: A follow-up study into the elementary school. *Journal of the Division for Early Childhood, 4,* 62–79.

Karnes, M., & Zehrbach, R. (1977). Alternative models for delivering services to young handicapped children. In J. Jordan, A. Hayden, M. Karnes, & M. Wood (Eds.), *Early childhood education for exceptional children* (pp. 20–65). Reston, VA: Council for Exceptional Children.

Lerner, J., Mardell-Czudnowski, C., & Goldenberg, D. (1981). *Special education for the early childhood years.* Englewood Cliffs, NJ: Prentice-Hall.

Safford, P. (1978). *Teaching young children with special needs.* St. Louis, Mosby.

Salvia, J., & Ysseldyke, J. (1985). *Assessment in special and remedial education* (3rd ed.). Boston: Houghton Mifflin.

Schweinhart, L., & Weikart, D. (1981). Effects of the Perry Preschool Program on youths through age 15. *Journal of the Division for Early Childhood, 4,* 29–39.

Select Committee on Children, Youth, and Families. (1985). *Opportunities for success: Cost effective programs for children.* Washington, DC: U.S. Government Printing Office.

Shearer, M., & Shearer, D. (1977). Parent involvement. In J. Jordan, A. Hayden, M. Karnes, & M. Wood (Eds.), *Early childhood education for exceptional children* (pp. 208–235). Reston, VA: Council for Exceptional Children.

Swan, W. (1981). Efficacy studies in early childhood special education: An overview. *Journal of the Division for Early Childhood, 4,* 1–4.

Tjossem, T. (1976). Early intervention: Issues and approaches. In T. Tjossem (Ed.), *Intervention strategies for high risk infants and young children* (pp. 3–33). Baltimore, MD: University Park Press.

Wood, M., & Hurley, O. (1977). Curriculum and instruction. In J. Jordan, A. Hayden, M. Karnes, & M. Wood (Eds.), *Early childhood education for exceptional children* (pp. 132–157). Reston: VA: Council for Exceptional Children.

DEBORAH C. MAY
*State University of New York,
Albany*

PRESCHOOL ASSESSMENT
PRESCHOOL SCREENING

PRESIDENT'S COMMITTEE ON MENTAL RETARDATION (PCMR)

The President's Committee on Mental Retardation (PCMR) is a federal agency that acts as advocate for the mentally retarded. Its interests are prevention, better services, the most unrestricted settings, public acceptance of the retarded, and full citizenship rights for this handicapped group. Through preparation of major resource documents and through national publicity, PCMR keeps the needs of the mentally retarded before agencies and people that can help them: the president, the public, federal and state agencies, and consumers and providers of services in the public and private sector. The PCMR reports regularly to the president, Cabinet members, agency officials, and legislators on the nation's progress in dealing with mentally retarded persons.

Inquiries to PCMR go to the Public Information Office. This office provides publications free of charge, on a single copy basis. Sample titles are *Mental Retardation and the Law; The Naive Offender;* and *International Directory of Mental Retardation Resources.*

JAMES BUTTON
*United States Department
of Education*

MENTAL RETARDATION

PREVENTION, PRIMARY

This term refers to efforts made to reduce the incidence or prevalence of handicapping conditions through the establishment of medical and social programs that attempt to change those conditions responsible for their development. During the past 30 years, several approaches have been emphasized that have resulted in significant progress in the prevention of handicapping conditions.

A number of programs have been developed to provide neonatal care for those children delivered at risk. Some of these programs have been effective in reducing various postnatal factors that result in retardation. For example, infant stimulation programs have been established in hospitals to facilitate the development of low-birth-weight or high-risk infants (Brown & Hepler, 1976). These programs use such measures as involving mothers in infant stimulation techniques, making infants in incubators more attractive to staff who interact with them by placing ribbons on them, and providing intensive follow-up services to both mothers and infants. These programs have been brief and the results somewhat time-limited, but they have resulted in increased attention to opportunities for preventive intervention models.

It is widely recognized that a small proportion of children are mentally retarded because of organic causes; the majority are retarded because of environmental and cultural deficiencies, poverty, and inadequate child-rearing approaches (Grossman, 1983). Massive social changes that address these causes must occur to achieve comprehensive prevention of mental retardation and other handicapping conditions.

The President's Committee on Mental Retardation set a goal of preventing the occurrence of 50% of all cases of mental retardation by the year 2000 (President's Committee on Mental Retardation, 1976). As a result, research has been done on virtually all known causes of mental retardation. Patton, Payne, and Beirne-Smith (1986) indicate that for each cause, a specific preventive measure has been found. The most fruitful approaches to prevention include carrier detection, prenatal monitoring, and

newborn screening. Combinations of these approaches appear to be more successful in preventing various handicapping conditions than the use of individual techniques (Sells & Bennett, 1977). Prevention is often approached within the framework of determining cause. The major causes appear to result from infections and intoxications, trauma or physical agents, disorders of metabolism and nutrition, gross brain disease, unknown prenatal influence, and chromosomal abnormalities (Grossman, 1983).

Preventive measures implemented during the preconception period can significantly reduce hereditary, innate, congenital, and other constitutional disorders. Adequate prenatal care and analysis for possible genetic disorders are two general approaches to prevention usually associated with the gestational period. Yet one out of every four women who gives birth in a hospital has never received prenatal care from a physician during her pregnancy (Koch & Koch, 1976). Anticipating potential problems that may occur at delivery can avert problems during the perinatal period. For example, anoxia (lack of oxygen to the brain that may cause mental retardation and other learning problems) is a condition that can be prevented (Kirk & Gallagher, 1979).

Environmental intervention, adequate nutrition, and avoidance of hazards constitute the bulk of preventive measures during the childhood period. For example, a high correlation between ingestion of lead in drinking water and mental retardation has been reported (Gearheart, 1980).

Blood-screening techniques can be used to identify some conditions (e.g., Tay-Sachs disease) transmitted through autosomal recessive genes or x-linked genes. Using several screening procedures, Thoene et al. (1981) identified seven metabolic disorders caused by an enzyme deficiency. Because of the low incidence rate of most conditions, carriers are so rare that general screening procedures would have to involve massive numbers of people to be effective (Westling, 1986). Thus genetic screening is most often used by those who have already had one child with a disorder or who are aware that the condition exists in their family.

Monitoring the fetus prior to birth has resulted in the identification of over 100 inherited disorders (Sells & Bennett, 1977). Amniocentesis (drawing some of the amniotic fluid surrounding the fetus for cellular examination) is used to detect three types of problems: those identified through the chromosomal structure, those identified through enzyme deficiencies, and neural tube defects. Milunsky (1976) indicated that women who are over 35, couples in which one parent is a balanced carrier of translocation, and couples who have already had one Down's syndrome child are the three groups that most frequently seek chromosomal analysis through amniocentesis. The use of fetoscopy permits the physician to insert a small tube through the mother's abdominal wall to examine parts of the fetus. This permits the determination of physical characteristics that may be useful in determining whether a disorder exists. Senography consists of the use of ultrasound waves to outline the fetus and identify structures indicative of handicapping conditions (e.g., spina bifada, microcephaly) through different densities. Rh incompatibility may be prevented through Rh gamma gloubulin injections for the Rh-negative mother after the birth of her first Rh-positive child or after a miscarriage.

Newborn screening tests permit the identification of many infants with inborn errors of metabolism (e.g., galactosemia, phenylketonuria). In some cases, mental retardation may be prevented by altering the diet (Carpenter, 1975). Hypothyroidism can also be detected through birth screening using the same blood samples used with phenylketonuria (Dussualt et al., 1975). Since some diagnostic indicators develop slowly during the first 6 months, the newborn screening should be followed with additional testing during later infant examinations.

Avoidance of certain substances (e.g., drugs, alcohol, X-rays) is the only current source of prevention for some disorders. Preconceptual vaccinations can fight some bacterial infections (e.g., rubella, syphilis). Yet it has been estimated that 25% of children, older girls, and young women in the United States are not protected against rubella (Gearheart, 1980). A Caesarean-section birth may be used with women who have a herpes virus at the time of delivery. Postnatal causes that can often be prevented include direct trauma to the head, cerebral hemorrhage, lesions on the brain, infections that cause conditions such as encephalitis and meningitis, and electric shock. Although controversy still surrounds the role that chronic malnutrition plays in mental development, there is evidence that it can result in a greater risk of infection and increased likelihood of disease from other agents (Westling, 1986).

REFERENCES

Brown, J., & Hepler, R. (1976). Care of the critically ill newborn. *American Journal of Nursing, 76,* 578–581.

Carpenter, D. G. (1975). Metabolic and transport anomalies. In C. H. Carter (Ed.), *Handbook of mental retardation syndromes* (3rd ed.). Springfield, IL: Thomas.

Dussault, H. H., Coulombe, P., Laberge, C., Letarte, J., Guyda, H., Khoury, K. (1975). Preliminary report on a mass screening program for neonatal hypothyroidism. *Journal of Pediatrics, 86,* 670–674.

Gearheart, B. R. (1980). *Special education for the 80s.* St. Louis: Mosby.

Grossman, H. J. (1983). *Classification in mental retardation.* Washington, DC: American Association on Mental Deficiency.

Kirk, S. A., & Gallagher, J. J. (1979). *Educating exceptional children* (3rd ed.). Dallas: Houghton Mifflin.

Koch, R., & Koch, J. H. (1976). We can do more to prevent the tragedy of retarded children. *Psychology Today, 107,* 88–93.

Milunsky, A. (1976). A prenatal diagnosis of genetic disorders. *New England Journal of Medicine, 295,* 377–380.

Patton, J. R., Payne, J. S., & Beirne-Smith, M. (1986). *Mental retardation* (2nd ed.). London: Merrill.

President's Committee on Mental Retardation. (1976). *Mental retardation: The known and the unknown.* Washington, DC: U.S. Government Printing Office.

Sells, C. J., & Bennett, F. C. (1977). Prevention of mental retardation: The role of medicine. *American Journal of Mental Deficiency, 82,* 117–129.

Thoene, J., Higgins, J., Krieger, I., Schmickel, R., & Weiss, L. (1981). Genetic screening for mental retardation in Michigan. *American Journal of Mental Deficiency, 85,* 335–340.

Westling, D. L. (1986). *Introduction to mental retardation.* Englewood Cliffs, NJ: Prentice-Hall.

LONNY W. MORROW
*Northeast Missouri State
University*

SUE ANN MORROW
*EDGE, Inc., Bradshaw,
Michigan*

GENETIC COUNSELING
INBORN ERRORS OF METABOLISM
PHENYLKETONURIA
PREMATURITY/PRETERM

PREVOCATIONAL SKILLS

Secondary handicapped students may have difficulty in learning vocational concepts because they have not mastered prerequisite basic skills that serve as the foundation for many vocational activities. Three areas closely related to vocational skills are reading skills such as vocabulary, comprehension, and the use of a glossary; mathematic skills such as time, measurement, and application of algorithms; communication skills, including listening, speaking, and writing.

Essential to learning vocational skills is a set of hands-on exploratory experiences that will help each individual to answer self-awareness questions and develop work values. Examples of hands-on experiences include setting up a printing press, practicing laboratory safety, and following directions. These prevocational hands-on activities help students to identify materials, tools, and processes, discover physical properties of materials, measure sizes and quantities, compute costs, and develop social skills (Phelps & Lutz, 1977).

A student's success in a vocational program is influenced by his or her readiness to participate. Readiness skills are often identified as prevocational knowledge and attitudes. Brolin and Kokaska (1979) identified three curriculum areas with 22 major competencies. The areas and skills are (1) daily living (i.e., managing family finances, caring for personal needs, and engaging in civic activities); (2) personal-social abilities (i.e., interpersonal relationships, problem solving, independence); (3) occupational guidance and preparation (i.e., knowing and exploring occupational possibilities, work habits, and behaviors; being able to seek, secure, and maintain satisfactory employment).

Several factors can be considered predictors of vocational development for handicapped individuals. These include achievement of basic academic skills, adaptive behavior, verbal manners and communication skills, performance on vocational checklists, and actual samples of work behavior (Forness, 1982). A closer look at these predictors indicates that assessing a handicapped individual's vocational potential be evaluating his or her academic and social skills within the context of a work-related situation is valuable. Skills learned in a classroom setting may not generalize when applied to work settings. One step toward achieving generalization of academic skills is to develop a technique to assess applied academic and social skills. Neff (1966) suggested four approaches to the evaluation of the work potential of handicapped individuals. They are the mental testing approach, the job analysis approach, the work sample approach, and the situational assessment approach.

REFERENCES

Brolin, D. E., & Kokaska, C. J. (1979). *Career education for handicapped children and youth.* Columbus, OH: Merrill.

Forness, S. R. (1982). Prevocational academic assessment of children and youth with learning and behavior problems. In K. P. Lynch, W. E. Kiernan, & J. A. Stark (Eds.), *Prevocational and vocational education for special needs youth.* Baltimore, MD: Brooks.

Neff, W. S. (1966). Problems of work evaluation. *Personnel and Guidance Journal of Mental Deficiency, 44,* 682–688.

Phelps, A. L., & Lutz, R. J. (1977). *Career exploration and preparation for the special needs learner.* Boston: Allyn & Bacon.

KAREN L. HARRELL
University of Georgia

VOCATIONAL EVALUATION
VOCATIONAL REHABILITATION
VOCATIONAL TRAINING OF THE HANDICAPPED

PRIMARY MENTAL ABILITIES TEST (PMA)

The Primary Mental Abilities Test (PMA; Thurstone & Thurstone, 1965) is a group-administered measure of both general intelligence and specific intellectual factors that the authors call primary mental abilities. In earlier versions of the PMA, six to eight primary mental abilities were identified. Subsequently, this number was reduced to the current five factors. There are six levels of the test (K–1, 2–4, 4–6, 6–9, 9–12, and adult). The adult test is identical to that for grades 9–12. No attempt was made to prepare adult norms, and no additional psychometric characteristics at the adult level are included in the documentation.

A description of the behaviors sampled by the five subtests of the PMA is provided by Salvia and Ysseldyke (1978). Verbal meaning assesses one's ability to derive meaning from words. Number facility assesses one's ability to work with numbers, to handle simple quantitative problems rapidly and accurately, and to understand and recognize quantitative differences. Reasoning requires a person to solve problems logically. Perceptual speed assesses quick and accurate recognition of similarities and differences in pictured objects or symbols. Spatial relationships assesses ability to visualize how parts of objects or figures fit together, what their relationships are, and what they look like when rotated in space. The presence of and emphasis given to each of the specific intellectual factors within the various levels reflect the judgment of the authors as to their relative importance within each grade level. Only one level (grades 4–6) includes all five factors; perceptual speed is omitted from levels 6–9 and 9–12 and reasoning is omitted from K–1 and 2–4.

The test has several technical limitations. Standardization of the scale was based only on geographic, age, and grade stratification; reliabilities of the subtests are not included for K–1 and are relatively low for the other levels (Salvia & Ysseldyke, 1978). The test-retest reliability estimates for total scores range between .83 and .95 and may be deemed satisfactory, while the reliability estimates for the levels vary considerably from one grade to another and frequently are too low to be used with confidence (Quereshi, 1972). As expected, the total score is superior to any of the subtest/factor scores in predicting grades in separate school subject areas (Milholland, 1965). The PMA was developed using techniques to demonstrate that there are several factors involved in intelligence and learning. Yet, the total score is superior to single factors in predicting achievement in any one subject area. This contradicts the theoretical underpinnings of the test itself.

Historically, the PMA occupied a prominent position in the development of cognitive tests. The original series, published between 1938 and 1941, was based on extensive factor analytic work and represented a major contribution to test construction. The high aspirations held for the PMA battery reflected in early reviews were never realized (Schutz, 1972). While the Thurstones continued to contribute to both multifactor science and technology after the PMA was commercially available, very little of this new knowledge and technology found its way back into subsequent PMA revisions. Thus the PMA soon became outstripped by competing tests in terms of technical quality and functional utility. Because of the technical superiority of other instruments assessing similar abilities, reviewers have questioned the continued use of the PMA (Quereshi, 1972; Schutz, 1972).

REFERENCES

Milholland, J. E. (1965). SRA Primary Mental Abilities, Revised. In O. K. Buros (Ed.), *The sixth mental measurements yearbook* (pp. 1048–1050). Highland Park, NJ: Gryphon.

Quereshi, M. Y. (1972). SRA Primary Mental Abilities (1962 ed.). In O. K. Buros (Ed.), *The seventh mental measurements yearbook* (pp. 1064–1066). Highland Park, NJ: Gryphon.

Salvia, J., & Ysseldyke, J. E. (1978). *Assessment in special and remedial education* (pp. 293–295). Boston: Houghton Mifflin.

Schutz, R. E. (1972). SRA Primary Mental Abilities (1962 ed.). In O. K. Buros (Ed.), *The seventh mental measurements yearbook* (pp. 1066–1068). Highland Park, NJ: Gryphon.

Thurstone, L., & Thurstone, T. (1965). *Primary Mental Abilities Test*. Chicago: Science Research.

JEFF LAURENT
THOMAS OAKLAND
University of Texas, Austin

PRIVATE SCHOOLS AND SPECIAL EDUCATION

Prior to the passage of the Education for All Handicapped Children Act of 1975 (PL 94-142), private schools that existed to provide services to handicapped children were mainly tuition-based, profit-making institutions that held the parents responsible for costs. With the passage of PL 94-142, it became the local education agency's responsibility to provide a free, appropriate, public education to all children regardless of severity of handicap.

Until 1977, handicapped children, especially those with severe handicapping conditions, had fewer, consistent options for receiving educational services. Although many school districts had developed programs, especially for the less severely handicapped, there were still areas of the United States where children remained at home without an education, were institutionalized without an education, or received private education at the parents' expense (Bajan & Susser, 1982).

After 1977, local education agencies began to quickly develop or expand their own programs to meet this new responsibility. There still remained those few students for whom appropriate services could not be provided, either because of the severity of their handicap or because of a lack of appropriate numbers of a specific handicapping condition within the local education agency. These are the students who were typically enrolled in private schools as of 1985. Public Law 94-142 also mandated that it was the local education agency's (LEA) responsibility to provide the tuition for those students that the LEA placed in private schools (McQuain, 1982). Although it is clear that the LEA must be responsible for paying the tuition for students who are in private placement as a result of LEA placement, it is unclear as to the responsibility for pay-

ment for those students who are in church-related or other private schools at the request of the parent or a social agency (Wylie, 1981). For example, if a child's handicapping condition necessitates placement in a residential school to provide education, the placement, including nonmedical care and room and board, becomes the responsibility of the LEA. If placement is for noneducational concerns, home or community problems, then the LEA is responsible only for the educational costs. It sometimes becomes extremely difficult to separate education from other needs (McQuain, 1982).

Some decisions have been made by the courts related to placement issues. A program must be state approved to receive tuition payments from the LEA (Grumet & Inkpen, 1982). If an appropriate program exists within the LEA for a child, the LEA will not be responsible for private tuition (McQuain, 1982). Parents are not entitled to reimbursement for tuition as a result of voluntary placement in nonapproved schools (Grumet & Inkpen, 1982), unless a clear case can be made that the program was appropriate and the LEA failed to take timely and appropriate action in evaluation or placement. The decision as to whether a child should attend a private school should involve the availability of an appropriate program in the LEA, the proximity of the program to home, the severity of the handicapping condition, and the provision of related services (Guarino, 1982). The LEA must ensure that all children in private placement receive the same rights and procedures that they would receive if in public placement (Grumet & Inkpen, 1982). Therefore, the LEA, in conjunction with the state education agency, has the responsibility to monitor the programs in the private sector.

Within the continuum of services concept, a private placement is seen as most restrictive because of the inability to mainstream. Therefore, being placed in a residential setting, a child must first receive the full benefit of opportunities provided within the LEA (Grumet & Inkpen, 1982). An excellent summary of the legal trends in financial responsibilities of LEAs was written by McQuain (1982).

Continued clarification of the law is needed in the area of provision of services on the premises of the private school. This area includes:

> authorization for the provision of services to private school handicapped children on the premises of the private school, use of public school personnel in private schools to deliver services, payment of wages to private school personnel for providing services in private schools outside their regular hours of duty, and loaning and use of equipment, acquired with federal funds, by private schools (Wylie, 1981, p. 50).

Audette (1982) described additional areas in which concerns must be addressed in the future. These include transportation, coordination of individual education plans, artificiality of environment of private placement, rising costs of placement, unanticipated placements, and due process issues.

REFERENCES

Audette, D. (1982). Private school placement: A local director's perspective. *Exceptional Children, 49*(3), 214–219.

Bajan, J. W., & Susser, P. L. (1982). Getting on with the education of handicapped children: A policy of partnership. *Exceptional Children, 49*(3), 208–212.

Grumet, L., & Inkpen, T. (1982). The education of children in private schools: A state agency's perspective. *Exceptional Children, 49*(3), 100–106.

Guarino, R. L. (1982). The education of handicapped children in private schools. *Exceptional Children, 49*(3), 198–199.

McQuain, S. (1982). Special education private placements: Financial responsibility under the law. *Journal of Educational Finance, 7*(4), 425–435.

Wylie, R. J. (1981). The handicapped child and private education. *Journal of Adventist Education, 8*(9), 35–36.

SUSANNE BLOUGH ABBOTT
Stamford, Connecticut

EDUCATION FOR ALL HANDICAPPED CHILDREN ACT OF 1975
MAGNET SCHOOLS
MAINSTREAMING

PRIVILEGED COMMUNICATION

Privileged communication is a legal term that is applied to the interactions between certain specific groups of professionals and their clients. Typically, these groups of professionals include physicians, lawyers, clergy, and psychologists. When an interaction between a professional and a client meets the criteria for being classified as privileged, such an interaction may not and should not be revealed to others, including the courts.

Privileged communication exists because courts and legislative bodies understand the need for certain types of professionals to allow their clients to interact freely without fear that what they say will later be a source of embarrassment or a source of evidence that may be used against them. For example, the clergy have argued strongly and successfully that their communications with people must be privileged and not revealed to anyone. Thus, when someone discloses to a clergyman that he or she has committed a crime, the goal is often to help the person through counseling rather than turn the person over to the police. If the criminal behavior later comes to light and the clergyman is called to testify in court, privileged communication can be used as a reason for not revealing the earlier confession. The clergy and other groups aruge that their ability to help others in the future would be impaired if they were forced to testify.

In the area of special education, it is unlikely that anyone, except possibly the school psychologist, would be able to use privileged communication as a way not to reveal what a student or parent has said to them. Although each state defines it differently, most educators have not been included in the groups that are entitled to invoke privileged communication. Typically, the only individuals who work in special education who can assure clients that communications will remain private are school psychologists who are licensed by the state as professional psychologists. This excludes virtually all school psychologists trained at a subdoctoral level. Most state statutes do not view communication between certified but unlicensed psychologists and their clients as privileged; thus, such communication must be disclosed in court when requested.

Even when an interaction is considered privileged communication, professionals may need to divulge what they have learned from a client if it is apparent that the client is a danger to himself or herself and others. According to the landmark court decision of *Tarasoff* v. *Regents of California* (1974), professionals must evaluate the harm that will result to the client if the information is revealed relative to the potential danger to society if the information is not revealed. According to the *Tarasoff* case:

> public policy favoring protection of the confidential character of patient-psychotherapist communication must yield to instances in which disclosure is essential to avert danger to others. The protective privilege ends where public peril begins. (p. 137)

Although the case concerned communication between a psychologist and a client, the logic can probably be applied to communications involving other groups of professionals.

In summary, privileged communication is a legal term that protects certain communications between professional groups and their clients. It does not apply to most individuals who work in educational settings. Thus it is a relatively safe assumption that communications between educators and students will have to be revealed in court if requested. The interested reader is referred to Reynolds, Gutkin, Elliott, and Witt (1984) for a more detailed discussion of the issues involved in privileged communication, confidentiality, and related topics.

REFERENCE

Reynolds, C. R., Gutkin, T. B., Elliott, S. N., & Witt, J. C. (1984). *School psychology: Essentials of theory and practice.* New York: Wiley.

JOSEPH C. WITT
Louisiana State University

CONFIDENTIALITY OF INFORMATION
PARENTS OF THE HANDICAPPED

PROBLEM SOLVING, CREATIVE

See CREATIVE PROBLEM SOLVING.

PROCEDUAL SAFEGUARDS

See DUE PROCESS.

PROCESS REMEDIATION

See REMEDIATION, DEFICIT-CENTERED MODELS OF.

PROCESS TRAINING

See ABILITY TRAINING.

PRODUCTION DEFICIENCY

Production deficiency is closely tied to mediation theory (Flavell, 1970). Mediation refers to the intervention of some process between the initial stimulating event and the final response (Reese & Lipsitt, 1970). Special education students are often unable to "mediate" or use other task-appropriate strategies as intermediate steps in the learning process (Torgersen, 1977). Such inability may be due to special education students being inactive learners lacking goal-directed motivation (Torgerson, 1977).

Additional research in this area has resulted in an alternative explanation to those previously mentioned; special education students' poor academic performance may reflect a production deficiency (Naron, 1978; Wong, 1980). A production deficiency suggests that a student may have the ability to use the mediation strategy or another strategy but fails to spontaneously and appropriately produce it (Wong, 1980). For these children, prompting and training in metacognition and related processes might prove helpful.

REFERENCES

Flavell, J. H. (1970). Developmental studies in mediated memory. In H. W. Reese & L. P. Lipsitt (Eds.), *Advances in child development and behavior.* New York: Academic.

Naron, N. K. (1978). Developmental changes in word attribute utilization for organization and retrieval in free recall. *Journal of Experimental Child Psychology, 25,* 279–297.

Reese, H. W., & Lipsitt, L. P. (1970). *Experimental child psychology.* New York: Academic.

Torgersen, J. K. (1977). The role of nonspecific factors in the task performance of learning disabled children: A theoretical assessment. *Journal of Learning Disabilities, 10,* 27–34.

Wong, B. Y. L. (1980). Activating the inactive learner: Use of questions/prompts to enhance comprehension and retention of implied information in learning disabled children. *Learning Disability Quarterly, 3,* 29–37.

JOHN R. BEATTIE
*University of North Carolina,
Charlotte*

MEDIATIONAL DEFICIENCY

PRO-ED, INC.

PRO-ED is a publishing company that deals in special and remedial education, counseling, rehabilitation, psychology, speech pathology, and audiology. The product line focuses on assessment materials, professional books, and monographs. In addition, PRO-ED publishes three journals: *Remedial and Special Education* (RASE), *Journal of Learning Disabilities* (JLD), and *Topics in Early Childhood Special Education* (TECSE). PRO-ED is a privately held corporation founded in 1977. In 1985 the company had approximately 500 active titles.

DONALD D. HAMMILL
PRO-ED, Inc., Austin, Texas

RASE
TECSE

PROFESSIONAL SCHOOL PSYCHOLOGY

Professional School Psychology is the official journal of Division 16 of the American Psychological Association. *Professional School Psychology* in intended as a forum to promote and maintain high standards of preparation for professional school psychologists and effective delivery of school psychological services. The journal publishes empirically and theoretically based papers intended to reflect a cross-section of school psychology and suitable for a broad readership. Papers that analyze, synthesize, reformulate, or offer an empirical or conceptual perspective to issues involving the underpinnings of the profession, the delivery and evaluation of services, ethical and legal aspects, and approaches to education and training are encouraged. Of special interest are articles that outline innovative professional procedures with rigorous, theoretical, and empirical support.

The type of manuscripts published in *Professional School Psychology* include theoretical pieces, literature reviews, models of professional practice, policy examinations, ethical/legal manuscripts, major addresses, interviews, proceedings from national or international conferences or symposiums, miniseries devoted to special topics in the field of school psychology, and reviews of books and materials. *Professional School Psychology* is published quarterly by Lawrence Erlbaum Associates.

THOMAS R. KRATOCHWILL
*University of Wisconsin,
Madison*

PROFESSIONAL STANDARDS FOR SPECIAL EDUCATORS

Professional standards for special educators are rules and guidelines governing the conduct of persons who work in special education. The development of competency standards is an attempt to increase the overall quality of service in the field and to strive for excellence in the profession. In 1966 the Council for Exceptional Children developed Professional Standards for Personnel in the Education of Exceptional Children. In 1979 the council approved Guidelines for Personnel in the Education of Exceptional Children. These standards did not include formal definable criteria for determining whether a teacher had acquired the necessary competencies. The most recent set of standards published by the council (*Exceptional Children*, 1983), consists of three policy statements focusing on common requirements for the practice of special education: Code of Ethics, Professional Practice, and Standards for the Preparation of Special Education Personnel. These statements describe the philosophical position of special education professionals, the skills the specialists should exhibit in their jobs, and how training organizations should best prepare future special educators.

The development of competency standards for special educators is important for a variety of reasons. One is to increase the consistency and quality of service across the special education field. Another is to require excellence so that it may translate into greater academic and social achievements for the handicapped students being served. Standards also serve as a way to measure the quality of performance of special educators. They help protect the profession from embracing techniques or skills that are based more on subjectivity than on empirical data. Heller (1983) suggested that if professionals in special education do not oversee themselves, someone else will.

Standards of professional competence for special educators describe expectations in two general categories of duties: those that are necessary for successful and ethical treatment of persons labeled with special needs, and those

that are necessary for the growth and stature of the field of special education. The specific details can be found in *Exceptional Children* (1983). Professionals have several obligations, including the use of their training to help those with special needs. Their methods must be appropriate and effective. Special educators must also use techniques to manage behavior that are ethical, humane, and consistent with existing rules and regulations. Aversive techniques may not be used except as a last resort. Professionals also serve the parents of exceptional children by communicating clearly and by soliciting and using their advice and information. Parents should be informed of all matters related to their particular situations and of the rights afforded them by law. Special educators should serve as advocates for the exceptional person in a variety of ways—changing government policy, monitoring adequacy of available resources, and protecting the individual rights of the special needs person. Special educators also have the responsibility of keeping abreast of new developments and findings in special education.

Professional standards exist to guide the conduct of special education professionals. One way to ensure that special educators are influenced by these standards is for all institutions that prepare special education teachers and professionals to provide for their students the most current standards and to incorporate those standards into the educational process (Standards for the Preparation of Special Education Personnel, 1983). At the state and national levels, any licensing or accreditation requirements in existence could be compared with the profession's standards and adjusted accordingly.

Once the development and implementation of the standards are completed, professionals in the field need to concentrate their efforts in three areas. First, the development of continuing or in-service education must address the competencies needed by professionals already in the field (Stedman, Smith, & Baucom, 1981). Second, as mentioned by Gersten (1985), efforts should focus on which teacher competencies actually make a difference to people with special needs (Englert, 1983). Interviewing experts to develop professional competencies (Zane, Sulzer-Azaroff, Handen, & Fox, 1982) is useful in developing a large number of skills and standards that seem logical, but such a strategy is insufficient in that it does not provide for a determination of whether such skills are functionally related to student improvement. Third, updating and changing of the standards must continue (Standards for the Preparation of Special Education Personnel, 1983). The validation process is one way that new skills and competencies will become known and incorporated into the standards as the nature of the field changes and the needs of the developmentally disabled shift over time. By validating them, updating as needed, and incorporating them into institutions that train special educators, the standards will become an integral part of the training of special educators and will achieve the original purpose for their development—producing qualified professionals and providing maximum improvement of persons with special needs.

REFERENCES

Englert, C. S. (1983). Measuring special education teacher effectiveness. *Exceptional Children, 50,* 247–254.

Gersten, R. (1985). Direct instruction with special education students: A review of evaluation research. *Journal of Special Education, 19,* 41–58.

Heller, H. H. (1983). Special education professional standards: Need, value, and use. *Exceptional Children, 50,* 199–204.

Standards for the preparation of special education personnel. (1983). *Exceptional Children, 50,* 210–218.

Stedman, D. J., Smith, R. R., & Baucom, L. D. (1981). Toward quality in special education programs. In D. Stedman & J. Paul (Eds.), *New directions for exceptional children: Professional preparation for teachers of exceptional children* (No. 8). San Francisco: Jossey-Bass.

Zane, T., Sulzer-Azaroff, B., Handen, B. L., & Fox, C. J. (1982). Validation of a competency-based training program in developmental disabilities. *Journal of the Severely Handicapped, 7,* 21–31.

THOMAS ZANE
Johns Hopkins University

ETHICS
TEACHER EFFECTIVENESS

PROFILE ANALYSIS

Profile analysis is the evaluation of scatter, or irregular performance, on the subtests and scales of a test. Whenever a profile of performance across specific areas is generated from a test, analysis of the profile is possible on a formal or informal basis. Thus, the patterns of scores from numerous intelligence, achievement, personality, aptitude, and vocational interest measures can be interpreted through the analysis of the relative positions of subtests and scales to each other (Goldstein & Hersen, 1984).

For a growing number of instruments, this process is facilitated through the availability of computerized programs for automated scoring and interpretation. Controversy surrounds this movement toward computer-assisted analysis, however, because of the wide-ranging quality of the available programs. Regardless of whether profile analysis is done with the assistance of these programs, the intent should be to evaluate areas of intraindividual strength and weakness (Sattler, 1982) and to use this information as hypotheses tht merit further evaluation and that offer clues to instructional programming.

Empirical support exists for the use of profile analysis with various instruments. Among personality measures, the Minnesota Multiphasic Personality Inventory (MMPI) has been the focus of numerous research efforts (Lewandowski & Graham, 1972), while the Wechsler scales have been the most closely scrutinized intelligence measures. Among the latter, the strongest support exists for the use of profile analysis with the Wechsler Intelligence Scale for Children-Revised (WISC-R), but only when careful consideration is given to three important caveats enumerated in Kaufman (1979), Sattler (1982), and Salvia and Ysseldyke (1981).

Of prime importance is that profile analysis is dependent on the presence of statistically significant differences among the subscales or among the subtests. Thus, before statements can be made about whether the examinee obtained higher or lower IQs, scaled scores, or subtest scores, significant differences among the subscales or the subtests must be present. Statistically significant differences among subtests or scales suggest that the differences are attributed to the abilities tapped by the respective subtests or scales rather than to measurement error.

Even with statistical differences, ideas generated must be viewed simply as hypotheses to be checked against other information about the examinee. Thus, a second caution is that profile analysis should be done with an understanding that uneven scores can be caused by many factors, including unreliability of the subtests, examiner/situational variability, background factors, physical disability, and minority group status (Sattler, 1982). In other words, experts agree that profile analysis is done only when the examinee's entire performance is evaluated to exclude the influence of other factors before specific strengths and weaknesses in cognitive ability are inferred. Moreover, when taken alone, uneven skill development does not allow one to make decisions about pathological conditions or the possible causes and cures of the uneven development. Thus, an understanding of the range of scores that exists among normal functioning children is necessary (Kaufman, 1976). Even when scatter is outside normal limits, however, it does not necessarily indicate the presence of pathology (Kaufman, 1979; Sattler, 1982).

Not only do the caveats apply to the WISC-R and other intelligence tests, they also provide a context for understanding the potential for misuse of profile analysis on tests that do not have a strong research base. Nevertheless, when done with careful consideration to statistically significant differences, other information about a child's functioning, and the extent of uneven skill development among normal functioning children, the analysis of profiles from intelligence tests and other instruments can assist in the process of uncovering clues to effective treatment, educational programming, or vocational placement.

REFERENCES

Goldstein, G., & Hersen, M. (1984). *Handbook of psychological assessment*. New York: Pergamon.

Kaufman, A. S. (1976). A new approach to the interpretation of test scatter on the WISC-R. *Journal of Learning Disabilities, 9*, 166–168.

Kaufman, A. S. (1979). *Intelligent testing with the WISC-R*. New York: Wiley.

Lewandowski, D., & Graham, J. R. (1972). Empirical correlates of frequently occurring two-point MMPI code types: A replicated study. *Journal of Consulting and Clinical Psychology, 39*, 467–472.

Salvia, J., & Ysseldyke, J. E. (1981). *Assessment in special and remedial education* (special ed.). New York: Houghton Mifflin.

Sattler, J. M. (1982). *Assessment of children's intelligence and special abilities*. Boston: Allyn & Bacon.

KATHLEEN D. PAGET
University of South Carolina

INTELLIGENCE TESTING

PROFILE VARIABILITY

Profile variability is an index of test scatter (individual variation in test scores between or within various psychological and educational tests) first defined by Plake, Reynolds, and Gutkin (1981). It is used as a diagnostic aid in determining the degree of intratest variability in an individual's performance on the subtests of any multiscale assessment device. A large degree of within test scatter has long been held to be an indicator of the presence of a learning disability (Chalfant & Scheffelin, 1969).

Test scatter has typically been determined by range (the highest minus the lowest score for an individual on a common family of tests), or by the number of test scores deviating at a statistically significant level from the individual's mean score on all tests administered (the latter sometimes is referred to as the number of deviant signs, or NDS). Profile variability is similar in some respects to range, but it is more accurate, more stable, and more powerful than older indexes of scatter. Profile variability encompasses data from all tests or subtests administered to an individual. It is not limited to the two most extreme scores as is the range.

Calculation of the index of profile variability is straightforward since it is the variance of a set of scores for one person on more than one measure, hence, the name profile variability. Profile variability for each member of a group or population can be estimated to be (Plake, Reynolds, & Gutkin, 1981):

$$S^2 = \sum_{j=1}^{k} \frac{(x_{ij} - \bar{x}_i)^2}{k - 1}$$

where S^2 = the index of profile variability

x_{ij} = the score of person i on test or subtest j

$\bar{x}_j$ = the mean score for person i on all tests (k) administered

k = the number of tests administered

The resulting value can then be compared with data taken from the standardization sample of a test or some other group to determine whether the variance of the individual's profile is an unusual or a common occurrence. In a research setting, it may also be of interest to know if the mean S^2 for one group differs at a statistically significant level from the mean S^2 for another group. A statistical test of the significance of the difference has been developed and is detailed in Plake, Reynolds, and Gutkin (1981).

Relatively little research on the clinical utility of S^2 has been completed as yet. However, of the various scatter indexes, profile variability is the most stable and the most mathematically sound.

REFERENCES

Chalfant, J. C., & Scheffelin, M. A. (1969). *Central processing dysfunctions in children*. (NINDS Monograph No. 9). Bethesda MD: U.S. Department of Health, Education, and Welfare.

Plake, B., Reynolds, C. R., & Gutkin, T. B. (1981). A technique for the comparison of profile variability between independent groups. *Journal of Clinical Psychology, 37*, 142–146.

CECIL R. REYNOLDS
Texas A&M University

PROFILE ANALYSIS
TEST SCATTER

PROFOUNDLY HANDICAPPED, COMPETENCIES OF TEACHERS OF

Students considered to be profoundly handicapped (PH) may include individuals who have been diagnosed and labeled as either profoundly mentally retarded, autistic, deaf-blind, severely multiply handicapped, or severely emotionally disturbed. In recent years, increased emphasis has been placed on determining the competencies or skills needed by teachers of these students (Burke & Cohen, 1977; Horner, 1977; Southeastern Regional Coalition, 1982).

The competencies that have been suggested in the professional literature, as necessary for teachers of PH students, can be divided into nine general areas (Whitten & Westling, 1985). These include (1) curriculum development or selection; (2) behavioral programming and behavior management; (3) working with parents; (4) assessment; (5) methods of instructional delivery; (6) medical aspects; (7) child development; (8) use of other professionals and paraprofessionals; and (9) characteristics of mental, emotional, and physical disabilities.

In addition to knowing how to teach, teachers must also know what to teach profoundly handicapped students. Teachers must be able to select or develop curriculum in a variety of content areas including self-help skills, sensory-motor development, social, and recreational skills.

Among the specific competency areas considered to be most important in the area of behavioral programming and management are development of task analyses, understanding of behavior modification techniques, and the ability to arrange and manage reinforcement contingencies and principles. In addition, within this area, the ability to develop strategies for appropriate acquisition, maintenance, and generalization of behaviors, and the ability to measure behavior precisely, are considered to be important teacher competencies.

The ability to involve parents in educational planning and to function as an effective parent trainer are often suggested as important competencies for teachers of profoundly handicapped students.

The ability to maintain an ongoing assessment of learning is important. Knowledge of instrumentation and procedures appropriate for screening, diagnosis, and educational assessment, and the ability to comprehend and interpret diagnostic reports, are necessary skills.

Instructional delivery is an additional competency area that includes the ability to develop or select instructional materials, the use of a high percentage of minutes per day for instruction, and the ability to facilitate skill acquisition.

Knowledge of medical aspects has been determined to be an important area of needed competence. The skills of using modified equipment, administering medication, and providing assistance to a student having a seizure are often necessary competencies.

An understanding of the normative developmental sequence and early academic learning processes is paramount in the education of profoundly handicapped students.

A frequently stated competency is the ability to communicate and work effectively with other professionals. Other skills include the ability to supervise paraprofessional personnel and the understanding and use of support services in the school and community.

The final area includes the specific competencies of understanding cognitive, language, social, motor, and behavioral development and knowledge of clinical syndromes. Although an abundance of competencies have been suggested for teachers of PH students, the majority of these statements are based on the opinions of the author(s), groups of professionals, or citations from the professional literature. Only five suggested competencies have been validated as a result of an established empirical link between the demonstration of a specific competency and gain in student achievement.

Four of the competency statements based on student gains involved the use of behavioral principles, while a fifth statement focused on instructional delivery. Statements based on empirically validated behavioral techniques include the ability to conduct task analyses (Fredericks, Anderson, & Baldwin, 1979), the ability to use behavior management techniques (Koegel, Russo, & Rincover, 1977), the use of successive approximation procedures (Katz, Goldberg, & Shurka, 1977), and the delivery of primary reinforcement (Whitten & Westling, 1985). In addition, according to research conducted by Fredericks et al. (1979), students of teachers who used a higher percentage of time each day for instruction achieved more than students of teachers who provided a lower percentage of instructional time.

While it appears that a considerable amount of attention has been focused on the delineation of competencies needed by teachers of profoundly handicapped students, as previously noted, the majority of the suggested competencies have been based on opinions (Thurman & Hare, 1979; Whitten & Westling, 1985). It is, therefore, important to determine empirically the skills that teachers of profoundly handicapped students should demonstrate so that the optimal functioning levels of these students may be achieved. According to Turner (1971), the highest criterion to judge effectiveness of teacher practices is to determine the effect to these practices on student learning over an extended period of time. Rather than basing the practices teachers use on opinion, it appears to be essential that the validity of the suggested teacher competencies be determined as a result of empirical research.

In reviewing the competency statements, it appears that many of those suggested may be applicable to all teachers and especially all special educators. However, teachers of profoundly handicapped students need to be much more proficient in their use. Sontag, Burke, and York (1973) noted an inverse relationship between the level of competence needed by the teacher and the functioning level of the student. Therefore, if profoundly handicapped students are to reach their optimal functioning levels, it is essential that their teachers demonstrate a higher level of competence than teachers of regular or other special students.

REFERENCES

Burke, P., & Cohen, M. (1977). The quest for competencies in serving the severely/profoundly handicapped: A critical analysis of personnel preparation programs. In E. Sontag, J. Smith, & N. Certo (Eds.), *Educational programming for the severely and profoundly handicapped* (pp. 445–465). Reston, VA: Council for Exceptional Children.

Fredericks, H. D., Anderson, R., & Baldwin, V. (1979). The identification of competency indicators of teachers of the severely handicapped. *American Association for the Education of the Severely/Profoundly Handicapped Review, 4,* 81–95.

Horner, R. D. (1977). A competency based approach to preparing teachers of the severely and profoundly handicapped: Perspective II. In E. Sontag, J. Smith, & N. Certo (Eds.), *Edu-*

cational programming for the severely and profoundly handicapped* (pp. 430–444). Reston, VA: Council for Exceptional Children.

Katz, S., Goldberg, J., & Shurka, E. (1977). The use of operant techniques in teaching severely retarded clients work habits. *Education & Training of the Mentally Retarded, 12*, 14–20.

Koegel, R. L., Russo, D. C., & Rincover, A. (1977). Assessing and training teachers in the generalized use of behavior modification with autistic children. *Journal of Applied Behavior Analysis, 10*, 197–205.

Sontag, E., Burke, P. J., & York, R. (1973). Considerations for serving the severely handicapped in public schools. *Education & Training of the Mentally Retarded, 8*, 20–26.

Southeastern Regional Coalition for Personnel Preparation to Work with Severely/Profoundly Handicapped. (1982). Developing personnel preparation programs to train personnel to teach severely handicapped individuals. *Teacher Education & Special Education, 5*(1), 46–51.

Thurman, S. K., & Hare, B. A. (1979). Training teachers in special education: Some perspectives circa 1980. *Education & Training of the Mentally Retarded, 14*, 292–295.

Turner, R. L. (1971). Levels of criteria. In B. Rosner (Eds.)., *The power of competency-based teacher education.* Washington, DC: U.S. Office of Education, National Center for Educational Research and Development.

Whitten, T. M., & Westling, D. L. (1985). Competencies for teachers of severely and profoundly handicapped: A review. *Teacher Education & Special Education, 8*(2), 104–111.

THOMAS M. WHITTEN
Florida State University

COMPETENCY TEST

MILDLY HANDICAPPED, TEACHER COMPETENCIES FOR PROFOUNDLY RETARDED

PROFOUNDLY RETARDED

Profound retardation is one of four levels of retardation defined by the American Association on Mental Deficiency. A profoundly retarded person's IQ score falls five or more standard deviations below the mean (Grossman, 1977). Scores will vary according to the test used (Stanford-Binet—19 and below; WISC—24 and below). The severity of retardation is such that it interferes with the total life-functioning ability of the individual. Consequently these individuals are in need of 24-hour care and supervision. They also need maximum intervention efforts on the part of many professionals and agencies owing to the multiplicity of the handicapping conditions within each individual.

The profoundly retarded make up the smallest subgroup within the area of mental retardation. Frequently, the term severely/profoundly retarded is used and the two groups are treated as one. Many severely retarded individuals can learn to take care of many of their basic needs if 24-hour supervision or assistance is available, but this is not the case for the profoundly retarded.

The profoundly retarded rarely use any spontaneous, intelligible speech. Occasionally, an individual will use "mama" or "da-da" indiscriminately. Other sensory deficits (impairments of vision and hearing and tactile defensiveness) and physical abnormalities are manifest. Another common characteristic of the profoundly retarded is the presence of stereotypic behaviors (e.g., rocking, biting of self, hand-flapping). Others are withdrawn or passive and incontinent. The life expectancy for the profoundly retarded is shorter than average, although recent advances in medicine have increased their life expectancy significantly.

The passage of PL 94-142 dramatically changed the lives of profoundly retarded school-age children and adolescents. The education of this population became the responsibility of the public schools, and some children who had never received any services began school. Multidisciplinary and transdisciplinary teams slowly began to address the issues at hand. In particular, the definition and application of the concept of least restrictive environment came to the fore. Other major issues included education versus training (Meyers, MacMillan, & Zetlin, 1979), the acceptance or rejection of the responsibility for physical or occupational therapy by the school, and questions involving the care of medically fragile students.

As a result of the implementation of PL 94-142, many new programs have developed for the profoundly retarded. Interest in critical issues such as improving strategies for teaching, creating better living environments, and studying training techniques to increase employability have increased. The development of approaches to improve socio-communicative behaviors and enhance nonspeech communication, including the use manual signing, graphic symbol systems, and microcomputers, has been reported.

More and more profoundly retarded individuals are being kept in their homes with support from community agencies as well as the public schools. The future should continue to improve life for these individuals, particularly as more is learned about facilitating their socio-communicative functions and techniques are further developed to bring aberrant behaviors under control.

REFERENCES

Grossman, H. J. (1977). *Manual on terminology and classification in mental retardation.* Washington, DC: American Association on Mental Deficiency.

Meyers, C. E., MacMillan, D. L., & Zetlin, A. (1979). The measurement of adaptive behavior. In N. R. Ellis (Ed.), *Handbook of mental deficiency: Psychological theory and research* (2nd ed., pp. 431–481). Hillsdale, NJ: Erlbaum.

ANNE CAMPBELL
Purdue University

AAMD CLASSIFICATION SYSTEMS
MENTAL RETARDATION

PROGRAM EVALUATION

Program evaluation in elementary school and secondary school education has been an area of considerable activity during the past 20 years. Program evaluation has been such an active area largely because of public concern about program accountability as well as a desire by school professionals to provide quality programs and services (Cronbach, 1982). Although no universal definition exists, program evaluation can be characterized by two essential activities: systematic, purposeful data collection relative to one or more important evaluation questions; and the use of evaluation information to judge whether a program is worthwhile (Rossi, Freeman, & Wright, 1985).

Numerous educational program evaluations have been conducted in school settings, with many of the evaluations focused on federally funded programs and projects such as Head Start, Follow-Through, and Chapter I (formerly Title I) programs. Essentially, these program evaluations have been summative in nature, whereby large numbers of students who received the program were compared with large groups of students with similar characteristics who did not receive the program or who received another program. The primary intent of these evaluations has been to determine program effectiveness and to decide whether the outcome justifies disseminating the program to other sites and students as part of public policy initiatives.

Large-scale educational program evaluation has been proven beneficial to federal and state policy makers in terms of aggregate data for decision-making purposes. Additionally, issues and methods have been clarified in important ways for those interested in evaluation design and measurement. Despite these gains in understanding, what does not seem to have been readily established is the direct and practical relevance of program evaluation to local level programs, especially small-size school districts. More specifically, local school professionals have voiced concern over how they can use program evaluation to help them develop and improve local offerings (Dunst, 1979; Kennedy, 1982).

In special education, program evaluation has become an area of avid interest and increasing activity at local school district levels nationwide, with collaborative efforts being undertaken among administrators, staff, and outside consultants. An important impetus to this avid interest and increasing activity at the local level was a two-day national conference on special education program evaluation held in St. Louis during December 1983 (Council of Administrators of Special Education, 1984). At that conference, which was jointly sponsored by the Council of Administrators of Special Education and the Office of Special Education and Rehabilitation Services, four proven models of local-level special education program evaluation were presented by their proponents. The invited audience of over 100 special education directors and supervisors from throughout the nation took part in workshops to learn about these practical approaches. Subsequent to the conference, local school district applicants were reviewed and the various models were field tested during 1984 at about 20 local sites (Associate Consultants, 1985).

Case study results of these field tests, along with empirical results from additional evaluations of local special education programs that occurred during 1985 and 1986 through state department initiatives, coupled with professional publications on special education program evaluation, have all coalesced to delineate and propose several important features and characteristics of this rapidly developing area. These features and characteristics are reflected in terms of the process of special education program evaluation, the foci of evaluation efforts, the methods, procedures, and instruments for conducting evaluations of special programs, and the enhancement of the use of evaluation information for program planning.

The process of special education program evaluation is best considered in the generic sense, i.e., as the systematic gathering of data about a program or service to answer one or more clearly articulated evaluation questions. For special education programs, the following evaluation questions usually have been raised by local level practitioners when planning an evaluation: (1) What were the characteristics of the students who were provided the program? (2) How was the program actually implemented? (3) Were program goals attained? (4) How did various individuals—teachers, parents, students—react to the program and its outcomes? (5) Was the program responsible for the outcome results? (6) Was the program worth the investment? Although it is not possible for all of these questions to be addressed in a particular evaluation, the questions are important in that the evaluation information gathered in response to them can lead to particular program planning actions.

The foci of special education program evaluation can be numerous, since a special education services delivery system includes a range of programs and services (Maher & Bennett, 1984). For instance, various instructional programs serving special needs learners can be the foci of evaluation efforts including programs such as resources rooms, self-contained classrooms, supplemental instructional programs, regular class mainstreaming programs and, of course, individualized education programs (IEPs). In the area of related services, a district's student counseling program, for example, can be the object of an evaluation as can other programs such as parent education programs or physical therapy services. Similarly, a special education program evaluation can focus on a staff development course or on an important, yet often neglected type of program, e.g., an assessment program such as preplacement evaluation. In deciding the evaluation questions to be addressed in relation to special education programs and services, a local-level team or committee approach has been found to be useful in selecting the most appropriate questions and in facilitating the involvement of staff in the evaluation endeavor (Maher & Illback, 1984).

Since diverse evaluation questions can be addressed in relation to various special programs and services, it is not surprising that a plan for special education program evaluation lists many kinds of methods, procedures, and instruments. At the local level, special education program evaluation plans seem to reflect not comparative group evaluation designs, as has been typical in regular education special evaluation, but special education evaluation plans characterized by a single case approach, where the program (e.g., resource room) is compared with itself over time (e.g., over a 2- to 3-year period) to determine whether it is effective (Tawney & Gast, 1984). Usually, evaluations include use of instruments and procedures that rely on teacher or staff retrospective judgment, especially through use of behavioral checklists and rating scales and parent and teacher interviews. Additionally, criterion-referenced testing and review of IEP goal attainment data have been commonly employed to answer important evaluation questions. Hence, both qualitative and quantitative data gathering approaches appear to be necessary to the conduct of practical and meaningful special education program evaluation.

An emphasis on the use of special education program evaluation information seems to have been a positive outgrowth of practitioners' desires to act on the information for program planning purposes. In this regard, it has been found important that written evaluation reports be kept brief, that they be written in the nontechnical language of the school audience for which it is intended, and that the narrative be augmented with clearly developed tables, graphs, figures, and other illustrations to emphasize important points. Most important, recommendations for program planning should be specific as to how to take the next steps and clear as to how the steps were derived. To facilitate use of the information, it has been found useful to hold group meetings or forums between evaluation personnel and target audiences.

REFERENCES

Associate Consultants. (1985). *Results of the field tests of the special education program evaluation models*. Washington, DC: Author.

Council of Administrators of Special Education. (1984). *Proceedings of the national conference on special education program evaluation*. Indianapolis, IN: Author.

Cronbach, L. J. (1982). *Designing evaluations of educational and social programs*. San Francisco: Jossey-Bass.

Dunst, C. J. (1979). Program evaluation and the Education for All Handicapped Children Act. *Exceptional Children, 46*, 26–31.

Kennedy, M. M. (1982). *Recommendations of the Division H Task Force on Special Education Program Evaluation*. Washington, DC: American Educational Research Association.

Maher, C. A., & Bennett, R. E. (1984). *Planning and evaluating special education services*. Englewood Cliffs, NJ: Prentice-Hall.

Maher, C. A., & Illback, R. J. (1984). A team approach to evaluating special services. In C. A. Maher, R. J. Illback, & J. E. Zins (Eds.), *Organizational psychology in the schools*. Springfield, IL: Thomas.

Rossi, P., Freeman, H., & Wright, L. (1985). *Evaluation: A systematic approach*. Beverly Hills, CA: Sage.

Tawney, J. W., & Gast, D. L. (1984). *Single subject research in special education*. Columbus, OH: Merrill.

CHARLES A. MAHER
Rutgers University

LOUIS J. KRUGER
Tufts University

SCHOOL EFFECTIVENESS

SUPERVISION IN SPECIAL EDUCATION

PROGRAMMED INSTRUCTION

Programmed instruction is a unique educational method based on principles emphasized by B. F. Skinner (1954, 1958). First, the use of positive reinforcement is preferable to punishment or lack of feedback. Second, positive reinforcement is more effective in producing behavioral changes if given frequently and immediately after each response. Last, there is value in presenting students with small chunks of information to learn that will eventually result in desired behaviors. Skinner sought to apply these principles through programmed learning and the use of teaching machines.

The development of an automated teaching machine by Pressley in the 1920s anticipated Skinner's work. Pressley's machine required students to read questions and then press buttons to answer (in multiple-choice format). The machine presented the next question in a sequence only after the student made the correct choice. Pressley's concept and technology were not readily accepted or widely used. Skinner (1958) attributed the limited use of Pressley's teaching machine to "cultural inertia" and the incomplete or inappropriate application of learning principles. Skinner developed another teaching machine that not only provided frequent and immediate feedback, but also presented the information to be learned in small, easily acquired segments that the student had to master before moving on to new material. The small steps increased the chances of a student's making a correct response, provided positive reinforcement and student motivation, and ensured student success at each step as well as at the final goal.

Programmed learning has been hailed as allowing truly individualized instruction permitting students to progress at their own pace. In many cases, it seems to be highly motivating to the student because of the immediacy of results, high density of reinforcement, and enjoyment from manipulating the machine (when a teaching machine is used). It has also been instrumental in showing how to teach complex tasks by breaking them down into small, teachable segments. In addition, when using teaching machines, teachers are freer to use their time in more productive ways than presenting information to students.

While the early application of programmed instruction used machines to present learning programs, programmed texts and workbooks soon followed. The increasing use of computers in special education has been revitalizing interest in variations of programmed instruction. An impressive characteristic of modern computers is the great degree of individualized instruction now possible for each student because of the development of branching programs (Rubin & Weisgerber, 1985). Students diagnosed as learning disabled and mentally retarded (mild to profound) have learned a variety of skills on computers, such as addition, subtraction, word recognition, and matching to sample (Richmond, 1983).

However, it is the application of learning principles and not the use of a computer that is the important issue. A computer does not automatically incorporate programmed instruction principles; in fact, much of the educational software in use today is to a large extent based on the traditional trial-and-error procedures that may result in academic failure in many children (LeBlanc, Hoko, Aangeenbrug, & Etzel, 1985). Integrating instructional principles of programmed learning into the development of educational methodologies, whether in software, textbooks, or other forms, is a way to maximize the chances for learning in special education students.

REFERENCES

LeBlanc, J. M., Hoko, J. A., Aangeenbrug, M. H., & Etzel, B. C. (1985). Microcomputers and stimulus control: From the laboratory to the classroom. *Journal of Special Education Technology, 7,* 23–30.

Richmond, G. (1983). Comparison of automated and human instruction for developmentally retarded preschool children. *Journal of the Association for the Severely Handicapped, 8,* 78–84.

Rubin, D. P., & Weisgerber, R. A. (1985). The center for research and evaluation in the application of technology to education. *Technological Horizons in Education, 12,* 83–87.

Skinner, B. F. (1954). The science of learning and the art of teaching. *Harvard Educational Review, 24,* 86–97.

Skinner, B. F. (1958). Teaching machines. *Science, 128,* 969–977.

THOMAS ZANE
Johns Hopkins University

COMPUTER MANAGED INSTRUCTION
COMPUTER USE WITH HANDICAPPED
DIRECT INSTRUCTION
OPERANT CONDITIONING

PROJECTIVE TECHNIQUES

See PERSONALITY ASSESSMENT.

PROJECT ON CLASSIFICATION OF EXCEPTIONAL CHILDREN

In the early 1970s, Nicholas Hobbs was asked to direct a systematic review of the classification and labeling practices for exceptional children. Sponsored by 10 federal agencies and organized by Elliot Richardson, then secretary of health, education, and welfare, this review had several objectives.

The first objective was to increase public understanding of the issues associated with labeling and classifying handicapped individuals. The second objective was to formulate a statement of rationale for public policy, including suggestions for regulatory guidelines. The third objective was to educate professionals who were ultimately responsible for the provision of services to the population of exceptional children (Hobbs, 1975a).

The results of this review, known as the Project on Classification of Exceptional Children, are reported in the publication *The Futures of Children* (Hobbs, 1975b). Included in this report is a list of recommendations that detail actions to be taken as well as who should be responsible for the implementation, the cost of service, and the length of time required to accomplish the project objectives.

Hobbs, a distinguished psychologist and educator, was generally opposed to the practice of labeling individuals. His major argument against labeling was that it is very limited in value. Hobbs pointed out that while the original intent of classification was to provide equal access and opportunity for the handicapped population, the process usually resulted in the transfer of the label or classification to a negative condition or description of the child. For example, a child who was classified within the category of mental retardation became known as a mental retardate.

Hobbs (1975b), citing the current practices of the time, warned:

categories and labels are powerful instruments for social regulation and control, and they are often employed for obscure, covert, or hurtful purposes: to degrade people, to deny them access to opportunity, to exclude "undesirables" whose presence in some way offends, disturbs familiar custom, or demands extraordinary effort. (p. 11)

One of the seven major recommendations to emerge from the project was the call to improve the classification system. Specifically, the project report suggested five ways to improve the existing process. The suggestions included (1) revision of the classification process; (2) constraints in the use of psychological testing; (3) improvements in early identification procedures; (4) safeguards in the handling of confidential records; and (5) provision of due process in identification and placement.

One finding of the project was that the current classification systems were inadequate. Citing arbitrary and outmoded conceptual guidelines, the members called for a comprehensive classification system that would be based on the needs of exceptional children. According to the general recommendations, the classification system should reflect the full range of conditions of children who need special services. Under this model, classification would emphasize the services required rather than the types of children served.

The specific recommendations of the project members included the formation of a national advisory committee for the purpose of establishing a comprehensive classification system. As a result of such a system, there would be increased understanding of the complexities of the characteristics and etiology of handicapping conditions. The changes proposed in the classification system were not regarded as an end product but rather as a vehicle for improving service and programming for handicapped individuals and their families.

Historically, there has been a great deal of controversy associated with the classification systems for handicapped populations. Since the introduction of the first special education textbook in the early 1920s, there has been a demand for more accurate classification systems (Kaufman & Hallahan, 1981).

Currently, there is little evidence in relevant literature that the recommendations resulting from the Project on Classification of Exceptional Children have been implemented on a national level. Individual agencies have made progress in several areas identified by the project report (e.g., improvement of diagnostic procedures, increases in services for the families of handicapped individuals, and protection of individuals' right to due process). However, the major recommendation calling for a national advisory panel that would help to establish policy and direct relevant research has yet to be realized.

REFERENCES

Hobbs, N. (Ed.). (1975a). *Issues in the classification of children* (Vols. 1, 2). San Francisco: Jossey-Bass.

Hobbs, N. (1975b). *The futures of children*. San Francisco: Jossey-Bass.

Kaufman, J. M., & Hallahan, D. P. (Eds.). (1981). *Handbook of special education*. Englewood Cliffs, NJ: Prentice-Hall.

FRANCINE TOMPKINS
University of Cincinnati

AAMD CLASSIFICATION SYSTEM
CLASSIFICATION SYSTEMS
LABELING

PROJECT RE-ED

The project on the Re-Education of Emotionally Disturbed Children (Project Re-ED) evolved after a 1953 study of mental health needs by the Southern Regional Education Board. The study indicated that there was great need for child mental health programs with demonstrated effectiveness, reasonable cost, access to a large talent pool of trained personnel, and potential for transfer of techniques to public schools. In 1956 the federal government sponsored a study of mental health programs in France and Scotland, where mental health services were provided by French *educateurs* and Scottish "educational psychologists" to children with desperate needs because of the effects of evacuation and other traumas resulting from World War II. The National Institute for Mental Health (NIMH) study group recommended a pilot project using trained personnel in the United States (Hobbs, 1983).

In 1961 a NIMH grant of $2 million was awarded to George Peabody College for Teachers (now part of Vanderbilt University) and the states of Tennessee and North Carolina. Nicholas Hobbs was the primary developer of the 8-year pilot project for moderately to severely disturbed children (ages 6 to 12) in residential centers in Nashville, Tennessee, and Durham, North Carolina. Centers were in residential areas and provided services to groups of 24 and 40, subdivided into groups of eight. Program planning emphasis was on health rather than illness, teaching rather than therapy, the present rather than the past, and the operation of a total social system of which the child is a part rather than intrapsychic processes alone. Initial planning was pragmatic rather than theoretical; the theory developed with project research and experience. Hobbs (1978) later commented that one of the important ideas in the planning and development of Project Re-ED was that there should be no orthodoxy or dogma, but a "colleagueship" of discovery guiding the activities of professional individuals working together closely.

Basic ideas underlying program development included (1) insight is a possible consequence but not a cause of behavioral change; (2) health and happiness must grow out of life as it is lived, not as talked about in the context of personality theory; and (3) emotional disturbance in children is not something within the child, but a symptom of a malfunctioning ecosystem. Teacher-counselors and liaison teachers were carefully selected and provided with condensed, highly functional training (master's level) and a dependable system of day-to-day consultation by highly trained and skilled professional personnel. Teachers were not expected to solve complex problems intuitively, but were trained in understanding psychodynamics of individual development and families. Training also included child development, remedial instruction, management of behavior, recreational skills, and use of consultants.

Hobbs believed that trust between children and adults is basic to reeducation and that training of the children should be designed to encourage development of self-confidence by ensuring success. Symptoms were treated directly (controlled) without emphasis on causality. Family and school contacts were maintained while children were in residence. By 1970 the age range was expanded to include adolescents and preschool children.

Follow-up studies of Project Re-ED children (Weinstein, 1974) indicated that although the reeducation program did not change the students into "normal" children, they were better adjusted than disturbed children who were not in the project. Since the average length of stay in centers was about 7 months (contrasted to several years in some other types of residential centers), it appears that the project met its goal, which was not to cure children, but to restore to effective operation the small social system of which the child is an integral part. Hobbs thought that Project Re-ED would be most likely to pay off when its concepts were applied in public schools. By 1983 about two dozen reeducation centers were established in nine states and several others were being planned. Professional consensus now is the Project Re-ED is a viable means of providing effective services to disturbed children.

REFERENCES

Hobbs, N. (1975). *The futures of children*. San Francisco: Jossey-Bass.

Hobbs, N. (1978). Perspectives on re-education. *Behavior Disorders, 3*(2), 65–66.

Hobbs, N. (1983). Project Re-Education: From demonstration project to nationwide program. *Peabody Journal of Education, 60*(3), 8–24.

Weinstein, L. (1974). *Evaluation of a program for re-educating disturbed children: A follow-up comparison with untreated children* (ERIC Document Reproduction Service No. ED-141-966). Washington, DC: U.S. Department of Health Education, and Welfare.

SUE ALLEN WARREN
Boston University

LIFE SPACE INTERVIEWING
RESIDENTIAL FACILITIES

PROJECT SUCCESS (PS)

Project Success (PS) is an academic and social remediation program for the college-bound specific language-handicapped or dyslexic student. The intent of the program is for the language-handicapped student to become language-independent as well as socially and psychologically adjusted to the new environment.

Becoming language-independent means that the dyslexic individual learns how to read and spell any word by relying on his or her own integrated knowledge of the phonemic structure of the American-English language. Students in PS acquire this knowledge initially by memorizing how the 50 phonemes and 26 letters can be employed to identify 271 sound symbol assignments for reading and 245 sound symbols assignments for spelling.

This total number of assignments for both reading and spelling are taught using a multisensory approach. The instructional methodology used is Nash's (1984) adaptation of the original Orton Gillingham, Tri-Modal, Simultaneous Multi-Sensory Instructional Procedure (OG, TM, SMSIP). This procedure trains the learner to use the senses simultaneously to memorize and to integrate up to 84% of all American-English words. In addition to reading and spelling remediation, the program remediates math and writing deficits. There is also a social habilitation program.

The written expression program concentrates on teaching the writing of sentences as outlined by Langan (1983). The social habilitation/remediation component of PS was developed to give students an opportunity to give back to fellow students what they have received in a therapeutic, personal, and productive way. As students go through the PS social component, they learn about the secondary characteristics associated with dyslexia. In addition, students have the opportunity to enhance their sense of self-awareness and to be more sensitive to the psychosocial implications of being dyslexic.

The project's arithmetic remediation component assumes that the carrying out of math functions is an exercise in decoding. Thus students who are deficient in math skills are taught to analyze a math problem into a sequence of sentences; each sentence is representative of a particular step or procedure associated with the solving of a particular math problem.

REFERENCES

Langan, J. (1983). *Sentence skills* (3rd ed.). New York: Holt, Rinehart, & Winston.

Nash, R. (1984). *Manual for remediating the reading and spelling deficits of elementary, secondary, and postsecondary students.* Oshkosh, WI: Robert T. Nash Language Training School.

ROBERT T. NASH
*University of Wisconsin,
Oshkosh*

READING DISORDERS

PROJECT TALENT

Project Talent was conceived in the late 1950s as an ambitious survey of American youth. A two-day battery of specially designed tests and inventories was administered to a 5% sample of high-school students from across the United States. The intention was to follow-up those tested at regular intervals, and through this process develop an information base about the processes by which men and women develop and use their abilities. The goals of Project Talent were to develop a national inventory of human resources; to achieve a better understanding of how young people choose and develop their careers; and to identify the educational and life experiences that are most important in preparing individuals for their life work (Flanagan et al., 1962).

The group tested included over 400,000 students, constituting a 5% probability sample of all students in grades 9, 10, 11, and 12 in public and nonpublic secondary schools in the United States in the spring of 1960. In addition, several supplemental samples were tested in 1960 to address special questions. These included a probability sample of all 15 year olds, whether or not they happened to be in the grade 9 to 12 range or, for that matter, in school. Also included were all high-school students in Knox County (Knoxville), Tennessee. Finally, over 10,000 students from 100 schools originally tested as ninth graders in 1960 were retested for two days as twelfth graders in 1963.

The Project Talent battery included a wide variety of aptitude and achievement tests, sample information in academic and nonacademic areas, and a questionnaire on vocational interests. There was also a personality inventory and a biographical questionnaire containing nearly 400 questions about school life, out-of-school activities, general health, plans, aspirations, home, and family. In addition, each of the more than 1000 participating junior and senior high schools provided information on its instructional and guidance programs, facilities, staffing, and student/community characteristics.

The original plan for Project Talent called for follow-up of those tested 1, 5, 10, and 20 years following the expected graduation of each class. There were subsequent modifications with follow-up surveys 1, 5, and 11 years following the year of class graduation. For example, the original twelfth-, eleventh-, tenth-, and ninth-grade students were surveyed in 1961 through 1963, respectively, when students in each sample were at the model age of 19 years. Surveys were by mail, with a random sample of nonrespondents intensively pursued (by questionnaire or, if necessary, interview) to allow the development of accurate population statistics.

Each of the follow-up surveys sought information on postsecondary education, career choices, work experiences, and family plans, and were timed to occur at key points in individuals' personal and career development. The first- and fifth-year follow-ups focused on the years in which the participants began to put their career choices into action, either through education, training, or direct job experience. Most individuals had completed their formal education, had entered the labor force, and had started their families at the time of the 11-year follow-up. The most recent survey focused on each individual's satisfaction with educational preparation, careers, and general quality of life.

Another more limited line of research involved the follow-back design. This approach was based on the fact that approximately 5% of those entering medical school in the mid 1960s, for example, were part of the Project Talent sample. It is possible to check names of those enrolling in medical school against the Project Talent files, and as a result have valuable precollege data on a random sample of those entering medical school.

The results of Project Talent are far more extensive than can be covered in this report. The body of knowledge includes technical reports and published articles by the Project Talent staff between 1962 and the present, as well as articles by researchers accessing the information through the Project Talent Data Bank. Many of these reports are in university libraries; others can be obtained through Publications Service, American Institutes for Research, P.O. Box 1113, Palo Alto, California 94302.

The initial report of results from the Project Talent staff was in 1964; it described the inventory of talent in the United States (Flanagan et al., 1964). One highlight from the one-year follow-up surveys was the tremendous amount of change in career plans. For example, those tested in 1960 were asked to indicate career plans. One year after high school graduation, more than half of those electing each of the career alternatives as high school seniors had changed their plans (Flanagan et al., 1966). Percentages were even lower for those graduating in 1961 to 1963. Of interest was the fact that changes were toward career choices more in line with abilities and interests.

Results of the fifth- (Flanagan et al., 1971) and the eleventh-year (Wilson & Wise, 1975; Wise, McLaughlin, & Gilmartin, 1977) follow-up studies have also been reported. An important finding from the eleventh-year follow-up was that nearly 25% of the men and women at age

29 still planned to obtain further education toward various degrees (Wise, et al., 1977).

The data collected in conjunction with Project Talent are available to scientists, stripped of identifying information and on a cost-recovery basis. The most comprehensive study done by an outside investigator using this data was that published by Christopher Jencks and his colleagues in the book *Inequality: A Reassessment of the Effect of Family and Schooling in America* (1972).

REFERENCES

Flanagan, J. C., Cooley, W. W., Lohnes, P. R., Schoenfeldt, L. F., Holdeman, R. W., Combs, J., & Becker, S. (1966). *Project Talent one-year follow-up studies*. Pittsburgh: Project Talent.

Flanagan, J. C., Dailey, J. T., Shaycoft, M. F., Gorham, W. A., Orr, D. B., & Goldberg, I. (1962). *Design for a study of American youth*. Boston: Houghton Mifflin.

Flanagan, J. C., Davis, F. B., Dailey, J. T., Shaycoft, M. F., Orr, D. B., Goldberg, I., & Neyman, C. A., Jr. (1964). *The American high school student*. Pittsburgh: American Institutes for Research.

Flanagan, J. C., Shaycoft, M. F., Richards, J. M., Jr., & Claudy, J. G. (1971). *Five years after high school*. Palo Alto, CA: American Institutes for Research.

Jencks, C., Smith, M., Acland, H., Bane, M. J., Cohen, D., Gintis, H., Heyns, B., & Michelson, S. (1972). *Inequality: A reassessment of the effect of family and schooling in America*. New York: Basic Books.

Wilson, S. R., & Wise, L. L. (1975). *The American citizen: 11 years after high school* (Vol. 1). Palo Alto, CA: American Institutes for Research.

Wise, L. L., McLaughlin, D. H., & Gilmartin, K. J. (1977). *The American citizen: 11 years after high school* (Vol. 2). Palo Alto, CA: American Institutes for Research.

LYLE F. SCHOENFELDT
Texas A&M University

PROSOPAGNOSIA

Prosopagnosia is a rare acquired defect in facial recognition that is a consequence of focal brain damage. Visual acuity remains intact. Individuals that develop prosopagnosia are unable to recognize faces as familiar and so do not know whose specific face they are seeing. This is true despite adequate ability to recognize the generic face. For example, a young patient who developed prosopagnosia was puzzled as to why all the actors on a favorite television program had been changed. The faces no longer looked familiar to her, nor could she recognize particular characters by sight. Similarly, she was unable to recognize pictures of members of her own family. This deficit in visual recognition of familiar faces occurs independently of any defect in language or cognition.

Prosopagnosia is often accompanied by other specific kinds of visual disturbances. Individuals with prosopagnosia usually have either a unilateral or bilateral visual field defect. That is, they are unable to see one portion of what ordinarily can be seen when the eyes are held fixed at mid position. This defect is secondary to brain damage or damage to the optic nerve radiations, not to eye damage. In addition, prosopagnosia frequently is accompanied by central achromatopsia, the acquired inability to perceive color as a consequence of central nervous system disease despite adequate retinal function. Visual agnosia also is often present. Visual agnosia is normal ability to see and perceive without the ability to give meaning to what one sees. Normal visual acuity, visual scanning, and visual perception must be demonstrable in an individual diagnosed with visual agnosia. Despite the adequacy of visual skills, the individual is unable to recognize what is seen. Difficulty in identification is not a consequence of deficits in language or cognition. Indeed, many of these patients can recognize objects once they touch them, or once their function is described to them.

Historically, there has been substantial contention about the localization of the brain lesion producing prosopagnosia. Initially, most authors identified the necessary lesion as restricted to the right hemisphere (Hecaen & Albert, 1978), as many of the individuals who had prosopagnosia had left-sided visual field defects indicative of right hemisphere pathology. Recent studies using both radiologic and autopsy findings suggest that prosopagnosia requires bilateral damage to the mesial and inferior visual association cortex (Damasio & Damasio, 1983; Damasio, Damasio, & Van Hoesen, 1982).

REFERENCES

Damasio, A. R., & Damasio, H. (1983). Localization of lesions in achromotopsia and prosopagnosia. In A. Kertesz (Ed.), *Localization in neuropsychology* (pp. 331–341). New York: Academic.

Damasio, A. R., Damasio, H., & VanHoesen, G. W. (1982). Prosopagnosia: Anatomic basis and behavioral mechanisms. *Neurology, 32*, 331–341.

Hecaen, H., & Albert, N. L. (1978). *Human neuropsychology*. New York: Wiley.

GRETA N. WILKENING
*Children's Hospital, Denver,
Colorado*

**VISUALLY IMPAIRED
VISUAL PERCEPTION AND DISCRIMINATION
VISUAL TRAINING**

PROSTHETIC DEVICES

A prosthesis is any additional device, or artificial appliance, to support or replace a missing part of the body. Prosthetics are the dental and surgical specialities concerned with the artificial replacement of missing parts of the body. Examples of prosthetic devices are artificial legs, dental bridges, wheelchairs, and long leg braces. Devices supporting hand or arm control for eating or drinking such as specialized drinking cups, a molded lower arm supports, or upper arm frames, are also examples of prosthetic devices.

Physical therapists and occupational therapists under the supervision of physiatrists are two of the professional groups that train persons in the use, care, and applications of a prosthetic device. A prosthetic device makes the world reachable for the handicapped by bringing the disabling condition to that point where it places the least restriction on the handicapped person.

Modern technology has not only added to the number of prosthetic devices, it has elevated their functional involvement to a considerable degree. The expanded use of microchips, lasers, and microcomputer technology has greatly expanded readers, laser canes, and opticons for the visually impaired. Technology capable of changing auditory signals into appropriate letters and reflecting them in eyeglasses, or capable of generally improving hearing aid quality, has been miraculous for the hearing impaired. Other important changes in signal systems that permit guided mobility for artificial limbs, stimulated by either movement or voice, now provide auto-regulating movement for the orthopedically handicapped and amputees.

Technology continues to push back the restrictions placed on the handicapped by disabilities. Rehabilitation engineering and rehabilitation technology are fields that, when connected to biomedical, electronic, and other areas of engineering, may well restore usable vision, hearing, ambulation, or upper arm control. The horizons of tomorrow are boundless in terms of the possibilities that technology offers in prosthetic development.

DAVID A. SABATINO
*West Virginia College of
Graduate Studies*

**OCCUPATIONAL THERAPY
PHYSICAL THERAPY**

PROTECTION AND ADVOCACY SYSTEM— DEVELOPMENTALLY DISABLED (P&A)

The protection and advocacy system (P&A) was established under federal legislation for the developmentally disabled (Section 113, PL 94-103). Each state or territory receiving funding from the Administration on Developmental Disabilities is required to have a P&A agency. The P&A agencies must be independent of any other state agency or governmental unit to ensure their ability to freely protect and advocate the rights of developmentally disabled (DD) individuals.

Activities of P&A staff may involve negotiation, administrative or legal remedies on behalf of clients seeking programs, services, or protection of clients' rights as DD citizens. The agency's staff is also responsible for information dissemination concerning the rights of DD clients. Activities include presentations and workshops for lay and professional groups on the rights of the disabled. Areas such as education, employment, transportation, housing, architectural barriers, and legal aid are concerns of a P&A agency. The P&A office for each state or territory may be located through the Office of the Governor or by contacting Commissioner, Administration on Developmental Disabilities, OHDS/HHS, Washington, DC 20201.

PHILIP R. JONES
*Virginia Polytechnic Institute
and State University*

PSEUDORETARDATION

The concept of pseudoretardation is best considered within the context of differences in *definitions of* mental retardation. Definitions that included criteria of incurability and a biological basis for the condition were prevalent until mid-century and are still used by some workers. Later definitions such as that of the American Association on Mental Deficiency (AAMD), Clausen's proposed definition emphasizing psychometric score, and Bijou's reinforcement history definition avoid the concept of pseudoretardation.

Probably the most commonly accepted definition of mental retardation before 1960 was specified by Doll (1941): "(1) social incompetence, (2) due to mental subnormality, (3) which has been developmentally arrested, (4) which obtains at maturity, (5) is of constitutional origin, and (6) is essentially incurable" (p. 215). With this definition it is difficult to explain cases in which an individual is functioning at a retarded level at one time in life but not at another.

Pseudoretardation may be thought of in two ways. First, there may simply be a diagnostic error; in this situation, correction (not a new clinical term) is needed. Second, there may be a condition of behavioral retardation that can be ascribed to some factors other than those usually believed to be antecedent conditions of true mental defect. Thus one could speak of true and false retardation. If criteria in the definition include constitutional origin and no such origin can be demonstrated, or if incurability is a criterion and a retarded individual becomes socially competent later, a concept of pseudoretardation is needed.

The AMD's Terminology and Classification Committee published a definition in 1959 that did not include the criteria of incurability or constitutionality. The AAMD definition placed focus on current functioning level and separated the etiological medical classification system from the definition (Heber, 1959). Defining retardation in terms of current functional level seems to provide for optimism and encourages allocation of monies and resources to ameliorate retardation.

Changing a definition does not avoid another problem associated with the concept of pseudoretardation—whether intelligence tests measure potential capacity or not. Like intelligence, potential is a hypothetical concept and must be inferred from that which can be observed. Some psychologists estimate potential intelligence while others prefer to present the data from tests and make predictions in terms of probabilities. The trend among psychologists today appears to be toward interpreting test scores as indexes of functioning and indicating probabilities rather than estimating potential. A retarded adult who is socially competent when living in the structured, prosthetic environment of a residential facility, but incompetent living alone in a city, would be classified as retarded in either setting rather than truly retarded in the city and falsely retarded in the institution.

The pseudoretardation concept and term are more commonly used today by those not working directly in the field of retardation. For example, pediatricians' reports about preschool programs use the term pseudoretardation to describe children who received medical and dental treatment and later obtained IQs above 70 on intelligence tests. In addition, some who accept the idea that functional level determines classification may say that a child is not retarded, but just tests that way when they wish to imply potential greater than current functioning. Such attitudes indicate that although terminology may change, the idea of pseudoretardation is still with us.

REFERENCES

Doll, E. A. (1941). The essentials of an inclusive concept of mental deficiency. *American Journal of Mental Deficiency, 46,* 214–219.

Heber, R. F. (1959). A manual on terminology and classification in mental retardation. *American Journal of Mental Deficiency, 64.*

SUE ALLEN WARREN
Boston University

AAMD CLASSIFICATION SYSTEM
MENTAL RETARDATION

PSYCHOANALYSIS AND SPECIAL EDUCATION

Until the beginning of the twentieth century, mental illness was believed to be the result of biological and organic factors residing within the individual. Sigmund Freud,

who was a practicing physician and neurologist at the turn of the century, began to doubt that the hysterical reactions he was treating in his patients had solely an organic basis. Freud formulated an alternative theory to the development of personality that has subsequently had a profound effect on the way the behavior of an individual is explained. From Freud's psychoanalytic point of view, the psychological processes are the primary determinants of emotionally disturbed behavior. Psychological processes include all mental operations, thoughts, emotions, desires, needs, and perceptions.

Psychoanalysis is a specialized technique in which the individual verbalizes all of his or her thoughts and feelings without censorship (Finch, 1960). Freud's theory holds that individuals are only minimally aware of the causes of their behavior. Behavior is propelled by unconscious forces that are too threatening to be part of the conscious. In treatment, patients are taught to free associate to understand the meaning of their behavior and become better acquainted with the unconscious. Eventually, basic conflicts emerge and are understood and dealt with by the individual. Psychoanalysis is a long, tedious, and complex process that has had limited use in the schools (Finch, 1960). It is based on a medical or disability model where the pathology is believed to reside within the individual. To educators who do not have extensive training in psychology or, more specifically, psychoanalysis, the process seems complex and mysterious. Teachers prefer to refer students with emotional problems to outside agencies or self-contained special education classes rather than to risk making a serious mistake that would do further damage to the student.

Newcomer (1980) discusses both the positive and negative contributions of psychoanalysis to special education. There is the notion in psychoanalytic theory that personality characteristics are determined by childhood events; thus, pathology would develop before a child arrives in school. The problems in school are caused by disorders that are within the child. Therefore the strategies for remediation focus on the child and the family rather than the school. This may result in the school having a passive role in resolution of the conflict.

In addition, because of the psychoanalytic belief that abnormal behaviors are symptoms of unconscious conflicts and that resolution lies in open expression, educators are encouraged to treat disturbed children carefully to avoid repressing their behavior. A nonrepressive environment often provides little structure, and the expectations for normal behavior are reduced. Teachers are encouraged to stop teaching content material until the child's behavior is stable (Newcomer, 1980). It is not clear that this is the most effective way to deal with abnormal behavior. However, there has been a longstanding close association between special education and psychoanalysis in terms of understanding and providing for the needs of students (Pajak, 1981). Psychoanalytic theory has promoted the idea that children do not always consciously plan and cannot always control their disruptive behaviors, but they do respond to internal conflicts (Newcomer, 1980). These beliefs have resulted in more understanding and less primitive treatment of children with emotional disturbance.

Significant contributions to psychoanalysis and special education have been made by Bruno Bettleheim and Fritz Redl (Haring & Phillips, 1962). Their approaches have been primarily permissive in nature, and school work is often used as a vehicle to assist the child in bringing the unconscious conflict to a conscious level of awareness. In general, special education programs have moved from child-directed, psychoanalytic models to more teacher-directed behavioral models where emphasis is primarily on academics and behavior control. Only a few states still require psychiatric evaluation for placement in special education classrooms (Mendelsohn et al., 1985). Public Law 94-142 mandates teaching students in the least restrictive environment. Therefore, the emphasis in special education is on teaching children appropriate and acceptable behavior in school, which is in conflict with the free and open expression advocated by Freud and his followers.

REFERENCES

Finch, S. M. (1960). *Fundamentals of child psychiatry.* New York: Norton.

Haring, N. G., & Phillips, E. L. (1962). *Educating emotionally disturbed children.* New York: McGraw-Hill.

Mendelsohn, S. R., Jennings, K. D., Kerr, M. M., Marsh, J., May, K., & Strain, P. S. (1985). Psychiatric input as part of a comprehensive evaluation program for socially and emotionally disturbed children. *Behavioral Disorders, 10*(4), 257–267.

Newcomer, P. L. (1980). *Understanding and teaching emotionally disturbed children.* Boston: Allyn & Bacon.

Pajak, E. F. (1981, Nov.). Teaching and the psychology of the self. *American Journal of Education,* 1–13.

Rezmierski, V., & Kotre, J. (1977). A limited literature review of theory of the psychodynamic model. In W. C. Rhodes & M. L. Tracy (Eds.), *A study of child variance: Vol. 1. Conceptual models* (pp. 181–258). Ann Arbor, MI: University Press.

NANCY J. KAUFMAN
University of Wisconsin, Stevens Point

CHILD PSYCHIATRY
PSYCHODRAMA
PSYCHOTHERAPY

PSYCHODRAMA

Psychodrama is a method of group psychotherapy devised and developed by Moreno (1946). Psychodrama requires a well-trained therapist, preferably one with special certification as a psychodramatist. Psychodrama consists of using dramatic techniques with clients who act out real-life situations, past, present, or projected, in an attempt to gain insight into their behavior and emotions. Psychodrama also provides the opportunity to practice specific behaviors in a supportive group atmosphere. The method of psychodrama integrates insight and cognitions with experiential, participatory involvement, taking advantage of the group therapy setting and using physical movement to bring nonverbal cues to the client's attention. This component of psychodrama can be crucial in therapy with individuals who have limited verbal skills, particularly children and delinquent adolescents (Blatner, 1973). Another significant advantage of psychodrama is its ability to convert the child or adolescent's urge to act out into a more constructive form of "acting in," with guided role playing.

Many production techniques have been devised since psychodrama was introduced, including the auxiliary ego, the double, and the soliloquy. Important to the success of psychodrama is a time for warm-up at the beginning of each session. Participants must also know that the dramatic qualities of the production are not being evaluated, nor are they crucial to the success of therapy. Trust and support of the group are far more important. The role of the director (the psychodramatist) is primarily one of keeping the action moving and helping to lead the participants toward a resolution of the problem situation presented. Keeping the audience (the remainder of the group) involved is also an important role for the director. Three phases will typically constitute a psychodrama, the warm-up phase, the action phase, and the discussion phase.

Psychodrama can be a particularly useful form of psychotherapy with children and adolescents with a variety of behavior disorders. It offers an opportunity for understanding and gaining insight, but it also offers a setting for the development of alternative behaviors and an opportunity for rehearsal in a realistic and supportive setting.

REFERENCES

Blatner, H. A. (1973). *Acting-in: Practical application of psychodramatic methods.* New York: Springer.

Moreno, J. L. (1946). *Psychodrama* (Vol. 1). New York: Beacon House.

CECIL R. REYNOLDS
Texas A&M University

SOCIODRAMA

PSYCHOEDUCATIONAL METHODS

Psychoeducational methods generally refer to the processes of psychological assessment and the subsequent design of remedial programs. Historically, special educators have attempted to develop a variety of psychoeducational methods, all with the goal of facilitating the learning of the exceptional child. This effort has been intensified in the years following the passage of federal and state special education laws mandating the link between psychoeducational assessment data and the development of instructional strategies in the form of the individualized educational plan (IEP).

Hundreds of different types of psychoeducational methods are currently in use. However, the choice of a particular psychoeducational method is often tied to the educator's assumptions or beliefs regarding the nature and etiology of a child's exceptionality (Quay, 1983; Ysseldyke & Mirkin, 1982).

One view of exceptionality is what Quay (1973) refers to as process dysfunction, which is based on the assumption that the child suffers from dysfunctions or impairments in processes that are necessary for learning. The viewpoint holds that the problem resides within the child and the cause of the child's learning problems is the particular dysfunction or deficit. These dysfunctions, according to Ysseldyke and Mirkin (1982), can be in any number of areas, including sensory processes (visual acuity), response processes (motor coordination), specific hypothetical internal processes (attention, visual-perception, and memory) or global hypothesized internal processes (intelligence, personality, and motivation).

Guided by the process dysfunction view of exceptionality, the psychoeducational assessment is geared toward identifying the specific nature of the dysfunction or deficit responsible for the learning problem and then the development of psychoeducational methods to "cure" the dysfunction. This particular view of exceptionality has been popular in special education and has led to the development of numerous types of psychoeducational methods.

Historically, psycholinguistic training programs (Kirk & Kirk, 1971; Minskoff, Wiseman, & Minskoff, 1972) tied to the Illinois Test of Psycholinguistic Abilities have represented some of the more popular psychoeducational methods. However, research investigating the effectiveness of these psycholinguistic training programs in facilitating the learning and increasing the academic achievement of exceptional children has been equivocal (Hammill & Larsen, 1974, 1978; Kavale, 1981; Lund, Foster, & McCall-Perez, 1978). Many of the criticisms have centered around the methodological flaws of the research investigating the effectiveness of the programs. The level of empirical support of these psycholinguistic training programs suggests they should be implemented only for research purposes.

Another popular psychoeducational method based on the process dysfunction view of exceptionality is the perceptual-motor training program. This program includes training in visual discrimination, spatial relations, visual memory, auditory-visual integration, and auditory-perceptual skills (Ysseldyke & Mirkin, 1982). Typical training activities include walking a balance beam, jumping and hopping, chalkboard drawing, copying geometric shapes, and moving arms and legs, as in "angels in the snow." Programs developed by Barsch (1967, 1968), Frostig and Horne (1964), Johnson and Myklebust (1967), and Kephart (1964) represent the better known psychoeducational methods in this area. Little empirical support exists for any relationship between perceptual-motor processes and academic achievement (Larsen & Hammill, 1975) or for the effectiveness of these types of psychoeducational methods in improving academic performance (Ysseldyke & Mirkin, 1982).

Psychoeducational methods based on modality training (Johnson & Myklebust, 1967; Lerner, 1981; Wepman, 1967) have also received little empirical support (Arter & Jenkins, 1977). Modality training rests on the assumption that a child may learn better through one modality than through another. In modality training, children are taught using their stronger modality, strengthening the modality of deficit, or a combination approach. An example of the combination approach would include a child who has a strong auditory but weak visual modality being taught reading using a phonetic as opposed to a whole word approach while strengthening the child's weaker visual skills with separate lessons.

Optometric vision training has been another commonly prescribed psychoeducational method, but there exists little empirical support for the training's improving academic achievement (Keogh, 1974). This was formally acknowledged when the American Academies of Pediatrics and Ophthalmology together with the American Association for Pediatric Ophthalmology and Strabismus (1984) issued a policy statement. The policy pertaining to children and adults with dyslexia or a related learning disability stressed the need for early medical, educational, and/or psychological evaluation and diagnosis, and for remediation with valid educational procedures. The groups explicitly included the statement that "no known scientific evidence supports claims for improving the academic abilities of dyslexic or learning disabled children with treatment based on visual training, including muscle exercises, or glasses (with or without bifocals or prisms)" (p. 2).

Psychoeducational methods have also been developed based on process dysfunctions in intellectual skills (Cutrona, 1975; Jacobson & Kovalinsky, 1969). As an example, expressive language skills are tapped on the vocabulary subtest of the Wechsler Intelligence Scale for Children-Revised. Psychoeducational methods developed to remediate this deficit include activities such as making extensive use of show-and-tell games at the younger age levels, playing crossword puzzles and Scrabble games, and making up stories after arranging pictures, at the older age levels. Other psychoeducational methods to remediate intellectual process dysfunctions draw from psychodynamic, perceptual, behavioral, and motivational theories in developing remedial programs. However, tasks on tests like the Wechsler represent only samples of behavior and inadequate performance on some of these samples should not automatically suggest the need to remediate those behaviors. Low scores should be viewed only as symptoms of problems that need to be corroborated to determine whether they represent global or pervasive deficits (Kaufman, 1979). Further, there is little empirical support that in isolation the psychoeducational methods designed to remediate deficits in cognitive skills are effective in facilitating academic learning (Ysseldyke & Mirkin, 1982).

Sensory integration (Ayres, 1972) and training in rhythm and balance (Rice, 1962) represent two additional psychoeducational methods designed to alleviate underlying dysfunctions. As is true for the other methods discussed, little evidence exists to support their use to improve academic achievement (Ysseldyke & Mirkin, 1982).

The opposite end of the continuum, in relation to views of the etiology of exceptionality, is represented by Quay's (1973) experience deficit notion. This viewpoint suggests that a student's learning problems are due not to deficits within the child but to the student's limited behavioral repertoire. The student's learning apparatus is intact and underlying process deficits are not assumed. The goal of the psychoeducational assessment guided by this notion of exceptionality is to identify experiential deficits and develop remedial or compensatory interventions or psychoeducational methods to eliminate them.

The task-analytic or skills-training approach represents a class of psychoeducational methods that is based on this experience deficit notion. Example methods include direct instruction (Carnine & Silbert, 1979) and precision teaching (Lindsley, 1971). Both of these methods focus on the academic and social skill requirements of the school program. They also share the characteristics of being sequential, systematic, and intensive, and are typically implemented in individualized or small group settings. Further, complex learning tasks are broken up into simpler component subskills so they can be taught more easily, using behavioral principles such as reinforcement and modeling. These various psychoeducational methods differ in the frequency and directness of their measurements. Precision teaching involves the continuous measurement of a student's performance in the mastery of academic or social skill objectives. The method also includes the direct assessment of skills that have been taught rather than the assessment of effectiveness through sampling from a larger domain. All of the task-analytic or skills-training psychoeducational methods are based on the assumption that the teacher cannot predict consistently the particular interventions that will be most effective with a particular child; therefore, the methods are used as tentative hypotheses that are always being tested and modified if necessary.

Compared with the other psychoeducational methods discussed, the task-analytic or skill-development approaches that use direct and continuous measurement tend to be the most effective in increasing academic achievement (Ysseldyke & Mirkin, 1982; Ysseldyke & Salvia, 1974). However, future research may indeed demonstrate that those who assess, develop, and implement psychoeducational methods for exceptional children should hold the belief that exceptionality is explained by an interaction view. Learning problems may well result from deficits resulting from process deficits and/or experiential deficits. However, most special educators exclusively use psychoeducational methods that are based on one or the other viewpoint (Ysseldyke & Mirkin, 1982). Special education needs more psychoeducational methods that rely on an interactive approach.

REFERENCES

American Academy of Pediatrics, American Academy of Ophthalmology. (1984). *Policy statement on learning disabilities, dyslexia, & vision.* San Francisco: Authors.

Arter, J. A., & Jenkins, J. R. (1977). Explaining the benefits and prevalence of modality consideration in special education. *Journal of Special Education, 11*, 281–298.

Ayres, A. J. (1972). *Sensory integration and learning disorders.* Los Angeles: Western Psychological Services.

Barsch, R. H. (1967). *Achieving perceptual-motor efficiency.* Seattle, WA: Special Child.

Barsch, R. H. (1968). *Enriching perception and cognition.* Seattle, WA: Special Child.

Carnine, D., & Silbert, J. (1979). *Direct instruction reading.* Columbus, OH: Merrill.

Cutrona, M. P. (1975). A psychoeducational interpretation of the Wechsler Intelligence Scale for Children-Revised (2nd ed.). Belleville, NJ: Cutronics.

Frostig, M., & Horne, D. (1964). *The Frostig program for the development of visual perception.* Chicago: Follett.

Hammill, D. D., & Larsen, S. C. (1974). The effectiveness of psycholinguistic training. *Exceptional Children, 41*, 5–14.

Hammill, D. D., & Larsen, S. C. (1978). The effectiveness of psycholinguistic training: A reaffirmation of position. *Exceptional Children, 44*, 402–412.

Jacobson, S., & Kovalinsky, T. (1969). *Educational interpretation of the Wechsler Intelligence Scale for Children-Revised (WISC-R).* Linden, NJ: Remediation Associates.

Johnson, D., & Myklebust, H. R. (1967). *Learning disabilities: Educational principles and practices.* New York: Grune & Stratton.

Kaufman, A. S. (1979). *Intelligent testing with the WISC-R.* New York: Wiley.

Kavale, K. (1981). Functions of the Illinois Test of Psycholinguists Abilities (IPTA): Are they trainable? *Exceptional Children, 47*, 496–513.

Keogh, B. K. (1974). Optometric vision training programs for children with learning disabilities: Review of issues and research. *Journal of Learning Disabilities, 7*, 36–48.

Kephart, N. C. (1964). Perceptual motor aspects of learning disabilities. *Exceptional Children, 31*, 201–206.

Kephart, N. C. (1971). *The slow learner in the classroom* (2nd ed.). Columbus, OH: Merrill.

Kirk, S. A., & Kirk, W. D. (1971). *Psycholinguistic learning disabilities: Diagnosis and remediation.* Urbana, IL: University of Illinois Press.

Larsen, S. C., & Hammill, D. D. (1975). The relationship between selected visual perceptual abilities to school learning. *Journal of Special Education, 9,* 281–291.

Lerner, J. S. (1981). *Children with learning disabilities* (3rd ed.). Boston: Houghton Mifflin.

Lindsley, O. R. (1971). Precision teaching in perspective: An interview with Ogden R. Lindsley. *Teaching Exceptional Children, 3,* 114–119.

Lund, K., Foster, G., & McCall-Perez, F. (1978). The effectiveness of psycholinguistic training. A re-evaluation. *Exceptional Children, 44,* 310–321.

Minskoff, E., Wiseman, D. E., & Minskoff, J. G. (1972). *The MWM program for developing language abilities.* Ridgewood, NJ: Educational Performance Associates.

Quay, H. C. (1973). Special education: Assumptions, techniques, and evaluative criteria. *Exceptional Children, 40,* 165–170.

Rice, A. (1962). Rhythmic training and board balancing prepares a child for learning. *Nation's Schools, 6,* 72.

Wepman, J. (1967). The perceptual bases for learning. In E. C. Friersen & W. B. Barbe (Eds.), *Educating children with learning disabilities: Selected readings.* New York: Appleton-Century-Crofts.

Ysseldyke, J. E., & Mirkin, P. K. (1982). The use of assessment information to plan instructional interventions: A review of the research. In C. R. Reynolds & T. B. Gutkin (Eds.), *The handbook of school psychology.* New York: Wiley.

Ysseldyke, J., & Salvia, J. (1974). Diagnostic perscriptive teaching: Two models. *Exceptional Children, 4,* 181–186.

MARK E. SWERDLIK
Illinois State University

ASSESSMENT
ETIOLOGY
MEASUREMENT
TASK ANALYSIS
TEACHING STRATEGIES

PSYCHOGENIC MODELS

Psychogenic models present causes of human behavior in terms of the psychological functioning of the individual. The cognitive and emotional aspects of personality are central to explaining behavior. The psychogenic approach emphasizes emotional distress as the root of deviant behavior (Bootzin, 1984). The model stands in contrast to the biogenic approach in placing little emphasis on the physiological factors underlying behavior.

Psychogenic models, however, emphasize factors internal to the individual as mechanisms of behavior. For example, personality integration is the central construct of psychological definitions of mental health (Freeman & Giovannoni, 1969). The effects of the ecology of the family or school are mediated by psychological factors, and changes in behavior result from improvements in psychological functioning. The psychogenic model may share with the biogenic model a tendency to blame the victim.

Balow (1979) noted that psychological models are compatible with special education practice because most educational interventions are based on psychological principles. The models, techniques, and measurements of special education are expressed typically in terms of psychological function of individual students.

REFERENCES

Balow, B. (1979). Biological defects and special education: An empiricist's view. *Journal of Special Education, 13,* 35–40.

Bootzin, R. (1984). *Abnormal psychology: Current perspectives* (4th ed.). New York: Random House.

Freeman, H., & Giovannoni, J. (1969). Social psychology and mental health. In G. Lindzey & E. Aronson (Eds.), *The handbook of social psychology.* (Vol. 5, 2nd ed. pp. 660–719). Reading, MA: Addison-Wesley.

LEE ANDERSON JACKSON, JR.
*University of North Carolina,
Wilmington*

BIOGENIC MODEL OF BEHAVIOR ETIOLOGY

PSYCHOLINGUISTICS

In the late 1950s, with the aid of workers in philosophy and anthropology and the earlier insights of distinguished scholars such as von Humboldt and Wundt, psychologists and linguists joined forces to study the content and organization of mature linguistic (i.e., phonological, syntactic, morphological, and semantic) knowledge. In addition, they studied the content and organization of mature communicative (e.g., conversational) competence, linguistic and communicative development, speech production and comprehension processes, memory for linguistic input, and the relationship between language and thought (Blumenthal, 1970; Foss & Hakes, 1978). Thus was born the science of psycholinguistics, which soon attracted the attention of workers in fields such as special education, speech-hearing-language disorders, reading, and second-language learning.

One of the factors responsible for this attraction in special education and related fields was the recognition of the need to describe and explain normal language acquisition when attempting to assess the language problems of, for example, mentally retarded or autistic children (Rosenberg, 1982). At the same time, however, basic researchers in psycholinguistics began to recognize that their theories of normal language acquisition and functioning could be illuminated by observations of language disorders in children and adults. The fact, for example, that there are rarely any qualitative differences between normal and language-disordered children in the course of language acquisition or in the structure of the language acquired suggests "that there are strong specifically linguistic biological constraints on first-language acquisition that limit significantly the manner in which a wide variety of insults can affect language competence and its development" (Rosenberg, 1984, p. 228).

As indicated, psycholinguistics has been influential in the field of special education, with its longstanding commitment to children with language and communicative disorders associated with mental retardation, hearing impairment, visual impairment, learning disabilities, and other handicaps. This influence has been apparent in work with handicapped children on the assessment and remediation of disorders of linguistic competence (Bloom & Lahey, 1978), on linguistic coding and reading ability (Vellutino & Scanlon, 1982), and, most recently, on the development of communicative competence (Donahue & Bryan, 1983). The work on communicative competence is the result of an increased emphasis in special education on preparing handicapped students for community living and mainstreaming.

Thus, progress has been made in the education of handicapped children in the areas of language and communication, although much remains to be done, particularly concerning the role of first-language competence in learning to read.

Recent applied psycholinguistic research that has particular implications for special education includes Abbeduto and Rosenberg (1980) who have shown that the conversational communicative competence of mildly retarded adults (and possibly moderately retarded adults as well) is mostly indistinguishable from that of normal adults. Therefore, although mentally retarded children tend to get off to a slow start in the area of conversational communicative competence, many of them may be able to catch up to their nonretarded peers. Such findings could inspire special educators to expand their efforts to facilitate communicative development in mentally retarded children.

An appreciable number of psycholinguists believe that a major factor in a child's ability to "crack the code" of the language he or she hears is the meanings inferred from the sensory input provided by nonlinguistic context. Therefore, blind children should be unable to master word meanings that require sight, and should be considerably delayed in other aspects of language development. However, as Landau and Gleitman (1985) have shown, blind children can learn a good deal about the meanings of such words, and their language development is only minimally delayed. Like sighted children, blind children bring to the task of language acquisition native resources or expectations that facilitate language acquisition independent,

to a significant extent, of sensory experience. Clearly, blind children should be encouraged by teachers and others to use their vocabulary of sight to whatever extent is possible, and to engage in age-appropriate language and communicative activities generally.

REFERENCES

Abbeduto, L., & Rosenberg, S. (1980). The communicative competence of mildly retarded adults. *Applied Psycholinguistics, 1*, 405–426.

Bloom, L., & Lahey, M. (1978). *Language development and language disorders.* New York: Wiley.

Blumenthal, A. L. (1970). *Language and psychology.* New York: Wiley.

Donahue, M., & Bryan, T. (1983). Conversational skills and modelling in learning disabled boys. *Applied Psycholinguistics, 4,* 251–278.

Foss, D. J., & Hakes, D. T. (1978). *Psycholinguistics.* Englewood Cliffs, NJ: Prentice-Hall.

Landau, B., & Gleitman, L. R. (1985). *Language and experience.* Cambridge, MA: Harvard University Press.

Rosenberg, S. (Ed.). (1982). *Handbook of applied psycholinguistics; Major thrusts of research and theory.* Hillsdale, NJ: Erlbaum.

Rosenberg, S. (1984). Disorders of first-language development: Trends in research and theory. In E. S. Gollin (Ed.), *Malformations of development: Biological and psychological sources and consequences.* NY: Academic.

Vellutino, F. R., & Scanlon, D. M. (1982). Verbal processing in poor and normal readers. In C. J. Brainerd & M. Pressley (Eds.), *Verbal processes in children.* NY: Springer-Verlag.

SHELDON ROSENBERG
University of Illinois, Chicago

LANGUAGE DISORDERS
LANGUAGE THERAPY

PSYCHOLOGICAL ABSTRACTS (PA)

Psychological Abstracts (PA) provides nonevaluative summaries of the world's literature in psychology and related disciplines. Over 950 journals, technical reports, monographs, and other scientific documents provide material for coverage in PA. *Psychological Abstracts* includes bibliographic citations or annotations that are used to cover books, secondary sources, articles peripherally relevant to psychology, or articles that can be represented adequately in approximately 30 to 50 words. Since 1967 the abstracts have been entered into machine-readable tapes that now provide the basis for the automated search and retrieval service known as Psychological Abstracts Information Service (PsychINFO).

As psychology has multiple roots in the older disciplines of philosophy, medicine, education, and physics, the vocabulary of psychological literature is characterized by considerable diversity. Each new generation of psychologists added to the vocabulary in attempting to describe their research and perceptions of behavioral processes. As a result, the American Psychological Association standardized the vocabulary by designing a Thesaurus of Psychological Index Terms in 1974, a few years after establishing the computerized version of PA. By 1967 there were over 800 terms that indexed psychological research and writing. In 1974, when the first *Thesaurus* was published, the index and terms were based on the frequency of the occurrence of single words in titles or abstracts in PA over the preceding years. The *Thesaurus* was revised in 1977 and 1982. Each entry in the *Abstracts* and the PsychINFO system is indexed for retrieval by one or more *Thesaurus* index terms, which reflect broader, narrower, and related terms that may describe content in the article. In addition, each article is identified as belonging to one of 16 major content categories and 64 subcategories.

Using these index and content classification terms enables the user to locate articles of interest for hand searchers of *PA* issues or for computerized retrieval from the PsychINFO system. Further information about PA or the PsychINFO system can be obtained from the American Psychological Association, 1200 Seventeenth Street, NW, Washington, DC 20036.

NADINE M. LAMBERT
*University of California,
Berkeley*

PSYCHOLOGICAL CLINICS

University psychological clinics are generally student training facilities that have a cooperative relationship with the surrounding community. The clinics provide undergraduate and graduate students in disciplines such as education, counseling, and psychology with an opportunity to apply their theoretical and technical knowledge in working with a variety of clients in a closely supervised practicum. Individuals from the communities surrounding the university psychological clinics are able to receive innovative, state-of-the-art evaluations and treatments at reasonable fees from professionals in training. Each clinic usually has a director who is responsible for the coordination and overall functioning of the clinic and each student's activities are generally scrutinized by one or more qualified supervisors (i.e., licensed psychologists, speech pathologists, or special educators). A number of types of services are usually offered in the psychological clinics, including: child assessment and treatment; parent training; family counseling; teacher consultation; program

evaluation; and organizational consultation. Therefore, the clinic provides clients with a wide array of psychological services and the students in training with exposure to a number of different approaches to a particular problem.

TIMOTHY L. TURCO
STEPHEN N. ELLIOTT
Louisiana State University

CHILD GUIDANCE CLINIC
COLLEGE PROGRAMS FOR DISABLED COLLEGE STUDENTS

PSYCHOLOGICAL CORPORATION

The Psychological Corporation is the world's oldest and largest commercial test publisher. It was founded in New York City in 1921 by three noted professors from Teachers College of Columbia University; James M. Cattell, Edward L. Thorndike, and Robert S. Woodworth. Over its 65-year history, the corporation's primary mission has been the application of principles of psychology and measurement to the solution of educational, clinical, industrial, and social problems. On the eve of its fiftieth anniversary, the Psychological Corporation merged with the test department of Harcourt, Brace, & World, and in 1975 it became a subsidiary of Harcourt Brace Jovanovich. Growth in development programs, services, and professional staff required the corporation to move from New York to Cleveland, Ohio, in 1983. The corporation continued to expand rapidly, employing over 200 people, including 50 psychologists specializing in measurement, child development, and education, by 1985. In 1986 the corporation relocated to permanent headquarters at 555 Academic Court, San Antonio, Texas 78204, with field offices in New York, Chicago, Atlanta, San Diego, Orlando, and Toronto.

The corporation is well known for high-quality educational and psychological tests. Names such as the Wechsler Intelligence Scales for Children-Revised, McCarthy Scales of Children's Abilities, Baley Scales of Infant Development, and Stanford Diagnostic Reading and Mathematics Tests are familiar to scholars throughout the world. The corporation also provides tests and services to many of the nation's largest companies, government agencies, and health care institutions, and holds contracts for large-scale assessment programs in English- and non-English-speaking countries worldwide. The corporation now publishes over 200 tests. In 1985 it inaugurated a computer software development program.

PAUL A. McDERMOTT
University of Pennsylvania

PSYCHOLOGICAL REPORTS

Psychological Reports is published bimonthly, two volumes a year, the first with issues in February, April, and June and the second with issues in August, October, and December. Between 2000 and 3000 pages are published annually. Approximately one-third of the articles come from outside the United States. The purpose of this journal is to encourage scientific originality and creativity in the field of general psychology for the person who is first a psychologist and then a specialist. It carries experimental, theoretical, and speculative articles; comments; special reviews; and a listing of new books and other materials received. Controversial material of scientific merit is welcomed. Multiple referees examine submissions. Critical editing is balanced by specific suggestions as to changes required to meet standards (Ammons & Ammons, 1962a).

The complete publication process requires as little as 8 to 12 weeks. Distribution of the journal is international. Abstracts appear in standard outlets (e.g., *Psychological Abstracts*), in numerous on-line services for special interest areas, and in journals with particular emphases. A survey made in 1985 (the thirty-first year of publication) showed that *Psychological Reports* appeared in the top 5% of psychology journals for number of citations of articles and number of refereed, selected archival articles published, and that it had held that position for the preceding decade. The journal has consistently maintained for 30 years a policy of being highly experimental, open to all defensible points of view, encouraging of new and often unpopular ways of looking at problems, and protective of authors by careful but open-minded refereeing and editing (Ammons & Ammons, 1962b).

REFERENCES

Ammons, R. B., & Ammons, C. H. (1962a). Permanent or temporary journals: Are PR and PMS stable? *Perceptual & Motor Skills, 14*, 281.

Ammons, C. H., & Ammons, R. B. (1962b). Permanent or temporary journals: PR and PMS become stable. *Psychological Reports, 10*, 537.

C. H. AMMONS
Psychological Reports/
Perceptual and Motor Skills,
Missoula, Montana

PSYCHOLOGY IN THE SCHOOLS

Psychology in the Schools began in 1964 with William Hunt serving as editor. He was followed briefly by B. Claude Mathis and then in 1970 by Gerald B. Fuller of Central Michigan University, who remains as editor. In an attempt to meet the practical needs of professionals in the field, this journal emphasizes an applied orientation. It addresses practicing school and clinical psychologists, guidance personnel, teachers, educators, and university faculty. Articles of preference clearly describe the relevancy of the research for these practitioners. However, occasionally important experimental and theoretical papers may be included.

The major areas of focus include (1) theoretical papers and interpretive reviews of literature when these relate to some aspect of school psychology; (2) opinions that are well formulated and presented; (3) treatment and remediation approaches; (4) evaluation of treatment and remediation or other program evaluations; (5) deviant or atypical features of the behavior of school children; (6) social or group effects on adjustment and development; (7) educational, intellectual, and personality assessments; (8) etiology and diagnosis; and (9) case studies. These areas are grouped into four categories within the journal: evaluation and assessment; educational practices and problems; strategies for intervention; and general topics.

GERALD B. FULLER
Central Michigan University

PSYCHOMETRICS

See MEASUREMENT.

PSYCHOMOTOR SEIZURES

The term psychomotor was introduced in 1938 by Gibbs and Lennox (Lennox & Lennox, 1960) to describe epileptic manifestations composed of various multiple psychic or motor activities. These manifestations are associated with spikes, sharp or slow waves on the electroencephalogram over the anterior area of the temporal lobe; therefore, the manifestations are also called temporal lobe seizures. According to the classification of the International League Against Epilepsy (1981), the seizures are partial, as they begin locally, and also complex, as they are associated with "a clouding of consciousness and complete or partial amnesia for the event" (Livingston, 1972). They may be followed by generalized tonic-clonic seizures.

Psychomotor seizures are more frequent in older children, adolescents, and young adults (Currie et al., 1971; Gastaut, 1953; Livingston, 1972). However, Holowach et al. (1961) and Chao et al. (1962) reported this kind of seizure in 11 and 15.7% of children with all types of epilepsy up to 15 years of age. The onset occurred before the age of 6 years in more than 50% and before the age of 3 years in almost 30%.

As in every partial seizure, the temporal lobe epilepsy may start with an aura that is the first subjective and remembered symptom of the seizure. This aura is indicative of the starting point of the fit, and sometimes of its spreading. In psychomotor epilepsy, the wide variety of symptoms, sensory, motor, or mental, are due to the structures encountered in the temporal lobe area, such as the temporal convolutions, the cortex in the fissure of Sylvius, the insula, the amygdaloid nucleus, the uncus, and the hippocampal zone. The International League Against Epilepsy (1985) proposes to classify the multiple clinical pictures into four subtypes: hippocampal (mesiobasal limbic or primary rhinencephalic psychomotor), amygdalar (anterior polaramygdalar), lateral posterior temporal, and opercular (insular) epilepsies. The symptoms may be motor, sensory, or psychic, appearing simultaneously or consecutively, but they present some clinical patterns (Chao et al. 1962; Gastaut, 1953; Holowach et al., 1961; Livingston, 1972).

Young children may, as an aura, run to their mother with fear or complain of gastric discomfort or unpleasant smell or taste before the loss of consciousness. The symptoms often start with an arrest of motion, with eye staring eventually followed by simple and/or complex automatisms such as repetitive oral movements (e.g., lip smacking, chewing, and swallowing). The motor activities, like rubbing the face, fumbling with buttons of clothing, or wandering around the room, appear purposive but inappropriate at the time. Speech may become incoherent or mumbled. Autonomic disturbances such as urination, vomiting, salivation, or flushing of the face may be present. Awareness is impaired and amnesia of the attack is a fairly constant finding. The episodes are not very frequent (from one to five per day to one to five per month) and usually brief, 2 to 3 minutes, but the return to consciousness is often gradual. Mental or psychic seizures are variable, but visual or auditory hallucinations are frequent and owed to connections with the vicinity. Affective manifestations such as fear or aggressiveness are frequently present. The attack may terminate in a grand mal seizure. The symptomatology is often associated with mental retardation, cerebral palsy, and hyperkinetic syndrome (as with any organic brain disorder of childhood).

In children the etiology is most often the result of a chronic, nonprogressive neurologic disease. The seizures may be due to previous insult to the brain in the neonatal period as in hypoxia, infection, trauma, or congenital malformations, but also to severe or prolonged seizures in early life or to febrile convulsions. Tumors are rare. Often, no definite cause can be established (Gomez & Klass, 1983). The most common abnormality is mesial temporal sclerosis (incisural sclerosis). The prognosis is better than previously thought (Lindsay et al., 1979; Staff, 1980), and treatment is mainly medical through drug therapy.

REFERENCES

Chao, D., Sexton, J. A., & Santos Pardo, L. S. (1962). Temporal lobe epilepsy in children. *Journal of Pediatrics, 60*, 686–693.

Currie, S., Heathfield, K. W. G., Henson, R. A., & Scott, D. F. (1971). Clinical course and prognosis of temporal lobe epilepsy: A survey of 666 patients. *Brain, 94*, 173–190.

Gastaut, H. (1953). So called "psychomotor" and "temporal" epilepsy—A critical review. *Epilepsia, 2*, 59–99.

Gomez, M. R., & Klass, D. W. (1983). Epilepsies of infancy and childhood. *Annals of Neurology, 13*, 113–124.

Holowach, J., Renda, Y. A., & Wapner, J. (1961). Psychomotor seizures in childhood. A clinical study of 120 cases. *Journal of Pediatrics, 59*, 339–346.

International League Against Epilepsy. (1981). Proposal for revised clinical and electroencephalographic classification of epileptic seizures. *Epilepsia, 22*, 489–501.

International League Against Epilepsy. (1985). Proposal for classification of epilepsies and epileptic syndromes. *Epilepsia, 26*, 268–278.

Lennox, W. G., & Lennox, M. A. (1960). *Epilepsy and related disorders*. Boston: Little, Brown.

Lindsay, J., Ounsted, C., & Richards, P. (1979). Long-term outcome in children with temporal lobe, seizures. *Developmental Medicine and Child Neurology, 21*, 285–636.

Livingston, S. (1972). *Comprehensive management of epilepsy in infancy, childhood and adolescence*. Springfield, IL: Thomas.

Staff. (1980). Prognosis of temporal lobe epilepsy in childhood. *British Medical Journal, 280*, 812–813.

HENRI B. SZLIWOWSKI
*Hôpital Erasme, Brussels,
Belgium*

ABSENCE SEIZURES
DRUG THERAPY
EPILEPSY
GRAND MAL EPILEPSY

PSYCHOMOTRICITY

An independent science firmly established in France, psychomotricity is based on the interdependence of physical, affective, and intellectual functions and thus covers a wide field that encompasses neurology, pedagogy, and psychoanalysis.

Numerous scientific ideas from various disciplines have contributed for more than a century to the elaboration of the concept of psychomotricity. Near the end of the nineteenth century, scientific achievements made it necessary to abandon Cartesian dualism, which separated body and mind and led to a mechanistic approach to the body. Instead, the integrative action of the nervous system and its role in the regulation of the organism interacting with its environment were stressed. Neurophysiologists started to examine the bases of tonus and movement (gamma loop and Renshaw recurrent circuit, cerebellum, subcortical nuclei, neocortex, etc). Penfield's center-encephalic theory of motor adjustment (counter to traditional associationism) underscored the importance of the basal centers and their integrating role, and of the vertical cortical-subcortical relationships.

Dupré, a neuropsychiatrist, described the syndrome of motor deficiency in relation to mental deficiency and compared it with the immature state of newborn babies (limb hypertonicity, enuresis, etc.). For the first time, motricity and intelligence were linked.

In *La naissance de l'intelligence chez l'enfant* (1936), Piaget stated that the first stage in the development of intelligence is the coordination of sensorimotor schemas (i.e., feeling and movement systems such as suction, sight, prehension, etc.) leading to adaptations and assimilations that enable the individual to reach a higher (preoperative) type of intelligence. Piaget's ideas were developed further. De Ajuriaguerra showed that the tonic state is used by the newborn baby as a mode of relation (e.g., crying hypertonicity, contentment hypotonicity). A structuring dialogue actually takes place between mother and child. Wallon studied the relationship between motricity and character (*L'enfant turbulent*, 1925). He described the body image as a progressive construction involving all our perceptive, motor, and affective experiences. Phenomenology, too, played a role in the coming about of psychomotricity. It gave birth to the gestalt theory, in which every physical or psychological phenomenon is seen as an indivisible whole known as the form. This theory helped shape the notions of body schema, behavior, and movement. According to Merleau-Ponty and Buytendijk, the different types of behavior are modalities of the *in-der-Welt-sein*, i.e., of mind and body as they interact continuously in the flow of life. Thus, in the phenomenal world body and mind were no longer separated and psychomotricity could enter the field.

Psychoanalysis also contributed to the elaboration of the concept. The body was defined as a scene of pleasure, and psychic development was divided into organic stages: oral, anal, phallic, and genital. Moreover, it was contended that an organic or perceptual-motor function could be used effectively only if it had been effectively invested. An emotional disorder can easily bring about physical dysfunctions such as conversion hysteria or organic neurosis. Reich stated that the social-emotional state of a person influences his or her tonic state (tension rings). The ethology of the child also played a role. Montagner gave a minute description of the child's behavior in the nursery and highlighted socio-affective correlations.

In France, psychomotricity was recognized as a discipline in the early 1960s. The first French Psychomotricity Charter (de Ajuriaguerra-Soubiran) was promulgated and a curriculum was created. A trade union and various publications came about.

As far as practice is concerned, a distinction is usually made between education, remedial work, and therapy. Education aims at stimulating the healthy child's psychomotor functions. This concept is slowly spreading in nursery schools. Remedial exercises aim at improving psychomotor symptomatology through a reprogramming of the neuromotor sphere. Model lessons by the well-known team of the Henri-Rousselle Hospital in Paris are available. Therapy aims at deblocking and developing the disturbed child's psychic structures through bodily and relational interaction with the therapist and mediatory objects. According to Aucouturier, technicity consists of working out sensorimotor pleasure and treatment of aggressive and fantasmatic productions. These various approaches are used primarily with children up to 7 years of age when symbolizing processes enable them to dissociate themselves from their bodily experiences. However, the concept of psychomotricity applies in theory to every stage of life.

REFERENCES

Piaget, J. (1936). *Le naissance de l'intelligence chez l'enfant*. Neuchatel: Delachaux et Niestlé.

Wallon, H. (1925). *L'enfant turbulent*. Paris: Alcan.

DANIELLE MICHAUX
*Vrije Universiteit Brussel,
Belgium*

PSYCHONEUROTIC DISORDERS

The term psychoneurotic as a description of childhood emotional disorders is associated with the psychoanalytic tradition of Sigmund Freud. It is a general term that has been applied to specific clinical syndromes, including phobias, anxiety reactions, obsessive-compulsive behavioral patterns, and hysterical or conversion disorders. Anxiety is postulated by all authorities as being the prime causal process in these clinical syndromes. Some authorities also include childhood and adolescent depressive reactions under the conceptual rubric of psychoneurotic disorders.

Obsessive-compulsive neurosis is characterized by recurrent thoughts or actions that the child feels he or she must think about or perform. To the objective outside observer, these appear to be irrational ideas and unnecessary or ridiculous behaviors. The obsessive child is seen as a highly anxious child whose obsessional thoughts and compulsive behaviors are a way to defend against intense anxiety. Unfortunately for the child, this cognitive and behavioral style never totally alleviates the anxiety and often leads to new problems in adapting to the social environment.

Virtually all people have occasional obsessive thoughts. A highly valued activity may lead to recurrent thoughts and excitement, or a catchy tune may roll over and over in one's head. Clinicians also observe a degree of compulsiveness in anxious children that, while of a significant proportion, does not occur with enough frequency or intensity to warrant the diagnosis of an obsessive-compulsive syndrome. For example, a 9-year-old boy was seen for an evaluation. Psychological tests revealed a clear compulsive style in executing a variety of cognitive and educational tasks. He was a slow worker with perfectionistic tendencies who functioned at a fairly high level academically and socially. His role in the family was that of a "pleaser." His sister had recently been discharged from a psychiatric hospital after a suicide attempt, and there was an inordinate amount of external stress on the family. It was clear that this child was developing a compulsive behavioral style in defense against the insecurity he felt as a member of this family system.

When the obsessive compulsiveness reaches a high degree, the child can become extremely dysfunctional. Obsessive compulsive children are haunted by extreme irrational thinking and ritualistic behavioral patterns. Kesler (1972) classifies obsessional fears experienced by such children into two types. The first is precautionary fear, which includes worries about one's health, safety, or cleanliness. The second is repugnant fears such as concern that one might engage in sexual abnormalities or some type of conspicuously taboo behavior. Kesler also suggests that compulsive acts can be dichotomized into those that are precautionary such as washing one's hands repeatedly to rid oneself of germs, and those that act as self-punishment such as compulsive counting or bed making.

It should be stressed that the diagnosis of this disorder is made only when the pattern leads to dysfunctional behavior and that a certain degree of compulsive traits are functional. Attention to cleanliness and detail can be very helpful in participation in the family and performing well in school. A bedtime ritual such as reading stories before bed is a beneficial quieting behavior at the end of the day. Few teachers complain about elementary school children who have their desks neatly organized each school day. Most authorities agree that the incidence of obsessive-compulsive disorders is extremely rare (Achenbach, 1974). It appears to be roughly equally distributed among both sexes (Templer, 1972).

Conversion reaction also is described as hysteria. It is most closely associated with the psychoanalytic tradition. Anxiety is presumed to be converted into physical complaints and illnesses. A hysterical syndrome can be contrasted with a psychosomatic disorder in that the former has no medical basis and may be totally contradicted by medical findings. The types of physical symptoms that may represent conversion reactions are almost limitless. Sometimes they mimic known physical diseases and specific organic dysfunctions such as blindness.

A clinical case demonstrates the unique form that conversion reactions can take. A 14-year-old girl was seen for the presenting complaint of a sudden onset of the inability to read normally. She was, in fact, reading backward in mirror-image form. Examinations by a neurologist and an ophthalmologist suggested there was no organic basis for the problem. The case was treated as a conversion reaction. Individual psychotherapy revealed a highly stressful family environment. The father suffered from a terminal illness. Emerging adolescent sexuality also was an issue. The girl was very afraid of growing up and was treated like a young child by the family. The inability to read was treated as a manipulation to avoid these developmental issues. Both the patient and her family denied that this was a psychologically caused symptom. Denial is common among hysterical syndromes. An unorthodox paradoxical treatment approach was employed whereby the girl was not allowed to read and was given the message by the parents that she needed to be more independent and grown up. After much hostility and acting out behavior by the patient, she did begin to read again. It is noteworthy that when stress again peaked several months later, the same symptoms resurfaced. They again remitted with treatment.

Most approaches to the study of psychoneurotic abnormalities follow either a psychoanalytic theory or a learning-behavioral approach. Each theoretical orientation has a substantial following and, at this point, there is no basis for rejecting or accepting the superiority of one approach over the other for the treatment of psychoneurotic dysfunction. Each of these two general theoretical frameworks also have application to the explanation and treatment of a wide range of abnormal behaviors.

The psychoanalytic approach is primarily based on Freud's theory of neurosis. According to this approach, psychoneurotic manifestations result from the individual's response to unconscious conflicts involving sexual and aggressive impulses. At the center of Freud's theory is his emphasis on defense mechanisms, particularly repression. In hysterical behavior, the affective arousal (presumed to be sexual in origin) is pushed out of consciousness and converted into somatic complaints. According to Freud, the obsessive-compulsive child, in contrast, is unable to convert anxiety into physical symptoms so repression is used to destroy the emotional link between an unacceptable idea and the feelings about it. The obsessive can be aware of the unacceptable idea, but manages to keep from thinking about it.

The sexual conflict that leads to neurotic symptoms was postulated by Freud to involve a conflict between the ego, or the child's emerging personality structure, and the libido, the unconscious psychological energy. Symptoms reflect this conflict between the ego and unacceptable ideas. Freud's theory, often labeled the libido theory, proposes that the effect of excitation can be displaced, discharged, or converted into other forms such as bodily or compulsive behaviors. For more complete descriptions of the psychoanalytic theory of neurosis, including Freud's revision of his theory in 1923, see Kesler (1972) or Achenbach (1974).

A learning theory approach discounts the importance of internal unconscious impulses or a personality structure. The learning theorist traces the cause of anxiety to specific environmental circumstances. The operant conditioning paradigm focuses on environmental or behavioral contingencies that reinforce symptomatic behavior (e.g., make it more likely to be repeated). Psychoneurotic symptoms emerge as a way of reducing the aversive effects of feeling anxious; in this way they reinforce the hysterical or obsessive-compulsive behaviors. The reinforced behavior can be generalized to different but similar situations. Thus the learning theory approach discusses complex associations that are learned as the child attempts to cope with anxiety.

Conversion reactions and obsessive-compulsive disorders have traditionally been treated with individual psychotherapy from a psychoanalytic approach. Behavioral approaches have been more frequently applied to the anxiety disorders such as phobias where their efficacy is well established. Noticeably fewer applications of behavioral therapy to obsessive-compulsive and conversion reactions have been reported. Psychodynamic individual therapy with children with these disorders is based on the intensity of the relationship between the child and the therapist. This approach attempts to examine the intrapsychic conflicts that produce the anxiety and then the psychoneurotic disorder. Play therapy is often used for younger children as part of the therapeutic process so that the child can express his or her conflicts through play. The Freudian approach emphasizes that the symptom must be removed by resolving the basic conflict. Otherwise, it is postulated that symptom substitution will occur where the intrapsychic conflict that is left unresolved will resurface in the form of a different pattern of abnormal behavior.

In contrast, behavior therapists reject the notion of symptom substitution and directly attack the symptom or problem behavior. Reinforcement contingencies may be set up by the therapist and implemented by the significant adults in the child's life. The problem behaviors would no longer be positively reinforced and may be negatively reinforced; more appropriate ways of responding would be positively reinforced with the goal that the child would learn new ways of coping with anxiety. For example, in the classroom setting, the teacher, after consultation with the therapist, would implement responses to compulsive behavior by the child that would encourage the child to be less perfectionistic and work at a greater rate of speed. The case of the 14-year-old with conversion reaction discussed at the beginning of the chapter illustrates a behavioral intervention following a psychodynamic formulation. The secondary gain from the conversion reaction behavior (i.e., failing to read) was eliminated. The child was not allowed to read and did not receive special tutoring at school. Emphasis was placed on normal social behavior involved with growing up and focus was shifted away from the symptom.

Family therapy is usually a valuable, if not necessary, adjunct to individual therapy for psychoneurotic children. The traditional psychoanalytic point of view would assign a separate therapist to work with the parents while the individual psychotherapist worked with the child. More often today, the same therapist works individually with the child and consults with the parents. Family therapy sessions may also be held. The behavior therapist often consults with the parents on specific behavioral interventions that they could make at home. In this way, the parents become collateral therapists. School consultation is frequently a valuable adjunct to effective intervention. The therapist can educate the teacher on the nature of the problem and give suggestions for appropriate responses. These teacher behaviors might include being more patient, as in the case of a conversion reaction or excessive compulsivity; specific behavioral interventions by the teacher can play an important role in changing behavior. Drug therapy is generally inappropriate for these disorders, as there is little evidence of biological causes. An exception would be if a parallel disorder, such as depression in an older adolescent, called for antidepressant medication.

REFERENCES

Achenbach, T. M. (1974). *Developmental psychopathology.* New York: Ronald.

Kesler, J. W. (1972). Neurosis in childhood. In B. B. Wolman (Ed.), *Manual of child psychopathology* (pp. 387–435). New York: McGraw-Hill.

Templer, D. (1972). The obsessive-compulsive neurosis: Review of research findings. *Comprehensive Psychiatry, 13,* 375–398.

WILLIAM G. AUSTIN
*Cape Fear Psychological
Services, Wilmington, North
Carolina*

ANXIETY DISORDERS
CHILDHOOD PSYCHOSIS
DEPRESSION
EMOTIONAL DISORDERS
SERIOUSLY EMOTIONALLY DISTURBED

PSYCHOPATHY

See SOCIOPATHY.

PSYCHOSIS, AMPHETAMINE

SEE AMPHETAMINE PSYCHOSIS.

PSYCHOSOCIAL ADJUSTMENT

Psychosocial adjustment refers to social and emotional functioning: the way a person relates to and interacts with other people in his or her environment. It is one noticeable area of difference between special needs students and those labeled normal. While problems in psychosocial development and intrafamily relations may contribute to later psychosocial difficulties (Erickson, 1963), a behavioral analysis position (Bryant & Budd, 1984) emphasizes the importance of environmental stimuli in reinforcing and maintaining appropriate social skills.

A number of remedial techniques have been used when an exceptional child exhibits psychosocial problems. Often parents can be taught to provide a more positive family environment and to more effectively communicate with their child. In school and during play, specific appropriate social behaviors, such as approaching other children, sharing, and playing social games, can be targeted for training and shaping using reinforcement techniques (Davies & Rogers, 1985). A high density of positive reinforcement for correct approximations of social contact may also be used to strengthen appropriate social relationships.

REFERENCES

Bryant, L. E., & Budd, K. S. (1984). Teaching behaviorally handicapped preschool children to share. *Journal of Applied Behavior Analysis, 17,* 45–56.

Davies, R. R., & Rogers, E. S. (1985). Social skills with persons who are mentally retarded. *Mental Retardation, 23,* 186–196.

Erickson, E. H. (1963). *Childhood and society* (2nd ed.). New York: Norton.

THOMAS ZANE
Johns Hopkins University

EMOTIONAL DISORDERS
FAMILY COUNSELING
SOCIAL SKILLS

PSYCHOSOMATIC DISORDERS

The somatic expression of anguish is a frequent phenomenon in childhood and adolescence. More than 90% of children between the ages of 3 and 18 years have established a psychological relationship with the surrounding world and expressed a confusion in a psychosomatic form at some time during their development. Somatic expression in childhood is always bound with anxiety either in reaction to a situation objectively traumatic or in relation to the perceptive distortion of an objectively nontraumatic situation. Somatic expression in the child in regard to the adult is specific and evolutionary in relation to the maturational stage of the child (affective and neurological). It is associated with a quantitative or qualitative deficiency in the parent/child relationship, most often with the mother.

Somatizations are frequent in the everyday life of a family, and are expressed through abdominal pain, headaches, fatigue, syncopal tendencies, and breathing difficulties without any objective clinical manifestation. The causes are multiple and often related to situational stress, e.g., divorce of the parents, death, academic examinations, personal crises, and approaching adolescence. Through somatic symptoms, the child frequently aims to provoke a modification in the family system by focusing the tension on himself or herself. Sometimes the child preserves the equilibrium of parents who are ready to break down. There is always a message in somatization; it is chosen consciously or unconsciously by the child in families where only this type of expression is tolerated. The underlying personality is not specific but is generally strong. The somatization is a means of expression limited in time and related to a difficult situation experienced by the child that could regress through verbal exchanges and dramatization. At times, somatization presents itself in a family context called psychosomatic and is characterized through a systematic avoidance of conflicts, enmeshment of roles, pseudomutuality, and functional rigidity. The treatment will then be systemic (familial). The somatization cannot be underestimated even if physical examination is normal; the symptoms are real. It is not a simulation, and the symptoms must be seriously taken into account and the context carefully analyzed.

Psychosomatic diseases of children differ from those of adults and result from the conjunction of various factors. A calendar of psychosomatic diseases exists: colic at 3 months, vomiting at 6 months, eczema between 8 and 12 months, breath-holding spells at 2 years, abdominal pain at 3 years, asthma at 5 years, headaches at 6 years, and Crohn's disease at adolescence. The development of a psychosomatic syndrome is associated with (1) a genetically fragile somatic background (repetitive infections); (2) a precocious inappropriate parent–child relationship (rejection, overprotection, aggression, anxiety); (3) physical stress (allergene) or psychological reactivation of a previous problem of anguish until compensated; and (4) a familial functioning of the psychosomatic type. According to age, the prevalent etiology, and the therapeutic possibilities, the treatment will be made along an organistic or psychological point of view, individually or familial, and symptomatic or global.

Every serious somatic disease is stressful for the child, the family, and those surrounding the child (teachers, grandparents, etc.). The factors of adaptation are related to the nature of the disease itself, to the child (age and personality), and to the possibilities of modification in the functioning of the family facing a distressing situation, e.g., new context of life, hospital, family doctor. Frequently the child uses the physical symptoms to express feelings of discomfort. The diabetic child cheats with treatment, the hemophiliac tempts the danger of bleeding, and the child with cystic fibrosis refuses treatment. The use of an organic symptom that does not have objective reality (e.g., pain in the appendicular region after appendectomy) is frequent and testifies to the nonrecognition of an underlying message by the family of the child: the organ is removed but the psychic suffering persists.

The psychosomatic symptomatology of the child is the borderline of the physical and the psychical, of the inborn and the acquired, of the personal and the relational, and of the conscious and the unconscious. The approach to such a symptomatology needs a great deal of empathy, tact, and comprehension of the global context of the child, the family, and the society surrounding the child. Special educators are in an optimal situation to assist in the diagnosis of these disorders because of the consistent daily observations made by all teachers. If physical complaints over a period of time alert the teacher to suspect a somatic disorder, the school psychologist and parents should be made aware of the situation. Referrals to support professionals in the community should be on hand to assist the family in diagnosis and treatment.

REFERENCES

Ajuriaguerra, J de. (1984). *Psychopathologie de l'enfant* (2nd ed.). Paris: Masson.

Kreisler, L. (1981). *L'enfant du désordre psychosomatique.* Toulouse: Privat Editeur.

Kreisler, L., Fain, M., & Soule, M. (1974). *L'enfant et son corps.* Paris: Presses Universitaires de France.

J. APPELBOOM-FONDU
HENRI B. SZLIWOWSKI
*Université Libre de Bruxelles,
Belgium*

**EMOTIONAL DISORDERS
FAMILY COUNSELING
PHYSICAL HANDICAPS
SCHOOL PHOBIA**

PSYCHOSURGERY

Psychosurgery is not an intervention that responds to a specific mental disorder. Instead, it is a neurosurgical procedure that was derived from observations made in animal aggression research (Fulton, 1949; Jacobsen, 1935) and applied to humans to control more violent psychiatric symptoms. Psychosurgical techniques were employed in the United States starting in the 1940s (Freeman & Watts, 1950). A variety of techniques that proceeded from gross frontal destruction by means of injections of alcohol into the frontal white matter (Kalinowsky, 1975) to sophisticated stereotaxic, electrically produced, ablative procedures (Kelly, Richardson, & Mitchell-Heggs, 1973) have been used. The location of lesions also has become more sophisticated. Initially, the goal of practitioners appeared to be to destroy enough anterior brain matter to create the desired effect, which was pacification of the patient. Contemporary techniques focus on greater localization of a lesion, hence avoiding large-scale brain destruction. Sites include parts of the limbic system, the anterior cingulum, and the posteromedial hypothalamus (Sano, Sekino, & Mayanagi, 1972).

The effectiveness of psychosurgery is straightforward. The issue is not one of vitiating the disorder but of limiting an individual's responsiveness to frightening and disturbing mental symptoms (Kalinowsky, 1975). Thus an individual is still likely to perceive threatening voices, but not react to them. Much like patients suffering the residuals of an accidental traumatic brain injury, leucotomized patients often were perceived by others as generally less spontaneous, more socially withdrawn, and more interpersonally distant. Psychosurgery has been used for schizophrenic conditions, obsessive compulsive neuroses, and affective disorders. As may be expected, given the more general effects of the lesions, psychosurgery with affective disorders produces the least favorable outcome. With the prevalence of psychotropic medications, the use of psychosurgery for behavioral management has diminished significantly.

Recent applications of neurosurgical procedures have noted success in dealing with pain (Culliton, 1976) and uncontrolled seizures (Spiers, Schomer, Blume, & Mesulam, 1985). The latter approach is the best example of what psychosurgery was intended to do; that is, to remove a brain area that is intimately involved in producing a disorder. The goal of surgical intervention with an uncontrolled epileptic disorder is to remove the brain tissue that is producing a seizure focus. Thus, the techniques used to identify that focus are as important as the surgical procedure itself. This last point draws the most clear distinction between earlier psychosurgical procedures and current methods. When performed to alleviate behavioral dysfunction, psychosurgery was essentially an approach to limit reactivity without affecting the underlying disorder; in contrast, when surgery is performed to alleviate uncontrolled seizures, the underlying cause is removed with changes in behavior following.

REFERENCES

Culliton, B. J. (1976). In R. N. De Jong, & O. Sugar (Eds.), *The year book of neurology and neurosurgery: 1978* Chicago: Year Book Medical.

Freeman, W., & Watts, J. W. (1950). *Psychosurgery.* Springfield, IL: Thomas.

Fulton, J. F. (1949). *Functional localization in the frontal lobes and cerebellum.* Oxford, England: Oxford University Press.

Jacobsen, C. F. (1935). Functions of frontal association areas in primates. *Archives of Neurology and Psychiatry, 33,* 558.

Kalinowsky, L. (1975). Psychosurgery. In A. M. Freedman, H. I. Kaplan, & B. J. Sadock (Eds.), *Comprehensive textbook of psychiatry–II* (pp. 1979–1982). Baltimore, MD: Williams & Wilkins.

Kelly, D., Richardson, A., & Mitchell-Heggs, N. (1973). Techniques and assessment of limbic leucotomy. In L. V. Laitinen & K. E. Livingston (Eds.), *Surgical approaches in psychiatry* (p. 201). Lancaster, England: Medical & Technical.

Sano, K., Sekino, H., & Mayanagi, Y. (1972). Results of stimulation and destruction of the posterior hypothalmus in cases with violent, aggressive, or restless behavior. In E. Hitchcock, L. Laitinen, & K. Vaernet (Eds.), *Psychosurgery* (p. 203) Springfield, IL: Thomas.

Spiers, P. A., Schomer, D. L., Blume, H. W., & Mesulam, M. (1985). Temperolimbic epilepsy and behavior. In M. Mesulam (Ed.), *Principles of behavioral neurology* (pp. 289–326). Philadelphia: Davis.

ROBERT F. SAWICKI
*Lake Erie Institute of
Rehabilitation, Lake Erie,
Pennsylvania*

ELECTROCONVULSIVE THERAPY
NEUROPSYCHOLOGY

PSYCHOTHERAPY WITH THE HANDICAPPED

Psychotherapy is defined as the application of psychological theories and principles to the treatment of problems of abnormal behavior, emotions, and thinking. The three major schools of psychotherapy are psychodynamic therapies, behavior therapies, and humanistic therapies.

The goal of psychodynamic, or insight, therapies is to help the client gain a sound understanding of his or her problems. Psychodynamic therapies are rooted in Freud's personality theory. Current behavioral and emotional problems are assumed to be the result of unconscious, intrapsychic conflicts and the unconscious mechanisms (i.e., defense mechanisms) employed to deal with them. It is a major goal of insight therapies to help bring this unconscious material into consciousness and thereby allow the client to exercise conscious, rationale control over his or her actions. Hostile and sexual impulses as well as other motives or needs not acceptable to the individual's conscious sense of morality exert an influence on behavior through the unconscious. Techniques used in classical psychoanalysis to accomplish the goal of insight include free association, interpretation, and transference. Through free association, the client is encouraged to say whatever comes into his or her mind, no matter how trivial, embarrassing, or illogical. The analyst minimizes his or her influence on the client's verbal associations by responding minimally and nondirectively. At critical times during the free association, the analyst provides interpretations of the verbalizations in an attempt to help the client gain insight.

Transference refers to the expected tendency on the part of the client to experience the therapist-client relationship as similar to the parent-child relationship. Because the origin of the client's problems is assumed to reside in early parent-child interactions, transference permits the client to resolve problems from the past in the context of a new relationship. It is hoped that in the process, the client will discover insight into his or her behavior. When the patient sees a replaying of the old role of helpless child, he or she realizes the possibility of assuming adult roles in relationships with significant others rather than being driven by old, unresolved feelings experienced in the original parent-child relationship. Psychoanalysis is a complex and time-consuming process (50 minutes per day for months or years). Scientific evidence of its effectiveness is inadequate compared with that on more recent behavior therapies. Contemporary psychodynamic therapists retain an appreciation for unconscious influences on behavior but use more direct and focused techniques to help the client gain insight and exercise more rational control. The goal is to help clients find more realistic and effective ways to cope with their emotional needs. The client is helped to accept emotional needs and to find ways to meet them within the demands of external reality.

Behavior therapies differ from psychodynamic therapies in several ways. First, the presenting problem is viewed as the appropriate focus for the treatment rather than assumed underlying causes in the client's intrapsychic life. Second, principles of learning derived from experimental psychology studies are applied to modifying maladaptive behaviors and cognitions. Maladaptive behaviors and cognitions are assumed to be learned, and they can be modified through the application of learning principles. Behavior therapists focus on the here and now rather than on the historical causes of a problem. Behavior therapy is a broad term encompassing a wide variety of therapeutic techniques. A basic tenet of behavior therapy is that different problems require different treatments. Furthermore, the selection of treatment procedures are based on empirical studies of the effectiveness of different procedures with similar problems.

Humanistic therapies also incorporate a wide range of techniques. Therapies with a humanistic orientation share a belief that each client is a unique individual striving for personal growth, or self-actualization. Carl Rogers' (1951) client-centered therapy is the best known example of the humanistic therapies. Key therapy techniques include the therapist's positive regard for the client and empathic, or reflective, listening. In reflective listening, the therapist is nondirective, serving as a mirror for the client, helping the client to sort out thoughts, attitudes, and feelings. It is assumed that the patient has the personal resources for solving his or her problem but needs the support of the therapist and an opportunity to see the problems more clearly.

The rationale for providing psychotherapy to handicapped pupils is that handicapped persons have the same or greater need for improved psychological functioning as nonhandicapped persons. Some pupils may not be able to focus their mental energies on learning because they are experiencing psychological stress and emotional confusion. When a child's emotional and behavioral problems interfere with his or her learning and social behavior, educational interventions need to be supplemented by interventions that focus on the interfering emotional and behavioral problems.

REFERENCE

Rogers, C. (1951). *Client-centered therapy: Its current practice, implications, and theory.* Boston: Houghton-Mifflin.

JAN N. HUGHES
Texas A&M University

**ADJUSTMENT OF THE HANDICAPPED
FAMILY COUNSELING
FAMILY THERAPY**

PSYCHOTROPIC DRUGS

The majority of drugs classified as psychotropic affect brain processes and thus indirectly produce behavioral changes. Their chemicals work by either increasing or decreasing the availability of specific neurotransmitters. The major classifications include hypnotics, major tranquilizers (antipsychotic agents), minor tranquilizers (antianxiety agents), stimulants, opiates, and psychedelics (hallucinogens). In most cases, these drugs increase or decrease activity level by producing effects on an individual's level of arousal. Potent psychedelic drugs add perceptual distortions to the more general effects.

Hypnotics are intended to produce drowsiness, enhance the onset of sleep, and maintain the sleep state (Katzung, 1982). These drugs produce a more profound depression on the central nervous system. They typically are referred to as barbiturates. Examples of this class of drugs are pentobarbital (Nembutal); secobarbital (Seconal); amobarbital (Amytal); and glutethimide (Doriden, Tuinal).

Barbiturates often are called "downers" because of their soporific action. Intoxication from barbiturates produces effects similar to those noted with alcohol. (For a complete review of barbiturate effects, see Blum, 1984, pp.

165–210). Of particular concern in the use of barbiturates is the tendency to produce physical dependence over time. Additionally, unless withdrawal is performed in graded steps under medical supervision, there is the possibility of mortality during sudden withdrawal.

Barbiturates are the drugs most involved in suicides, including accidental suicides (automatisms). The latter refers to a state of confusion during which an individual who habitually uses sedatives is unsure whether a pill has been ingested and proceeds to take additional pills (Ray, 1972).

Tranquilizers are intended to diminish the discomfort associated with anxiety states. Stimulants are intended to combat fatigue and have been used with children to limit hyperactivity. Moderate doses of stimulants (amphetamines) have been prescribed as adjuncts to weight reduction programs. Examples of these drugs are amphetamines (Benzedrine), caffeine (coffee, cola), cocaine, dextroamphetamine (Dexedrine), methamphetamine (Methedrine), methylphenidate (Ritalin), and nicotine (tobacco).

Stimulants may be drunk (coffee), smoked (tobacco), inhaled (cocaine), ingested (amphetamines of various types), or injected (amphetamines). Though the following effects are seen most often in amphetamine abuse, they also are evident in relative degrees with the abuse of any of the stimulants. After use, the individual experiences a mild flush, which in the case of injectable amphetamines is compared to sexual orgasm. Feelings of euphoria, invulnerability, absence of boredom, and unlimited energy follow. Since abusers are likely to build up a tolerance for a specific drug, increased dosages or drug mixtures are used to create the "high." Continued abuse of a stimulant appears related both to the wish to recreate the high and to the desire to avoid the fatigue and depression that occur during withdrawal.

Negative side effects of chronic abuse include malnutrition, insomnia, impulsiveness, defective reasoning, delusional thinking, hallucinations, and paranoia (Blum, 1984). Owing to the affective lability of abusers, the associated hyperactivity, and the significant paranoia, abuse of amphetamines tends to set up conditions in which violence may occur.

Opiates are intended to provide relief from pain and appear to mimic natural analgesics (endorphins). Historically, morphine was used not only to provide relief from extreme pain, but also for diarrhea, cough, anxiety, and insomnia (Katzung, 1982). Examples of drugs in this class include opium, morphine, codeine, heroin, dihydromorphine (Dilaudid), and meperidine (Demerol).

Of particular concern with this class of drug is that, along with tolerance for a specific drug, physical dependence also occurs. Though central nervous system depressants, opiates produce feelings of euphoria in persons who are experiencing either physical or emotional pain (Leavitt, 1982). Persons appear to start abusing opiates secondary to situational stress, unenlightened treatment for severe pain, and comradeship (Blum, 1984). Chronic abuse produces periods of nausea, vomiting, constipation, respiratory inefficiency, and limited pain awareness. The latter produces additional effects since abusers are unaware of physical distress (Leavitt, 1982). Mortality rates among heroine addicts under 30 are approximately 8 times that of nonaddicts (Leavitt, 1982).

Psychedelics have been used in various research programs, from perceptual research to brainwashing techniques (Leavitt, 1982). They have no consistent, specified therapeutic value. Some, like peyote, have been used in religious ceremonies because they bring on visions (hallucinations). It is this hallucinogenic property that makes these drugs attractive to abusers.

REFERENCES

Blum, K. B. (1984). *Handbook of abusable drugs.* New York: Gardner.

Katzung, B. G. (1982). *Basic & clinical pharmacology.* Los Altos, CA: Lange Medical.

Leavitt, F. (1982). *Drugs and behavior.* New York: Wiley.

Ray, O. S. (1972). *Drugs, society and human behavior.* St. Louis: Mosby.

ROBERT F. SAWICKI
*Lake Erie Institute of
    Rehabilitation, Lake Erie,
    Pennsylvania*

**DRUG ABUSE
DRUG THERAPY
HALLUCINOGENS
TRANQUILIZERS**

PSYC SCAN

During the past decade, a vast amount of information, traditionally available only in print, has been placed into computer-readable and retrievable form. Consequently, psychologists, special educators, and researchers have at their disposal a wealth of knowledge that has been classified, summarized, and stored for easy, quick, inexpensive retrieval by computer. Psyc SCAN is a service of Psyc INFO, which is part of the Psychological Abstract Information Services Department of the American Psychological Association.

Psyc SCAN provides computer-readable information and publications in various areas that are important to professionals involved in special education: applied, clinical, and developmental psychology, learning/communication disorders (LD) and mental retardation (MR). On a quarterly basis, Psyc SCAN offers subscribers an effective

and efficient way of keeping up to date on practice and research in their fields by providing citations and abstracts from recently published journal articles.

Abstracts in the applied, clinical, and developmental psychology sections of Psyc SCAN are derived from a set of core journals. When a publication is selected for one of these three areas, all relevant articles are summarized and listed by journal title along with complete citation, abstract, and index terms.

Abstracts in the LD/MR section of Psyc SCAN likewise are published quarterly and offer a practical way of keeping abreast of clinical and educational literature in the field. For this section, however, material is taken from all of the approximately 13,000 serial publications covered by the Psyc INFO Data Base. As such, each issue is arranged by three broad areas: learning disorders, communication disorders, and mental retardation; they are further subdivided into theories, research, and assessment and educational issues. All entries in this section contain full bibliographic citations, index terms, and abstracts.

Additional information about Psyc SCAN and related services can be obtained from Psyc INFO Services, American Psychological Association, 1400 North Uhle Street, Arlington, VA 22011.

CHARLES A. MAHER
Rutgers University

LOUIS J. KRUGER
Tufts University

**COMPUTER ASSISTED INSTRUCTION
SPECIALNET**

PUBLIC LAW 93-112

See EDUCATION FOR ALL HANDICAPPED CHILDREN ACT OF 1975.

PUBLIC LAW 93-380

See BUCKLEY AMENDMENT.

PUBLIC LAW 94-103

Also known as the Developmentally Disabled Assistance and Bill of Rights Act of 1975, PL 94-103 requires that the states and territories of the United States have in effect (after October 1, 1977) a protection and advocacy system for the developmentally disabled in order to qualify for federal funds for developmental disabilities programs. The law requires these systems to

> protect and advocate the rights of persons with developmental disabilities . . . to pursue legal, administrative, and other appropriate remedies, and to be independent of any state agency which (sic) provides treatment, services, or habilitation to persons with development disabilities.

According to a lengthy analysis by Sales, Powell, and Duizend (1982), this was the first time that Congress conditioned the receipt of federal funds on the development of a system to advocate for and protect the rights of a specific class of individuals.

PL 94-103 does not define advocacy for the states, although the rules and regulations for the law, developed by the Department of Health, Education, and Welfare (DHEW) provides guidelines for determining whether advocacy has been achieved. Advocacy was defined under the DHEW guidelines as "speaking for, pleading for, supporting, advising, espousing the rights of or interceding on behalf of persons with developmental disabilities before any public or private individuals, agencies, organizations, or institutions serving such people."

No method for establishing an advocacy system is specified in either the law or the subsequent DHEW guidelines. States may choose to establish an advocacy system through legislation or other means.

REFERENCE

Sales, B. D., Powell, D. M., & Duizend, R. V. (1982). *Disabled persons and the law*. New York: Plenum.

CECIL R. REYNOLDS
Texas A&M University

CIVIL RIGHTS OF THE HANDICAPPED ADVOCACY FOR HANDICAPPED CHILDREN

PUBLIC LAW 94-142

See EDUCATION FOR ALL HANDICAPPED CHILDREN ACT OF 1975;

PUBLIC LAW 95-561

The Gifted and Talented Children's Education Act of 1978 was added, by PL 95-561, as Part A of Title IX of the Elementary and Secondary Education Act. The statute and its companion regulations describe gifted and talented children as individuals from birth through 18 years of age who require special educational services or activities because they possess demonstrated or potential abilities that give evidence of high performance capability in areas such as intellectual, creative, specific academic, or leadership ability, or in the performing and visual arts.

Financial assistance was provided under the Gifted and Talented Children's Education Program through two types of awards. Each state educational agency was eligible for a grant to plan, develop, operate, and improve programs for gifted and talented children. Eligible public or private organizations, agencies, or institutions also could compete for awards to conduct personnel training, model projects, information dissemination, or research.

On August 13, 1981, this funding program was consolidated into a block grant under Chapter 2 of the Education and Consolidation Improvement Act of 1981. States and localities may use the block grant funds, as appropriate, for continued services to gifted and talented children.

SHIRLEY A. JONES
*Virginia Polytechnic Institute
and State University*

PUBLIC LAW 98-527

See DEVELOPMENTAL DISABILITIES ACT.

PUBLIC SCHOOLS AND SPECIAL EDUCATION

Interest in both special education and public schools in the mid 1980s is providing an unprecedented opportunity for educators to analyze and develop programs sharply contrasting from those of the past 50 years. Such evaluation and interest in developing effective schools has arisen from several major forces. First, concern is growing for the implementation of programs that truly enhance the academic and social skills of the nation's youth. Second, popular and accepted conceptions about handicapping conditions have changed, as have those toward the responsibilities of special and regular education. The result of this has been a drastic change in the procedures used in classifying students, in part as a function of the research providing an empirical critique of current practice, but also as a function of the consequences of such practice. Third, the relationship between special and regular education has been questioned both in terms of the content and the outcomes. These three forces have provided a major impetus behind the current efforts at designing our educational system.

As Ysseldyke and Algozzine (1983) have noted, the general goals and objectives of American education include instruction in basic skills, inculcation of social principles in a democratic society, and provision of the opportunity to develop to the greatest potential possible. While there is little disagreement about the value of these goals, considerable controversy abounds regarding the procedures for attainment of such goals. Ysseldyke and Algozzine (1983) cite data from the Children's Defense Fund that indicate problems in the lack of attendance for a significant number of students, and refer to *The Literacy Hoax* (Cooperman, 1978), which provides data on the decline in achievement scores through the 1960s and 1970s.

Recently, criticsm has been generated with the report from the National Commission on Excellence in Education, *A Nation at Risk: The Imperative for Educational Reform* (1983). Following its publication, a series of task forces and commissions were assembled to review and/or evaluate the educational process in America's schools (Gross & Gross, 1985). Despite differing focuses, methods, and proposals, the consistent message in all of the reports is that reform of our schools is both necessary and imperative if the social benefits conferred through education are to be maintained. Critical areas addressed in all reports include: (1) curriculum and course content, (2) students' attitudes toward and needs in learning, and (3) teachers and teaching, including expectations and demands.

In part, the disagreement in procedures for educating the nation's youth is a function of the failure of schools to adequately address the great diversity present in the classrooms. While education is meant to be appropriate and applicable to all students regardless of background, race, sex, or creed, it is clear that success or failure in the schools is not uniform for all students. As reported nearly 20 years ago in the Equality of Educational Opportunity (Coleman, 1966) public education is not equal in most regions of the country. Recently, this concern for equality has expanded beyond a concern for race and has also addressed the inclusion of the handicapped.

The ideal that an appropriate education should be available to all children has profoundly influenced the direction of education in our country, especially the education of handicapped students. Special education services in public schools emerged in response to this ideal. However, the commitment to providing "education for all" is a recent development (Ysseldyke & Algozzine, 1983). In fact, the right of any citizen to a free and appropriate education began in the mid-1970s as a consequence of PL 94-142, the Education for All Handicapped Act. Up to the late nineteenth century, only a very small percentage of the population enjoyed the benefits of a formal education (Lilly, 1979).

The early nineteenth century marked the beginning of special education in the United States. Special education in the 1800s was characterized by residential programs that were narrowly categorical in their orientation. The programs served students with visual or hearing impairments, who were severely emotionally disturbed, or who were moderately to severely mentally retarded. Residential schools comprised the primary mode of service delivery in special education and those whose problems were less severe in nature and not as obvious in appearance often were overlooked.

Initially, the goals of many residential programs, especially for the mentally retarded, were highly optimistic. However, it was apparent by the early 1900s that earlier hopes of curing mental retardation were not realistic. Consequently, the residential institutions became more custodial than educational and it was assumed that residents would spend the rest of their lives in the sheltered environments of the institutions.

The development of intelligence tests in France, and their subsequent translation into English, were two of the most significant events of the early twentieth century with respect to special education in the United States. As a result, mildly retarded students were identified and special education services expanded. Perhaps more important, the emphasis on intelligence testing created the assumption that learning problems were centered in the individual, rather than due to an interaction between the individual and the school environment. Unfortunately, this assumption still is held by some to this day.

The period between 1920 and 1960 can be viewed as one of rapid expansion for special education. Public school education programs for those with behavior disorders emerged in the 1920s. Previously, programs for children with severe emotional disturbance had been primarily residential. The 1930s witnessed the development of special classes within public schools for children who were judged too disruptive for the regular classroom, but who did not score low enough on tests of intelligence to qualify as mildly mentally retarded. This period saw a dramatic increase in special classes for the mildly retarded, who eventually came to be called educable mentally retarded. The result was a virtual explosion during the decade between 1950 and 1960 in regard to the number of classes available and the number of children served.

Many university programs were founded in the area of special education in the 1950s. Such programs were responsible for training personnel for special education teaching positions and were especially important because of the emphasis on research. To some extent, the research of this period questioned ineffective or inefficient practices and prevented these practices from becoming a permanent part of the special education service delivery system.

Although few states adopted mandatory special education legislation in the 1950s, state involvement in special education finance and planning grew rapidly during the decade. In the 1960s, the federal government emerged as a major influence in the financing and policymaking of special education. The federal government provided grants to state agencies, universities, and colleges for the training of special education teachers. Federal support also consisted of grants for demonstration projects and research into the education of the handicapped. An additional type of federal support was direct aid to states for the initiation, improvement, and expansion of special education services. This type of federal support exhibited the greatest rate of growth in the 1970s.

In the late 1960s, the category of learning disabilities was added to a few states lists of disabilities eligible to receive special education services. This new category was established because a number of children were in need of special services, but neither exhibited the behavioral aberrance necessary to be considered emotionally disturbed nor scored low enough on intelligence tests to qualify as mentally retarded. This new category permitted the extension of special education services to children who previously had been neglected. The brief history of the field of learning disabilities has been characterized by a series of controversies regarding its definition, labeling practices, and the provision of services.

The 1960s saw an increase in the number of states mandating special education services for handicapped children. An extensive search for the most effective, comprehensive, and cost efficient system of special education was initiated by the establishment of special education as a right of all children.

The tools used as the primary determiner of mental retardation, intelligence tests, were the subject of heated controversy during the 1960s and 1970s. The tests were criticized as racially and socioeconomically biased. Indeed, it was obvious that special classes for the educable mentally retarded contained disproportionate numbers of minority and economically disadvantaged children. Controversy also raged about the efficacy of various types of special education services that were being provided to children. Much of the discussion centered on the advisability of special class placement for children labeled educable mentally retarded or behavior disordered (Lilly, 1979).

One of the greatest problems confronting the development of special education programs is the rapid expansion of services to more students. In the latest available report to Congress, the number of handicapped individuals being served in the public schools has risen to more than 4.3 million. A great percentage of these students, more than 1.8 million of them, has been identified as "learning disabled" (U.S. Department of Education, 1986). In part, this may be a function of the reluctance of school personnel to identify individuals as retarded, given the litigation that has occurred since *Larry P. v. Riles* in 1976.

In the late 1970s, Congress funded five research centers throughout the country to investigate the practices and procedures in use with learning disabled students. At one of these centers, the Institute for Research on Learning Disabilities at the University of Minnesota, a 6-year in-

vestigation was initiated to document the state of the art in assessment practices. In summarizing the results from the university's research program, Ysseldyke and Thurlow (1983) state that

1. Considerable variability exists in the assessment practices and classification criteria used by schools.

2. The instruments used in the assessment process are, for the most part, technically inadequate.

3. Generally, students are placed in special education programs because of a deficit between ability and achievement.

4. Current criteria for identifying learning disabled students are inadequate and inaccurate.

5. Classification decisions often are unrelated to the data generated during the assessment process.

6. Decision makers do not use assessment data reliably to identify students as learning disabled.

7. The focus of most teams is on reporting of data, with little time spent on integrating the data or attending to instructional interventions.

8. Professional opinions about the definition and prevalence of learning disabilities are discordant.

9. The most important determinant in placement in special education is the referral itself. Once a student is referred, the probability of assessment is 92%; once assessed, the probability of placement is 73%.

10. Placement in special education often does not result in substantive changes in educational programs that are different from those programs implemented in regular education.

Litigation pertaining to education began on a small scale during the 1960s, and evolved to a major area of concern among the special education community during the 1970s. In the 1960s, advocates for and parents of handicapped children first used the legal system to ensure the protection of the children's rights in the special education placement process. The area of special education litigation expanded greatly during the 1970s, and the courts became a primary arena for change in the field of special education.

An extremely significant legislative mandate emerged in response to the educational litigation of the 1960s and early 1970s. The adoption of PL 94-142, the Education for All Handicapped Children Act of 1975, which became fully effective October 1, 1977, has had a profound effect on assessment procedures and the delivery of psychological and educational services for minority group children. Two of the most important changes mandated by the law have been the establishment of due process procedures in each state to safeguard the rights of handicapped children and their parents or guardians in the provision of special education services, and the requirement of an individualized educational program (IEP). The IEP must include statements documenting the child's current level of performance, short term objectives, annual goals, educational services to be provided, the child's participation in regular education programs, anticipated length of the services, date of service initiation, and progress evaluation procedures (Lilly, 1979).

Legal action has been effective in drawing attention to a number of relevant issues such as nondiscriminatory testing and the use of multiple measures on the evaluation and placement of children. Furthermore, litigation can be recognized for encouraging our society to expect free appropriate public education for all children. This expectation has become well established and is widely pursued by the field of special education and our society as a whole.

The emphasis on litigation, and the still present inequities in the way students are identified and served in special education, has resulted in a renewed effort to more precisely determine the procedures for assessing and placing students in special education. The problem with current assessment and placement practices has had great impact on the provision of equal opportunity to all students. The most dramatic effect has been in the over-identification of minority children and males. The Office for Civil Rights (OCR) of the U.S. Department of Education has revealed that these two groups of students have been overrepresented in special education. Given this problem, the Panel on Selection and Placement of Students in Programs for the Mentally Retarded was established in 1979 to provide an analysis of factors responsible for such disproportionate placement and to identify procedures that would overcome such factors.

In addressing the issue of overrepresentation, the panel recast the issue to consider why such disproportionate placement was a problem, and focused on the validity of the assessment procedures and the quality of instruction. Based on an extensive review of current law and educational theory and practice, the panel proposed six major components for inclusion in an assessment system:

1. Multiple educational interventions should be attempted in the regular classroom prior to the referral for placement in specialized classrooms, including the use of effective instructional procedures.

2. Measurement systems should be used that validly assess the functional needs of the individual and are related to manipulatable factors in the educational environment.

3. If students are to be labeled, it is imperative that as a consequence of the labels, distinctive educational practices are prescribed and result in improvements that otherwise would not be attainable in the regular classroom.

4. Data must be collected that demonstrate systematic implementation of high quality and effective special instruction which produce results not attainable in the regular classroom.

5. A student's placement in special education should be reviewed on an annual basis, and retention should be based on the failure of meeting specified educational objectives with all efforts made to achieve these objectives.

6. Systematic and regular monitoring of placement practices should be conducted at the local, state, and national levels to ensure equitable and effective program development for various groups of children.

As intimated in this report, current practice in the delivery of special education programs is being reformulated. In part, this modification is based upon the lack of empirical support for the present procedures. As noted by Tindal (1985), the effectiveness of special education has been consistently questioned over the past 20 years by a number of reviewers. Most of these reviewers have found little evidence clearly indicating superior achievement gains as a result of special education. However, the methodology of the research in these efficacy studies has been sufficiently poor to question the validity of the findings.

In a related review by Epps and Tindal (in press), the analysis of special education programs was expanded to include not only the achievement outcomes, but also the definition of program components. In particular, this review investigated the differences between special and regular education programs in the content and context of instruction. Several studies were reviewed utilizing the process-product research paradigm, in which classrooms are observed in terms of organization and teacher behaviors and students' performance is monitored for gains in achievement. The major conclusion was that few, if any, differences exist between the two environments. Instruction has been defined in substantially the same manner in both special and regular education. Students receive approximately the same amounts of time and are required to engage in many of the same behaviors in receiving instruction. The only clear difference to emerge in the manner in which instruction is defined in special education is that students are instructed in one to one setting rather than the small or large group settings.

In response to both of these issues, the lack of markedly different or superior instruction in special education, increasing interest has been expressed in reformulating the delivery of special education. The major model has continued to be the cascade of services originally proposed by Deno (1970) and revamped by Reynolds and Birch (1982). In the original cascade, seven levels of service were delineated, demarcated primarily on the basis of setting or physical arrangements: (1) observation and assessment in level one, (2) indirect services only in level two, (3) primary placement in regular education in level three, (4) primary placement in special education in level four, (5) full-time placement in special education in level five, (6) residential placement with inhouse school program (in district) in level six and, (7) residential placement with inhouse school program (out of district) in level seven.

In a new conception of the cascade model, Reynolds and Birch (1982) focus on the development of diversified environments and staff within the regular classroom. Thus, any given regular education class may contain various specialized staff and learning centers. Students are placed in specialized environments for limited periods of time. Such a conceptualization places a premium on the regular classroom environment as the least restrictive environment.

Implementation of this system generally has acknowledged the importance of consultants to regular classroom teachers. The consultation's content includes assessment procedures, development of individualized instructional procedures, and evaluation of program outcomes. Two models of consultation have been developed and field tested successfully over the past ten years; The Vermont Consulting Teacher out of the University of Vermont (Knight, Meyers, Paolucci-Whitcomb, Hasazi, & Nevin, 1981), and the Resource Consulting Teacher out of the University of Illinois (Idol-Maestas, 1981, 1983). In both models, the emphasis has been on the development of sensitive measurement and assessment systems that focus on behavioral dimensions having relevance for both student performance in the classroom and the development of effective instructional strategies. Service is indirect, in that instructional programs are developed in the regular classroom. Finally, student progress is frequently evaluated for determining when and what to change.

In summary, current practice in the assessment and placement of students in special education generally has been judged inappropriate. Little justification exists for continuing many of the current practices, providing a major impetus for redefining the relationship between special and regular education programs. One new direction being proposed, in response to both empirical practices as well as legal mandates, is the implementation of special education programs within regular education environments. In this system, specialized staff serve as consultants in the development of IEPs. By implementing such an approach, special education would indeed become a part of, rather than be apart from, the public schools.

REFERENCES

Cooperman, P. (1978). *The literacy hoax: The decline of reading, writing, and learning in the public schools and what we can do about it.* New York: Morrow.

Coleman, J. (1966). *Equality of educational opportunity.* Washington, DC: U.S. Government Printing Office.

Deno, E. (1970). Special education as developmental capital. *Exceptional Children, 37,* 229–337.

Epps, S., & Tindal, D. (in press). The effectiveness of differentiated programming in severely mildly handicapped students: Placement options and instruction programming, In M. Wong, M. Reynolds, & H. Walberg, (Eds.), Oxford England: Pergamon Press.

Gross, R., & Gross, B. (1985). *The great school debate: Which way for American education.* New York: Simon & Schuster.

Idol-Maestas, L. (1983). *Special educator's consultation handbook.* Rockville, MD: Aspen.

Knight, M., Meyers, H., Paolucci-Whitcomb, P., Hasazi, S., & Nevin, A. (1981). A four year evaluation of consulting teacher service. *Behavior Disorders, 6,* 92–100.

Lilly, M. S. (1979). *Children with exceptional needs.* Chicago: Holt, Rinehart, & Winston.

National Commission on Excellence in Education. (1983). *A nation at risk: The imperative for educational reform.* Washington, DC: Government Printing Office.

Reynolds, M., & Birch, J. (1982). *Teaching exceptional children in all America's schools* (revised ed.). Reston, VA: Council for Exceptional Children.

Tindal, G. (1985). Investigation the effectiveness of special education: Analysis of methodology. *Journal of Learning Disabilities, 18,* 101–112

U.S. Department of Education. *To assure the free appropriate public education of all handicapped children: Seventh annual report to Congress on the implementation of Public Law 94-142: The Education for All Handicapped Children Act.* Washington, DC: Department of Education.

U.S. Department of Education (1986). *Annual Report to Congress on Implications of PL 94-142.* Washington, DC: Author.

Ysseldyke, J., & Algozzine, B. (1983). *Critical issues in special and remedial education.* Boston: Houghton-Mifflin.

Ysseldyke, J., & Thurlow, M. (1983). *Identification/classification research: An integrative summary of findings.* (Research Report No. 142). Minneapolis: University of Minnesota Institute for Research on Learning Disabilities.

GERALD TINDAL
KATHLEEN RODDEN-NORD
University of Oregon

ASSESSMENT
CASCADE MODELS OF SPECIAL EDUCATION
EDUCATION FOR ALL HANDICAPPED CHILDREN ACT OF 1975
INDIVIDUAL EDUCATION PLAN
LEAST RESTRICTIVE ENVIRONMENT

PUERTO RICO, SPECIAL EDUCATION IN

Special education services in Puerto Rico are administered under the legislative provisions of PL 94-142, which are reflected in territorial law concerning the handicapped. Before PL 94-142, there were few services. Since the legislation there has been greater consistency and continuity of services, improvement and expansion of personnel preparation, reduction of negative attitudes, and increasing movement of children toward the mainstream (Smith-Davis, Burke, & Noel, 1984).

Until a few years ago, the handicapped population in Puerto Rico was generally served in self-contained classes at the elementary level. Since 1979 programming has shifted to the mild and moderately handicapped, to mainstreaming, and to programs at intermediate and secondary levels. Prevocational and vocational centers for the handicapped have also been established (Smith-Davis, Burke, & Noel, 1984).

During the 1981–1982 school year, about 28,000 handicapped children were served on the island. Earlier, Olivares (1979) had estimated that three times that number required some form of special education services and that many children remained unserved partly because they were protected too well by overanxious families.

Teacher certification policies in Puerto Rico are primarily noncategorical, with categorical certification reserved for those serving low-incidence populations. Smith-Davis et al. (1984) report that the University of Puerto Rico, which has had a special education program since 1965, and the Inter-American University, both offer undergraduate and graduate programs in special education. The University of the Sacred Heart and the Catholic University of Puerto Rico offer primarily undergraduate programs. In addition, two American universities, Fordham University–Puerto Rico Campus, and New York University's extension program offer graduate training at campuses on the island. All of these institutions offer adequate programs learning disabilities, mental retardation, emotional disorders, and behavioral disorders. However, formal programs on the severely retarded and multiply handicapped are inadequate although some course work is available. The Department of Education carries on a vigorous in-service program at both local and regional levels and employs tuition assistance and other means to retrain and recertify practitioners.

Special education practices in Puerto Rico must be interpreted in light of the school system, which is highly centralized. It is organized into a central office responsible for all administrative and policy decisions, and six educational regions, each under a director appointed by the secretary of education (who is appointed by the governor at cabinet level). Each region is subdivided into districts run by superintendents. Within this structure, special education is largely centralized. It is directed by a special education director and is divided into four units: administrative, curricular, academic, and vocational. Regional special education supervisors are appointed to each region. Thus there are six plus two supervisors, one each for prevocational and vocational programs (Brown, 1977).

Unlike the United States, where Puerto Ricans are a linguistic minority, in Puerto Rico they are the majority. Consequently, all services and instructional aids and materials for special education are in Spanish. It is important that U.S. special educators be aware that Puerto Rico,

through the governor's office and other agencies, is ready to offer technical assistance in these areas to anyone who requests it (Cruz, 1979).

REFERENCES

Brown, F. M. (1977, August). *Southeast Area Learning Resource Center: Final technical report, Sept. 1, 1974 through May 31, 1977*. Washington, DC: Bureau of Education for the Handicapped.

Cruz, D. (1979, June). Outreach problems in Puerto Rico. In G. Dixon & D. Bridges (Eds.), *On being Hispanic and disabled: The special challenge of an underserved population*. Chicago: Illinois State Board of Vocational Education and Rehabilitation.

Olizares, G. (1979, June). Hispanic and disabled. In G. Dixon & D. Bridges (Eds.), *On being Hispanic and disabled: The special challenge of an underserved population*. Chicago: Illinois State Board of Vocational Education and Rehabilitation.

Smith-Davis, J., Burke, P. J., & Noel, M. M. (1984). *Personnel to educate the handicapped in America: Supply and demand from a programmatic viewpoint*. College Park, MD: Maryland University College of Education.

H. ROBERTA ARRIGO
Hunter College, City University
of New York

LATIN AMERICA AND THE CARRIBEAN, SPECIAL EDUCATION IN

MEXICO, SPECIAL EDUCATION IN

PUNISHMENT

Punishment, defined functionally, occurs when the presentation of an aversive consequence contingent on the emission of a behavior reduces the subsequent rate of that behavior. It is a commonly employed operant conditioning procedure. As Alberto and Troutman (1986) state, "Any stimulus can be labeled a punisher if its contingent application results in a reduction of the target behavior. A punisher, like a reinforcer, can be identified only by its effect on behavior—not on the nature of the consequent stimulus" (p. 245). Thus the mere application of an aversive stimulus (such as a spanking) or removal of a positive stimulus (such as a token or money) cannot be termed a punishment procedure unless a reductive effect on the target behavior occurs. Unfortunately, this reductive effect on behavior by a consequent stimulus is seldom evaluated in everyday use, thus resulting in inappropriate and ineffective use of the punishment procedure.

Although punishment may involve the removal of a positive stimulus, it is most commonly applied by parents and teachers as the application of an aversive stimulus contingent on a behavior in order to reduce that behavior (Walker & Shea, 1984). A common example of this form would be physical or corporal punishment. Although the application of aversive stimuli has been documented as an effective procedure in reducing self-injurious behaviors (Dorsey et al., 1980; Sajwaj, Libet, & Agras, 1974) and severe aggressive behaviors toward others (Ludwig et al., 1969), its use in the form of physical punishment is not generally advocated by most professionals in the field of behavior management as the preferred means of reducing inappropriate behaviors. Besides legal, humane, and ethical concerns, there are a multitude of other disadvantages associated with the use of punishment:

> In the long run, it could cause people to punish more often and to harm themselves and their victims by injuring them, if the punishment is physical, or by impairing social relationships and promoting aggression or escape, self-blame, imitative aggression, and other harmful side-effects. (Sulzer-Azaroff & Mayer, 1986, p. 146)

REFERENCES

Alberto, P. A., & Troutman, A. C. (1986). *Applied behavior analysis for teachers* (2nd. ed.). Columbus, OH: Merrill.

Dorsey, M. F., Iwata, B. A., Ong, P., & McSween, T. E. (1980). Treatment of self-injurious behavior using a water mist: Initial response suppression and generalization. *Journal of Applied Behavior Analysis, 13*, 324–333.

Kerr, M. M., & Nelson, M. N. (1983). *Strategies for managing behavior problems in the classroom.* Columbus, OH: Merrill.

Ludwig, A. M., Marx, A. J., Hill, P. A., & Browning, R. M. (1969). The control of violent behavior through faradic shock. *Journal of Nervous & Mental Disease, 148*, 624–637.

Sajwaj, T., Libet, J., & Agras, S. (1974). Lemon juice therapy: The control of life-threatening rumination in a six-month old infant. *Journal of Applied Behavior Analysis, 7*, 557–563.

Sulzer-Azaroff, B., & Mayer, G. R. (1986). *Achieving educational excellence using behavioral strategies.* New York: Holt, Rinehart, & Winston.

Walker, J. E., & Shea, T. M. (1984). *Behavior management: A practical approach for educators* (3rd ed.). St. Louis: Mosby.

Louis J. LaNunziata
University of North Carolina,
Wilmington

APPLIED BEHAVIOR ANALYSIS
AVERSIVE STIMULUS
NEGATIVE PUNISHMENT
PUNISHMENT, POSITIVE

PUNISHMENT, POSITIVE

Punishment is a procedure in which the presentation of a stimulus contingent on a behavior reduces the rate of emission of the behavior (Azrin & Holz, 1966). Punishment, like reinforcement, is defined by its effect on behavior. Numerous behavior change techniques used by psychologists and educators can be classified as punishment techniques (e.g., timeout, response cost, overcorrection, verbal reprimands, and electric shock; Axelrod & Apsche, 1983).

The use of adjectives such as "positive" and "negative" are most frequently associated with reinforcement techniques, but occasionally have been employed to further define punishment techniques. Behaviorists use these adjectives to describe the contingent presentation of a stimulus (positive) or the contingent removal of a stimulus (negative). These terms should *not* be interpreted as value judgments synonymous with "good" and "bad." Therefore, *positive punishment* is the contingent presentation of an aversive stimuli for a misbehavior or rule violation. Spanking a child for fighting with a peer is a classic example of positive punishment. Socially more acceptable examples of positive punishment include undertaking a noxious task such as cleaning a restroom (i.e., the aversive stimulus) contingent on messing it up. *Negative punishment* is the contingent removal of a positive stimulus. Common examples of negative punishment techniques include response cost or timeout.

REFERENCES

Axelrod, S., & Apsche, J. (1983). *The effects of punishment on human behavior.* New York: Academic.

Azrin, N. H., & Holz, W. C. (1966). Punishment. In W. A. Honig (Ed.), *Operant Behavior: Areas of research and application.* (pp. 380–447). New York: Appleton.

Stephen N. Elliott
Louisiana State University

PUNISHMENT

PURDUE PERCEPTUAL-MOTOR SURVEY (PPMS)

The Purdue Perceptual-Motor Survey (PPMS) (Roach & Kephart, 1966) was developed to enable qualitative observations of problem areas of perceptual-motor development. Subtests include walking board, jumping, identification of body parts, imitation of movements (following the examiner's arm movements), obstacle course, Kraus Weber (requiring the child to raise first the upper and then the lower torso while prone), angels in the snow (differentiation of arms and legs in various patterns), chalkboard (e.g., drawing simple to complex patterns), ocular pursuits (visual tracking), and visual achievement forms (a paper and pencil copying task).

The theoretical and practical implications of the scale are described in Kephart (1971). The major assumptions, now controversial (Hammill, 1982), are that higher levels of learning are dependent on a motor base of achievement, and that perceptual-motor interventions are important for the remediation of academic deficits.

The norms are based on data from 200 children in grades one through four. Means and standard deviations are provided by grade. Test-retest reliability was .95 (n = 30, one-week interval). A validation study compared the performance of a sample of 97 nonachieving children with the normative sample (mentally retarded children were excluded). With one exception, items differentiated between groups.

REFERENCES

Hammill, D. D. (1982). Assessing and training perceptual-motor skills. In D. D. Hammill & N. R. Bartel, *Teaching children with learning and behavior problems* (3rd ed., pp. 379–408). Boston: Allyn & Bacon.

Kephart, N. C. (1971). *The slow learner in the classroom* (2nd ed.). Columbus, OH: Merrill.

Roach, E. G., & Kephart, N. C. (1966). *The Purdue Perceptual-Motor Survey*. Columbus, OH: Merrill.

DAVID W. BARNETT
University of Cincinnati

PERCEPTUAL AND MOTOR SKILLS

PUTAMEN

The putamen is the largest nucleus of the basal ganglia (caudate nucleus, putamen, globus pallidus, claustrum and amygdala) that function in background motor control via the extrapyramidal motor system (Carpenter & Sutin, 1983). The putamen also houses receptor sites for the dopamine containing neurons projecting from the substantia nigra. (The nigrastriatal system with the striatum is the putamen and candate nucleus.) The putamen is located lateral to the thalamus and internal capsule but medial to the external capsule and inner aspect of the Sylvian fissure (see Figure 1 under CAT scan of the brain for depictions of its location). Since dopamine is an essential neurotransmitter for both normal motor and mental functioning, damage to the putamen may result in a wide spectrum of neurobehavioral changes. The prototype disorder of the basal ganglia that best exemplifies these motor and mental changes is Huntington's chorea. In Huntington's chorea there are specific motor deficits characterised by uncontrolled choreic movements as well as progressive dementia (Heilman & Valenstein, 1985). The disruption of any part of the nigrastriatal system will affect dopamine production and will have significant neurobehavioral effects. These are discussed in the section on the substantia nigra. Recent research has also implicated a greater role of the basal ganglia in language function than had been suspected (Segalowitz, 1983).

REFERENCES

Carpenter, M. B., & Sutin, J. (1983). *Human neuroanatomy* (8th ed.). Baltimore, MD: Williams & Wilkins.

Heilman, K. M., & Valenstein, E. (1985). *Clinical neuropsychology*. New York: Oxford University Press.

Segalowitz, S. J. (1983). *Language functions and brain organization*. New York: Academic.

ERIN D. BIGLER
Austin Neurological Clinic,
University of Texas, Austin

HUNTINGTON'S CHOREA
SUBSTANTIA NIGRA

PYGMALION EFFECT

According to Rosenthal and Jacobson (1966, 1968), one of the possible relationships between prophecies and events can be described as the pygmalion effect. The central concept behind the pygmalion effect is that of the self-fulfilling prophecy. That is, people behave in ways that increase the likelihood that their predictions and expectations will be realized. One person's expectation of another person's behavior becomes an accurate prediction as a result of its having been made.

Rosenthal and Jacobson (1966, 1968) applied this concept to children who performed poorly in school. "If school children who perform poorly are those expected by their teachers to perform poorly, one cannot say in the normal school situation whether the teacher's expectation was the cause of the performance or whether she simply made an accurate prognosis based on her knowledge of past performance by the particular children involved" (1968, p. 19). To test this, Rosenthal and Jacobson (1966, 1968) designed an experiment that rested on the premise that some deficiencies (and therefore some remedies) may lie in the attitudes of teachers toward children labeled disadvantaged. They established an expectation that some five pupils in each classroom in a school might demonstrate superior academic performance. The names of these children were chosen randomly. The treatment was simply to give their names to their new teachers. The only real difference between the children pointed out as gifted and the undesignated control group was in the minds of the teachers. The children in the treatment group (for whom the teachers expected superior academic gains) demonstrated superior academic achievement.

Early researchers (Gottlieb & Budoff, 1972; Jones, 1972; Lilly, 1970) in the area of attitudes toward children labeled mildly retarded looked at what is expected of those who carry the label and how this expectation affects performance. Labels may engender specific behavioral expectations, particularly on the part of teachers. These expectations, in turn, may be reflected in the teacher's behavior toward the labeled child, and eventually in the child's level of performance.

Much concern about the pygmalion effect in special education was stimulated by minority groups who pointed out the disproportionate numbers of their children in special classes (*Larry P.* v. *Riles; Diana* v. *California Board of Education; Lora* v. *Board of Education of the City of New York*). The concern was focused on the consequences of special class placement as seen in the child's rejection by teachers, parents, and peers, poor self-image, and poor prospects for post school adjustment and employment.

REFERENCES

Gottlieb, J., & Budoff, M. (1972). Attitudes toward school by segregated and integrated retarded children. *Studies in Learning Potential, 2,* 1–10.

Jones, R. L. (1972). Labels and stigma in special education. *Exceptional Children, 38,* 553–564.

Lilly, M. S. (1970). Special education: A teapot in a tempest. *Exceptional Children, 36,* 43–48.

Rosenthal, R., & Jacobson, L. (1966). Teacher expectancies: Determinants of pupils IQ gains. *Psychological Reports 19,* 115–118.

Rosenthal, R., & Jacobson, L. (1968). *Pygmalion in the classroom.* New York: Holt, Rinehart, & Winston.

CAROLE REITER GOTHELF
*Hunter College, City University
of New York*

LABELING
TEACHER EXPECTANCIES

Q

Q-SORT

The Q-sort is a technique used to implement Q-methodology, a set of philosophical, psychological, statistical, and psychometric ideas propounded by William Stephenson (1953). The Q-sort was developed as a research tool, in particular a tool for exploring and testing theoretical formulations (e.g., about the existence of different educational philosophies). However, its use has been extended to both clinical assessment and to program evaluation.

The Q-sort is a way of rank-ordering objects. The objects ranked usually take the form of statements written on cards (though real objects, such as works of art, have been subjected to the Q-sort also). The sorter is given a set of cards—usually between 60 and 120—and instructed to distribute them into a fixed number of piles arranged along some continuum (e.g., approval to disapproval). The sorter is required to put a specified number of cards in each pile, resulting in a normal or quasi-normal distribution. This distribution permits the use of conventional statistical techniques, including correlation, analysis of variance, and factor analysis, in analyzing the results.

The results of the Q-sort typically are used to draw inferences about people (not the objects they are ranking) for theoretical, clinical, or program evaluation purposes. For example, a preliminary theory about the existence of two opposing educational philosophies can be tested by creating a set of statements reflecting each philosophy, having the combined set sorted on an "approval-disapproval" continuum, and analyzing the results to determine if there are groups of people who rank-order the statements in the same way. In the clinical setting, the patient's sort can be compared with those associated with known pathological syndromes. Finally, in program evaluation, sorts made before and after a program can be compared with one another or with a criterion sort meant to represent the desired outcome of the program.

Q-methodology is not universally accepted in the research community (Kerlinger, 1973). Criticisms of Q are based primarily on the fact that it cannot be used easily with large samples and on its violation of the statistical assumption of independence (i.e., the response to one item should not be affected by the response to any other). However, even with these liabilities, Q is regarded by many as a useful tool for particular research and applied purposes.

REFERENCES

Kerlinger, F. N. (1973). *Foundations of behavioral research* (2nd ed.). New York: Holt, Rinehart, & Winston.

Stephenson, W. (1953). *The study of behavior.* Chicago: University of Chicago Press.

RANDY ELLIOT BENNETT
MARY LOUISE LENNON
Educational Testing Service
Princeton, New Jersey

FACTOR ANALYSIS
MEASUREMENT
PHILOSOPHIES OF SPECIAL EDUCATION
RESEARCH IN SPECIAL EDUCATION

QUADRIPLEGIA

Quadriplegia is often referred to as paralysis from the neck down. Although this definition may be accurate for certain conditions, it is also misleading. A more accurate description of quadriplegia is a nonspecific paralysis or loss of normal function in all four limbs of the body. The condition most often affects motor skills but also may affect sensory awareness. Quadriplegia may result from damage to or dysfunction of the brain (e.g., cerebral palsy, stroke, traumatic head injury), spinal cord (e.g., spinal cord injury, amyotrophic lateral sclerosis), or peripheral structures (e.g., muscular dystrophy, multiple sclerosis). The condition also may occur as a result of tumor, toxic chemicals, congenital abnormalities, or infection. The term sometimes includes quadriparesis, which is considered a weakness or incomplete paralysis of the four extremities. Quadriplegia is not generally associated with the head or neck, but it may involve these structures in some conditions (e.g., cerebral palsy).

The specific skills or functions that are lost or impaired for persons with quadriplegia may vary considerably and depend largely on the individual's primary impairment. For example, a person who experiences quadriplegia as a result of a spinal cord injury experiences a loss of sensation and movement below the level of the injury. When the injury occurs at the level of the third cervical vertebra (C3), the person has essentially no sensation or functional use of the body below the neck. On the other hand, a person with a C5 injury has some active movement available at the elbow (flexion and supination) and shoulder (abduction and external rotation), but most other movements are lost. In the latter stages of the Duchenne's form of muscular dystrophy, a person may be able to use the fingers to write, type, or manipulate other small objects. Because of progressive weakness in the large muscles of the body, people with this type of quadriplegia are unable to move their arms at the shoulder or wrist. Unlike quadriplegia from spinal cord injury, sensation in this type of impairment remains intact. Children with quadriplegia owed to cerebral palsy are almost always able to move the joints in their upper extremities. They usually experience normal tactile sensation, but they may have abnormal kinesthetic sensation. Because of abnormal changes in muscle tone in various groups of muscles, movements are either very rigid and stiff, uncoordinated, or limp and flaccid. Children with quadriplegic cerebral palsy also may experience abnormal muscle tone and movement patterns in their neck or facial muscles in addition to involvement in all four extremities.

The specific treatment, education, or other intervention for persons with quadriplegia also is dependent on the impairment that causes this condition. A team approach using multidisciplinary, transdisciplinary, or interdisciplinary models is essential in the care and management of an individual with quadriplegia. Team members may include physicians, nurses, teachers, physical therapists, occupational therapists, speech pathologists, rehabilitation engineers, family members, attendants, and, as often as possible, the affected individual. Sometimes individuals with quadriplegia need considerable assistance for even the most routine activities (e.g., eating a meal), while others are able to live independently, pursue a career, and raise a family.

Although quadriplegia usually results in extensive disability, a variety of electronic and nonelectronic devices may be used to facilitate more normal experiences or abilities. Electrically powered wheelchairs, specially designed passenger vans, adapted eating utensils, augmentative communication systems, and personal hygiene and grooming devices are only a few examples that may be used to compensate for impaired skills. These technologic advances have fostered a more independent lifestyle for many people with quadriplegia, but some advocates for people with disabilities would argue that social changes also are needed to permit the greatest level of independence. Elimination of environmental and attitudinal barriers and affirmative action for employment often are identified as essential components of a productive and satisfying life. References illuminating etiology, definition and management are cited below for further reading.

REFERENCES

Bobath, B. (1985). *Abnormal postural reflex activity caused by brain lesions* (3rd ed.). Rockville, MD: Aspen Systems.

Bobath, B., & Bobath, K. (1975). *Motor development in the different types of cerebral palsy*. London: Heinemann Medical Books.

Ford, J., & Duckworth, B. (1974). *Physical management for the quadriplegic patient*. Philadelphia: Davis.

Miller, B., & Keane, C. (1983). *Encyclopedia and dictionary of medical nursing and allied health* (3rd ed.). Philadelphia: Saunders.

Nagel, D. A. (1975). Traumatic paraplegia and quadriplegia. In E. E. Bleck & D. A. Nagel (Eds.), *Physically handicapped children—A medical atlas for teachers* (pp. 209–214). New York: Grune & Stratton.

Trombly, C. A. (1983). Spinal cord injury. In C. A. Trombly (Ed.), *Occupational therapy for physical dysfunction* (2nd ed., pp. 385–398). Baltimore, MD: Williams & Wilkins.

DANIEL D. LIPKA
*Lincoln Way Special Education
Regional Resource Center,
Louisville, Ohio*

ACCESSIBILITY OF BUILDINGS

QUAY, HERBERT C. (1927–   )

Born in Portland, Maine, Herbert C. Quay received his BS (1951) and MS (1952) in psychology from Florida State University. He received his PhD (1958) in clinical psychology from the University of Illinois. Currently, he is chairman of the department of psychology, director of the program in applied social sciences, and professor of psychology and pediatrics at the University of Miami.

Quay has questioned the traditional classification system of special education categories. In 1971 he discovered that the number, rather than the type, of behavior symptoms was more effective in identifying psychopathology in a child. This finding acknowledges that most children exhibit most behaviors labeled pathologic at some point in their development without becoming pathological themselves (Werry & Quay, 1971). He also found that an assessor's theory of development and pathology was a factor in how that assessor diagnosed a child (Quay, 1973). That is, if an assessor believed in a theory of process dysfunctions, there would be a different diagnosis than from an assessor who believed in experiential deficits.

By using factor analysis, Quay developed the Behavior Problem Checklist (Quay, 1977). This is a three-point scale to rate traits of problem behaviors in children and adolescents. Quay advocated the checklist to differentiate dimensions of deviance, select treatment programs, and determine systematic differences among children with divergent patterns of deviance.

Quay has been listed in *Who's Who in the World*, *Who's Who in America*, *American Men of Science*, and *Leaders in Education*.

REFERENCES

Quay, H. C. (1973). Special education: Assumptions, techniques, and evaluative criteria. *Exceptional Children, 40,* 165–170.

Quay, H. C. (1977). Measuring dimensions of deviant behavior: The behavior problem checklist. *Journal of Abnormal Child Psychology, 5,* 277–287.

Werry, J. S., & Quay, H. C. (1971). The prevalence of behavior symptoms in younger elementary school children. *American Journal of Orthopsychiatry, 41,* 136–143.

E. Valerie Hewitt
Texas A&M University

QUAY-PETERSON REVISED PROBLEM BEHAVIOR CHECKLIST

See behavior problem checklist revised.

QUESTIONNAIRES IN SPECIAL EDUCATION

Questionnaires are often used for gathering research data in special education. They are relatively inexpensive, can assure anonymity, and can be used with relative ease by novice researchers as well as seasoned professionals.

Pride (1979) has observed that the mail questionnaire in particular is useful in obtaining data from distant populations. It reaches subjects too busy to be interviewed, enables targeting subgroups of respondents, and is conducive in format to framing responses in a manner suitable for statistical analysis. The mail questionnaire can also "eliminate interviewer bias to questions that are sensitive or embarrassing when posed by an interviewer" (Pride, 1979, p. 59).

As popular survey research tools questionnaires (whether mailed, completed by telephone, or administered in person) require careful design. The design process includes separate decisions about (1) the kind of information sought (e.g., attitudinal, behavioral), (2) the question structure (e.g., open-ended, close-ended with ordered categories), and (3) the actual choice of words (Dillman, 1978, pp. 79–80). Every investigation presents special requirements and different problems. Oppenheim (1966), Dillman (1978), and Sudman and Bradburn (1982) provide thorough discussions about the many factors to be considered when designing questionnaires and detailed recommendations for writing and presenting questions.

Despite the fact that the mail survey is, in many cases, the most feasible approach for retrieving data from large, widely dispersed samples, many researchers have expressed concern about its methodological rigor and adequacy. This concern is based largely on the grounds of seriously deficient response rates. "The most common flaw is nonresponse of a size or nature which makes the answers nonrepresentative of the total sample and thus the total

universe" (Erdos, 1970, p. 142). Returns of less than 40 or 50% are common. Additionally, there are limitations on the nature of data that may be obtained and the quality of responses to many mail questionnaires.

Kanuk and Berenson (1975) confirmed that, despite the proliferation of research studies (well over 200) reporting techniques to reduce nonresponse bias, "there is no strong empirical evidence favoring any techniques other than follow-up and the use of monetary incentives" (p. 451). Research on the topic generally has been narrowly focused, poorly integrated, and contradictory. Erdos (1970) and Dillman (1978) represent the few attempts to improve response rates to mail questionnaires from the perspective of addressing the entire mail survey process.

Dillman's recommendations offer a fully integrated, planned sequence of procedures and techniques that are designed to increase response rates and that are fully adaptable to research problems in special education. His total design method (TDM) attempts to present mail surveys in such a way that respondents develop proprietary attitudes toward the research project in which they are being asked to participate. Based on the tenets of motivational psychology, Dillman has postulated that the process of designing and sending a questionnaire, and getting respondents to complete it in an honest manner and return it, is a special kind of social exchange. His highly prescribed method and related strategies are designed to minimize the costs for responding, maximize the rewards for doing so, and establish trust that those rewards will be delivered. Readily adaptable in its present form, the TDM also provides a useful frame of reference against which the design aspects of each mail survey research problem may be considered.

REFERENCES

Dillman, D. (1978). *Mail and telephone surveys: The total design method.* New York: Wiley.

Erdos, P. L. (1970). *Professional mail surveys.* New York: McGraw-Hill.

Kanuk, L., & Berenson, C. (1975). Mail survey and response rates: A literature review. *Journal of Marketing Research, 12,* 440–453.

Oppenheim, A. N. (1966). *Questionnaire design and attitudes measurement.* New York: Basic Books.

Pride, C. (1979). Building response to a mail survey. *New Directions for Institutional Advancement, 6,* 59–69.

Sudman, S., & Bradburn, N. M. (1982). *Asking questions.* San Francisco: Jossey-Bass.

Lawrence S. Cote
Pennsylvania State University

RESEARCH IN SPECIAL EDUCATION

QUIGLEY, STEPHEN P. (1927–   )

Born in Belfast, Northern Ireland, Stephen P. Quigley received his BA (1953) in psychology from the University of

Denver. He received his MA (1954) in speech and hearing disorders and his PhD (1957) in speech science and psychology from the University of Illinois. Currently, he is professor of education and speech and hearing science at the University of Illinois, Urbana–Champaign.

Quigley's main interests have been in communication, language, and the educational development of hearing-impaired children. He worked on Chomsky's idea that careful manipulation of stimulus-response could produce more effective insights into language acquisition. With this background, he developed the Test of Syntactical Abilities (1978), a standardized test for the diagnosis and assessment of the syntactical abilities of deaf children.

His *Language and Deafness* (1984) emphasizes a need for every deaf child to have a fluent and intelligible communication system. He has discovered that many deaf children enter school without any well-developed first language. Without this first language, whether it be oral, written, or sign, it is impossible to examine the child's language development. Quigley has also seen that all children develop language structures similarly, but that the rate of development is much slower for a deaf child (Quigley, Power, & Steinkamp, 1977). Without understanding basic syntax, deaf children have difficulties in understanding and producing figurative language (Quigley, 1982). Quigley advocates the development of reading materials for deaf children that recognize the needs of these children but that are not overly specialized.

REFERENCES

Quigley, S. P. (1982). Reading achievement and special reading materials. *Volta Review, 84*(5), 95–106.

Quigley, S. P., & Paul, P. V. (1984). *Language and deafness.* San Diego, CA: College Hill.

Quigley, S. P., Power, D. J., & Steinkamp, M. W. (1977). The language structure of deaf children. *Volta Review, 79*(2), 73–84.

Quigley, S. P., Steinkamp M., Power, D., & Jones, B. (1978). *Test of syntactical abilities.* Beaverton, OR: Dormac.

E. VALERIE HEWITT
Texas A&M University

R

RACIAL BIAS IN TESTING

See CULTURAL BIAS IN TESTING.

RACIAL DISCRIMINATION IN SPECIAL EDUCATION

The right to education, nondiscriminatory treatment, equal protection, and due process protection for all handicapped children was established by Congress with the Education Amendments of 1974 and the Education For All Handicapped Children Act of 1975. Prior to this national policy, more than 36 court cases throughout the country brought convincing documentation that racially and culturally discriminatory practices existed in special education. Racially and culturally diverse school children continue to be disproportionately represented in special education programs while local and state education officials attempt to improve testing and classification procedures.

Racially and culturally biased identification and placement procedures in special education were initially disputed in *Hobson v. Hansen* (1967). Judge J. Skelly Wright found that the ability grouping track system in the public schools of the District of Columbia deprived black disadvantaged and handicapped students of "their right to equal educational opportunity with white and more affluent public school children" (401). Relying on factual findings of discrimination, the Court ordered the track system abolished in 1969. Subsequently, seven black exceptional children labeled as either behavior problems, mentally retarded, emotionally disturbed, or hyperactive, sued the District of Columbia Public Schools for failing to provide them with special education while providing such education to other children (*Mills v. Board of Education, District of Columbia*, (1972). Holding "that Constitutional rights must be afforded citizens despite the greater expense involved" (p. 876), the court's decree established (1) standards and procedures for an "appropriate educational program," (2) a required "comprehensive plan" for identification and notification of exceptional students and their parents, and (3) "alternative program of education, placement in a regular public school class with appropri-

ate ancillary services is preferable to placement in a special class" (p. 880).

In California, nine Mexican-American students in *Diana v. State Board of Education* (1970) and six black students in *Larry P. v. Riles* (1972) alleged that they were being misplaced in special classes for the educable mentally retarded on the basis of inappropriate tests and testing procedures that ignored their cultural and racial learning experiences. Both cases were brought to the Northern California Federal District Court and documented statewide, the statistically significant overrepresentation of minorities in special education. *Diana's* stipulated settlement agreement (1973) established testing procedures in the student's primary language, retesting of Mexican-American and Chinese-American students currently in classes for the retarded, and a mandate for a state developed and appropriate standardized intelligence test.

Judge Peckham in *Larry P.* cited California's historical racial discriminatory use of Intelligence Quotient (I.Q.) tests against blacks and issued a preliminary injunction in 1972 against the San Francisco Unified School District. The injunction prevented the use of intelligence tests for placement purposes and ordered the elimination of the disproportionate placement of black children in special classes for the educable retarded. Similarly, a statewide order on December 13, 1974, by the court and a state imposed moratorium in January, 1975, stopped all IQ testing of the educable mentally retarded for the purposes of placement (1979, p. 931, n.4). The decision was affirmed in 1984.

Matti T. v. Holladay was a class action suit filed on April 25, 1975 on behalf of 26 handicapped students from seven local school districts in Mississippi against state and local school officials. The suit challenged the policies and practices in special education. The plaintiffs in *Matti T.* claimed that the schools used racially and culturally discriminatory procedures in the identification, evaluation, and education placement of handicapped children. Evidence showed that three times as many black children than white children were placed in educable retarded classes and conversely, twice as many white children than black children were placed in higher costs and more integrated specific learning disability classes. The court ordered an agreement decree on January 26, 1979, requiring the state to substantially reduce the racial disparity by

1982 by establishing new identification practices and monitoring and enforcement procedures.

Isaac *Lora v. Board of Education of the City of New York*, in June 1975, represented all black and hispanic students assigned to special day schools for emotionally disturbed in New York City. Citing statistically significant disparities between minorities and white students with the same problems, the class of plaintiffs alleged discriminatory testing and that "the special day schools are intentionally segregated dumping grounds for minorities forced into inadequate facilities without due process" (1978, p. 1214). Following lengthy proceedings, appeals, and recommendations of a national "Lora Advisory Panel," a conciliatory agreement produced nondiscriminatory standards and procedures in 1984.

REFERENCES

Diana v. Board of Education, No. C-70-37 RFP (N.D. Cal. Jan. 7, 1970, June 18, 1973, and Order of May 27, 1974).

Hobson v. Hansen, 269 F. Supp. 401 (D.D.C. 1967), *Smuck v. Hobson*, 408 F.2d. 175 (D.C. Cir. 1969).

Larry P. v. Riles, 343 F. Supp. 1306 (N.D. Cal. 1972), 502 F.2d. 963 (9th Cir. 1974), 495 F. Supp. 926 (N.D. Cal. 1979), aff'd. 9th Cir., Jan. 23, 1984 (EHLR 555:304, Feb. 3, 1984).

Lora v. Board of Educ. of City of New York, 456 F. Supp. 1211 (E.D.N.Y. 1978), 623 F.2d. 248 (2d Cir. 1980), 587 F. Supp. 1572 (E.D.N.Y. 1984).

Mattie T. v. Holladay, No. DC-75-31 (N.D. Miss. Jan. 26, 1979), EHLR 551:109, Apr. 1, 1979.

Mills v. Board of Education of District of Columbia, 348 F. Supp. 866 (D.D.C. 1972).

LOUIS SCHWARTZ
Florida State University

DIANA *v.* BOARD OF EDUCATION
EDUCATION FOR ALL HANDICAPPED CHILDREN ACT OF 1975
HOBSON *v.* HANSEN
LARRY P.
SPECIAL EDUCATION, LEGAL REGULATIONS OF
MATTIE T. *v.* HOLLADAY
MILLS *v.* BOARD OF EDUCATION

RASE

See REMEDIAL AND SPECIAL EDUCATION.

RATIO IQ

A ratio intelligence quotient or ratio IQ is a score from a test of intelligence (or cognitive or mental ability). Now obsolete as a statistical term, it is still a useful concept for interpreting current levels of mental functioning and, to a limited extent, for predicting future mental development. The ratio IQ has been replaced by most authors of mental ability tests with a standard score such as a deviation IQ.

At the turn of the century, and for the next several decades, tests of mental ability were administered to children of several different chronological ages. The average number of items answered correctly at each age level was recorded. Then the number of items answered correctly by a given child could be compared with the average performance of children of various ages. Such scores were known as a mental age (MA) or age equivalent (AE). Such scores made it possible to say that a particular child of a given age performed on the test as a typical 4 year old, or another as a typical 6 year old, or another as an 8 year old, etc., but MAs describe only present status.

The concept of a mental quotient to indicate the rate of cognitive development was introduced by William Stern in a paper to the German Congress of Psychology in Berlin in April 1912. With the Stanford Revision and Extension of the Binet-Simon Intelligence Scale in 1916, Lewis Terman introduced the term intelligence quotient and its abbreviation, IQ, as a prediction of the rate of future mental development (based on the rate of previous accomplishment). Early IQs were simply the ratio of the mental age to the chronological age, multiplied by 100 to eliminate the decimals (i.e., IQ = MA/CAx 100). However, mental ages represent ordinal not interval data and therefore the distance between two ages, e.g., 4 and 6, is not necessarily the same as between two other ages, e.g., 12 and 14. Also, test authors have not been able to construct tests with equal variability at each age level. As a result, the standard deviation of scores is not the same at each age and, therefore, the same ratio IQ obtained at different age levels may not be equal to the same percentile rank. (A ratio IQ that equals or exceeds 3% of the population might be 75 at one age, 68 at another, and 60 at another.) Whereas the statistical properties of a ratio IQ present too many difficulties for its use to be continued except as a concept for interpretation, the simplicity of the concept is still helpful in explaining performance to many consumers. With an IQ of 65, one can say that a 10-year-old child is functioning mentally much like most 6 to 7 year olds and is exhibiting about two-thirds of a year of mental growth each year. The concept of ratio IQ and mental age seem almost nonsensical when applied to adults. Since ratio IQs represent only ordinal scaling, they can neither be multiplied, divided, added, or subtracted across ages and are obsolete for most needs in diagnostic settings.

JOSEPH L. FRENCH
Pennsylvania State University

DEVIATION IQ
INTELLIGENCE QUOTIENT

RAVEN'S MATRICES

The Standard Progressive Matrices and the Colored Progressive Matrices (Raven, 1938–1983) are a collection of figures that resemble swatches removed from a wallpaper pattern. The test requires the examinee to locate the swatch that best fits the removed pattern. The test is purportedly an excellent measure of g factor intelligence (general intellectual ability) (Marshalek, Lohman, & Snow, 1983). The matrices tests have recieved wide use around the world because of their easy administration, nonverbal format, and high correlations with traditional measures of intelligence and achievement. The progressive matrices have been used in hundreds of psychological studies internationally.

Since the progressive matrices (developed in the United Kingdom) originated in a psychometric era known for providing examiners with minimal information on standardized sample characteristics, technical adequacy, item construction and use, rationale and theory, and potential uses and misues of instruments, the progressive matrices manuals provide little information in these areas. Additionally, Levy and Goldstein (1984), editors of *Tests in Education*, the British equivalent of the *Buros Mental Measurements Yearbook*, note that the British have lagged behind the Americans in the care that psychologists have used in the development of psychoeducational assessment measures. However, the large number of studies compiled on the progressive matrices attest to the instruments' use and value.

The matrices are appropriate for individuals ages 5 through adult and are printed both in color (ages 5 to 11) and standard black and white versions (ages 6 and over). The test provides only percentile ranks as an individual's reported score, but even these are not complete; the manual reports performance levels only at the 5, 10, 25, 50, 75, 90, and 95th percentiles. Thus the test only approximates levels of performance. As such, the matrices are useful for the rough assessment of the nonverbal reasoning abilities of individuals 5 years and above. Because of the many deficiencies in the tests' manuals and standardized samples, it is best used as an assessment tool for research purposes and those occasional clinical instances in which an estimate of an individual's intellectual abilities are needed.

REFERENCES

Marshalek, B., Lohman, D. F., & Snow, R. (1983). The complexity continuum in the radex and hierarchical models of intelligence. *Intelligence, 7*, 107–127.

Levy, P., & Goldstein, H. (1984). *Tests in education: A book of critical reviews*. London: Academic.

BRUCE A. BRACKEN
LINDSAY S. GROSS
*University of Wisconsin,
Milwaukee*

"g" FACTOR THEORY
INTELLIGENCE
INTELLIGENCE TESTING

RAY ADAPTATION OF THE RAY WECHSLER INTELLIGENCE SCALE FOR CHILDREN— REVISED

Ray (1979) adapted the Wechsler Intelligence Scale for Children-Revised (WISC-R) performance scales for an intelligence test designed especially for the hearing impaired. He introduced a set of simplified verbal instructions and added more practice items in an attempt to provide standardized test administration techniques to increase a deaf child's comprehension and performance. Therapists who are unskilled in American Sign Language are able to administer the test. In addition to Ray's version of instructions, several different techniques exist for nonverbal administration (Sullivan, 1982). Seven scores are yielded in the adaptation: picture completion, picture arrangement, block design, object assembly, coding, mazes, and total. Administration time averages about 45 minutes.

The adaptation was normed on 127 hearing-impaired children from 6 to 16 years old. The sample used was not representative of the deaf school-age population, including no low-verbal deaf children and no multiply handicapped children (Sullivan, 1985). Norms provided in Ray's test should be regarded with caution, and thought should be given to other deaf norms developed. The WISC-R performance scales can be a suitable alternative to the Hiskey-Nebraska if the Anderson and Sisco norms are used with a total communication approach for administration (Phelps & Ensor, 1986). Genshaft (1985) thinks that the most useful improvement in the adaptation would be separate, representative norms for deaf children.

REFERENCES

Genshaft, J. L. (1985). Review of the WISC-R: For the deaf. In J. V. Mitchell, Jr. (Ed.), *The ninth mental measurements yearbook* (Vol. 2). Lincoln: University of Nebraska.

Phelps, L., & Ensor, A. (1986). Concurrent validity of the WISC-R using deaf norms and the Hiskey-Nebraska. *Psychology in the Schools, 23*, 138–141.

Ray, S. (1979). *An adaptation of the Wechsler Intelligence Scale for Children—Revised for the deaf*. Natchitoches: Northwestern State University of Louisiana.

Sullivan, R. M. (1982). Modified instructions for administering the WISC-R performance scale subtests to deaf children (Appendix B). In J. M. Sattler (Ed.), *Assessment of children's intelligence and special abilities* (2nd ed.). Boston: Allyn & Bacon.

Sullivan, P. M. (1985). Review of the WISC-R: For the deaf. In J.

V. Mitchell, Jr. (Ed.) *The ninth mental measurements yearbook* (Vol. 2). Lincoln: University of Nebraska Press.

LISA J. SAMPSON
Eastern Kentucky University

DEAF
WECHSLER INTELLIGENCE SCALE FOR CHILDREN—
REVISED

REACTION TIME

The time required for a person to respond to a stimulus was one of the most frequent measures of human behavior by early psychologists. Indeed, E. G. Boring, a historian of psychology, characterized the late nineteenth century as the period of "mental chronometry." During this period Galton first used reaction time to an auditory stimulus as a measure of intelligence; similar reaction-time items were incorporated into several early intelligence tests. When reaction time was found to have negligible correlation with seemingly more valid measures of intelligence, however, interest in it waned. In retrospect, it appears that the failure of reaction time may have been due to unreliable measurement and other methodological difficulties. It is now recognized that a large number of trials are required to obtain a reliable average reaction time for an individual person.

As the computer analogy has come to dominate cognitive psychology in recent years, there has been a resurgence of interest in reaction time. The goal of current reaction time research is to measure the time required for the brain to perform a variety of elementary cognitive tasks. From such information it may be possible to infer how the mind is functioning.

Basically, the procedure is to measure reaction time in a task that requires a simple mental operation. The complexity of the mental operation is then increased, and the increase in reaction time is used as a measure of the time required for the brain to process the increased complexity. The following three basic paradigms have been frequently used.

Hick (1952) measured the increase in time required to choose among several visual or auditory stimuli as the number of stimuli increased. The time required is a log function of the number of stimuli, which can be interpreted as the amount of information involved in the choice. Thus the brain appears to be making a block-wise comparison among the various stimuli.

Sternberg (1966) presented subjects with a set of digits followed by a probe digit; the subjects then indicated whether the probe digit was included in the set. This task appears to measure speed of scanning short-term memory. Reaction time increases linearly with the number of items in the set, suggesting a sequential scanning mechanism.

Posner (1969) asked subjects to indicate whether two letters were the same or different, with similarity being first defined as physical similarity, in which *A* and *a* are different, and then as semantic similarity, in which *A* and *a* are the same. The latter task requires considerably more time than the first, since the letters must be identified, evidently by a search of long-term memory.

Jensen (1980) has studied the relationship of individual differences in time required to perform these elementary cognitive tasks to scores on traditional psychometric tests of intelligence. The surprising finding is that, with careful measurement and allowing for certain sources of error, about half of the variance in psychometric intelligence test scores is predictable from the several measures of speed of mental processing. If this provocative finding turns out to be easily replicated by other investigators, it will establish a major link between psychometric intelligence and its biological substrate.

REFERENCES

Hick, W. (1952). On the rate of gain of information. *Quarterly Journal of Experimental Psychology, 4*, 11–26.

Jensen, A. R. (1980). Chronometric analysis of intelligence. *Journal of Social & Biological Structures, 3*, 103–122.

Posner, M. I. (1969). Abstraction and the process of recognition. In G. H. Bower & J. T. Spense (Eds.), *The psychology of learning and motivation* (Vol. 3, pp. 43–100). New York: Academic.

Sternberg, S. (1966). High speed scanning in human memory. *Science, 153*, 652–654.

ROBERT C. NICHOLS
DIANE JARVIS
State University of New York, Buffalo

CULTURE FAIR TESTS
"g" FACTOR THEORY
INTELLIGENCE TESTING
SPEARMAN'S HYPOTHESIS OF BLACK/WHITE
    DIFFERENCES

READABILITY AND READABILITY FORMULAS

Readability refers to the difficulty level of a passage of text, and is often presented as a grade level number. Typically, reading curricula are designed to match the readability level of stories to the grade level in which the materials are to be used. Textbooks often are described in terms of their readability level. Various readability formulas are used to determine these readability levels.

Klare (1982) provides a general definition of a readability formula: "a predictive device that uses counts of word and sentence variables in a piece of writing to provide a quantitative, objective index of style difficulty" (p.

1522). More than 200 formulas have been published since the first one was developed in the 1920s.

To predict the readability level of a complete text, formulas typically are applied to 100-word samples drawn randomly from throughout the text. Formulas generally are based on regression equations, using weighted scores for word and sentence counts to predict a comprehension score that roughly corresponds to a tested reading grade level. Formulas either rely on word lists or counts of syllables that estimate semantic difficulty (Klare, 1982).

The analogy of a thermometer is often used to explain readability and its limitations (Klare, 1982, 1984). Just as a thermometer is an index of the warmth of a room, particular characteristics of words and sentences index reading difficulty, but do not necessarily cause it. Altering words and sentences in a text may change the readability level, but may not make the text any more comprehensible, just as holding a lighted match under a thermometer will change the temperature reading but will not substantially warm the room.

As Duffelmeyer (1985) notes, a formula's reliance on word length as an index of difficulty can be misleading. Although there is a high correlation between average word length and prose difficulty, long words (more than six letters) in very easy reading materials are often plurals or variations of simple roots (e.g., schools, run*ning*) and should not be weighted as much as words of equal length that involve more complex concepts.

Formulas also do not necessarily adequately capture aspects of text familiarity and complexity. Familiar words make reading easier because they are easier to recall from memory; yet, the familiarity or processing difficulty of a word for a particular reader is not defined by the statistical frequency of that word. For example, an unfamiliar word is easier to process if it appears in a familiar story. And more familiar words may be less precise in communicating the author's meaning.

Similarly, measures that rely on sentence length as an index of difficulty assume that the demand on working memory increases as the length of clauses or sentences increases. The number of words does not accurately reflect the amount of effort expended by readers, however, since readers chunk together text segments. Dividing long sentences in a passage into shorter ones will reduce the readability level of the passage, but may make the text more difficult to understand. The elimination of words connecting ideas—such as *because*, *since*, and *then*—places greater demands on the reader to draw inferences about the relationships between those ideas.

Beck and her colleagues (Beck, McKeown, Omanson, & Pople, 1984) argue that "readability formulas are at best, useless, and at worst, misleading, for assisting in the development of readable texts" (p. 263). They found that traditional readability formulas do not adequately describe what makes a text more or less comprehensible. When two stories from basal readers were revised to improve their

coherence (story events were organized and clarified, and connections in the text were made more apparent), readability levels increased by one grade level even though the revised stories were more easily comprehended and recalled than the original ones with lower readability levels.

Davison (1984) notes that making changes in text to conform to readability formulas may

> seriously distort the logical relations between the parts of the text, sentences, or paragraphs; and may disrupt the presentation of ideas. . . . The less information is expressed explicitly in the words and syntactic structures of the text, the more load is placed on the ability to make inferences and to use background information. (p. 124)

Davison (1984) also notes that "it is possible—and in some cases *probable*—that a text may be simplified to the point of being readable at a particular level as measured by readability formulas without being *comprehensible*" (p. 128). Similarly, the Commission on Reading (Anderson Hiebert, Scott, & Wilkinson, 1985) suggests that "it is quite possible to write a disorganized text, full of incomprehensible sentences, and still achieve a desired readability score" (p. 64).

Variability in readability levels of different sections within the same basal reader also has been noted (Fuchs, Fuchs, & Deno, 1982). Fuchs et al. examined how many simple passages from basal texts were required to obtain a consistent readability level for those texts. From 5 to 14 passages had to be sampled at every reading level before the readability scores for any two passages agreed with the mean readability levels established for each text. More than half of the 19 textbooks included in the study required sampling of 10 or more passages before two or more representative passages could be identified.

A related study (Fuchs, Fuchs, & Deno, 1984) examined the usefulness of six readability formulas in predicting the relative difficulty of three passages, with difficulty measured as students' reading scores (number of words read aloud correctly in 1 minute). Rank orderings of passage difficulty based on the formulas did not agree with the students' reading scores on the passages.

Many common readability measures are available in microcomputer format. A program may consist of a single procedure or as many as eight procedures. Kennedy (1985) provides information on nearly a dozen such programs. Duffelmeyer (1985) contends that although computer programs compute formulas quickly and easily, teacher judgment still is required to assess the conceptual difficulty of the material.

REFERENCES

Anderson, R. C., Hiebert, E. H., Scott, J. A., & Wilkinson, I. A. G. (1985). *Becoming a nation of readers: The report of the Com-*

mission on Reading. Champaign, IL: Center for the Study of Reading.

Beck, I. L., McKeown, M. G., Omanson, R. C., & Pople, M. T. (1984). Improving the comprehensibility of stories: The effects of revisions that improve coherence. *Reading Research Quarterly, 19*(3), 263–277.

Davison, A. (1984). Readability—Appraising text difficulty. In R. C. Anderson, J. Osborn, & R. J. Tierney (Eds.), *Learning to read in American schools: Basal readers and content texts* (pp. 121–139). Hillsdale, NJ: Erlbaum.

Duffelmeyer, F. A. (1985). Estimating readability with a computer. Beware the aura of precision. *Reading Teacher, 38*(4), 392–394.

Fuchs, L. S., Fuchs, D., & Deno, S. L. (1982). Reliability and validity of curriculum-based Informal Reading Inventories. *Reading Research Quarterly, 18*(1), 6–26.

Fuchs, L. S., Fuchs, D., & Deno, S. L. (1984). Inaccuracy among readability formulas: Implications for the management of reading proficiency and selection of instructional materials. *Diagnostique, 9*(2), 86–95.

Kennedy, K. (1985). Determining readability with a microcomputer. *Curriculum Review, 25*(2), 40–43.

Klare, G. R. (1982). Readability. In H. E. Mitzel (Ed.), *Encyclopedia of educational research* (5th ed., pp. 1520–1531). New York: Free Press.

Klare, G. R. (1984). Readability. In P. D. Pearson (Ed.), *Handbook of reading research* (pp. 681–744). New York: Longman.

Linda J. Stevens
University of Minnesota

READING
READING DISORDERS
READING IN THE CONTENT AREAS

READABILITY FORMULAS

Readability formulas are employed to predict the readability level of text. To develop these formulas, researchers select a criterion index of text difficulty and a set of predictor variables or indicators of text structure and relate the criterion index and set of predictor variables through application of multiple regression. This statistical procedure identifies formulas that best predict the criterion index. With the selection of easily calculated predictor variables, estimating text difficulty is relatively simple.

Perhaps because of the comparative simplicity of this approach, the use of formulas has proliferated. Nevertheless, research demonstrates the often dramatic inaccuracy of readability formulas in predicting passage difficulty (Britton & Lumpkin, 1977; Fuchs, Fuchs, & Deno, 1982; Fuchs, Fuchs, & Deno, 1984). This imprecision may be explained in the following ways. First, formulas have been derived and refined to predict difficulty estimates of criterion passages for which there is little evidence to support

the correctness of text readability designations (Fitzgerald, 1980). Second, formulas rely on surface characteristics of text rather than on passage content and student characteristics, despite evidence that pupils' familiarity with the content of text influences passage difficulty (Kemper, 1983; Pearson, 1974–1975). Recently, some progress has been made in developing formulas that move beyond the surface structure of text and that predict more valid criterion indices of text difficulty (Kemper, 1983).

However, until more appropriate procedures for predicting readability are developed to account for text content and student characteristics, special education diagnosticians and practitioners should interpret cautiously reading assessments based on basal texts or tests that have been developed with readability formulas. This caveat may be especially relevant for work with handicapped pupils whose background information may be influenced by their handicapped experience and may be different from that of the norm (Fuchs et al., 1984).

REFERENCES

Britton, G. E., & Lumpkin, M. C. (1977). Computerized readability verification of textbook reading levels. *Reading Improvement, 14*, 193–199.

Fitzgerald, G. G. (1980). Reliability of the Fry sampling procedures. *Reading Research Quarterly, 15*, 489–503.

Fuchs, L. S., Fuchs, D., & Deno, S. L. (1982). The reliability and validity of curriculum-based informal reading inventories. *Reading Research Quarterly, 18*, 6–26.

Fuchs, L. S., Fuchs, D., & Deno, S. L. (1984). Inaccuracy among readability formulas: Implications for the measurement of reading proficiency and selection of instructional material. *Diagnostique, 9*, 86–97.

Kemper, S. (1983). Measuring the inference load of a text. *Journal of Educational Psychology, 75*, 391–401.

Pearon, P. D. (1974–1975). The effects of grammatical complexity on children's comprehension, recall, and conception of certain semantic relations. *Reading Research Quarterly, 10*, 155–192.

Lynn S. Fuchs
Douglas Fuchs
Peabody College, Vanderbilt University

BASAL READERS
MULTIPLE REGRESSION

READING

Reading is the process of deriving meaning from print. While people have been reading as long as language has been written down, at no other time in recorded history has interest in reading, both from a research and practical standpoint, been greater (Anderson, R., Hiebert, Scott, &

Wilkerson, 1984). In the past 15 years, there has been a concerted effort to understand how the reading process occurs and to translate that knowledge into materials and strategies that more effectively teach reading. Reading educators, long concerned with reading research and its implementation, have recently been joined by cognitive, educational, and developmental psychologists, linguists, and sociolinguists in the attempt to unravel the mysteries of reading.

Although the word reading characterizes any meaningful interaction between an individual and print, we can subdivide reading into four basic types. Each of these types is differentiated by the purpose for which the reading act is undertaken. The four types of reading to be discussed are developmental reading, studying, functional reading, and recreational reading.

Developmental reading can be described as the activity undertaken for the purpose of learning how to read. During the colonial period, the *Bible*, the *Psalter*, and other religious materials were used to teach children to read. A century later, the McGuffey readers were published. These readers were the forerunners of the graded readers in use today, and their appearance paralleled the development of graded schools. Several decades ago, children learned to read with the assistance of the "Dick and Jane" books. With such familiar phrases as, "See Dick. See Jane," school-aged children across the United States entered the world of formal reading instruction. Today, much of the formal reading instruction in the early elementary grades is still devoted to developmental reading, although the commercially produced reading materials far outdistance their predecessors both in their extensiveness and their sophistication. However, the effectiveness of the current basal series and current instructional methodologies to produce better readers remains the source of great controversy (Anderson, et al., 1984).

As students progress through elementary school, developmental reading remains an integral part of their schooling, with the goal of increasing reading proficiency. Although developmental reading was confined to elementary grades in years past, it is now common to find developmental reading courses being offered at the college level. The rationale for this upward trend in developmental reading is the presence of larger numbers of college students who have not reached proficiency in reading, and who still require some instruction in learning how to read.

In the upper elementary grades, and throughout formal schooling, developmental reading is joined by another type of reading: studying. According to Anderson (1979), studying is a special form of reading that is concerned with the accomplishment of some instructional goal. The type of reading engaged in during studying is special for various reasons.

While the material used for developmental reading is mainly narrative text (i.e., storylike text), the kind of text students most often study is expository in nature. In terms of its demands on comprehension and recall, expository text appears to possess certain disadvantages over narrative text in that it has no identifiable elements such as plot, character, and setting. In addition, expository text is frequently less colorful, and filled with more technical language. Therefore, the task of studying may be more difficult than other forms of reading because expository text may be more difficult and less motivational to read. Not only is the text used in studying potentially more difficult to process, but when students study expository text it is often with the realization that they will be tested on the content; that fact is likely to make the studying experience less enjoyable.

Because of its nature, studying requires individuals to employ specialized learning and study skills (Weinstein, Goetz, & Alexander, in press). In addition to the well known SQ3R method (Robinson, 1970), there are such cognitive strategies as note-taking, outlining, paraphrasing, imaging, and rereading that might enhance student performance. Some of the other study strategies that have been looked at by researchers in recent years are lookbacks (Alexander, Hare, & Garner, 1984; Garner, et al., 1984), elaborative or generative processes (Wittrock, 1983), and cooperative learning strategies (Dansereau, in press; Dansereau, et al., 1979).

While developmental reading and studying are the forms of reading most directly associated with school, there is another form of reading that arises from real-world needs. This form of reading is called functional or survival reading. When we read road signs or find our way on a map, follow a recipe, or order from a menu, we are employing functional reading. Simply stated, functional reading is the reading that is required to accomplish some personal as opposed to instructional goal.

It is disheartening to note that there are many individuals in the United States who cannot even read well enough to make sense of the critical print around them. They cannot read the road signs along the road, or follow a recipe, fill out a job application, or read the dosage on a medicine bottle. Individuals who lack even this limited reading proficiency are called functionally illiterate. According to government estimates, they number in the tens of millions in the United States.

The final form of reading, recreational, is internally motivated. This form of reading is sometimes described as reading for enjoyment. Recreational reading serves no other goal than the reader's entertainment. When you read the comics, a novel, or poetry for pleasure, then you are engaging in recreational reading. There appears to be a strong relationship between the amount of recreational reading individuals engage in and their performance on other types of reading tasks such as studying. Because of this relationship, programs such as Sustained Silent Reading (SSR; McCracken, 1971) were developed to encourage schoolchildren to read more often. The hope of such programs is that students will begin to read more often and, ultimately, more effectively.

Whether developmental, for study, functional, or recreational, reading remains a complex and much investigated cognitive process. Although most reading researchers and educators would agree that reading is an extremely complex activity involving written language, there is much debate as to how the reading process takes place. Of course, how individuals view the reading process will directly affect the aspects of reading that they emphasize, as well as the instructional materials or strategies they select. Because of its overall importance, therefore, it seems worthwhile to consider the predominant perspectives of the reading process.

According to Smith (1979), reading as a communications task is basically concerned with two types of information. The first of these is visual information. Visual information is linguistic in nature, that aspect of reading that we can see on the printed page. It is comprised of words, spaces, sentences, paragraphs, and so on. In Smith's words, visual information is that part of reading that disappears when the lights are turned off. The second type of information critical in the reading process is nonvisual or metalinguistic information, that knowledge about language and about the world that makes print meaningful. The views of reading that we will discuss place differential importance on visual and nonvisual information.

The top-down view of reading, for example, weighs the nonvisual information most heavily. Advocates of this perspective (e.g., Goodman & Goodman, 1979) believe that it is the reader's prior knowledge that makes print comprehensible. Without appropriate knowledge, the individual is helpless to convert written language into meaning.

To illustrate, consider how impossible a task it would be to read in a foreign language that you did not know. From this example it can be argued that you need to know a language before you can learn to read it, just as young children learn to speak long before they learn to read. Similarly, consider how difficult it would be to read a technical report on a subject, such as hydronuclear reactors, unless you already possessed some knowledge of that subject.

Those who hold to a top-down view approach the instruction of reading with the assumption that the acquisition of reading is a natural by-product of development. Given the right environment and the right stimulation, the child will easily and quickly move from oral to written language. Within that framework, it is the teacher's function to surround children with print by reading to them, letting them manipulate books, and engaging them in related language activities such as writing or speaking. As a consequence, one would expect that in a "top-down classroom," there would be much creative writing, storytelling, and listening activities planned.

In the early elementary grades the Language Experience Approach (Hall, 1981), a method of using students' dictated stories as the basis of reading instruction, would be the primary basis for teaching reading. Another characteristic of a top-down classroom would be that it would be devoid of skills instruction; that is, teachers would not focus on any unit of language smaller than the whole word. In this view it is assumed that students participating in holistic language activities, like reading and writing, would acquire such basic reading skills such as knowing letter names or vowel sounds.

A very different, if not opposite, view is taken by those advocating a bottom-up approach to the reading process. Those holding a bottom-up view of reading believe that most everything that an individual needs to be able to read can be found on a page of text. To these individuals, the visual or linguistic information is significantly more important in the reading process than anything the reader brings to the task.

In other words, it is believed that if reading is carefully broken down into teachable skills, ordered from simpler to more complex, and if individuals master those skills, then reading will result. The impact of this approach can be seen each day in reading classrooms across the country. Look at any scope and sequence chart for a commercial basal reading series and you will find evidence of the bottom-up perspective. These basals, which are the primary tools of reading instruction, are systematically organized according to a hierarchy of reading skills. Much of the instructional time in reading classes is devoted to the presentation of these specified reading skills.

In sharp contrast to the top-down view previously described, those advocating a bottom-up model of reading do not assume that the acquisition of reading is natural. To the contrary, it would appear that it is predominantly through consistent, ordered skill instruction that an individual learns to read effectively. In the bottom-up model, the teacher's role is instructive rather than facilitative. As noted previously, the basal series provides the structure and the content for teachers taking primarily a skills-acquisition approach to reading instruction.

What the previous two views represent in many ways are the two extreme positions on a continuum that describes the reading process. At one end is the top-down position, which stresses nonvisual information almost to the exclusion of visual information. In the other position we find the bottom-up view, which focuses almost exclusively on visual or linguistic information. In actuality, most existing interpretations of the reading process fall somewhere between these two extremes.

According to the interactive model, the successful accomplishment of any reading task requires some interaction between both visual and nonvisual information (Smith, 1979). The degree to which the reading act is more or less dependent on either source of information is a consequence of many factors, including the reader's existing knowledge of the subject being read, the reason for reading, interest in the subject, and the system of evaluation.

For example, if you were reading a familiar nursery

rhyme such as "Hey, Diddle-Diddle" for pleasure, you would require very little visual or linguistic information. If, however, you were reading a manual for preparing your income taxes, or studying a difficult chapter in your statistics textbook for an exam, then it is likely that you would focus much more heavily on the text. In each case, the reader is the same individual, but what is read and why it is read differ. Consequently, the reading process engaged in differs as well.

An individual's purpose for reading is directly linked to the type of reading (i.e., developmental, for study, functional, or recreational) engaged in. Likewise, an individual's purpose for reading impacts the nature of the process that occurs. Regardless of the type or view of reading, one fact remains clear: in an information-processing age, the ability to read well is an essential life skill. Further, reading and the investigation of the reading process will continue as long as there is written language.

REFERENCES

Alexander, P. A., Hare, V. C., & Garner, R. (1984). Effects of time, access, and question type on the response accuracy and frequency of lookbacks in older, proficient readers. *Journal of Reading Behavior, 16,* 119–130.

Anderson, R. C., Hiebert, E. H., Scott, J. A., & Wilkerson, I. A. G. (1984). *Becoming a nation of readers.* Champaign, IL: University of Illinois, Center for the Study of Reading.

Anderson, T. H. (1979). Study skills and learning strategies. In H. F. O'Neil & C. D. Spielberger (Eds.), *Cognitive and affective learning strategies* (pp. 77–98). New York: Academic.

Dansereau, D. F. (in press). Cooperative learning strategies. In C. E. Weinstein, E. T. Goetz, & P. A. Alexander (Eds.), *Learning and study strategies: Issues in assessment, instruction, and evaluation.* New York: Academic.

Dansereau, D. F., McDonald, B. A., Collins, K. W., Garland, J. C., Holley, C. D., Diekhoff, G. M., & Evans, S. H. (1979). Evaluation of a learning strategy system. In H. F. O'Neil & C. D. Spielberger (Eds.), *Cognitive and affective learning strategies* (pp. 3–44). New York: Academic.

Garner, R., Hare, V. C., Alexander, P. A., Haynes, J., & Winograd, P. (1984). Inducing use of a text lookback strategy among unsuccessful readers. *American Educational Research Journal, 21,* 780–798.

Goodman, K. S., & Goodman, Y. M. (1979). Learning to read is natural. In L. B. Resnick & P. A. Weaver (Eds.), *Theory and practice of early reading* (Vol. 1, pp. 137–154). Hillsdale, NJ: Erlbaum.

Hall, M. (1981). *Teaching reading as a language experience* (3rd ed.). Columbus, OH: Merrill.

McCracken, R. A. (1971). Initiating sustained silent reading. *Journal of Reading, 14,* 582–583.

Robinson, E. P. (1970). *Effective study* (2nd ed.). New York: Harper & Row.

Smith, F. (1978). *Understanding reading* (2nd ed.). New York: Holt, Rinehart & Winston.

Smith, F. (1979). Conflicting approaches to reading research and instruction. In L. B. Resnick & P. A. Weaver (Eds.), *Theory and practice of early reading.* (Vol. 2, pp. 31–42). Hillsdale, NJ: Erlbaum.

Weinstein, C. E., Goetz, E. T., & Alexander, P. A. (in press). *Learning and study strategies: Issues in assessment, instruction, and evaluation.* New York: Academic.

Wittrock, M. C. (1983, April). *Generative reading comprehension.* Address presented at the annual meeting of the American Educational Research Association, Montreal.

PATRICIA A. ALEXANDER
Texas A&M University

READING DISORDERS
READING REMEDIATION

READING AND EYE MOVEMENTS

Cognitive processes may be inferred from observation of a reader's eye movements (Pavlidis, 1985; Rayner, 1985). The reading process requires that readers focus their eyes on a relatively small region of the visual field. The eyes do not make a continuous sweep across the visual field. Instead, they make a series of jumps and pauses from left to right, across the line of print. Each pause is called a fixation. When the eye is fixated, the print is processed. A jump is called a visual saccade (interfixation movement). During the saccade, vision is blurred and detailed processing of the print is not possible. A backward movement and pause is made when a reader fails to process the print during the fixation. The good reader is assumed to have more regular, fewer, and shorter fixations than the poor reader, as well as fewer regressions.

'It has been asserted that poor reading can be improved by training eye movement patterns (Getman, 1985). The nature of the relationship between eye movement behavior and reading has been fraught with controversy. Empirical evidence supporting the efficacy of this training with the reading disabled is sparse. Tinker (1958) reviewed studies in which the performance of poor readers was compared before and after such training. The studies that he reviewed suggest that poor readers could be taught to make more efficient eye movements, but that reading ability remained unchanged.

Evidence that eye movements cause reading disabilities is meager. Rayner (1985) reviewed the characteristics of eye movements during reading and concluded that eye movements are not a cause of reading problems. Rather, eye movement characteristics appear to reflect the difficulty that readers have in reading; they are caused by the reading disturbance and not vice versa.

REFERENCES

Getman, G. N. (1985). A commentary on vision training. *Journal of Learning Disabilities, 18,* 505–512.

Pavlidis, G. T. (1985). Eye movements in dyslexia: Their diagnostic significance. *Journal of Learning Disabilities, 18*, 42–
50.

Rayner, K. (1985). The role of eye movements in learning to read
and reading disability. *Remedial & Special Education, 6*, 53–
59.

Tinker, M. A. (1958). Recent studies of eye movements in reading.
Psychological Bulletin, 55, 215–231.

HARRISON C. STANTON
Texas A&M University

READING DISORDERS

READING DISORDERS

It is an understatement to say that the process of reading
is complex. Those who have sought to model the reading
process serve as evidence of this complexity (LaBerge &
Samuels, 1974). However, it is also true that most individuals will master the demanding skill of reading without much difficulty, and in spite of the instructional methods by which they are taught. For many, it would seem,
the acquisition of reading appears to be more or less second
nature; i.e., an easy and relatively unmemorable feat
(Smith, 1978). Yet there are those for whom the task of
reading is anything but second nature. For these individuals, attempts to acquire even rudimentary reading skills
seem destined to fail. Rather than being "reading-able,"
these are the reading disabled. It is the purpose of this
discussion to look more closely at this reading disabled
population and to consider potential sources of their reading failures.

Before we deal specifically with sources of reading failure, it is important that this examination of reading disorders be placed into a historical framework. By dealing
briefly with the historical perspective, the reader may
come to understand some of the controversy that underlies
present thinking in the area of reading disorders.

References to reading failures can be traced as far back
as the early seventeenth century. The earliest published
studies of reading disorders, appearing around the turn of
the twentieth century, were undertaken by people in the
medical profession. In 1896, W. Pringle Morgan, a British
ophthalmologist, published what is credited as the first
report of a reading disorder. In this report, Morgan presented a detailed account of a young man who could not
read despite seemingly adequate intelligence. Morgan
speculated that the youth suffered from "congenital word
blindness." The explanation of reading failure articulated
by Morgan was followed by a series of clinical studies published by Hinshelwood (1917). In his internationally recognized book, Hinshelwood, a Scottish eye surgeon, investigated the role of the brain in congenital word
blindness.

The research of British medical professionals like Morgan and Hinshelwood, although generally stimulating little interest among most educators and psychologists at
home and abroad, did influence the work of others. Notable
among this work was Orton's (1925) studies of hemispheric
imbalance. Orton, a neurologist, felt that the principal
symptom of reading disorders was strephomymbolia, or
severe reversals of language symbols. He felt that this condition was attributable to the lack of cerebral dominance.
This pattern of letter reversal, which is often associated
with the condition of dyslexia, remains a popular indicator
of reading problems.

Two important outcomes of the early medical writings
on reading disabilities were evident. First, a medical perspective of reading disorders became firmly established.
As a consequence of this perspective, which is still evident
in certain circles today, the causes of reading problems
were primarily sought among neurological factors. In
other words, the focus of reading disorders was seen as
within the reader (Lipson & Wixson, 1986): a neurological
deficit that prevented the reader from successfully completing the reading act.

Even today, those who do not embrace the strongly neurological or psychoneurological view of reading problems,
as projected in the early medical writings, cannot dismiss
the lasting impression made by early medical research on
the identification and treatment of reading disorders. To
illustrate, we need only look at the language of reading
assessment. In a clinical setting, in order to provide remediation (improvement) of reading difficulties, the client
(reader) is diagnosed (tested), and an instructional treatment (program) is prescribed (developed).

The second outcome of the early medical influence in
reading disorders was that it led to the development of
scientific instruments that would be useful in isolating the
source of reading problems. For example, in 1914 Thorndike developed a group test of reading ability, and in 1915
Gray followed with an oral reading test. As the number
of such assessment tools grew, so did the concern for the
improvement of the identified disorder or remediation. Diagnostic instruments became components of early clinical
programs, established most often in conjunction with medical schools, and for the purpose of determining the cause
of reading problems (etiology).

Initially, the diagnosis of reading disorders consisted
of an extensive battery of physical, neurological, and language assessments that often entailed the individual's admission into a hospital. Today, while these more extensive
diagnostic screenings are still administered, particularly
in medically related clinics, briefer, more educationally
related screenings have become far more prevalent. These
school-based assessments focus heavily on reading
achievement and aptitude measures, and only slightly on
the physical characteristics of the reader such as visual

discrimination and visual acuity and even less on the neurological factors.

Further, at the school level, most initial decisions about students' reading abilities or disabilities are made on the basis of group testings administered by classroom teachers, not by individual tests administered by trained specialists as in the case of clinical programs. These variations in tests and testing procedures between school-based and medically based reading programs are indicative of fundamental differences between such programs with regard to reading disorders. As noted, the neurological view of reading disorders focuses on deficits within the reader. Alternative perspectives in reading disorders center attention elsewhere.

Even from the beginning, with the work of Morgan and others, there have been those who have preferred to look outside the reader for factors contributing to reading failure. Some have sought to place the blame for reading problems squarely on the shoulders of the instruction these readers received (Judd, 1918; Uhl, 1916). For example, Judd (1918) contended that the emphasis on phonics instruction in education led to confusion in the reader's eye fixations, thus producing reading disability. Gray (1922) also put the burden for reading failure outside the reader and inside the educational system. As with those holding strongly to neurological views of reading disorders, those, like Judd and Gray, holding as strongly to instructional explanations for reading failures found only limited support.

In contrast to either view, the predominant approach to reading disorders is an interaction of the two positions, reflecting a position somewhere between the two extremes. Within this more moderate perspective, failure to read can be not only a consequence of neurological deficits or of misguided instruction, but reading failure can be attributed to multiple factors that include physical, emotional, and social conditions. For the remainder of this discussion, we will examine each of these potential contributors to reading failure.

Reading is a complex mental activity that involves the acquisition, manipulation, and retrieval of language symbols by the reader. As discussed, when a failure to read exists, there is the tendency to examine that failure in terms of its etiology or cause. Familiar terms such as brain injury, damage, dysfunction, and neuropsychological disorder reflect a neurological etiology. Harris and Sipay (1980) summarize the symptoms of neurological problems as encompassing (1) a history of a difficult birth, perhaps involving prolonged labor, an instrumental delivery, or deformity of the head; (2) prenatal conditions or premature birth; (3) poor balance or general awkwardness; (4) marked language delay; (5) attention deficit, or (6) a history of seizures or brief lapses in consciousness.

According to Spache (1976), there has been a resurgence in emphasis on neurological factors over the past two decades. This resurgence may be accounted for, in part, by the increased awareness of the brain and brain functioning provided by expanding technology. However, Spache cautions that even though brain damage can result in such evident conditions as aphasias, cerebral palsy, or mental retardation, "it appears that almost any failure to learn to read is now being interpreted, by some medical and/or reading specialists, as proof of the presence of brain damage or dysfunction" (p. 177).

Among the most common neurologically related reading disorders are alexia, partial or total loss of reading ability, dyslexia, deficit language production, and learning disability, reading underachievement. Because of the widespread application of the labels of dyslexia and learning disability, we will consider these conditions in more depth.

Dyslexia is certainly one of the most widely applied and perhaps one of the most misused labels for reading problems. References to dyslexic conditions, which can be linked all the way back to Morgan's writings on congenital word blindness and Orton's research on strephomymbolia, have continued to appear with regularity in the literature. Although a multitude of definitions of dyslexia do exist, the root of the word relates to word distortion, and it is frequently associated with letter or word reversals. Critchley (1970) identified two types of dyslexia: developmental and symptomatic. Developmental dyslexia, in his opinion, has an organic source, while symptomatic dyslexia may be influenced by a variety of factors, both organic and psychiatric.

Despite the popularity of the term, many, principally in the educational community, prefer to believe that such a condition as dyslexia does not exist. While it seems likely that the word dyslexia is too easy and invalidly applied by the general populace, it is equally difficult to discount the number of individuals who display an inability to encode, or to manipulate, written language.

Some of the same characteristics that apply to the condition of dyslexia apply as well to the condition of learning disability (LD). According to PL 94-142, a specific learning disability is "a disorder in one or more of the basic psychological processes" required to understand language. "The term includes such conditions as perceptual handicaps, brain injury, minimal brain dysfunction, dyslexia, and developmental aphasia" (p. 65083, 1977).

Beyond this legal definition, however, there is ample disagreement about the nature, identification, and treatment procedures for learning disabilities. What is most interesting about LD is that in many ways the condition is primarily an educational problem. What frequently unites the vast numbers of students labeled LD is that there is a significant gap between perceived potential and demonstrated performance. In addition, there is no apparent cause for the significant gap between potential and performance. This gap may be related to a combination of affective and cognitive factors, and may be reflected both in learning and behavioral problems within the learner.

Often, teachers and specialists struggle to bring the LD student's performance up to potential through the application of medical and educational treatments.

While important, neurological factors such as those discussed here account for relatively few of the reading problems encountered in classrooms (Harris & Sipay, 1980). Other factors such as physical ones, may also contribute to reading difficulties.

Reading, as we have observed, is a mental undertaking. Beyond its purely neurological aspects, however, the act of reading is very much a sensory activity, relying heavily on visual and auditory stimuli. There are several sensory deficits that can have an immediate and significant effect on an individual's acquisition and maintenance of reading proficiency. Several of those deficits will be examined in this section.

Although the terms sight and vision are frequently used interchangeably, there are semantic differences in these terms that become important in a discussion of reading disorders. Basically, the word sight refers to the eye's response to light. By comparison, the word vision implies that there is some interpretation of the information transmitted by the eye to the brain. In reading disability research, the term visual acuity is employed to represent the state of having good sight. Visual discrimination refers to the individual's ability to interpret minute differences between and among visual stimuli. During reading, the learner's eyes must not only see and discriminate among single stimuli but most also make saccadic movements or smooth left-to-right progressions and sweeps from line to line of text. The eyes are also required to pause and focus periodically in the reading process. These periodic pauses are called fixations.

Without a doubt, clear and appropriate visual access to the printed page facilitates the individual's ability to process written language. When visual acuity is impaired, the process of reading is diminished, at best, or made extremely difficult, at worst. What precisely is the effect of various visual defects on reading performance? Reviews of the research present inconclusive evidence on the relationship of visual defects of reading performance (Harris & Sipay, 1980; Spache, 1976). Several factors that can account for the inconsistent findings of this research include (1) variations in what supposedly similar tests are actually measuring; (2) the brief and unreliable nature of visual tests; (3) the lack of comparability in the ages and visual development of subjects; and (4) the adaptability of learners.

There are many visual problems that can impede the reading process. Among the most common visual deficiencies are nearsightedness (myopia), farsightedness (hyperopia), and astigmatism; all are refractive errors or abnormalities in eye shape. In one longitudinal study of the role of vision defects (Kelley, 1957), it was found that myopia increased with age and was correlated with high achievement, whereas hyperopia was correlated with poor reading

performance. These findings have been supported in other studies of the relationship of visual defects to reading performance (Grosvenor, 1970; Terman, 1925).

When functioning during the reading process, the eyes must make several critical adjustments, and difficulties in performing these adjustments can interfere with the reading process. For example, the muscles of the eyes must operate together in a coordinated fashion, focusing and centering on the visual target in such a way as to produce a single, clear image. When functioning effectively, the eyes allow us to perceive the depth or thickness of a visual target (stereopsis). This muscular balance of the eyes is referred to as binocular coordination, and the process of centering the visual stimuli is labeled fusion.

At times, there can be a muscular imbalance preventing the eyes from operating in a coordinated way. In certain cases, one eye may assume dominance over the other eye (amblyopia), a condition commonly referred to as lazy eye. If binocular coordination is impaired, there may be occurrences of heterophoria, or a muscular resistance to fusion. When this condition is mild, the reader sees a blurred image, but when severe, two images may actually be seen. In the milder cases of heterophoria, one eye may turn inward (esophoria), or outward (exophoria), or may focus higher than the other (hyperphoria). In more severe cases, the eyes appear crossed or "walleyed." This extreme form of binocular imbalance is known as strabismus. In general, partial fusion with its blurring effect is more problematic to readers than complete lack of fusion. For the most part, readers with milder cases of muscular imbalance can accommodate well, except when they experience fatigue, tension, or headaches; when extreme, the individual trends to ignore one eye.

While reading, particularly oral reading, depends on auditory skills, few severe reading problems can be directly linked to auditory factors. However, in our discussion of reading disorders, several auditory classifications should be considered. Those categories are auditory acuity, auditory discrimination, and auditory memory. Auditory acuity refers the state of having good hearing. Auditory discrimination involves the recognition of minute differences in speech sounds. Students' appropriate production of speech sounds is dependent on their ability to hear such differences. Many early reading programs stress phonic analysis, which relies on students' ability to recognize and reproduce the common sound-symbol patterns in language. Consequently, deficits in auditory acuity or discrimination would place the child at a disadvantage.

Also of importance in the reception of auditory stimuli is the individual's ability to mask or eliminate extraneous noises in the environment. As most of us know, the classroom, where so much information is transmitted auditorily, is anything but noise-proof. Focusing on important information in the classroom demands that the learner mask out sounds that would otherwise interfere with the acquisition of salient information. Overall, however, auditory deficits play a much less critical role in reading disorders than the visual or neurological conditions already discussed.

Beyond the visual or auditory factors presented, there are other physical conditions that may contribute to reading problems. Among those conditions are illnesses, general awkwardness, glandular problems, poor nutrition, and allergies. It must be noted, however, that there is little direct evidence that such conditions significantly affect reading performance. For example, illnesses tend to come into play in reading problems when students suffer from prolonged or chronic ailments. Yet, in most instances, prolonged illnesses prevent the learner from attending school, and it is this lack of school attendance that contributes most to reading failures. General awkwardness is not, itself, a factor in reading problems, but it is of importance in that it is frequently a symptom of minimal brain dysfunction. Further, while glandular abnormalities can result in such physical abnormalities as dwarfism and obesity, there is limited understanding of the effects of endocrine treatment on reading disorders. The effect of malnutrition on reading disorders is also difficult to pinpoint since this condition is also closely tied to low socioeconomic status.

To this point we have been discussing neurological and physical factors that impact reading performance. There are also less easily measured factors within the individual that may influence the reading process. Among these less measurable factors are psychosocial characteristics of the reader. Even from the beginning of work in the area of reading disorders, writers such as Orton (1925) and Gray (1922) have contended that good readers are socially and emotionally different from poor readers. Good readers have been seen as not only good at reading skills, but good at psychosocial adjustment. By comparison, disabled readers have been categorized by such descriptors as restless, withdrawn, or introverted (Robinson, 1953).

That certain psychosocial behaviors have been frequently related to poor reading performance is widely accepted. However, the significance of emotional and social factors in causing reading disorders is unclear. Do certain psychosocial behaviors result in reading failure? Does the presence of reading problems have certain emotional or social effects on the learner? Do certain emotional or social behaviors and reading problems develop simultaneously? These questions remain unanswered by the existing literature.

In part, we know little about the relationship of psychosocial conditions and reading disorders because the techniques for gathering data in these areas are somewhat unreliable. For example, teacher observation, which may be employed to gather information on a learner's emotional or social behavior, can be biased. Further, teachers generally conduct observations without the benefit of training. Interviews may also be used to collect data on these factors. Yet, even when these interviews are per-

formed by training specialists, there is little assurance that what the learner says is an accurate reflection of the internal state. Personality measures are another tool for assessing an individual's emotional and social condition. While such measures may provide a better understanding of the condition of the learner than observations and interviews, the reliability of these measures is still a point of contention.

Although failing to produce consistent differences between disabled and able readers, research (Harris, 1971; Harris & Sipay, 1980) has generated various aspects of psychosocial behavior that may contribute to reading problems. For example, Harris and Sipay (1980) delineate the following characteristics as related to reading problems:

Conscious refusal to learn

Overt hostility

Negative conditioning to reading

Displacement of hostility

Resistance to pressure

Clinging to dependency

Quick discouragement

Success seen as dangerous

Extreme distractibility or restlessness

Absorption in a private world

Harris and Sipay's characteristic of exteme distractibility and restlessness as indicative of reading problems relates to the work on attention deficit disorders in the literature on learning disabilities. Since the research of Bandura (1969) and Gibson (1969), the importance of attention to learning has been widely accepted. It would appear that LD students, for whom there is a gap between potential and academic performance, suffer from a developmental lag with regard to attention (Ross, 1976). Often, LD students are unable to sustain attention to task, and the effect is decreased learning. To assist LD students in improving reading performance, Bateman (1979) has suggested that instructional programs (1) attend to relevant phoneme features; (2) increase the number of repetitions to mastery; and (3) use reinforcement.

Currently, several of the psychosocial characteristics listed by Harris and Sipay (e.g., quick discouragement and negative conditioning) are being more closely examined in the literature on achievement motivation (Dweck & Bempechat, 1983; Nicholls, 1983; Weiner, 1983). Achievement motivation can be distinguished from other forms of motivation by its purpose, which involves an increase in learner competence. Dweck and Bempechat (1983) describe the importance of achievement motivation to learning as follows:

Motivational factors can have pronounced and far-reaching effects on children's learning and performance. They determine such critical things as whether children see or avoid challenges and whether they persist in the face of obstacles—in short, whether children actually pursue and master the skills they value and are capable of mastering. (p. 239)

In his research on achievement motivation, Nicholls (1983) has identified two types of motivation, labeled ego-involvement and task-involvement. In ego-involvement motivation, it is the individual who is the focus of attention. For the ego-involved, learning is of little value in and of itself, except as a personal reflection of worth. In the task-involvement form of achievement motivation, the task becomes the focal point and the individual exerts effort on the task primarily for the sake of learning. The task-involved student will view success as the result of effort applied to learning tasks, and failure as the need to increase that effort. By comparison, the ego-involved student will view academic success or failure in a personal light, as something removed from the task. Because of this attitude, ego-involved students seem less likely to seek help when confronted with a difficult task because they would be admitting that they lack the necessary ability (Ames, 1981).

There are also those in reading classes who have given up any chance of increased competence, for whom learning represents little more than an unbroken chain of failure and frustration. These individuals suffer from a condition called learned helplessness. Because the learned helpless expect failure to occur, they seem unwilling to exert the effort that may be required to achieve in the reading classroom. Indeed, they are so conditioned to failure that they that may be uncomfortable with successful learning experiences. Observations in remedial reading classrooms reveal many who attribute their reading problems to personal failure, and who have chosen to abandon any attempts to gain competence in reading. Such motivational conditions are apt to make improvements in reading performance unlikely.

Two important points need to be made with regard to psychosocial behaviors and reading disorders. First, reading, as it occurs in the context of schooling, remains a social activity. The reader must not only process text to meet personal ends, but must interpret and verify understanding of text for teachers and peers in a way that is seen as appropriate. Therefore, whether or not social and emotional factors are significant in a causal way, they will continue to be related to reading performance. Second, schools tend to see themselves in the business of teaching reading skills, not of treating emotional and social problems. Consequently, in few classrooms or clinics are the emotional and social needs of the problem reader given serious attention. It would seem that those working with problem readers often feel that the emotional and social conditions of these individuals will be taken care of when the specific reading problems are dealt with. Others, however, would argue that to treat only the reading problem without treating the concomitant emotional and social concerns would result in only partial and temporary gains in learner performance. Continued research in the area of psychosocial factors is necessary if we are to understand how best to improve the performance of disabled readers.

REFERENCES

Ames, C. (1981). Competitive versus cooperative reward structures: The influence of individual and group performance factors on achievement attributions and affect. *American Educational Research Journal, 18,* 273–287.

Bandura, A. (1969). *Principles of behavior modification.* New York: Holt, Rinehart, & Winston.

Bateman, B. (1979). Teaching reading to learning disabled and other hard-to-teach children. In L. B. Resnick & P. A. Weaver (Eds.), *Theory and practice in early reading* (Vol. 1, pp. 227–259). Hillsdale, NJ: Erlbaum.

Critchley, M. (1970). *The dyslexic child.* Springfield, IL: Thomas.

Dweck, C. S., & Bempechat, J. (1983). Children's theories of intelligence: Consequences for learning. In S. G. Paris, G. M. Olson, & H. W. Stevenson (Eds.), *Learning and motivation in the classroom* (pp. 239–256). Hillsdale, NJ: Erlbaum.

Gibson, E. J. (1969). *Principles of perceptual learning and development.* Englewood Cliffs, NJ: Prentice-Hall.

Gray, C. T. (1922). *Deficiencies in reading ability: Their diagnosis and remedies.* Boston: Heath.

Gray, W. S. (1915). *Oral reading paragraph test.* Bloomington, IN: Public School.

Grosvenor, T. (1970). Refractive state, intelligence test scores and academic ability. *American Journal of Optometry & Archives of American Academy of Optometry, 47,* 355–360.

Harris, A. J. (1971). Psychological and motivational problems. In D. K. Bracken & E. Malmquist (Eds.), *Improving reading ability around the world* (pp. 97–103). Neward, DE: International Reading Association.

Harris, A. J., & Sipay, E. R. (1980). *How to increase reading ability* (7th ed.). New York: Longman.

Hinshelwood, J. (1917). *Congenital word-blindness.* London: Lewis.

Judd, C. H. (1918). *Reading: Its nature and development* [Educational Monograph No. 10]. Chicago: University of Chicago.

Kelley, C. R. (1957). *Visual screenings and child development: The North Carolina Study.* Raleigh, NC: Department of Psychology, North Carolina State College.

LaBerge, D., & Samuels, S. J. (1974). Toward a theory of automatic information processing in reading. *Cognitive Psychology, 6,* 292–323.

Lipson, M. Y., & Wixson, K. K. (1986). Reading disability research: An interactionist perspective. *Review of Educational Research, 56,* 111–136.

Morgan, W. P. (1896). A case of congenital word-blindness. *British Medical Journal, 2,* 1612–1614.

Nicholls, J. G. (1983). Conceptions of ability and achievement motivation: A theory and its implications for education. In S. G. Paris, G. M. Olson, & H. W. Stevenson (Eds.), *Learning and motivation in the classroom* (pp. 211–237). Hillsdale, NJ: Erlbaum.

Orton, S. T. (1925). Word-blindness in school children. *Archives of Neurology & Psychiatry, 14,* 582–615.

Robinson, H. M. (1953). Personality and reading. In A. E. Traxler (Ed.), *Modern educational problems* (pp. 87–99). Washington, DC: American Council on Education.

Ross, A. O. (1976). *Psychological aspects of learning disabilities and reading disorders.* New York: McGraw-Hill.

Smith, F. (1978). *Reading without nonsense.* New York: Teachers College Press.

Spache, G. D. (1976). *Investigating the issues of reading disabilities.* Boston: Allyn & Bacon.

Terman, L. M. (1925). Genetic studies of genius. *Mental and physical traits of 1000 gifted children.* Stanford, CA: Stanford University Press.

Thorndike, E. L. (1914). The measurement of ability in reading. *Teachers College Record, 15,* 207–227.

Uhl, W. L. (1916). The use of the results of reading tests as bases for planning remedial work. *Elementary School Journal, 17,* 266–275.

Weiner, B. (1983). Some thoughts about feelings. In S. G. Paris, G. M. Olson, & H. W. Stevenson (Eds.), *Learning and motivation in the classroom* (pp. 165–178). Hillsdale, NJ: Erlbaum.

PATRICIA A. ALEXANDER
Texas A&M University

AMBLOYOPIA
DEVELOPMENTAL DELAY
DYSLEXIA
DYSPEDAGOGIA
LEARNED HELPLESSNESS
READING REMEDIATION

READING IN THE CONTENT AREAS

For over at least half a century, reading and curriculum specialists have claimed that every teacher is a teacher of reading. Many books, articles, and research reports have been published during this period and courses in teaching reading in the content areas are offered in many colleges of education. Despite these efforts, content teachers have typically maintained that they are teachers of subject matter and not teachers of reading. In a comprehensive and critical review of the research in reading in the content areas, Dupois (1984) concludes that content teachers know too little about reading in general and reading in their subjects in particular. She further reports that teachers feel "helplessness and frustration in the face of students who cannot read classroom materials" (p. 1).

This frustration is further amplified when students are labeled as special or disabled. Teachers feel especially helpless in their attempts to deal with the reading needs of the special student, assuming they lack some vital prerequisite training or technique. Yet what has been re-

peatedly revealed in research studies is the need for good holistic language teaching for students of all ability levels, rather than separate programs for special populations.

Specialists have a vital role to play in the field of special education, but it is not in the creation of separate programs focused on subskills of language; these programs often are less of a solution than a perpetuation of a problem with a child's reading. One major role of the special education specialist is that of collaborator and consultant to the content teacher in mainstream classrooms. The purpose of this relationship is to strengthen the regular classroom teacher as he or she plans to more fully involve special children in the intellectual and social life of the classroom.

Recently, 27 national organizations of teachers, supervisors, administrators, and lay groups endorsed a statement called "The Essentials Approach: Rethinking the Curriculum for the 80's" (1981), which proclaims the interdependence of skills and content as well as interdependence of knowledge in the several content areas. Interdependence of skills and content refers to the learner's use of reading, writing, talking, and thinking in learning literature, social studies, science, and math. The "Essentials" consortium argued that teachers will teach their subjects more effectively if they teach students the special reading, writing, and study strategies for acquiring and critically responding to knowledge in their disciplines. Ultimately, such a concerted effort will prepare students for a lifetime of learning but helping to make them independent learners. Clearly, the direction proposed is not limited to the relationship between reading and learning but rather extends to writing, studying, talking, and thinking.

The "Essentials" consortium warned against two related practices in many schools that stand in the way of fostering the interdependence principle. The first faulty practice defines basic skills by what can be measured at a time when tests are severely limited in what they can measure. Related to this is the practice of teaching the skills identified by such tests in isolation from significant content, i.e., from texts that look like the tests rather than real content texts. In short, reading skill has been fragmented away from the content areas and further fragmented into discrete subskills. Goodlad (1983) documented this state of the schools, which he characterized as being preoccupied with lower intellectual processes and boredom of epidemic proportions. The problem is exacerbated in special and mainstream classrooms for special educational populations, where it has been erroneously believed that there needs to be more emphasis on isolated subskills to remediate the poor reading skills of these students.

In 1985, the Commission on Reading of the National Academy of Education published *Becoming A Nation of Readers* (Anderson et al., 1985), which synthesized current sociopsycholinguistic theory and research on learning to read and reading to learn. This document provides a theoretical rationale for teachers who would implement the "Essentials" approach.

Reading is not defined as a product or as a set of subskills to be tested but rather as "a process for constructing meaning from written texts . . . a complex skill requiring the coordination of a number of interrelated sources of information" (p. 7). Those sources lie in the reader, in the text, in fellow students, and in the teacher. Readers bring to the reading task knowledge of the world, of language, of strategies for reading various texts, and of their teachers' purposes and expectations. They also bring their own interests and purposes. Texts present world knowledge in special ways; for example, literary texts have different conventions and structures from informational texts. They vary in purpose, content, and style. Fellow students constitute a community of comprehenders. Through interaction they can share relevant prior knowledge, text knowledge, and reading strategies.

The role of teachers is to orchestrate these interrelated sources, developing productive transactions among readers and texts that lead to more efficient strategies for information processing by students. Information processing involves such active mental searches as drawing on prior knowledge, predicting, questioning, elaborating, transforming, structuring, restating, summarizing, synthesizing, reflecting, and critically evaluating. In practical terms, content teachers can teach reading and study by modeling strategies that incorporate one or more of these searches by having students practice strategies in pairs and in small groups as well as on their own and by having students reflect on and share their experiences with each other in using the strategies.

Two lists of such strategies follow. They were developed by Botel (1984) at the University of Pennsylvania for preparing teachers and reading specialists. The first list includes strategies for reading and comprehending literary texts; the second includes strategies for reading and comprehending expository texts. These strategies are no less vital for the special education student than the regular student. It will be noted that these strategies enable students to experience reading at their own levels.

Strategies for Reading, Writing, and Studying Library Texts

Before Reading
Brainstorming
What questions, ideas or experiences were suggested by the title and opening paragraph(s) or verse?
Write or Talk and Write
Write nonstop about what comes to mind as you think about the title.
Write whatever questions come to mind as you think about the title.

Recall a related remembered experience; share it; write it.
Take notes on the way of life of a character from another culture (categories: family relationships, sources of food, beliefs about nature, housing, community, recreation, education).

While Reading
If you do not understand something, put a mark in the margin and go on.
Picture in your mind's eye what happens in the story

After Reading
Personal Responding
What stands out for you in the selection?
Retelling
Retell history from the point of view of different characters.
Tell the story to someone in the family, to a friend, to a younger person, etc.
Vocabulary Development
Write key words or expressions and define them in context.
Write words the writer uses to describe a character; then write a brief paragraph about the character using these words.
Write synonyms for key words.
Writing
Prepare questions you would ask if you could interview a character.
Write a journal entry about an important event as if you were the character who experienced it.
Write notes as if you were one of the characters.
Write an eyewitness or reporter's account of a scene as it might appear in a newspaper.
Making Tests
Prepare tests on content studied using the same form found in standardized and other tests.
Illustrating
Draw a floor plan of a major setting.
Illustrate a scene.
Make a map or graphic diagram of a key concept or relationship.
Illustrate key words and expressions.
Show the story or episode in a four-frame cartoon.
Dramatizing
Plan a "Reader's Theater."
Plan a panel discussion as if you were characters in the story.
Plan an informal dramatization.
Plan a debate.
Compare similarities and differences between your culture and that of a character.

Strategies for Reading, Writing, and Studying Expository Texts

Before Reading
Brainstorming

List words and phrases you associate with the title; see if your items can be grouped or chunked.

What questions are suggested by the title or opening paragraphs?

What questions would you hope would be answered by the selection?

Previewing

Read the headings and first and last paragraphs; then say or recite briefly what they suggest about the text.

Based on your review, what are the main questions that the author probably set out to answer in the selection?

Making Tests

Prepare tests on content studied using the same form found in standardized and criterion-referenced tests.

While and After Reading

Personal Responding

What stands out for you in the selection?

Taking Notes

Turn headings into questions and answer them.

Underline one or two key words in each paragraph.

Write a question for each paragraph or section.

Make marginal notes.

Make a map or graphic diagram of a key concept or relationship.

Develop Vocabulary

Write key words and expressions and define them in context.

Reread and Recite

Reread only the key words and write them from memory.

Reread only the key words and write a summary.

As noted earlier, Dupois reported that content teachers know little about teaching reading of their subject. Adaptation of the two lists of strategies in teaching subject matter should correct that problem. That leaves the problem of students who cannot read texts on their own. These students would benefit greatly from having the material read to them while others in the class read silently. But they can also benefit from involvement with classmates in the learning of the strategies, in particular when they are practiced and reflected on collaboratively.

Beyond the learning of strategies for comprehending texts, students in the content areas should be reading a variety of periodicals and library books independently to broaden their perspectives, deepen their knowledge, and excite their interest in the content. Self-selected independent reading provides another way of accommodating the varying reading levels in a classroom (Anderson, et al., 1985; Botel, 1981). Librarians and professional associations of content teachers are excellent sources for such reading. In social studies, the Children's Book Council

(1984) produces an excellent list. Earle (1976) prepared a list of high-interest materials for the math classroom.

It is clear that reading in the content areas today deals with how teachers can organize and plan for instruction so as to relate the basic academic competencies (language processes of not only reading, but also writing, listening, and speaking) to learning the basic academic subjects. That is true for all students, including special education students in mainstream classrooms as well as in learning centers.

In summary, from the point of view of special education, the proposed ways of teaching content reading would have the effect of providing for more learning and less isolation and fragmentation, less stigmatization and separation from peers, less isolation of teachers, and less fragmentation of language.

REFERENCES

Anderson, R. C., Hiebert, E. H., Scott, J. A., Wilkinson, I. A. G., (1985). *Becoming a nation of readers: The report of the Commission on Reading*. Washington, DC: National Institute of Education.

Botel, M. (1981). *A Pennsylvania comprehensive reading/communication arts plan*. Harrisburg: Pennsylvania Department of Education.

Botel, M. (1984). *Comprehending texts: Subskills or strategies*. Philadelphia: Graduate School of Education, University of Pennsylvania.

Children's Book Council. *Notable children's trade books in the field of social studies*. New York: Author.

Dupois, M. M. (Ed.). (1984). *Reading in the content areas: Research for teachers*. Newark, DE: International Reading Association.

Earle, R. A. (1976). *Teaching reading and math*. Newark, DE: International Reading Association.

Goodlad, J. I. (1983). What some schools and classrooms teach. *Educational Leadership, 40*(7), 8–19.

Mercier, L. Y. (Ed.). (1981). *The essentials approach: Rethinking the curriculum for the 80's*. Washington, DC: U.S. Department of Education, Basic Skills Improvement Program.

Morton Botel
University of Pennsylvania

READING DISORDERS
READING REMEDIATION

READING REMEDIATION

Reading can be described as an essential and highly complex cognitive activity. As a cognitive task, the outcomes of the reading act require the successful completion of many simple and complex linguistic skills (Perfetti, 1983). To illustrate, consider the task of reading aloud the word *dog*. To accomplish this seemingly simple task, a reader must know the letters of the alphabet, must have internalized the sound/symbol patterns common to the English language, and must be able to decode or sound out the word accurately. Decoding alone can be a troublesome venture in the English language, where exceptions appear to outnumber phonetic rules. Further, if an understanding of dog is also required, then the reader must relate the abstract symbols and sounds to the concept of dog stored in long-term memory.

If many skills are required to read and understand a single word, then the skills necessary to make sense of the previous paragraph are far more extensive. It is therefore not surprising that some individuals never acquire reading proficiency. Those individuals who consistently experience difficulties in processing print are part of a population of learners who require special instruction. This special instruction is referred to as reading remediation.

Reading remediation is a branch of language instruction that is concerned with the identification and treatment of reading problems. The following text will examine factors that contribute to reading difficulties, consider how the cycle of remediation occurs, discuss levels of reading diagnosis, survey principles that should guide effective diagnosis, and review profiles of problem readers.

Even before an individual is asked to read, there are factors that are likely to enhance or inhibit reading performance. Rupley and Blair (1983) identify two broad categories of variables that relate to reading performance: functional and facilitative factors. Functional factors are those variables that actually pertain to reading. Sight vocabulary, reading rate, and oral language development are examples of functional factors. In many ways, these functional variables are the outcome of other variables that are not directly part of the reading performance but contribute to it. These variables are called facilitative factors, and they are of particular importance in reading remediation. Facilitative factors fall under such broad headings as physical, cognitive, and emotional characteristics. Within each of these broad areas there are conditions that can significantly influence reading performance.

For example, among physical characteristics, we know that gender, visual and auditory ability, and general health influence reading performance. Whether owed to genetic or environmental factors, or a combination of both, females tend to have an advantage over males in language acquisition and early language proficiency. Males' linguistic disadvantage may be a partial explanation for the disproportionate number of boys enrolled in remedial reading classes.

It is also clear that individuals who suffer from visual or auditory impairments will have more difficulty in acquiring proficiency in written language. The ability to see and hear adequately are basic to reading. Among young children, many suspected reading problems can be traced to visual or auditory impairments, many of which are correctable. Once the vision or hearing problem has been cor-

rected, many young children go on to acquire reading proficiency. Consequently, analysis of reading problems frequently begins with vision and hearing screening. In these screenings, visual and auditory acuity and discrimination are tested.

Cognitive factors also contribute significantly to the reading process. As we will see in the discussion of reader profiles, the cognitive ability an individual brings to the reading act is a major determinant of the level of proficiency expected. While there is no one-to-one correspondence between intelligence and reading ability, the relationship between the two is strong indeed. Cognitive factors may be assessed by means of achievement or intelligence test data, or school performance records.

Similarly, an individual's emotional well-being can positively or negatively affect the ability to read. The significant influence of affective factors on learning has been the topic of recent research (McCombs, in press; Palmer & Goetz, in press), and should not be ignored in the evaluation of reading problems. Learners who have the cognitive potential may lack the desire or commitment that is required to do well in reading. Parent/student interviews and self-concept and personality tests may be used to gather information on the emotional condition of a reader.

When a reading problem is suspected, it is prudent first to determine whether existing physical, cognitive, and emotional as well as socioeconomic, cultural, or educational factors are potential sources of the problem. The systematic assessment of functional and facilitative factors is part of reading diagnosis, which, in turn, is a major component in the remediation cycle.

Much of the language of reading remediation is borrowed from medical science. The medical influence is particularly apparent in the cycle of reading remediation. This cycle is comprised of three phases: diagnosis, prescription, and treatment.

The diagnosis or data-collection phase of the remediation cycle refers to the systematic assessment of existing conditions: a search for evidence that might indicate the source of a reader's problems. It is in this phase that information about the reader and reading performance is gathered and analyzed. Knowledge about the reader may be collected in a spontaneous fashion within the classroom, or it may be amassed through a formal and extensive procedure.

On the basis of careful diagnosis, the second phase of the cycle, the prescription or program-specification phase, is put into place. Prescription is the delineation of the appropriate instructional treatment to be administered. It is expected that a carefully prescribed instructional program will ameliorate the reader's problems. As with the diagnostic procedure, the instructional plan may be informal or formal in nature. An informal prescription might entail little more than the teacher's specification of instructional objectives that seem appropriate for a reader. A formal prescription, by comparison, may be an elaborate instructional program to be administered by a specialist within a clinic or resource room.

Finally, there is the treatment or program-implementation phase of the cycle. In this phase, the prescribed instructional treatment is carried out and its effectiveness evaluated. From the knowledge gained during instruction and evaluation, additional information about the reader and reading performance is gathered. Based on these new data, a revised diagnosis may be rendered and the remediation cycle begins anew. This remediation cycle forms the basis of reading instruction, whether it occurs in the regular classroom or in the resource room (Cheek & Cheek, 1980).

Diagnosis can take place at several levels of complexity. Those levels, in order of increasing formality, are informal, classroom, and clinical diagnosis (Wilson & Cleland, 1985). In the previous section, the data gathering was apt to be part of the more extensive form of clinical reading diagnosis. Meeting the needs of most readers does not often require that diagnosis reach such a formal level, however. Rather, clinical diagnosis should be the last stage is the diagnostic procedure. For the most part, serving the needs of the reader entails only the first two levels in the sequence of diagnosis, informal, and classroom diagnosis.

Informal diagnosis is an ongoing process that takes place continuously in the regular reading classroom. This stage of diagnosis encompasses the teacher's monitoring of reading instruction to determine whether that instruction is appropriate for the learner. If found inappropriate or ineffective, the instruction should be adjusted in some fashion to suit more adequately the learner's needs and capabilities.

For example, let us say that a teacher asks a child to read aloud from a basal reader. The teacher finds that the child's oral reading is poor, containing many errors and little expression. Based on this informal assessment, the teacher adjusts instruction by telling the child to read the basal passage silently first before reading it aloud. After an opportunity to practice the basal passage, the teacher finds that the reading is smooth and expressive. In this instance, the teacher engaged in informal diagnosis and altered the instruction accordingly. The results in this case were successful.

What if the minor adjustments in reading instruction were not successful in improving the situation? What would the teacher do next? In the second stage of diagnosis, the teacher would conduct some testing within the classroom in an attempt to identify the nature of the reading problem. Classroom diagnosis may involve the use of teacher-made or commercial tests that can be administered and interpreted by teachers who have no specialized knowledge of reading or assessment. Perhaps, as in the preceding case, the teacher constructs a cloze test (Tierney, Readence, & Dishner, 1980) from the basal text. From this cloze test, the teacher determines that the reading book that the child has been assigned is too difficult. The teacher then moves the child to a more appropriate reading group and the problem with oral reading seems to disappear.

Should the classroom teacher's attempts to identify or remediate the reading problem fail, then it is time to call in a specialist. It is at this point in the diagnostic sequence that a clinical assessment of the reading problem should be conducted. Following the assessment of facilitative factors, a battery of reading tests are given. Among the reading skills frequently tested in a clinical diagnosis are sight vocabulary, oral reading, silent reading, listening comprehension, and word analysis skills. The information amassed in diagnosis permits the clinical specialist to ascribe a remediation program for the learner that is likely to improve reading performance.

Because of the major role that diagnosis plays in the remediation cycle, it is imperative that the assessment provides valid and reliable information. Bond and Tinker (1973) have outlined some guiding principles for clinical diagnosis that should result in the more effective remediation of reading problems. Many of these principles can also be applied to informal and classroom diagnosis.

1. Diagnosis should be directed toward formulating methods of improvement.
2. Diagnosis should involve more than an appraisal of reading skills and abilities.
3. Diagnosis should be efficient and effective.
4. Diagnosis should be continuous.
5. Diagnosis should seek to identify patterns of behavior.

According to the first of these principles, it is important to remember that diagnosis is not an end in itself. It is conducted to provide accurate information from which effective remediation can be developed. Without the other components of prescription and treatment, diagnosis would be an isolated and meaningless undertaking. Further, for diagnosis to be effective it must be beyond the assessment of reading alone and examine the learner in a more holistic fashion. That is, the physical, cognitive, emotional, socioeconomic, and educational characteristics of the learner must also be part of the decision-making process.

Another pragmatic concern in the diagnostic procedure is that the amount of testing and the instrumentation be appropriate for the individual case under examination. For example, if a physical condition is suspected as the primary cause for existing reading problems, and if visual/auditory screening confirms that situation, then further testing may prove costly and unwarranted. Likewise, it would be essential to employ valid and reliable measures to determine physical factors and to have those measures administered and evaluated by qualified individuals.

Diagnosis should generally be an ongoing process. Once information has been gathered and an instructional program prescribed, the effects of the prescribed program should be assessed. Even as it pertains to clinical diagnosis, no diagnosis is final and the treatment prescribed on the basis of formal assessment should be periodically reviewed and revised. It is important to remember that converging evidence is essential for an effective diagnosis. One piece of information is, under most circumstances, insufficient for building a remediation program that will lead to improvement for the learner. Patterns of scores are more likely to convey a more accurate view of the reader's strengths and needs.

Not only do scores produce certain patterns, but the diagnostic data across readers also tend to fall into certain patterns. It is on the basis of these diagnostic patterns that several commonly encountered reader profiles have been generated (Bond & Tinker, 1973; Harris & Sipay, 1980). Gifted readers are individuals who manifest normal or above normal intelligence and who possess reading skills that are markedly above grade level. Although the definition of markedly above grade level may vary somewhat, a rule of thumb for determining a significant difference is two years above grade level. It is important to note that the gifted reader may or may not be gifted in other domains. That is, the learner may be advanced in reading skills but average in math or science. Therefore, a gifted reader with reading skills that are significantly above grade level may have an intelligence only slightly above average. For example, Ruth is a fourth grader with a measured intelligence of 125. According to diagnosis, Ruth's sight vocabulary was 6–8 (grade equivalent of sixth grade, eighth month), oral reading 6–3, silent reading 7–1, and listening comprehension 7–5. As these scores indicate, Ruth's overall reading performance is well above the fourth-grade level. We would say that Ruth appears to be a gifted reader.

The needs of the gifted reader may be served within the context of the regular reading class or within a specific gifted program. However, if mainstreamed in the regular reading classroom, it is expected that these proficient readers will be provided with reading materials and instruction that is commensurate with their demonstrated abilities. In many schools, these advanced readers are grouped for reading instruction so that the teacher can more effectively provide them with appropriate instruction.

Underachievers are similar to gifted learners in that they demonstrate exceptional cognitive potential. However, they may fail to demonstrate reading skills that approach their potential. Dave, for example, is Ruth's fourth-grade classmate. Dave's IQ is estimated to be 140, yet he is performing just barely at grade level in reading class. His sight vocabulary is 4–6, silent reading and listening comprehension 4–1, and oral reading 3–8. While Dave's reading scores are not significantly below his grade level,

they are significantly below his potential. Although further diagnosis is appropriate in this case, Dave would be classified as a reading underachiever at this level.

The underachieving reader is often the most difficult case to identify. Primarily because reading performance is near grade level, many classroom teachers do not recognize or attend to the gap between the underachiever's potential and performance. Further, prescribing and treating the underachiever is a complex undertaking; reading problems may be tied to any number of emotional, physical, neurological, social, or cultural factors that cannot be easily detected or treated.

Sometimes there are those learners who do fairly well in reading but who have a problem in one or two skills areas. This type of reader possesses a specific skills deficiency, the most common problem-reader profile. For the most part, these skill-deficient readers remain in the regular classroom with help provided by the reading teacher.

When reading assistance is given in the context of the classroom and is administered by the classroom teacher, it is labeled a corrective reading program. Jake is a case in point. Jake is also in Ruth's fourth grade class. Although he usually does well in reading, Jake has problems with his listening comprehension. As part of his corrective reading program, Jake's teacher works with him on a weekly basis to improve his listening skills. In this way, it is hoped that Jake's listening skills can be brought in line with his other reading skills.

Some readers' problems are not as limited or as easily treated as Jake's. There are those cases in which a learner with normal intelligence performs well below grade level on the majority of reading skills. For example, another fourth grader, Betsy, has an IQ of 101, but her reading grade equivalency scores are as follows: sight vocabulary, 1–5; oral reading, preprimer; silent reading 1–3; listening comprehension 2–0. The remediation program required to meet the needs of this type of problem reader is referred to as a remedial reading program. Because of the serious nature of the reading problems being treated, remedial reading programs become the responsibility of a reading specialist or resource teacher. Regular classroom teachers rarely have the training to deal effectively with remedial readers, nor can they provide these individuals the highly individualized attention they need to remediate their reading problems.

The determination to place a learner in a remedial reading program is often the result of a group decision-making process similar to that followed for other categories of special learners. While the primary responsibility for reading remediation falls to the reading specialist, the remediation program can and should involve parents, outside specialists, content-area teachers, and school administrators. Both long- and short-term goals are established for the reader, focusing on cognitive, metacognitive, and affective needs. Progress toward these goals are carefully documented, so that accurate evaluation of the program and the learner is possible.

The last reader profile is that of the slow learner. Like the remedial reader, the slow learner demonstrates reading skills that are far below grade level. However, unlike the remedial reader, the slow learner's reading performance is commensurate with cognitive ability. In other words, the slow learner is basically performing up to his or her potential. Victor, who is also in Ruth's classroom, has reading scores similar to Betsy's. However, when he was tested by the school psychologist, it was found that Victor's IQ is 85. Victor's reading scores appear to correspond to his cognitive ability. Because of the specialized treatment they require, slow learners may be assigned to a reading specialist or resource teacher for remediation.

As long as there is the complex process of reading there will be learners who encounter difficulties and who will require special reading instruction. It is the purpose of effective reading remediation programs to provide appropriate instruction to those learners for whom proficient reading is a goal yet to be achieved.

REFERENCES

Bond, G. L., & Tinker, M. A. (1973). *Reading difficulties: Their diagnosis and correction* (3rd ed.). Englewood Cliffs, NJ: Prentice-Hall.

Cheek, M. C., & Cheek, E. H. (1980). *Diagnostic-prescriptive reading instruction*. Dubuque, IA: Brown.

Harris, A. J., & Sipay, E. R. (1980). *How to increase reading ability* (7th ed.). New York: Longman.

McCombs, B. L. (in press). Motivational skills training: Combining metacognitive, cognitive, and affective learning strategies. In C. E. Weinstein, E. T. Goetz, & P. A. Alexander (Eds.), *Learning and study strategies: Issues in assessment, instruction, and evaluation*. New York: Academic.

Palmer, D. J., & Goetz, E. T. (in press). Selection and use of study strategies: The role of the studier's beliefs about self and strategies. In C. E. Weinstein, E. T. Goetz, & P. A. Alexander (Eds.), *Learning and study strategies: Issues in assessment, instruction, and evaluation*. New York: Academic.

Perfetti, C. A. (1983). Individual differences in verbal processes. In R. F. Dillon & R. R. Schmeck (Eds.), *Individual differences in cognition* (Vol. I, pp. 65–104). New York: Academic.

Rupley, W. H., & Blair, T. R. (1983). *Reading diagnosis and remediation: Classroom and clinic* (2nd ed.). Boston: Houghton Mifflin.

Tierney, R. J., Readence, J. E., & Dishner, E. K. (1980). *Reading strategies and practices: A guide for improving instruction*. Boston: Allyn & Bacon.

Wilson, R. M., & Cleland, C. S. (1985). *Diagnostic and remedial reading for classroom and clinic* (5th ed.). Columbus, OH: Merrill.

Patricia A. Alexander
Texas A&M University

REALITY THERAPY

Reality therapy is a recently developed method of psychotherapy that stresses the importance of clients learning more useful behaviors to deal with their current situations. Reality therapy stresses internal motivation, behavior change, and development of the "success identity." In terms of philosophical or theoretical stance, reality therapy can be described as strongly cognitive or rational in its approach, appealing to the client's reason and emphasizing the possibility of meaningful change, not just in feelings, but in behavior. The therapist takes an active, directive role as teacher, but remains supportive and nonpunitive.

William Glasser, a physician, developed the theory of reality therapy over a period of years beginning with his psychiatric training. Both Glasser's reaction against traditional psychoanalytic psychotherapy and his experiences in working with delinquent youths at a California school for girls probably played major roles in the development of reality therapy (Belkin, 1975).

Glasser (1965) sees the individual as motivated internally by need to belong, to be loved, and to be a successful, worthwhile person. Control is seen as a major element in the human system: the individual works to control the environment so that internal, personal needs can be met. The individual's interface with the reality of his or her current life situation is the arena of action. Therefore, reality therapy stresses personal commitment, change in behavior, responsibility and the here and now. The individual's past history is not seen as particularly significant, and the medical model or orthodox concept of mental illness has no place in this approach (Corey, 1986).

The therapist is viewed as a coach or instructor who provides clients with assistance and encouragement in evaluating the usefulness of their current behavior in satisfying their needs. Where the appropriateness of change is recognized, the therapist assists in the development and execution of plans for remediation. Development of the client's strengths and feelings of self-worth leading to a success identity is a key responsibility of the therapist.

Reality therapy is basically a didactic activity, by which the client develops an understanding of reality and learns to act responsibly and effectively in accordance with that reality. A summary of the techniques and procedures of reality therapy is provided by Corey (1986), based on his adaptation and integration of material from several sources. Corey discusses eight steps in therapy: create a relationship, focus on current behavior, invite clients to evaluate their behavior, help clients develop an action plan, get commitment, refuse to accept excuses, refuse to use punishment, and refuse to give up.

Glasser has promoted the acceptance of his approach by numerous presentations and publications. In *Reality Therapy: A New Approach to Psychiatry* (1965), *Stations of the Mind* (1981), and *Take Effective Control of Your Life* (1984), Glasser develops his theoretical approach to psychotherapy and demonstrates its application to clinical cases. Glasser's *Schools Without Failure* (1969) applies the concepts of reality therapy to the school setting. *Positive Addiction* (1976) treats a different, but related, theme; it also has met with wide public acceptance.

Reality therapy has grown in popularity and influence. It is particularly well received in schools and the criminal justice system, and with counselors who work to rehabilitate handicapped individuals. This psychotherapeutic approach lends itself to short-term, direct, and active therapy.

REFERENCES

Belkin, G. S. (1975). *Practical counseling in the schools*. Dubuque, IA: Brown.

Corey, G. (1986). *Theory and practice of counseling and psychotherapy* (3rd ed.). Monterey, CA: Brooks/Cole.

Glasser, W. (1965). *Reality therapy: A new approach to psychiatry*. New York: Harper & Row.

Glasser, W. (1969). *Schools without failure*. New York: Harper & Row.

Glasser, W. (1976). *Positive addiction*. New York: Harper & Row.

Glasser, W. (1981). *Stations of the mind*. New York: Harper & Row.

Glasser, W. (1984). *Take effective control of your life*. New York: Harper & Row.

ROBERT R. REILLEY
Texas A&M University

PSYCHOSOCIAL ADJUSTMENT
PSYCHOTHERAPY

RECATEGORIZATION (OF WISC-R SCORES)

Since the publication of the Wechsler Intelligence Scale for Children (WISC) and its revision, the WISC-R, psychoeducational assessors have attempted to develop and use a variety of interpretive methods. These methods are intended to maximize the diagnostic information the test yields. Efforts also have been made to investigate characteristic subtest patterns to aid in differentiating various groups of atypical learners.

In addition to Wechsler's theory of the verbal-performance dichotomy, factor-analytic research has aided in the interpretation of WISC-R data. Kaufman (1975) factor analyzed the WISC-R standardization sample data at ages $5\frac{1}{2}$ to $16\frac{1}{2}$ (N = 2000 per age group), employing two- and three-factor solutions. The factor structure that emerged was similar across age levels. The three factors identified included (1) verbal comprehension, comprised of vocabulary (V), information (I), comprehension (C), and similarities (S); (2) perceptual organization, including block design (BD), object assembly (OA), picture completion (PC), picture arrangement (PA), and mazes (M); and (3) freedom from distractibility, comprised of arithmetic (A), digit span (DS), and coding (COD).

The verbal and performance IQs represent good estimates of the verbal comprehension and perceptual organization factors. The freedom from distractibility factor can be associated with distractibility or anxiety, short-term memory, symbolic facility, sequencing, or attention-concentration (Kaufman, 1979). Other factor-analytic research has generally confirmed the existence of three factors found to be stable across sexes (Reynolds & Gutkin, 1980) for normal (Reschly & Reschly, 1979) and referred children (Gutkin & Reynolds, 1980). To aid the practitioner in the interpretation of the factor scores, Gutkin (1978) calculated the reliability of the three factors for each WISC-R age group and developed formulas to convert the WISC-R factor scores into deviation IQs.

In a further effort to make WISC-R data more meaningful, several clinically derived subtest groupings have been developed. Based in part on the results of factor-analytic studies, Bannatyne's (1971, 1974) recategorization represents one of the more popular and extensively researched groupings. Initially, Bannatyne suggested that this recategorization had greater psychological meaning and diagnostic use than those based soley on factor-analytic results such as the verbal-performance dichotomy.

With modifications suggested by Rugel (1974), Bannatyne proposed a WISC-R subtest recategorization consisting of four groups. Acquired knowledge included the child's combined performance on the subtests of I, A, and V. Spatial ability was based on combined performance on PC, BD, and OA, and related to the child's ability to recognize spatial relationships and to manipulate objects either directly or symbolically in multidimensional space. The spatial grouping also related logically to the factor of perceptual organization. Bannatyne's sequencing grouping was identical in composition to the third factor identified in factor-analytic research, freedom from distractibility, and was composed of the examinee's combined performance on A, DS, and COD. The conceptual category represented the fourth grouping, and was related to general language use and function. It also closely resembled the verbal comprehension factor. The conceptual category was composed of the child's combined performance on S, V, and C correlated with the child's ability to use concepts and engage in abstract reasoning.

Bannatyne's recategorization groupings have been investigated as an aid in diagnosing a variety of exceptionalities. Overall, the recategorization system has been found to be ineffective in improving the differential diagnosis of exceptional children (Kavale & Forness, 1984). However, the recategorization system can be useful in understanding a particular child's strengths and weaknesses, including styles and methods of information processing (Kaufman, 1979; Reynolds, 1981).

Kaufman (1979) has also developed a number of informal guidelines to determine relative strengths and weaknesses for various WISC-R subtest groupings and methods for conducting comparisons among them. Subtest groupings proposed by Kaufman include reasoning or problem solving based the child's composite performance on S, A, and C, versus recall, comprised of the subtests of I, V, and DS. WISC-R subtests (I, A, C) composed of long stimuli or lengthy questions are contrasted with performance on subtests (S, V, DS) that include brief test stimuli or questions. Other groupings of subtests include those requiring responses with much verbal expression (S, V, C) compared with those whose responses demand little verbalization for successful performance (I, A, DS). Also as part of Kaufman's WISC-R recategorization, a comparison is suggested among those subtests that are comprised of meaningful item content (PC, PA, OA) and those that include abstract stimuli (BD, COD). Performance on nonverbal subtests that demand no essential motor activity by the examinee (PC, PA) is contrasted with performance on those subtests that demand responses that are highly dependent on coordination (BD, OA, COD, mazes).

Kaufman further suggested a grouping related to mode of processing information by comparing those subtests requiring right brain processing (PC, OA) with those demanding more integrated functioning (PA, BD, COD). In addition, the WISC-R Performance Scale can be recategorized along the dimension of information processing with the subtests related to simultaneous processing (PC, BD, OA) compared with the subtests requiring successive processing (PA, COD). Another grouping consists of those subtests that require the child to imitate or reproduce models (BD, COD) contrasted with other performance subtests that demand more problem solving. A final subtest grouping suggested by Kaufman was based on Guilford's theory, with subtests tapping cognition (PC, BD, OA, mazes) compared with those related to convergent production (PA, COD).

Grossman (1985) facilitated working with both the Bannatyne and Kaufman recategorized subtest groupings by providing formulas to compute standardized deviation quotients and standard errors of measurement for the various subtest combinations. He also provided data to determine statistically significant discrepancies between pairs of subtest combinations.

Lutey (1977) has also developed a system of interpreting a subject's relatively strong and weak areas of cognitive functioning through WISC-R subtest recategorization. Her system is based on the derivation of a variety of scores founded in part on factor-analytic research, clinical research findings, and Lutey's own attempts to resolve ambiguities in the design of other recategorization systems. A lesser known recategorization scheme has been proposed by Witkin, Dyk, Faterson, Goodenough and Karp (1974). Their categories include verbal comprehension (I, V, C), analytic-field approach (OA, PC, BD), and attention-concentration (A, DS, COD). The verbal comprehension grouping represents a variation of the verbal comprehension factor and Bannatyne's conceptual category. The analytic-field category is equivalent to Bannatyne's spatial grouping and the attention-concentration category relates to Bannatyne's sequential grouping. All of the various recategorization systems are helpful in generating working hypotheses for the WISC-R test user. These hypotheses must then be confirmed or refuted with further diagnostic assessment.

REFERENCES

Bannatyne, A. (1971). *Language, reading, and learning disabilities*. Springfield, IL: Thomas.

Bannatyne, A. (1974). Diagnosis: A note on recategorization of the WISC scaled scores. *Journal of Learning Disabilities, 7,* 272–237.

Grossman, F. M. (1985). Interpreting clinically derived WISC-R subtest groupings: A statistical approach. *Journal of Psychoeducational Assessment, 3,* 89–96.

Gutkin, T. B. (1978). Some useful statistics for the interpretation of the WISC-R. *Journal of Consulting & Clinical Psychology, 46,* 1561–1563.

Gutkin, T. B., & Reynolds, C. R. (1980). Factorial similarity of the WISC-R for Anglos and Chicanos referred for psychological services. *Journal of School Psychology, 18,* 34–39.

Kaufman, A. S. (1975). Factor analysis of the WISC-R at 11 age levels between 6½ and 16½ years. *Journal of Consulting & Clinical Psychology, 43,* 135–147.

Kaufman, A. S. (1979). *Intelligent testing with the WISC-R*. New York: Wiley.

Kavale, K. A., & Forness, S. R. (1984). A meta-analysis of the validity of Wechsler scale profiles and recategorizations: Patterns or parodies. *Learning Disability Quarterly, 7*(2), 136–156.

Lutey, C. (1977). *Individual intelligence testing*. Greeley CO: Author.

Reschly, D., & Reschly, J. E. (1979). Validity of WISC-R factor scores in predicting achievement and attention for sociocultural groups. *Journal of School Psychologists, 17,* 355–361.

Reynolds, C. R. (1981). A note on determining significant discrepancies among category scores on Bannatyne's regrouping of WISC-R subtests. *Journal of Learning Disabilities, 14,* 468–469.

Reynolds, C. R., & Gutkin, T. B. (1980). Stability of the WISC-R factor structure across sex at two age levels. *Journal of Clinical Psychology, 36,* 775–777.

Rugel, P. R. (1974). WISC subtest scores of described readers: A review with respect to Bannatyne's recategorization. *Journal of Learning Disabilities, 1,* 57–64.

Witkin, H. A., Dyk, R. B., Faterson, H. G., Goodenough, D. R., & Karp, S. A. (1974). *Psychological differentiation*: Potomac, MD: Erlbaum.

MARK E. SWERDLIK
Illinois State University

FACTOR ANALYSIS
FREEDOM FROM DISTRACTIBILITY
WECHSLER, DAVID
WISC/WISC-R

RECEPTIVE LANGUAGE DISORDERS

A language disorder in which there is a severe loss or impairment in the understanding or use of language owing to brain injury or dysfunction is known as aphasia. This disorder may be dichotomized into expressive or motor aphasia, in which the ability to form speech is impaired, and receptive or sensory aphasia, in which the ability to comprehend the spoken word is affected. In adults, aphasia is acquired through brain damage and results in cessation or regression from a prior ability to use language. In children, language disorders may be acquired as a result of brain injury, or they may be developmental in nature. That is, because of abnormal development or injury to the language centers of the central nervous system prenatally, perinatally, or postnatally during the first year, the child has difficulty in developing normal understanding and use of language (Gaddes, 1980). This condition is also known as a primary or congenital language disorder (Deuel, 1983). When the dysfunction in the language centers of the brain is mild, it may be referred to as a learning disability.

Although many parts of the brain are active and interrelated in language and speech, certain areas are of greater importance to specific language functions (Benson, 1983). In 1874, Carl Wernicke, a German neurologist, identified the superior lateral surface of the left temporal lobe as the cortical area for decoding oral speech. Geschwind (1972) stressed the importance of subcortical bundles of neural fibers that connect distant cortical areas. However, the precise boundaries of important cortical areas remain vague owing to considerable interindividual variation and the fact that most brain lesions are not highly localized (Benson, 1983; Gaddes, 1980). Although the left hemisphere is dominant for language in most right-handed individuals, those who are left-handed or ambidextrous may have right hemisphere or bilateral language functions (Lezak, 1983). Some experts believe that comprehension of spoken language is more likely to have bi-

lateral representation than other language functions (Benson, et al., 1973).

Receptive language disorders may be classified in several ways. Johnson and Myklebust (1967) discuss a generalized deficit in auditory learning in which a child hears but does not interpret. Other children, less affected, can interpret nonverbal, social sounds, but cannot relate the spoken word to an appropriate unit of experience. In cases of less severe receptive language deficits, the inability to comprehend may be limited to abstract language or to specific parts of speech. Benson (1983) cites four clinically distinguishable comprehension disturbances and suggests a neuroanatomical locus of pathology for each. These are (1) receptive disturbances, involving comprehension and repetition of spoken language; (2) perceptive disturbances (also known as Wernicke's aphasia), in which comprehension of written and spoken language is involved; (3) semantic disturbances, characterized by an inability to understand the meaning of spoken and written language despite relatively normal ability to repeat spoken language; and (4) syntactic disturbances, involving difficulties with syntactical structures and sequencing. Benson emphasizes that there is much overlap among these comprehension problems, and they are rarely found in isolation.

Receptive language disorders frequently are observed in conjunction with other disabilities. In the developmental hierarchy of language outlined by Myklebust (1954), expressive language follows and is dependent on inner and receptive language. In a similar way, reading and written language are dependent on the acquisition of earlier levels of language. Therefore, it is not surprising that reading, writing, and the problem-solving areas of arithmetic may be affected by receptive language disorders. Johnson and Myklebust (1967) suggest that auditory cognitive skills, including discrimination, rhyming, and blending, often are correlates of receptive language disorders. Such skills are prerequisite to the success of an auditory-phonetic reading program and indicate the need for a global language approach to instruction.

To remediate receptive language disorders, it is necessary to create a match between the auditory symbol and a meaningful unit of experience. Although Myklebust (1971) stresses the importance of comprehensive diagnostic testing to determine a profile of strengths and weaknesses on which highly individualized remediation may be based, he acknowledges certain similarities common to all instructional programs. Johnson and Myklebust (1967) list several of these principles to be incorporated into successful remediation. The first is that training should begin early. Benson (1983) suggests the presence of residual language competency in the nondominant hemisphere that slowly decreases with age. The plasticity of a young brain may allow language function to be taken over by the nondominant hemisphere or be shared bilaterally. Other principles of remediation suggested by Johnson and Myklebust include (1) input precedes output (comprehension precedes expression); (2) auditory symbol and unit of experience are simultaneous; (3) repetition is used; and (4) vocabulary is carefully selected. Myklebust (1971) cautions against the indiscriminate use of a multisensory motor approach. In some cases, such a remedial approach may result in overloading and have a negative effect on attention, orientation, and motivation. McGinnis (1963) gives a detailed description of additional remedial procedures.

REFERENCES

Benson, D. F. (1983). The neural basis of spoken and written language. In H. R. Myklebust (Ed.), *Progress in learning disabilities* (Vol. 5, pp. 3–25). New York: Grune & Stratton.

Benson, D. F., Sheremata, W. A., Buchard, R., Segarra, J., Price, D., & Geschwind, N. (1973). Conduction aphasia. *Archives of Neurology, 28,* 339–346.

Deuel, R. K. (1983). Aphasia in childhood. In H. R. Myklebust (Ed.), *Progress in learning disabilities* (Vol. 5, pp. 29–43). New York: Grune & Stratton.

Gaddes, W. H. (1980). *Learning disabilities and brain function: A neuropsychological approach* (2nd ed.). New York: Springer-Verlag.

Geschwind, N. (1972). Language and the brain. *Scientific American, 226*(4), 76–83.

Johnson, D. J., & Myklebust, H. R. (1967). *Learning disabilities: Educational principles and practices.* New York: Grune & Stratton.

Lezak, M. D. (1983). *Neuropsychological assessment* (2nd ed.). New York: Oxford University Press.

McGinnis, M. A. (1963). *Aphasic children: Identification and education by the association method.* Washington, DC: Alexander Graham Bell Association for the Deaf.

Myklebust, H. R. (1954). *Auditory disorders in children: A manual for differential diagnosis.* New York: Grune & Stratton.

Myklebust, H. R. (1971). Childhood aphasia: Identification, diagnosis, remediation. In L. E. Travis (Ed.), *Handbook of speech pathology and audiology* (pp. 1203–1217). New York: Appleton-Century-Crofts.

BARBARA S. SPEER
*Shaker Heights City School
District, Shaker Heights,
Ohio*

APHASIA
AUDITORY DISCRIMINATION
AUDITORY PERCEPTION
DEVELOPMENTAL APHASIA

RECIPROCAL DETERMINISM

Throughout the history of the behavioral sciences and human service professions, there have been a number of theoretical models proposed to provide insights for understanding, predicting, and manipulating human behavior. The most traditional perspective is commonly referred to as the medical model. Within this framework, human behavior is viewed as emanating primarily from forces that are internal to the individual (e.g., personality, IQ, neurological characteristics, hormonal activity). This orientation evolved from psychodynamic views of psychopathology and advances in the field of medicine. The work of Sigmund Freud (1943) provides a classic example of this perspective. A behavioral model developed in reaction to the medical model and as a result of the research and theory generated by leading behaviorists such as Skinner (1938, 1953). In contrast to the medical model, the behavioral model places primary emphasis on the influence of the immediate external environment (e.g., reinforcement, punishment) as a means for understanding human behavior. Recently, an ecological model of human behavior has emerged. Prompted largely by the work of Barker (1965), this set of principles focuses on the impact of the broad external environment (e.g., behavior settings, organizational policies, social norms) on the behavior of persons who function within that environment.

Reciprocal determinism is a model of human behavior that effectively synthesizes the medical, behavioral, and ecological models into a single integrated perspective. Proposed by Bandura (1978) as a result of his extensive theoretical and empirical work on social learning theory, reciprocal determinism postulates that human activity is a function of the mutual and reciprocal interactions that occur between a person's behavior (B), cognitive and other internal events related to the person (P), and the external environment (E). The model hypothesizes that human behavior results from an ongoing interaction among the B, P, and E factors in each person's life. According to this point of view, meaningful insight into a person's behavior is best attained if one can discern (1) the salient B, P, and E factors operating on and within that individual and (2) how those factors interact and influence each other.

The reciprocal determinism model holds important theoretical and practical insights for special educators. Consider, for example, the hypothetical case of a fourth-grade boy who has developed reading difficulties. Approaching this child's problem from a medical model perspective would lead special educators to examine the IQ, neurological status, health, etc. Those who subscribe to a behavioral model would focus primarily on information such as the nature of classroom interactions with teachers, peers, and academic materials during reading lessons. If special educators were to use the ecological model, it would lead them to consider the nature of the school's reading program, the district's resources in the area of reading, the home environment, etc. From the perspective of reciprocal determinism, however, special educators can see that each of these pieces of information may be important and that none should be overlooked.

Even more significant, the reciprocal determinism

model highlights that one cannot really understand the causal factors behind children's educational and psychological difficulties without understanding how the B, P, and E factors affect each other. For example, the behavior of this hypothetical child in reading class (B) is continuously affected by his intellectual abilities (P), which are in turn either heightened or diminished as a function of the school's academic programs and his home environment (E), which are themselves influenced by how the child behaves both in and out of school (B). By sensitizing special educators to this dynamic interaction among B, P, and E forces, reciprocal determinism provides a comprehensive framework within which children's problems can be conceptualized, assessed, diagnosed, and treated (Reynolds, Gutkin, Elliott, & Witt, 1984).

REFERENCES

Bandura, A. (1978). The self-system in reciprocal determinism. *American Psychologist, 33*, 344–358.

Barker, R. G. (1965). Explorations in ecological psychology. *American Psychologist, 20*, 1–14.

Freud, S. (1943). *A general introduction to psychoanalysis.* Garden City, NY: Garden City.

Reynolds, C. R., Gutkin, T. B., Elliott, S. N., & Witt, J. C. (1984). *School psychology: Essentials of theory and practice.* New York: Wiley.

Skinner, B. F. (1938). *The behavior of organisms.* New York: Appleton-Century-Crofts.

Skinner, B. F. (1953). *Science and human behavior.* New York: Macmillan.

TERRY B. GUTKIN
University of Nebraska, Lincoln

BANDURA A.
BEHAVIORAL MODIFICATION
ECOLOGICAL ASSESSMENT .
ECOLOGICAL EDUCATION OF THE HANDICAPPED
HUMANISTIC SPECIAL EDUCATION

RECORDING FOR THE BLIND (RFB)

Recording for the Blind (RFB) is an organization that was founded in 1951 for the purpose of recording textbooks at no charge for persons unable to use ordinary print, whether because of visual, perceptual, or physical conditions. Kirchner and Simon (1984), in a study conducted in 1982–1983, stated that RFB serves over 7300 students in higher education; 57% of the students served are visually impaired.

Recording programs such as RFB are invaluable to the education of visually impaired learners. Other service organizations provide audio-formatted materials for this population (Ferrell, 1985). The Talking Book Program,

sponsored by the American Printing House for the Blind, is a source of materials for parents and teachers serving visually impaired students. American Printing House also distributes the variable speech control cassette recorder to be used with their audio cassettes. The National Library Service for the Blind and Physically Handicapped, of the Library of Congress, offers free library services to visually impaired persons. The Library of Congress also lends special talking book record and cassette players to applicants. Many of the materials available from these organizations are popular leisure books, magazines, religious materials, and newspapers.

Addresses for these organizations are:

American Printing House for the Blind
1839 Frankfort Avenue
Louisville, KY 40206

National Library Service for the Blind and Physically Handicapped
Library of Congress
Washington, DC 20542

Recording for the Blind, Inc.
215 E. 58th Street
New York, NY 10022

REFERENCES

Ferrell, K. (1985). *Reach out and teach: Meeting the training needs of parents of visually and multiply handicapped young children.* New York: American Foundation for the Blind.

Kirchner, C., & Simon, Z. (1984). Blind and visually handicapped college students—Part I: Estimated numbers. *Journal of Visual Impairment & Blindness, 78*, 78–81.

VIVIAN I. CORREA
University of Florida

BLIND .
VERSABRAILLE

RECREATION, THERAPEUTIC

Therapeutic recreation is a form of play or physical activity that is used to improve a variety of behaviors that may occur in the cognitive, emotional, social, and physical domains. These activities include games, dancing, horseback riding, and a wide range of other individual and group games and sports.

The intellectual domain may be influenced through gross and fine motor movement activities. There are many theories of cognitive development occurring in sequential order in which motor abilities are the basis for higher thought processes (Kephart, 1960; Piaget, 1950). Theoretically, motor skills help to develop higher skill levels in handicapped persons by increasing memory, language, and problem solving (Major & Walsh, 1977). Forms of recreation may be used as an alternate to more traditional teaching methods. Humphrey (1976) used games and dancing to aid in reversal difficulties, sequencing difficulties, left and right directionality, and improvement in following direction skills. Physical movement helped to present concepts and skills in a more concrete form. Through imitation and role playing, children were able to use intellectual concepts they had already learned and developed (Yawkey, 1979).

Other forms of learning may be influenced by physical activities and games that have the objective of increasing motivation and attention span. Naville and Blom (1968) stressed educational achievements of concentration, willpower, and self-control through movement.

Emotions can be influenced through recreational activities, which may help individuals improve self-concepts and self-confidence. Being aware of one's body and feeling good about one's self can be associated with the pleasure of recreation. Socially, organized group activities may offer social skills learning through structured interpersonal play. Individuals have opportunities to work together, follow leaders, engage in appropriate behaviors, and develop various forms of self-expression. Recreation can be used not only as a medium for communication but also to help integrate the handicapped with the nonhandicapped and teach activities to decrease isolation.

Physically, recreational activities have endless limits. Movement may help individuals increase coordination and range of motion of body movement. For example, water sports, swimming, or water therapy can be extremely valuable to a variety of handicapped children and youths, as can free motion activities such as creative dance. These activities can increase physical strength and flexibility; having a strong, attractive body correlates with a positive self-image.

Specific programs such as bowling, folk dancing, and even competitive sports have incorporated recreational activities as therapy for different populations; a good example of one of these programs is the Special Olympics for various groups of handicapped students. Jacques-Dalcroze (1930) first developed eurhythmics for the blind to increase self-confidence and expression through music and rhythm. Gollnitz (1970) developed a rhythmic-psychomotor therapy that combined movement, music, and rhythm for individuals with psychic and developmental disorders. Lefco (1974) followed the idea of the integration of the body and mind when she used dance therapy to promote mental and physical well being. The Cove Schools in Racine, Wisconsin, and Evanston, Illinois, were designed for brain-injured students to provide play experiences that may have been missed because of slow rates of development. The Halliwick method deals with the swimming ability of the physically handicapped. Norway has a horseback riding school for the disabled. Mann, Berger, and Proger (1974) offer a comprehensive review of the research on the influence of physical education on the cognitive, physical, affective, and social domains in which movement was significant in helping the handicapped with different variables in these areas.

In summary, therapeutic recreation includes structured physical and social activities that are designed to have as objectives the enjoyment of leisure time, improved movement, and development of physical strength and social skills. Recreation, adaptive physical education, and physical activities increase or improve social, physical, and mental abilities.

REFERENCES

Gollnitz, G. (1970). Fundamentals of rhythmic-psychomotor music therapy: An objective-oriented therapy for children and adolescents with developmental disturbances. *Acta Paedopsychiatrica. The International Journal of Child Psychiatry, 37*, 130–134.

Humphrey, J. H. (1976). *Improving learning ability through compensatory physical education.* Springfield: IL: Thomas.

Jacques-Dalcroze, E. (1930). *Eurhythmics: Art and education.* London: Chatto & Windum.

Kephart, N. (1960). *The slower learner in the classroom.* Columbus, OH: Merrill.

Lefco, H. (1974). *Dance therapy.* Chicago, IL: Nelson-Hall.

Major, S., & Walsh, M. (1977). *Learning activities for the learning disabled.* Belmont, CA: Fearon-Pitman.

Mann, L., Berger, R., & Proger, B. (1974). Physical education intervention with the exceptional child. In L. Mann & D. A. Sabatino (Eds.), *The second review of special education.* NY: Grune & Stratton.

Naville, S., & Blom, G. E. (1968). *Psychomotor education: Theory and practice.* Denver, CO: University of Colorado Medical Center.

Piaget, J. (1950). *Psychology of intelligence.* New York: Harcourt & Brace.

Yawkey, T. D. (1979). More in play as intelligence in children. *Journal of Creative Behavior, 13*, 247–256.

DONNA FILIPS
Steger, Illinois

EQUINE THERAPY
RECREATIONAL THERAPY
RECREATION FOR THE HANDICAPPED

RECREATIONAL READING
FOR THE HANDICAPPED

According to most dictionaries, recreation is an agreeable art, a pastime, or a diversion that affords relaxation and enjoyment. However, most handicapped students would not link recreation with reading because books symbolize failure and emotional distress (Schanzer, 1973). Therefore, the goal of education should be to encourage students to be independent readers who regularly choose to read. For this to occur, it is necessary for teachers, librarians, and parents to become involved.

Teachers are likely to be the only reading models for many students (Smith, Smith, & Mikulecky, 1978). Therefore, they should be active reading models, talking about what they have been reading and allowing students to see them carrying personal books or magazines. In the classroom, free reading time, when everyone reads without the threat of book reports or lengthy comprehension checks, should be scheduled (Smith, Smith, & Mikulecky, 1978). Teachers should be sure to have large classroom libraries of recreational reading materials. However, standard, off-the-shelf novels or biographies present frustrating hurdles such as reading level, subject matter, and length (Hallenbeck, 1983). Therefore, such books should be didactic, with important words repeated several times. The themes should relate closely to the lives of the students and the sentences should be short with simple verb tenses. In addition, pronouns should be placed near the nouns that they modify and characters should be human beings, not abstract things or ideas. Finally, the style of writing should be conversational (Slick, 1969). This will help to eliminate the selection of reading material that is too difficult.

To halt deterioration of positive reading attitudes, teachers should talk to students about their reading habits and interests, observe what they read, and get to know their interests so appropriate suggestions can be made (Smith, et al., 1978). In addition, reading-attitude measures and interest inventories are desirable since there is much intrinsic motivation in reading about something relevant and familiar. When vocabulary and concepts are known, rate may increase with excitement, and the likelihood of a successful, pleasurable experience is high (Smith et al., 1978). When reading material is matched to interests, students tend to comprehend from one to two grade levels above tested reading levels (Estes & Vaughn, 1973, cited in Smith et al., 1978). Matching students with reading materials dealing with life interests helps to initiate lifelong reading habits (Smith et al., 1978). To encourage students to read past the school experience, reading must be motivated outside the classroom by curiosity; pleasure and excitement at the new; practicality; prestige and social status with peers; escape and vicarious experiences; expansion and reinforcement of present attitudes and interests; and reflection of personal situations and dilemmas (Smith et al., 1978). Teachers can create this desire to read by conferencing with students about what they have read; by allowing students to conference with one another, and by engaging in motivational activities such as brief oral readings to students and games and gimmicks such as book auctions. (Smith et al., 1978).

Librarians can also be helpful in encouraging recreational reading among handicapped students because they come in contact with all students in an average school week. The librarian should remove all stumbling blocks so that special education students feel free to use the library. For example, the borrowing period may have to be adjusted because these students may need more time to complete a book. In addition, it is important to eliminate the frustration of book selection by establishing a one-to-one relationship with the student and having enough high-interest low-reading-level books available. As special education students begin to frequent the library, praise and commendation should be given. In addition, individual guidance and personal service are needed. It would also be helpful for the librarian to supply the special education class with a list of the new books in the library so that students can request a particular book when visiting the library. Finally, it is helpful to have students act as library aides to assure them that they are needed, are helpful, and are appreciated (Slick, 1969).

For many students, reading takes place at school or not at all. If reading is to become an enjoyable and lifelong experience, it is necessary for reading to occur at home. However, pressure from the parents to read is not the answer since pressure violates the spirit of free reading (Haimowitz, 1977). As early as the 1940s in Japan, there were two home reading programs. One was a 20-minute mother-child reading process in which parents and children sat for 20 minutes a day and the children read to the mothers. The second was scheduled reading hours once a week in which everyone in the family read (Smith et al., 1978). Programs such as these and others initiated by PTA groups and community groups can be helpful in encouraging recreational reading among handicapped students.

REFERENCES

Haimowitz, B. (1977, December). Motivating reluctant readers in inner-city classes. *Journal of Reading, 21*, 227–230.

Hallenbeck, M. J. (1983, March). A free reading journal for secondary LD students. *Academic Therapy, 18*, 479–485.

Schanzer, S. S. (1973, Fall). Independent reading for children with learning disabilities. *Academic Therapy, 9*, 109–114.

Slick, M. H. (1969, April 10). *Recreational reading materials for special education students.* Pittsburgh: University of Pittsburgh, School of Library Science. (ERIC Document Reproduction Service No. ED 046 173)

Smith, C. B., Smith, S. L., & Mikulecky, L. (1978). *Teaching reading in secondary school content subjects: A book-thinking process.* New York: Holt, Rinehart, & Winston.

CAROLINE D'IPPOLITO
*Eastern Pennsylvania Special
Education Resources Center,
King of Prussia,
Pennsylvania*

HIGH INTEREST–LOW VOCABULARY READING

LIBRARY SERVICES FOR THE HANDICAPPED READING

RECREATIONAL THERAPY

Recreational activities are necessary for the total well-being of any individual. They provide an important source of pleasure and relaxation. Most individuals learn how to use recreational activities from a lifetime of learning how to play. But as with other skill areas, the handicapped often experience difficulties in using free time appropriately. They may have been sheltered during much of their developmental period, or their disability may have prohibited them from acquiring the skills necessary for participation in recreational activities. Consequently, many handicapped individuals will require intentional and systematic instruction if they are to acquire those skills. In that regard, recreational therapy is a planned intervention process developed to promote the growth and development of recreational skills and leisure-time activities.

Recreational therapy attempts to eliminate or minimize an individual's disability. It uses recreation to assist the handicapped in changing certain physical, emotional, or social characteristics so they may pursue leisure activities and live as independently as possible (National Recreation and Park Association, 1978). Recreational therapy is also concerned with helping the handicapped participate in activities with the nonhandicapped as much as possible. This integration allows the handicapped to move into the recreational mainstream and become more involved in community recreational activities. In addition to helping the handicapped to engage in recreational activities, recreational therapy also provides other benefits. A second advantage of the program is that appropriate recreational and leisure-time skills can lead to increased physical development, socialization skills, and even cognitive and language development (Schulz & Turnbull, 1984). Therefore, recreational therapy may be recommended to help the handicapped to maintain their physical skills, interact socially, and increase academic progress.

REFERENCES

National Recreation and Park Association. (1978). *The therapeutic recreator.* In W. L. Heward & M. D. Orlansky (1980). *Exceptional children.* Columbus: Charles E. Merrill.

Schulz, J. B., & Turnbull, A. P. (1984). *Mainstreaming handicapped students. A guide for classroom teachers* (2nd ed.). Boston: Allyn & Bacon.

LARRY J. WHEELER
*Southwest Texas State
University*

EQUINE THERAPY
OCCUPATIONAL THERAPY

RECREATION FOR THE HANDICAPPED

Recreation for the handicapped includes individual and group programs of outdoor, social, sports, or educational activities conducted during leisure time. Such programs conducted in medically supervised institutions are identified as therapeutic recreation while those conducted in schools and the community are called community programs (Pomeroy, 1983). The overall goal of recreation programs is to enable each handicapped person the right to participate at the lowest effective care level as independently as abilities and disabilities permit (Stein, 1985).

Recreation services for the handicapped should be distinguished from therapeutic recreation. The latter is a means of intervention to bring about desired changes. In schools, therapeutic recreation is medically prescribed and programmed by recreational therapists. In contrast, the purpose of recreation programs for the handicapped is to provide these students with opportunities to realize their leisure and recreational needs whether on an individual or group basis. Recreation programs in schools or communities for handicapped students are voluntary in nature and programmed by recreational leaders.

Prior to 1960, most recreation programs for the handicapped were segregated or held in institutions (Robinson & Skinner, 1985). Since 1960 legislative forces and concerned professional organizations have sought to deinstitutionalize and desegregate such programs. With the enactment of PL 94-142, recreation came to be considered as a related service in the schools. During the late 1970s the federal government provided grants to colleges and universities to set up training programs for recreation therapists and adapted physical education teachers and for the development of regional information and resource centers (Robinson & Skinner, 1985). Private organizations such as Wheelchair Sports and the Association for the Help of Retarded Children have also been active in promoting recreational programs in schools and communities.

Although only 5 to 10% of all handicapped persons are being reached by existing park and recreation service providers, the prognosis for the future appears to be positive. Statutes to promote barrier design, and the changing attitudes of service providers and participants, seem to indicate a trend toward more handicapped people availing themselves of school or community recreation programs.

Delineated on the basis of the degree of supervision required, there are four types of recreation programs for the handicapped. First, there are special programs limited to persons with specific disabilities, e.g. blind, deaf, or physically disabled persons. These programs often revolve around a single activity for the purposes of fun, socialization, and skill development. Second, there are semiintegrated services that allow the handicapped to mix with the nonhandicapped in activities that lend themselves to integration. Third, some communities have a buddy system where handicapped persons participate with nonhandicapped persons in the same activities and programs; scouting and Camp Fire Girls have used the buddy system extensively in their programs. The fourth type of program is one that provides opportunities for total integration in all activities, as is the case in many national parks and recreation areas.

The major categories of recreational activities for the handicapped listed by Russell (1983) are sports and games, hobbies, music, outdoor recreation, mental and literary recreation, arts and crafts, dance, and drama.

Handicapped programs at the national and international levels are usually of a competitive nature. Examples of these include the Para-olympics, which meets every 4 years in a different part of the world and has four disability groups: deaf, amputee, cerebral palsy, and paraplegic competition. Wheelchair Sports, sponsored by the National Wheelchair Athletic Association, provides competition in track, basketball, and weightlifting. The National Handicapped Sports and Recreation Association promotes sports and recreational activities through 29 regional offices across the United States.

Most state and regional programs are part of national structures such as the Special Olympics program. Some state programs are resident or day camps or outdoor activity centers. There are very few recreation centers that exclusively serve the handicapped. The majority are in large urban areas e.g., the Anchor Program in New York City and the Recreation Center for the Handicapped in San Francisco.

Many schools, colleges, and communities sponsor local recreational programs for the handicapped. Community swim programs seem to be the most popular and widespread. Hunter College in New York City conducts a recreation program for mentally retarded and physically disabled teenagers from the city, most of whom are minorities.

REFERENCES

Pomeroy, J. (1983). Community recreation for persons with disabilities. In E. Pan, T. Backer, & C. Vosh (Eds.), *Annual review of rehabilitation* (pp. 241–291). St. Louis: Mosby.

Robinson, F., & Skinner, S. (1985). *Community recreation for the handicapped.* Springfield, IL: Thomas.

Russell, R. (1983). *Planning programs in recreation.* St. Louis: Mosby.

Stein, J. (1985). Mainstreaming in recreational settings. *Journal of Physical Education, Recreation & Dance,* 5(56), 25–27.

THOMAS BURKE
Hunter College, City University
of New York

EQUINE THERAPY
GAMES FOR THE HANDICAPPED
MUSIC THERAPY
OLYMPICS

REDL, FRITZ (1902–   )

Born in Klaus, Austria, Fritz Redl received his PhD in psychology from the University of Vienna in 1925; he received further training from the Wiener Psychoanalysis Institute from 1925 to 1936. With the rise of the Nazis in Europe, Redl came to the United States in 1936 and first worked for the Rockefeller Foundation in the field of adolescence. He has been a Pinkerton guest professor in the School of Criminal Justice, New York State University, Albany, and a visiting professor, Department of Child Psychiatry, University of Utrecht, Holland. Currently, he is distinguished professor emeritus at Wayne State University.

Fritz Redl

Redl wanted to explore the reasons why children's behavioral controls deteriorate, how children defend themselves in an adult world, and how to prevent, or treat, as necessary, the disorganization created when a child's behavior control system becomes maladaptive. Redl believed that studying the severely disturbed child helps illuminate the common techniques used by the average, normal child. In the process of his studies, he developed the Detroit Group Project for clinical group work with children; this project became a summer camp for children from low-income groups. Redl also developed Pioneer House, a residential program to study and treat the delinquent, severely aggressive child. His work has been documented in Redl and Wineman's *The Aggressive Child* (1957).

Redl has lectured throughout the United States on education, mental health, group work, and group therapy. He has been a Ford Foundation fellow and has been included in *Who's Who in America.*

REFERENCE

Redl, F., & Wineman, D. (1957). *The aggressive child.* New York: Free Press.

E. VALERIE HEWITT
Texas A&M University

LIFE-SPACE INTERVIEWING

REFERRAL PROCESS

Referral is the process by which potentially handicapped or gifted students are identified for comprehensive individual evaluation by school officials. The identification of students for evaluation is a federally mandated activity for which all school districts and state education departments must have specific policies and procedures (U.S. Office of Education, 1977, sections 121a.128 and 121a.220). The law holds districts and state departments responsible for identifying all handicapped children within their jurisdictions who require special education or related services, including those in the care of other public and private agencies.

It is reported that some 3 to 5% of the school-age population are referred each year (Algozzine, Christenson, & Ysseldyke, 1982). Of those referred, about three-fourths are placed in special education. While these averages may characterize the nation as a whole, individual districts may vary widely in the percentage of students referred, evaluated, and placed.

Students can be referred in one of two major ways (Heller, Holtzman, & Messick, 1982). The first is through the systematic efforts of school districts, community agencies, or government institutions. For example, districts may use very low or very high performance on annually administered achievement tests to refer students. Similarly, hospitals may screen newborns for referral to early intervention programs. Finally, state education departments may conduct print and electronic media campaigns and establish toll-free hotlines aimed at encouraging the referral of handicapped or gifted students currently not receiving services.

The second major referral mechanism involves the efforts of individuals who know the child. Such individuals include the child's teachers, parents, and physician. Of these individuals, the large majority of referrals appear to emanate from teachers (Heller, Holtzman, & Messick, 1982). The advent of PL 94-142, however, has increased the involvement of others both in and outside the school (Bickel, 1982).

Referrals made by teachers (and other individuals) are generally personal decisions based on subjective criteria. As such, these decisions are open to a variety of influences. The specific factors that influence teacher referrals are difficult to identify with any certainty (Bickel, 1982). However, research suggests that teachers are influenced by several considerations. One consideration is program availability; if no program exists to meet the student's needs, or if no room is available in an existing program, referral is unlikely. Second, teachers seem hesitant to refer if there is a large backlog in assessment. Such backlogs cause teachers to consider referral a meaningless action. Third, parents may influence the process. Teachers may hesitate to refer children whose parents would be likely to react in a hostile manner, or be quick to refer those whose parents exert positive pressure. Finally, eligibility criteria affect the decision. For example, some states and districts require that teachers refer students for placement in a specific program such as one for educable mentally retarded pupils. Hence, teachers may be encouraged to refer only children with particular characteristics.

In addition to these factors, other influences on referral undoubtedly exist (Ysseldyke & Algozzine, 1984). Teachers' decisions likely are affected by their own beliefs about what constitutes normal child development and proper behavior, and by the extent to which a given child violates those assumptions. The referral decision is also governed by the teacher's skills in dealing with deviations; those who are less adept in handling learning or behavioral differences may be more likely to refer.

It should be clear, then, that a great amount of personal discretion exists in the referral process (Bickel, 1982). Such discretion allows substantial variation in referral practice within and across districts, suggesting that referral often depends as much on what class or school a child attends as on actual learning capabilities and performance. Because of this personal discretion, there is a tendency to refer children who disrupt school routines and those with more severe, easily verifiable problems.

The subjectivity inherent in the referral process has social and ethical implications. First, there is the possibility that substantial numbers of children are being referred inappropriately. Inappropriate referral is problematic because it wastes valuable resources; creates backlogs in assessment, thereby denying services to those truly in need; and subjects children to the potential stigma of special education placement and to education in an environment that may not meet their needs.

Second, inappropriate referral may disproportionately affect particular social groups. For many years, disproportionate placements of minority children and of males in programs for educable mentally retarded (EMR) students have been documented (Heller, Holtzman, & Messick, 1982). The reasons for these disproportionate placements are many and complex. While these placements are not necessarily inappropriate, their existence raises the question of whether teacher referrals, too, are disproportionate.

Relatively little research has been conducted on the topic of disproportionate referral. Those studies that do exist have used two basic methodologies. Some investigators have analyzed existing referral data to determine whether disproportionate numbers of students from particular groups are referred. Other researchers have presented different groups of teachers with simulated data describing a student and have asked them to make referral decisions. The data received by the groups differed only in the social group membership assigned to the student. While no definitive conclusions can be drawn, the studies have shown a tendency toward higher rates of referral for minorities even though these students presented problems that appeared little different from those of their majority peers (Bickel, 1982).

Concern regarding both the possibility that children are being inappropriately referred and disproportionate placement of minority students in special education has led many school districts to refine their referral processes. These refinements have primarily occurred with respect to teacher referrals. Such referrals were originally passed directly through to the pupil evaluation team. Most refinements have focused on inserting checks and balances into this teacher-to-evaluation team pathway.

The most immediately useful refinement probably has been the introduction of consultation (Zins & Curtis, 1984). Consultation may be provided by a resource teacher, school psychologist, or other specialist. The aim of consultation is to help the teacher deal with the student in the regular classroom. The consultant may work with the teacher to develop, apply, and evaluate the effects of alternative instructional or behavior management strategies (Bennett, 1981).

A second type of referral refinement requires the provision of extensive evidence to support the need for referral. The aim of this evidence is to rule out deficiencies in the learning environment as explanations for failure. Failures of the educational system should be discounted first, lest they be interpreted erroneously as failures of the child (Messick, 1984).

Reporting the findings of the National Research Council Panel on Selection and Placement of Students in Programs for the Mentally Retarded, Messick, (1984) suggests the provision of four kinds of evidence. First, evidence should be offered that the school is using effective programs and curricula. This evidence should support the effectiveness of those programs and curricula not just for students in general, but for the ethnic, linguistic, or socioeconomic group from which the referred students actually come. Second, evidence should be presented that the student in question has been adequately exposed to the curriculum. It should be documented that the student was not absent regularly from school and that the teacher implemented the curriculum effectively. Third, objective evidence should be offered that the child has not learned what was taught (e.g., through criterion-referenced tests, systematic behavioral recordings, student work samples). Finally, documentation should be provided to show that systematic efforts were made to correct the problem such as introducing remedial approaches, changing the curriculum materials, or trying a new teacher.

A third refinement is the review of referral requests. Review seems to be conducted most often at the building level. In this system, teacher referrals are reviewed by the principal—or by a committee consisting of the principal, guidance counselor, or other building staff—before being forwarded to the pupil evaluation team. The review is de-

signed to encourage teachers and principals to make greater attempts to deal with problem situations within the regular classroom and local school, and, as a result, to limit the occurrence of inappropriate referrals.

The three refinements described—consultation, evidence, and review—are the major elements of a prereferral intervention model. While many variations on this model exist, prereferral intervention has become an important component in the referral process, helping to ensure that those students referred are truly the ones most in need of special education services.

REFERENCES

Algozzine, B., Christenson, S., & Ysseldyke, J. (1982). Probabilities associated with the referral to placement process. *Teacher Education & Special Education, 5,* 19–23.

Bennett, R. E. (1981). Assessment of exceptional children: Guidelines for practice. *Diagnostique, 7,* 5–13.

Bickel, W. E. (1982). Classifying mentally retarded students: A review of placement practices in special education. In K. A. Heller, W. H. Holtzman, & S. Messick, *Placing children in special education: A strategy for equity.* Washington, DC: National Academy.

Heller, K. A., Holtzman, W. H., & Messick, S. (1982). *Placing children in special education: A strategy for equity.* Washington, DC: National Academy.

Messick, S. (1984). Placing children in special education: Findings of the National Academy of Sciences Panel. *Educational Researcher, 13*(3), 3–8.

U.S. Office of Education. (1977). Education of handicapped children: Implementation of Part B of the Education of the Handicapped Act. *Federal Register, 42*(163), 42474–42518.

Ysseldyke, J. E., & Algozzine, B. (1984). *Introduction to special education.* Boston: Houghton Mifflin.

Zins, J. E., & Curtis, M. (1984). Building consultation into the educational service delivery system. In C. A. Maher, R. J. Illback, & J. E. Zins (Eds.), *Organizational psychology in the schools: A handbook for professionals.* Springfield, IL: Thomas.

RANDY ELLIOT BENNETT
MARY LOUISE LENNON
Educational Testing Service,
Princeton, New Jersey

EDUCATION FOR ALL HANDICAPPED CHILDREN ACT OF 1975
PREREFERAL INTERVENTIONS

REFLEX

A reflex is an automatic connection between a stimulus and a response. One example is the knee-jerk reflex. Another is the reflexive constriction of the pupil in response to light.

Historically, the concept of the reflex has captured the

imagination of many theorists who wished to emphasize the mechanical nature of behavior. René Descartes proposed a hydraulic model to account for the behavior of nonhuman animals. The Russian physiologist Ivan Sechenov (1863/1965) argued that all behavior, including that of humans, is reflexive (meaning that it is determined). Ivan Pavlov and other theorists of learning have used such terms as conditioned reflex to imply that even learned behaviors are mechanically determined and that they can be described as stimulus-response connections.

Certain human reflexes can be observed only in infancy (Peiper, 1963). For example, infants reflexively grasp any object placed firmly in the palm of the hand. Newborns grasp an elevated bar tightly enough to support their own weight, at least briefly. If someone strokes the sole of an infant's foot, the infant extends the big toe and fans the others (this is known as the Babinski reflex). If someone touches an infant's cheek, an infant who is awake will often, but not always, turn toward the stroked cheek and begin to suck.

Infant reflexes are suppressed in older children and adults, but the connections responsible for the reflexes are not destroyed. The infant reflexes may return as a result of brain damage, especially damage to the frontal lobes of the cerebral cortex. Neurologists often test for the presence of the Babinski reflex or the grasp reflex as a means of detecting possible dysfunction of the frontal lobes. The infant reflexes may also return temporarily as a result of interference with cerebral activity, such as that caused by an epileptic seizure, excessive levels of carbon dioxide, or certain drugs (Paterson & Richter, 1933).

REFERENCES

Paterson, A. S., & Richter, C. P. (1933). Action of scopolamine and carbon dioxide on catalepsy produced by bulbocapnine. *Archives of Neurology & Psychiatry, 29,* 231–240.

Peiper, A. (1963). *Cerebral function in infancy and childhood.* New York: Consultants Bureau.

Sechenov, I. (1863/1965). *Reflexes of the brain.* Cambridge, MA: MIT.

JAMES W. KALAT
North Carolina State University

BEHAVIORISM
BEHAVIOR MODIFICATION
DEVELOPMENTAL MILESTONES

REGIONAL MEDIA CENTERS FOR THE DEAF

In 1959 the U.S. Office of Education implemented a program, under PL 85-905, to provide captioned films and related media to assist in bringing deaf persons into the mainstream of American life. The program featured the development and dissemination of highly specialized media services and products through four regional media centers. In the 1960s, 13 special education instructional media centers were established in addition to the four regional centers for the deaf. By the end of that decade, those 17 centers had been consolidated into four area learning resource centers (ALRCs). The ALRCs conducted activities related to educational media and technology for all handicapped persons, but specialized centers within the ALRC structure provided educational media and technology services for deaf persons. In 1972 the National Center on Education Media and Materials for the Handicapped replaced the ALRCs.

Currently, the Media Services and Captioned Films Program under Part F of the Education of the Handicapped Act includes support for the captioning and lending of films, for educational media and materials centers, and for projects in educational media and technology research, production, distribution, and training. Deaf individuals remain the principal focus of the program, although its scope has broadened to benefit persons with other disabilities.

SHIRLEY A. JONES
*Virginia Polytechnic Institute
and State University*

REGIONAL RESOURCE CENTERS (RRCs)

The Regional Resource Centers (RRCs) were created by the Elementary and Secondary Education Act, Title 6, of 1965. They were intended to assist state educational agencies (SEAs) in the implementation of special education services at a time when special education was just beginning to be recognized as a national concern. The RRCs were intended to help SEAs and local educational agencies (LEAs) in the development of special education services and resources by serving as agents in planning, programming, service delivery, training, and the creation of instructional materials.

The actual operations of the RRCs proceeded through a variety of agencies, including state educational departments, universities, and LEAs. The funding was not as generous as originally intended because the federal government envisioned RRCs as a nationwide enterprise. In the first funding cycle (1970–1974), Pennsylvania established an RRC whose services were directed statewide. Other RRCs, however, had multistate service areas; e.g., the Southwest Regional Resource Center served Arizona, Colorado, Nevada, New Mexico, and the Bureau of Indian Affairs. In multistate agencies, the major modes of service were information, consultation, and in-service training. In state-limited programs such as that of Pennsylvania, it was easier to focus services on specified state needs. For example, Pennsylvania used its funds to create diagnostic-prescriptive programs and to help fund classes to validate them (National Association of State Directors of Special Education, 1976).

A later round of funding of RRCs (1974–1977) resulted in some states being refunded and others funded for the first time. While some states such as New York and Pennsylvania, maintained statewide services, efforts were being made to move to multistate and regional operations. Thus, the Southeastern Regional Resource Center at Auburn University, in Montgomery, Alabama, was given the responsibility for Alabama, Florida, Georgia, Louisiana, Mississippi, Puerto Rico, South Carolina, and the U.S. Virgin Islands. Separate agencies were split off from the RRCs to assist in the provision of instructional resources to special educators. These were the Area Learning Resource Centers. By 1983, with legislative amendments to the Education of the Handicapped Act, the RRCs became a matter of discretionary support and funding on the part of states. They were adopted in various forms by state educational agencies or subsumed by the SEAs into other entities.

REFERENCE

National Association of State Directors of Special Education. (1976). *A survey of opinions of state directors of special education on Regional Resource Centers: Report.* Washington, DC: Bureau of Education for the Handicapped.

DON BRASWELL
Research Foundation,
City University of
New York

SPECIAL EDUCATION, FEDERAL IMPACT ON SPECIAL EDUCATION PROGRAMS

REGRESSION (STATISTICAL)

Regression is a term widely used in behavioral research (multiple regression). It has come to mean both a statistical technique and a statistical phenomenon. The phenomenon or artifact of statistical regression is addressed here. Simply, regression is a way to say that two behaviors or variables are not perfectly related to each other. For example, high school performance and freshman year grade point average (GPA) typically correlate about .5. Regression refers to the fact that when a researcher uses one variable to predict the other (high school performance to predict freshman GPA), the predicted score will be less extreme than the predictor score. In the example just given, a predicted freshman GPA will be .5 times the high

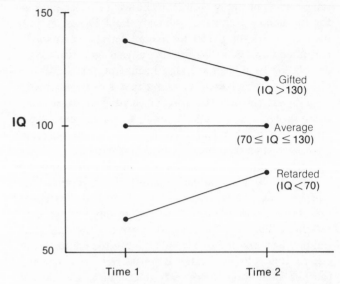

Examples of hypothetical regression effects between two testings for groups of children with IQs at three levels.

school rank in standard deviation units. A student one standard deviation above average on high school performance will be predicted to be one-half standard deviation above average for his or her class in GPA at the end of the freshman year.

The phenomenon was noted by Galton (and others before him) in his studies of human characteristics in the nineteenth century. He termed it regression to the mean, since the expected or predicted performance is always closer to the mean in standard deviations than is the predictor. Galton showed that sons of tall fathers were less extreme in their tallness than their fathers. Note that regression does not describe the actual performance, only its relative extremity. Thus the sons, through better nutrition, were generally taller than their fathers. They were generally, however, less extreme. Also, the regression phenomenon is a statistical condition applied to groups of scores. While we can use the prediction for an individual, we cannot specify that every individual will be less extreme, only that on average, the cases to which the prediction applies will be less extreme. Thus sons of 6-ft fathers who, let us say, are one standard deviation above average, may average 6 ft, 1 in. (which is .7 standard deviations above average height of the sons), but they are not uniformly the same height. Some may be under 6 ft in height, others well over 6 ft. Their average is 6 ft, 1 in.

The significance of regression for special education is that the clients tend to be extreme in some way. Special education students by definition score differently, often extremely, on tests or observation scales with respect to the entire population of students. Thus when a second measure is made on the students, they will be observed, through regression, to be less extreme (see Figure, for example). Sometimes this artifact is confused with instructional or program improvement. Hopkins (1968), in a classic paper on the topic, detailed the problem for special educators. He pointed out that in attempting to test the effects of treatments for special education students, the students are sometimes matched with nonspecial education students. Matching is a keyword that should always force the researcher or reader to consider regression effect. In such studies, the special education students, having been selected as extreme on one test, will exhibit regression on another test, perhaps the posttest in a research study. Their matched control group, also extreme owing to matching, will also show regression on the posttest. Unless the two groups have identical population means (a highly unlikely condition), they will show different amounts of regression, so that the difference between the groups found on the posttest may be due entirely to differential regression. Thus matching is a poor substitute for techniques such as randomization in comparative research. Similarly, single group designs, in which one treatment group is measured before and after treatment, is at risk to show regression effects. While the regression effect can be estimated in some situations, such designs are poor substitutes for carefully planned experimental designs.

REFERENCES

Hopkins, K. D. (1968). Regression and the matching fallacy in quasi-experimental research. *Journal of Special Education, 3*, 329–336.

VICTOR L. WILLSON
Texas A&M University

REGULAR CLASS PLACEMENT

See MAINSTREAMING.

REHABILITATION

The term rehabilitation refers to any process, procedure, or program that enables a disabled individual to function at a more independent and personally satisfying level. This functioning should include all aspects—physical, mental, emotional, social, educational, and vocational—of the individual's life. A disabled person may be defined as one who has any chronic mental or physical incapacity caused by injury, disease, or congenital defect that interferes with his or her independence, productivity, or goal attainment. The range of disabilities is wide and varied, including such conditions as autism, mental retardation,

muscular dystrophy, and a variety of neurological and orthopedic disorders. These disparate conditions may appear singly or in concert. Clearly, the process that is designed to assist persons in obtaining an optimal level of functioning is a complex one.

The complexity of the rehabilitation process necessitates a team approach that involves a range of professionals almost as broad and varied as the types of conditions addressed. Goldenson, Dunham, and Dunham (1978) discuss no fewer than 39 rehabilitation specialists in their handbook. Their list includes such diverse professions as orientation and mobility training, genetic counseling, biomedical engineering, and orthotics and prosthetics, in addition to numerous medical, mental health, therapeutic, and special education fields. In view of the potential involvement of such an array of professionals, it becomes particularly important to remember that the rehabilitation process is not one that is done to or for disabled persons, but rather one that is done with disabled persons and often their families as well. If a person is to become as fully functional as his or her abilities will allow, a process that fosters dependence is a self-defeating one.

It is necessary for the professionals involved in the rehabilitation process to function as a team rather than as separate individuals. McInerney and Karan (1981) have pointed out that without information sharing and cooperative integration, the rehabilitation process will not fit the needs of the client. The client should not be expected to fit the needs of the service delivery system. As rehabilitation is a process, not an isolated treatment, a continuum of services must be provided to give the disabled person assistance in all aspects of life. A program that is cohesive in approach, regardless of the number of professionals involved, is essential. In addition, these services must alter to meet the client's changing needs.

REFERENCES

Goldenson, R. M., Dunham, J. R., & Dunham, C. S. (Eds.). (1978). *Disability and rehabilitation handbook*. New York: McGraw-Hill.

McInerney, M., & Karan, O. C. (1981). Federal legislation and the integration of special education and vocational rehabilitation. *Mental Retardation, 19,* 21–24.

LAURA KINZIE BRUTTING
*University of Wisconsin,
Madison*

REHABILITATION COUNSELING
VOCATIONAL TRAINING OF THE HANDICAPPED

REHABILITATION ACT OF 1973

The Rehabilitation Act of 1973 authorizes comprehensive vocational rehabilitation services designed to help physically and mentally handicapped persons become employable. The act also authorizes service projects for persons with special rehabilitation needs. For severely handicapped persons without apparent employment potential, the act authorizes services to promote independent living. Training programs are provided to help ensure a supply of skilled persons to rehabilitate handicapped persons. The act also authorizes a research program, a national council to review federal policy regarding handicapped persons, and a compliance board to help enforce accessibility standards for the handicapped.

The act authorizes state grants for comprehensive services designed to enable handicapped individuals to become employable. Each state receives an allotment of federal funding that must be matched on a 20% state to 80% federal ratio. Federal funds are allotted on the basis of population and per capita income, with the lower per capita income states receiving a relatively higher allotment on a per capita basis.

Funds are authorized for various service projects for handicapped persons. These projects include funds for programs to serve the severely handicapped, migrant workers, American Indians, and other groups with special needs. Support is provided for training of rehabilitation personnel. State grants and discretionary funds are authorized for independent living services. A client assistance program is required in each state to help clients and applicants obtain services funded under the act.

The National Council on the Handicapped is composed of 15 members appointed by the president. The council establishes general policies for the National Institute on Handicapped Research, advises the president and Congress on the development of programs carried out under the Rehabilitation Act, and reviews and evaluates federal policy regarding programs for the handicapped.

The Architectural and Transportation Barriers Compliance Board was authorized to ensure compliance with the Architectural Barriers Act of 1968 and to promote accessibility for handicapped individuals. The board is composed of 11 members from the general public (five of whom must be handicapped individuals) and 11 representatives of federal agencies.

The National Institute on Handicapped Research administers funds for the rehabilitation research programs. The institute, through a federal interagency committee, is responsible for the coordination of all major federal research related to handicapped persons.

JAMES BUTTON
United States Department of Education

REHABILITATION ACT OF 1973, SECTION 504 OF

REHABILITATION ACT OF 1973, SECTION 504 OF

Section 504 of what is commonly called the Rehabilitation Act is frequently cited as an important precursor to the passage of *PL 94-142* two years later (Bersoff, 1982). Section 504, among other things, protects the rights of handicapped children and precludes discrimination in employment and education. The stipulations of the Rehabilitation Act apply to the programs receiving federal financial assistance.

The Rehabilitation Act was cited in the noted *Larry P.* vs. *Riles* decision by Judge Peckham in 1979. This decision cited the state as being in noncompliance with Section 504 in its use of intelligence tests for making placement decisions in special education. Certainly, the Rehabilitation Act of 1973 has had an important impact on special education practice by encouraging more sophisticated and humane treatment of handicapped children.

REFERENCE

Bersoff, D. N. (1982). The legal regulation of school psychology. In C. R. Reynolds & T. B. Gutkin (Eds.), *The handbook of school psychology*. New York: Wiley.

RANDY W. KAMPHAUS
Eastern Kentucky University

LARRY P.

REHABILITATION LITERATURE

Rehabilitation Literature is a bimonthly journal published by the National Easter Seal Society. It is principally an educational service journal that abstracts articles published elsewhere and reviews books, journals, films, treatment programs, etc. dealing with the rehabilitation of all types of human disabilities. At least one original feature article appears in each issue. It is written at a level for professional personnel and students training to become professional service providers in all disciplines concerned with the rehabilitation of persons with handicapping conditions.

This abstracting and review journal receives wide circulation among rehabilitation workers and is well regarded in the field. It has been in continuous publication since January 1940; it was taken over by the National Easter Seal Society in 1959. *Rehabilitation Literature* has taken the position that, as an educational service of a large charitable organization, up to 100 reproductions of articles may be made without permission provided they are for free distribution within an organization or classroom. Other rights of reproduction have been reserved. Frequent topics of interest to special educators appear in nearly every issue, bridging such broad areas as stuttering, learning disabilities, aphasias, spina bifida, reading, and general techniques in special education.

CECIL R. REYNOLDS
Texas A&M University

REISMAN, FREDRICKA KAUFFMAN (1930–   )

Fredricka Kauffman Reisman received her BA in psychology (1952), her MS in education (1963), and her PhD in math education (1968), all from Syracuse University. Her main fields of interest are mathematics education, the integration of computing into the assessment and instruction of mathematics, the preparation of teachers, and diagnostic teaching. Her work has emphasized the prevention of learning difficulties rather than prescription or remediation. Reisman believes teachers need to be aware of learner and content characteristics and the design of instructional environments that use modern technology.

Fredricka Kauffman Reisman

Reisman has been included in several of the Who's Who in America series. Reisman's published works include *A Guide to the Diagnostic Teaching of Arithmetic, Teaching Mathematics: Methods and Content, Sequential Assessment in Mathematics Inventories: K–8 (SAMI)*, and *Becoming a Teacher: Grades K–8.*

REFERENCES

Reisman, F. K. (1981). *Teaching mathematics: Methods and content* (2nd ed.). Boston: Houghton Mifflin.

Reisman, F. K. (1982). *A guide to the diagnostic teaching of arithmetic* (3rd ed.). Columbus, OH: Merrill.

Reisman, F. K. (1986). *Sequential assessment in mathematics inventories K–8*. San Antonio, TX: Psychological Corporation.

Reisman, F. K., & Payne, B. (1987). *Becoming a teacher: Grades K–8*. Columbus, OH: Merrill.

E. VALERIE HEWITT
Texas A&M University

REITAN-INDIANA NEUROPSYCHOLOGICAL TEST BATTERY FOR CHILDREN (RINTBC)

The Reitan-Indiana Neuropsychological Test Battery for Children (RINTBC; ages 5 through 8), along with the Halstead Neuropsychological Test Battery for Children (ages 9 through 14) and the Halstead Neuropsychological Test Battery for Adults (ages 15 and older), constitute a global battery commonly referred to as the Halstead-Reitan Neuropsychological Test Battery. Each of these three batteries was devised as a tool for the assessment of brain-behavior relationships. The RINTBC was developed after it became apparent that many of the items on the battery for older children were too difficult for children below the age of 9 (Reitan, 1979).

The developmental research for the RINTBC, conducted at the Neuropsychology Laboratory of the Indiana University Medical Center, began in the mid-1950s. R. M. Reitan, a student of W. C. Halstead, modified several of the tests from Halstead's original adult battery (Halstead, 1947), and also created six new tests to complete this battery for young children. The modified tests include children's versions of the Category Test, Tactual Performance Test, Sensory-Perceptual Disturbances Tests, Finger Oscillation Test, and Aphasia Screening Test. New tests include the Color Form Test, Progressive Figures Test, and Matching Picture Tests; these were designed to measure cognitive flexibility and concept formation. The Target Test and the Individual Performance Test assess reception and expression of visuo-spatial relationships, while the Marching Test measures gross motor coordination (Reitan, 1979). The RINTBC customarily is supplemented by the Reitan-Klove Lateral Dominance Examination, the Reitan-Klove Sensory-Perceptual Examination, Strength of Grip, the Wechsler Preschool and Primary Scale of Intelligence, and the Wide Range Achievement Test (Reitan, 1974).

Reitan and Davison (1974) present a review of research that has demonstrated that the RINTBC effectively differentiates brain-damaged from normal functioning children, provided the test is administered and interpreted properly by trained professionals.

REFERENCES

Halstead, W. C. (1947). *Brain and intelligence*. Chicago: University of Chicago Press.

Reitan, R. M. (1974). Psychological effects of cerebral lesions in children of early school age. In R. M. Reitan & L. A. Davison (Eds.), *Clinical neuropsychology: Current status and applications* (pp. 53–89). New York: Hemisphere.

Reitan, R. M. (1979). *Manual for the administration of neuropsychological test batteries for adults and children*. Tucson, AZ: Reitan Neuropsychology Laboratories.

Reitan, R. M., & Davison, L. A. (1974). *Clinical neuropsychology*, New York: Hemisphere.

GALE A. HARR
*Maple Heights City Schools,
Maple Heights, Ohio*

HALSTEAD-REITAN NEUROPSYCHOLOGICAL TEST
BATTERY
NEUROPSYCHOLOGY

RELATED SERVICES

The Education for All Handicapped Children Act of 1975 (PL 94-142) holds education agencies responsible not only for the provision of special education services, but for the delivery of related services as well. Related services are defined as "transportation, and such developmental, corrective, and other supportive services . . . as may be required to assist a handicapped child to benefit from special education." (Section 4a).

Among the services specifically included within the related services definition are speech pathology and audiology, psychological services, medical services (for diagnostic and evaluation purposes only), physical and occupational therapy, recreation, and counseling. However, because the phrase "other supportive services . . . as may be required" is included in the law, the precise definition of related services remains the subject of debate.

Disputes regarding the type and extent of related services required under PL 94-142 have been the focus of a series of court cases, including the first Supreme Court decision on federal special education law. Litigation has involved questions of eligibility, definition, and financial responsibility. All three issues were addressed in *Hendrick Hudson Board of Education* v. *Rowley*. In this case, the Supreme Court ruled that a high-achieving deaf student need not be provided a sign language interpreter at the school district's expense, given her demonstrated ability to benefit from the educational program already provided. While the Court's decision focused on the narrow issue of one student's right to a particular related service, it suggested that the term "related services" need not be interpreted broadly to mean any service that would improve the quality of a handicapped child's education.

In the subsequent case of *Irving Independent School District* v. *Tatro*, definition was again at issue, with the focus on medical services required by the law. Medical services are defined in the law as those services provided by a physician for diagnostic and evaluation purposes. The school district argued that catheterizing a student (inserting a tube to drain the bladder) several times daily constituted a nondiagnostic medical service and therefore was not a related service for which the district was responsible. However, the Supreme Court ruled that catheterization is included within the related services definition because it is a simple nonmedical procedure that can be administered by a school nurse. As such, the Court felt that catheterization was representative of the other supportive services needed to provide "the meaningful access to education that Congress envisioned" ("Court Backs Catheterization," 1984).

A major issue underlying both Supreme Court cases is financial responsibility. Related services are expensive to provide and school districts are struggling to define the limits of their fiscal responsibility. Interpreting the *Rowley* decision, U.S. District Judge John A. Nordberg said, "the Court recognized the unfairness of imposing large financial burdens on states on the basis of broad interpretation of ambiguous language in funding statutes" ("Students Have," 1983). Even with a conservative interpretation of what constitutes related services, state and local education agencies often find themselves in a difficult financial position.

Dealing with the financial ramifications of providing related services is a continuing challenge. In its *Seventh Annual Report to Congress* (1985), the United States Department of Education described effective policies developed to provide related services in cost-efficient ways. One strategy has been to pool resources among local education agencies to make a range of related service specialists available to students. Another has been to seek third-party funding from public and private insurance providers. A third approach involves establishing joint funding and cooperative programming arrangements among education and human service agencies. For example, a school district and local mental health agency agree that the mental health agency will provide and assume the related services costs for the district's seriously emotionally disturbed children (Maher & Bennett, 1984). Each of these arrangements exemplifies efforts to share financial responsibility and work cooperatively to improve the quality of related services available to handicapped children.

REFERENCES

Court backs catheterization, limits fees in handicap cases. (1984). *Education of the Handicapped, 10*(14), 1–3.

Maher, C. A., & Bennett, R. E. (1984). *Planning and evaluating special education services*. Englewood Cliffs, NJ: Prentice-Hall.

Students have no right to free psychiatric care, court rules. (1983, Aug. 24). *Education of the Handicapped, 9*(17), 7–8.

U.S. Department of Education. (1984). *Seventh annual report to Congress on the implementation of the Education of the Handicapped Act*. Washington, DC: U.S. Government Printing Office.

MARY LOUISE LENNON
RANDY ELLIOT BENNETT
*Educational Testing Service,
Princeton, New Jersey*

DIAGNOSIS IN SPECIAL EDUCATION
EDUCATION FOR ALL HANDICAPPED CHILDREN ACT OF 1975
INTERPRETERS FOR THE DEAF
SPEECH-LANGUAGE SERVICES

RELIABILITY

Test reliability refers to the precision of a test as a measuring device. What is the likelihood of obtaining similar results on a second administration of a test? If test results are to be meaningful and useful, precision of measurement is a highly desirable characteristic for the test or measurement procedure used. Test users must evaluate carefully information about test reliability provided in a test manual to determine the reliability of a test for its stated purpose.

Two types of statistical evidence of reliability are usually reported in test manuals: the reliability coefficient and the standard error of measurement. The reliability coefficient is a general indicator of test precision and is useful when making comparisons among tests. The standard error of measurement, on the other hand, is useful when interpreting the test score of an individual because it permits a statement of confidence to be placed in the particular score (Anastasi, 1982). Both aspects of test reliability will be discussed, along with certain principles that merit careful consideration in the interpretation of reliability data.

Gulliksen (1950) notes that a basic definition underlying reliability states that an obtained test score (X_0) is composed of two parts: a true score (X_t) portion and error (X_e) (Formula 1):

$$X_0 = X_t + X_e$$

Formula 1 can be rewritten in terms of the variation among individuals, or variance (s^2), attributable to these sources (Formula 2):

$$s_0{}^2 = s_t{}^2 + s_e{}^2$$

Formula 2 states that the variance that occurs among observed, or obtained, scores ($s_0{}^2$) equals the true score variance ($s_t{}^2$) plus the error variance ($s_e{}^2$). Reliability (r_{xx}) is defined as the ratio of total variance attributable to true scores to the total variance of observed scores (Formula 3):

$$r_{xx} = \frac{s_t{}^2.}{s_0{}^2}$$

The r_{xx} in Formula 3 indicates that the reliability coefficient is actually a type of correlation coefficient. In practice, the reliability coefficients for most published tests cluster in the .80s and .90s (Anastasi, 1982). If, for example, a standardized reading test for grade six reported a reliability coefficient of .90, this would mean that 90% of the variance among individuals was true variance, with 10% attributable to error. Obviously, the smaller the error, the greater the confidence in the accuracy of the test scores.

There are several procedures for estimating reliability. Readers of test manuals will encounter several types of reliability coefficients: test-retest, alternate forms, split-half, and internal consistency are the most common. Each of these permits different sources of error to be reflected in the test scores. Each type of reliability coefficient is estimated from either a single test administration or from

two test administrations separated by a brief time interval (Thorndike & Hagen, 1977).

Test-retest reliability is determined by administering the same test twice, with an intervening time interval, and then correlating the scores. Differences in individual scores on the two testings would be attributed to the differential effects of factors specific to each test session. Alternate-forms reliability is estimated by administering two parallel test forms on separate occasions, with an intervening time interval, and then correlating the scores. Differences in individual scores on the two testings would be attributed both to differential factors affecting performance on each test occasion, and to different samples of content used in each test form. Alternate-forms reliability provides the most rigorous estimate of reliability (Thorndike & Hagen, 1977). Both test-retest and alternate-forms reliability require two separate test administrations; however, it is possible to estimate reliability from a single administration of a test. Split-half reliability estimates are obtained by dividing a test into two equivalent half-tests and correlating the results. Actually, the results are based on tests half as long as the total test and must be corrected to full-length estimates by use of the Spearman-Brown formula to adjust for test length. Individual score differences would be attributed to differences in the two content samples. Internal consistency reliability is estimated from item performance. Sources of error variance reflected include content and heterogeneity of the construct or trait measured by the test (Anastasi, 1982).

Reliability coefficients must be interpreted cautiously because a number of factors may affect their magnitude. Among these influences are the range of ability present in the group used to estimate reliability, the ability level of the group, and the extent to which test scores are dependent on speed or rate of work (Anastasi, 1982).

The size of a reliability coefficient is directly related to the range or extent of individual differences present in the group used to obtain reliability estimates. If, for example, an easy mathematics test were administered to a group of mathematicians, the reliability coefficient would be low owing to the fact that all the mathematicians would probably achieve perfect scores. There is little or no variability in a group such as this; hence, the reliability coefficient would be near zero. In a related sense, reliability coefficients may differ for groups different in overall ability or other demographic characteristics. The composition of a particular group must always be described clearly to sharpen the meaning of a particular reliability coefficient (Anastasi, 1982).

One additional consideration needing careful attention is the extent to which test scores are influenced by speed or rate of work. To the extent that a test is a speed test, the reliability coefficient will be spuriously high if reliability is estimated from a single test administration, such as that used to estimate split-half or internal-consistency reliability. Alternate-forms reliability or some variant of this procedure is recommended for tests dependent on speed (Anastasi, 1982). Most educational tests are power tests that do not depend on speed but allow ample time for most examinees to answer items appropriate to their ability.

The standard error of measurement (SEM), which is obtained from a reliability coefficient, is useful in the interpretation of individual test scores. If it were possible to test an individual many times with the same test and ignore any practice effects, the scores could be expected to vary owing to measurement error. The SEM indicates the extent to which an individual's test score could be expected to deviate from his or her unknown "true" test score. If it is assumed that the various observed test scores are distributed normally around the person's "true" score, then it becomes possible to specify that the observed score is expected to be within the range ± 1 SEM about two times out of three, or ± 2 SEMs 95 times out of 100. The SEM is computed from Formula 4:

$$\text{SEM} = S_x\sqrt{1 - r_{xx}},$$

where S_x = the standard deviation of scores on measure X, and

r_{xx} = the obtained reliability coefficient

Once the SEM is obtained, it becomes possible to construct confidence bands that portray realistically the amount of error associated with a particular test score (Anastasi, 1982). For example, if the corrected split-half reliability coefficient for a 50-item reading comprehension test given in grade six were found to be .91, and the standard deviation of raw scores was observed to be 10, then the SEM (using Formula 4) is 3.0. If a particular pupil obtains a raw score of 35, it becomes possible to state with 68% certainty that the pupil's "true" reading score occurs within the range 35 $\pm$ 3, or 32–38; the obtained score ± 1 SEM is used for most types of test score interpretation (Mehrens & Lehmann, 1984). If the test user wants a greater degree of certainty, it is possible to use ± 2 SEM. Thus, in the same example it is possible to state with 95% certainty that the pupil's "true" score occurred within the range 35 $\pm$ 6, or 29–41. Establishing confidence bands such as these is highly recommended because it represents a sound way to take account of measurement error in the interpretation of test results.

REFERENCES

Anastasi, A. (1982). *Psychological testing* (5th ed.). New York: Macmillan.

Gulliksen, H. (1950). *Theory of mental tests.* New York: Wiley.

Mehrens, W. A., & Lehmann, I. J. (1984). *Measurement and evaluation in education and psychology.* New York: CBS College.

Thorndike, R. L., & Hagen, E. P. (1977). *Measurement and evaluation in psychology and education.* New York: Wiley.

GARY J. ROBERTSON
American Guidance Service,
Circle Pine, Minnesota

ASSESSMENT
MEASUREMENT

RELIGIOUS EDUCATION FOR THE HANDICAPPED

Religious education for the handicapped refers to the moral and spiritual education of children with disabilities. It can be traced to l'Abbé de l' Epée and other ordained ministers who established schools for handicapped children with the specific purpose of bringing their students to the knowledge of God. Parents have also been instrumental in procuring religious education for their handicapped children by demanding that these children be given religious instruction and taught to participate in religious activities. Both priests and parents have insisted that handicapped children have the same need for spiritual development as other children and that they have the right to an equal place in the church or synagogue (Ellis, Ellis, & Warren, 1984).

The 1980s have seen a growing focus on the religious needs of handicapped individuals, as evidenced by the designation of the year 1983 as the International Religious Year of Persons with Disabilities (Ellis, Ellis, & Warren, 1984). There have been a number of church groups throughout the country that have adopted resolutions, or issued pastoral or policy statements, related to ministering to persons with handicapping conditions. In addition, a questionnaire concerning religion and handicapped persons was sent by the President's Committee on Employment of the Handicapped to 24 religious groups having a million or more members.

Issues in the religious education of handicapped persons include the integration of individuals with disabilities into the church/synagogue community; the sparseness of literature on special religious education; church/synagogue accessibility (architecture, attitudes, communication, awareness); formation programs for the religious educators of children with special needs; organizational considerations; and effective teaching techniques. There is also the issue of the unique position of the church or synagogue in informing, educating, and motivating people to become involved in facilitating the transition of the severely disabled from social isolation to full participation in the community (Hawkins-Shepard, 1984).

Curriculum materials for the religious education of children with special needs are available (Hall, 1982), as well as suggestions for the adaptation of regular religious education curricula (Paul, 1983) and advice about religious education for parents and teachers of handicapped children (Hall, 1982; Paul, 1983).

Common difficulties concerning religious education for handicapped learners include complaints that religious development is a neglected area in the lives of handicapped children; that too few churches and synagogues provide programs on a national, regional, or local level for the religious involvement of handicapped individuals; and that many churches separate handicapped worshippers into special groups in special parts of the church or only provide opportunities for participation in part of the total worship experience (Denton, 1972).

REFERENCES

Denton, D. (1972). Religious services for deaf people. *Journal of Rehabilitation of the Deaf, 6*, 42–46.

Ellis, H., Ellis E., & Warren, G. T. (Feb. 1984). An open letter to pastors and parents. *The Exceptional Parent, 14* (1), 39.

Hall, S. (1982). Into the Christian community: Religious education with disabled persons. Washington, DC: National Catholic Educational Association.

Hawkins-Shepard, C. (1984). Bridging the gap between religious education and special education. *Proceedings of the 1984 National Convention of the Council for Exceptional Children*, Washington, DC.

Paul, J. (1983). *The exceptional child: A guidebook for churches and community agencies.* Syracuse, NY: Syracuse University Press.

ROSEMARY GAFFNEY
Hunter College, City University of New York

PRIVATE SCHOOLS AND SPECIAL EDUCATION
PRIVILEGED COMMUNICATION

REMEDIAL AND SPECIAL EDUCATION (RASE)

In 1982, PRO-ED, a publishing company, purchased the journal *Exceptional Education Quarterly* from Aspen Systems Corporation. Two years later, in 1984, the name of the journal was changed to *Remedial and Special Education* (RASE) and the issues printed were increased to six per year. That same year, PRO-ED acquired two additional journals, *Topics in Learning and Learning Disabilities* (from Aspen) and *The Journal for Special Educators* (from the American Association of Special Educators); these were also merged into RASE. The journal is devoted to topics involving the education of persons for whom typical instruction is not effective. Emphasis is on interpretations of research literature and on recommendations for the practice of remedial and special education. All articles printed have been peer reviewed.

DONALD D. HAMMILL
PRO-ED, Inc., Austin, Texas

PRO-ED

REMEDIAL INSTRUCTION

The term remediation is derived from the word *remedy*, meaning a correction, repair, or cure of something that is awry. Medicines are medical remedies. Remedies in education are called remediations (Ysseldyke, & Algozzine, 1984).

Remedial teaching has been distinguished from developmental teaching and from corrective teaching. As usually construed, developmental teaching is the type of instruction given to the majority of students attending regular classes (Otto & McMenemy, 1966; Rupley & Blair, 1983).

Developmental instruction in the modern classroom is likely to be guided by clearly defined instructional objectives. Thus developmental reading instruction has been described as "a systematic guided series of steps, procedures or actions intended to result in learning or in the reaching of a desired goal" (Harris & Hodges, 1981, p. 157).

Corrective and remedial instruction both are forms of academic assistance provided to students who need special help in various areas of instruction. When that assistance is offered by the classroom teacher within a regular classroom setting to students who are deficient in some particular skills or not achieving up to expectations in particular subject matters, help is identified as corrective instruction. Corrective instruction is given when the type of learning problem, or its degree, is not judged as severe enough to require specific types of remediation. Remedial instruction is usually given to students with more severe or persistent academic difficulties. Usually it is provided by a specialist in a particular skill or content area and in circumstances apart from the child's regular classroom. Remedial instruction often suggests a learning disability; indeed, remedial instructors often act as learning disability specialists.

Arbitrary standards often are set for eligibility for corrective or remedial services: within 2 years of grade expectation the child may be given corrective instruction, but beyond 2 years the child will receive remedial instruction.

While developmental and corrective as well as remedial instruction attempt to individualize according to students' needs, remedial instruction is most likely to address a student and his or her problems diagnostically and to offer intensive interventions (Reisman, 1982). Thus remedial instruction is likely to be provided to students whose academic deficiencies or disabilities appear so severe or specialized as to require more precise, intense, or individualized assistance.

In remedial instruction the distinction may be made between skill remediation and ability or process remediation. The first attempts to correct or strengthen particular academic skills such as decoding in reading, carrying in two column addition, and not writing out silent sounds in spelling. In the second, efforts are made to correct presumed deficits in cognitive processes such as perception, memory, and attention. A popular current process approach is that of teaching learning-handicapped children to more effectively use cognitive strategies in learning and school performance (Mann & Sabatino, 1985).

Since special education is based on individualized intensive interventions addressed to students who, because of their handicapping conditions, may not be able to keep up with their nonhandicapped peers, the notion of remediation, from a special educator's point of view, may be redundant. Indeed, the special education resource room, whether in regular or special education, is likely to be a place where remedial education is offered. Cawley (1984) believes that carefully controlled curricular approaches to the problems of learning-disabled students are likely to be more effective than traditional diagnostic-prescriptive remedial methods so often emphasized in remediation.

Remedial reading is the most frequently offered form of remedial or corrective help provided in grade school, both elementary and secondary. Remedial mathematics, writing, etc., also go on in regular education settings, but they are less likely to be carried out by remedial specialists. Remedial instruction is often provided at the college level as well as during the earlier grades. It is most often required by students who, either because of poor earlier preparation, problems in managing English, or specific cognitive deficits, require specialized help to succeed in higher education. Many colleges and other institutions of higher learning provide remedial writing.

REFERENCES

Cawley, J. F. (1984). Preface. In J. F. Cawley (Ed.), *Developmental teaching of mathematics for the learning disabled.* Rockville, MD: Aspen.

Harris, T. L., & Hodges, R. E. (Eds.). (1981). *A dictionary of reading and related terms* Newark, DE: International Reading Association.

Mann, L., & Sabatino, D. A. (1985). *Foundations of cognitive processes.* Rockville, MD: Aspen.

Otto, W., & McMenemy, R. A. (1966). *Corrective and remedial reading.* Boston: Houghton Mifflin.

Reisman, F. (1982). *A guide to the diagnostic teaching of arithmetic.* Columbus, OH: Merrill.

Rupley, W. H., & Blair, T.R. (1983). *Reading diagnosis and remediation: Class & clinic.* Boston: Houghton Mifflin.

Ysseldyke, J. E., & Algozzine, B. (1984). *Introduction to special education.* Boston: Houghton Mifflin.

LESTER MANN
*Hunter College, City University
of New York*

DIAGNOSTIC PRESCRIPTIVE TEACHING
DIRECT INSTRUCTION
READING, REMEDIAL

REMEDIAL READING

According to Smith (1965), the term remedial reading first appeared in the professional literature in a 1916 journal article by W. H. Uhl; however, like so many of the terms in the field of reading, the term remedial reading has no universally agreed on operational definition. The amount of confusion that exists with respect to the term was expressed well some 15 years ago by Goldberg and Schiffman (1972), who noted:

> Some educators refer to the problem category as remedial, strephosymbolia, associative learning disability, specific reading or language disability, congenital word blindness, primary reading retardation, or developmental dyslexia. One school district may refer to all retarded readers as remedial; another agency, in the same community, may use the term remedial for a small group of children with specific learning disabilities. (pp. 156–157)

Goldberg and Schiffman go on to point out that, because of the widely varying definitions, estimates of the percent of students requiring remedial reading instruction vary from as low as 1% to as high as 20%.

A Dictionary of Reading and Related Terms (Harris & Hodges, 1981) provides a realistic, though somewhat vague, definition of the term remedial reading:

> Any specialized reading instruction adjusted to the needs of a student who does not perform satisfactorily with regular reading instruction.
>
> Intensive specialized reading instruction for students reading considerably below expectancy.

Before examining this definition, it might be helpful to quickly introduce two reading terms that are frequently contrasted with the term remedial reading; they are developmental reading, and corrective reading. Developmental reading refers to instruction that is designed for and offered to the average child who is acquiring reading skills at an average rate. Group instruction, centering around the use of basal readers, is the typical approach to developmental reading instruction.

Corrective reading is a term usually applied to instruction that is offered to children who are essentially average intellectually, but who are slower than average in the rate at which they are acquiring reading skills; however, the disparity between where they are expected to be reading, usually based on age, grade placement, and intelligence, is not large. The difficulties that they are encountering are mild enough so that with some adjustments, the responsibility for their reading instruction can be assumed by a regular classroom teacher.

While it seems fairly easy to separate developmental reading from remedial reading, the distinction between corrective and remedial reading is not so clear. The first definition offered by Harris and Hodges would make the two indistinguishable; however, even the second definition offers no clear criteria for separating the two. Harris and Sipay (1985) list four characteristics that distinguish corrective from remedial programs. The first characteristic relates to where the treatment takes place. Remedial reading usually takes place in a special classroom or even in a special clinic. The second characteristic relates to who provides the treatment. Corrective instruction is usually offered by a classroom teacher while remedial instruction is within the province of a reading or learning disabilities specialist. Third is the number of children treated in a session. Group size is smaller for remedial instruction or is on a one-to-one basis. The final characteristic is the severity of the problem. Otto and McMenemey (1966) sum up this definitional problem when they write:

> In terms of diagnostic and instructional techniques, the distinction between actual corrective and remedial instruction is often one of degree rather than kind. Strictly remedial techniques tend to be more intensive and more highly individualized but usually not intrinsically different from corrective techniques. (pp. 38–39)

Some authors have tried to bring objectivity to the definition of remedial reading by defining it as referring to children who are reading 2 or more years below grade level. Unfortunately, this simple approach is fraught with problems. To begin with, years with regard to reading skill development are not equal interval units. Reading skills tend to develop rapidly during grades 1 through 3 and to develop at a negatively accelerating rate thereafter. A child who at the end of grade 2 has acquired no reading skills (hence is 2 years behind) is very different from an grade 8 student who has acquired grade 6 skills. Even Otto and McMenemy (1966), who are among the few professionals who attempt to justify the adoption of a 2-year criterion for defining a remedial reader, are quick to point out that it is "clearly unrealistic" in the early grades and that "slavish application of such an arbitrary criterion would be unfortunate" (p. 37).

A second major problems in adopting a 2-year disparity between where a child is expected to be in reading skill acquisition and where that child actually is relates to the method for calculating that disparity. In most cases, the disparity is based on a difference between actual, measured reading achievement of a student and the level he or she should have attained based on some measure of capacity to learn, usually an intelligence test. Unfortunately, there is no agreed on method for calculating the amount of disparity between expectancy and achievement. Stauffer, Abrams, and Pikulski (1978) have shown how widely different results will be achieved depending on the formula used to calculate the expected level of reading achievement. In addition, tests of intelligence and of reading can yield widely differing results depending on the tests used.

Yet another problem in defining remedial reading lies in the enormous overlap between the concepts of learning disabilities and remedial reading. Given our present level of diagnostic sophistication, distinguishing between these two classifications appears to depend almost totally on arbitrary local definitions or regulations or on funding considerations. Lewis (1983) presents an excellent summary of some of the major considerations that need to be taken into account in providing instruction for the student who is severely disabled in reading, regardless of whether that student is labeled as a remedial reader or as a child with a learning disability. The article is also excellent in providing evidence that challenges some widely held misconceptions about students who have severe reading problems.

The confused situation relative to the use of the term remedial reading and related terms, described by Goldberg and Schiffman earlier, continues to exist today; in fact, the confusion may be exacerbated by the introduction of even more terms.

While there are apparently no clear-cut ways to diagnostically differentiate among remedial readers, the learning disabled, corrective readers, dyslexics, etc., one might wonder if there are any instructional methods or materials that are unique to remedial reading. Textbooks dealing with this topic imply that there are. For example, Bond, et al. (1984) indicate that there are four important elements of remedial instruction: it is individualized; it encourages the reader; it uses effective teaching procedures; and it enlists cooperative efforts. While these elements are important to remedial reading, they are also important to all reading instruction. These authors go on to suggest that basal readers, the hallmark of developmental reading instruction, are a primary source of materials for remedial reading.

A careful reading of discussions of remedial reading suggests that the principles of teaching reading are the same regardless of whether we are concerned with remedial or developmental readers. The basic consideration is that remedial reading to based on a careful assessment of what the reader knows and needs to learn in terms of reading skills and that instruction then be at an appropriate level of challenge. Many of the techniques are similar to those used for teaching reading to achieving readers. For example, Rude and Oehlkers (1984) describe how a language experience approach to teaching reading, which centers around the use of reading materials that are dictated by the reader and written by the teacher, can be used for remedial reading; the language experience approach is also a major developmental technique for teaching reading. Nevertheless, there are three approaches that might be considered specifically designed for use in remedial reading.

The first approach is the use of high interest-low vocabulary materials. These materials are books, usually designed as a series, that are specifically written to appeal to the interests of older children, but that use a limited vocabulary. Harris and Sipay (1985) include a list of over 90 such series.

In the Fernald V-A-K-T approach, the letters V-A-K-T stand for visual, auditory, kinesthetic, and tactile. The approach was devised by Grace Fernald (1943) to treat children with learning problems. In this approach, children learn to read by using all four senses; they see words written by a teacher, they pronouce and hear those same words; they trace the written copy of the words so as to receive tactile and kinesthetic stimulation. The technique, which is highly prescribed, forces the learner to pay full attention to the word learning process. See Johnson (1966) and Stauffer, Abrams, and Pikulski (1978) for descriptions of this approach.

The Orton-Gillingham approach stresses the importance of learning phonics as the major reading skill. Students learn sounds for letters and are taught to blend the sounds to make words. This, too, is a highly structured and prescribed approach. It also uses multiple sensory stimuli. It is based on the work of an influential neurologist, Samuel T. Orton. The technique is fully described by Orton (1966) and Gillingham and Stillman (1966).

REFERENCES

Bond, G. L., Tinker, M. A., Wasson, B. B., & Wasson, J. B. (1984). *Reading difficulties: Their diagnosis and correction* (5th ed.). Englewood Cliffs, NJ: Prentice-Hall.

Fernald, G. M. (1943). *Remedial techniques in basic school subjects.* New York: McGraw-Hill.

Gillingham, A., & Stillman, B. W. (1966). *Remedial training for children with specific difficulty in reading, spelling, and penmanship* (7th ed.). Cambridge, MA: Educators Publishing Service.

Goldberg, H. K., & Schiffman, G. B. (1972). *Dyslexia: Problems of reading disabilities.* New York: Grune & Stratton.

Harris, A. J., & Sipay, E. R. (1985). *How to increase reading ability* (5th ed.). White Plains, NY: Longman.

Harris, T. L., & Hodges, R. E. (Eds.). (1981). *A dictionary of reading and related terms.* Newark, DE: International Reading Association.

Johnson, M. S. (1966). Tracing and kinesthetic techniques. In J. Money (Ed.), *The disabled reader.* Baltimore, MD: Johns Hopkins University Press.

Lewis, R. B. (1983). Learning disabilities and reading: Instructional recommendations from current research. *Exceptional Children, 50*(3) 230–240.

Orton, J. L. (1966). The Orton-Gillingham approach. In J. Money (Ed.), *The disabled reader.* Baltimore, MD: Johns Hopkins University Press.

Otto, W., & McMenemy, R. A. (1966). *Corrective and remedial reading: Principles and practices.* Boston: Houghton Mifflin.

Rude, R. T., & Oehlkers, W. J. (1984). *Helping students with reading problems.* Englewood Cliffs, NJ: Prentice-Hall.

Smith, N. B. (1965). *American reading instruction.* Newark, DE: International Reading Association.

Stauffer, R. G., Abrams, J. C., & Pikulski, J. J. (1978). *Diagnosis,*

correction and prevention of reading disabilities. New York: Harper & Row.

JOHN J. PIKULSKI
University of Delaware

BASAL READERS
FERNALD METHOD
HIGH INTEREST-LOW VOCABULARY MATERIALS
ORTON-GILLINGHAM METHOD
READING
READING DISORDERS

REMEDIATION, DEFICIT-CENTERED MODELS OF

Deficit-centered models for the remediation of children's learning problems have been the predominant model, though certainly not the only model, of special education worldwide throughout the twentieth century. Deficit-centered remediation focuses on the identification of underlying process deficiencies on the part of the child; it then directs any subsequent intervention at the remediation of these process deficiencies. The assumption of such programs is that once the underlying deficit has been remediated (fixed, removed, or cured), academic learning will occur at a more or less normal pace. Deficit-centered remediation has undergone numerous facelifts since the 1930s, although the strong influence of Samuel T. Orton, is felt in most of these programs even today.

One of the more recent, and most notable, examples of deficit-centered remediation is the Illinois Test of Psycholinguistic Abilities (ITPA; Kirk, McCarthy, & Kirk, 1971) and its accompanying curriculum, interventions, and training materials. (Perhaps a more popularly known deficit-centered program, and also one of the most heavily refuted and ineffective, is the Doman and Delacato program at the Institute for the Achievement of Human Potential. This is the approach that calls on the concept of neurological organization and treatment through patterning among other activities.) The ITPA focuses on the identification and assessment of basic psycholinguistic processes such as auditory reception, auditory sequential memory, visual sequential memory, auditory association, etc. If a deficit appears in one or more of these areas, a remedial program is then prescribed (Kirk & Kirk, 1971). For example, if a child is referred for a reading program and found to have an auditory reception deficit (determined on the ITPA by the child's inability to respond correctly at an age-appropriate level to such questions as, Do bananas fly? Do barometers congratulate? Do chairs sit?), exercises might be prescribed for the child aimed at practicing the hearing and discrimination of similar sounds (e.g., noting the differences between pin and pen, pet and let, then and tin, dot and spot). The child also might be given practice in the following of instructions. Once these activities are mastered, the deficit-centered model argues, learning to read would proceed more or less normally since the cognitive processing (or central process) dysfunction that was the stumbling block to reading has been removed.

Many other assessment techniques and programs exist to identify weaknesses or deficits in cognitive processes for subsequent intervention. Some of the approaches that emphasize treating the child's greatest area of weakness in cognitive processing include those of Ayres (1974), Bannatyne (1980), Ferinden and Jacobson (1969). Frostig and Horne (1964), Kephart (1963), and Vallett (1967). The efficacy of deficit-centered models has been the subject of considerable scrutiny by researchers in psychology and special education for some time. Unfortunately, support for the effectiveness of deficit-centered remediation programs for the remediation of academic deficits is nil, particularly when reading and math are the academic problem areas (Glass & Robbins, 1967; Mann, 1979; Reynolds, 1981a, 1981b; and Ysseldyke & Mirkins, 1982). Perceptual and visual-motor functioning can be improved by deficit-centered remediation programs (Myers & Hammill, 1976), but there is, as yet, no documentable generalization for the remediation of the learning problems that trigger the referral.

Other, related areas of research have repeatedly noted potentially major limiting factors in the application of deficit-centered models. Findings from the fields of neurology, genetics, and related areas demonstrate neurological (Adams & Victor, 1977; Hartlage, 1975; Hartlage & Givens, 1982; Kolb & Whishaw, 1980; Levine, Brooks, & Shonkoff, 1980) or genetic bases (Adams & Victor, 1977; Hartlage & Hartlage 1973a, 1973b) for many learning problems in which deficit-centered models or remediation had been thought to be appropriate as the primary method of intervention. From the point of view of many contemporary neuropsychological models, the deficit-centered process approach to remediation is doomed to failure because it takes damaged, dysfunctional, or undeveloped areas of the brain and focuses training specifically on those areas. Not only does our existing knowledge of neurology predict failure for such efforts, but the efforts will not withstand empirical scrutiny.

Hartlage and Reynolds (1981) have criticized deficit-centered models of remediation as potentially harmful to children. The emotional trauma that may accompany the treatment approach of Doman and Delacato has been widely discussed and the method has been condemned (Levine, Brooks, & Shankoff, 1980). While it is unlikely that other deficit-centered models are as emotionally damaging, it is likely (though unproven) that making children work and practice for lengthy periods process skills in which they are deficient (in some cases, years) without noticeable academic gains is emotionally damaging, particularly to the child's self-esteem, motivation, and the likelihood of continuing in school. Glass (1981), in a meta-analysis of the effectiveness of what were deficit-centered

models of remediation, reported that a significant number had net negative effects on academic skills—that is, many deficit-centered remediation programs resulted in less academic gains than no special education program at all. In some instances, then, doing nothing is superior to a deficit-centered approach to remediation, when only academic skills are considered.

Recently, cognitive psychologists have become interested in children's information-processing strategies and have made great strides in understanding how children organize, store, and manipulate stimuli. Concomitant with the revival of interest in cognitivism have been attempts to assess "new" cognitive deficits and provide remedial strategies. Haywood and Switzky (1986), among others, propose that through such techniques as Feuerstein's (1979) Learning Potential Assessment Device (known popularly as the LPAD), deficiencies in children's cognitive processes can be identified and targeted for remediation. Conceptually, this new "cognitive science" approach is no different from the approaches of the past—only the names of the processes thought to be deficient are new. The new deficit-centered models have been the subject of debate (Gresham, 1986; Haywood & Switzky, 1986; Reynolds, 1986), and there is evidence that, through the use of a like set of materials, children's scores on tests such as Raven's Matrices (a nonverbal test of intelligence) improve.

However, many of the specific abilities included in the cognitive science models of deficit-centered remediation are covered overtly in prior models and implicitly in many training programs. The cognitive science models do give us some new abilities to train, notably thinking skills and strategies such as metacognition, regrouping, rehearsal, and various methods of classification, but merely leave us with new labels for others. The intelligence test score improvement reported by Feuerstein, Haywood, and others (Haywood & Switzky, 1986) likely is due to teaching the test, and generalizability to other tests or to academic skills is not in evidence. As with deficit-centered remediation programs throughout the twentieth century, the new cognitive science model is narrow and highly task-specific in its effects. While improvements in these characteristics of children's thinking are desirable, they are not desirable at the neglect of the academic deficiencies that trigger the referral.

There is no evidence that deficit-centered remediation programs aid in such real-world tasks as learning to read, write, or cipher. They remain popular largely on the basis of rational, intuitive appeal and personal testimony or anecdotal data. However, occasional children do improve without treatment and the same percentage or less improve under deficit-centered remediation. As Mann (1979) periodically reminds us, we are better off training or teaching for the task at hand, not for the latest process. In assessing the new cognitive science approach to remediation, we are forced to conclude, as has Mann (1979) in his review of process training, "The new scientific pedagogy was going to revitalize education, provide individual prescriptive correctives for learning problems, reclaim the cognitively impaired. Down with models of general intellectual incompetency! Down with medical models of noneducational etiology!" (pp. 529, 538). "The promised land was at hand. Alas, neither Moses nor we ever crossed to the other side" (Mann, 1979, p. 539). Process is not a useless variable, however. It is crucial to consider in the diagnosis of learning disabilities as well as certain other disorders; efforts to use process approaches to remediate academic problems seem better built on strength models of remediation than on deficit-centered models.

Strength Models of Remediation

Strength models of remediation also invoke the concept of cognitive or intellectual processes and often measure them in the same way. The resulting approach and techniques differ greatly, however. Strength models argue that the best remedial approach for a child who cannot read is to teach the child reading, not metacognition, rehearsal strategies, auditory reception, or grouping and classification.

In strength models of remediation, direct instruction is encouraged in the area(s) of academic or behavioral difficulty. However, instruction is formatted around the child's best developed processes, taking advantage of the child's best intellectual abilities and avoiding those processes that are poorly developed, dysfunctional, or inept in this function. As Reynolds (1981b) describes this method, "The strength model is based on processes that are sufficiently intact so as to subserve the successful accomplishment of the steps in the educational program, so that the interface between cognitive strengths [determined from the assessment process] . . . and the intervention is the cornerstone of meaningfulness for the entire diagnostic-intervention process" (p. 344). In Lurian terminology, this would denote the need for locating a complex functional system within the brain that operates well enough to be capable of taking control and moderating the learning process necessary to acquire the academic skills in question.

This view is hardly new, though it is largely untested. Woodrow (1919) suggested teaching to cognitive strengths on the basis of scientific psychology and the interpretation of "laws" of factor analysis, while attempting to reconcile the views of Spearman and of Thurstone (Mann, 1979). Woodrow (1919) observed that "sometimes a high order of intelligence is accompanied by defects which make it imperative to use . . . the stronger faculties" (p. 293). More directly and in reference to the mildly mentally retarded, Woodrow (1919) argued that since "Their most valuable asset is rote memory. . . . Its training should, therefore, form a conspicuous part in their education" (pp. 285–286). Today we hope to use the stronger faculties in developing instructional strategies, as Woodrow also proposed, rather than in training the stronger processes to become even

stronger; the latter is not an unlikely side effect of strength models of remediation, however.

Strength models do not tell us specifically what to teach children, as do deficit-centered models. The latter tells us to teach the specific process that has been found to be deficient. In strength models, the specifics of what to teach come from a detailed task analysis or a diagnostic achievement test that delineates precisely what academic skills are problematic for the child. The strength model of remediation tells us how to teach: how the material best can be organized and presented so that learning has the best opportunity to occur (Reynolds, 1985). The specific techniques of strength models of remediation have been elaborated in a variety of sources, as has validity evidence for the approach (Gunnison & Kaufman, 1982; Hartlage & Reynolds, 1981; Reynolds, 1981a, 1981b, 1985). Building on strengths has intuitive appeal as well. Deficit models focus on the child's weakest, least developed areas of cognitive processing, the areas in which failures have been experienced most frequently. The stress, anxiety, and self-denigration that may be fostered can be intolerable for many children. Using the child's strengths as building blocks for the acquisition of academic skills or even the remediation of behavioral disorders increases the probability of more positive and successful experiences, reducing stress and alleviating anxiety. Strength models of remediation may have other emotional benefits for children as well.

A strength model of remediation also can serve as a meeting ground for a variety of divergent theoretical models in use in the remediation of a child's problems. One can easily blend cognitive, behavioral, neuropsychological, and psycheducational models in a strength approach. Behavioral and psychoeducational models that focus on academic skill delineation through task analysis or diagnostic achievement testing are needed to tell us specifically what to teach; cognitive and neuropsychological models that focus on how the child best thinks and processes information tell us how to organize, present, and teach the content and behaviors; behavioral models, particularly positive reinforcement programs using operant techniques, are best at giving the child reason, purpose, and motivation, the why of learning. Of the various processing theories from which to build the how, to implement strength models of remediation, the neuropsychological model seems the most promising (Reynolds, 1981b, 1985), and a blending of this model with others has been proposed on several occasions.

An Illustrative Example

Recently, authors have advocated the use of behavioral principles in conjunction with neuropsychological techniques for the remediation of academic problems (Horton, 1981; Reynolds, 1981a, 1985). Others have presented exemplary case studies that recommend inclusion of behavior management techniques based on the unique patterns of cognitive strengths within a given child (Hartlage, 1981; Hartlage & Telzrow, 1983). The focus in all cases is on assessing as accurately as possible the various dysfunctional or intact neuropsychological processing systems for the child using a variety of assessment devices integrated with data from numerous other sources (e.g., teachers, parents, physicians). The goal is then to design a behavior management program (usually in conjunction with an academic remediation program) that emphasizes the child's particular strengths.

Although this approach seems almost matter of fact in terms of face validity, what actually occurs in schools is usually quite contrary to this model. The following hypothetical case can illustrate how a remediation program might be designed for a given child, based first on a deficit-centered model and second on a strength model.

Tina is an eight-year-old female who is experiencing problems learning to read. The teacher describes her as immature, distractible, and unable to follow classroom instruction. Results of a complete evaluation reveal that Tina possesses average to above average intellectual abilities with significant weakness in her auditory and visual sequencing abilities. She seems to exhibit above average visuo-spatial skills. A classroom observation reveals that she appears to be daydreaming when the teacher gives the morning's assignments and she is frequently reprimanded for talking while she attempts to get information from her peers. Achievement data indicate that she is functioning significantly below her ability in reading, exhibiting almost no knowledge of grapheme-phoneme relationships. Auditory comprehension of material is excellent.

The resultant educational plan based on a traditional deficit-centered model might proceed as follows: Tina would go to a resource room for 45 minutes, 3 days a week, for drill in phonics. This is in addition to the 30 minutes she spends each day in her regular reading program where phonics is also heavily emphasized. In addition, once a week Tina is provided with training in auditory sequencing skills. A behavior management system is designed whereby she stays in from recess when she has not completed assignments as instructed by the teacher. If this fails, she also stays after school to complete assignments.

On adoption of a strength model perspective, a radically different plan would be designed for Tina. Based on the identical assessment information, the emphasis would shift to capitalizing on Tina's strong visuo-spatial skills while bypassing her weaknesses in auditory sequencing to the maximum extent possible. Therefore, Tina may still benefit from additional reading instruction with a resource teacher but the emphasis of the techniques would be quite different. It is probable that for a child with deficient auditory sequencing abilities, a strong phonics program to teach reading would prove futile and subsequently frustrating to the child and the teacher. Under the strength model, one would incorporate techniques into the reading program that would allow Tina to use her stronger visuo-spatial abilities. Look-say, rebus, and language ex-

perience stories with pictures are all reading programs that have techniques to emphasize visuo-spatial skills and deemphasize sequencing skills. Context would be emphasized. That is not to say that strength models demand an emphasis on one system to the exclusion of the other, but rather in preference to it.

Another obvious recommendation would be to have Tina sit as close to the teacher as possible and for the teacher to provide additional visual cues whenever giving oral directions to the class. Writing the directions on the board, having Tina copy them and then illustrate them, might be helpful in maintaining her attention. Tina also might benefit from direct instruction in the use of visual imagery for remembering sight words, following direction, etc.

As for the appropriate behavior management technique, it is possible that simply changing the classroom environment and the demands of the activities would result in an increase in work completed and a reduction in the time spend off task. Strategies that emphasize verbal understanding or memory of specific rules should be avoided. Techniques that provide Tina with visual representation of her behavioral progress (e.g., charting amount of tasks completed) might be the most effective for her. These recommendations may be more difficult to implement only in that they require more creative teachers and support staff. There are, as yet, no purely canned programs or specific techniques for strength models of remediation, since the approach is relatively new and requires great individualization of instruction. It does appear to be worth the effort. Student characteristics should affect the choice of an instructional method. As obvious as this seems, given the tremendous differences observed among children in the depth and breadth of their learning when exposed to a common method, this is clearly not the case in regular or special education at present (Hayes & Jenkins, 1986). Convenience and the needs of administrators all too often dictate the choice of curriculum and methods in special education instruction. Allowing students' characteristics to drive this process under a strength approach to implementing differential instruction offers far greater promise than current practice.

REFERENCES

Adams, R. D., & Victor, M. (1977). *Principles of neurology*. New York: McGraw-Hill.

Ayres, A. J. (1974). *Sensory integration and learning disorders*. Los Angeles: Western Psychological Services.

Bannatyne, A. (1980, September). *Neuropsychological remediation of learning disorders*. Paper presented at the NATO/ASI International Conference on Neuropsychology and Cognition, Augusta, GA.

Ferinden, W. E., & Jacobson, S. (1969). *Educational interpretation of the Wechsler Intelligence Scale for Children (WISC)*. Linden, NJ: Remediation Associates.

Feuerstein, R. (1979). *The dynamic assessment of retarded performers. The learning potential assessment device, theory, in-*

struments and techniques. Baltimore, MD: University Park Press.

Frostig, M., & Horne, D. (1964). The Frostig program for the development of visual perception. Chicago: Follett.

Glass, G. V., & Robbins, M. P. (1967). A critique of experiments on the role of neurological organization in reading performance. Reading Research Quarterly, 3, 5–52.

Glass, G. V. (1981, September). Effectiveness of special education. Paper presented at the Working Conference of Social Policy and Educational Leaders to Develop Strategies for Special Education in the 1980s, Wingspread, Racine, WI.

Gresham, F. (1986). On the malleability of intelligence: Unnecessary assumptions, reifications, and occlusion. School Psychology Review, 15, 261–262.

Gunnison, J., & Kaufman, N. L. (1982, August). Cognitive processing styles: Assessment and intervention. In Assessment and diagnostic—prescriptive intervention: Diversity and perspective. Symposium conducted at the annual meeting of the American Psychological Association, Washington, DC.

Hartlage, L. C. (1975). Neruopsychological approaches to predicting outcome of remedial educational strategies for learning disabled children. Pediatric Psychology, 3, 23–28.

Hartlage, L. C. (1981). Clinical application of neuropsychological test data: A case study. School Psychology Review, 10, 362–366.

Hartlage, L. C., & Reynolds, C. R. (1981). Neuropsychological assessment and the individualization of instruction. In G. W. Hynd & J. E. Obrzut (Eds.), Neuropsychological assessment of the school-aged child: Issues and procedures. New York: Grune & Stratton.

Hartlage, L. C., & Telzrow, C. F. (1983). Neuropsychological assessment. In K. D. Paget & B. A. Bracken (Eds.), The psychoeducational assessment of preschool children. New York: Grune & Stratton.

Hartlage, P. L., & Givens, T. S. (1982). Common neurological problems of school age children. In C. R. Reynolds & T. B. Gutkin (Eds.), The handbook of school psychology, New York: Wiley.

Hartlage, P. L., & Hartlage, L. C. (1973a). Comparison of hyperlexic and dyslexic children. Neurology, 23, 436–437.

Hartlage, P. L., & Hartlage, L. C. (1973b). Dermatoglyphic markers in dyslexia. Paper presented at the annual meeting of the Child Neurology Society, Atlanta, GA.

Hayes, M. C., & Jenkins, J. R. (1986). Reading instruction in special education resource rooms. American Educational Research Journal, 23, 161–190.

Haywood, H. C., & Switzky, H. N. (1986). The malleability of intelligence: Cognitive processes as a function of polygenic experiential interaction. School Psychology Review, 15(2), 245–255.

Horton, A. M. (1981). Behavioral neuropsychology in the schools. School Psychology Review, 10, 367–373.

Kephart, N. C. (1963). The brain injured child in the classroom. Chicago: National Society for Crippled Children and Adults.

Kirk, S. A., & Kirk, W. D. (1971). Psycholinguistic learning disabilities: Diagnosis and remediation. Urbana: University of Illinois Press.

Kirk, S. A., McCarthy, J., & Kirk, W. D. (1971). Illinois Test of Psycholinguistic Abilities. Urbana: University of Illinois Press.

Kolb, B., & Whishaw, I. Q. (1980). Fundamentals of human neuropsychology. San Francisco: Freeman.

Levine, M. D., Brooks, R., & Shonkoff, J. P. (1980). A pediatric approach to learning disorders. New York: Wiley.

Mann, L. (1979). On the trail of process. New York: Grune & Stratton.

Myers, P., & Hammill, D. (1976). Methods of learning disorders (2nd ed.). New York: Wiley.

Reynolds, C. R. (1981a). The neuropsychological basis of intelligence. In G. Hynd & J. Obrzut (Eds.), Neuropsychological assessment of the school aged child: Issues and procedure. New York: Grune & Stratton.

Reynolds, C. R. (1981b). Neuropsychological assessment and the habilitation of learning: Considerations in the search for the aptitude x treatment interaction. School Psychology Review, 10, 343–349.

Reynolds, C. R. (1985, August). Putting the individual into the ATI. Paper presented at the annual meeting of the American Psychological Association, Los Angeles.

Reynolds, C. R. (1986). Transactional models of intellectual development, yes. Deficit models of process remediation, no. School Psychology Review, 15, 256–260.

Vallett, R. E. (1967). The remediation of learning disabilities: A handbook of psychoeducational resource programs. Palo Alto, CA: Fearon.

Woodrow, H. (1919). Brightness and dullness in children. Philadelphia: Lippincott.

Ysseldyke, J., & Mirkin, P. K. (1982). The use of assessment information to plan instructional intervention: A review of research. In C. R. Reynolds & T. B. Gutkin (Eds.), The handbook of school psychology. New York: Wiley.

CECIL R. REYNOLDS
Texas A&M University

JULIA A. HICKMAN
University of Texas, Austin

FROSTIG, MARIANNE
ILLINOIS TEST OF PSYCHOLINGUISTIC ABILITIES
INFORMATION PROCESSING
KAUFMAN ASSESSMENT BATTERY FOR CHILDREN
NEUROLOGICAL ORGANIZATION
LEARNING POTENTIAL ASSESSMENT DEVICE
ORTON, SAMUEL T.
PERCEPTUAL TRAINING
SEQUENTIAL AND SIMULTANEOUS COGNITIVE
 PROCESSING

REMEDIATION, STRENGTH MODELS OF

See REMEDIATION, DEFICIT-CENTERED MODELS.

RENZULLI, JOSEPH S. (1936–)

Joseph S. Renzulli received the BS (1958) from Glassboro State College, the MEd (1962) from Rutgers University, and the EdD (1966) in educational psychology from the University of Virginia. He is currently professor of educational psychology and director of the Teaching the Talented Program at the University of Connecticut.

Renzulli's work has been focused on developing ways to identify high potential and to develop educational models to maximize giftedness. He designed the Enrichment Triad Model (Renzulli, 1984), which includes general exploratory activities, group training activities, and individual and small-group investigators of real problems.

Joseph S. Renzulli

Renzulli has devised the Revolving Door Identification Model (1981), which provides a flexible approach to identifying high potential in young people. In addition, the Schoolwide Enrichment Model (1985), a plan for general schoolwide enrichment, applies practices developed for serving the gifted and talented into a system that not only serves the highly able, but also provides a general upgrading of the curriculum for all students.

Among his many professional activities, Renzulli has served as president of the Association for the Gifted (1974–1975). In addition, he was recipient of the National Association for Gifted Children Distinguished Scholar Award (1984).

REFERENCES

Renzulli, J. S., Reis, S. M., & Smith, L. H. (1981). *The revolving door identification model.* Mansfield Center, CT: Creative Learning.

Renzulli, J. S. (1984). The triad/revolving door system: A research based approach to identification and programming for the gifted and talented. *Gifted Child Quarterly, 28,* 163–171.

Renzulli, J. S. (1985). *The Schoolwide Enrichment Model.* Mansfield Center, CT: Creative Learning.

ANN E. LUPKOWSKI
Texas A&M University

REPEATED READING

Repeated reading is a remedial reading technique designed to improve fluency and indirectly increase comprehension. The method is based largely on the teaching implications of automatic information processing theory in reading (LaBerge & Samuels, 1974). In automaticity theory, fluent readers are assumed to decode text automatically; attention is therefore free for comprehension. Nonfluent, word-by-word readers, on the other hand, must focus excessive amounts of attention on decoding, making comprehension difficult. The purpose of repeated reading is to make decoding of connected discourse automatic, thus fluency is increased and the reader is able to concentrate on comprehension.

The method involves multiple oral rereadings of connected discourse until a prescribed level of fluency is attained. Samuels' (1979) method, intended as a supplement to developmental reading programs, consists of multiple rereadings of a short passage of from 50 to 200 words, depending on the skill of the student. Reading speed and number of word recognition errors are recorded for each repetition. When the fluency criterion is reached, the student moves on to a new passage.

Chomsky (1976) proposes a similar method. In this variation, students listen to a tape recording of a storybook while following the text. Students read and listen repeatedly to the text until oral reading fluency is achieved. In addition to reported gains in fluency and comprehension, the method of repeated reading is said to promote more positive attitudes toward reading in that it virtually ensures a successful reading experience (Kann, 1983).

Moyer (1982) offers a theoretical rationale for the potential effectiveness of the method with disabled readers. She suggests that for some poor readers, the amount of repetition/redundancy offered by traditional reading programs is insufficient to permit the acquisition of reading. Repeated reading of entire passages, however, maximizes redundancy at all levels of written expression. Thus readers are given much practice in using syntactic and semantic cues, as well as in acquiring knowledge of graphophonemic word structure.

REFERENCES

Chomsky, C. (1976). After decoding: What? *Language Arts, 53,* 288–296.

Kann, R. (1983). The method of repeated readings: Expanding the neurological impress method for use with disabled readers. *Journal of Learning Disabilities, 16,* 90–92.

LaBerge, D., & Samuels, S. J. (1974). Toward a theory of automatic information processing in reading. *Cognitive Psychology, 6,* 293–323.

Moyer, S. B. (1982). Repeated reading. *Journal of Learning Disabilities, 15,* 619–623.

Samuels, S. J. (1979). The method of repeated readings. *Reading Teacher, 32,* 403–408.

TIMOTHY D. LACKAYE
*Hunter College, City University
of New York*

READING
READING REMEDIATION

RESEARCH IN SPECIAL EDUCATION

Research in special education is the means through which knowledge and methods of treatment are acquired and verified for application to persons exhibiting special needs. Such research encompasses a wide range of methodologies, data collection and analysis techniques, subjects, and issues. Although all special education research contributes to the ever increasing knowledge base of the field, all are different to some extent. Research ranges from case studies to single subject and group designs. Each method differs from the others in terms of ease of use, confidence and validity of results obtained, and generality of findings.

Through the process of research, advances are made in what is known about disabilities and how to prevent and treat them through education and training. The importance of research methodology in validating the findings of research must be emphasized. Many hypotheses related to developmental disabilities are advanced in the form of anecdotal reporting and logical analyses. But these hypotheses are speculative and before being applied to the special education field, they must be subjected to verification through research. Only by careful study through controlled research designs can research findings be considered useful and applied to persons other than those involved in the research study.

Special education research is usually applied research; in other words, it is conducted primarily in the places where handicapped persons live, work, and attend school. For example, research has been conducted in group homes, sheltered workshops, resource rooms, and the community. Although less rigorous than research in the experimental laboratory, special education research has the advantage of being relevant to and practical for the subjects involved; that is, the issues studied are usually of high priority for the well-being of the people involved because of their functional relevance. Through rigorously applied research programs, professionals in special education can confirm observations by testing hypotheses on persons with special needs and verifying known effects with different populations. In the long view, research provides a solid foundation of knowledge from which to progress and maintain the intellectual vitality of special education (Drew, Preator, & Buchanan, 1982).

Observation of phenomena is inherent in all research and particularly in special education research Naturalistic observation is one way to collect information about subjects. With this technique, the researcher observes a person (or group of people) and makes extensive records of the subject's behaviors. The purpose is to be as descriptive as possible to provide a post-hoc analysis of possible mediating factors. For example, Currin and Rowland (1985) assessed the communication ability of persons who were labeled profoundly handicapped. These researchers videotaped interactions among adult teachers and 15 nonverbal youths and then divided the communications behaviors exhibited by the subjects into eight categories. The researchers provided no training or other intervention. Such a naturalistic account is important because it can provide an accurate description of specific skills in a certain population. This description can, in turn, later be used as a base from which to provide more precise analyses or from which to guide subsequent interventions. Authors of the majority of articles published from 1983 to 1985 in four major special education research journals used naturalistic observation for collecting and reporting their respective information.

Another important characteristic of research is that of systematically manipulating variables and observing the effects of such manipulations on other variables. Typically, a researcher wants to measure accurately how the dependent variable (e.g., subject behaviors targeted for change) is affected when the subject is exposed to the independent variable (one or more factors manipulated by the researcher). Some examples of dependent variables in special education research are number of words read, frequency of correct expressive signs made, number of problems solved, percentage of inappropriate social behaviors exhibited, and frequency of interruptions. Some examples of independent variables in research are teacher praise, repetition of task, removal of child from activity, use of a particular prompting strategy, and administration of drugs.

A third characteristic of most research is use of an experimental method to determine the extent to which independent variables are functionally related to changes in dependent variables. Researchers carefully design how and when their subjects are exposed to independent variables. Experimental designs minimize the possibility that uncontrolled, extraneous factors play a part in changing dependent variables. Research that is not adequately designed to decrease the impact of extraneous factors must be viewed with caution (Sidman, 1960).

A final characteristic of research concerns analysis of findings. Typically, researchers have used statistical methods to determine whether their results demonstrate a strong (significant) change. Whether the research compares a pre- and postintervention difference, or whether the results obtained from one subject exposed to an independent variable is compared with those of another subject who is not exposed, the intent of the analysis is to assess the degree of difference and make a statement as to whether such a difference could be expected by chance. Statistical methods used in special education research include *t*-tests, analysis of variance, analysis of covariance, and regression analysis. Numerous authors have addressed the role of statistics and research (e.g., Edwards, 1985; Galfo, 1983). In addition, researchers can determine whether their work has caused an observable practical change in their subjects. This determination is termed functional or clinical significance. For example, assume that a researcher is testing a new method for teaching handicapped students to tell time. For those subjects who learn to use a clock during their daily routine, a definite functional skill has been learned regardless of whether or not a statistical test indicates statistical significance.

A research design describes the manner in which subjects are exposed to independent variables. Researchers must structure their designs to meet basic criteria that permit confidence in results obtained by the research. All researchers must control for extraneous variables entering into and possibly affecting the research outcome. In other words, the dependent variables measured by the researcher must be affected only by variables manipulated by the researcher. Campbell and Stanley (1963) proposed eight factors that may cause changes in dependent measures regardless of the effect of the independent variables studied. These eight threats to the validity of research follow:

1. *History*. Experiences (in addition to the independent variable) of the subjects. For example, assume that a student is a subject in a research project focusing on peer tutoring to increase appropriate social skills. If the peer tutor becomes ill and misses 3 days of the study, causing the subject to be in training for a fewer number of sessions than the other subjects, this will threaten the validity of the results.

2. *Maturation*. Uncontrolled changes in subjects. For example, handicapped infants may become fatigued and lose attentiveness over a few hours or late in the day. Behavior changes owed to weariness, hunger, or aging illustrate a maturation threat.

3. *Testing*. The effect of taking a first test on subsequent tests. For example, students who repeatedly take a test improve their test scores over time.

4. *Instrumentation*. Changes in the devices measuring behavior of subjects. For example, mechanical items such as a video camera or cumulative recorder may fail to operate properly. Human observers may be-

come bored or fatigued and as a result unknowingly alter their scoring.

5. *Statistical Regression*. Subjects selected for inclusion in a study because of extreme scores on some test or measure. For example, assume some learning-disabled students are selected for a research study on improving reading. These particular students are selected because of their low scores on a reading achievement test given as a pretest measure. The experimental treatment is applied and then a posttest is given (the same reading achievement assessment). Any increases in posttest scores cannot be assumed to be related to the experimental manipulation because there is a tendency for low scores on a test to increase on subsequent testing.

6. *Selection*. Subjects for experimental and control groups. If a project involves the comparision of two subject groups, the research results may be a function of the subjects being different initially rather than a function of the experimental manipulation. For example, assume that a school district receives financial support to hire extra vocational counselors and trainers to work with handicapped students for a year in vocational training. At the end of the year, the superintendent of the district decides to assess whether the extra staff made a positive impact on the vocational success of the students. The administrator arranges for a standard vocational assessment to be given to all of the vocational students who received the assistance, and to students in another district who did not. Differences in the assessment scores may be due to a basic difference between the students of the two districts.

7. *Experimental Mortality*. Losing subjects from a research study. For example, researchers frequently group subjects along relevant variables such as age, sex, and handicapping condition. If several subjects in one group drop out of the study for any reason, any results of the research showing a difference between the two groups may be due to the loss of the subjects rather than an effect of the independent variable.

8. *Selection-Maturation Interaction, Etc*. A combination of any of the previous factors.

According to Campbell and Stanley, if a researcher arranges the experimental design to minimize the possibility of the mentioned potential alternative explanations, then any changes in the dependent measures can be confidently assumed to be due to the experimental intervention.

A second criterion for all research designs concerns the extent to which results can generalize (be applied directly) to other subjects or conditions. In special education particularly, the results of research need to be relevant to persons similar to those involved in the particular research project. Campbell and Stanley recognized four factors that reduce confidence in generalizing the results of a research study to special needs persons not participating in that study or in settings other than the experimental one:

1. *Effect of Testing.* Subjects who are tested may be affected by testing and thus react differently than an untested population. For example, assume that handicapped students are enlisted as subjects in a research project testing the impact of an innovative procedure for increasing spelling accuracy. The subjects are given a preintervention spelling test followed by treatment. Finally, the subjects complete a posttest. The subjects may do better than other students simply because they were given a spelling test before the intervention.

2. *Effect of Selection of Subjects and Experimental Variable.* Subjects may be more or less sensitive to the experimental intervention than other students. For instance, a special education classroom may be used extensively by special education researchers for research purposes. If the students in such a classroom are frequently involved as research subjects, and if there are constant visitors and observers in the classroom, then these students may be more or less sensitive to any experimental manipulations than students in other special education classes.

3. *Effect of Experimental Arrangements.* Conditions of the research itself may affect subjects in a special way. For example, this threat exists when students from several classes are randomly selected to be in an experimental group and are taken to a new classroom for the study. Subjects who are in an unfamiliar environment with unfamiliar people may react differently to experimental procedures than those in their familiar surroundings.

4. *Multiple-Treatment/Interference of Previous Treatments.* Previous treatments may have effects on subjects that are unknown and when working with humans as subjects, locating experimentally naive individuals can be extremely difficult. For example, some researchers study the effect of different variations of a prompting strategy known as stimulus-delay on academic skills. If they were to use the same subjects repeatedly in different experiments, over time these subjects might become familiar with the stimulus-delay method and do better or worse than subjects not initially exposed.

It is important to note that to the greatest extent possible, research in special education must meet these concerns of generalization. The importance of educational research lies both with the improvement of the particular subjects

in a research project and the belief that the results and knowledge gained from the research can be applied to other persons with special needs.

All research projects involve either one or more subjects. Single-subject and group designs are labels that describe the primary categories used in special education. The majority of published articles between 1983 and 1985 in four journals devoted exclusively to research on special needs incorporated a group experimental design, either random or matched. A variety of single-subject designs were used as well.

Typically, a single-subject design involves one subject being exposed to all of the experimental conditions involved in the research. One unique characteristic of such designs is that an individual is compared with his or her own performance only. The measurement of behavior takes place before and repeatedly during the intervention. This permits a comparison of an individual's performance at regular points in time. Such within-subject analyses (Sulzer-Azaroff & Mayer, 1977) potentially yield richer information on the performance of individuals than the traditional experimental and control group designs that stress comparing average scores of large groups of subjects. Single-subject designs are particularly useful with both mildly and severely handicapped persons.

The single-subject designs are withdrawal of treatment, alternating treatment, and multiple baseline. Each is relatively easy to use in a classroom, has strong validity, and has been proven useful in many classroom situations. These designs are adaptable for use when targeting academic and social behavior, when attempting to increase or decrease a response, or when working with a single student or groups.

The withdrawal of treatment evaluation technique typically involves four distinct phases. First, the researcher measures the subject's performance on the target skill prior to a formal attempt at changing the instructional method (baseline). In some cases, the baseline consists of a previous intervention or teaching method other than the intervention of interest. Once this phase is completed, the experimenter intervenes with the independent variable(s) selected. There is frequent measurement of subject performance, usually either per lesson or daily. After the period of time during which the subject's performance stabilizes, the experimenter terminates the intervention and continues to measure the subject's behavior during this second baseline phase. Finally, the researcher reinstates the instruction and continues to measure performance.

Correa, Poulson, and Salzberg (1984) used this design to test the effects of a graduated prompting procedure on the behavior of toy grasping in a two-year-old visually impaired and mentally retarded youngster. The general procedure involved the presentation of a noise-making toy in front of the child and the opportunity for the child to grasp it with no assistance. If the child did so within 10 seconds, he was given praise and the opportunity to manipulate the toy. The experimenters first conducted a series of baseline trials and found that the child touched the toy only when assisted. During the first treatment condition, unassisted touching of the toy increased to a mean of 7% of the trials. Although the following return-to-baseline phase resulted in no unassisted touching of the toy, the subsequent treatment condition increased touching once again to a mean of approximately 18%.

The rationale and strength of this design are apparent. If there is improvement in performance during the times in which the intervention is in effect, and deterioration in performance during the baseline conditions, then the researcher can have confidence that the teaching is the factor resulting in the learning. Such a research design demonstrates experimental control of behavior (Hersen & Barlow, 1976) and minimizes the possibility that uncontrolled factors are responsible for the changes in the subject's performance. On the other hand, there are times when a withdrawal of treatment design is not used (Tawney & Gast, 1984). Ethical concerns may contraindicate withdrawing an intervention if the target behavior is very important (e.g., aggression toward peers), or if a clear, clinically significant change in behavior occurs in the first intervention phase. Methodological concerns may also argue against the use of this design when the target behavior is one that, once learned, is not likely to return to preintervention levels (e.g., learning addition).

The alternating treatments design involves the exposure of the subject to two or more different treatment strategies for the same behaviors. The treatments are alternated over time. Although obtaining a baseline measure of the behavior is desirable, the researcher need not do this because the primary variable of interest is observed changes in the behavior with respect to the different treatments.

An important characteristic of this design is the use of teacher instructions or cues to signal the student as to which intervention is in effect. Typically, the design is used as follows. The researcher first develops the different strategies and selects a means for notifying the subject of each. The researcher also determines a schedule of when each treatment is to be used. The schedule must allow for each treatment to be used an equal number of times in random order. Once the research begins, the experimenter alternates the conditions, measures the subject's behavior, and records it separately for each treatment.

Barrera and Sulzer-Azaroff (1983) used such a design to compare two different language training programs (oral and total communication) in an attempt to improve expressive labeling of three autistic children. Each day, subjects were exposed to both training programs, but the sequence in which they were used alternated randomly. The experimenter signaled which treatment was in use by providing either vocal cues only (oral communication training) or vocal and gestural cues (total communication).

With this design, a teacher can immediately start to remediate a behavior rather than waiting for the rate of behavior to stabilize during a baseline period. In addition, this design can be used with behaviors irreversible once learned. However, this design is unusual in that it does not reflect the "natural" form of classroom instruction whereby one treatment strategy is used consistently over a period of time. There is also the possibility that the subject might be affected by the sequence of the various treatments. Last, a behavior that changes slowly will not be discovered with this design owing to the frequent switching of independent variables.

The multiple baseline design involves measurement of multiple target behaviors, subjects, or situations. The targeted responses, for example, may be from one subject, different behaviors of several subjects, or one behavior exhibited by a subject in different situations. After obtaining baseline measures, the researcher applies the intervention to just one behavior while continuing to collect baseline data on the others. The intervention is subsequently applied to the remaining targets in a successive fashion. This design objectively demonstrates the success of intervention if a target response changes only when the intervention is applied to it.

The multiple baseline design can be used in a variety of different situations. First, it is excellent for use when teaching a student similar behaviors. For example, Haring (1985) used such a design when teaching students labeled moderately/severely handicapped to play with different toys. Haring first noted that the children exhibited no appropriate play with any of four different toys. He then trained the children to play correctly with one toy while noting whether spontaneous play occurred with any of the other three toys. Although the child learned to play correctly with the trained toy, there was no generalized play to the other three toys. The children played correctly only after receiving direct training with the other toys.

Such a design is used across individuals and situations in the same manner as with behaviors. Foxx, McMorrow, and Mennemeier (1984) trained two groups of three adults labeled mildly and moderately retarded to exhibit appropriate social skills such as being polite and responding to criticism. After obtaining a preintervention assessment on all subjects, they taught one group while assessing the other. After several sessions, the subjects in the second group received the training. A multiple baseline across settings is used in a similar fashion. Instead of targeting different behaviors or students, the teacher assesses one behavior of a single student in different situations (e.g., at recess, lunch, in reading class, etc.) and applies the intervention in one setting at a time.

There are limitations associated with the multiple baseline design (Tawney & Gast, 1984). One concerns repeated testing during the baseline conditions; this could potentially continue for many sessions, especially for the third or fourth behavior (or setting or person). Such a lengthy assessment period precludes training and increases the potential for student frustration. However, this problem is minimized by either providing some type of treatment during baseline—so that the student receives some intervention, albeit not the one of interest—or by collecting baseline assessment infrequently. For example, although a minimum of three assessments is recommended, they could be done at random points throughout the baseline phase. Another disadvantage concerns measuring several behaviors or the behaviors of several different subjects, possibly even in different settings. Such a demanding requirement could be time-consuming and impractical in some situations.

There are several research methodologies incorporating a group design approach such as random group, matched group, counterbalanced, and norm-referenced.

In the random group design, subjects are randomly selected from a defined population and assigned to two groups. Both groups are given the same pretest. One group is then given the experimental treatment while the other group is given either no treatment or a treatment that will be compared with the experimental treatment. Finally, both groups are given the same posttest. Wang and Birch (1984) used the random group design when comparing the instructional effectiveness of two different remedial programs for handicapped students. A total of 179 children were randomly assigned to either a part-day resource room or a full-day class representing an adaptive learning environments model (ALEM). Dependent measures consisted of scores from standardized achievement tests, student attitude surveys, and classroom processes. The results indicated that on the average, students in the ALEM class progressed more than students in the part-day resource room.

Another design, matched group, involves subjects in both groups being matched as closely as possible with each other. The matching can occur on variables such as age, sex, learning histories, or intelligence. The variables along which the matching will occur depend on the purposes of the research. For example, Jago, Jago, and Hart (1984) matched subjects in the experimental and control groups along the dimensions of age and etiology of disability. Pretesting, experimental manipulation, and posttesting are done in a manner similar to that in the random group design.

Counter-balanced design involves subjects being exposed to identical experimental interventions but in a different sequence. For example, Carr and Durand (1985) assessed the rate of disruptive behavior exhibited by four developmentally disabled children in four conditions: (1) an easy task with constant teacher attention, (2) a difficult task with constant teacher attention, (3) an easy task with limited teacher attention, and (4) a difficult task with limited teacher attention. Each child was observed in each of these four situations, but in a varying sequential order. For example, one child was exposed to easy task/limited attention, easy task/constant attention, and difficult task/constant attention. A second child was observed in the order of difficult task/constant attention, easy task/constant attention, and easy task/limited attention.

With the norm-referenced design, only one group of subjects is exposed to the experimental intervention and standardized tests are used for pretest and posttest assessments. The results are then compared with results obtained by the standardization for that particular test; in other words, the standardization sample serves as the control group. For example, Gersten and Maggs (1982) assessed cognitive and academic changes in a group of moderately retarded children and adolescents over a 5-year period. The dependent measure was the score of the Stanford-Binet Intelligence Test. The independent measure was the DISTAR Language Program. After almost 5 years of language training, the subjects were given the Stanford-Binet and postexperimental scores were compared with preexperimental scores on the same test. The researchers found that the subjects were gaining points on their IQ scores faster than the population of children used to standardize the test. The norm-referenced design has serious problems since seldom will the research sample match a test's standardization sample or all key variables. Standardization samples of tests are just not good control groups.

Group designs are particularly useful when testing the effectiveness of a treatment package or when addressing questions concerning the magnitude of an effect in terms of the number of people positively or negatively affected. They are the design of choice when testing for a general effect. However, giving treatment to one group of subjects and withholding treatment from another group can be ethically questionable. This is a particular concern in the context of educational treatment, but it can be minimized by offering the control group a treatment different from the experimental intervention, or perhaps the treatment in use prior to the experimental intervention. Another limitation concerns the practical difficulty of finding a sufficient number of matched subjects. Special needs people have unique strengths and disabilities, and finding truly matched subjects may be difficult to achieve.

One other disadvantage with some group designs concerns the portrayal of results in statistical means (averages). One can determine a general outcome when experimental and control group averages are compared, but any analysis of the effect the experimental intervention has on individuals is difficult. Reporting averages ignores the number of subjects positively affected, negatively affected, or not affected at all.

A unique problem with a norm-referenced design is that virtually all of the standardized tests developed to date have used nonhandicapped persons for standardization. Using the results of such a group to assess handicapped subjects is questionable. However, tests (e.g., the American Association of Mental Deficiency Adaptive Behavior Scales) are being developed using a developmentally disabled population for standardization purposes. This could make the use of norm-referenced designs more valid.

Research conducted in special education has increased knowledge in the field and at the same time raised new questions. One important concern is the ethical conduct of the special educator while doing research. Experimenters who use humans as subjects have the responsibility of providing stringent safeguards to protect the health and well-being of their subjects. Professionals in special education must be particularly sensitive to these concerns in that developmentally disabled subjects may not be capable of understanding the issues involved in the research and thus may not be able to give truly informed consent.

Research safeguards to protect subject rights do exist and professionals must abide by them. Kelty (1981) summarized several key guidelines for researchers to consider when planning studies using humans. Generally, these involve informed consent on the part of the subject so that the subject truly understands the purpose of the study, any risks benefits to the subject, and the option to volunteer or to withdraw so that there is maximum possibility for benefit with minimum possibility of harm.

A standard component of research studies is a description of reliability procedures to verify that the primary data collector is accurate in recording the responses of the subjects. Unfortunately, few researchers present a similar case verifying that an experimental treatment is actually applied as proposed. This issue has been termed integrity of treatment (Salend, 1984) and is crucial for confidence in research results. For example, if an experimenter inadvertently implements a different intervention than the one planned, relating the proposed experimental method to the results would be erroneous. Integrity of treatment may be verified with little extra effort on the part of the research designers. As reported in Zane, Handen, Mason, and Geffin (1984), the integrity check can be made part of the traditional reliability check. The reliability scorer notes whether the person implementing the experimental program uses the correct intervention and scores the subject response correctly. By presenting both sets of data, readers can judge to what extent the proposed intervention is actually implemented.

What are some recognized areas of special education in which more research could profitably be done? One area is diagnosis. Techniques that accurately assess the etiology of a person's deficits and discovery of the youngest age at which a true diagnosis can be achieved for various handicapping conditions would have a significant impact. Another area concerns the success of mainstreaming. Ideally, a solid research base should exist to support mainstreaming as well as to delineate ways of making it more successful. Several important questions can be addressed. What is the optimal class ratio of children labeled normal and developmentally disabled? How does mainstreaming affect the individual student in terms of academic and social success? What affect is there, if any, on the students labeled normal? Answers to these questions obtained from systematic research will shed light on the future direction of mainstreaming and lead to even further improvements for disabled people.

One final research area to pursue concerns the extent to which practitioners in the field actually apply the findings from special education research (Englert, 1983). The purpose of research is to provide information that can be used to improve the lives of special needs persons. To what extent do the techniques and knowledge of special education professionals reflect the most recent research findings? If research findings are not being used by teachers and other special education professionals, the reasons must be sought and corrected. Such a discrepancy may be due to limited access to sources of research findings, a possible lack of skills training, or research that is not useful to practitioners. Whatever the reason(s), research findings must make their way to the people who can use them to enhance the lives of special needs people.

REFERENCES

Barrera, R. D., & Sulzer-Azaroff, B. (1983). An alternating treatment comparison of oral and total communication training programs with echolalic autistic children. *Journal of Applied Behavior Analysis, 16,* 379–394.

Campbell, D. T., & Stanley, J. C. (1963). *Experimental and quasi-experimental designs for research.* Chicago: Rand McNally College.

Carr, E. G., & Durand, V. M. (1985). Reducing behavior problems through functional communication training. *Journal of Applied Behavior Analysis, 18,* 111–126.

Correa, V. I., Poulson, C. L., & Salzberg, C. L. (1984). Training and generalization of reach-grasp behavior in blind, retarded young children. *Journal of Applied Behavior Analysis, 17,* 57–69.

Currin, F. M., & Rowland, C. M. (1985). Communicative assessment of nonverbal youths with severe/profound mental retardation. *Mental Retardation, 2,* 52–62.

Drew, C. J., Preator, K., & Buchanan, M. L. (1982). Research and researchers in special education. *Exceptional Education Quarterly, 2,* 47–56.

Edwards, A. L. (1985). *Multiple regression and the analysis of variance and covariance.* New York: Freeman.

Englert, C. S. (1983). Measuring special education teacher effectiveness. *Exceptional Children, 50,* 247–254.

Foxx, R. M., McMorrow, M. J., & Mennemeier, M. (1984). Teaching social/vocational skills to retarded adults with a modified table game: An analysis of generalization. *Journal of Applied Behavior Analysis, 17,* 343–352.

Galfo, A. J. (1983). *Educational research design and data analysis.* New York: University Press of America.

Gersten, R. M., & Maggs, A. (1982). Teaching the general case to moderately retarded children: Evaluation of a five-year project. *Analysis & Intervention in Developmental Disabilities, 2,* 329–334.

Haring, T. G. (1985). Teaching between class generalization of toy play behavior to handicapped children. *Journal of Applied Behavior Analysis, 18,* 127–139.

Hersen, M., & Barlow, D. H. (1976). *Single-case experimental designs: Strategies for studying behavior change.* New York: Pergamon.

Jago, J. L., Jago, A. G., & Hart, M. (1984). An evaluation of the total communication approach for teaching language skills to developmentally delayed preschool children. *Education & Training of the Mentally Retarded, 19,* 175–182.

Kelty, M. F. (1981). Protection of persons who participate in applied research. In G. T. Hannah, W. P. Christian, & H. B. Clark (Eds.), *Preservation of client rights: A handbook for practitioners providing therapeutic, educational, and rehabilitative services.* New York: Free Press.

Salend, S. J. (1984). Integrity of treatment in special education research. *Mental Retardation, 6,* 309–315.

Sidman, M. (1960). *Tactics of scientific research.* New York: Basic Books.

Sulzer-Azaroff, B., & Mayer, G. R. (1977). *Applying behavior-analysis procedures with children and youth.* New York: Holt, Rinehart, & Winston.

Tawney, J. W., & Gast, D. L. (1984). *Single subject research in special education.* Columbus, OH: Merrill.

Wang, M. C., & Birch, J. W. (1984). Comparison of a full-time mainstreaming program and a resource room approach. *Exceptional Children, 51,* 33–40.

Zane, T., Handen, B. L., Mason, S. A., & Geffin, C. (1984). Teaching symbol identification: A comparison between standard prompting and intervening response procedures. *Analysis & Intervention in Developmental Disabilities, 4,* 367–377.

THOMAS ZANE
Johns Hopkins University

MEASUREMENT
MULTIPLE BASELINE DESIGN
MULTIPLE REGRESSION
REGRESSION (STATISTICAL)

RESIDENTIAL FACILITIES

Residential facilities in America have been provided a variety of labels, including school, hospital, colony, prison, and asylum. Both the role and the labels that institutions for the handicapped have taken on have been reflective of the social and cultural climate of the time (Wolfensberger, 1975). The periods that had major influence on residential institutions have been characterized as follows: early optimism, 1800–1860; disillusionment, 1860–1900; reconsideration, 1920–1920; ebb and flow, 1930–1950; new reconsideration, 1950–1960; and enthusiasm, 1960–1970 (Cegelka & Prehm, 1982).

In the United States no public provisions were made for residential placement and care for the handicapped until the 1800s. Prior to that time handicapped individuals were placed in a variety of settings. These ranged from poorhouses to charitable centers. Such institutions provided no systematic attempts at rehabilitation or training of the handicapped. Rather, they served as facilities that stored and maintained handicapped and other persons. It has been estimated that as late as 1850, 60% of the inhabitants of all institutions in the United States were deaf, blind, insane, or mentally retarded (National Advisory Committee for the Handicapped, 1976).

The first residential institution designed for handicapped individuals was established in 1817. That year the American Asylum for the Education and Institution of the Deaf was established in Hartford, Connecticut. In 1819 a second school, for the blind, was established in Watertown, Massachusetts; it was named the New England Asylum for the Blind. During this period and continuing until the Civil War, a number of eastern states established residential schools for the deaf, blind, orphaned, and mentally retarded (National Advisory Committee for the Handicapped, 1976).

The development of residential institutions for the mentally retarded in the United States began in the 1840s. The growth of such institutions was strongly influenced by the work of Johann Guggenbuhl in Switzerland. In 1848 Samuel Howe convinced the Massachusetts Legislature to allocate funds for the establishment of the first public setting for individuals with retardation. That same year Harvey Wilbur founded the first private institution for treating retarded persons. These institutions were designed to provide education and training to mildly, and occasionally to moderately, handicapped children and adolescents. After the Civil War, residential institutions fell into disfavor. However, the latter portion of the century was marked by continued growth, both in numbers of facilities and numbers of individuals within those facilities. As the nineteenth century came to a close, it became clear that institutions were not accomplishing training that would lead to the reintegration of handicapped individuals into the community. By 1900, 7000 handicapped individuals were housed in institutions. During this time, the role of residential institutions changed significantly. Their emphasis shifted from training to prevention of retardation through systematic segregation of the mentally retarded from society (Wolfensberger, 1975).

The view of institutions held by state legislatures and the general public fluctuated until after World War II. By this time institutions were overcrowded and understaffed. The effects of the baby boom in the late 1940s and the early 1950s placed further pressures on these settings. After World War II, a growing acknowledgment of the existence and needs of the exceptional person was experienced by the nation. This awareness was fostered by parental pressures, returning servicemen's needs, professional enthusiasm, and the availability of public and private funding. These factors led to a reevaluation of procedures, research, and a new understanding of the handicapped and the role of institutions in their treatment, care, and training. By 1969, 190,000 handicapped individuals were housed in institutions (Cegelka & Prehm, 1982).

By the 1970s a new view of the dangers and inadequacies of institutions was recognized. The courts played a major role in bringing this realization to the fore. *Watt* v. *Stickney* (1972) affirmed mentally retarded persons' right to treatment. *Lessard* v. *Schmidt* (1972) ensured due process for institutionalized individuals. *Souder* v. *Brennan* (1973) outlawed involuntary servitude of institutionalized persons. The federal government also caused major reforms with the passage of Title XIX (Medicaid) provisions in 1971. These provisions brought institutions under the same controls and review processes as other service providers for the handicapped. A nationwide push to return handicapped individuals to the community was experienced. Deinstitutionalization became a social, fiscal, and moral goal within each of the states. Between the late 1960s and the early 1980s, the number of handicapped persons being served by public residential institutions declined by over 50,000. At the same time, staff-to-client ratios improved along with the physical quality of many institutions.

To facilitate the deinstitutionalization process, community-based alternatives were developed and expanded during the 1970s and 1980s. During the same period, a number of small institutions (less than 100 residents) were built. Small group homes, foster placements, semiindependent residences, and nursing homes were heavily relied on to handle individuals leaving institutional placements and as alternatives to initial placement in large residential institutions. Although anticipated, few of the older large institutions were closed and many of the handicapped stayed within those larger institutions. Changes in the nation's economic stability during the late 1970s and early 1980s also led to many difficulties in realizing the successful integration of the majority of handicapped persons into the community (Cegelka & Prehmn, 1982).

Current data concerning residential institutions for individuals with mental retardation reveal a clear picture of institutions in general throughout the United States. In summary, facilities with 15 or fewer residents increased over 500% from 1977 to 1982; they are continuing to increase. Each year in the recent past, 17% of residential facilities have closed or moved, displacing approximately 2.7% of all retarded individuals. The large institutions are far more stable. Within these institutions (generally exceeding 300 clients), the profoundly retarded make up the largest portion of residents. In public institutions, staff-to-client ratio is approximately 1.6 to 1. In these facilities, the direct-care staff ratio is .82 to 1 and the clinical staff ratio is .32 to 1. On the other hand, in community-based residential facilities, the functioning level of the individuals served is notably higher while at the same time staff ratios are notably lower (Hill et al., 1985; Eplle, Jacobson, & Janicki, 1985).

From this data, general conclusions may be drawn concerning the future of residential institutions. First, large residential facilities will continue to provide services for the handicapped. These institutions will serve greater numbers of increasingly involved persons. This will be done at an increased actual dollar cost per resident. Community-based residential programs will grow as alternative residential settings for handicapped individuals.

These community-based programs will provide services to the majority of previously unserved handicapped individuals. Such settings will provide financially and morally appropriate residential services to a large percent of all handicapped individuals, thus reducing, but not eliminating, the need for larger residential institutions in the latter part of the twentieth-century (Giffth, 1985).

REFERENCES

Cegelka, P. T., & Prehm, H. J. (1982). *Mental retardation.* Columbus, OH: Merrill.

Eplle, W. A., Jacobson, J. W., & Janicki, M. R. (1985). Staffing ratios in public institutions for persons with mental retardation. *Mental Retardation, 23*, 115–124.

Giffth, R. G. (1985). Symposium: Residential institutions. *Mental Retardation, 23*, 105–106.

Hill, B. K., Bruininks, R. H., Lakin, K. C., Hauber, F. A., & McGuire, S. P. (1985). Stability of residential facilities for people who are mentally retarded 1977–82. *Mental Retardation, 23*, 108–114.

National Advisory Committee for the Handicapped. (1976). *The unfinished revolution: Education for the handicapped, 1976 annual report.* Washington, DC: U.S. Government Printing Office.

Wolfensberger, W. (1975). *The origin and nature of our institutional models.* Syracuse, NY: Human Policy.

ALAN HILTON
Seattle University

HISTORY OF SPECIAL EDUCATION
PHILOSOPHY OF EDUCATION FOR THE HANDICAPPED

RESOURCE ROOM

The resource room concept gained popularity following the *Hobsen* v. *Hansen* litigation, which declared tracking systems illegal and required reevaluation on a regular basis. This litigation was a forerunner for mainstreaming and the concept of least restrictive alternative (environment). This model of service delivery allows the handicapped child to remain in the educational mainstream as much as possible. With the passage of PL 94-142, and further emphasis on the least restrictive alternative, the resource room has gained even further popularity. There are over 100,000 resource room teachers in the United States today. Professional special educators have consistently cited the importance of the resource room concept and have noted its viability as a promising alternative to placement in self-contained classes or regular classes without support services (Fimian, Zaback, & D'Alonzo, 1983; Kasik, 1983; Learner, 1985; Marsh, Price, & Smith, 1983; Meyen, 1982; Reger, 1973; Sabatino, 1972; Sindelar & Deno, 1978; Wiederholdt, 1974).

Usually, students attending resource rooms are identified as mildly handicapped (4 to 6% of the total school population). Resource rooms are a widespread means of service delivery for the mildly handicapped, and are gaining acceptance for use with gifted exceptional children.

There are voluminous data available on the definition of resource rooms (Chaffin, 1974; Deno; 1973; Fox, et al. 1973; Hammil & Wiederholdt, 1972; Kasik, 1983; Lilly, 1971; Reger, 1972, 1973; Sabatino, 1972; Wiederholdt, 1974). According to Kasik (1983), a resource room is a place where special education students attend for less than 50% of their school day for support services. The student remains in the regular classroom for the majority of the academic instruction. The resource room is staffed by a resource room teacher. Attendance in the resource room is determined by a multidisciplinary staff according to the student's individual needs. Students are scheduled into specific time slots to attend the resource room, where they receive remedial instruction from a trained specialist in their deficit areas. A resource room should be well equipped with a wide variety of instructional materials. Individualized instruction may include perceptual training, language development, motor training, social and emotional development, and academic skills development. Resource room class size should be small. A recommended caseload per teacher would be no more than 20 students at any one time. Class sessions are either individual or in small groups of up to five students per session. They are a minimum of 20 minutes and a maximum of 45 minutes in length. The resource room should have the same comfortable characteristics of a regular classroom such as at least 150 square feet, adequate lighting, ventilation, and temperature control. The resource room should be easily accessible to teachers and students and possess adequate storage space for folders and materials. In general, the resource room should provide a positive learning environment.

Placement in the resource room is intended to be of short duration (Kasik, 1983). As students progress toward specified goals, they are returned to full-time placement in the regular classroom. Return to the regular classroom should progress through a gradual phasing out of support services. The resource room is to be considered as one type of service delivery within the continuum of services available.

REFERENCES

Chaffin, J. D. (1974). Will the real mainstreaming program please stand up! *Focus on Exceptional Children, 5*(6), 1–18.

D'Alonzo, B. (1983). *Educating adolescents with learning and behavior problems.* Rockville, MD: Aspen Systems.

Deno, E. (1973). *Instructional alternatives for exceptional children.* Reston, VA: Council For Exceptional Children.

Fox, W. L., Egnar, A. N., Polucci, P. E., Perelman, P. F., & McKenzie, H. S. (1972). An introduction to regular classroom approaches to special education. In E. Deno (Ed.), *Instructional alternatives for exceptional children.* Reston, VA: Council For Exceptional Children.

Hammill, D. D., & Wiederholdt, L. (1972). *The resource room: Rationale and implementation.* Ft. Washington, PA: Journal of Special Education Press.

Kasik, M. M. (1983). Analysis of the professional preparation of the resource room teacher. *Dissertation Abstracts International.* (University Microfilms International No. DAO 56766).

Learner, J. (1985). *Learning disabilities: Theories, diagnosis, and teaching strategies* (4th ed.). Boston: Houghton Mifflin.

Lilly, M. S. (1971). A training based model for special education. *Exceptional Children, 37,* 747–749.

Marsh, G. E., Price, B. J., & Smith, T. E. C. (1983). *Teaching mildly handicapped children: Methods and materials: A generic approach to comprehensive teaching.* St. Louis: Mosby.

McLaughlin, J. A., & Kelly, D. (1982). Issues facing the resource teacher. *Learning Disability Quarterly 5,* 58–64.

Meyen, E. L. (1982). *Exceptional children and youth* (2nd ed.). Chicago: Love.

Reger, R. (1972). Resource rooms: Change agents or guardians of the status quo? *Journal of Special Education. 6,* 355–360.

Reger, R. (1973). What is a resource room program? *Journal of Learning Disabilities, 6,* 609–614.

Sabatino, D. A. (1972). Resource rooms: The renaissance in special education. *Journal of Special Education, 6,* 235–348.

Sindelar, P. T., & Deno, E. (1978). The effectiveness of resource room programming. *Journal of Special Education, 12,* 17–28.

Wiederholdt, J. L. (1974). Planning resource rooms for the mildly handicapped. *Focus on Exceptional Children, 5*(8), 1–10.

MARIBETH MONTGOMERY KASIK
Governors State University

LEAST RESTRICTIVE ENVIRONMENT
RESOURCE TEACHER
SELF-CONTAINED CLASSROOM

RESOURCE TEACHER

Much of the research literature calls for resource rooms to be staffed by highly trained special educators who are personable, demonstrate good human interactional skills, and are prepared professionally in the diagnosis and remediation of single or multiple groups of handicapped children. Wallace and McLoughlin (1979) identify the resource teacher's main role as including assessment, instructional planning, teacher evaluation, and liaison-consultant duties. Learner (1985) describes the resource teacher as a highly trained professional who is capable of diagnosing the child, planning and implementing the teaching program, assisting the classroom teacher, providing continuous evaluation of the student, and conducting in-service sessions with other educators and the community. Sabatino (1981) states that the role of the resource teacher includes direct service to individuals and small groups of children, consultant services to classroom teachers, and responsibility for assessment and delivery of individualized programs. Kasik (1983) states that the resource teacher needs to be well organized, flexible, self-directed, and effective in time management. Paroz, Siegenthaler, and Tatum (1977) suggest that the resource teacher be actively involved with the total school community, including students and staff members. They add that the "teacher's role is open ended and limited only by time, talent, and acceptance of the teacher by the school administration and staff" (p. 15). The resource teacher is a trained specialist who works with, and acts as a consultant to, other teachers, providing materials and methods to help children who are having difficulties within the regular classroom. Usually, the resource teacher works with the mildly handicapped population in a centralized resource room where appropriate materials are housed.

Some of the most common responsibilities a resource teacher will probably be asked to undertake have been identified by Sabatino (1982). The resource teacher will conduct and participate in screening for children with learning disabilities, determine the nature of their learning, and prepare final reports for each referral. Instruction will be provided individually or in small groups. The resource teacher will prepare lessons for use when a child cannot function within the framework of the regular lesson. Students will participate in the resource room until they are integrated full time or until successful transition is complete. Schedules should include six or seven sessions daily, except on Fridays, which should be half a day. This allows the teacher to complete reports, observations, parent meetings, consultations, etc. Consultation with classroom teachers and other pupil services personnel should be consistent. The resource teacher should serve as a resource person and provide supportive assistance for all classroom teachers. Observation in the regular classroom and conferences with regular class teachers and parents about pupil progress should be continuous. In addition to meeting with teachers, the resource teacher may be required to prepare in-service materials and supervise the work of paraprofessionals and volunteers. Despite these suggestions, there is no consistency within the field regarding actual practice.

There are four different types of resource room teachers: (1) categorical, (2) noncategorical, (3) itinerant (or mobile), and (4) teacher-consultant. Categorical programs serve one specific population; noncategorical programs may serve one or more populations. The itinerant resource room teacher travels from one building to another and usually does not have an assigned room from which to work. The teacher-consultant resource room teacher provides consultation to regular class teachers, parents, and other service delivery personnel.

REFERENCES

Kasik, M. M. (1983). Analysis of the professional preparation of the special education resource room teacher. *Dissertation Abstracts International*, (University Microfilms International No. DAO 56766).

Learner, J. (1985). *Learning disabilities: Theories, diagnosis, and teaching strategies* (4th ed.). Boston: Houghton Mifflin.

Paroz, J., Siegenthaler, L., & Tatum, V. (1977). A model for a middle school resource room. *Journal of Learning Disabilities, 8*, 7–15.

Sabatino, D. A. (1981). Overview for the practitioner in learning disabilities. In D. A. Sabatino, T. L. Miller, & C. R. Schmidt (Eds.), *Learning disabilities: Systemizing teaching and service delivery*. Rockville, MD: Aspen.

Sabatino, D. A. (1982). An educational program guide for secondary schools. In D. A. Sabatino & L. Mann (Eds.), *A handbook of diagnostic and prescriptive teaching*. Rockville, MD: Aspen Systems.

Wallace, G., & McLoughlin, J. A. (1979). *Learning disabilities: Concepts and characteristics* (2nd ed.). Columbus, OH: Merrill.

MARIBETH MONTGOMERY KASIK
Governors State University

DIAGNOSTIC PRESCRIPTIVE TEACHING
RESOURCE ROOM

RESPITE CARE

Respite care complements special education in providing support to families of handicapped children. Respite care may be defined as temporary care given to a disabled or otherwise dependent individual for the purpose of providing relief to the primary caregiver (Cohen & Warren, 1985). The concept of respite care is generally associated with intermittent services, although this term is also sometimes used to refer to regularly scheduled services occurring once or twice a week.

Respite care programs first appeared in the mid 1970s in response to the deinstitutionalization movement. Deinstitutionalization meant that many families who would probably have placed their disabled children in institutions, either out of choice or as a result of professional advice, no longer had the option to do so. In addition, some children who had been placed in institutions in earlier years were being returned to their families. Thus a substantial number of parents now had to cope with the care needs of their severely handicapped children each day. The natural breaks that parents of nonhandicapped children experience when their children sleep at a friend's home, or visit with relatives, or go to camp were usually not available. It was virtually impossible to obtain paid babysitters and even relatives were reluctant to assume this responsibility. The primary caregiver, usually the mother, found it impossible to engage in normal activities such as shopping, caring for medical and dental needs, or seeing friends. Parents rarely had time for each other or for their other children. Families experienced severe problems in coping.

The cries of parents for help were heard by some professionals. Other parents, receiving no help from the service field, organized themselves and initiated respite care programs while continuing to bring their plight to the attention of service agencies. It was not until the late 1970s that professionals recognized the importance of respite care services. Parents were the primary advocates for these services prior to that time.

Respite care is a family-support service, designed to improve family functioning and help normalize families of the disabled. This service is of particular importance to families with weak natural support systems, poor coping skills, or strenuous care demands. Difficulty in care provision may reflect the severity of the behavioral problems or the extensiveness of the physical and health care needs of the disabled person. Primary caregivers use the relief provided through respite care services to rest, meet their own medical needs, improve relationships with other family members, and engage in some of the common personal or social activities that other adults are able to enjoy (e.g., visiting with a friend, taking a vacation, going shopping).

Models of respite care may vary along several dimensions such as where the service is provided, what the content/nature of the care is, who provides the care, how the service is administered, and how much time is allotted. The most important variation in models is whether services are provided in the home or in some other setting. In-home services are preferred by a majority of families. In-home services are economical and minimize the adjustments that must be made by the disabled individual and the family. These services may be of short duration, as when the parents go to a movie, or for a period of a week or two when parents take a vacation. In-home services may be provided by a sitter with only a few hours of training or by a homemaker/home health aide with substantial training.

About 40% of families experience a strong need to have their disabled members temporarily out of the home (Cohen & Warren, 1985). Out-of-home services may be provided on evenings, weekends, and holidays, or for continuous periods up to 30 days. These services may be provided in a respite care facility, in a residential facility that reserves some beds for temporary care, or in the home of the respite care provider. Services based in the home of the provider are personalized and economical. They can help expand the social/community experiences of the disabled child, and they allow for the development of an ongoing relationship between the provider family and the disabled child.

Babysitting and companionship are the major ingredients of respite care services that are of brief duration. Personal care and nursing care may be required when the client has severe physical or health problems. Social/recreational programming is usually a major component of longer respite care episodes.

Respite care services are often funded through state mental retardation/developmental disabilities agencies, with families obtaining services either directly through local offices of these agencies or through community programs supported by funds from these state sources. The provision of respite care services is uneven from state to state and from region to region within states. States that have made strong efforts to provide sufficient respite care services of good quality include Massachusetts, California, Washington, and most recently, Ohio. Funding problems remain the greatest impediment to the provision of adequate respite care services. In light of funding limitations, parent co-ops and volunteer models of respite care have become popular. Such programs are low in cost and are congruent with the zeitgeist of the 1980s that emphasizes self-help and alternatives to government provision.

REFERENCE

Cohen, S., & Warren, R. D. (1985). *Respite care: Principles, programs, and policies.* Austin, TX: PRO-ED.

SHIRLEY COHEN
*Hunter College, City University
of New York*

DEINSTITUTIONALIZATION

RESPONSE GENERALIZATION

Response generalization occurs when the effects of reinforcement or punishment of one response increase or decrease, respectively, functionally similar behaviors. Such generalization is an implicit goal of teaching because learning would be of little value if it affected only a specific response. Unfortunately, as Baer (1981) has emphasized, such generalization is not automatic and may be restricted in some handicapped children and adults, particularly retardates (Robinson & Robinson, 1976).

For generalization to occur, it may need to be trained explicitly. Techniques for training generalization may be found in Baer (1981) and Sulzer-Azeroff and Mayer (1977).

REFERENCES

Baer, D. M. (1981). *How to plan for generalization.* Lawrence, KA: H & H Enterprises.

Robinson, N. M., & Robinson, H. B. (1976). *The mentally retarded child* (2nd ed.). New York: McGraw-Hill.

Sulzer-Azeroff, B., & Mayer, G. R. (1977). *Applied behavior analysis procedures with children and youth.* New York: Holt, Rinehart, & Winston.

ROBERT T. BROWN
LISSEN SIMONSEN
*University of North Carolina,
Wilmington*

GENERALIZATION
TRANSFER OF LEARNING

RESTRAINT

See PHYSICAL RESTRAINT.

RETARDATION

See CULTURAL-FAMILIAL RETARDATION; SEE MENTAL RETARDATION.

RETENTION IN GRADE

Retention in grade or nonpromotion has been an issue of interest to educators since the turn of the century. The first comprehensive study of pupil progress was done by Ayres (1909) in his book *Laggards in Our Schools*. Literally hundreds of articles and studies have argued the pros and cons of nonpromotion. Since 1975 the number of students retained in grade has been on the increase. A great deal of this increase appears to be related to the establishment of performance standards in skill subjects. In 1979 and 1980 about half of the first, second, and third graders in Washington, DC, were retained in a grade because they failed to meet the new reading and math standards.

The results of studies conducted over the years on retention have generally borne mixed results. The quality of those studies has also been suspect (Jackson, 1975). Jackson concluded that studies that compared promoted students with nonpromoted students were biased in favor of promotion because promoted students did better than those retained. Using a technique called meta-analysis, Holmes and Matthews (1984) analyzed 44 studies that compared retained students with those promoted. In 18 of the studies they found matched subject designs that used control factors such as IQ, achievement, socioeconomic status, sex, and grades. The studies they analyzed used a variety of dependent means to evaluate the effects of nonpromotion. Included were academic achievement, personal adjustment, self-concept, and attitude toward school. On all variables, nonpromotion resulted in negative effects. The average size of effect for all variables was −.38. This means that students who were promoted performed about one-third of a standard deviation better than those who were retained.

The results from variable to variable were surprisingly consistent. For academic achievement, the size of effect was .44, for personal adjustment it was .27, for self-concept .19, and for attitude toward school .16. All differences showed a more positive performance for students who were promoted than for those who were retained. The outcomes seem to demonstrate that the potential for negative effects far outweighs the benefits for nonpromotion. Based on the preceding evidence, there would need to be compelling evidence to warrant a retention decision. It appears that simple retention in the absence of other planned supportive services produces negative consequences.

REFERENCES

Ayres, L. P. (1909). *Laggards in our schools*. New York: Russell Sage Foundation.

Holmes, C. T., & Matthews, K. M. (1984). The effects of nonpromotion in elementary and junior high school pupils: A meta-analysis. *Review of Educational Research, 54*(2), 225–236.

Jackson, G. B. (1975). The research evidence in the effect of grade retention. *Review of Educational Research, 45*, 438–460.

ROBERT A. SEDLAK
University of Wisconsin, Stout

DEVELOPMENTAL DELAYS
PREREFFERAL INTERVENTIONS

RETICULAR ACTIVATING SYSTEM

The reticular activating system is the mass of cells in the brain stem associated with arousal, wakefulness, attention, and habituation. Its dysfunction may be associated with the hyperactivity and attention deficits often observed in brain-damaged children.

The major function of the reticular system is to provide for cortical activation via its connections through the diffuse thalamic projection system. If the reticular system is significantly impaired, as in severe head trauma, coma results. However, even with less severe impairment, wakefulness, perception (Livingston, 1967), or cognitive functions are attenuated. The second major function is through the posterior hypothalamus, an area that provides a similar activating influence on the limbic system (Feldman & Waller, 1962; Iwamura & Kawamura, 1962; Routtenberg, 1968).

Specific investigations of the dual arousal systems have revealed different functions of each. Damage to the reticular system attenuates its cortical activation effects but does not impair behavioral arousal. In contrast, damage to the posterior hypothalamus impairs arousal but cortical activation remains (Feldman & Waller, 1962; Kawamura, Nakamura, & Tokizane, 1961; Kawamura & Oshima, 1962). Because of their anatomical proximity and the neuronal interconnections between the posterior hypothalamus and the reticular system, it is likely that both systems will become impaired by injury or disease, although one system may be affected to a greater extent. This may account for some of the variability observed in brain-impaired children.

REFERENCES

Feldman, S., & Waller, H. (1962). Dissociation of electrocortical activation and behavioral arousal. *Nature, 196,* 1320.

Iwamura, G., & Kawamura, H. (1962). Activation pattern in lower level in the neo-, paleo-, archicortices. *Japanese Journal of Physiology, 11,* 494–505.

Kawamura, H., Nakamura, Y., & Tokizane, T. (1961). Effect of acute brain stem lesions on the electrical activities of the limbic system and neocortex. *Japanese Journal of Physiology, 11,* 564–575.

Kawamura, H., & Oshima, K. (1962). Effect of adrenaline on the hypothalamic activating system. *Japanese Journal of Physiology, 12,* 225–233.

Livingston, R. (1967). Brain in circuitry relating to complex behavior. In G. Quarton, T. Melnechuk, & Schmitt, F. (Eds.), *The neurosciences: A study program.* New York: Rockefeller University Press.

Routtenberg, A. (1968). The two arousal hypothesis: Reticular formation and limbic system. *Psychological Review, 75,* 51–80.

CHARLES J. LONG
GERI R. ALVIS
University of Tennessee,
Memphis
Memphis State University

ATTENTION DEFICIT DISORDER
BRAIN DAMAGE
HYPERKINESIS

RETINITIS PIGMENTOSA (RP)

Retinitis pigmentosa (RP) was first described in the mid 1800s. The term pigmentary retinal dystrophy is more accurate, as retinitis suggests an inflammation of the retina although none is present. The condition is often hereditary and characterized by a progressive deterioration of retinal photoreceptor cells and associated layers of pigment epithelium and choroid (Krill, 1972). Clinical features include spiculated clumping of pigment in association with retinal vessels, pallor (atrophy) of the optic disk and thinning of the retinal vessels. The condition is always bilateral in familial cases, but sporadic unilateral cases have been reported. Pigmentary changes typically become noticeable during the first decade of life, and begin as fine dots that gradually assume the spidery bone corpuscle appearance. Unusual pigmentary distributions may be noted, including central and sector defect patterns. The pigment flecks may be sparse or absent (i.e., RP *sine pigmenti*) (Tasman, 1971).

Three basic modes of inheritance are recognized: autosomal recessive, autosomal dominant, and sex linked. The recessive form is the most common, the sex linked form often the most disabling. Approximately 40% of patients reveal no hereditary pattern. Ocular associations include posterior polar cataract, glaucoma, myopia, and keratoconus. Extraocular associations include deafness and neurologic and endrocrine abnormalities such as oligophrenia, ophthalmoplegia, sphingolipidoses, Friedreich's ataxia, amyotrophic lateral sclerosis (Lou Gehrig's disease), and progressive muscular atrophy. Perhaps the best known syndrome in the differential diagnosis of RP is that of Laurence-Moon-Biedl, encompassing mental retardation, hypogenitalism, polydactyly, shoulder and hip girdle obesity, retinal changes, and a recessive inheritance pattern. Less common RP syndromes include Refsum's (polyneuritis, cerebellar ataxia, atypical pigmentary degeneration, cardiac anomalies, paresis of the lower extremities, and autosomal recessive pattern) and Bassen and Kornzweig's (spinocerebella degeneration, low blood cholesterol, celiac disease, and beta-lipoprotein deficiency). Hallgren's and Cockayne's syndromes are autosomal recessive disorders associated with RP and deafness; Hallgren's with cerebellar ataxia and Cockayne's a progeria-like dwarfism (Walsh & Hoyt, 1969).

Attempts at treatment have been disappointing. Current theory suggests the disease represents an abnormal sensitivity to light, with light being the agent leading to retinal photoreceptor degeneration. Occlusion of one eye, in an attempt to slow the progress of the disease, has been attempted with equivocal results. Injections of extracts from placental tissues have been tried in the past with no effect.

This disease tends not to affect school performance until late in its course. Clues for educators may include walking into objects (constricted or "gun-barrel" visual field defects), night blindness, and other defects such as hearing loss and degenerative central nervous system disease. Constriction of the visual field may make location of material on a chalkboard difficult. Braille instruction is typically ineffective unless no useful vision is present.

REFERENCES

Krill, A. E. (1972). *Hereditary retinal and choroidal diseases.* Hagerstown, MD: Harper & Row.

Tasman, W. (1971). *Retinal diseases in children.* New York: Harper & Row.

Walsh, F. B., & Hoyt, W. F. (1969). *Clinical neuro-ophthalmology.* Baltimore: MD: Williams & Wilkins.

GEORGE R. BEAUCHAMP
Cleveland Clinic Foundation,
Cleveland, Ohio

RETROLENTAL FIBROPLASIA (RLF)

Retrolental fibroplasia (RLF) was first recognized in the early 1940s, with the first literature description published in 1942. Over the ensuing decade, many unrelated and sometimes conflicting etiologies for the disease were considered. Among these were water miscible vitamins, iron, oxygen, cow's milk, and abnormal electrolytes, all of which have been shown in positive association to the incidence of RLF. Experimental evidence implicated vitamin E deficiency as a possible cause. Other factors that have been associated with RLF are viral infections, hormonal imbalances, premature exposure of infant eyes to light, and vitamin A deficiency in the mother. The observation that the incidence of the disease increases in direct relation to the duration and exposure of premature infants to oxygen was reported first in 1952. A controlled study was completed in 1954; it established oxygen as the most likely etiologic agent for the condition. The rise of this disease, called by some an epidemic, closely parallels the development of the ability to effectively concentrate oxygen administration to infants in incubators (Silverman, 1980).

The importance of oxygen concentration monitoring became apparent as experimental evidence of the early 1950s accumulated. Ambient oxygen levels were limited whenever possible to 40%, and measurements of oxygen concentration in the blood were made. This did not entirely resolve the issue for several reasons: the disease occurred in the absence of supplemental oxygen therapy; it occurred when 40% oxygen was administered "appropriately"; and this level of supplemental oxygen often was not sufficient to relieve the respiratory distress syndrome that often accompanies prematurity. The important relationship between arterial blood oxygen (PO_2), the respiratory distress syndrome, and retrolental fibroplasia is now well established. However, numerous attempts to monitor and control arterial blood oxygen (PO_2) have been fraught with great difficulties, both technical and physiologic.

Approximately 10% of infants under 2500 g birth weight are afflicted with the respiratory distress syndrome, accounting for approximately 40,000 infants per year in the United States; the incidence of RLF blindness following oxygen administration is a small percentage of the group, perhaps 2%. Recognizing this, many authors now designate this disease retinopathy of prematurity (ROP).

An appreciation of the clinical stages of the disease accompanied experimental evidence concerning its pathophysiology. Evidence suggests that high arterial oxygen levels cause vasospastic constriction of developing peripheral retinal vasculature, inciting the elaboration of vasoproliferative factors. New vessels grow in a mound-like elevation, typically in the temporal peripheral retina (Tasman, 1971). Such neovascularization either may proceed or spontaneously regress. With resolution of the active process, cicatrization (scarring) occurs, which on contraction may drag the retina temporally. If traction is sufficient, perpherial retinal detachment occurs. When the entire retina becomes detached and drawn into a fibrous cicatrix (scar) behind the lens, the disease has reached its most advanced stage, representing the clinical picture for which the disease was named. Additional ocular sequelae include myopia; vitreous opacification; and a variety of retinal changes, including chorioretinal atrophy, pigmentary retinopathy, and retinal folds. Based on these observations, clinical characterization of the disease recently has been reviewed and a proposed international classification published.

The relationship of oxygen therapy to neurological outcome also was studied. In general, neurologic outcome is inversely related to ocular outcome; that is, spastic diplegia incidence falls and retrolental fibroplasia rises with increased duration of oxygen treatment. Thus, there is a desire to prevent neurologic events following cyanotic attacks (secondary to cardiorespiratory insufficiency) by extending treatment with oxygen; this then increases the risk of RLF.

The full spectrum of consequences of RLF blindness to the child, family, social agencies, school, and community is beginning to be fully considered. Affected individuals tend not to see loss of sight as a major burden. Preconceptions, paternalism, and insensitivity of authorities in the visually oriented world often constrict the lives of those who wish to see this same world nonvisually. A number of factors—medical, legal, and societal—tend to perpetuate the stereotype that the blind wish to shed in their desire to move toward independence. Thus the complexity of this disease at several levels—visual, neurological, personal, and social—is only now being appreciated.

The visually disabling forms of RLF may impact on school performance by limiting sensory input, the degree of disability reflecting the severity of disease. Teachers may observe "blindness" where disability is severe. When bilateral retinal blindness is present, braille instruction is required. The educator should be aware of the complexity of problems for individuals with this condition.

REFERENCES

Silverman, W. A. (1980). *Retrolental fibroplasia: A modern parable*. New York: Grune & Stratton.

Tasman, W. (Ed.). (1971). *Retinal diseases in children*. New York: Harper & Row.

GEORGE R. BEAUCHAMP
*Cleveland Clinic Foundation,
Cleveland, Ohio*

REVERSALS IN READING AND WRITING

The term reversals is usually associated with reading or writing disabilities. Reversals are difficulties characterized in either reading or writing by reversing letters, numbers, words, or phrases (e.g., *saw* for *was*, *p* for *q*), or what some have referred to as mirror reading or writing.

In Orton's first theoretical papers on reading disabilities (1925, 1928), he suggested that such reversal problems were due to poorly established hemispheric dominance. Orton (1928) cited the following examples of strephosymbolia (literally, twisted symbols): (1) difficulty discriminating *b* and *d*; (2) confusion with words like *ton* and *not*;

(3) ability to read from mirror images; and (4) facility at writing mirrorlike images. Orton further stipulated that these reversal problems were not caused by mental retardation. Other investigators have since promoted the concept of developmental lag in perceptual abilities as causally related to reading disorders (Bender, 1957; Fernald, 1943).

As a result of this initial work, a variety of programs were developed that attempted to remediate reading disabilities by treating perceptual problems (Forness, 1981). For example, Kephart (1960) focused on the use of motor activities for developing perceptual skills. Additionally, programs such as Barsch's (1965) movigenic curriculum and Delacato's (1966) patterning techniques promoted the evolutionary progression that was seen as a necessary prerequisite for complete perceptual development. Frostig and Horne (1964) developed a visual perceptual program to remediate these difficulties, while Gillingham and Stillman (1960) prescribed the language triangle approach of combining the visual, auditory, and kinesthetic modes for teaching reading and writing.

Empirical support that reversals are due to perceptual deficits has been equivocal. It has been seen that many beginning readers reverse letters and words (Gibson & Levin, 1980). In fact, more than one half of all kindergarten students typically reverse letters (Gibson & Levin, 1980). This is considered a part of the normal component of discrimination learning when children first acquire reading skills. Gibson and Levin (1980) cite research that indicates that normal children continue to make reversal errors until the age of eight or nine. It was also found that single letter reversals account for only a small percent of total reading errors exhibited by poor readers. In addition, it has been questioned whether such reversals in learning-disabled students indicate underlying perceptual problems rather than, for example, linguistic problems (Gupta, Ceci, & Slater, 1978).

Remedial programs based on visual motor perceptual training have generally not resulted in reading improvement (Keogh, 1974). Later research efforts have suggested that reversal problems can be remediated with the use of behavioral techniques. Hasazi and Hasazi (1972) reported an instance in which digit reversals (e.g., 12 for 21) of an 8-year-old boy were remediated by means of contingent teacher attention. With respect to letter reversals, Carnine (1981) provided evidence that discriminations that reflect differences in spatial orientation only (e.g., b, d) are best taught singly. In other words, a student should be taught to discriminate b from nonreversible letters first, followed by the separate introduction of the letter d. Some specific instructional techniques are provided by Hallahan, Kauffman, and Lloyd (1985).

REFERENCES

Barsch, R. H. (1965). *A movigenic curriculum* (Publication No. 25). Madison, WI: Wisconsin State Department of Instruction.

Bender, L. A. (1957). Specific reading disability as a maturational lag. *Bulletin of the Orton Society, 7,* 9–18.

Carnine, D. W. (1981). Reducing training problems associated with visually and auditorily similar correspondences. *Journal of Learning Disabilities, 14,* 276–279.

Delacato, C. H. (1966). *Neurological organization and reading.* Springfield, IL: Thomas.

Fernald, G. (1943). *Remedial techniques in basic school subjects.* New York: McGraw-Hill.

Forness, S. R. (1981). *Recent concepts in dyslexia: Implications for diagnosis and remediation.* Reston, VA: Council for Exceptional Children.

Frostig, M., & Horne, D. (1964). *The Frostig program for the development of visual perception: Teacher's guide.* Chicago: Follett.

Gibson, E. J., & Levin, H. (1980). *The psychology of reading.* Cambridge, MA: MIT Press.

Gillingham, A., & Stillman, B. W. (1960). *Remedial training for children with specific disability in reading, spelling, and penmanship.* Cambridge, MA: Educator's.

Gupta, R., Ceci, S. J., & Slater, A. M. (1978). Visual discrimination in good and poor readers. *Journal of Special Education, 12,* 409–416.

Hallahan, D. P., Kauffman, J. M., & Lloyd, J. W. (1985). *Introduction to learning disabilities* (2nd ed.). Englewood Cliffs, NJ: Prentice-Hall.

Hasazi, J. E., & Hasazi, S. E. (1972). Effects of teacher attention on digit-reversal behavior in an elementary school child. *Journal of Applied Behavior Analysis, 5,* 157–162.

Keogh, B. K. (1974). Optometric vision training programs for children with learning disabilities: Review of issues and research. *Journal of Learning Disabilities, 7,* 219–231.

Kephart, N. C. (1960). The slow learner in the classroom. Columbus, OH: Merrill.

Orton, S. T. (1925). Word-blindness in school children. *Archives of Neurology and Psychiatry, 14,* 581–615.

Orton, S. T. (1928). Specific reading disability-strephosymbolia. *Journal of the American Medical Association, 90,* 1095–1099.

THOMAS E. SCRUGGS
MARGO A. MASTROPIERI
Purdue University

AGRAPHIA
DYSGRAPHIA
HANDWRITING

REVERSE MAINSTREAMING

Reverse mainstreaming is a procedure that involves introducing nonhandicapped students into special classrooms to work with severely handicapped students. The purpose is to maximize integration of severely handicapped and nonhandicapped students. Mainstreaming, a more familiar concept, refers to the integration of the handicapped into the nonhandicapped classroom to enable each individual to participate in patterns of everyday life that are close to the mainstream. Reverse mainstreaming is, as the name suggests, a procedure carried out in reverse of mainstreaming but striving for the same goals. Reverse mainstreaming can be used with all severe handicaps.

The primary use of reverse mainstreaming has been with the severely and profoundly mentally handicapped and the autistic. Until the early 1970 these severely handicapped students were educated in segregated environments that had only handicapped individuals. These environments included institutions and special education schools. Mildly mentally handicapped students, on the other hand, were more likely to be educated in closer proximity to nonhandicapped peers.

There has been widespread acceptance in the past 15 years of the philosophy of normalization. This philosophy implies that the handicapped should be able to live as similarly as possible to the nonhandicapped. Public Law 94-142, adopted in 1978, required that the handicapped be educated as similarly as possible to the nonhandicapped. For the mildly mentally handicapped, this has resulted in considerable integration into nonhandicapped classrooms. For the severely mentally handicapped, this has meant placement in buildings occupied by the nonhandicapped. It is frequently unrealistic to expect the severely mentally handicapped to participate in regular classrooms because of their low functioning levels and special needs. In these cases, in order to maximize interactions, special educators arrange for nonhandicapped students to participate in the classrooms of the handicapped as volunteers, or "peers"; hence, mainstreaming in reverse.

The implementation of reverse mainstreaming requires cooperation and communication between teachers of the handicapped and the nonhandicapped. They must work together to prepare the nonhandicapped "peers" who will participate. Poorman (1980), who started Project Special Friend in a central Pennsylvania community, recommends using slides of the handicapped children followed by discussions about their characteristics and behaviors and about the role of the peers. Topics include communication skills, handicaps, realistic expectations, and dealing with inappropriate behaviors. Opportunities should be provided for the nonhandicapped students to interact in a social way with their special friends.

Poorman (1980) outlines a sequential program, moving from introductions through free play activities to instructional activities in the reverse mainstreaming setting. Almond, Rodgers, and Krug (1979) provide a detailed presentation of techniques for training peer volunteers to work with severely handicapped autistic students. The volunteers initiate individualized educational programs on a one-to-one basis under the supervision of special educators. They participate in the classroom of the severely handicapped on a weekly schedule. Donder and Nietupski (1981) describe how reverse mainstreaming can be implemented to maximize social integration on the playground.

In all these instances, nonhandicapped students are introduced into the classroom and playground environment of the severely handicapped in order to maximize interactions between the handicapped and the nonhandicapped. This procedure has been shown to lead to increased learning of preacademic skills and socially appropriate behavior by the handicapped. It also contributes to greater acceptance of the handicapped by their nonhandicapped peers. While sharing goals and accomplishments with mainstreaming, the procedure is still mainstreaming in reverse—bringing the mainstream into the classrooms and the lives of the severely handicapped.

REFERENCES

Almond, P., Rodgers, S., & Krug, D. (1979). A model for including elementary students in the severely handicapped classroom. *Teaching Exceptional Children, 11,* 135–139.

Donder, D., & Nietupski, J. (1981). Nonhandicapped adolescents teaching playground skills to their mentally retarded peers: Toward a less restrictive middle school environment. *Education & Training of the Mentally Retarded, 16,* 270–276.

Poorman, C. (1980). Mainstreaming in reverse with a special friend. *Teaching Exceptional Children, 12,* 136–142.

NANCY L. HUTCHINSON
BERNICE Y. L. WONG
Simon Fraser University

LEAST RESTRICTIVE ENVIRONMENT
MAINSTREAMING
PEER RELATIONSHIPS

REVISED CHILDREN'S MANIFEST ANXIETY SCALE (RCMAS)

See CHILDREN'S MANIFEST ANXIETY SCALE.

REVISUALIZATION

Revisualization has been defined as the active recall of the visual image of words, letters, and numbers (Johnson & Myklebust, 1967). Deficiencies in revisualization prevent students from picturing the visual form of printed material, and are related to difficulty in spelling and writing. By contrast, good spellers are able to compare their productions against an auditory or visual image when checking their spelling.

In terms of memory functioning, recall tends to be the area most substantially impaired for children with revisualization deficits, while recognition is somewhat less affected. Therefore, activities such as dictated spelling tests, number sequencing, and drawing from memory are often extremely difficult for students with revisualization deficits. Such deficits will be less apparent when matching and multiple choice activities are employed.

Johnson and Myklebust (1967) have listed closure and visual sequential memory as two component subprocesses that are deficient in children who cannot revisualize printed material. Closure is the extrapolation of a whole from an incomplete gestalt. Children who have problems with closure are unable to supply missing details and, as such, are less able to code visual information for later retrieval. Deficiencies in visual sequential memory, the recall of images in order, impairs children's ability to remember the order and position of letters within words and words within sentences.

Instructional materials and techniques have been designed to help children compensate for deficits in closure and sequencing by capitalizing on their intact perceptual processes (Johnnson & Myklebust, 1967). Thus, training materials that use well-formed, heavily outlined letters have been recommended for circumventing closure problems. Sequencing deficits have been remediated by using different print sizes or colors. Multisensory techniques have also been suggested for remediating revisualization deficits. Other methods specify the use of initial consonant cues, verbal labels, verbal mediators, and categorization strategies (Peters & Cripps, 1980).

McIntyre (1982), reporting on research with learning-disabled children, criticizes the reliance on visual memory in Myklebust and Johnson's approach, and contends that reading is a verbal skill. On the other hand, Dodd (1980) has reported that deaf children, relying stricty on visual coding, are able to recognize regular spelling patterns. Peters and Cripps (1980), consolidating the two positions, state that words that have regular sound-letter associations can be coded verbally, but that irregular words must be revisualized.

REFERENCES

Dodd, B. (1980). The spelling abilities of profoundly prelingually deaf children. In U. Firth (Ed.), *Cognitive processes in spelling.* London: Academic.

Johnson, D. J., & Myklebust, H. R. (1967). *Learning disabilities.* New York: Grune & Stratton.

McIntyre, T. C. (1982). *Dyslexia: The effects of visual memory and serial recall.* (ERIC Document Reproduction Service No. ED 227 603).

Peters, M. L., & Cripps, C. (1980). *Catchwords: Ideas for teaching spelling.* New South Wales, Australia: Harcourt Brace Jovanovich Group (Australia) PTY., Limited.

GARY BERKOWITZ
Temple University

IMAGERY
VISUAL TRAINING

REYE'S SYNDROME

Reye's syndrome is an acute, frequently fatal disease of childhood. It is given the name of the Australian pathologist, R. D. K. Reye, who described the characteristics of this syndrome in the early 1960s. It is a rare condition with a reported risk of 1 to 2 per 100,000 children per year (Kolata, 1985). The onset of Reye's syndrome frequently follows an upper respiratory or gastrointestinal viral infection, such as may be associated with influenza B or chicken pox (*Mosby's*, 1983; Silberberg, 1979). Recovery from these relatively mild symptoms may appear to be under way when the life-threatening symptoms of Reye's syndrome ensue. These symptoms include persistent vomiting, fever, disturbances of consciousness progressing to coma, and convulsions. A characteristic posture (flexed elbows, clenched hands, extended legs) may be identified in some patients (Magalini, 1971). Deep, irregular respiration may occur, sometimes leading to respiratory arrest. The pathology associated with Reye's syndrome includes massive edema (swelling) of the brain and fatty infiltration of the liver and kidneys (Magalini, 1971; Silberberg, 1979).

The etiology of Reye's syndrome is unknown. A number of findings, including increased incidence following influenza B outbreaks and the localization of a virus in some Reye's patients, suggest a viral infection as the precipitating factor (Silberberg, 1979). Some studies have reported a link between aspirin given as a therapeutic agent during influenza or chicken pox and the subsequent development of Reye's syndrome. A study of 29 children with Reye's syndrome and 143 controls reported "children with chicken pox or flu who take aspirin may be 25 times more likely to get Reye's syndrome than those who do not" (Kolata, 1985, p. 391). In January 1985, Margaret Heckler, secretary of the Department of Health and Human Services, requested that manufacturers of aspirin include warning labels on aspirin products (Kolata, 1985). Further studies of the link between aspirin and Reye's syndrome are being conducted.

The course of Reye's syndrome is variable. A high percentage of afflicted children die. Estimates of mortality range from 25 to 50%, although more recent figures are consistent with the lower figure, probably as a result of enhanced medical management (Kolata, 1985; Silberberg, 1979). Survivors of Reye's syndrome frequently display significant neurologic sequelae, including mental retardation, seizures, hemiplegia, or behavior problems including hyperactivity and distractibility (Culbertson et al., 1985; Silberberg, 1979). There is evidence of an age effect on outcome for survivors of Reye's syndrome, with younger children exhibiting more severe impairment (Culbertson et al., 1985; Hartlage, Stovall, & Hartlage, 1980).

Although Reye's syndrome is an extremely rare condition, it is of relevance for educators since it afflicts children exclusively and is associated with sometimes devastating impairment. Because of the suspicion of an association between aspirin and Reye's syndrome, school officials should exercise caution in the use of aspirin with children. Survivors of Reye's syndrome may require special education or related services, which should be determined following a multifactored evaluation.

REFERENCES

Culbertson, J. L., Elbert, J. C., Gerrity, K., & Rennert, O. M. (1985, February). *Neuropsychologic and academic sequelae of Reye's syndrome.* Paper presented to the International Neuropsychological Society, San Diego.

Hartlage, L. C., Stovall, K. W., & Hartlage, P. L. (1980). Age related neuropsychological sequelae of Reye's syndrome. *Clinical Neuropsychology, 21,* 83–86.

Kolata, G. (1985). Study of Reye's-aspirin link raises concerns. *Science, 227,* 391–392.

Magalini, S. (1971). *Dictionary of medical syndromes.* Philadelphia: Lippincott.

Mosby's medical and nursing dictionary (1983). St. Louis: Mosby.

Silberberg, D. (1979). Encephalitic complications of viral infections and vaccines. In P. B. Beeson, W. McDermott, & J. B. Wyngaarden (Eds.), *Cecil textbook of medicine* (pp. 836–839). Philadelphia: Saunders.

CATHY F. TELZROW
*Cuyahoga Special Education
Service Center, Maple
Heights, Ohio*

ENCEPHALITIS

REYNOLDS, CECIL R. (1952–   )

Before receiving his BA in psychology in 1975 from the University of North Carolina at Wilmington, Cecil Reynolds was a professional baseball player with the New York Mets organization for five years. He received his MEd in psychometrics in 1976, his EdS in school psychology in 1977, and his PhD in educational psychology in 1978, all from the University of Georgia. There his mentors were Alan S. Kaufman and E. Paul Torrance, both of whom have continued to influence Reynolds heavily.

Reynolds went to the University of Nebraska, where he became assistant professor in 1978. He remained there until 1981, during which time he was acting director and then associate director of the Buros Institute of Mental Measurement. Reynolds was responsible for moving the Buros Institute to Nebraska and was the first director of the Institute to succeed its founder, Oscar K. Buros, who had served as its director from 1928 until his death in 1978. Reynolds came to Texas A&M University as associate professor in 1981 and became director of the Doctoral School Psychology Training Program, which he led to

Cecil R. Reynolds

American Psychological Association accreditation in 1985. He gained the rank of professor in 1985.

Reynolds' primary interests are in measurement, particularly as related to the practical problems of individual assessment and diagnosis. He also has worked in childhood emotional disturbance and is the author of the Revised Children's Manifest Anxiety Scale (Reynolds & Richmond, 1985). He is best known in school psychology for his work in the area of the cultural test bias hypothesis (Reynolds, 1983). He is on the editorial board of more than 10 major journals, including *School Psychology Review, Journal of School Psychology, Journal of Learning Disabilities,* and *Journal of Special Education.* He has published more than 200 scholarly and professional papers and is author or editor of eight books. He is senior editor, with Terry Gutkin, of *The Handbook of School Psychology,* and is editor of the Plenum book series, Perspectives on Individual Differences.

In 1983 he chaired the U.S. Department of Education, Special Education Programs Work Group on Critical Measurement Issues in Issues in Learning Disabilities. The report of this task force (Reynolds, 1984) and several related works (Reynolds, 1981; Reynolds & Stowe, 1985) have been instrumental in developing practical but psychometrically sound models of severe discrepancy analysis in learning disabilities diagnosis. He is the youngest recipient of the American Psychological Association (APA) Division of School Psychology's Lightner Witmer Award and has also received early career awards from the Division of Educational Psychology and the Division of Evaluation and Measurement of the same association.

Reynolds also has been active politically. He served a 3-year stint on the executive board of the National Association of School Psychologists and as vice president of the Division of School Psychology of the APA. In 1986 he was elected to a 2-year term as president of the National Academy of Neuropsychologists. He is a frequent speaker at state and regional professional meetings throughout the United States and Canada.

REFERENCES

Reynolds, C. R. (1981). The fallacy of "two years below grade level for age" as a diagnostic criterion for reading disorders. *Journal of School Psychology, 19*, 250–258.

Reynolds, C. R. (1983). Test bias: In God we trust, all others must have data. *Journal of Special Education, 17*, 214–268.

Reynolds, C. R. (1984). Critical measurement issues in learning disabilities. *Journal of Special Education, 18*, 451–476.

Reynolds, C. R., & Richmond, B. O. (1985). *Revised–children's manifest anxiety scale.* Los Angeles: Western Psychological Services.

Reynolds, C. R., & Stowe, M. (1985). *Severe discrepancy analysis.* Philadelphia: TRAIN.

RAND B. EVANS
Texas A&M University

BUROS INSTITUTE OF MENTAL MEASUREMENT
KAUFMAN, ALAN S.
REVISED CHILDREN'S MANIFEST ANXIETY SCALE
SEVERE DISCREPANCY ANALYSIS
TORRANCE, E. PAUL

REYNOLDS, MAYNARD C. (1922–   )

A native of Doyan, North Dakota, Maynard Reynolds received his BS in education from Moorhead State University in 1942. He obtained his graduate degrees in educational psychology at the University of Minnesota after World War II, receiving his MA in 1947 and his PhD in 1950. After brief teaching assignments at the University of Northern Iowa and Long Beach State University, he returned to the University of Minnesota, first as the di-

Maynard C. Reynolds

rector of the Psychoeducational Clinic, then as the chairman of the Department of Special Education, and, more recently, as professor of educational psychology and special education.

In the 1950s Reynolds became involved in the development of programs for exceptional students and issues concerning the diagnosis of such children. In the 1960s Reynolds became the international president of the Council of Exceptional Children (CEC). Later, as the first chair of CEC's Policy Commission, he was increasingly active in advancing the concept that every child has a right to an education. Since the passage of PL 94-142, the Education for All the Handicapped Children Act, Reynolds has led national programs in technical assistance systems relating to changes in special education programs. From 1978 to 1984, with James Ysseldyke and Richard Weinberg, Reynolds also helped in Network, a technical assistance effort in the field of school psychology.

Reynolds has been included in *Who's Who in America* and *American Men and Women of Science.* He has been given the J. E. Wallace Wallin Award by the CEC for service to handicapped children and the Mildred Thomson Award by the American Association on Mental Deficiencies.

Some of his principal publications include a text, *Teaching Exceptional Children in All America's Schools,* and several articles, including "Categories and Variables in Special Education" (1972), "A Framework for Considering Some Issues in Special Education" (1962), and "A Strategy for Research" (1963).

REFERENCES

Reynolds, M. C. (1962). A framework for considering some issues in special education. *Exceptional Children, 28*, 367–370.

Reynolds, M. C. (1963). A strategy for research. *Exceptional Children, 29*(5), 213–219.

Reynolds, M. C., & Balow, B. (1972). Categories and variables in special education. *Exceptional Children, 38*(5), 357–366.

Reynolds, M. C., & Birch, J. W. (1982). *Teaching exceptional children in all America's schools* (2nd ed.). Reston, VA: Council for Exceptional Children.

E. VALERIE HEWITT
Texas A&M University

RH FACTOR INCOMPATIBILITY (ERYTHROBLASTOSIS FETALIS)

Rh factor incompatibility between mother and fetus results from a fetus with an Rh positive blood type within a mother whose blood is Rh negative. Simply stated, the mother develops antibodies that attack and destroy the red blood cells of the fetus or neonate. This condition is known as erythroblastosis fetalis and is classified as a blood disease of the fetus or neonate (Benson, 1978).

The appearance of Rh negative blood types is about 15% in the white population and about 5% in the black. Fifty-five percent of white males are heterozygous carriers of the Rh negative blood type. These data indicate that Rh incompatibility occurs three times more often in the white population.

The condition occurs following the introduction of Rh positive fetal blood into the Rh negative blood of the mother. This may occur during pregnancy, at the time of delivery, or as a result of trauma or abortion. Once the mother has been sensitized to the fetal blood, her body begins to manufacture increasingly larger amounts of the Rh antibody. Small amounts of fetal blood can now trigger massive antibody production.

Fortunately, two factors help prevent this from occurring. First, the antibody production does not usually occur at a serious level during the first pregnancy, but only after birth. Second, 55% of white males are heterozygous for the Rh factor, increasing the possibility of producing an Rh negative fetus and eliminating the incompatibility problem. Finally, the capacity of an Rh negative mother to be sensitized to the antigen is variable; some produce the antibody quickly and subject the first pregnancy to risk; others never develop the antibody and can bear several Rh positive children without problem (Behrman & Vaughan, 1983).

In most cases, the condition is immediately determined at birth by the presence of jaundice. In less severe cases, treatment may include planning an earlier delivery, phototherapy, and an exchange transfusion to remove the antibody-attacked red blood cells from the infants blood (Butts & Puls, 1981). In severe cases, termed hydrops fetalis, the reaction includes numerous body systems and may result in the death of the infant.

The risk of developing this condition can be minimized by screening all Rh negative mothers at regular prenatal intervals for the immunization from Rh positive antigens (Butts & Puls, 1981). "The risk of initial sensitization of Rh negative mothers has been reduced from 10–20% to less than 1% by injection of human anti-D globulin (RhoGam) within 72 hours of delivery or abortion" (Behrman & Vaughan, 1983).

REFERENCES

Behrman, R., & Vaughan, V. (1983). *Nelson textbook of pediatrics* (12th ed.). Philadelphia: Saunders.

Benson, R. (Ed.). (1978). *Current obstetric and gynecologic diagnosis and treatment* (2nd ed.). Los Altos, CA: Lange Medical.

Butts, P., & Puls, K. (1981). *Diseases: The nurses' reference library series*. Philadelphia: Intermed Communications.

JOHN E. PORCELLA
Rhinebeck Country School,
Rhinebeck, New York

RIGHT-HANDEDNESS

Right-handedness is a species-specific characteristic of humans (Hicks & Kinsbourne, 1978). Additionally, right-handedness, also called dextrality, can be considered universal in that 90% of the human population is right-handed (Corballis & Beale, 1983). Since the majority of individuals prefer using their right hands, and are also more skilled with their right hands, more positive properties and values have come to be associated with the right than with the left. For example, throughout history the right has represented the side of the gods, strength, life, goodness, light, the state of rest, the limited, the odd, the square, and the singular. The left has been signified by the polar opposites of these characteristics. Maleness also has been traditionally associated with the right, providing symbolic expression of the universality of male dominance (Needham, 1974).

Although people classify themselves as right-handed or left-handed, handedness more accurately spans a continuous range from extreme right-handedness through mixed-handedness or ambidexterity to extreme left-handedness (Corballis & Beale, 1976). Investigators always have been curious about the abundance of right-handedness and the rarity of the various degrees of nonright-handedness. However, studies of historical records and artifacts have revealed enough inconsistencies in incidence to preclude any simple choice between culture or biology to explain the origin of handedness. Consequently, combinations of these various nature and nurture explanations have been invoked. Harris (1980) provides an interesting and detailed account of these various theories.

Corballis and Beale (1983), in an extensive study of the neuropsychology of right and left, have argued that right-handedness is biologically rather than culturally determined. They cite the fact that right-handedness always has been universal across diverse and seemingly unrelated cultures; moreover, although right-handedness itself is not manifest until late in the first year of life, it is correlated with other asymmetries that are evident at or before birth. They acknowledge that there are environmental pressures to be right-handed and that some naturally left-handed individuals may be compelled to use their right hands for certain tasks, but suggest that these very pressures have their origins in the fundamental right-handedness of most human beings.

Today the relationship between right-handedness and the unilateral representation of language in the left cerebral hemisphere is well documented. Case studies linking the side of brain damage and the incidence of aphasia, or language impairment, have revealed that approximately 98% of right-handers use the left hemisphere of their brain for language. A similar conclusion has been drawn from studies in which linguistic functioning has been impaired in 95% of the right-handers whose left cerebral hemispheres were injected with sodium amobarbitol, a momentarily incapacitating drug.

The hemisphere of the brain used for language in left-handers is more variable. Two-thirds of left-handers have demonstrated the use of their left hemisphere. Almost half of the remaining left-handers use their right hemispheres for speech, while the remainder have some capacity for speech in both hemispheres (Rasmussen & Milner, 1975). In view of these data, many investigators suggest that both right-handedness and left cerebral dominance for language are genetically controlled expressions of some underlying biological gradient. This relationship further reveals the significance of right-handedness in the unique cognitive functioning of the human species.

REFERENCES

Corballis, M. C., & Beale, I. L. (1976). *The psychology of left and right*. Hillsdale, NJ: Erlbaum.

Corballis, M. C., & Beale, I. L. (1983). *The ambivalent mind*. Chicago: Nelson-Hall.

Harris, L. J. (1980). Left-handedness: Early theories, facts, and fancies. In J. Herron (Ed.), *Neuropsychology of left-handedness* (pp. 3–78). New York: Academic.

Hicks, R. E., & Kinsbourne, M. (1978). Human handedness. In M. Kinsbourne (Ed.), *Asymmetrical function of the brain* (pp. 267–273). New York: Cambridge University Press.

Needham, R. (Ed.). (1974). *Right and left: Essays on dual symbolic classification*. Chicago: University of Chicago Press.

Rasmussen, T., & Milner, B. (1975). Clinical and surgical studies of the cerebral speech areas in man. In K. J. Zulch, O. Creutzfeldt, & G. Galbraith (Eds.), *Otfried Foerster symposium on cerebral localization*. Heidelberg: Springer-Verlag.

GALE A. HARR
*Maple Heights City Schools,
Maple Heights, Ohio*

CEREBRAL DOMINANCE
LEFT BRAIN, RIGHT BRAIN

RIGHT TO EDUCATION

The right to education refers to the legal concept that justifies a school-aged person's freedom to receive educational services. The conceptual and legal development of this right has occurred in conjunction with an increasing societal concern for individuals who exhibit exceptional educational needs. These changing social attitudes have been reflected in judicial decisions and legislative efforts that have substantiated the right of all school-aged children and youths to receive educational services.

The U.S. Constitution, although not explicit in its guarantee of the right to education, has been cited as the fundamental justification for the provision of educational services. Specifically, the right to education has been implied from the Fourteenth Amendment, which states in its equal protection clause, "a state may not pass laws, nor act in any official way, so as to establish for a group of citizens benefits or penalties which other citizens do not receive." Thus, this amendment requires that, where educational

services are available, such services must be available to all on an equivalent basis.

Early court cases that addressed the right of the exceptional needs learner to receive educational services did not reflect this interpretation. Generally, litigation in this area prior to the 1950s resulted in exclusionary educational policies (e.g., *Watson* v. *Cambridge,* 1883; *Beattie* v. *Board of Education,* 1919). However, with the onset of the increasing civil rights awareness apparent in the early 1950s, right to education court cases evidenced a more positive trend. Some of the more influential court cases that have related to the development of the right to education concept for the exceptional needs learner include *Brown* v. *Board of Education of Topeka* (1954), *Pennsylvania Association for Retarded Citizens* v. *the Commonwealth of Pennsylvania* (1971), and *Mills* v. *Board of Education of the District of Columbia* (1972).

The *Brown* case dealt with the rights of a class of citizens (blacks in the South) to attend public schools in their community on a nonsegregated basis. The major issues in this case were suspect classification (i.e., classification by race) and equal protection. In a unanimous decision for the plaintiff, the Supreme Court emphasized the social importance of education and also ruled that education must be made available on equal terms to all.

The *Pennsylvania Association for Retarded Citizens (PARC)* case dealt more specifically with the educational rights of exceptional needs learners. Citing the Fourteenth Amendment right to due process and equal protection, the judge in this case ruled that Pennsylvania statutes permitting denial or postponement of entry to public schools by mentally retarded children were unconstitutional. The terms of the settlement reached in this case included provision of due process rights to the plaintiffs and identification and placement in public school programs of all previously excluded children.

More general in its plaintiff class, the *Mills* case challenged the exclusion of mentally retarded, epileptic, brain-damaged, hyperactive, and behavior-disordered children from public schools. Finding for the plaintiffs, the court required the defendants to provide full public education or "adequate alternatives." These alternatives could only be provided after notice and a reasonable opportunity to challenge the services that had been given. The progression from *Brown* (1954) to *PARC* (1971) to *Mills* (1972) reflects an increasing sophistication in the awareness of the educational needs of individuals with exceptional learning characteristics. This more complete view of the educational needs and rights of exceptional individuals is also apparent in recent legislation.

Two major legislative efforts that have addressed the educational rights of exceptional needs learners are the Rehabilitation Act of 1973, Section 504, and PL 94-142. Section 504 of the Rehabilitation Act of 1973 is particularly important because it deals with all programs that receive federal funds. This legislation mandates nondiscrimination on the basis of handicapping conditions if these funds are to continue.

Public Law 94-142 embodies the intent of all legislation that it follows in its highly specific delineation of the educational rights of exceptional needs learners. This law requires that all individuals, regardless of handicapping condition or its degree, be offered a free appropriate education at public expense. Public Law 94-142 further specifies that these services must be delivered in the least restrictive environment appropriate for the individual child.

The right to education for children and youths with exceptional learning characteristics has resulted from changing societal views of the needs and rights of these individuals. These attitudes have been reflected in increased litigation questioning the adequacy, availability, and appropriateness of the educational services offered this group. The outcome of these cases has established a legal basis for a right to education. This litigation has in turn led to legislation developed to ensure that right. For a comprehensive discussion of the right to education for the exceptional needs learner (see Wortis, 1978).

REFERENCES

Beattie v. *State Board of Education of Wisconsin*. (1978). In J. Wortis (Ed.), *Mental retardation and developmental disabilities*. New York: Brunner/Mazel.

Watson v. *Cambridge, Mass*. (1978). In J. Wortis (Ed.), *Mental retardation and developmental disabilities*. New York: Brunner/Mazel.

Wortis, J. (Ed.). (1978). *Mental retardation and developmental disabilities*. New York: Brunner/Mazel.

J. TODD STEPHENS
*University of Wisconsin,
Madison*

BROWN *v.* BOARD OF EDUCATION
EDUCATION FOR ALL HANDICAPPED CHILDREN ACT OF 1975
MILLS *v.* BOARD OF EDUCATION
PAR *v.* COMMONWEALTH OF PENNSYLVANIA

RIGHT TO TREATMENT

The term right to treatment refers to the legal concept that justifies an individual's freedom to receive therapeutic and/or curative services. Initially developed as an extension of litigation that targeted the availability of medically oriented services for institutionalized individuals, recent legal interpretations of this right have been broadened to include the right to habilitation and the right to education.

The development of the right to treatment reflects a trend of change in societal attitudes about providing services for individuals with exceptional learning or behav-

ioral characteristics. As attitudes have changed, concerned individuals have organized systematic efforts to ensure the availability of these services. These changes have resulted in litigative and legislative efforts that have addressed both the availability and adequacy of treatment for institutionalized people.

The three major court cases that shaped the legal interpretation of the right to treatment are *Rouse* v. *Cameron* (1968), *Wyatt* v. *Stickney* (1970), a class-action suit, and *New York Association for Retarded Citizens* v. *Rockefeller* (1972). In these cases constitutional amendments and state laws were interpreted as requiring treatment services for institutionalized persons. The first court case that dealt with the right of an institutionalized person to receive treatment was *Rouse* v. *Cameron* (1968). In this case, a man was institutionalized for 4 years after having been found not guilty, by reason of insanity, of a misdemeanor. While institutionalized, Rouse did not receive treatment. Citing constitutional rights (due process, equal protection, freedom from cruel and unusual punishment) and basing the decision on state law, the court ruled that confinement for treatment purposes when treatment was not made available was equivalent to imprisonment. Rouse was subsequently freed.

The *Wyatt* v. *Stickney* case (1970) was a class-action suit filed on behalf of the residents of three residential facilities in Alabama. The case was exhaustive in its pursuit of information and remedies. In the final ruling, standards were delineated with regard to treatment, habilitation, freedom from restraint, and a host of other treatment considerations. The court-ordered remedies included development of appropriate staff ratios, individual habilitation plans, and the delineation of specific procedures for treatment. Thus according to the rulings of *Wyatt* (1970), not only must treatment be available, but such treatment must also be supported by sufficient staff and planning.

Following the initial hearing of Wyatt, the *New York Association for Retarded Citizens* (NYARC) filed a petition against the then governor of the state, Nelson Rockefeller (*NYARC* v. *Rockefeller*, 1972) requesting relief from the overcrowded and inhumane conditions at the Willowbrook state institution. Citing the constitutional right to due process, the judge in this case ruled for immediate reduction of the resident population and appropriate development of community-based programs. Thus the *NYARC* case indicated that in addition to the right to receive adequate services in humane conditions, residents must also be considered as members of a society to which they should be allowed reasonable access.

Each of these cases represents a litigative response to either a complete lack of treatment availability, ineffective delivery of treatment, or use of inappropriate treatment. The decisions in these cases reflect an expanding awareness of the legal right of institutionalized individuals not only to receive treatment, but to be allowed access to systematically planned programming that meets the varied needs of the resident. For a more detailed discussion of the right to treatment, see *Wortis* (1978).

REFERENCE

Wortis, J. (Ed.). (1978). *Mental retardation and developmental disabilities*. New York: Brunner/Mazel.

J. TODD STEPHENS
*University of Wisconsin,
Madison*

RIGHT TO EDUCATION
WYATT *v.* STICKNEY

RIMLAND, BERNARD (1928–   )

Bernard Rimland earned his BA (1950) and MA (1951) at San Diego State University, and his PhD in experimental psychology in 1954 from Pennsylvania State University. On the diagnosis of his eldest son as autistic, Rimland began extensive research that led to his neural theory of infantile autism, as described in his prize-winning book. He founded the National Society for Autistic Children in 1965, and established the Institute for Child Behavior Research in San Diego in 1967. He currently serves as director of the institute, a nonprofit organization providing parents and professionals worldwide with information on etiology and treatment of severe behavior disorders in children.

Rimland was an early advocate of the use of behavior modification as well as a pioneer researcher on the effects of nutrition on behavior and mental health. In his massive review of the literature on autism in the early 1960s, Rimland found no scientific support for the widely held psychoanalytic theories that blamed supposedly unloving families for the child's severe disorder. Discarding the psychoanalytic explanation, Rimland advocated a neurophysiological cause of autism, involving, in part, possible dysfunction of the brain stem reticular formation. The reticular formation plays an important role in perception. Autistic children seem to have difficulty in distinguishing boundaries between themselves and their surrounding world. This perceptual malfunction may be the result of impaired reticular functioning. Rimland's treatments of choice are behavior modification and megavitamin therapy. Research by Rimland and others has shown some promising results for megavitamin therapy in autism and other childhood disorders.

Rimland's major publication is *Infantile Autism: The Syndrome and Its Implications for a Neural Theory of Behavior*, which won him the 1963 Appleton-Century-Crofts Award for a Distinguished Contribution to Psychology. In addition, he has published and contributed to over 100 journal articles and served as coeditor of *Modern Therapies*.

In addition to being honorary board member and founder of the National Society for Autistic Children, Rimland also serves on 32 advisory boards for publications, research organizations, and schools for children with severe behavior disorders. He also has served as vice president for the Academy of Orthomolecular Psychiatry and the Orthomolecular Medical Society.

MARY LEON PEERY
Texas A&M University

RITALIN

Ritalin (methylphenidate) is a widely used stimulant drug that has been found to improve the cognitive deficits and behavioral difficulties of hyperactive children. It has been estimated that nearly half a million children in the United States are being treated with Ritalin for hyperactivity each year (Gadow, 1983), although the exact extent of use is difficult to determine, primarily because there is no federal agency maintaining centralized records. The efficacy of Ritalin has been thoroughly documented in the pediatric psychopharmacology literature, particularly in the areas of classroom behavior, sustained attention, and impulse control.

The major side effects of Ritalin are anorexia and insomnia when taken late in the day. There have been some isolated cases reported in the literature of dyskinetic episodes after Ritalin administration; these episodes disappeared as the drug effect wore off. Short-term side effects with stimulants tend to be minor and easily reversed; insomnia and anorexia are usually temporary. Although a depression in growth rate and state-dependent learning have been posited (Ross & Ross, 1982), subsequent attempts to prove this effect have not been successful. The absorption rates of orally administered Ritalin have been surprisingly low, and differences have been observed in children's abilities to absorb individual doses. However, important information about optimal dosage levels to enhance cognitive performance has been obtained (Brown & Sleator, 1979).

Despite the notable short-term efficacy of Ritalin for the cognitive and behavioral difficulties of hyperactive children, results have been less than encouraging regarding school achievement (Brown, Wynne, & Medenis, 1985). In addition, follow-up studies have yielded inconsistent data with regard to finding a reemergence of symptomatology upon the cessation of Ritalin therapy (Ross & Ross, 1982). Despite these disappointing findings, the use of Ritalin has become the treatment of choice among the majority of physicians who treat hyperactive children.

REFERENCES

Brown, R. T., & Sleator, E. K. (1979). Methylphenidate in hyperkinetic children: Differences in dose effects on impulsive behavior. *Pediatrics, 64,* 408–411.

Brown, R. T., Wynne, M. E., & Medenis, R. (1985). Methylphenidate and cognitive therapy: A comparison of treatment approaches with hyperactive boys. *Journal of Abnormal Child Psychology, 13,* 69–87.

Gadow, K. (1983). Effects of stimulant drugs on academic performance in hyperactive and learning disabled children. *Journal of Learning Disabilities, 16,* 290–299.

Ross, D. M., & Ross, S. A. (1982). *Hyperactivity: Current issues, research and theory* (2nd ed.). New York: Wiley-Interscience.

RONALD T. BROWN
*Emory University School of
Medicine*

ATTENTION DEFICIT DISORDER-HYPERACTIVITY
MEDICAL MANAGEMENT

ROBERTS APPERCEPTION TEST FOR CHILDREN (RATC)

The Roberts Apperception Test for Children (RATC) is a personality assessment technique designed for children ages 6 to 15. The RATC is an attempt to combine the flexibility of a projective technique with the objectivity of a standardized scoring system. Similar to the Thematic Apperception Test and the Children's Apperception Test, the RATC consists of a set of drawings designed to elicit thematic stories. The test consists of 27 cards, 11 of which are parallel forms for males and females. Thus 16 cards are administered during testing, which takes 20 to 30 minutes.

The RATC is said to have significant benefits over similar projective measures (McArthur & Roberts, 1982). The test manual is well designed and includes substantial information on psychometric properties of the test, administration, and scoring, as well as several case studies. The picture drawings were designed specifically for children and young adolescents, and depict scenes designed to elicit common concerns. For example, specific cards portray parent/child relationships, sibling relationships, aggression, mastery, parental disagreement and affection, observation of nudity, school, and peer relationships. The test has a standardized scoring system, with scores converted to normalized T scores based on data from a sample of 200 well-adjusted children. The following information may be obtained from the RATC:

1. *Adaptive Scales.* Reliance on others, support for others, support for the child, limit setting, problem identification, resolution.

2. *Clinical scales.* Anxiety, aggression, depression, rejection, lack of resolution.

3. *Critical Indicators.* Atypical response, maladaptive outcome, refusal.

4. *Supplementary Measures.* Ego functioning, aggression, levels of projection.

A recent review of the RATC in the *Ninth Mental Measurements Yearbook* (Sines, 1985) describes four unpublished validity studies and concludes that the psychometric properties of the test are unimpressive. In perhaps the most substantial of these studies, 200 well-adjusted children were compared with 200 children evaluated at guidance clinics. The normal children scored higher than the children at clinics on all eight adaptive scales; however, the two groups could not be reliably differentiated on the clinical scales for anxiety, aggression, and depression.

Overall, the RATC appears to be a useful, well-designed projective technique for children and young adolescents. The standardized scoring system, while lacking in evidence compared with purely objective measures of personality, appears to be relatively satisfactory compared with similar projective techniques.

REFERENCES

McArthur, D., & Roberts, G. (1982). *Roberts Apperception Test for Children: Test Manual.* Los Angeles: Western Psychological Services.

Sines, J. (1985). The Roberts Apperception Test for Children. In J. Mitchell (Ed.), *The ninth mental measurements yearbook.* Lincoln, NE: Buros Institute.

FRANCES F. WORCHEL
Texas A&M University

CHILD PSYCHOLOGY
PERSONALITY ASSESSMENT

ROBINSON, HALBERT B. (1925–1981) and ROBINSON, NANCY M. (1930–   )

Nancy and Hal Robinson are known for their work with mentally retarded children, early child care, and gifted children. A text they wrote together, *The Mentally Retarded Child: A Psychological Approach* (1976), was influential in defining the field of mental retardation and emphasizing its research base. In 1966 Hal Robinson, with Ann Peters, founded the Frank Porter Graham Child Development Center at the University of North Carolina (Robinson & Robinson, 1971). In 1969 he became professor of psychology at the University of Washington. The Robinsons subsequently edited the *International Monograph Series on Early Child Care,* nine national descriptions of early child care options, including that of the United States (Robinson, Robinson, Wolins, Bronfenbrenner, & Richmond, 1974).

Hal Robinson also served as the principal investigator of the Child Development Research Group (CDRG, now the Center for the Study of Capable Youth) at the University of Washington (UW) in Seattle (1974–1981). Among the CDRG's programs were the Child Development Preschool (now independent of the UW), which focused on the identification of, development of, and curriculum for children with advanced intellectual and academic skills (Roedell, Jackson, & Robinson, 1980), and the UW Early Entrance Program, which admits to the university middle-school-age students who are ready for university-level work before entering high school (Robinson & Robinson, 1982).

The Robinsons are recipients of many awards including the Education Award from the American Association on Mental Deficiency (1982). Nancy Robinson is professor of psychiatry and behavioral sciences at the University of Washington and editor of the *American Journal of Mental Deficiency*. Since 1981, after Hal's death in a scuba accident, she has been director of the Child Development Research Group.

REFERENCES

Robinson, H. B., & Robinson, N. M. (1971). Longitudinal development of very young children in a comprehensive day care program: The first two years. *Child Development, 42,* 1673–1683.

Robinson, H. B., Robinson, N. M., Wolins, M., Bronfenbrenner, U., & Richmond, J. B. (1974). Early child care in the United States. In H. B. Robinson & N. M. Robinson (Eds.), *International monograph series on early child care*. London: Gordon & Breach.

Robinson, N. M., & Robinson, H. B. (1976). *The mentally retarded child: A psychological approach* (2nd ed.). New York: McGraw-Hill.

Robinson, N. M., & Robinson, H. B. (1982). The optimal match: Devising the best compromise for the highly gifted student. In D. H. Feldman (Ed.), *Developmental approaches to giftedness and creativity*. San Francisco: Jossey-Bass.

Roedell, W. C., Jackson, N. E., & Robinson, H. B. (1980). *Gifted young children*. New York: Teachers College, Columbia University.

ANN E. LUPKOWSKI
Texas A&M University

ROBOTICS

A robot is a programmable multifunctional device that is capable of performing a variety of tasks, manipulations, and locomotions. Robots come in one of four configurations: rectangular, cylindrical, spherical, and anthropomorphic articulated (Yin & Moore, 1984). These electronic devices have five characteristics that set them apart from other devices: mobility, dexterity, payload capacity, intelligence, and sensory capability. The characteristics are found singly or in combination; however, at present there is no single system that integrates all of the characteristics.

Industrial robots are known for their payload capacity. For example, the large electronic arms used on the automotive assembly lines in Japan are capable of lifting enormous weights and performing the same routines tirelessly. Other robots are recognized for their sensory capability (e.g., to sense temperature or to recognize patterns). Educational robots usually have mobility and dexterity. For example, the Heath Company's robot Hero can be told to go forward, backward, left, or right. Hero's arm and hand can manipulate objects. The arm's five axes allow him to wave, gesticulate, lift objects, and drop them. Hero also speaks 64 phonemes, which means the robot can be programmed to speak almost any language. Hero can also respond to light, sound, and objects (Slesnick, 1984).

Turtle Tot is a small robot that can be programmed by young children to count, draw pictures, and move at various angles. A machine that has greater dexterity but less mobility is the Rhino XR II, which is used in college-level engineering classes. The arm is a five-axis manipulator that has a hip, shoulder, elbow, and hand. The hand is capable of pitch, roll, and grip (Shahinpoor & Singer, 1985).

In special education, robots offer the potential to perform two basic functions. First, they can serve as an extension of the teacher by interacting with students and providing instruction in a fascinating area of technology. Second, robots can be controlled by students to meet their personal needs and objectives. For handicapped individuals, robotics can help alleviate many of the restrictions imposed by limited mobility and dexterity. For the orthopedically disabled in particular, robotics may compensate for missing or impaired human functions (Kimbler, 1984). In the future, robotics may help compensate for visual and auditory disabilities. Scientists are working on robots that will respond to voice commands and have computerized vision.

REFERENCES

Kimbler, D. L. (1984, June). *Robots and special education: The robot as extension of self.* Paper presented at Special Education Technology Research and Development Symposium, Washington, DC.

Shahinpoor, M., & Singer, N. (1985). A new instructional laboratory. *T.H.E. Journal, 13,* 54–56.

Slesnick, T. (1984). Robots and kids. *Classroom Computer Learning, 4,* 54–59.

Yin, R. K., & Moore, G. B. (1984). *Robotics, artificial intelligence, computer simulation: Future applications in special education.*

(Contract No. 300-84-0135). Washington, DC: U.S. Department of Education.

ELIZABETH MCCLELLAN
*Council for Exceptional
Children, Reston, Virginia*

COMPUTER-ASSISTED INSTRUCTION
COMPUTER USE WITH THE HANDICAPPED

ROBOTICS IN SPECIAL EDUCATION

Robotics in special education serves two potential functions. First, robotics can operate as an auxiliary to education by providing novel instruction to students, increasing motivation, and acting as an extension of the teacher in an instructional role. These auxiliary educational functions can be found in robots and robotic educational systems available today. They have been put to productive, albeit limited, use in special education. Little research has been conducted to test the efficacy of such uses.

A second, and perhaps potentially more dramatic, use of robotics for the handicapped concerns the robot as an extension of self. The robot is controlled by the individual to meet his or her personal needs and objectives and to control the environment. These functions demand a robot capable of a high level of sophistication in its logic and actions, a level not currently available in a single robotics unit (Kimbler, 1984). Nevertheless, the potential of the robot as an extension of the handicapped individual has prompted speculation concerning relevant applications and preliminary work on requisite performance characteristics.

Speculation on the usefulness of robotics has focused on handicapped conditions that limit mobility, dexterity, and interaction with the environment (Kimbler, 1984). The robot has been conceptualized as providing missing or impaired human functions under the direction of the disabled individual. Remote control devices have been used in this manner to some extent, and individual robots have been employed in restricted environments to perform limited functions such as serving meals. However, these applications have required modification of the environment. Ideally, the capacity of the robot would be more generalized; it would perform its functions by interacting with existing environments. A second major type of disability for which robotics applications have been conceptualized is sensory impairments, including visual and auditory disabilities. In these cases, the robot would provide sensory interaction as a mobile, dextrous adaptive device, permitting individuals to perceive the environment and then to operate on the setting directly or to control the robot to interact for them.

To support these functions, certain performance char-acteristics are necessary. For example, mobility under internal control to accomplish external demands is required. This movement needs to be smooth, to vary in speed from very slow to quick, and to react to novel environments through sensory systems. Robotics for these purposes require both payload, or strength and manipulation for that which needs to be carried, and dexterity dimensions to support varied and precise functions. The intelligence of the robot must allow reception and transmission of information through sensory apparatus, coordination of basic motion with its command and sensory input, communication in a conversational mode, and adaptation to new settings and uses. Finally, the robot must combine these characteristics with reasonable size; for acceptable and practical use, the robot must approximate the size of an average adult but maintain adequate bulk, stability, and power.

The robot that meets these requirements is complex and beyond current capabilities. Nevertheless, research on machine intelligence, performance characteristics, and integration proceeds. Work on artificial intelligence, expert systems, real-time computing, sensing capabilities, environmental mapping, conversational input and output, and power sources continues. The present state of technology in each of these areas supports feasibility of the robotic extension but requires packaging into a single working unit (Kimbler, 1984). Additionally, philosophical issues related to the cost of such technology must be addressed before applications of robotics to improve the ability of the handicapped to function in uncontrolled environments can be realized (Blaschke, 1984).

REFERENCES

Blaschke, C. (1984). *Market profile report: Technology and special education.* Falls Church, VA: Project Tech Mark, Education TURNKEY Systems.

Kimbler, D. L. (1984). Robots and special education: The robot as extension of self. In T. S. Hasselbring (Ed.), Toward the advancement of microcomputer technology in special education, *Peabody Journal of Education, 62,* 67–76.

LYNN S. FUCHS
*Peabody College, Vanderbilt
University*

ROCHESTER METHOD

The Rochester method is an oral, multisensory procedure for instructing deaf children in which speech reading is simultaneously supplemented by finger spelling and auditory amplification. The language of signs is wholly excluded from this procedure of instruction. (Quigley & Young, 1965).

The Rochester method was established by Zenos Westervelt at the Rochester School for the Deaf, in Rochester, New York, in 1878. Westervelt was convinced that finger spelling was the best means of teaching deaf children grammatically correct language. He believed that the easy visibility of finger spelling could help in lip reading as well as in speech instruction (Levine, 1981). The Rochester method is directly related to the method used by Juan Pablo Bonet of Spain. He advocated the use of a combination of a one-handed alphabet and speech in his book *The simplification of sounds and the art of teaching mutes to speak*, published in 1620. This method had a resurgence in the Soviet Union in the 1950s under the name neo-oralism, and in the United States in the 1960s (Moores, 1982).

Various studies have assessed the effectiveness of the Rochester method as an educational tool. Reviewing these, Quigley and Paul (1984) reported that, in general, researchers concluded that deaf children exposed to the Rochester method performed better than comparison groups in finger spelling, speech reading, written language, and reading. They also found that, when good oral techniques are used in conjunction with finger spelling, there are no detrimental effects to the acquisition of oral skills.

REFERENCES

Levine, E. (1981). *The ecology of early deafness*. New York: Columbia University Press.

Moores, D. (1982). *Educating the deaf: Psychology, principles and practices*. Boston: Houghton Mifflin.

Quigley, S., & Paul, P. (1984). *Language and deafness*: San Diego, CA: College-Hill.

Quigley, S., & Young, J. (Eds.). (1965). *Interpreting for deaf people*. Washington, DC: U.S. Department of Health, Education, and Welfare.

ROSEMARY GAFFNEY
*Hunter College, City University
of New York*

**DEAF
SIGN LANGUAGE TRAINING
TOTAL COMMUNICATION**

ROEPER REVIEW

The *Roeper Review*, published since 1977 by the Roeper City and Country School, is a journal on the education of gifted students. It originated as an information periodical for parents whose children attended the Roeper City and County School. The journal has three purposes: (1) presenting philosophical, moral, and academic issues that are related to the lives and experiences of gifted and talented persons; (2) presenting various views on those issues; and

(3) translating theory into practice for use at school, at home, and in the general community (Staff, 1983, p. ii).

The audience and authors for *Roeper Review* include practicing teachers and administrators, teacher-educators, psychologists, and scientists. They are served by in-depth coverage of important topics in each issue. Some examples of issues discussed in past editions are teacher education for gifted education, social studies education for the gifted, special subpopulations among gifted students, and perceptions of gifted students and their education. The mailing address is *Roeper Review*, Box 329, Bloomfield Hills, MI 48013.

REFERENCE

Staff. (1983). Statement of purpose. *Roeper Review, 6*, ii.

ANN E. LUPKOWSKI
Texas A&M University

ROGER, HARRIET B. (1834–1919)

Harriet B. Roger began the first oral school for the instruction of the deaf in the United States in 1863 when she accepted a deaf child as a private pupil in her home. With published accounts of the instruction of the deaf in Germany to guide her, she taught herself how to instruct the child. Her success in this undertaking led to the admission of other deaf children. One of these was Mabel Hubbard, who became Mrs. Alexander Graham Bell and whose father, a prominent lawyer, obtained legislation for the creation of an oral school for the deaf in Massachusetts. Hubbard formed this school by moving Rogers' school to Northampton, where, in 1867, they established the Clarke School for the Deaf, the second purely oral school for the deaf in the United States (the Lexington School for the Deaf having opened in New York City earlier that year). Rogers, the first teacher and the instructional leader of the Clarke School, remained there until her retirement in 1886.

REFERENCE

Lane, H. (1984). *When the mind hears*. New York: Random House.

PAUL IRVINE
Katonah, New York

ROOS, PHILIP (1930–   )

Born in Brussels, Belgium, Philip Roos received a BA in psychology and a BS in biology and premedical sciences (1949); he did postgraduate study in statistics, clinical and

Philip Roos

child psychology, at Stanford University. He received his PhD in clinical psychology (1954) from the University of Texas. He is currently president of Roos and Associates, Hurst, Texas (a consulting firm providing training to business and industry). He also maintains a private clinical practice of psychology.

Roos advocates the early use of behavior modification with severely and profoundly retarded institutionalized persons as well as with mildly retarded adolescents with behavior disorders (Roos & Oliver, 1970). He has developed the Developmental Model for programming persons with mental retardation. This model emphasizes the potency of expectations in working with handicapped individuals and the impact of the interpersonal environment in shaping individual development. It is the basis for many of the current programs for the mentally retarded and is incorporated in many national accreditation standards for agencies working with the mentally retarded.

Roos is an active member of the advocacy movement, wanting to help parents of handicapped children deal with their emotional and practical frustrations (Roos, 1983). He has helped individualize services to, and establish the rights of, the handicapped. Currently, he is engaged in human relations training within agencies and organizations. Roos has been included in *Who's Who in the World*, *American Men and Women of Science*, and *Who's Who in Health Care*.

REFERENCES

Roos, P. (1983). Advocate groups of the mentally retarded. In J. L. Matson & J. Mulick (Eds.), *Comprehensive handbook of mental retardation*. New York: Pergamon.

Roos, P., & Oliver, M. (1970). Evaluation of operant conditioning with institutionalized retarded children. *American Journal of Mental Deficiency, 74*, 325–330.

E. VALERIE HEWITT
Texas A&M University

RORSCHACH

The Rorschach, developed by Hermann Rorschach in 1921, is generally regarded as the most widely used projective personality assessment technique (Lubin, Wallis, & Paine, 1971). Five distinct scoring systems developed following Rorschach's death in 1922. Exner's Comprehensive Rorschach System (Exner, 1974, 1978; Exner & Weiner, 1982) has provided the fragmented Rorschach community with a common methodology, language, and literature; it is one of the most frequently used systems.

The Rorschach test stimuli consist of 10 inkblots, half achromatic and half with different degrees of color. Cards are presented individually to subjects, who are allowed to give as many responses as they wish describing "what the cards might be." Determinants that are scored include location, form, color, shading, movement, and quality and quantity of responses. Information obtained from the scored protocol includes personality state and trait characteristics, coping style, extent and quality of self-focus, quality of reality testing, likelihood of suicidal ideation or schizophrenia, depression, maturity, and complexity of psychological operations. Scoring and interpretation of the Rorschach, which is time-consuming and detailed, requires that the examiner be thoroughly trained in Rorschach assessment.

Criticisms of the Rorschach include the length of the time needed for administration, scoring and interpretation, and the fact that accurate usage is highly dependent on the clinical skills of the administrator. When used to gather descriptive clinical information, the Rorschach is considered to be an empirically valid instrument (Maloney & Glasser, 1982; Parker, 1983). Gittelman-Klein (1978) has presented an in-depth review of the validity of projective techniques, with positive results.

REFERENCES

Exner, J. E. (1974). *The Rorschach: A comprehensive system. Vol. 1. Basic foundations*. New York: Wiley.

Exner, J. E. (1978). *The Rorschach: A comprehensive system. Vol. 2: Current research and advanced interpretation*. New York: Wiley.

Exner, J. E., & Weiner, I. B. (1982). *The Rorschach: A comprehensive system. Vol. 3: Assessment of children and adolescents*. New York: Wiley.

Gittelman-Klein, R. (1978). *Validity of projective tests for psychodiagnosis in children*. In R. L. Spitzer & D. F. Klein (Eds.), *Critical issues in psychiatric diagnosis*. New York: Raven.

Lubin, B., Wallis, R. R., & Paine, C. (1971). Patterns of psychological test usage in the United States: 1935–1969. *Professional Psychology, 2*, 70–74.

Maloney, M. P., & Glasser, A. (1982). An evaluation of the clinical utility of the Draw-A-Person test. *Journal of Clinical Psychology, 38*, 183–190.

Parker, K. A. (1983). A meta-analyses of the reliability and validity of the Rorschach. *Journal of Personality Assessment, 47,* 227–231.

Constance Y. Celaya
Frances F. Worchel
Texas A&M University

ROSWELL-CHALL DIAGNOSTIC READING TEST OF WORD ANALYSIS SKILLS, REVISED AND EXTENDED

The Roswell-Chall Diagnostic Reading Test was developed to evaluate the word analysis and word recognition skills of pupils reading at the first- through fourth-grade levels. It may also be used with pupils who are reading at higher levels where there is a suspicion of decoding and word recognition difficulties or for research and program evaluation.

Two comparable forms of the test are available. Each is individually administered. The test has 10 main subtests and 4 extended evaluation subtests. All of the subtests or only those deemed appropriate may be given. The following skills are measured: high-frequency words, single consonant sounds, consonant diagrams, consonant blends, short vowel words, short and long vowel sounds, rule of silent e's, vowel diagrams, common diphthongs and vowels controlled by *r*, and syllabication (and compound words). The extended evaluation subtests include naming capital letters, naming lower-case letters, encoding single consonants, and encoding phonetically regular words.

The test takes approximately 10 minutes to administer, score, and interpret. Score interpretations are provided in the manual. The test has good reliability and validity. Users should be concerned about the size and somewhat limited nature of the norm sample, therefore, the administrator should be knowledgeable in the kinds of skills needed in most individual testing situations and, in order to interpret the test accurately, be a relatively skilled reading clinician.

REFERENCES

Manual of instructions: Roswell-Chall Diagnostic Reading Test of Word Analysis Skills, Revised and Extended. (1978). LaJolla, CA: Essay.

Ronald V. Schmelzer
Eastern Kentucky University

ROUSSEAU, JEAN J. (1712–1778)

Jean Jacques Rousseau, French-Swiss philosopher and moralist, revolutionized child-rearing and educational

Jean J. Rousseau

practices with the publication, in 1762, of *Emile*, a treatise on education in the form of a novel. Rousseau contended that childhood is not merely a period of preparation for adulthood to be endured, but a developmental stage to be cherished and enjoyed. He enjoined parents and educators to be guided by the interests and capacities of the child, and was the first writer to propose that the study of the child should be the basis for the child's education. Probably every major educational reform since the eighteenth century can be traced in some way to Rousseau, and indebtedness to him is clear in the works of Pestalozzi, Froebel, Montessori, and Dewey. An eloquent writer, Rousseau's works on man's relationship with nature, as well as his writings on social, political, and educational matters, were major contributions to the literature of his day.

REFERENCES

Boyd, W. (1963). *The educational theory of Jean Jacques Rousseau.* New York: Russell & Russell.

Rousseau, J. J. (1969). *Emile.* New York: Dutton.

Paul Irvine
Katonah, New York

RUBELLA

Postnatal rubella (German measles) is a relatively mild viral infection that is generally inconsequential. It was first differentiated from measles and scarlet fever by German workers in the latter part of the eighteenth century. German scientists termed the disease *Roethelm*. According to *Black's Medical Dictionary*, the term German measles has no geographical reference but rather comes from the word germane, meaning akin to. Rubella comes from the Latin word *rubellus* meaning red (*Black's*, 1984).

The postnatal rubella virus is transmitted through contact with blood, bodily waste excretions, nasopharyngeal secretions of infected persons, and, possibly, contact with contaminated clothing (*Professional Guide to Diseases*, 1984). Humans are the only known host for the rubella virus and the period of communicability lasts from about 10 days before the rash appears until about 5 days after it appears. When acquired postnatally, rubella is a self-limited viral infection. It appears most frequently in the late winter or spring, particularly in large urban communities. Rubella is distributed worldwide. Although major epidemics occur in intervals ranging from 10 to 30 years, sizable epidemics may occur every 6 to 9 years (Alford, 1976). The factors responsible for the continuation of the epidemics is unknown.

It is believed that the rubella virus enters the body through the upper respiratory tract, is transmitted to the blood system, and results in low levels of viral production from 9 to 11 days. After this time, virimic seeding results in viral excretion from the nasopharynx, urine, cervix, and feces. After the incubation period of 14 to 21 days, a red rash erupts. Enlargement of the lymph nodes, most easily identified on the face or the neck, is a hallmark of a rubella infection. The rash, which typically begins on the face, rapidly spreads to the trunk and other parts of the body. The rash may be accompanied by a low-grade fever (99 to rarely higher than 104). In adults, the rash may also be accompanied by headaches, joint pains, and conjunctivitis.

Because of the mild nature of rubella acquired postnatally, there is little concern for active treatment. The rash rarely requires topical ointments but aspirin may be taken to ease the discomfort associated with fever and body pains. Children or adults with postnatal rubella should be isolated owing to the threat of infecting newly pregnant mothers.

Congenital rubella is a concern because of the 20 to 30% chance of damage to the fetus when a mother contracts the infection during the first trimester of pregnancy (Bonwick, 1972). Catastrophic damaging effects were first reported by Sir Norman Gregg, an Australian ophthalmologist, 1941. The classic congenital rubella syndrome as described by Gregg consists of fetal anomalies, ocular defects, and hearing impairment. Mental retardation was also shown to be a common result of early damage to the fetus.

Shortly after the rubella virus was isolated in 1961, the first epidemic since 1940, and the last major epidemic to date, struck the United States. The results of the epidemic are reported by Rudolph and Desmond, 1972:

> Some 30,000 pregnancies ended in miscarriage or stillbirth, and between 20,000 to 30,000 infants suffered from various defects . . . 8000 cases of deafness, 3600 cases of deafness and blindness, 1800 cases of mental retardation, and 6600 other malformations . . . 5000 therapeutic abortions and 2000 excess neonatal deaths. (p. 4)

It appears that circulation of the virus in the blood of the infected mother during the incubation period of her postnatal infection is the initial step in contraction of congenital rubella by the fetus. The virus is transferred from the mother's bloodstream to the placenta and then often to the fetal bloodstream. Although the exact reasons for this are not known, it is apparent that the earlier in the pregnancy the mother contracts the viral infection, the more pervasive the damage to the fetus. It is also apparent that congenital rubella is very different from postnatal rubella in that the former is widely disseminated throughout the body of the fetus.

Extensive investigations during the last 20 years have characterized congenital rubella as having pathologic potential much greater than was first assumed by Gregg. For instance, it is now hypothesized that congenital rubella, in addition to being responsible for the anomalies previously reported, may also be responsible for numerous abnormalities that appear later in life. These include dental problems, anemia, encephalitis, giant cell hepatitis, dermatitis, and diabetes.

Active prevention seems the key to reducing the impact of congenital rubella, as once the damage has been done in utero there appears to be little hope of reversing the effects. Of course, corrective surgery can be performed in cases where the fetus suffers cardiac damage or has cataracts, and hearing aids can be given to the hearing-impaired child, but the damage is not reversible.

Passive immunization procedures such as large doses of gamma globulin have been shown to be ineffective in preventing damage to the fetus once the mother has contracted the virus. Chemotherapeutic procedures also have proven inadequate as protection against the devastating effects of congenital rubella (Alford, 1976).

An active immunization program seems to hold the best promise to date to reducing the spread of rubella to pregnant females. Immunization with live virus vaccine RA27/3 is used in the United States. This preventive program is aimed at vaccinating large numbers of infants and young children in the hopes of reducing circulation of the virus in the general population and thus protecting females in the childbearing years. Some have advocated that all young girls between 11 and 14 years should be vaccinated if they have not had the disease. It is also advocated now that all young women of childbearing age who have not had the disease and who are not pregnant be vaccinated. In Europe immunization programs are directed toward young married women. This approach is not without its risks and questions (Alford, 1976). Certain guidelines for administering the vaccine are available (*Professional Guide to Diseases*, 1984).

Often the psychological impact of giving birth to a handicapped child can be as damaging as the virus itself. Parents of children with congenital rubella can obtain help and advice from the National Association for Deaf, Blind and Rubella Handicapped, 12 A Rosebery Avenue, London, England ECIR 4TD.

REFERENCES

Alford, C. A. (1976). Rubella. In J. S. Remington, & J. O. Klein (Eds.), *Infectious diseases of the fetus and newborn infant*. Philadelphia: Saunders.

Black's medical dictionary (1984). Totowa, NJ: Barnes & Noble.

Bonwick, M. (1972). *Rubella and other intraocular viral diseases in infancy*. Boston: Little, Brown.

Professional guide to diseases. (1984). (pp. 384–386). Springhouse, PA: Springhouse.

Rudolph, A. J., & Desmond, M. M. (1972). Clinical manifestations of the congenital rubella syndrome. In M. Bonwick (Ed.), *Rubella and other intraocular viral diseases in infancy*. Boston: Little, Brown.

JULIA A. HICKMAN
University of Texas, Austin

CATARACTS
CONGENITAL DISORDERS
MENTAL RETARDATION

RURAL SPECIAL EDUCATION

Approximately 67% of the 16,000 public school districts in the United States are classified as rural because of sparse population or geographic location (Sher, 1978). According to Helge (1984), educational characteristics of rural areas are distinctly different from those of urban areas. Rural areas have higher poverty levels and serve greater percentages of handicapped children. Populations in rural areas are increasing, however, their tax bases are not. Education costs more in rural areas than in nonrural areas because of transportation requirements and scarce professional resources.

Because of the remoteness of the areas, assessing the effectiveness of special education services to handicapped and gifted children has been difficult. One reason for this, according to the director of the National Rural Research Project (Helge, 1984) has been the absence of a consistently applied definition of the term rural among federal agencies, educators, and professional organizations. The definition that is most commonly used is the one developed for the 1978 to 1983 research projects funded by the U.S. Office of Special Education Programs and conducted by the National Rural Research and Personnel Preparation Project. This definition reads:

> A district is considered rural when the number of inhabitants is fewer than 150 per square mile or when located in counties with 60% or more of the population living in communities not larger than 5000 inhabitants. Districts with more than 10,000 students and those within a Standard Metropolitan Statistical Area (SMSA), as determined by the U.S. Census Bureau, are not considered rural. (p. 296)

The National Rural Research and Personnel Preparation Project was funded (to be conducted in four phases from 1978 to 1981)

> to investigate state and local educational agencies nationwide in order to determine problems and effective strategies for implementing Public Law 94-142; and to develop profiles of effective special education delivery systems and strategies, given specific rural community and district subcultural characteristics. (p. 296)

Phase I, conducted during 1978 and 1979, focused on identifying facilitating and hindering factors that operate to determine the success or failure of rural local educational agency compliance with PL 94-142. Results of this phase showed that problems identified by state educational agencies were grouped in three categories: (1) staffing problems (recruiting and retaining qualified staff); (2) attitudinal variables (resistance to change, suspicions of outside interference, and long distances between schools); and (3) problems based on rural geography (fiscal problems, difficult terrain and economic conditions). Phase II, conducted during 1979 and 1980, was designed to develop profiles interrelating community characteristics and school district characteristics with service delivery options proven viable in other local education agencies with similar characteristics. Phase III (1980) involved using Phase I and II data to develop interdisciplinary models of personnel preparation for effective service delivery to rural subcultures. Phase IV, conducted in 1980 and 1981, was designed to field test and disseminate the modules for use in preservice and in-service training programs (Helge, 1981).

A series of in-service training modules have been developed with topics that range from stress reduction to alternate rural service delivery systems. In addition, several preservice modules are presently being field tested in universities across the country. Topics of the modules include alternate instructional arrangements and delivery systems for low-incidence handicapped students in rural America; Warren Springs, Mesa: a rural preservice simulation; solving rural parent-professional related dilemmas; working with parents of rural handicapped students; involving citizens and agencies of rural communities in cooperative programming for handicapped students; working with peer professionals in rural environments; creative resource identification for providing services to rural handicapped students; solving educational dilemmas related to school administration; and personal development skills and strategies for effective survival as a rural special educator. These modules are available through the American Council on Rural Special Education.

In a report on the state of the art of rural special education (Helge, 1984), it was noted that major service delivery problems remained basically the same as in the initial study done in 1979. These problems were associated with funding inadequacies, difficulties in recruiting and retaining qualified staff, transportation inadequacies, problems with providing services to low-incidence handicapped populations, and inadequacies of preservice training. In addition, many of these inadequacies were seen as future problems.

In an effort to focus on rural special education and the identified service delivery problems, the American Council on Rural Special Education was founded in 1981. This nonprofit national membership organization is an outgrowth of the National Rural Development Institute, headquartered at Western Washington University in Bellingham. The organization is composed of approximately 1000 rural special educators and administrators, parents of handicapped students, and university and state department personnel. The specific purposes of the organization are to enhance direct services to rural individuals and agencies serving exceptional students; to increase educational opportunities for rural handicapped and gifted students; and to develop a system for forecasting the future for rural special education and planning creative service delivery alternatives.

The American Council on Rural Special Education (ACRES) serves as an advocate for rural special education at the federal, state, regional, and local levels; provides professional development opportunities, and disseminates information on the current needs of rural special education. The ACRES has established a nationwide system to link educators and administrators needing jobs with agencies having vacancies. The ACRES Rural Bulletin Board communicates to interested agencies information regarding rural special education issues and promising practices through SpecialNet, the electronic communication system operated by the National Association of State Directors of Special Education. ACRES publishes a quarterly newsletter and a journal, the *Rural Special Education Quarterly*. These publications include up-to-date information on issues facing handicapped students in rural America, problem-solving strategies, pertinent legislation and conferences, and articles on rural preservice and in-service strategies. The ACRES also holds an annual conference each year in the spring, usually at the institute's headquarters. The conferences feature presentations to enhance services to rural handicapped and gifted children, media displays, curriculum materials, and hardware and software exhibits.

REFERENCES

Helge, D. I. (1981). Problems in implementing comprehensive special education programming in rural areas. *Exceptional Children, 47*, 514–524.

Helge, D. I. (1984). The state of the art of rural special education. *Exceptional Children, 50*, 294–305.

Sher, J. P. (1978). A proposal to end federal neglect of rural schools. *Phi Delta Kappan, 60*, 280–282.

CECELIA STEPPE-JONES
*North Carolina Central
University*

RUSH, BENJAMIN (1745–1813)

Benjamin Rush, physician, teacher, reformer, and patriot, began medical practice in Philadelphia in 1769. He taught chemistry at the College of Philadelphia, and published the first American textbook on that subject. During the Revolutionary War, he served as surgeon-general of the Army and published a textbook on military medicine that was still in use at the time of the Civil War. Following his military service, Rush returned to the practice of medicine in Philadelphia, where he established the first free dispensary in the United States. He is believed to be the first physician to relate smoking to cancer and to advocate temperance and exercise to promote good health. An outspoken advocate of humane treatment for the mentally ill, in 1812 Rush published a work that would influence medical education for generations to come, *Medical Inquiries and Observations Upon the Diseases of the Mind*.

Despite his accomplishments as a physician, political and social issues were Rush's major interests. He was a member of the Continental Congress and a signer of the Declaration of Independence. He was active in the movement to abolish slavery, and was influential in the ratification of the federal Constitution in Pennsylvania. He involved himself in a number of educational causes, advocating improved education for girls and proposing a comprehensive system of public schools that would offer science and practical subjects as well as traditional academics.

REFERENCES

Hawke, D. (1971). *Benjamin Rush*. New York: Bobbs-Merrill.

Rush, B. (1962). *Medical inquiries and observations upon the diseases of the mind*. New York: Hafner.

PAUL IRVINE
Katonah, New York

RUTTER, MICHAEL (1933–   )

On completing his basic medical training at the University of Birmingham, England (1955), Michael Rutter took residencies in internal medicine, neurology, and pediatrics. His training in general and in child psychiatry was

Michael Rutter

done at the Maudsley Hospital, London. Away on fellowship study for a year (1961–1962), Rutter returned to work in the Medical Research Council Special Psychiatry Research Unit. Since 1965 Rutter has served as professor and head of the Department of Child and Adolescent Psychiatry at the University of London's Institute of Psychiatry, and as a private practitioner.

Rutter's major fields of interest show a strong interdisciplinary approach and include interviewing skills, schools as social institutions, stress resistance in children, developmental links between childhood and adult life, psychiatric epidemiology, and infantile autism. As a teacher and a researcher, his work centers on building bridges between the areas of child development and clinical child psychiatry.

Rutter's major published contributions include *Child and Adolescent Psychiatry: Modern Approaches, Depression in Young People: Developmental and Clinical Perspectives*, "Resilience in the Face of Adversity: Protective Disorders," "The Treatment of Austic Children," and "Child Psychiatry: The Interface Between Clinical and Developmental Research." His publications number some 21 books, 49 chapters, and 145 research articles and associated works.

In 1979 Rutter served as a fellow at the Center for Advanced Study in the Behavioral Sciences at Stanford. He was appointed honorary director of the Medical Research Council Child Psychiatry Unit at the Institute of Psychiatry (1984), is an honorary fellow of the British Psychological Society and the American Academy of Pediatrics, and an honorary member of the American Academy of Child Psychiatry. In addition, Rutter serves on the editorial board of the *Journal of Autism and Developmental Disorders* (as European editor) as well as on eight other journals.

REFERENCES

Rutter, M. (1985a). Resilience in the face of adversity: Protective factors and resistance to psychiatric disorders. *British Journal of Psychiatry, 147*, 598–611.

Rutter, M. (1985b). The treatment of autistic children. *Journal of Child Psychology & Psychiatry, 26*, 193–214.

Rutter, M. (1986). Child psychiatry. The interface between clinical and developmental research. *Psychological Medicine, 16*, 151–169.

Rutter, M., & Hersov, L. (Ed.). (1985). *Child and adolescent psychiatry: Modern approaches*. Oxford, England. Blackwell.

Rutter, M., Izard, C., & Read, P. (1986). *Depression in young people: Developmental and clinical perspectives*. New York: Guilford.

MARY LEON PEERY
Texas A&M University

S

SABATINO, DAVID A. (1938–   )

David A. Sabatino received his BS (1960), MA (1961), and PhD (1966) from Ohio State University. Currently, he is director of the School Psychology Division of Behavioral Studies at West Virginia College of Graduate Studies.

Sabatino considers learning disabilities to be an information-processing disability. He believes the problem is complex and that appropriate educational plans require input from any service provider that can help a particular handicapped child (Sabatino, Miller, & Schmidt, 1981). He does not believe that any one professional, of any single discipline, can have the answers or meet the needs of all children. Sabatino believes that the child's parents should be partners with the various professionals in the process of helping the child, sharing information freely.

Sabatino finds that increasing numbers of handicapped children are being neglected and that the secondary schools are ill-equipped to manage the influx. He finds that secondary schools stress mastery of a topic rather than a students' growth and learning. If the student has not developed a learned helplessness in elementary school, Sabatino believes the child will develop learned helplessness without an appropriate, effective secondary school program. He therefore advocates functional teaching that will teach any child what is necessary to know in order to function at a basic academic level. For example, if a child does not know how to read, Sabatino believes one should teach the child to read rather than label the child (Sabatino & Lanning-Ventura, 1982). Sabatino advocates writing practical material that can be used for in-service training or by a teacher who wants to know what to do in class each day.

REFERENCES

Sabatino, D. A., & Lanning-Ventura, S. (1982). Functional teaching, survival skills and teaching. In D. A. Sabatino & L. Mann (Eds.), *A handbook of diagnostic and prescriptive teaching.* Rockville, MD: Aspen.

Sabatino, D. A., Miller, T. L., & Schmidt, C. R. (1981). *Learning disabilities: Systemizing teaching and service delivery.* Rockville, MD: Aspen.

E. Valerie Hewitt
Texas A&M University

SAFETY ISSUES IN SPECIAL EDUCATION

Accountability, malpractice, due process, and liability insurance are all terms familiar to special educators. For teachers to gain protection from legal situations it is critical that children's safety become a high priority. In particular, physically impaired and severely handicapped children are more prone to accidents, medical emergencies, and injuries. Therefore, teachers must take certain precautions to protect students and staff from unnecessary risks. Specifically, educators must consider many facets of the classroom program in order to create safe environments for children. Four major areas related to safety must be considered: (1) basic first aid skills, (2) emergency weather and fire drill procedures, (3) safe classroom environments, and (4) parent consent and involvement in classroom activities.

Many states require teachers to obtain certification in first-aid procedures before they are eligible to obtain a teaching certificate. In particular, teachers should be trained in cardiopulmonary resuscitation (CPR) and antichoking procedures such as the Heimlich maneuver. For teachers working with children who have seizures, a clear understanding of first-aid procedures for managing seizures is critical. Furthermore, basic instruction on poison management, eye injuries, and contusions must be included in first-aid programs. In the same context, children on medication such as Ritalin, Phenobarbital, and Dilantin, must be carefully monitored for signs of over or under dosage. Teachers should never be left solely responsible for dispensing any medications to children without the assistance of a physician or school nurse.

Emergency weather and fire drill procedures should be clearly posted in all classrooms. For teachers in certain areas of the country, where tornados and hurricanes are likely, extra efforts must be taken to understand the civil defense procedures for the school. For teachers of the physically handicapped, visually impaired, and nonambulatory severely impaired, procedures should be established with the school principal for added assistance during civil defense drills and fire drills.

Much has been written on designing school facilities and classroom environments for handicapped students (Abend, Bednor, Froehlinger, & Stenzler, 1979; Birch & Johnstone, 1975; Forness, Gutherie, & MacMillan, 1982;

Hutchins & Renzaglia, 1983; Zentall, 1983). Environmental designing of classrooms also involves a safety aspect for children in special education. For example, many classrooms for physically handicapped or blind students should have adequate storage space for bulky equipment (e.g., wheelchairs, walkers) and materials (e.g., braillers, books, canes). A classroom that is organized and neat ensures safety for children. Cabinets within the classroom holding harmful materials should be inaccessible to students in the classroom. Rossol (1982) discusses the possible hazards to students in special education using art materials.

Many of the activities developed for handicapped students involve out-of-school visits such as field trips, community-based training, and recreation/leisure trips. Parental consent would be critical if liability issues arose from one of these activities. Additionally, behavioral intervention programs that might appear intrusive (e.g., time-out, physical restraint, withholding food) must be discussed by the educational team and parents prior to implementation of any such procedures. Each school or district should have policies regarding corporal punishment. Those policies must be understood by all special education teachers and all parents.

In conclusion, safety in special education is a topic that is rarely found in the literature, yet it has enormous implications for teachers working with handicapped children. Although much of what has been discussed is commonsense, it is important to remind teachers of the many safety aspects in special education.

REFERENCES

Abend, A., Bednor, M., Froehlinger, V., & Stenzler, Y. (1979). *Facilities for special education services.* Reston, VA: Council for Exceptional Children.

Birch, J., & Johnstone, B. (1975). *Designing schools and schooling for the handicapped.* Springfield, IL: Thomas.

Forness, S., Guthrie, D., & MacMillan, D. (1982). Classroom environments as they relate to mentally retarded children's observable behavior. *American Journal of Mental Deficiency, 3,* 259–265.

Hutchins, M., & Renzaglia, A. (1983). Environmental considerations for severely handicapped individuals: The needs and the questions. *Exceptional Education Quarterly, 4,* 67–71.

Rossol, M. (1982). *Teaching art to high risk groups.* (ERIC Document Reproduction Service No. ED 224 182)

Zentall, S. (1983). Learning environments: A review of physical and temporal factors. *Exceptional Education Quarterly, 4,* 90–115.

VIVIAN I. CORREA
University of Florida

ACCESSIBILITY OF PROGRAMS
LIABILITY OF TEACHERS IN SPECIAL EDUCATION
MEDICALLY FRAGILE STUDENT
RITALIN

SALVIA, JOHN (1941–   )

Born in St. Louis, Missouri, John Salvia received a BA (1963) in education and an MEd (1964) in history from the University of Arizona. He received his EdD (1968) in special education, with a minor in educational psychology, from Pennsylvania State University. Currently, he is a professor of special education in the Division of Education and Communication Disorders, Pennsylvania State University.

Early in his professional career, Salvia was a teacher of the educable mentally retarded, becoming interested in colorblindness in these children (Salvia, 1969). Later, he became interested in assessment in special education. *Assessment in Special and Remedial Education* (Salvia & Ysseldyke, 1978) was written to provide basic information on the assessment process and its resulting data to people who use the information, and need to understand it, but do not generate it. Salvia also is interested in various areas of the assessment process, especially the factors that may or may not bias the outcome of an assessment (Salvia & Meisel, 1980; Duffy, Salvia, Tucker, & Ysseldyke, 1981).

Salvia has been involved in a children's TV workshop and has been a visiting professor at the University of Victoria, British Columbia, Canada. He was a Fulbright fellow at the University of Sao Paulo, Sao Paulo, Brazil. He has been included in *Leaders in Education.*

REFERENCES

Duffy, J. B., Salvia, J., Tucker, J., & Ysseldyke, J. (1981). Nonbiased assessment: A need for operationalism. *Exceptional Children, 47*(6), 427–434.

Salvia, J. (1969). Four tests of color vision: A study of diagnostic accuracy with the mentally retarded. *American Journal of Mental Deficiency, 74*(3), 421–427.

Salvia, J., & Meisel, C. J. (1980). Observer bias: A methodological consideration in special education research. *Journal of Special Education, 14*(2), 261–270.

Salvia, J., & Ysseldyke, J. E. (1978). *Assessment in special and remedial education.* Boston: Houghton Mifflin.

E. VALERIE HEWITT
Texas A&M University

SAPIR, SELMA GUSTIN (1916–   )

Born in New York City, Selma Gustin Sapir received her BS (1935) in education and psychology from New York University, her MA (1956) in psychology from Sarah Lawrence College, and her EdD (1984) in applied clinical psychology from Teachers College, Columbia University. She organized and directed the Learning Disability Laboratory, Bank Street College, New York, a child service

Selma Gustin Sapir

demonstration center and interdisciplinary training project.

Having already developed the Sapir Dimensions of Learning (1980), the Sapir Learning Lab Language Scale (1979), the Sapir Self-Concept Scale (1967), and the Sapir Development Scale (1966), Sapir has most recently developed a new treatment model based on child developmental research (Sapir, 1985). Her idea is to combine psychological theory and practices with educational treatment models for the treatment of learning-disabled children. Her model emphasizes that development is a continuing process. As a child matures, the child's functioning changes. When one dimension (social, emotional, or cognitive) changes, there is a growth in other areas. Sapir believes that one must know the norms of development to understand and recognize its deviations.

Sapir has developed graduate programs related to special education/learning disabilities in Mayaguez, Puerto Rico, and Mons, Belgium. As a Fulbright professor, she organized a psychology clinic for special children and their families in Mexico City. She was invited to participate in a NATO conference on neuropsychology and accepted an appointment to the New York Academy of Science. She is also a nongovernmental advisor to the United Nations, representing the International Council of Psychologists.

REFERENCE

Sapir, S. G. (1985). *The clinical teaching model: Clinical insights and strategies for the learning disabled child.* New York: Brunner/Mazel.

E. VALERIE HEWITT
Texas A&M University

SARASON, SEYMOUR B. (1919–   )

Born in Brooklyn, New York, Seymour B. Sarason received his BA from the University of Newark in 1939 and his MA (1940) and PhD (1942) in psychology from Clark University. Sarason's first professional position was as chief psychologist at the Southbury (Connecticut) Training School for the Mentally Retarded. Sarason joined the psychology department at Yale University in 1946.

Sarason's major efforts have been in attempting to broaden society's conceptualization of the needs of the mentally retarded. He advocates that there is more to be learned about an individual, especially one labeled retarded, from noncontrived, naturally occurring situations than from a score on a test given in an artificial situation. Sarason raises questions about the reasons for segregated classrooms for the mentally retarded child and the issue of institutionalization versus mainstreaming.

Sarason's major publications include *Psychological Problems in Mental Deficiency, Psychology Misdirected,* and *Education Handicap, Public Policy and Social History: A Broadened Perspective on Mental Retardation.*

Sarason has been a past president of the Division of Clinical Psychology of the American Psychological Association. He has also received Distinguished Contributions Awards from the American Association on Mental Deficiency and the Divisions of Clinical and Community Psychology of the American Psychological Association.

REFERENCES

Sarason, S. B. (1969). *Psychological problems in mental deficiency* (4th ed.). New York: Harper & Row.

Sarason, S. B. (1981). *Psychology misdirected.* New York: Free Press.

Sarason, S. B., & Doris, J. (1979). *Educational handicap, public policy, and social history: A broadened perspective on mental retardation.* New York: Free Press.

E. VALERIE HEWITT
Texas A&M University

SATTLER, JEROME M. (1931–   )

Born in New York City, Jerome M. Sattler received his BA from the City College of New York in 1952. He went on to the University of Kansas and earned his MA in 1953 and PhD in psychology in 1959. As a professor of psychology at San Diego State University, Sattler's research has led him to become an authority in the areas of intelligence testing, racial experimenter effects, ethnic minority testing, and racial factors in counseling and psychotherapy. His introductory text, *Assessment of Children's Intelligence and Special Abilities*, is a standard textbook used in the field of school psychology and clinical psychology and remains a classic reference text in the field of special education.

Sattler was an expert witness and consultant to the California Attorney General's Office for the case of *Larry*

P. et al. v. *Wilson Riles et al.*, from September 1977 to April 1978; this was a landmark case in the area of cultural bias in assessment. In addition, he is a member of the developmental team, which includes R. E. Thorndike and E. Hagen, that revised the Stanford-Binet Intelligence Scale into the fourth revision, published in 1986.

Sattler was a Fulbright lecturer at the University of Kebangsaan, Malaysia, from 1972 to 1973, and an exchange professor, Katholicke Universiteit, Instituut voor Orthopedagogiek, Nijmegen, the Netherlands, from 1983 to 1984. In 1979 he was elected a fellow of the American Psychological Association. Sattler has published over 85 articles in the field of psychology and has been a special reviewer for over 30 books, articles, and grant proposals, as well as an editor for such journals as the *Journal of Consulting and Clinical Psychology*, *Psychology in the Schools*, the *Journal of Psychoeducational Assessment*, and *Psychological Reports*.

REFERENCE

Sattler, J. M. (1982). *Assessment of children's intelligence and abilities* (2nd ed.). Boston: Allyn & Bacon.

E. VALERIE HEWITT
Texas A&M University

SCALES OF INDEPENDENT BEHAVIOR (SIB)

The Scales of Independent Behavior (SIB; Bruininks, Woodcock, Weatherman, & Hill, 1984) were published as a comprehensive measure of adaptive and maladaptive behavior. Individually administered through structural interview, the SIB covers a wide range with norms available from infancy through mature adult (40+ years). The SIB was primarily designed to assess adaptive behavior and to provide program planning information. It assesses skills needed to function independently in home, social, and community settings. The SIB norms were equated statistically to the Woodcock-Johnson Psycho-Educational Battery (Woodcock & Johnson, 1977), thus allowing normative comparisons of scores across instruments. This permits users to evaluate an individual's adaptive behavior in comparison with others at the same age and at the same level of intellectual functioning.

The 14 adaptive behavior subscales contain 226 items and are organized into four clusters of behavior domains (motor skills, social interaction and communication skills, personal living skills, and community living skills). Information derived from these four clusters can be summarized into a measure of broad independence as a full-scale score. A short form also is provided, as well as an early development (ED) scale. The ED scale is designed for use with individuals whose developmental level is below approximately $2\frac{1}{2}$ years of age, making it particu-

larly useful for assessing the development of very young children and severely and profoundly handicapped children and adults. Adaptive behavior items are scored on a four-point rating scale (range 0–3). The respondent evaluates the individual on each task, based on the requirement of independent performance. Basal and ceiling rules are provided to facilitate adaptive testing and administration of the SIB is easily learned. Administration time is estimated at 45 to 60 minutes.

In addition to evaluating adaptive behavior, a problem behavior scale is included to help identify maladaptive behaviors that may limit personal and community adjustments. This scale includes eight major categories organized into four clusters of maladaptive behavior indices (general maladaptive, internalized maladaptive, asocial maladaptive, and externalized maladaptive). Behaviors are rated according to frequency of occurrence and severity. The respondent is also asked to describe the usual management responses to the behaviors identified.

Various derived and cluster scores can be obtained from the SIB; they are similar to those in the Woodcock-Johnson scoring system. Age-based standard scores are provided with a mean of 100 and standard deviation of 15. Adjusted adaptive behavior scores are available if the user wishes to evaluate the individual's independence in relation to level of intellectual functioning (as measured by the Woodcock-Johnson broad cognitive ability cluster score), in addition to age.

Not included with the test kit, but important for knowledgeable use of the SIB, is a technical manual entitled *Development and Standardization of the Scales of Independent Behavior* (Bruininks et al., 1985), which describes the standardization sample and provides reliability and validity information. Normative data for the SIB were drawn from a stratified random sample of 1764 persons, ranging in age from infancy to 40+ years. Additional technical data were collected on over 1000 handicapped and nonhandicapped individuals.

Reliability and validity of the SIB appear sound. Internal consistency reliability estimates were calculated across all subscores using the split-half procedure, corrected by the Spearman-Brown formula. Median corrected split-half reliabilities are mostly in the high .70s and .80s. Median cluster score reliabilities fall mostly in the high .80s and .90s. Special studies were conducted to analyze the reliability of the SIB with handicapped samples, with median coefficients across samples and age levels ranging mostly in the .90s. Numerous comparative studies were conducted to establish construct validity for the SIB. Results of the studies indicate that the SIB adaptive behavior scores strongly differentiate among more severely handicapped people and their nonhandicapped peers. Differences in adaptive behavior are less frequently found among mildly handicapped and nonhandicapped peers. In addition, further studies indicate that the moderately to severely retarded and the behaviorally disordered produced significantly greater negative maladaptive behavior indices than their normal counterparts. The SIB technical manual reports that SIB scores correlate well with scores on the AAMD Adaptive Behavior Scale: School Edition (ABS-SE; Lambert, 1981). For example, the SIB broad independence score correlated .81 with the ABS-SE overall comparison score.

REFERENCES

Bruininks, R. H., Woodcock, R. W., Weatherman, R. F., & Hill, B. K. (1984). *Scales of Independent Behavior*. Allen, TX: DLM Teaching Resources.

Bruininks, R. H., Woodcock, R. W., Weatherman, R. F., & Hill, B. K. (1985). *Development and standardization of the Scales of Independent Behavior*. Allen, TX: DLM Teaching Resources.

Lambert, N. (1981). *AAMD Adaptive Behavior Scale: School Edition*. Monterey, CA: Publishers Test Service.

Woodcock, R. W., & Johnson, M. B. (1977). *Woodcock-Johnson Psycho-Educational Battery*. Allen, TX: DLM Teaching Resources.

KATHRYN A. SULLIVAN
Texas A&M University

ADAPTIVE BEHAVIOR

SCALES OF ORDINAL DOMINANCE

See ORDINAL SCALES OF PSYCHOLOGICAL DEVELOPMENT.

SCANDINAVIA, SPECIAL EDUCATION IN

The Scandinavian nations, Denmark, Norway, and Sweden, and nearby Finland have been in the vanguard with respect to their concern for the social welfare of their citizens. While they have not been free of the social turmoil that characterizes much of the world today, there has been general consensus that individuals with special needs need special care. In particular, this appears to be true in Denmark and Sweden. The nations of Scandinavia have been characterized by exemplary care in many ways. One reason is that the population is homogeneous in nature. The conflicts that often arise from cultural, ethnic, or racial differences are relatively mild in Scandinavia. The Scandinavian countries are relatively small in population, lending themselves to easier management than larger nations, such as Great Britain.

The world, and the United States in particular, began to pay close attention to Scandinavian endeavors and innovations on behalf of handicapped individuals during the 1960s. President Kennedy sent missions to study and report on programs for the mentally retarded in Scandinavia and the Netherlands. Wolfensberger reported positively on Scandinavian concepts and practices in several articles (1964a, 1964B, 1965). Vail (1968) published a book in which programs for the mentally retarded and mentally ill in Scandinavia were praised. The Committee on Mental Retardation's report on residential care (Kugel & Wolfensberger, 1968) called attention to Scandinavian normalization principles and practices. The Scandinavian concept of normalization was to affect American attitudes and practices dramatically. It contributed to the notion of least restrictive environment at all ages and for all handicapped persons. The news from Scandinavia on a variety of fronts made it apparent that there was much that was good and innovative—by any standards—in Scandinavian educational programs and methods (Juul, 1978, 1980, 1985).

The Swedish medical system is perhaps the most efficient in the world with respect to serving handicapped children. More than 99% of Swedish children receive free voluntary checkups during their preschool years. This health examination includes screening for hearing and vision and for cognitive development and behavior disorders. Each child is assigned a permanent code number. The child's health record is accessible through a national registry bank.

As is the case in most European countries, education for the handicapped in Scandinavia is likely to emphasize social and artistic endeavors at levels beyond those typical of American schools. Thus at the Sogn School in Oslo, Norway, art and other handiwork is emphasized (Juul, 1980). The lekotek or toy library movement was started in Sweden in 1963 by Blid (1971) and Stensland (1964, 1974). Two parents of handicapped children created library centers to evaluate children's developmental needs and teach parents how to use toys and equipment and materials to stimulate their children's learning. The libraries were able to lend toys to handicapped children. These lekoteks spread through Denmark, Finland, Sweden, and other European countries; they have been hailed as a success in the United States (deVincentis, 1984).

The Scandinavians have been interested in facilitating of the transition of handicapped students into the world of adulthood. The strong social welfare systems that characterize Scandinavian countries make this transition somewhat easier and less threatening than in other countries. Norway has carried out experimental secondary programs. Sweden has reported a number of innovative approaches in this area including the use of escorts, a group dynamic method, and computerized job procurement. Of major importance in a nation such as Sweden is the accommodation to and the accommodation of the labor policies, because they play dominant roles in politics (National Swedish Board of Education, 1984).

In vocational education the Scandinavians have distinguished themselves overall. The Swedish AMU vocational training center in Upsala is world famous. It is a multipurpose training operation seeking to improve the employability of disabled young people. Not only does it provide them with training for a number of different types of employment, it also offers opportunities for retraining to meet changing job market situations.

Scandinavian countries have been leaders in transition training for the handicapped. For almost 150 years they have maintained folk high schools, special institutions that are intended to help young people make effective transitions from adolescence to adulthood. These schools differ greatly in their philosophies and curricular orientations, as well as in the types of students that they serve. Some of these schools address the needs and problems of handicapped and disadvantaged youths. One of these schools, the Kjesater Folk High School in Sweden (Zielnok & Kignell, 1975), was found to have some students interested in creative arts, as well as a considerable number of mentally retarded students and some deaf ones. Run by the Swedish Scouting Association, it also provides courses that prepare Scout leaders to work with the handicapped. The Peder Moret Folk High School in Norway, which started operations in 1976, serves both mentally retarded and nonretarded resident students, all with their own rooms but sharing other facilities. Juul (1985) studied folk schools in Denmark, Finland, Norway, and Sweden and has suggested that folk high schools can serve as models for the education and integration of handicapped youths.

Teacher preparation institutions in Scandinavia include the State Graduate School for Special Education in Oslo, Norway. This school has extremely high admission standards, exceeded only by those for the colleges of medicine and law. It has served as a model for Norway and neighboring countries.

The use of voluntary agencies has been high in Scandinavian countries. The Society and Home for Disabled (1974) in Denmark operates hospitals, orthopedic clinics, children's homes, and boarding and vocational schools. It also designs and constructs orthopedic and prosthetic devices. Indeed, Scandinavian contributions to prosthetic development is impressive. The Swedish Scouting Association has backed the development of lekotek and the Kjesäter Folk High School for the handicapped. The Norwegian Red Cross is known for its initiative in creating special education opportunities.

Scandinavian countries have been leaders in integrating handicapped individuals into society. In Denmark's public schools, special education is an integral part of regular education. Unlike the United States, there are no specific special education budgets, though students who have special needs receive special help. In the same spirit, Denmark passed into law, as of January 1, 1979, provisions to decentralize services for the administration of programs for the handicapped. This law dissolved a variety of specific agencies serving the handicapped on the premise that the handicapped are best served if they are not labeled as handicapped as a prerequisite for receiving help and if

they receive service from agencies that also help nonhandicapped persons.

REFERENCES

Blid, E. (1971). *Leka, o..va, la..ra* Stockholm: Bonniers.

deVincentis, S. (1984, April). *Swedish play intervention for handicapped children.* Paper presented at the annual convention of the Council for Exceptional Children, Washington, DC.

Faber, N. W. (1968). *The retarded child.* New York: Crown.

Juul, K. D. (1978). European approaches and innovations in serving the handicapped. *Exceptional Children, 44,* 322–330.

Juul, K. D. (1980). Special education in Western Europe and Scandinavia. In L. Mann & D. A. Sabatino (Eds.), *The fourth review of special education.* New York: Grune & Stratton.

Juul, K. D. (1985). The Scandinavian folk high school: A model for the education and integration of handicapped youth. *Exceptional Children, 32,* 121–127.

Kugel, F. B., & Wolfensberger, W. (Eds.). (1968). *Changing patterns of residential services for the mentally retarded.* Washington, DC: President's Committee on Mental Retardation.

National Swedish Board of Education. (1984). *Transition from school to work for handicapped adolescents: Swedish position report to the OECD/CERI Project concerning the education of handicapped adolescents—Innovative approaches in the transition to adult and working life.* Stockholm: Department for Coordination and Planning, Information and Documentation Section.

Stensland, J. K. (1964). *The child in the glass ball.* Nashville, TN: Abingdon.

Stensland J. K. (1974). A center for play rehabilitation as an indispensable part of the medical and educational care of handicapped and sick children. *Paediatrician, 3,* 315–320.

Vail, D. J. (1968). *Mental health systems in Scandinavia.* Springfield, IL: Thomas.

Wolfensberger, W. (1964a). Some observations on European programs. *Mental Retardation, 2,* 280–285.

Wolfensberger, W. (1964b). Teaching and training of the retarded in European countries. *Mental Retardation, 2,* 331–337.

Wolfensberger, W. (1965). General observations on European countries. *Mental Retardation, 2,* 331–337.

Zielnok, W., & Kignell, E. (1975). Behinderte belegen kurse an einer Schwedischen Heim-Volkschule. *Lebenshilfe, 14,* 98–104.

DON BRASWELL
*Research Foundation, City
University of New York*

FRANCE, SPECIAL EDUCATION IN
WESTERN EUROPE, SPECIAL EDUCATION IN

SCAPEGOATING

A scapegoat is generally defined as a person or group that bears the blame for the mistakes of others. Typically, this is manifested as a group singling out an individual for unfair attack. In schools such systematic victimization of one child by a group of others can isolate the child from the social life of the class and cause the child to feel unworthy of inclusion in the peer group. At times handicapped children may be scapegoats, particularly those with low self-esteem, which is usual with handicapped children owing to academic, emotional, or physical problems (Gearheart, 1985).

Allan (1985) has reported that the scapegoating of one child by others is a common problem facing teachers and counselors. The scapegoats suffer from social isolation and poor self-concept. This type of environment can only have a negative effect on learning. This is especially true for children in classes for the handicapped. However, the disruptiveness caused by scapegoating is not only destructive to the scapegoat, but also to children who fear that they may become the next victim. These children may develop coping strategies to avoid that possibility. Such strategies may include ingratiating themselves with class leaders, mistreating scapegoats to prove that they are not scapegoats themselves, and refusing to associate with former friends who are now scapegoats.

Nonhandicapped children require help with social skills as they interact with handicapped peers in mainstreamed classrooms. One problem that may arise is the calling of names, which can be dealt with in a variety of ways. Salend and Schobel (1981) described one strategy that they implemented with a fourth-grade class. Discussion included the meaning of names, how names differ, and the positive and negative consequences of names. The last topic included a discussion of the negative effects of nicknames and the importance of considering another person's reaction to the nickname. It is obvious that educators must seriously consider the effects of scapegoating and must continue to develop strategies to counteract the negative effects of scapegoating on handicapped children.

REFERENCES

Allan, C. L. (1985). Scapegoating: Help for the whole class. *Elementary School Guidance and Counseling, 18,* 147.

Gearheart, B. R. (1985). *Learning disabilities.* St. Louis: Times Mirror/Mosby College Pub.

Salend, S. J., & Schobel, J. (1981). Coping with namecalling in the mainstream setting. *Education Unlimited, 3*(2), 36–38.

JOSEPH M. RUSSO
*Hunter College, City University
of New York*

SELF-CONCEPT
SOCIAL SKILLS

SCHAEFER, EARL S. (1926–   )

A native of Adyeville, Indiana, Earl S. Schaefer received his BA in psychology from Purdue University (1948). His MA (1951) and PhD (1954) degrees in psychology were earned at the Catholic University of America. Currently, he is a professor in the Department of Maternal and Child Health, School of Public Health, University of North Carolina. He is also senior investigator at the Frank Porter Graham Child Development Center, University of North Carolina.

Schaefer's early research on parent attitudes resulted in the Parental Attitude Research Instrument (Schaefer & Bell, 1958). He has continued that early work (Schaefer & Edgerton, 1985) in a study of parental modernity in beliefs and values correlated with child intellectual development. Schaefer is now involved in a study of low-income mothers and children that indicates that grade retention in kindergarten can be predicted from maternal characteristics and behavior during pregnancy and the child's infancy. Schaefer's major educational goals are to contribute to programs designed to foster child improvement.

REFERENCES

Schaefer, E. S., & Bell, R. Q. (1958). Development of a parental attitude research instrument. *Child Development, 29,* 339–361.

Schaefer, E. S., & Edgerton, M. (1985). Parent and child correlates of parental modernity. In E. Sigel (Ed.), *Parental belief systems.* Hillsdale, NJ: Erlbaum.

E. VALERIE HEWITT
Texas A&M University

SCHIEFELBUSCH, RICHARD L. (1918–   )

A Kansas native, Richard L. Schiefelbusch received his BS from Kansas State Teachers College in 1940, his MA from the University of Kansas in 1947, and his PhD from Northwestern University in 1951. He has taught speech pathology at the University of Kansas since 1946. In 1955 he was appointed director of the Bureau of Child Research, University of Kansas, a position he still holds. Through

Richard L. Schiefelbusch

these two positions, he has been able to work in the field of speech pathology as well as psychology.

Much of Schiefelbusch's work with the Bureau of Child Research has been in the area of language and communications programs for mentally retarded children. He has been instrumental in discovering and developing effective applied behavior analysis techniques for severely retarded children. Studies done through the bureau were designed to alter the range of educational and social activities of institutionalized children. Schiefelbusch was able to demonstrate that children who had no previous history of educational success could be included in productive instructional programs. New techniques of treatment and training in useful language and social skills were made available to severely and multiply handicapped children.

Schiefelbusch has authored numerous books and articles, including *Language Perspectives: Acquisition, Retardation and Intervention; Language Intervention Strategies*; and *Nonspeech Language and Communication: Analysis and Intervention*. In 1975 he was given a special award by the American Association for Mental Deficiency, and in 1976 he received the honors of the association from the American Speech and Hearing Association. In 1981 he was selected for *Who's Who in America*, and in 1984 was awarded the National Distinguished Service Award by the Association for Retarded Citizens.

REFERENCES

Schiefelbusch, R. L. (Ed.). (1978). *Language intervention strategies*. Baltimore, MD: University Park Press.

Schiefelbusch, R. L. (Ed.). (1980). *Nonspeech language and communication: Analysis and intervention*. Baltimore, MD: University Park Press.

Schiefelbusch, R. L., & Bricker, D. (Eds.). (1981). *Early language: Acquisition and intervention*. Baltimore, MD: University Park Press.

Schiefelbusch, R. L., & Lloyd, L. L. (Eds.). (1974). *Language perspectives: Acquisition, retardation and intervention*. Baltimore, MD: University Park Press.

Schiefelbusch, R. L., & Pickar, J. (Eds.). (1984). *Communicative competence: Acquisition and intervention*. Baltimore, MD: University Park Press.

E. VALERIE HEWITT
Texas A&M University

SCHOOL ATTENDANCE OF HANDICAPPED

School attendance of the handicapped, and of all children, is affected by the following factors: motivational level, home and community problems, levels of stress, academic underachievement, rate of failure, negative self-concept, social difficulties, external directedness, improper school placement, inconsistent expectations by parents and teachers, aversive elements in the school environment, and skill deficiences (Grala & McCauley, 1976; Schloss, Kane, & Miller, 1981; Unger, Douds, & Pierce, 1978). Absenteeism is learned; as it becomes habitual, it increases and continues to reinforce itself (Stringer, 1973).

Since it is difficult to develop effective intervention strategies in academic, social, emotional, and vocational areas if children are not in school, attendance becomes a parallel goal to the successful completion of the handicapped student's individual educational plan (IEP). Various authors (Jones, 1974; Schloss, Kane, & Miller, 1981; Unger, Douds, & Pierce, 1978) have suggested programs for motivating or changing patterns of behavior of special education students to assist in increasing their school attendance.

Jones (1974) described the Diversified Satellite Occupations Program and Career Development, which allows the student to register in a less structured school setting from the one he or she normally attends, provides a curriculum with an emphasis on occupational guidance for all ages, and shortens the school day. The program was successful in decreasing truancy.

Schloss, Kane, and Miller (1981) evaluated factors related to adverse aspects of attending school and pleasant aspects of staying at home. An intervention program was individually developed to assist the student in increasing the amount of satisfaction received from going to school, decreasing the amount of satisfaction gained from staying home, and actively teaching skills that enhance the student's ability to benefit from going to school. Not only did school attendance improve, but test scores also increased. Unger, Douds, and Pierce (1978) described a program that taught students the skills necessary to succeed in school. Each student's attendance pattern was examined, reasons for truancy evaluated, and individual lessons devised. Students' attendance and attitudes toward school both improved.

Since school attendance for handicapped children is mandated by the Education for All Handicapped Children Act of 1975 (PL 94-142), it is extremely important that absenteeism be evaluated constantly by the local educational agency and that steps be undertaken to remediate the situation on an individual basis whenever possible.

REFERENCES

The education for all handicapped children act (PL 94-142); Rules and regulations for implementation of Part B (1977, Aug. 23). *Federal Register*. 42474–42514.

Grala, R., & McCauley, C. (1976). Counseling truants back to school: Motivation combined with a program for action. *Journal of Counseling Psychology, 23,* 166–169.

Jones, H. B. (1974). *Dropout prevention: Diversified Satellite Occupations Program and Career Development. Final report*. Washington, DC: Bureau of Adult, Vocational, and Technical Education.

Schloss, P. J., Kane, M. S., & Miller, S. (1981). Truancy intervention with behavior disordered adolescents. *Behavior Disorders, 6*(3), 175–179.

Stringer, L. A. (1973). Children at risk 2. The teacher as change agent. *Elementary School Journal, 73*(8), 424–434.

Unger, K. V., Douds, A., & Pierce, R. M. (1978). A truancy prevention project. *Phi Delta Kappan, 60*(4), 317.

SUSANNE BLOUGH ABBOTT
*Bedford Central School District,
Mt. Kisco, New York*

PARENTS OF THE HANDICAPPED

EDUCATION FOR ALL HANDICAPPED CHILDREN ACT OF 1975

SCHOOL EFFECTIVENESS

School effectiveness is a term adopted in the late 1970s to refer to a body of research on identifying effective schools and the means for creating more of them. The movement to research effective schools has been driven largely by three principal assumptions. According to Bickel (1983), these are that: (1) it is possible to identify schools that are particularly effective in teaching basic skills to poor and minority children; (2) effective schools exhibit identifiable characteristics that are correlated with the success of their students and these characteristics can be manipulated by educators; and (3) the salient characteristics of effective schools form a basis for the improvement of noneffective schools.

Bickel (1983) has traced the origins of the school effectiveness movement to three factors. The first is the backlash that developed in response to the Coleman studies (and like research) of the 1960s. These studies left the unfortunate impression that differences among schools were irrelevant in the education of poor and minority children. The second basis, according to Bickel, was the general psychological climate of the 1970s. Principals, teachers, parents, and others seemed ready for a more positive, hopeful message, one that said schools could make a difference and that effective schools did exist in the real world. The final factor described by Bickel is the readiness of the educational research community to accept the findings that to date include such intuitively appealing variables as strong instructional leadership, an orderly school climate, high expectations, an emphasis on basic skills, and frequent testing and monitoring of student progress.

MacKenzie (1983) has noted broad, rapid agreement on the dimensions and fundamental elements of what constitutes effective schools. The Table, adapted from MacKenzie's (1983) excellent review, lists these various elements; however, as MacKenzie has discussed, the listing of attributes is truly misleading in this instance. The characteristics of effective schools are largely interactive, producing a circumstance that promotes learning that goes

Dimensions of Effective School Research and Corresponding Elements of Effective Schools

---

Leadership Dimensions

Core Elements

1. Positive overall school and organizational climate
2. Activities focused toward clear, attainable, relevant, and objective goals
3. Teacher-directed classroom management
4. Teacher-directed decision making
5. In-service training designed to develop effective teaching

Facilitating Elements

1. Consensus among teachers and administrators on goals and values
2. Long-range planning
3. Stability of key staff
4. District-level support for school improvement

Efficacy Dimensions

Core Elements

1. Expectations for high achievement
2. Consistent press for excellence
3. Visible rewards for academic excellence
4. Group interaction in the classroom
5. Autonomy and flexibility to implement adaptive practices
6. Total staff involvement in school improvement
7. Teacher empathy, rapport, and interaction with students

Facilitating Elements

1. Emphasis on homework and study
2. Acceptance of responsibility for learning outcomes
3. Strategies to avoid nonpromotion of students
4. Deemphasis on ability grouping

Efficiency Dimensions

Core Elements

1. Amount and intensity of time engaged in learning
2. Orderly school and classroom environments
3. Continuous assessment, evaluation, and feedback
4. Well-structured classroom learning activities
5. Instruction driven by content
6. Schoolwide emphasis on basic and on higher order skills

Facilitating Elements

1. Opportunities for individualized work
2. Number and variety of opportunities to learn
3. Reduced class size

Source: After MacKenzie, 1983.

far beyond a summation of the parts. The effectiveness of a school cannot be predicted by determining the mere presence or absence of each of these factors—they must be assessed as they interact within the school under observation.

As can be seen from the elements of school effectiveness given in the Table, making schools particularly good learning environments is a total system effort. Elements are listed that affect the district level, building level, and classroom level. It is difficult to point to any one level as being the most crucial, even though schools are hierarchically arranged; however, if there is one level that deserves more emphasis, it is the classroom. The individual classroom is where instruction takes place; it will always be the key to the educational process. The classroom is affected by many elements that cannot be ignored. MacKenzie (1983) emphasizes:

> The classroom as a learning environment is nested in the larger environment of the school, which is embedded in a political-administrative structure through which it relates to the surrounding community. . . . It will be difficult if not impossible to provide effective classroom teaching in a disorderly, disorganized, and disoriented school environment, and it may be nearly as difficult to organize good schools in an atmosphere of political and managerial indifference. (p. 9) (Also see Purkey and Smith, 1982.)

Effective schools may have been thought, intuitively, by some to bring all students to some designated average level of performance. However, instead of causing students to cluster tightly about some central tendency, effective schools expand the differences among students rather than restrict them. Rich, facilitative environments enhance the results of ability differences, allowing the maximum possible levels of growth; deprived, restrictive environments slow and constrain growth. This does not mean that group differences will necessarily increase. If schools and instruction are particularly effective for all groups, as should be the case, then the overall level of achievement should increase for all groups along with the within group dispersion.

Attempts to implement the results of school effectiveness research to create more effective schools are few as yet. The best known project to date is New York City's School Improvement Project. Clark and McCarthy (1983) have described this effort in detail, discussing the various barriers encountered, the problems of true implementation, and the various failures of the project. However, as Clark and McCarthy note emphatically, when the school effectiveness findings were able to be implemented in a manner true to the model, student achievement increased.

As promising as the school effectiveness literature appears to be, and even with the consensus on the core elements of school effectiveness, a variety of valid criticisms have been offered. These have been summarized and reviewed by Rowan, Bossert, and Dwyer (1983). The technical properties of the research have been criticized as (1) using narrow, limited measures of effectiveness that focus only on instructional outcomes; (2) using design that allows an analysis of relational variables from which cause

and effect cannot be inferred; and (3) making global comparisons on the basis of aggregate data, without assessing intraschool variations in organizational climate or outcomes across classes within schools. Rowan, Bossert, and Dwyer (1983) also caution that the effect sizes present in this line of research are questionable. They have argued that the traditional methods of research in school effectiveness resemble "fishing expeditions" that spuriously inflate the probability of finding significant results. Despite these and other problems, the school effectiveness movement has rekindled optimism that schools can be organized and restructured to enhance student performance. As yet, the application of the methods and concepts of the school effectiveness literature have not been applied to special education programs. Special education programs are typically excluded from the data in such studies and desperately need to be assessed. It remains to be seen whether special education programs that can be identified as particularly effective in educating the handicapped are affected by the same variables and with the same form of interaction as are regular education programs. The time to apply the concepts and research methods of school effectiveness to special education is past due. It holds much promise for understanding what makes special education effective and how to effect such changes.

REFERENCES

Bickel, W. E. (1983). Effective schools: Knowledge, dissemination, inquiry. *Educational Researcher, 12*, 3–5.

Clark, T. A., & McCarthy, D. P. (1983). School improvement in New York City: The evolution of a project. *Educational Researcher, 12*, 17–24.

MacKenzie, D. E. (1983). Research for school improvement: An appraisal of some recent trends. *Educational Researcher, 12*, 5–19.

Purkey, S. C., & Smith, M. S. (1982). Too soon to cheer? Synthesis of research on effective schools. *Educational Leadership, 40*, 64–69.

Rowan, B., Bossert, S. T., & Dwyer, D. C. (1983). Research on effective schools: A cautionary note. *Educational Researcher, 12*, 24–32.

CECIL R. REYNOLDS
Texas A&M University

SPECIAL EDUCATION PROGRAMS
TEACHER EFFECTIVENESS

SCHOOL FAILURE

There are many reasons why children fail in school. In some cases, failure may be due to circumstances within the child's environment. In other cases, school failure may be the result of a physical problem originating before, during, or after birth. This section identifies and discusses some of the chief causes of failure in school.

Failure in school often occurs when children come from

environments characterized by economic hardship, deprivation, neglect, trauma, divorce, death, foster parenting, drug abuse, poor school attendance, or lack of adequate instruction. Cultural differences also contribute to school failure. When a language other than English is used in the home and children are limited in English proficiency, they do poorly in school. The cultural values held by students also affect how they perceive their school, their teachers, and their peer group. For example, students' values determine how much they will be motivated in class, how they perceive and respond to authority, and whether they will be highly competitive or more responsive to a cooperative approach to learning. When values differ widely from one culture to another, what is valued in one culture may serve as a barrier to learning in another (Saville-Troike, 1978).

Children who exhibit behavior problems in the classroom also experience school failure. Some children have conduct disorders in which they disrupt the class, constantly irritate the teacher, do not follow directions, are easily distracted, are impulsive, or fail to attend. Other students who are fearful, anxious, withdrawn, or immature have difficulty in responding freely in the classroom and fail to learn to the limits of their abilities. Children whose self-esteem is so low that they believe they are of little worth often learn to be helpless. These children stop trying in school because they think they cannot learn. When children with behavior problems do not conform to the standards of the school environment, they may become socially aggressive, reject the values of the school and society, and come into conflict with authorities. A student may openly confront teachers and administrators, begin using drugs or alcohol, join gangs, break laws, steal, and eventually be expelled from or drop out of school (Knoblock, 1983; Long, Morse, & Newman, 1980; Quay & Werry, 1979).

Children with physical handicaps whose participation in routine activities is limited may fail in school unless the learning environment is modified to meet their needs. Physical handicaps include disorders of the heart and lungs; muscular or skeletal conditions; and disorders of the brain, spinal cord, or the nerve network that reaches all parts of the body. Conditions such as cerebral palsy, spinal cord injury, paralysis, epilepsy, or diseases such as arthritis, cancer, cystic fibrosis, diabetes, or muscular dystrophy can result in physical handicaps that cause failure in school (Bigge, 1982).

Children who have difficulty in seeing and hearing often fail in school. Although 1 child in 10 enters school with some degree of visual impairment, most of these problems can be corrected and have no effect on educational development. One child out of a thousand, however, has visual impairments so severe they cannot be corrected. Children who are hard of hearing or deaf have difficulty in learning to understand language. This causes difficulty in learning to speak, read, and write the English language (Barraga, 1983).

Mental retardation results in school failure. Mental retardation may range in severity from mild to moderate to severe to profound. Delayed mental development can contribute to failure in language acquisition and use, achievement in academic subjects, social adjustment, and becoming a self-supporting adult (Mittler, 1981).

Specific learning disabilities can result in failure in school. A learning disability is a dysfunction in one or more of the psychological processes that are involved in learning to read, write, spell, compute arithmetic, etc. In some cases, a child may have an attention disability and may not be able to direct attention purposefully, failing to selectively focus attention on the relevant stimuli or responding to too many stimuli at once. A memory disability is the inability to remember what has been seen or heard. Perceptual disabilities cover a wide range of disorders in which a child who has normal vision, hearing, and feeling may experience difficulty in grasping the meaning of what is seen, heard, or touched. An example is a child who has difficulty in seeing the directional differences between a "d" and a "b," or who requires an excessive amount of time to look at a printed word, analyze the word, and say the word. Thinking disabilities involve problems in judgment, making comparisons, forming new concepts, critical thinking, problem solving, and decision making. A disability in oral language refers to difficulties in understanding and using oral language. All of these specific learning disabilities might cause difficulty in learning to read, write, spell, compute arithmetic, or adopt appropriate social-emotional behaviors (Kirk & Chalfant, 1984).

REFERENCES

Barraga, N. (1983). *Visual handicaps and learning* (rev. ed.). Austin, TX: Exceptional Resources.

Bigge, J. (1982). *Teaching individuals with physical and multiple disabilities* (2nd ed.). Columbus, OH: Merrill.

Kirk, S. A., & Chalfant, J. C. (1984). *Academic and developmental learning disabilities.* Denver, CO: Love.

Knoblock, P. (1983). *Teaching emotionally disturbed children.* Boston: Houghton Mifflin.

Long, N., Morse, W., & Newman, R. (Eds.). (1980). *Conflict in the classroom: The education of emotionally disturbed children* (4th ed.). Belmont, CA: Wadsworth.

Mittler, P. (Ed.). (1981). *Frontiers of knowledge in mental retardation: Vol. 1. Social educational and behavioral aspects; Vol. 2. Biomedical aspects.* Baltimore, MD: University Park Press.

Quay, H., & Werry, J. (Eds.). (1979). *Psychopathological disorders of childhood* (2nd ed.). New York: Wiley.

Saville-Troike, M. (1978). *A guide to culture in the classroom.* Rosslyn, VA: National Clearinghouse for Bilingual Education.

JAMES CHALFANT
University of Arizona

EMOTIONAL DISORDERS
LEARNED HELPLESSNESS

LEARNING DISABILITIES
MENTAL RETARDATION

SCHOOL PHOBIA

School phobia has been the subject of hundreds of research studies and dozens of literature reviews over the past four decades. The phenomenon was first described in 1932 when Broadwin distinguished a type of school refusal from truancy by an anxiety component. The term school phobia was coined in 1941 (Johnson, Falstein, Szurek, & Svendson, 1941). A common definition of school phobia cited in the more recent literature includes the following characteristics:

Severe difficulty in attending school often amounting to prolonged absence.

Severe emotional upset shown by such symptoms as excessive fearfulness, undue temper, misery or complaints of feeling ill without obvious organic cause on being faced with the prospect of going to school.

Staying at home during school hours with the knowledge of the parents at some stage in the course of the disorder.

Absence of significant antisocial disorder, such as stealing, lying, wandering, destructiveness, or sexual misbehavior. (Berg, Nichols, & Pritchard, 1969, p. 123).

In contrast to school phobia, truancy is characterized by behaviors that are the opposite of the last two behaviors.

Contemporary writers who use the term school refusal generally describe it with the same set of characteristics that defines school phobia. An exception is the American Psychiatric Association's (1980) classification system (DSM-III), which describes school refusal as one possible concomitant of separation anxiety disorder, while reserving the term school phobia for a fear of the school situation even when parents accompany the child.

The occurrence of school phobia is relatively rare when one considers the abundance of literature devoted to it. Estimates of the incidence of school phobia range from 3.2 to 17 per 1000 schoolchildren (Kennedy, 1965; Yule, 1979). The wide discrepancy may be due in part to the age at which children are sampled. Prevalence is thought to peak at three different ages: 5 to 7, on entry or shortly after entry to school; 11, around the time children change schools; and 14, often concomitant with depression (Hersov, 1977). Many writers consider school phobia to occur in three girls for every two boys (Wright, Schaefer, & Solomons, 1979). However, this ratio has not appeared in several studies of school phobics reported in the literature (Baker, & Wills, 1978; Berg et al., 1969; Hersov, 1960; Kennedy, 1965).

The causes of school phobia have been couched in psychoanalytic, psychodynamic, and social learning theory terms. The psychoanalytic focus frames school phobia within a mutually dependent and hostile parent-child relationship. Some psychoanalysts believe that the unconscious conflict resulting from this relationship leads the child to want to protect the mother, and hence, not leave her. Other psychoanalysts indicate that the conflict surrounding the hostile-dependent relationship with mother is displaced onto the school situation, which becomes the manifest phobic object. In any case, both agree that separation anxiety plays a key role in school phobia (Atkinson, Quarrington, & Cyr, 1985; Kelly, 1973).

An alternative theory that was intended to explain the occurrence of school phobia at later ages was postulated by Leventhal and Sills (1964). Kelly (1973) labeled this theoretical approach, which focuses on the school phobic's unrealistic self-image, as "nonanalytic psychodynamic." According to Leventhal and Sills (1964):

These children commonly overvalue themselves and their achievements and then try to hold onto their unrealistic self-image. When this is threatened in the school situation, they suffer anxiety and retreat to another situation where they can maintain their narcissistic self-image. This retreat may very well be a running to a close contact with mother. (p. 686)

Others have used the term fear of failure in referring to this theory (Atkinson et al., 1985).

Behavioral theories account for school phobia in terms of both classical and operant conditioning. The former model explains school phobia as a conditioned anxiety response elicited by the school situation or some other school-related event. For instance, an often cited case (Garvey & Hegrenes, 1966) involved a boy whose mother repeatedly told him as he was leaving for school that she might die while he was gone. Eventually, the thought of going to school led to fear of his mother's death. The operant model assumes that internal or environmental cues both trigger and maintain the school phobic behavior.

Atkinson et al. (1985) argued that the three perspectives differ more in focus than in substance because all can account for school phobia as a fear of separation, of the school situation, or of failures in school. For example, the child whose unrealistic self-image leads to a fear of failure in the school situation may be reinforced by parents for not attending school. Similarly, separation anxiety may be a component of school phobia triggered by a traumatic school event.

Coolidge, Hahn, and Peck (1957) were the first to describe subtypes of school phobia. Based on differences within a fairly small sample of 27 school phobics, they discussed neurotic and characterological types. The former were characterized by sudden onset after several years of normal school attendance while the latter were described as more severely disturbed, with the fear of school being only one fear among many in a generally fearful personality. Subsequent investigations by Kennedy (1965) and Hersov (1960) confirmed the general distinction between an acute form and a more pervasive disturbance. Kennedy (1965) elaborated 10 criteria that distinguished type 1 (neurotic) from type 2 (characterological) school phobics based on a sample of 50 children aged 4 to 16. Generally, the former was characterized by acute onset, a first episode, intact family relations, and occurrence in younger children. Type 2 was characterized as being chronic, often accompanied by a character disorder, unstable parental relationship, incipient onset, and a history of prior episodes.

Family relations have been investigated as a separate correlate of school phobia. Hersov (1960) described three patterns of parent-child relationships that characterized his sample of 50 school phobic children aged 7 to 16 years:

An overindulgent mother and an inadequate, passive father dominated at home by a willful, stubborn, and demanding child who is most often timid and inhibited in social situations.

A severe, controlling, and demanding mother who manages her children without much assistance from her passive husband; a timid and fearful child away from home and a passive and obedient child at home, but stubborn and rebellious at puberty.

A firm, controlling father who plays a large part in home management and an overindulgent mother closely bound to and dominated by a willful, stubborn, and demanding child, who is alert, friendly, and outgoing away from home. (p. 140)

The first two relationship types have been considered to be subtypes of characterological school phobia while the third seems more characteristic of the neurotic type (Atkinson et al., 1985). It should be noted that categorization based on a sample of 50 children needs further validation before conclusions are drawn about parent-child correlates. The same caution holds for Kennedy's classification system, particularly of type 2 school phobia, which was based on six children.

As Atkinson et al. (1985) noted in their review, the construct of school phobia is too heterogeneous to be described by a simple dichotomy. They examined five variables related to school phobia, some of which overlap more than others—extensiveness of disturbance, source of fear, mode of onset, age, and gender of the child. The extensiveness of fear can be conceptualized along a continuum with the dichotomies of neurotic/characterological or type 1/type 2 at the end points. Generally, acute or sudden onset is characteristic of type 1 and chronic or gradual onset is characteristic of type 2. When researchers have operationalized acute mode of onset as the occurrence of school phobia after 3 or more years of trouble-free attendance, other correlates emerge. For instance, chronic onset tended to be associated more than acute onset with poor premorbid adjustment, dependency on parents, low self-esteem, and a poor prognosis.

Similarly, source of fear, age, and gender do not bear a one-to-one correspondence with the dichotomous classifications. Generally, four sources of fear have been reported that correspond to the etiological approaches—fear of maternal separation, fear of something or someone at school, fear of failure, and a generally fearful disposition. Atkinson et al. (1985) conclude that the fear sources are not mutually exclusive, and that fears surrounding separation may coincide with more general fearfulness. They caution, however, that conclusions relating the extensiveness of disturbance to a specific fear source are premature based on current studies. In contrast, extent of disturbance and age appear to be related, with older children generally exhibiting more severe disturbance. While Kennedy differentiated type 1 from type 2 phobics in part on age differences, there is no consistent finding that type 1 or acute type is more typical of younger children.

Both psychological and pharmacotherapy have been employed for children experiencing school phobia. We focus here on psychological interventions only. The interested reader is referred to Gittelman and Koplewicz (in press) for an overview of pharmacotherapy of childhood anxiety disorders. Early treatments of school phobia stemmed from the psychoanalytic tradition and focused on resolving the mutual hostile-dependent relationship between the school phobic child and his or her parents. Typically, parallel treatment was carried out on mother and child, with one therapist using play therapy with the child and another therapist "treating" the mother. Johnson et al. (1941) describe treatment as "a collaborative dynamic approach . . . to relieve the guilt and tension in both patients" (p. 706). Treatment of eight cases reported in their seminal study of school phobia lasted from 5 months to over a year. There does not appear to be consensus among the psychoanalytic clinicians on whether gradual or immediate return is preferable.

The treatment that emerged from Leventhal and Sills' (1967) psychodynamic theory involves "outmaneuvering" the child. Unlike the psychoanalytic approach, rapid return rather than insight is the primary goal of treatment. Once parents are helped to see their complicity in maintaining school avoidance, the parent who is likely to stand firm is chosen to carry out the plan, which is essentially immediate, forced return to school. Kennedy (1965) also advocates forced return to school and described successful treatment of 50 cases of type 1 school phobia. He identified the following six components as essential to successful treatment: (1) good professional public relations; (2) avoidance of emphasis on somatic complaints; (3) forced school attendance; (4) structured interview with parents; (5) brief interview with child; and (6) follow-up (p. 287).

During the past 20 years a proliferation of behavioral treatments of school phobia have occurred. Yule (1979) and Trueman (1984) provide critical reviews of the behavioral treatment of school phobia. Trueman (1984) reviewed 19 case studies between 1960 and 1981 that used behavioral treatments based on classical, operant, or a combination of those techniques. Of the eight studies reviewed that used techniques based on classical conditioning, six used reciprocal, one used implosion, and one used emotive imagery. Six of the studies involved boys aged 10 to 17; two studies involved girls aged 8 and 9. Trueman noted considerable variation among the reciprocal inhibition treatments, making conclusions difficult concerning the most efficacious component. Additionally, he noted the difficulty in distinguishing between systematic densensitization and shaping.

Among the 10 case studies reviewed by Trueman that used operant procedures, five involved boys aged 7 to 12 and five involved girls aged 6 to 14. The change agents varied among studies as well as the specific techniques and the criteria for success. Thus comparisons between procedures are hard to make. The procedures included training parents in positive reinforcement methods, contingency contracting, prompting and shaping, and school-based contingencies. Until more well-controlled group and single case studies are conducted with uniform criteria for success, no firm conclusions can be drawn as to the relative effectiveness of available treatments for school phobia.

REFERENCES

American Psychiatric Association. (1980). *Diagnostic and statistical manual of mental disorders (3rd ed.)*. Washington, DC: Author.

Atkinson, L., Quarrington, B., & Cyr, J. J. (1985). School refusal: The heterogeneity of a concept. *American Journal of Orthopsychiatry, 55*, 83–101.

Baker, H., & Wills, U. (1978). School phobia: Classification and treatment. *British Journal of Psychiatry, 132*, 492–499.

Berg, I., Nichols, K., & Pritchard, C. (1969). School phobia—Its classification and relationship to dependency. *Journal of Child Psychology & Psychiatry, 10*, 123–141.

Broadwin, I. T. (1932). A contribution to the study of truancy. *American Journal of Orthopsychiatry, 2*, 252–259.

Coolidge, J., Hahn, P., & Peck, A. (1957). School phobia: Neurotic crisis or way of life. *American Journal of Orthopsychiatry, 27*, 296–306.

Garvey, W. P., & Hegrenes, J. R. (1966). Desensitization techniques in the treatment of school phobia. *American Journal of Orthopsychiatry, 36*, 147–152.

Gittelman, R., & Koplewicz, M. S. (in press). Pharmacotherapy of childhood anxiety disorders. In R. Gittelman (Ed.), *Anxiety disorders in children*. New York: Guilford.

Hersov, L. A. (1960). Refusal to go to school. *Child Psychology & Psychiatry, 1*, 137–145.

Hersov, L. A. (1977). School refusal. In M. Rutter & L. Hersov (Eds.), *Child psychiatry: Modern approaches* (pp. 455–486). Oxford, England: Blackwell.

Johnson, A. M., Falstein, E. J., Szurek, S. A., & Svendsen, M. (1941). School phobia. *American Journal of Orthopsychiatry, 11*, 702–711.

Kelly, E. W. (1973). School phobia: A review of theory and treatment. *Psychology in the Schools, 10*, 33–42.

Kennedy, W. A. (1965). School phobia: Rapid treatment of fifty cases. *Journal of Abnormal Psychology, 70*, 285–289.

Leventhal, T., & Sills, M. (1964). Self-image in school phobia. *American Journal of Orthopsychiatry, 34*, 685–694.

Leventhal, T., Weinberger, G., Stander, R. J., & Stearns, R. P. (1967). Therapeutic strategies with school phobics. *American Journal of Orthopsychiatry, 37*, 64–70.

Trueman, D. (1984). The behavioral treatment of school phobia: A critical review. *Psychology in the Schools, 21*, 215–223.

Wright, L., Schaefer, A., & Solomons, G. (1979). *Encyclopedia of pediatric psychology*. Baltimore, MD: University Park Press.

Yule, W. (1979). Behavioral approaches to the treatment and prevention of school refusal. *Behavioral Analysis & Modification, 3*, 55–68.

JANET A. LINDOW
THOMAS R. KRATOCHWILL
University of Wisconsin,
Madison

RICHARD J. MORRIS
University of Arizona

CHILDHOOD NEUROSIS
PHOBIAS AND FEARS
SEPARATION ANXIETY AND THE HANDICAPPED

SCHOOL PSYCHOLOGY

Psychology is devoted to the goals of describing and explaining human behavior and promoting conditions that foster human development and welfare. School psychologists generally share these goals and strive to apply psychological theories, concepts, and techniques to facilitate growth and development through education and schools. The birth of psychology occurred about 100 years ago in Germany. Psychologists began working in U.S. schools about 20 years later as child study departments and clinics began to form.

An estimated 25,000 school psychologists presently serve in many of the nation's 15,300 school districts. While many school psychologists have teaching experience or an undergraduate degree in psychology, neither is a prerequisite in most states. School psychologists' median age is about 40, slightly more are females than males, and 9 to 10 years of experience as a school psychologist is typical. The median yearly salaries for school psychologists employed 9 to 10 months and with 10 to 14 years of work experience at the doctoral level is $26,000; at the subdoctoral level, it is $22,500 (Stapp & Fulcher, 1981).

The number of school psychology programs and students has increased during the last decade (Fagan, 1985). An estimated 2200 students graduate yearly from more than 200 school psychology programs (Brown & Lindstrom, 1978). Students seeking a specialist's degree frequently take 2 years of graduate work plus a full-time, yearlong internship. Those seeking a doctoral degree frequently take 3 years of graduate work and devote 1 or more years each to an internship and a dissertation. Thus, with 3 to 5 years of graduate preparation, school psychologists tend to be the most highly educated behavioral scientists employed by the schools.

Some (Brown, 1982) view school psychology as a profession separate and independent from the professions of psychology and education; others (Bardon, 1982) view school psychology as a specialty within the profession of psychology. In fact, most school psychologists straddle the professions of psychology and education. They provide many services that are unique and drawn from psychology as well as education. A comprehensive study of the expertise of school psychologists (Rosenfeld, Shimberg, & Thornton, 1983) found the practice of school psychology to be similar to the practice of clinical and counseling psychology. In fact, school psychologists devote considerable attention to assessment and organizational issues.

School psychological services differ between communities. Their character is influenced by many conditions: federal and state laws and policies; local institutional traditions, policies, and practices; financial resources and practices governing allocation; availability of psychologists and the nature of their professional preparation; and national, state, and local professional standards. Furthermore, the services often differ for elementary and secondary grades. Although the nature of their services differ, many school psychologists are guided by a scientist-practitioner model (Cutts, 1955), which holds that applications of psychology should be supportable empirically or theoretically and derived from a body of literature that is held in high esteem. Professionals are expected to have good command of this literature discussing the theoretical, empirical, and technical components of their specialties.

A comprehensive review of the school psychology literature (Ysseldyke, Reynolds, & Weinberg, 1984) identified the following 16 domains as ones in which school psychology has expertise: classroom management, classroom organization and social structure, interpersonal communication and consultation, basic academic skills, basic life skills, affective/social skills, parent involvement, systems development and planning, personnel development, individual differences in development and learning, school-community relations, instruction, legal, ethical, and professional issues, assessment, multicultural concerns, and research and evaluation.

While school psychology is a dynamic specialty and one not easily categorized or described, its work in five broad areas is described briefly. School psychologists frequently conduct psychoeducational evaluations of pupils needing special attention. The evaluations typically consider a student's cognitive (i.e., intelligence and achievement), affective, social, emotional, and linguistic characteristics,

and use behavioral, educational, and psychological (including psychoneurological and psychoanalytic) techniques.

School psychologists also participate in planning and evaluating services designed to promote cognitive, social, and affective development. Their services can include teaching, training, counseling, and therapy. While their principal focus frequently is on individual pupils, they also work individually with parents, teachers, principals, and other educators.

School psychologists also offer indirect services to pupils through educators, parents, and other adults. Their indirect services typically involve in-service programs for teachers, parent education programs, counseling, consultation, and collaboration. Their consultative and collaborative activities involve them with groups composed of students, teachers, parents, and others. Their work as members of the education staff enables them to effect important changes in organizations by working on broad and important issues that impact classrooms, school buildings, districts, communities, corporations, or a consortium of districts and agencies.

School psychologists' knowledge of quantitive methods commonly used in research and evaluation often surpasses that of other educational personnel. Thus they frequently are responsible for conceptualizing and designing studies, collecting and analyzing data, and integrating and disseminating findings.

School psychologists also may supervise pupil personnel and psychological services. In this capacity, they are responsible for conceptualizing and promoting a comprehensive plan for these services, for hiring and supervising personnel, for promoting their development, and for coordinating psychological services with other services in the district or community.

School psychology, like other professions, has developed and promulgated a number of standards that exemplify the profession's values and principles and that serve the needs of service providers, clients, educators, society, and legal bodies (Oakland, 1986). These standards, as described by the American Psychological Association, are included in *Psychology as a Profession* (1968), "Guidelines for Conditions of Employment of Psychologists" (1972), *Ethical Principles in the Conduct of Research with Human Subjects* (1973), *Standards for Educational and Psychological Testing* (1985), *Criteria for Accreditation of Doctoral Training Programs and Internships in Professional Psychology* (1980), *Ethical Principles of Psychologists* (1981a), and "Specialty Guidelines for the Delivery of Services by School Psychologists" (1981b). The National Association of School Psychologists standards are included in *Standards for the Provision of School Psychological Services* (1984b), *Standards for Training and Field Placement Programs in School Psychology* (1984c), *Standards for Credentialing in School Psychology* (1978), and *Principles for Professional Ethics* (1984a).

Most school psychologists work in the schools or within other organizational structures (e.g., mental health clinics, juvenile courts, guidance centers, private and public residential care facilities). State certification is important for these school psychologists. Forty-nine states presently certify school psychologists—an increase of 42 since 1946. Many school psychologists also want the option to practice privately. Although those who have doctoral degrees typically can be licensed by their states as psychologists, those holding subdoctoral degrees typically have been denied a license to practice psychology independently and increasingly are seeking the right to be licensed and to practice privately.

Five professional journals are devoted to advancing the knowledge and practice of school psychology: *Journal of School Psychology, Professional School Psychology, Psychology in the Schools, School Psychology International*, and *School Psychology Review*. An additional 16 secondary and 26 tertiary journals add to the literature (Reynolds & Gutkin, 1982). Persons interested in further information about school psychology are encouraged to consult the professional journals, *The Handbook of School Psychology* (Reynolds & Gutkin, 1982), and the many textbooks discussing school psychology (Whelan & Carlson, 1980).

REFERENCES

American Psychological Association. (1968). *Psychology as a profession*. Washington, DC: Author.

American Psychological Association. (1972). Guidelines for conditions of employment of psychologists. *American Psychologist, 27*, 331–334.

American Psychological Association. (1973). *Ethical principles in the conduct of research with human subjects*. Washington, DC: Author.

American Psychological Association. (1977). *Standards for providers of psychological services* (revised ed.). Washington, DC: Author.

American Psychological Association. (1980). *Criteria for accreditation of doctoral training programs and internships in professional psychology*. Washington, DC: Author.

American Psychological Association. (1981a). *Ethical principles of psychologists* (revised ed.). Washington, DC: Author.

American Psychological Association. (1981b). Specialty guidelines for the delivery of services by school psychologists. *American Psychologist, 36*, 639, 670–682.

American Psychological Association. (1985). *Standards for educational and psychological testing*. Washington, DC: Author.

Bardon, J. (1982). The psychology of school psychology. In C. R. Reynolds & T. B. Gutkin (Eds.), *The handbook of school psychology* (pp. 1–14). New York: Wiley.

Brown, D. (1982). Issues in the development of professional school psychology. In C. R. Reynolds & T. B. Gutkin (Eds.), *The handbook of school psychology* (pp. 14–23). New York: Wiley.

Brown, D. T., & Lindstrom, J. P. (1978). The training of school psychologists in the United States: An overview. *Psychology in the Schools, 15*, 37–45.

Cutts, N. E. (Ed.). (1955). *School psychology at mid-century*. Washington, DC: American Psychological Association.

Fagan, T. (1985). Quantitative growth of school psychology in the United States. *School Psychology Review, 14*, 121–124.

National Association of School Psychologists. (1978). *Standards for credentialing in school psychology*. Washington, DC: Author.

National Association of School Psychologists. (1984a). *Principles for professional ethics*. Washington, DC: Author.

National Association of School Psychologists. (1984b). *Standards for the provision of school psychological services*. Washington, DC: Author.

National Association of School Psychologists. (1984c). *Standards for training and field placement programs in school psychology*. Washington, DC: Author.

Oakland, T. (1986). Professionalism within school psychology. *Professional School Psychology, 1*, 9–27.

Reynolds, C. R., & Gutkin, T. B. (1982). *The handbook of school psychology*. New York: Wiley.

Rosenfeld, M., Shimberg, B., & Thornton, R. (1983). *Job analysis of licensed psychologists in the United States and Canada*. Princeton, NJ: Educational Test Service.

Stapp, J., & Fulcher, R. (1981). *Salaries in psychology*. Washington, DC: American Psychological Association.

Whelan, T., & Carlson, C. (1980). Books in school psychology: 1970 to present, *Professional School Psychology, 1*, 283–293.

THOMAS OAKLAND
University of Texas, Austin

EDUCATIONAL DIAGNOSTICIAN

PSYCHOLOGY IN THE SCHOOLS

SCHOOL PSYCHOLOGY DIGEST

See SCHOOL PSYCHOLOGY REVIEW.

SCHOOL PSYCHOLOGY REVIEW

School Psychology Review is the official journal of the National Association of School Psychologists (NASP); it was founded in the winter of 1972. The primary purpose of the *Review* is "to provide a means for communicating scholarly advances in research, training, and practice that can affect the delivery of school psychological services." The *Review* is a refereed, quarterly publication with an editor and appointed editorial advisory board. Publication priorities include original research, reviews of theoretical and applied topics, case studies, and descriptions of intervention techniques useful to psychologists working in educational settings. Scholarly reviews of books, tests, and other psychological materials also are published occasionally. Portions of three annual issues are reserved for guest edited miniseries on themes relevant to NASP membership. These solicited theme issues differentiate the *Review* from other major school psychology journals.

Until 1980, *School Psychology Review* was titled *The School Psychology Digest*. The change in name was accompanied by an evolution from primarily publishing condensations of previously published articles or invited articles to the publication of original reviews, research, and case studies. Today, the *Review* enjoys the largest circulation (9500 readers) of any of the journals representing the field of school psychology, and it is one of the most widely distributed journals in the entire discipline of psychology.

Five individuals have served as editor of the *Review*. The founding editor was John Guidubaldi of Kent State University. He was followed by Liam Grimley (Indiana State University), Daniel Reschly (Iowa State University), George Hynd (University of Georgia), and Stephen N. Elliott (Louisiana State University).

A content analysis of the *Review* since 1980 indicates that approximately 30% of the articles concern professional issues in school psychology, 25% concern interventions for academic and behavior problems of children, and 20% involve testing and measurement issues. The remaining 25% of articles cover a wide array of topics including program evaluation, psychological theories, and special education practices. *School Psychology Review* is published by NASP and is a benefit of membership; it may also be purchased separately. Generally, over 65 articles appear in each volume. Back issues are available. Starting with Volume 14, cumulative author, subject, and title indexes are published.

STEPHEN N. ELLIOTT
Louisiana State University

SCHOOL RECORDS

School records constitute three types of documents: information collected and kept by the teacher or administrator; directory information; and psychological, psychiatric, or test data. Historically, school records were considered to be cumulative records. The cumulative record was intended to be a collection of information about a student that constituted a picture of the student's development—physically, academically, and socially. Cumulative records contained data that included personal information and family background; medical and health information; school entry information; grades; transcripts from other schools; schoolwide test results; personality and behavior trait ratings; school activities; anecdotal records; and autobiographical written papers (Allen, 1944).

In 1974 PL 98-380, Title V, the Family Education and Privacy Rights Act, defined educational records to mean

those records, files documents, and other material which (i) contain information directly related to the student; and (ii) are maintained by an educational agency or institution or by a person acting for such agency or institution.

The intent of the law was to allow the inspection of a student's educational records by the parents or legal guardians and to maintain the privacy of those records.

The law specifies that the records kept by the teacher, administrator, or other educational personnel "which are in the sole possession of maker thereof and which are not accessible or revealed to any other person except a substitute" are not included in what the law considers educational records. Anecdotal or privately kept notes and records of the teacher, supervisor, or other educational personnel are not subject to parental inspection as long as they are kept by the author and are not revealed to others in staffings or used to make placement decisions. The law also excludes records and notes kept by a physician, psychiatrist, therapist, or other professional or paraprofessional who may be employed by the agency or institution, on or off the campus, that are used in a professional capacity or in the normal course of business and that are not available to anyone other than those persons providing treatment and are used only for that purpose.

The law also defines a class of educational records as directory information. This class includes the following information: the student's name; address; telephone listing; date and place of birth; major field of study; participation in officially organized activities or sports; weight and height for members of athletic teams; dates of attendance; degrees and awards received; and most recent previous educational agency or institution attended. The law directs agencies or institutions to publicly announce the information that will be listed as directory information and allows parents the right to request that any or all such information not be released without the parents' prior consent.

The law specifies a third class of information that may not be gathered without prior consent of the parents or student (if over 18). This includes psychiatric or psychological information when the primary purpose is to reveal information concerning political affiliations; mental or psychological problems potentially embarrassing to the student or family; sexual behavior and attitudes; illegal, antisocial, self-incriminating, or demeaning behavior; critical appraisals of other individuals with whom respondents have close family relationships; legally recognized priviliged relationship such as those of lawyers, physicians, or ministers; or income other than that required by law to determine eligibility for participation in a program or for receiving financial assistance under such program.

The law specifies that no funds will be made available

to any agency or institution that has a policy or practice of permitting the release of educational records or personally identifiable information other than directory information about a student without written prior consent of the parents to any individual, agency, institution, or organization. Those persons authorized to access educational records without prior written consent include school officials within the educational institution or agency, including teachers who have legitimate educational interests; officials of other schools or school systems that the student seeks to enroll in; and miscellaneous government officials acting in an official capacity. The law allows for research and accreditation access to student educational records when such studies will not permit personal identification of students and their parents and when the information is destroyed when no longer needed for the purpose for which it was collected.

The release of educational records other than directory information can be done only with the written consent of the student's parents, specifying the records to be released and to whom, the reasons for the release, and a copy of the records to be released. The records can also be released in compliance with a judicial order or pursuant to a lawfully issued subpoena on condition that the parents and students are notified of all such orders or subpoenas in advance of the compliance.

Parents and students over 18 years old have the right to review and receive copies of educational records within a reasonable amount of time on written request. The educational agency or institution must also inform parents and students over 18 years old of their rights under this law. Parents or students over 18 years old also have the right to review all instructional material, including teachers' manuals, films, tapes, and other supplementary instructional materials that will be used in connection with any research or experimental program or project that is designed to explore or develop new or unproven teaching methods or techniques.

REFERENCE

Allen, W. C. (1944). Development of cumulative record system. *Handbook of Cumulative Records* (Bulletin No. 5). Washington, DC: U.S. Office of Education.

DANIEL R. PAULSON
University of Wisconsin, Stout

CONFIDENTIALITY OF INFORMATION
PRIVILEGED COMMUNICATION

SCHOOL STRESS

Stress is the nonspecific response of the human body to a demand. It is not simply nervous tension but a physiological response of the body. Stress occurs in all living organisms and is with us all the time (Selye, 1976). Stress comes from mental, emotional, and physical activity. Whereas stress can add flavor and excitement to life, too much stress can seriously affect physical and mental well being. In school, as elsewhere, stressors can be helpful and harmful. Children need enough stress to be effective but not so much that the result is debilitating.

School stress results from the impact of the school environment on children. Physical stress is accompanied by feelings of pain and discomfort, but physical stress is seldom a major factor in school stress. In schools the stressors are most often psychological and result in emotional reactions with accompanying physiological changes in the body.

In school stress, the demands usually result from significant others in the school, i.e., teachers and peers, or those who are expectant about school activities (e.g., parents). School stress is dependent on cognitive processes that lead to emotional reactions and a form or style of coping behavior. The coping behavior may or may not be effective, or the coping behavior may only appear to be effective. When this is the case, the body has changed from a state of alarm and is in the resistance stage. When in the resistance stage, one's ability to deal effectively with other stressors is reduced. Resistance can be maintained only so long before physical or psychological problems occur (Selye, 1976). In the stage of resistance, the person is much more susceptible than when not defensive. In reacting to stress, individuals usually try harder with the coping skills they have or search for other techniques, but when stress is prolonged or is particularly frustrating, it may cause distress physically or mentally. If the stimuli continue to be perceived as stressful, the individual's reaction can be as debilitating as prolonged physical stress in other situations.

Some children are bothered much more than others by what appear to be the same stressors. The intensity of the demand as perceived by the individual and whether the individual is able to manage the stress are the most important factors.

As defined by the culture, schools are places where children are formed into groups for instruction in those topics deemed important by parents and adults responsible for education. As such, schools are social melting pots in which not only achievement in basic education is expected, but in which pressing social problems are expected to be solved.

Teachers and principals often represent authority and generate the stress that goes with reacting to authority figures. They, and/or parents, often press children to achieve more (sometimes much more) than they are able to produce. School stress often comes from a lack of perceived success, but stress may come from any segment of the environment. Stress can come from those things that are novel, intense, rapidly changing, or challenging the limits of a child's tolerance. Some children pressure class-mates to keep up (or to not work very hard regardless of what adults say), to speak as they do, to appear as they do, to disclose secret thoughts, etc. Sometimes stress comes from crowding, racial imbalance, the opposite sex, or facing separation from one or both parents or certain friends. Whether in school or out, many children are pressured to perform competitively. Some children thrive on pressure, others wilt and withdraw.

School stress can be prevented by intervening in the environment to eliminate or modify stress-producing situations before they have a chance to affect children; by intervening with children to protect them from the impact of stressors by building up their resistance and personal strength (i.e., self-concept); by intervening with children to increase their tolerance for stress; and by putting children who are adversely affected by stress in an environment that minimizes stress (Phillips, 1978). There are many techniques and strategies that can be used with children suffering from school stress. Most involve a focus on learning and motivational processes.

REFERENCES

Phillips, B. (1978). *School stress and anxiety.* New York: Human Sciences.

Selye, H. (1976). *The stress of life.* New York: McGraw-Hill.

JOSEPH L. FRENCH
Pennsylvania State University

SCHOOL PHOBIA
STRESS AND THE HANDICAPPED STUDENT

SCHOPLER, ERIC (1927–   )

Eric Schopler received his BA (1949) from the University of Chicago. He received an MA (1955) in psychiatric social work from the School of Social Service Administration, and his PhD (1964) in clinical child development from the Committee on Human Development, University of Chicago. He is currently professor of psychology in psychiatry and director and founder of the Division for Treatment and Education of Autistic and Related Communication Handicapped Children (TEACCH), University of North Carolina, Chapel Hill.

Early experiences helped convince Schopler that parents are victims of their child's developmental disorder (Schopler, 1971). Schopler advocates having parents and professionals collaborate as cotherapists (Schopler & Reichler, 1971) with teachers (Schopler, Reichler, & Lansing, 1980) for the most effective consequences for the developmentally handicapped child.

Schopler believes in an effective statewide program, with unified parent-professional collaboration that focuses

Eric Schopler

on family adaptation, school adjustment, and community relations. TEACCH includes both strong research and professional training components. Publications have been translated into five languages and the TEACCH program has served as a national and international model. In recognition of his contributions, Schopler has received the American Psychiatric Association (APA) Gold Achievement Award (1972), the University of North Carolina's O. Max Gardner Award for Outstanding Contribution to Human Welfare (1985), and the APA Award for Distinguished Public Service (1985).

REFERENCES

Schopler, E. (1971). Parents of psychotic children as scapegoats. *Journal of Contemporary Psychology, 4,* 17–22.

Schopler, E., & Reichler, R. J. (1972). Parents as cotherapists in the treatment of psychotic children. In S. Chess & A. Thomas (Eds.), *Annual progress in child psychiatry and child development.* New York: Brunner/Mazel.

Schopler, E., Reichler, R. J., & Lansing, M. (1980). *Individualized assessment and treatment for autistic and developmentally disabled children. Vol 2: Teaching strategies for parents and professionals* (2nd ed.). Baltimore, MD: University Park Press.

E. VALERIE HEWITT
Texas A&M University

SCOLIOSIS

Scoliosis, a lateral curvature of the spine, is the most common type of spinal deformity. Functional scoliosis results from poor posture or a difference in length of the legs. It is not progressive and usually disappears with exercise. Structural scoliosis, however, is a more severe form, involving rotation of the spine and structural changes in the vertebrae (Ziai, 1984).

Most cases of structural scoliosis are idiopathic—of unknown cause (Benson, 1983). Idiopathic scoliosis occurs most frequently in adolescent females during the growth spurt, ages 12 to 16. If untreated, the condition progresses rapidly throughout the spinal growth period (ages 15 to 16 for girls and ages 18 to 19 for boys). Scoliosis can also accompany neuromuscular disorders such as cerebral palsy and muscular dystrophy, or can develop as a result of infection, trauma, or surgery.

Early diagnosis of scoliosis is essential to prevent progression of the curvature. Treatment varies with the type of scoliosis, the age of the child, and severity of deformity. Mild curvatures require only observation, while more pronounced curvatures require bracing and exercise. In severe cases, surgery is required. Recent treatment approaches have also included electrostimulation (Benson, 1983) and use of biofeedback techniques (Ziai, 1984).

REFERENCES

Benson, D. R. (1983). The spine and neck. In M. E. Gershwin & D. L. Robbins (Eds.), *Musculoskeletal diseases of children* (pp. 469–538). New York: Grune & Stratton.

James, J. I. P. (1976). *Scoliosis* (2nd ed.). Edinburgh, Scotland: Churchill Livingstone.

Ziai, M. (Ed.). (1984). *Pediatrics* (3rd ed.). Boston: Little, Brown.

CHRISTINE A. ESPIN
University of Minnesota

CEREBRAL PALSY
MUSCULAR DYSTROPHY

SCOPE AND SEQUENCE

Scope and sequence information play an important role in the special education of exceptional individuals. In academic areas where curriculum is not readily available, the use of scope and sequence information and task analysis provides the special educator with ways of determining a set of skills (Hargrave & Poteet, 1984).

To provide appropriate programs, special educators need a clear understanding, in the form of a sequence of skills, of what each of the academic domains include. This array of skills is referred to as scope and sequence information. Scope and sequence charts provide schemata of an instructional domain. Scope refers to those skills that are taught; sequence refers to the order in which they are taught. Sequences may be determined from the work of others or may be synthesized by the special educator from experience (Wehman & McLaughlin, 1981).

Scope and sequence charts vary in structure and format among special educators and programs. Scope and sequence information provide a link between assessment and the specification of instructional goals and objectives (Wehman & McLaughlin, 1981). It is essential in developing individual educational programs. Knowledge of the scope and sequence of skills provides the teacher with a clearer profile of those skills that the student has acquired and those that he or she still needs to acquire (Mercer & Mercer, 1985).

REFERENCES

Hargrave, L. J., & Poteet, J. A. (1984). *Assessment in special education*. Englewood Cliffs, NJ: Prentice-Hall.

Mercer, C. D., & Mercer, A. R. (1985). *Teaching students with learning problems*. Columbus, OH: Merrill.

Wehman, P., & McLaughlin, P. J. (1981). *Program development in special education*. New York: McGraw-Hill.

ANNE M. BAUER
University of Cincinnati

SCOUTING AND THE HANDICAPPED

The scouting movement for boys and girls has made a significant effort to involve youths with handicaps. All levels of scouting have provisions to mainstream scouts in community units and to develop specialized troops for youngsters with severe disabilities or unusual needs. Scouting organizations catering to members with given disabilities are capable of designing adapted activities. For example, Stuckey and Barkus (1986) reported that the Boy Scout Troop of the Perkins School for the Blind went on a special camping trip at the Philmont Scout Ranch in New Mexico.

The national scout offices coordinate their efforts with a variety of organizations serving and advocating for the handicapped. Leadership training materials that deal with issues in scouting for handicapped members and guidelines on adapting scouting activities are available, as are materials such as taped scout handbooks. A number of adapted merit badge programs allow impaired scouts to earn an award while knowing that they have truly met the requirements for a badge.

Scouting offers youths many opportunities for developing motor, cognitive, and social skills, increasing self-esteem and a sense of achievement, and obtaining a feeling of enjoyment. Boy Scout and Girl Scout programs have worked toward making these benefits available to all youths. Many publications and other materials are available to interested persons from the national offices of Girl Scouts and Boy Scouts and from various local scout executives.

REFERENCE

Stuckey, K., & Barkus, C. (1986). Visually impaired scouts meet the Philmont challenge. *Journal of Visual Impairment & Blindness, 80*, 750–751.

LEE A. JACKSON, JR.
*University of North Carolina,
Wilmington*

RECREATION, THERAPEUTIC

SECONDARY SPECIAL EDUCATION

The wide acceptance of special education programs in public schools is evidenced by the steady growth of programs at the elementary level since the 1960s as well as an emphasis on preschool intervention. The development of programs at the secondary level, however, is not as widespread. Scranton and Downs (1975) surveyed school systems to determine the scope of special education services available in the United States. Of 37 reporting states, 40% of the districts offered elementary programs while only 9% offered programming at the secondary level. Perhaps the clearest indication of the lack of emphasis on secondary programming in all areas of special education is the practice of most states of not differentiating between the certification of elementary and secondary teachers.

The characteristic of secondary special education programming that distinguishes it from elementary programming is the emphasis on acquisition of knowledge in content areas. Few teachers in secondary settings have any formal training in teaching basic skills. More important, few secondary teachers are experienced in the methods of adapting curriculum or implementing accommodation techniques for students lacking in skills necessary for the attainment of course work. Elementary programs are expected to prepare students with basic skills sufficient for more advanced pursuits in secondary programs. However, secondary teachers are seldom willing or able to assume responsibility for remediation of basic academic deficiencies. Secondary training and interest is frequently specific to subject areas or vocational skills rather than reading skills, number concepts, or underlying factors in school settings that may interfere with student performance.

Special education practice at the secondary level must account for different competencies and a different orientation than would be expected at the elementary level. The practitioner at the elementary level is able to communicate easily with regular classroom teachers because they share common training and a similar purpose in the instruction of basic language and math skills. The most common type of service delivery system in the elementary school seems to be the resource room. This arrangement is a natural extension of the regular classroom, with activities integrated with regular school curriculum. The result is a high degree of continuity from one area to another. Several problems are associated with using this approach at the secondary level. Teachers tend to be divided by areas of specialization and do not focus on individual differences of learners as readily as at the elementary level. This often results in the misinterpretation or misunderstanding of the value and nature of special education programming (Ysseldyke & Algozzine, 1984). This approach

is not usually successful because it fails to involve many regular education classroom teachers and disregards the realities of the advanced secondary curriculum. The efforts of the special education practitioner should, therefore, be directed toward immediate problems of the learner and provide for close interaction with teachers and the specific course of study for each student.

Because few models for service delivery of secondary special education services exist, and university training programs have traditionally prepared teachers with an elementary emphasis, many secondary systems have relied on the elementary resource room as a model for service delivery. If the school adopts the philosophy of providing assistance only in the acquisition of basic skills in language and mathematics, then the traditional elementary model might be useful. If the school recognizes, however, the special demands and circumstances of the exceptional student as well as the unique problems associated with the onset of adolescence, then different programming is needed (Marsh, Gearheart, & Gearheart, 1978).

Lerner (1976) asserts that a secondary service delivery system in special education must account for several options in programming. For some students it may be desirable to offer a self-contained classroom, while for others a special resource room may be more beneficial because the teacher can act as a liaison between the regular education teacher, counselor, student, and parent. The school also may offer a variety of specially designed courses for students with learning problems. Lerner holds that resource room teachers in high school must be familiar with the entire curriculum of the school to be successful in remediating and programming for exceptional students. This familiarity would enable the teacher to assist the students in a variety of courses rather than in the remediation of specific academic skills. Remediation must be tied closely to what happens in the mainstream classroom.

Goodman and Mann proposed a different model in 1976. They theorized a basic education program at the secondary level that restricts the activities of the teacher to instruction of mathematics and language arts. Enrollment of students would be limited to those who lacked sixth-grade achievement. The goal for the secondary teacher in special education would be to remediate students to a sixth-grade level to allow for mainstreaming into regular education classes.

Program options, in fact, lie somewhere between the two extremes, with decisions regarding the thrust of programming often dictated by local custom and philosophy. The main objective should be to provide a system of instruction that reduces the complexity without sacrificing quality. A carefully balanced program should include the provision for specific remediation as well as assistance in addressing course work through the accommodation of individual needs. Equal opportunity should allow each student to benefit from academic training and career education to the fullest extent possible. Insufficiency in reading should not deny a student the opportunity to participate and learn in an academic class; nor should it limit the student to training that leads to entry-level skills in low-status jobs. The verbal bias evidenced in the instruction of many schools should not limit the pursuits of intelligent but inefficient learners.

REFERENCES

Goodman, L., & Mann, L. (1976). *Learning disabilities in the secondary school.* New York: Grune & Stratton.

Lerner, J. W. (1976). *Children with learning disabilities* (2nd ed.). Boston: Houghton Mifflin.

Marsh, G. E., Gearheart, C., & Gearheart, B. (1978). *The learning disabled adolescent.* St. Louis: Mosby.

Scranton, T., & Downs, M. (1975). Elementary and secondary learning disabilities programs in the U.S.: A survey. *Journal of Learning Disabilities, 8*(6), 394–399.

Ysseldyke, J. E., & Algozzine, B. (1984). *Introduction to special education.* Boston: Houghton Mifflin.

CRAIG D. SMITH
Georgia College

RESOURCE ROOM
RESOURCE TEACHER
VOCATIONAL TRAINING

SECTION 504 OF THE 1973 REHABILITATION ACT

See REHABILITATION ACT OF 1973.

SEEING EYE DOGS

See ANIMALS FOR THE HANDICAPPED.

SEGUIN, EDOUARD (1812–1880)

Edouard Seguin, who demonstrated to the world that mentally retarded individuals can be educated, studied medicine under Jean Marc Gaspard Itard in Paris, and applied the training methods of that famous physician and teacher to the education of the mentally retarded. In 1837 Seguin established the first school in France for the mentally retarded, with remarkable success. In 1848 he moved to the United States, where he practiced medicine, served as director of the Pennsylvania Training School, and acted as adviser to numerous state institutions. He was a founder and first president of the Association of Medical Officers of American Institutions for Idiotic and Feeble-Minded Persons, now the American Association on Mental Deficiency.

Seguin's methods, which provided the foundation for the movement for the education of the mentally retarded in the United States, were based on a number of principles: that observation of the child is the foundation of the child's education; that education deals with the whole child; that the child learns best from real things; that perceptual training should precede training for concept development; and that even the most defective child has some capacity for learning. Seguin incorporated art, music, and gymnastics into the educational program, and emphasized the use of concrete materials in the classroom.

Seguin's influence on the early development of special education services can hardly be overstated. Samuel Gridley Howe, who was responsible for the formation of the first state school for mentally retarded children in the United States, obtained much of his methodology directly from Seguin. Maria Montessori gave credit to Seguin for the principles on which she based her system of education. Today, more than a century after his death. Seguin's influence is evident in the methods being used to instruct children with learning handicaps.

REFERENCES

Kanner, L. (1960). Itard, Seguin, Howe—Three pioneers in the education of retarded children. *American Journal of Mental Deficiency, 65,* 2–10.

Seguin, E. (1907). *Idiocy and its treatment by the physiological method.* New York: Teachers College, Columbia University.

Talbot, E. *Edouard Seguin: A study of an educational approach to the treatment of mentally defective children.* New York: Teachers College, Columbia University.

PAUL IRVINE
Katonah, New York

SEIZURES

See EPILEPSY; Also see SPECIFIC SEIZURE TYPE.

SELF-CARE SKILLS

Self-care skills (e.g., toileting, eating, dressing, grooming) represent one of the skill domains in the broader set of domains that constitute adaptive behavior (language, socialization, self-direction, vocational preparation, etc.).

Adaptive behavior as defined by the American Association on Mental Deficiency (AAMD) classification system is "the effectiveness or degree to which an individual meets standards of personal independence and social responsibility expected for age and cultural groups" (Grossman, 1977). Adaptive behavior and level of measured intelligence (IQ) are jointly considered in the determination of level of retardation and are used to determine placement in programs.

There are two principal methods of assessing self-care skills. One method involves the administration of standardized instruments such as the Adaptive Behavior Scale published by the AAMD to assess adaptive and maladaptive behaviors. A profile of an individual's skills can be derived and compared with those of the group of persons labeled mentally retarded across the various skill domains. This will determine global skill levels and a person's relative standing in skill development in comparison with a group norm based on age and IQ. The other method involves the use of criterion-referenced assessment approaches. Task analytic assessment involves breaking a skill into the series of discrete steps necessary to perform the skill. The level of performance can be scored for each step to indicate how much of a skill has been mastered. Self-care behaviors can be defined (e.g., errors in using a spoon) and then counted so that progress can be determined. Criterion-referenced measures are useful for assessing the performance of specific skills to evaluate instructional efforts.

Watson and Uzzell (1981) describe the success of initial efforts to systematically train self-care skills through the use of operant conditioning methods that are based on the reinforcement of the performance of desired skills or behaviors. In the early 1960s, basic self-care skills such as toileting, eating, and dressing were first taught to institutionalized persons. Backward chaining (i.e., a method of skill sequencing that gradually requires the person to finish a skill from progressively earlier points in the task sequence) and reinforcement of desired performance were the first methods employed. Further improvements in the efficiency and efficacy of training self-care skills were obtained through the introduction of graduated guidance and systematic prompting. These procedures included the use of visual, verbal, and physical guidance prompts.

During the 1960s and 1970s, many mentally retarded persons were deinstitutionalized and placed in community-based residential programs. Forward chaining (a method of skill sequencing in which the person is required gradually to perform more of the component behaviors leading toward task completion) and whole-task strategies (a method of training in which the person is provided concurrent instruction on all steps of a task) are other methods that have been used successfully for teaching self-help skills. Snell (1983), in an excellent review of self-care skills training research, provides examples of each of the previously identified procedures.

Recently, the focus of self-care skills training has expanded to include the more advanced skills necessary for community living such as toothbrushing, bathing and showering, menstrual hygiene, clothing purchase and care, shopping skills, nutritional eating, home safety, and housekeeping (Wehman, Renzaglia, & Bates, 1985). In these efforts, consumers and professionals have begun to emphasize the skill requirements of subsequent environments as being the primary rationale for curriculum development (Brown et al., 1979). Self-care skills training programs must emphasize maintenance of skills over time and generalization of skills beyond the instructional setting (Cuvo & Davis, 1983). As researchers, practitioners, and consumers have become more critical in their evaluations of self-care skills training programs, the focus has expanded from isolated skill acquisition to demonstrations of generalized development of functional skill sequences in naturalistic settings (Freagon & Rotatori, 1982).

REFERENCES

Brown, L., Branston, M. B., Hamre-Nietupski, S., Pumpian, I., Certo, N., & Gruenewald, L. (1979). A strategy for developing chronological-age-appropriate and functional curricular content for severely handicapped adolescents and young adults. *Journal of Special Education, 13*, 81–90.

Cuvo, A. J., & Davis, P. (1983). Behavior therapy and community living skills. In M. Hersen, R. M. Eisler, & P. M. Miller (Eds.), *Progress in behavior modification* (Vol. 14). New York: Academic.

Freagon, S., & Rotatori, A. F. (1982). Comparing natural and artificial environments in training self-care skills for group home residents. *Journal of the Association for Persons with Severe Handicaps, 8*, 73–86.

Grossman, H. (Ed.). (1977). *Manual of terminology and classification in mental retardation*. Washington, DC: American Association on Mental Deficiency.

Meyers, C. E., Nihira, K., & Zetlin, A. (1979). The measurement of adaptive behavior. In N. R. Ellis (Ed.), *Handbook of mental deficiency*. Hillsdale, NJ: Erlbaum.

Snell, M. E. (1983). Self-care skills. In M. E. Snell (Ed.), *Systematic instruction of the moderately and severely handicapped*. Columbus, OH: Merrill.

Watson, L. S., & Uzzell, R. (1981). Teaching self-help skills to the mentally retarded. In J. L. Matson & J. R. McCartney (Eds.), *Handbook of behavior modification with the mentally retarded*. New York: Plenum.

Wehman, P., Renzaglia, A., & Bates, P. (1985). *Functional living skills for the moderately and severely handicapped*. Austin, TX: Pro-Ed.

HAROLD HANSON
PAUL BATES
Southern Illinois University

ADAPTIVE BEHAVIOR
SOCIAL BEHAVIOR
TASK ANALYSIS

SELF-CONCEPT

Self-concept is an individual's evaluation of his or her own abilities and attributes. It includes all aspects of an individual's personality of which he or she is aware. Although some authors have drawn distinctions between self-concept and self-esteem (Damon & Hart, 1982), the terms are frequently used interchangeably. Several theoretical models of self-concept exist in the literature. For example, Coopersmith (1967) has suggested that four factors contribute to an individual's self-concept: significance (feeling of being loved and approved of by important others), competence (ability to perform tasks considered important), virtue (adherence to moral and ethical principles), and power (the degree to which an individual is able to exert control over self and others). Recently, Harter (1982) found that self-concept can be broken down into three specific components, cognitive, social, and physical competence, and a general self-worth factor.

Children with a positive self-concept are described as imaginative, confident in their own judgments and abilities, assertive, able to assume leadership roles, less preoccupied with themselves, and able to devote more time to others and to external activities. Children with a negative self-concept are described as quiet, unobtrusive, unoriginal, lacking in initiative, withdrawn, and doubtful about themselves (Coopersmith, 1967). School progress and academic achievement are influenced by self-concept, as is vocational choice. Unfortunately, much of the research on the effects of self-esteem has been subject to methodological and theoretical criticism (Damon & Hart, 1982; Wylie, 1979).

Self-concept begins to develop early in life, with children as young as 18 to 24 months able to discriminate between self and others (Lewis & Brooks-Gunn, 1979). As children's thought processes become less concrete and more abstract, there are corresponding changes in self-concept. Younger children (e.g., 9 year olds) tend to describe themselves in categorical terms (name, age, gender, physical attributes, etc.), while older children take an increasingly abstract view, describing their personal and interpersonal traits, attitudes, and beliefs (Montemayor & Eisen, 1977). There is not, however, any consistent evidence of age-related changes in the level of self-esteem (how positively or negatively one views oneself). The one exception to this is a temporary decline in self-esteem around the time children enter their teens (Simmons et al., 1979).

A number of factors influence an individual's self-concept. Parents appear to play a particularly important role (Coopersmith, 1967). Children with high self-esteem tend to have parents who themselves have high self-esteem and who are warm, nurturing, and accepting of their children while setting high academic and behavioral standards. They set and enforce strict limits on their children and are fair, reasonable, and consistent in their use of discipline.

Parents of low self-esteem children alternate unpredictably between excessive permissiveness and harsh punishment. A close relationship with the same-sex parent is typical among high self-esteem children. Findings of higher self-esteem in only children and first-born children suggest that parental attention is important. Other factors associated with high self-esteem include academic success, the presence of a close friendship, and the perceived opinions of others. Physical attractiveness and height are unrelated to self-esteem (Coopersmith, 1967).

Instruments to measure self-concept include the Piers-Harris Children's Self-Concept Scale (Piers, 1969), the Coopersmith Self-Esteem Inventory (Coopersmith, 1967), the Perceived Competence Scale for Children (Harter, 1982), and the Preschool and Primary Self-Concept Scale (Stager & Young, 1982).

REFERENCES

Coopersmith, S. (1967). *Antecedents of self-esteem*. San Francisco: Freeman.

Damon, W., & Hart, D. (1982). The development of self-understanding from infancy through adolescence. *Child Development, 53,* 841–864.

Harter, S. (1982). The perceived competence scale for children. *Child Development, 53,* 87–97.

Lewis, M., & Brooks-Gunn, J. (1979). *Social cognition and the acquisition of self.* New York: Plenum.

Montemayor, R., & Eisen, M. (1977). The development of self-conceptions from childhood to adolescence. *Developmental Psychology, 13,* 314–319.

Piers, E. V. (1969). *The Piers Harris Children's Self-Concept Scale.* Nashville, TN: Counselor Recordings and Tests.

Simmons, R. G., Blyth, D. A., Van Cleave, E. F., & Bush, D. M. (1979). Entry into early adolescence: The impact of school structure, puberty, and early dating on self-esteem. *American Sociological Review, 44,* 948–967.

Stager, S., & Young, R. D. (1982). A self-concept measure for preschool and early primary grade children. *Journal of Personality Assessment, 46,* 536–543.

Wylie, R. C. (1979). *The self-concept: Theory and research on selected topics* (Vol. 2, revised ed.). Lincoln: University of Nebraska Press.

ROBERT G. BRUBAKER
Eastern Kentucky University

DEPRESSION
EMOTIONAL LABILITY
SELF-MANAGEMENT
SOCIAL SKILLS

SELF-CONTAINED CLASS

The first self-contained special classes were established in the late 1800s and early 1900s as public school classes for the moderately retarded, deaf, hard of hearing, blind, emotionally disturbed, and physically handicapped. Esten (1900) states that special classes for the mentally retarded were established to provide slow learners with more appropriate class placement. A self-contained classroom for the handicapped can be defined as one that homogeneously segregates different children from normal children. Children are usually segregated along categorical groupings. As a result of Dunn's (1968) article on the detrimental aspects of self-contained placements for the mildly handicapped, students receiving special education in self-contained classes today are usually "low-incidence," exhibiting more severe problems. However, Kirk and Gallagher (1983) report gifted students are also grouped into special classes according to interests and abilities.

A self-contained class is a place where special education students spend more than 50% of their school day and receive most of their academic instruction. Typically, caseloads are small, ranging from 5 to 10 students in a class. A wide variety of instructional materials are available to the students. The self-contained class provides the opportunity for highly individualized, closely supervised, specialized instruction. The self-contained classroom is usually taught by one trained teacher who is certified according to the categories served. The self-contained classroom may be categorically specific (serving one population) or cross-categorically grouped (serving multicategorical populations).

Major purposes of a self-contained class as outlined by Sabatino, Miller, and Schmidt (1981) include providing the student with the social and personal adjustment skills necessary to promote school success, and maintaining a constant structure within the instructional environment to reduce distractibility, hyperactivity, restlessness, poor attention span, and control over the rate of information flowing to the learner. Additionally, the purposes include teaching the basic academic and social skills necessary for success in life and making cooperative arrangements based on adequate communication with parents (p. 321). As students demonstrate proficiency in specific skill areas, they are mainstreamed into regular classes. It is possible that a student may be assigned to a self-contained classroom and receive additional resource room assistance. Usually, students are mainstreamed into regular education for nonacademic subjects such as music, physical education, and art, or academic areas of proficiency.

REFERENCES

Dunn, L. M. (1968). Special education for the mildly handicapped: Is much of it justifiable? *Exceptional Children, 35,* 5–22.

Esten, R. A. (1900). Backward children in the public schools. *Journal of Psychoaesthenics, 5,* 10–16.

Kirk, S. A., & Gallagher, J. J. (1983). *Educating exceptional children* (4th ed.). Boston: Houghton Mifflin.

Sabatino, D. A., Miller, T. L., & Schmidt, C. R. (1981). *Learning* *disabilities: Systemizing teaching and service delivery.* Rockville, MD: Aspen Systems.

MARIBETH MONTGOMERY KASIK
Governors State University

GROUPING OF CHILDREN
LEAST RESTRICTIVE ENVIRONMENT
RESOURCE ROOM
SPECIAL CLASS

SELF-CONTROL CURRICULUM

The self-control curriculum is a product of the work of Fagen, Long, and Stevens (1975). They contend that emotional and cognitive development are closely related and therefore both need to be addressed simultaneously in the instructional process. They hold that learning is impaired when learners have negative feelings about themselves. Fagen et al. believe that in many cases of behavior disorders there is an inability on the part of the individual to exert self-control. The self-control curriculum has as its goals the development of self-control and positive feelings.

There are eight enabling skills in the self-control model. Four of these are in the cognitive area and four in the affective area. The eight skills are:

1. *Selecting.* Paying attention to directions/instruction.
2. *Storing.* Remembering directions/instructions.
3. *Sequencing and ordering.* Organizing materials/work areas to perform work.
4. *Anticipating Consequences.* Realizing that behavior has consequences and predicting those consequences.
5. *Appreciating Feelings.* Expressing feelings by words and actions.
6. *Managing Frustrations.* Behaviorally maintaining control in stressful situations.
7. *Inhibiting and Delaying.* Delaying actions and reflecting on consequences of possible actions even when excited.
8. *Relaxing.* Consciously relieving bodily tension.

The curriculum has pupil activities and guidelines for teachers for developing more lessons in each unit. The activities involve games, discussions, and role-playing activities. The position taken in the curriculum is that self-control must be taught just as any other subject. General recommendations throughout the curriculum are to proceed from easy to difficult, to proceed in small steps, to use repetition and provide practice, to make activities enjoyable, reinforce efforts, and provide opportunities to practice skills in new situations and settings.

REFERENCE

Fagen, S. A., Long, N. J., & Stevens, D. (1975). *Teaching children self-control*. Columbus, OH: Merrill.

Robert A. Sedlak
University of Wisconsin, Stout

SELF-MONITORING
SOCIAL BEHAVIOR OF THE HANDICAPPED
SOCIAL SKILLS TRAINING

SELF-FULFILLING PROPHECY

See PYGMALION EFFECT.

SELF-HELP TRAINING

The skill areas typically included under the domain of self-help are toileting, eating, dressing, and personal hygiene. An obvious reason for training the developmentally disabled in these skills is that there are widespread self-help skill deficits among this population. Another reason is that the acquisition of these skills represents a critical step in the developmental process. Once the skills are acquired, the caregiver's time devoted to the routine maintenance of the developmentally disabled person is reduced. The acquisition of self-help skills can have meaningful social consequences. It can increase the possibility of gaining access to valued places and activities.

Probably the most significant development in the training of self-help skills is the application of behavior modification procedures. This has been referred to as one of the most influential factors in improving the care and training of the developmentally disabled in the last 20 years (Whitman, Sciback, & Reid, 1983).

Research in each of the self-help skill training areas has undergone a similar developmental sequence (Reid, Wilson, & Faw, 1980). Early research demonstrated that caregivers, after receiving in-service training, could train a number of developmentally disabled individuals in self-help skills. Even though this research lacked experimental rigor, it did show the usefulness of behavior modification and stimulated further research. Contemporary research has focused on individual skills and has been more methodologically rigorous. There has also been an effort by Azrin et al. (Azrin & Fox, 1971; Azrin & Armstrong, 1973; Azrin, Schaeffer, & Wesolowski, 1976) to develop an intensive training approach that is more comprehensive than previous approaches. Intensive training is intended to produce rapid learning that is resistant to extinction.

Each self-help skill area has some unique characteristics that have affected the direction of research and training in that particular area (Reid et al., 1980). Training in independent toileting has become more complex and focuses on a more naturally occurring sequence of toilet behaviors. Automatic devices are being used to signal trainers when a trainee is about to have a toileting accident or has eliminated into the toilet. Nighttime toileting skills have also been trained to reduce the frequency of enuresis (bed wetting).

It is believed that training independent eating through behavior modification procedures has been relatively successful because food is an inherent reinforcer. In addition to focusing on the acquisition of independent eating skills, researchers and practitioners have attempted to eliminate or reduce inappropriate mealtime behaviors (e.g., eating too quickly and stealing food).

As in training eating skills, dressing has focused on acquisition of appropriate skills and the reduction of inappropriate behaviors (e.g., public disrobing). The generalization of dressing skills to other contexts has been an issue when developing training programs because training typically occurs when dressing is not naturally required. Maintenance over time has also been an important training issue because dressing is less inherently reinforcing than toileting and eating.

It is unusual that little research has been conducted on personal hygiene skills considering their importance in improving independent functioning and helping the developmentally disabled to gain community acceptance. A current development in training personal hygiene skills is a packaged approach called independence training (Matson, DiLorenzo, & Esveldt-Dawson, 1981). This approach expands on the typical behavioral training strategy by having trainees evaluate their own progress (self-monitor) and give each other feedback.

There are several areas of concern for future research and practice (Whitman et al., 1983). Often there is a discrepancy between the development of an effective training technology and its day-to-day application by caregivers. Consequently, it is important to understand what factors contribute to caregivers' willingness to carry out training. A component analysis of the multifaceted training strategies, like the intensive training package, could assist practitioners in selecting the most effective and efficient training. As increasing numbers of developmentally disabled people live and work in the community, it will be necessary to train more advanced and complex skills in community contexts. It will also be necessary to determine the social validity of certain self-help skills, particularly in the areas of dressing and personal hygiene. By assessing social validity, practitioners will know what to teach in order to bring a skill into a socially acceptable range. Finally, effective and practical self-help training procedures need to be developed for the physically disabled.

REFERENCES

Azrin, N. H., & Armstrong, P. M. (1973). The "mini-meal." A method for teaching eating skills to the profoundly retarded. *Mental Retardation, 11*, 9–13.

Azrin, N. H., & Fox, R. M. (1971). A rapid method of toilet training the institutionalized retarded. *Journal of Applied Behavior Analysis, 4*, 89–99.

Azrin, N. H., Schaeffer, R. M., & Wesolowski, M. D. (1976). A rapid method of teaching profoundly retarded persons to dress by a reinforcement guidance method. *Mental Retardation, 14*, 29–33.

Matson, J. L., DiLorenzo, T. M., & Esveldt-Dawson, K. (1981). Independence training as a method of enhancing self-help skills acquisition of the mentally retarded. *Behavior Research Therapy, 19*, 399–405.

Reid, D. H., Wilson, P. G., & Faw, G. D. (1980). Teaching self-help skills. In J. L. Matson & J. A. Mulick (Eds.), *Handbook of mental retardation* (pp. 429–442). New York: Pergamon.

Whitman, T. L., Sciback, J. W., & Reid, D. H. (1983). *Behavior modification with the severely and profoundly retarded: Research and application.* New York: Academic.

JOHN O'NEILL
Hunter College, City University of New York

FUNCTIONAL SKILLS
HABILITATION
REHABILITATION

SELF-INJURIOUS BEHAVIOR

Self-injury is one of the most unusual and probably least understood form of aberrant behavior. It may take a variety of forms, including biting, head banging, face slapping, pinching, or slapping. Such behavior has been reported to affect approximately 4 to 5% of psychiatric populations. Approximately 9 to 17% of normal young children (9 to 36 months of age) also exhibit self-injurious behavior (Carr, 1977).

Carr (1977) has reviewed the hypothetical causes of self-injurious behavior. These include positive reinforcement (seeking of attention), negative reinforcement (attempting to escape), sensory input (gaining stimulation), and psychogenic (psychosis) and organic (genetic and biological) factors. Carr was able to support each of the hypotheses, except for the psychogenic and the organic, by restrospectively applying research to each of the causal explanations. Since then, Evans and Meyer (1985) have proposed one additional hypothesis, an absence of appropriate skills, which research appears to substantiate. Each of these hypotheses warrants examination because of the effect they have on the selection of interventions.

Prior to the mid-1960s, self-injurious behavior was thought to be a product of insane persons with deranged or psychotic minds (Lovaas, 1982). This thinking shaped the model mental health professionals used to intervene with persons who exhibited self-injurious behavior. This dictated the extensive reliance on psychotherapy, drugs, and physical restraint for control.

Through a series of unrelated, yet complementary, studies, researchers were able to demonstrate that self-injurious behavior is regulated by the same laws that affect other human behaviors. The data from these early studies clearly point to the validity of applying the learning theory model to the treatment of self-injurious behavior (Lovaas, 1982).

The etiology of self-injurious behavior has been in debate for some time. There appears to be an organic basis for some self-injurious behavior. There are data to support the contention that self-injurious behaviors are seen in the Lesch-Nyhan and de Langhe syndromes, which are both genetically caused. In Lesch-Nyhan syndrome, a rare form of X-linked cerebral palsy found in only males, there is repetitive biting of the tongue, lips, and fingers. It is thought that this behavior is biochemically related. Considerable research has gone into finding a chemical cure for these characteristics. In de Lange syndrome, which is also genetic in origin, a broad variety of self-injurious behaviors have been reported. A biochemical association has not been presented. Other organic origins of self-injurious behavior have been identified. These include elevated pain thresholds and painful and prolonged infections of the middle ear. The data on organic causes of self-injurious behavior are contradictory, and limited chemical and medical mediations have been found. Although there is limited substantiation of organic causes of self-injurious behavior, awareness that there is a possibility of such causal factors, even in a small percentage of the handicapped population, is important. Those who deal directly with handicapped individuals should recognize that medical screening is necessary at the onset of any treatment program, and in some cases medical intervention may be appropriate (Carr, 1977; Evans & Meyer, 1985).

The positive reinforcement hypothesis can be easily explained as the individual seeking attention through the use of self-injurious behavior. The caregivers, in turn, reinforce such behavior and allow it to continue or progress in intensity. Under such conditions, behavioral interventions that remove reinforcement (e.g., extinction or time out) from the individual would possess a high probability of being successful (Carr, 1977).

The negative reinforcement hypothesis is explained by the use of self-injurious behavior to escape demands being placed on the individual. By exhibiting this form of aberrant behavior, the handicapped person is often allowed by the caregiver or teacher to refrain from participating in a required activity. Appropriate treatment for self-injurious behavior exhibited under these conditions should include interventions that focus on continued demand. In so doing the individual is not allowed to escape the demand (Carr, 1977).

The sensory input hypothesis is based on finding behaviors that provide the handicapped person with input into sensory receptors that under average conditions receive limited amounts of stimulation. An example might be found in a blind student who eye gouges. Self-injurious behavior becomes self-reinforcing and in turn self-maintaining. Interventions for behavior motivated in this manner have taken several different directions, including limiting the input that the self-injurious behavior provides the individual. This is done by modifying the environment (e.g., by using padding or placing adaptive devices on the individual). Another intervention that has been successful is the provision of increased amounts of stimulation from other sources (e.g., a vibrator; Carr, 1977).

The absence of alternative skills hypothesis rests on the concept that the handicapped person has extremely limited skills. Self-injurious behavior is part of a behavior system of an individual who lacks appropriate behavior to meet functional needs. This hypothesis is probably a subset of one or more of the preceding explanations of self-injurious behavior; however, it implies a somewhat different treatment. Part of the intervention strategy for self-injurious behavior caused by lack of skills would include teaching appropriate skills to replace the self-injurious ones (Evans & Meyer, 1985).

Iwata et al. (1982) have provided the practitioner with a method for functionally analyzing self-injurious behavior. Using this method it is possible to identify the specific motivational factors causing self-injury in many handicapped persons. Employing this approach requires observing the individual in four situations: under negative reinforcement, social attention, play, and alone. Mean levels of self-injurious behavior across each situation are determined. Specific patterns of behavior are manifested in a specific setting that often clearly reflects a specific motivational cause for the behavior.

As previously noted, medical interventions are occasionally appropriate and successful in reducing or eliminating self-injurious behavior. Psychotherapy and other psychological methods have also been used to treat self-injurious behavior. Clearly, the most successful and effective interventions have been behaviorally based. Such interventions should be selected on a least-restrictive model and monitored by systematic data collection procedures. Behaviorally based intervention strategies include the use of punishment. Punishment has been shown to be highly successful, at least on a short-term basis, for the treatment of self-injurious behavior. In cases of chronic self-injurious behavior, where life or irreversible damage is threatened, steps as drastic as electrical shock have been used (Lovaas, 1982). These procedures are generally used

to suppress serious self-injurious behavior until other approaches can replace them.

Self-injurious behavior poses many problems to the practitioner in its treatment. Although often misunderstood, recent work has provided both a theoretical explanation and a new direction for finding practical, effective, treatment methods for self-injurious behavior.

REFERENCES

Carr, E. (1977). The motivation of self-injurious behavior: A review of some hypothesis. *Psychological Bulletin, 84*, 800–816.

Evans, I. M., & Meyer, L. H. (1985). *An educative approach to behavior problems.* Baltimore, MD: Brooks.

Iwata, B. A., Dorsey, M. F., Slifer, K. J., Bauman, K. E., & Richman, G. S. (1982). Toward a functional analysis of self-injury. *Analysis and Intervention in Developmental Disabilities, 2* 3–20.

Lovaas, O. I. (1982). Comments on self-destructive behaviors. *Analysis and Intervention in Developmental Disabilities, 2*, 115–124.

ALAN HILTON
Seattle University

APPLIED BEHAVIOR ANALYSIS
SELF-STIMULATION
STEREOTYPIC MOVEMENT DISORDERS

SELF-MANAGEMENT

Self-management, also termed self-control, self-regulation, and self-direction, refers to actions intended to influence one's own behavior. Individuals are taught techniques that can be used in a deliberate manner to change their thoughts, feelings, or actions. Students who engage in self-management may, for example, work longer, complete more problems, make fewer errors, engage in fewer aggressive outbursts, or behave appropriately when an adult is not present.

The traditional approach in education has emphasized external management of programming by the teacher. As noted by Lovitt (1973), "Self-management behaviors are not systematically programmed [in the schools] which appears to be an educational paradox, for one of the expressed objectives of the educational system is to create individuals who are self-reliant and independent" (p. 139). Although frequently effective, use of external management procedures has several potential disadvantages (Kazdin, 1980). Implementation of procedures may be inconsistent as teachers may miss instances of behavior, or there may be problems with communication between change agents in different settings. A teacher may become a cue for particular behaviors, resulting in limited generalization to other situations in which that teacher is not present. Other potential disadvantages of external procedures include limited maintenance of behavior change, excessive time demands placed on educators, and the philosophic concern that the student has minimal involvement in the behavior change process.

Self-management procedures offset the concerns associated with external control and offer the possibility of improved maintenance and generalization of behavior change. The focus of self-management in special education is on teaching students to become effective modifiers of their own behaviors through use of such procedures as self-monitoring, self-evaluation, self-consequation, and self-instruction. Although each of these is discussed separately, in practice they frequently have been combined in self-management packages.

Self-monitoring refers to the observation, discrimination, and recording of one's own behavior. A child in the classroom, for example, may record on an index card each math problem completed. Self-monitoring has been demonstrated to have both assessment and therapeutic use with exceptional students who present a wide range of social and academic behaviors. Common problems associated with using self-monitoring as an assessment procedure include the inaccuracy and reactivity (spontaneous behavior change) of self-monitoring, both of which may result in a distorted picture of the initial levels of behavior. When self-monitoring is used as a treatment strategy, however, reactive effects are desired and inaccuracy may not interfere with obtaining this desired reactivity.

Self-evaluation, or self-assessment, is the comparison of one's own behavior against a preset standard to determine whether performance meets this criterion. Standards may be self-imposed or externally determined. In one study, special education students were asked to rate their behavior as "good," "okay," or "not good" when a timer rang at the end of 10-minute intervals. As is typical, self-evaluation was used as one component of a more comprehensive package; this resulted in reductions in disruptive behavior and increases in academic performance in these students (Robertson, Simon, Pachman, & Drabman, 1979).

Self-consequation refers to the self-delivery of positive consequences (self-reinforcement) or aversive consequences (self-punishment) following behavior. Self-reinforcement is preferred over self-punishment when possible and frequently is used in combination with other procedures. As an example, continued low levels of disruptive behavior or increased on-task behavior have been observed in special education students when self-reinforcement procedures were added to multicomponent programs (Shapiro & Klein, 1980).

Self-instruction is a process of talking to oneself to initiate, direct, or maintain one's own behavior. Children with attention deficit disorder, for example, may be taught specific coping self-statements that compete with such classroom problems as distractibility, overactivity, and off-task behavior. Typical training components include cognitive modeling, overt and covert rehearsal, graded practice on training tasks, and performance feedback (Meichenbaum, 1977).

Self-management training frequently combines these and other procedures in multicomponent self-management packages. In one example, disruptive developmentally disabled individuals were taught skills of self-monitoring, self-evaluation, self-consequation, and self-instruction that successfully reduced their chronic and severe conduct difficulties in a vocational training setting (Cole, Gardner, & Karan, 1985; Cole, Pflugrad, Gardner, & Karan, 1985).

Although total self-management is not possible for many special education students, most can be taught to be more self-reliant. Further, evidence suggests that self-management procedures are at least as effective as similar externally managed procedures in facilitating positive behavior change and in ensuring maintenance of this behavior change. Thus, in addition to its therapeutic effects, self-management offers economic, philosophic, legal, and professional benefits for use in special education.

REFERENCES

Cole, C. L., Gardner, W. I., & Karan, O. C. (1985). Self-management training of mentally retarded adults presenting severe conduct difficulties. *Applied Research in Mental Retardation, 6,* 337–347.

Cole, C. L., Pflugrad, D., Gardner, W. I., & Karan, O. C. (1985). *The self-management training program: Teaching developmentally disabled individuals to manage their disruptive behavior.* Champaign, IL: Research.

Kazdin, A. E. (1980). *Behavior modification in applied settings* (rev. ed.). Homewood, IL: Dorsey.

Lovitt, T. C. (1973). Self-management projects with children with behavioral disabilities. *Journal of Learning Disabilities, 6,* 15–28.

Meichenbaum, D. (1977). *Cognitive-behavior modification: An integrative approach.* New York: Plenum.

Robertson, S. J., Simon, S. J., Pachman, J. S., & Drabman, R. S. (1979). Self-control and generalization procedures in a classroom of disruptive retarded children. *Child Behavior Therapy, 1,* 347–362.

Shapiro, E. S., & Klein, R. D. (1980). Self-management of classroom behavior with retarded/disturbed children. *Behavior Modification, 4,* 83–97.

CHRISTINE L. COLE
*University of Wisconsin,
Madison*

ATTENTION DEFICIT DISORDER
COGNITIVE BEHAVIOR MODIFICATION
SELF-CONTROL CURRICULUM
SELF-MONITORING

SELF-MONITORING

Self-monitoring is one component of a more general process variously known as self-management, self-regulation, or self-control. The process of self-monitoring first involves a person's recognizing that a need exists to regulate his or her behavior. To recognize this need, the person must be observing his or her behavior and comparing it with some preset standard. This self-observation and assessment then combines with recording the behavior to create the self-monitoring component (Shapiro, 1981). Other components in the self-management process can include self-reinforcement, standard setting, self-evaluation, and self-instruction. These components have been used in various combinations with self-monitoring to modify many different types of behaviors (e.g., overeating, temper outbursts, negative statements, attending to task) in the developmentally disabled (Cole, Gardner, & Karan, 1983).

It has been shown that many different types of developmentally disabled individuals are capable of self-monitoring a range of behaviors in various settings. However, at least some of these individuals, particularly the mentally retarded, need training to acquire self-monitoring skills (Litrownik, Freitas, & Franzini, 1978; Shapiro, McGonigle, & Ollendick, 1980).

Self-monitoring among nondevelopmentally disabled people has a reactive or therapeutic effect: those behaviors being monitored tend to change in a desirable direction (McFall, 1977; Nelson & Hayes, 1981). The studies that have assessed the use of self-monitoring in developmentally disabled populations have also found therapeutic effects. For example, mentally retarded individuals have shown increases in the percent of housekeeping chores completed (Bauman & Iwata, 1977), the frequency of appropriate classroom verbalizations (Nelson, Lipinski, & Boykin, 1978) and the productivity of work (Zohn & Bornstein, 1980). Therapeutic decreases have also occurred in face-picking, head-shaking (Zegiob, Klukas, & Junginger, 1978), and tongue-protrusion behaviors (Rudrud, Ziarnik, & Colman, 1984). However, some studies conducted with the developmentally disabled (Horner & Brigham, 1979; Shapiro & Ackerman, 1983) have found the desirable effects of self-monitoring to be short-term or nonexistent, which is consistent with some research conducted on the nondisabled (Kazdin, 1974).

The variable results obtained with self-monitoring are probably due to several intervening factors that can impact on the reactivity or therapeutic value of self-monitoring (Nelson, 1977). The following comments are only suggestive, because the empirical evidence is limited and most of the supporting research has been done with non-developmentally disabled people. First, a behavior's valence or a person's desire to change the behavior can affect reactivity. Positively valenced behaviors tend to increase and negatively valenced behaviors to decrease. Generally, reactivity is enhanced by the frequency of self-monitoring; however, there are situations where the act of monitoring can interfere with reactivity, particularly with positively valenced behaviors. Reactivity also tends to be augmented when the recording device is visible and apparent to the person doing the self-monitoring. In addition, if several behaviors are monitored concurrently, the likelihood of change in any of them is suppressed. Finally, training in self-monitoring seems to enhance reactivity, particularly if the behavior is negatively valenced.

REFERENCES

Bauman, K. E., & Iwata, B. A. (1977). Maintenance of independent housekeeping skills using scheduling plus self-recording procedures. *Behavior Therapy, 8,* 554–560.

Cole, C. L., Gardner, W. I., & Karan, O. C. (1983). *Self-management training of mentally retarded adults with chronic conduct difficulties.* Madison WI: University of Wisconsin, Rehabilitation Research and Training Center, Waisman Center on Mental Retardation and Human Development.

Horner, R. H., & Brigham, T. A. (1979). The effects of self-management procedures on the study behavior of two retarded children. *Education & Training of the Mentally Retarded, 14,* 18–24.

Kazdin, A. E. (1974). Self-monitoring and behavior change. In M. J. Mahoney and C. E. Thoresen (Eds.), *Self-control: Power to the person.* Monterey, CA: Brookes/Cole.

Litrownik, A. J., Freitas, J. L., & Franzini, L. R. (1978). Self-regulation in mentally retarded children: Assessment and training of self-monitoring skills. *American Journal of Mental Deficiency, 82,* 499–506.

McFall, R. M. (1977). Parameters of self-monitoring. In R. B. Stuart (Ed.), *Behavioral self-management.* New York: Brunner/Mazel.

Nelson, R. O. (1977). Methodological issues in assessment via self-monitoring. In J. D. Cone & R. P. Hawkins (Eds.), *Behavioral assessment: New directions in clinical psychology.* New York: Brunner/Mazel.

Nelson, R. O., & Hayes, S. C. (1981). Theoretical explanations for reactivity in self-monitoring. *Behavior Modification, 5,* 3–14.

Nelson, R. O., Lipinski, D. P., & Boykin, R. A. (1978). The effects of self-recorders' training and the obtrusiveness of the self-recording device on the accuracy and reactivity of self-monitoring. *Behavior Therapy, 9,* 200–208.

Rudrud, E. H., Ziarnik, J. P., & Colman, G. (1984). Reduction of tongue protrusion of a 24-year-old woman with Down's syndrome through self-monitoring. *American Journal of Mental Deficiency, 88,* 647–652.

Shapiro, E. S. (1981). Self-control procedures with the mentally retarded. In M. Hersen, R. M. Eisler, & P. M. Miller (Eds.), *Progress in behavior modification.* New York: Academic.

Shapiro, E. S., & Ackerman, A. (1983). Increasing productivity rates in adult mentally retarded clients: The failure of self-monitoring. *Applied Research in Mental Retardation, 4,* 163–181.

Shapiro, E. S., McGonigle, J. J., & Ollendick, T. H. (1980). An analysis of self-assessment and self-reinforcement in a self-managed token economy with mentally retarded children. *Applied Research in Mental Retardation, 1,* 227–240.

Zegiob, L., Klukas, N., & Junginger, J. (1978). Reactivity of self-monitoring procedures with retarded adolescents. *American Journal of Mental Deficiency, 83,* 156–163.

Zohn, C. J., & Bornstein, P. H. (1980). Self-monitoring of work performance with mentally retarded adults: Effects upon work productivity, work quality, and on-task behavior. *Mental Retardation, 18,* 19–25.

JOHN O'NEILL
*Hunter College, City University
of New York*

**IMPULSE CONTROL
SELF-CARE SKILLS
SELF CONTROL CURRICULUM
SELF-MANAGEMENT**

SELF-SELECTION OF REINFORCEMENT

When the student involved in a contingency management program is permitted to choose a reinforcer or determine the cost of a reinforcer relative to a target behavior, the technique of self-selection of reinforcement is being used. It is one of several self-management methods. It may be used in isolation or in combination with self-recording or self-evaluation (Hughes & Ruhl, 1985). However, a recording and evaluation system (controlled by either the teacher or the student) must be in operation prior to implementing self-selection of reinforcement.

As with other self-management techniques, self-selection of reinforcement appears to be more effective with students previously exposed to a systematic, externally controlled reinforcement system. Consequently, it may function as a helpful transition step for students being weaned from externally controlled systems. Studies (Dickerson & Creedon, 1981; Rosenbaum & Drabman, 1979) have indicated that student-selected reinforcers are more effective than those selected by the teacher. This may be true because students are more capable of identifying what is of value to them and what they are willing to work for.

According to Hughes and Ruhl (1985), the following considerations and steps are helpful when teaching students to use self-selection of reinforcement:

1. Begin with a system of externally controlled contingencies.

2. Verify student understanding of ongoing recording and evaluation procedures and directly reteach if student understanding is in doubt.

3. List available reinforcers and have the student identify one for which he or she is willing to work.

4. Determine stringent performance standards for obtaining reinforcement with the student.

5. Establish a time or signal for administration of the reinforcer.

Stringent performance standards for reinforcement (i.e., those requiring a high rating or frequency for all, or almost all, evaluation periods) are important because they result in significantly better performance results than do lax standards (Alberto & Troutman, 1982). Because students tend to set performance standards that are more lenient than those established by teachers (Flexibrod & O'Leary, 1973, 1974; Frederiksen & Frederiksen, 1975), students should be prompted to set vigorous criteria. Verbal prompts, providing examples and rationales and praising acceptable performance standards, will assist the student in determining appropriate criteria. Examples of criteria for reinforcement include obtaining a specified number of tokens or time intervals with low rates of occurrence of an inappropriate behavior.

Regardless of who is recording or evaluating the behavior, a method for communicating the time for reinforcement should be established. For example, the self-selected reinforcement might come at the end of an academic period, after reading five pages of a text, or at the end of the school day when the school bell rings.

REFERENCES

Alberto, P. A., & Troutman, A. C. (1982). *Applied behavior analysis for teachers: Influencing student performance.* Columbus, OH: Merrill.

Dickerson, A. E., & Creedon, C. F. (1981). Self-selection of standards by children: The relative effectiveness of pupil-selected and teacher-selected standards of performance. *Journal of Applied Behavior Analysis, 141,* 425–433.

Flexibrod, J. J., & O'Leary, K. D. (1973). Effects of reinforcement on children's academic behavior as a function of self-determined and externally imposed contingencies. *Journal of Applied Behavior Analysis, 6,* 241–250.

Flexibrod, J. J., & O'Leary, K. D. (1974). Self-determination of academic standards by children: Toward freedom from external control. *Journal of Educational Psychology, 66,* 845–850.

Frederiksen, L. W., & Frederiksen, C. B. (1975). Teacher-determined and self-determined token reinforcement in a special education classroom. *Behavior Therapy, 6,* 310–314.

Hughes, C. A., & Ruhl, K. L. (1985). Learning activities for improving self-management skills. In B. Algozzine (Ed.), *Educators' resource manual for management of problem behaviors in students.* Rockville, MD: Aspen.

Rosenbaum, M. S., & Drabman, R. S. (1979). Self-control training in the classroom. *Journal of Behavior Analysis, 12,* 467–485.

KATHY L. RUHL
Pennsylvania State University

**APPLIED BEHAVIOR ANALYSIS
BEHAVIOR MODIFICATION
CONTINGENCY CONTRACTING
POSITIVE REINFORCEMENT**

SELF-STIMULATION

Self-stimulation, also called stereotypic behavior, includes "highly consistent and repetitive motor posturing behaviors which are not outer directed in the sense of being explicitly disruptive and harmful to others" (Forehand & Baumeister, 1976, p. 226). Examples of self-stimulatory behavior include flapping the hands at the wrists, light gazing, excessive laughing, repetitive humming, head weaving, twirling in circles, hand staring, spinning or banging objects, finger posturing, and masturbation. Approximately two-thirds of the individuals living in institutions exhibit self-stimulatory behaviors (Snell, 1983).

Another class of self-stimulation is self-injurious behavior. This occurs when a person repeats a behavior that causes injury to himself or herself. Examples of self-injurious behaviors are eye gouging, head banging, self-biting, scratching or pinching, and face slapping. It has been estimated that between 4 and 10% of the institutionalized population engages in some form of self-injurious behavior (Snell, 1983).

Many variables can influence the frequency of self-stimulatory behavior. Environments interpreted as aversive may reinforce self-stimulatory behavior as a means of escape. A second variable that may influence self-stimulatory behavior is the reinforcing characteristic of the behavior itself. Self-stimulatory behavior is intrinsically reinforcing, and because it feels good, it increases the likelihood that the behavior will reoccur. Additionally, attention from others when the person is self-stimulating may increase the behavior's occurrence.

Ecological variables can also influence self-stimulatory behavior. For example, the number of people in the environment, the specific setting, the materials used for instruction, and the amount of nonstructured time available can influence the frequency of self-stimulation. In the past, institutions' characteristic lack of programming and staff contributed to the acquisition of self-stimulatory behaviors. Additionally, self-stimulatory behaviors are characteristic of persons with autism and severe and multiple handicaps.

Although not always disruptive to others in the environment, self-stimulatory behavior disrupts the individual's learning environment, precludes participation in normalized educational, vocational, and leisure activities, and, in the case of self-injurious behavior, poses a threat to physical well-being. Self-stimulatory behaviors, especially self-injurious behaviors, are high priorities for intervention.

Intervention techniques need to be carefully evaluated to determine their potential for alleviating a particular individual's self-stimulatory behavior. Before any behavioral or environmental intervention is begun, the medical status of the individual must be evaluated. Physical discomfort may be responsible for the self-stimulatory behavior. If no medical factors are revealed, other approaches should be explored.

The framework for selecting intervention techniques to reduce self-stimulatory behavior involves evaluating techniques along a continuum of least intrusive and most natural to most intrusive and least natural. According to Snell (1983), the degree of intrusiveness can be determined by evaluating

the extent to which the procedure can be applied in the natural environment without interfering with learning, the necessity for involving artificial or prosthetic devices, the amount of staff time required, the potential for abuse of the technique, the potential for increasing appropriate behaviors as alternatives to the aberrant behavior, and the degree to which the people required to carry out the program feel comfortable with the techniques selected. (p. 325)

According to Alberto and Troutman (1982), the techniques of first choice are those that apply a positive approach to behavior reduction; i.e., strategies of differential reinforcement. The technique of second choice would be the use of extinction procedures or the withdrawing of reinforcers that maintain the behavior. Third choice employs a punishing consequence, in that a desirable stimulus is contingently removed in order to decrease behavior. Fourth choice is the application of unconditional or conditional aversive stimuli.

Interventions that have aversive consequences (e.g., physical punishment, noxious odors and liquids, electric shock) are interventions of last resort. These interventions may be justifiable when self-injurious behaviors are life-threatening and all other less intrusive techniques have failed. In cases where aversive techniques are used, continuous program monitoring is critical both for programming and for ethical and legal justification.

REFERENCES

Alberto, P. A., & Troutman, A. C. (1982). *Applied behavior analysis for teachers*. Columbus, OH: Merrill.

Forehand, R., & Baumeister, A. (1976). Decelaration of aberrant behavior among retarded individuals. In M. Hersen, R. M. Eisler, & P. M. Miller (Eds.), *Progress in behavior modification*, 2. New York: Academic.

Foxx, R. M. (1982). *Decreasing behaviors of severely retarded and autistic persons*. Champaign, IL: Research Press.

Snell, M. E. (1983). *Systematic instruction of the moderately and severely handicapped*. Columbus, OH: Merrill.

CAROLE REITER GOTHELF
Hunter College, City University of New York

AUTISTIC BEHAVIOR
SELF-INJURIOUS BEHAVIOR

SEMMEL, MELVYN I. (1931–   )

Born in New York City, Melvyn I. Semmel received his BS (1955) and his MS (1957) in special education from City

College, City University of New York. He received his EdD (1963) in special education with a minor in psychology from George Peabody College. Currently, he is professor and program leader of special education at the Graduate School of Education, University of California, Santa Barbara.

Semmel's early teacher training led him into involvement with teacher preparation and coordinating research on special education methods. In 1968 he pioneered the development of the Computer-Assisted Teacher Training System (CATTS). He is still actively involved in computer-assisted educational practices (Semmel, in press).

In the 1970s Semmel was director of the Center for Innovation in Teaching the Handicapped (CITH), a research and development center for alternative teacher training methods and instructional materials, including games, simulations, and multimedia training packages. In 1976 the National Society for Performance and Instruction named CITH the outstanding organization of the year. Currently, as professor and program leader, Semmel is director of the Special Education Research Laboratory, which contains both a microcomputer technology and a teacher training laboratory. The laboratory focuses on topics such as microcomputers with handicapped learners, new models for research teaching, and the development of cognitively oriented interventions for the severely emotionally disturbed.

Semmel has written over 100 books, research papers, and chapters related to special education and educational psychology. He has been listed in *Who's Who Biographical Record* and has been elected as a life member and fellow of the American Association on Mental Deficiency for 30 years of continuous contribution to the field. Semmel is also a fellow of Divisions 15 and 33 of the American Psychological Association.

REFERENCE

Semmel, M. I. (in press). Special education administrators' policies and practices on microcomputer acquisition, allocation, and access for mildly handicapped children: Interfaces with regular education with et al. *Exceptional Children*.

E. VALERIE HEWITT
Texas A&M University

SENF, GERALD M. (1942–   )

Gerald M. Senf graduated, with honors, in 1964 from Yale University with a BA in psychology. He then received his MA, in 1966, in experimental psychology and his doctorate, in 1968, in the fields of experimental and clinical psychology, both from the University of California, Los Angeles.

Senf has been assistant professor of psychology at the University of Iowa, associate professor of psychology at the University of Illinois, evaluation research director at the Leadership Training Institute in Learning Disabilities, and associate professor of special education at the University of Arizona. From 1977 to 1986, Senf served as editor in chief of the *Journal of Learning Disabilities*.

Senf is the author of numerous research papers in the area of cognitive functioning; he also has authored chapters concerned with this topic and with research methodology in the field of learning disabilities. His principal interests have centered around information-processing skills and memory among the learning disabled (Senf, 1969, 1972, 1976, 1981, 1986). He is the coauthor of a screening test, coeditor of three books, and developer of computer programs for the learning disabled.

REFERENCES

Senf, G. M. (1969). Development of immediate memory for bisensory stimuli in normal children and children with learning disorders. *Developmental Psychology Monograph, 1* (Pt. 2).

Senf, G. M. (1972). An information integration theory and its application to normal reading acquisition and reading disability. In N. D. Bryant & C. E. Kass (Eds.), *Leadership Training Institute in Learning Disabilities* (Vol. 2). Tucson: University of Arizona Press.

Senf, G. M. (1976). Some methodological considerations in the study of abnormal conditions. In R. Walsh & W. T. Greenough (Eds.), *Environment as therapy for brain dysfunction*. New York: Plenum.

Senf, G. M. (1981). Issues surrounding the diagnosis of learning disabilities: Child handicap versus failure of the child-school interaction. In T. R. Kratochwill (Ed.), *Advances in school psychology* (Vol. 1, pp. 83–131). Hillsdale, NJ: Erlbaum.

Senf, G. M. (1986). LD research in sociological and scientific perspective. In J. K. Torgesen & B. Wong (Eds.), *Psychological and educational perspectives on learning disabilities*. San Diego, CA: Academic.

ROBERTA C. STOKES
Texas A&M University

JOURNAL OF LEARNING DISABILITIES

SENSORINEURAL HEARING LOSS

A sensorineural hearing loss is a hearing impairment resulting from a pathological condition in the inner ear or along the auditory nerve (VIII cranial nerve) pathway from the inner ear to the brain stem. If the pathological condition or site of lesion is confined to the inner ear or cochlea, it is known as an inner ear or cochlea hearing loss. If the site of lesion is along the auditory nerve (as is the case with an acoustic nerve tumor), it is known as a retrocochlear hearing loss. Several audiological, medical, and radiological special tests have been developed to assist in the diagnosis of whether a sensorineural hearing loss is due to a cochlear or retrocochlear site of lesion.

An individual with a sensorineural hearing loss has reduced hearing sensitivity and lacks the ability to discriminate speech sounds, especially when listening in a noisy environment. Tinnitus is a common symptom of a sensorineural hearing loss. Tinnitus is any sensation of sound in the head heard in one or both ears. It may be described as a hissing, whistling, buzzing, roaring, or a high-pitched tone or noise. Dizziness is also a symptom of sensorineural hearing loss; it can range from light-headedness to a severe whirling sensation known as vertigo, that leads to nausea.

A sensorineural hearing loss can occur in varying degrees ranging from mild-moderate to severe-profound. The degree of sensorineural hearing loss is determined by averaging the decibel amount of hearing loss across the frequencies needed to hear and understand speech or the speech frequencies (500, 1000, and 2000 Hz). Individuals with a mild to severe hearing loss are usually classified as being hard of hearing, while individuals with a profound hearing impairment are classified as deaf. A sensorineural hearing loss can occur in just one ear (unilateral) or in each ear (bilateral). If the hearing loss occurs in each ear, one ear may be more affected than the other.

A sensorineural hearing loss can be caused by many factors, including genetic diseases (dominant, recessive, or sex-linked), diseases acquired during pre-, peri-, and postnatal periods, and childhood diseases. Adults can obtain sensorineural hearing loss from noise exposure, diseases, medication, and the aging process. Many sensorineural hearing losses are due to unknown etiology. A sensorineural hearing loss also may be part of a syndrome that affects the individual in other ways. A congenital sensorineural hearing loss is one that has existed or has an etiology from birth; an adventitious hearing loss is one that occurred after birth and in most cases is due to injury or disease. If the sensorineural hearing loss occurred prior to the development of speech and language skills, it is known as prelingual; if it occurred after the development of speech and language skills, it is known as postlingual.

In children having sensorineural hearing losses, about half the cases are due to genetic causes and half to acquired causes. Meningitis and prematurity are the leading acquired causes of sensorineural hearing loss in children. For adults, the leading cause of sensorineural hearing loss is the aging process, known as presbyacusis, and excessive exposure to noise. Typically, the sensorineural hearing loss from presbyacusis or noise exposure is a progressive reduction of high frequency (1000 to 8000 Hz) hearing sensitivity that causes problems in understanding speech.

It is important that individuals with a sensorineural hearing loss have audiological and otological diagnosis and management. In almost all cases, there is no medical treatment for sensorineural hearing loss from a cochlear site of lesion. However, a retrocochlear lesion from a tumor, or some other growth along the auditory nerve may benefit from an operation. Almost always, retrocochlear lesions occur in adults and are unilateral.

Children and adults with cochlear sensorineural hearing loss can benefit through the use of hearing aids. Most children are fitted with a hearing aid for each ear (binaural amplification) and require auditory and speech reading training, speech and language therapy, and academic tutoring. Adults are usually fitted with either a hearing aid on one ear (monaural) or with binaural amplification. Generally, adults do not need specialized training; however, many adults benefit from speech-reading therapy. References for in depth discussion of sensorineural hearing loss are cited below.

REFERENCES

Gerber, S. E., & Mencher, G. T. (1980). *Auditory dysfunction.* San Diego, CA: College-Hill.

Jerger, J. (1984). *Hearing disorders in adults.* San Diego, CA: College-Hill.

Schubert, E. D. (1980). *Hearing: Its function and dysfunction.* New York: Springer-Verlag.

Schuknecht, H. F. (1974). *Pathology of the ear.* Cambridge, MA: Harvard University Press.

Wolstenholmer, G. E. W., & Knight, J. (1970). *Sensorineural hearing loss.* London: J. & A. Churchill.

THOMAS A. FRANK
Pennsylvania State University

DEAF
DEAF EDUCATION

SENSORY EXTINCTION

Sensory extinction is a procedure developed by Rincover (1978) for reducing various pathological behaviors in developmentally disabled children. It has been used to suppress self-stimulation (Maag, Wolchik, Rutherford, & Parks, 1986; Rincover, 1978), compulsive behaviors (Rincover, Newsom, & Carr, 1979), and self-injury (Rincover & Devaney, 1981). In a sensory extinction paradigm, stereotypy is considered operant behavior maintained by its sensory consequences. For example, repetitive finger flapping might be conceptualized as being maintained by the specific proprioceptive feedback it produces, while persistent delayed echolalia may be maintained by auditory feedback.

Sensory extinction involves masking, changing, or removing certain sensory consequences of behavior. If the sensory reinforcement received is removed, the behavior will be extinguished. For example, if a child continuously spins a plate on a table, a piece of carpet could be placed on the table to remove the auditory feedback resulting from this behavior. Similarly, the stereotypic behavior of a child who ritualistically switches a light on and off could be extinguished by either removing the visual feedback (if seeing the light were reinforcing) or removing the auditory feedback (if hearing the light switch click were reinforcing).

When sensory extinction is used to suppress stereotypy, the preferred sensory consequences of the behavior can be used to teach appropriate behaviors. For example, the child who spins plates could be taught to spin a top instead, since this would provide the same sensory consequences as the maladaptive behavior. Rincover, Cook, Peoples, and Packard (1979) found that children preferred to play with toys that provided sensory reinforcement similar to the sensory reinforcement previously found in the stereotypy.

While sensory extinction is a procedure in which multiple components are altered at the same time (Maag et al., 1986), it remains unclear as to the extent to which stimulus modality is an important factor (Murphy, 1982). Maag et al. found that isolating the sensory consequences for some forms of behavior can be impractical and/or time-consuming. In addition, Maag et al., point out that a cumbersome apparatus is sometimes necessary to mask some types of sensory feedback. This apparatus may restrict the child's ability to participate in activities and also be socially stigmatizing. Therefore, although sensory extinction may represent a viable set of procedures for reducing stereotypy, it should be assessed thoroughly to determine the appropriateness of this intervention for particular children.

REFERENCES

Maag, J. W., Wolchik, S. A., Rutherford, R. B., & Parks, B. T. (1986). Response covariation of self-stimulatory behaviors during sensory extinction procedures. *Journal of Autism & Developmental Disorders 16,* 119–132.

Murphy, G. (1982). Sensory reinforcement in the mentally handicapped and autistic child: A review. *Journal of Autism & Developmental Disorders, 12,* 265–278.

Rincover, A. (1978). Sensory extinction: A procedure for eliminating self-stimulatory behavior in developmentally disabled children. *Journal of Abnormal Child Psychology, 6,* 299–310.

Rincover, A., Cook, R., Peoples, A., & Packard, D. (1979). Sensory extinction and sensory reinforcement principles for programming multiple adaptive behavior change. *Journal of Applied Behavior Analysis, 12,* 221–233.

Rincover, A., & Devaney, J. (1981). The application of sensory extinction principles to self-injury in developmentally disabled children. *Analysis & Intervention in Developmental Disabilities, 4,* 67–69.

Rincover, A., Newsom, C. D., & Carr, E. G. (1979). Using sensory extinction procedures in the treatment of compulsive-like behavior of developmentally disabled children. *Journal of Consulting and Clinical Psychology, 47,* 695–701.

ROBERT B. RUTHERFORD, JR.
Arizona State University

BEHAVIOR MODIFICATION
SELF-STIMULATION

SENSORY INTEGRATIVE THERAPY

Sensory integrative therapy is a technique for the remediation of sensory integrative dysfunction developed by A. Jean Ayres (Ayres, 1972). Sensory integrative dysfunction is believed by Ayres and others (Quiros, 1976; Silberzahn, 1982) to be at the root of many learning disorders. Ayres uses the term sensory integrative dysfunction to describe children whose learning problems are due to the failure of the lower levels of the brain (particularly the midbrain, brain stem, and vestibular system) to use and organize information effectively. The principal objective of sensory integrative therapy is to promote the development and the organization of subcortical brain mechanisms as a foundation for perception and learning. Treatment procedures consist of the use of gross motor activities and physical exercise to achieve this goal. Sensory integrative therapy has gained its greatest popularity among occupational therapists.

The five key features of sensory integrative dysfunction follow (Silberzahn, 1982):

1. *Developmental Apraxia.* This is a problem in motor planning and is part of a complex that includes deficits in tactile functions. According to Ayres (1972), the fundamental problem lies in the difficulty in recognizing the time and space aspects of sensation and the relationships among body parts that are necessary for cortical planning of events.

2. *Tactile Defensiveness.* This represents a defensive or hostile reaction to tactile stimuli and it part of a complex believed, in sensory integrative therapy, to include hyperactivity, distractibility, and discrimination problems in most major sensory modalities.

3. *Deficits in Interhemispheric Integration.* These deficits are manifest in problems integrating the two sides of the body. Ayres (1972) believes these deficits are common in children with reading problems and that they can be shown clinically as the child tends to use each side of the body independently and avoids crossing the midline.

4. *Visual and Space Perception Deficits.* These problems are typically associated with a more extensive problem that involves inadequate integration of vestibular, proprioceptive, tactile, and visual stimuli at the level of the brain stem. Developmental apraxia may also result.

5. *Auditory-Language Deficits.* These deficits are a result of problems in areas 3 and 4 and disrupt written and spoken language.

Sensory integrative therapy attempts to remediate these problems through the development of perception and learning via the enhancement of organizations and sensations at the brain stem level. Motor activities are the principal therapeutic media and center around activities that require the child to adapt and organize a variety of sensory motor experiences while taking an active role in each process. Coordinated use of the two sides of the body is promoted.

Carefully controlled studies of the outcome of sensory integrative therapy are lacking, particularly in regard to improvements in academic skills. The therapy is a deficit-centered approach to remediation, though not strictly a process approach. However, it seems unlikely that learning disabilities can be corrected through the use of gross motor activities and physical exercise.

REFERENCES

Ayres, A. J. (1972). *Sensory integration and learning disorders.* Los Angeles: Western Psychological Services.

Quiros, J. B. de. (1976). Diagnosis of vestibular disorders in the learning disabled. *Journal of Learning Disabilities, 9,* 39–47.

Silberzahn, M. (1982). Sensory integrative therapy. In C. R. Reynolds & T. B. Gutkin (Eds.), *The handbook of school psychology,* New York: Wiley.

CECIL R. REYNOLDS
Texas A&M University

AYRES, A. J.
DEFICIT MODELS OF REMEDIATIONS

SENSORY MOTOR INTEGRATION

Inherent to sensory motor integration is the relationship between learning and central nervous system functioning. Normal learning requires normal central nervous system functioning. However, Ayres (1975) believes that children with learning and behavior problems do not possess intact or properly functioning central nervous systems. Lerner (1985) notes that some children are unable to process information properly because of tactile, proprioceptive (systems within the body such as the digestive or nervous), or vestibular (systems enabling one to detect motion) processing disorders. Consequently, these children are unable to function in normal academic or social settings.

Therapeutic intervention using sensory motor integration theories includes activities designed to stimulate the tactile, proprioceptive, and vestibular systems. Ayres (1975) notes that treatment for tactile imbalances might include activities that concentrate on stimulating the senses through touching and rubbing different surfaces. Activities designed to stimulate the proprioceptive system include the use of scooter boards. Finally, vestibular sys-

tem stimulation is carried out through activities such as swinging, spinning, and being rolled on a large ball. The activities described are often used in a clinical setting by occupational and physical therapists.

REFERENCES

Ayres, A. J. (1975). *Sensory integration and learning disorders.* Los Angeles: Western Psychological Services.

Lerner, J. (1985). *Learning disabilities: Theories, diagnosis and teaching strategies.* Boston: Houghton Mifflin.

JOHN R. BEATTIE
*University of North Carolina,
Charlotte*

OCCUPATIONAL THERAPY
SENSORY INTEGRATIVE THERAPY

SEPARATION ANXIETY AND THE HANDICAPPED

Separation anxiety is defined by Bowlby as anxiety about losing, or becoming separated from, someone loved. It is the usual response to a threat or some other risk of loss. This fear of abandonment can not only create intense anxiety, it can arouse anger of an intense degree, especially in older children and adolescents, and cause dysfunction (Bowlby, 1982). Adverse separation experiences have at least two kinds of effects: They make the individual more vulnerable to later adverse experiences and they make it more likely that the individual will have such experiences (Bowlby, 1982).

In infants and young children, separation anxiety is a normal part of the developmental process; it is related to the formation of positive attachment behavior. Sears (1972) says that attachment is completed during the second half of the first year of life, while separation anxiety appears after the child reaches 6 months of age. Ainsworth (1972) also states that an attachment if formed when definitive separation causes anxiety, although Yarrow (1972) believes that environmental conditions that influence the strength of positive attachment behaviors determine the strength and character of response to separation anxiety.

By observing the pattern of behavior shown in unfamiliar situations and in the episodes of reunion after separation, a child's response can be used in assessment procedures to measure the degree of positive attachment. Some danger signals of attachment quality include greater than average separation anxiety, shadowing of the caregiver, ignoring the caregiver, and continuing impulse-driven darting away, provoking the caregiver to pursuit (Mahler, 1979). Ainsworth (1979) identified eight patterns, but classed responses into three main groups. Group

A was anxious/avoidant, where on separation, the child rarely cried and during reunion the child mingled proximity-seeking with avoidant behaviors, ignoring the caregiver. Group B was securely attached, but distressed by separation and seeking contact with the caregiver on reunion. Group C was anxious/resistant, and intensely distressed by separation and ambivalent about reunion episodes. In normal infants, it appears that differences in attachment behavior are attributable to caregiver behavior.

When the quality of attachment is poor, all subsequent development of personal relationships may be in jeopardy. In later development, Ainsworth (1979) found the securely attached infants more cooperative and affectively positive toward caregivers and other familiar adults, and more competent and sympathetic in interaction with peers. They were more curious, self-directed, and ego-resilient. Group A infants continued to be more aggressive, noncompliant, and avoidant, while group C emerged as more easily frustrated, less persistent, and generally less competent.

The presence of a handicap can put significant stress on the attachment process, increasing the vulnerability of both the infant and the caregivers (Ulrey, 1981). By viewing the attachment-separation process as a system, it follows that any change will produce disequilibrium, with different implications for various handicaps. A child with motor deficits may be at increased risk because the infant may not be able to adjust to the physical comforting offered by the parents, possibly minimizing parental contact. Abnormal muscle tone may influence the child's activity level and facial movements, affecting the child's emotional expressiveness, while other motor deficits may make it impossible for the child to physically move away from the caregivers, delaying the separation process. A visually handicapped child will develop attachments more slowly than a sighted child, but, once formed, attachments persist longer, delaying separation. Children with impaired hearing may also be at increased risk for disruption of the attachment process (Ulrey, 1981). A caregiver's anxiety about a child who is handicapped may make it difficult for appropriate interaction with the child to provide the stimulation necessary to form a quality attachment.

REFERENCES

Ainsworth, M. D. S. (1972). Attachment and dependency: A comparison. In J. L. Gerwitz (Ed.). *Attachment and dependency* (pp. 97–139). New York: Winston/Wiley.

Ainsworth, M. D. S. (1979). Infant-mother attachment. *American Psychologist, 34,* 932–937.

Bowlby, J. (1969). *Attachment and loss: Vol. 1. Attachment.* New York: Basic Books.

Bowlby, J. (1982). Attachment and loss: retrospect and prospect. *American Journal of Orthropsychiatrics, 52,* 664–678.

Mahler, M. S. (1979). *The selected papers of Margaret S. Mahler, M. D.: Vol. 2. Separation-individuation.* New York: Aronson.

Sears, R. R. (1972). Attachment, dependency and frustration. In J. L. Gerwitz (Ed.), *Attachment and dependency* (pp. 1–28). New York: Winston/Wiley.

Ulrey, G. (1981). Emotional development of the young handicapped child. In N. J. Anastasiow (Ed.), *Socioemotional development: New directions for exceptional children* (No. 5, pp. 33–52). San Francisco: Jossey-Bass.

Yarrow, L. J. (1972). Attachment and dependency: A developmental perspective. In J. L. Gerwitz (Ed.), *Attachment and dependency* (pp. 81–96). New York: Winston/Wiley.

CATHERINE O. BRUCE
*Hunter College, City University
of New York*

BORDERLINE PERSONALITY DISORDER
CHILD-CARETAKER
SCHOOL PHOBIA

SEQUENCED INVENTORY OF COMMUNICATION DEVELOPMENT (SICD)

The Sequenced Inventory of Communication Development (SICD) (Hedrick, Prather, & Tobin, 1975) was designed to test receptive and expressive preverbal and verbal communication skills of children between the ages of 4 months and 4 years. The test consists of a kit of objects and pictures, an examiner's manual, and test forms. The items include both direct observations of the child and parental reports; many items are adaptations from other tests and scales such as the Denver Developmental Screening Test (Frankenberg & Dodds, 1967). In 1984 the authors made available a revised instruction manual, additional profile forms, and a test manual. The new manuals and forms make this test considerably easier to administer and score. The new test forms organize the items into the areas of phonologic, semantic, syntactic, pragmatic, and perceptual skills.

The standardization sample was small, including 252 children, 21 at each of 12 age levels, all from the Seattle, Washington, area. Test time is approximately 30 to 75 minutes. Reported test-retest and interexaminer reliabilities are high. Measures of validity include moderate correlations with other language tests. Strengths of the test include good reliability, a thorough manual, and applicability to very young children with the option of using parent reports for many items. Weaknesses include limited standardization and the need for considerable experience with the test before mastering the administration and scoring procedures.

REFERENCES

Darley, F. L. (1979). *Evaluation of appraisal techniques in speech and language pathology.* Reading, MA: Addison-Wesley.

Frankenberg, W. K., & Dodds, J. B. (1967). Denver Developmental Screening Test. *Journal of Pediatrics, 71,* 181–191.

Hedrick, D. L., Prather, E. M., & Tobin, A. (1975). *Sequenced Inventory of Communication Development.* Seattle: University of Washington Press.

MARGO E. WILSON
Lexington, Kentucky

VERBAL DEFICIENCY
VERBAL SCALE IQ

SEQUENTIAL AND SIMULTANEOUS COGNITIVE PROCESSING

Sequential and simultaneous are two of many labels used to denote two primary forms of information coding processes in the brain. These coding processes are the primary functions of Luria's (1973) Block II of the brain (the parietal, occipital, and temporal lobes, also known as the association areas of the brain). They have been proposed as fundamental integration processes in Das, Kirby, and Jarman's (1979) model of Luria's fundamental approach to human information processing. Other labels commonly used to distinguish these forms of processing include successive versus simultaneous (Das et al., 1979), propositional versus appositional (Bogen, 1969), serial versus multiple or parallel (Neisser, 1967), and analytic versus gestalt/holistic (Levy, 1972).

No matter what label is applied, the descriptions of the processes corresponding to each label appear to be defining similar processes though some minor distinctions may exist. Thus sequential processing is defined as the processing of information in a temporal or serial order. Using this coding process, analysis of information proceeds in successive steps in which each step provides cues for the processing of later steps. This type of processing is generally employed, e.g., when an individual repeats a series of numbers that have been orally presented. Each stage of processing is dependent on the completion of the immediately preceding stage.

Simultaneous coding processes are used when all the pieces of information or all the stimuli are surveyable at one time and are thus available for processing at one time; i.e., at the analysis of parts of information can take place without dependence on the parts' relationship to the whole. When an individual discerns the whole object with only parts of the picture available, this is usually accomplished using simultaneous processing. The Figure presents an example of a strongly simultaneous processing task. See if you can determine what is pictured. Even with many of the parts missing and the pictured figure only in silhouette form, most individuals beyond the age of 10 to 12 years will recognize the figure to be a man on horse-back. Some will have great difficulty or take a long time to recognize the figure; this is true especially if one takes a step-by-step approach to determining the identity of the picture, looking at individual pieces and trying to add them as a simple sum of the separate parts. While not impossible, such an approach is more difficult.

In the literature, several assumptions regarding these two forms of processing are presented. First, sequential and simultaneous processing are not hierarchical. That is, one form of processing does not appear to be more complex than the other. Both appear to require the transformation of stimulus material before synthesis of the information can occur (Das et al., 1979).

Second, determining whether to process information sequentially or simultaneously is not solely dependent on the presentation mode of the stimuli to be processed (e.g., visual or auditory). Rather, the form of processing used appears to be more dependent on the cognitive demands of the task and the unique sociocultural history and genetic predisposition of the individual performing the task (Das et al., 1979; Kaufman & Kaufman, 1983). This may become habitual and individuals do develop preferred styles of information processing.

Third, sequential and simultaneous processing have been indirectly linked to various areas of the brain, but psychologists do not agree on the exact location of each of these functions. Some contend that processing abilities are best associated with the two hemispheres of the brain (Gazzaniga, 1975; Reynolds, 1981), with sequential processing being a left hemisphere function and simultaneous processing being a right hemisphere function. Luria (1973), on the other hand, located successive or sequential processing as a function of the frontal regions of the brain, with simultaneous processing carried out in the occipital-parietal or rear sections of the brain.

These forms of processing have traditionally been measured in nonbrain-damaged individuals with a battery of standardized tests, the components of which are certainly less than pure measures of process. Evidence of simultaneous processing abilities has been inferred from individuals' performance on such instruments as Raven's Progressive Matrices (Raven, 1956), Memory-for-Designs (Graham & Kendall, 1960), and Figure Copying (Ilg & Ames, 1964). Each of these tasks places a premium on visuo-spatial skills and the synthesis of information for successful performance.

Sequential processing abilities have typically been inferred from observing an individual's performance on such tasks as Digit Span (a purely auditory task), Visual Short-Term Memory, and Serial or Free Recall. It is apparent that it is not the mode of presentation but rather the cognitive demands of the task that are the major determining factors in what cognitive processing style is used.

Recently, the Kaufman Assessment Battery for Children (K-ABC; Kaufman & Kaufman, 1983) was introduced into psychological and educational circles. This in-

An example of a task that might be used to assess an individual's simultaneous cognitive processing skills; what do you think is pictured here? (The answer is in the text)

strument was designed as an individually administered intelligence test for children ages 2½ and 12½; it is composed of several subtests that according to factor analytic data, measure sequential and simultaneous processing abilities. Focused on process rather than content as the major distinction of how children solve unfamiliar problems, this instrument has resulted in more controversy and discussion than any intelligence test in recent history (Reynolds, 1985).

Controversy has arisen over the Kaufmans' assertion that knowledge about a child's information-processing abilities, as measured on the K-ABC, in conjunction with other sources of data, can more easily translate into educational programming for children with learning or behavioral problems than traditionally had been possible from data gathered on other, content-based intelligence tests. Primarily employing an aptitude × treatment interaction (ATI) paradigm (Cronbach, 1975) and the habilitation philosophy of neuropsychology (Reynolds, 1981), the Kaufmans propose using knowledge regarding a child's individual strengths in information processing (e.g., simultaneous processing) as the foundation for any remedial plans thus developed. The notion of a strength model of remediation is in direct contrast to the deficit-centered training models that have dominated special education remedial plans for years, but that have proven largely ineffective in improving academic abilities (Ysseldyke & Mirkin, 1982).

Although preliminary data seem encouraging regarding the efficacy of using knowledge of a child's individual processing style to remediate learning or behavioral difficulties (Gunnison, Kaufman, & Kaufman, 1983), the data are not sufficient to support this assumption unequivocably. Much research remains to be done in this area, but for now the role of sequential and simultaneous processing in educating children with special needs certainly seems worth exploring.

REFERENCES

Bogen, J. E. (1969). The other side of the brain: Parts I, II, & III. *Bulletin of the Los Angeles Neurological Society, 34*, 73–203.

Cronbach, L. J. (1975). Beyond the two disciplines of scientific psychology. *American Psychologist, 30*, 116–125.

Das, J. P., Kirby, J. R., & Jarman, R. F. (1979). *Simultaneous and successive cognitive processes.* New York: Academic.

Gazzaniga, M. S. (1975). Recent research on hemispheric lateralization of the human brain: Review of the split brain. *UCLA Educator, 17*, 9–12.

Graham, F. K., & Kendall, B. S. (1960). Memory-for-Designs Test: Revised general manual. *Perceptual & Motor Skills, 43*, 1051–1058.

Gunnison, J., Kaufman, N. L., & Kaufman, A. S. (1983). Reading remediation based on sequential and simultaneous processing. *Academic Therapy, 17*, 297–307.

Ilg, F. L., & Ames, L. B. (1964). *School readiness: Behavior tests used at the Gesell Institute.* New York: Harper & Row.

Kaufman, A. S., & Kaufman, N. (1983). *The Kaufman Assessment Battery for Children.* Circle Pines, MN: American Guidance Service.

Levy, J. (1972). Lateral specification of the human brain: Behavioral manifestations and possible evolutionary basis. In J. A. Kiger (Ed.), *Biology of behavior.* Cornallis: Oregon State University Press.

Luria, A. R. (1973). *The working brain: An introduction to neuropsychology.* London: Penguin.

Neisser, W. (1967). *Cognitive psychology.* New York: Appleton-Century-Crofts.

Raven, J. C. (1956). *Coloured progressive matrices: Sets A, Ab, B.* London: H. K. Lewis.

Reynolds, C. R. (1981). Neuropsychological assessment and the habilitation of learning: Considerations in the search for the aptitude × treatment interaction. *School Psychology Review, 10*, 343–349.

Reynolds, C. R. (Ed.) (1985). K-ABC and controversy [Special issue]. *Journal of Special Education, 18*(3).

Ysseldyke, J., & Mirkin, P. (1982). The use of assessment information to plan instructional interventions: A review of the research. In C. R. Reynolds & T. B. Gutkin (Eds.), *The handbook of school psychology.* New York: Wiley.

Julia A. Hickman
University of Texas, Austin

INFORMATION PROCESSING

KAUFMAN ASSESSMENT BATTERY FOR CHILDREN
PERCEPTUAL TRAINING
REMEDIATION, DEFICIT-CENTERED MODELS OF

SEQUENTIAL ASSESSMENT OF MATHEMATICS INVENTORIES (SAMI)

The Sequential Assessment of Mathematics Inventories (SAMI) is a diagnostic mathematics assessment system for students in grades kindergarten through eight. The standardized 1985 publication is comprised of eight subtests, each of which measures a curriculum "strand" of mathematics content and operations that spans several grade levels. These eight strands include mathematical language, ordinality, number and notation, computation, measurement, geometric concepts, mathematical applications, and word problems. The standardized inventory has four components: (1) the manual, comprised of information needed to administer, score, and interpret the test, as well as normative and technical data on the test; (2) the easel, containing all items that include oral directions to be read aloud to the student; (3) the student response booklet, containing all items to which the student is asked to indicate the answer in writing; and (4) the record form, which allows the test administrator to record students' performance and construct performance summaries. The standardized inventory, designed for use primarily by school psychologists, educational diagnosticians, and special education teachers, is individually administered and takes from 20 to 60 minutes, depending on the age and mathematics competence of the student. A parallel testing/teaching program for classroom use, called the *SAMI Informal Inventory*, is scheduled for publication in 1987.

REFERENCES

Reisman, F. K. (1985). *Sequential assessment of mathematics inventories: Standardized inventory.* Columbus, OH: Merrill.

Reisman, F. K., & Hutchinson, T. A. (1985). *Sequential assessment of mathematics inventories: Standardized inventory. Examiner's manual.* Columbus, OH: Merrill.

Fredricka K. Reisman
Drexel University

ASSESSMENT
MATHEMATICS, LEARNING DISABILITIES IN

SEQUENTIAL PROCESSING

See SEQUENTIAL AND SIMULTANEOUS COGNITIVE PROCESSING.

SERIOUSLY EMOTIONALLY DISTURBED

The term seriously emotionally disturbed has been defined by federal legislation as a condition with one or more of the following characteristics occurring to a marked degree and over a long period of time: (1) inability to learn not explainable by health, intellectual, or sensory factors; (2) inability to develop or maintain appropriate interpersonal relationships with students and teachers; (3) inappropriate behaviors or feelings in normal circumstances; (4) a pervasive mood of depression; (5) a tendency to develop physical symptoms or fears in response to personal or school difficulties (PL 94-142). According to the legislative definition, the term specifically includes childhood schizophrenia but specifically excludes children who are socially maladjusted except when the maladjustment is accompanied by serious emotional disturbance.

Although autism was originally included as a form of serious emotional disturbance, in the most recent publication of the *Diagnostic and Statistical Manual of Mental Disorders* (DSM-III), autism was removed from classification as a psychosis and defined as a pervasive developmental disorder. This reclassification of autism was based on recent research that has established clear differences between autism and the childhood psychoses on a variety of dimensions, including symptomatology, age of onset, family history of psychopathology, language ability, intellectual functioning, and socioeconomic status. There is no support for the early hypothesis that autism is the result of parent-child interactions that are mechanical and lacking in warmth. Most currently accepted theories of autism posit an innate defect in central nervous system (CNS) arousal, although the nature of the defect is a subject of debate. The CNS deficiency is thought to interfere with the accurate perception and organization of stimuli and to make it impossible for the child to interact effectively with the environment.

The prevalence of childhood psychoses is difficult to reliably measure because of definitional issues and other methodological problems. Most prevalence studies have not distinguished between autism and childhood schizophrenia or have dealt with autism exclusively. The most commonly cited prevalence estimate for childhood schizophrenia is somewhat lower than that for autism (which is 5 per 10,000 children; Kolvin, 1971a). All epidemiological studies of childhood psychoses report a sex ratio favoring males (Werry, 1979).

Current theories of the etiology of schizophrenia posit that schizophrenia develops from an interaction between the presence of a biological predisposition to the disorder and environmental or psychosocial stressors. The assumption is that a biological predisposition is a necessary, but not sufficient, prerequisite, and that external influences such as perinatal insults or significant emotional stressors can sometimes play a major role in symptom development (Dawson & Mesibov, 1983).

There is substantial evidence that genetic factors play a role in the development of schizophrenia. Approximately 12% of the children of schizophrenic parents develop schizophrenia, compared with about 1% of the general population. Twin studies and adoption studies also support the notion of an inheritable biological predisposition for schizophrenia. Schizophrenics also have an increased rate of other forms of neuropsychiatric disturbance in their families, with depression and suicide represented at a high rate (Dawson & Mesibov, 1983).

Evidence of other biological factors in schizophrenia includes the presence of temporal lobe epilepsy at a rate greater than that found in the general population. In one study, approximately 12% of childhood schizophrenics also had temporal lobe epilepsy (Kolvin, Ounsted, & Roth, 1971). In the same study, 15% of the schizophrenic children had unequivocal evidence of brain damage and 30% had suggestive evidence of brain damage.

The onset of schizophrenic symptoms is related to a precipitating event in about half of the cases in which no evidence of organic impairment exists and about 30% of the organically related cases. Examples of precipitating events that have been related to symptom onset include a death in the family and sexual assault (Kolvin, Ounsted, Richardson, & Garside, 1971). The presence of a precipitating event is associated with better outcome (Eggers, 1978.

The major symptoms of childhood schizophrenia are similar to those found in adult schizophrenics. One study of childhood schizophrenics reported that 80% experienced hallucinations and 60% exhibited a formal thought disorder (Kolvin, Ounsted, & Roth, 1971). The presence of hallucinations becomes more likely with age, however, and among schizophrenic children younger than 10 years they are found infrequently (Eggers, 1978). When hallucinations are reported, it is imperative that the child be scheduled for a thorough neurological evaluation to rule out seizures or some other organic problem. The symptoms of childhood schizophrenia develop after a period of relatively normal development and almost never occur before the age of 5 years. However, most children who later develop symptoms of childhood schizophrenia were considered premorbidly odd by the parents or were described as having personality problems prior to developing schizophrenic symptomatology (Eggers, 1978; Kolvin, 1971b). Indeed children between 3 and 6 years of age diagnosed as psychotic usually are found to have clear-cut organic symptoms (Kolvin, Ounsted, Humphrey, & McNay, 1971).

Before the age of 10 years, specific symptoms that characterize childhood schizophrenia include loss of contact with reality, loss of interest in usual activities, and speech disturbances with neologisms and disintegration of speech. The children seem to retreat into their own world, become moody, anxious, cold, and distrustful. They develop a lack of social inhibition and may exhibit public defecation or masturbation. Some lose their sense of identity and begin to identify themselves with animals, other people, or objects. Their coldness may at times reach extreme levels with behaviors such as torturing of pets occurring in some cases (Eggers, 1978).

When onset occurs after the age of 10 years, the symptoms more closely resemble those of adult schizophrenics, with the majority showing hallucinations, delusions, and/ or a formal thought disorder. Hypochondriacal symptoms and paranoid ideation are common, with religious and depressive themes occurring frequently. Hallucinations are usually auditory, but visual hallucinations become increasingly common. Delusions become increasingly elaborate and systematized. The symptoms picture become more like those of adult schizophrenics with increasing age of onset. Notably rare in childhood schizophrenia are the motor stereotypies and abnormal resistance to change that are characteristic of autistic children (Eggers, 1978; Kolvin, 1971b).

The mean IQ level of childhood schizophrenics generally falls in the range of one standard deviation below the population mean. Approximately 40% of childhood schizophrenics are reported to have IQs of less than 90 (Kolvin, 1971a). This, also, is in marked contrast to autism, in which 50% of the children have IQs of less than 50 and fall into the mentally deficient range of intellectual functioning.

The prognosis for childhood schizophrenics is more positive than that for autistic children. Good to complete recovery 15 years later was found in one study for half of a group of children who had developed schizophrenic symptoms between the ages of 7 and 13 years (Eggers, 1978). The best prognosticators of positive outcome were higher IQ, acute rather than chronic process, and good premorbid personality functioning. Family factors, including the presence or absence of a disturbed parent, and particular schizophrenic symptoms, were unrelated to the outcome.

A variety of treatment techniques for schizophrenia have been employed. Drug treatment can provide some relief for certain symptoms, such as insomnia and thought disorder, but it has not been found to have specific antipsychotic properties (Campbell, 1973). Behavior therapy, also, has been found useful in the management of specific schizophrenic behaviors. Milieu therapy, family therapy, residential child-centered therapy, and intensive long-term, individual psychoanalysis have all been employed in the treatment of schizophrenic children. While case studies suggest that all of these methods are potentially useful in the treatment of schizophrenia, well-controlled studies comparing the outcome with different methods are virtually nonexistent.

The current approach to treatment is combined drug treatment, psychotherapy, and educational intervention in the management and treatment of schizophrenic children. A highly structured educational program has been found to yield the greatest improvement in psychotic children when compared with programs with less structure (Bartak & Rutter, 1973; Rutter & Bartak, 1973; Schopler,

1974). Thus, in an educational setting, psychotic children are likely to fare best when provided with a predictable environment based on clearly defined rules and expectations.

REFERENCES

American Psychiatric Association (1980). *Diagnostic and statistical manual of mental disorders* (3rd ed.). Washington, DC: Author.

Bartak, L., & Rutter, M. (1973). Special educational treatment of autistic children: A comparative study. I. Design of study and characteristics of units. *Journal of Child Psychology & Psychiatrics, 14,* 161–179.

Campbell, M. (1973). Biological interventions in psychoses of childhood. *Journal of Autism & Childhood Schizophrenia, 3,* 347–373.

Dawson, G., & Mesibov, G. (1983). Childhood psychoses. In C. E. Walker & M. C. Roberts (Eds.), *Handbook of clinical child psychology.* New York: Wiley.

Eggers, C. (1978). Course and prognosis of childhood schizophrenia. *Journal of Autism & Childhood Schizophrenia, 8,* 21–36.

Kolvin, I. (1971a). Psychoses in childhood—A comparative study. In M. Rutter (Ed.), *Infantile autism: Concepts, characteristics, and treatment.* Edinburgh: Livingstone.

Kolvin, I. (1971b). Studies in childhood psychoses. I. Diagnostic criteria and classification. *British Journal of Psychiatry, 118,* 381–384.

Kolvin, I., Ounsted, C., Humphrey, M., & McNay, A. (1971). The phenomenology of childhood psychoses. *British Journal of Psychiatry, 118,* 385–395.

Kolvin, I., Ounsted, C., Richardson, I. M., & Garside, R. F. (1971). Studies in childhood psychoses. III. The family and social background in childhood psychoses. *British Journal of Psychiatry, 118,* 396–402.

Kolvin, I., Ounsted, C., & Roth, A. (1971). Studies in childhood psychoses. V. Cerebral dysfunction and childhood psychoses. *British Journal of Psychiatry, 118,* 407–414.

Rutter, M., & Bartak, L. (1973). Special educational treatment of autistic children: A comparative study. II. Follow-up findings and implications for services. *Journal of Child Psychology & Psychiatry, 14,* 241–270.

Schopler, E. (1974). Changes of direction with psychotic children. In A. Davids (Ed.), *Child personality and psychopathology: Current topics* (Vol. I). New York: Wiley.

Werry, J. S. (1979). The childhood psychoses. In H. C. Quay & J. S. Werry (Eds.), *Psychopathological disorders of childhood* (2nd ed.). New York: Wiley.

FAITH L. PHILLIPS
DIANE J. WILLIS
University of Oklahoma Health Sciences Center

CHILDHOOD PSYCHOSIS
CHILDHOOD SCHIZOPHRENIA
EMOTIONAL DISORDERS

SERVICE DELIVERY MODELS

Service delivery models are programs, processes, and safeguards established to ensure a free, appropriate public education for handicapped children and youths. The models that have been developed for the delivery of services to handicapped school-aged children generally reflect in their form and operation the influence of at least three factors: (1) the statutory requirements and congressional intent of PL 94-142, the Education for All Handicapped Children Act, the 1983 amendments of that act in PL 98-199, and the U.S. Office of Education regulations (1977) for the implementation of that act; (2) the nature of the particular state or local education agency providing the services in terms of physical size, population distribution, and, to some extent, the available fiscal and human resources; and (3) the specific needs of the children being served. PL 94-142 (1977) and PL 98-199 (1983) require that handicapped children to the degree possible be educated with nonhandicapped children and that removal from the regular education environment occur "only when the nature or severity of the handicap is such that education in regular classes with the use of supplementary aids and services cannot be achieved satisfactorily" (PL 98-199, Section 1412). The regulations for the Act elaborate on this condition and refer to a "continuum of alternate placements" (U.S. Office of Education, 1977, Section 121a.551) that must include instruction in regular classes with access to resource room services or itinerant instruction if necessary, special classes, special schools, home instruction, and instruction in hospitals and institutions. The regulations also require assurance that the "various alternative placements included under Section 121a.551 are available to the extent necessary to implement the individualized education program for each handicapped child" (Section 121a.552). The congressional intent clearly was to ensure the design of models for the delivery of services to meet the instructional needs of each handicapped child rather than to allow assignment of a handicapped child to whatever special education services happen to be available at the time, unless those services also happen to meet the needs of the particular child as detailed in that child's individual education plan (IEP).

The continuum of alternative placements as listed in the U.S. Department of Education regulations together with the language of PL 94-142 suggest the basic models for the delivery of special education and related services. Reynolds (1962) originally laid out a chart showing various organizational patterns for instruction. His work was later modified by Deno and illustrates a cascade of services for handicapped children (Reynolds & Birch, 1982). The placements as shown in Figure 1 can be classified according to the amount of direct intervention provided by someone other than the regular classroom teacher; the more direct services necessary, the more a child moves away from the first level placement, the regular classroom. As the triangular shape of the illustration might suggest,

more children with special needs should be found in regular classrooms with access to consultant or itinerant support or resource room assistance and fewer in the special classes, special schools, residential schools, or placements outside the school setting.

Public Law 94-142 and its regulations intend for regular class placement to be the goal for handicapped students. There will always be some students whose educational needs cannot be met in the regular class, however, without some adaptations, special equipment and/or materials, or extra help (Cartwright, Cartwright, & Ward, 1985). Because the regular class teacher may not be adequately trained to make those adaptations, secure the special equipment or materials, or provide the specialized instruction, full-time regular class placement for some children may be enhanced by the provision of consulting teachers who collaborate with regular class teachers. One of the earliest models for a teacher consultant program was developed by the University of Vermont and the Vermont State Department of Education (Fox et al., 1973). The teacher consultant works directly with the classroom teacher (rather than with students) to determine what instructional strategies and/or materials and other adaptations or adjustments might improve learning, bring inappropriate behavior under control, or create an atmosphere conductive to cooperative learning for all the children in the class. The skills required for the teacher consultant include problem solving, communication, public relations, and collaboration (Haight, 1984; Salend, 1984), in addition to a recognition of and respect for the knowledge and skills the regular classroom teacher already has acquired and brings to the consultation.

Some children, for example, those with sensory impairments, may thrive in the regular classroom if their special needs are met with the help of supportive services from itinerant teachers who can work directly with the handicapped students as well as provide consultation and assistance for the classroom teachers. While the children may be taken out of the regular class for periods of specialized instruction, for example orientation and mobility, typing, signing, language development, listening skills, or Optacon, the primary responsibility for instruction remains with the regular class teacher.

A resource room program can enable some children who need more intensive instruction in some or all of the basic skills, or whose behavior at times goes beyond what is appropriate or tolerable in the regular class, to remain in the regular class except for limited periods of time each day or week. The resource room model has been particularly popular for learning-disabled students, although students with other handicapping conditions also profit from additional help provided by resource room teachers. Some resource room programs are organized by disability area while others, particularly in more recent years, accommodate children with a variety of handicapping conditions but whose instructional needs are similar.

Placement in a special class for all or part of the school

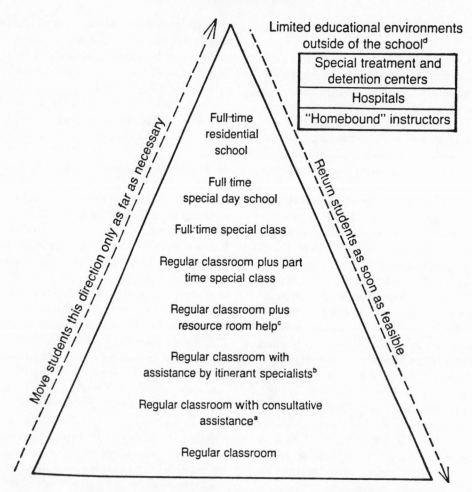

Figure 1. The original special education cascade. *Source*: Reynolds, M. C. and Birch, J. W. (1982). *Teaching exceptional children in all America's schools*. Reston, VA: Council for Exceptional Children, 39.

[a]Consultative assistance might be offered, for example, by school psychologists, consulting teachers, resource room teachers, supervisors or others. The term *consultative* denotes only *indirect* services and no *direct* service or instruction to the child by the consultant.

[b]Itinerant specialists commonly include speech and hearing therapists and mobility instructors for the blind, for example. They offer some *direct* instruction to the students involved.

[c]A resource classroom is a special station in a school building that is manned by a resource teacher who usually offers some direct instruction to selected students but also usually offers consulting services to regular teachers. Sometimes resource teachers are categorical (such as resource teacher for the blind) but increasingly resource teachers are employed for a more generic, noncategorical role.

[d]This special set of environments is included here in set-aside fashion because usually students are placed in these settings for reasons other than educational. For example, they go to detention centers on court orders for reason of conviction for some criminal offense; or they go to hospitals or are held at home because of health problems. Special educators often work in these *limited* environments and some degree of specialization in education is required. But, in the main, there is strong preference, from an educational point of view, for return of the students to regular school environments as soon as feasible.

day is considered necessary for some children. Frequently, the deciding factors for resource room, part-time special class, or full-time special class placement are the amount of time the handicapped child can benefit from time in the regular class and the severity of the needs of that child. Interestingly, there seems to be considerable overlap in the types of students, the amount of time spent in the regular class, and the ways teachers actually use their time in resource room classes, self-contained special classes, and even residential classes, at least for emotionally disabled students (Peterson, Zabel, Smith, & White, 1983). This suggests some inconsistencies in determining appropriate placement for children and in defining responsibilities for special and regular education personnel.

Some handicapped children are placed in special schools for their daily instructional programs. Such children, by the nature of their placement, have limited access to participation in social, academic, extracurricular, or spontaneous activities with nonhandicapped children. These children are, therefore, to be placed in special schools and residential settings only when the severity of their conditions warrants such placement and only for so long as that placement is necessary. The same holds true for those students in settings such as hospitals, treatment centers, and detention facilities that are outside the educational system.

The overriding principle in selecting appropriate placement for a handicapped child who needs special education and related services is that of the least restrictive environment. No one placement or service delivery system described here can be cited as the best for all handicapped children, and that includes the regular classroom. Rather, selection must be made on the basis of what setting permits the implementation of the IEP designed for a given child and allows for meaningful involvement with nonhandicapped children, if possible in the same community

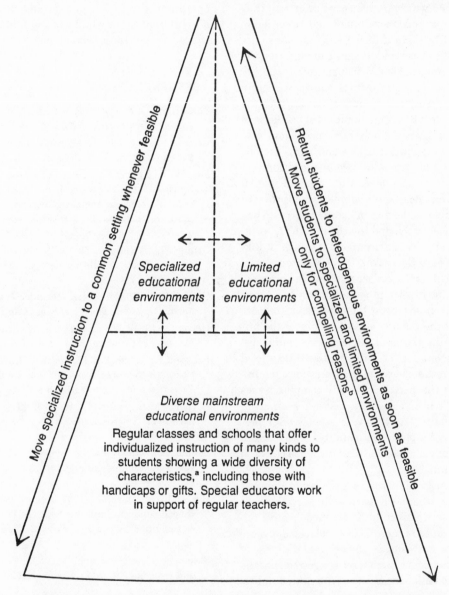

[a]It is assumed that no educational "place" is impervious to change and development and that through good efforts many of the varieties of specialized and intensive forms of education can be moved into a developing mainstream.

[b]Here, as in the case of the original cascade, it is assumed that students should be removed from the mainstream only for limited periods and compelling reasons; that their progress should be monitored carefully and regularly; and that they should be returned to the mainstream as soon as feasible. All students start their schooling in the mainstream and have a *place* there at all times, even though they may be located in a special setting for some period of time.

Figure 2. The instructional cascade. *Source*: Reynolds, M. C., and Birch, J. W. (1982). *Teaching exceptional children in all America's schools*. Reston, VA: Council for Exceptional Children, 47.

where the handicapped child would attend school if there were no handicapping condition necessitating a special education program.

While the service delivery models described represent the typical programs available for handicapped children, or those that should be available by law and regulation, the specific character of any particular program will be determined in part by the nature of the geography, size, population distribution, and resources available in the child's district of residence. Rural areas have special challenges to face, among which are transportation, length of time en route to programs, recruitment and retention of qualified personnel to serve children with low-incidence handicaps, smaller tax base, and in some communities, the power of tradition (Helge, 1984). Urban areas face another set of challenges that typically include transportation in densely populated areas, desegregation issues, and the problems that develop when large numbers of people with little in common must interact under crowded conditions.

In addition to these special urban and rural factors, there is the impact that access to special education programs in private schools can have. The laws and regulations are clear that handicapped children must be provided appropriate free public education in approved private day and residential schools only, and in accord with the principle of the least restrictive environment (Grumet & Inkpen, 1982; U.S. Office of Education, 1977). If parents wish their handicapped child to attend a private school program and place their child in that program themselves, then except for special circumstances, the parents are responsible for the cost of their child's education. But if the private day or residential school placement is recommended as the appropriate one for the child by the child's local school district, then the education program must be provided at no cost to the parents. Already complex issues regarding private school placement become even more complicated when out-of-state private schools offer programs considered appropriate for children with certain types of needs as, for example, multihandicapped children or deaf-blind children.

In summary, the cascade of service delivery models emphasizes the place where children with special needs might be assigned for instruction. These models have collected criticism because of their focus on placement more than program content. Reynolds, the original designer of the placement cascade, and Birch have suggested that the next step be an instructional cascade as illustrated in Figure 2. Inherent in the instructional cascade is the goal of equipping the regular classroom to be a learning environment where the diverse needs of many children, including handicapped, gifted, and handicapped gifted learners, can be accommodated (Reynolds & Birch, 1982).

Service delivery models in the context of special education have changed over the years as laws, court decisions, local needs, parental pressures, fiscal and human resources, and community concerns have made their influence felt. Ysseldyke and Algozzine (1982) have suggested that change will continue but primarily in response to economic needs. More recently, Crowner (1985) has presented a taxonomy of special education finance and an analysis of funding bases, formulas and types and sources of funds for special education. The balance between congressional intent and legal necessity, local control, fiscal reality, and administrative expediency is delicate at best. For the benefit of all children currently in school and those to come, efforts must continue to be directed at designing and operating service delivery systems that meet the needs of all children, those who have conditions requiring special education and those who do not.

REFERENCES

Cartwright, G. P., Cartwright, C. A., & Ward, M. E. (1985). *Educating special learners* (2nd ed.). Belmont, CA: Wadsworth.

Crowner, T. T. (1985). A taxonomy of special education finance. *Exceptional Children, 51*(6), 503–508.

Fox, W. L., Egner, A. N., Paolucci, P. E., Perelman, P. F., McKenzie, H. S., & Garvin, J. S. (1973). An introduction to a regular classroom approach to special education. In E. Deno (Ed.), *Instructional alternatives for exceptional children.* Reston, VA: Council for Exceptional Children.

Grumet, L., & Inkpen, T. (1982). The education of children in private schools: A state agency's perspective. *Exceptional Children, 49*(3), 200–206.

Haight, S. L. (1984). Special education teacher consultant: Idealism versus realism. *Exceptional Children, 50*(6), 507–515.

Helge, D. (1984). The state of the art of rural special education. *Exceptional Children, 50*(4), 294–305.

Peterson, R. L., Zabel, R. H., Smith, C. R., & White, M. A. (1983). Cascade of services model and emotionally disabled students. *Exceptional Children, 49*(5), 404–408.

Reynolds, M. C., & Birch, J. W. (1982). *Teaching exceptional children in all America's schools.* Reston, VA: Council for Exceptional Children.

Salund, S. J. (1984). Factors contributing to the development of successful mainstreaming programs. *Exceptional Children, 50*(5), 409–416.

U.S. Office of Education (1977, August 23). Education of handicapped children: Implementation of Part B of the Education of the Handicapped Act. *Federal Register, 42*(163), 42474–42518.

Ysseldyke, J., & Algozzine, B. (1982). *Critical issues in special and remedial education.* Boston: Houghton Mifflin.

MARJORIE E. WARD
Ohio State University

CASCADE MODEL OF SPECIAL EDUCATION
EDUCATION FOR ALL HANDICAPPED CHILDREN ACT OF 1975
LEAST RESTRICTIVE ENVIRONMENT
RESOURCE ROOM
SELF-CONTAINED CLASSROOM

SEVERE DISCREPANCY ANALYSIS (SDA)

Severe Discrepancy Analysis (SDA) is a computer program developed by Reynolds and Stowe (1985) to assist in the diagnosis of learning disabilities. The program provides an analysis of the severe discrepancy component of the federal definition of learning disabilities, which is also one of the most prevalent of the five major components of definitions of learning disabilities nationwide. The program also strongly recommends that all remaining aspects of the definition be assessed prior to arriving at a diagnosis of learning disabilities.

The program performs the two fundamental analyses recommended in the Federal Work Group Report on Critical Measurement Issues in Learning Disabilities (Reynolds, 1984): it assesses (1) the statistical significance of the difference between the child's score on an aptitude measure and an achievement measure and (2) the relative frequency of occurrence of the difference between the child's current achievement level and the average achievement level of all other children at the same IQ level. These two analyses and the principles underlying them are explained in detail in Reynolds (1984, 1985).

The SDA is available for use on the Apple II series, the Commodore 64, and IBM and IBM-compatible computers. It requires a disk drive and needs approximately 2 minutes per case to perform the various analyses. It will allow the adjustment of cutoff scores but defaults to the values recommended in the Federal Work Group Report. The program is designed for use with all major tests of achievement and aptitude that provide standard scores. Any future tests may be easily accommodated and can be entered by the user if standard scores are available. Grade equivalents and related types of scores cannot be used (Reynolds, 1981).

REFERENCES

Reynolds, C. R. (1981). The fallacy of "two years below grade level for age" as a diagnostic criterion for reading disorders. *Journal of School Psychology, 19*, 350–358.

Reynolds, C. R. (1984). Critical measurement issues in learning disabilities. *Journal of Special Education, 18*, 451–476.

Reynolds, C. R. (1985). Measuring the aptitude-achievement discrepancy in learning disability diagnosis. *Remedial & Special Education, 6*, 37–55.

Reynolds, C. R., & Stowe, M. (1985). *Severe discrepancy analysis.* Philadelphia: TRAIN.

CECIL R. REYNOLDS
Texas A&M University

GRADE EQUIVALENTS
LEARNING DISABILITIES, PROBLEMS IN DEFINITION OF
LEARNING DISABILITIES, SEVERE DISCREPANCY
   ANALYSIS IN

SEX DIFFERENCES IN LEARNING ABILITIES

Popular stereotypes and epidemiological research both suggest that boys have more learning and adjustment problems than girls. Boys are more readily referred for psychological services than girls with similar problems (Caplan, 1977). In addition, boys of all ages are more likely than girls to be evaluated or treated for learning problems (Eme, 1979). The reasons for apparent gender differences are widely debated. Some suggest that (1) boys are at some biological or developmental disadvantage that affects learning and adjustment (Ullian, 1981); (2) classrooms, teachers, or professionals are less tolerant of boys than girls (Pleck, 1981); and (3) the problems manifested by girls are perceived differently or considered to be less important. This debate leads one to question whether recognizable gender differences exist in children's learning abilities.

Many persons believe the cognitive abilities of boys and girls differ. The common notion is that boys have better developed quantitative abilities while girls are better in verbal areas. After reviewing literature on psychological gender differences, Maccoby and Jacklin (1974) conclude that three cognitive gender differences are well established: girls have greater verbal ability than boys, while boys have better visual-spatial and mathematical ability than girls. The authors further conclude that gender differences in verbal ability emerge after age 11, gender differences in quantitative (i.e., mathematical) abilities emerge at around 12, and gender differences in spatial ability emerge in adolescence.

Other investigations report gender differences in verbal and spatial abilities at earlier ages than those reported by Maccoby and Jacklin. A number of researchers have found that females as early as age 1 month and throughout the preschool years show some slight verbal advancement over males, an advancement that appears stronger and more reliable after age 10 or 11 (McGuinness & Pribram, 1979; Oetzel, 1966; Petersen & Wittig, 1979). While sex differences are seen more clearly during and after adolescence, male superiority in spatial performance may appear as early as age 6 (Harris, 1978; McGuinness & Pribram, 1979). The magnitude of differences between males and females depends in part on the type of spatial skill. Maccoby and Jacklin (1974) distinguish visual nonanalytic spatial skills (i.e., those solved without the use of verbal mediation) from visual analytic spatial skills (i.e., those solvable with verbal mediation). Postpubescent males score consistently higher than females on most spatial abilities, particularly nonanalytic visualization abilities (Maccoby & Jacklin, 1974; Petersen & Wittig, 1979).

Generalizations regarding gender differences in verbal, spatial, and quantitative areas do not go unchallenged. After reviewing the evidence on cognitive gender differences used by Maccoby and Jacklin, Sherman (1978) reported the magnitude of the gender differences to be very small. Hyde (1981) also concludes from a meta-analysis of the data used by Maccoby and Jacklin that the gender differences in verbal ability, quantitative ability, visual-spatial ability, and field articulation are small. Sex differences appear to account for no more than 5% of the population variance. In general, gender differences in verbal ability are smaller and gender differences in spatial ability are larger. Hyde questions whether statistically significant sex differences in cognitive abilities are practically significant. In other words, the common notion that girls are better at verbal tasks while boys excel in spatial or mathematical areas largely is meaningless in terms of educational implications. Moreover, a close review of literature examining gender differences is likely to lead readers to conclude that boys and girls exhibit similarities more frequently than differences.

Do sex differences exist in school achievement? The evidence is contradictory. Few gender differences in learning were found in a five-year longitudinal study of students ages 5 through 9 (Anastas & Reinherz, 1984). However, a review of the cross-national data on gender differences in achievement found that boys' mathematics achievement is higher than that of girls at both the elementary and secondary levels, that boys score higher in all areas of science, and that girls have higher achievement in verbal areas involving reading comprehension and literature (Fennema, 1982).

Assuming achievement is affected by opportunities to learn (e.g., participation in courses, amount of instruction), and that boys generally have more opportunities to learn mathematics and science than girls (Finn, Dulberg, & Reis, 1979), we may conclude that girls perform lower in math and science because of fewer opportunities in these areas rather than intrinsic factors. While research infrequently has considered the extent to which differences in socialization and educational experiences may account for differential performance and attainment, many social scientists believe most or even all sex differences in ability and achievement are due to differing cultural and social opportunities and expectations for boys and girls (Levine & Ornstein, 1983). Still, we know little about the origins of sex differences. When gender differences appear, we should be cautious in speculating about their etiologies.

REFERENCES

Anastas, J. W., & Reinherz, H. (1984). Gender differences in learning and adjustment problems in school: Results of a longitudinal study. *American Journal of Orthopsychiatry, 54,* 110–122.

Caplan, P. (1977). Sex, age, behavior and school subject as determinants of report of learning problems. *Journal of Learning Disabilities, 10,* 314–316.

Eme, R. (1979). Sex differences in childhood psychopathology: A review. *Psychological Bulletin, 86,* 574–593.

Fennema, E. (1982, March). *Overview of sex-related differences in mathematics.* Paper presented at the annual meeting of the American Educational Research Association. New York.

Finn, J. D., Dulberg, L., & Reis, J. (1979). Sex differences in educational attainment: A cross-national perspective. *Harvard Educational Review, 49,* 477–503.

Harris, L. J. (1978). Sex differences in spatial ability: Possible environmental, genetic, and neurological factors. In M. Kinsbourne (Ed.), *Asymmetrical function of the brain.* London: Cambridge University Press.

Hyde, J. S. (1981). How large are cognitive gender differences? A meta-analysis using w^2 and d. *American Psychologist, 36,* 892–901.

Levine, D. U., & Ornstein, A. C. (1983). Sex differences in ability and achievement. *Journal of Research & Development in Education, 16,* 66–72.

Maccoby, E. E., & Jacklin, C. N. (1974). *Psychology of sex differences.* Stanford, CA: Stanford University Press.

McGuinness, D., & Pribram, K. H. (1979). The origins of sensory bias in the development of gender differences in perception and cognition. In M. Bortner (Ed.), *Cognitive growth and development.* New York: Brunner/Mazel.

Oetzel, R. (1966). Classified summary of research on sex differences. In E. E. Maccoby (Ed.), *The development of sex differences.* Stanford, CA: Stanford University Press.

Petersen, A. C., & Wittig, M. A. (1979). Sex differences in cognitive functioning: An overview. In M. A. Wittig & A. C. Petersen (Eds.), *Sex-related differences in cognitive functioning: Developmental issues.* New York: Academic.

Pleck, J. (1981). *The myth of masculinity.* Cambridge, MA: MIT Press.

Sherman, J. (1978). *Sex-related cognitive differences: An essay on theory and evidence.* Springfield, IL: Thomas.

Ullian, D. (1981). Why boys will be boys: A structural perspective. *American Journal of Orthopsychiatry, 51,* 493–501.

THOMAS OAKLAND
JEFF LAURENT
University of Texas, Austin

HEMISPHERIC ASYMMETRY, SEX DIFFERENCES IN

SEX EDUCATION OF THE HANDICAPPED

Many professionals and parents believe the sexual needs of the handicapped should be met (Craft & Craft, 1981; Fitz-Gerald & Fitz-Gerald, 1979; Love, 1983). The principle of normalization promoted in the United Nations Declaration of Rights of the Mentally Handicapped (United Nations, 1971) underscores this belief. The declaration states that handicapped people have the same basic rights as other citizens of the same country and the same age. In the United States, normalization is espoused in the Rehabilitation Act of 1973 (PL 93-380) and the Education of All Handicapped Children Act of 1975 (PL 94-142), which provide for the individualized education of the handicapped in accordance with the requirement of the least restrictive environment.

The advocacy of mainstreaming in school and the movement away from custodial institutional care and toward community living supply the impetus for focusing on the sexual rights of the handicapped (Bass, 1974; Jacobs, 1978; Shindell, 1975; Thornton, 1979). In conjunction with the philosophy of protecting basic human rights, sex education is advocated to achieve the same ends for the handicapped as for the nonhandicapped: to develop sexually fulfilled persons who understand themselves, their values, and resulting behaviors (Harris, 1974; Reich & Harshman, 1971). Moreover, many persons agree with Kempton (1977) that sex education is bound to the practical tasks of improving the social and sexual functions of the handicapped. The need to moderate educational goals on the bases of age, gender, type of handicap and severity of handicap is inherent in the nature of sex education of the handicapped.

Alongside the demands for individualization of instruction is a humanistic approach that advocates meeting the needs of persons while deemphasizing labels (Johnson, 1981). In contradiction to the rationale given in the past, this outlook maintains that sex education should not only respond to critical sexual problems as they arise, or to conditioning that seeks to prevent all sexual experiences (Craft & Craft, 1978, 1980; Edmonson & Wish, 1975; Gordon, 1971a, 1971b; Kempton, 1977, 1978). Implied in the normalization philosophy is the goal of working for the good of all by securing individual freedom since, with teaching, training, and the availability of specific support services, the handicapped are more likely to blend into society.

Notwithstanding the fact that the philosophy of normalization has impacted the literature, the topic of sex education for the handicapped is fraught with controversy. Issues and concerns presently being raised include improvement of curricula and resources, training and preparation of teachers, assessment of the effects of teaching, and involvement of the parents in sex education.

Great strides have been made in the individualization of sex education (Johnson & Kempton, 1981). A wealth of curriculum guides exists that identifies programs to meet the varied needs of the handicapped (see Edmonson, 1980, for a 30-reference list of programs and materials available for the blind, deaf, retarded, and emotionally impaired). Adapted sex education enables even the severely retarded to improve their sexual knowledge (Edmonson, 1980). However, outdated sex laws and repressive social attitudes often prevent the optimal development and employment of instructional resources (Sherwin, 1981). Teaching materials aimed at compensating for specific handicaps (e.g., genital models for use with the blind) can run afoul of obscenity laws. Also, few legal principles protect sex

educators, counselors, or therapists (Sherwin, 1981). Audiotactual sex education programs for blind children have been implemented successfully with the use of models, but touching the human body is seen as problematic (Knappett & Wagner, 1976; Tait & Kessler, 1976). Sex education programs for blind children should take into account the sexual taboos of our culture (Torbett, 1974). Fortunately, according to Johnson (1981), this negativism is lifting somewhat as judged by a shift from a position of elimination regarding the acceptance of the sexuality of the handicapped to a position of toleration. The recent evolution toward a more permissive attitude regarding sexual expression for recreational rather than procreational purposes has been conducive to this change. Still, sodomy laws in many states condemn all sexual activity as illegal except vaginal intercourse within marriage. These laws deny nonprocreative sex as a legitimate right. For a given handicapped person, this form of sexual expression may be the only one possible. In light of such social taboos and legal restraints, the development of appropriate programming to suit the individual needs of the handicapped is constrained.

Minimal attention is paid to sex education during the preparation of teachers for the handicapped. A recent survey indicated that, while 61% of student teachers in special education courses received some preparation in sex education, this preparation was either an elective option or a few hours of coverage subsumed under a different topic such as methods of teaching (May, 1980). This is regrettable since sex education courses in special education could help teachers overcome their discomfort in dealing with this subject (Blom, 1971). Professionals can increase their comfort with sexual matters as well as improve attitude and knowledge levels as a result of systematic training in sexuality and disability (Chubon, 1981). Kempton (1978) has proposed training professionals to provide services, as well as develop policies, regarding the sexual rights of the handicapped. She advises (1977) that successful programs be broadly conceived to prepare for skills for living in society.

A major obstacle to sex education of the handicapped has been the denial of their sexuality by parents and teachers, who are concerned that education could trigger sexual experimentation and appetite (Craft, 1983). However, experts in this field (Gordon, 1975; Kempton, 1978) have argued that sex education results in improved social behavior, increased self-respect, more openness, and fewer guilt feelings. On the other hand, withholding information fails to deter sexual activity, causes confusion, needless fears, inappropriate behaviors, and unwanted consequences such as pregnancy.

In spite of this authoritative stance, advocates for sex education have provided little evidence that sex education has changed sexual behavior patterns or identified the valid expectations and limitations of their procedures (Balester, 1971). The literature that examines specific sex education programs for the handicapped mainly presents theorizations rather than scientific data (Vockell & Mattick, 1972). Teaching the handicapped is a complex task owing to such factors as low cognitive abilities and academic skill, short attention span, and secondary handicaps of a sensory, physical, emotional, or behavioral nature. Therefore, restraints in setting educational goals have been recommended (Watson & Rogers, 1980). However, programs that facilitate specific abilities (e.g., contraceptive use or knowledge of sexually transmitted diseases) seem to represent too modest a first step toward devising an educational technology of sexual instruction that will empirically appraise the limits of sexual development and social awareness in this diverse population.

While many parents are interested in sex education for their handicapped youngsters, their sexual conservatism may severely limit the nature of the curriculum. For example, parents of sensorially impaired students give the highest rating to teaching less controversial topics such as cleanliness, knowledge of one's own body, venereal disease, dating, reproduction, pregnancy, marriage, and feelings about self and others. They frequently resist instruction regarding contraceptives, sexual intercourse, sexual deviancy, incest, divorce, masturbation, abortion, sterilization, and pornography (Love, 1983). Parental cooperation and support are crucial to program development and to the transfer of skills from school to home and community settings. Thus it remains essential to involve the parents in cooperative educational efforts by securing their agreement with expectations of instruction (Hamre-Nietupski & Ford, 1981; Kempton, 1975).

Normalization frequently entails the sexual development of the handicapped to enable them to assume more normal lives. While there has been progress in designing and offering sex education programs for the handicapped, several areas of concern have hampered their acceptance. These include (1) constraints imposed on the design and implementation of curricula owing to legal and social restraints that pertain to sexual taboos; (2) neglect by teacher training institutes in the preparation of professionals in special education who are trained in sex education; (3) problems in assessing the effects of teaching because of the nature of affective instructional goals interacting with a diversity of abilities in this population; and (4) conservatism on the part of parents that tends to place limitations on expectations of instruction. These problems hinder but do not preclude change. Models for the successful institutionalization of sex education for the handicapped exist elsewhere, as in Sweden (Grunewald & Linner, 1979). Public policy regarding sex education for the handicapped is desirable given the obvious needs in this area (Craft, 1983). The handicapped should understand their sexuality, should be safe from sexual exploitation, and should become responsible in their sexual behavior (Craft, 1983).

REFERENCES

Balester, R. J. (1971). Sex education: Fact and fancy. *Journal of Special Education, 5,* 355–357.

Bass, M. S. (1974). Sex education for the handicapped. *Family Coordinator, 23,* 27–33.

Blom, G. E. (1971). Some considerations about the neglect of sex education in special education. *Journal of Special Education, 5,* 359–361.

Chubon, R. A. (1981). Development and evaluation of a sexuality and disability course for the helping professions. *Sexuality & Disability, 4,* 3–14.

Craft, A. (1983). Sexuality and mental retardation: A review of the literature. In A. Craft & M. Craft (Eds.), *Sex education and counseling for mentally handicapped people.* Baltimore, MD: University Park Press.

Craft, A., & Craft, M. (1980). Sexuality and the mentally handicapped. In G. B. Simon (Ed.), *Modern management of mental handicap: A manual of practice.* Lancaster England MTP Press.

Craft, A., & Craft, M. (1981). Sexuality and mental handicap: A review. *British Journal of Psychiatry, 139,* 494–505.

Craft, M., & Craft, A. (1978). *Sex and the mentally handicapped* London: Routledge & Kegan Paul.

Edmonson, B. (1980). Sociosexual education for the handicapped. *Exceptional Education Quarterly, 1,* 67–76.

Edmonson, B., & Wish, J. (1975). Sex knowledge and attitudes of moderately retarded males. *American Journal of Mental Deficiency, 80,* 172–179.

Fitz-Gerald, D., & Fitz-Gerald, M. (1979). Sexual implications deaf-blindness. *Sexuality & Disability, 2,* 212–215.

Gordon, S. (1971a). Missing in special education. Sex. *Journal of Special Education, 5,* 351–354.

Gordon, S. (1971b). Okay, let's tell it like it is (instead of just making it look good). *Journal of Special Education, 5,* 379–381.

Gordon, S. (1975). Workshop: Sex education for the handicapped. In M. S. Bass & M. Gelof (Eds.), *Sexual rights and responsibilities of the mentally retarded.* Proceedings of the Conference of the American Association on Mental Deficiency, Washington, DC: AAMD.

Grunewald, K., & Linner, B. (1979). Mentally retarded: Sexuality and normalization. *Current Sweden, 237–239.*

Hamre-Nietupski, S., & Ford, A. (1981). Sex education and related skills: A series of programs implemented with severely handicapped students. *Sexuality & Disability, 4,* 179–193.

Harris, A. (1974). What does "sex education" mean? In R. Rogers (Ed.), *Sex education: Rationale and reaction.* Cambridge, England: Cambridge University Press.

Jacobs, J. H. (1978). The mentally retarded and their need for sexuality education. *Psychiatric Opinion, 15,* 32–34.

Johnson, W. R. (1981). Sex education for special populations. In L. Brown (Ed.), *Sex education in the eighties.* New York: Plenum.

Johnson, W. R., & Kempton, W. (1981). *Sex education and counseling of special groups.* Springfield, IL: Thomas.

Kempton, W. (1975). Sex education: A cooperative effort of parent and teacher. *Exceptional Children, 41,* 531–535.

Kempton, W. (1977). The mentally retarded person. In H. Gochros & J. Gochros (Eds.), *The sexually oppressed.* New York: Association.

Kempton, W. (1978). The rights of the mentally ill and mentally retarded: Are sexual rights included? *Devereux Forum, 13,* 45–49.

Knappett, K., & Wagner, N. N. (1976). Sex education and the blind. *Education of the Visually Handicapped, 8,* 1–5.

Love, E. (1983). Parental and staff attitudes toward instruction in human sexuality for sensorially impaired students at the Alabama Institute for Deaf and Blind. *American Annals of the Deaf, 128,* 45–47.

May, D. C. (1980). Survey of sex education coursework in special education programs. *Journal of Special Education, 14,* 107–112.

Reich, M., & Harshman, H. (1971). Sex education for the handicapped youngsters, reality or repression? *Journal of Special Education, 5,* 373–377.

Sherwin, R. (1981). Sex and the law on a collision course. In W. R. Johnson (Ed.), *Sex in life.* Dubuque, IA: Brown.

Shindell, P. E. (1975). Sex education programs and the mentally retarded. *Journal of School Health, 45,* 88–90.

Tait, P. E., & Kessler, C. (1976). The way we get babies: A tactual sex education program. *New Outlook for the Blind, 70,* 116–120.

Thornton, C. E. (1979). A nurse-educator in sex and disability. *Sexuality & Disability, 2,* 28–32.

Torbett, D. S. (1974). A humanistic and futuristic approach to sex education for blind children. *New Outlook for the Blind, 68,* 210–215.

United Nations. (1971). *Declaration of general and special rights of the mentally handicapped.* New York: UN Department of Social Affairs.

Vockell, E. L., & Mattick, P. (1972). Sex education for the mentally retarded: An analysis of problems, programs, and research. *Education & Training of the Mentally Retarded, 7,* 129–134.

Watson, G., & Rogers, R. S. (1980). Sexual instruction for the mildly retarded and normal adolescent: A comparison of educational approaches, parental expectations and pupil knowledge and attitude. *Health Education Journal, 39,* 88–95.

JACQUELINE CUNNINGHAM
THOMAS OAKLAND
University of Texas

SEX DISTURBANCES IN THE HANDICAPPED
SOCIAL BEHAVIOR OF THE HANDICAPPED
SOCIAL DEVELOPMENT
SOCIAL ISOLATION
SOCIAL SKILLS TRAINING

SEX INFORMATION AND EDUCATION COUNCIL OF THE UNITED STATES (SIECUS)

The Sex Information and Education Council of the United States (SIECUS) is a nonprofit, voluntary health organization dedicated to the establishment and exchange of information about human sexual behavior. The council is funded primarily by foundation grants and individual contributions. The SIECUS provides information and responds to requests for consultation from churches, communities, school boards, and any other national or international health or educational organizations interested in establishing or improving their sex education programs. As a part of this concern, SIECUS developed a policy and resource guide concerning sex education for the mentally retarded individual (SIECUS, 1971).

The guide begins by observing that the mentally retarded individual has sexual feelings similar to those of all humans, but that because of possible confusion and misunderstanding, the mentally retarded student may need sexual guidance and education to understand sex and his or her own sexuality. The SIECUS provides instructional, curricular, and counseling information in the guide that will be useful in helping the mentally retarded individual to achieve this understanding. Finally, information is provided regarding printed materials, films and filmstrips, tapes, and other teaching aids that may be useful in sex education for the mentally retarded individual.

REFERENCE

SIECUS. (1971). *A resource guide in sex education for the mentally retarded.* New York: Author.

JOHN R. BEATTIE
University of North Carolina, Charlotte

SEX RATIOS IN SPECIAL EDUCATION

As concern grows about sexual bias in society and its effect on children, attention is focusing on the classroom. Sex bias in education is of particular concern to the field of special education. Research indicates that more males than females are served in special education programs, and that the sex label has been recognized as having a profound impact on the education of handicapped children. Gillespie and Fink (1974) report that the mere identification of exceptional children as either male or female results in arbitrary practice and discriminatory judgments, and in intervention decisions that limit opportunities for personal and vocational development of those children and youths.

There is a belief among educators that boys are more

in need of special services than girls; consequently, more male students are provided with special education services. Boys are much more likely to be referred and treated in all the major areas of exceptionality; they are more likely to be identified as exhibiting reading problems, learning disabilities, and mental retardation (Gillespie & Fink, 1974). However, female students are shown to be more in need of special education assistance on the basis of standardized test data (Sadker, Sadker, & Thomas, 1981).

Caplan (1977) suggests that girls with learning disabilities are less likely than learning-disabled boys to be identified as learning disabled or to participate in special education programs. It is generally accepted among special educators that the male to female ratio in special education is about 3:1. Norman and Zigmond (1980) confirm that learning disabilities usually are identified as a male disorder; they find a ratio of 3.7:1. The authors report that the ratio is similar to the 3:1 ratio suggested by Kirk and Elkins (1975) and the 4.6:1 ratio reported by Lerner (1976).

Rubin and Balow (1971), in a longitudinal study of 967 kindergarten through third grade students, discovered that educationally defined behavior problems were exhibited by 41% of the children participating in their study. When results were reported by sex, the number of boys far exceeded the number of girls; boys were reported to have more attitude and behavior problems, to be receiving more special services, and to be repeating more grades. The authors suggested that teachers accept only a narrow range of behaviors, and that deviations outside this range are viewed as cause for intervention.

Further evidence for the disproportionate number of males in special education comes from a study reported in Young, Algozzine, and Schmid. McCarthy and Paraskevopoulos (1969) examined behavior patterns of average, emotionally disturbed, and learning-disabled children, and found that boys outnumbered girls 8:1 in the emotionally disturbed sample and 9:1 in the learning-disabled sample.

Mirkin, Marston, and Deno (1982) investigated the referral-placement process and discovered that males were referred far in excess of females; however, this was true only for teacher judgment referrals. For referrals based on academic screening using curriculum-based tasks, no significant differences were found in the number of males versus females referred for special education. Furthermore, females who had been referred by teachers were rated as more problematic than the females referred by the screening tests.

A variety of theories have been proposed to account for the sex ratio discrepancy in special education. Caplan (1977) suggested that the boy/girl learning problem report ratio is aggravated by behavioral differences. Caplan and Kinsbourne (1974) discovered that girls who fail in school tend to behave in socially acceptable ways, but their male counterparts tend to react punitively and aggressively. On the basis of this discovery, the authors suggested that because teachers view aggression as the most disturbing type of behavior, they would be more likely to notice boys who are failing in school than their well-behaved, silent female counterparts. Consequently, boys would be more likely to be recognized as needing special attention, if only to get them out of the classroom.

Further support for the claim of behavioral differences as the cause of the unbalanced sex ratio in special education can be found in a 1979 study by Schlosser and Algozzine, who attempted to determine whether behaviors more characteristic of boys are viewed by teachers as more disturbing than behaviors associated with girls. They found significant differences between the "disturbingness" of male-associated behaviors and those more typical of girls. The authors suggested that if boys exhibit more of the behaviors that are bothersome to teachers, the likelihood is greater that their behavior will be perceived as more disturbing and of greater concern than that of girls.

It also has been suggested that this ratio may be further aggravated by a societal bias that boys' academic achievement is more important than that of girls (Caplan, 1977). Physiological explanations for the higher incidence of males in special education also have been offered; several categories of exceptionality such as that of learning disabilities have been explained on the basis of sex-linked genetic traits (Rossi, 1972). However, according to Singer and Osborn (1970), there are no known physiological causes to explain the higher number of males treated for mental retardation. Singer and Osborn explain the high ratio of males to females receiving treatment as stemming from sociocultural expectations such as behavior differences and less societal tolerance for boys with academic problems.

Whatever the cause of the unbalanced ratio of males to females in special education, it is apparent that a bias exists. Special educators must recognize this discrepancy, establish its causes, and make the delivery of special education services more equitable.

REFERENCES

Caplan, P. J. (1977). Sex, age, behavior and school subject as determinants of report of learning problems. *Journal of Learning Disabilities, 5,* 314–316.

Caplan, P. J., & Kinsbourne, M. (1974). Sex differences in response to school failure. *Journal of Learning Disabilities, 4,* 232–235.

Gillespie, P. H., & Fink, A. H. (1974). The influence of sexism on the education of handicapped children. *Exceptional Children, 41,* 155–161.

Mirkin, P., Marston, D., & Deno, S. L. (1982). *Direct and repeated measurement of academic skills: An alternative to traditional screening, referral, and identification of learning disabled students* (Research Report No. 75). Minneapolis: University of Minnesota, Institute for Research on Learning Disabilities.

Norman, C. A., & Zigmond, N. (1980). Characteristics of children labeled and served as learning disabled in school systems affiliated with child service demonstration centers. *Journal of Learning Disabilities, 13*(9), 16–21.

Rossi, A. O. (1972). Genetics of learning disabilities. *Journal of Learning Disabilities, 5*, 489–496.

Rubin, R., & Balow, B. (1971). Learning and behavior disorders: A longitudinal study. *Exceptional Children, 38*, 293–299.

Sadker, D., Sadker, M., & Thomas, D. (1981). Sex equity and special education. *Pointer, 26*(1), 33–37.

Schlosser, L., & Algozzine, B. (1979). The disturbing child: He or she? *Alberta Journal of Educational Research, 25*(1), 30–36.

Singer, B. D., & Osborn, R. W. (1970). Special class and sex differences in admission patterns of the mentally retarded. *American Journal of Mental Deficiency, 75*, 162–190.

Young, S., Algozzine, B., & Schmid, R. (1979). The effects of assigned attributes and labels on children's peer accepted ratings. *Education & Training of the Mentally Retarded, 12*, 257–261.

KATHLEEN RODDEN-NORD
GERALD TINDAL
University of Oregon

PRE-REFFERAL INTERVENTION
See **SEX DIFFERENCES IN LEARNING DISABILITIES**

SEXUAL DISTURBANCES IN HANDICAPPED CHILDREN

Most of the research and study concerning sexual disturbances in handicapped individuals has focused on those persons with physical disabilities and/or mental retardation in institutional settings. Sexual problems also exist in other special populations but they are less well documented.

Monat (1982) outlines a number of problems found in the mentally retarded population, including excessive and harmful masturbation, same-sex mutual masturbation, opposite-sex mutual masturbation, bestiality (especially in rural areas), sodomy, indecent exposure, child sexual abuse, lewd and lascivious behavior, and statutory rape. Undesired pregnancy is also a problem with the mentally retarded, though not necessarily a sexual disturbance.

The approaches recommended today for dealing with sexual disturbances in the mentally retarded ask that professionals who attempt to intervene be both knowledgeable about sex and sexuality and comfortable with this knowledge and their own sexuality. Recognition must be given to differing levels of cognitive ability with the mentally retarded population that lead to variable levels of conceptual understanding and to the likelihood of different sexual behaviors and problems at different levels of functioning. In the past, especially in residential facilities, excessive reliance on moralization, punishment, and sterilization (Haavik & Menninger, 1981) colored attempts to deal with sexual matters. Current approaches generally focus on staff training for desensitization, concrete sex education (including on birth control, marriage, and parenthood), the dispelling of sexual myths, the importance of personal choice and responsibility, the appropriateness of personal social behavior, and the concept of privacy. The staff needs to follow through and review to be certain learning has occurred and the information has been retained. Sex counseling, which is designed to deal with the values and feelings surrounding sexuality, is now more readily available to complement sex education (which is more concerned with the transfer of relevant information).

In examining sexual disturbances, the type of living environment involved is important. With the present preference for community living and independence for the handicapped, greater emphasis must be placed on appropriate community behavior, the legality of different sexual behaviors, personal choices, and the acceptance of responsibility. The handicapped adolescent or adult moving to a less restrictive setting must be aware of the dangers of venereal disease, acquired immune deficiency syndrome (AIDS), and pimps and prostitutes (Monat, 1982). For some, especially those leaving certain residential facilities or protected home settings, community living arrangements, community-based training centers, or job sites of any type may offer the first true coeducational experiences. It has been shown that the knowledge of even noninstitutionalized mentally retarded young men and women is often severely limited (Brantlinger, 1985).

Often it is expected that formerly institutionalized persons will encounter problems with homosexuality in the community. Though this may be the case in a few situations, it is often the limited choice of partners that leads to the designation of certain behaviors as homosexual in nature. This is similar to the situation found in prisons and other same-sex institutions. West (1979) characterized the observed sexual behavior of institutionalized severely retarded adolescents and adults as essentially normal and appropriate, though sometimes socially improper. He noted that the residents' "sexual activity was very often the only spontaneous cooperative mutual behavior observed and the only interresident interaction apart from aggression."

Attitudes have always played a large part in viewing the sexuality of the handicapped. Sexual disturbances or problems of physically handicapped individuals, especially those with essentially normal intelligence whose physical disability resulted from postnatal accident, injury, or trauma, have been something of an exception among the general handicapped population. Professionals, and probably society in general, seem more willing to recognize the sexual rights of this group and to provide the understanding, support, and even the aids or prostheses to help them regain normal sexuality (Thorn-Gray &

Kern, 1983). This view is markedly different than that found when dealing with mentally retarded persons.

Where education has been unsuccessful in preventing sexual disturbances or counseling has been ineffective in eliminating inappropriate sexual behaviors, a variety of behavioral approaches have been found to be successful in individual cases. Hurley and Sovner (1983) describe case reports on the effective use of response cost procedures, aversive conditioning, overcorrection, in vivo desensitization, and positive reinforcement in dealing with problems such as exhibitionism, public masturbation, public disrobing, and fetishism. Assaultive and inappropriate interpersonal sexual behaviors were successfully eliminated in an adolescent male with Down's syndrome through a combination of differential reinforcement of other behaviors and naturalistic social restitution. The control of this behavior was able to be generalized to the student's teachers (Polvinale & Lutzker, 1980).

Sexual problems noted in learning-disabled populations have often been attributed to conceptual difficulties, disinhibition, or inadequate impulse control. Insights into sex-related difficulties in blind and visually impaired persons can be found in Mangold and Mangold (1983) and in Welbourne et al. (1983). Information on sex and deafness can be found in *Sexuality and Deafness* (Gallaudet College, 1979).

REFERENCES

Brantlinger, E. A. (1985). Mildly mentally retarded secondary students' information and attitudes toward sexuality and sex education. *Education & Training of the Mentally Retarded, 20,* 99–108.

Gallaudet College. (1979). *Sexuality and deafness.* Washington, DC: Outreach Services.

Haavik, S. F., & Menninger, K. A. (1981). *Sexuality, law, and the developmentally disabled person: Legal and clinical aspects of marriage, parenthood and sterilization.* Baltimore, MD: Brookes.

Hurley, A. D., & Sovner, R. (1983). Treatment of sexual deviation in mentally retarded persons. *Psychiatric Aspects of Mental Retardation Newsletter, 2*(4), 13–16.

Mangold, S. S., & Mangold, P. N. (1983). The adolescent visually impaired female. *Journal of Blindness & Visual Impairment, 77*(6), 250–255.

Monat, R. K. (1982). *Sexuality and the mentally retarded.* San Diego, CA: College-Hill.

Polvinale, R. A., & Lutzker, J. R. (1980). Elimination of and inappropriate sexual behavior by reinforcement and social restitution. *Mental Retardation, 18*(1), 27–30.

Thorn-Gray, B. E., & Kern, L. H. (1983). Sexual dysfunction associated with physical disability: A treatment guide for the rehabilitation practitioner. *Rehabilitation Literature, 44*(5–6), 138–144.

Wellbourne, A., Lifschitz, S., Selvin, H., & Green, R. (1983). A comparison of the sexual learning experiences of visually im-

paired and sighted women. *Journal of Blindness & Visual Impairment, 77*(6), 256–261.

West, R. R. (1979). The sexual behaviour of the institutionalised severely retarded. *Australian Journal of Mental Retardation, 5,* II–L3.

JOHN D. WILSON
*Elwyn Institutes,
Elwyn, Pennsylvania*

**MASTURBATION, COMPULSIVE
MENTAL RETARDATION
SELF STIMULATION**

SHELTERED WORKSHOPS

The concept of the sheltered workshop was introduced in the United States in 1838 by the Perkins Institute for the Blind. The early workshop programs that followed provided sheltered employment for those whose handicapping conditions precluded competitive employment.

Federal involvement with sheltered workshops came about 100 years later. In an effort to help sheltered workshops compete with other businesses for contracts, the 1938 amendments to the Vocational Rehabilitation Act (PL 75-497) allowed workshops to pay below-minimum wages to employees.

With the passage of the Vocational Rehabilitation Act of 1943 (PL 78-113), persons with mental retardation and mental illness were considered eligible for rehabilitation services. This initiated a change in rehabilitation programs in the United States. For the first time, there was recognition of persons who had never been employed.

The Vocational Rehabilitation Act amendments of 1965 (PL 89-333) expanded the definition of "gainful employment" to include not only competitive but also sheltered employment. There was an emphasis on the provision of services that would lead toward gainful sheltered employment for more severely handicapped individuals. According to Snell (1983):

> Sheltered employment is when an individual is receiving subsidized wages or working for less than minimum wage, with handicapped co-workers at a job that provides limited advancement to competitive work settings and that is organized primarily for therapeutic habilitation or sheltered production. (p. 504)

The Rehabilitation Act of 1973 (PL 93-112) and the continuation amendments of 1974 (PL 93-516) emphasized the provision of services that would lead toward gainful sheltered employment for persons with severe handicaps.

Special education programs help prepare young adults with disabilities to work in sheltered workshops. According to Bigge (1982), the special education curriculum should include work evaluation, work adjustment, work experience, vocational skills, and on-the-job training programs.

The sheltered workshop is the most widely used type of vocational training facility for adults with handicaps. Sheltered workshops can be classified into three general types: regular program workshops; work activities centers; and adult day programs. Regular program workshops (or transitional workshops) provide therapies and work intended to foster readiness for competitive employment. The Department of Labor requires that workers earn no less than 50% of minimum wages. Work activities centers (WACs) provide training, support, and extended employment in a sheltered environment to more severely handicapped adults. A wage ceiling of 50% of minimum wage has been set for WACs clients. The Fair Labor Standards Act, as amended in 1966, defines regular program workshops and work activities centers. Both are monitored by the Department of Labor. Adult day programs, managed by state developmental disabilities agencies, provide nonvocational services such as socialization, communication skills, and basic work orientation. The primary goal of adult day programs is the acquisition of basic living skills, leading to a decrease in maladaptive behavior and movement toward more vocationally oriented programs.

A sheltered workshop operates as a business. It generally engages in one of three types of business activities: contracting, prime manufacturing, or reclamation. In contracting, there is an agreement that a sheltered workshop will complete a specified job within a specified time for a given price. Workshops bid competitively for each job. Prime manufacturing is the designing, producing, marketing, and shipping of a complete product. A reclamation operation is one in which a workshop purchases or collects salvageable material, performs a reclamation operation, and then sells the reclaimed product.

REFERENCES

Bigge, J. L. (1982). *Teaching individuals with physical and multiple disabilities* (2nd ed.). Columbus, OH: Merrill.

Heward, W. L., & Orlansky, M. D. (1984). *Exceptional children.* (2nd ed.). Columbus, OH: Merrill.

Lynch, K. P., Kiernan, J. A., & Stark, J. A. (1982). *Prevocational and vocational education for special needs youth.* Baltimore, MD: Brookes.

Mori, A. A., & Masters, L. F. (1980). *Teaching the severely mentally retarded.* Germantown, MD: Aspen.

Schreerenberger, R. C. (1983). *A history of mental retardation.* Baltimore, MD: Brookes.

Snell, M. A. (1983). *Systematic instruction of the moderately and severely handicapped* (2nd ed.). Columbus, OH: Merrill.

CAROLE REITER GOTHELF
Hunter College, City University of New York

VOCATIONAL REHABILITATION
VOCATIONAL TRAINING OF THE HANDICAPPED

SIBLINGS OF THE HANDICAPPED

Siblings of the handicapped have received little research attention compared with the literature available on the effects of a handicapped child on parents (Crnic, Friedrich, & Greenberg, 1983; Drew, Logan, & Hardman, 1984; Trevino, 1979). The available research, however, suggests that nonhandicapped siblings are a population at risk for behavioral problems, the degree to which is influenced by a number of variables and factors (Crnic et al., 1983; Gargiulo, 1984; Trevino, 1979). Specific factors that appear to interact and contribute to sibling adjustment include the number of normal siblings in the family (Powell & Ogle, 1985), the age and gender of siblings (Crnic et al., 1983; Grossman, 1972), and parental response and attitude toward the handicapped child (Trevino, 1979). Trevino (1979) reports that prospects for normal siblings having difficulty in adjusting increase when (1) there are only two siblings in the family, one who is handicapped and one who is not; (2) the nonhandicapped sibling is close in age to or younger than the handicapped sibling or is the oldest female child; (3) the nonhandicapped child and the handicapped child are the same sex; and (4) the parents are unable to accept the handicap. Schwirian (1976), Farber (1959), and Cleveland and Miller (1977) found that the female sibling's role demanded more parent-surrogate duties as she was expected to help care for the disabled child when she was at home. In addition, sibling literature emphasizes healthy and honest parental attitudes and behaviors toward the handicapped child as essential to the siblings positive growth and development.

Grossman (1972) found that socioeconomic status (SES) can also affect sibling responses to a handicapped child. Middle-class families and those from higher SES families tended to be more financially secure and better prepared to use outside resources such as respite care services, thus lessening a youngster's responsibility of caring for a handicapped sibling.

The emotional responses of siblings of the handicapped have been reported to include hostility, guilt, fear, shame, embarrassment, and rejection. Crnic et al. (1983) found that the presence of a retarded child has a detrimental effect on a nonretarded sibling's (particularly a female's) individual functioning. This involves high degrees of anxiety, conflicts with parents, and problems in social and interpersonal relationships. On the other hand, Farber (1960) reported, after an extensive study, that many siblings adopted life goals toward dedication and sacrifice (Crnic et al., 1983).

Although the concerns of siblings vary according to the

nature and degree of severity of their handicapped sibling's disability, key concerns, such as how to deal with parents, what to tell friends, and what kind of future they can expect for their handicapped sibling, appear to be similar across types of impairments (Murphy, 1979). If the needs and concerns of siblings are not met, they may result in problems and negative feelings.

The psychological and behavioral problems that may result from having a handicapped sibling is a reality that must be dealt with by parents and professionals. Siblings can benefit from the experience of having a handicapped sibling if they are introduced to the situation in an understanding and compassionate way. Siblings and parents should seek support from family counselors, religious organizations, nonprofit agenices, and sibling support groups that focus on the individual needs, attitudes, concerns, and feelings of the nonhandicapped sibling. Teachers should be alerted to the child's family situation to provide additional support and information.

REFERENCES

Cleveland, D. W., & Miller, N. (1977). Attitudes and life commitments of older siblings of mentally retarded adults; An exploratory study. *Mental Retardation, 15,* 38–41.

Crnic, K. A., Friedrich, W. N., & Greenberg, M. T. (1983). Adaptation of families with mentally retarded children: A model of stress, coping and family ecology. *American Journal of Mental Deficiency, 88,* 125–139.

Drew, C. J., Logan, D. R., & Hardman, M. L. (Eds.). (1984). *Mental retardation: A life cycle approach* (3rd ed.). St. Louis: Times/ Mirror Mosby.

Farber, B. (1959). Effects of a severely mentally retarded child on family integration. *Monographs of the Society for Research in Child Development, 24,* (whole No. 71).

Farber, B. (1960). Family organization and crisis: Maintenance of integration in families with a severely retarded child. *Monographs of the Society for Research in Child Development, 25,* 1–95.

Gargiulo, R. M. (1984). Understanding family dynamics. In R. M. Gargiulo (Ed.), *Working with parents of exceptional children* (pp. 41–64). Boston: Houghton Mifflin.

Grossman, F. K. (1972). *Brothers and sisters of retarded children: An exploratory study* Syracuse, NY: Syracuse University Press.

Murphy, A. T. (1979). Members of the family: Sisters and brothers of the handicapped. *Volta Review 81,* 352–354.

Powell, T. H., & Ogle, P. A. (1985). *Brothers and sisters in the family system.* Baltimore, MD: Brookes.

Schwirian, P. M. (1976). Effects of the presence of a hearing impaired pre-school child in the family on behavior patterns of older "normal" siblings. *American Annals of the Deaf, 121,* 373–380.

Trevino, F. (1979). Siblings of handicapped children: Identifying those at risk. *Social Casework: Journal of Contemporary Social Work, 62,* 488–493.

MARSHA H. LUPI
*Hunter College, City University
of New York*

FAMILY RESPONSE TO HANDICAP

RESPITE CARE

SICARD, ABBÉ ROCHE AMBROISE CUCURRON (1742–1822)

Abbé Roche Ambroise Cucurron Sicard, educator of the deaf, studied with Abbé Epée at the National Institution for Deaf-Mutes in Paris and, in 1782, opened a school for the deaf at Bordeaux. Sicard succeeded Epée at the National Institution and, except for a few years during the French Revolution, served as its director until his death in 1822. Sicard made many improvements in Epée's educational methods. His most important publication was a dictionary of signs, a work begun by Epée.

The beginning of education for the deaf in the United States was greatly influenced by Sicard. He invited Thomas Gallaudet, who was planning the first school for the deaf in the United States, to observe the methods employed at the National Institute in Paris, with the result that Gallaudet became proficient in Sicard's methods. In addition, Sicard provided Gallaudet with his first teacher, Laurent Clerc.

REFERENCES

Bender, R. E. (1970). *The conquest of deafness.* Cleveland, OH: Case Western Reserve University Press.

Lane, H. (1984). *When the mind hears.* New York: Random House.

PAUL IRVINE
Katonah, New York

SICKLE-CELL DISEASE

Sickle-cell disease is an inherited blood disorder that occurs as two conditions, sickle-cell anemia (SCA) and sickle-cell trait (SCT). Sickle-cell anemia is the more serious of the two conditions; it can be defined as an abnormality of the hemoglobin molecule, the oxygen-carrying protein in the red blood cells. Oxygen-carrying red blood cells are usually round and flexible. Under certain conditions, the red blood cells of a person with sickle-cell anemia may change into a crescent or sickle cell. This unusual shape causes the cells to adhere in the spleen and other areas, leading to their destruction. This results in a shortage of red blood cells, which has serious consequences for the individual with SCA (Haslam & Valletutti, 1975; March of Dimes, 1985). These consequences include fever, abdominal discomfort, bone pain, damage to the brain, lungs, and kidneys, and, for some, death in childhood or early adulthood (Haslam & Valletutti, 1975; March of Dimes, 1985; National Association for Sickle Cell Disease [NASCD], (1978). Individuals with SCA will experience episodes of pain known as sickle-cell crisis. During these periods, the sickled cells become trapped in tiny blood vessels. This blocks other red blood cells behind them, which lose oxygen and become sickle-shaped, totally blocking the vessels. When the bone marrow inadequately produces red blood cells, the child experiences an aplastic crisis and requires blood transfusion (Weiner, 1973). These crises and their effects vary greatly from person to person. Most people with SCA enjoy reasonably good health much of the time (March of Dimes, 1985; NASCD, 1978).

Sickle-cell anemia occurs when a sickle-cell gene is inherited from each parent. A person with sickle-cell anemia has sickle cells in the bloodstream and has sickle-cell disease. The second condition, sickle-cell trait (SCT), occurs when a sickle-cell gene is inherited from one parent and a normal gene from the other. A person with sickle-cell trait does not have sickle cells in the bloodstream and does not have sickle-cell disease. Persons with SCT may pass the sickle-cell gene on to their offspring (March of Dimes, 1985; NASCD, 1978; Whitten, 1974). As an autosomal recessive disorder, children of parents who both carry the sickle-cell gene have a 50% chance of inheriting SCT, a 25% chance of being a carrier, and a 25% chance of having SCA (Whitten, 1974).

In the United States, sickle-cell disease occurs most frequently among blacks and Hispanics of Caribbean ancestry. About 1 in every 400 to 600 blacks and 1 in every 1000 to 1500 Hispanics inherit sickle-cell disease (March of Dimes, 1985). Approximately 1 in 12 black Americans carry a gene for sickle-cell trait (NASCD, 1978). Less commonly affected peoples include those whose ancestors lived in countries bordering on the Mediterranean Sea (Greeks, Maltese, Portuguese, Arabians; NASCD, 1978).

There is no known cure for sickle-cell anemia. However, a number of new therapies for reducing the severity and frequency of crises are being tried (March of Dimes, 1985; Weiner, 1973). A blood test for sickle-cell anemia and its trait is readily available; it is called hemoglobin electrophoresis. There is also a prenatal test to determine whether the fetus will develop sickle anemia or be a carrier.

The child with SCA may need to be placed in an educational program that is geared to his or her physical capabilities. Since many individuals with SCA tire easily, children should be encouraged to participate in most school activities of other children their age with the understanding that they may rest more frequently. If communication between the child and family has been open and honest concerning SCA, then the child can develop healthy social attitudes and self-reliance (NASCD, 1978).

REFERENCES

Haslam, R. M. A., and Valletutti, P. J. (1975). *Medical problems in the classroom.* Baltimore, MD: University Park Press.

March of Dimes, (1985). *Genetics series: Sickle cell anemia.* White Plains, NY: Author.

National Association for Sickle Cell Disease. (1978). *Sickle cell disease: Tell the facts, quell the fables.* Los Angeles: Author.

Weiner, F. (1973). *Help for the handicapped child.* New York: McGraw-Hill.

Whitten, C. F. (1974). Fact sheet on sickle cell trait and anemia. Los Angeles: National Association for Sickle Cell Disease.

MARSHA H. LUPI
Hunter College, City University of New York

GENETIC DISORDERS

SIDIS, WILLIAM JAMES (1898–1944)

William James Sidis was a famous child prodigy of the early twentieth century who came to a tragic end after leading a short, largely unfulfilled life. Sidis's history and early demise are often cited in early literature opposing acceleration and other aspects of special education for the intellectually gifted. Much of Sidis's life has been distorted in various informal accounts. Montour (1977) has characterized the use of Sidis's story to deny acceleration to intellectually advanced children as the Sidis fallacy. Simply stated, the Sidis fallacy denotes "early ripe, early rot."

In 1909, at the age of 11, Sidis entered Harvard College. A year later he lectured on higher mathematics at the Harvard Mathematical Club. Sidis had performed remarkably in intellectual endeavors throughout his life. By Montour's (1977) account, by the age of 3 he read fluently with good comprehension; he was writing with a pencil 6 months later. By age 4, Sidis was a fluent typist. When he was 6, Sidis could read English, Russian, French, German, and Hebrew; he learned Latin and Greek shortly thereafter. At the age of 8, Sidis passed the entrance exam at the Massachusetts Institute of Technology, developed a new table of logarithms employing base 12 instead of base 10, and passed the Harvard Medical School exam in anatomy. He was well qualified to enter Harvard at that time but was denied entrance based on his age. Sidis earned his BA in 1914, although it has been reported that he completed his work for the degree 2 years earlier. Sidis pursued some graduate study in several fields, including a year in law school, but never earned an advanced degree. He spurned academia after an unsuccessful year as a professor at Rice University at age 20. He became sullen, cynical, and withdrawn from society (Montour, 1977). Sidis chose to live as a loner, working at low-level clerical jobs until his death in 1944, at the age of 46, from a stroke.

Sidis's academic contributions were limited to two books. In 1926 he published *Notes on the Collection of Transfers*. A more serious volume, published in 1925 (but written in 1919 and 1920, *The Animate and Inanimate*, was devoted to a proof of James's theory of reserve energy.

Sidis's turn against academia and his choice to drop out of society seems related to his intellectual talent and precocity only in the most indirect fashion; it was certainly not a result of his academic acceleration. Montour (1977) argues credibly that it was the result of a rebellion against an overbearing, domineering, but emotionally barren father who rejected Sidis at the first sign of any weakness. Although the Sidis's case is often cited in opposition to academic acceleration, there is little to support such a position on the basis of Sidis's history. In fact, far more cases of successful acceleration are present with outcomes strongly supportive of acceleration programs. Norbert Wiener (a classmate of Sidis), John Stuart Mill, Merrill Kenneth Wolf, David Noel Freedman, and John Raden Platt are but a few of many such successes (Montour, 1977). Indeed, educational acceleration will be the method of choice for the education of many intellectually precocious youths.

"It was not extreme educational acceleration that destroyed William James Sidis emotionally and mentally, but instead an interaction of paternal exploitation and emotional starvation" (Montour, 1977, p. 276). The events of Sidis's life are often exaggerated and misstated. The Sidis fallacy has restricted the education of the gifted and persists in some educational programs even today; it is yet another myth that afflicts programs for the gifted.

REFERENCES

Montour, K. (1977). William James Sidis, the broken twig. *American Psychologist, 32,* 265–279.

Sidis, W. J. (1925). *The animate and inanimate.* Boston: Badger.

Sidis, W. J. (1926). *Notes on the collection of transfer.* Philadelphia: Dorrance.

CECIL R. REYNOLDS
Texas A&M University

**ACCELERATED PLACEMENT OF GIFTED CHILDREN
STUDY OF MATHEMATICALLY PRECOCIOUS YOUTH**

SIDIS FALLACY

See SIDIS, WILLIAM JAMES.

SIECUS

See SEX INFORMATION AND EDUCATION COUNCIL OF THE UNITED STATES.

SIGHT-SAVING CLASSES

For much of the present century it was common to educate children with low vision in "sight-saving classes". This was done in public schools as well as in residential facilities. Such classes for partially sighted children were begun in public schools as far back as 1913 (Livingoton, R.).

The notion behind these sight-saving classes was that a low-vision child's residual vision would be damaged by overuse. The emphasis, thus, was on conserving the child's vision as far as possible. This meant that children whose vision was impaired but still usable were removed from presumably visually stressful situations by reducing visual demands made on them. Some were even educated in dark rooms or blindfolded. The situation today is dramatically altered. It is now believed that all children, including visually handicapped ones, benefit from using their visual abilities as much as possible.

REFERENCE

Livingston, R. (1986). Visual impairments. In N. G. Haring, & L. McCormick (Eds.), *Exceptional children and youth* (4th ed., pp. 398–429). Columbus, OH: Merrill.

MARY MURRAY
*Journal of Special Education,
Ben Salem, Pennsylvania*

**LOW VISION
PARTIALLY SIGHTED**

SIGNING

See SIGN LANGUAGE.

SIGN LANGUAGE

Sign language is a general term that refers to any gestural/visual language that makes use of specific shapes and movements of the fingers, hands, and arms, as well as movements of the eyes, face, head, and body. There is no international system that is comprehensible to all deaf people. There exists a British Sign Language, a Spanish Sign Language, an Israeli Sign Language, and probably a sign language in every country where deaf people have needed to communicate among themselves rapidly, efficiently, and visually without the use of pad and pencil.

American Sign Language, sometimes called Ameslan or ASL, was created over the years by the deaf community in the United States. In American Sign Language, one hand shape frequently denotes a concept. American Sign Language must be differentiated from finger spelling or dactylology, which is the use of hand configurations to denote the letters of the alphabet. In finger spelling, one hand shape stands for one letter. Sometimes finger spelling is used to spell out the English equivalent for a sign (especially proper nouns) when ASL is used. In ASL, interpreters frequently finger spell the word for a technical or uncommon sign the first time it is used during a conference. Finger spelling with speech and speech reading for additional acoustic and visual cues is called the Rochester method (Quigley & Paul, 1984).

Total communication is the use of signs, finger spelling, speech, speech reading, and, in reality, any and all modes of communication to ensure effective communication with hearing-impaired people. Although it is possible for ASL to be used as the manual component of total communication, the two terms are not synonymous.

Signed English, developed in the 1960s under the direction of Harry Bornstein of Gallaudet College, is a manually coded system of English used in conjunction with speech. It was devised to facilitate the acquisition of English by young deaf children. It incorporates special signs to indicate affixes (prefixes like un-, and suffixes like -s and -ment) and verb tense. Signed English is basically an educational tool used in some schools for deaf students. Its use of the specific tense and affix markers slows down the communication process considerably (Schlesinger & Namir, 1978).

Research into the linguistic nature of American Sign Language has shown that the grammar of ASL, like the grammar of all languages, consists of a finite set of rules with which an infinite number of sentences can be created or generated. Deaf children and hearing children of deaf parents who use ASL acquire these rules in much the same way that hearing children abstract linguistic rules from the spoken language to which they are exposed (Bellugi & Klima, 1985). Courses in sign language are offered in many colleges, schools for deaf students, centers for continuing education, and some public libraries.

REFERENCES

Bellugi, U., & Klima, E. (1985). The acquisition of three morphological systems in American Sign Language. In F. Powell (Ed.), *Education of the hearing-impaired child*. San Diego, CA: College Hill.

Quigley, S., & Paul, P. (1984). *Language and deafness*. San Diego, CA: College Hill.

Schlesinger, I., & Namir, L. (1978). *Sign language of the deaf*. New York: Academic.

ROSEMARY GAFFNEY
Hunter College, City University of New York

ROCHESTER METHOD
LIPREADING/SPEECHREADING
TOTAL COMMUNICATION

SIMULTANEOUS PROCESSING

See SEQUENTIAL AND SIMULTANEOUS COGNITIVE PROCESSING.

SINGLE-SUBJECT RESEARCH DESIGN

Increasingly, researchers are recognizing the importance of single-case investigations for the development of a knowledge base in psychology and education. Single-case time series designs involve observations before, during, and after interventions in order to describe changes in selected dependent variables. The development of time-series methodology, especially single-subject design, has been advantageous for researchers for several reasons. First, single-case research designs provide an important knowledge base that is unobtainable through traditional large-N between-group designs in clinical research. Single-subject designs are uniquely suited to evaluation of treatments involving a single client, a characteristic that is important given that it often is impossible to conduct group comparative outcome studies because of the limited number of subjects for a particular type of disorder or problem.

Another major advantage of single-case designs is that they provide an alternative to traditional large-N group designs about which various ethical and legal considerations are often raised (Hersen & Barlow, 1976). These concerns include the ethical objections of withholding treatment from clients in a no-treatment control group or randomly assigning clients to a particular treatment type.

Single-subject designs have been important in promoting the development of a measurement technology that can be used repeatedly throughout the intervention process. For example, various outcome measures such as direct observation, rating scales and checklists, self-monitoring, standardized tests, and psychophysiological recordings, can be used as ongoing measures of client functioning over the course of a research program. Such repeated measures taken over time allow for an analysis of individual variability as well as monitoring of potential response covariation within a single client. Perhaps the most important aspect of repeated measurement technology is its flexibility in the modification of treatment if the data indicate that this modification is necessary.

Single-case research strategies have also provided options for practitioners to be involved in research and evaluation of practice. There are differences of opinion, however, as to how feasible it is to implement well-controlled designs while providing clinical services. Carefully constructed single-case designs are usually difficult to implement (Kratochwill & Piersel, 1983). The use of a particular design may compromise the on-line clinical intuition of the therapist, yielding either a threat to internal validity of the evaluation or less appropriate treatment of the client. Finally, while clinicians may be concerned with the potential threats to being most responsive to patient needs, others may take the position that formal evaluation increases efficacy of the intervention itself (Barlow, Hayes, & Nelson, 1984). By implementing careful observation and measurement of behavior change, the therapist can measure type and degree of improvement and also know whether the treatment is responsible for change. The issues are readily subject to debate.

As single-subject strategies become more prevalent in the educational literature, it becomes important to discuss some design types. Three basic design types have been described in the literature (Barlow et al., 1984); they include within-, between-, and continued-series strategies.

In within-series designs, changes observed within a series of data points across time on a single measure or set of measures are analyzed. Each data point is analyzed in the context of those that immediately precede and follow it. Each consistent condition constitutes a phase in the series. Phases also are evaluated in the context of phases that precede and follow them. The researcher establishes internal validity in within-series designs by replicating effects of the independent variable across the phases.

One type of within-series design is the withdrawal procedure, that is used to assess whether responses are maintained under different conditions rather than to demonstrate the initial effects of an intervention in altering behavior (Kazdin, 1982). Typically, an A-B-A-B paradigm is used in which the intervention is introduced following a baseline, withdrawn for a phase, and then reintroduced. The withdrawal design seems best suited for evaluating the controlling effects of a reversible procedure, that is defined as one that would not produce a permanent change in the dependent variable. Withdrawal of the procedure would result in a return to baseline measures.

An example of the A-B-A-B withdrawal design is offered by Powers and Crowel (1985). They studied the effectiveness of a positive practice overcorrection procedure to decrease stereotypic vocal behavior produced by an 8-year-old autistic male. A baseline level of the child's percent of 10-second intervals of stereotypic vocalizations was obtained over 9 days. Treatment was then introduced and implemented for 7 days, withdrawn for 17 days, and reimplemented for 7 more days. Figure 1 illustrates the effects of the positive practice overcorrection procedure on the stereotypic vocalizations produced by the subject. During the initial baseline, the vocalizations averaged about 69%. During treatment, the percent of intervals of stereotypic vocalizations decreased to an average of about 17%. Withdrawal of the treatment resulted in a return to initial baseline levels of vocalizations, while reintroduction of the treatment resulted in another decrease in average levels of the stereotypic behavior.

Since the A-B-A-B design is generally not appropriate for irreversibe procedures (Hersen & Barlow, 1976), there are a number of considerations regarding its use. First, ethical decisions need to be made regarding withdrawal of treatment in any therapy program. Complicated decisions need to be made regarding the relative importance and overall advantages of obtaining reliable data about treatment efficacy as against withdrawing treatment from the client. Second, practical limitations may prevent one's choice of an A-B-A-B design. Often there is not enough time to institute two or more withdrawal phases. A third issue pertains to one's philosophy of intervention. In remediation of certain disorders, it might be argued that the client will not reverse to previous states once an intervention is introduced.

The withdrawal design might also be implemented in evaluating components of a treatment package. Specific aspects of a particular approach may be investigated by manipulating one variable at a time between adjacent phases in a withdrawal design. This type of strategy has been described in detail by several authors in their discussions of interaction designs (Barlow et al., 1984; Kratochwill, 1978; McReynolds & Kearns, 1983). Interaction designs examine the interactions of two or more variables over time in a basic within-series procedure. The purpose is to evaluate additive, subtractive, and interactive effects of individual components of a treatment.

If the researcher is interested in the effect of two independent variables but without evaluation of the individual contributions of B and C, the design would follow the classic A-B-A design, but it would specify the existence of the two variables. The design would be represented as A-BC-A-BC. However, if the investigator is interested in the relative contribution of B and C, and the interactive effects of both, each variable must be evaluated alone and in conjunction with the other. The design may be repre-

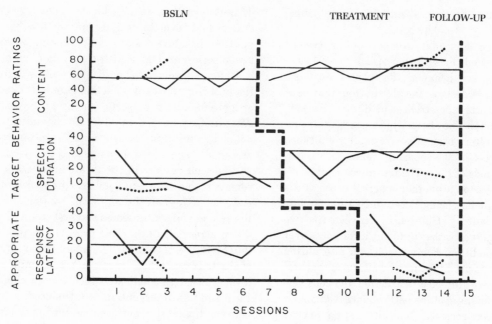

Figure 1. BSLN treatment follow-up.

sented as A-B-BC-B-BC. In this format, the effect of B alone is tested as well as the effect of BC together.

It should be noted that only one variable is manipulated at a time and each variable to be evaluated must be adjacent to the rest. Unless the components are in adjacent phases (e.g., B-BC-B) the investigator cannot determine the effects of either component alone. For example, if one used an A-B-BC-A-B design, comparison of the behavior in B with the behavior in BC is confounded because of the intervening A phase. An A-B-A-B-BC design is often mistakenly interpreted as revealing interactive and relative effects. The final two phases (B-BC) form an uncontrolled A-B design and, therefore, are descriptive rather than experimental.

The interaction design may be time consuming since all the phases need to be completed. Also, there is a threat of sequence effects as one phase follows another. To control for order effects, the researcher would need to increase the number of subjects and implement counterbalancing and replication.

Other variations of the withdrawal design may be applicable. Maintenance of a behavior may be studied following a successful treatment package. A sequential withdrawal design might be implemented in which different components of the treatment package are gradually withdrawn while observations are made to see whether the behavior is maintained. A partial withdrawal design is another strategy that is used to evaluate maintenance. It consists of withdrawing a component of the treatment package from one of several different baselines, or from one of several subjects. This design would be readily applicable to many situations where one is interested in whether target behaviors measured during treatment are

likely to be maintained if the treatment package or components are withdrawn.

Another within-series procedure is the changing criterion design. This design can be used to evaluate the effects of treatment on a single gradually acquired behavior. It is appropriate for studying the effectiveness of shaping behavior. The effect of the intervention is demonstrated by showing that behavior changes gradually over the course of treatment. Rather than withdrawing or withholding treatment, the design uses several subphases within the intervention phase. In each subphase a different criterion for performance is specified. When performance meets the criterion, more stringent criteria are set. This is done repeatedly over the course of the design.

During the baseline phase a single behavior is monitored until a stable response rate is achieved. Baseline data are used to establish an initial criterion level and treatment is initiated and continued until the target behavior stabilizes at that level. Both reinforcement schedules and criterion levels are then increased. The remainder of the phase progresses in a steplike manner, with each criterion adjustment more closely approximating a terminal level.

Many aspects and variations of the design are important in its use, including phase length, number and magnitude of criterion shifts, directionality of change, and potential data ambiguity. This design is most appropriate for behaviors acquired gradually; it does not require withdrawal or reversal of treatment. Only one behavior is selected for treatment, allowing inferences to be made about the efficacy of the treatment for that specific behavior. Possible confounding because of order effects and counterbalancing is also avoided in this design. This design is well suited for examining generalization across settings, subjects, and time.

Between-series designs allow comparisons of two or more treatments or conditions in order to examine relative effectiveness on a given behavior. There are two basic types of between-series designs: the alternating treatment design and the simultaneous treatment design (Barlow, Hayes & Nelson, 1984). The alternating treatment design involves the rapid alternation of two or more conditions. It exposes the subject to the separate treatment components for equal periods of time. The treatment may be alternated from one session to another or across two sessions each day, with sequence being determined randomly or through counterbalancing. Differences between the two treatments are examined rather than any differences over time within one condition. For example, an alternating treatment design was used to study the effects of teacher-directed versus student-directed instruction and cues versus no cues for improving spelling performance (Gettinger, 1985). Nine children received four alternating experimental treatments during a 16-week spelling program. The two cuing procedures (cues vs. no cues) were alternated weekly while the student-directed and teacher-directed components were alternated biweekly. Mean pretest, posttest, and retention scores were obtained for each treatment condition; they indicated improved spelling accuracy for all four conditions. The data also demonstrated that a student-directed procedure incorporating visual and verbal cues produces the highest posttest accuracy scores.

The simultaneous treatment design differs from the alternating treatment design in that the treatments (or conditions) are available simultaneously. The purpose of the design is to measure subject "preference" rather than the treatment efficacy (Barlow et al., 1984). For example, a simultaneous treatment design might be employed to determine which type of reinforcement is most preferred by a client. That particular reinforcement could then be incorporated into a remediation program.

Potential problems exist for the use of these designs in some areas of research. The interactive effects of two treatments or conditions would be difficult to ascertain, especially in patients exhibiting cognitive or language deficits. Carryover or generalization effects of one intervention may confound inferences that might be made with regard to the other treatment or condition. Both alternating treatment and simultaneous treatment designs depend on showing changes for a given behavior across sessions or time periods. The need for behavior to shift rapidly dictates both the type of interventions and the behaviors that can be studied in multiple treatment designs. Interventions suitable for these designs may need to show rapid effects initially and to have little or no carryover effects when terminated. If the effects of the first intervention linger after it is no longer presented, the intervention that follows would be confounded by the previous one.

In addition to alternating and simultaneous treatment designs, one other strategy has been employed when withdrawal and reversal designs are not feasible. These are multiple baseline designs that combine within and between series strategies with regard to inference.

The methodology for multiple baseline designs is relatively straightforward. Baseline data are collected on two or more units (e.g. subjects, settings, behaviors, or time). After performance is stable for all the units, treatment is applied to the first; measurements continue to be taken across all. The researcher's expectation is that changes will be seen quickly in the treated unit while the others remain stable at baseline levels. After performance again stabilizes across all the units, the treatment is applied to the second and continued on the first. Data continue to be taken across all units. This process is repeated until all units have been treated. The effect of the intervention is evaluated on whether the series remains stable at baseline levels until treatment, at which time a change is seen. Each time an intervention is introduced, a test is made between the level of performance during the intervention and the projected level of the previous baselines. A unique feature of this design is the testing of predictions across different units; these units serve as control conditions to evaluate what changes can be expected without the application of the treatment.

An example of the use of a multiple baseline design is offered in Figure 2, that illustrates the results of a study designed to test the effectiveness of social skills training for improving the social behaviors of a 17-year-old deaf female (Lemanek & Gresham, 1984). A multiple baseline design across behaviors was used to examine the effect of treatment on three dependent variables (duration of communications, response latency, and content).

Figure 2 illustrates the baseline measures across all three dependent variables, with treatment initiated on the first behavior (content) at session seven. Baseline measures continued to be taken on the second and third behaviors (speech duration and response latency). Treatment was then initiated on the second behavior, and at session 11, on the third behavior. Visual inspection of the data indicates a slight improvement in appropriate content during treatment. Speech duration increased significantly from baseline to treatment. Decreases in response latency occurred from baseline throughout treatment and follow-up.

Several variations of the multiple baseline design are often used, applying the strategy across subjects, or across situations, settings, and time (Kazdin, 1982). In the variation across subjects, baseline data are gathered for a specific behavior across two or more subjects. A selected treatment is then applied in sequence across the matched subjects, just as in the multiple baseline across behaviors. Preferably, the subjects are exposed to identical environmental conditions. In the variation across settings, a treatment variable is applied sequentially to the same behavior in the same subject across different and independent set-

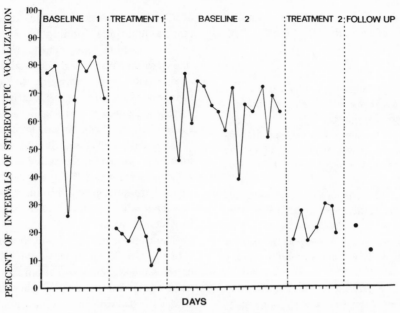

Figure 2. BSLN treatment follow-up 1 and 2.

tings. The same procedures apply for introducing the treatment after the stabilization of behavior across each setting for each baseline.

Many issues that are important to the implementation of this design are beyond the scope of this presentation. However, among the more salient are that at least two baselines should be used and that more are preferable. Issues such as length of phase and counterbalancing are important in these designs as well, and should be taken into account. It also should be noted that the use of this design across subjects or behaviors could result in withholding treatment from a particular subject for a longer period of time than might be judged clinically appropriate.

In multiple baseline designs across behaviors, the assumption is that the targeted behaviors are independent from one another. In some disorders, it is reasonable to assume that targeted behaviors may covary. As a result, the controlling effects of the treatment variables are subject to question.

A particular problem with implementing many single-case time-series designs in applied settings is the amount of time required for appropriate baseline measures. Often the subject cannot handle a long treatment session, or is frustrated by repeated attempts at a difficult treatment. A balance must be reached between the amount of data needed to demonstrate experimental control and the practical aspects of working with the client. One design that has been offered to alleviate this problem is the multiple-probe design. This design is a combination of multiple baseline design and probe procedures.

A probe is defined as an intermittent assessment of selected target behaviors under nontreatment conditions. The nature of the probes depends on behaviors being investigated and practical considerations. There are three primary features of the multiple-probe design. First, there is an initial probe of every step in a chain or successive approximation. Second, a probe is conducted on each step in the treatment sequence after criterion is achieved on any one step. Third, a series of probes or real baselines are conducted immediately before the initiation of treatment on any given step in the sequence. Only probes following the completion of all prerequisite steps and immediately before intervention are considered a true measure of the subject's ability to perform a given step.

Experimental control can be shown despite less baseline data as long as the pretreated probe and true baseline data are stable and a consistent change with introduction of treatment is shown. Graphic representation of the data would resemble that of multiple baseline studies. Probes and true baselines along the abscissa can be examined to determine whether the behavior remained stable until intervention was initiated at each step in the training sequence.

In the multiple-probe design, similar but independent behavior must be chosen to maintain experimental control, as the design is not appropriate for studying steps that are truly interdependent. The multiple-probe design avoids problems of extinction, fatigue, and distraction that can occur as a result of continuous baseline testing. The design is a potentially efficient means of evaluating the effects of training on sequential steps in a treatment program for behaviors that are not totally interdependent.

Time-series designs, especially single-subject investigations, are increasingly recognized as important methodologies for the evaluation of the efficacy of treatment. Within-, between-, and combined-series designs each provide internally valid methods for answering questions regarding the effects of a particular treatment, or the relative effects of different treatments or conditions. The use of single-subject time-series designs offers the educational researcher a valid way of answering questions about the nature of the intervention offered clients.

REFERENCES

Barlow, D. H., Hayes, S. C., & Nelson, R. O. (1984). *The scientist practitioner: Research and accountability in clinical and educational settings*. New York: Pergamon.

Gettinger, M. (1985). Effects of teacher-directed versus student-directed instruction and cues versus no cues for improving spelling performance. *Journal of Applied Behavior Analysis, 18,* 167–171.

Hersen, N., & Barlow, D. H. (1976). *Single case experimental designs: Strategies for studying behavior change.* New York: Pergamon.

Kazdin, A. E. (1982). *Single-case research designs: Methods for clinical and applied settings.* New York: Oxford University Press.

Kratochwill, T. R. (Ed.) (1978). *Single-subject research: strategies for evaluating change.* New York: Academic.Kratochwill, T. R., & Piersel, W. C. (1983). Time-series research: Contributions to empirical clinical practice. *Behavioral Assessment, 5,* 165–176.

Lemanek, K. L., & Gresham, P. M. (1984). Social skills training with a deaf adolescent. Implications for placement and programming. *School Psychology Review, 13,* 385–390.

McReynolds, L., & Kearns, K. (1983). *Single subject experimental designs in communicative disorders.* Baltimore, MD: University Park Press.

Powers, M. D., & Crowel, R. L. (1985). The educative effects of positive practice overcorrection: Acquisition, generalization, and maintenance. *School Psychology Review, 14,* 360–372.

EDYTHE A. STRAND
THOMAS R. KRATOCHWILL
University of Wisconsin,
Madison

APPLIED BEHAVIOR ANALYSIS RESEARCH IN SPECIAL EDUCATION

SIX-HOUR RETARDED CHILD

The term 6-hour retardate first appeared in the report of the Conference on Problems of Education of Children in the Inner City (President's Committee on Mental Retardation, 1969). The conference was charged with developing a new set of recommendations regarding the problems of mentally retarded children living within the ghettos of U.S. cities. After reviewing the papers of the 92 participants, 7 major recommendations were developed: (1) provide early childhood stimulation education as part of the public education program; (2) conduct a study of histories of successful inner-city families who have learned to cope effectively; (3) restructure education of teachers, administrators, and counselors; (4) reexamine present systems of intelligence testing and classification; (5) commit substantial additional funding for research and development in educational improvement for the disadvantaged; (6) delineate what constitutes accountability and hold the school accountable for providing quality education for all children; and (7) involve parents, citizens, citizen groups, students, and general and special educators in a total educational effort. However, one outcome overshadowed all of these recommendations. It was the conclusion that "we now have what may be called a 6-hour retarded child— retarded from 9 to 3, 5 days a week, solely on the basis of an IQ, without regard to his adaptive behavior, which may be exceptionally adaptive to the situation and community in which he lives."

The concept of the 6-hour retarded child has survived into the late 1980s. Today many psychologists and educators have accepted as a given that children identified as mildly retarded during the school-age years manifest retarded functioning only in the school setting, and that outside of school, during childhood and in their work lives as adults, they function successfully. Often their retardation is invisible to their employers, families, neighbors, and friends.

The conclusion of the conference participants was not inconsistent with case studies and some published reports of the adult lives of the mildly retarded. Although observations of the mildly retarded as children led many to believe that as adults they would fail in community adaptation, many investigators observed a high proportion of the adult retarded who achieved satisfactory adjustment, even when a variety of criteria were used.

The results of these early conclusions were confounded by subsequent reports showing that success in adult adaptation was equivocal, at best. The challenge of a more definitive portrayal of the adult lives of the mildly retarded was undertaken by the Socio-Behavioral Research Group at UCLA, who produced several informative studies of mildly retarded children as adults. Edgerton (1984) and Koegel and Edgerton (1984) used a holistic natural approach rather than measures of discrete adult outcomes. They conducted extensive ethnographic participant research studies of several aspects of the adult behavior of individuals who had been mildly retarded as children.

One of their studies centered on the functioning of blacks who had been classified as educable mentally retarded (EMR) as children, an adult sample of those who were the object of concern in the 1969 Conference on Problems of Education of Children of the Inner City. They identified 45 residents in a black community who had attended EMR classes and who represented the broad range of competencies and lifestyles found among mildly retarded adults in the black community. The 12 subjects who were selected for their study satisfied one criterion: field researchers, during the course of their first visits, expressed serious doubt that they were, in fact, retarded. These 12 individuals, when compared with the remainder of the sample, clearly led more normal lives. They had mean IQ scores of 62, 33% were married, and 42% were competitively employed. For 1 year a staff of black ethnographic field researchers maintained regular contact with the 12 participants, visiting them for 1 to 4 hours a day on an average of 12 separate occasions. The visits took place in homes, at work sites, and schools, during leisure activities, shopping expeditions, and job searches. Both parents and subjects were interviewed regarding any limitations they perceived, as well as their experiences in various aspects of their adult lives.

Although the adult lives of the participants were varied, none of them had "disappeared" into his or her community as a normal person. All 12 were seen by others close to them as limited or handicapped and most of the 12 participants acknowledged their own limitations. The participants continued to be troubled by the same problems that characterized them during their formal schooling—problems with reading, numerical concepts, and everyday tasks such as shopping, applying for jobs, traveling around the city, eating out in restaurants, making ends meet, etc.

Their problems transcended those associated with academic or intellectual pursuits. Their case histories included difficulties arising from poor judgment, vulnerability to exploitation and victimization, need for help in rearing their children, and an inability to comprehend satisfactorily their everyday experiences.

This study and several others of the adult lives of mildly retarded adults raise serious doubts regarding the efficacy and use of the concept of the 6-hour retarded child. The lives of these participants sometimes paralleled those of the nonretarded in the community, but never completely. Even though they were no longer receiving services as adults, they continued to face the same kinds of problems they did as children.

The contrast between the expectancies of the conference participants in 1969 and some of the recent studies such as the work by Edgerton et al. suggests that regular and special education programs should attend to preparing children with limited potential for the roles they will engage in as adults. Moreover, no one concerned about the future of the mildly retarded pupil can be content in the belief that their problems exist only in school, and that outside of this setting they function as capably as their age mates.

REFERENCES

Edgerton, R. B. (Ed.). (1984). *Lives in process: Mildly retarded adults in a large city*. Washington, DC: American Association on Mental Deficiency.

Koegel, P., & Edgerton, R. B. (1984). Black "six hour retarded" children as young adults. In R. B. Edgerton (Ed.), *Lives in process: Mildly retarded adults in a large city*. Washington, DC: American Association on Mental Deficiency.

President's Committee on Mental Retardation. (1969). *The six hour retarded child*. Washington, DC: Bureau of Education for the Handicapped, Office of Education, U.S. Department of Health, Education, and Welfare.

NADINE M. LAMBERT
*University of California,
Berkeley*

**EDUCABLE MENTALLY RETARDED
MENTAL RETARDATION**

SKEELS, HAROLD M. (1901–1970)

Harold M. Skeels, pioneer researcher in the field of mental retardation, was responsible for a large number of studies of institutional populations during the 1930s and early 1940s. These studies showed that children placed in unstimulating institutional environments failed to develop normally, and that the longer they remained, the greater their deficits became. Skeels reached the conclusion that it is possible to improve intellectual functioning through early stimulation, and he advocated early adoption as an alternative to institutionalization. His findings set off a nature-nurture controversy, and Skeels and his associates were the targets of vehement attacks.

Harold M. Skeels

Following service in the armed forces during World War II, and subsequent employment with the U.S. Public Health Service and the National Institute of Mental Health, Skeels made a follow-up study of some of the subjects of his earlier research. The results showed dramatically the long-term effects of differences in childhood environments. By the time his report was published, many of Skeels's concepts from the 1930s had become commonplace: adoption at an early age had become routine, institutional placements were decreasing, and a variety of early childhood services had been developed, including some programs, like Head Start, aimed specifically at early stimulation of disadvantaged and handicapped children.

REFERENCES

Crissey, M. S. (1970). Harold Manville Skeels. *American Journal of Mental Deficiency, 75*, 1–3.

Skeels, H. M. (1966). Adult status of children with contrasting early life experiences. *Monograph of the Society for Research in Child Development, 33*, 1–65.

Skeels, H. M., & Dye, H. B. (1939). A study of the effects of differential stimulation. *Proceedings of the American Association on Mental Deficiency, 44*, 114–136.

PAUL IRVINE
Katonah, New York

HEAD START
NATURE VERSUS NURTURE

SKILL TRAINING

The skill training model rests on the premise that assessment of a student's performance should focus on classroom tasks. Such assessment is usually tied to some hierarchy of skills. Instruction, then, follows directly from the results of the hierarchial assessment, and often uses direct instruction skills (Mercer, 1983).

Skill training is a commonly used approach in special education. It provides the teacher with an opportunity to evaluate specific skills, skills that are of immediate and direct concern to classroom instruction. The skill training process usually begins with the administration of a criterion-referenced or teacher-made assessment device. The analysis of the results of the assessment provides the teacher with additional information that is specifically related to classroom interventions. That is, the analysis, focusing on a hierarchy of skills, helps to pinpoint the specific error the student is making, allowing a more precise instructional decision to be made. This instructional decision will usually result in the teacher using some direct instructional technique, concentrating the teaching efforts on a specific academic skill. Pupil progress is continuously measured to ensure that instruction continues to focus on appropriate skills. On mastery of one skill, the teacher and student progress to the next hierarchial skill.

REFERENCE

Mercer, C. D. (1983). *Students with learning disabilities* (2nd ed.). Columbus, OH: Merrill.

JOHN R. BEATTIE
University of North Carolina,
Charlotte

MASTERY LEARNING

SKINNER, BURRHUS FREDERICK (1904–   )

Burrhus Frederick Skinner received his BA (1926) in literature from Hamilton College and his MA (1930) and PhD (1931) in psychology from Harvard University. He remained at Harvard for the next five years working in W. J. Cozier's laboratory, and was a Junior Fellow in the Society of Fellows of Harvard University from 1933 to 1936.

In 1936, Skinner joined the Psychology Department at the University of Minnesota where he wrote his first and probably most important book, *The Behavior of Organisms* (1938) that described the results of years of research using white rats in an operant conditioning chamber. The function of the word "operant," then as now, was to identify behavior traceable to reinforcing contingencies rather than to eliciting stimuli. In the tradition of objective behaviorism, Skinner believed that speculations about what intervenes between stimulus and response or between response and reward to be superfluous. Skinner also wrote his novel, *Walden Two* (1948), at the University of Minnesota, which was a blueprint for a utopia based on behavioral principles. He was chairman of the department of psychology at Indiana University from 1945 to 1948. In the fall 1947, he was appointed William James Lecturer at Harvard University and joined the department of psychology as professor in 1948: he is currently Professor Emeritus.

Skinner advanced behaviorism by distinguishing between two types of behavior, respondent and operant, and showing how various contingencies of reinforcement can be employed to modify or control any kind of behavior. He raised a storm of controversy by posing the application of these principles in *Beyond Freedom and Dignity* (1971) where he interprets concepts of freedom, value, and dign-

Burrhus Frederick Skinner

ity in objective terms. He also suggests the design of a society in which the behavior of citizens would be shaped and controlled by planned systems of rewards (reinforcements).

The basic principles of operant conditioning described by Skinner have been applied in two main areas in special education, programmed learning and behavior modification. Both areas allow the special educator to analyze and develop a plan of instruction for learning or behavior that is systematic and situation specific.

Skinner has extended his studies to verbal behavior, psychotic behavior, instructional devices, and the analysis of cultures.

REFERENCES

Skinner, B. F. (1938). *The behavior of organisms: An experimental analysis*. New York: Appleton-Century.

Skinner, B. F. (1948). *Walden two*. New York: Macmillan.

Skinner, B. F. (1971). *Beyond freedom and dignity*. New York: Bantam.

ELAINE FLETCHER-JANZEN
Texas A&M University

BEHAVIOR MODIFICATION
OPERANT CONDITIONING

cation involves the arrangement of contingencies of reinforcement to ensure effective learning. Skinner (1968) noted that although students obviously learn outside the classroom without such systematic procedures, "teachers arrange special contingencies which expedite learning, hastening the appearance of behavior which would otherwise be acquired slowly or making sure of the appearance of behavior which might otherwise never occur" (p. 65). Operant techniques have been applied in classrooms more than in any other setting and have been extremely successful in improving a variety of academic and social behaviors in diverse student populations (Kazdin, 1978).

REFERENCES

Kazdin, A. E. (1978). *History of behavior modification: Experimental foundations of contemporary research*. Baltimore, MD: University Park Press.

Skinner, B. F. (1953). *Science and human behavior*. New York: Free Press.

Skinner, B. F. (1968). *The technology of teaching*. Englewood Cliffs, NJ: Prentice-Hall.

CHRISTINE L. COLE
University of Wisconsin,
Madison

BEHAVIOR MODIFICATION
CONDITIONING
OPERANT CONDITIONING
SKINNER, B. F.

SKINNER'S FUNCTIONAL LEARNING MODEL

B. F. Skinner's functional learning model, known as operant conditioning, describes the relationship between behavior and the environmental events that influence it. The basic principles of operant conditioning include reinforcement, punishment, extinction, and stimulus control. These principles describe the functionality of events that precede or follow behavior. Reinforcement, for example, serves the function of increasing the strength of behavior. Skinner (1953) described two types of reinforcement. Positive reinforcement refers to the presentation of an event, commonly called a reward, following behavior. For example, a teacher smiles and says, "Good work" following completion of a child's assignment. Negative reinforcement refers to the removal of an event presumed to be unpleasant following behavior. For example, a child's aggressive behavior may cause a teacher to remove an unpleasant request. In both cases, the effect of reinforcement is the same—the child is more likely to engage in that behavior (assignment completion or aggressive behavior) under similar conditions in the future.

The application of operant conditioning to special edu-

SLINGERLAND SCREENING TESTS

The Slingerland screening tests are comprised of four forms with designated grade levels (Form A, grades 1 and 2; Form B, grades 2 and 3; Form C, grades 3 and 4; Form D, grades 5 and 6) (Slingerland & Ansara, 1974; Slingerland, 1974). There are eight subtests for Forms A, B, and C that may be either group or individually administered. These subtests require the students to copy letters and words from a board, copy from a page, perform visual matching exercises by selecting a stimulus word from an array of distractor words with various letter reversals, copy words presented in flashcard fashion, write dictated words, and detect initial and final sounds. For children that exhibit difficulties with portions of the eight subtests, there are individually administered auditory tests designed to assess auditory perception and memory. The student is asked to repeat individual words and phrases, to complete sentences with a missing word, and to retell a story. With the exception of additional subtests assessing personal orientation, Form D is comparable to the other three forms of the test. As noted by Fujiki (1985), the purpose of the Slingerland is not to identify linguistically handicapped children, but to assess auditory, visual, and motor skills associated with learning to read and write.

Local norms are advocated to interpret the results of students' test performance. This recommendation is necessary because of the notable omission of adequate normative data. Also absent in the manuals is an adequate discussion of reliability, stability, or validity.

REFERENCES

Fujiki, M. (1985). Review of Slingerland Screening Tests for identifying children with specific language disabilities. In J. V. Mitchell (Ed.), *The ninth mental measurements yearbook* (Vol. 2, pp. 1398–1399). Lincoln, NE: University of Nebraska Press.

Slingerland, B. H. (1974). *Teacher's manual to accompany Slingerland Screening Tests for Identifying Children with Specific Language Disability-Revised Edition* (Form D). Cambridge, MA: Educators.

Slingerland, B. H., & Ansara, A. S. (1974). *Teacher's manual to accompany Slingerland Screening Tests for Identifying Children with Specific Language Disability-Revised Edition* (Forms A, B and C). Cambridge, MA: Educators.

JACK A. CUMMINGS
Indiana University

ASSESSMENT
BASIC ACHIEVEMENT SKILLS
LANGUAGE DISORDERS

SLOSSON INTELLIGENCE TEST (SIT)

First published in 1961 by Slosson Educational Publications, the Slosson Intelligence Test (SIT) is a highly verbal, brief screening measure of intelligence intended to approximate the lengthier Stanford-Binet Intelligence Scale. A second edition was published in 1981. The SIT is a popular screening measure used by many special educators. Unfortunately, its use for any purpose is largely unsupportable on psychometric grounds and its status as a brief screening test precludes use in placement decisions.

The 1981 norming sample was drawn entirely from the New England states, and no attempt was made to select children randomly or to otherwise mimic the general population with whom the test is intended to be used. Attempts were made to develop deviation IQs that are equated to Stanford-Binet (1972 norms) IQs. Even this effort was seriously flawed as many extrapolations were made as well as interpolations between extrapolations. Internal consistency reliability estimates are not reported and the few reliabilities given are likely inflated owing to collapsing across four and five age ranges.

With the publication of the Stanford-Binet Fourth Re-

vision in 1985, any remaining justification for the use of the SIT is eliminated. Given the number of well-standardized, sophisticated, and psychometrically sound measures of intelligence now available, there are no longer any reasons for the use of poorly normed scales. Whenever a brief screening measure of intelligence is desired, the use of short forms of major scales such as the WISC-R and the K-ABC is best.

CECIL R. REYNOLDS
Texas A&M University

DEVIATION IQ
KAUFMAN ASSESSMENT BATTERY FOR CHILDREN
STANFORD-BINET INTELLIGENCE TEST
WECHSLER INTELLIGENCE SCALE FOR CHILDREN—
  REVISED

SLOW LEARNER

Historically, the slow learning child has been described in numerous ways. Ingram's (1960) book, the *Education of the Slow-Learning Child*, discussed the education of the educable mentally retarded child. Johnson (1963) noted that "slow learners compose the largest group of mentally retarded persons" (p. 9). Today, however, the term slow learner most accurately describes children and adolescents who learn or underachieve, in one or more academic areas, at a rate that is below average yet not at the level considered comparable to that of an educable mentally retarded student. Intellectually, slow learners score most often between a 75 and a 90 IQ—between the borderline and low-average classifications of intelligence.

It is unusual to find the slow learner discussed in the standard special education textbook. Indeed, slow learners are not special education students. There is no PL 94-142 label or definition of slow learner, and these students are not eligible for any monies or services associated with that law. When slow learners receive additional supportive services, it is typically in the regular classroom or in remedial classes that may be supported by federal title funds or programs. These remedial classes are not conceptualized as alternative educational programs; they are used to reinforce regular classroom curricula and learning. Some slow learners are inappropriately labeled learning disabled to maintain the enrollment (and funding) of some special education classrooms, or because they would otherwise fail in the regular classroom, despite not having special education needs.

There is no consensus on a diagnostic or descriptive profile that characterizes the slow learner. Indeed, there is very little contemporary research with samples specifically labeled as slow learners. Many slow learners are now described by their specific academic weaknesses; research and/or remedial programs are applied to these academic areas—not to the slow learner labels. Because of this shift in emphasis, earlier research describing slow learners as being from low socioeconomic and minority family backgrounds, academically and socially frustrated, and devalued by teachers and peers, and as having low self-concepts, may or may not still apply (Cawley, Goodstein, & Burrow, 1972).

REFERENCES

Cawley, J. F., Goodstein, H. A., & Burrow, W. H. (1972). *The slow learner and the reading problem.* Springfield, IL: Thomas.

Ingram, C. P. (1960). *Education of the slow-learning child* (3rd ed.). New York: Ronald.

Johnson, G. O. (1963). *Education for slow learners.* Englewood Cliffs, NJ: Prentice-Hall.

HOWARD M. KNOFF
University of South Florida

CLASSIFICATION, SYSTEMS OF EDUCABLE MENTALLY RETARDED

SNELLEN CHART

The Snellen chart is a measuring device used to determine an individual's central distance visual acuity. The chart contains eight rows of letters of the alphabet in graduated sizes. There is a version for young children and for people who cannot read that replaces the alphabet with the letter E in different orientations and sizes. The letter sizes on the chart correspond to the estimate of the ability of a typical person to read the material. It is constructed so that at a distance of 20 ft, a person reading the figures on the chart corresponding to what a normal eye sees at 20 ft is said to have 20/20 vision (Bryan & Bryan, 1979). A person with 20/20 vision and both eyes working in a co-ordinated fashion is considered to be normally sighted. When a person sees at 20 ft what a normal person sees at 70 ft or 200 ft, that person has 20/70 or 20/200 vision. Individuals who have low vision or who are visually limited may be legally blind (visual acuity of 20/200 or less), or partially sighted (visual acuity between 20/70 and 20/200; DeMott, 1982).

The Snellen chart is widely used as a screening device for detecting eye problems because of the ease and speed with which it can be administered, its low cost, and its wide range of applicability. When compared with the Orthorater vision tester, Johnson and Caccamise (1983) found the Snellen chart to be an "acceptable, less expensive alternative" (p. 406). It can be used with young children as well as adults. However, because the Snellen measures only central visual acuity, it should be combined with other procedures in screening. The Snellen chart gives no indication of near-point or peripheral vision, convergence ability, fusion ability, or muscular imbalance.

Bryan and Bryan (1979) list three shortcomings of the Snellen chart:

1. It is not a good predictor of competence in visual processing of objects and tasks.
2. It does not tell how a child uses vision in terms of discriminating light or darkness, estimating size, or determining spatial location.
3. The results are not translatable into educational programs. Children with the same visual acuity may respond differently to school tasks, and, therefore, require different programming.

Getman (1985) argues that visual acuity is not the only criteria for measuring acquisition of basic visual skills. He estimates that 80% of the assignments in contemporary classrooms are visually centered and that every child should have the opportunity to improve all of the visual skills on which success will pivot. However, DeMott (1982) holds that the most important initial screening device for detecting eye problems is one that measures central visual acuity. Combining results from the Snellen chart with other screening measures is important for early diagnosis and remediation of eye problems.

REFERENCES

Bryan, J. H., & Bryan, L. H. (1979). *Exceptional Children.* Sherman Oaks, CA: Alfred.

Getman, G. N. (1985). A commentary on vision-training. *Journal of Learning Disabilities, 18*(9), 505–512.

DeMott, R. M. (1982). Visual impairments. In N. G. Haring (Ed.), *Exceptional children and youth.* Columbus, OH: Merrill.

Johnson, D. D., & Caccamise, F. (1983). Hearing impaired students: Options for visual acuity screening. *American Annals of the Deaf, 128*(3), 402–406.

Kirk, S. A. (1962). *Educating exceptional children.* Boston: Houghton Mifflin.

NANCY J. KAUFMAN
University of Wisconsin, Stevens Point

VISUAL ACUITY VISUALLY IMPAIRED

SOCIAL BEHAVIOR OF THE HANDICAPPED

Evidence from Lerner (1985) and Stephens, Hartman, and Lucas, (1983) has clearly documented that many exceptional children experience difficulty in the area of social skills. This difficulty could range from mild problems to severe disorders. Minskoff (1980) considers social perceptual difficulties as among the more serious problems of learning-disabled children. Drew, Logan, and Hardman

(1984) indicate that retarded students often have a higher incidence of emotional problems than nonretarded students. Lerner (1985) identified six characteristics of social behavior that are common among disabled children and youths: (1) lack of judgment, (2) difficulties in perceiving others, (3) problems in making friends, (4) poor self-concept, (5) problems involving family relationships, and (6) social difficulties in the school setting.

In most instances, children who are receiving special education services have more than one problem and disabilities produce different behaviors in different children (Cartwright, Cartwright, & Ward, 1984). Bloom (1956) proposes a system whereby all education-related activities would fall into three major domains—affective, psychomotor, and cognitive. Cartwright et al. (1984) define the affective domain as the social domain; this deals with an individual's social abilities, such as establishing and maintaining satisfactory interpersonal skills, displaying behavior within reasonable social expectations, and making personal adjustments. Social skills and the ability to get along with others are just as important to the handicapped student as they are to the nonhandicapped student. In fact, these social skills are even more critical to the person who is handicapped because the handicapped are often compared with the norm and must compete for grades, social status, and employment.

Wallace and Kauffman (1986) indicate that social behavior development is inseparable from the student's acquisition of academic skills and that "inappropriate behavior limits the student's chances for success in school: conversely, school failure often prompts undesirable behavior" (p. 165). Wallace and Kauffman (1986) strongly suggest that the remediation of students' social behavior problems is just as important as the remediation of their academic problems.

Social skills have been hard to define and even more difficult to measure according to Wallace and Kauffman (1986), and Strain, Odom, and McConnell (1984). Direct observation is perhaps one of the most reliable methods used in assessment of social skills problems. Other procedures used to assess competence in social behavior are self-reporting and screening instruments, clinical judgment, analysis of antecedent events, interviews, sociometric procedures, behavior and rating scales. However, when assessing an individual's social skills, one must be aware of the situations and circumstances in which the behavior occurs. Social and emotional problems may not be the primary difficulties facing most exceptional children; nevertheless, except for behavior-disordered or seriously emotionally disturbed students, these problems are present.

Eleas and Maher (1983) suggest that well-adjusted children have certain social and academic skills that many mildly handicapped students do not possess. Such skills as sensitivity to others' feelings, goal-setting persistence, and an adequate behavior repertoire are just a few men-

tioned. Many more social skills deficits that often plague handicapped students such as poor self-concept, withdrawal, rejection, and attention problems, compound the academic problems. School personnel need to address these social skill problems of the handicapped student. Mercer and Mercer (1985) indicate that teachers can "help foster the student's emotional development as well as the acquisition of social skills" (p. 132). Wallace and Kauffman (1986) and Mercer and Mercer (1985) believe that direct instruction may be the best method for remediating problems associated with social skills deficits. In addition to direct instruction, there are instructional materials and kits available commercially that are designed for teaching social skills. However, many of these kits have little validity data and vary widely in terms of the populations with which they have been used.

Perhaps social competence might be a better term to describe the skills necessary to get along with others. Schulman (1980) defines social competence as "getting along with people, communicating with them and coping with the frustrations of social living" (p. 285). Nearly all of us need to feel accepted and socially competent. However, many handicapped students and adults have difficulty, to some degree, in developing those skills necessary for adequate social acceptance.

REFERENCES

Bellach, A. S. (1983). Recurrent problems in the behavior assessment of social skills. *Behavior Research & Therapy, 21,* 29–41.

Bloom, B. (1956). *Taxonomy of educational objectives: The classification of educational goals.* New York: Longman.

Cartwright, C. P., Cartwright, C. A., & Ward, M. E. (1984). *Educating special learners.* Belmont, CA: Wadsworth.

Eleas, M. J., & Maher, C. A. (1983). Social and effective development of children: A programmatic perspective. *Exceptional Children, 4,* 339–346.

Drew, C. J., Logan, D. R., & Hardman, M. L. (1984). *Mental retardation: A life cycle approach* (3rd ed.). St. Louis: Mosby.

Lerner, J. (1985). *Learning disabilities: Theories, diagnosis, and teaching strategies* (4th ed.). Boston: Houghton Mifflin.

Mercer, D. D., & Mercer, A. R. (1985). *Teaching students with learning problems* (2nd ed.). Columbus, OH: Merrill.

Minskoff, E. H. (1980). Teaching approach for developing nonverbal communication skills in students with social perception deficits. *Journal of Learning Disabilities, 13,* 118–126.

Schulman, E. D. (1980). *Focus on retarded adults: Programs and services.* St. Louis: Mosby.

Stephens, T. M., Hartman, A. C., & Lucas, V. H. (1983). *Teaching children basic skills: A curriculum handbook* (2nd ed.). Columbus, OH: Merrill.

Strain, P. S., Odom, S. L., & McConnell, S. (1984). Promoting social reciprocity of exceptional children: Identification, target behaviors selection, and intervention. *Remedial & Special Education, 1,* 21–28.

Wallace, G., & Kauffman, J. M. (1986). *Teaching students with learning and behavior problems* (3rd ed.). Columbus, OH: Merrill.

HUBERT R. VANCE
East Tennessee State University

ADAPTIVE BEHAVIOR
SOCIAL SKILLS
SOCIAL SKILLS TRAINING
SOCIOGRAM

SOCIAL COMPETENCE

See ADAPTIVE BEHAVIOR.

SOCIAL DARWINISM

Social Darwinism, a social philosophy that was developed in the latter half of the nineteenth century, was based on the application of Darwin's principles of natural selection and survival of the fittest to the problems of society. Mental retardation, insanity, epilepsy, alcoholism, and other disorders were explained in terms of heredity, genetics, and Darwinian principles. Adams (1971) describes social Darwinism as follows: "the people of above average intelligence by previous standards become the norm in the next evolutionary phase, and the slow ones drop back to become the social casualties of the new order." Social Darwinism was also associated with attempts to interpret mental retardation as deviance rather than incompetence (Farber, 1968).

When Western Europe and North America became industrialized, environmental conditions that hindered the intellectual development of normal children resulted. Industrialization also led to health hazards that were responsible for the birth of biologically deficient children. At the same time, correlations were found between intellectual and social deficits that stimulated a variety of explanatory efforts. According to the principle of social Darwinism, human deficiencies were caused by evolutionary obstacles or the degeneration of genetic matter. The historical perspective of social Darwinism and its relation to the eugenics movement are central to understanding the treatment of disabled individuals from the 1850s to the 1950s.

In the 1850s, even before Darwin published his findings and theories, Morel speculated that all varieties of mental illnesses were related and were due to hereditary factors. Noting an association between mental retardation and sterility, he further postulated that these illnesses became more profound with each succeeding generation, leading ultimately to sterility and extinction. Morel suggested that mental illnesses were caused by physical diseases, alcoholism, and social environments, and called for more adequate food, housing, and working conditions as preventive measures. Concurrently, with evidence of a genetic, inheritable component of intelligence mounting, mental health professionals were becoming convinced that institutional segregation of the disabled was necessary, thus abandoning their efforts to return handicapped individuals to the community. Darwinism reached a height of popularity in England in the 14-year period from 1858 to 1872, but its effects were felt until the turn of the century. In the United States, Darwinian doctrine provided justification for the existing status structure prior to and during the Civil War. Darwinian proponents contended that foreigners and members of lower socioeconomic levels were distinct races that were inferior and might justifiably be subjugated. However, the North's victory strengthened the position of the anti-Darwinian proponents (Farber, 1968).

The optimism that characterized the treatment and care of the disabled in the early portion of the nineteenth century began to disappear in the latter half of the century. Institutions began moving away from treatment programs, replacing them with basic care and maintenance services. The emphasis on rehabilitation and education degenerated into support for terminal institutional placement (Hardman, Drew, & Egan, 1984). In the early portion of the twentieth century, with the introduction of mental tests, researchers found that a large proportion of prison inmates could be classified as feebleminded. Mentally retarded women were believed to be promiscuous, burdening society with many illegitimate offspring. It was estimated that criminals and unmarried mothers constituted 40 to 45% of the mentally retarded population. Furthermore, Tredgold and his followers contended that 90% of mental deficiency was due to hereditary factors. The feebleminded were regarded as unable to sustain gainful employment and a danger to the community and the "race." The solutions that were proposed most often were segregation and sterilization (Farber, 1968).

The "eugenic scare" of the early 1900s has been described as a shift in focus from the protection of the mentally handicapped from a cruel and exploitative society to the protection of society from contamination by inferior mental stock (Adams, 1971). With social Darwinism setting the stage, the eugenic movement was fed by the alarming increase in pauperism, vagrancy, alcoholism, and delinquency in society, and the association of low mentality and sociopathic behavior within identified families (e.g., the Jukes and the Kallikaks) whose genetic lines had been traced. The eugenic position was manifested in legislation for sterilization and the proposal to extend custodial care to all the retarded in the United States during their childbearing years. The first sterilization law was passed in Indiana in 1907, followed by similar legislation in seven other states soon thereafter (Adams, 1971).

By the 1920s, pessimistic forecasts appeared to have been vindicated in England, where the incidence of mental deficiency was sharply increasing. Although eugenicists strove to win the debate on mental deficiency during the period from 1900 to 1940, their efforts were hindered by their inability to identify the unfit, to prove causation, and to limit fertility (Macnicol, 1983). In reality, the concept of total social control over the retarded was never much more than an idea, and neither wholesale institutional commitment nor sterilization was implemented. Providing institutional care to segregate a large portion of society at public expense proved to be highly impractical. Nevertheless, by associating mental defects with genetic factors, the social forces that were causing pathological living conditions among the poor were neglected and the economic causes for social maladjustment were ignored (Adams, 1971). Recently, the negative side effects of involuntary sterilization of retarded persons have been documented. Low self-esteem, feelings of failure, a sense of helplessness, and social isolation have all been associated with forced sterilization (Roos, 1975).

Social Darwinism and related social movements have had a profound impact on the treatment of the mentally retarded and other disabled individuals. However, not all of the effects of the social Darwinism movement were negative. Its popularity, along with the development of special educational services, has been credited with providing an impetus for the systematic study of the prevalence of mental retardation (Farber, 1968).

REFERENCES

Adams, M. (1971). *Mental retardation and its social dimensions.* New York: Columbia University Press.

Farber, B. (1968). *Mental retardation: Its social context and social consequences.* Boston: Houghton Mifflin.

Hardman, M. L., Drew, C. I., & Egan, M. W. (1984). *Human exceptionality: School, society, and family.* Boston: Allyn & Bacon.

Macnicol, J. (1983). Eugenics, medicine and mental deficiency: An introduction. *Oxford Review of Education, 3,* 177–180.

Roos, P. (1975). Psychological impact of sterilization on the individual. *Law & Psychology Review, 1,* 45–56.

GREG VALCANTE
University of Florida

EUGENICS
HEREDITY
JUKES AND THE KALLIKAKS

SOCIAL DEVELOPMENT

Social skill development of handicapped individuals is essential for successful integration into community life (Goldstein, 1969). According to Turner, Hersen, and Bel-

lack (1978), intellectually deficient individuals are noted for their extremely limited social skill repertoires and excessive rates of socially unacceptable behavior. Follow-up studies conducted with mentally retarded adults have consistently revealed that social skill deficits interfere significantly with a person's vocational success and community integration (Stanfield, 1973). In addition to mentally retarded populations, emotionally disturbed and learning-disabled populations are also recognized as having social skill deficits. These skill deficits often result in handicapped individuals being actively avoided. As a result of being avoided by nonhandicapped peers, the handicapped individual's exposure to appropriate peer models is reduced. Consequently, many handicapped persons spend a great deal of time in isolation or in contact with similarly handicapped peers. Both outcomes are equally void of optimal social skill building experiences and contribute to a perpetuation of inadequate social functioning.

The importance of social skill development is widely accepted and the inadequacies of handicapped populations in this area are well substantiated. With the increasing trend toward deinstitutionalization and integration of handicapped persons with nonhandicapped individuals in the least restrictive community environment, the development of appropriate social behaviors must be a priority (Gresham, 1981). However, until recently, few research efforts were directed toward the identification of intervention strategies that promote development.

One of the problems that has detracted from a concentrated investigation of social development has been the lack of agreement on an overall conceptualization of social behavior. Developmental theorists have examined the play behavior of nonhandicapped children and identified a series of stages or levels that are assumed to be related to more sophisticated social skill acquisition (Parten, 1932). Parten identified eight levels of social behavior on the basis of his observations of the play behavior engaged in by normal preschool children. These observations revealed that children typically engage in particular play behaviors at certain ages. For example, normal infants show little awareness of others around them while older preschoolers actively interact with each other. The categories or levels of this analysis have been confirmed by other researchers; they include autistic behavior, unoccupied behavior, independent play, observing behavior, attempted interaction, parallel play, associative play, and cooperative play.

Although developmental analysis has provided categories of social behavior that are useful for general assessment activities, this analysis has proven inadequate for the identification of specific training objectives that are required in specific interpersonal contexts. The developmental literature fails to specify clearly the frequency of behavior at various developmental levels, appropriate time and place for social behavior, appropriate chronological age for specific behaviors, and strategies for adjusting the normal developmental sequence for handicapped learners. Furthermore, developmental analyses have emphasized play skill development and have not given adequate attention to the range of behaviors that are included in a broader conceptualization of social development. Given the limitations associated with this approach, other theorists and researchers have provided taxonomies of social development that include a hierarchy of skills that contribute to social-interpersonal effectiveness in a variety of different settings (Gambrill & Richey, 1975; Goldstein, 1969; Stephens, 1978).

According to Goldstein (1969), social competence is comprised of two basic characteristics: the ability to think critically and the ability to act independently. An individual's ability to think critically refers to the accuracy of his or her perceptions of the facts in a social situation. In more precise terminology, thinking critically can be described as the ability to discriminate and decode social stimuli. The second basic characteristic, acting independently, refers to the range of verbal and nonverbal behaviors that are required for a person to be well assimilated in society (Goldstein, 1969). Goldstein's taxonomy is organized around these two basic characteristics.

Another taxonomy of social skill development was proposed by Gambrill and Richey (1975). These authors used factor analysis procedures to identify 11 categories of social behavior content that have been included in social skill development programs. These categories or factors are initiating interactions, confronting others, giving negative feedback, responding to criticism, turning down requests, handling service situations, resisting pressure to alter one's consciousness, engaging in "happy talk," complimenting others, admitting personal deficiencies, and handling bothersome situations. Virtually all interpersonal situations can be categorized into one of these skill categories.

Normative analysis has been suggested as a method for identifying specific social-interpersonal behaviors that contribute to a person's overall social development. A normative analysis is accomplished by determining the social skills that are performed typically by nonhandicapped persons in a particular setting. This analysis may include the frequency and duration of social responses in relation to specific interpersonal contexts. The goals and objectives that evolve from this analysis reflect those skills that will enable a person to function as normally as possible. By teaching a handicapped individual to behave according to social norms, the chances of that person successfully functioning in community life are maximized.

In the past few years, a treatment regimen involving verbal instruction, modeling, behavior rehearsal, and response feedback has been used to teach social skills to both normal and psychiatric populations (Rich & Schroeder, 1976). Since some individuals may need to learn how and when to engage in particular interpersonal behaviors (Hersen & Bellack, 1977), the previously noted combination of instructional components may be essential for ongoing social development.

REFERENCES

Gambrill, E., & Richey, C. (1975). An assertive inventory for use in assessment and research. *Behavior Therapy, 6,* 550–561.

Goldstein, H. (1969). Construction of a social learning curriculum. *Focus on Exceptional Children, 1,* 1–10.

Gresham, F. (1981). Social skills training with handicapped children: A review. *Review of Education Research, 51,* 139–176.

Hersen, M., & Bellack, A. S. (1977). Assessment of social skills. In A. R. Ciminero, K.S. Calhann, & H. E. Adams (Eds.), *Handbook for behavioral assesment.* New York: Wiley.

Parten, M. B. (1932). Social participation among pre-school children. *Journal of Abnormal & Social Psychology, 27,* 243–269.

Rich, A. R., & Schroeder, H. E. (1976). Research issues in assertiveness training. *Psychological Bulletin, 83*(6), 1081–1096.

Stanfield, J. S. (1973). Graduation: What happens to the retarded child when he grows up. *Exceptional Children, 39,* 548–552.

Stephens, T. M. (1978). *Social skills in the classroom.* Columbus, OH: Cedars.

Turner, S. M., Hersen, M., & Bellack, A. S. (1978). Social skills training to teach prosocial behaviors in an organically impaired and retarded patient. *Journal of Behavior Therapy & Experimental Psychiatry, 9,* 253–258.

PAUL BATES
Southern Illinois University

ACTIVITY, THEORY OF
SOCIAL LEARNING THEORY
SOCIAL SKILLS

SOCIAL INTEGRATION OF HANDICAPPED IN SCHOOL

See MAINSTREAMING.

SOCIAL ISOLATION

Social isolation has been subsumed under the rubric of social skills or social competence. The problem of defining social isolation in children, specifically, is consonant with the problem of defining social skills or social competence in general. Children labeled as social isolates do not appear to constitute a homogeneous or clearly defined group, and several descriptors have been used in the literature as labels (e.g., shy, isolated, withdrawn, anxious-withdrawn). Social isolation is a behavior pattern that occurs across various categories of children such as the autistic, mentally retarded, schizophrenic, and normal.

There is a lack of agreement among investigators regarding the specific behaviors that need to be performed to indicate social skillfulness or competence, and the appropriate behaviors that are not performed, or the inappropriate behaviors that are performed, that indicate a lack of social skillfulness or competence. The contribution of several variables such as age, sex, social status, and situationally specific factors, in determining the presence or absence of social competence is poorly understood. Also, the criterion measures used to assess social isolation (behavioral observations, peer sociometric ratings, teacher ratings) may affect what is labeled as social isolate behavior (Conger & Keane, 1981). These criterion measures may not tap the same dimensions of behavior and may identify different subtypes of children (Gottman, 1977). The behaviors that have been selected as indicators of social isolate behavior have not been empirically determined. They have been chosen on the basis of the face validity of their relationship to the behavior pattern of social isolation, and single measures of social isolation typically have been employed (Conger & Keane, 1981). Additionally, little or no relationship has been found between the two main types of criterion measures used to assess social isolate behavior when they have been compared (i.e., global peer sociometric ratings of acceptance or rejection and behavioral observations of rate of discrete social interactions; Gottman, 1977).

The principal approaches in the conceptualization of social isolation in childhood have been in terms of withdrawal indicated by low rates of social interaction relative to other children and rejection or lack of acceptance by peers (Gottman, 1977). These two groups of social isolates may represent different populations; however, the infrequent use of both methods of assessment with the same groups of children does not allow for a determination of how well these measures agree on or discriminate among different subtypes of children. Also, given the lack of agreement on what behaviors or lack of behaviors are related to social isolation, it is unclear whether low rates of social interaction imply a lack of social skills or a lack of exhibiting social skills that the child possesses. In terms of peer acceptance or rejection, it is not clear whether this is based on a lack of social skills or on behaviors perceived as negative by peers such as aggressiveness. The grouping together of various behaviors within the category of social isolate behavior obscures assessment and intervention efforts and reduces the likelihood of heterogeneous grouping.

The development of positive social relationships with peers is an important developmental achievement. Typically, social interaction increases and relationships become more stable as children grow older (Asher, Oden, & Gottman, 1977). Thus social isolation may represent a significant deviation in social development. Gronlund (1959) reports that 6% of a sample of grades 3 to 6 had no classroom friends, and 12% had only one friend. A study of elementary age problem children identified 13.95% of the children referred by teachers for psychological services as withdrawn (Woods, 1964; as cited in Woods, 1969). Strain,

Cook, and Apolloni (1977) estimate that 15% or more of children referred for psychological services exhibit social withdrawal as a major presenting symptom. Once a pattern of withdrawal behavior is established, it may persist through childhood and adolescence (Branson, 1968). The evidence for the carryover of social isolation into adulthood is beset with methodological problems and conflicting results that limit generalizations. It does appear, however, that adults with certain psychiatric disabilities were socially isolated as children, but that not all socially isolated children develop psychiatric disabilities as adults (Strain et al., 1977). Hops, Walker, & Greenwood (1979) note that children referred for psychological services because of social isolate behavior appear to lead quiet, retiring lives, with some restriction in social contacts.

Intervention approaches used with socially withdrawn children increasingly emphasize the training of social skills. Social learning procedures (Coombs & Slaby, 1977) have constituted major treatment methods for teaching social skills to socially isolated children (Conger & Keane, 1981; Hops, 1983). The use of instructional packages with multiple components appears to be the best method for teaching social skills. The packages may include a combination of shaping, modeling, coaching, and reinforcement. Cognitively oriented interpersonal problem-solving interventions have also been employed; they emphasize the training of cognitive processes to mediate performance across a range of situations rather than discrete behavioral responses to various situations (Urbain & Kendall, 1980). The cognitive-behavioral approach uses many of the same instructional methods as the social learning approach, but it focuses on teaching problem-solving strategies and verbally mediated self-control (e.g., self-instruction).

The evidence to date suggests that interventions have demonstrated modest to moderate effects in teaching social skills to socially isolated children. Also, there are problems in establishing training effects that generalize beyond the treatment setting and maintain over time. Given the importance of positive social relationships with peers, efforts need to be continued to overcome conceptual, methodological, and assessment problems. Advances in these areas may further improve intervention efforts with children for whom peer relationships are problematic.

REFERENCES

Asher, S. R., Oden, S. C., & Gottman, J. M. (1977). Children's friendship in the school setting. In L. G. Katz (Ed.), *Current topics in early education* (Vol. 1). Norwood, NJ: Ablex.

Bronson, W. C. (1968). Stable patterns of behaviors: The significance of enduring orientations for personality development. In J. P. Hill (Ed.), *Minnesota symposia on child psychology* (Vol. 2). Minneapolis, University of Minnesota Press.

Conger, J. C. & Keane, P. (1981). Social skills intervention in the treatment of isolated or withdrawn children. *Psychological Bulletin, 90*(3), 478–495.

Coombs, M. L., & Slaby, D. (1977). Social skills training with children. In B. B. Lahey & A. E. Kazdin (Eds.), *Advances in clinical child psychology* (Vol. 1). New York: Academic.

Gottman, J. M. (1977). Toward a definition of social isolation in children. *Child Development, 48*, 513–517.

Gronlund, N. E. (1959). *Sociometry in the classroom.* New York: Harper.

Hops, H. (1983). Social skills training for socially withdrawn/isolate children. In P. Karoly & J. J. Steffen (Eds.), *Improving children's competence.* Lexington, MA: Lexington.

Hops, H., Walker, H. M., & Greenwood, C. R. (1979). PEERS: A program for remediating withdrawal in school. In L. A. Hamerlynck (Ed.), *Behavioral systems for the developmentally disabled: In school and family environments.* New York: Brunner/Mazel.

Strain, P. S., Cooke, T. P., & Apolloni, T. (1976). *Teaching exceptional children: Assessing and modifying social behavior.* New York: Academic.

Urbain, E. S., & Kendall, P. C. (1980). Review of social-cognitive problem-solving interventions with children. *Psychological Bulletin, 88*(1), 109–143.

HAROLD HANSON
PAUL BATES
Southern Illinois University

SOCIAL BEHAVIOR
SOCIAL BEHAVIOR OF THE HANDICAPPED
SOCIOGRAM

SOCIALIZATION

Socialization refers to a complex set of skills that are required to interact effectively with other people. According to Hersen and Bellack (1977), the socially skilled individual is one who has the "ability to express both positive and negative feelings in an interpersonal context without suffering consequent loss of social reinforcement." These authors also emphasize that socialization encompasses the use of social skills in a variety of interpersonal contexts, coordination of verbal and nonverbal behaviors, and differential responding to the unique aspects of particular interpersonal situations.

The direct instruction of behaviors designed to facilitate one's socialization has an interesting history. In the 1930s personality theorists (e.g., Lewin, 1939) were stressing the importance of interpersonal situational determinants of behavior. Out of this backdrop emerged the first direct instructional therapy for interpersonal relations' inhibitions (Salter, 1949). The originator of this therapy, Andrew Salter, wrote a book entitled *Conditioned Reflex Therapy.* In this book Salter developed the position that "excitation" may be directly trained to overcome an individual's inhibitions (passiveness). With increased exci-

tation, Salter's subject was more spontaneous, spoke with feeling, and stood up to others.

Conditioned reflex therapy was not a popular clinical technique until it reemerged in 1958 under a different name and slightly different emphasis. Wolpe (1958) introduced the term assertiveness as a replacement for excitation because of the confusion in the layperson's mind between excitation and excitability. Wolpe's therapy emphasized the role of assertiveness training in reciprocal inhibition. By using modeling and behavioral rehearsal, Wolpe arranged for his clients to engage in behaviors that previously had been sources of debilitating anxiety for them. The successful experiences that these clients had during assertiveness training served a deconditioning function for the previously associated anxiety.

Wolpe's work was conducted with individuals who presumably had the necessary social skills in their repertoires, but who were prevented from using them because of maladaptive anxiety. The social skills involved in Wolpe's assertiveness training included all socially acceptable expressions of personal rights and feelings (Wolpe & Lazarus, 1966).

As the success of Wolpe's assertiveness training procedures became known, clinicians began to apply these techniques to a wider range of interpersonal behaviors and to a more diverse subject population. The modeling, rehearsal, and feedback components of assertiveness training have been found useful for facilitating the development of socialization-related behaviors. However, as clinicians have begun to apply these procedures with chronic psychiatric and mentally retarded populations, some of the assumptions of Wolpe's assertiveness have been questioned.

With chronic psychiatric patients and mentally retarded individuals, one cannot assume that relieving anxiety alone will enable them to function effectively in social situations. These populations may need to learn what to do, how to do it, and when to do it (Hersen & Bellack, 1977). According to Goldfried and D'Zurilla, ineffective socialization responses may be due to any one or a combination of the following four conditions: Inhibition of effective responses due to anxiety; Deficit in effective responses; Inhibition of cognitive problem-solving operations; and Actual deficit in cognitive problem-solving operations. With each of these conditions, an educative approach, involving verbal directions, modeling, behavior rehearsal, feedback, and natural environment practice, has proven useful (Hersen & Bellack, 1977). In these socialization-training initiatives, verbal instructions have been used to specifically direct the desired social action or content of a response. Following verbal instruction, an explicit model demonstration of the target behavior is provided to show how the skill is to be performed. Once the person has had the opportunity to observe a modeled demonstration, he or she is encouraged to rehearse by practicing the desired socialization behavior several times.

Contingent on demonstrating particular aspects of the target response, feedback is used to reinforce appropriate behavior and correct inappropriate responses. If the targeted socialization skill is being taught in a classroom environment, it is highly desirable to have the person practice in the natural environments in which the behavior is to be used. The treatment regimen described has been used to improve a variety of socialization behaviors involving handicapped and nonhandicapped individuals (Gresham, 1981).

REFERENCES

Gresham, F. (1981). Social skills training with handicapped children: A review. *Review of Educational Research, 51*, 139–176.

Hersen, M., & Bellack, A. S. (1977). Assessment of social skills. In A. R. Ciminero, K. S. Calhann, & H. E. Adams (Eds.), *Handbook for behavioral assessment*. New York: Wiley.

Lewin, K. (1939). Field theory and experiment in social psychology: Concepts and methods. *American Journal of Sociology, 44*, 868–896.

Wolpe, J. (1958). *Psychotherapy by reciprocal inhibition*. Stanford, CA: Stanford University Press.

Wolpe, J., & Lazarus, A. A. (1966). *Behavior therapy techniques*. New York: Pergamon.

PAUL BATES
Southern Illinois University

SOCIAL BEHAVIOR
SOCIAL ISOLATION
SOCIAL SKILLS

SOCIAL LEARNING THEORY

Social learning theory is one of the most well known and most influential models for understanding human behavior. In explaining this theory, it is helpful to describe what it is not, because social learning theory grew out of a reaction to other theoretical orientations. First, social learning theory does not view human behavior as purely a result of internal cognitive thoughts or feelings. Freud, for example, viewed human behavior as mediated by thoughts, wishes, self-concepts, impulses, etc. Neither does social learning theory view behavior as strictly a function of environmental events. Thus social learning theory is not a model of human behavior based strictly on the principles of operant conditioning developed by B. F. Skinner. Skinner and others believe that behavior is purely a function of environmental events.

Social learning theory does, however, provide an integration of previous theories such as Freud's and Skinner's. Although social learning theory is closely related to Skinner's principles of operant conditioning, the major difference is the incorporation of internal events as controlling stimuli. Social learning theorists recognize that an individual's thoughts and feelings have a significant impact on behavior.

Social learning theory is a term that has been applied to the views of a relatively wide range of theorists and researchers. Without question, the theorist who has done the most to conceptualize and advance the ideas of social learning theory is Albert Bandura. At the core of Bandura's (1978) version of social learning theory is the concept of reciprocal determinism. Reciprocal determinism, as a model of human behavior, conceptualizes behavior as a continuous reciprocal interaction between an individuals thoughts, behaviors, and environmental factors.

This triadic model views human functioning as a three-way interaction among behavior (B), cognitions and other internal events that affect perceptions and actions (P), and a person's external environment (E). An interesting aspect of this view is that each element of the triad affects the other two elements. Thus not only do internal and environmental events affect behavior, but behavior also affects internal events and the environment in reciprocal fashion. As Bandura (1978) suggests:

> Cognitive factors partly determine which external events will be observed, how they will be perceived, and how information they convey will be organized for future use . . . . An act therefore includes among its determinants self-produced influences . . . . By their actions, people play a role in creating the social milieu and other circumstances that arise in their daily transactions. (p. 345)

Because social learning theory has incorporated internal variables (e.g., thoughts and feelings) that are not directly observable, it has been criticized by professionals who hold a strongly behavioristic theoretical stance. Similarly, the emphasis within social learning theory on environmental factors has caused it to be dismissed by individuals who have a strong cognitive, biological, or Freudian view of human behavior. Despite being in disfavor with the radical behaviorists and the pure cognitivists, social learning theory has enormous appeal to a wide variety of professionals. The reason for this appeal is the breadth of coverage. Social learning theory is seen by many as being very comprehensive in its ability to handle a diverse range of human experiences and problems.

A key component in most social learning theories is observational learning, which is based on the process of modeling. Through modeling children learn a wide array of complicated skills such as language and social interaction. Moreover, these skills are learned without reinforcement. This is in stark contrast to behavioral theory, which posits that complex behaviors are learned through the reinforcement of gradual changes in molecular response patterns. Teachers make use of observational learning many times a day. For example, some teachers will verbally reinforce a child who is behaving appropriately. Other children nearby see the type of behavior that is being reinforced and attempt to imitate. Social learning theorists maintain that it would be impossible to learn all of the tasks involved in the socialization process if each one had to be acquired by the step-by-step process hypothesized by the radical behaviorists.

Another key aspect of social learning theory is the concept of internal dialogues. These dialogues, or internal speeches, are used by people to learn information (e.g., to rehearse a phone number), for self-instruction (e.g., "Now what is it I am supposed to do first?"), and for self-reinforcement (e.g., "Boy, that was a great effort"). Internal speech, especially self-reinforcement, has been used extensively with special education children. For example, with children who are hyperactive and distractible, a major goal is to help them become more reflective. Thus interventions have been developed that teach children to talk to themselves in specific ways. Children are taught to stop and think about what they are supposed to do, to do the task carefully, to check the accuracy of the task, and to reinforce themselves verbally for good work.

Social learning theory is an extremely broad conceptualization of human behavior. The interested reader is referred to Bandura (1978) for a general discussion of social learning theory and to Reynolds, Gutkin, Elliott, and Witt (1984) or Wood, Spence, and Rutherford (1982) for discussions specific to special education.

REFERENCES

Bandura, A. (1978). The self-system in reciprocal determinism. *American Psychologist, 33*, 344–358.

Reynolds, C. R., Gutkin, T. B., Elliott, S. N., & Witt, J. C. (1984). *School psychology: Essentials of theory and practice.* New York: Wiley.

Wood, F. H., Spence, J., & Rutherford, R. B. (1982). An intervention program for emotionally disturbed students based on social learning principles. In R. L. McDowell, G. W. Adamson, & F. H. Wood (Eds.), *Teaching emotionally disturbed children.* Boston: Little, Brown.

JOSEPH C. WITT
Louisiana State University

BANDURA, A.
IMPULSE CONTROL
MEDIATIONAL DEFICIENCIES
MEDIATORS
OBSERVATIONAL LEARNING
RECIPROCAL DETERMINISM

SOCIAL MATURITY

See ADAPTIVE BEHAVIOR.

SOCIAL SECURITY

Social Security is based on the concept of providing income and health maintenance programs for families in such instances as retirement, disability, poor health, or death. In general, to be eligible for Social Security a person must first pay into Social Security by working and allowing a certain amount of income to be deducted from earnings. Sixteen percent (over 3 million people) of the population in the United States receive Social Security checks. Individuals over 65 (about 25 million) are covered under health insurance called Medicare. In the category of disability, the number receiving benefits are about 3 million.

The Social Security Act of 1935 consisted of three broad areas: (1) Social Security insurance, which included old age, survivors, disability, and hospital insurance (DASDHI), unemployment insurance, workman's compensation, compulsory temporary disability insurance, and railroad retirement system and railroad unemployment and temporary disability insurance; (2) government sponsorship of government or farm workers under civil service retirement, national service life insurance, federal crop insurance, public assistance (which is based on need), and veterans benefits; and (3) social assistance (welfare), which includes public assistance, national assistance, old-age assistance, unemployment assistance, and social pension programs that provide cash payments and other benefits to individuals based on need. Owing to the many changes in our society since 1935 such as demographic shifts, changes in values and attitudes, and inflation the Social Security system has been revised.

To be considered disabled under Social Security law a person must have a physical or mental condition that prevents that person from doing any substantial gainful work. The condition must be expected to last for at least 12 months, or expected to result in death. Examples of such conditions include diseases of the heart, lungs, or blood vessels that have resulted in serious loss of heart or lung reserves or serious loss of function of the kidneys; diseases of the digestive system that result in severe malnutrition, weakness, and anemia; and damage to the brain that has resulted in severe loss of judgment, intellect, orientation, or memory. Children of individuals who are eligible disabled persons can receive benefits if they are under 18 or 19, still in high school full time, or disabled before age 22, unmarried, and living at home. If an individual is blind, there are special considerations such as a disability freeze on income averaging for retirement purposes. In addition, blind persons between the ages of 55 and 65 on disability are classified under different work interpretations. This is based on the concepts of gainful and comparable employment. Work situations must require skills and abilities that are comparable to those of the individual's previous work history. If, however, the person is disabled before 22 and the parents are paying into Social Security, they can receive disability benefits.

In order to qualify, the person must be unable to work in gainful employment and the person under whose credits they are applying must be retired, disabled, deceased, or fully insured under Social Security.

Another federal program administered by the Social Security Administration for low-income individuals is Supplemental Security Income (SSI). Supplemental security income is not based on work credits. Eligibility is based on age (over 65), income guidelines, and disability at any age for persons who earn below a specific income. In general, individuals living in institutions are not eligible for SSI unless they are classified under the four exceptions listed by the Social Security Administration (1986):

1. A person who lives in a publicly operated community residence that serves no more than 16 people may be eligible for SSI payments.

2. A person who lives in a public institution primarily to attend approved educational or vocational training provided in the institution may be eligible if the training is designed to prepare the person for gainful employment.

3. If a person is in a public or private medical treatment facility and Medicaid is paying more than half the cost of his or her care, the person may be eligible, but the SSI payment is limited to no more than $25 per month.

4. A person who is a resident of a public emergency shelter throughout a month can receive SSI payments for up to 3 months during any 12-month period. (pp. 9–10)

To receive SSI under a disability option, the individual must have a physical or mental disability that prevents him or her from gainful employment. The disability must be one that will last at least 12 months or be expected to end in death. For individuals under age 18, the decision is based on whether the disability would not allow the person to work if he or she were an adult. In terms of income requirements, in 1986 the resource limits (such as stocks, bonds, savings accounts, etc.) were $1700 for a single person and $2550 for a couple. The income limits for a federal payment were $336 a month for a single person and $504 a month for a couple.

JANICE HARPER
*North Carolina Central
University*

DISABILITY
LEGISLATION REGARDING THE HANDICAPPED
REHABILITATION
SOCIOECONOMIC STATUS

SOCIAL SKILLS

According to Foster and Ritchey (1979), social skills are "those responses, which within a given situation, prove effective, or in other words, maximize the probability of producing, maintaining or enhancing positive effects for the interactor" (p. 626). Examples of such positive effects include friendship and acceptance in a peer group.

Social skills are necessary to form and sustain relationships with others. They may be acquired through gradual learning and are largely influenced by a variety of social agents (institutions and individuals) present in the culture. The process by which members of society learn these skills is called socialization. Children must develop a complete system of cues in order to determine which skills are appropriate in a situation. According to Page and Garwood (1983), children learn to control and direct their own behavior in ways that are rewarding and help them accomplish goals. Although the content of social skills varies across cultures, the processes by which these skills are acquired are universal and are not culturally dependent (Page & Garwood, 1983).

A child's social skill development can deviate from that which is expected for a variety of reasons. According to Page and Garwood (1983), conditions that influence the course of the development of social skills can be hereditary, maturational, or environmental. Adults become concerned about children's social interactions when they conflict with societal expectations, deviate from developmental norms, or demonstrate sudden changes in style of interaction with others.

Historically, the field of special education has emphasized social competence both in defining and understanding handicapping conditions. According to Gresham (1981), social skills may be conceptualized as part of the construct of social competence. Social competence includes both social skills and adaptive behavior. According to Snell (1983), social competence is a "complex set of verbal and nonverbal behaviors emitted in response to the unique stimuli of specific interpersonal situations. These behaviors include social skills requiring interaction with other people as well as isolated skills that occur within a situation in which other people are present" (p. 315). Adaptive behavior "is defined as the effectiveness or degree with which individuals meet the standards of personal independence and social responsibility expected for age and cultural group" (Grossman, 1983, p. 1). According to Gresham (1981), the focus of adaptive behavior is self-sufficiency; the focus of social skills is interpersonal functioning and social acceptance.

According to Polloway, Payne, Patton, and Payne (1985), children with handicapping conditions may experience a variety of adjustment problems and may display a variety of socially inappropriate behaviors that will interfere with their overall development. Instruction must respond to these needs as personal/social characteristics are major determinants of success in mainstream situations. Gresham (1982) reviewed studies dealing with the social skills of children with handicapping conditions. He concluded that the failure of mainstreaming was due to the children's lack of requisite social skills critical for peer acceptance. This was compounded by the fact that once children were mainstreamed, there were no provisions to support the development of social skills.

Leland (1977) suggests that the ability of people who are mentally retarded to succeed in their communities is partially a function of their ability to maintain "social invisibility" (i.e., to avoid standing out). To be considered socially competent, the individual must engage in socially appropriate behavior and refrain from engaging in socially inappropriate behavior. According to Snell (1983), a social skills curriculum that will ultimately enable an individual to attain social competence should include social decoding (the ability to discriminate relevant cues); social communication; nonverbal behavior; and independent social skills (the ability to walk into a store or sit in the park). Within these skill areas are steps that range from greeting another person to developing a relationship with a member of the opposite sex.

According to Snell (1983), the first step in designing a program to train social skills is to prioritize objectives. The instructor must analyze the environments in which the student interacts to determine the necessary skills for successful performance. This should be followed by an assessment of the individual to determine individualized social skill objectives and provide a baseline for the ongoing evaluation of the effectiveness of specific instructional procedures.

Snell (1983) emphasizes the appropriateness of criterion-referenced assessment techniques to this situation. In criterion-referenced assessment, the standards for the successful performance of social skills under specific conditions must be described in measurable terms. The student is evaluated relative to his or her progress in meeting the established criteria.

Instructional strategies appropriate for use in social skills training programs include the manipulation of antecedent variables as well as the systematic arrangement of consequences. The manipulation of antecedent variables includes such techniques as integrating individuals with handicapping conditions with individuals without handicapping conditions in a variety of social settings; using appropriate social leisure materials; scheduling opportunities for social interaction; and using strategies of task analysis, response prompting, chaining, and contingent reinforcement, as well as combinations of verbal, gestural, and physical cues and corrections (Snell, 1983; Wehman, 1979).

According to Snell (1983), the systematic arrangement of consequences is frequently used to maintain and strengthen social skills. This might include the use of response feedback and external reinforcements as well as self-reinforcement. Most programs to train social skills employ various combinations of antecedent and consequence arrangements (Snell, 1983). Additionally, Matson and Andrasik (1982) demonstrated that social skills can be generalized beyond the training setting with proper instruction.

REFERENCES

Foster, S. L., & Ritchey, W. L. (1979). Issues in the assessment of social competence in children. *Journal of Applied Behavior Analysis, 12*, 625–638.

Gresham, F. M. (1981). Social skills training with handicapped children: A review. *Review of Educational Research, 51*, 139–176.

Gresham, F. M. (1983). Social skills assessment as a mainstreaming placement decisions. *Exceptional Children, 49*, 331–386.

Grossman, H. J. (1983). *Classification in mental retardation.* Washington, DC: American Association on Mental Deficiency.

Heber, R. (1959). *A manual of terminology and classification in mental retardation.* Willimantic, CT: American Association on Mental Deficiency.

Leland, H. (1977). Theoretical considerations of adaptive behavior: In W. A. Coulter and H. W. Morrow (Eds.), *The concept and measurement of adaptive behavior within the scope of psychological assessment.* Austin: Texas Regional Resource Center.

Matson, J., & Andrasik, F. (1982). Training leisure-time and social-interaction skills to mentally retarded adults. *American Journal of Mental Deficiency, 86*, 533–542.

Page, D., & Garwood, S. G. (1983). Developments in social behavior. In S. G. Garwood (Ed.), *Educating young handicapped children.* Rockville, MD: Aspen.

Polloway, E., Payne, J., Patton, J., & Payne, R. (1985). *Strategies for teaching retarded and special needs learners.* Columbus, OH: Merrill.

Snell, M. E. (1983). *Systematic instruction of the moderately and severely handicapped.* Columbus, OH: Merrill.

Wehman, P. (1979). Teaching recreation skills to severely and profoundly handicapped persons. In E. Edgar & R. York (Eds.), *Teaching the severely handicapped* (Vol. 4). Seattle, WA: American Association for the Education of Persons with Severe Handicaps.

CAROLE REITER GOTHELF
Hunter College, City University of New York

ADAPTIVE BEHAVIOR
SOCIAL COMPETENCE
SOCIAL DEVELOPMENT
SOCIOGRAM

SOCIAL SKILLS AND THE HANDICAPPED

Social skills involve the behaviors that are employed in successful and appropriate interactions with others. These skills appear to have bases in social cognition such as social perception and social reasoning (Renshaw & Asher, 1983). Further, social behaviors are a developmental phenomenon and can be influenced by intervention (Gresham & Nagle, 1980; Ladd, 1981; Oden & Asher, 1983).

Socialization, in the sense of the development of interactional skills and the facilitation of interaction with others, is most important for the student who is handicapped (Gresham, 1981; Kingsley, Viggiano, & Tout, 1981). Schools and classrooms are social environments. Social skills are needed to function most effectively within the classroom and to profit fully from instructional activities that occur in an interactional context. Perhaps even more important, the normalization of handicapped persons involves their preparation to function as normally as possible within the recurring day-to-day life situations of their culture (Wolfensberger, 1974). The need to interact effectively with others is fundamental to an individual's functioning normally in society. Beyond the interactional skills needed in school settings, it is important that a pupil have the skills to participate effectively in general social exchanges and to conduct himself or herself appropriately in various social settings.

Handicapped persons are at risk of isolation from their nonhandicapped school peers (Bryan, 1978; Reese-Dukes & Stokes, 1978; Vacc, 1972). This risk of isolation from and rejection by peers extends to the mentally retarded (Reese-Dukes & Stokes, 1978), the pupil with learning problems (Bryan, 1978), and the behaviorally disordered pupil (Vacc, 1972).

Beyond the risk of social isolation, efforts to mainstream handicapped children, to increase their social contact with nonhandicapped peers, may encounter the barrier of negative teacher attitudes toward the handicapped. Brophy and Good (1974) have raised the general issue of the relationship between teacher attitudes and instructional efficacy, while McMillan, Jones, and Meyers (1976) have discussed the positive relationship between teacher attitudes and the effectiveness of the instruction of mainstreamed handicapped pupils. Shapiro (1975) has suggested that the mainstreaming of handicapped pupils may be facilitated by in-service development efforts that are directed at both informational and attitudinal goals. Further, Shapiro has discussed the importance of having school administrators, particularly principals, reach these goals.

REFERENCES

Brophy, J., & Good, T. (1974). *Teacher-student relationships, courses and consequences.* New York: Holt, Rinehart, & Winston.

Bryan, T. H. (1978). Social relationships and verbal interactions of learning disabled children. *Journal of Learning Disabilities, 11,* 58–66.

Gresham, F. M. (1981). Social skills training with handicapped children: A review. *Review of Educational Research, 51,* 139–176.

Gresham, F. M., & Nagle, R. J. (1980). Social skills training with children: Responsiveness to modeling and coaching as a function of peer orientation. *Journal of Consulting & Clinical Psychology, 18,* 718–729.

Kingsley, R. F., Viggiano, R. A., & Tout, L. (1981). Social perception of friendship, leadership, and game playing among EMR special and regular class boys. *Education & Training of the Mentally Retarded, 16,* 201–206.

Ladd, G. W. (1981). Effectiveness of a social learning method for enhancing children's social interaction and peer acceptance. *Child's Development, 52,* 171–178.

MacMillan, D. L., Jones, R. L., & Meyers, C. E. (1976). Mainstreaming the mentally retarded: Some questions, cautions, and guidelines. *Mental Retardation, 14,* 3–10.

Marland, S. (1972). *Education of the gifted and talented.* Report to the Congress of the United States by the U.S. Commissioner of Education. Washington, DC: U.S. Government Printing Office.

Oden, S., & Asher, S. R. (1983). Children's goals and strategies for social interaction. *Merrill-Palmer Quarterly, 23,* 29–44.

Reese-Dukes, J. L., & Stokes, E. H. (1978). Social acceptance of elementary educable mentally retarded pupils in the regular classroom. *Education & Training of the Mentally Retarded, 13,* 356–361.

Renshaw, P. D., & Asher, S. R. (1983). Children's goals and strategies for social interaction. *Merrill Palmer Quarterly, 29,* 353–374.

Shapiro, J. (1975). *The effects of staff development on mainstreaming.* Doctoral Dissertation, Univ. of Illinois, Champaign/Urbana.

Siperstein, G. N., Bak, J. J., & Gottlieb, J. (1977). Effects of group discussion on children's attitudes toward handicapped peers. *Journal of Educational Research, 7,* 131–134.

Vacc, N. A. (1972). Long-term effects of special class intervention for emotionally disturbed children. *Exceptional Children, 39,* 15–22.

Wolfensberger, W. (1974). *Normalization.* Toronto, Canada: National Institute of Mental Retardation.

LeRoy Clinton
Boston University

SOCIAL SKILLS
SOCIAL SKILLS TRAINING

SOCIAL SKILLS TRAINING

Social skills training is a method of teaching children effective coping strategies. It is used as an intervention to manage disruptive behavior, a method to prevent future disruptions, and a tool to foster emotional growth in children (Gresham & Elliott, 1984). The adjustment problems of many handicapped children have been related to social skills deficits; social skills training attempts to address these dysfunctional areas. Drawing from behavioral, cognitive, and humanistic theories of psychology, social skills training employs an educational approach to remediating behavior problems.

Social skills have been described in various terms. Eisenberg and Harris (1984) have defined them as a set of developmentally related abilities that contribute to an overall level of social competence. The component skills include role or perspective taking, interpersonal problem solving, moral judgment, self-control, and communication facility. Kratchowill and French (1984) view social skills as learned verbal and nonverbal behaviors that are performed within a specific social context. Gerber (1983) has discussed social skills in relation to an individual's social perceptual accuracy (i.e., the ability to understand subtle nuances and define critical elements in the social environment). Rathjen (1984) defines social skills within the context of an aggressiveness-shyness continuum, and views adjustment in relation to an individual's awareness of socially accepted limits.

An individual's social skills determine important social outcomes such as peer acceptance and ascribed personality characteristics. Those children with poor self-control may learn inappropriate social strategies because their behavior leads to peer rejection (Gresham & Elliott, 1984). Socially incompetent children are reported to continue having socialization difficulties through adulthood (Rathjen, 1984).

In a review of a number of social skills training programs, Baskin and Hess (1980) reported that programs designed with cognitive and behavioral objectives were effective in increasing children's understanding of social causation, improving peer relations, decreasing discipline referrals, and improving behavioral adjustment ratings made by teachers. Successful training programs appear to balance content flexibility with skill sequence and structure (Shure & Spivack, 1981). They stimulate thought and discussion around the types of interpersonal problems with which participants can identify. Effective programs also allow for repetition and practice of learned skills. Meichenbaum (1983) states that training materials should be drawn from the child's natural play environment when possible. He also finds that children are able to incorporate material when they brainstorm as a group. Finally, program effectiveness is enhanced when trainers are highly energetic and capable of acting at the child's level.

A number of social skills training programs are available as commercial packages; others are offered as models and techniques. Shure and Spivack (1981) designed a program to improve behavior-disordered children's interpersonal cognitive problem solving skills. Children are trained to examine their behavior in terms of possible outcomes. They are then guided to consider alternate behaviors that might be substituted for the present one. Next, predicted outcomes for these alternate behaviors are explored. Finally, the children are taught to weigh the various outcomes in terms of desirability and to choose the behavior most likely to produce the desired effect.

Cognitive behavior modification (CBM), a technique developed by Donald Meichenbaum, is an approach to social skills training that has been used with impulsive, aggressive, and hyperactive children (Meichenbaum, 1983). The CBM focuses on generalizable strategies that children can use across a variety of situations. The training consists of guided rehearsal and modeling, in which the children work with a mediating adult to establish covert verbal control over their disruptive behaviors. The turtle technique, a method based on CBM, has been found effective in reducing impulsive children's aggressive responses to frustration (Schneider, 1974). This procedure teaches children to respond to a verbal cue by relaxing, pausing, and implementing problem-solving techniques such as visualizing the consequences of a proposed action and its alternatives.

Elardo and Cooper (1977) developed AWARE, a four-step social skills training program. First, children are helped to formulate rules for their group meetings. Next, they are taught to become more aware of their feelings and the feelings of others. Third, the children are encouraged to explore unique aspects of their own personalities and to recognize the uniqueness of others. Finally, the children are encouraged to explore real-life difficulties and to solve them in a peaceful and mutually beneficial manner. The teacher's duties in the AWARE program include leading discussions, carrying through ideas in daily practice, asking questions, and providing a warm and supportive environment.

Handicapped students with inadequate social perception need training in basic interpersonal skills (Speer & Douglas, 1981). They may need to learn appropriate social gestures such as smiling and making eye contact. Learning-disabled children may also need instruction in interpreting and labeling facial expressions, and in moderating their verbal behavior. Language-deficient children must be taught appropriate verbal responses in social conversation. Communication training for language-impaired youngsters should teach them to be aware of four critical factors: personalities and roles of the participants, setting, topic, and objectives (Minskoff, 1982). Reality therapy, an approach to social skills training that stresses the relationship between behavior and natural consequences, has been used to encourage emotionally disturbed children to use more effective interpersonal strategies (Fuller & Fuller, 1982).

Social skills training has also been used with retarded children. Meisgeier (1981) has outlined a program stressing problem solving, personal responsibility, and communication skills. Students are taught to replace aggressive behaviors with assertive ones. The program consists of a series of structured success experiences stressing positive self-statements and relaxation.

Social skills training has been employed to increase the probability of mainstreaming effectiveness, and to help nonhandicapped children learn to accept their handicapped peers (Gresham, 1982). Gresham suggests that social skills assessments be included in all mainstreaming decisions.

As critics (Gerber, 1983) have argued that social skills training takes up valuable academic learning time, Shure and Spivack (1981) suggest that evaluation components be integrated into all social skills training programs to judge student growth and program effectiveness. One commonly used instrument is the Means-Ends Problem Solving measure (Platt, Spivack, and Bloom, 1971). This consists of a set of hypothetical social problems in which children are required to formulate a variety of possible solutions. Ratings can be made on the quantity and quality of these proposed solutions. Another popular evaluation approach uses sociometric procedures. Sociometric data are gathered by asking peers to rate each other in terms of popularity and desirability. Behavior rating scales also offer a means of assessing social skills. These scales attempt to define skills in terms of observable behavior, and are usually completed by the classroom teacher.

REFERENCES

Baskin, E. J., & Hess, R. D. (1980). Does affective education work? A review of seven programs. *Journal of School Psychology*, *18*(1), 40–50.

Eisenberg, N., & Harris, J. D. (1984). Social competence: A developmental perspective. *School Psychology Review*, *13*(3), 267–277.

Elardo, P., & Cooper, M. (1977). *AWARE: Activities for social development*. Menlo Park, CA: Addison-Wesley.

Fuller, G. B., & Fuller, D. L. (1982). Reality therapy: Helping LD children make better choices. *Academic Therapy*, *17*(3), 269–277.

Gerber, M. M. (1983). Learning disabilities and cognitive strategies: A case for training or constraining problem solving: *Journal of Learning Disabilities*, *16*(5), 255–260.

Gresham, F. M. (1982). Misguided mainstreaming: The case for social skills training with handicapped children. *Exceptional Children*, *48*(5), 422–433.

Gresham, F. M., & Elliott, S. M. (1984). Assessment and classification of children's social skills: A review of methods and issues. *School Psychology Review*, *13*(3), 292–301.

Kratchowill, T. R., & French, D. C. (1984). Social skills training for withdrawn children. *School Psychology Review*, *13*(3), 339–341.

Meichenbaum, D. (1983). Teaching thinking: A cognitive-behavioral perspective. In S. Chipman and J. Segal (Eds.), *Thinking and learning skills: Current research and open questions*. Hillsdale, NJ: Erlbaum.

Meisgeier, C. (1981). A social/behavioral program for the adolescent student with serious learning problems. *Focus on Exceptional Children*, *13*(9), 1–13.

Minskoff, E. H. (1982). Training LD students to cope with the everyday world. *Academic Therapy*, *17*(3), 311–316.

Platt, J. J., Spivack, G., & Bloom, M. R. (1971). *Means-ends problem solving procedure (MEPS): Manual and tentative norms*. Philadelphia: Hahnemann Medical College and Hospital.

Rathjen, D. P. (1984). Social skills training for children. Innovations and consumer guidelines. *School Psychology Review*, *13*(3), 302–310.

Schneider, M. R. (1974). Turtle technique in the classroom. *Teaching Exceptional Children*, 7, 22–24.

Shure, M. B., & Spivack, G. (1981). The problem solving approach to adjustment: A competency-building model of primary prevention. *Prevention in Human Services*, *1*(1–2), 87–103.

Speer, S. K., & Douglas, D. R. (1981). Helping LD students improve social skills. *Academic Therapy*, *17*(2), 221–224.

GARY BERKOWITZ
Temple University

BEHAVIOR MODELING
DEVELOPING UNDERSTANDING OF SELF AND OTHERS

SOCIAL VALIDATION

In an educational context, social validation is the philosophy of providing psychological services that emphasize the importance of the student's or teacher's subjective opinions about intervention methods. Social validity differs from the statistical notion of validity in several aspects. Statistical validity refers to how well treatment results correlate with an objective set of criteria or other treatment methods. Social validity is concerned with the subjective opinions of teachers, parents, and/or students and how these subjective opinions affect the overall treatment outcomes. In social validity it is assumed "that if the participants don't like the treatment then they may avoid it, or run away, or complain loudly. And thus, society will be less likely to use our technology, no matter how potentially effective and efficient it might be" (Wolf, 1978, p. 206).

Social validity can be assessed on at least three levels (Wolf, 1978). First, we can evaluate the social significance of the treatment goals. Here we consider whether desired outcomes are of any real value to teachers, students, or society in general. The second level of assessment of social validity questions the social appropriateness of the treatment procedures. At this level, teachers and students are asked how acceptable the treatment methods are (i.e., whether the results of the treatment justify the methods used). "Judgements of acceptability include whether a treatment is appropriate for the problem, whether it is fair, reasonable, or intrusive, and whether it is consistent with conventional notions of what treatment should be" (Kazdin, 1980, p. 330). The treatment acceptability paradigm has been used with students and teachers in clinical settings (Kazdin, French, & Sherick, 1981); university settings (Kazdin, 1980); and primary and secondary school settings (Elliott, Witt, Galvin, & Moe, 1986; Turco, Witt, & Elliott, in press). In the final level of social validation evaluation, teachers and students report their satisfaction with the methods used (i.e., How important are the effects of the treatment methods? Are the teachers and students satisfied with the results, even the unplanned ones?; Wolf, 1978).

Consumer satisfaction differs from treatment acceptability mainly in the timing of the measurements. Treatment acceptability requires teachers and students to judge treatments before they begin. Consumer satisfaction requires teachers and students to judge treatments during the treatment or after the treatment is over. In applied behavior analysis, it is believed that the outcomes of treatments are easily judged based on behavioral changes from baseline measurements. However, according to the social validity paradigm, the usefulness of school interventions can only be judged by the subjective evaluations of the teachers and students participating in the treatment program.

REFERENCES

Elliott, S. N., Witt, J. C., Galvin, G. A., & Moe, G. L. (1986). Children's involvement in intervention selection: Acceptability of interventions for misbehaving peers. *Professional psychology: Research and practice, 17* (3), 235–241.

Kazdin, A. E. (1980). Acceptability of alternative treatments for deviant child behavior. *Journal of Applied Behavior Analysis, 13*, 259–273.

Kazdin, A. E., French, N. H., & Sherick, R. B. (1981). Acceptability of alternative treatments for children: Evaluations by inpatient children, parents, and staff. *Journal of Consulting and Clinical Psychology, 49*, 900–907.

Turco, T. L., Witt, J. C., & Elliott, S. N. (in press). Factors influencing teachers' acceptability of classroom interventions for deviant student behavior. *Monograph on secondary behavioral disorders.* Reston, VA: Council for Exceptional Children.

Wolf, M. M. (1978). Social validity: The case for subjective measurement or how applied behavior analysis is finding its heart. *Journal of Applied Behavior Analysis, 11*, 203–214.

TIMOTHY L. TURCO
STEPHEN N. ELLIOTT
Louisiana State University

APPLIED BEHAVIOR ANALYSIS
TEACHER EXPECTANCIES

SOCIAL WORK

Social work in special education traditionally falls within the realm of the school social worker. The functions performed by social workers within the school include individual and family casework, individual and group work with students, and community liaison services. School social workers have stated their goals as helping students to maximize their potential, developing relationships between the school and other agencies, and offering a perspective of social improvement in the education of students (Costin, 1981).

In 1975, PL 94-142 mandated free and appropriate education for all students; social work falls under the section providing for related services (Hancock, 1982). The school social worker often participates as a member of an interdisciplinary team, and in some states assumes a permanent position on a child study team. Local boards of education determine the specific roles of team members (Winters & Easton, 1983). As a team member, the social worker may be responsible for gathering family information, coordinating team meetings, developing individualized educational programs, and monitoring services.

The school social worker often participates in the evaluation of students who are being considered for special education. In this regard, the case history is an extremely important tool that the social worker uses to gain environmental, developmental, social, and economic information about the student.

To work effectively with a special population, the school social worker must have several basic competencies. Dickerson (1981) includes counseling, crisis intervention, knowledge of related services, and understanding of adapted curricula and techniques as required skills. To be effective, the school social worker must also hold the belief that special-needs children are entitled to the same rights and privileges as those afforded to their mainstreamed peers.

Often, family members of the disabled need support from the social worker in their efforts to program for their impaired youngsters. The primary goal of the social worker in providing services to family members of the handicapped is to help them face and accept the limiting condition (Dickerson, 1981). The family is encouraged to follow through on recommendations designed to enhance their child's functioning. The social worker helps the family to recognize that the problem is real and that it can be helped by the development of an accepting, positive attitude about the child.

The school social worker may provide a number of different services to the family. Hancock (1982) writes that one role for the school social worker is to support parents in their efforts to become more active participants in school decisions regarding their children. Social workers may contribute information regarding home versus institutional care for severely impaired children. The social worker may also provide direct counseling services to the family, or act as a link to other supportive services. For example, parents might be encouraged to find a support or advocacy group. Ensuring that families receive the financial support to which they are entitled is another important function.

Pupil services such as counseling, sex education, prevocational development, and child advocacy are often performed by the school social worker. As an advocate, the social worker attempts to create systemic changes that improve the quality of the impaired child's school life. The social worker may assume responsibility for shaping a school system's attitudes to reflect more adaptive, relevant, and socially responsible positions (Lee, 1983).

School social workers may be responsible for developing communication links within the school so that teachers, administrators, and other staff can exchange information necessary for student programming. They may also plan in-service workshops in areas related to student welfare. Future trends in special education social work will continue to expand the systems approach to service delivery. To this end, an increase in coordinator and liaison roles for special education social workers is predicted (Randolph, 1982).

REFERENCES

Costin, L. B. (1981). School social work as specialized practice. *Social Work, 26*, 36–44.

Dickerson, M. O. (1981). *Social work practice and the mentally retarded.* New York: Free Press.

Hancock, B. L. (1982). *School social work.* Englewood Cliffs, NJ: Prentice-Hall.

Lee, L. J. (1983). The social worker in the political environment of a school system. *Social Work, 28*(4), 302–307.

Randolph, J. L. (1982). School social work can foster educational growth for students. *Education, 102*, 260–265.

Winters, W. G., & Easton, F. (1983). *The practice of social work in the schools.* New York: Free Press.

GARY BERKOWITZ
Temple University

MULTIDISCIPLINARY TEAMS
PERSONNEL TRAINING IN SPECIAL EDUCATION

SOCIODRAMA

Sociodrama is a group-therapy technique developed by J. L. Moreno (1946) as an extension of a group-therapy technique, also devised by Moreno, known as psychodrama. (Moreno is often credited with having initiated group therapy in Vienna just after the beginning of the twentieth century.) Though he developed the technique, Moreno did little with sociodrama, preferring to continue his efforts in the development and application of psychodrama. E. Paul Torrance, a psychodramatist who studied with Moreno, later reconceptualized and refined sociodrama as a group problem-solving technique based on Moreno's early work but also incorporating the creative problem-solving principles of Torrance (1970) and Osborn (1963). Sociodrama can be used with all ages from preschool through adulthood.

The primary uses of sociodrama, largely reflecting Torrance's interests and influence, have been in primary prevention of behavior problems with the disadvantaged and other high-risk populations. Sociodrama has also been used in specific treatment programs with adolescents who engage in socially deviant behaviors and with status offenders. Sociodrama seems particularly helpful in introducing and teaching new social behaviors as well as in improving the problem-solving skills of the youngsters involved, giving them more behavioral options.

During sociodrama, a problem or conflict situation that is likely to be common to the group is derived from group discussion. Members of the group are cast into roles, which they play as the situation is acted out. Many production techniques are brought into play to facilitate solution of the conflict; these include the double, the soliloquy, direct presentation, mirror, and role reversal.

The director's role is to keep the action moving in the direction of a resolution, or, preferably, multiple resolutions of the conflict. Each session should end with a series of potential resolutions that can be discussed by the group. Appropriate behaviors can also be practiced. By teaching participants to brainstorm alternative behaviors and to rehearse for real-life problem situations, sociodrama has proved a useful method for treatment and prevention of behavior problems in children and adolescents. Torrance (1982) provides a more detailed presentation of the techniques of sociodrama.

REFERENCES

Moreno, J. L. (1946). *Psychodrama.* Beacon, NY: Beacon House.

Osborn, A. F. (1963). *Applied imagination* (3rd ed.). New York: Scribner's.

Torrance, E. P. (1970). *Creative learning and teaching.* New York: Dodd, Mead.

Torrance, E. P. (1982). Sociodrama: Teaching creative problem-solving as a therapeutic technique. In C. R. Reynolds & T. B. Gutkin (Eds.), *The handbook of school psychology,* New York: Wiley.

CECIL R. REYNOLDS
Texas A&M University

GROUP THERAPY
PSYCHODRAMA

SOCIOECONOMIC IMPACT OF DISABILITIES

There is a well-established relationship between parents' socioeconomic status and children's school performance. Caldwell (1970) reports that many of the children from lower socioeconomic classes live in restricted and nonstimulating environments. As a result, low socioeconomic profile is one factor that is significantly related to poor cognitive functioning. There are many more children from lower socioeconomic classes with poor cognitive functioning than from higher socioeconomic classes.

An investigation analyzing the extent to which parental social status influences the decisions made in reference to potentially handicapped students was conducted by Ysseldyke et al. (1979). Individuals involved in decision making were given identical data on students referred for evaluation. All data were samples of normal or average performance. The decision makers were told in half of the cases that the child's father was a bank vice president and the mother a real estate agent. The other half were told that the child's father was a janitor at the bank and the mother a clerk at a local supermarket. As a result of knowledge of the parents' socioeconomic status, the decision makers made different placement and classification decisions for the children.

There are many factors associated with socioeconomic status that are considered contributing factors to some disabilities. These include poor health care, inadequate pre- and postnatal care, improper diet, and lack of early stimulation. Zachau-Christiansen and Ross (1975) state that infants from lower socioeconomic families are at greater risk for experiencing or being exposed to conditions that may hinder development. These conditions include low birth weight and maternal infections during pregnancy. Kagan (1970) discusses other psychological differences between lower class and more privileged children. The differences are evident during the first 3 years of life and tend to remain stable over time. Variables include language, mental set, attachment, inhibition, sense of effectiveness, motivation, and expectancy of failure. All of the factors play a crucial role in influencing school performance. Deficits in any of these areas limits the child's ability in various cognitive skills. Young children raised in an environment lacking in stimulation and healthy interaction with adults will often be retarded in motor, language, cognitive, and social skills.

Lack of proper nutrition can negatively affect the maturation of the brain and central nervous system. Malnutrition affects brain weight and tends to have lasting effects on learning and behavior. It has a very damaging effect during the first 6 months of life owing to the rate of brain cell development during this period. In the area of mental retardation and learning disabilities, the majority of the students tend to be from lower socioeconomic status homes and racial and cultural minorities. In many cases, the poor achievement of the socioculturally different individual is related to lack of proper nutrition and medical care. Kavale (1980) reports that almost all complications of prenatal life, pregnancy, labor and delivery, and postnatal diseases that are potentially damaging to the infant's brain development are disproportionately high among low socioeconomic groups.

Many other correlates of low socioeconomic status are associated with poor school learning. Some of these correlates are delayed development of language; greater impulsivity; lower intelligence on standard intelligence tests that predict success in standard curricula; lower parental educational levels; families with children over five; poor home climate; lack of variety in sensory stimuli; minimal encouragement of scholastic success within the home; and less time spent on tasks in the classroom and on homework.

An area that is crucial to academic performance is language development. Jensen (1968) lists several factors associated with language development as sources of social class differences and intellectual achievement. In the lower classes, early vocalization by infants is less likely to be rewarded; the child is less likely to have a single mother-child relationship in the early years; there is less verbal interaction and verbal play in response to early vocalizations; and speech tends to be delayed. In the early stages of speech, there is less shaping of speech sounds, in which parents reinforce approximations of adult speech, and much vocal interaction with slightly older siblings whose own speech is only slightly more advanced and who do not systematically shape behavior.

According to MacMillian (1982), the physical environment of lower class homes tends to be related to cultural familial retardation. When compared with middle-class households, lower class households tend to have the father absent from the home, crowded living conditions, poor nutrition and medical care, large family size, dilapidated living environment, and high ratio of children to adults. These factors have a negative impact on the child and his or her social, emotional, and educational adjustment. In many instances, the lower classes are less likely to vote and participate in political or social activities. The trend for the upper and middle classes is to send their children to private schools, while lower class children attend public schools.

The psychological environment of the lower classes may also depress the aspiration levels of children and expose them to an attitude of helplessness. Zigler (1970) reviewed the literature on social class variations in behavior and determined certain factors that show differences in social class members:

1. While parents of all social classes wanted their children to be honest, happy, obedient, and dependable, middle-class parents emphasized internal standards (such as honesty, self-control, and curiosity) while

lower-class parents emphasized qualities that would assure respectability (such as obedience, neatness, and cleanliness).

2. Lower class children are more likely to perceive parents and other adults as predominantly hostile; they also show a greater readiness to experience guilt.

3. Lower class parents and children are more inclined to vent hostility in overt acts of aggression. However, the findings are mixed; while most studies report higher aggression in lower class children, a few find no differences or higher aggression in middle-class children.

4. Middle-class parents appear to emphasize achievement and success to a greater extent than lower class parents.

MacMillian (1982) has emphasized the dangers of class stereotyping. Determining socioeconomic status and the relationship between the ratings and developmental outcomes can be misleading; there are some exceptions to every rule. An example would be the idea that only middle-class parents have high expectations for their children. There are many lower class parents who also have high expectations for their children. The major concern should be placed on the overall impact of socioeconomic factors in preventing or enhancing the possibility of physical, social, emotional, and intellectual disabilities.

REFERENCES

Caldwell, B. (1970). The rationale for early intervention. *Exceptional Children*, 36, 717–727.

Jensen, A. R. (1968). Social class, race, and genetics: Implications for education. *American Educational Research Journal*, 5, 1–412.

Kagan, J. (1970). On class differences and early development. In V. Denenberg (Ed.), *Education of the infant and young child*. New York: Academic.

Kavale, K. A. (1980). Learning disability and cultural-economic disadvantage: The case for a relationship. *Learning Disability Quarterly*, 3, 97–112.

MacMillian D. L. (1982). *Mental retardation in school and society*. (2nd ed.). Boston: Little, Brown.

Ysseldyke, J. E., Algozzine, B., Regan, R., Potter, M., Richey, L., & Thurlow, M. L. (1979). *Psychoeducational assessment and decision making: A computer-simulated investigation* (Research Report No. 32). Minneapolis: University of Minnesota Institute for Research on Learning Disabilities.

Zachau-Christiansen, B., & Ross, E. M. (1979). *Babies: Human development during the first year*. Chichester, England: Wiley.

Zigler, E. (1970). Social class and the socialization process. *Review of Educational Research*, 40, 87–110.

JANICE HARPER
*North Carolina Central
University*

**GIFTED AND TALENTED MINORITIES
SOCIOECONOMIC STATUS**

SOCIOECONOMIC STATUS (SES)

Davis (1986) defines socioeconomic status (SES) as a person's position in the community. There are many factors involved in determining SES. These factors include income, employment, location and cost of home, and social status of the family. Socioeconomic status influences various behavior patterns. For example, the number of children, the year and model of the family car, and the number of vacations per year will vary according to SES.

Society places a high value on wealth and material possessions. There is a tendency to rank individuals based on their wealth and power within the community. It becomes important to let people know how wealthy one may be. This is done by displaying status symbols. It is assumed that the upper class displays their wealth with such status symbols as a Rolls Royce or Mercedes Benz. Wealth is highly correlated with education, income, and occupation. Studies of social classes in the United States report five or six classes. Hodges (1964) has developed a system of six social classes. The first is the upper-upper class, which represents 1 to 2% of the community. This group includes people with wealth, power, and a family name that is prominent. Individuals can only be born into this class, with the exception of a few marrying into it. The lower-upper class also represents 1 to 2% of the community. This class does not have a prominent family name and their money is fairly new. However, they have wealth and power. The upper-middle class represents 10 to 12% of the community. These people have college degrees, are usually professionals and successful merchants. The lower-middle class represents 33% of the community. These people are usually small business people, salespeople, clerks, and forepeople. They tend to have average income and education, with high value placed on family, religion, thrift, and hard work. The upper-lower class also represents 33% of the community. These people are blue-collar workers who may not be high-school graduates. In many cases they are employees rather than employers. The lower-lower class represents 15 to 20% of the population. These people are unskilled workers. They tend to marry young and have many children. Many are not high-school graduates and may frequently be unemployed.

Socioeconomic status has a direct relationship to the length and quality of life. The lower-lower classes do not live as long as members of the upper class. The poor are more likely to suffer from chronic and infectious diseases and are less likely to see a physician or a dentist. This may be a result of lack of money to pay for medical expenses. However, it has also been found that minor illnesses such as fevers, have a low priority in poverty-stricken homes. Other factors such as child-rearing practices, are affected by socioeconomic status of the family. Middle-class parents tend to be more permissive, while lower class parents are more rigid (Bassis, Gelles, & Levine, 1980).

Kohn (1969) states that middle-class mothers value self-control, dependability, and consideration, while lower class mothers value obedience and the ability to defend oneself. The middle-class family raises the child in an environment where achievement and getting ahead are encouraged. The lower class family raises the child in an environment that emphasizes the immediate and the concrete. The child is taught to shy away from the new or unfamiliar. According to Boocock (1972), the family characteristic that is the most powerful predictor of school performance is socioeconomic status. More specifically, the higher the socioeconomic status of the family, the higher the child's academic achievement. Socioeconomic status also predicts the number and type of extracurricular activities the child will be involved in and social and emotional adjustment to school. Other areas highly correlated with socioeconomic status include grades, achievement test scores, retentions at grade level, course failures, truancy, suspensions from school, dropout rates, college plans, and total amount of schooling.

REFERENCES

Bassis, M. S., Gelles, R. J., & Levine, A. (1980). *Sociology: An introduction* (2nd ed.). New York: Random House.

Boocock, S. S. (1972). *An introduction to the sociology of learning.* Dallas: Houghton Mifflin.

Davis, W. E. (1986). *Resource guide to special education* (2nd ed.). Boston: Allyn & Bacon.

Hodges, H. M. (1964). *Social stratification* Cambridge, MA: Schenkman.

Kohn, M. (1969). *Class and conformity.* Homewood, IL: Dorsey.

JANICE HARPER
North Carolina Central University

SOCIOECONOMIC IMPACT OF DISABILITIES

SOCIOGRAM

A sociogram (Moreno, 1953) is a graphic display of interpersonal relationships within a group. It is considered one of the most common sociometric techniques used by teachers. In most instances, a sociometric test is administered to a group of children by asking each child who he or she would like to work with on a particular activity. The sociogram displays a diagram of students with whom other students prefer to study, play, or work. It also displays a diagram of students who are rejected and tend to be isolates. Each child is asked such questions as, With which three students would you prefer to study? Which three students do you like best? Which two students do you prefer to play with at recess? Which three students are your best friends? The students' responses to these types of questions are used to construct the sociogram.

There are two types of sociograms: the graphic and the target diagram. The graphic sociogram assigns initial letters of the alphabet (such as A, B, C) to the most popular students. These students appear in the center of the chart. The isolates are assigned middle letters (such as H, I, J), and appear on the edges of the diagram. Stanley and Hopkins (1972) listed the limitations of this chart as difficulty in reading with 30 or more students and requiring a great deal of practice to learn the most effective placement. The target diagram consist of circles, with the most popular students placed in the center and the isolated students placed on the outer edges. According to Stanley and Hopkins (1972), this diagram is more productive for teachers with large classrooms.

The information obtained from a sociogram can be used for screening students who may be isolated, socially immature, and unhappy. Once this information has been obtained from the sociogram, the teacher may begin to ask questions to determine why some students are considered isolates and often rejected. This information can assist the teacher with assigning students to groups for class projects and making changes in classroom relationships. It may also alert the teacher to the possibility of an existing or potential handicapping condition.

REFERENCES

Moreno, J. L. (1953). *Who shall survive? Foundations of sociometry, group psychotherapy, and sociodrama* (2nd ed.). New York: Beacon House.

Stanley, J. C., & Hopkins, K. D. (1972). *Educational and psychological measurement and evaluation.* Englewood Cliffs, NJ: Prentice-Hall.

JANICE HARPER
North Carolina Central University

SOCIAL SKILLS
SOCIAL SKILLS AND THE HANDICAPPED

SOCIOMETRIC TECHNIQUES WITH THE HANDICAPPED

Sociometric techniques originated by Moreno (1953) are a set of questions used to determine the social organization of a group. There are various types of sociometric techniques that are used with the handicapped. The two most common forms are peer nomination and roster and rating methods. Most peer nomination techniques ask questions such as, With whom would you most like to study? Who would you most like to sit with at lunch? Who would you most enjoy working with on an art project? Who would you most enjoy being with during break? (Mercer & Mercer, 1981 p. 109).

Other forms of peer nomination techniques may ask students questions relating to attitudes and behavior: Which students are very popular? Which students does the teacher like most? Which students cause a lot of trouble? Which students are selfish? (Mercer & Mercer 1981 p. 110). The rating scales usually lists all students in the class along with the rating scale (e.g., 1 = low and 10 = high) and ask each student to rate each person in the class. A score is determined for each child based on the average of their ratings.

Another common sociometric technique is the use of the sociogram, which is a visual display of the interrelationships within a group. The sociogram clearly shows which child is popular and which child is isolated by their positions on a diagram. There are teacher-made sociometric techniques and commercially produced sociometric techniques. The commercially produced techniques include the Ohio Social Acceptance Scale, which is designed for children in grades three through six. There are six headings: (1) my very best friends; (2) my other friends; (3) not friends, but okay; (4) don't know them; (5) don't care for them; (6) dislike them. The children are asked to write the names of their classmates under each of the headings (Wallace & Larsen 1978).

Another commercial technique is the Peer Acceptance Scale, which is used to obtain social status scores of children. This test uses stick figures of two children playing ball together, which is labeled friend; two children at a blackboard, which is labeled all right; and two children with their backs to each other, which is labeled wouldn't like. The students are read a list of names of classmates they are familiar with and asked to circle the figure that best describes how they feel about the student (Goodman, Gottlieb, & Harrison, 1972). The information from these sociometric techniques may be helpful to the teacher for the following activities: (1) assigning instructional groups and peer tutors; (2) planning affective development activities; (3) identifying potential groups; (4) predicting interpersonal difficulties within the group; and (5) measuring change in social adjustment (Marsh, Price, & Smith, 1983, p. 51).

With handicapped children social acceptance is considered a very important aspect of school adjustment and educational achievement. Sociometric techniques may help the teacher determine whether the handicapped child is accepted by his or her nonhandicapped peers. If the child is not accepted, the next step is to decide which interventions will help to improve the child's social status.

REFERENCES

Goodman, H., Gottlieb, J., & Harrison, H. (1972). Social acceptance of EMRs integrated into a nongraded elementary school. *American Journal of Mental Deficiency, 76,* 412–417.

Marsh, G. E., Price, B. J., & Smith, T. E. (1983). *Teaching mildly handicapped children: Method and materials.* St. Louis: Mosby.

Mercer, C. D., & Mercer A. R. (1981). *Teaching students with learning problems.* Columbus, OH: Merrill.

Moreno, J. L. (1953). *Who shall survive? Foundations of sociometry, group psychotherapy and sociodrama* (2nd ed.). New York: Beacon House.

Wallace, G., & Larsen, S. (1978). *Educational assessment of learning problems: Testing for teaching.* Boston: Allyn & Bacon.

JANICE HARPER
*North Carolina Central
University*

**SOCIAL SKILLS
SOCIOGRAM**

SOCIOPATHY

Sociopathy is a diagnostic label applied to adults of 18 years or older who exhibit a lifelong pattern of conduct problems or antisocial behavior. About 1800, Philippe Pinel coined the term *manie sans délire* to designate those individuals who exhibit deviant social behavior but lack many of the cardinal manifestations of a mental disorder such as delusions, hallucinations, or bizarre behavior. The category was narrowed when Prichard used the term moral insanity in the mid-nineteenth century. By the turn of the twentieth century, the label psychopathic inferiority was introduced by Koch; it is still reflected in the current usage of psychopathic personality disorder, psychopathic character, and psychopath. The *Diagnostic and Statistical Manual* (DSM) which was published in 1952, substituted the term sociopathic personality to underscore the etiological importance of environmental factors and to rid the concept of its moralistic flavor. The subsequent two editions of the DSM have favored the term antisocial personality disorder.

Behavioral characteristics of sociopaths can be observed in their work history, drug use (including alcohol), social and familial relationships, and illegal activities. Sociopaths frequently show a checkered employment history with significant unemployment, absenteeism, or frequent job changes. Their functioning as parents is often inadequate as evidenced by gross financial, medical, and emotional neglect of their children. An arrest record is not uncommon since sociopaths fail to accept norms. In addition, they exhibit difficulty in maintaining close relationships and interpersonal affairs and are often exploitive and blatantly manipulative. Sociopaths are remarkable for their lack of empathy and an absence of genuine remorse or guilt for their transgressions. Many sociopaths display a superficial charm and are highly skilled in conveying the appearance of sincerity; this makes them all the more successful in "conning" others. Some successful politicians, professionals, and businesspeople evidence aspects of sociopathy but are not likely to meet the current DSM-III criteria for classification, particularly in the areas of employment history, poor school achievement, and delinquency. DSM-III has been criticized for bringing the criteria for antisocial personality dangerously close to criminality in general (Davison & Neale, 1982). Contrary to popular myth, sociopaths are not of superior intelligence. Also, chronic criminal activity during adolescence or adulthood is not necessarily indicative of sociopathy. However, a random sample of the prison population would yield a higher percentage of sociopaths than would a random sample of the general population; that is why much of the research on sociopathy is conducted in prisons. The disorder is much more frequently diagnosed in males.

The most valid predictor of sociopathy is antisocial behavior in childhood. Fighting, stealing, persistent lying, delinquency, and chronic violations of rules at home serve as markers for the disorder. The term incorrigible is an apt description of the budding sociopath. Conduct problems at school are chronic. It is not uncommon for these children to have a sociopathic father. In fact, irrespective of socioeconomic status, the more family relatives that display antisocial behavior, the greater the likelihood that the child will engage in antisocial acts (Robins, 1972).

As is true for most psychological disorders, specific patterns of parenting or family dynamics have not been clearly identified as leading to sociopathy. Nonetheless, several authors have noted two styles of child rearing that may contribute to the development of the syndrome (Meyer, 1980). One consists of cold, aloof parents that fail to demonstrate, and thus inculcate, a sense of empathy and a capacity for intimacy. The other parental style is characterized by a lack of consistency in administering reinforcement and punishment. The child then fails to learn abstract rules of right and wrong and instead responds to short-term consequences, fails to trust, and does not react to interpersonal consequences such as disapproval. In addition, exposure to an antisocial adult, usually a male, provides a model for nonnormative behavior.

Unfortunately, there is no widely accepted, experimentally based theory of sociopathy. Several biological and behavioral correlates have been observed but they have not as yet been integrated into a formulation that accounts for the development of the disorder. There is suggestive evidence that a biological predisposition may be of etiological significance. Research in Denmark by Hutchings and Mednick (1974) with criminals, and Schulsinger (1972) with sociopaths, revealed a higher rate of criminality and sociopathy in biological relatives. Research in the United States with adopted children has shown similar results (Cadoret, 1978; Crowe, 1974).

During the 1960s it was hypothesized that males who possessed an extra male Y chromosome were predisposed to violent activity. In fact, lawyers for the mass murderer Richard Speck tried unsuccessfully to use the XYY syndrome as the basis for an insanity plea. Ten years later, a large-scale study in Denmark (Witkin, et al., 1976) found the prevalence of this syndrome to be 2.9 per thousand. Of 12 XYY men, 5 (42%) had already been convicted of criminal offenses. Only 9.3% of a comparison group of XY men had been convicted of a crime. This would seem to lend support to the XYY syndrome hypothesis. However, it was found that only one of the XYY men had been convicted of a violent crime. Moreover, the average IQ of XYY males is lower than that of XY males. Thus it is plausible that men with subnormal intelligence are predisposed to criminal activity or are less successful in escaping apprehension for illegal activities.

Several studies have found electroencephalogram (EEG) abnormality in 31 to 58% of sociopaths. The most common abnormality is nonlocalized slow-wave activity, typical of infants and young children (Ellingson, 1954). Among extremely impulsive and aggressive sociopaths, temporal lobe EEG abnormalities have been found and positive spikes of 6 to 8 cycles per second (cps) and 14 to 16 cps have been observed (Hill, 1952; Syndulko, 1978). These data are difficult to interpret as causal factors in sociopathy because not all sociopaths show such brain wave activity. Perhaps there are subtypes of this personality disorder that when identified will allow for a different etiological theory of each type. Nevertheless, Hare (1970) has speculated that slow wave brain activity is indicative of a dysfunction in behavioral inhibitory mechanisms. This is consistent with the belief that sociopaths have difficulty in learning from experience, and despite social or physical punishment continue their maladaptive behavior.

Based on early observations by Cleckley (1976) that sociopaths are seldom anxious, manifest a cool demeanor in the face of threat, and seem not to be regulated by the social consequences of their misbehavior, Lykken (1957) hypothesized that the sociopath's low level of anxiety is responsible for a lack of behavioral inhibition. In one study, in an experimental task, subjects were required to learn a sequence of 20 correct lever presses. Feedback was delivered that indicated when a response was correct or incorrect; some of the incorrect lever presses were followed by shock. Since the threat of shock induces anxiety and anxiety usually facilitates the learning of avoidance behavior, it was predicted that sociopaths would be less successful in learning to avoid the electric shock. When compared with a group of college students and nonsociopathic prison inmates, the results supported the hypothesis. Sociopaths received significantly more shocks than college students and their inmate counterparts, although the latter comparison only approached significance. A replication study by Schachter and Latané (1964) found clear differences among the groups, providing further support for the hypothesis. Moreover, when sociopaths were injected with adrenalin, their avoidance learning improved. Anxiety is mediated by the sympathetic branch of the autonomic nervous system and the effects of adrenalin mimic sympathetic activity, thus creating an increase in anxiety, particularly when the subject is unaware that he is receiving adrenalin, as was true in the study (Schachter & Singer, 1962).

An interesting study by Schmauk (1970) qualifies these findings by showing that sociopaths do not evidence impaired avoidance learning when the punisher is loss of money rather than shock. Thus it appears that the failure to learn from experience notion needs to be revised. While behavioral consequences such as physical punishment and social disapproval have less effect in controlling the behavior of sociopaths in comparison with nonsociopaths, consequences that are meaningful within the value system of the sociopath serve as effective motivators and do control their behavior, albeit the means used to avoid these punishers or acquire reinforcers may be antisocial.

Despite the protestations of some that sociopathy is a wastebasket category, the concept is considered meaningful by most clinicians (Gray & Hutchinson, 1964) and is reliably diagnosed. Indeed, interrater agreement for this disorder exceeds that commonly found for most other categories in the *Diagnostic and Statistical Manual* (Spitzer, Cohen, Fliess, & Endicott, 1967). No doubt the definitional criteria for antisocial personality will continue to shift, most likely in the direction of subtypes, as researchers continue to bring this complex syndrome into focus. It is hoped that these efforts will also lead to effective measures for prevention and treatment. With the exception of isolated reports (Meyer, 1980), the most optimistic prognostic statement is that the sociopathic behavior pattern seems to lessen as the person reaches middle age.

REFERENCES

Cadoret, R. J. (1978). Psychopathology in adopted-away offspring of biologic parents with antisocial behavior. *Archives of General Psychiatry, 35,* 176–184.

Cleckley, H. (1976). *The mask of insanity* (5th ed.). St. Louis: Mosby.

Crowe, R. R. (1974). An adoption study of antisocial personality. *Archives of General Psychiatry, 31,* 785–791.

Davison, G. C., & Neale, J. M. (1982). *Abnormal psychology.* New York: Wiley.

Ellingson, R. (1954). Incidence of EEG abnormality among patients with mental disorders of apparently nonorganic origin: A criminal review. *American Journal of Psychiatry, 111,* 263–275.

Gray, H., & Hutchinson, H. C. (1964). The psychopathic personality: A survey of Canadian psychiatrists' opinion. *Canadian Psychiatric Association Journal, 9,* 450–461.

Hare, R. D. (1970). *Psychopathy: Theory and research.* New York: Wiley.

Hill, D. (1952). EEG in episodic psychotic and psychopathic behavior: A classification of data. *EEG & Clinical Neurophysiology, 4,* 419–442.

Hutchings, B., & Mednick, S. A. (1974). Registered criminality in the adoptive and biological parents of registered male adoptees. In S. A. Mednick, F. Schulsinger, J. Higgins, & B. Bell (Eds.), *Genetics, environment and psychopathology.* New York: Elsevier.

Lykken, D. T. (1957). A study of anxiety in the sociopathic personality. *Journal of Abnormal and Social Psychology, 55,* 6–10.

Meyer, R. G. (1980). The antisocial personality. In R. H. Woody (Ed.), *Encyclopedia of clinical assessment.* San Francisco: Jossey-Bass.

Robins, L. N. (1972). Follow-up studies of behavior disorders in children. In H. C. Quay & J. S. Werry (Eds.), *Psychopathological disorders in childhood.* New York: Wiley.

Schachter, S., & Latané, B. (1964). Crime, cognition, and the autonomic nervous system. In D. Levine (Ed.), *Nebraska symposium on motivation.* (Vol. 12). Lincoln: University of Nebraska Press.

Schachter, S., & Singer, J. E. (1962). Cognitive, social and physiological determinants of emotional state. *Psychological Review, 69,* 379–399.

Schmauk, F. J. (1970). Punishment, arousal, and avoidance learning in sociopaths. *Journal of Abnormal Psychology, 76,* 443–453.

Schulsinger, F. (1972). Psychopathy: Heredity and environment. *International Journal of Mental Health, 1,* 190–206.

Spitzer, R., Cohen, J., Fliess, J., & Endicott, J. (1967). Quantification of agreement in psychiatric diagnosis: A new approach. *Archives of General Psychiatry, 17,* 83–87.

Syndulko, K. (1978). Electrocortical investigations of sociopathy. In R. D. Hare & D. Schalling (Eds.), *Psychopathic behavior: Approaches to research.* New York: Wiley.

Witkin, H. A., Mednick, S. A., Schulsinger, F., Bakkestrom, E., Christiansen, K. O., Goodenough, D. R., Hirschhorn, K., Lundsteen, C., Owen, D. R., Philip, J., Rubin, D. B., & Stocking, M. (1976). Criminality in XYY and XXY men. *Science, 193,* 547–555.

Laurence G. Grimm
University of Illinois, Chicago

SOFT (NEUROLOGICAL) SIGNS

Neurological soft signs are defined by Shaffer, O'Connor, Shafer, and Prupis (1983) as "non-normative performance on a motor or sensory test identical or akin to a test of the traditional neurological examination, but a performance that is elicited from an individual who shows none of the features of a fixed or transient localizable neurological disorder" (p. 145). Some sources (e.g., Buda, 1981; Gaddes, 1985) suggest soft signs have a strong age-related component, in that many of the behaviors judged to represent soft signs in children of a certain age would be considered within the range of normal behavior for chronologically younger children. The term is contrasted with hard neurological signs, which are medically documented symptoms of neurologic disease.

The concept of neurological soft signs developed during the 1960s in conjunction with the description of the minimal brain dysfunction (MBD) syndrome (Spreen et al., 1984). Although there were behavioral differences observed in children described as having MBD syndrome, hard neurologic findings were not demonstrated in the population. The vague, inconsistent behaviors that were observed were called soft neurological signs. To be considered a soft sign, Shaffer et al. (1983) state there should be no association between the observed behavior and a positive history of neurologic disease or trauma. Furthermore, clusters of neurological soft signs should not be pathognomonic of neurologic disease or encephalopathy. Soft signs, by definition, are not indicative of specific central nervous system pathology. Soft signs are not additive in the traditional sense: "the presence of more than one soft sign does not make a hard sign" (Spreen et al., 1984, p. 246).

The generalizability of data from studies of neurological soft signs has been complicated by inconsistency across studies in the specific signs tested. Soft signs have been categorized into three different types: those that may suggest immaturity or developmental delay; those that are mild expressions of classic hard neurological signs, which are difficult to elicit and may be inconsistent; and behaviors that may be associated with nonneurologic causes (Spreen et al., 1984). Testing a population of children for soft signs of the type associated with the first category may identify a different subgroup than would testing for signs associated with the others.

Nearly 100 different neurological soft signs have been identified (Spreen et al., 1984). Such signs encompass a wide variety of behaviors, including attention, concentration, fine motor speed, activity level, and affect. Gaddes (1985) lists the following as among the most common neurologic soft signs: motor clumsiness, speech and language delays, left-right confusion, perceptual and perceptual-motor deficits, and deficient eye-hand coordination. Soft signs may occur in conjunction with hyperactivity and spe-

cific learning disabilities, but the presence should not be considered pathognomonic of these conditions (Gaddes, 1985).

The relationship between neurologic soft signs and learning and behavior disorders in children has been investigated widely. In a comprehensive review of studies of children conducted prior to 1983, Shaffer et al. (1983) reported these investigations demonstrated consistent relationships between neurological soft signs and IQ scores, as well as diagnosed psychiatric disturbances and behavior problems. The authors described a study of 456 children participating in the Collaborative Perinatal Project of the National Institute of Neurological and Communicative Disorders and Stroke (NINCDS). The subjects were examined for the presence or absence of 18 neurological soft signs at age 7. Specific signs included movement disorders (e.g., tics, tremors, mirror movements) and coordination difficulties (e.g., dysmetria, dysdiadochokinesia). Subjects were rated blind on 15 behaviors (e.g., fearfulness, verbal fluency, cooperativeness, attention span). As in previous studies, the authors reported increased incidence of cognitive dysfunction, learning problems, and behavior disorders in children who exhibited neurologic soft signs.

The etiology of neurological soft signs has not been delineated clearly, and it is likely there are multiple causes. Soft signs may constitute one end of a continuum of neurologic signs, and thus may be a result of mild central nervous system impairment. For other individuals, soft signs may represent a genetic variation (Shaffer et al., 1983). The high incidence of neurologic soft signs in the general population suggests that caution should be exercised when interpreting their significance.

REFERENCES

Buda, F. B. (1981). *The neurology of developmental disabilities*. Springfield, IL: Thomas.

Gaddes, W. H. (1985). *Learning disabilities and brain function: A neuropsychological approach* (2nd ed.). New York: Springer-Verlag.

Shaffer, D., O'Connor, P. A., Shafer, S. Q., & Prupis, S. (1983). Neurological "soft signs": Their origins and significance for behavior. In M. Rutter (Ed.), *Developmental neuropsychiatry* (pp. 144–163). New York: Guilford.

Spreen, O., Tupper, D., Risser, A., Tuokko, H., & Edgell, D. (1984). *Human developmental neuropsychology*. New York: Oxford University Press.

CATHY F. TELZROW
*Cuyahoga Special Education
Service Center, Maple
Heights, Ohio*

**LATERALIZATION
NEUROPSYCHOLOGY
VISUAL-MOTOR AND VISUAL-PERCEPTUAL PROBLEMS**

SOMPA

See SYSTEM OF MULTICULTURAL PLURALISTIC ASSESSMENT.

SONICGUIDE

The Sonicguide is a mobility aid and environmental sensor for the visually handicapped. It operates on the principle of reflected high-frequency sound, which, when converted into audible stereophonic signals, provides the user with information about the distance, position, and surface characteristics of objects within the travel path and immediate environment. The user learns to locate and identify objects up to a distance of approximately 5 meters.

A transmitter in the center of a spectacle frame radiates ultrasound (high-frequency sound inaudible to the human ear) in front of the wearer. When the ultrasound hits an obstruction such as a wall, a person, or a tree, it is reflected to the aid and received by two microphones below the transmitter. The microphones transform the reflected signals into electrical signals, which are shifted to a much lower range of frequency and converted into audible sounds by two small earphones in the arms of the spectacle frame. The sounds are then directed to each ear by small tubes. These tubes do not interfere with normal hearing and the user learns to integrate the sounds of the Sonicguide with natural sounds to enhance a concept of the environment. The microphones are deflected slightly outward so that sounds produced by objects to either side of the user will be louder in the ear nearer to the object. This process of sound localization occurs in normal hearing and therefore is a natural indication of direction. The pitch of the signal indicates the approximate distance of a reflecting object; it is highest at the maximum range of the aid and gradually reduces as the object comes closer. By interpreting the comparative loudness at each ear of the signal and its pitch and tonal characteristics, the user is able to judge the direction, distance, and surface qualities of reflecting objects.

The electronics of the aid are contained in a control box that is attached by a cable to the spectacle frame. The battery that powers the aid is attached under the control box and the complete unit can be carried in a pocket, at the belt, or on a shoulder strap. The aid's sensors are built into a spectacle frame to encourage the user to develop the same head movements and posture as a sighted person. When the skills of the aid are mastered, safer and more confident travel and a heightened awareness of the environment is assured. In outdoor situations, the device is to be used in conjunction with a long cane or guide dog, unless the area of travel is both familiar and free from hazards at ground level, which the Sonicguide may not detect.

MONIQUE BAUTERS
*Centre d'Etude et de
Reclassement,
Brussels, Belgium*

**BLIND
ELECTRONIC TRAVEL AIDS
VISUAL TRAINING**

SOUTH AMERICA

See MEXICO, SPECIAL EDUCATION IN.

SOVIET EDUCATION

Soviet Education is a journal of English-language translations that started publication in 1959. It made Soviet education literature available through English-language translations for the first time. The founding editors of *Soviet Education* were Myron Sharpe, Murray Yanowitch, and Fred Ablin. From 1967 through 1969, Seymour Rosen served as editor, followed by Harold Noah in 1970. The editorial load was shared with Beatrice Szekely, who assumed the full role of editor in the late 1970s.

A topical journal, *Soviet Education* draws material from Russian-language books and works in teacher training texts, educational psychology, sociology, comparative education, and educational administration. The journal tends to focus on educational policy issues. It is published monthly.

ROBERTA C. STOKES
CECIL R. REYNOLDS
Texas A&M University

SOVIET UNION AND EASTERN EUROPE, SPECIAL EDUCATION IN THE

The Soviet Union is comprised of 15 constituent republics: Armenia, Azerbajdzan, Belorussia, Estonia, Georgia, Kazakhstan, Kirgisia, Latvia, Lithuania, Moldavia, Russia, Tadzikistan, Turkmenia, Ukraine, and Uzbekistan.

Administration of special education in the Soviet Union is centralized within the All-Union (Vse-Souznaya) Ministry of Education in Moscow. Each of the 15 republics has its own ministry of education and a department of special education. The ministries of education of the republics are responsible to the Ministry of Education of the USSR. The scope and the degree of comprehensiveness of special education services is not identical in each one of the Soviet republics.

In Russia, toward the end of the nineteenth century and the beginning of the twentieth century, there were sporadic individual attempts to develop programs for handicapped children. The noted neuropathologist Bechtiarev was interested in the education of exceptional children and suggested pedagogical reflexology as a name for this field. However, a relatively small number of mentally retarded, deaf, and blind children were cared for by religious or private organizations prior to the end of World War I (1918).

During the first few years following the Russian revolution, a strong movement based on European influences emerged among Soviet educators. This movement, described as pedology, attempted to identify and assess individual differences in abilities. Among supporters of pedology were such noted Soviet psychologists as Vygotsky and Blonsky. In the early 1930s, strong opposition to pedology developed, led by Makarenko and Medinsky. On July 4, 1936, the Central Committee of the Communist Party of the Soviet Union decreed that pedology was founded on pseudoscientific and anti-Marxist theses (Shore, 1947).

The central goal of Soviet education, as emphasized by Soviet educators, is successful rearing of a new member of the communist society. The field of special education has been traditionally divided into four areas: oligophrenopedagogy (education of the mentally retarded); surdopedagogy (education of the deaf); typhlopedagogy (education of the blind); and logopedagogy (education of those who need speech correction). Discussion of developmentally delayed children is a relatively recent phenomena in the Soviet literature. Research with this population began in 1965 at the Scientific Research Institute of the Academy of Pedagogical Sciences (Holowinsky, 1983).

The service delivery network for exceptional children extends from nursery and kindergarten through vocational and adult continuing education. There exists an elaborate system of registration of infants and young children with high risk of handicapping conditions. Any developmental abnormalities are noted at the time of birth in the delivery room. Special schools group children according to chronological age and degree of severity of impairment.

In addition to special schools for the mentally retarded, blind, and deaf, there are also auxiliary schools for the mildly handicapped. The program in an auxiliary school is arranged in such a way that a youngster is expected to reach an eighth-grade competency level after 12 years of schooling. There is heavy emphasis on vocational training in auxiliary schools. Language stimulation and speech correction with exceptional children has been significantly

increased since 1976, the curriculum has been extended from 4 to 18 hours per week. New programs began in 1974 for developmentally delayed children, and the first residential school for such children was established in 1980.

Since 1976 a special class limit of 12 has been set for children with auditory, visual, and speech defects, and 16 for the mentally retarded. Physical exercise has a prominent place in the curriculum for exceptional children.

A typical curriculum for the moderately retarded is described by Kuzmitskaya (1977). The curriculum includes nine objectives: (1) personal communication, (2) orientation to place of residence, (3) knowledge of primary occupations of residents of towns and villages, (4) basic ideas of commerce, (5) familiarity with basic food preparation, (6) knowledge of available health services in the neighborhood, (7) use of the post office, telephone, telegraph, and radio, (8) knowledge of available recreation facilities in the neighborhood, and (9) basic familiarity with work habits and schedules.

Preschool education of the handicapped has developed considerably in the past decade. In 1970 there were 700 preschool facilities in the Soviet Union in which more than 11,000 handicapped children were educated (Filkina, 1977). In 1976 there existed 1580 preschool facilities with 49,648 children. As of 1982 there were preschool facilities providing care, training, and education to over 140,000 exceptional children. The following types of preschool facilities are in existence: kindergartens with full-day curriculums; residential homes for children; preschool groups attached to special schools; and special groups for various categories of exceptional children within kindergartens for normal children (Noskova & Mironova, 1982).

There have been special education developments in various Soviet republics. The first school for blind children in Armenia opened in 1922. In 1928 the first auxiliary school opened in Erevan (capital city of Armenia). There was particular growth of special education programs in Armenia in 1960s and 1970s (Minasian, 1970).

Since the 1970s, the programs for developmentally delayed children have been put in place in Byelorussia (Gaiduk, Slepovitch, & Asanova, 1984). The first class for children with this classification opened in Vitebsk in 1974. By 1982 there were 74 classes for children classified as developmentally delayed in Belorussia. Development of special education services began in Kazakhstan early in the 1970s. As of the late 1970s, approximately 26,000 exceptional children of school and preschool age attended various programs including 77 special classes. The defectological department of the Kazakh Pedagogical Institute is heavily involved in in-service training (Lutskina & Grushevskaya, 1985).

Special education in Lithuania originated in the nineteenth century. The first school for deaf children opened in Vilnious in 1805. The first auxiliary school for the mentally retarded opened in Vilnious in 1923; another opened in Kaunus in 1931. As of the 1970s (Machikhina, 1975), there were 35 auxiliary schools in existence in Lithuania, providing education to over 7000 exceptional children in first through eighth grades. The section of defectology within the Lithuanian Scientific Research Institute of Pedagogy was organized in 1970 (Karvelis, 1979). The first program for the severely retarded was organized in Moldavia in 1946 (Pavlova, 1978), and the first auxiliary school for the mildly mentally retarded opened in the early 1950s. In 20 years (1950–1970), 37 additional schools were organized for the mildly retarded, three evening schools for the deaf, one school for the blind, and 13 speech correction clinics within the public schools.

Sixty-eight special schools are operating in Uzbekistan; they serve over 18,000 children (Gordienko, 1985). Additionally, there are 85 special classes within the public schools. It is reported that in 5 years (1971–1976), programs for preschool handicapped in Uzbekistan increased fourfold. Nearly 3000 special educators are working in special schools; 520 of them have defectological preparation. Specialists for Uzbekistan are trained at defectological institutes in Moscow, Leningrad, Kiev, Sverdlowsk, and Minsk.

In the Soviet Union approaches to the assessment of exceptional children differ significantly from the psychometric approaches generally accepted in the United States and Western Europe. In the absence of standardized tests of intelligence, assessment and classification of exceptional children has been based on a variety of informal techniques. Evaluation data include medical history, interviews with parents and siblings, and informal psychoeducational evaluation based on comprehension of written stories and description of pictorial material. Assessment practices in the Soviet Union reveal three trends. The pedology movement was replaced in the 1930s by an antitesting policy followed more recently by a reassessment of psychodiagnostic practices. In the late 1970s and early 1980s, a strong interest in psychodiagnosis was revealed (Holowinsky, 1984).

In the Soviet Union, professional personnel preparation for work with exceptional children is carried out at two types of facilities. Special education teachers are usually trained at 2-year teacher training institutes. Those trained at the universities are referred to as defectologists. After graduation, in-service training is usually organized. Prior to the revolution, preparation of special educators was sparodic based on short-term in-service training. In 1918 a department of pathological pedagogy was organized in Leningrad; the State Institute of a Defective Child was organized in Moscow in 1920; and in 1921, the Pedagogical Institute of Child's Abnormalities. These two institutes joined in 1924 and reorganized into the defectological section of the Pedagogical Department of the Moscow Second State University. The Moscow State Pedagogical-Defectological Institute was organized in 1938. From 1959 to 1981, 10 additional defectological departments were organized: Shauley (1960), Minsk (1961), Sverdlovsk (1962), Irkutsk (1963), Slavyansk (1966),

Tashkent (1967), Tartu (1968), Lyepay (1969), Kishinev (1970), and Alma-Ata (1979; Lapshin & Zhivina, 1981). The curriculum to train defectologists was reorganized in 1963; it includes a 4-year sequence of full-time study. Courses of study include introduction to defectology, physics, chemistry, biology, anatomy, psychopathology, neuropathology of children, geography, pedagogical psychopathology, developmental psychopathology, sexual psychopathology, and clinical practice (Zhivina, 1974). In keeping with the Soviet Union's position that political indoctrination is an integral part of professional preparation, defectologists are required to study historical materialism, political economy, and political education. As of 1976, a Council of Defectology was formed within the Ministry of Education of the USSR. Medico-pedagogical committees were formed to facilitate cooperation between educators and physicians.

Guidelines for future preparation of teacher-defectologists were published in a directive of the Central Committee of the Communist Party of the Soviet Union. The document states that Soviet specialists should know, among other information, foundations of theoretical disciplines to the extent necessary to enable them to make pedagogical and administrative decisions; the disciplines of psycho-pedagogical areas including pedagogy, psychology, developmental physiology, neuropathology, anatomy, physiology, pathology of hearing, speech, and vision, genetics, and clinical oligophrenia; and basic tenets of teaching children with physical and cognitive deviations as well as the methodology of teaching basic subjects.

Research with exceptional children in the Soviet Union is conducted at the Institute of Defectology of the Academy of Pedagogical Sciences in Moscow and at leading Soviet universities. Soviet defectologists publish their research in *Defectologia* and *Voprosy Psykhologii* (Problems of Psychology). Achievements have been made in the areas of mental retardation (Luria, 1963; Pevzner, 1961); developmental disabilities (Pevzner & Rostiagaylova, 1981); cerebral palsy (Kalizhniuk & Sapunova, 1975; Mastiukova, 1973); auditory disorders (Moskovina, Bertyn, & Opolinsky, 1979); visual handicaps (Kozakov, 1975; Solntseva, 1979); and speech disorders (Karpukhina, 1980; Kononova, 1968; Popova, 1968; Lozbiakova, 1973; Luria, 1966; Mastiukova, 1979; Tsvetkova, 1972).

In the Ukraine, isolated attempts to provide help to handicapped children were recorded as early as the eleventh century. It is reported (Yarmachenko, 1968) that at that time, a home was established for blind, deaf, physically disabled, and orphaned at the Kiev-Pechersk monastery. Systematic instruction of blind children began in the nineteenth century when several schools were organized throughout the Ukraine (Chernyhiv, 1892; Kamenets-Podilsky, 1885; Kharkiv, 1886; Kiev, 1840; Lviv, 1851; Odessa, 1887; Poltava, 1894). A noted Ukrainian scholar-educator, A. M. Shcherbyna (1874–1934), is considered one of the founders of Soviet defectology. His most noted activity as an educator was associated with the Kiev

Pedagogical Institute, where in 1929 a special education department was organized (Zolotnyckaya, 1977).

Sokolansky is also recognized as a noted special educator of the 1920s. He developed in Kharkiv a program for the education of deaf, blind, and mute children. In the 1930s, Makarenko acquired prominence as an educator; he contributed significantly to the development of the collective concept in Soviet educational literature. The child's collective is viewed as an integral part of society. Makarenko viewed collective as meaning not just as an assembly or a group of individuals interacting together, but as a goal-directed constellation of personalities responsive to their organizational structure.

Special education in the Ukraine covers such traditional categories as the blind, visually handicapped, deaf, hard of hearing, mentally retarded, and severely speech impaired. Acceptable terms for intellectual subnormality are *rozumova vidstalist* or *umove nedorozvynennia*, translated as intellectual backwardness and mental retardation.

Children entering an auxiliary school are divided into two groups based on higher or lower cognitive abilities. During the 1978–1979 school year, individualized instruction was introduced into auxiliary schools serving mentally retarded children. Yeremenko (1976) described individualized instruction as a new approach to the education of mentally retarded children, calling it one of the most pressing needs currently confronting defectologists.

Starting with the 1981–1982 school year, new curriculum guides for special schools of all types were adopted. Since 1982 new types of schools for the developmentally delayed have been organized. By 1984 six such schools became operational. Currently, there are 369 residential schools serving over 77,000 children. There are also 51 schools, 798 programs, and 13 homes caring for preschool children. Assessment practices with exceptional children in the Ukrainian SSR parallel those currently accepted through the Soviet Union.

While standardized testing is as yet unknown in the Ukraine, recently attention has been paid to the assessment of exceptional children. The Psychological Institute in Kiev, in collaboration with the Institute of Pedagogy, recently published *Principles of Assessment and Education of Atypical Children*. Likewise, in 1978 Bleykher and Burlachuk (Rozhdestvenskaya, 1979) published a book in Kiev that describes the psychological diagnosis of intelligence and personality and reviews both the theory and practice of psychological diagnosis.

An important activity in the selection and placement of children is exercised by the Central Medico-Pedagogical Commission established within the Ukraine's Research Institute of Psychology. Members of the commission are providing consultation for parents of exceptional children and for teachers of special schools. Defectological departments exist in Kiev and Slavyansk. The department in Kiev was established in 1920 as a medico-pedagogical section within the department of social education at the Kiev State Pedagogical Institute. In 1939 the section became a separate department. At present, the Kiev State Pedagogical Institute contains 8 departments with 19 specialties. In 1965 the department of defectology was divided into two departments: the department of the education of the deaf and speech impaired and the department of oligophreno-pedagogy (Bondar & Sosenko, 1983).

Prominent research in the area of developmental and educational psychology was conducted in the late 1920s and early 1930s in Kharkiv. Noted researchers of that time were, among others, Vygotsky and Zaporozhets, and later Zinchenko.

Currently, research with exceptional children is being conducted at the Ukraine's Institute of Psychology and at various universities. In 1955 a department of special psychology was established at the institute under the direction of Stadnenko. The institute is noted for its efforts in learning research and mental development (Proskura, 1969). Research focuses include pathological and psychopathological correlates of behavior and cognitive activity of mentally retarded children (Yeremenko, 1977); child psychopathology; psychology of mentally retarded children; education of the mentally retarded; and mental development of youngsters in special schools. Research and scholarly studies are publsihed in *Defectologia* (Defectology), *Voprosy Psikhologii* (Problems of Psychology), and *Radianska Shkola* (Soviet School).

REFERENCES

Bondar, V. I., & Sosenko, N. F. (1983). Training of defectology specialists in Kiev Pedagogical Institute. *Defectologia, 4,* 69–71.

Filkina, L. M. (1977). Actual extent of pre-school upbringing of atypical children and several problems of its further development. *Defectologia, 1,* 3–11.

Gaiduk, F. M., Slepovitch, E. S., & Asanova, N. K. (1984). Practice of organizing service for developmentally backward children in Byelorussian SSR. *Defectologia, 2,* 32–35.

Gordienko, E. A. (1985). Status of education of abnormal children in Uzbek SSR. *Defectologia, 1,* 34–39.

Holowinsky, I. Z. (1983). Research on developmentally delayed children in the Soviet Union. *Journal of Special Education, 3*(17), 365–369.

Holowinsky, I. Z. (1984). Assessment of cognitive skills in the USSR: Historical trends and current developments. *Journal of Special Education, 4*(18), 541–545.

Hroza, T. A. (1985). History of education of visually impaired children in Ukrainian SSR. *Defectologia, 2,* 69–76.

Kalizhniuk, E. S., & Sapunova, Y. V. (1975). Disturbance of visual-spatial perception of C.P. pre-school children and several methods of its remediation. *Defectologia, 6,* 17–24.

Karpukhina, P. P. (1980). Differential approach to studying children during the onset of stuttering. *Defectologia, 1,* 66–70.

Karvelis, V. J. (1979). Progress of special education in Lithuania. *Defectologia, 1,* 33–38.

Kononova, I. M. (1968). Vocal reactions in children during the first year of life and their relationship to various patterns of behavior. *Voprosy Psikhologii*, *5*, 119–127.

Kozakov, A. A. (1975). Application of a photo-electrical instrument presenting color information to the blind. *Defectologia*, *1*, 71–75.

Kuzmitskaya, M. I. (1977). Preparation of trainable retardates to practical life (home and social adaptation). *Defectologia*, *5*, 89–91.

Lapshin, V., & Zhivina, A. (1981). Sixty years of higher defectological education in the USSR and the role of defectological department of the Lenin Pedagogical College of Moscow in training of diplomate defectologists. *Defectologia*, *6*, 78–81.

Lozbiakova, M. I. (1973). Pronunciation of speech sounds in five-year-olds. *Defectologia*, *1*, 69–76.

Luria, A. R. (1963). *The Mentally retarded child*. New York: Pergamon.

Luria, A. R. (1966). *Higher cortical functions in man*. New York: Basic Books.

Lutskina, R. K., & Grushevskaya, M. G. (1985). Third republican science-practical conference of Kazakhstan defectologists. *Defectologia*, *4*, 91–92.

Machikhina, V. F. (1975). The experience of the ministry of education of the Lithuanian SSR in managing special schools. *Defectologia*, *6*, 3–8.

Machikhina, V. F. (1977). Development of special education in the Kazakh SSR. *Defectologia*, *4*, 4–9.

Mastiukova, Y. M. (1973). On the development of cognitive activity in C.P. children. *Defectologia*, *6*, 24–30.

Mastiukova, Y. M. (1979). Speech disorders in students with a hyperkinetic form of cerebral palsy and medical reasons for speech therapy. *Defectologia*, *3*, 24–31.

Minasian, A. M. (1970). Education of handicapped children in the Armenian Soviet Socialist Republic. *Defectologia*, *1*, 25–34.

Moskovina, A. G., Bertyn, G. P., & Opolinsky, E. S. (1979). The problems of the origin of hearing disorders in children. *Defectologia*, *2*, 6–12.

N. N. (1983). New curriculum—An important factor of defectologists' training advancement in pedagogical institutes. *Defectologia*, *5*, 3–6.

Noskova, L. V., & Mironova, S. A. (1982). Social system of preschool upbringing of abnormal children in Kazakh SSR. *Defectologia*, *6*, 58–62.

Pavlova, N. (1978). Silver jubilee of the first auxiliary school of Moldavia. *Defectologia*, *2*, 87–88.

Pevzner, M. S. (1961). *Oligophrenia: Mental deficiency in children*. New York: Consultants Bureau.

Popova, M. I. (1968). Some features of speech manifestation in children of the first half-year of the second year of life. *Voprosy Psikhologii*, *4*, 116–122.

Proskura, O. V. (1969). The role of teaching in the formation of seriation actions in preschool children. *Voprosy Psikhologii*, *15*, 37–45.

Rozhdestvenskaya, M. (1979). Psychological diagnosis of intelligence and personality. *Defectologia*, *5*, 89–90.

Shore, M. (1947). *Soviet education: its psychology and philosophy*. New York: Philosophical Library.

Solntseva, L. I. (1979). Creation of multi-sensory bases for compensation of blindness in early childhood. *Defectologia*, *5*, 61–68.

Tsvetkova, L. S. (1972). Basic principles of a theory of reeducation of brain-injured patients. *Journal of Special Education*, *2*, 135–146.

Yarmachenko, N. D. (1968). Upbringing and education of deaf children in Ukrainian SSR. *Radianska Shkola* (Soviet School), 6–8.

Yeremenko, I. H. (1976). On differential instruction in auxiliary schools. *Defectologia*, *4*, 56–63.

Yeremenko, I. H. (1977). Conditions and perspectives of scientific research in the field of defectology in Ukrainian SSR. *Defectologia*, *5*, 12–20.

Zhivina, A. I. (1974). Major stages of development of special education teacher training in the USSR. *Defectologia*, *2*, 68–75.

Zolotnyckaya, R. (1977). A. M. Shcherbyna, educator of the blind. *Defectologia*, *2*, 90–92.

Ivan Z. Holowinsky
Rutgers University

LURIA, A. R.
SOVIET EDUCATION
THEORY OF ACTIVITY
VGOTSKY, L. S.

SPACHE DIAGNOSTIC READING SCALE

See DIAGNOSTIC READING SCALE.

SPAN OF APPREHENSION

See PERCEPTUAL SPAN.

SPASTICITY

Spasticity is a type of cerebral palsy involving a lack of muscle control. Spastic children make up the largest group of the cerebral palsied, constituting 40 to 60% of the total.

Another term that has been used to refer to spastic cerebral palsy is pyramidal. This term was coined because the nerves involved are shaped like pyramids. Spastic cerebral palsy is produced by damage sustained to the nerve cell that is found in the motor cortex. The motor cortex is the gray matter of the brain containing nerve cells that initiate motor impulses to the muscles. The nerve cells have tracts that extend from the neuron in the cortex to the spinal cord. These cells eventually connect with nerve tracts that innervate the limb so that muscle movement can be carried out. If these nerve cells or tracts are injured, spasticity results.

Because spasticity can affect one or all four extremities, it is subdivided into several types. Monoplegia involves one extremity only, either an arm or leg. This type is extremely rare. Triplegia involves the impairment of three extremities; it is an unusual occurrence. Hemiplegia means that the abnormality is confined to half of the body, either the right or left side with the arm more involved than the leg. This is the most common locus of involvement. Bilateral hemiplegia or double hemiplegia involves weakness or paralysis of both sides of the body with the arms compromised more than the legs. Another type, quadriplegia, occurs in all four extremities with more disability of the legs than the arms. Diplegia means that all four limbs are affected, with minimal involvement of the arms. Paraplegia is neurologic dysfunction of the legs only. Spastic hemiplegias are the most common group, representing approximately 40% of the total cerebral palsied population, while spastic quadriplegias represent 19% of the total (Capute, 1978).

In mild cases, the spastic child has an awkward gait and may extend his or her arms for balance. In moderate cases, the child may bend the arms at the elbow and hold both arms close to the body with the hands bent toward the body. The legs may be rotated inwardly and flexed at the knees; this causes a "scissoring gait." In severe cases, the child may have poor body control and be unable to sit, stand, and walk without the support of braces, crutches, a walking frame, or other support (Kirk & Gallagher, 1979).

REFERENCES

Capute, A. (1978). Cerebral palsy and associated dysfunctions. In R. Haslam & P. Valletutti (Eds.), *Problems in the classroom* (pp. 149–163). Baltimore, MD: University Park Press.

Kirk, S., & Gallagher, J. (1979). *Educating exceptional children*, (3rd ed.). Boston: Houghton Mifflin.

CECELIA STEPPE-JONES
*North Carolina Central
University*

**CEREBRAL PALSY
PHYSICAL DISABILITIES**

SPEARMAN, C. E. (1863–1945)

C. E. Spearman grew up in an English family of established status and some eminence; he became an officer in the regular army. He remained in the army until the age of 40, attaining the rank of major. He then obtained his PhD in Wundt's laboratory at Leipzig in 1908 at the age of 45. He was appointed to an academic position at University College, London, where he remained for the rest of his career.

Spearman is known for his theory of general intelligence and for a number of contributions to statistical methodology, including factor analysis, the Spearman rank correlation, and the Spearman-Brown prophecy formula. Spearman's primary interest was in the study of general intelligence, which he preferred to call g. His methodological innovations were directed toward the better definition and measurement of g.

Spearman conceived of intelligence as a general capability involved in the performance of almost all mental tasks, although he saw some tasks as more dependent on g than others. Thus the variance of any mental test may be divided into two parts: a part associated with individual differences in g and a part specific to the test in question. Since the correlation coefficient indicates the proportion of shared variation of two variables, Spearman was able to develop methods of analyzing a matrix of correlations among tests to determine the presence of a general factor and to calculate the g loading for a test, its correlation with the underlying general factor. The conception of intelligence as g provided an objective method of defining intelligence and of evaluating the adequacy of any proposed measure of intelligence.

Spearman's original two-factor theory (Spearman, 1904) included only g and a factor specific to each task. Subsequently, he expanded the theory to include group factors, which are factors common to a group of tasks independent of g. However, his major emphasis was always on g (Spearman, 1927). Subsequent development and mathematical refinement of factor analysis by Thurstone and others emphasized the group factors; g became obscured in the correlation among the primary factors. Today g is recognized as a second order factor accounting for the correlations among the primaries. There is still disagreement concerning its importance.

REFERENCES

Spearman, C. E. (1904). "General intelligence" objectively determined and measured. *American Journal of Psychology, 15,* 201–293.

Spearman, C. E. (1927). *The abilities of man: Their nature and measurement.* London: Macmillan.

ROBERT C. NICHOLS
DIANE JARVIS
*State University of New York,
Buffalo*

**g FACTOR THEORY
INTELLIGENCE
REACTION TIME**

SPEARMAN'S HYPOTHESIS OF BLACK/WHITE DIFFERENCES

C. Spearman (1863–1945), in commenting on a study by Pressey and Teter (1919) in which 10 diverse mental tests were administered to large samples of black and white American children, noted that the mean difference between the races "was most marked in just those [tests] which are known to be most saturated with *g*" (Spearman, 1927, p. 379). The smallest racial difference was on a test of rote memory, the largest on a test of verbal ingenuity.

This observation attracted no special attention until 1985, when Arthur Jensen published an extensive analysis of all available relevant data as a test of what he referred to as Spearman's hypothesis. Jensen distinguished between strong and weak forms of the hypothesis, a distinction not made by Spearman.

> The strong form . . . holds that the magnitudes of the black-white differences (in standard score units) on a variety of tests are directly related to the tests' *g* loadings, because black and white populations differ only on *g* and on no other cognitive factors. The weak form of the hypothesis holds that the black-white difference in various mental tests is predominantly a difference in *g*, although the populations also differ, but to a much lesser degree, in certain other ability factors beside *g*. (Jensen, 1985, p. 198)

To test Spearman's hypothesis, Jensen, in a systematic search of the recent literature, found 11 studies containing appropriate data: comparisons of large unselected black and white samples on six or more diverse tests of ability. Jensen reanalyzed the data from these studies to obtain general factor (μg) loadings for the tests and compared these loadings with the size of the group differences. He concluded that

> all the evidence reviewed clearly substantiates Spearman's hypothesis (in its weak form). Every set of reasonably suitable data that I have been able to find is consistent with the hypothesis, and I have not been able to find any set of data . . . that contradicts the hypothesis. (Jensen, 1985, p. 206)

Jensen's article was accompanied by 27 commentaries by knowledgeable professionals in the field. Nine of the commentaries explicitly regarded the hypothesis to be borne out by the evidence, two expressed doubts, three suggested that the results might be due to some artifact of the methodology, and the remaining 13 expressed no definite opinion regarding Spearman's hypothesis.

REFERENCES

Jensen, A. R. (1985). The nature of the black-white difference on various psychometric tests: Spearman's hypothesis. *Behavioral & Brain Sciences, 8,* 193–219.

Pressey, S. L., & Teter, G. F. (1919). A comparison of colored and white children by means of a group scale of intelligence. *Journal of Applied Psychology, 33,* 447–514.

Spearman, C. (1927). *The abilities of man.* New York: Macmillan.

ROBERT C. NICHOLS
DIANE JARVIS
*State University of New York,
Buffalo*

ASSESSMENT
CULTURAL BIAS IN TESTS
CULTURE FAIR TESTS
"*g*" FACTOR THEORY
INTELLIGENCE TESTING

SPECIAL CLASS

The first special classes were established in the late 1800s and early 1900s as public school classes for the moderately retarded, deaf, hard of hearing, blind, emotionally disturbed, and physically handicapped. Esten (1900) stated that special classes for mentally retarded were established to provide slow-learning children with more appropriate class placement.

A special classroom for the exceptional can be defined as one that homogeneously segregates different children from normal children. Children are usually segregated along categorical groupings. As a result of Dunn's (1968) article on the detrimental aspects of special class placements for the mildly handicapped, students receiving special education in self-contained special classes today are usually those with more severe problems. However, Kirk and Gallagher (1983) report gifted exceptional students are also grouped into special classes according to interests and abilities. As low-incidence students demonstrate proficiency in specific skill areas, they are mainstreamed into regular classes.

Other types of service delivery for special education students (e.g., resource rooms) do not fall under the label special class. Resource rooms usually provide service for high-incidence populations. Special classes, on the other hand, usually service low-incidence populations. In addition, there are four different types of resource rooms: categorical, serving one population; noncategorical, serving more than one population; itinerant; and teacher-consultant. There is usually only one type of special class, self-contained.

REFERENCES

Dunn, L. M. (1968). Special education for the mildly handicapped: Is much of it justifiable? *Exceptional Children, 35,* 5–22.

Esten, R. A. (1900). Backward children in the public schools. *Journal of Psychoaesthenics, 5,* 10–16.

MARIBETH MONTGOMERY KASIK
Governors State University

RESOURCE ROOM
SELF-CONTAINED CLASS

SPECIAL EDUCATION, EFFECTIVENESS OF

See EFFECTIVENESS OF SPECIAL EDUCATION.

SPECIAL EDUCATION, FEDERAL IMPACT ON

The impact of the federal government on special education occurs through two independent, but overlapping, functions: (1) the administration and development of programs, and (2) the compliance monitoring of state education agencies. The administration and development of programs involves the disbursement of discretionary grants and contracts as well as the disbursement of formula grant funds under Part B of the Education of the Handicapped Act (EHA-B). Discretionary grants are awarded to individuals and organizations in states and territories on a competitive basis. Depending on the specific program for which awards are made, these funds are to be used for research, program/materials development, technical assistance, demonstration, or training. During fiscal year 1984, a total of 1393 projects were funded at a cost approaching $128 million. For the most part, these projects do not directly serve handicapped children and youths, but rather, are intended to support existing programs, demonstrate new or more effective ways of delivering services, train special education and related services personnel, or increase our knowledge of current or promising components of special education (i.e., research efforts). The exceptions are those programs that provide direct services to handicapped students from low-incidence populations (e.g., the severely handicapped). The following listing shows each state's special education discretionary grant awards by number and amount:

State	Project Funded	Amount of Award
Alabama	18	$2,301,217
Alaska	8	1,044,429
Arizona	32	2,552,115
Arkansas	18	1,087,615
California	92	8,704,465
Colorado	30	2,612,831
Connecticut	19	2,054,977
Delaware	4	337,480
District of Columbia	52	4,450,890
Florida	21	1,606,250
Georgia	14	951,538
Hawaii	10	1,036,998

State	Project Funded	Amount of Award
Idaho	10	767,362
Illinois	60	4,764,667
Indiana	16	1,232,766
Iowa	18	1,158,505
Kansas	48	4,000,908
Kentucky	27	2,303,544
Louisiana	14	1,113,381
Maine	12	953,874
Maryland	35	3,654,093
Massachusetts	49	5,473,855
Michigan	21	1,733,371
Minnesota	33	3,456,357
Mississippi	9	892,176
Missouri	18	1,327,303
Montana	8	658,383
Nebraska	15	1,202,747
Nevada	7	501,900
New Hampshire	6	453,462
New Jersey	12	1,338,001
New Mexico	14	1,218,336
New York	101	9,709,821
North Carolina	47	4,695,712
North Dakota	7	522,012
Ohio	40	4,294,553
Oklahoma	6	406,182
Oregon	69	5,776,276
Pennsylvania	55	4,903,651
Rhode Island	5	432,261
South Carolina	9	604,632
South Dakota	4	492,133
Tennessee	37	3,644,771
Texas	38	3,988,970
Utah	47	3,915,102
Vermont	18	1,760,917
Virginia	53	6,378,876
Washington	54	4,781,095
West Virginia	13	946,860
Wisconsin	27	2,231,075
Wyoming	3	256,329
American Samoa	2	122,867
Guam	4	452,513
Northern Marianas	1	104,958
Puerto Rico	1	94,496
Trust Territories	1	92,031
Virgin Islands	1	85,000

In addition to discretionary grant awards and contracts, states also receive annual funds based on the total number of handicapped children and youths receiving special education and related services. The history of funding for this entitlement program, termed the EHA-B state grant program, is shown in the table below:

Fiscal Year	Total Amount Available	Child Count	Per-Child Average
1977	$251,769,927	3,485,000	$72
1978	566,030,074	3,561,000	159

Fiscal Year	Total Amount Available	Child Count	Per-Child Average
1979	804,000,000	3,700,000	217
1980	874,500,000	3,803,000	230
1981	874,500,000	3,941,000	222
1982	931,008,000	3,990,000	233
1983	1,017,900,000	4,053,000	251
1984	1,068,875,000	4,094,000	261
1985	1,135,145,000	4,113,312	276

Each state education agency (SEA) must distribute at least 75% of the total funds to local education agencies to be used directly for the education of handicapped students. The remaining funds may be used by the SEA, with some portion going toward administrative costs. Thus federal funds are used to offset some of the additional costs associated with educating handicapped students.

Federal funds also are available under Chapter 1 of ECIA (formerly PL 89-313) to provide for the educational needs of handicapped students in state-operated or state-supported schools. These students have been presumed to be more severely handicapped, and thus more costly to provide for, than handicapped students served in local educational agencies. An abbreviated funding history of this program is shown below:

Fiscal Year	Total Amount Available	Eligible Children	Per-Child Allocation
1977	$121,590,937	201,429	$604
1978	132,492,071	223,804	592
1979	143,353,492	225,660	635
1980	145,000,000	233,744	620
1981	152,625,000	243,708	626
1982	146,520,000	242,616	604
1983	146,520,000	245,785	596
1984	146,520,000	247,119	593
1985	150,170,000	249,656	587

Federal funds are available to expand services to preschool handicapped children. Termed the Incentive Grant Program (authorized under Section 619 of EHA-B), this program provides formula grants to states based on the number of handicapped children, ages 3 through 5, receiving special education and related services, although these funds may be used for handicapped children ages birth through 5. The funding history of this program is:

Fiscal Year	Total Amount Available	Child Count	Per-Child Amount
1977	$12,500,000	197,000	$63
1978	15,000,000	201,000	75
1979	17,500,000	215,000	81
1980	25,000,000	232,000	108
1981	25,000,000	237,000	105
1982	24,000,000	228,000	105
1983	25,000,000	242,000	103
1984	26,330,000	253,000	104
1985	29,000,000	259,483	112

Thus one of the primary ways special education is impacted by the federal government is through a direct infusion of funds that assist state and local educational agencies in offering special education and related services, or through efforts that further state and local programs (discretionary grants and contracts).

The second major area in which the federal government impacts special education is through compliance monitoring. Section 616 of EHA-B (as well as Section 74.85 of the Education Department's General Administrative Regulations) provides for the monitoring of state education agencies to ensure compliance with provisions of Sections 612 and 613 of the Education of the Handicapped Act.

To accomplish this objective, special education programs engage in program administrative reviews that involve on-site and off-site reviews of information. Where deficiencies are found, corrective actions are requested from the SEA. The corrective actions report includes a description of the steps to be taken by the SEA, timelines for completion, and the documentation to be submitted verifying that deficiencies have been corrected. Should substantial noncompliance be noted, the U.S. Department of Education is authorized to withhold federal funds. Considerable leeway exists within the department's administration of its compliance monitoring efforts to ensure that each state receives funding. Nevertheless, the possibility that a state may not receive federal funds can be persuasive in altering special education programs in that state. Thus this is one further way in which special education is impacted.

MARTY ABRAMSON
University of Wisconsin, Stout

DEMOGRAPHY OF SPECIAL EDUCATION
POLITICS AND SPECIAL EDUCATION
SPECIAL EDUCATION PROGRAMS

SPECIAL EDUCATION, GENERIC

See GENERIC SPECIAL EDUCATION.

SPECIAL EDUCATION, HISTORY OF

See HISTORY OF SPECIAL EDUCATION.

SPECIAL EDUCATION, HUMANISTIC

See HUMANISTIC SPECIAL EDUCATION.

SPECIAL EDUCATION, JOURNAL OF

The Journal of Special Education is published quarterly by Buttonwood Farms Inc., a nonprofit organization chartered to provide services and products relating to the education of handicapped children.

The *Journal of Special Education* began publishing in October 1966, at a time when modern day special education was still in its infancy and there were few independent publications. It was known in the beginning for its willingness to serve as a forum for controversial issues, even during periods when consensus rather than discussion was preferred on many issues and on many grounds. A number of the journal's special issues have become classics.

The *Journal of Special Education*, by choice, has chosen to be an elitist publication holding to the highest standards of scholarship. As such, it has continued to be respected by the professional community. It assumes a broad perspective as to what constitutes special education and has encouraged the emergence of new points of view in the field.

Representing no particular professional organization, nor ideology of research or practice, the *Journal of Special Education* has sought to sustain a nondoctrinaire position relative to the field it serves and is considered by many the flagship of special education publishing.

LESTER MANN
Hunter College, City University of New York

SPECIAL EDUCATION, LEGAL REGULATION OF

Regulations are the formal, explicit guidelines by which a public law (or statute) is administered. Regulatory content carries the weight of law and provides both the interpretive framework and the strict operational standards by which federal programs are managed and evaluated, program eligibility is defined, and funding is distributed.

The most significant piece of federal special education legislation to date was signed into law in 1975 as PL 94-142, the Education for All Handicapped Children Act. The regulations governing the various subchapters incorporated in the Education of the Handicapped Act (EHA) are identified in the 34 code of federal regulations (CFR), parts 300.1 through 338.39. Specifically, the programs and regulations administering each program follow.

Part 300: Assistance to States for the Education of Handicapped Children

Part 301: Preschool Incentive Grants
Part 305: Regional Resource Center
Part 307: Services for Deaf-Blind Children and Youth
Part 309: Handicapped Children's Early Education Program
Part 315: Auxiliary Activities
Part 318: Training Personnel for the Education of the Handicapped
Part 320: Recruitment of Personnel and Dissemination of Information
Part 324: Research in the Education of the Handicapped
Part 326: Secondary Education and Transitional Services for Handicapped Youth
Part 330: Captioned Films Loan Service for the Deaf Program
Part 331: Education Media Loan Service for the Handicapped Program
Part 332: Education Media Research, Production, Distribution, and Training
Part 333: Centers for Educational Media and Materials for the Handicapped Program
Part 338: Postsecondary Education Program for Handicapped Persons

The Education of the Handicapped Law Report (1984) and the U.S. Congress (1984) have published comprehensive reviews of the regulations, including interpretive comments that clarify the basic regulatory provisions. These documents can be reviewed at your local public or university library.

In addition to the EHA regulations cited, there are two additional sets of regulations that have a substantial impact on the provision of services to disabled individuals. These are Section 504 of the Rehabilitation Act of 1973 and Chapter I of the Education Consolidation and Improvement Act of 1981. The former legislation deals primarily with protections against discrimination (on the basis of handicap) in programs and services. The administration of these regulations at the federal level is under the guidance of the U.S. Department of Education, Office of Civil Rights. The Chapter I (formerly PL 89-313) regulations are currently being revised by the U.S. Department of Education. They cover the provision of services to handicapped children and youths placed in state-operated or state-supported programs.

REFERENCE

National Council on the Handicapped. (1986). *Toward independence.* Washington, DC: U.S. Government Printing Office.

GEORGE JAMES HAGERTY
Stonehill College

EDUCATION FOR ALL HANDICAPPED CHILDREN ACT OF 1975

SPECIAL EDUCATION, ON-LINE DATABASES FOR

See ON-LINE DATA BASE FOR SPECIAL EDUCATION.

SPECIAL EDUCATION, PHILOSOPHERS OPINIONS ABOUT

See PHILOSOPHY OF EDUCATION FOR THE HANDICAPPED.

SPECIAL EDUCATION, PROFESSIONAL STANDARDS FOR

See PROFESSIONAL STANDARDS FOR SPECIAL EDUCATORS.

SPECIAL EDUCATION, RACIAL DISCRIMINATION IN

See RACIAL DISCRIMINATION IN SPECIAL EDUCATION.

SPECIAL EDUCATION, SUPERVISION IN

See SUPERVISION IN SPECIAL EDUCATION.

SPECIAL EDUCATION, TEACHER TRAINING IN

The training and practice of special educators have undergone rapid development and change over the past three decades. In recognition of the small number of individuals who were prepared to conduct research and train teachers to educate the retarded, PL 85-926 was passed in 1958. With the passage of this law, funds were allocated to establish university, doctoral-level training programs in the area of mental retardation. These training programs, along with a robust postwar economy, resulted in a decade characterized by a proliferation of programs for exceptional children (Tawney & Gest, 1984). The need for trained individuals to run public and private school programs has preceded a clear understanding of what and how to teach children with various handicapping conditions. The first special education curricula were watered-down or slowed-down adaptations of regular class programs; they underscored the absence of empirical data in the field. Training, for the most part, focused on how to control children's behavior. The hope was that a child controlled was a child ready to learn.

The 1970s saw a continuance of the optimism of the 1960s and a period of advocacy and activism. Public Law 94-142, a civil rights bill for the handicapped, guaranteed a "free and appropriate" education for exceptional children. At the same time, it called on special educators to document, as precisely as possible, children's progress. For the first time in public education, teachers were called on to be accountable. Practically, concerns for accountability meant that the field moved to replace the generalized curricula of the 1960s with more individualized curricula focused on matching instructional strategies to individual learner characteristics. Tawney and Gest (1984) pointed out that "the cumulative effect of the developmental efforts of the 1970s, then, was to set the stage for a new era of intensive programming for handicapped students in the 1980s" (p. 5). Problems with a worsening economy in the late 1970s, however, shifted attention from the problems of the handicapped to more personal priorities.

The reality of the 1980s is essentially economic in character. Given the increase in the number of children being served (from 1976–1977 to 1982–1983, the number of identified handicapped children increased by more than 500,000, to 4,298,427—a 16% increase [Keogh, 1985]), and the fact that federal, state, and local budgets do not have unlimited resources, the 1980s have become a period of retrenchment and uncertainty in special education. There is a clear and pressing need to increase the number of teachers qualified to work with handicapped children, but at the same time newly trained teachers are being asked to do more with less. Teachers in special education are being called on to be more resourceful, more organized, and more precise in creating, planning, and executing instructional interventions.

In addition to these broad political and economic factors, the quantity and quality of research in human learning and development and pedagogy has had an impact on the preparation of teachers for handicapped pupils. Out of the massive research and development efforts with handicapped and nonhandicapped children that began in the 1960s, special educators have acquired a substantial base of knowledge concerning effective instructional practices. With this large and growing body of information and the complex roles that special education teachers are currently being asked to assume, effective training of special educators in the 1980s will require greater breadth and depth of preparation than ever before.

While there is a lack of agreement concerning specific knowledge and skills that teachers of the handicapped should possess, there is a growing consensus among regular and special educators concerning the general characteristics of a professional teacher and the framework for teacher preparation programs. The general parameters include the following. First, teachers need a firm foundation in general literacy and in the basic disciplines of the humanities, liberal arts, and sciences as prerequisite to entering the teaching profession (Denemark & Nutter, 1980). Second, special education teachers must be well versed in general education requirements as well as those specific to special education; i.e., they must be education generalists as well as education of the handicapped specialists (Reynolds, 1979). Their training should include acquiring knowledge of school development, basic academic skill curricula, instructional methods, including the effective use of computer-assisted instruction, and instructional and behavioral management strategies.

Third, as a key to participation in mainstreaming efforts, special education teachers must function as team members and as consultants, providing expertise to the general education faculty on questions concerning handicapped pupils (Reynolds, 1979). Fourth, regardless of the nature and severity of a pupil's disability, all special education teachers must possess effective communication skills to work with parents of handicapped children. These include a working knowledge of the motivational, cognitive, and social consequences associated with their pupils' handicapping conditions. Special educators should also be able to assess pupils' current levels of functioning, select and implement instructional strategies based on youngsters' learning characteristics, and evaluate the effectiveness of their instructional procedures.

Lastly, teacher training programs should provide extensive practical experience for their students. This practical experience should be initiated early in the students' training, with greater amounts of professional practice provided as students progress through the program (Scannell & Guenther, 1981). As researchers have recognized that the first year of teaching is critical for the maintenance and development of effective teaching skills, a yearlong paid and supervised internship has been recommended as the culminating training experience of a preservice program. For student-teachers to gain the most from these practica, they should be closely monitored and effective models of teaching should be provided. Training that includes the previously noted components cannot be provided in an undergraduate teacher preparation program. The American Association of Colleges of Teacher Education Commission of Education for the Profession argues that the presently constituted teaching profession is, at best, a semiprofession (Howsam, Corrigan, Denemark, & Nash, 1976). The commission recommends a 5-year initial teacher preparation program combining the bachelor's and master's degrees, plus a sixth year of supervised internship to improve the quality of teacher education.

Such an effort would enhance the profession of teaching and lead to outstanding pupil achievement. In view of these collective recommendations, it appears that preparation of special education teachers will require the extension of teacher education into graduate training.

Unfortunately, due to declining enrollments in teacher preparation programs and reductions in university budgets, few university faculties have decided to make their programs more rigorous by incorporating the recommendations of leaders in the area of teacher education and special education. However, one of the training programs that has attended to these requirements is the Generic Special Education Teacher Training Program at Texas A&M University (Palmer, Anderson, Keuker, Hall, & Parrish, 1985). This program prepares teachers to work with handicapped pupils evidencing mild to moderate learning and behavior problems. Specifically, teachers are trained to work with children identified as emotionally disturbed, learning disabled, and mildly retarded.

The training program at Texas A&M University occurs in two phases. The first phase is a 4-year program in education leading to a bachelor's degree in educational curriculum and instruction without teacher certification. During this first phase, students complete their general education requirements, including a number of humanities and social science elective courses. In addition, their professional elementary education course work, with the exception of student teaching and the majority of special education course work, is completed within the bachelor's degree program. During the senior year, students are required to apply for and be accepted into the graduate special education program within the department of educational psychology. This graduate phase of the program occurs during the fifth and sixth years of the student's training. The fifth year includes completion of special education course work, graduate course work related to tests and measurement, educational statistics, and consultation and directed teaching in elementary and special education. At the successful completion of the fifth year, students are recommended for a provisional elementary or secondary certificate with a special education specialization. The sixth year of training consists of advanced graduate education courses and a full-time 1-year internship. On successful completion of this sixth year, students receive a master's degree in educational psychology.

Attrition of special education teachers has been a major concern nationally. Moreover, lack of quality in preservice training has been related to teacher attrition rates. While programs such as the one at Texas A&M University have just recently been initiated, it is hoped that they will meet current personnel needs and have a long-term effect on teacher shortages. That is, with the extensive course work, practica, and internship training required in this program, graduates will be better prepared to meet the challenges and demands of special education instruction. As a consequence, they may continue to teach handicapped youngsters for a longer period of time and in a more effective manner.

REFERENCES

Denemark, G., & Nutter, N. (1980). *The case for extended programs of initial teacher preparation*. Washington, DC: ERIC Clearinghouse on Teacher Education.

Howsam, R. B., Corrigan, D. C., Denemark, G. W., & Nash, R. J. (1976). *Education as a profession: Report of the Bicentennial Commission on Education for the Profession of Teaching of the American Association of Colleges for Teacher Education*. Washington, DC: American Association of Colleges for Teacher Education.

Keogh, B. K. (1985). *Learning disabilities: Diversity in search of order*. Paper prepared for the Pittsburgh Research Integration Project, University of Pittsburgh.

Palmer, D. J., Anderson, C., Hall, R., Keuker, J., & Parrish, L. (1985). *Preparation of special educators: Extended generic special education training program* (Report to the U.S. Department of Education, Special Education Programs, Division of Personnel Preparation).

Reynolds, M. (1979). *A common body of practices for teachers: The challenge of Public Law 94-142 to teacher education*. Minneapolis, MN: The National Support System Project.

Scannell, D., & Guenther, J. E. (1981). The development of an extended program. *Journal of Teacher Education, 32*, 7–12.

Tawney, J. W., & Gest, D. L. (1984). *Single subject research in special education*. Columbus, OH: Merrill.

DOUGLAS J. PALMER
ROBERT HALL
Texas A&M University

HUMAN RESOURCE DEVELOPMENT
TEACHER BURNOUT
TEACHER EFFECTIVENESS

SPECIAL EDUCATION, TELECOMMUNICATION SYSTEMS IN

See TELECOMMUNICATION SYSTEMS IN SPECIAL EDUCATION.

SPECIAL EDUCATION AND POLITICS

See POLITICS AND SPECIAL EDUCATION.

SPECIAL EDUCATION IN CANADA

See CANADA, SPECIAL EDUCATION IN.

SPECIAL EDUCATION INSTRUCTIONAL MATERIALS CENTERS (SEIMCS)

More than a decade before the passage of the Education for All Handicapped Children Act, the United States Office of Education recognized that one of the main obstacles to education of quality for handicapped students was the dearth of appropriate instructional materials and services both for the students and for those responsible for their education (Alonso, 1974). The federal government hoped to have established a network of service centers to address this problem by 1980.

The initiation of this effort began in 1963, when two projects were funded—one at the University of Southern California and the other at the University of Wisconsin—to serve as demonstration models for the development and dissemination of effective instructional materials and methods. From this modest beginning was to come 13 regional special education instructional materials centers (SEIMCs); four regional media centers for the deaf and hearing impaired (RMCs); a Clearinghouse on Handicapped and Gifted Children in the Educational Resources Information Center (ERIC) Network; an Instructional Materials Reference Center at the American Printing House for the Blind; and a National Center on Education Media and Materials for the Handicapped (NCEMMH).

The role of SEIMCs, some of which in various funding periods were also called regional Resource Centers (RRCs) and Area Learning Resource Centers (ALRCs), would change somewhat over the decade of their existence. During the experimental phase, which ran from 1964 to 1966, the two centers were expected to develop appropriate materials and methods for handicapped children, transform them into workable curricula, and disseminate the results, along with other information, to the field. The early centers were also charged with the exploration of new technologies for instructional purposes as well as for information dissemination (Langstaff & Volkmor, 1974).

The official scope of the centers was not strictly defined by the government. It was acknowledged that needs varied widely from one service area to another, and each program was encouraged to respond to its local situation appropriately and to take full advantage of the special strengths of its staff. In general, however, the activities tended to break down into three categories. The first involved identifying, collecting, evaluating, circulating, and, when necessary, developing or stimulating the development of instructional materials. The second category consisted of field services of various sorts: the training of teachers in the choice, evaluation, and use of instructional media and materials; coordination activities that established or improved the delivery of services to special educators and their students; and technical assistance to state departments of education to ensure the institutionalization of ongoing support services within each state. Finally, the centers were all involved to some extent in the systematic dissemination of information regarding current research, methods, and materials for special education.

Federal funding for the SEIMCs was intended only as seed money to help defray the considerable costs of starting up such a large-scale service network. A survey of the centers conducted in 1973 (Trahan, 1973) indicated that over two-thirds of the centers were supported by state and local funding in addition to federal grants. This would suggest that there was a commitment to continuing support services after the federal funding for the SEIMCs ended in 1974. Readers are encouraged to contact their state offices of special education for further information.

REFERFENCES

Alonso, L. (1974). *Final technical report of the Great Lakes region special education instructional materials center* Washington, DC: Bureau of Education for the Handicapped. (ERIC Document Reproduction Service No. ED 094 507).

Langstaff, A. L., & Volkmor, C. B. (1974). *Instructional materials center for special education: Final technical report* Washington, DC: Bureau of Education for the Handicapped. (ERIC Document Reproduction Service No. ED 107 086).

Trahan, M. (1973). Special education instructional materials centers: An assessment. *Bureau Memorandum, 15*(1), 28–30.

JANET S. BRAND
Hunter College, City University of New York

ON-LINE DATABASES FOR SPECIAL EDUCATION
SPECIAL NET

SPECIAL EDUCATION IN SWITZERLAND

See SWITZERLAND, SPECIAL EDUCATION IN.

SPECIAL EDUCATION IN THE SOVIET UNION AND EASTERN EUROPE

See SOVIET UNION AND EASTERN EUROPE, SPECIAL EDUCATION IN THE.

SPECIAL EDUCATION IN THE UNITED KINGDOM

See UNITED KINGDOM, SPECIAL EDUCATION IN THE.

SPECIAL EDUCATION PROGRAMS (SEP)

In 1982 Special Education Programs (SEP) succeeded the Office of Special Education as the primary federal agency responsible for overseeing federal initiatives in the education of the handicapped. Although SEP's mission has basically remained the same since the creation of the Bureau of Education for the Handicapped in 1966, its organizational structure has changed. Special Education Programs is divided into five divisions.

The Division of Assistance to States (DAS) has four areas of responsibility. Its primary function is to monitor the extent to which states are implementing the requirements of PL 94-142 and PL 89-313 state-operated programs. The DAS is also SEP's liaison with the Office for Civil Rights when parent complaints are received. The DAS provides technical assistance to states either directly through its program officers or through a national network of regional resource centers. Finally, DAS oversees the awarding of grants to centers that serve the deaf-blind.

The Division of Innovation and Development (DID) carries out SEP's mission for generating new information to help the handicapped. The DID administers several grant competitions. Field-initiated research allows any investigator to suggest a project and student projects are the most widely known. The DID has the U.S. Department of Education's responsibility for conducting the PL 94-142, Section 618, evaluation of the implementation of programs for the handicapped whose results appear in the *Annual Reports to Congress* (U.S. Department of Education, 1986).

The Division of Personnel Preparation administers grant programs to prepare special educators and related services personnel, parents of handicapped children, and doctoral-level professionals, among others, to serve the needs of handicapped students.

The Division of Educational Services is responsible for grant projects that develop model programs in the areas of early childhood education, youth employment, services for the severely handicapped, transitional services for students changing their least restrictive environment placement, and captioning of films for the hearing impaired.

The Division of Program Analysis and Planning has responsibility for managing the planning and budgetary processes within SEP. It also coordinates the efforts of other divisions when changes are proposed and made to regulations in the administration of PL 94-142, PL 89-313, and the various grant and contract programs.

The current address of SEP is U.S. Department of Education, Special Education Programs, 400 Maryland Avenue, SW, Washington, DC 20202.

REFERENCE

U.S. Department of Education. (1986). *Eighth annual report to Congress on the implementation of Public Law 94-142: The Education for All Handicapped Children Act.* Washington, DC: Author.

ROLAND K. YOSHIDA
Fordham University

OFFICE OF SPECIAL EDUCATION

SPECIALNET

SpecialNet, the largest education-oriented computer-based communication network in the United States, is operated by the National Association of State Directors of Special Education. SpecialNet makes it possible for its more than 2000 subscriber agencies to use the system to send electronic mail (messages, forms, reports, questions, and answers) instantaneously to one or many participants. The system also contains electronic bulletin boards, which are topical displays of various information bases, administered by content experts around the country. Nearly 30 such bulletin boards are currently available; they include coverage of personnel development, early childhood education, computers and other technologies, program evaluation, promising practices, federal news, gifted education, parent programs, educational policy, vocational education, and many other topics.

SpecialNet can be accessed on any computer or terminal, either of which must be equipped wiih an inexpensive modem (telephone hookup). Access through a local or toll-free 800 number is available nationwide via the GTE Telenet public data network, through which SpecialNet information is transmitted and stored. Access to SpecialNet is obtained through an annual subscription fee. Further charges accrue for on-line time spent accessing the system. SpecialNet may be contacted at 2021 K Street, NW, Suite 315, Washington, DC 20006.

JUDY SMITH-DAVIS
*Counterpoint Communications
Company, Reno, Nevada*

SPECIAL EDUCATION INSTRUCTIONAL MATERIALS CENTERS
ON-LINE DATA BASES FOR SPECIAL EDUCATION

SPECIAL OLYMPICS

See OLYMPICS, SPECIAL.

SPECIAL SERVICES IN THE SCHOOLS (SSS)

Published by Haworth Press (New York City), *Special Services in the Schools* (*SSS*) is a quarterly, refereed journal with an applied focus. It is now in its fourth volume. The *SSS* is intended to be read by multidisciplinary professional audiences who provide special services in schools and related educational settings, including school psychologists, guidance counselors, consulting teachers, social workers, and speech and language clinicians. It is the journal's policy to disseminate available information of direct relevance to these professionals. As such, information published in *SSS* includes reviews of relevant research and literature, descriptions and evaluations of programs, viewpoints on latest trends in policy development, and guidelines for designing, implementing, and evaluating special service programs.

The issues of the journal are organized in a sequence whereby thematic and general issues alternate. Thematic issues have focused on topics such as microcomputers and exceptional children, health promotion strategies, new directions in assessment of special learners, and international perspectives on facilitating cognitive development of children. Articles in general issues have included topics such as evaluation of programs of children of divorce, staff stress and burnout, curricula and programs for pregnant and parenting adolescents, and involving parents in the education of their handicapped children.

Articles are aimed at being informative and instructive to special educators, psychologists, counselors, nurses, social workers, speech and language clinicians, physical and occupational therapists, and school supervisors and administrators. The material is intended to assist these professionals in performing a wide range of service delivery tasks. These include:

Assessing individual pupils and groups to determine their special educational needs

Designing individualized and group programs

Assisting regular and special classroom teachers in fostering academic achievement and functional living for special students

Enhancing the social and emotional development of pupils through preventive and remedial approaches

Helping school administrators to develop smoothly functioning organizational systems

Fostering the physical well being of special students

Involving parents and families in special programs

Educating and training school staff to more effectively educate special needs students

Manuscripts that focus on the topical areas and service delivery tasks noted are routinely considered for publication. All manuscripts undergo blind review by editorial consultants.

CHARLES A. MAHER
Rutgers University

LOUIS J. KRUGER
Tufts University

SPECIFIC LEARNING DISABILITIES

See LEARNING DISABILITIES.

SPEECH

In the context of special education, the word speech may have two different meanings. Sometimes, it is used to refer to the whole of linguistic skills. Such is the case in compounds such as speech pathologist and speech therapy. In other cases, the meaning is narrower, with the word referring to spoken language. The use of the word speech to denote the whole of verbal abilities is indicative of the cardinal importance of spoken language. Oral language is by far the most frequently used form of verbal communication. It is also the first linguistic ability to be acquired by the child.

Speech (i.e., spoken language) is produced by means of the speech organs. These organs make up parts of the respiratory system and the digestive tract. Usually, expiratory air is used to generate audible speech sounds. If air from the lungs activates the larynx, voiced sounds such as vowels or voiced consonants are produced. If the vocal cords are kept apart and consequently do not vibrate during exhalation, egressive air is turned into voiceless consonants (such as /s/ or /f/). Speech movements are rapid, complex, and finely timed sequences of gestures. Therefore, it takes the child several years to learn to perform them.

Since speech is ordinarily produced on exhalation, air is taken in just prior to starting to speak. Inspiration is caused by a contraction of the diaphragm and of the external intercostal muscles. When it contracts, the diaphragm flattens out and goes down. When the external intercostals contract, they lift up the rib cage. A membrane called parietal pleura is attached to both the diaphragm and the rib cage. When the diaphragm goes down and the rib cage goes up, the parietal membrane follows them. This enlarges the interpleural space, which is the closed space between the parietal membrane and the visceral membrane. The latter membrane enwraps each of the two lungs. Because the interpleural space becomes larger, the pressure in this space drops. Residual air (even after the most forcible expiration possible, some air remains in the lungs; this air is called residual) forces the expansible lungs to dilate so that the visceral pleura can

follow the parietal pleura and annihilate the negative pressure in the interpleural space. In the expanded lungs the pressure is now negative and external air flows in via the nose (or mouth), larynx, and trachea to annihilate it (Kaplan, 1971).

Once the diaphragm starts to relax, the lower part of the parietal pleura is sucked upward by the retractile lungs. Similarly, the upper part of the pleura is sucked downward once the external intercostals start to relax. The retraction of the lungs increases the air pressure in them and air escapes via the upper respiratory tract. If, at some point, the relaxation pressure becomes insufficient to produce audible speech, expiratory muscles, mainly the internal intercostals, are used to draw the rib cage further in (Perkins & Kent, 1985).

On its way out, egressive air passes the larynx. This organ comprises a vertical tube in which a V-shaped horizontal narrowing, called the glottis, is found. The sides of the glottis are formed by two ligaments, which together with the muscle fibers behind them constitute the vocal folds. If the vocal folds are approximated during expiration, the glottis is closed and the air can no longer flow out of the trachea. As a result, the air pressure in the trachea increases. At some point, the pressure is such that it blows the vocal folds apart. Some air escapes through the glottis. As a consequence, the pressure in the trachea diminishes. Moreover, a Bernoulli effect is created in the glottis. The Bernoulli effect is the negative pressure on the sides of a bottleneck when a gas or a liquid flows through it. The glottis forms a bottleneck between the trachea and the pharynx. As a consequence, when air escapes through the glottis, the vocal folds are sucked toward one another. The Bernoulli effect and the temporary decrease in tracheal air pressure enable the elastic vocal folds to come together again. Since the glottis is now closed again, pressure builds up in the trachea until it blows the vocal cords apart, etc. In this way, the column of pulmonary air is divided into a quick succession of puffs that are fired into the supraglottal cavities (pharynx, mouth, and nasal cavity). The puffs of air hit the air mass present in the supraglottal cavities, causing it to vibrate. These vibrations, leaving the mouth of the speaker, propagate themselves in the air until they reach the ears of a listener, who perceives them as voice. The form of the individual vocal waves varies with the form of the supraglottal cavities (Zemlin, 1968). In this way, it is possible to produce vocal waves that sound like /a/, /u/ or any other vowel.

The puffs of air from the larynx not only hit the mass of air in the supraglottal cavities, but also move it forward. This forward movement can be used to form consonants. These consonants are voiced since their generation is synchronous with voice production. If, on the contrary, the vocal folds are kept in an abducted position and consequently do not vibrate, air from the lungs flows directly into the supraglottal cavities, where it can be molded into voiceless consonants. The shaping of the vocal waves and the molding of egressive air into speech sounds is performed by the articulators. The main articulators are the tongue and the velum. The latter moves upward and shuts off the nasal cavity from the oropharyngeal cavity during articulation of oral sounds. In English, most speech sounds are articulated with the velum in a raised position. Failure of the velum to occlude the passage of air to the nose results in hyperrhinolalia, i.e., nasalized speech.

REFERENCES

Kaplan, H. (1971). *Anatomy and physiology of speech*. New York: McGraw-Hill.

Perkins, W., & Kent, R. (1985). *Textbook of functional anatomy of speech, language, and hearing*. Philadelphia: Taylor & Francis.

Zemlin, R. (1968). *Speech and hearing science: Anatomy and physiology*. Englewood Cliffs, NJ: Prentice-Hall.

YVAN LEBRUN
School of Medicine, V.U.B.,
Brussels, Belgium

LANGUAGE DISORDERS
SPEECH DISORDERS

SPEECH, ABSENCE OF

Many children use their first recognizable word at age one and by two are using some type of sentence. When a child has not started speaking by age two, parents often become concerned about the child's development. However, it is not unusual for the normally developing child not to use his or her first word until some time after the second birthday. However, if a child has no speech by age five, there is almost certain to be a serious problem (Bloodstein, 1984).

The most common cause of a lack of speech is mental deficiency. While many children exhibiting severe retardation have the potential to develop some language, those with a profound deficiency are likely to have no speech throughout their lives (Robinson & Robinson, 1976). It is not known how many individuals of this type exist because many are institutionalized. Mental deficiency sometimes may be due to genetic factors. In more instances, however, identified brain injuries are the known cause of mental retardation. Children with mental deficiency who do develop language do so in much the same manner as normal children but slower (Naremore & Dever, 1975). They do, however, tend to exhibit limitations in their vocabulary and syntax usage.

Another possible cause of a child exhibiting no speech is congenital deafness. When a child is born with a profound hearing loss there is generally a failure on the part of the child to develop speech without special intervention. A number of children are born with hearing loss, but they are not so severe that the child cannot use hearing for the development of speech and language. However, the profoundly deaf child experiences severe problems in developing speech because the child has no way of monitoring his or her own speech production. Surprisingly, the profoundly deaf child's difficulty with hearing is often not noticed until the child is about age two and has not spoken his or her first word. This is due in part to the fact that many hearing-impaired children appear to go through the babbling stage in much the same way that hearing children do.

Once a hearing loss is identified, most hearing handicapped children are fitted with a hearing aid. If the child has more than a 90 dB loss, he or she probably will not learn speech and language through hearing alone. The speech and language training of some children begins with the oral method, where language instruction is carried out primarily by requiring the child to lip read and speak. During the last 10 to 15 years, language instruction for deaf children has changed. Now many deaf children are exposed to a sign language system once they are identified. School systems generally maintain speech instruction. For children who are born with a profound hearing loss, however, only a small percentage attain speech that is intelligible to a stranger. However, many do attain a fairly high level of intelligibility to those who are familiar with the speech patterns of deaf individuals. It is important to make a distinction between speech and language when referring to hearing-impaired children because many profoundly deaf children acquire language without having usable speech.

Another cause of absence of speech is cerebral palsy (Cruickshank, 1976). Cerebral palsy is caused by brain damage occurring at or near the time of birth. Cerebral palsy can be of the type and of such severity that the child will not have sufficient control of the speech mechanism to produce intelligible speech. Some children, as their speech mechanism matures, can learn to produce intelligible speech with the help of specialists. However, some children can communicate only through other means such as language boards and computers. Because of the physical disability and difficulty in communicating, the intelligence of the child with cerebral palsy is often considerably underestimated.

Another problem that can cause an absence of speech is the presence of psychotic disturbances, specifically childhood schizophrenia and early infantile autism (Churchill, 1978). Typically, the child with schizophrenia appears to develop normally for the first few years of life, and then begins to regress, losing all language and speech. Schizophrenia, characterized by periods of remission, has been found to be resistant to treatment and most individuals worsen over time. Unlike schizophrenia, autism seems to be present in the child from birth. Autistic infants withdraw from social contact, not looking into the eyes of adults and not leaning on the person carrying them. As they grow, their behavior appears to become even more bizarre. The autistic tend to treat people as objects. Obsessive behavior is common, with play appearing to be stereotyped. A large percentage of these children fail to develop language. Language usage that does develop can be quite deviant. Some autistic children have been known to speak fully formed sentences, but only once or twice in their lifetimes. Others develop what is known as echolalic speech, where they parrot back what is spoken to them. These utterances do not appear to be used meaningfully. Other children do use some sentences meaningfully, but these seem to be memorized strings of words and are often simple demands. A few autistic children eventually attain a fair degree of speech and language. Most, however, never speak and eventually require institutionalization or close supervision in community living and job settings.

There are some children who do not develop speech but the exact reasons seem unclear. It has been argued that some of these children have an unidentified form of brain damage. These children have been labeled aphasic because adults with known brain damage without speech are often labeled aphasic (Eisenson, 1972). However, many practitioners consider such a label misleading because there is often no clinical evidence that actual brain damage exists. Most speech and language practitioners are more comfortable using the term specific language deficit. These so-called language-impaired children often display difficulties in both using and understanding language.

Social deprivation can also be a cause of language acquisition problems. However, deprivation must be extremely severe for the child to acquire no speech whatsoever. Human beings appear to have a strong predisposition for learning language. Only minimal conditions of exposure to language need be present for the child to learn to speak. However, there are a few isolated cases of children who apparently have had no exposure to language and therefore do not develop language (Fuller, 1975). It would also appear that in some cases where a child is consistently deprived of attention, severe language delay may occur. In the past, some children who were institutionalized received no attention except for feeding and being kept clean. In such situations, some children experienced severe delays in the acquisition of language.

Occasionally, a clinician will see a child who understands language but does not speak at all. No cause can be found. For some time it was thought that these children were suffering from maternal overprotection. Because the mother anticipated the child's needs, the child did not learn to speak. Recently, however, clinicians have expressed doubt about attributing the lack of language usage to the behavior of the mother. While it is true that the mother will often respond to the nonverbal cues of the child, it is generally recognized that the mother does this to alleviate severe frustration on both their parts. The mother's behavior is now seen more as a response than as a cause. Children exhibiting this disorder frequently develop normal language over a period of time.

In the past, many children who did not acquire speech were institutionalized, receiving little or no educational services. With the advent of PL 94–142, however, many of these children now live at home and are provided schooling on a regular basis. Likewise, those children who are institutionalized receive educational services. The result has been a marked improvement in the communication skills of a number of these children.

REFERENCES

Bloodstein, O. (1984). *Speech pathology: An introduction*. Boston: Houghton Mifflin.

Churchill, D. (1978). *Language of autistic children*. New York: Wiley.

Cruickshank, W. M. (1976). *Cerebral palsy: A developmental disability* (3rd ed.). Syracuse, NY: Syracuse University Press.

Eisenson, J. (1972). *Aphasia in children*. New York: Harper & Row.

Fuller, C. W. (1975). Maternal deprivation and developmental language disorders. *Speech & Hearing Review. A Journal of New York State Speech & Hearing Association, 7*, 9–23.

Naremore, R. C., & Dever, R. B. (1975). Language performance of educable mentally retarded and normal children at five age levels. *Journal of Speech & Hearing Research, 18*, 92.

Robinson, N. M., & Robinson, H. B. (1976). *The mentally retarded child* (2nd ed.). New York: McGraw-Hill.

CAROLYN L. BULLARD
Lewis and Clark College

AUTISM
ELECTIVE MUTISM
MUTISM
SPEECH AND LANGUAGE HANDICAPS
SPEECH THERAPY

SPEECH AND LANGUAGE HANDICAPS

A handicap refers to a condition that prevents or restricts normal achievement. It may include an anatomical, physiological, or mental deficiency. A young child or adult whose speech or language is difficult to understand is said to have a limitation in function, or a handicap. The child who has difficulty producing several of the sounds of the language is said to have a phonological (articulatory) disorder. There is evidence that delayed phonological development that is extensive in nature may be associated with a broader more encompassing language disorder and with difficulties in learning to read and other cognitive abilities.

A deaf child may have difficulties with broader aspects of speech, the suprasegmentals or prosodic characteristics. These features cut across more than one sound and include frequency or pitch, intensity or loudness, duration, rhythm, and timing. Other terms frequently used are intonation or the variation in frequency over an utterance, and stress or emphasis, which includes frequency, intensity, and duration. For example, in the sentence "I have a blue ball," when the stress is placed on blue, typically, the length of the vowel (in blue) is increased and intensity and frequency are also increased to signify that the ball is blue and not red. It is not necessary, however, to have all three parameters increased to increase stress. Only two of the three parameters, say duration and intensity, may increase and frequency may not vary at all. In the case of the deaf individual, he or she may stress all the syllables equally, use abnormal pitch variation in an utterance, or use an abnormally loud or soft vocal effort depending on the type of hearing loss.

Aspects of language with which individuals may have difficulty are semantics (the lexicon, morphology, or structure of words) and pragmatics (how language is used). Difficulties with the language lexicon or semantics of the language represent problems in identifying the words of the language and their meanings. It involves the ability to perceive a sequence of sounds that are uttered such as "thatisabigcat" and the ability to segment or divide the sequence into meaningful words of the language.

Syntax or grammar is another aspect of language with which children or adults with language disorders may have difficulty. The grammar represents knowledge of the rules that govern how words are put together to form sentences. In the sentence "The man hid the boy," the sequence of words is important to conveying the intent of the speaker. The speaker must understand that the word preceding the verb is the agent or the one performing the action and the word following the verb is the object, the person, or thing being acted on. The following sentence is syntactically anomalous because none of the syntactic rules are being followed: "The jumped swift the deer fence."

Phonological and morphological rules that govern language are those that determine how speech sounds change meaning and how the smallest meaningful units such as prefixes, suffixes, and infixes provide more specificity to the meaning of language. This involves the ability to differentiate between the utterances "The boy runs away" and "The boys ran away."

In addition to producing and understanding language, the individual must learn the appropriate use of language or the pragmatics of language. The choice of utterance is governed by the context of the interaction and the social roles of the speaker and listener. For example, in urban language studies by Labov (1966), Shuy, Baratz, and Wol-

fram (1969), and Shuy, Wolfram, and Riley (1967), two main social variables that govern language use were identified: the social class of the speaker and the formality of the speaking situation. The inability to select the appropriate message for the social situation will lead to problems in language use.

Individuals with speech and language disorders can manifest problems in phonology/morphology, syntax, semantics, and pragmatics. These aspects of language, while separate, are constantly interacting so that it is not unreasonable to assume that an individual may have difficulty in several of these areas of speech and language simultaneously.

REFERENCES

Labov, W. (1966). *The social stratification of language in New York City*. Washington, DC: Center for Applied Linguistics.

Leonard, L. B. (1982). Early language development and language disorders. In G. H. Shames & E. H. Wigg (Eds.), *Human communication disorders: An introduction* (pp. 221–257). Columbus, OH: Merrill.

Shriberg, L. (1980). Developmental phonological disorders. In T. J. Hixon, L. D. Shriberg, & J. H. Saxman (Eds.), *Introduction to communication disorders* (pp. 263–309). Englewood Cliffs, NJ: Prentice-Hall.

Shuy, R. W., Baratz, J. C., & Wolfram, W. A. (1969). *Sociolinguistic factors in speech identification* (NIMH Research Project No. MH-15-48-01). Washington, DC: Center for Applied Linguistics.

Shuy, R. W., Wolfram, W. A., & Riley, W. K. (1967). *Linguistic correlates of social stratification in Detroit speech* (USOE Cooperative Research Project No. 6-1347). Michigan State University.

HARVEY R. GILBERT
Pennsylvania State University

COMMUNICATION DISORDERS
LANGUAGE DEFICIENCIES AND DEFICITS
LANGUAGE DISORDERS
SPEECH

SPEECH DISORDERS

Speech disorders are included among communication disorders in the American Speech and Hearing Association's (ASHA) definition of such disorders as "impairments in articulation, language, voice, or fluency (Comprehensive Assessment and Service (CASE) Information System, 1976, p. 26). A hearing impairment may also be classified as a communication disorder if it impairs either speech or language.

Speech is defined as disordered or impaired (Van Riper, 1978; Perkins, 1977) if it interferes with an individual's ability to communicate, calls unfavorable attention to the speaker, or causes social problems of some sort. Most specialists distinguish between language disorders and other forms of speech disorders. Speech represents the way in which language is orally expressed. Speech problems involve difficulties in oral expression (i.e., in producing sounds properly), in effectively managing the rhythm and flow of speech production, or in using the voice effectively while speaking. Language involves the mastery of the symbols and rules of language. Language problems involve difficulties in understanding, managing, or expressing the language symbols and rules that are used in communicating. Someone who has speech difficulties may not have language difficulties, e.g., a child who stutters. Someone with language difficulties may not have additional speech problems, e.g., a receptive aphasia stroke victim. While distinct, speech and language are closely related. Thus a child may suffer from either speech or language disorders, or both together. Language disorders are complicated by speech problems.

Some types of speech disorders are clearly organic in nature (i.e., caused by physical or neurological problems), as might be encountered in cerebral palsy. Other types of speech disorders are functional in nature, e.g., they can be the consequences of incorrect or inappropriate learning, as some experts posit in the case of stuttering. The importance of correct diagnosis is obvious, since the nature of the efforts to improve an individual's speech may take a different direction depending on the cause of the speech disorder. Three major types of speech disorders may be distinguished in addition to language disorders (Culatta & Culatta, 1985; McCormick, 1986). These are articulation disorders, voice disorders, and fluency disorders. Misarticulation, which means abnormal production of phonemes, may result from a number of different causes such as hearing impairments, oral structural disorders, and neuromuscular defects. Voice disorders involve deviations of voice loudness and pitch and of voice quality. They can result from physical abnormalities such as abnormal growths in the larynx, or they can be the consequence of vocal abuse, as from using the vocal mechanisms incorrectly. Fluency disorders include stuttering.

It is important to keep the speaker's cultural background, education, and age in mind when attempting to assess whether or not speech disorders or impairments are involved. Such factors clearly determine what is to be considered as normal for the speaker. The importance of speech disorders, or speech difficulties of any kind, should not be minimized in light of the importance that oral communication holds in everyone's life.

REFERENCES

Comprehensive Assessment and Service (CASE) Information System. (1976). Washington, DC: American Speech-Language-Hearing Association.

Culatta, R., & Culatta, B. K. (1985). Communication disorders. In W. H. Berdine & A. E. Blackhurst (Eds.), *An introduction to special education* (pp. 145–181). Boston: Little, Brown.

McCormick, L. (1986). Communication disorders. In N. G. Haring & L. McCormick (Eds.), *Exceptional children and youth* (4th ed.) (pp. 201–231). Columbus, OH: Merrill.

Perkins, W. H. (1977). *Speech pathology.* St. Louis: Mosby.

Van Riper, C. (1978). *Speech correction: Principles and methods* (6th ed.). Englewood Cliffs, NJ: Prentice-Hall.

LESTER MANN
*Hunter College, City University
of New York*

**LANGUAGE DISORDERS
SPEECH
VOICE DISORDERS**

SPEECH-LANGUAGE PATHOLOGIST

Speech-language pathologist is the accepted title of a professional who studies normal speech and language and who provides a program of diagnosis and treatment to individuals with communication disorders. Among other titles used are speech correctionist, speech and language clinician, speech and language therapist, speech teacher, and speech clinician.

The speech-language pathologist must have knowledge of normal anatomy, physiology, neurology of the mechanisms underlying speech and language, and how individuals with disorders of speech and language deviate from the normal population. The speech pathologist must also have knowledge of linguistics, developmental psychology, learning theory, abnormal psychology, principles of motivation, and reinforcement. He or she must have clinical and interviewing skills, the ability to evaluate behavioral phenomena, and knowledge of scientific methods. He or she must be able to work closely with professionals from several disciplines (such as audiology, psychology, otolaryngology, neurology, plastic surgery, pediatrics, prosthodontics, and orthodontics).

Speech and language pathologists are employed in a wide variety of locations. Approximately 35% of speech-language pathologists work in the public school systems, with 3% in preschools and 8% in special schools (schools for the deaf or institutions for mentally retarded individuals). About 8% work in universities and about 26% work in nonuniversity clinics and hospitals, rehabilitation centers, community speech and hearing centers, nursing homes, and home health agencies. About 9% are employed in other settings. More and more professionals are choosing to go into private practice (9% are now in full-time private practice) or into an association with other professional groups such as psychologists, counselors, or medical professionals.

The American Speech-Language-Hearing Association (ASHA) sets the standards for colleges and universities in the training of speech-language pathologists and audiologists. It issues a Certificate of Clinical Competence (CCC). Of the 42,000 plus members of ASHA, most hold the CCC in either speech pathology or audiology.

Speech-language pathologists are viewed as clinicians, scientists, or clinical or applied scientists. The role of the clinician is to rehabilitate or habilitate individuals who have speech and language disorders. This is accomplished through appropriate diagnostic and treatment programs.

The scientist draws on knowledge from many different disciplines (e.g., biology, physiology, engineering, physics, psychology, linguistics, education, statistics, research design, neurology). He or she applies this information to obtain a better understanding of the normal processes of speech, language, and hearing. How is speech produced and understood? What is the role of the brain in language learning and language processing?

The applied or clinical scientist bridges the gap between the clinical world and the research laboratory. He or she must have a scientific as well as a clinical background. Not only must these scientists be knowledgeable about clinical procedures, but they also must have expertise concerning the communicatively disordered population being studied. The task of the clinical research is to better understand the disorder being studied and to advance the diagnostic and treatment process through research. What can be done to restore the normal voice quality of an individual whose soft palate is paralyzed because of a neuromuscular disease such as myasthenia gravis? What is the best method for controlling the presence of hypernasality in this individual: the use of a prosthetic appliance, surgical intervention, or medication?

REFERENCES

Matthews, J. (1982). The professions of speech-language pathology and audiology. In G. H. Shames & E. H. Wigg (Eds.), *Human communication disorders: An introduction* (pp. 3–20). Columbus, OH: Merrill.

Skinner, P. H. (1985). Speech and hearing. In P. H. Skinner & R. L. Shelton (Eds.), *Communication in speech-language and hearing: Normal processes and disorders* (pp. 1–19). New York: Wiley.

HARVEY R. GILBERT
Pennsylvania State University

COMMUNICATION DISORDERS
SPEECH AND LANGUAGE HANDICAPS
SPEECH THERAPY

SPEECH-LANGUAGE SERVICES

The provision of services to children and adults who have speech and/or language disabilities is a complex problem.

According to Cleland and Swartz (1982), delivery of services includes such factors as funding, transportation, and consumer resistance, in addition to problems of keeping service providers up to date in the latest techniques and tools.

Speech and language services are provided in a variety of settings, but always by professionals trained as speech pathologists having appropriate certification or a state license. All clinically certified speech-language pathologists are capable of providing a complete range of services. Some choose to specialize, but all have knowledge across a variety of speech and language disorders.

The greatest number of speech pathologists are employed in school settings, ranging from preschool through high school. Services provided include: screening for speech and hearing disorders, diagnosis, treatment, and referral for more complex disorders. Since children make up the caseload in public schools, the majority of disorders treated are those concerning speech, language, voice, and stuttering.

Many hospitals provide speech and language services. Speech clinics are usually established in rehabilitation departments. Speech-language pathologists work with occupational and physical therapists to treat people with physical disorders. Sometimes hospitals also provide services for children, thus offering an alternative to the free services of public schools.

There are speech-language clinics in many large metropolitan areas. Some of these clinics are private; others are associated with hospitals or universities. These clinics usually provide a wide range of services while at the same time being used as a training base for future speech-language professionals.

Privately funded or publicly funded health service agencies may also provide speech-language services. These agencies provide speech-language services to people from low socioeconomic backgrounds. Speech clinicians employed by these agencies usually are itinerant: they go to the home of the client to provide the speech-language service. Clinics run by these agencies also provide a wide range of clinical services.

There is a trend for speech-language pathologists to establish their own speech-language services rather than work for a school, hospital, clinic, or public agency. These individuals set up offices and see clients there. Occasionally, they hire other speech pathologists and enlarge their caseloads to the point where they can call their practice a clinic. Again, services are provided across the full range of speech and hearing disorders. Occasionally, speech-language pathologists are employed by industry. In these settings, the pathologists usually serve a diagnostic function only.

In summary, speech-language services cover a wide range of diagnostic and therapeutic treatments in a variety of settings. These settings include public schools, hospitals, private speech clinics, university speech clinics, health service agencies, and private practices.

REFERENCES

Cleland, C. C., & Swartz, J. D. (1982). *Exceptionalities through the lifespan.* New York: Macmillan.

Perkins, W. H. (1978). *Human perspectives in speech and language disorders.* St. Louis: Mosby.

Van Riper, C. (1979). *A career in speech pathology.* Englewood Cliffs, NJ: Prentice-Hall.

FREDERICK F. WEINER
Pennsylvania State University

SPEECH THERAPISTS
SPEECH THERAPY

SPEECH SYNTHESIZER

A speech synthesizer is an electronic device that attempts to duplicate the human voice. Essentially, it allows a machine to talk to a human being. Of course, a human being must program the synthesizer and tell it what to say.

There are two different techniques for producing speech output that account for almost all the current synthesizer designs. The first is called linear predictive coding (LPC), which attempts to make an electronic model of the human voice. It creates tones much like those of the human vocal folds. These tones are passed through a set of filters that shape the tones into sounds the way that the articulators (tongue, lips, teeth, etc.) shape tones into sounds. This is a popular technique because it requires only enough computer memory to store the filter configurations and therefore is relatively inexpensive to make. Sound quality is acceptable but not realistic because the modeling of the voice is not exact enough to duplicate all the subtle vocal characteristics of human speech. The result is a machine-like speech quality.

The second method of producing speech is referred to as digitized speech. Actually, digitized speech is not synthesized speech. In digitized speech, the sound waves of the speech signal rather than the throat positions are recorded. These waves are then digitized—converted to digital codes and played back when needed. The advantage to this method is that the speech quality is good, sounding like a high-quality tape recorder. The disadvantage is that great amounts of memory are required to store the speech waves. The amount of memory required is practical only for the largest computers and all but impractical for microcomputers or small hand-held devices.

Aside from the industrial application of speech synthesizers, the synthesizers are being used as communication devices for nonspeaking handicapped individuals and to prompt handicapped individuals using remediation software.

FREDERICK F. WEINER
Pennsylvania State University

AUGMENTATIVE COMMUNICATION SYSTEMS
COMPUTER USE WITH THE HANDICAPPED

SPEECH THERAPY

Speech therapy comprises all activities that are carried out to modify communicative behaviors. Originally, the term speech therapy was used to cover all activities needed to remediate speech and language behaviors. The term language therapy should be used when remediation of language behaviors is desired. Therapy for any communication problem involves a diversity of methods and techniques. These techniques have been developed through clinical experience, research, and different theories. For example, because there is a diversity of opinion as to why stuttering occurs, there are many different approaches to stuttering therapy.

Diagnostic testing precedes therapy. Collection of sufficient data is necessary before therapy takes place. Diagnostic activity should also become an integral part of the therapy, with the clinician continuing to evaluate the communication disorder. The clinician is continually testing and observing the patient's response to therapy. Changes can be made in the original diagnosis as well as in the original therapy plan. Therapy and diagnosis are strongly interrelated, with diagnosis continuing throughout the therapy process and with therapy dependent on the diagnostic outcome.

Therapy is based on the anatomical and physiological aspects of the speech problems. However, understanding speech and language disorders is more complex than just understanding the structural and functional aspects. The psychosocial aspects of the patient must be of concern to the therapist also. The patient's attitude toward the communication process, his or her perception of the disorder, and the therapy situation itself are all important.

The clinician must have knowledge in a variety of areas (e.g., learning theory, reinforcement techniques, and child development). According to Flower (1984), there are three main activities used to modify communicative behavior. The first is mastery of the specific components of normal communication. Understanding these components would help improve the production and comprehension of speech and language. Stress is also placed on the efficient production of speech and language. The second activity is to provide alternative communication procedures or devices when communicative impairments are not remediable. For example, when intelligible speech is not possible, as in an individual with dystonia (a degenerative neuromuscular disorder affecting, among other things, the speech articulators), alternative or assistive devices using artificial or synthesized speech may be required. Sign language may also be taught when intelligible speech cannot be mastered. Other assistive devices include language boards, hearing aids, palatal appliances, and artificial larynges used following removal of the larynx.

The third activity introduced into therapy is the modification of attitudes toward better communication. The patient's attitude toward the process of communication or toward certain communication situations may be more adverse than the communication disorder itself. For example, a stutterer may be fearful of talking over the telephone and stuttering severity may increase substantially when the telephone is used in the communication process. The individual who has had his or her larynx removed has difficulty many times in learning to use the esophagus as the new noise source. This person may withdraw totally from any communicative interaction. One's attitude toward communication, therefore, is essential for effective and efficient communication and must be part of a total therapy program.

According to Flower (1984), therapy involves more than just the achievement of normal communication or some approximation to it. The broad nature of therapy goals will influence the type of patient seen, the therapy approach used, expectations for therapy, and accountability in the therapy process.

REFERENCES

Flower, R. M. (1984). *Delivery of speech-language pathology and audiology services.* Baltimore, MD: Williams & Wilkins.

Meitus, I. J. (1983). Approach to the diagnostic process. In I. J. Meitus & B. B. Weinberg (Eds.), *Diagnosis in speech-language pathology* (pp. 3–29). Baltimore, MD: University Park.

HARVEY R. GILBERT
Pennsylvania State University

AUGMENTATIVE COMMUNICATION SYSTEMS
SPEECH AND LANGUAGE HANDICAPS
SPEECH-LANGUAGE PATHOLOGIST

SPELLING DISABILITIES

Spelling is a traditional element of the elementary school curriculum and an integral part of the writing process. The primary goal of spelling instruction for both handicapped and nonhandicapped students is to make the act of correctly spelling words so automatic that it requires only a minimal amount of conscious attention. If students master the ability to spell words with maximum efficiency and minimum effort, it is assumed that they will be able to devote more of their attention, and consequently more of their effort, to higher order writing processes such as purpose, content, and organization (Graham, 1982).

It is commonly believed that the majority of students who are labeled handicapped exhibit spelling problems. This is particularly the case for handicapped students with academic difficulties. For instance, MacArthur and Graham (1986) found that learning-disabled students made spelling errors in approximately 1 out of every 10 words that they used when writing a short story. Although similar spelling difficulties have been reported for other handicapping conditions (Graham & Miller, 1979), it is important to note that our present understanding of spelling difficulties and handicapped students' development of spelling skills is incomplete.

One development of particular interest in the area of spelling disabilities is the formulation of various systems for classifying spelling problems. Poor spellers who are also poor readers have frequently been classified as dyslexic, while poor spellers who possess normal reading skills have been labeled dysgraphic. In addition, many of the classification schemes presently available represent an attempt to interpret various spelling errors and difficulties as evidence of neurological dysfunction.

Spelling instruction for the handicapped has, in large part, been based on the use or modification of traditional spelling procedures and techniques. Although handicapped students may not progress as rapidly through the spelling curriculum or master all of the skills taught to normally achieving students, their spelling programs commonly emphasize the traditional skills of (1) mastering a basic spelling vocabulary; (2) determining the spelling of unknown words through the use of phonics and spelling rules; (3) developing a desire to spell words correctly; (4) identifying and correcting spelling errors; and (5) using the dictionary to locate the spelling of words. There is considerable controversy, however, surrounding the issue of which skills should receive primary emphasis. Some experts, for example, recommend that a basic spelling vocabulary should form the core of the spelling program, while others have argued that spelling instruction should take advantage of the systematic properties of English orthography and stress the application of phonics and spelling rules (Graham, 1983).

Although spelling instruction for handicapped students has received little attention in the research literature, experts generally agree that these students should be taught a systematic procedure of studying unknown spelling words. Effective word study procedures usually emphasize careful pronunciation of the word, visual imagery, auditory and/or kinesthetic reinforcement, and systematic recall (Graham & Miller, 1979). Additional instructional procedures that are considered desirable for use with handicapped students include using a pretest to determine which words a student should study; presenting and testing a few words on a daily basis; interspering known and unknown words in each spelling test; requiring students to correct their spelling tests under the guidance of a teacher; periodically reviewing to determine whether spelling skills have been maintained; and using spelling games to promote interest and motivation.

A final point concerns the use of behavioral and cognitive procedures. Although the evidence is not yet conclusive, spelling procedures based on behavioral and/or cognitive principles appear to be particularly effective with handicapped students. McLaughlin (1982) found, for example, that the spelling accuracy of students in a special class improved as a result of group contingencies. In terms of cognitive procedures, Harris, Graham, and Freeman (1986) found that strategy training improved learning disabled students' spelling performance and, in one study condition, improved their ability to predict how many words would be spelled correctly on a subsequent test.

REFERENCES

Graham, S. (1982). Composition research and practice: A unified approach. *Focus on Exceptional Children, 14*, 1–16.

Graham, S. (1983). Effective spelling instruction. *Elementary School Journal, 83*, 560–568.

Graham, S., & Miller, L. (1979). Spelling research and practice: A unified approach. *Focus on Exceptional Children, 12*, 1–16.

Harris, K., Graham, S., & Freeman, S. (1986). *The effects of strategy training and study conditions on metamemory and achievement.* Paper presented at the American Educational Research Association, San Francisco.

MacArthur, C., & Graham, S., (1986). *LD students' writing under three conditions: Word processing, dictation, and handwriting.* Paper presented at the American Educational Research Association, San Francisco.

McLaughlin, T. (1982). A comparison of individual and group contingencies on spelling performance with special education students. *Child and Family Behavior Therapy, 4*, 1–10.

STEVE GRAHAM
University of Maryland

WRITING REMEDIATION
WRITTEN LANGUAGE OF THE HANDICAPPED

SPERRY, ROGER W. (1913–   )

Roger W. Sperry was born in Hartford, Connecticut, on August 20, 1913. He attended Oberlin College, receiving a BA in 1935 in English and an MA in psychology in 1935. He then went to the University of Chicago, obtaining a PhD in zoology in 1941. During World War II, Sperry worked with Karl Lashley, first as a National Research Council fellow at Harvard University (1941–1942) and then at the Yerkes Laboratory of Primate Biology in Florida (1942–1946). He was also involved during those years with an Office of Scientific Research and Development project on nerve injuries.

In 1946 he went to the University of Chicago as assistance professor of anatomy and became associate professor of psychology in 1952. In 1954 Sperry went as Hixon Professor of Psychobiology to the California Institute of

Roger W. Sperry

Technology. He became trustee professor emeritus in 1984.

Sperry's early research in the 1930s was on nerve plasticity. He determined that nerve fibers are not functionally interchangeable, but are connected in the brain for specific functions. He also did pioneering work on the development of this functional specificity, showing the orderly way in which nerves are able to grow selectively to connect with specific targets in the central nervous system. This work resulted in Sperry's theory of chemoaffinity, giving new insight into the way in which neural networks mediating different forms of behavior could be inherited and grown directly into the developing brain prior to any function.

Sperry is perhaps best known for his work on split brain preparation. He and his associates demonstrated the significance of the communication between the hemispheres at the corpus callosum. In 1981 Sperry shared the Nobel Prize in Medicine/Physiology for his research on the separate hemispheres in human split brain patients.

REFERENCES

Sperry, R. (1952). Neurology and the mind-brain problem. *American Scientist, 40*, 291–312.

Sperry, R. (1982). Some effects of disconnecting the cerebral hemispheres. *Science, 217*, 1223–1226, 1250.

RAND B. EVANS
Texas A&M University

SPINA BIFIDA

Spina bifida (myelomeningocele) is a congenital abnormality present at birth. The defect begins early in embryogenesis (the first 30 days of gestation), as the central nervous system is developing, with a failure of the spinal cord to close over the lower end (Haslam & Valletutti, 1975). Without such closure, normal development of the spinal column cannot occur; the spinal cord and covering membranes bulge out and block further development.

It is a fairly common developmental anomaly present in .2 to .4 per 1000 live births (Haslam & Valletutti, 1975). The risks increase dramatically to 1/20 to 1/40 following the birth of one affected infant. It is possible to test for spina bifida through amniocentesis. The amniotic fluid is analyzed by testing for abnormally high alpha fetal protein and acetyl cholinesterase levels. Both are normally present in the fetal cerebrospinal fluid, which, in myelomeningocele, leaks into the amniotic fluid (Behrman & Vaugh, 1983).

Detection at birth is due to the presence of a large bulging lesion or swelling, with or without a skin covering, at the lower part of the back (lumbosacral region). It is the damage to or the defect of the spinal cord that results in a variety of handicapping conditions. Eighty percent of children with spina bifida have hydrocephalus, a condition caused by the accumulation of fluid in the ventricles of the brain (Haslam & Valletutti, 1975). If left untreated, hydrocephalus can result in severe mental retardation. Treatment consists of diverting the cerebrospinal fluid to some other area of the body, usually the atria of the heart or the abdominal cavity (Wolraich, 1983).

Paraplegia resulting from the disruption of the motor tracts from the brain to the muscles at the spinal cord level leads to weakness and paralysis of muscles. The degree of paralysis depends on the location and extent of spinal cord damage. Bladder and bowel control is often absent and may present one of the biggest obstacles to a child's participation in a regular school program.

Children with spina bifida will require extensive medical, orthopedic, and educational services. This is often expensive and time consuming, creating frustration and financial hardship for the family. Educational programming for these children must consider the need for personnel trained in toileting techniques and physical therapy. While some children wtih spina bifida may require a self-contained special education class setting, others who are less severely impaired cognitively may be able to perform successfully in a mainstream classroom with support services.

REFERENCES

Behrman, R. E., & Vaughn, V. C. (1983). Defects of closure tube. In W. B. Nelson (Ed.), *Nelson's textbook of pediatrics* (pp. 1560–1561). Philadelphia: Saunders.

Haslam, R. A., & Valletutti, P. J. (1975). *Medical problems in the classroom: The teacher's role in diagnosis and management.* Baltimore, MD: University Park Press.

Wolraich, M. (1983). Myelomeningocele. In J. A. Blackman (Ed.), *Medical aspects of developmental disabilities in children birth*

to three: A resource for special service providers in the educational setting. Iowa City: University of Iowa.

MARSHA H. LUPI
*Hunter College, City University
of New York*

HYDROCEPHALUS

SPINAL CORD INJURY

Damage to the spinal cord frequently, but not always, result in paralysis or paresis to the extremities. The specific impairment or dysfunction that occurs in the extremities depends on the corresponding spinal level and the severity of the injury. In some situations, the injury may be only temporary and the individual may not experience any permanent effects. More often, the injury results in permanent damage and loss of function in the involved extremities.

The most common causes of spinal cord injury are accidents in or about the home, falls, bullet wounds, sports injuries, or motor vehicle accidents. The injury is often associated with fractured bones of the spinal column but also may occur from dislocation of one or more of these bones on the other. When the spinal cord is damaged, the nervous pathways between the body and the brain are interrupted. All forms of sensation (e.g., proprioception, touch, temperature, pain) and muscular control are typically lost below the level of the damage. Although nerves outside the spinal cord may be repaired or heal spontaneously, damaged nerves within the spinal cord will not regenerate. If the injury is low on the spinal cord (usually below the first thoracic vertebra), only the lower extremities are involved. This type of injury is called paraplegia. If the injury is higher on the spinal cord (cervical level), all four extremities and the trunk may be involved; this condition is referred to as quadriplegia. Injury to the highest levels of the cervical spine may cause death because of the loss of innervation to the diaphragm. Occasionally, only one side of the cord is damaged. This type of condition is called Brown-Sequard syndrome. Loss of proprioception and motor paralysis occur on the same side as the injury, while loss of pain, temperature, and touch sensations occur on the opposite side.

Immediate treatment after a spinal injury or suspected injury is immobilization. Immobilization prevents further shearing of the spinal column, which may result in further or more permanent damage to the spinal cord. If there is any doubt about a possible spinal cord injury, the injured person should not be moved until trained assistance arrives. Once the injured person has been transported to an appropriate medical facility, the course of treatment varies, depending on the nature of the injury.

During the initial stage of spinal cord trauma, autonomic and motor reflexes below the level of the injury are suppressed. This flaccid paralysis is called spinal shock and may last from several hours to 3 months. As the spinal shock recedes, spinal reflexes return in a hyperactive state. This spasticity or muscular hypertonicity may vary initially at different times of the day or in response to different stimuli, but it becomes more consistent within one year of the injury. The most common form of acute treatment is traction to the spinal column to bring about a realignment and healing of the fractured or displaced vertebrae. Special beds may be used to permit people in traction to be turned from their back to their abdomen, thereby reducing the chance of pressure sores (decubitus).

Artificial ventilation usually is necessary for persons with injuries at or above the level of the third cervical vertebra (C3). Decreased respiratory capacity is present in injuries from C4 through T7 (the seventh thoracic vertebra), making coughing difficult and often necessitating suctioning when the patient gets a respiratory infection. Dizziness or blackout may occur from pooling of blood in the abdomen and lower extremities when a person is first brought to an upright position following a period of immobilization. This is a normal reaction and is avoided through the aid of a reclining wheelchair or a tilt table that allows gradual adjustment to a full upright position. Numerous other secondary conditions or complications may occur for several months or years following a spinal cord injury. These include muscle contracture or shortening, loss of sexual functioning in males, impaired bowel or bladder control, kidney or urinary tract infections, or psychological reactions, to name but a few.

Rehabilitation procedures begin within a few days of the injury and usually continue for several weeks or months after the healing process is complete. The general goal of rehabilitation is to improve the physical capacities and develop adapted techniques to promote as independent a lifestyle as possible. Educational performance for a person with a spinal cord injury is hampered only by the individual's physical limitations. Persons with high-level injuries may require numerous assistive devices such as an electronic typewriter with mouthstick or mechanical page turner. Persons with low-level injuries may not require any specialized assistance to benefit from education. Counseling to help a person adjust to new physical impairments and to develop future vocational pursuits may also be in order.

REFERENCES

Hanak, M., & Scott, A. (1983). *Spinal cord injury: An illustrated guide for health care professionals.* New York: Springer-Verlag.

Long, C. (1971). Congenital and traumatic lesions of the spinal cord. In T. H. Krusen, F. H. Kottke, & P. M. Ellwood (Eds.), *Handbook of physical medicine and rehabilitation* (2nd ed., pp. 475–516). Philadelphia: Saunders.

Trombly, C. A. (1984). Spinal cord injury. In C. A. Trombly (Ed.), *Occupational therapy for physical dysfunction* (3rd ed.). Baltimore: Williams & Wilkins.

Wilson, D. J., McKenzie, M. W., Barber, L. M., & Watson, K. L. (1984). *Spinal cord injury: A treatment guide for occupational therapists.* Thorofare, NJ: Slack.

DANIEL D. LIPKA
*Lincoln Way Special Education
Regional Resource Center,
Louisville, Ohio*

**PARAPLEGIA
QUADRIPLEGIA**

SPINOCEREBELLAR DEGENERATION

See FRIEDREICH'S ATAXIA.

SPITZ, HERMAN (1925–)

Herman Spitz was born on March 2, 1925, in Paterson, New Jersey. He is a noted psychologist and researcher in the field of mental retardation. Currently director of research at the E. R. Johnstone Training and Research Center, Bordentown, New Jersey, Spitz obtained his BA at Lafayette College (1948) and PhD at New York University (1955). He was an assistant psychologist (1951–1955) and chief psychologist (1955–1957) at Trenton State Hospital. Since 1957, Spitz has been affiliated with the E. R. Johnstone Training and Research Center, initially as a research associate (1957–1962), and since 1962 as the director of research. In 1975 Spitz received the Brian E. Tomlison Award for outstanding achievement in the field of psychology. He is the author of over 90 publications in various professional books and journals as well as a consulting editor for the *American Journal of Mental Deficiency* and *Memory and Cognition.* His major contributions are in information processing, cognitive strategies, and problem solving of the mentally retarded. In recognition of his research contributions, Spitz has been invited as a lecturer and/or consultant by numerous institutions, including Alabama University, Columbia University, George Peabody College for Teachers, and Medical Research Council, London.

REFERENCE

American Men of Science. (1962) (10th ed.). Tempe, AZ: Jaques
    Cattell.

IVAN Z. HOLOWINSKY
Rutgers University

SPITZ, RENE ARPAD (1887–1974)

Rene Arpad Spitz, educated in his native Hungary and in
the United States, was a leading representative of psychoanalysis in the United States. He served on the faculty
of the New York Psychoanalytic Institute, was professor
of psychiatry at City College, City University of New York
and the University of Colorado, and was clinical professor
of psychiatry at Lenox Hill Hospital in New York City.
The author of some 60 monographs and papers, Spitz is
best known for his extensive studies of infant development.

REFERENCES

Spitz, R. A. (1962). *A genetic field theory of ego formation.* New
    York: International Universities Press.
Spitz, R. A., & Cobliner, W. G. (1966). *The first year of life.* New
    York: International Universities Press.

PAUL IRVINE
Katonah, New York

SPLINTER SKILL

See IDIOT SAVANT.

SPLIT-BRAIN RESEARCH

The technique of cerebral commissurotomy (split-brain
surgery) was first introduced by Van Wagenen in 1940 as
a surgical solution for severe and intractible forms of epilepsy. Van Wagenen performed the operation on approximately 2 dozen cases, hoping to be able to restrict the
abnormal electrical activation characteristic of epilepsy to
a single hemisphere. Unfortunately, the early operations
were not successful and the procedure was largely aban-
doned until the early 1960s, when it was taken up by Roger
Sperry working in collaboration with Joseph Bogen and
Philip Vogel (Beaumont, 1983). The refined operation
proved to be effective in many cases and, more important
from scientific perspective, the procedure allowed a unique

opportunity to study cerebral organization. Sperry's work
with split-brain patients was deemed so important that he
shared the Nobel Prize in Medicine in 1984. This award
appropriately reflects the tremendous advances that were
made in the neurosciences following this seminal work.

The technique of cerebral commissurotomy involves the
complete section of the corpus callosum, including the anterior and hippocampal commissures in the massa inter-
media. This technique effectively isolates each half of the
cortex and prevents transfer of information from one side
of the brain to the other. Despite the operation's dramatic
nature, postsurgical patients appear to function quite
well. Fairly sophisticated testing procedures are necessary
to isolate and identify the effects of surgery.

Detailed study of postsurgical split-brain patients reveals that, in fact, a number of problems do exist for these
patients (Springer & Deutsch, 1981). The patients frequently report trouble with associating names and faces.
This may be due to the differential loci for naming and
facial recognition, with the assignment of names occurring
in the left hemisphere and the recognition of faces more
intimately linked to the right hemisphere. Patients also
report difficulty with geometry, and many complain of
memory loss. Finally, many postsurgical patients report
cessation of dreaming; however, this has not been supported empirically and these patients continue to show
REM sleep postsurgically.

Sperry has consistently maintained that the operation
produces two separate minds within one body, each with
its own will, perception, and memories. This is supported
by numerous anecdotes of conflict between the hemispheres or between the body parts controlled by the respective hemispheres. These reports, albeit fascinating,
are largely anecdotal and appear to be somewhat exaggerated. In general, while early studies and writers emphasized the division and uniqueness of the two hemispheres, recent research has been devoted to how the brain
works as a whole and how the hemispheres cooperate in
transferring information back and forth. Zaidel (1979) has
compared performance of each hemisphere operating singly with performance of the brain operating as a whole.
He has found that much better results are evident when
the brain is working as a whole with the hemispheres serving in tandem. In addition, it is important not to forget
that both cortical structures are intimately linked to an
integrated subcortical substrate with a number of linked
bilateral structures.

Eccles (1977) has reviewed the split-brain research and
has argued that it suggests consciousness is intimately
linked to speech and therefore must reside in the dominant
left hemisphere. However, all such generalizations from
split-brain research are limited by the fact that the brains
studied are clearly pathological specimens and may not
represent normal cognitive functioning.

One of the interesting findings that has emerged from
split-brain research is that rudimentary language percep-

tion skills have been associated with the right cerebral hemisphere. Recognition of nouns by the right hemisphere appears to be easier than recognition of verbs (Gazzaniga, 1970). This difference is especially marked when a rapid response is required. If patients are given maximum time to respond, the noun-verb distinction is less apparent.

Levy and her colleagues have completed a number of studies with split-brain patients employing chimeric stimulae (Levy, Trevarthen, & Sperry, 1972). These are stimulus items that are composed by joining two half-stimuli. The stimuli are presented in such a way that each half goes to the isolated contralateral hemisphere. On the basis of these studies, Levy has argued that the left hemisphere is best described as analytic while the right is best described as holistic.

Split-brain patients make ideal subjects for dichotic listening experiments in which different stimuli are presented simultaneously in each ear. In addition, for those patients who receive a commissurotomy, divided visual field studies can be employed with less concern for saccadic eye movements. However, considerable experimental skill is necessary to avoid the phenomenon of cross-cuing. This occurs when a patient deliberately or inadvertently develops strategies for delivering information to both hemispheres simultaneously. For example, a subject who is palpating a comb may rub the teeth of the comb with the left hand. Although the tactile information will reach only the right hemisphere in the split-brain patient, the associated sound goes to both ears and may reach the left hemisphere and allow for linguistic identification.

Increasingly, neurosurgeons are performing partial commissurotomies with good success. These procedures allow still more detailed information about the localization of transference fibers in the corpus callosum. For example, it has become clear that somatosensory information is transmitted via the anterior corpus callosum while the rear portion, the splenium, transfers visual information.

The work done to date on split-brain patients may offer important clues to help the teacher better understand and educate the child with special needs. Levy (1982) has used split-brain data to develop a model of handwriting posture; Obrzut and Hynd (1981) have applied these findings on cerebral lateralization to children with learning disabilities; and Hartlage (1975) has developed a plan for predicting the outcome of remedial educational strategies based on a model of cerebral lateralization. Perhaps it is only through understanding how each half of the brain works that we will ever approach an understanding how it works as a whole.

REFERENCES

Beaumont, J. G. (1983). *Introduction to neuropsychology*. New York: Guilford.

Eccles, J. C. (1977). *The understanding of the brain* (2nd ed.). New York: McGraw-Hill.

Gazzaniga, M. S. (1970). *The bisected brain*. Englewood Cliffs, NJ: Prentice-Hall.

Hartlage, L. C. (1975). Neuropsychological approaches to predicting outcome of remedial educational strategies for learning disabled children. *Pediatric Psychology, 3*, 23–28.

Levy, J. (1982). Handwriting posture and cerebral organization: How are they related? *Psychological Bulletin, 91*, 589–608.

Levy, J., Trevarthen, C., & Sperry, R. W. (1972). Perception of bilateral chimeric figures following hemispheric disconnection. *Brain, 95*, 61–78.

Obrzut, J. E., & Hynd, G. W. (1981). Cognitive development and cerebral lateralization in children with learning disabilities. *International Journal of Neuroscience, 14*, 139–145.

Springer, S. P., & Deutsch, G. (1981). *Left brain, right brain*. San Francisco: Freeman.

Zaidel, E. (1979). Performance on the ITPA following cerebral commissurotomy and hemispherectomy. *Neuropsychologia, 17*, 259–280.

DANNY WEDDING
Marshall University

CEREBRAL DOMINANCE
LEFT BRAIN, RIGHT BRAIN

SPORTS FOR THE HANDICAPPED

The origin of sports adapted to the needs of the handicapped can be traced to the end of World War II, when thousands of physically handicapped veterans joined already existing groups of people with congenital and traumatic handicaps. In 1948 Stoke Mandeville Hospital in Aylsburg, England, first introduced an organized wheelchair sports program for patients; the first international games were held there in 1952 (Wehman & Schleien, 1981). This use of sports in rehabilitation was the stimulus for the growth of the international sports for the disabled movement that is prevalent today (DePauw, 1984).

From the beginning it was apparent that adaptations of rules and equipment were going to be necessary for sports programs, and many of the adaptations were the result of the imaginative efforts of the participants themselves. In addition, the participants joined together with others who needed the same adaptations, and through their activities were able to participate within the wider community. For some disabled persons, a sports program means competition; in other situations, the aim of sports is to meet therapeutic needs; for others the objective of sports involvement is to fulfill leisure-time pursuits (Adams et al., 1982).

Currently, federal mandates regulate physical education services and sports opportunities for individuals with disabilities. Public law 94-142 requires a free appropriate public school education, which includes instruction in physical education, in the least restrictive environment.

Public law 93-112, Section 504, specifies nondiscrimination on the basis of handicap, and states that equal opportunity and equal access must be provided for handicapped persons, specifically including physical education services, intramurals, and athletics. The most direct mandate for sports opportunities is the Amateur Sports Act of 1978 (PL 95-606) (DePauw, 1984).

As a result of this law, the U.S. Olympic Committee initiated a Handicapped in Sports Committee, which changed its name to the Committee on Sports for the Disabled (COSD) in 1983 (DePauw, 1984). Committee membership consists of two representatives from each major national organization in the United States offering sports opportunities for disabled individuals. At least 20% of COSD members must be, or have been, actively participating disabled athletes.

There are seven organizations designated as members of COSD. The National Association of Sports for Cerebral Palsy is a program of United Cerebral Palsy providing competitive sports opportunities for individuals with cerebral palsy and similar physically disabling conditions (Adams, 1984). The American Association for the Deaf sanctions and promotes state, regional, and national basketball, softball, and volleyball tournaments, the World Games for the Deaf, the AAD Hall of Fame, and the Deaf Athlete of the Year (Ammons, 1984). The National Handicapped Sports and Recreation Association is unique in the world of sports groups in that its members possess a variety of physical and mental disabilities (Hernley, 1984). The National Wheelchair Athletic Association organizes and conducts competition in seven different Olympic sports, and also in wheelchair slalom, involving a race against time over a series of obstacles to challenge a competitor's wheelchair handling and speed skills (Fleming, 1984). The United States Amputee Athletic Association has grown from a small group of competitors in 1981 to a national organization which sponsors annual games (Bryant, 1984). The major purpose of the U.S. Association for Blind Athletes is to develop individual independence through athletic competition without unnecessary restrictions (Beaver, 1984).

Founded in 1968 by Eunice Kennedy Shriver, the first International Special Olympics was a single track and field event with about a thousand participants. Today over 1 million mentally handicapped children and adults from around the world take part in Special Olympics; it is the biggest sports event in which handicapped children are likely to be involved. Sports activities range from events in swimming, gymnastics, and bowling, to basketball, track and field, and soccer. Racewalking has been adopted as a new sport, and equestrian sporting events are now being offered as demonstration sports.

Sports activities for the handicapped are sponsored by many nonschool groups, however, guarantees of equal opportunities for disabled students require that educators give more attention to school-sponsored sports programs. Unique and innovative approaches are needed so that these individuals can participate in sports within the schools. One possibility is to have special sections for the disabled as part of regular track, swimming, and gymnastic meets. It also may be possible to mix people with different handicapping conditions with able-bodied individuals in some sports programs.

REFERENCES

Adams, C. (1984). The National Association of Sports for Cerebral Palsy. *Journal of Physical Education, Recreation & Dance, 55*, 34–35.

Adams, R. C., David, A. N., McCubbin, J. A., & Rullman, L. (1982). *Games, sports and exercises for the physically handicapped* (3 rd ed.). Philadelphia: Lea & Febiger.

Ammons, D. C. (1984). American Athletic Association for the Deaf, *Journal of Physical Education, Recreation and Dance, 55*, 36–37.

Beaver, D. P. (1984). The United States Association for Blind Athletes. *Journal of Physical Education, Recreation & Dance, 55*, 40–41.

Bryant, D. C. (1984). United States Amputee Athletic Association. *Journal of Physical Education, Recreation, and Dance, 55*, 40–41.

DePauw, K. P. (1984). Commitment and challenges, sport opportunities for athletes with disabilities. *Journal of Physical Education, Recreation & Dance, 55*, 34–35.

Fleming, A. (1984). The National Wheelchair Association. *Journal of Physical Education, Recreation & Dance, 55*, 38–39.

Hernley, R. (1984). National Handicapped Sports and Recreation Association. *Journal of Physical Education, Recreation & Dance, 55*, 38–39.

Wehman, P., & Schleien, S. (1981). *Leisure programs for handicapped persons, adaptations techniques and curriculum.* Baltimore, MD: University Park Press.

Catherine O. Bruce
*Hunter College, City University
of New York*

OLYMPICS, SPECIAL
RECREATIONAL THERAPY

STAFF DEVELOPMENT

Staff development represents the professional growth of persons toward observable and measurable objectives that benefit an organization and its members. Professional and personal growth are necessary if an organization is to maintain its performance standards, develop a feeling of pride, stimulate its membership, and generate a creative work environment, all of which contribute to personal and corporate well being.

Staff development is necessary to improve the product of an organization by raising the skill level and awareness of the human resources of that organization. In the public schools, the product is education. Teachers design and deliver the product; students consume; and the public evaluates the product based on their observations of its effects on the consumers (children). Education must be accepted as meaningful and pertinent to the children before they learn. The motivating and technical skills of teachers, as salespersons, are vital to the success of the enterprise. The delivery of the product—instruction—requires teacher performance, materials, physical plant, technology, and student motivation. These variables determine the amount of the product the consumers buy or, in some cases, refuse. The teacher's skills, as those of the producer and delivering agent, are the key input in the process. Because of the importance of those skills, development of the staff as a key resource should be continuous and planned, as with any of the other resources of an organization. Development must be perceived as required, meaningful, and attainable by the staff.

Initial planning may begin by determining the needs of the organization and its membership. Needs surveying instruments are designed for that purpose. A staff development plan will fulfill those preferred needs that have been identified. The staff may contribute by assembling a list of requirements that can be collectively prioritized with regard to an organization's needs. This allows for all staff to feel a part of the planning process. Communication of the results of the needs survey should follow.

Another component of basic staff development is the creation of a supportive environment. To establish this environment there are several desirable elements that an administrator should provide, including teaching assignments, scheduling, released time, and special instructional supplies. Administrators must also be sensitive to personal needs and personalities of the staff, supporting them with concern, sincerity, and other humanizing factors. Developing support groups among teachers, organizing functional committees, and being a public relations agent for the school are indicative of a supportive environment. Praising and supporting teachers in the community when adversarial situations are apparent is also important in providing a supportive environment.

The administration should develop a plan for the enhancement of the school's staff resource. The plan may encompass several areas: curriculum; instruction; personal skills; licensure; advanced education; stress management; work environment; administrative support; school, home, community relations; student management; and school organization. Once the needs of the organization have been identified, each staffer's part in the scheme is drawn up and agreed to. The individual's role is contracted for and evaluated in the routine teacher evaluation process. Methods for enhancing the skill level of the organization may include professional in-service training, team teaching, internships, remedial plans of development, individual guided education units, school visitations, outside instruction, and role modeling.

Once needs are identified, a positive environment established, and a plan designed and implemented, monitoring of the professional staff is recommended. Positive feedback to personnel regarding their teaching performance is essential for it identifies the organizational expectations. Monitoring/supervising can be the same activity. Being visible, asking curriculum-directed questions, acknowledging instructional changes, encouraging staff reviews and faculty support groups, organizing creative instructional changes, providing evaluative feedback, and holding teacher conferences are all supervisory techniques under the heading of monitoring. Classroom visitations are important to monitoring. These activites deliver a clear message of administrative interest. When these components are addressed, an environment of trust develops. The teaching staff becomes more accepting of staff development programs once positive staff development has occurred in the school among the staff.

Need identification, planning and implementation, support and monitoring are basic staff development and personal growth activities. Before the typical staff development plans are initiated, these components should be communicated to and experienced by the staff. Teaching personnel need to know their needs have been identified by the administration as part of the organization's requirements. They should realize that the administration wants to provide a supportive, positive, professional working environment and that a system of consistent, fair, sincere supervision/monitoring is in place. Before outside resources are brought to the organization, in-house staff development should be established on a continuing basis. Staff development strategies can fall on deaf ears unless teachers are in an accepting, creative, and productive atmosphere cultivated by involvement in the building's own program.

The administrator is the key person in preparing the staff for a resourceful plan, but only after the staff has been provided the opportunity for in-house planning and leadership. The assets of an organization, human and physical, must be known. A development system can allow for a committee of teachers to help decide in-service and other needs. As the human resources are assessed, staff should be placed in positions where personal/professional talents are best used. An extension of the effort can complete the plan for achievement of the overall objective of the organization.

ANN SABATINO
Hudson, Wisconsin

**PERSONNEL TRAINING IN SPECIAL EDUCATION
SUPERVISION IN SPECIAL EDUCATION**

STANDARD DEVIATION

The standard deviation is a measure of the dispersion of sample or population scores around the mean score. It is the most important and most widely used measure of dispersion for quantitative variables when the distribution is symmetric. We compute the standard deviation for a population of n scores by first averaging squared deviations of scores (X) from the mean population (μ) using Equation 1:

$$\sigma^2 = \frac{\sum_{i=1}^{n} (X_i - \mu)^2}{n} \qquad (1)$$

This yields the variance of the scores, σ^2. The square root of this value, σ, is the population standard deviation. For a sample of n scores, the variance is computed using Equation 2:

$$s^2 = \frac{\sum_{i=1}^{n} (X_i - \overline{X})^2}{n - 1} \qquad (2)$$

where $\overline{X}$ is the mean sample score. Here we use $(n - 1)$ as the divisor instead of n because this produces an unbiased sample estimate of σ^2. Dividing by n produces a biased estimate. The square root of this value, s, is the standard deviation of the scores in the sample; i.e., the average dispersion of the scores around the mean score.

This measure of dispersion is widely used in the behavioral sciences to describe the spread of scores around the mean score when the distribution of scores is normal. Then we can state the proportion of scores that fall above or below any given value or between any two values by first converting the value(s) to z score units using

$$z_i = \frac{X_i - \overline{X}}{s} \quad \text{or} \quad z_i = \frac{X_i - \mu}{\sigma} \qquad (3)$$

for a sample or population. For example, for a sample of scores with computed statistics $\overline{X} = 40$ and $s = 5$, the value $X_i = 50$ is two standard deviations above the mean. Thus from a normal table, we find that 97.72% of the scores fall below 50 while 0.28% are larger than 50.

The size of the standard deviation also indicates the relative spread of two comparable distributions. For example, given that $s = 3$ for males and $s = 5$ for females on a given test, where the mean score, 15, is the same for either group, we can tell that the female scores span a wider range than the male scores, with 16% of the females scoring at least 20 while only 5% of the males obtain this score or higher.

In addition to describing a distribution of scores, the standard deviation is used widely in inferential statistics for describing the spread of the sampling distribution. For example, the standard deviation of the sampling distribution of the sample mean, $\overline{X}$, is given by $(\sigma/\sqrt{n})$, where σ is defined in Equation 2. We may also obtain the standard deviation of the sample proportion, variance, correlation coefficient, or any other statistic. When so used, the standard deviation is called the standard error of estimate of the statistic. Further, in regression estimation procedures, the standard deviation of the errors of prediction is used to judge the precision of the predicted values. This measure is called the standard error of estimate of prediction. In measurement, we define the standard deviation of the errors of measurement, the standard error of measurement, and use it to infer the value of true scores (Hopkins & Stanley, 1981). Further information on the standard deviation is found in the following references.

REFERENCES

Glass, G. V., & Hopkins, K. D. (1984). *Statistical methods in education and psychology* (2nd ed.). Englewood Cliffs, NJ: Prentice-Hall.

Hays, W. L. (1981). *Statistics* (3rd ed.). New York: Holt, Rinehart, and Winston.

Hopkins, K. D., & Stanley, J. C. (1981). *Educational and psychological measurement and evaluation* (6th ed.). Englewood Cliffs, NJ: Prentice-Hall.

Kirk, R. E. (1984). *Elementary statistics* (2nd ed.). Monterey, CA: Brooks/Cole.

GWYNETH M. BOODOO
Texas A&M University

CENTRAL TENDENCY
NORMAL CURVE EQUIVALENT

STANDARDS FOR EDUCATIONAL AND PSYCHOLOGICAL TESTING (SEPT)

The Standards for Educational and Psychological Testing (SEPT) is a joint effort of the American Psychological Association, the American Educational Research Association, and the National Council on Measurement in Education. The most recent revision of these standards (Committee to Review the Standards for Educational and Psychological Testing, 1985) is an update of the 1974 standards. It represents an evolution of formal standards for testing, beginning with the Technical Recommendations for Psychological Tests and Diagnostic Techniques published by the American Psychological Association in 1954. The document is now under continuing review by the committee and will undergo periodic revision. Information on and copies of the most recent SEPT are available from the American Psychological Association.

The SEPT is divided into four major sections: technical standards for test construction and evaluation; professional standards for test use; standards for particular applications (including testing language minorities and testing individuals with handicapping conditions); and standards for administrative procedures. The principal purposes for the SEPT are to provide criteria for the evaluation of tests, testing practices, and the effects of test use. While these evaluations depend on the judgment of professionals with appropriate training and certification/licensure for the use and construction of test, the SEPT provides the key frame of reference and ensures that all relevant areas are addressed in making such judgments. Tests and testing are rapidly changing and the SEPT does not provide precise numbers or cutoffs for meeting the various standards. Rather, the SEPT requires that specific types of information be reported so that appropriate evaluations can be made on the basis of evidence and not various fallacies such as the "expert opinion" or appeal to authority.

The SEPT sets several relatively specific requirements for evaluating new tests or testing programs. The SEPT states that:

> When judging the short-term acceptability of a test or program under development or redevelopment, the test user should determine that the test is on a par with readily available alternatives. In addition, the test developers or publishers should determine that (1) advertising for a test or program recommends only applications supported by a test's research base; (2) necessary cautions are given in the manual or elsewhere to encourage sufficiently limited reliances on test results, particularly when the use of the new test will have significant impact on the test takers; and (3) there is clear indication of continuing and significant improvement in the research base directed toward observation of the standards. (p. 3)

While spelling out the responsibilities of the test author and test publishers, the SEPT is prominent in pointing out that the ultimate responsibility for appropriate test use lies with the users of the test.

Though all sections of the SEPT are relevant to the testing of children and adolescents for special education placement and program planning, the 1985 SEPT, for the first time, places special emphasis on this process by devoting an entire chapter to testing people who have handicapping conditions. Several components of these standards, if actually applied, have major implications for practice as it now exists. Much data that are not widely available will be required to be collected and reported under these new standards. Validity and reliability evidence regarding testing of individuals with specific handicapping conditions, and the effects of modifications in testing procedures on reliability and validity evidence, will be necessary and likely will have to be collected by practitioners in their daily practice.

The SEPT is a document that all test users and consumers of test results should have intimate knowledge of and should apply in practice. Tests not reporting the required information or conforming to the standards should not be used because their appropriateness cannot be evaluated adequately.

REFERENCE

Committee to Review the Standards for Educational and Psychological Testing. (1985). *Standards for educational and psychological testing*. Washington, DC: American Psychological Association.

CECIL R. REYNOLDS
Texas A&M University

BUROS MENTAL MEASUREMENT YEARBOOK
TEST IN PRINT

THE STANFORD-BINET INTELLIGENCE SCALE

The Stanford-Binet Intelligence Scale has a longer history and tradition, and a larger volume of scientific literature associated with it, than any other test in the English language. Designed as a measure of intelligence for children, the first edition, developed by Lewis Terman in 1916, was a revision of the Binet-Simon Scale. The 1916 Stanford-Binet Intelligence Scale was notable for its systematic standardization and for the introduction of the concept of intelligent quotient (IQ), which was arrived at by dividing mental age (MA) by chronological age (CA). Subsequent revisions in 1937 and 1960 (Terman & Merrill, 1937) brought with them improved standardization procedures, alternate forms, extended age ranges (from 2 to 18), and replacement of the old ratio IQ with a normalized standard score of mean 100 and standard deviation of 16. The Fourth Edition was published in 1985. While covering the same age range, it differs from previous editions in that it includes many new items that cover four broad groups of cognitive abilities. It also provides a profile of subtest scores in addition to an overall IQ score.

The Stanford-Binet Intelligence Scale was highly influential in stimulating the development of clinical psychology in the United States. It demonstrated the use of standardized mental measurement in education, industry, and the military (for classification), leading to the development of many other types of tests and to an acceptance of testing by the public.

REFERENCES

Terman, L. M., & Merrill, M. A. (1937). *Measuring intelligence*. Boston: Houghton Mifflin.

Terman, L. M., & Merrill, M. A. (1960). *Stanford Binet Intelligence Scale*. Boston: Houghton Mifflin.

Thorndike, R. L., Hagen, E. P., & Sattler, J. M. (1985). *The Stanford Binet Intelligence Scale —Revised*. Chicago: Riverside.

LIZANNE DeSTEFANO
*University of Illinois,
Urbana-Champaign*

ASSESSMENT
BINET, A.
INTELLIGENCE TESTING
MENTAL RETARDATION

STANFORD DIAGNOSTIC MATHEMATICS TEST (SDMT)

The purpose of the Stanford Diagnostic Mathematics Test (SDMT) is to assess reliably pupils who typically score below the fiftieth percentile. It was designed to contain a significantly greater proportion of easy items than the typical achievement test. Hence, low-achieving and remedial pupils should find the SDMT less frustrating and less threatening.

The SDMT has four color-coded levels covering first grade through community college. There are numerous instructional objectives organized into three separate tests of number system and numeration, computation, and applications. Empirical norms are provided through fall and spring standardizations. There were no attempts to assess special education pupils.

Interpretation in both machine and hand-scoring formats emphasizes criterion-referenced measurement. The Instructional Placement Report lists the skills assessed, the raw score out of number possible, and the progress indicator. For each skill, the pupil receives a progress indicator of + (proceed without specific remediation) or − (remediation is needed before progressing in the regular instructional sequence).

Instructional follow-up includes traditional offerings in the *Handbook of Instructional Techniques and Materials*. In addition, there is a software system (PRISM, Math 1) with drills, practices, and end-of-instructional-sequence tests specifically tied to SDMT objectives.

REFERENCE

Beatty, L. S., Madden, R., Gardner, E. F., & Karlsen, B. (1984). *Stanford Diagnostic Mathematics Test*. New York: Psychological Corporation.

Thomas F. Hopkins
*Center for Behavioral
Psychotherapy, White Plains,
New York*

ARITHMETIC INSTRUCTION
ASSESSMENT
MATHEMATICS, LEARNING DISABILITIES AND

STANFORD DIAGNOSTIC READING TEST: THIRD EDITION (SDRT)

The Stanford Diagnostic Reading Tests (SDRT) are group tests designed to diagnose a pupil's specific strengths and weaknesses in reading. They are useful as a screening device for further diagnosis or as a tool for placing students into groups based on their instructional needs. The tests include four levels: red (grades 1 and 2 and low-achieving pupils in grade 3); green (grades 3 and 4 and low-achieving pupils in grade 5); brown (grades 5 through 8 and low-achieving high-school students); and blue (grades 9 through 12 and community-college students).

The tests view reading as comprised of four major components: decoding, vocabulary, comprehension, and rate. These areas are measured at each of the four levels. The red level (working time: 105 minutes) measures skills in auditory discrimination, phonetic analysis, auditory vocabulary, word recognition, and comprehension of short sentences and paragraphs. The green level (114 minutes) measures skills in auditory discrimination, phonetic and structural analysis, auditory vocabulary, and literal and inferential comprehension. The brown level (108 minutes) measures skills in phonetic and structural analysis, auditory vocabulary, literal and inferential comprehension of textual, functional, and recreational reading material, and reading rate. The blue level (116 minutes) measures skills in phonetic and structional analysis, reading vocabulary, literal and inferential comprehension of textual, functional, and recreational reading material, word parts, reading rate, and skimming and scanning.

Users may score the test by hand or by machine; a scoring service is available. To assist in interpreting and using the tests several materials are available, including *The Manual for Interpreting and Using Test Results* and the PRISM software systems, which are tied specifically to SDRT objectives.

The third edition of SDRT is one of the most comprehensive and well-developed screening tests for reading available today. All forms of the test have excellent reliability and validity. Accurate interpretation requires specialized knowledge in diagnostic and clinical practices in reading.

REFERENCES

Manual for interpreting: Stanford diagnostic reading test (1985). Cleveland, OH: Harcourt Brace Jovanovich.

Stanford diagnostic reading test. (1978). In O. K. Buros (Ed.), *The eighth mental measurement yearbook* (Vol. 2, pp. 1297–1300). Highland Park, NJ: Gryphon.

Ronald V. Schmelzer
Eastern Kentucky University

READING

STANLEY, JULIAN C. (1918–   )

Julian C. Stanley received his BS (1937) from Georgia Southern College and his EdM (1946) and EdD (1950) from

Julian C. Stanley

(Ed.), *Handbook of research on teaching* (pp. 171–246). Chicago: Rand McNally.

Stanley, J. C., Keating, D. P., & Fox, L. H. (1974). *Mathematical talent: Discovery, description, and development.* Baltimore, MD: Johns Hopkins University Press.

ANN E. LUPKOWSKI
Texas A&M University

STUDY OF MATHEMATICALLY PRECOCIOUS YOUTH

Harvard University in experimental educational psychology. Stanley is widely recognized for his work in test theory, experimental design (Campbell & Stanley, 1963), and statistics, although he is known best for his study of gifted students. Currently, he is director of the Study of Mathematically Precocious Youth (SMPY) and a professor of psychology at Johns Hopkins University.

Stanley's interest in the intellectually talented began in 1938 in a tests and measurements course at the University of Georgia. He pursued his career as a research-methodologist in education until a grant from the Spencer Foundation enabled him to create SMPY at Johns Hopkins in 1971 (Benbow & Stanley, 1983; Stanley, Keating, & Fox, 1974). The SMPY has as its goals identifying mathematically able youngsters and enabling them to learn mathematics and other related subjects faster and better than they might in the usual school curriculum. Many youngsters who participate in SMPY score at least 700 on the mathematics portion of the Scholastic Aptitude Test before age 13; only about 1 in 10,000 youngsters under age 13 score that high. The talent search concept now covers all the United States. Talent searches are conducted at the Center for the Advancement of Academically Talented Youth at Johns Hopkins and at programs at Duke University, Northwestern University, the University of California (Berkeley), the University of Denver, and the University of Washington.

Known nationally and internationally, Stanley has been a Fulbright research scholar (University of Louvain, 1958–1959) and a Fulbright-Hays lecturer (Australia and New Zealand, 1974). He served as president of the American Educational Research Association (AERA) in 1965–1966 and has been the recipient of many awards, including the AERA Award for Distinguished Contributions to Research in Education (1980).

REFERENCES

Benbow, C. P., & Stanley, J. C. (1983). *Academic precocity: Aspects of its development.* Baltimore, MD: Johns Hopkins University Press.

Campbell, D. T., & Stanley, J. C. (1963). Experimental and quasi-experimental designs for research on teaching. In N. L. Gage

STEINART'S DISEASE (MYOTONIC DYSTROPHY)

Steinart's disease (myotonic dystrophy) appears to be caused by an autosomal dominant characteristic that results in varying degrees of mental retardation, poor muscle development, bilateral facial paralysis, and general muscular wasting. Overt myotonic does not usually occur in early infancy. Most often, it manifests itself in late childhood or adolescence. Many children display behavioral characteristics of suspiciousness and moroseness and are asocial and submissive in treatment needs. Mental retardation is often present; although it may vary from mild to severe, it tends to be severe, particularly with early onset of the disease (Carter, 1978).

The older toddler or young child with myotonic dystrophy may have muscular weakness and wasting with psychomotor delay, drooping eyelids, and an open, drooling mouth. Cataracts are present in most individuals. High-arched palates and weak tongues are seen, as is an open, drooling mouth, even in older children. Children often have difficulty in feeding and swallowing. Abnormal curvature of the neck and back is seen. Atrophy of the extremities is often seen and clubfoot may be present. Premature baldness is also seen. Hypogonadism causes premature loss of libido or impotence in affected males. Nasal speech and articulation problems are common, as are vision problems associated with cataracts. Diabetes, heart arrhythmias, and cardiac abnormalities may be present, as well as increased incidence of diabetes mellitus (Lemeshaw, 1982).

Educational planning will often include categorical placement in an educable class; however, this disorder may not manifest itself until much later in life. For this reason, educational placement will vary with the individual. Health problems may affect education and physical education programs. Speech services will commonly be needed, as will vision services. Orthopedic defects will often necessitate physical and occupational therapy as well as specialized adaptive educational materials. With young children having swallowing and feeding problems, an aide may be required.

REFERENCES

Carter, C. (Ed.). (1978). *Medical aspects of mental retardation.* (2nd. ed.). Springfield, IL: Thomas.

Lemeshaw, S. (1982). *The handbook of clinical types in mental retardation.* Boston: Houghton Mifflin.

Menolascino, F., & Egger, M. (1978). *Medical dimensions of mental retardation.* Lincoln: University of Nebraska Press.

SALLY L. FLAGLER
University of Oklahoma

DIABETES
MENTAL RETARDATION
MUSCULAR DYSTROPHY

STELAZINE

Stelazine is the trade name for the generic antipsychotic agent Trifluoperazine. It is of the class of drugs known as phenothiazines and demonstrates many of the expected side effects. The piperazine subgroup of phenothiazines is very potent in its actions. In relation to Thorazine (Chlorpromazine), the dose/response ratio is approximately 20 to 1. Stelazine also appears to be more long-acting than Thorazine; thus fewer administrations are necessary to maintain therapeutic blood level.

In addition to the general side effects produced by phenothiazines, the piperazine subgroup has been related to a consistent pattern of extrapyramidal symptoms called the Rabbit syndrome, owing to distinctive facial movements (Bassuk & Schoonover, 1977). These side effects are reported most commonly in women over age 45. Characteristic symptoms include tremor of the lips and masticatory muscles that resembles a rabbit chewing. In contrast to tardive dyskinesia, tongue movements do not appear to be involved.

REFERENCE

Bassuk, E. L., & Schoonover, S. C. (1977). *The practitioner's guide to psychoactive drugs.* New York: Plenum Medical.

ROBERT F. SAWICKI
*Lake Erie Institute of
Rehabilitation, Lake Erie,
Pennsylvania*

THORAZINE

STEREOTYPIC BEHAVIORS

Stereotypic behaviors are variously defined in the literature. Terms are used to describe animal as well as human behaviors in developmental stages and in some abnormal or pathological situations (Berkson, 1983). Stereotyped behaviors are highly persistent and repetitious motor or posturing behaviors that seem to have little or no functional significance (Baumeister & Forehand, 1973). They are rhythmic movements that are coordinated and apparently intentional. They are repeated in the same fashion for long periods, often an hour or more at a time (Mitchell & Etches, 1977). Stereotyped movements are voluntary, brief, or prolonged habits or mannerisms that often are experienced as pleasurable (American Psychiatric Association, 1980). Sometimes present in children of normal intelligence, they are most common among individuals with mental retardation or autism. The stereotyped behaviors, mainly seen in infancy and early childhood, may persist into adolescent and adult life, especially in institutionalized retarded persons.

The most typical movements are head rolling, head banging, and body rocking. Other rhythmic repetitive movements have been described as foot kicking, hand shaking, hand rotation, finger and toe sucking, lip biting, and tooth grinding. Nail biting is frequently associated with emotionally disturbed children. According to Sallustro and Atwell (1978) and Mitchell and Etches (1977), head rolling from side to side on the pillow occurs mainly before the infant falls asleep, but it also may be seen during sleep and while awake; it is usually encountered in early infancy up to the first 2 to 3 years of life. Head banging, seen more often in the sitting position but sometimes on hands and knees or even standing, typically starts toward the end of the first year. It sometimes follows head rolling and ceases before the age of 4 years. The child repeatedly and monotonously bangs the head against the pillow or the bars of the cot, and sometimes against a wall or the floor. This generally occurs before sleep, but it may be seen at any time of the day or night, may continue for an hour or longer, and may alternate with other rhythmic movements. Body rocking, the most frequent stereotyped behavior, is a slow, rhythmical backward and forward swaying of the trunk, usually while in the sitting position, beginning in the first year of life (Sallustro & Atwell, 1978). It can persist in normal children, but it is very common in children and adults with Down's syndrome or other types of mental handicaps.

Various theories and opinions are presented in the literature regarding the origin, the mechanisms, and the significance of repetitive stereotyped behaviors. Rhythmicity is a characteristic and fundamental attribute of all life. Thelen (1979) showed in her studies of the development of normal infants during their first year of life that groups of stereotypies involving particular parts of the body or postures have characteristic ages of onset and peak performance and decline, and are highly correlated with motor development. As maturation enlarges processing capacity, repetitive behaviors are normally inhibited or incorporated into more complex behavior patterns. For many authors, the stereotypic behaviors represent a developmental disorder, as they are already seen in normal infants in relation to motor growth and maturity but they remain longer in the repertoire and persist into adolescent and adult life in mentally defective individuals. Their maintenance in some normal children might be due to personal or familial predisposition to rhythmic patterns, as head rolling and body rocking sometimes are present in one of the parents and are more frequent among other members of the family. However, the transformation of natural repetitive movements into pathological stereotypies is not clearly understood.

Many other authors believe that the movements are deliberate and purposeful, pleasurable, and self-stimulatory in character (Berkson, 1983), and that they supply compensatory satisfaction by relief of sensory monotony, body tension, discomfort, apprehension, frustration, anger, or boredom. None of the hypotheses presented explain why some of the stereotypies, like head banging and biting, are self-injurious and dangerous to the individual's well being, while others are not (e.g., head rolling, body rocking, complex hand and finger movements).

The true significance of these movements is still unknown as to their anatomical and functional levels. Their high frequency among severely mentally handicapped children suggests the failed development of cortical control and that most of these movements are probably infracortical in origin. The element of volition appears to indicate participation of the cerebral cortex in their initiation and maintenance. La Grow and Repp (1984) have reviewed various treatments and strategies used to suppress the stereotyped patterns from the behavior repertoire.

REFERENCES

American Psychiatric Association. (1980). *Diagnostic and statistical manual of mental disorders* (3rd ed.). Washington, DC: Author.

Baumeister, A. A., & Forehand R. (1973). Stereotyped acts. In N. R. Ellis (Ed.), *International review of research in mental retardation* (Vol. 6). New York: Academic. p. 55–96.

Berkson, G. (1983). Repetitive stereotyped behaviors. *American Journal of Mental Deficiency, 88,* 239–246.

La Grow, S. J., & Repp, A. C. (1984). Stereotypic responding: A review of intervention research. *American Journal of Mental Deficiency, 88,* 595–609.

Mitchell, R. G., & Etches, P. (1977). Rhythmic habit patterns (stereotypies). *Developmental Medicine and Child Neurology, 19,* 545–550.

Sallustro, F., & Atwell, C. W. (1978). Body rocking, head banging, and head rolling in normal children. *Journal of Pediatrics, 93,* 704–708.

Thelen, E. (1979). Rhythmical stereotypies in normal human infants. *Animal Behavior, 27,* 699–715.

HENRI B. SZLIWOWSKI
Hôpital Erasme, Brussels,
Belgium

JEANNIE BORMANS
Center for Developmental
Problems, Brussels, Belgium

AUTISM
MENTAL RETARDATION
SELF-INJURIOUS BEHAVIOR
SELF-STIMULATION

STEREOTYPIC MOVEMENT DISORDERS

Some individuals with handicaps or emotional disturbance may lack appropriate social interaction skills and engage in excessive behavior patterns such as rocking, head weaving, finger flapping, hand staring, and head banging. Little is known of the causes of these abnormal behavior problems, whether they be physical, psychological, or environmental. Kirk (1972) points out possible causes such as dysfunction of the central nervous system, discrepancies between an individual's capabilities and environmental demands, early home experiences, and social and economical aspects of the individual's environment. Studies have shown a relationship between a high level of this behavior and the restriction of the environment the individual lives in. Forehand and Baumeister (1970) believe the movement patterns may be linked to environments that are tense, discomforting, lacking opportunities to manipulate objects, lacking visual stimulation, and confining, such as to cribs and beds in residential institutions. These stereotypic movements have been associated with different handicaps such as severe and profound retardation, autism, and emotional disturbance.

An individual's handicap is greatly accentuated by these behavior patterns, which must be modified. The behavior needs to be less visual; for example, who finger flaps could be taught to do it behind the back so that it looks more like a nervous habit, or be taught to eliminate the excessive movement. Many techniques in the form of behavior management have been employed as intervention (Reese, 1978). The first step is to identify the target behavior and note the events that occur before the behavior and the consequences following the behavior to see if these events trigger or maintain the behavior. This analysis is used to design the program by manipulating the events to affect the behavior.

There are a number of behavior modification techniques that can be used as intervention. Not only should the program concentrate on eliminating the undesirable behavior, but it should focus on replacing it with an appropriate behavior. Elimination can be done by techniques such as punishment (Gardner, 1969), overcorrection (Foxx & Azrin, 1973), shock treatment (Lovaas, 1973), extinction (Williams, 1959), satiation (Ayllon, 1963), response cost (Kazdin, 1972), or time-out (Leitenberg, 1965).

Intervention is more effective by teaching a behavior that is incompatible with the inappropriate one. Techniques such as positive reinforcement of appropriate behavior (Mulhern & Baumeister, 1969), shaping and modeling (Reese, 1978), chaining (Pierrel & Sherman, 1963), and negative reinforcement (Azrin & Powell, 1969) may be used. Drugs may be another alternative (Berksen, 1965).

Undesirable behaviors can be controlled and eliminated using these interventions and individuals can be taught appropriate social interaction skills. These programs have helped the handicapped to eliminate some of the characteristics that alienate them from the normal public and helped them to live better lives.

REFERENCES

Ayllon, T. (1963). Intensive treatment of psychotic behavior by stimulus satiation and food reinforcement. *Behavior Research & Therapy, 1,* 53–61.

Azrin, N. H., & Powell, J. (1969). Behavioral engineering: The use of response priming to improve prescribed medication. *Journal of Applied Behavior Analysis, 2,* 39–42.

Berksen, G. (1965). Stereotyped movements of mental defectives VI: No effect of amphetamine or a barbituate. *Perceptual Motor Skills, 21,* 698.

Forehand, R., & Baumeister, A. A. (1970). Effect of frustration in stereotyped body rocking; Follow up. *Perceptual and Motor Skills, 31,* 894.

Foxx, R. M., & Azrin, N. H. (1973). Dry pants: A rapid method of toilet training children. *Behavior Research & Training, 11,* 435–442.

Gardner, W. I. (1969). Use of punishment procedures with the severely retarded: A review. *American Journal of Mental Deficiency, 74,* 86–103.

Kazdin, A. E. (1972). Response cost: The removal of conditioned reinforcers for therapeutic change. *Behavior Therapy, 3,* 533–546.

Kirk, S. A. (1972). *Educating exceptional children.* Boston: Houghton Mifflin.

Leitenberg, H. (1965). Is time-out from positive reinforcement an aversive event? A review of experimental evidence. *Psychological Bulletin, 64,* 428–441.

Lovaas, O. I. (1973). *Behavioral treatment of autistic children.* NJ: General Learning.

Mulhern, T., & Baumeister, A. A. (1969). An experimental attempt to reduce stereotype by reinforcement procedures. *American Journal of Mental Deficiency, 74,* 69–74.

Pierrel, R., & Sherman, J. G. (1963, February). Barnabus, the rat with college training. *Brown Alumni Monthly,* pp. 8–12.

Reese, E. P. (1978). *Human operant behavior, analysis and application.* Dubuque, IA: Brown.

William, C. D. (1959). The elimination of tantrum behavior by extinction procedures. *Journal of Abnormal & Social Psychology, 59,* 269.

DONA FILIPS
Steger, Illinois

APPLIED BEHAVIOR ANALYSIS
BEHAVIOR MODIFICATION
SELF-STIMULATION

STEREOTYPISM

People generally are classified and fit into molds or groups that have certain attributable characteristics. With handicapped individuals, the characteristics especially focused on are disabilities rather than abilities. Labeling an individual or fitting a person into a specific handicapped group or category according to certain characteristics has a few advantages and many disadvantages. The traditional handicapping labels are basically used to explain a medical problem or to aid in educational intervention, but the result generally is stereotyping of individuals, which may lead to misleading and inhumane side effects.

Throughout history, we can see that the treatment and attitudes toward those persons classified as different or abnormal have slowly changed (Kirk, 1972). Frampton and Gall (1955) recognized three stages: pre-Christianity, when the handicapped were mistreated, neglected, or killed; the Christian era, when they were pitied and protected; and the present era. In recent years, the handicapped are being accepted, educated, and integrated more and more into society.

During the early years (before present enlightenment), terms such as idiot, mad, crazy, moron, and imbecile were used to describe people who differed from the norm (Snell, 1978). These terms carried negative connotations and caused great misconceptions of what handicapped individuals are really like. People were actually afraid of these individuals because of the mystery surrounding their handicaps. The fear was due partly to lack of knowledge about the causes of these deviations and partly to lack of exposure to individuals with these characteristics. At first, the handicapped were put away in institutions, basements, or closets. Later, they were allowed to be kept in homes but away from schools. Even when education programs became prominent, the special education classrooms were in environments different from other children's. The first special education classrooms in regular schools were in the basement or away from the regular students.

Today, misconceptions arise from stereotyping the handicapped. Although many visually handicapped individuals have no mental retardation, the term visually handicapped often carries the connotation that these individuals are physically disabled and severely mentally deficient (Hollinger & Jones, 1970). Goffman (1963) and Edgerton (1967) write extensively of the negative stereotypes and stigmata associated with the mentally retarded. People with cerebral palsy may have an IQ of average or above average, but their physical rigidity and slurred speech often make people talk to them as if they were unable to understand. The hearing impaired have fought against the stereotype of being deaf and dumb. People interacting with blind individuals believe they have to talk loudly in order to be heard. Learning-disabled students are frequently associated with the retarded even though their mental capacities are generally average or above.

The emotionally disturbed are thought to be crazy or mad.

The misconceptions have caused many sociological, economic, and other types of barricades for the handicapped. These individuals have been denied access to a life that is as normal as possible, not only in the physical environment but also in the social environment. Many of the handicapped are still isolated, laughed at, and criticized. Their problems may be increased because of added emotional stress.

We have come a long way toward bringing positive images of the handicapped to the fore. The Special Olympics, media reports of accomplishments of individuals physically or mentally disabled, and improved school programs have helped to eliminate some barriers. Making the public more knowledgeable about definitions of handicapping terminology has improved public opinion. Movies or television shows about deformed or retarded individuals have switched to positive and inspiring messages. As the exceptional person becomes more prevalent in restaurants, stores, schools, etc., the public becomes educated.

A reversal of roles would be an ideal way for the general public to learn about and relate to individuals with handicapping conditions. Spending a few hours in a wheelchair, with a blindfold on, or with mittens on, would help one to see what it is like to be handicapped. It would be important for one to experience the difficulties of having the handicap and to feel the stares and other negative attitudes of those more fortunate.

School intervention has changed greatly for the better. Education programs are now a great source for informing the public. Mainstreaming has helped regular classroom students to better understand special education students; mainstreaming has also helped special education students to develop feelings of belonging and self-worth. Exposure to the regular classroom student has given the special education student a model from which to learn.

If less negative labels were used, and if the educational programs were fit to the handicapped individual's needs, there would be less stereotyping (Reger, Schroeder, & Uschold, 1968). It is hoped that as the positive trends continue to grow, the stigmata will be replaced with understanding and acceptance.

REFERENCES

Frampton, M. E., & Gall, E. D. (1955). *Special education for the exceptional* MA: Porter Sargent.

Goffman, E. (1963). *Notes on the measurement of spoiled identity.* Englewood Cliffs, NJ: Prentice-Hall.

Hollinger, C. S., & Jones, R. L. (1970). Community attitudes toward slow learners and mental retardates: What's in a name? *Mental Retardation, 8,* 19–13.

Kirk, S. A. (1972). *Educating exceptional children.* Boston: Houghton-Mifflin.

Reger, R., Schroeder, W., & Uschold, K. (1968). *Special education children with learning problems.* New York: Oxford University Press.

Snell, M. E. (1978). *Systematic instruction of the moderately and severely handicapped.* Columbus, OH: Merrill.

DONNA FILIPS
Steger, Illinois

ATTITUDES TOWARD THE HANDICAPPED
FAMILY RESPONSE TO A HANDICAPPED CHILD
HISTORY OF SPECIAL EDUCATION

STERN, WILLIAM (1871–1938)

William Stern, German psychologist and pioneer in the psychology of individual differences, introduced the concept of the intelligence quotient, in 1912. This quotient, used to express performance on intelligence tests, is found by dividing the subject's mental age as determined by the test performance by the chronological age and multiplying by 100. In the United States, the intelligence quotient, or IQ was used by Lewis M. Terman in his 1916 Stanford Revision of the Binet Scales.

REFERENCES

Murchison, C. (Ed.). (1961). *A history of psychology in autobiography.* New York: Russell & Russell.

Stern, W. (1914). *The psychological methods of intelligence testing.* Baltimore, MD: Warwick & York.

PAUL IRVINE
Katonah, New York

STIGMATIZATION

See LABELING.

STIMULANT DRUGS

Stimulant drugs are a commonly used class of medications for the treatment of inattention, impulsivity, and restlessness in school-age children and adolescents, and, less often, for the treatment of narcolepsy and drowsiness or disorders of arousal in the elderly. Children and adolescents having an attention deficit disorder (American Psychiatric Association, 1980) are the ones most often given these medications because of the significant effects of the drugs on sustained attention. The drugs are so named because of their stimulation of increased central nervous system activity, presumably by way of their effects on dopamine and norepinephrine production, and reuptake at the synaptic level of neuronal functioning (Cantwell & Carlson, 1978). The drugs may also have effects on other central neurotransmitters as well as on peripheral nervous system activity. The changes in central neurotransmitter activity result in increased alertness, arousal, concentration, and vigilance or sustained attention, as well as reductions in impulsive behavior and activity or restlessness that is irrelevant to particular tasks (Barkley, 1977, 1981). While a number of substances such as caffeine fall into this class of medications, those most typically used with children and adolescents are methylphenidate (Ritalin), d-amphetamine (Dexedrine), and pemoline (Cylert). Despite similar behavioral effects and side effects, the mechanism of action of each of these stimulants is somewhat different, and that for pemoline is not well specified.

The stimulants are relatively rapid in their initiation of behavioral changes and in the time course over which such changes are maintained. Most stimulant drugs, taken orally, are quickly absorbed into the bloodstream through the stomach and small intestine and pass readily across the blood-brain barrier to affect neuronal activity. Behavioral changes can be detected within 30 to 60 minutes after ingestion and may last between 3 and 8 hours, depending on the type of stimulant and preparation (regular or sustained release) employed. Traces of medication and their metabolites in blood and urine can be detected up to 24 hours after ingestion, perhaps corresponding to the clinical observation of persisting side effects after the desired behavioral effects are no longer noticeable.

Approximately 70% or more of children over 5 years of age, adolescents, and young adults display a positive behavioral response to the stimulants. Children below age 3 are much less likely to respond well to medication, and the drugs have not been approved by the Food and Drug Administration for children younger than 6 years. The best predictor of a positive response is the degree of inattention before treatment, while that for a poor response is the presence and severity of pretreatment anxiety and emotional disturbance (Barkley, 1976; Loney, 1986; Taylor, 1983).

The medications are taken one to three times per day, with some children taking them only on school days while others remain on medication throughout the week. Medication is often discontinued during summer vacations from school to permit a rebound in appetite and growth that may have been mildly suppressed during treatment. Children having more severe, pervasive, and persistent behavioral disorders, however, may remain on medication throughout the year. The average length of treatment with stimulants is typically 3 to 5 years, but this may increase in the future because of reports of equally positive effects with adolescents and young adults having significant inattention, impulsivity, and restlessness (Woods, 1986).

The most commonly experienced side effects are diminished appetite, particularly for the noon meal, and insomnia, although these are often mild, diminish within several weeks of treatment onset, and are easily managed by reductions in dose where problematic. Increases in blood pressure, heart rate, and respiration may occur, but they are typically of little consequence (Hastings & Barkley, 1978). Other side effects of lesser frequency are irritability, sadness or dysphoria, and proneness to crying, especially during late afternoons, when the medication is "washing out" of the body (Cantwell & Carlson, 1978). Some children experience heightened activity levels during this washout phase. Headaches and stomach aches are infrequently noted and, like all side effects, appear to be dose related. Temporary suppression of growth in height and weight may be noted in some children during the first 1 to 2 years of treatment with stimulants, but there appear to be few lasting effects on eventual adult stature. Between 1 and 2% of children and adolescents may experience nervous tics while on stimulant medication, but these diminish in the majority of cases with reduction in dose or discontinuation of medication. A few cases of Gilles de la Tourette's syndrome (multiple motor tics, vocal tics, and, in some cases, increased utterance of profanities) have been reported after initiation of stimulant medication (Barkley, 1987). Children with a personal or family history of motor/vocal tics should use these drugs only with caution because of the possible emergence or exacerbation of their tic conditions, observed in more than 50% of such children.

The medications appear to improve fine motor agility, planning, and execution, as well as reaction time, speech articulation (in children having mild delays in fine motor control of speech), and handwriting, in some children. Increases in academic productivity, short-term memory, simple verbal learning, and drawing and copying skills frequently are noted, but little, if any, change is seen on tests of intelligence, academic achievement, or other complex cognitive processes (Barkley, 1977). Despite generally positive behavioral improvements in most children with attention deficit disorder taking stimulants, these drugs have shown little, if any, significant, lasting effect on the long-term outcome of such children in late adolescence or young adulthood once medication has been discontinued.

REFERENCES

American Psychiatric Association. (1980). *Diagnostic and statistical manual of mental disorders* (3rd ed.). Washington, DC: Author.

Barkley, R. (1976). Predicting the response of hyperactive children to stimulant drugs: A review. *Journal of Abnormal Child Psychology, 4*, 327–348.

Barkley, R. (1977). A review of stimulant drug research with hyperactive children. *Journal of Child Psychology & Psychiatry, 18*, 137–165.

Barkley, R. A. (1981). *Hyperactive children: A handbook for diagnosis and treatment.* New York: Guilford.

Barkley, R. A. (1987). Tic disorders and Tourette's syndrome. In

E. Mash & L. Terdal (Eds.), *Behavioral assessment of childhood disorders* (2nd ed.). New York: Guilford.

Cantwell, D., & Carlson, G. (1978). Stimulants. In J. Werry (Ed.), *Pediatric psychopharmacology*. New York: Brunner/Mazel.

Hastings, J., & Barkley, R. (1978). A review of psychophysiological research with hyperactive children. *Journal of Abnormal Child Psychology, 7*, 413–447.

Loney, J. (1986). Predicting stimulant drug response among hyperactive children. *Psychiatric Annals, 16*, 16–22.

Taylor, E. (1983). Drug response and diagnostic validation. In M. Rutter (Ed.), *Developmental neuropsychiatry* (pp. 348–368). New York: Guilford.

Woods, D. (1986). The diagnosis and treatment of attention deficit disorder, residual type. *Psychiatric Annals, 16*, 23–28.

RUSSELL A. BARKLEY
*University of Massachusetts
Medical Center*

ATTENTION DEFICIT DISORDER
DOPAMINE
HYPERACTIVITY
NOREPINEPHRINE
RITALIN
TOURETTE'S SYNDROME

STIMULUS DEPRIVATION

Stimulus deprivation refers to an increase in reinforcer effectiveness that occurs following a reduction in the availability of or access to that reinforcing event. The effectiveness of reinforcers, especially of primary reinforcers such as food, depends greatly on the deprivation state of the individual. Using edible reinforcers with a student who has just returned from lunch probably will not be as effective as using the same reinforcers immediately prior to lunch, when the student is more likely to be in a state of deprivation for food. Most stimulus events serve as effective reinforcers only if the individual has been deprived of them for a period of time prior to their use. In general, the longer the deprivation period, the more effective the reinforcer (Martin & Pear, 1983).

The magnitude or amount of a reinforcer required to change behavior is less when the individual is partially deprived of the event (Kazdin, 1980). For example, students who are temporarily deprived of teacher attention may require less attention to maintain behavior than students who have frequent access to teacher attention. If a potential reinforcer is provided in limited quantities, thus creating a partial state of deprivation, that event is more likely to maintain its effectiveness as a reinforcer.

A state of deprivation may be created intentionally by the educator to increase the value of reinforcing events. This procedure is especially valuable with events that previously were effective reinforcers but temporarily show a satiation effect. Using the principle of deprivation, the reinforcer is withheld or reduced in availability for a period of time as a means of increasing the state of deprivation. If free time, listening to music, or a particular edible item show satiation effects, the teacher may wish to reduce or remove these for a period of time. As students become deprived, these reinforcers can once again be introduced with increased effectiveness.

Ethical and legal issues should be considered prior to use of a deprivation procedure. Major objections typically focus on deprivation of essential primary reinforcers (e.g., food, water, shelter, human contact) on the basis that it constitutes a violation of basic human rights. As noted by Kazdin (1980), however, deprivation is a natural part of human existence. All people are, in some ways, deprived by society of self-expression in such areas as free speech and sexual behavior. Certainly, special education students who demonstrate academic and behavioral difficulties frequently are deprived of access to employment or other economic opportunities as a result of their characteristics. Thus the negative effects of social deprivation that special education students normally experience as a result of their deficits must be weighed against any temporary negative effects associated with stimulus deprivaton used as a treatment strategy (Baer, 1970). A decision to use deprivation, or any other aversive technique, requires careful consideration of the kind of deprivation, the duration of the program, the availability of alternative treatment strategies, and the demonstrable benefits resulting from its use (Kazdin, 1980). As a precautionary measure when using a deprivation procedure, an individual should never be completely deprived of the reinforcing event for a lengthy period of time.

Fortunately, intentional deprivation of reinforcers usually is not necessary, as the natural deprivation that occurs in the course of an individual's daily activities often is sufficient to increase reinforcer effectiveness. Since children in the classroom, for example, do not have unlimited access to free time, they normally experience a mild form of deprivation during the course of a school day. As another example, when using small amounts of edible reinforcers to increase appropriate responding, the only deprivation required may be the natural deprivation that occurs between meals. Thus a variety of events may serve as effective reinforcers simply as a result of natural deprivation without the introduction of more formal deprivation procedures.

REFERENCES

Baer, D. M. (1970). A case for the selective reinforcement of punishment. In C. Neuringer & J. L. Michael (Eds.), *Behavior modification in clinical psychology*. New York: Appleton-Century-Crofts.

Kazdin, A. E. (1980). *Behavior modification in applied settings* (revised ed.). Homewood, IL: Dorsey.

Martin, G., & Pear, J. (1983). *Behavior modification: What it is and how to do it* (2nd ed.). Englewood Cliffs, NJ: Prentice-Hall.

CHRISTINE L. COLE
University of Wisconsin,
Madison

BEHAVIOR MODIFICATION
OPERANT CONDITIONING
STIMULUS SATIATION

STIMULUS SATIATION

Stimulus satiation refers to the reduction in reinforcer effectiveness that occurs after a large amount of that reinforcer has been obtained (usually within a short period of time). Thus an event that initially shows reinforcing qualities may become ineffective or even aversive for a period of time if experienced too frequently or excessively. Teacher praise may be effective the first few times if it is provided in the morning, but may gradually diminish in value with additional use during the day. Treats and certain activities may be highly reinforcing if used sparingly but may lose their effectiveness if used frequently. The special educator should be sensitive to the principle of satiation and provide alternative reinforcing events when loss of effectiveness is noted (Gardner, 1978).

Satiation is especially common with primary reinforcers such as food. These reinforcers, when provided in excessive amounts within a short period, may lose their reinforcing properties relatively quickly. To prevent or delay satiation, only a small amount of the reinforcer should be provided at any one time. Satiation of primary reinforcers is usually temporary, as these events regain their reinforcing value as deprivation increases.

Secondary reinforcers such as praise, attention, and recognition are less likely than primary reinforcers to be influenced by satiation effects. The category of secondary reinforcers called generalized reinforcers is least susceptible to satiation. This is due to the fact that the reinforcers themselves (e.g., tokens, grades, money) can be exchanged for a variety of other reinforcing events called back-up reinforcers. Thus satiation of generalized reinforcers is not likely to occur unless the individual becomes satiated with the items or events offered as back-up reinforcers. The greater the number and range of back-up reinforcers available, the less likelihood that satiation will occur (Kazdin, 1980). This would suggest that teachers consider the use of tokens, exchangeable for a wide variety of back-up reinforcers, when tangible events are required to ensure effective learning and behavior (Gardner, 1978).

The principle of satiation may also be used as an intervention tactic to reduce the value of events that appear to serve as reinforcers for maladaptive behavior. In a stimulus satiation procedure, the individual is provided with a reinforcing event with such frequency or in such large quantities that the event loses its reinforcing qualities for a period of time; the result is that the behavior maintained by that reinforcer is weakened. In a frequently cited example, Ayllon (1963) used a stimulus satiation procedure with a hospitalized psychiatric patient who hoarded large numbers of towels in her room. Although many efforts had been made to discourage hoarding, these had proved to be unsuccessful and the staff had resorted to simply removing on a regular basis the towels she had collected. With the stimulus satiation procedure, the staff provided her with large numbers of towels without comment. After a few weeks, when the number of towels in her room reached 625, she began to remove a few and no more were given to her. The patient engaged in no towel hoarding during the subsequent year.

The purpose of such a stimulus satiation procedure is to reduce or remove the reinforcing qualities of the event serving to maintain the maladaptive behavior. In the Ayllon study (1963) this loss of reinforcer effectiveness was reflected in the patient's comments: "Don't give me no more towels. I've got enough. . . . Take them towels away. . . . Get these dirty towels out of here" (p. 57). Apparently, as the number of towels increased to an excessive level, they were no longer reinforcing and even became aversive to her.

Although long-term maintenance of behavior change was obtained in this case, the effects of stimulus satiation procedures typically are temporary. This is especially true if the reinforcer is highly valuable to the individual. Educators can enhance the effects of a satiation procedure by ensuring that, during the interim period in which the maladaptive behavior is absent or of low strength, other more appropriate replacement behaviors are taught and strengthened (Gardner, 1978).

REFERENCES

Ayllon, T. (1963). Intensive treatment of psychotic behaviour by stimulus satiation and food reinforcement. *Behaviour Research & Therapy, 1,* 53–61.

Gardner, W. I. (1978). *Children with learning and behavior problems: A behavior management approach* (2nd ed.). Boston: Allyn & Bacon.

Kazdin, A. E. (1980). *Behavior modification in applied settings* (revised ed.). Homewood, IL: Dorsey

CHRISTINE L. COLE
University of Wisconsin,
Madison

APPLIED BEHAVIOR ANALYSIS
BEHAVIOR MODIFICATION
STIMULUS DEPRIVATION

STRABISMUS, EFFECT ON LEARNING OF

Strabismus, also called heteropia, is a visual condition in which the two eyes are not parallel when viewing an object. While one eye is fixed on an object, the other eye will be directed elsewhere. Strabismus can be classified in two ways. The first concerns the angle of separation. In concomitant strabismus, the angle of separation is fixed; in noncomitant strabismus the angle between the eye that is fixed and the deviant eye varies. Strabismus also can be classified as to whether the visual paths of the two eyes converge or diverge (Harley & Lawrence, 1977).

The effect of strabismus on learning is closely tied to its age of onset. If it occurs later in childhood, after other visual reflexes have developed, it can result in double vision (diplopia), which can be stressful and lead to learning disabilities. Lipton (1971) noted significant correlations between strabismus and neurotic traits, character disorders, and learning problems. Haskell (1972), on the other hand, showed no relationship between strabismus and academic achievement.

If the onset of strabismus occurs before the age of two, the effects are not as severe because other visual reflexes are not as developed. However, early onset of strabismus can lead to the development of ambliopia, a condition in which the brain suppresses the signals coming from the deviant eye. If not corrected, the brain can permanently lose the ability to process a 20/20 image from this eye.

Some form of strabismus occurs in approximately 5% of all children. The percentage increases to 40 to 50% for children with cerebral palsy; it is noted in as many as 60% of the children who are visually impaired at birth as a result of their mother's having contracted rubella during pregnancy.

Strabismus can be corrected through lenses if it is detected early in a child's life. Additionally, some doctors recommend eye exercises as a way to correct the condition. This recommendation is controversial. Eden (1978) notes that strabismus often starts early in life, before the child is capable of following any rigorous exercise schedule. Once the child is capable of following such a schedule, permanent visual damage may already have occurred. In school, close work should be limited for students with strabismus, and these students should be given frequent rest periods.

REFERENCES

Eden, J. (1978). *The eye book.* New York: Viking.

Harley, R. K., & Lawrence, G. A. (1977). *Visual impairment in the schools.* Springfield, IL: Thomas.

Haskell, S. H. (1972). Visuoperceptual, visuomotor, and scholastic skills of alternating and uniocular squinting children. *Journal of Special Education, 6,* 3–8.

Lipton, E. L. (1971). Remarks on the psychological aspects of strabismus. *Sight-Saving Review, 4,* 129–138.

THOMAS E. ALLEN
Gallaudet College

AMBLIOPIA
BLIND

STRAUSS, ALFRED A. (1897–1957)

Alfred A. Strauss was born in Germany and received his medical degree and subsequent training in psychiatry and neurology there. He left Germany in 1933, became visiting professor at the University of Barcelona, and helped to establish Barcelona's first child guidance clinics. In 1937 Strauss joined the staff of the Wayne County (Michigan) School, where he served as research psychiatrist and director of child care. In 1947 Strauss founded the Cove School in Racine, Wisconsin, a residential institution that gained an international reputation for its pioneering work with brain-injured children. Strauss served as president of the school until his death.

Alfred A. Strauss

Strauss made major contributions in the areas of diagnosis and education of brain-injured children. He developed tests for diagnosing brain injury. His studies of children without intellectual deficit who showed characteristics of brain injury in learning and behavior resulted in the first systematic description of a new clinical entity, minimal brain dysfunction. His 1947 book, *Psychopathology and Education of the Brain-Injured Child,* written with Laura Lehtinen, was the major guide for many of the numerous school programs for minimally brain-injured children that came into existence during the 1950s and 1960s.

REFERENCES

Gardiner, R. A. (1958). Alfred A. Strauss, 1897–1957. *Exceptional Children, 24,* 373.

Lewis, R. S., Strauss, A. A., & Lehtinen, L. E. (1960). *The other child.* New York: Grune & Stratton.

Strauss, A. A., & Kephart, N. C. (1955). *Psychopathology and education of the brain-injured child.* (Vol. 2). New York: Grune & Stratton.

Strauss, A. A., & Lehtinen, L. E. (1947). *Psychopathology and education of the brain-injured child.* (Vol. 1). New York: Grune & Stratton.

PAUL IRVINE
Katonah, New York

BIRTH INJURIES

STRAUSS SYNDROME

The term Strauss syndrome was coined by Stevens and Birch (1957) to focus on an expanded set of behavioral characteristics of children who could not learn and did not easily fit into other classification systems. It also extended the work of a leading pioneer in the field, Alfred Strauss. Strauss's ideas regarding the education of brain-injured, perceptually handicapped children were presented in works coauthored first with Laura Lehtinen (1947) and later with Newell Kephart (1955).

The term Strauss syndrome was introduced to describe the brain-injured child who evidenced (1) erratic and inappropriate behavior on mild provocation; (2) increased motor activity disproportionate to the stimulus; (3) poor organization of behavior; (4) distractibility of more than an ordinary degree under ordinary conditions; (5) persistent hyperactivity; and (6) awkwardness and consistently poor motor performance (Stevens & Birch, 1957).

Despite the importance of the works of Strauss et al., it became apparent that their description of the brain-injured child pertained only to a certain portion of the total group having neurogenic disorders of learning. Major objections to the term brain-injured child were presented by Stevens and Birch (1957). They concluded that:

1. The term is an etiological concept and does not appropriately describe the symptom complex. This is important because the condition that prevails is viewed in terms of symptoms rather than etiology.

2. The term is associated with other conditions, some of which have no relation to the symptom complex commonly referred to as brain injury.

3. The term does not help in the development of a sound therapeutic approach.

4. The term is not suited for use as a descriptive one since it is essentially a generic expression, the use of which results in oversimplification (p. 349).

REFERENCES

Stevens, G., & Birch, J. (1957). A proposal for clarification of the terminology used to describe brain-injured children. *Exceptional Children, 23*, 346–349.

Strauss, A., & Kephart, N. (1955). *Psychopathology and education of the brain-injured child* (Vol. 2). New York: Grune & Stratton.

Strauss, A., & Lehtinen, L. (1947). *Psychopathology and education of the brain-injured child* (Vol. 1). New York: Grune & Stratton.

CECELIA STEPPE-JONES
North Carolina Central University

BRAIN DAMAGE
ETIOLOGY
LEARNING DISABILITIES
LESIONS
MINIMAL BRAIN DYSFUNCTION

STRENGTH MODELS OF REMEDIATION

See REMEDIATION, DEFICIT-CENTERED MODELS OF.

STREPHOSYMBOLIA

Strephosymbolia is a Greek term that literally means twisted symbol. Originally used by Samuel T. Orton, strephosymbolia is most commonly used in discussions regarding dyslexia. Orton and others noticed that when certain children read, they often reverse letters, syllables, or words. These children see all parts of a word, but not in the accepted order. So, instead of "pebbles," a strephosymbolic child might see "pelbbse" (Johnson, 1981). This twisting of reading material is viewed as a primary symptom of dyslexia (Clarke, 1973).

Orton believed that strephosymbolia resulted from a failure to establish cerebral dominance in the left hemisphere of the brain (Lerner, 1985). The reversals that resulted from the lack of cerebral dominance were due to failure to erase memory images from the nondominant side of the brain (Kessler, 1980). These memory images were projected to the dominant side of the brain as mirror images, resulting in the reversals of letters and/or words (Kessler, 1980).

Currently, Orton's theory has little credibility as there has been no substantiation that mirror images are projected onto the brain (Kessler, 1980). Mercer (1983) notes that these difficulties are referred to as severe reading disabilities and are treated according to the specific difficulty.

REFERENCES

Clarke, L. (1973). *Can't read, can't write, can't talk too good either.* New York: Walker.

Johnson, C. (1981). *The diagnosis of learning disabilities*. Boulder, CO: Pruett.

Kessler, J. W. (1980). History of minimal brain dysfunction. In H. E. Rice & E. D. Rice (Eds.), *Handbook of minimal brain dysfunction: A critical review*. New York: Wiley.

Lerner, T. (1985). *Learning disabilities: Theories, diagnosis and teaching strategies* (4th ed.). Boston: Houghton Mifflin.

Mercer, C. D. (1983). *Students with learning disabilities* (2nd ed.). Columbus, OH: Merrill.

JOHN R. BEATTIE
*University of North Carolina,
Charlotte*

**DYSLEXIA
READING DISORDERS**

STRESS AND THE HANDICAPPED STUDENT

Stress results when physical and psychological demands on an individual exceed personal coping skills. Stress is activated when a threat to security, self-esteem, or safety is perceived. Schultz (1980) suggests that stress is often triggered by environmental interactions, which may be more problematic for handicapped children than for non-handicapped ones. Handicapped children may also develop stress reactions to personal thoughts.

In regard to the development of stress, Schultz has suggested a pattern of (1) occurrence of an event, (2) internal assignment of the meaning of the event, and (3) occurrence of internal and external responses to the event depending on the assigned meaning.

Rutter (1981) suggests resilience is demonstrated by young people who succeed despite stress, but that children who have handicapping conditions may be constitutionally less resilient. Particularly stressful periods for handicapped children include school entry, change of school, and last years of school. The uncertainties present during these periods are exacerbated because of the handicapped child's lack of resilience (Kershaw, 1973).

Low-achieving individuals demonstrate more stress than their better achieving peers. Lower functioning handicapped students are subject to more stress in childhood than higher functioning individuals (Westling, 1986). This increased stress may be due to social rejection and parental overprotection concurrent with the children's reduced capacity for coping with various situations.

Mainstreaming may produce increased stress in the handicapped student. Tymitz-Wolf (1984) analyzed mildly mentally handicapped students' worries about mainstreaming as related to academic performance, social interactions, and the transitions inherent in split placement. A range of worries were reported in all three areas, with worries concerning transitions being the most prevalent.

Schultz (1980) contends that stress-management programs for handicapped students should emphasize instruction in adaptive coping skills, including relaxation train-ing. Relaxation training has been used to decrease stress in learning-disabled students (Omizo, 1981).

REFERENCES

Kershaw, J. D. (1973). *Handicapped children in the ordinary school: Stresses in children*. New York: Crane & Russak.

Omizo, M. M. (1981). Relaxation training and biofeedback with hyperactive elementary school children. *Elementary School Guidance & Counseling, 15*(4), 329–332.

Rutter, M. (1981). Stress, coping, and development: Some issues and some questions. *Journal of Child Psychology & Psychiatry, 22*, 323–356.

Schultz, E. (1980). Teaching coping skills for stress and anxiety. *Teaching Exceptional Children, 13*(3), 12–15.

Tymitz-Wolf, B. (1984). An analysis of EMR children's worries about mainstreaming. *Education & Training of the Mentally Retarded, 19*, 157–168.

Westling, D. L. (1986). *Introduction to mental retardation*. Englewood Cliffs, NJ: Prentice-Hall.

ANNE M. BAUER
University of Cincinnati

**SELF-CONCEPT
SOCIAL SKILLS**

STRONG-CAMPBELL INTEREST INVENTORY

The 1985 revised edition of the widely used Strong-Campbell Interest Inventory (SVIB-SCII) is currently distributed by Consulting Psychologists Press. Its used in high schools as an aid in making curricular and occupational choices.

The new edition retains the use of Holland's six general occupational themes and the 23 basic interest scales. Changes include the addition of 17 vocational/technical occupations (34 scales) and 6 new professions (12 scales). Currently, there are 106 occupations in the profile represented by 207 occupational scales. There are also measures of academic comfort and introversion-extroversion.

The revised edition continues the tradition of solid empirical support for the SVIB-SCII. The instrument was normed on a final sample of 48,000 chosen by special selection criteria from over 140,000 protocols. The manual also reports on some research with rehabilitation populations.

The SVIB-SCII is machine-scored only. A profile report and an interpretive report are provided. In addition, there is a microcomputer system available in IBM and Apple versions.

An exciting innovation is the availability of PATH-FINDER. PATHFINDER is a career exploration program that uses the technologies of laser videodisc and microcomputer to guide students through customized interpretations of their SVIB-SCII results.

REFERENCE

Stanford University. (1985). *Strong-Campbell Interest Inventory* (rev. ed.). Palo Alto: CA: Author.

THOMAS F. HOPKINS
*Center for Behavioral
Psychotherapy, White Plains,
New York*

**HABILITATION
VOCATIONAL REHABILITATION**

STRUCTURE OF INTELLECT

J. P. Guilford (1967), in his work *The Nature of Human Intelligence*, developed a model of intelligence based on his factor analysis of human intellect. The structure of intellect theory (SI) grew out of experimental applications of the multivariate method of multiple-factor analysis. The basic research was carried out on a population of young adults but successive investigations have substantiated Guilford's initial findings with subject samples ranging in age from 5 to 15 years. Implications from this theory and its concepts have led to many new interpretations of already known facts of general significance in psychology.

The major aim of the structure of intellect theory is to give the concept of intelligence a firm, comprehensive, and systematic theoretical foundation. A second aim is to put intelligence within the mainstream of general psychological theory. For his frame of reference, Guilford has chosen what he terms a morphological, as opposed to hierarchical, model. His model, which he also refers to as the "three faces of intellect," includes three categories along with their subclassifications. The three dimensions are content, referring to types of information that are discriminable by the individual; products, the outcomes of intellectual operations; and operations, referring to the primary kinds of intellectual activities or processes.

The model or cube is a three-dimensional diagram. The operations dimension is broken down into five subclassifications: evaluation, convergent production, divergent production, memory, and cognition. The six types of products are units, classes, relations, systems, transformations, and implications. The four types of content are figural, symbolic, semantic, and behavioral. The complete schema is diagrammed as an array of 120 (5 × 4 × 6) predicted cells of intellectual abilities. The 120 types of abilities are derived from the intersection of the three-way classification system. Of the 120 discrete factors, at least 82 have been demonstrated; others are still under investigation.

Although Guilford's model has not been widely used, it has pointed to a theory that has been lacking from the beginning of the era of mental testing—i.e., to give the concept of intelligence a firm, comprehensive, and systematic theoretical foundation. Guilford maintains that a firm foundation must be based on detailed observation; that the theory itself should include all aspects of intelligence; and that the result must be systematic, embracing numerous phenomena within a logically ordered structure. The outcome is his structure of intellect.

REFERENCE

Guilford, J. P. (1967). *The nature of human intelligence.* New York: McGraw-Hill.

CECELIA STEPPE-JONES
*North Carolina Central
University*

**INTELLIGENCE
INTELLIGENCE TESTING**

STUDY OF MATHEMATICALLY PRECOCIOUS YOUTH (SMPY)

The Study of Mathematically Precocious Youth (SMPY) was officially begun on September 1, 1971, by Julian Stanley. Stanley had become intrigued by a 13½-year-old boy who scored extremely well on several standardized mathematics tests. A fear that students such as this one might fail to be identified and appropriately served led Stanley to devise the SMPY at Johns Hopkins University.

The SMPY is geared to the top 1 to 3% of mathematics students in U.S. junior high schools (Johnson, 1983). These students often display swift and comprehensive reasoning, an inclination to analyze mathematical structure, a tendency to deal in the abstract, and an untiring approach to working on mathematics (Heid, 1983). Indeed, students accepted into SMPY are so mathematically advanced that they must score at least 700 on the math portion of the Scholastic Aptitude Test (SAT-M) before their thirteenth birthday (Stanley & Benbow, 1983). Allowances are made for those students who are over 13 years of age. They must score an additional 10 points on the SAT-M for each month of age over 13 years. For example, a student who is 13 years, 2 months, must score at least 720 on the SAT-M before being considered for the SMPY (Stanley & Benbow, 1983).

Once the students have been selected, the goal of the program is to accelerate learning in mathematics. Stanley & Benbow (1982) note that there is no sense in allowing precocious students to languish in slow-paced math classes. Math classes, they feel, should be taught according to individual students' abilities and achievements. Consequently, precocious students should spend less time in math classes, allowing for potential concentration on related topics such as physics (Tursman, 1983). Additionally, by spending less time in math class, mathematically precocious students would spend less time in school. This would allow them to take college courses while still in high school and to enter college at an earlier age (Stanley & Benbow, 1982). This is a goal of SMPY and is strongly emphasized by Stanley as a way to get these students quickly into the work force.

The SMPY is essentially a summer program. Students are identified, evaluated, and selected for the program throughout the year. Once selected, students participate in an eight-week program, meeting one day a week for slightly less than 5 hours per day. Throughout the instruction, the student-teacher ratio never exceeds 1:5 (Stanley, 1980). All instructors are former SMPY graduates and usually range in age from 13 to 20. During this approximately 35-hour program, students will typically demonstrate mastery of material 2 school years beyond where they began (Stanley, 1980).

To achieve such dramatic results, SMPY uses a "diagnostic testing followed by prescriptive instruction" method of instruction (Stanley, 1980; Stanley & Benbow, 1983). An evaluation determines what the student does not know. The instructors then help the student learn the information without taking an entire course (Stanley & Benbow, 1982).

REFERENCES

Heid, M. K. (1983). Characteristics and special needs of the gifted students in mathematics. *Mathematics Teacher, 76,* 221–226.

Johnson, M. L. (1983). Identifying and teaching mathematically gifted elementary school children. *Arithmetic Teacher, 30,* 55–56.

Stanley, J. C. (1980). On educating the gifted. *Educational Researcher, 9,* 8–12.

Stanley, J. C., & Benbow, C. P. (1982). Educating mathematically precocious youth: Twelve policy recommendations. *Educational Researcher, 11,* 4–9.

Stanley, J. C., & Benbow, C. P. (1983). SMPY's first decade: Ten years of posing problems and solving them. *Journal of Special Education, 17,* 11–25.

Tursman, C. (1983). Challenging gifted students. *School Administrator, 40,* cover, 9–10, 12.

JOHN R. BEATTIE
*University of North Carolina,
Charlotte*

ACCELERATION OF GIFTED CHILDREN
ADVANCED PLACEMENT PROGRAM
GIFTED AND TALENTED CHILDREN

STUTTERING

Stuttering effects the fluent, smooth flow of speech emitted by a speaker. Stutterers present a wide variety of symptoms, both visible and hidden. Overtly, they prolong or repeat sounds and repeat words or phrases. In addition, they may demonstrate secondary behaviors such as eye blinking, head jerking, facial grimaces, and muscular tension. Covertly, stutterers may substitute words, avoid situations, or reply with incorrect information to avoid saying certain words.

This complex disorder has perplexed victims and their families as well as professionals since stuttering was first described. It is still not known what causes stuttering and effective treatment has been elusive. Several etiological theories have been put forth (Van Riper, 1971).

The theory of cerebral dominance states that a child is predisposed to stutter because neither side of the brain is dominant in controlling motor activities associated with speaking. This theory evolved from the observation that many children who stutter are left-handed or have converted from left-handed to right-handed. It led to clinical management techniques involving the use of rigidly programmed unilateral motor activities. Although the theory has few followers today, some evidence does exist to support lack of cerebral dominance in some stutterers.

Another theory views stuttering as an inherited predisposition. An early view within this theory was that stuttering was a convulsive disorder related to epilepsy, with instances of stuttering being seizures that could be triggered by emotional stress. Other support for predisposition as a cause of stuttering comes from reports of blood-sugar imbalance in stutterers and differences in basal metabolism and brain waves. Support for the predisposition view comes from the relatively high frequency of stuttering that runs in families.

A popular theory of the etiology of stuttering in the early 1940s was the diagnosogenic-semantogenic theory. Wendell Johnson, the main proponent of this theory, noticed that many children, as they develop speech, experience a period of "normal disfluency." Johnson suggested that if the parents diagnosed the normal disfluency as stuttering, and the child accepted the diagnosis, the chid became a stutterer. Parents and child then responded to the idea of the handicap rather than the actual speaking behavior. Prevention was seen in counseling parents to avoid diagnosing and treatment was based on changing a stutterer's faulty beliefs.

Psychiatrists have viewed stuttering as need for oral gratification, need for anal gratification, covert expression of hostility, a device for gaining attention and sympathy, or an excuse for failure. The views are collectively considered under the topic neurotic theories. Research investigations of these views have been few. Most evidence comes from case reports of a therapist working with a stutterer.

Another theory of stuttering is that it is learned behavior. One view is that an originally unconditioned breakdown in speech fluency becomes associated with a speaker's anxiety about talking. The person then begins to stutter in anxiety-provoking situations and thus becomes classically conditioned. Another view is that stuttering is an approach-avoidance conflict. The stutterer is seen in conflict between the desire to speak and the desire not to speak.

There is a general developmental pattern of stuttering. In the first phase, stuttering is episodic and in response to pressure in the environment. Speech is characterized by repetitions of words or syllables at the beginning of utterances. In the second phase, stuttering becomes more chronic and the child views himself or herself as a stutterer. Disfluency becomes more frequent, especially during conditions of excitement or rapid speech. In the third phase, the stutterer begins to attach fear to certain situations, words, or sounds. The child begins to anticipate stuttering but does little to avoid speaking. In phase four, the stutterer develops fears and fearful anticipation of stuttering. He or she avoids and feels embarrassed by his or her speech.

There are as many treatment approaches to the elimination of stuttering as there are theories concerning the etiology of stuttering. Some of the popular methods (Bloodstein, 1975) include (1) behavior modification, wherein disfluencies are negatively reinforced or fluency is positively reinforced; (2) syllable-timed speech, where the stutterer is asked to speak in a rhythmic sing-song manner that usually produces fluency; (3) speaking with delayed-auditory feedback or masking noise (when a stutterer is deprived of auditory feedback when speaking, he or she is usually more fluent); (4) use of gentle onset, wherein the stutterer is taught to start laryngeal voicing before attempting to speak; and (5) counseling, wherein the therapist attempts to improve the stutterer's self-image.

REFERENCES

Bloodstein, D. (1975). *A handbook on stuttering.* Chicago: National Easter Seal Society for Crippled Children and Adults.

Goldiamond, I. (1964). Stuttering and fluency as manipulable operant classes. In L. Krasner & L. P. Ullman (Eds.), *Research in behavior modification: New Developments and their clinical applications.* New York: Holt, Rinehart, & Winston.

Sheehan, J. G. (1970). *Stuttering: Research and therapy.* New York: Harper & Row.

Van Riper, C. (1971). *The nature of stuttering.* Englewood Cliffs, NJ: Prentice-Hall.

Van Riper, C. (1973). *The treatment of stuttering.* Englewood Cliffs, NJ: Prentice-Hall.

FREDERICK F. WEINER
Pennsylvania State University

SPEECH AND LANGUAGE HANDICAPS
SPEECH INSTRUCTION
SPEECH THERAPY

SUBSTANCE ABUSE

Substance abuse has become the popular phrase to describe the use and abuse of, and dependence on or addiction to, psychoactive substances, including alcohol. This term replaces the now outdated traditional one, drug abuse, which did not include alcoholic beverages. The professional community more frequently uses the term substance abuse to describe the phenomenon of alcohol and other drugs used in society as a social/medical issue. The term substance abuser is used to describe a person who inappropriately uses legal substances or illegal compounds. Readers will also find the term chemical dependency in the literature, but this term is used almost exclusively to describe those persons who are psychologically or physiologically dependent on a mood altering compound, and not simply using or abusing it (Ray, 1978).

The phenomenon of substance abuse describes that aspect of human behavior that involves the use of mood- or mind-altering substances, both chemical and organic. Chemical substances are compounds that are synthesized in a laboratory such as barbiturates, tranquilizers, synthetic narcotics, and hypnotics, to name a few. These compounds require the use of chemical techniques to achieve usable potential. Other compounds are found in nature and require little or no processing to be usable by humans. Examples of these are marijuana, opium, peyote, psilocybin mushrooms, and cocoa leaves. It should be noted that some organics such as opium and cocoa leaves may be chemically processed into semisynthetic compounds to make them more usable or ingestable; heroin and cocaine, respectively, are examples.

As the term has changed to describe more accurately the phenomenon, the nonmedical use of psychoactive compounds has increased nationally at an unprecedented rate. America has had other periods when the use and abuse of psychoactive compounds reached alarming or epidemic proportions. Morphine addiction was prevalent at the turn of the century owing to the widespread use of the drug as an analgesic during and immediately after the Civil War. Alcohol was prohibited at one time in our society because of its detrimental effects, only to be legalized and taxed some years later when continued use by large numbers of citizens made Prohibition infeasible. The introduction of large numbers of "wonder" drugs, and a general reliance on medication to solve minor everyday pains, has developed over the past 25 years. Concurrent with this trend has been a widespread reliance on other psychoactive compounds to enhance social or recreational activities. The generation of the 1960s made recreational drug and alcohol use an integral part of leisure time, a practice still prevalent in the social activities of the youth of today (Cohen, 1983).

Substance abuse is included in the third edition of the *Diagnostic and Statistical Manual of Mental Disorders* (DSM-III; American Psychiatric Association, 1980) as an identifiable mental health problem. The manual notes in its introduction that with regard to any mental health problem, the issue is the classification of disorders, not persons. Substance use disorders are conceptualized as significant psychological or behavioral patterns that occur in individuals. Associated with these patterns is either a painful symptom (distress) or impairment in specific areas of functioning (disability). The DSMfiII further states that substance use disorders focus on the more or less regular use of substances that affect the central nervous system. The manual discriminates between abuse and dependency, but does not specifically define use. Use, per se, is not clinically significant until it creates distress or disability for the individual.

Key concepts in understanding substance abuse include tolerance and withdrawal. Tolerance indicates that the user's body has become chemically dependent on a substance such that larger amounts are required to produce the user's desired outcome. The usual dose of the substance fails to achieve its usual effect. Depending on the substance being used, if an individual is tolerant to a drug and does not take the regular amount used, withdrawal may be experienced. Withdrawal is a condition in which the user has physical signs and symptoms of distress. Based on the user's body weight and size, the potency of the substance used, and the duration of use, the symptoms can be mild, moderate, or severe. The presence of tolerance and the resulting withdrawal symptoms distinguish substance abuse from substance dependence. It should be noted that symptoms of distress can be physical or psychological, again depending on the class of substance being used. Compounds like alcohol, barbiturates, narcotics, and some tranquilizers cause severe impairment in physical and psychological functioning. Compounds like marijuana, LSD, and some types of stimulants create psychological distress but no physical distress.

The proliferation of legal medicines and over-the-counter substances (cough syrups, cold pills, sleep and diet aids), and a growing reliance on alcohol and other illegal compounds (cocaine, marijuana) for social lubrication, will likely result in a continued upward trend in substance use and abuse, resulting in greater numbers of chemically dependent persons. Although modern medicine has given society many wonderful cures and processes to arrest pain and discomfort, the advent of psychoactive compounds, both legal and illegal, continues to be a major scourge on American culture.

REFERENCES

American Psychiatric Association. (1980). *Diagnostic and statistical manual of mental disorders* (3rd ed.). Washington, DC: Author.

Cohen, S. (1983). *The alcoholism problems.* New York: Haworth.

Ray, O. S. (1978). *Drugs, society and human behavior* (2nd ed.). St. Louis: Mosby.

L. Worth Bolton
*Cape Fear Substance Abuse
Center, Wilmington,
North Carolina*

**CHEMICALLY DEPENDENT YOUTH
DRUG ABUSE**

SUBSTANTIA NIGRA

The substantia nigra houses the cell bodies of dopamine containing neurons that project to the striatum (putamen and caudate nucleus). This the so-called nigrostriatal pathway is the major dopamine pathway in the brain. The substantia nigra is a midbrain structure and is darkly pigmented, hence its name (i.e., black substance or black body). The nigrostriatal pathway is an important pathway in the extrapyramidal motor system, which controls background movement. Because of the importance of dopamine in the regulatory control of motor as well as emotional functioning, the nigrostriatal system has been implicated in a variety of neurobehavioral disorders (Andreasen, 1984). In particular, a breakdown of normal functioning of the dopaminergic system has been strongly implicated in schizophrenia (Andreasen, 1984). Also, other lines of investigation have suggested that dopamine plays a role in hyperactivity and attention deficit disorder (Shaywitz, Shaywitz, Cohen, & Young, 1983). The motor maladroitness frequently seen in learning-disabled children may be related in some fashion to basal ganglia/nigrostriatal irregularities (Duane, 1985; Rudel, 1985). The prototype neurologic disorder with primary substantia nigra involvement, and hence dopamine loss, is Parkinson's disease (Kolb & Whishaw, 1985).

REFERENCES

Andreasen, N. C. (1984). *The broken brain.* Cambridge, England: Harper & Row.

Duane, D. (1985). Written language underachievement: An overview of the theoretical and practical issues. In F. H. Duffy & N. Geschwind (Eds.), *Dyslexia: A neuroscientific approach to clinical evaluation.* Boston: Little, Brown.

Kolb, B., & Whishaw, I. Q. (1985). *Fundamentals of human neuropsychology.* New York: Freeman.

Rudel, R. G. (1985). The definition of dyslexia: Language and motor deficits. In F. H. Duffy & N. Geschwind (Eds.), *Dyslexia: A neuroscientific approach to clinical evaluation.* Boston: Little, Brown.

Shaywitz, S. E., Shaywitz, B. A., Cohen, D. J., & Young, J. G. (1983). Monoaminergic mechanisms in hyperactivity. In M. Rutter (Ed.), *Developmental neuropsychiatry.* New York: Guilford.

Erin D. Bigler
*Austin Neurological Clinic
University of Texas, Austin*

**DOPAMINE
PUTAMEN**

SUBTEST SCATTER

Subtest scatter refers to the variability of an individual's subtest scores. The highs and lows of the profile indicate strengths and weaknesses on specific subtests. Differences between composite scores for an individual also are termed scatter. While the term subtest scatter may be aptly applied to any multiple subtest battery of basic skills, reading achievement, adaptive behavior, or other tests, the term has been popularized by its association with intellectual assessment. Exactly what role scatter has in diagnosing and differentiating among populations has not been determined. Is scatter a valid indicator for diagnostic purposes, or is it limited to identifying a subject's abilities and achievements in various areas? The believers in the significance of scatter have developed several diagnostic schemes that can be used to differentiate among populations.

Kaufman (1979) points out that scatter, significant differences in abilities measured by the Wechsler Intelligence Scale for Children (WISC-R), occurs frequently in the normal population. On the basis of this finding, he emphasizes the importance of being certain that the intersubtest variability is indeed rare in comparison with that of normal children before associating the scatter with abnormality. However, certain characteristic scatter has been consistently found for specific groups. Low scores on arithmetic, coding, information, and digit span subtests of the WISC-R have been shown to characterize the performance of many groups of learning-disabled children. However, categorization and profiles of WISC-R scores were reported to have no clinical significance in a recent meta-analysis (Kavale & Forness, 1984). It was concluded that learning disabilities are more likely to be indicated by intraindividual differences than by set profiles.

Bannatyne (1971) suggests that close to 30% of reading-disabled children have a characteristic profile based on subtest scatter. There is a distinct ordering of scores on the WISC-R, spatial (Sp) conceptual (C) sequential (Sq). Because of a familial pattern of reading difficulties, the conclusion was reached that a genetic dyslexic subtype could be identified by the Sp > C > Sq profile. Further investigation into this profile showed that it held for reading-disabled children, but it was not unique to a genetic dyslexic subtype (Decker & Corley, 1984). It has not, however, shown much relationship to other cognitive abilities or academic achievement scores. The profile may be common in reading-disabled groups, but when applied to individual children, it has little diagnostic validity.

Scatter has been applied to problems other than learning disabilities. Different types of mental deficiencies have been described in terms of scatter (Roszkowski & Spreat, 1982). Organically caused mental deficiency exhibited more scatter in Wechsler Adult Intelligence Scale (WAIS) scores than environmentally caused deficiency, but not to a significant degree. Greater scatter may be linked to lower functioning individuals. Large amounts of scatter on intelligence tests can also be associated with high degrees of maladaptive behaviors (Roszkowski & Spreat, 1983) and social-emotional problems (Greenwald, Harder,

& Fisher, 1982). Thus scatter can be associated with behavioral, emotional, and organic disorders, as well as with the more commonly thought of learning disabilities.

There may be evidence linking scatter to various disorders, but it is questionable whether it is strong enough to warrant its use as a diagnostic tool. The greatest portion of the evidence says no (Kavale & Forness, 1984). Subtest scatter may be useful in specifying particular strengths and weaknesses of an individual's performance, and in educational intervention planning. Caution is needed with interpretation of scatter and profile analysis, and flexibility is recommended when selecting tests for a particular population (Kamphaus, 1985).

REFERENCES

Bannatyne, H. (1971). *Language, reading, and learning disabilities*. Springfield, IL: Thomas.

Decker, S. A., & Corley, R. P. (1984). Bannatyne's "genetic dyslexic" subtype: A validation study. *Psychology in the Schools, 21*, 300–304.

Greenwald, D. F., Harder, D. W., & Fisher, L. (1982). WISC scatter and behavioral competence in high-risk children. *Journal of Clinical Psychology, 38*, 397–401.

Kamphaus, R. W. (1985). Perils of profile analysis. *Information/Edge: Cognitive Assessment & Remediation, 1*, 1–4.

Kaufman, A. S. (1979). *Intelligence testing with the WISC-R*. New York: Wiley.

Kavale, K. A., & Forness, S. (1984). A meta-analysis of the validity of Wechsler scale profiles and recategorizations: Patterns or parodies? *Learning Disability Quarterly, 7*, 136–156.

Roszkowski, M., & Spreat, S. (1982). Scatter as an index of organicity: A comparison of mentally retarded individuals experiencing and not experiencing concomitant convulsive disorders. *Journal of Behavioral Assessment, 4*, 311–315.

Roszkowski, M., & Spreat, S. (1983). Assessment of effective intelligence: Does scatter matter? *Journal of Special Education, 17*, 453–459.

LISA J. SAMPSON
Eastern Kentucky University

FACTOR ANALYSIS
PROFILE ANALYSIS
TEST SCATTER
WISC-WISC-R

SUICIDE

Suicide is rare in children, comprising only .02% of the known deaths by suicide in the United States in 1976.

However, during adolescence the rate increases sharply—from 0.8 per 100,000 among 10 to 14 year olds to 7.6 per 100,000 among 15 to 19 year olds (Weiner, 1982). These rates appear to be increasing at an alarmingly rapid rate: from 1962 to 1972 the suicide rate per 100,000 increased by almost 80% among 15 to 24 year olds, in contrast to an increase of approximately 10% in the general population (*Vital Statistics of the United States,* 1963–1976).

The origins of suicide in children and adolescents have been cited as (1) lack of stable support in a home or family situation; (2) family problems that lead the young person to feel powerless and without control of his or her own life; (3) lack of supportive social relationships; and (4) inability to successfully solve problems (Weiner, 1982). Clearly, these factors, singly or in concert, are likely to affect many exceptional children and youths, particularly those who experience institutionalization or social stigmatization. In addition, there are clear parallels between these factors and theories of learned helplessness and depression. Seligman (1975) has defined learned helplessness as the belief that one's actions do not affect or shape one's destiny. It has been further hypothesized that children who grow up with the sense of having little control over their own lives typically feel unable to cope with problem situations and become depressed (Dweck, 1977; Miller & Seligman, 1975).

Recent research dealing with affective disorders among the mentally retarded suggests low levels of social support do lead to depression and learned helplessness within this group (Reiss & Benson, 1985). Reynolds and Miller (1985), in an initial investigation, found educable mentally retarded (EMR) adolescents to be more depressed than their nonretarded peers. In addition, higher than normal rates of suicide have been reported among other exceptional groups, including persons with alcohol and drug abuse problems, for which children and adolescents are at increasingly high risk (Farmer, 1978; McIntire & Angle (1980), and mental illness (Dunham, 1978), a disorder for which the retarded are at high risk (Lewis & MacLean, 1982; Szymanski, 1980).

These factors clearly indicate that exceptional youths constitute a high-risk group for suicide, particularly during mid to late adolescence. Age, the social/familial conditions and absence of control that often develop in consonance with physical or developmental disorders (e.g., living away from home, lack of a supportive peer group, not being involved in making decisions affecting one's life), and the coexistence of additional problems such as mental illness, each place the exceptional child at high risk. For the individual for whom several risk factors occur, the possibility of depression and/or suicide is magnified proportionally.

To reduce the risk of suicide among exceptional children and adolescents, intervention must occur on a basic level, addressing those needs that have been identified as preceding learned helplessness, depression, and suicide.

The construction of stable family or familylike support groups, the involvement of the exceptional individual in planning and control of his or her own life, assistance in forming supportive peer and social relationships, training in problem solving and coping skills, and appropriate treatment for related disorders such as alcohol, drug abuse, or mental illness should substantially reduce the risk of suicide in this population.

REFERENCES

Dunham, C. S. (1978). Mental illness. In R. M. Goldenson, J. R. Dunham, & C. S. Dunham (Eds.), *Disability and rehabilitation handbook.* New York: McGraw-Hill.

Dweck, C. S. (1977). Learned helplessness: A developmental approach. In J. G. Schulterbrandt & A. Raskin (Eds.), *Depression in childhood.* New York: Raven.

Farmer, R. H. (1978). Drug-abuse problems. In R. M. Goldenson, J. R. Dunham, & C. S. Dunham (Eds.), *Disability and rehabilitation handbook.* New York: McGraw-Hill.

Lewis, M. H., & MacLean, W. E., Jr. (1982). Issues in treating emotional disorders. In J. L. Matson & R. P. Barrett (Eds.), *Psychopathology in the mentally retarded* (pp. 1–36). New York: Grune & Stratton.

McIntire, M. S., & Angle, C. R. (1980). *Suicide attempts in children and youth.* New York: Harper & Row.

Miller, W., & Seligman, M. E. P. (1975). Depression and learned helplessness in man. *Journal of Abnormal Psychology, 84,* 228–238.

Reiss, S., & Benson, B. A. (1985). Psychosocial correlates of depression in mentally retarded adults: I. Minimal social support and stigmatization. *American Journal of Mental Deficiency, 89,* 331–337.

Reynolds, W. M., & Miller, K. L. (1985). Depression and learned helplessness in mentally retarded and nonmentally retarded adolescents: An initial investigation. *Applied Research in Mental Retardation, 6,* 295–306.

Seligman, M. E. P. (1975). *Helplessness: On depression, development, and death.* San Francisco: Freeman.

Szymanski, L. S. (1980). Individual psychotherapy with retarded persons. In L. S. Szymanski & R. E. Tanguay (Eds.), *Emotional disorders of mentally retarded persons.* Baltimore, MD: University Park Press.

Vital Statistics of the United States, 1963–1976. Rockville, MD: U.S. Department of Health, Education, and Welfare.

Weiner, I. B. (1982). *Child and adolescent psychopathology.* New York: Wiley.

LAURA KINZIE BRUTTING
J. TODD STEPHENS
*University of Wisconsin,
Madison*

DEPRESSION
EMOTIONAL DISORDERS
LEARNED HELPLESSNESS

SULLIVAN, ANN

See MACY, ANN SULLIVAN.

SULLIVAN PROGRAMMED READING

The Sullivan Programmed Reading system comprises an individualized programmed workbook approach to teaching reading to students in grades one through three. The sequence of the three-year system extends from Reading Readiness through Series III, with diagnostic prescriptive teaching aids and student activities that are designed to optimize individual pacing. Pupils systematically progress from letter discrimination to word recognition or to reading sentences and stories. The first ten weeks of the program are spent in the development of a basic vocabulary and the acquisition of skills that are necessary for the use of programmed material. This part of the series is teacher directed or oriented and must be done as a class or group. Afterward, the program allows each pupil to progress according to his or her own rate of learning. The pupil is provided with a minimal amount of information, a problem is posed, a response is solicited, and the response is corrected or reinforced. The child makes the response, then checks his or her answer against the correct response that is revealed as a slider moves down the page to reveal the next frame (Hafner & Jolly, 1972; Moyle & Moyle, 1971; Scheiner, 1969; Sullivan Associates, 1968).

The Reading Readiness and Programmed Readers Series I, II, and III provide sequential instruction in consonants, vowels, sight words, punctuation, suffixes, contractions, possessives, capitals, and comprehension. Placement tests indicate at which point in the series to enter a pupil who begins in the system after first grade. The Programmed Reading Program is comprised of 23 levels, with one book per level. Pupils progress through each book and are expected to pass an end-of-book test before proceeding to the next book. A total of 3266 words are introduced in the complete program (Hafner & Jolly, 1972; Sullivan Associates, 1968).

The following components of the Sullivan Associates system may be ordered as kits or separately. Reading Readiness consists of two kits, each of which contain two full-color, 72-page Big Books, two comprehensive teacher guides, two hour-long tape cassettes, a set of Webstermasters, and a wire easel and alphabet strips. On completion of the prereading stage, the child should master (1) the names of letters; (2) how to write letters; (3) the sounds that represent letters; (4) left to right sequencing; (5) the concept that words are formed from groups of letters; and (6) the ability to read the words *yes* or *no* in sentences. Series I, II, and III Programmed Readers Books 1 to 23 provide logical linguistic progression, constant reinforcement, colorful art, and stimulating story content. By the end of the eighth book in Series I, 14 vowels and 23 consonant classes will have been mastered; in addition, children will know approximately 450 words phonetically and 10 sight words. On completion of Series III, 25 more vowels and consonant classes, a total of 3200 new words, and 40 more sight words, will have been mastered.

Two sets of seven filmstrips that are primarily designed to introduce the readers to new words supplement Books 1 to 14. Each filmstrip reviews material from the previous level and presents new vocabulary and characters. Three sets of Activity Books reinforce ideas provided by the programmed series through cutout patterns for characters, puppets, and games. Webstermasters allow duplications to supplement each series of programmed readers. Read and Think Series are provided for Series I and II and are to be read after completion of the programmed text to motivate children to read for enjoyment. Achievement tests (criterion-referenced) measure student progress in terms of predetermined behavioral objectives for each series. There is an item-by-item analysis of the skills tested and specific remediation for each item that is missed. Word cards and response booklets allow pupils to write their answers using a wax pencil or crayon, making the tests reusable. Teachers' guides are organized by book, skill, and unit. An overview of decoding and comprehension information, and a listing of the sound-symbol and vocabulary progression and content summary, are outlined. Each grade also contains a reading aloud, dictation, creative writing, and test section for each book level, and specific item-by-item instructions for both with remediative recycling options (Sullivan & Associates, 1968). For uses with exceptional children, see Lerner (1985).

REFERENCES

Hafner, L., & Jolly, H. (1972). *Patterns of teaching reading in the elementary school.* New York: Macmillan.

Lerner, J. (1985). *Learning disabilities: Theories, diagnosis and teaching strategies* (4th ed.). Dallas: Houghton Mifflin.

Moyle, D., & Moyle, L. (1971). *Modern innovations in the teaching of reading.* London: University of London Press.

Scheiner, L. (1969). *An evaluation of the Sullivan Reading Program (1967–1969) Rhoads Elementary School,* Washington D.C.: U.S. Department of Health, Education and Welfare. (ERIC Document Reproduction Service ED 002 362).

Sullivan Associates. (1968). *Sullivan Associates programmed reading Sullivan Press.* New York: McGraw-Hill.

FRANCES T. HARRINGTON
Radford University

READING DISORDERS
READING REMEDIATION

SUMMER SCHOOL FOR THE HANDICAPPED

Extended-year programs for individuals with handicapping conditions have been a highly debated issue for many years. The position of many individuals is that extended school year programs are needed for students with handicapping conditions to prevent the loss of existing skills, accelerate the acquisition of new skills, and provide recreational programming and respite care for the parents. There are several main questions for which there are no appropriate answers: (1) Do extended school year programs accomplish instructional objectives and, if so, how much? (2) If students do learn something, is it additive to what is learned during the school year? (3) Do students without extended school years lose skills or do they increase maladaptive (i.e., irritant) responding? (4) Do students without extended school years catch up to students who do experience extended school year programming and thus negate the effect of the extended year? (5) If students with extended school years do have additive learning, is the cost effectiveness of that learning acceptable? (6) What types of extended school years (e.g., school, school plus recreational, recreational, short programs, long programs) have what types of effects, and what are the desired effects (e.g., retention, gain, degree of gain)? (7) What are the "doability" variables (e.g., What teachers and aides will be involved? Is burnout an issue? Who will supervise? (8) How will documentation be provided? (9) Is there student burnout, etc.

There are some other questions that do have answers. First, do handicapped students have a right to a public education? Public Law 94-142, and Section 504 of the Rehabilitation Act of 1973, have defined the right of handicapped children to a free appropriate public education. Second, do specific classes of handicapped students have a right to an extended school year? The courts have substantiated the right of specific classes of handicapped children to extended (over 180-day) school year programs in a number of court cases (e.g., *Armstrong* v. *Kline*, 1979). Additional cases are currently pending throughout the United States. Therefore, while there is growing educational and legal support for extended-year programming, many questions still need to be addressed.

Empirical support for the current policy on extended-year programs for individuals with handicaps is difficult to find in the literature. Browder, Lentz, Knoster, and Wilansky (1984) found that the primary methodology for determining both eligibility for and effectiveness of extended-year programs was the subjective judgments of teachers and parents (Bahling, 1980; McMahon, 1983). This information, while not surprising, does not provide empirical support for extended school year programming. Ellis (1975a) studied the effects of a summer program on possible regression of 16 multihandicapped blind children, and found that none of the students had regressed in eight target skill areas (e.g., communication skills). In a second study, Ellis (1975b) examined the skill levels of 145 physically and neurologically handicapped students and found a significant improvement in skill areas for the summer program participants. In contrast, Edgar, Spence, and Kenowitz (1977), in a study that examined the findings of 18 summer programs, found that the data (e.g., teacher observations, rating scales) did not strongly support the premise that such programs facilitated the maintenance of skills. However, these results are possible when there is not a coherence between the school year objectives and those of the summer program. Therefore, there are conflicting data concerning the effectiveness of extended-year programming in either maintaining or extending the learning repertoire of handicapped students.

In a recent study, Zdunich (1984) reported on data gathered on extended-year programs in Canada. This study examined the effects of four types of summer programming (short programs, high-structure, low-structure, and medium-structure programs). A control group that received no summer programming was also used in the study. While the study's sample size was relatively small (overall $n = 186$), its results were interesting. First, the study found that maladaptive behaviors had been significantly reduced only in the high- and medium-structure programs and that students in the other conditions increased maladaptive responding. Second, skill development (e.g., communication, self-help, fine motor skills) was significantly greater in high- and medium-structure programs. Other types of summer experiences showed relative maintenance of skills with some small amount of skill regression. In addition, the skill acquisition data held constant over the following academic year. The study also examined many variables related to each of these two major concerns. It should provide a substantial increase in our database on the educational and social impact of extended school year programming.

REFERENCES

Bahling, E. (1980). *Extended school year program, Intermediate Unit #5, June–August, 1980*. Paper presented at the annual international convention of Council for Exceptional Children, Philadelphia. (ERIC Document Reproduction Service No. 208 609).

Browder, D. M., Lentz, F. E., Knoster, T., & Wilansky, C. (1984). *A record based evaluation of extended school year eligibility practice*. Unpublished manuscript.

Edgar, E., Spence, W., & Kenowitz, L. (1977). Extended school year for the handicapped: Is it working? *Journal of Special Education, 11*, 441–447.

Ellis, R. S. (1975a). Summer pre-placement program for severely multihandicapped blind children. *Summer 1975, Evaluation Report*. New York City Board of Education. (ERIC Document Reproduction Service No. ED136489).

Ellis, R. S. (1975b). Summer education program for neurologically and physically handicapped children *Summer 1975, Evaluation Report*. New York City Board of Education. (ERIC Document Reproduction Service No. ED136489).

McMahon, J. (1983). Extended school year programs. *Exceptional Children, 49*, 457-460.

Zdunich, L. (1984). *Summer programs for the severely handicapped*. Edmonton, Alberta, Canada: Alberta Education.

LYLE E. BARTON
Kent State University

TUTORING

SUPERVISION IN SPECIAL EDUCATION

Current emphasis in special education is on the employment of a program administrator specifically for exceptional children. Other titles used are special education director and supervisor of exceptional children's programs. For most states, the administrator or director of special education must have an academic degree at the master's level in the education of exceptional children or a related field. Owing to the nature of the position, it is also helpful if this person completes the requirements for a supervisor's or administrator's certificate in addition to the master's degree in special education. The educational program for the preparation of exceptional children's program administrators is basically the same as for preparing general school administrators. The major difference in their preparation is in the specific exceptional children's program content requirement.

The exceptional children's program administrator has been identified by the North Carolina Division for Exceptional Children as

> one who plans, develops, coordinates, supervises, administers, and evaluates the effectiveness of local educational agency's educational programs. The program administrator provides guidance and leadership to all exceptional children program personnel. The role is performed under the general supervision of the superintendent or designee. The program administrator maintains a cooperative relationship with principals, other school personnel, other related service agencies, and parents. The administrator is responsible for maintaining the program within local, state, and federal guidelines, rules, regulations, and laws which govern exceptional children.

Program administrators should have competencies in the administration of exceptional children's programs, including assessment; planning and implementing programs; budgeting; communicating with parents, central office staff, principals, other service providers, and state and local agencies; staff development; and program evaluation. Another area of expertise necessary for program administrators is the application of school law adminis-

tration of exceptional children's programs. This includes knowledge of legislation about the handicapped as it relates to PL 94-142; other state and federal statutes; confidentiality guidelines; due process procedures; procedures for auditing and evaluating compliance; authority of the hearing officer; and schools' responsibility for various placements, transportation, suspension and expulsion, related services, competency tests, and evaluations.

Program administrators should be well versed in supervision of instruction centered around personnel management. He or she should be able to interview and select qualified exceptional children's teachers, observe and evaluate teachers to identify teaching strengths and weaknesses, and develop professional growth plans for teachers and support staff. The administrator should be able to design instructional units that specify performance objectives, instructional sequences, learning activities, and materials and evaluation processes, and prepare an educational plan that includes curriculum content and level, activities, alternative teaching strategies, and evaluation of learning outcomes. The program administrator should also be able to evaluate the quality, utility, and availability of learning resource materials.

REFERENCES

Comprehensive system of personnel development report. (1984, August). Raleigh: Division for Exceptional Children, North Carolina Department of Public Instruction.

Competencies and guidelines for approved teacher education programs. (1983, September). Raleigh: Division for Exceptional Children, North Carolina Department of Public Instruction.

CECELIA STEPPE-JONES
North Carolina Central University

ADMINISTRATION OF SPECIAL EDUCATION
POLITICS, SPECIAL EDUCATION AND

SUPPORTED EMPLOYMENT

Supported employment is a vocational alternative that has been described in rules published by the U.S. Department of Education in the *Federal Register* (June 18, 1985) as "paid work in a variety of integrated settings, particularly regular work sites, especially designed for severely handicapped individuals irrespective of age or vocational potential." Traditionally, individuals with severe disabilities have been served in day activity centers in which the intended goal is to prepare these clients for vocational rehabilitation services and, ultimately, employment. However, this readiness model of service delivery has not prepared these individuals successfully for vocational rehabilitation services or employment. Supported employment provides employment opportunities to those individuals with mental and physical disabilities so severe that they are not eligible for vocational rehabilitation services.

Supported employment (Will, 1985) includes four characteristics that differentiate it from vocational rehabilitation services and traditional methods of providing day activity services. First, the service recipients are those typically served in day activity centers who do not have the potential for unassisted competitive employment and thus are ineligible for vocational rehabilitative services. Second, ongoing support, which is unavailable in a traditional day activity program, as well as supervision and ongoing training is involved. Supported employment is not designed to lead to unassisted competitive work as are vocational rehabilitation programs. Third, the employment focus of supported employment provides the same benefits typically obtained by people from work (e.g. income, security, mobility, advancement opportunities, etc.). It does not seek to identify and teach prerequisite skills and behaviors needed for employment as is usually done in day activity centers. Last, there is flexibility in support strategies to assist individuals with severe disabilities in obtaining and maintaining employment. This may include the provision of a "job coach" by a community agency. The coach provides training and supervision at an individual's work site, direct support to employers to offset training and special equipment costs, or salary supplements to coworkers who provide regular assistance in the performance of personal care activities while at work.

Federal initiatives have provided the impetus for the development of supported employment programs. These programs vary according to client characteristics, community resources, and employment opportunities. Options for supported employment are flexible owing to the wide range of community jobs and the variety of ways to provide support to individuals with severe diabilities (McCarthy, Everson, Moon, Barcus, 1985). The features common to various supported employment program options are emphasis on paid employment, ongoing support and training that enables individuals with severe handicaps to get and keep a job, and social integration in which these individuals are provided with opportunities to work and interact with coworkers, supervisors, and other nondisabled individuals (Password, 1985). Examples of four supported employment options are enclaves, mobile work crews, specialized industrial programs, and supported competitive employment. A brief discussion of each follows.

An enclave is an industry-based option that relies on private and public sector cooperation to create an organizational structure that supports the employment of individuals with severe disabilities. While a wide range of alternatives is possible with this service model, an enclave is a group of individuals with disabilities who are provided training and support by a third-party public organization among nonhandicapped workers in a private company.

Rhodes and Valenta (1985) describe the ideal enclave as having the following characteristics. Enclave employees are located in physical proximity to coworkers and represent approximately 1% of the total work force. Enclave employees perform the same work, have the same work routines (work hours, breaks, lunch), and are supervised in the same manner as their nonhandicapped coworkers. They are employed by the host company and arrive at work via car pools with coworkers or public or company transportation. Finally, the support organization maintains low visibility and intervenes only when necessary to maintain and support employment.

Mobile work crews are community-based employment groups that usually involve four to six individuals and a crew supervisor working together on various job sites (Bourbeau, 1985). As the title indicates, these work crews operate out of a vehicle and move from one work site to the next. The work performed by the crews is specific to community needs any may entail a variety of jobs such as janitorial work or grounds maintenance (Bourbeau, 1985). Since the job site is in the community, integration and interaction is fostered (interaction with people in the community, eating in community restaurants, etc.).

Another supported work option is described by O'Bryan (1985), the benchwork model. This model was developed at the University of Oregon in 1973 as a small, nonprofit business and since has been replicated at 17 sites. The benchwork model shares many of features and constraints with traditional sheltered workshops, although it is designed for persons with more severe disabilities. The major differences are the size and location of the operation. Only 15 individuals with severe or profound disabilities are employed. The location in the community close to stores and restaurants provides the opportunity for regular participation in the surrounding community. Training in skills that relate to a typical working day are provided with the major foci on those skills necessary to experience the regular daily, weekly, and monthly rhythms of the community. One of the major constraints, however, is that job security, benefits, and integration depend on the organization's commercial success.

The fourth option, a supported competitive employment program, has been defined by Wehman (1985) as real work at the federal minimum wage at a job with predominantly nonhandicapped workers. The provision of specialized assistance in locating an appropriate job, intensive job-site training, and permanent ongoing support at the level required by the individual are components of this option.

Supported work options have been initiated at state and local levels to meet the vocational needs of individuals with severe disabilities. The purpose of these work options is to provide these individuals with real work opportunities and the support necessary for them to keep their jobs. The assumption is that all persons, regardless of the severity of their disabilities, have the ability to work as long as appropriate, ongoing services are provided.

REFERENCES

Bourbeau, P. E. (1985). Mobile work crews: An approach to achieve long-term supported employment. In P. McCarthy, J. Everson, S. Moon, & M. Barcus (Eds.), *School-to-work transition for youth with severe disabilities* (pp. 151–166). Richmond, VA: Rehabilitation Research and Training Center, Virginia Commonwealth University.

McCarthy, P., Everson, J., Moon, S., & Barcus, M. (Eds.). (1985). *School-to-work transition for youth with severe disabilities.* Richmond, VA: Rehabilitation Research and Training Center, Virginia Commonwealth University.

O'Bryan, A. (1985). The specialized training program (STP) benchwork model. In P. McCarthy, J. Everson, S. Moon, & M. Barcus (Eds.), *School-to-work transition for youth with severe disabilities* (pp. 183–194). Richmond, VA: Rehabilitation Research and Training Center, Virginia Commonwealth University.

Password. (1985, Autumn). *Office of Special Education and Rehabilitative Services (OSERS) News in Print, 1*(1), 2.

Rhodes, L. E., & Valenta, L. (1985). Enclaves in industry. In P. McCarthy, J. Everson, S. Moon, & M. Barcus (Eds.), *School-to-work transition for youth with severe disabilities* (pp. 129–149). Richmond, VA: Rehabilitation Research and Training Center, Virginia Commonwealth University.

Wehman, P. (1985). Supported competitive employment for persons with severe disabilities. In P. McCarthy, J. Everson, S. Moon, & M. Barcus (Eds.), *School-to-work transition for youth with severe disabilities* (pp. 167–182). Richmond, VA: Rehabilitation Research and Training Center, Virginia Commonwealth University.

Will, M. (1985, Autumn). Supported employment programs: Moving from welfare to work. *Office of Special Education and Rehabilitative Services (OSERS) News in Print, 1*(1), 8–9.

EILEEN F. MCCARTHY
*University of Wisconsin,
Madison*

TRANSITION
VOCATIONAL REHABILITATION

SUPPORTED WORK

Supported work was a term first used to describe a national Manpower Development Research Corporation demonstration project designed to provide transitional work training for hard-to-employ individuals (Krauss & MacEachron, 1982). However, supported work, in the context of special education (Rehabilitation Research and Training Center at Virginia Commonwealth University and the Specialized Training Program at the University of Oregon, 1985) has come to refer to a form of employment that has all the usual outcomes (e.g., wages, benefits, job security), rather than a service designed to develop vocational skills. Supported work involves providing a person with the ongoing support necessary to obtain and maintain a job in a socially integrated context where relationships can develop with people who do not have disabilities and who are not paid caregivers.

There seems to be considerable flexibility built into the supported work model to accommodate a range of outcomes in terms of amount of wages earned and degree of integration. Acceptable outcomes can range from one disabled person working for more than minimum wage in a setting with no other disabled workers to a group of disabled individuals performing bench work for less than minimum wage in a setting that allows social integration only during lunch and breaks.

Supported work has emerged as a viable alternative for severely disabled adults because of dissatisfaction with adult day programs and sheltered workshops. The growth in adult day programs has been enormous because of the movement toward deinstitutionalization and community-based programs. From 1964 to 1980 the number of programs in the United States grew from 65, serving approximately 3200 people, to 1989, serving over 105,000 (Bellamy, Sheehan, Horner & Boles, 1980). However, these programs do not typically provide vocational services even though research (Bellamy, Peterson, & Close, 1975; Gold, 1972; O'Neill & Bellamy, 1978) has clearly shown that severely disabled individuals are capable of performing diverse vocational skills. Other research has shown that many severely disabled individuals can perform real work in integrated settings at competitive wage rates (Bellamy, Inman, & Yates, 1978; Wehman et al., 1982), yet sheltered workshops or work activity programs, even though they do provide vocational services, have generally not been capable of providing meaningful work in integrated settings for substantive wages (Whitehead, 1979).

There are documented and theoretical benefits associated with supported work for both clients and society. The most obvious and direct benefit for clients is that they earn considerably more money when engaging in supported work (Rhodes & Valenta, 1985) that provides the resources necessary to access a community's recreational activities where integrated social interaction is likely to occur. Supported work also increases the likelihood of developing integrated social relationships with nondisabled coworkers. Society benefits in terms of a net cost savings owing to lower Social Security payments, lower costs of alternative programming, and the payment of income and sales taxes (Hill & Wehman, 1983).

REFERENCES

Bellamy, G. T., Inman, D., & Yates, J. (1978). Evaluation of a procedure for production management with the severely retarded. *Mental Retardation, 17,* 37–41.

Bellamy, G. T., Peterson, L., & Close, D. (1975). Habilitation of the severely and profoundly retarded: Illustrations of competence. *Education & Training of the Mentally Retarded, 10,* 174–186.

Bellamy, G. T., Sheehan, M. R., Horner, R. H., & Boles, S. M. (1980). Community programs for severely handicapped adults: An analysis. *Journal of the Association for the Severely Handicapped, 5,* 307–324.

Gold, M. W. (1972). Stimulus factors in skill training on a complex assembly task: Acquisition, transfer and retention. *American Journal of Mental Deficiency, 76,* 517–526.

Hill, M., & Wehman, P. (1983). Cost benefit analysis of placing moderately and severely handicapped individuals into competitive employment. *Journal of the Association for the Severely Handicapped, 8,* 30–38.

Krauss, M. W., & MacEachron, A. E. (1982). Competitive employment training for mentally retarded adults: The supported work model. *American Journal of Mental Deficiency, 86,* 650–653.

O'Neill, C., & Bellamy, G. T. (1978). Evaluation of a procedure for teaching saw chain assembly to a severely retarded woman. *Mental Retardation, 16,* 37–41.

Rehabilitation Research and Training Center at Virginia Commonwealth University and the Specialized Training Program at the University of Oregon. (1985). *Perspectives on supported work* (Vol. 2). Richmond, VA: Author.

Rhodes, L. E., & Valenta, M. A. (1985). Industry-based supported employment: An enclave approach. *Journal of the Association for Persons with Severe Handicaps, 10,* 12–20.

Wehman, P., Hill, M., Goodall, P., Cleveland, P., Brooke, V., & Pentecost, J. (1982). Job placement and follow-up of moderately and severely handicapped individuals after three years. *Journal of the Association for the Severely Handicapped, 7,* 5–16.

Whitehead, C. (1979). Sheltered workshops in the decade ahead: Work, wages or welfare. In G. T. Bellamy, G. O'Connor, & O. C. Karan (Eds.), *Vocational rehabilitation of severely handicapped persons: Contemporary service strategies.* Baltimore, MD: University Park Press.

JOHN O'NEILL
Hunter College, City University of New York

ADULT HANDICAPPED
ADULT PROGRAMS FOR THE DISABLED
SHELTERED WORKSHOPS
VOCATIONAL REHABILITATION

SURROGATE PARENTS

Public Law 94-142, the Education for All Handicapped Children Act, included parental participation as a major component in the educational planning for handicapped children. The purpose of including parents was to ensure that the rights of the child and the parents are protected. This component of PL 94-142 officially recognized the parents as a crucial and viable force in the life of their child

and required their input in the educational planning and decision-making process. However, there are instances when a handicapped child's parents, for various reasons, are unable to represent him or her in the educational decision-making process. This is when the public agency responsible for educating the child appoints a surrogate parent. According to federal regulations, a surrogate parent is appointed when (1) no parent can be identified; (2) the public agency, after reasonable efforts, cannot discover the whereabouts of a parent; or (3) the child is a ward of the state under the laws of that state (*Federal Register,* 1977 p. 42496).

Surrogate parents are individuals who are responsible for ensuring that the handicapped child receives a free appropriate education in the least restrictive environment. The surrogate parents' role is limited to the educational needs of the child. Specifically, the role of the surrogate parents, based on the federal regulations, relates to

(1) The identification, evaluation, and educational placement of the child. . . .

(2) The provision of a free appropriate education to the child. . . . The public agency may select a surrogate parent in any way permitted by state law. The public agencies shall insure that a person selected as surrogate has no interest that conflicts with the interests of the child he or she represents; and has knowledge and skills that ensure adequate representation of the child. The person who is appointed as a surrogate parent cannot be an employee of the public agency that is directly involved in the education and care of the child. (*Federal Register,* 1977 p. 42496)

Shrybman (1982) listed the following rights of surrogate parents:

1. Review all written records regarding the child's education
2. Take part in the evaluation and development of the individual education plan (IEP)
3. Reject, accept, or recommend changes in the IEP
4. Request and/or initiate a second evaluation
5. Initiate mediation, hearing, or appeals procedures
6. Receive legal help at no cost if such assistance is necessary in the furtherance of the surrogate's responsibilities
7. Monitor the child's program
8. Recommend changes in the pupil's placement
9. Take advantage of all the rights afforded to natural parents in the special education decision-making process (pp. 267–268)

Each state is required to develop specific requirements for the selection of the surrogate parents. Once the need has been proven by the local agency, the criteria and responsibilities are specifically defined. A surrogate parent does not have to be a professional person; however, it is important that the surrogate have a general knowledge of state and federal laws relating to the handicapped. In addition, knowledge of the rules and regulations of the public school system and specific information about the child's handicap and educational needs are crucial areas. The state is responsible for education and training of the surrogate parent to ensure adequate representation of the child.

The surrogate parent has many responsibilities that must be understood and explained by the local agency. Knowledge of these responsibilities are essential if the educational needs of the child are to be met in the least restrictive environment. A surrogate parent may be dismissed from his or her role if the local agency determines that the roles and responsibilities outlined by federal and state regulations have been neglected, or the well being of the child is at risk. Shrybman (1982) listed the responsibilities of surrogate parents of handicapped children: to attend any training program the local agency offers; to be sure there are no areas of interest that conflict with their responsibilities to the child; to be involved in identification, evaluation, program development, initial placement, review placement, and reevaluation; to be knowledgeable of the child's educational needs, wishes, and concerns; to maintain confidentiality of all records; to be aware of support provided by human services in the community; and to be sure the child is receiving special education in the least restrictive environment.

REFERENCES

Federal Register. (1977). Washington, DC: U.S. Government Printing Office.

Shrybman, J. A. (1982). *Due process in special education*. Rockville, MD: Aspen.

JANICE HARPER
North Carolina Central University

EDUCATION FOR ALL HANDICAPPED CHILDREN ACT OF 1975
PARENT EDUCATION
PARENTS OF THE HANDICAPPED

SURVIVAL SKILLS

Survival skills are essential components of functional teaching. Many educators use the terms survival skills and functional teaching synonymously. Heward and Orlansky (1984) define functional skills as skills that are "frequently demanded in a student's natural environment" (p. 340). Cassidy and Shanahan (1979) suggest the term survival emphasizes the need to develop skills that

will help individuals to attain personal goals and social responsibilities. A few examples of survival skills include balancing a checkbook, riding a bus, completing a job application, reading a menu, and shopping for groceries.

Sabatino (1982) emphasized the importance of the functional curriculum model to prepare the handicapped youth for a vocational career. Examples of survival skills from this model include a word list from a driver's manual, social skills training, and using technical terms to understand career information. McDowell (1979) further stressed the need for handicapped adolescents to exhibit specific behaviors to help them function successfully in today's society and on the job. These behaviors include showing respect for others, demonstrating good manners, knowing when certain behaviors are appropriate, and learning to accept and follow directions.

Sabatino and Lanning-Ventura (1982) state that there is an important question that must be addressed by teachers of educationally handicapped students at the secondary level. When should the educational program focus on survival skills and not on overcoming educational handicaps? The answer to this question should be based on the individual characteristics of the student. However, functional teaching is most appropriate when the chances for academic gains are limited.

An essential component of survival skills in the area of reading is selection of materials. Cassidy and Shanahan (1979) identified the three basic critera for selection as relevance, necessity, and frequency. Relevance implies considering the student's age, current level of functioning, and geographical area when selecting materials. In terms of geographical area, using materials such as a phone book or a bus schedule from a student's hometown is more appropriate than using commercial materials. Necessity suggests selecting materials that are representative of tasks required in the real world. Frequency deals with the number of times the student will deal with the materials selected. Activities such as reading menus and container labels occur often in the real world.

Potential strengths of the functional curriculum model identified by Alley and Deshler (1979) include the following: (1) students are equipped to function independently, at least over the short term in society; (2) students may be better prepared to compete for specific jobs on graduation from high school; and (3) instruction in the functional curriculum may have particular relevance for the high school junior or senior who is severely disabled (p. 50).

REFERENCES

Alley, G., & Deshler, D. (1979). *Teaching the learning disabled adolescent: Strategies and methods*. Denver: Love.

Cassidy, J., & Shanahan, T. (1979). Survival skills: Some considerations. *Journal of Reading, 23*, 136–40.

Heward, H. L., & Orlansky, M. D. (1984). *Exceptional children*. Columbus OH: Merrill.

McDowell, R. L. (1979, May). *The emotionally disturbed adolescent* (PRISE Reporter, No. 3) (pp. 1–2). King of Prussia, PA: Pennsylvania Resource and Information Center for Special Education.

Sabatino, D. A. (1982). An educational program guide for secondary schools. In D. A. Sabatino & L. Mann (Eds.), *Diagnostic and prescriptive teaching*. Rockville, MD: Aspen.

Sabatino, D. A., & Lanning-Ventura, S. (1982). Functional teaching: Survival skills and tutoring. In D. A. Sabatino & L. Mann (Eds.), *Diagnostic and prescriptive teaching*. Rockville, MD: Aspen.

JANICE HARPER
*North Carolina Central
University*

FUNCTIONAL INSTRUCTION
FUNCTIONAL SKILLS

SWEDEN, SPECIAL EDUCATION IN

In the beginning of the nineteenth century, the first faint attempts toward special education of handicapped pupils were made. First, there came an interest in the education of deaf and blind children. In the middle of the nineteenth century, special education for mentally retarded children started, and in 1879, the first remedial class for slow learners was created. In 1942 the first central directives for arranging remedial classes were issued.

The education of handicapped children can be divided into three stages of development: (1) the undifferentiated stage; (2) the stage of differentiation; and (3) the stage of integration.

In stage (1), handicapped children were educated together regardless of age or handicapping condition, therefore attempts at support were inadequate. During stage (2), the handicapped child was educated in special classes or special schools that offered more systematic observations of the child. There were classes for slow learners, hearing- or vision-impaired pupils, and physically disabled pupils, and observation classes for pupils with adjustment difficulties and behavioral disturbances. In addition, remedial reading and extended reception classes were offered. One drawback, however, was that the child in a special class was isolated from nonhandicapped children and placed in an overprotected environment.

With the introduction of the 9-year compulsory school in 1969 (age group 7 to 16 years), special education became more adjusted to the individual capacity of the pupil; this meant an integration (stage 3). The pupil was to get individual teaching according to individual capacity within the framework of the class.

In the compulsory school curriculum of 1980 it is stated that the school should develop toward "one school for everybody," and that the school should have the responsibility for pupils with disabilities and for those who belong to different minorities. The remedial teaching of these pupils by the special teacher should be only one part of a teamwork required, which includes all the personnel within the work unit and parents and recreation instructors outside the framework of the school. Special education is defined as an interdisciplinary branch of knowledge.

Within the school management area, there is a division into joint classes; these classes plan the support for pupils with difficulties. Pupil case conferences establish the measures to be taken with the pupil and his or her parents. The team identifies the problems and sets up the remedial program and later the evaluation. The school psychologist and the special teacher do the assessment and testing together. The social worker studies the social relations and the school doctor and nurse are responsible for the health of the child.

There are several ways of delivering special education in Sweden. Small groups for pupils who need special support for a short while can be arranged. A student can study special subjects for a longer period than normal. A pupil can get help with homework at school if he or she cannot do it at home. In addition, conversation groups on different subjects can be organized. A student with severe learning disabilities might need more than one semester (the school year in Sweden consists of two semesters) in a special group. Special education groups are arranged for pupils with severe physical handicaps; pupils with social and emotional disturbances; and pupils with other severe learning disabilities.

The special teacher can be attached to one or more joint classes. There can also be a special teacher for one school or for one school management area, or attached to a special education group or to a special day school. The role of the remedial teacher is of great importance. This person contributes above all to the planning of the education with in-depth knowledge about functionally handicapped pupils and the effects of different environmental factors and intervention programs on improving the possibilities for development and learning.

Special education is given to certain pupils who cannot participate in ordinary school work because of long-term illness or handicap. Their teaching takes place in a hospital, in the home, or at some other suitable place.

Because of adjustment difficulties, language problems, and isolation, learning disabilities may arise for immigrant children. It is of great importance for the school not only to make these children work well at school but also to make them feel part of the community. They are given auxiliary lessons in the Swedish language and also in their native language.

There are special schools for deaf children, for children with severe vision impairment, and for children with severe speech and language retardation. Most of the pupils that are functionally handicapped, however, go to ordinary classes or, in some cases, to special teaching groups within the local compulsory school. Generally, physically disabled children can attend an ordinary school, but for some of them special measures must be taken. They can also be educated in special classes or in special teaching groups placed in the regional habilitation center. Medical care, speech therapy, physiotherapy, instruction in the activities of daily living, and occupational therapy are included in the training program.

For certain handicaps (mainly for physically disabled pupils and visually impaired pupils), the school offers a personal assistant to help students transport themselves. However, the personal assistant must stress self-help and not overprotection.

For severely visually impaired children, there are two governmental schools, but most of those children attend local compulsory schools. Their teachers take an extra training course to be able to care for them adequately. There are several governmental special schools for severely hearing-impaired children with extended school attendance (10 years). The local school offers education in special groups with only hearing-impaired students in classrooms with special equipment.

There is one governmental special school for children with severe speech defects and audially impaired children with behavioral and other difficulties. However, most of the children with speech problems attend ordinary schools and are given remedial teaching by the speech therapists already in preschool. If the speech-retarded child has not been normalized by the age of compulsory school, he or she will be given special education as long as it is needed.

For children who have learning difficulties because of mental retardation, the county council takes care of the organization of special schools, which include preschools, 10-year compulsory schools, or, for those who are severely handicapped, schools for training of sensory development and social and practical skills or vocational schools. Some of the best pupils are able to be integrated in the ordinary compulsory schools with, for example, personal assistants.

Special education also includes preschools for children with different handicaps. Recently the first preschool for severely language-retarded children was started in Sweden.

The government gives grants for special education of handicapped children. Of the maximum special resource of 0.3 period per week per student for special education, 0.24 period per week per student was used during the school year of 1983–1984.

In order to have a holistic approach to special education in Sweden, the teachers need more in-depth knowledge of different subjects. The future special teacher must be able to act as a coordinator within the school management area and must attend to the allocation of resources, assessment, the psychosocial environment of the school, and collaboration with other authorities such as the police, social services, and child psychiatric clinics.

REFERENCES

Arte, H., Berglund, L. (1985). *Specialpedagogik*. Lund, Sweden: Studentlitteratur.

Emanuelsson, I. (1983). *Verksamhet bland elever med svårigheter eller arbete med elevers svårigheter*. Stockholm: Skolöverstyrelsen.

Holmberg, L. (1983). *Om en speciallärares vardag: Analys av en dagbok*. Lund, Sweden: CWK Gleerup.

Jönsson, T., Karlerö, L.-I. (1977). *Specialundervisning*. Stockholm: Liber/Utbildningsförlaget.

Skolöverstyrelsen. (1980). *Läroplan för grundskolan*. Stockholm: Liber.

Skolöverstyrelsen. (1982a). Kommentarmaterial Lgr 80. *Elever med funktionshinder*. Stockholm: Liber.

Skolöverstyrelsen. (1982b). Kommentarmaterial Lgr 80. *Hjälp till elever med svårigheter*. Stockholm: Liber.

Skolöverstyrelsen. (1985). *En skola för alla*. Att arbeta förebyggande och stödjande. Stockholm: Liber.

BRITT-INGER FEX
University of Lund

WESTERN EUROPE, SPECIAL EDUCATION IN

SWITZERLAND, SPECIAL EDUCATION IN

Special education in Switzerland has a long tradition. It has been strongly developed in the past two or three decades, not according to a coherent federal conception, but in a pragmatic way corresponding to the cantonal laws. Therefore, the system of special education varies from canton to canton. Switzerland has neither a national ministry of education nor a national welfare department. The Federal Disability Insurance, founded in 1960, has, through its extensive financial support, certain influence on the special education system.

Early education of handicapped children can be extended from birth to kindergarten or start of school. There is no obligation to report these children. Early recognition depends on doctors and locally organized institutions in touch with parents. A teacher of special education who specialized in early education takes charge of the child with developmental problems. In some services, there are also other specialists such as physiotherapists or occupational therapists. Specialized services for particular handicaps exist for blind and/or deaf children, but most services are open to those with different handicaps. Normally, the teacher goes to the child's home and works there with the child and the parents once or twice a week. At the age of 4, 5, or 6, the handicapped child goes for 1 or 2 years with nonhandicapped peers to the normal kindergarten or to the special kindergarten for the severely handicapped. Although kindergarten is optional throughout the country, most of the children attend it. For slightly handicapped children, early education and education in the special kindergarten is paid for by the canton or private funds. The Disability Insurance helps finance severely handicapped children.

School attendance is compulsory from the age of 6 years up to 15. If a child needs special help, he or she may get additional teaching or ambulatory treatment, or may attend a special class within the regular school or a special school. Special classes admit children with relatively minor handicaps; i.e., children who are slow learners, who are mildly emotionally disturbed, who are crippled or have health problems, who have problems owing to a foreign language background, who have perceptual or speech disorders, or who are taught in hospitals. The special classes are under the authority of the cantonal department of education. Special schools are managed partly by private organizations and partly by the state (canton), supported by the Federal Disability Insurance. They are open to more severely handicapped children; i.e., the mentally retarded, blind, visually impaired, deaf, hearing impaired, and severely speech-impaired. There exist about 500 special schools that offer special education for about 18,000 pupils (average size is 36 pupils per special school).

Special education takes place either within regular school buildings or in separate ones, including residential facilities. In practice, more and more children are living at home and attend school just for the day. In the 1983–1984 school year, 4.2% of the 771,000 pupils in compulsory schools (primary and secondary level) were in special classes or schools. But this percentage varies frrom region to region in accordance with local segregation practice and philosophy and the availability of itinerant school services. These services offer an array of different counseling and therapeutic possibilities, i.e., speech and language therapy, therapy pertaining to specific learning disabilities, psychomotor therapy, psychotherapy, rhythmics, ergotherapy, and physiotherapy. At the present time, much thought is being given to the broadening of itinerant services so that the number of special classes in the regular schools can be made smaller.

Vocational training of the handicapped is based on the federal law regarding vocational training and the law regarding the Disability Insurance. According to these regulations and to the capabilities of the handicapped person, there is the possibility of taking normal vocational training (i.e., apprenticeship) or of having an individualized vocational program that takes into consideration the handicap(s) involved. If the handicap is so severe that special provision is necessary, the handicapped youngster goes to a rehabilitation center or sheltered workshop. The rehabilitation center usually trains only those young handicapped persons who will be able to work in open industry afterward. In Switzerland open industry is not forced by law to employ handicapped people. The sheltered workshop offers ongoing work as well as a certain amount of vocational training. Young people normally will stay in the sheltered workshop, but they can work in open industry whenever circumstances allow. Handicapped adults live in their own apartments, in their parents' homes, in small groups of handicapped people, in homes built especially for elderly handicapped people, or in existing institutions such as homes for old people.

Specialists in special education receive their higher education either at an institute of the university, at a private training institute, or in special courses organized by the cantons. Most candidates are teachers who wish to specialize through a two- or three-year program leading to a diploma. The university institutes offer formal study with traditional academic degrees.

ALOIS BÜRLI
*Swiss Institute for Special
Education, Lucerne,
Switzerland*

WESTERN EUROPE, SPECIAL EDUCATION IN

SYDENHAM'S CHOREA

Sydenham's chorea is more commonly known as St. Vitus' Dance, but it also may be called minor chorea, rheumatic chorea, or acute chorea. It is generally regarded as an inflammatory complication of rheumatic fever, tonsillitis, or other infection; it also can be associated with pregnancy (chorea gravidarum). The condition is most prevalent in young girls between the ages of 5 and 15 and more common in temperate climates during summer and early fall. The condition has declined substantially in recent years owing to a similar decline in rheumatic fever. It is characterized by involuntary choreic movements throughout the body and occurs in about 10% of rheumatic attacks.

Choreic movements are rapid, purposeless, short lasting, and nonrepetitive. The movements usually begin in one limb and flow to many different parts of the body; they may resemble athetoid cerebral palsy. Fidgety behavior, clumsiness, dropping of objects, facial grimacing, awkward gait, and changes in voice or slurred speech are common symptoms that may occur at onset. A month or more may pass before medical attention is sought because these symptoms initially may be mild. Anxiety, irritability, and emotional instability also may occur because of the uncontrolled movements. The involuntary motions disappear during sleep and occasionally are suppressed by rest, sedation, or attempts at voluntary control. Sydenham's chorea is nonfatal and recovery usually occurs within 2 to 6 months. Recurrence may happen two or three times over a period of years in almost one-third of the people affected.

Differential diagnosis depends on ruling out other causes through history and laboratory studies. There are no characteristic laboratory abnormalities, and pathologic studies suggest scattered lesions in the basal ganglia, cerebellum, and brain stem. No deficits in muscle strength or sensory perception are found during neurologic examination. The course of the impairment is variable and difficult to measure because of its gradual diminution.

There is no specific treatment, but some medications (phenobarbital, diazepam, perphenazine, or haloperidol) can be effective in reducing chorea. In most situations, the person with Sydenham's is encouraged to return to school or work, even if residual symptoms continue. In severe cases, protection from self-injury by using restraints may be necessary. The prognosis for recovery is variable but the condition inevitably subsides. Reassurance that the condition is self-limiting and eventually will decline without residual impairment is in order for people with Sydenham's, their families, teachers, and classmates. Behavioral problems, mild motor abnormalities, and poor performance in psychometric testing have been reported after the chorea dissipates.

REFERENCES

Berkow, R. (Ed.). (1982). *Merck Manual* (14th ed.) (pp. 87–88). Rahway, NJ: Merck, Sharp, & Dohme Research Laboratories.

Bird, M. T., Palkes, H., & Prensky, A. L. (1976). A follow-up study of Sydenham's chorea. *Neurology, 26,* 601–606.

Fahn, S. (1985). Neurologic and behavioral diseases. In J. Wyngaarden & L. Smith, Jr. (Eds.), *Cecil textbook of medicine* (17th ed., pp. 2074–2075). Philadelphia: Saunders.

Magalini, S., & Scarascia, E. (1981). *Dictionary of medical syndromes* (2nd ed., pp. 882–883). Philadelphia: Lippincott.

Merritt, H. H. (1979). *A textbook of neurology* (6th ed.). Philadelphia: Lea & Febiger.

Nuasieda, P. A., Grossman, B. J., Koller, W. C., Weiner, W. J., & Klawans, H. L. (1980). Sydenham's chorea: An update. *Neurology, 30,* 331–334.

DANIEL D. LIPKA
Lincoln Way Special Education Regional Resource Center, Louisville, Ohio

CHOREA
HUNTINGTON'S CHOREA

SYNAPSES

The synapse is the structure that mediates the effects of a nerve impulse on a target cell, permitting communication among nerve cells, muscles, and glands. It is a synapse that joins the terminal end of an axon of one neuron with the dendrites or cell body of another. The synapse was first described by Sir Charles Sherrington in 1897. The word itself means connection.

Messages arrive at the synapse in the form of action potentials. Synaptic potentials are triggered by action potentials; they in turn trigger subsequent action potentials, continuing the neural message on to its destination. While action potentials vary in frequency, they do not vary in form or magnitude. It is the synaptic potential that is responsible for variance in the nervous system.

The synaptic terminals on the end tips of axons take on various forms such as ball-like endings (boutons), nobs, spines, and rings. These terminals almost, but not quite, make contact with a part of another neuron (usually a dendrite or occasionally an axon or cell body). The space between the terminal of one neuron and the other neuron is called the synaptic cleft. This cleft is miniscule, typically on the order of about 200 angstroms. Transmission time across the synaptic cleft is approximately .3 to 1.0 msec.

Synaptic transmission can be electrical or chemical, although the former is uncommon in the mammalian brain (Gazzaniga, Steen, & Volpe, 1979). With chemical transmission, one cell, the presynaptic, secretes molecules that cross a synaptic cleft and join with a postsynaptic cell. The presynaptic cell endings contain mitochondria and synaptic vesicles that hold various neurotransmitters. The neurotransmitter substances are released in tiny packettes called quanta. These substances can serve excitatory or inhibitory purposes, and not all are currently identified. However, major excitatory neurotransmitters include acetylcholine, noradrenalin, seratonin, and dopamine. Important inhibitory transmitters include gamma-amino-butric acid (GABA) and glutamate. Specific receptor molecules that receive these neurotransmitters have been identified on the postsynaptic cell.

Synapses generally are classified as axiodendritic or axiosomatic. The typical pattern is axiodendritic; this pattern occurs when an axon meets a dendrite. Somewhat less common is the axiosomatic pattern, in which an axon meets a cell body.

REFERENCES

Barr, M. D. (1979). *The human nervous system: An anatomic viewpoint* (3rd ed.). New York: Harper & Row.

Gazzaniga, M., Steen, D., & Volpe, B. T. (1979). *Functional neuroscience.* New York: Harper & Row.

DANNY WEDDING
Marshall University

DENDRITES
DOPAMINE

SYNTACTIC DEFICIENCIES

See CHILDHOOD APHASIA, EXPRESSIVE LANGUAGE DISORDERS; LANGUAGE DEFICIENCIES AND DEFICITS.

SYSTEMS OF CLASSIFICATION

A system of classification can be developed in an effort to identify individuals as members of one of the major handicapping conditions (e.g., learning disabilities), or it may be used to provide a subclassification within a major area of exceptionality (e.g., Down's syndrome as a subcategory of mental retardation). Contemporary special education services rely heavily on the classification of general handicapping conditions and, to lesser extent, on subclassifications.

The historical origins of the use of classification systems are dominated by two events. First, special education represents a unique educational development derived from the discipline of psychology. As such, it emerged in light of that discipline's intense interest in the measurement and study of individual differences. Subsequent refinements in measurement, including the development of classification systems based on reliable individual differences, were transferred to special education practice in the first part of the twentieth century. A second related influence arose from the attempts of early special educators to provide a science of treatment. That is, the study of individual differences led to the acceptance of a nosological orientation in treatment. Long practiced in medicine, the nosological orientation presumes that disorders can be isolated with reference to etiology, that etiology can ultimately be treated, and that subsequent cases can be similarly addressed (i.e., treatment proceeds from symptom to diagnosis of etiology to specification of treatment). In this approach, the development of a precise system of classification and subclassification is essential.

Possibly the most influential classification system now in effect is that provided within PL 94-142 (Education of All Handicapped Children Act of 1975). Ysseldyke and Algozzine (1984) indicate that through this legislation, the U.S. Department of Education recognizes 11 categories of exceptionality, although some states recognize more or less categories. In most states, the categories represent an effective determinant of service: If an individual is not a member of the specified handicapping condition, services are not mandated. Thus, systems of classification, and related entry procedures, are essential in the selection process that ultimately determines entrance to special education.

A number of subclassification systems exist within the broad categories of exceptionality. Most of these attempt to suggest, if not prescribe, the general course of diagnosis and treatment. Two well-known systems typify this approach. The *Diagnostic and Statistical Manual of Mental Disorders* (third edition; DSM III) is a psychiatrically derived classification system for use with children and adults with emotional disorders. The DSM III is the standard classification system within mental health facilities in the United States, though it has far less official influence in public education. In DSM III, disorders are grouped into five major divisions (intellectual, behavioral, emotional, physical, and developmental). Each division is further partitioned into specific disorders as defined by rigid diagnostic criteria. Individuals thus receive codes that indicate the diagnosed handicaps.

A second classification system is used in the diagnosis and treatment of mental retardation. The American Association on Mental Deficiency classification system (Grossman, 1983) is based on a number of factors, including intelligence and adaptive behavior. In this system, the degree of retardation is specified as mild, moderate, severe, or profound. The intent of the system is clearly to specify training needs.

It is erroneous to conclude that these two well-accepted classification systems are acceptable to all agencies, that alternatives are nonexistent, or that particular systems are not revised over time. For example, DSM III is in the third substantially revised edition and tends not to be used in schools; alternatives such as Quay's (1964) system are often favored. Nor is there a paucity of systems. MacMillan (1982) reports at least 10 systems have been used in the twentieth century with the mentally retarded. Of these, four are now in common use. Clearly, classification systems are modified in response to the influence of social pressures, research bases, and professional opinions.

A number of theoretical and pragmatic pitfalls are evident in current classification systems. Three are particularly germane. First, the fact that multiple classification systems exist and are endorsed by various agencies creates opportunities for classification and service provision irregularities. Second, there is question as to whether behavioral diagnostic techniques possess the necessary reliability and validity to provide precise classification; error in measurement and misassignment to categories is possible (Salvia & Ysseldyke, 1985). Third, the significance of classification systems based on etiology may prove to be less important to the behavioral than the medical sciences. That is, treatment links have generally not been established between etiological diagnosis and behavioral treatment. Such links may prove difficult or impossible to achieve (Neisworth & Greer, 1975).

Despite these criticisms, classification systems remain an important consideration for special education. Kauffman (1977) provided a rationale for the continuation of attempts to classify behavior: classification is a fundamental aspect of any developing science of behavior; classification is of importance in organizing and communicating information; and classification systems, if scientifically investigated, may ultimately assist in the prediction of behavior and offer insights into the preferred method of treatment. As noted by Kauffman (1977), the alternative to continued development of classification systems is "an educational methodology that relies on attempts to fit interventions to disorders by random choice, intuition, or trial and error" (p. 27).

REFERENCES

American Psychiatric Association. (1980). *Diagnostic and statistical manual of mental disorders* (3rd ed.). Washington, DC: American Psychiatric Association.

Grossman, H. J. (Ed.). (1983). *Manual on terminology and classification in mental retardation* (3rd ed.). Washington, DC: American Association on Mental Deficiency.

Kauffman, J. M. (1977). *Characteristics of children's behavior disorders.* Columbus, OH: Merrill.

MacMillan, D. L. (1982). *Mental retardation in school and society* (2nd ed.). Boston: Little, Brown.

Neisworth, J. T., & Green, J. G. (1975). Functional similarities of learning disabilities and mild retardation. *Exceptional Children, 42*, 17–21.

Quay, H. C. (1964). Dimensions of personality in delinquent boys as inferred from factor analysis of case history data. *Child Development, 35*, 479–484.

Salvia, J., & Ysseldyke, J. E. (1985). *Assessment in special and remedial education* (3rd ed.). Boston: Houghton Mifflin.

Ysseldyke, J. E., & Algozzine, B. (1984). *Introduction to special education.* Boston: Houghton Mifflin.

TED L. MILLER
*University of Tennessee,
Chattanooga*

DIAGNOSTIC AND STATISTICAL MANUAL OF MENTAL DISORDERS (DSM III)
LEARNER TAXONOMIES

SYSTEM OF MULTICULTURAL PLURALISTIC ASSESSMENT (SOMPA)

The System of Multicultural Pluralistic Assessment (SOMPA) (Mercer & Lewis, 1979) was designed to provide a comprehensive measure of the cognitive abilities, perceptual-motor abilities, sociocultural background, and adaptive behavior of children ages 5 through 11 years. It employs three models of assessment and attempts to integrate them into a comprehensive assessment: (1) the medical model, defined as any abnormal organic condition interfering with physiological functioning; (2) the social system model, determined principally from labeling theory and social deviance perspectives taken from the field of sociology, which attempts to correct the "Anglo conformity" biases of the test developers who have designed IQ tests for the last 80 years; and (3) the pluralistic model, which compares the scores of a child with the performance levels of children of a similar ethclass (that is, the same demographic, socioeconomic, and cultural background) correcting for any score discrepancies with the white middle class. English and Spanish language versions of the scale are available.

The SOMPA is a complex and somewhat innovative

system of assessment designed to ameliorate much of the conflict over assessment in the schools. The senior author, Mercer, a sociologist, conceptualized SOMPA in the late 1960s and early 1970s from her work in sociology's labeling theory and her sociological surveys and studies of mental retardation, particularly mild mental retardation, as a sociocultural phenomenon. The SOMPA has been extensively reviewed and debated (Humphreys, 1985; Nuttall, 1979; Reynolds, 1985; Reynolds & Brown, 1984; Sandoval, 1985). Unfortunately, presentation of the SOMPA for clinical application as opposed to pure research appears to have been premature. Major conceptual and technical issues pertaining to the scale have not been resolved adequately, even considering that a complete resolution of most of these issues is not possible. As a result, the SOMPA has contributed to the controversy over assessment practices in the schools rather than moved the field closer to a resolution. Even though controversy frequently can be stimulating to a discipline, in many ways, SOMPA has polarized the assessment community.

One of the major conceptual problems of the SOMPA centers around its primary underlying assumption. Mercer developed the SOMPA in response to her acceptance of the cultural test bias hypothesis. Briefly stated, this hypothesis contends that all racial, ethnic, socioeconomic, or other demographically based group differences on mental tests are due to artifacts of the tests themselves and do not reflect real differences. According to Mercer and Lewis, this is due to the extent of Anglocentrism (degree of adherence to white middle-class values, norms, and culture) apparent in most, if not all, mental measurements. In accepting this hypothesis as fundamentally correct, Mercer relies primarily on the mean differences definition of bias, which states that any differences in mean levels of performance among racial or ethnic groups on any mental scale is prima facie evidence of bias. The principal purpose of the SOMPA is to remove this bias by providing a correct estimate of intellectual abilities, an estimated learning potential (ELP). While adding a "correction factor" to the obtained IQs of disadvantaged children is not a new idea, the SOMPA corrections are unique in their objectivity and in having a clearly articulated, if controversial, basis. The corrections are based on the child's social-cultural characteristics and equate the mean IQs of blacks, whites, and Hispanics with varying other cultural characteristics such as family structure and degree of urban acculturation.

Unfortunately for the SOMPA, its underlying assumption that mean differences among sociocultural groups indicate cultural bias in tests is the single most rejected of all definitions of test bias by serious psychometricians researching the cultural test bias hypothesis (Jensen, 1980; Reynolds, 1982). The conceptual basis for the SOMPA is far more controversial than it appears in the test manuals and is indeed open to serious question. If other approaches to the cultural test bias hypothesis had demonstrated the existence of bias, then the need for a resolution to the problem such as proposed by Mercer would remain tenable. However, the large body of evidence regarding the cultural test bias hypothesis, gathered primarily over the last decade, has failed to substantiate popular claims of bias in the assessment of native-born, ethnic minorities. For the most part, the psychometric characteristics of well-designed and carefully standardized tests of intelligence such as the Wechsler scale have been shown to be substantially equivalent across ethnic groups (Jensen, 1980; Reynolds, 1982).

If this argument is dismissed and Mercer's contentions regarding test bias accepted, other serious conceptual issues remain. The ELP, a regression-based transformation of Wechsler IQs, is said to provide a good estimate of the child's innate intelligence or potential to profit from schooling. Such a claim is difficult to support under any circumstances. It is unlikely that we will ever be able to assess innate ability since environment begins to impact the organism at the moment of conception. We are left only with the possibility of observing the phenotypic construct. Furthermore, as of this writing, no evidence exists relating ELP to any other relevant criteria (Reschly, 1982).

Others have noted substantial agreement in criticisms of the SOMPA ELP, particularly regarding its construct validity (Humphreys, 1985; Reschly, 1982). Humphreys, (1985) argues that "Estimated learning potential is a thoroughly undesirable construct. Many people want to hear and believe the misinformation furnished by ethclass norms, but this is dangerous for it solves no real problems. It is conceivable, of course, that several generations from now black and Hispanic performance on standard tests of intelligence and achievement might equal the white majority. In this limited sense, ethclass norms might not misinform, but an inference that requires 50 years or more to validate helps little in dealing with today's children. They need higher scores on measures of reading, listening, writing, computing, mathematics, and science, not ethclass IQs" (p. 1519). The ELP may in fact be misleading and result in a denial of special education services to children who are seriously at risk of academic failure or already experiencing such failure. As Reschly has stated, "All of the direct uses of ELP at present and in the foreseeable future are questionable" (p. 242). Equally controversial, even in Mercer's home field of sociology, is labeling theory, another important concept in the establishment of the need for a system like SOMPA. If we accept the contention that false negatives are more desirable than false positives in the diagnosis of mental retardation, a check on the utility function tells us that it would most likely be best to diagnose no children as mentally retarded since the incidence in Mercer's model in particular is far less than 3%.

Technical problems are also evident in the development and application of the concept of ELP. As noted, the ELP is a regression-based transformation of Wechsler IQs to a scale with a mean of 100 and standard deviation of 15 independent of a child's sociocultural characteristics. These transformations are made on the basis of the SOMPA sociocultural scales. Based on data derived during the norming of the SOMPA, regression equations were derived for determining the ELP. The stability of these regression equations and their generalizability to children outside the standardization sample have been called into question. Since the SOMPA was not normed on a stratified random sample of children nationwide, but rather on a sampling restricted to California, generalizability studies received some priority on the measure's publication. Regression equations derived from samples from other states, notably Texas and Arizona, have not been at all similar to the original equations; even the multiple R between the various sociocultural variables and Wechsler IQ varies substantially (i.e., from .30 to .60 in some cases) across states and across ethnic groups (Reschly, 1982). Given the state of contemporary applied psychometrics and the sophisticated normative sampling of such scales as the Wechsler series and the recent Kaufman Assessment Battery for Children, the failure to provide an adequate standardization sample for the SOMPA is inexcusable and not characteristic of the publisher.

The reliability of the ELP will also be dependent to a large extent on the stability of the sociocultural scales from which the corrections to the obtained Wechsler IQs are derived. The stability of these scores has been seriously questioned in at least one recent study. Over a 4-year period, Wilkinson and Oakland (1983b) report test-retest correlations that range from .39 to the high .90s across scales. Within scales and across demographic groupings such as race, sex, and socioeconomic status, the correlations also vary considerably, pointing up the real possibility of bias in the SOMPA. Apparently the ELP can change dramatically for individual children over a 4-year period (given that half of the stability coefficients reported for the SOMPA sociocultural scales are below .80), a result that seems antithetical to the entire concept of the ELP.

Stability of other SOMPA scales that should be relative stable has also been questioned. The SOMPA health history inventory shows test-retest reliability coefficients ranging from −.08 (!) to .96. Considerable differences are evident within scales across demographic groupings as well. The trauma scale shows a stability coefficient of .23 for males and .74 for females (Wilkinson & Oakland, 1983a). Prepostnatal scores show a stability of .78 for whites and .96 for blacks, a scale that should remain highly stable since the SOMPA begins at age 5 years.

These are but a few of the conceptual and technical issues plaguing the SOMPA. Much work was needed on the SOMPA prior to its presentation for practical application, work that was not done. The conceptual issues in particular needed clarification. Nevertheless, the SOMPA does have one component that may be useful.

There are relatively few good measures of adaptive behavior available to clinicians. The Adaptive Behavior Inventory for Children (ABIC), developed to accompany the SOMPA as an integral part of the scale, is one of the promising current adaptive behavior measures for children ages 5 to 11 years. Though lengthy, somewhat cumbersome, and suffering from a lack of high-quality normative data, the ABIC may be useful in a comprehensive assessment, especially when mental retardation or emotional disturbance are viable possibilities. However, the scaling of the ABIC does leave something to be desired. The use of a scaled score system with a mean of 50 and a standard deviation of 15 adds to the difficulty of using the whole system; a well-known or common scale such as T-scores (mean = 50, standard deviation = 10), or an IQ-based scale (mean = 100, standard deviation = 15), would have enhanced its interpretability. Though Mercer and Lewis recommend that only the complete SOMPA should be used, the ABIC is able to stand on its own and can (and should) be abstracted from the SOMPA and used in the assessment of adaptive behavior. Those who do not wish to violate the author's recommendation in this regard should consider the AAMD Adaptive Behavior Scale, public school version, or the 1984 revision of the Vineland Social Maturity Scales (VABS) as excellent alternatives. The ABIC does need much more validity data, however, and until it is available, these alternative measures may be more desirable; though the VABS was published in 1984, it already has more available data than the ABIC.

On another level, the SOMPA must be questioned as an assessment system for children especially. The SOMPA is designed primarily as a means of providing a fairer scheme of classifying children into diagnostic categories. It has clearly not been validated adequately for this purpose. However, a more far-reaching concern to the clinician working with children experiencing school failure is the development of programs for the habilitation of learning. The SOMPA, outside of the ABIC, provides no real clues to the development of such interventions. This is especially damaging to practical applications of the SOMPA since it requires a substantial investment of professional time to be properly administered. The commitment of so much time and effort to an assessment system that does not provide considerable help with the development of individual educational programs cannot be justified in any kind of cost-benefit analysis. The emphasis on prevention-intervention-habilitation is more in keeping with the needs of the field.

The SOMPA cannot be recommended for use at this time. Its conceptual, technical, and practical problems are simply too great. Nevertheless, it was an innovative, gallant effort at resolving the conflict over assessment practices in the schools. Current evidence would point to failure; however, it may serve as a springboard in some ways for future assessment systems if we attend to the problems inherent in this scale.

REFERENCES

Humphreys, L. G. (1985). Review of System of Multicultural Pluralistic Assessment. In J. V. Mitchell (Ed.). *Ninth mental measurements yearbook*. Lincoln, NE: Buros Institute.

Jensen, A. R. (1980). *Bias in mental testing*. New York: Free Press.

Mercer, J., & Lewis, J. (1979). *System of Multicultural Pluralistic Assessment*. New York: The Psychological Corporation.

Nuttall, E. V. (1979). Review of System of Multicultural Pluralistic Assessment. *Journal of Educational Measurement, 16*, 285–290.

Reschly, D. J. (1982). Assessing mild mental retardation: The influence of adaptive behavior, sociocultural status, and prospects for nonbiased assessment. In C. R. Reynolds & T. B. Gutkin (Eds.), *The handbook of school psychology*. New York: Wiley.

Reynolds, C. R. (1982). The problem of bias in psychological assessment. In C. R. Reynolds & T. B. Gutkin (Eds.), *The handbook of school psychology*. New York: Wiley.

Reynolds, C. R. (1985). Review of System of Multicultural Pluralistic Assessment. In J. V. Mitchell (Ed.), *Ninth mental measurements yearbook*. Lincoln, NE: Buros Institute.

Reynolds, C. R., & Brown, R. T. (Eds.). (1984). *Perspectives on bias in mental testings*. New York: Plenum.

Sandoval, J. (1985). Review of System of Multicultural Pluralistic Assessment. In J. V. Mitchell (Ed.), *Ninth mental measurements yearbook*. Lincoln, NE: Buros Institute.

Wilkinson, C. Y., & Oakland, T. (1983a, August). *Stability of the SOMPA's health history inventory*. Paper presented to the annual meeting of the American Psychological Association, Anaheim, CA.

Wilkinson, C. Y., & Oakland, T. (1983b, August). *Stability of the SOMPA's sociocultural modalities*. Paper presented to the annual meeting of the American Psychological Association, Anaheim, CA.

CECIL R. REYNOLDS
Texas A&M University

ADAPTIVE BEHAVIOR
CULTURAL BIAS IN TESTING
MERCER, JANE R.
VINELAND ADAPTIVE BEHAVIOR SCALES

T

TACHISTOSCOPE

The tachistoscope, or t-scope, is an instrument for presenting visual stimuli for very brief times at a controlled level of illumination (Stang & Wrightsman, 1981). The t-scope may be a self-contained unit or mounted on a slide projector.

Often the goal of tachistoscopic presentation is to determine the threshold at which subjects verbally report recognition of a stimulus. Research using the tachistoscope also has been carried out concerning the existence of subliminal perception where stimuli are said to affect behavior below the conscious threshold of perception.

Reading involves very briefly viewing words; the tachistoscopic task was broadly assumed to mimic the requirements faced by skilled readers. Despite questions of the applicability of t-scope research to everyday reading tasks, a variety of components of reading have been examined in the presence of varying speeds of presentation and levels of illumination. The threshold of word recognition can be determined and models of skilled reading can be constructed (Carr & Pollatsek, 1985; Gough, 1984; Mewhort & Campbell, 1981). The performance of skilled and disabled readers can be compared to determine the differences that might be diagnostically significant (Pirozzollo, 1979).

REFERENCES

Carr, T., & Pollatsek, A. (1985). Recognizing printed words: A look at current models. In D. Besner, T. G. Waller, & G. E. Mackinnon (Eds.), *Reading research: Advances in theory and practice* (Vol. 5, pp. 2–82). Orlando, FL: Academic.

Gough, P. B. (1984). Word recognition. In P. D. Pearsen, (Ed.), *Handbook of reading research* (pp. 225–291). New York: Longman.

Mewhort, D. J. K., & Campbell, A. J. (1981). Toward a model of skilled reading performance: An analysis of performance in tachistoscopic tasks. In G. E. Mackinnon & T. G. Waller (Eds.), *Reading research: Advances in theory and practice* (Vol. 1.3, pp. 39–118). New York: Academic.

Pirozzolo, F. J. (1979). *The neuropsychology of developmental reading disorders.* New York: Praeger.

Stang, D., & Wrightsman, L. (1981). *Dictionary of social behavior and social research methods.* Monterey, CA: Brooks–Cole.

LEE ANDERSON JACKSON, JR.
*University of North Carolina,
Wilmington*

PERCEPTUAL SPAN

TALENTED CHILDREN

See SPECIFIC TALENT, E.G., ACADEMICALLY TALENTED CHILDREN.

TALKING BOOKS

Talking books are books recorded on vinyl disks or, more often the case in recent years, on cassette tapes that are used principally by the blind. These modified records are played on special talking book machines and recorded on modified machines as well. Talking books and the modified recorders are available to all visually impaired students registered through the American Printing House for the Blind. Severely reading impaired students with a diagnosis of dyslexia may also qualify for the use of talking books.

STAFF

AMERICAN PRINTING HOUSE FOR THE BLIND

TASK ANALYSIS

Task analysis is a teaching strategy that encompasses the breaking down and sequencing of goals into teachable subtasks. Moyer and Dardig (1978) noted it is a critical component of the behavioral approach and it serves a dual role in the instruction of learners with handicaps. First, it serves an effective diagnostic function by helping teachers pinpoint a student's individual functioning levels on a specific skill or task. Second, it provides the basis for sequential instruction, which may be tailored to each child's pace of learning. A thorough task analysis results in a set of subtasks that form the basic steps in an effective program.

Task analysis has been acclaimed to be an effective strategy for the mildly handicapped learner (Bateman, 1974; Siegel, 1972; Tawney, 1974). Gold (1976) applied this technique to the education of severely handicapped learners with great success and Williams, Brown, and Certo (1975) stated that task analysis is critical to teachers of severely handicapped learners since programmatic steps must be sequenced with precision and care.

According to Mithaug (1979), the procedures that define task analysis have evolved from Frederick Taylor's work measurement studies and Frank and Lillian Gilbreth's motion studies conducted in the late 1800s. Motion analysis was the precursor of today's task analysis, although many elements critical to motion analysis have not been included in the educational applications of task analysis. The term task analysis came into increasing use during the 1950s, whenever tasks were identified and examined for their essential components within the workplace. This foreshadowed subsequent applications of task analysis to teach individuals with disabilities in the late 1960s.

Guidelines for designing and implementing task analysis programs have been suggested (Moyer & Dardig, 1978; Siegel, 1972). These are:

Limit the scope of the main task

Write subtasks in observable terms

Use terminology at a level understandable to potential users

Write the task in terms of what the learner will do

Focus attention on the task rather than the learner

In choosing a method of task analysis, Moyer & Dardig (1978) noted that all tasks, whether from the psychomotor, cognitive, or affective domains, can be broken down into simple units of performance. However, there is no foolproof strategy for selecting the appropriate method of analysis for a given task. It is helpful first to identify the domain of the learning task and then to apply the appropriate task analysis procedure. They suggest several possible methods of task analysis that may be adopted by the special education teacher:

1. Watch a master perform. This requires watching and writing down all the steps that are required to perform the task as it is performed by someone adept at it.

2. In a variation of the first method, have the teacher perform the task, making note of the required steps. Sometimes this is difficult in that performing the task may interfere with recording the steps.

3. Work backward from the terminal objective, making note of the required steps.

4. Brainstorm. This entails writing down all the component steps without regard to order. Then, once all steps have been identified, arrange them into some logical order.

5. Make the conditions under which the task is completed progressively more simple. As the learner gains proficiency, slowly change the simplified conditions (e.g., trace name; gradually remove the model: dark model, light model, dotted model, etc.).

The ability to analyze tasks, a skill that can be acquired by any teacher, enables the detection of trends in a student's performance and the modification of task components during an instructional session (Junkala, 1973). Thus it is an extremely effective instructional method and diagnostic tool in special education.

REFERENCES

Bateman, B. D. (1974). Educational implications of minimum brain dysfunction. *Reading Teacher, 27*, 662–668.

Gold, M. C. (1976). Task analysis of a complex assembly task by the retarded blind. *Exceptional Children, 43*, 78–84.

Junkala, J., (1973). Task analysis: The processing dimension. *Academic Therapy, 8*(4), 401–409.

Mithaug, D. E. (1979). The relation between programmed instruction and task analysis in the pre-vocational training of severely and profoundly handicapped persons. *AAESPH Review, 4*(2), 162–178.

Moyer, J. R., & Dardig, J. C. (1978). Practical task analysis for special educators. *Teaching Exceptional Children, 11*(1), 16–18.

Siegel, E. (1972). Task analysis and effective teaching. *Journal of Learning Disabilities, 5*, 519–532.

Tawney, J. W. (1974). *Task analysis.* Unpublished manuscript, University of Kentucky.

Williams, W., Brown, L., & Certo, N. (1975). Basic components of instructional programs for the severely handicapped students. *AAESPH Review, 1*(1), 1–39.

EILEEN F. MCCARTHY
*University of Wisconsin,
Madison*

BEHAVIOR ASSESSMENT
BEHAVIOR MODIFICATION
BEHAVIORAL OBJECTIVES

TAT

See THEMATIC APPERCEPTION TEST.

TAXONOMIES

Taxonomy is the science of systematics. It incorporates the theory and practice of classification, or sorting and ordering significant similarities and differences among members of a system to facilitate precise communication about members, enhance understanding of the interrelationships among members, and suggest areas where additional relationships might be discovered. Early attempts to design taxonomies date back to the third century BC and Aristotle's efforts to classify animals as warm- or cold-blooded. Theophrastus, Aristotle's pupil, concentrated on a system for sorting plants. In the eighteenth century in Sweden, Linnaeus designed a classification system for botany that has seved as a basis for almost all subsequent systems.

Among the more commonly used taxonomies today are the Library of Congress and Dewey Decimal systems for the classification of books and the taxonomies developed for the classification of plants and animals. The latter contains categories that permit the identification of individual organisms according to species, genus, family, order, class, phylum, and kingdom.

In the late 1940s, members of the American Psychological Association who were concerned about the problems of precise communication among college examiners and researchers involved in testing and curriculum development began work on the classification of educational objectives. The result was the preparation of taxonomies of educational objectives or intended student outcomes in the cognitive, affective, and psychomotor domains (Bloom, 1956; Harrow, 1972; Krathwohl, Bloom, & Masia, 1964). The major classes in these three taxonomies are presented in Figure 1. All three reflect an emphasis on the intended outcomes of instruction and the student behaviors that would demonstrate achievement of each outcome.

Stevens (1962) developed a taxonomy for special education that focuses on physical disorders. He observed that classification systems then in use were typically based on a medical model with an emphasis on disease, etiology, and symptomatology. His intent was to improve communication regarding educationally relevant attributes or somatopsychological or body disorders and the special education procedures students with such disorders might require. Stevens stressed the differences among the terms impairment, disability, and handicap and provided for attributes that carried significance for planning special education programs. Figure 2 lists Stevens' classes.

More recently the World Health Organization (WHO) has published its *International Classification of Impairments, Disabilities, and Handicaps* (1980). This publication relates consequences of disease to circumstances in which disabled persons are apt to find themselves as they interact with others and adapt to their physical surroundings. The purpose of WHO's efforts, which are summarized in Figure 3, was to prepare a taxonomy that would ease

Cognitive Domain
1. Knowledge
2. Comprehension
3. Application
4. Analysis
5. Synthesis
6. Evaluation

Affective Domain
1. Receiving/attending
2. Responding
3. Valuing
4. Organization
5. Characterization

Psychomotor Domain
1. Reflex movement
2. Basic fundamental movement
3. Perceptual abilities
4. Physical abilities
5. Skilled movements
6. Nondiscursive movements

Figure 1. Taxonomies of educational objectives for the cognitive, affective, and psychomotor domains (Bloom, 1956; Harrow, 1972; Krathwohl, Bloom, & Masia, 1964).

the production of statistics regarding the consequences of disease, facilitate the collection of statistics useful in planning services, and permit storage and retrieval of information about impairments, disabilities, and handicaps (WHO, 1980).

Ultimately, taxonomies should be comprehensive, improve communication, stimulate thought, and be accepted by professionals in the field for which they were designed (Bloom, 1956). Whether the taxonomies available for spe-

1. *Somatopsychological variants*
   1.1 Handicap
   1.2 Disability
   1.3 Impairment
2. *Educationally significant attributes of somatopsychological disorders*
   2.1 Nature of condition
   2.2 Nature of therapeutic process
   2.3 Psychological aspects
   2.4 School considerations
   2.5 Cultural considerations
   2.6 Etc.
3. *Special education procedures*
   3.1 Modification of laws
   3.2 Finance
   3.3 Instructional modifications
   3.4 Noninstructional services
   3.5 Administrative modifications
   3.6 Ancillary services
   3.7 Etc.

Figure 2. Taxonomy in special education for children with body disorders (Steven, 1962).

Impairments
1. Intellectual
2. Other psychological
3. Language
4. Aural
5. Ocular
6. Visceral
7. Skeletal
8. Disfiguring
9. Generalized, sensory, and other

Disabilities
1. Behavior
2. Communication
3. Personal care
4. Locomotor
5. Body disposition
6. Dexterity
7. Situational
8. Particular skill
9. Other activity restrictions

Handicaps
Survival roles
1. Orientation
2. Physical independence
3. Mobility
4. Occupational
5. Social integration
6. Economic self-sufficiency
Other handicaps
7. Other handicaps

Figure 3.   WHO classification of impairments, disabilities, and handicaps (WHO, 1980).

cial educators lead to the achievement of these goals remains to be seen.

REFERENCES

Bloom, B. S. (Ed.). (1956). *Taxonomy of educational objectives: The classification of educational goals: Handbook I. Cognitive domain.* New York: McKay.

Harrow, A. J. (1972). *A taxonomy of the psychomotor domain: A guide for developing behavioral objectives.* New York: McKay.

Krathwohl, D. R., Bloom, B. S., & Masia, B. B. (1964). *Taxonomy of educational objectives: Classification of educational goals: Handbook II. Affected domain.* New York: McKay.

Stevens, G. D. (1962). *Taxonomy in special education for children with body disorders.* Pittsburgh, PA: Department of Special Education and Rehabilitation, University of Pittsburgh.

World Health Organization. (1980). *International classification of impairments, disabilities, and handicaps.* Geneva, Switzerland: Author.

MARJORIE E. WARD
The Ohio State University

BLOOM, BENJAMIN S.
CLASSIFICATION, SYSTEMS OF

TAY-SACHS SYNDROME

Tay-Sachs disease is a disorder of fat metabolism that results in loss of visual function and progressive mental deterioration. It is one of a variety of demyelinating diseases of the nervous system characterized by cerebral macular degeneration. The disorder is named after Warren Tay, an English physician (1843–1927), and Bernard Sachs, an American neurologist (1858–1944). The disorder is transmitted by an autosomal recessive gene and is found with dramatically increased frequency among Jewish infants of eastern European origin. Approximately 90% of cases of Tay-Sachs syndrome can be traced to Lithuanian or Jewish ancestry.

The disorder typically first manifests itself in infants between the ages of 4 and 8 months. Early signs include an abnormal startle response to acoustic stimulation, delay in psychomotor development or regression with loss of learned skills (e.g., loss of the ability to roll over), spasticity, and cherry red spots in the retinas, the result of degeneration of retinal ganglion cells. Head size typically increases in the second year while the cerebral ventricles remain relatively normal. There are frequently tonic-clonic seizures and blindness may occur. Infants typically become weak and apathetic. Death usually occurs at 3 to 5 years. At autopsy, the appearance of the brain is one of widespread atrophy. Treatment is aimed at the symptoms of the disease with anticonvulsant medications used to suppress seizures.

REFERENCE

Adams, R. A., & Victor, N. (1977). *Principles of neurology.* New York: McGraw-Hill.

DANNY WEDDING
Marshall University

CONGENITAL DISORDERS

TEACCH

Treatment and Education of Autistic and related Communication handicapped Children (TEACCH) is a unique program offering comprehensive services, research, and professional training for autistic children of all ages, and their families, in the state of North Carolina. TEACCH is a division of the psychiatry department of the University of North Carolina School of Medicine, Chapel Hill.

The program was founded in 1966 by Eric Schopler and Robert J. Reichler as a research project supported in part by the National Institute of Mental Health. Its purpose was to investigate the following misconceptions about autism: (1) that the syndrome is primarily an emotional disorder that causes children to withdraw from their hostile and pathological parents; (2) that these parents are educationally privileged and from an upper social class; and (3) that autistic children had potential for normal or better intellectual functioning. The research results clarified these misconceptions by demonstrating that autism is a developmental disability rather than an emotional illness; that parents come from all social strata and, like their children, are the victims rather than the cause of this disability; and that in spite of peak skills, mental retardation and autism can and do coexist.

These empirical research findings led to the development of the TEACCH program based on the following principles:

1. Parents should be collaborators and cotherapists in the treatment of their own children.
2. Treatment should involve individualized teaching programs using behavior theory and special education.
3. Teaching programs should be based on individualized diagnosis and assessment.
4. Implementation should be by psychoeducational therapists or teachers who function as generalists rather than specialists in a technical field such as physical therapy or speech therapy. Treatment outcome is evaluated according to the interaction between improved skills and environmental adjustments to deficits.

The TEACCH program provides comprehensive services, including professional training and research efforts that are integrated with clinical services. Training is provided for various specialists, including teachers, psychologists, psychiatrists, pediatricians, speech pathologists, and social workers. The main emphasis is on the involvement of parents in all facets of the program directed toward adjustment in all areas of the child's life—home, school, and the community.

Home adjustment is facilitated at five regional TEACCH centers, each located in a city housing a branch of the state university system to facilitate both research and training. The centers' main function is to provide diagnosis and individualized assessment involving family and school. Parents are trained to function as cotherapists using behavior management and special education techniques. The centers' staff provide professional training and consultation.

School adjustment is fostered through special education classrooms in the public schools that include four to eight children with a teacher and an assistant teacher. These classrooms (about 54 currently) are under TEACCH direction according to individual school contracts. TEACCH functions often include hiring teachers, intensive in-service training of teachers, diagnosis and placement of children, and ongoing classroom consultation for behavior problems and special curriculum issues.

Community adaptation is facilitated through parent groups. Each center and class has a parent group affiliated with the North Carolina Society for Autistic Adults and Children, and a chapter of the National Society. The main goal of this collaboration is to improve community understanding of the client's special needs and to develop new and cost-effective services. In recent years, this involved services for the older age group, including group homes, respite care, summer camps, vocational training, social skills training, and the development of a learning-living community program.

The outcome studies of various TEACCH services have shown that autistic children learn better in a structured setting, and that with appropriate training, parents become effective in teaching and managing their own children. Such gains carry over into the home situation. Moreover, when the North Carolina rate of institutionalized autistic children is compared with the rate reported from other states and countries, it is less than one-fifth, demonstrating that a strong community support program can improve the quality of life for handicapped children and adults at a fraction of the cost incurred by institutional warehousing.

ERIC SCHOPLER
*University of North Carolina,
Chapel Hill*

AUTISM
FILIAL THERAPY
JOURNAL OF AUTISM AND DEVELOPMENTAL
    DISORDERS

TEACHER BURNOUT

Increased public demands on education have produced additional pressures and stresses on teachers. Needle, Griffin, Svendsen, and Berney (1981) report that teaching ranks third in the hierarchy of stressful professions. Studies conducted by teachers' unions and other educational agencies support the notion that many teachers are currently "burning out" (Cichon & Koff, 1980; Wilson & Hall, 1981). Special educators in particular may be at high risk for burnout and its consequences (Bradfield & Fones, 1985).

Burnout has been defined in a variety of ways in the literature during its nearly 10-year history (Gold, 1985). Weiskopf (1980) defines burnout by its relationship to six categories of stress often found at the teaching work place. They include work overload, lack of preceived success, amount of direct contact with children, staff-child ratio, program structure, and responsibility for others. Freudenberger (1974) and Maslach (1977) find the general theme of burnout to be "emotional and/or physical exhaustion resulting from the stress of interpersonal contact." It can be viewed as a gradual process with stages ranging from mild to severe (Spaniol & Caputo, 1979).

Burnout seems to affect people working in the human social services professions particularly because of the degree of intimacy that they experience with their clients and the extended period of time that they work with them. Moreover, many of the recipients of human services do not respond to the efforts of professionals, causing disillusionment and frustration (Pines & Maslach, 1977). This may be particularly true for special education teachers because of the unique nature of their teaching responsibilities (Bradfield & Fones, 1985).

Many causes for burnout in the helping professions have been proposed. In education, occupational burnout may arise from the failure of the work environment to provide the teacher with the support and encouragement needed and expected (Needle, Griffin, Svendsen, & Berney, 1981). Bensky et al. (1980) point out that often teachers are not given clearly defined job descriptions and receive additional job responsibilities for which they are unprepared or to which they are unaccustomed. Role ambiguity, if not clarified as part of the education process, is likely to lead to an increase in job-related stress and dissatisfaction (Coates & Thoresen, 1976; Greenberg & Valletutti, 1980). Many teachers have cited violence, vandalism, disruptive students, inadequate salaries, lack of classroom control, lack of job mobility, and fear of layoffs as reasons for burnout (Gold, 1985).

The effects of burnout vary from individual to individual depending on such variables as personality, age, sex, and family history. Physiological manifestation may include such reactions as migraine headaches, ulcers, diarrhea, muscle tension, and heart disease. Emotional manifestations include such reactions as depression, anxiety, irritability, and nervousness. Behavioral manifestations generally include excessive smoking or overeating (American Academy of Family Physicians, 1979).

The ways in which teachers may manifest specific responses to burnout on the job is cause for concern. Spaniol and Caputo (1979) have formulated a list of symptoms that may indicate that a teacher is experiencing burnout: a high level of absenteeism, lateness for work, a low level of enthusiasm, decline in performance, lack of focus, a high level of complaints, lack of communication, and a lack of openness to new ideas.

The implications of teacher burnout are grave and broadly based. They include the individual's own personal dissatisfaction, his or her family's unhappiness, chronic health problems, problems with colleagues and school administrators, and, ultimately, ineffective teaching. Sparks and Ingram (1979) reported that the teachers from whom students learn the most are reasonable, relaxed, enthusiastic, and interested in their students. Teachers who are consistently feeling stressed have been described as irritable, tense, humorless, depressed, self-involved, and unable to perform their job well. In general, Needle et al.

(1981) found that job stress affects the classroom environment, the teaching/learning process, and the attainment of educational goals and objectives.

To reduce the possibility of teacher burnout, teachers must be provided with knowledge and information on effective methods of coping with stress in the environment. One popular method has been involvement in stress management workshops (Betkouski, 1981). These workshops have been effective in providing teachers with strategies for coping with stress such as forming support groups, reviewing exercise and nutrition patterns, developing hobbies and interests outside the work environment, and practicing relaxation techniques (Shannon & Saleeby, 1980). The prevention of burnout in teaching, however, must first and foremost involve a serious commitment to improving the quality and circumstances under which teachers work.

REFERENCES

American Academy of Family Physicians. (1979). *A report on the lifestyles/personal health in different occupations: A study of attitudes and practices.* Kansas City: Research Forecasts.

Bensky, J., Shaw, S. F., Gouse, A. S., Bates, H., Dixon, B., & Beane, W. (1980). Public law 94-142 and stress: A problem for educators. *Exceptional Children, 47*(1), 24–29.

Betkouski, M. (1981 March). On making stress work for you: Strategies for coping. *Science Teacher, 48,* 35–37.

Bradfield, R. H., & Fones, D. M. (1985). Stress and the special teacher: How bad is it? *Academic Therapy, 20*(5), 571–577.

Cichon, D. J., & Koff, R. H. (1980, March). Stress and teaching. *National Association of Secondary School Principals Bulletin,* 91–103.

Coates, T. J., & Thoresen, C. E. (1976). Teacher anxiety: A review with recommendations. *Review of Educational Research, 46,* 159–184.

Freudenberger, H. J. (1974). Staff burn-out. *Journal of Social Issues, 30*(1), 159–165.

Gold, Y. (1985). Burnout: Causes and solutions. *Clearinghouse, 58,* 210–212.

Greenberg, S. F., & Valletutti, P. J. (1980). *Stress and the helping professions.* Baltimore, MD: Brookes.

Maslach, C. (1977). Job burnout: How people cope. *Public Welfare, 36,* 61–63.

Needle, R., Griffin, T., & Svendsen, R., & Berney, M. (1981). Occupational stress: Coping and health problems of teachers. *Journal of School Health, 51,* 175–181.

Pines, A., & Maslach, C. (1977, April). *Detached concern and burnout in mental health professions.* Paper presented at the 2nd National Conference on Child Abuse and Neglect, Houston, TX.

Shannon, C., & Saleeby, D. (1980). Training child welfare workers to cope with burnout. *Child Welfare, 59*(8), 463–468.

Spaniol, L., & Caputo, J. (1979). *Professional burnout: A personal survival kit.* Boston: Human Services Associates.

Sparks, D., & Ingram, M. J. (1979). Stress prevention and management: A workshop approach. *Personnel & Guidance Journal, 59,* 197–200.

Weiskopf, P. A. (1980). Burn-out among teachers of exceptional children. *Exceptional Children, 47*(1), 18–23.

Wilson, C. F., & Hall, D. L. (1981). *Preventing burnout in education*. La Mesa, CA: Wright Group.

MARSHA H. LUPI
Hunter College, City University of New York

TEACHER EFFECTIVENESS
TEACHER EXPECTANCIES

TEACHER CENTERS (TC)

A teacher center represents a centralized setting that facilitates teacher development, in-service programs, and the exchange of ideas (Hering, 1983). Initially, TCs were funded directly with federal dollars. The basis for this funding was the passage in 1976 of PL 94-482. Approximately 110 TCs were directly supported by the federal government. However, as noted by Edelfelt in 1982, "The categorical assignment of funds for teacher centers . . . [was] terminated in the fiscal year 1982 federal budget" (p. 393). The majority of TCs have continued as a result of their funding from other local and state sources. Their continuation supports the contention that the original concepts that premised their initiation are still valid.

A primary factor that led to the origination of TCs in the United States in the mid-1970s was the interest of teachers in being in charge of their own in-service training and to keep up with new educational trends and curricular concepts. The idea was that TC in-service programs were to depart from the traditional and standard in-service programs, e.g., one-time sessions on a given topic such as discipline or learning activities for the talented and gifted. In contrast, the intent of established TC in-service programs was to be innovative and to influence professional development; those goals are still desirable today.

Another of the original precepts was that TCs would have a full-time director who was both an administrator and a teacher. The director would then become the nucleus of a governing board that was to consist of local citizens. Boards with an efficient mix of leadership, inspiration, and idealism were and are in a position effectively to institute needed changes. Weiler (1983) has outlined a blueprint for the establishment of new TCs that make needed changes possible.

Researchers (Commission on Reading, 1984; Committee on Education and Labor, 1984; Kozal, 1984; Tunley, 1985; Zorinsky, 1985) estimate that 12 to 18% of the teenage and adult population groups are functionally illiterate. There are 25 to 40 million Americans who are handicapped with depressed literacy skills in the primary academic areas of reading, writing, and arithmetic. This instructional need is one that active TCs can legitimately embrace through the initiation of planned in-service programs that retrain teachers to be more efficient in their instruction.

Beyond the need for TC to endorse direct instructional intervention to improve the efficiency of classroom instruction, Hering (1983) identified a composite of five major functions that TCs can attend to: (1) assist teachers in their more immediate awareness of changes in instructional knowledge as it appears in educational literature; (2) assist teachers to be more efficient in meeting the social educational goals of students that society expects its nation's schools to attend to; (3) assist teachers to be more effective in their classrooms in attending to their students' developmental and remedial instructional needs; (4) assist teachers in achieving increased social and psychological competence; and, (5) assist teachers as a faculty group to be more responsible to the needs of the group.

The history of TCs (Edelfelt, 1982) has had its share of developmental setbacks. However, as Hering (1983) has pointed out, TCs that work toward a quality program of instruction for all students will simultaneously attain from the community and the school board recognition of the worth and the work of teachers. Teacher centers that are influential in achieving quality instruction for any one group or classification of students have the probability of doing the same for any other group or classification of students, including the special education student.

REFERENCES

Commission on Reading. (1984). *Becoming a nation of readers*. Washington, DC: U.S. Department of Education.

Committee on Education and Labor. (1984). *Illiteracy and the scope of the problem in this country*. Washington, DC: U.S. Government Printing Office.

Edelfelt, R. A. (1982, September). Critical issues in developing teacher centers. *Education Digest, 48,* 28–31.

Hering, W. M. (1983). *Research on teachers' centers: A summary of fourteen research efforts*. Washington, DC: National Institute of Education.

Kozal, J. (1984). *Illiterate america*. Garden City, NY: Doubleday.

Tunley, R. (1985, September). America's secret shame. *Reader's Digest*, 104–108.

Weiler, P. (1983, September). Blueprint for a teacher center. *Instructor, 93,* 146–148.

Zorinsky, E. (1985). The National Commission on Illiteracy Act. *Congressional Record, 131*(41). Washington, DC: U.S. Government Printing Office.

ROBERT T. NASH
University of Wisconsin, Oshkosh

IN SERVICE TRAINING OF SPECIAL EDUCATION TEACHERS
INSTRUCTIONAL MEDIA CENTER

TEACHER EDUCATION AND SPECIAL EDUCATION

Teacher Education and Special Education is the official journal of the Teacher Education Division (TED) of the Council for Exceptional Children (CEC). The purposes of *Teacher Education and Special Education* are to support goals of the TED, and to stimulate thoughtful consideration of the critical issues that are shaping the future of teacher education.

The journal is published four times a year and the first issue of each volume is a potpourri issue that includes articles dealing with a wide range of topics. The second issue focuses on either preservice, in-service, or doctoral preparation. The third issue focuses on a topic of timely interest in personnel preparation. The last issue focuses on research and/or evaluation activities related to personnel preparation.

Each manuscript is screened by the editor and then sent to issue reviewers. The editor reserves the right to make minor changes that will not alter the content of the article. *Teacher Education and Special Education* is sent to all members of the TED of the Council for Exceptional Children; the dues are $10 per year.

Rebecca Bailey
Texas A&M University

COUNCIL FOR EXCEPTIONAL CHILDREN

TEACHER EFFECTIVENESS

Over the last 12 years, field-based studies have been conducted on the teaching process that related specific teaching behaviors to student achievement outcomes. The results of these studies have appeared in professional literature only within the last 8 years (Crawford et al., 1978; Anderson, Evertson, & Brophy, 1979; Fisher et al., 1978; Good & Grouws, 1977, 1979; Stallings, Needles, & Strayrook, 1979). In general, these studies have found that there is a common set of process variables that can be observed or documented in effective teachers across grade and subject areas. It is further indicated that less effective teachers do not demonstrate these same behaviors to the appropriate degree.

The body of this research clearly speaks to a technology of teaching, making it increasingly clear that teachers and what they do are important determinants of student achievement. We know that effective teachers (1) optimize academic learning time; (2) reward achievement in appropriate ways; (3) use interactive teaching practices; (4) hold and communicate high expectations for student performance; and (5) select appropriate units of instruction.

There are, of course, exceptions to these and other principles, and as such, teachers need to be adaptable. The research does not say that there is one best system of teaching but rather that the teacher must constantly be analyzing the feedback from students and performance data and making decisions to modify the instruction. Therefore, the findings from the teacher effectiveness studies and related research should be viewed as road maps with the teacher constantly making decisions regarding the best route to pursue and sometimes alter the selected route based on new information. In general, the literature strongly addresses the need to train teachers as accurate decision makers.

Changing teachers' behaviors has not been found to be as difficult a task as first believed (Good, 1979). Studies have examined the amount of intervention needed to create a change that will affect teacher effectiveness (Coladarci & Gage, 1984; Good, 1979; Mohlman, Coladarci, & Gage, 1982). Coladarci and Gage (1984) found that there is a lower limit in regard to how little can be done while still achieving a meaningful change in behavior. Periodic direct observation of teachers appears to be one component that facilitates adoption of the practices. An enthusiastic presentation of the information to the teachers and a spirit of support for the practices also appear to be important. Mohlman et al. (1982) found that teacher acceptance of change to the use of effective teaching practices was based on (1) teaching recommendations being stated in explicit, easily understood language; (2) a philosophical acceptance of the suggested practice on the part of the teacher; and (3) teachers' perceived view of the cost in terms of time and effort and a belief that the investment in time and effort was worth the payoff in expected student achievement.

Mohlman et al. (1982) also found that teacher acceptance of the innovations is more important than understanding of the innovations. One other finding from the research is that teachers who were trained in effective teaching practices either by workshop, summaries, or workbooks are much more likely to use these practices in their classrooms than teachers who were not provided with such information.

Various authors have separated the major components of effective teaching practices into different configurations. One possible organization places these practices under the domains of management, decision making, time utilization, and instruction, all of which interact with each other and result in the development of a supportive classroom climate. These domains and their subdomains are based on the experimental and correlational research reported regularly in journals on studies involving instructional strategies.

Effective teachers use effective classroom management. Effective classroom management means (1) organizing the physical classroom to minimize disruptions; (2) establishing teaching rules and procedures and adhering to those rules and procedures; and (3) anticipating problem situations and having action plans to prevent problems or deal with them when they occur.

Management has repeatedly been demonstrated as a critical element of effective teaching in major studies, including *The First Grade Reading Group Study* (Evertson et al., 1981) and *The Study of a Training Program in Classroom Organization and Management for Secondary School Teachers* (Fitzpatrick, 1982). Management inclues the establishment and teaching of rules and procedures, specification of consequences, physical organization of the classroom, and behaviors on the part of the teacher that prevent disruptive behavior. Good room management eliminates potential distractions for students and minimizes opportunities for students to disrupt others. Students' desks are arranged so that students can easily see instructional displays and visuals and so that students can be easily monitored by the teacher. Students are seated so as to eliminate "action zones." These zones are created when students select seating locations. There is a tendency in self-selection for high-ability learners to sit together in the front and low-ability students to sit at the back or side. The more effective teacher will intermingle with these students. When hand raisers are spread throughout the room, it will enable the teacher to spread his or her attention more evenly and become sensitized to low responders.

Rules govern student behaviors such as talking and respect for property. Effective teachers have only three to six rules stated in generic language. These are posted and taught through examples to students at the beginning of the school year. Merely posting rules is less effective than posting and teaching the rules. Established procedures and routines are time-saving mechanisms. When procedures are established, students know when to use the bathroom, how to head papers, how to distribute and collect assignments, how to ask for help, and so on. Without such established procedures, time is lost in explanations, or students disrupt the classroom by not knowing the procedures.

Consistency in enforcing the rules is a hallmark of effective teachers. Effective teachers have a hierarchy of consequences they follow to maintain the rules. Eye contact, moving closer to a student, or a pointed finger might be the first level of intervention. Withholding a privilege, assigning detention, conferencing with a student, or having a student restate a broken rule might be the second level. Contacting parents, behavioral contracting, or outside assistance might constitute the third level. In all cases, the teacher should remain calm when enforcing a rule.

Prevention of problems is largely brought about by advanced planning. A teacher can help prevent behavior problems by staying in close proximity to students while frequently teaching and monitoring them. A teacher should plan positive comments that can be used with students to establish a positive mood. Finally, a teacher should formulate plans to handle hypothetical disciplinary situations.

One major reason why management is such a critical variable in the teaching process is because of its relationship to instructional time. Instructional time is highly related to academic achievement. Walberg's (1982) review of studies involving time and achievement found correlation ranges from .13 to .71 with a median of .41. Ninety-five percent of the 25 studies reviewed as "time-on-learning" reported positive effects. Instructional time is lost for members of a class where students are disruptive, procedures are not readily available for teaching, and students do not understand the behavioral expectations of the teacher.

Decision making is generally an unobservable phenomenon, but the products of the decision are observable. Teachers regularly make decisions on content, time allocations, pacing, grouping, and class activities. If the content is not taught, then students generally do not learn. The literature uses the term "opportunity to learn" when describing this phenomenon. According to Berliner (1985), teachers make content decisions based on (1) the amount of effort required to teach the subject, (2) the perceived difficulty for the students, and (3) the teacher's personal feelings of enjoyment. In making content decisions, knowledge of the subject discipline appears to be of importance. The teacher's philosophy also enters into content decisions. Research from teacher effectiveness studies shows wide variability between the subject matter content covered by teachers of the same subject and grade.

Time allocation decisions involve time allotted across the school day and within a curriculum area. Observational studies on teacher behavior indicate that less than 1% of the time available in reading classes focuses on the teaching of reading comprehension (Pearson & Gallagher, 1983). Fisher et al. (1978) found some teachers of the same grade level allocated 16 minutes of instruction in math each day while others were allocated 51 minutes. The basic principle that evolves from this data is that teachers' time allocation decisions can affect students' opportunity to learn.

Pacing involves the rate at which a teacher covers the course or subject material. The more material that is covered, the more opportunity to learn is given; hence, each student attains a higher achievement level. The corollary to the pacing principle is that students need to be learning the material at the pace that is followed. More effective teachers solicit regular feedback from students by frequent tests and questioning; they use that information to gauge the pace of the instruction. Sometimes the textbooks impose a pace. Why do students learn to spell 20 new words each week? Because the textbooks are set up to teach 20 words a week. Some students could learn 40, others only 10. Teachers need to be aware of how materials may put limitations on pacing.

If grouping is to be done, the teacher must base the

grouping on objective criteria related to a valid achievement measure and must frequently reassess the value of the grouping. A problem inherent in grouping is the possible increased gap that can be created among different groups based on a difference in pacing. Grouping decisions cannot be taken lightly, and alternatives to grouping and differential pacing might be explored by teachers prior to a grouping decision. Teachers need to understand the consequences of grouping decisions as reflected in subsequent student achievement.

Appropriate use of time is a third component in a teaching effectiveness model. Research by Stallings et al. (1979), and Walberg (1979), and many others has revealed that time use is more important than time per se. Time can be conceptualized according to the activities being conducted. Berliner (1984) has identifed the following components of time: allocated time, engaged time, time related to outcome, and academic learning time. Academic learning time (ALT) is most related to student achievement. The key is to increase the amount of ALT within the time allocated for instruction. Strategies related to room arrangement, minimizing transition time, and teaching material at the conceptual level of students all need to be addressed to increase ALT. Research on effective teachers reveals that they plan the use of their school day, allocate a greater percent of the school day to the basic subjects, and teach in groups so that students can get more instructional time. They spend 50% of their reading periods actually engaged in reading instruction. They use short periods of time (not over 30 seconds) to assist individual students with problems in seat work. They circulate among the students doing seat work to ensure a high degree of on-task behavior.

Most research on teacher effectiveness has been done with students in the elementary grades; some has been done at the junior high or secondary level. All have come to similar conclusions about effective teaching (Lightfoot, 1981; Stallings, 1981). MacKinzie (1983) has noted, however, that while the core principles are the same, their expression in actual practice are different. High-school faculties are content specialists who hold little investment in basic skills.

Teaching strategies are the final component of the model. They represent a wide variety of specific procedures. These strategies are based on basic principles of learning and the interaction of those principles with student characteristics. Teaching requires explanation, elaboration, and clarification. Sequence, order, modeling, appropriate practice, goal setting, basic concept development, feedback, questioning, and a host of procedures and learning principles can be collapsed under this heading. The critical feature is to train teachers in the effective use of these procedures and in making decisions on when to best use each.

Effective teachers practice effective instruction a large percentage of the day. Instruction requires explanation, demonstration, and clarification. Effective instruction requires that material be explained and reviewed so that new material can be linked to old. Using demonstration and practice while focusing attention on the relevant dimension of a concept is a teaching art. The science of instruction followed by effective teachers is comprised of modeling, questioning, providing prompts and cues, providing feedback, and providing opportunities to practice newly learned skills. Students in classes taught by effective teachers know the goals and the expectations of the teachers for meeting those goals. Finally, research substantiates that effective teachers are people who believe they can make a difference in student achievement.

REFERENCES

Anderson, L. M., Evertson, C. M. & Brophy, J. E. (1979). An experimental study of effective teaching in first-grade reading groups. *Elementary School Journal, 79*, 193–222.

Berliner, D. C. (1984). The half-full glass: A review of research in teaching. In P. L. Hosford (ed.), *Using What We Know about Teaching*. Alexandra, VA: Association for Supervision and Curriculum Development.

Caladarci, T., & Gage, N. L. (1984). Effects of minimal intervention on teacher behavior and student achievement. *American Educational Research Journal, 21*(3), 539–555.

Crawford, et al. (1978). *An experiment on teacher effectiveness and parent assisted instruction in the third grade* (3 vols.). Stanford, CA: Center for Educational Research at Stanford.

Emmer, E., Evertson, C., Sanford, J., Clements, B., & Worsham, M. (1982). *Organizing and managing the junior high classroom*. Austin: Research and Development Center for Teacher Education, University of Texas.

Evertson, C., Emmer, E., Clements, B., Sanford, J., Worsham, M. & Williams, E. (1981). *Organizing and managing the elementary school classroom*. Austin: Research and Development Center for Teacher Education, University of Texas.

Fisher, et al. (1978). *Teaching behaviors, academic learning time, and student achievement: Final report of Phase III-B, Beginning Teacher Evaluation Study (Technical Report V-1)*. San Francisco: Far West Regional Laboratory for Educational Research and Development.

Fitzpatrick, K. (1981). *Successful management strategies for the secondary classroom*. Downers Grove, IL.

Good, T. & Grouws, D. (1977). Teaching effects: A process-product study in fourth-grade mathematics classrooms. *Journal of Teacher Education, 28*, 49–54.

Good, T. L. (1979). Teacher effectiveness in the elementary school: What we know about it. *Journal of Teacher Education, 30*, 52–64.

Good, T. L., & Grouws, D. A. (1979). The Missouri mathematics effectiveness project. *Journal of Educational Psychology, 71*, 355–382.

Lightfoot, S. L. (1981). Portraits of exemplary secondary schools: Highland Park. *Daedalus, 110*(4), 59–80.

Mackinzie, D. E. (1983). Research for school improvement: An appraisal of some recent trends. *Educational Researcher, 12*(4), 5–17.

Mohlman, G., Caladarci, T., & Gage, N. L. (1982). Comprehension

and attitude as predictors of implementation of teacher training. *Journal of Teacher Education, 33*, 31, 36.

Pearson, P. D. & Gallagher, M. C. (1983). The instruction of reading comprehension. *Contemporary Educational Psychology, 8*,
317–344.

Stallings, J. A. (1981). *What research has to say to administrators
of secondary schools about effective teaching and staff development.* Paper presented at the Conference Creating the Conditions for Effective Teaching, Center for Educational Policy
and Management, Eugene, OR.

Stallings, J., Needles, M. & Strayrook, N. (1979). *The teaching of
basic reading skills in secondary schools, Phase I and Phase
II.* Menlo Park, CA: Stanford Research Institute.

Walberg, H. J. (1979). *Educational environments and effects: Evolution, policy, and productivity.* Berkeley, CA: McCutchon.

Walberg, H. J. (1982). What makes schooling effective? A synthesis and a critique of three national studies. *Contemporary
Education: A Journal of Reviews, 1*(1), 22–34.

ROBERT A. SEDLAK
University of Wisconsin, Stout

TEACHER BURNOUT
TEACHER EXPECTANCIES
TEACHING STRATEGIES

TEACHER EXPECTANCIES

The general area of teacher expectancies involves investigating the effects of teachers' perceptions, beliefs, or attitudes about their students. Rosenthal and Jacobson
(1968) tested kindergarten through fifth-grade children
and then randomly identified some of them by telling their
teachers that they had the greatest potential to show significant academic achievement over the school year. Results demonstrating that these children made significantly greater IQ gains than the control groups were
interpreted to suggest that the teachers' expectations for
the higher potential children influenced their teaching interactions with them, positively affecting the children's
learning, as manifested in the higher scores. These results
and interpretations were rejected by some owing to methodological flaws; e.g., the failure to measure the teachers'
changed expectations and their teaching interactions.
Later studies (Hall & Merkel, 1985) failed to replicate
these results and indicated that teachers base their expectations for the most part on criteria relevant to academic performance and that they do not bias children's
education.

With respect to the handicapped, teacher expectations
have been discussed mostly in conjunction with the effects
of labeling. Within this field, there is a fear that children's
special education labels will cause teachers, parents, and
others to lower their expectations for these children's academic and social development. The term self-fulfilling
prophecy has been used to describe teachers' expectations
and resulting instructional interactions that reinforce
handicapped children to act in a manner consistent with

the stereotypical characteristics of their handicap. There
is the possibility that these children will have difficulty
in learning because "they are handicapped," and may master skills only up to a level popularly ascribed to their
handicap. This self-fulfilling prophecy, then, might lower
teachers' and others' expectations for handicapped children, lower the children's expectations for themselves, and
significantly limit the educational opportunities for them
because they are not exposed to more advanced work or
complex learning situations.

The research investigating teacher expectancies with
handicapped individuals has been inconclusive. While
some studies have demonstrated that labels do affect
teacher perceptions and expectations of handicapped children, others have shown no significant negative effects.
MacMillan (1977) appropriately concludes:

> Although it [the evidence] does not demonstrate convincingly
> that calling attention to people with [for example] intellectual
> deficiencies by giving them special attention is always a bad
> thing, the controversy over labeling should make us all more
> sensitive to its potential hazards. (p. 245)

Hobbs (1975), who coordinated a national study on the
effect of labels and their resulting expectancy effects, similarly noted no simple solution to the issues as long as
labels are required for entrance into special education programs and for the reimbursement of federal and state
funds to finance these programs. What appears necessary
at this time are ways to minimize the potential expectancy
effect of labels while permitting their continued use in the
field.

REFERENCES

Hall, V. C., & Merkel, S. P. (1985). Teacher expectancy effects
and educational psychology. In J. B. Dusek (Ed.), *Teacher expectancies* (pp. 67–92). Hillsdale, NJ: Erlbaum.

Hobbs, N. (1975). *The future of children.* San Francisco: Jossey-
Bass.

MacMillan, D. L. (1977). *Mental retardation in school and society.*
Boston: Little, Brown.

Rosenthal, R., & Jacobson, L. (1968). *Pygmalion in the classroom.*
New York: Holt, Rinehart, & Winston.

HOWARD M. KNOFF
University of South Florida

PYGMALIAN EFFECT

TEACHING EXCEPTIONAL CHILDREN (TEC)

Teaching Exceptional Children (*TEC*) is a professional
journal that is a joint production of the Council for Exceptional Children Information Center and the Instructional Materials Centers Network for Handicapped Children and Youth. It was first published in 1968 and now
has a circulation of 70,000.

Edited by June B. Jordan, TEC's objective is "to disseminate practical and timely information to classroom

teachers working with exceptional children and youth." Published quarterly the journal deals with various topic areas such as practical classroom procedures for use with the gifted and handicapped, educational-diagnostic techniques, evaluation of instructional material, new research findings, and reports of educational projects in progress.

The *TEC* is designed to garner feedback from readers and allow for professional input through features such as "The Teacher Idea Exchange," "Questions and Answers," "Teacher Write In," and "Letters to the Editor."

Information concerning subscriptions or manuscripts should be referred to Publication for Council for Exceptional Children, 1920 Association Drive, Reston, VA 22091.

RICK GONZALES
Texas A&M University

COUNCIL FOR EXCEPTIONAL CHILDREN

TEACHING STRATEGIES

Teaching strategies are those activities that are conducted by a teacher to enhance the academic achievement of students. A teaching strategy is based on a philosophical approach that is used in conjunction with a learning strategy. Teachers generally choose a particular approach based on their educational background and training, their personal beliefs, the subject being taught, the characteristics of the learner, and the degree of learning required.

Training backgrounds of special educators can range from the behavioral to the process-oriented. Teachers with behavioral backgrounds will use approaches that are task specific and focus on observable behaviors. Those coming from a process background are more inclined to follow approaches that focus on underlying processes. They try to treat the hypothesized cause of the problem or deficit rather than the observable behavior. Approaches such as perceptual-motor training or cognitive training may be followed by teachers with process orientations. Perceptual-motor training approaches are controversial and have questionable effectiveness in regard to academic achievement (Arter & Jenkins, 1979; Sedlak & Weener, 1973). Cognitive training approaches focus on thinking skills and learning how to learn rather than specific content skills. The research on this approach is promising. Examples of behavioral approaches are direct instruction and applied behavior analysis. These approaches focus on identifying the specific content to be taught and teaching that content in a systematic fashion using a prescribed system of learning strategies. There are also subject specific approaches. For example, in reading, some of the different approaches available are the linguistics approach, phonics, sight word, Fernald, multisensory, language experience, and the neurological impress method. These approaches focus on the organization of the materials needed for instruction and also prescribe, in some cases, specific strategies to be used.

In addition to an approach, the application of a learning strategy to a situation is needed to create a teaching strategy. A learning strategy becomes a teaching strategy when the teacher systematically plans, organizes, and uses a learning strategy with a student to achieve a specific outcome. In many texts, these learning strategies are referred to as generic strategies or principles of instruction. These strategies generally are used in conjunction with a particular phase of learning (e.g., acquisition, retention, or transfer), or for a particular type of learning (e.g., discrimination, concept, rule, problem solving). Generic strategies used for the acquisition phase include giving instruction (verbal, picture, modeling or demonstration, reading), revealing objectives to the learner, providing appropriate practice on a skill, providing feedback to the learner, organizing material into small steps and in sequential order, checking on student comprehension through questions, and offering positive and negative examples of concepts.

The generic strategies that can be used to maintain skills already acquired are overlearning, reminiscence, and spaced review. To teach for transfer, multiple examples of the application of the skill or concept are needed, along with teaching the skill with the appropriate cues in the setting in which it is to be practiced. Gradually fading artificial cues and relying on natural cues in the environment is another strategy used by teachers to facilitate transfer. Some other examples of teaching strategies are the use of mnemonics, peer teaching, assigned homework, graded homework, cooperative learning, mediated instruction, and computer-assisted instruction. In strategies such as these, a variety of learning strategies are organized and used.

REFERENCES

Arter, J. A., & Jenkins, J. R. (1979). Differential diagnosis—Prescriptive teaching: A critical appraisal. *Review of Educational Research, 49,* 517–555.

Sedlak, R. A., & Weener, P. (1973). Review of research on the Illinois Test of Psycholinguistics Abilities. In L. Mann & D. Sabatino, (Eds.), *The first review of special education.* Philadelphia: JSE.

ROBERT A. SEDLAK
University of Wisconsin, Stout

ABILITY TRAINING
APPLIED BEHAVIOR ANALYSIS
DIRECT INSTRUCTION
MNEMONICS

TECHNIQUES: A JOURNAL FOR REMEDIAL EDUCATION AND COUNSELING

Techniques originated in July 1984 with Gerald B. Fuller and Hubert Vance as coeditors. The journal provides multidisciplinary articles that serve as an avenue for communication and interaction among the various disciplines concerned with the treatment and education of the exceptional individual and others encountering special problems in living. The orientation is primarily clinical and educational, and reflects the various types of counseling, therapy, remediation, and interventions currently employed. The journal does not mirror the opinion of any one school or authority but serves as a forum for open discussion and exchange of ideas and experiences.

The specific sections in *Techniques* represent the following content areas:

1. *Educational and Psychological Materials.* This section helps the professional to keep current by evaluating, critiquing, comparing, and reviewing educational, counseling, and psychological materials (e.g., programs, kits) that are being proposed or used in applied settings.
2. *Research Studies.* This section offers empirical research, case studies, and discussion papers that focus on specific counseling, therapy, and remediation techniques that cut across various disciplines.
3. *Practical Approaches in the Field.* This section provides a description of hands-on techniques or approaches that the author(s) have used and found to be successful within their field.
4. *Parent Education.* This section provides comprehensive treatment of such topics as disruptive children and youths, single-parent families, reconstituted families, and prevention and treatment of child abuse and neglect.
5. *Bibliotherapy.* This is a compilation of books that are useful for the child and parent as well as the practitioner. The topics are practical and address such issues as divorce, self-concept, and drug abuse.
6. *What's New in the Field.* This section provides current information in the areas of remedial programs and counseling techniques, and includes reviews of current software programs.

GERALD B. FULLER
Central Michigan University

TECHNOLOGY FOR THE DISABLED

If there is one word that summarizes the impact of technology in the last 15 years, it is zeitgeist, the spirit of the time. The inculcation of silicon chips and microprocessors into our everyday lives has irrevocably changed us from an industrial society to an informational society (Toffler, 1982). If disabled persons are to fully function in this society, they must have access to the myriad technologies that can improve communication, information processing, and learning. While technological advances are making inroads in the reduction of the impact of motoric, sensory, and cognitive disabilities, the real potential is yet to be met. The following section is an introduction to some of the technologies that are currently affecting the lives of

disabled persons. It also offers an overview of some of the technologies that have yet to fulfill their promise.

The computer is second only to the printing press in its impact on the way in which humans acquire and distribute information. As computers are reduced in size and cost, their impact is multiplied geometrically. The computer has two characteristics that are particularly significant for disabled individuals: (1) as hardware decreases in size, it generally increases in capacity; and (2) the more sophisticated computers become, the easier they are to use. These characteristics are very important for handicapped individuals in several respects. First, as computers become smaller, they also become more portable. For example, hand-held microcomputers can be attached to wheelchairs to improve mobility. Second, as computers become easier to use, they are more accessible to the handicapped. For example, reducing the number of keystrokes required to perform certain computer functions has greatly facilitated their use.

Microprocessor-based technology facilitates communication in two ways: as a compensatory device for sensory disabilities and as an assistive device for individuals whose physical impairments make communication difficult. Examples of compensatory devices include talking computer terminals that can translate text into speech (Stoffel, 1982); special adaptive devices for microcomputers that can provide visual displays of auditory information by translating sound into text (Vanderheiden, 1982); and Cognivox, an adaptive device for Apple personal computers that combines the capabilities of voice recognition and voice output (Murray, 1982).

For individuals with motoric disabilities, communication aids have been developed that allow them to operate computers with single-switch input devices. These devices may be as simple as game paddles and joysticks or as sophisticated as screen-based optical headpointing systems. Keyboard enhancers and emulators help individuals with restricted movement by reducing the number of actuations necessary for communication. For example, Minispeak is a semantic compaction system that can produce thousands of clear, spoken sentences with as few as seven keystrokes (Baker, 1982). Adaptive communication devices can also be linked with microcomputers to help the disabled control their living environments (e.g., by running appliances, answering the telephone, or adjusting the thermostat).

The term telecommunication means communication across distance. It is a means of storing text and pictures as electronic impulses and transmitting them via telephone line, satellite, coaxial cable, or broadcast transmission. Telecommunication offers several advantages over traditional means of communication. First, telecommunication is relatively inexpensive when spread across time and users. Also, telecommunicating helps alleviate the problems associated with geographic remoteness or the isolation imposed by limited mobility. Information-gathering and dissemination need not be limited to schools. It can occur in the home or office; a local area network (LAN) can link several microcomputers or terminals to a computer with expanded memory. Such a system permits several operators to use the same software and data simultaneously. A wide-area network links computers from distant geographic regions. Examples of this networking capability can be found in several states where all of the local agencies are linked to the state agency. Statewide systems greatly reduce the time and paperwork necessary for compliance with special education legislation.

SpecialNet is another example of a wide-area network. The 2500 subscribers use it primarily to access electronic bulletin boards and to send messages through electronic mail. Electronic bulletin boards function much the same as traditional corkboards found in most schools. Users can post messages to obtain information, or they can read messages to find out the latest information about a given topic. For example, the employment bulletin board on SpecialNet posts vacancies in special education and related services. The Request for Proposals (RFP) bulletin board has information on the availability of upcoming grants and contracts. The exchange bulletin board is for users to post requests for information. Electronic mail, as the name implies, is a system whereby computer users can send and receive messages through their computers. On the SpecialNet system, each subscriber is given a special name that identifies his or her mailbox; with the aid of word processing and telecommunication software, users can send short or long documents in a matter of seconds.

In addition to capabilities offered by electronic bulletin boards and electronic mail, individuals with telecommunication hookups have access to information from large electronic libraries that store, sort, and retrieve bibliographic information. For example, the Educational Resources Information Center (ERIC), operated by the Council for Exceptional Children, is the largest source of information on handicapped and gifted children. Other important sources of information are the Handicapped Exchange (HEX), which contains information on handicapped individuals, and ABLEDATA, which is a catalog of computer hardware, software, and assistive devices for the handicapped.

Another important form of telecommunication is teletext, a one-way transmission to television viewers. Teletext uses the vertical blanking interval (VBI), the unused portion of a television signal, to print information on television screens. Current applications of teletext include news headlines, weather forecasts, and information on school closings. Closed captioning is a form of teletext that allows hearing-impaired individuals to see dialogue (JWK International, 1983). Experiments are now under way to use teletext to transmit instructional material. Broadcasters can transmit public domain software into homes and schools that have microcomputers and special transmission decoding devices.

A videodisk is a tabletop device that is interfaced with a monitor to play video programs stored on 12-inch disks. When interfaced with a microcomputer, the videodisk becomes interactive, and thus becomes a powerful instructional tool. Part of the videodisk's power comes from its storage capacity; it can hold 54,000 frames of information, including movies, filmstrips, slides, and sound. When com-

bined with the microcomputer's branching capacity, videodisks allow students to move ahead or go back according to the learner's needs. Information can also be shown in slow motion or freeze frame. One of the earliest educational videodisks was the First National Kidisc, a collection of games and activities for children. The California School for the Deaf in Riverside also developed a system to use the videodisk to teach language development and reading. With this system, students use light pens to write their responses on the screen (Wollman, 1981). In the past, videodisk technology has been very expensive because of the cost in developing the disks. Now, however, educators and other service providers can have customized disks made at relatively low cost.

Artificial intelligence refers to the use of the computer to solve the same types of problems and to make the same kinds of decisions faced by humans (Yin & Moore, 1984). Because scientists do not fully understand how humans solve problems and make decisions, they have debated whether true artificial intelligence is possible. So far, the closest they have come is the development of expert systems, natural systems, and machine vision. Expert systems are computer programs that use knowledge and inference strategies to solve problems. The systems rely on three kinds of information: facts, relations between the facts, and methods for using the facts to solve problems (D'Ambrosio, 1985). An example of an expert system is Internist, which makes medical diagnoses. Natural language processing is the use of natural speech to communicate with computers and to translate foreign language texts. Machine vision takes advantage of sensory devices to reproduce objects on the computer screen. These technological applications, like many others, offer potential benefits to disabled individuals, but their use for physical or cognitive prostheses hinges on the commitment of vast resources for their development.

A robot is a device that can be programmed to move in specified directions and to manipulate objects. What distinguishes a robot from other technologies and prosthetic devices is its capacity for locomotion. Robotic arms can pick up and move objects, assemble parts, and even spray paint. Robots of the future will not only be able to move, they will also be able to sense the environment by touch, sight, or sound. More important, the robot will be able to acquire information, understand it, and plan and implement appropriate actions (Yin & Moore, 1984). While robots offer great potential as prosthetic devices for the disabled, their current use is limited primarily to research and manufacturing. To some extent, robots are being used in classrooms to teach computer logic.

REFERENCES

Baker, B. (1982). Minispeak: A semantic compaction system that makes self-expression easier for communicatively disabled individuals. *Byte, 7,* 186–202.

D'Ambrosio, B. (1985). Expert systems—Myth or reality? *Byte, 10,* 275–282.

JWK International. (1983). *Teletext and videotex* (Contract No.

300-81-0424). Washington, DC: Special Education Programs Office.

Murray, W. (1982). The Cognivox V10-1003: Voice recognition and output for the Apple II. *Byte, 7,* 231–235.

Pfaehler, B. (1985). Electronic text: The University of Wisconsin experience. *T.H.E. Journal, 13,* 67–70.

Stoffel, D. (1982). Talking terminals. *Byte, 7,* 218–227.

Toffler, A. (1982). *The third wave.* New York: Bantham.

Vanderheiden, G. (1982). Computers can play a dual role for disabled individuals. *Byte, 7,* 136–162.

Wollman, J. (1981). The videodisc: A new educational technology takes off. *Electronic Learning, 1,* 39–40.

Yin, R. K., & Moore, G. B. (1984). *Robotics, artificial intelligence, computer simulation: Future applications in special education.* Washington, DC: U.S. Department of Education.

ELIZABETH MCCLELLAN
*Council for Exceptional
Children, Reston, Virginia*

COMPUTER USE WITH THE HANDICAPPED
ROBOTICS
SPECIALNET

TECSE

See EARLY CHILDHOOD SPECIAL EDUCATION, TOPICS IN.

TEGRETOL

Tegretol is most often referred to in the literature as carbamazepine, its generic name. It is a drug that is effective as an anticonvulsant and as a specific analgesic for trigeminal neuralgia. It is efficacious in the treatment of simple and complex partial seizures with or without secondary tonic-clonic seizures (often known as grand mal seizures) (Henriksen, Johannessen, & Munthe-Kaas, 1983). Absence seizures do not appear to be responsive to Tegretol. Though an effective drug, there has been concern about possible hematologic reactions; consequently, many physicians are hesitant to use it (Huf & Schain, 1980). There is some indication that these hematologic side effects are less common than had been thought (Henriksen, et al., 1983; Huf & Schain, 1980).

Because Tegretol is intoxicating and produces less sedation than other anticonvulsant medication (Dodrill, 1981), children treated with Tegretol may be less likely to experience difficulties with attention and concentration (Schain, 1983) and the associated behavioral and learning problems. There has been some suggestion (Rodin et al., 1976) that Tegretol might have some psychotropic antidepressant effects, but it is not clear whether the drug itself is responsible or whether this reflects cessation of other more sedating medication (Dodrill, 1981). Side effects other than the hematologic ones are rare (Dreifuss, 1983) but include allergic reactions, lethargy, ataxia, dy-

plopia, irritability, and gastrointestinal symptoms (Henrikson et al., 1983).

REFERENCES

Dodrill, C. B. (1981). Neuropsychology of epilepsy. In S. B. Filskov & T. J. Boll (Eds.), *Handbook of clinical neuropsychology* (pp. 366–395). New York: Wiley.

Dreifuss, F. E. (1983). *Pediatric epileptology: Classification and management of seizures in the child.* Boston: Wright.

Henriksen, O., Johannessen, S. I., & Munthe-Kaas, A. W. (1983). How to use carbamazepine. In P. L. Morselli, C. E. Pippenger, & J. K. Penry (Eds.), *Antiepileptic drug therapy in pediatrics* (pp. 237–244). New York: Raven.

Huf, R., & Schain, R. J. (1980). Long term experiences with carbamazepine (Tegretol) in children with seizures. *Journal of Pediatrics, 97,* 310–312.

Rodin, E. A., Rim, C. F., Kitno, H., Louis, R., & Rennick, P. N. (1976). A comparison of the effectiveness of Primidone versus carbamazepine in epileptic outpatients. *Journal of Nervous & Mental Disease, 163,* 41–46.

Schain, R. J. (1983). Carbamazepine and cognitive functioning. In P. L. Morselli, C. E. Pippenger, & J. K. Penry (Eds.), *Antiepileptic drug therapy in pediatrics* (pp. 189–192). New York: Raven.

GRETA N. WILKENING
*Children's Hospital,
Denver, Colorado*

ABSENCE SEIZURES
ANTICONVULSANTS
GRAND MAL SEIZURES

TELECOMMUNICATION DEVICES FOR THE DEAF (TDDs; TTYs)

Telecommunication devices for the deaf (TDDs or TTYs) make communication by telephone available to the hearing-impaired population by providing video or printed modes of communication across regular phone lines. Using a modem, or acoustic coupler, a TDD user types out a message to another user. This message either moves across a video display screen or is typed on a roll of paper. In this fashion, conversations can be held and information exchanged as far as telephone wires extend.

A TDD uses a regular or slightly modified keyboard. Some special terminology is used to facilitate ease of transmission. GA, for go ahead, indicates to one user that the other is waiting for a reply. SK, for stop keying, denotes the completion of a conversation. Often a Q is typed to imply a question.

The number of TDDs in public and private use is increasing rapidly. Public service agencies such as libraries, schools, and airlines are using TDDs to enable the hearing-impaired population to use their services (Low, 1985). Police and fire departments use TDDs to ensure the safety of hearing-impaired individuals. The TDD has been hailed as a great contributor to the independence of hearing-impaired persons.

REFERENCE

Low, K. (1985). Telecommunication devices for the deaf. *American Libraries, 16*, 746–747.

MARY GRACE FEELY
School for the Deaf, New York, New York

DEAF
ELECTRONIC COMMUNICATION AIDS

TELECOMMUNICATIONS SYSTEMS IN SPECIAL EDUCATION

The use of telecommunication technology for special education mirrors the explosion of technology in society. In the same way that commercial electronic network services such as Compu-Serve and The Source have become widely known to the general public, SpecialNet is becoming known as an electronic mail service and information source for special educators. Similarly, transformation of the telephone system from copper to fiber optic wire will facilitate rapid data transmission for any use, including perhaps transfer of data on special education students as they move from district to district.

Certain types of telecommunication technologies (e.g., computer-assisted instruction) delivered over telephone lines from a central location, as in the University of Illinois' PLATO system, are being made obsolete as modifications are made for personal computers, thus reducing the costs of instruction delivery. Other technologies involving electronic memory and telephone transmission are expanding, notably ABLEDATA, a bibliographic source of information on assistive devices for the disabled.

Telecommunications technology, currently in a period of rapid change, may transform special education practice in much the same way that it is transforming communication worldwide. However, in contrast to other technologies developed specifically for the disabled, special education will benefit from technological advances for all citizens. Thus the average modern family may use a personal computer, modem, and telephone line as a link to specialized news sources, stock quotes and discount brokers, specialized electronic news services, and targeted mailboards or electronic mailboxes. Disabled persons, using the same systems, may communicate with other persons with similar interests, scan specialized information sources, work in competitive employment from their homes, and avail themselves of services provided for all citizens. Special educators in public schools and higher education may use telecommunications for much the same purposes, targeting their efforts toward the acquisition of information from rapidly expanding specialized information networks.

JAMES W. TAWNEY
Pennsylvania State University

COMPUTER-ASSISTED INSTRUCTION
ELECTRONIC COMMUNICATION AIDS

TEMPERAMENT

Individual differences in temperament have been recognized for centuries. The Greeks talked of four basic dispositions, Kretschmer (1925) and Sheldon (1942) related personality to body types, and Eysenck (1967) linked constitutional and personality variables. Yet, the notion of constitutional contributions to behavior received only limited formal attention from American psychologists and educators until relatively recently. Major impetus to the study of temperament has come from the work of psychiatrists Alexander Thomas and Stella Chess and their colleagues (Thomas & Chess, 1977; Thomas, Chess, Birch, Hertzig, & Korn, 1963), but independent support for the notion of temperament may be found in pediatric and psychiatric research (Carey, 1981, 1982, 1985a; Graham, Rutter, & George, 1973; Rutter, 1964; Rutter, Tizard, & Whitmore, 1970), in longitudinal studies of development (Lerner & Lerner, 1983; Werner & Smith, 1982), in research on infants (Bates, 1980, 1983; Rothbart & Derryberry, 1981) and on child-family interactions (Dunn & Kendrick, 1982; Hinde, Easton, Meller, & Tamplin, 1982; Stevenson-Hinde & Simpson, 1982), in twin studies (Goldsmith & Gottesman, 1981; Matheny, Wilson, & Nuss, 1984; Wilson, 1983; Wilson & Matheny, 1983), and in work in behavioral genetics (DeFries & Plomin, 1978; Plomin, 1982; Torgersen, 1982). At the present time, temperament is an important area of concern from both research and applied perspectives. Its relevance to special education and the development and adjustment of handicapped children is increasingly recognized.

Definitions. Although intuitively appealing, temperament has somewhat different definitions, depending on the investigator. Thomas and Chess (1977) view temperament as a stylistic variable. They consider that temperament describes how an individual behaves, not what an individual does or how well he or she does it. Thomas and Chess identified nine dimensions of temperament or behavioral style: activity level, adaptability, approach/withdrawal, attention span and persistence, distractibility, intensity of reaction, quality of mood, rhythmicity (regularity), and threshold of responsiveness. The dimensions were derived in part from Thomas and Chess's clinical observations, and were formalized in major longitudinal research, the New York Longitudinal Study (NYLS). In Thomas and Chess's view, these temperamental variations are, in part, constitutional in base.

The constitutional or biological anchoring of temperament is apparent in other definitions. Buss and Plomin (1975, 1984) propose that to be considered a temperament, a behavioral predisposition must meet criteria of developmental stability, presence in adulthood, adaptiveness, and presence in animals, and must have a genetic component. They define four dimensions that, in their view, meet these criteria: emotionality, activity, sociability, and impulsivity. Rothbart and Derryberry (1981), based primarily on their studies of human infants, suggest that temperament is best conceptualized as individual differences in reactivity and regulation that are presumed to be constitutionally based. Their formulation emphasizes arousal (or excitability) and the neural and behavioral processes that regulate or modulate it, a formulation consistent with that of Strelau (1983). Goldsmith and Campos (1986) adopt a somewhat different perspective, defining temperament as individual variation in emotionality, including differences in the primary emotions of fear, anger, sadness, pleasure, etc., as well as in a more general arousal; they consider both temperament and intensive parameters. It should be noted that a major definitional issue relates to distinctions between temperament and personality (Goldsmith & Campos, 1982; Rutter, 1982). Many investigators consider temperament a constitutional and genetic component of personality. This view is well reflected in the definition that emerged from the 1980 New Haven Temperament Symposium: "Temperament involves those dimensions of personality that are largely genetic or constitutional in origin, exist in most ages and in most societies, show some consistency across situations, and are relatively stable, at least within major developmental areas" (Plomin, 1983, p. 49). Thus, despite differences in specific components and in emphases, there is some consensus that temperament is an individual difference that has its basis in biological or constitutional makeup, has some stability across setting and time, and is linked to differences in behavioral or expressive styles.

Measurement. Adequacy of measurement has been a persistent problem for researchers of temperament (Hubert, Wachs, Peters-Martin, & Gandour, 1982; Plomin, 1982; Rothbart, 1981; Rothbart & Goldsmith, 1985; Rutter, 1982). Rothbart and Goldsmith (1985) note that the three most commonly used data-gathering techniques for infant temperament studies are questionnaires, home observations, and laboratory observations. With older children there has been reliance primarily on parent, caretaker, or teacher reports gathered through interviews or questionnaires. Measures designed for use with adults (Burks & Rubenstein, 1979; Guilford & Zimmerman, 1949; Lerner, Palermo, Spiro, III, & Nesselroade, 1982) are usually self-report formats. In addition to issues of psychometric adequacy of scales, individual investigators have developed measuring instruments and techniques that are consistent with their own conceptualizations of temperament. Thus scales differ in the number of dimensions identified and in the content of those dimensions. As an example, the Thomas and Chess scale taps nine dimensions, the Buss and Plomin (EASI) scale taps four. Similarly, behavior ob-

servations in natural and laboratory settings vary according to project and investigator. The consequence has been continuing concern about constructs and measures (Baker & Velicer, 1982; Bates, 1980, 1983; Plomin, 1982; Rothbart, 1981; Thomas, Chess, & Korn, 1982; Vaughn, Deinard, & Egeland, 1980; Vaughn, Taraldson, Crichton, & Egeland, 1981). Given the importance of Thomas and Chess's influence on this field, and the relevance of their work to clinical and educational practice, their questionnaires will be described in more detail.

Thomas and Chess developed a Parent Temperament Survey (PTS) and a Teacher Temperament Survey (TTS). The PTS contains 72 items, 8 for each of the 9 hypothesized dimensions of temperament. The TTS, similar in format, contains 64 items (the dimension of rythmicity is not included). Items were selected to describe behavioral expressions of the various temperament dimensions (e.g., "When first meeting new children, my child is bashful"; from the TTS: "Child will initially avoid new games and activities, preferring to sit on the side and watch"). Items are rated 1 (hardly ever) to 7 (almost always). Dimensional scores (means of the items in each dimension) are assumed to be independent. Factor studies and qualitative analyses within the NYLS suggested three temperamental constellations that described two-thirds of the sample: the easy child, characterized as regular or rhythmic, positive in approach to new stimuli, adaptable to change, and mild or moderately intense and positive in mood; the difficult child, described as irregular, negative in response to new stimuli, low or slow in adaptability, and intense, often negative in mood; and the slow-to-warm-up child, viewed as mildly intense in reactivity, slow to adapt, but given time, positive in involvement.

A number of investigators have modified the PTS and TTS but have maintained Thomas and Chess's conceptual framework. Keogh, Pullis, and Cadwell (1980, 1982) reduced both parent and teacher scales to 23 items each, and identified simpler factor structures. The three primary factors in the TTS were task orientation, personal-social flexibility, and reactivity, an essentially negative factor. The PTS yielded two multidimensional factors and two single-dimension factors: social competence and reactivity, and mood and persistence. These factors are generally consistent with those identified by Windle and Lerner (1985) in their life-span research and with those defined by Martin and his colleagues (Martin, 1984a; Paget, Nagle, & Martin, 1984) in work with schoolchildren. Also working within the Thomas and Chess framework, Carey, Fox and McDevitt (1977) have done extensive scale development. Their questionnaires cover infancy through the elementary school years and include the Infant Temperament Questionnaire (ITQ; Carey, 1970; Carey & McDevitt, 1978), the Toddler Temperament Scale (Fullard, McDevitt, & Carey, 1978), the Behavioral Styles Questionnaire (McDevitt & Carey, 1978), and the Middle Childhood Temperament Questionnaire (Hegvik, McDevitt, & Carey, 1982). These instruments are similar in format, describe behaviors that are age and setting appropriate, and have good reliability and internal consistency. Each scale contains approximately 100 items and requires about 30 minutes for a parent to complete. Thus there are a number of instruments designed to capture parents' and teachers' views of children's temperamental characteristics. Despite their clinical appeal and usefulness, many of the questionnaires have been challenged on a number of counts: lack of independence of items and dimensions, item unreliability or bias, unknown factorial organization across developmental periods, or situational specificity of behaviors. Clearly, there are real and continuing uncertainties in the measurement of temperament that mandate caution in interpreting temperament findings. Yet, there is also considerable consistency of findings across studies and approaches, which argues for the robustness of temperament variables.

Clinical Applications. There are increasing numbers of reports of the importance of temperament in pediatric and psychiatric settings. Pediatricians Carey (1981, 1985a, 1985b, 1985c) and Weissbluth (1982, 1984; Weissbluth et al.,; Weissbluth, Brouillette, Kiang, & Hunt, 1985; Weissbluth & Green, 1984) emphasize that temperament is an influence on children's development and adjustment, specifically linking infants' temperamental characteristics to a variety of pediatric problems (e.g., colic, sleep difficulties). In recent work, Carey (1985b) suggests that temperament may also be viewed as an outcome or consequence of various clinical conditions e.g., pre-, post-, and perinatal conditions or insults. From psychiatric and psychological perspectives, there has also been a continuing interest in temperament as a predisposing factor for behavioral and emotional or adjustment problems (Barron & Earls, 1984; Cameron, 1977; Chess & Korn, 1970; Earls, 1981; Graham et al., 1973; Rutter, 1964; Thomas & Chess, 1977; Thomas, Chess, & Birch, 1968). Maziade et al., (1985) found difficult temperament predicted psychiatric diagnosis in later childhood, and Kolvin, Nichol, Garside, Day, and Tweddle (1982) reported relationships between temperament and aggression in clinic referred boys. Although the processes linking temperament and problems in behavior and adjustment are not yet explicit, there appears to be enough evidence to infer a relationship.

Educational Applications. The formal application of temperament constructs to educational practice is relatively recent but is growing. As part of the NYLS, Gordon and Thomas (1967) reported that children's temperament influenced teachers' estimates of their school abilities, and Carey, Fox, and McDevitt (1977) identified relationships between parents' ratings of children and adjustment in school. A number of investigators report relationships between temperamental patterns and academic performance in school (Chess, Thomas, & Cameron, 1976; Hall & Cadwell, 1984; Hegvik, 1984, 1986; Keogh, 1982a; Keogh & Pullis, 1980; Lerner, 1983; Lerner, Lerner, & Zabski, 1985; Martin, 1984b, 1986; Martin, Nagle, & Paget, 1983; Pullis, 1979; Pullis & Cadwell, 1982; Skuy, Snell, & Westaway, 1985). It should be noted that in general, there are nonsignificant or marginally significant relationships between temperament and cognitive ability as indexed by

IQ (Keogh, 1982a, 1982c; Pullis, 1983), although Martin (1985) identified moderate and significant relationships between temperament attributes of adaptability, approach/withdrawal, and persistence and IQ in a sample of grade 1 pupils. Overall, the evidence suggests that temperament and cognitive ability are partially independent contributors to educational achievement.

In addition to achievement in academic content, there is considerable evidence to suggest that temperamental variations are related to children's personal and social adjustment in school. Billman (1984), Carey et al. (1977), Chess et al. (1976), Feuerstein and Martin (1981), Hall and Keogh (1978), Keogh (1982a, 1982b, 1982c), Kolvin et al. (1982), Lerner (1983), Lerner et al. (1985), Martin (1985), Paget et al. (1984), Terestman (1980), and Thomas and Chess (1977) have linked children's temperament and behavior and adjustment problems. The impact of temperament may be particularly powerful where children have other handicapping or problem conditions (Keogh, 1982c), although there are temperamental differences within groups of handicapped children (Hanson, 1979. Field and Greenfield (1982) suggest that temperament patterns may be associated with particular handicapping conditions, and Chess, Korn, and Fernandez (1971) report a high number of behavior disorders related to difficult temperament patterns in a group of young congenital rubella children; the latter findings were consistent with the relationship between temperament and behavior problems in a group of mentally delayed children (Chess & Korn, 1970). In a series of ongoing studies, (Keogh, Bernhemier, Pelland, and Daley, 1985) confirmed links between developmentally delayed children's temperament and their behavior problems and adjustment. Lambert and Windmiller (1977) found strong correlations between selected temperament attributes and hyperactivity in a large group of at-risk elementary school children. There also is some tentative evidence linking temperament to adjustment and achievement problems of learning-disabled pupils (Keogh, 1983; Pullis, 1983; Scholom & Schiff, 1980).

Temperament may contribute to school achievement and adjustment in several ways (Keogh, 1986). It may be a factor in a generalized response set; i.e., some temperaments may fit well with the complex and changing demands of school whereas others do not. Temperament may affect a child's specific preparation for learning by allowing activity and attention to be modulated and directed easily and quickly. Temperament may interact with particular subject matter to facilitate or impede learning. Individual differences in temperament are also significant contributors to children's personal-social adjustment in school. Intuitively, at least, interpersonal problems have a strong foundation in child-peer and child-teacher interactions. Thus, personal style, or temperament, may be a major factor in problem behavior. If the relationship between children's temperament and their achievement and behavioral adjustment in school is considered within Thomas and Chess's "goodness of fit" notion, then both child characteristics and setting or task demands and conditions must be taken into account. Goodness of fit has important implications for identification, diagnosis, intervention, and treatment.

REFERENCES

Baker, E. H., & Velicer, W. F. (1982). The structure and reliability of the Teacher Temperament Questionnaire. *Journal of Abnormal Child Psychology, 10*(4), 531–546.

Barron, A. P., & Earls, F. (1984). The relation of temperament and social factors to behavior problems in three-year-old children. *Journal of Child Psychology & Psychiatry, 25*(1), 23–33.

Bates, J. E. (1980). The concept of difficult temperament. *Merrill-Palmer Quarterly, 26*(4), 299–319.

Bates, J. E. (1983). Issues in the assessment of difficult temperament: A reply to Thomas, Chess, and Korn. *Merrill-Palmer Quarterly, 29*(1), 89–97.

Billman, J. (1984, October). *The relationship of temperament traits to classroom behavior in nine year old children: A follow-up study.* Paper presented at the Conference on Temperament in the Educational Process, St. Louis, MO.

Burks, J., & Rubenstein, M. (1979). *Temperament styles in adult interaction: Application in psychotherapy.* New York: Brunner/Mazel.

Buss, A. H., & Plomin, R. (1975). *A temperament theory of personality development.* New York: Wiley.

Buss, A. H., & Plomin, R. (1984). *Temperament: Early developing personality traits.* Hillsdale, NJ: Erlbaum.

Cameron, J. R. (1977). Parental treatment, children's temperament, and the risk of childhood behavioral problems: Initial temperament, parental attitudes, and the incidence and form of behavioral problems. *American Journal of Orthopsychiatry, 48*, 140–147.

Carey, W. B. (1970). A simplified method for measuring infant temperament. *Journal of Pediatrics, 77*, 188–194.

Carey, W. B. (1981). The importance of temperament-environment interaction for child health and development. In M. Lewis & L. A. Rosenblum (Eds.), *The uncommon child.* New York: Plenum.

Carey, W. B. (1982a). Clinical use of temperament data in pediatrics. In R. Porter & G. M. Collins (Eds.), *Temperament differences in infants and young children* (pp. 191–205). London: Pitman.

Carey, W. B. (1985a). Clinical use of temperament data in pediatrics. *Developmental & Behavioral Pediatrics, 6*(3), 137–142.

Carey, W. B. (1985b). Interactions of temperament and clinical conditions. In M. Wolraich & D. K. Routh (Eds.), *Advances in developmental and behavioral pediatrics* (Vol. 6, pp. 83–115). Greenwich, CT: JAI.

Carey, W. B. (1985c). Temperament and increased weight gain in infants. *Development & Behavioral Pediatrics, 6*(3), 128–131.

Carey, W. B., Fox, M., & McDevitt, S. C. (1977). Temperament as a factor in early school adjustment. *Pediatrics, 60*(4), 621–624.

Carey, W. B., & McDevitt, S. C. (1978). Revision of the Infant Temperament Questionnaire. *Pediatrics, 61*, 735–739.

Chess, S., & Korn, S. (1970). Temperament and behavior disorders in mentally retarded children. *Archives of General Psychiatry, 23*, 122–130.

Chess, S., Korn, S. & Fernandez, P. (1971). *Psychiatric disorders of children with congenital rubella.* New York: Brunner/Mazel.

Chess, S., Thomas, A., & Cameron, M. (1976). Temperament: Its significance for early schooling. *New York University Education Quarterly, 7*(3), 24–29.

DeFries, J. C., & Plomin, R. (1978). Behavioral genetics. *Annual Review of Psychology, 29*, 473–515.

Dunn, J., & Kendrick, C. (1982). Temperamental differences, family relationships, and young children's responses to change within the family. In R. Porter & G. M. Collins (Eds.), *Temperamental differences in infants and young children* (pp. 87–105). London: Pitman.

Earls, F. (1981). Temperament characteristics and behavior problems in three-year-old children. *Journal of Nervous & Mental Disease. 169*, 367–387.

Eysenck, H. J. (1967). *The biological basis of personality.* Springfield, IL: Thomas.

Feuerstein, P., & Martin, R. P. (1981, April). *The relationship between temperament and school adjustment in four-year-old children.* Paper presented at the annual meeting of the American Educational Research Association, Los Angeles.

Field, T., & Greenberg, R. (1982). Temperament ratings by parents and teachers of infants, toddlers, and preschool children. *Child Development, 53*, 160–163.

Fullard, W., McDevitt, S. C., & Carey, W. B. (1978). *The Toddler Temperament Scale.* Unpublished manuscript, Temple University, Philadelphia.

Goldsmith, H. H., & Campos, J. J. (1982). Toward a theory of infant temperament. In R. M. Emde & R. J. Harmon (Eds.), *The development of attachment and affiliative systems* (pp. 161–193). New York: Plenum.

Goldsmith, H. H., & Campos, J. J. (1986). Fundamental issues in the study of early temperament: The Denver twin temperament study. In M. E. Lamb & A. L. Brown (Eds.), *Advances in developmental psychology* (pp. 231–283). Hillsdale, NJ: Erlbaum.

Goldsmith, H. H., & Gottesman, I. I. (1981). Origins of variation in behavioral style: A longitudinal study of temperament in young twins. *Child Development, 52*, 91–103.

Gordon, E. M., & Thomas, A. (1967). Children's behavioral style and the teacher's appraisal of their intelligence. *Journal of School Psychology, 5*(4), 292–300.

Graham, P., Rutter, M., & George, S. (1973). Temperamental characteristics as predictors of behavior disorders in children. *American Journal of Orthopsychiatry, 43*(3), 328–339.

Guilford, J. P., & Zimmerman, W. (1949). *The Guildford-Zimmerman Temperament Survey.* Beverly Hills, CA: Sheridan Supply.

Hall, R. J., & Cadwell, J. (1984, April). *Temperament influences on cognition and achievement in children with learning disabilities.* Paper presented at the annual conference of the American Educational Research Association, New Orleans, LA.

Hall, R. J., & Keogh, B. K. (1978). Qualitative characteristics of educationally high-risk children. *Learning Disability Quarterly, 1*(2), 62–68.

Hanson, M. J. (1979). A longitudinal description study of the behaviors of Down's syndrome infants in an early intervention program. *Monographs of the Center on Human Development.* Eugene, University of Oregon.

Hegvik, R. L. (1984, October). *Three year longitudinal study of temperament variables, academic achievement, and sex differences.* Paper presented at the Conference on Temperament in the Educational Process, St. Louis, MO.

Hegvik, R. L. (1986, May). *Temperament and achievement in school*. Paper presented at the sixth occasional Temperament Conference, Pennsylvania State University.

Hegvik, R. L., McDevitt, S. C., & Carey, W. B. (1982). The middle childhood temperament questionnaire. *Developmental & Behavioral Pediatrics, 3*, 197–200.

Hinde, R. A., Easton, D. F., Meller, R. E., & Tamplin, A. M. (1982). Temperamental characteristics of 3–4 year olds and mother-child interactions. In R. Porter & G. M. Collins, *Temperamental differences in infants and young children* (pp. 66–86). London: Pitman.

Hubert, N. C., Wachs, T. D., Peters-Martin, P., & Gandour, M. J. (1982). The study of early temperament: Measurement and conceptual issues. *Child Development, 53*, 126–132.

Keogh, B. K. (1982a). Children's temperament and teachers' decisions. In R. Porter & G. M. Collins (Eds.), *Temperamental differences in infants and young children*. (pp. 269–279). London: Pitman.

Keogh, B. K. (1982b). *Temperament and school performance of preschool children* (Technical report, Project REACH). Los Angeles: University of California, Los Angeles.

Keogh, B. K. (1982c). Temperament: An individual difference of importance in intervention programs. *Topics in Early Childhood Special Education, 2*(2), 25–31.

Keogh, B. K. (1983). Individual differences in temperament: A contribution to the personal-social and educational competence of learning disabled children. In J. D. McKinney & L. Feagens (Eds.), *Current topics in learning disabilities* (pp. 33–55). Norwood, NJ: Ablex.

Keogh, B. K. (1986). Temperament and schooling: What is the meaning of goodness of fit? In J. V. Lerner & R. M. Lerner (Eds.), *New directions for child development: Temperament and social interaction in infants and children*. San Francisco: Jossey-Bass.

Keogh, B. K., Bernheimer, L., Pelland, M., & Daley, S. (1985). *Behavior and adjustment problems of children with developmental delays* (Technical report). Los Angeles: University of California, Los Angeles, Graduate School of Education.

Keogh, B. K., & Pullis, M. E. (1980). Temperamental influences on the development of exceptional children. In B. K. Keogh (Ed.), *Advances in special education: Vol. 1. Basic constructs and theoretical orientations* (pp. 239–276). Greenwich, CT: JAI.

Keogh, B. K., Pullis, M. E., & Cadwell, J. (1980). *Project REACH* (Technical report). Los Angeles: University of California, Los Angeles.

Keogh, B. K., Pullis, M. E., & Cadwell, J. (1982). A short form of the Teacher Temperament Quesionnaire. *Journal of Educational Measurement, 29*(4), 323–329.

Kolvin, I., Nicol, A. R., Garside, R. F., Day, K. A., & Tweddle, E. G. (1982). Temperamental patterns in aggressive boys. In R. Porter & G. M. Collins (Eds.), *Temperamental differences in infants and young children* (pp. 252–268). London: Pitman.

Kretschmer, E. (1925). *Physique and character*. New York: Harcourt.

Lambert, N. M., & Windmiller, M. (1977). An exploratory study of temperament traits in a population of children at risk. *Journal of Special Education, 11*(1), 37–47.

Lerner, J. V. (1983). The role of temperament in psychosocial adaptation in early adolescents: A test of a "goodness of fit" model. *Journal of Genetic Psychology, 143*, 149–157.

Lerner, J. V., & Lerner, R. M. (1983). Temperament and adaptation across life: Theoretical and empirical issues. In P. B. Baltes & O. G. Brim (Eds.), *Lifespan development and behavior* (Vol. 5). New York: Academic Press.

Lerner, J. V., Lerner, R. M., & Zabski, S. (1985). Temperament and elementary school children's actual and rated academic performance: A test of a "goodness of fit" model. *Journal of Child Psychology and Psychiatry, 26*, 125–136.

Lerner, R. M., Palermo, M., Spiro, A., & Nesselroade, J. (1982). Assessing the dimensions of temperamental individuality across the life-span: The dimensions of temperament survey (DOTS). *Child Development, 53*, 149–160.

Martin, R. P. (1984a). *The Temperament Assessment Battery* (TAB). Atlanta: University of Georgia, Department of School Psychology.

Martin, R. P. (1984b, October). *A temperament model for education*. Paper presented at the Conference on Temperament in the Educational Process, St. Louis, MO.

Martin, R. P. (1985, July). *Child temperament and educational outcomes: A review of research*. Paper presented at the Symposium on Temperament, Leiden, the Netherlands.

Martin, R. P. (1986, May). *Context influences on the expression of temperament*. Paper presented at the sixth occasional Temperament Conference, Pennsylvania State University.

Martin, R. P., Nagle, R., & Paget, K. (1983). Relationships between temperament and classroom behavior, teacher attitudes, and academic achievement. *Journal of Psychoeducational Assessment, 1*, 377–386.

Matheny, A. P., Jr., Wilson, R. S., & Nuss, S. M. (1984). Toddler temperament: Stability across settings and over ages. *Child Development, 55*, 1200–1211.

Maziade, M., Caperaa, P., Laplante, B., Boudreault, M., Thivierge, J., Cote, R., & Boutin, P. (1985). Value of difficult temperament among 7-year-olds in the general population for predicting psychiatric diagnosis at age 12. *American Journal of Psychiatry, 142*(8), 943–946.

McDevitt, S. C., & Carey, W. B. (1978). The measurement of temperament in 3–7 year old children. *Journal of Child Psychiatry & Psychology, 19*(3), 245–253.

Paget, K. D., Nagle, R. J., & Martin, R. P. (1984). Interrelationships between temperament characteristics and first-grade teacher-student interactions. *Journal of Abnormal Child Psychology, 12*(4), 547–560.

Plomin, R. (1982). Behavioral genetics and temperament. In R. Porter & G. M. Collins (Eds.). *Temperamental differences in infants and young children* (pp. 155–167). London: Pitman.

Plomin, R. (1983). Childhood temperament. In B. B. Lahey & A. E. Kazdin (Eds.), *Advances in clinical child psychology* (Vol. 6, pp. 45–92). New York: Plenum.

Pullis, M. E. (1979). *An investigation of the relationship between children's temperament and school adjustment*. Unpublished doctoral dissertation, University of California, Los Angeles.

Pullis, M. E. (1983). *Temperament influences of teachers' decisions in regular and mainstreamed classes*. Paper presented at the meeting of the American Educational Research Association, New York.

Pullis, M. E., & Cadwell, J. (1982). The influence of children's temperament characteristics on teachers' decision strategies. *American Educational Research Journal, 19*(2), 165–181.

Rothbart, M. K. (1981). Measurement of temperament in infancy. *Child Development, 52*, 569–578.

Rothbart, M. K., & Derryberry, D. (1981). Development of individual differences in temperament. In M. E. Lamb & A. L. Brown (Eds.), *Advances in developmental psychology* (Vol. 1, pp. 37–86). Hillsdale, NJ: Lawrence Erlbaum.

Rothbart, M. K., & Goldsmith, H. H. (1985). Three approaches to the study of infant temperament. *Developmental Review, 5,* 237–260.

Rutter, M., (1964). Temperament characteristics in infancy and the later development of behavior disorders. *British Journal of Psychiatry, 110,* 651–661.

Rutter, M. (1982). Temperament: Concepts, issues and problems. In R. Porter & G. C. Collins (Eds.), *Temperamental differences in infants and young children* (pp. 1–19). London: Pitman.

Rutter, M., Tizard, J., & Whitmore, K. (1970). *Education, health, and behavior: Psychological and medical study of childhood development.* New York: Wiley.

Scholom, A., & Schiff, G. (1980). Relating infant temperament to learning disabilities. *Journal of Abnormal Child Psychology, 8,* 127–132.

Sheldon, W. (1942). *The varieties of temperament: A psychology of constitutional differences.* New York: Harper.

Skuy, M., Snell, D., & Westaway, M. (1985). Temperament and the scholastic achievement and adjustment of black South African children. *South African Journal of Education, 5*(4), 197–202.

Stevenson-Hinde, J., & Simpson, A. E. (1982). Temperament and relationships. In R. Porter & G. M. Collins (Eds.), *Temperamental differences in infants and young children* (pp. 51–65). London: Pitman.

Strelau, J. (1983). *Temperament-personality-activity.* New York: Academic Press.

Terestman, N. (1980). Mood quality and intensity in nursery school children as predictors of behavior disorder. *American Journal of Orthopsychiatry, 50,* 125–138.

Thomas, A., & Chess, S. (1977). *Temperament and development.* New York: Brunner/Mazel.

Thomas, A., Chess, S., & Birch, H. G. (1968). *Temperament and behavior disorders in children.* New York: New York University Press.

Thomas, A., Chess, S., Birch, H. G., Hertzig, M., & Korn, S. (1963). *Behavioral individuality in early childhood.* New York: New York University Press.

Thomas, A., Chess, S., & Korn, S. J. (1982). The reality of difficult temperament. *Merrill-Palmer Quarterly, 28*(1), 1–20.

Torgersen, A. M. (1982). Influence of genetic factors on temperament development in early childhood. In R. Porter & G. M. Collins (Eds.), *Temperamental differences in infants and young children* (pp. 141–154). London: Pitman.

Vaughn, B., Deinard, A., & Egeland, B. (1980). Measuring temperament in pediatric practice. *Journal of Pediatrics, 96,* 510–514.

Vaughn, B., Taraldson, B., Crichton, L., & Egeland, B. (1981). The assessment of infant temperament: A critique of the Carey Infant Temperament Questionnaire. *Infant Behavior & Development, 40,* 1–17.

Weissbluth, M. (1982). Plasma progesterone levels, infant temperament, arousals from sleep, and the sudden infant death syndrome. *Medical Hypotheses, 9,* 215–222.

Weissbluth, M. (1984). Sleep duration, temperament, and Conners' ratings of three-year-old children. *Developmental & Behavioral Pediatrics, 5*(3), 120–123.

Weissbluth, M., Brouillette, R. T., Kiang, L., & Hunt, C. E. (1982). Clinical and laboratory observations: Sleep apnea, sleep duration and infant temperament. *Journal of Pediatrics, 101*(2), 307–310.

Weissbluth, M., & Green, O. C. (1984). Plasma progesterone concentrations and infant temperament. *Developmental & Behavioral Pediatrics, 5*(5), 251–253.

Weissbluth, M., Hunt, C. E., Brouillette, R. T., Hanson, D., David, R. J., & Stein, I. (1985). Respiratory patterns during sleep and temperament ratings in normal infants. *Journal of Pediatrics, 106*(4), 688–690.

Werner, E. E., & Smith, R. S. (1982). *Vulnerable, but invincible: A longitudinal study of resilient children and youth.* New York: McGraw-Hill.

Wilson, R. S. (1983). The Louisville twin study: Developmental synchronies in behavior. *Child Development, 54*(2), 298–316.

Wilson, R. S., & Matheny, A. P. (1983). Assessment of temperament in infant twins. *Developmental Psychology, 19,* 172–183.

Windle, M., & Lerner, R. M. (1985). *Reassessing the dimensions of temperamental individuality across the life span: The Revised Dimensions of Temperament Survey* (DOTS-R). Unpublished manuscript, Johnson O'Connor Research Foundation, Chicago.

BARBARA KEOGH
University of California, Los Angeles

BODY IMAGE
HYPERACTIVITY
LEARNED HELPLESSNESS
PERSONALITY ASSESSMENT
TEACHER EXPECTANCIES

TEMPER OUTBURST

The temper outburst or temper tantrum, as it may be referred to more frequently, is familiar to any professional who works with children. The temper tantrum occurs more frequently among younger children who exhibit a variety of learning, physical, or emotional problems. In almost every instance where a temper tantrum occurs, it is obvious to the attending adults that the child is attempting to gain some personal objective(s) through this staged outburst.

The temper tantrum is usually easily recognizable because it is characterized by explosive kinds of behavior. Such behaviors as cursing, kicking, hitting, biting, destruction of property, and related behaviors that may be dangerous to those around as well as to furnishings. The wild rage and anger, the intense yelling and crying signify a child that is out of control emotionally. It often appears that the usual defenses of the child have fallen apart and that he or she can only vent intense, uncontrollable rage.

In general, the temper outburst seems to occur only when the child is in the presence of an adult in charge. Typically, this behavior may occur in the presence of the parent, but it may also occur with teachers or in an institutional setting with child-care workers. Trieschmann, Whittaker, and Bendro (1969) present a comprehensive treatment of the nature, causes, and possible treatments for temper tantrums. In general, the authors view the temper tantrum as an effort by the child to gain control and deal with developmental problems.

In many instances, the parent or child-care worker reports that there seems to be no reason for or warning that the child is going to erupt into wild, uncontrollable anger. However, most educators and psychologists who have made a thorough investigation of children's temper tantrums discover that there are precipitating or contingent factors. For example, the child usually exhibits tantrum behavior only around adults and always around other people. Usually, the child receives an intense amount of attention, albeit negative. In fact, adults present will often need to exhibit a great deal of attention (e.g., restraint) to prevent the child from hurting others or from destroying property. Mullen (1983) provides an extensive description of the occurrences of temper tantrums among children institutionalized in a youth development center. Some of these children are strong teenagers who can, and do, inflict injury on professional child-care workers. A temper outburst in this setting is characterized by fear on the part of other children and the staff. In all cases, the person having a temper tantrum captures the attention of others.

Less attention has been paid to temper tantrums in the literature in the last 10 years; that may be due in part to our success in extinguishing this behavior in some children. The key to its elimination often appears to be the reduction of attention from significant others following the temper tantrum. Graham and Doubleday (1984) report that children from ages 6 to 11 agree that anger is an emotion that they can control. This was in contrast to pity and guilt, for example, which they believed they could not control. Relying on the notion of self-control for temper tantrums, many professionals have succeeded in extinguishing temper tantrums completely. Zarski (1982) reports on the successful elimination of temper tantrums by a 5-year-old cerebral palsied child. This behavior began with the parents in their efforts to get the child to develop greater physical strength and skills. The successful plan of extinction was to tell the child that it was all right to have tantrums but that he must always have them in one specific room. The child was always taken to that room and encouraged to continue to have the tantrums while he was there. Within 2 months, the temper outbursts stopped completely. Carlson, Arnold, Becker, and Madsen (1968) report similar success with an 8-year-old girl in an elementary classroom. Her chair was placed in the back

of the room and she was held in the chair (which she resented) until the temper outburst subsided. All other children in the classroom were rewarded for not noticing her outbursts. Her behavior improved although the temper outbursts were not completely controlled that year. Although psychologists and educators continue to expand their understanding and techniques for controlling temper tantrums, they remain an attempt by children to gain control in certain social situations.

REFERENCES

Carlson, C. S., Arnold, C. R., Becker, W. C., & Madsen, C. H. (1968). The elimination of tantrum behavior of a child in an elementary classroom. *Behavioral Research & Therapy, 6,* 117–119.

Graham, S., & Doubleday, C. (1984). The development of relations between perceived controllability and the emotions of pity, anger, and guilt. *Child Development, 55,* 561–565.

Mullen, J. K. (1983). Understanding and managing the temper tantrum. *Child Care Quarterly, 12,*59–70.

Trieschmann, A. E., Whittaker, J. K., & Bendro, L. K. (1969). *The other 23 hours: Child care work in a therapeutic milieu.* Chicago: Aldine.

Zarski, J. A. (1982). The treatment of temper tantrums in a cerebral palsied child: A paradoxical intervention. *School Psychology Review, 11,* 324–328.

BERT O. RICHMOND
University of Georgia

BEHAVIOR MODIFICATION
BEHAVIOR OBSERVATION
RESTRAINT

TERATOGEN

The word teratogen drives from the Greek *teras,* signifying a marvel, prodigy, or monster; thus, by definition, a teratogen is an agent that causes developmental malformations or monstrosities (Duke-Elder, 1963). The causes can be environmental, genetic, multifactorial, maternal-fetal, or unknown. Environmental agents include drugs and similar agents (e.g., alcohol, anticonvulsants, cigarettes, LSD), hormones, infections (e.g., cytomegalic inclusion disease, influenza, mumps, rubella, syphilis, toxoplasmosis), radiation, mechanical trauma, hypotension (low blood pressure), vitamin deficiency or excess (hypervitaminosis A), and mineral deficiency (zinc). Genetic causes include chromosomal abnormality (e.g., Down's syndrome, trisomy 13) and various hereditary patterns—sporadic, dominant, recessive, and polygenetic. Maternal-fetal interactions are exemplified by advanced maternal age and maternal hypothyroidism. Finally, a variety of dysmorphic syndromes are undetermined as to etiology. Many congenital abnormalities may be detected prior to birth. The primary means for such diagnosis has been through amniocentesis. Additionally, imaging systems such as ultrasonography demonstrate relatively gross abnormalities late in development (Spaeth, Nelson, & Beaudoin, 1983).

The timing of development helps to clarify the spectrum of associated malformations. Injuries prior to the fifteenth day of gestation affect development of primary germ layers; such abnormalities are usually so global that survival of the fetus is unusual. Between weeks two and seven, insults cause major abnormalities that affect whole organ systems. Following the first trimester (the period of differentiation of organ detail and organ interrelationship), abnormalities tend to be more limited and specific. While timing of embryonic or fetal insult relates closely to manifest anomaly, certain substances may cause varying malformations, though the time of insult is constant.

REFERENCES

Duke-Elder, S. (1963). *System of ophthalmology: Vol. III, Part 2. Congenital deformities*. St. Louis, MO: Mosby.

Spaeth, G. L., Nelson, L. B., Beaudoin, A. R. (1983). Ocular teratology. In T. D. Duane & E. A. Jaeger (Eds.), *Biomedical foundations of ophthalmology* (Vol. 1, pp. 6–7). Hagerstown, MD: Harper & Row.

GEORGE R. BEAUCHAMP
*Cleveland Clinic Foundation,
Cleveland, Ohio*

CENTRAL NERVOUS SYSTEM GENETIC VARIATIONS

TERMAN, LEWIS M. (1877–1956)

Lewis M. Terman received his PhD in education and psychology from Clark University, where he studied under G. Stanley Hall. Experienced as a schoolteacher, principal, and college instructor, in 1910 he joined the faculty of Stanford University, where he served as head of the psychology department from 1922 until his retirement in 1942.

With an interest in mental tests dating from his graduate studies at Clark University, Terman became a leading figure in the newly born testing movement, developing dozens of tests during his career. The best known and most widely used of his tests were the Stanford-Binet tests of intelligence, which he adapted from the Binet-Simon Scale of Intelligence in 1916 and revised in 1937. He also developed the Army Alpha and Beta tests (the first group intelligence tests) for use in classifying servicemen during World War I. With the publication of the Stanford-Binet

Lewis M. Terman

tests in 1916, Terman introduced the term intelligence quotient (IQ), a term that quickly became a part of the general vocabulary.

In 1921 Terman initiated the first comprehensive study of gifted children. His staff tested more than 250,000 schoolchildren to identify 1,500 with IQs above 140. This sample of boys and girls was studied intensively and followed up periodically in a study that continues today. Terman found that, contrary to the popular belief at the time, children with high IQs tend to be healthier, happier, and more stable than children of average ability. In addition, they are more successful in their personal and professional lives. Terman, who can be credited with founding the gifted child movement, used his findings to promote the provision of special educational programs for able students.

REFERENCES

Fancher, R. E. (1985). *The intelligence men*. New York: Norton.

Hilgard, E. (1957). Lewis Madison Terman: 1877–1956. *American Journal of Psychology, 70*, 472–479.

Murchison, C. (Ed.). (1961). *A history of psychology in autobiography*. New York: Russell & Russell.

PAUL IRVINE
Katonah, New York

STANFORD-BINET INTELLIGENCE SCALE

TERMAN'S STUDIES OF THE GIFTED

In 1911, while at Stanford University, Lewis M. Terman began a systematic collection of data on children who achieved exceptionally high scores on the Stanford-Binet Intelligence Test. In the early 1920s, working with Melita Oden, he administered the Stanford-Binet test to students referred to by teachers as being "highly intelligent." Studies of their traits and the extent to which they differed from unselected normal children were begun in 1925.

Terman's subjects were in a 1500-child sample (800 boys and 700 girls) that was in the top 1% of the school population in measured intelligence; i.e., they possessed tested IQs of 140 or higher (Terman & Oden, 1925).

Terman and Oden (1951) summarized the characteristics of the students in their gifted sample as (1) slightly larger, healthier, and more physically attractive; (2) superior in reading, language usage, arithmetical reasoning, science, literature, and the arts; (3) superior in arithmetical computation, spelling, and factual information about history and civics (though not as markedly as in the areas covered in (2); (4) spontaneous, with a variety of interests; (5) able to learn to read easily, and able to read more and better books than average children; (6) less inclined to boast or overstate their knowledge; (7) more emotionally stable; (8) different in the upward direction for nearly all traits.

Follow-up studies in 1947, 1951, and 1959 were completed to obtain a comparison between promise and performance. Follow-up studies by other authors have obtained less "perfect" findings, in that not all of the subjects were found to be geniuses in the sense of transcendent achievement in some field (Feldman, 1984). Recent studies have supported Terman's findings on emotional stability (Schlowinski & Reynolds, 1985), spontaneity and creativity in play (Barnett & Fiscella, 1985), and reading aptitude (Anderson, Tollefson, & Gilbert, 1985).

The entire set of data sources for Terman's original group is maintained in closed files at Stanford University. It is estimated that less than half of the coded responses of this source of data have been transferred to tabulation sheets.

REFERENCES

Anderson, M. A., Tollefson, N. A., & Gilbert, E. C. (1985). Giftedness and reading: A cross sectional view of differences in reading attitudes and behavior. *Gifted Child Quarterly, 29*(4), 86–189.

Barnett, L. A., & Fiscella, J. (1985). A child by any other name. . . . A comparison of the playfulness of gifted and nongifted children. *Gifted Child Quarterly, 29*(2), 61–66.

Feldman, D. H. (1984). A follow-up of subjects scoring about 180 IQ in Terman's "Genetic Studies of Genius." *Exceptional Children, 50*(6), 518–523.

Schlowinski, E., & Reynolds, C. R. (1985). Dimensions of anxiety among high IQ children. *Gifted Child Quarterly, 29*(3), 125–130.

Sears, P. S. (1979). The Terman genetic studies of genius, 1922–1972. In A. H. Passow (Eds.), *The gifted and talented*. Chicago: National Society for the Study of Education.

Terman, L. M., & Oden, M. H. (1925). *Genetic studies of genius: Mental and physical traits of a thousand gifted children*. Stanford, CA: Stanford University Press.

Terman, L. M., & Oden, M. H. (1951). The Stanford studies of the gifted. In P. A. Witty (Ed.), *The gifted child*. Boston: D. C. Heath.

ANNE M. BAUER
University of Cincinnati

GIFTED CHILDREN
GIFTED CHILDREN AND READING

TERMAN'S STUDIES ON GENIUS

Lewis Terman, the American psychologist most noted for his development of the Stanford-Binet Intelligence Scale, published five volumes on the study of genius between the years 1925 and 1959. In 1921, Terman, a professor of education at Stanford University, began the longitudinal study of 1528 gifted California children. Primary-aged children who had obtained an IQ score of 140 or higher on the Stanford-Binet were included, as were high-school students who had scored in the top percentile on the Terman Group Test. The average age of the students was 11. In addition to intelligence scores, data were collected on a number of other variables such as socioeconomic status (SES), personality, and school performance. The major purpose of the study was to identify the factors that appeared along with intelligence, and to track the life experiences of these exceptionally bright individuals (Treffinger, Pyryt, Hawk, & Houseman, 1979).

Terman and Oden (1959) offered a summary of the characteristics of the gifted child. They reported that a higher than average proportion of the gifted children came from economically advantaged families. These children were also physically superior in terms of weight and health, and averaged 2 to 3 years above grade level on standardized achievement tests. However, they tended to be instructed at their chronologically determined grade levels. The gifted children learned to read easily and read more books than their peers. Preferences for play reflected typical gender trends. Many of the gifted children pursued leisure activities more typical of considerably older children. Terman and Oden (1959) concluded that these children surpassed their nongifted peers in almost every area tested. However, they cautioned that gifted children were also as different from one another as they were from children in the average group.

Some popularly held beliefs have paired high IQ with emotional instability. However, these exceptionally bright children grew into adulthood with no greater incidence of serious mental illness than is typical of individuals outside this range of intelligence (Oden, 1968). As adults they reported better health and lower mortality rates than were found in the general population.

Terman's gifted subjects maintained their intellectual ability throughout adulthood (Oden, 1968). Seventy-one percent of the men and sixty-seven percent of the women obtained college degrees, with sixty-eight percent of the men and twenty-four percent of the women holding at least one advanced degree. Eighty-six percent of the men were employed in professional or white-collar occupations. Publication credits included over 2500 articles, 200 books, and 350 patents. Forty-two percent of the women held full-time jobs, with the majority employed as teachers or secretaries. Women in professional roles tended to be highly successful. Similar achievement patterns were reported in a more recent study of a different sample of gifted adults (Powell, 1983).

More than four-fifths of the adult gifted subjects reported two or more avocational pursuits (Terman & Oden, 1959). They were active in professional and social organizations, and more than 90% reported that they usually or always vote. Their children were found to have an average IQ of 132.

Oden (1968) examined differences between the most and least successful gifted men in Terman's study. Success had been defined by Terman and Oden (1959) as including goal realization, a happy home life, economic comfort, social helpfulness, and peace of mind. Successful men were more likely to come from intact, higher SES families in which initiative and academic success were valued. A strong positive correlation was found between education and life success. Sears and Barbee (1977) reported that most of the women in Terman's study experienced life satisfaction, and that working women tended to be somewhat higher in this dimension. Other factors correlating in a positive direction with their success were education, health, early parental support, and self-confidence. Interestingly, no significant differences were seen between subjects with IQs over 180 and those scoring in the 140–150 range in terms of life success (Feldman, 1984).

REFERENCES

Feldman, D. H. (1984). A follow up of subjects scoring above 180 IQ in Terman's "Genetic Studies of Genius." *Exceptional Children, 50*(6), 518–523.

Oden, M. H. (1968). The fulfillment of a promise: 40 year follow up of the Terman gifted group. *Genetic Psychology Monographs, 77*, 3–93.

Powell, P. M. (1983). Educational and occupational attainments in two intellectually gifted samples. *Gifted Child Quarterly, 27*(2), 73–76.

Sears, P. S., & Barbee, A. H. (1977). Career and life satisfaction among Terman's gifted women. In J. C. Stanley, W. C. George, & C. H. Solano (Eds.), *The gifted and the creative: A fifty year perspective.* Baltimore, MD: Jonhs Hopkins University Press.

Terman, L. M., & Oden, M. H. (1959). The gifted group at midlife. *Genetic studies of genius* (Vol. 5). Stanford, CA: Stanford University Press.

Treffinger, D. J., Pyryt, M. C., Hawk, M. M., & Houseman, E. D. (1979). Education of the gifted and talented: Implications for school psychology. In G. D. Phye and D. J. Reschly (Eds.),

School psychology: Perspectives and issues. New York: Academic.

GARY BERKOWITZ
Temple University

GIFTED AND TALENTED CHILDREN
TERMAN, LEWIS M.

TEST ANXIETY

Test anxiety is such a universal phenomenon that it hardly requires general definition. In school, on the job, or for various application procedures, tests are required. Performance on a test can impact negatively on the test-taker. Thus an essential component for an anxiety arousal state exists when the individual is placed in a test-taking situation. Test situations are specific and thus present an opportunity to investigate the nature of anxiety.

Test anxiety is usually regarded as a particular kind of general anxiety. Ordinarily, it refers to the variety of responses—physiological, behavioral, and phenomenal (Sieber, 1980)—that accompany an individual's perceptions of failure. The person experiencing test anxiety often has a fear of failure as well as a high need to succeed. Both the fear of failure and the drive for success may be internalized. In some instances, either may seem more of a desire on the part of the test-taker to please a parent or other significant individual. Regardless of the originating causes of test anxiety, it can be a debilitating state of arousal.

One of the major challenges for theorists and researchers on test anxiety is to ascertain why anxiety appears to motivate some persons yet limits seriously the performance of others. Findings from several researchers suggest that the individual's expectations of success or failure on a test are strongly correlated to the development of test anxiety (Heckhausen, 1975; Weiner, 1966). For example, it may be argued that those who are low in motivation to succeed attribute failure to a lack of ability whereas those who are high in motivation to succeed see failure as emanating more from a lack of effort. Heckhausen (1975) cites data showing that those persons with a high fear of failure tend to attribute success more to good luck than those persons with a high expectation of success. Thus, for those who expect to succeed, anxiety may be more of a motivating force than for those who fear failure. For the latter group, initial anxiety may become a debilitating form of test anxiety.

Another avenue of investigation seeks to understand the affective value of test-taking in the context of its social significance. For some persons, test anxiety is heightened if it occurs where there is an observer of the test-taking performance (Geen, 1979; Geen & Gange, 1977). Test anxiety may then be heightened if there are judges, monitors, or others with whom the test-taker must interact. Some persons may, therefore, find an oral or observed performance type of test more anxiety producing than a written test. For such persons, it appears that test anxiety is more a response to their need for and perceptions of social approval than it is to an internalized need to demonstrate competence.

In summary, much of the available research and numerous self-reports suggest that test anxiety is a recurring problem for children and adults. Moreover, test anxiety often appears to inhibit the usual maximal level of performance of the individual. Thus if a test situation is to be used as an effective means of assessing human potential, it is important that we understand more fully the origin of test anxiety as well as its impact on individual performance.

REFERENCES

Dew, K. M. H., Galassi, J. P., & Galassi, M. D. (1984). Math anxiety: Relation with situational test anxiety, performance, physiological arousal, and math avoidance behavior. *Journal of Counseling Psychology, 31,* 480–583.

Geen, R. G. (1979). The influence of passive audiences on performance. In P. Paulus (Ed.), *The psychology of group influence.* Hillsdale, NJ: Erlbaum.

Geen, R. G., & Gange, J. J. (1977). Drive theory of social facilitation: Twelve years of theory and research. *Psychological Bulletin, 84,* 1267–1288.

Heckhausen, H. (1975). Fear of failure as a self-reinforcing motive. In I. G. Sarason & C. D. Spielberger (Eds.), *Stress and anxiety* (Vol. 2). Washington, DC: Hemisphere.

Sieber, J. E. (1980). Defining test anxiety: Problems and approaches. In I. G. Sarason (Ed.), *Test anxiety: Theory, research, and applications.* Hillsdale, NJ: Erlbaum.

Weiner, B. (1966). The role of success and failure in the learning of easy and complex tasks. *Journal of Personality & Social Psychology, 3,* 339–344.

BERT O. RICHMOND
University of Georgia

ANXIETY
STRESS AND THE HANDICAPPED STUDENT

TEST EQUATING

Test equating is a technique for making the characteristics of two tests similar or identical, if possible, so that an individual's scores on the two tests mean the same thing. This process is accomplished currently through statistical means. There are two different problems associated with test equating. One is the problem of equating scores on two tests that were designed to be of the same difficulty, for the same kind of student, with the same content. This

is called horizontal equating. The other problem is how to equate tests that were designed for different populations, often younger and older students, in which the content overlaps. In this case, one test will be hard for the younger students and the other will be quite easy for the older. This is called vertical equating.

Horizontal equating, while by no means completely solved as a statistical problem, is the better developed and studied of the two. The problem is best stated as follows: For a student with ability A, the relative placement of his or her score on test 1 is identical to the relative score on test 2 if the two tests have been perfectly equated. Mathematically, the two frequency distributions must be equal in normalized form. This means that a youngster's score on test 1 is the same number of standard deviations from the mean and exceeds the same percent of other scores as on test 2. There are three major techniques for achieving horizontal equating.

The first method of horizontal equating is called the equipercentile method. It is the most widely used and seems to be the most robust method under a variety of conditions. Simply put, observed score distributions are matched for percentile points. That is, the score at the first percentile point in test 1 is equated to the score at the first percentile point for test 2. This is done for all percentile points up to 99 or perhaps 99.9. There is a smoothing of the equated scores so that there are no abrupt jumps in scores from one percentile to the next. This procedure has been shown by Petersen, Marco, and Stewart (1982) to be not as good as linear equating, the next technique covered, in which the tests are similar and linear in relationship to each other. When there is a nonlinear relationship between the tests, the equipercentile technique is superior. This case is not common.

Linear equating is the application of a straight line equation of the form $Y = aX + b$. The parameters are functions of the means and standard deviations of the two tests (Braun & Holland, 1982). Not surprisingly, it works best when there is just a simple linear relation between true test scores.

The third technique for equating tests horizontally consists of a number of related techniques grouped under the heading item-characteristic curve (ICC) techniques. These techniques generally make somewhat stronger assumptions about the nature of the test and the test-taker than do the other two methods. They are based on a model that allows estimation of a test-taker's ability. $T1$ on test 1 and $T2$ on test two. These two scores then are equated, and the observed score from which they have been estimated can be calculated. Thus we can begin with either test, estimate the student's underlying ability on the test, and use that ability score on the other test to calculate an equivalent observed score. Since the procedure works both ways, it is hoped that the tests give similar results between calculated and actual observed scores. In general, such procedures have proven inferior to linear or equipercentile methods for large-scale standardized tests, which are carefully constructed. The ICC methods may be better for smaller, experimentally oriented tests, but their restriction to large samples makes this a rare usage.

Vertical equating is a more difficult problem, conceptually and statistically. The primary techniques used have been based on ICC models. They have not proven satisfactory to date. If two tests are given to a student, one that is hard for him or her and one that is easy (or easier), the ICC methods tend to overpredict ability score on the easy test and underpredict it on the hard test (Kolen, 1981).

REFERENCES

Braun, H. I., & Holland, P. W. (1982). Observed-score test equating: A mathematical analysis of some ETS equating procedures. In P. W. Holland & D. B. Rubin (Eds.), *Test Equating* (pp. 9–49). New York: Academic.

Kolen, M. J. (1981). Comparison of traditional and item response theory methods for equating tests. *Journal of Educational Measurement, 19,* 279–293.

Petersen, N. S., Marco, G. L., & Stewart, E. E. (1982). A test of the adequacy of linear score equating models. In P. W. Holland & D. B. Rubin (Eds.), *Test Equating* (pp. 71–135). New York: Academic.

VICTOR L. WILLSON
Texas A&M University

ASSESSMENT
MEASUREMENT

TEST FOR AUDITORY COMPREHENSION OF LANGUAGE, REVISED (TACL-R)

The TACL-R is a revision of the 1971 and 1973 versions of the Test for Auditory Comprehension of Language (TACL) (Carrow, 1973). The TACL-R is a test of receptive language that examines comprehension of the following forms and constructions: word classes and relations (including adjectives, nouns, and verbs); morphological forms (such as prepositions, pronouns, noun number and case, verb number and tense, and suffixes); and a variety of elaborated sentences. The three sections are comprised of 40 items each, for a total of 120 items. The test requires the child to point to one of three pictures in response to the examiner's stimulus. Basals and ceilings for each section make the overall time needed for test administration approximately 10 to 20 minutes.

The test is normed for ages 3 to 10, an extension of 2 years over the TACL. The standardization sample totaled 1003 subjects, stratified by family vocation, ethnic origin, age, gender, and geographical distribution. There were approximately 100 subjects per age level. This standardization is an improvement over the smaller and geographi-cally limited sample used for the TACL. Scores can be reported as percentile ranks, standard scores, and age equivalents. The TACL-R reports high correlations for test-retest reliability and split-half reliability. Validity data are extensively reported in the examiner's manual (Carrow-Woolfolk, 1985) and include moderate correlations with selected tests of language.

REFERENCES

Carrow, E. (1973). *Test for Auditory Comprehension of Language.* Austin, TX: Learning Concepts.

Carrow-Woolfolk, E. (1985). *Test for Auditory Comprehension of Language, Revised.* Allen, TX: DLM Teaching Resources.

MARGO E. WILSON
Lexington, Kentucky

AUDITORY PROCESSING

TEST OF LANGUAGE DEVELOPMENT (TOLD)

The Test of Language Development (TOLD) is an individually administered test designed to measure the expressive and receptive language skills of children ages 4-0 to 8-6 (TOLD-P) and students ages 8-6 to 12-11 (TOLD-I). The TOLD-P is comprised of seven subtests that assess listening (R) and speaking (E) skills in each of three linguistic feature domains. The semantic domain is assessed with picture vocabulary (R)—pointing to the picture that represents a spoken word—and oral vocabulary (E)—defining the meaning of stimulus words. The syntactic domain is assessed with grammatic understanding (R)—pointing to pictures that match sentences dictated by the examiner; sentence imitation (E)—repeating verbatim spoken sentences; and grammatic completion (E)—providing the missing word in a spoken sentence. The phonologic domain is assessed by word discrimination (R)—determining whether two spoken words are the same or different; and word articulation (E)—identifying by name objects shown in picture form.

The TOLD-I is comprised of five subtests that assess listening and speaking proficiency in two language feature domains. The semantic domain is assessed by characteristics (R)—determining the validity or truth of simple, spoken statements, and generals (E)—verbalizing how three spoken words are alike. The syntactic domain is assessed by grammatic comprehension (R)—recognizing incorrect grammar in spoken sentences; sentence combining (E)—forming compound or complex sentences from two or more simple sentences spoken by the examiner; and word ordering (E)—constructing meaningful sentences from words spoken in a random sequence.

Raw scores on the TOLD are converted to standard

scores, percentiles, and language-age scores (TOLD-P only) for each subtest. Speaking, listening, semantic, and syntactic composite "quotients" are obtained by summing the appropriate subtest standard scores.

The TOLD is an instrument that is widely used by speech therapists and educational diagnosticians who need to obtain a normative comparison of a child's language skills. Reviewers have generally found the norms and reliability of the tests to be adequate, but caution against the use of TOLD with children for whom English is not the primary language or with children who typically speak nonstandard variations of English (Allen, 1985).

REFERENCE

Allen, D. V. (1985). Review of the Test of Language Development. In J. V. Mitchell, Jr. (Ed.), *The ninth mental measurements yearbook* (pp. 1574–1575). Lincoln, NE: University of Nebraska Press.

GEORGE MCCLOSKEY
*American Guidance Service,
Circle Pines, Minnesota*

LANGUAGE DISORDERS

TEST OF NONVERBAL INTELLIGENCE (TONI)

The Test of Nonverbal Intelligence (TONI) (Brown, Sherbenou, & Dollar, 1982) was designed to serve as a language-free measure of cognitive ability or intelligence. It is to be administered individually or in small groups of up to five subjects for ages 5-0 to 85-11. The TONI is both quick and relatively easy to administer, requiring only 15 to 30 minutes.

The standardization sample consisted of 1929 subjects between 5-0 and 85 years, 11 months from 28 states. The sample closely approximates the 1980 Census data (*Statistical Abstract of the United States*, 1980).

The test consists of two alternate forms that yield a single raw score that is converted to a deviation score with a mean of 100 and a standard deviation of 15. No subscales are present. Percentile ranks are provided.

The items constituting each form represent a variety of problem-solving formats that increase in difficulty as the test progresses. The subject is required to look at a set of figures with one missing, determine the rule operating, and choose the correct figure that completes the set from a multiple-choice format of responses. The rules may be any one or a combination of five as outlined in the test manual. They include simple matching, five types of analogies, classifications, intersections, and progressions. No verbalization is allowed during the administration. The examiner pantomimes the instructions and the subject points to the desired response. The pantomime instructions are an excellent idea and should be incorporated more often into supposedly nonverbal tests (Clark & Reynolds, 1983).

Reliability and validity data appear acceptable for the most part. Reliability studies in the manual provide data that meet acceptable criteria for establishing the stability of the scores obtainable with TONI at most age levels. The only exception occurs at the 5- and 6-year-old levels, where internal consistency reliability estimates fail to reach the .80 level. The user is further cautioned against using TONI as a sole diagnostic instrument for the evaluation of intellectual function owing to the lack of convincing data establishing construct validity.

The TONI should be considered a useful tool in the context of a larger battery of tests evaluating intellectual functioning when extensive knowledge of nonverbal functioning is desired. It should not, however, be used as a group administered device until further data are available regarding correct administrative procedures and reliability and validity information is presented for this form of administration.

REFERENCES

Brown, L., Sherbenou, R. J., & Dollar, S. J. (1982). *Test of nonverbal intelligence*. Austin, TX: Pro-Ed.

Clark, J., & Reynolds, C. R. (1983). *Review of Test of Nonverbal International Journal of Clinical Neuropsychology*, 20–22.

Statistical Abstracts of the United States. (1980). Washington, DC: U.S. Department of Commerce, Bureau of the Census.

JULIA A. HICKMAN
University of Texas, Austin

INTELLIGENCE TESTING

TEST OF WORD FINDING (TWF)

The Test of Word Finding (TWF; German, 1986), published in April 1986, is a nationally standardized, individually administered, diagnostic tool for the assessment of word-finding skills in children ages 6 years, 6 months through 12 years, 11 months. The test is composed of five subtests: picture naming: nouns; picture naming: verbs; picture naming: categories; description naming; and sentence completion: naming. It is divided into two forms. The primary form, composed of 80 items, is principally normed for use with grades 1 and 2. The intermediate form, with 90 items, is normed primarily for use with children in grades 3 through 6.

The TWF is intended to be used by speech therapists, school psychologists, language pathologists, and related staff in the diagnosis and evaluation of one of the dysphasias, specifically an expressive dysphasia known as dysnomia (dysnomia means dysfunction in naming—or word finding). At the time of this writing, the TWF is the only formal, standardized measure of word finding available. Clinicians have relied for years on clinical judgment and informal assessment techniques to assess the presence or absence and relative severity of word-finding problems. The TWF attempts to standardize these procedures and, in addition, to lead the clinician to the development of an intervention program. Intervention strategies are classified into three categories: remediation, compensatory programming, and self-awareness.

Materials for the TWF are well designed and include two manuals, a technical manual and an administration, scoring, and interpretation manual, and a test book, which is contained in a familiar easel-kit format (such as the K-ABC or PIAT). For a first standardized effort in this field, the TWF is notably well prepared. The technical manual presents adequate data for the most part on the theory underlying the scale and much traditional information on construct, content, and criterion-related validity. Though significant portions of the technical manual will be abstruse to the nonpsychometrician, most well-trained psychologists and others knowledgeable about measurement and statistics will find sufficient information to allow an accurate appraisal of the TWF for a variety of applications. One of the greatest drawbacks to the TWF is its marginally acceptable levels of reliability. Although high reliability is needed and more extensive validity information desirable, the TWF is the best available measure for assessing dysnomic related expressive dysphasias.

REFERENCE

German, D. J. (1986). *Test of word finding*. Allen, TX: DLM Teaching Resources.

CECIL R. REYNOLDS
Texas A&M University

APHASIA
LEARNING DISABILITIES

TEST SCATTER

Individuals who take intelligence, achievement, and other educational and psychological tests seldom, if ever, earn precisely the same score on all tests or even on the subparts of one test. This variation in performance across tests by individuals is known as test scatter. There are three principal measures of test scatter present in the testing literature: the range, the number of deviant signs, and profile variability.

The range is simply the highest minus the lowest score for an individual on a battery of tests once the scores have been placed on a common scale such that the means and standard deviations are equal. The Wechsler Intelligence Scale for Children-Revised (WISC-R) has 10 regularly administered subtests and two supplementary subtests. As one index of test scatter, one might locate the highest subtest score and the lowest subtest score for a particular child and then subtract the two. The resulting number is the range. The range for a particular child can be compared with the average range of scores for individuals in the standardization sample of the tests or some other relevant reference group to determine the degree of "usualness" of the observed range of scores. Sometimes, as with the WISC-R verbal and performance scales, a range will be calculated with only two scores.

The number of deviant signs (NDS) refers to the number of subtests or other component parts or a battery of tests that deviate at a statistically significant level (typically, $p \le .05$) from the mean score of the individual across all tests taken or at least all of those used in the comparisons. Six subtests constitute the WISC-R verbal scale. It may be of interest of know whether the number of subtests that differ significantly from a child's own mean subtest score is unusual or whether it is a common occurrence to show so many strengths and weaknesses in an ability profile. Normative comparisons would again be made.

Profile variability is another prominent index of test scatter and one that appears to be the most stable. Profile variability is simply the variance of a set of scores for one individual, i.e., the average squared deviation from the mean score of all the scores.

Since perhaps the inception of the field of learning disabilities, learning-disabled (LD) children have been characterized as having a large or unusual amount of intra- and intertest scatter (Chalfant & Scheffelin, 1969). Until the mid-1970s, this assumption was made largely in ignorance of the degree of test scatters that characterizes the test performance of normal children. Although normative data on test scatter for the WISC had been presented as early as 1960, these data went largely ignored until Kaufman's studies of the WISC-R were published in 1976 (Kaufman, 1976a, 1976b). Prior to his examination of test scatter for the 2200 normal children in the WISC-R standardization sample, myths regarding such indexes abounded.

In an informal survey, Kaufman (1976a) reported that when asked to estimate the range of subtest scores on the WISC-R for normal children, most practicing psychologists and other diagnosticians suggested a range of only two to four points. The mean range for normal children in the WISC-R standardization sample turned out to be more than seven points, more than twice the typical estimate. A similar phenomenon occurred with regard to verbal-performance IQ differences on the WISC-R.

Conventional diagnostic beliefs, prior to the publication of Kaufman's work, held that a verbal-performance IQ difference of 15 points or more was a primary indication of learning disability. Even Wechsler (1974) indicated that

Percentage of Normal Children Obtaining WISC-R V-P Discrepancies of a Given Magnitude or Greater, by Parental Occupation

Size of V–P Discrepancy (Regardless of Direction)	Parental Occupation					
	Professional and Technical	Managerial, Clerical, Sales	Skilled Workers	Semiskilled Workers	Unskilled Workers	Total Sample
9	52	48	48	46	43	48
10	48	44	43	41	37	43
11	43	40	39	36	34	39
12	40	35	34	31	29	34
13	36	33	31	28	26	31
14	32	29	29	25	24	28
15	29	25	26	21	22	24
16	26	22	22	19	19	22
17	24	19	18	15	16	18
18	20	16	16	14	15	16
19	16	15	13	12	14	14
20	13	13	12	10	13	12
21	11	11	8	9	10	10
22	10	9	7	7	9	8
23	8	8	6	6	8	7
24	7	7	5	5	6	6
25	6	6	4	4	5	5
26	5	5	3	3	4	4
27	4	4	2	2	3	3
28–30	3	3	1	1	2	2
31–33	2	2	<1	<1	1	1
34+	1	1	<1	<1	<1	<1

Source: Kaufman, Alan S. Intelligent testing with the WISC-R. © 1979, New York: Wiley.

this degree of scatter was of clinical significance and deserving of follow-up study. At it turns out, approximately 35% of the population of normal children have a verbal-performance IQ difference of 12 or more points, representing a statistically significant difference between the two scores, and 24%, or nearly one out of four, of normal children demonstrate a difference of 15 or more points. These data are extremely similar to those reported in 1960 for the WISC.

A complete tabulation of Kaufman's (1979) findings regarding verbal-performance IQ differences is presented in the Table.

Since these seminal studies, a number of authors have investigated test scatter for normal children on such widely used tests as the Wechsler Preschool and Primary Scale of Intelligence (Reynolds & Gutkin, 1981) and the Kaufman Assessment Battery for Children (Chatman, Reynolds, & Willson, 1983). It is now clear that normal children exhibit much variation in their abilities, exploding the myth of the normal child's "flat" ability profile and that only exceptional children show large amounts of test scatter.

Large amounts of scatter in the profiles of normal children do not negate the importance of variation in children's test scatter. If the differences among a child's test scores are large enough to be considered real (reliable),

then chances are that real differences exist among the child's cognitive skills and abilities, differences that mandate attention and that have relevance to the development of instructional strategies. Unusual differences among test scores will continue to have diagnostic use as well, but only when determined with regard to normative standards.

REFERENCES

Chalfant, J. C., & Scheffelin, M. A. (1969). *Central processing dysfunctions in children* [NINDS Monograph No. 9]. Bethesda, MD: U.S. Department of Health, Education, and Welfare.

Chatman, S. P., Reynolds, C. R., & Willson, V. L. (1983). Multiple indexes of test scatter on the Kaufman Assessment Battery for Children. *Journal of Learning Disabilities, 17,* 523–531.

Kaufman, A. S. (1976a). A new approach to the interpretation of test scatter on the WISC-R. *Journal of Learning Disabilities, 9,* 160–168.

Kaufman, A. S. (1976b). Verbal-performance IQ discrepancies on the WISC-R. *Journal of Consulting & Clinical Psychology, 44,* 739–744.

Kaufman, A. S. (1979). *Intelligent testing with the WISC-R.* New York: Wiley-Interscience.

Reynolds, C. R., & Gutkin, T. B. (1981). Test scatter on the WPPSI: Normative analyses of the standardization sample. *Journal of Learning Disabilities, 14,* 460–464.

Wechsler, D. (1974). *Wechsler intelligence scale for Children-revised*. New York: The Psychological Corporation.

CECIL R. REYNOLDS
Texas A&M University

PROFILE VARIABILITY
VERBAL-PERFORMANCE IQ DISCREPANCIES

TESTS IN PRINT (TIP)

Tests in Print (*TIP*) (Buros, 1961; Buros, 1974; Mitchell, 1983) are volumes that provide a comprehensive index of commercially available educational and psychological tests in English-speaking countries. The volumes contain descriptive information about each test (e.g., the age or grade levels for which the test is designed, author, publishing company, scale scores); literature related to the specific test; an index to all reviews of the test in previous Buros *Mental Measurements Yearbooks* (MMY); and references to test descriptions and related literature cited in previous *Tests in Print* volumes.

The most current *Tests in Print III* (Mitchell, 1983) contains 2672 descriptions of commercially available tests; 12,170 references for specific tests; an alphabetical listing of test names; a directory of 565 publishers with addresses and an index to their tests; a title index showing both in-print and out-of-print tests since previous listings; a name index for test authors, reviewers, and authors of references; and a classified subject index for quickly locating tests in particular areas (e.g., achievement, personality).

The following is a reproduction of an entry from *Tests in Print III*. Each element is listed separately and is explained with a notation.

[772]	Entry number *not* page number
Early School Personality Questionnaire	Test name
Ages 6–8	Group for which test is intended
1966–76, c1963–76	Publication dates
ESPQ	Common acronym
13 first-order factor scores (reserved vs. warmhearted, dull vs. bright, affected by feelings vs. emotionally stable . . .), 4 second-order factor scores (extraversion, anxiety, tough poise, independence)	Scores available from test.
Richard W. Coan and Raymond B. Cattell	Test authors
Institute for Personality and Ability Testing, Inc.*	Publisher

For additional information and reviews by Jacob O. Sines and Robert L. Thorndike, see 8:540 (8 references); see also T2:1163 (3 references); for a review . . .	Cross-references to previous MMY and TIP entries
REFERENCES 1–7. See P:66 8–15. See 7:71	
16–18. See T2:1163 19–26. See 8:540 27. HARRIS, W. J., KING, D. R., & DRUMMOND, R. J. Personality variables of children nominated as emotionally handicapped by classroom teachers. Psychology in the Schools, 1978, 15, 361–363.	Recent research reports Concerning use of the ESPQ

REFERENCES

Buros, O. K. (1961). *Tests in print*. Highland Park, NJ: Gryphon.

Buros, O. K. (1974). *Tests in print II*. Highland Park, NJ: Gryphon.

Mitchell, J. V., Jr. (1983). *Tests in print III*. Lincoln, NE: Buros Institute of Mental Measurements.

JANE CLOSE CONOLEY
University of Nebraska, Lincoln

BUROS MENTAL MEASUREMENTS YEARBOOK

TESTS

See SPECIFIC TEST.
Also See MEASUREMENT.

TEST-TEACH-TEST PARADIGM (TTT-P)

The Test-Teach-Test Paradigm (TTT-P) is representative of an instructional concept that is similar to the concept of teaching students how to read by using the phonics approach. To conceptualize the TTT-P, we need to review some other terms: direct instruction, model-lead-and test, criterion assessment, criterion instruction, and appropriate practice.

Fundamentally, the TTT-P represents an instructional sequence. The portrayal that follows (Nash, 1985) is an adaptation of the instructional sequencing suggested by Bateman (1971) and Engelmann and Bruner (1969). In the course of this portrayal, some of the other terms referred to will be employed. The instructional concept and postures of both Bateman and Engelmann are regarded by many as representing a kind of pioneering methodology of the 1970s that distinguished special education instruction from regular education.

A. *The initial testing part of the TTT-P*

In a reading test with beginning second-grade students, all of the students misread the word *blew*.

B. *The teaching part of the TTT-P*

1. The teacher begins by saying, "We are going to learn to read the word *blew* by use of sounds using a simultaneous multisensory instructional procedure."

2. Next, the teacher directs the students to copy down the word that has been written out on the blackboard in front of the students.

3. Then the teacher models for the students what it is that they are to do.

   a. The teacher states that this word has three sounds. The teacher says the sounds, /b/, /l/, and /ew/, and simultaneously underlines each of them while doing so, *b l ew*.

   b. Next the teacher, using a lead says, "We, all of us, will now individually underline the three sounds that this word has—simultaneously saying the sound of the letter or letters as we do so." The teacher and the students all together and in an audible voice do so, *b l ew*.

   c. Then the teacher, using an intervening test, says, "Your turn—reunderline each sound saying each sound out loud as you do so." The students do so, *b l ew*.

   d. Next the teacher, using another model, says, "I will now loop and say in an audible voice the sounds in this word, *b l ew*.

   e. Then, using another lead, the teacher says, "We will now all together loop and say the sounds in this word." Students and teacher do so, *b l ew*.

   f. Next the teacher, using another intervening test, says, "Your turn, now all by yourself you loop and say out loud the sounds in this word." The students do so, *b l ew*.

   g. Next the teacher, using another lead, says, "We will now underline and say the word rapidly." The teacher and the students do so, *b l ew*.

   h. Then the teacher, using another intervening test, says, "Your turn—now all by yourself, you are to underline and say the word rapidly." The students do so, *b l ew*.

   i. Last, the teacher says, "All of you have just read the word *blew* correctly."

C. *The test part of the TTT-P*

This last phase or step in the TTT-P is the simplest part to do and can be attended to in a number of ways. Using our example word, a teacher could offer repeated appropriate practice experiences in reading this particular word.

The process of the TTT paradigm as exemplified can be replicated across any and all instruction, be it initial or advanced, across any and all tasks, with spelling as one of the more obvious ones. In the course of doing so, the teacher will automatically be involved with these additional concepts (Nash, 1986):

1. Direct instruction. The precise identification of what the student is to learn and how he or she is going to do so.

2. Model-lead-and test. While carrying out any given bit of instruction, the teacher can model what the student is to do and simultaneously follow this with a lead; i.e., doing the task with the student. At this point, the teacher can employ a simple test of what it is that the student knows.

3. Criterion assessment (CA). Both of the test parts of the TTT-P are examples of CA. The first part tests what it is the teacher is to teach if the student fails the test; the second test of the TTT-P is simply a reaffirmation and check on what the teacher intended to teach.

4. Criterion instruction (CI). The teaching part of the TTT-P represents CI because there is an intended 1:1 correlation between the first test and the subsequent needed instruction.

5. Appropriate practice. In the execution of the instruction associated with the TTT-P, the teacher will be implementing the model-lead-test concept automatically and involving the student in the necessary practice.

Instruction that implements the concepts reviewed is instruction that guarantees student success. These patterns can be repeated as often as student errors dictate.

REFERENCES

Bateman, B. D. (1971). *The essentials of teaching.* Sioux Falls, SD: Adapt.

Engelmann, S., & Bruner, E. (1969). *Distar reading* Chicago: Science Research.

Nash, R. T. (1986). *Manual for remediating the reading and spelling deficits of elementary, secondary and post-secondary students.* Flossmoor, IL: Language Prescriptions, Inc.

Nash, R. T. (1985). Remediation courses, Project Success, University of Wisconsin-Oshkosh. Unpublished raw data.

ROBERT T. NASH
University of Wisconsin,
Oshkosh

DIAGNOSTIC-PRESCRIPTIVE TEACHING

THALIDOMIDE AND THALIDOMIDE SYNDROME

Thalidomide is the best known human teratogen. It was among the first drugs for which teratogenicity was established. Effective as a sedative and a tranquilizer, it is an example of a teratogen that had positive effects on the mother but devastating consequences for the embryo.

Teratogenicity became suspected with the birth of a relatively large number of babies with phocomelia and a variety of other deformities in Europe in the late 1950s and early 1960s. Phocomelia (seal-flipper limbs) is a condition in which arms and/or legs are drastically shortened or absent and fingers/toes extend from the foreshortened limbs or the trunk. Never approved for distribution in the United States, thalidomide was widely distributed in Europe, where it is estimated to have affected over 7000 individuals. It was withdrawn from the market in late 1961 (Moore, 1982). Teratogenicity was unusually high: over 90% of women who took thalidomide during a particular period in pregnancy had infants with some type of defect (Holmes, 1983).

Thalidomide is the only drug whose timing of harmful effects has been well established, causing defects only if taken by the mother when the embryo was 34 to 50 days old; earlier or later consumption had no adverse effects (Holmes, 1983). Individual defects can be traced to particular days when the mother took the drug. The specificity of the embryo's age for thalidomide effects provides a particularly dramatic example of a critical period.

The particular complex of effects is sometimes termed the thalidomide syndrome (Landau, 1986). Phocomelia is the most common and pronounced sign, but absent or deformed ears and digits are common, and malformations of forehead, heart, and digestive system occasionally occur. Generally, overall intelligence is unaffected, but some language deficits have been reported (Holmes, 1983; Landau, 1986; Moore, 1982). Because thalidomide has teratogenic but not mutagenic qualities, thalidomide-syndrome individuals would be expected to have normal children.

REFERENCES

Holmes, L. B. (1983). Congenital malformations. In R. E. Behrman & V. C. Vaughn (Eds.), *Nelson textbook of pediatrics* (12th ed.) Philadelphia: W. B. Saunders. (pp. 311–317).

Landau, S. I. (1986). *International dictionary of medicine and biology.* New York: Wiley.

Moore, K. L. (1982). *The developing human* (3rd. ed.). Philadelphia: Saunders.

ROBERT T. BROWN
University of North Carolina,
Wilmington

EARLY EXPERIENCE AND CRITICAL PERIODS
ETIOLOGY
TERATOGENS

THEIR WORLD

Their World is the annual publication of the Foundation for Children with Learning Disabilities (FCLD). The FCLD was founded in 1977 and began publication of *Their World* in 1979. The publication is presented each year at FCLD's annual benefit in New York City. *Their World* is a public awareness vehicle, intended to educate the public about learning disabilities generally while emphasizing the accomplishments of the learning disabled. *Their World* publishes real-life stories about the way families cope with learning-disabled children. *Their World* supports after school, summer, athletic, and creativity programs as a support network for the learning disabled and their families. The publication is distributed to over 75,000 parents, educators, legislators, and professionals each year.

CECIL R. REYNOLDS
Texas A&M University

FOUNDATION FOR CHILDREN WITH LEARNING DISABILITIES

THEMATIC APPERCEPTION TEST (TAT)

The Thematic Apperception Test (TAT) is a projective assessment instrument developed by Henry Murray (1938) as a means of investigating his theory of personality. Designed for use with subjects ages 7 and older, TAT has become one of the most widely used assessment techniques. The test materials consist of 31 black and white pictures depicting characters in various settings. Each picture is designed to elicit particular themes or conflicts. Subsets of pictures (typically 8 to 10) are selected for administration depending on the individual's age and sex and the nature of the presenting problem. Subjects are asked to tell a story about each picture as it is presented. Typical instructions stress that subjects use their imagination and include in their response a description of what the characters in the scene are doing, thinking, and feeling, the preceding events, and the outcome. Responses are recorded verbatim by the examiner. An inquiry is usually conducted after all pictures have been presented.

The TAT has also been presented in group form; this requires the subject to provide written responses. Murray and others (Groth-Marnat, 1984) have devised scoring systems for TAT; however, in clinical practice, such systems are rarely used (Klopfer & Taulbee, 1976). Variations on the TAT include the Children's Apperception Test and the Senior Apperception Test (Bellack, 1975), which include stimulus materials believed to be more relevant to children and the elderly, respectively.

REFERENCES

Bellack, L. (1975). *The TAT, CAT and SAT in clinical use* (3rd ed.). New York: Grune & Stratton.

Groth-Marnat, G. (1984). *Handbook of psychological assessment.* New York: Van Nostrand Reinhold.

Klopfer, W. G., & Taulbee, E. S. (1976). Projective tests. In M. R. Rosenzweig & L. W. Porter (Eds.), *Annual review of psychology, 17,* 543–567.

Murray, H. A. (1938). *Explorations in personality.* New York: Oxford University Press.

ROBERT G. BRUBAKER
Eastern Kentucky University

EMOTIONAL DISORDERS
PERSONALITY ASSESSMENT

THEORY OF ACTIVITY

The theory of activity is a general theoretical paradigm for psychological and developmental research that has its historical roots in work carried out in the Soviet Union between 1925 and 1945 by L. S. Vygotsky, A. R. Luria, A. N. Leont'ev, and their colleagues (Leont'ev 1978, 1981; Minick, 1985; Wertsch, 1981, 1985). Activity theory is among the most important intellectual forces in contemporary Soviet psychology, providing a unifying conceptual framework for a wide range of psychological theory, research, and practice. As a consequence of linguistic, political, and conceptual barriers, however, it was only in the late 1970s that psychologists and social scientists in Western Europe and the United States began to become aware of activity theory.

The theory of activity is the product of an effort by Vygotsky's students and colleagues to extend the theoretical framework Vygotsky had developed between 1925 and his death in 1934. Vygotsky had been concerned with two fundamental limitations in the psychological theories of his time. First, he felt that many psychologists had underestimated or misrepresented the influence of social and cultural factors on human psychological development. He was particularly concerned with the failure to clarify the mechanisms of this influence. Second, Vygotsky felt that the disputes between the traditional psychology of mind and the behaviorist theories that were emerging in the 1920s reflected a widespread tendency in psychology and philosophy to represent mind and behavior in conceptual isolation from one another rather than as connected aspects of an integral whole (Davydov & Radzikhovskii, 1985; Minick, in press). Vygotsky's work and the subsequent emergence of activity theory were attempts to develop a theoretical paradigm that would overcome these limitations in existing theory.

A central premise of the theory of activity is that human psychological development is dependent on a process in which the individual is drawn into the historically developed systems of social action that constitute both society and the life of the mature adult. Within this framework, psychological development or change is dependent on the individual's progressively more complete participation in social life. Modes of organizing and mediating cognitive activity are mastered and the relationship to the external world of objects and people is defined in this process.

Three additional characteristics of activity theory are also extremely important to any effort to understand it. First, the concepts, constructs, and laws that provide the basic content of psychological theory developed within this framework and that determine how psychological characteristics and their development are conceptualized are represented and defined in such a way that a connection is consistently maintained between psychological characteristics and the organization of social action (Minick, 1985). For example, Leont'ev (1978) defines personality as a system of hierarchically related goals and motives that derives its structure from (1) the objective relationships among the actions that constitute the social system; (2) the objective relationships among the actions that constitute the life of the individual; and (3) the subjective relationships among these actions that are defined by the individual's values and beliefs. With this approach to the definition of scientific constructs in psychology, it becomes impossible to conceptualize the psychological characteristics of the individual or the laws of psychological functioning and development apart from the organization of concrete social systems and the individual's place in them (Minick, 1985). This can be contrasted with theoretical frameworks in which key constructs are defined in ways that conceptually isolate the psychological (e.g., reversible operations, traits, or associative networks) and the social (e.g., social roles, social norms, or social organization).

Second, the goal-oriented action serves as the central analytic object in activity theory (Davydov & Radzikhovskii, 1985; Leont'ev, 1978; Zinchenko, 1985). To analyze psychological characteristics and psychological processes in connection with socially organized action systems, one has to identify an appropriate analytic unit for the development of theory and research. As a basic unit both of the psychological life of the individual and of the organization of society, the goal-oriented action has assumed this role in activity theory.

Third, the theory of activity is based on a schema that emphasizes the importance of considering three levels of analysis in studying the goal-oriented action and the psychological processes that function and develop in connection with it (Leont'ev, 1978). At the level of activities, general yet socially and culturally defined motives are considered. For example, there are important differences in the organization of actions and goals in western systems of formal schooling and in more traditional apprenticeship systems. In formal schooling, education and learning are the motives that provide the general organizing framework for concrete goal-oriented actions. In apprenticeship, these motives are subordinated to the economic motives connected with the production of products for use or sale. At the level of operations, the impact of the object world on the way an action is carried out is considered. Under different conditions, a single set of motives may lead to the emergence of different concrete goals or to different ways of performing actions in order to realize those goals. This system of analytic levels (i.e., activity-motive, action-goal, and operation-condition) has provided activity theory with a useful framework for analyzing psychological functioning and development without losing sight of its connections with the physical and social environment in which it occurs.

As a general perspective on psychology and psychological development, the theory of activity has had an important impact on theory and practice in the broad domain of special education in the Soviet Union. While a detailed discussion of the nature of this impact is impossible in this context, a useful illustration is available in the English translation of a recent volume by Alexander Meshcheryakov in which he reviews his work with deaf and blind children (Meshcheryakov, 1979).

REFERENCES

Davydov, V. V., & Radzikhovskii, L. A. (1985). Vygotsky's theory and the activity-oriented approach in psychology. In J. V. Wertsch (Ed.), *Culture, communication, and cognition: Vygotskian perspectives* (pp. 35–65). New York: Cambridge University Press.

Leont'ev, A. N. (1978). *Activity, consciousness, and personality.* Englewood Cliffs, NJ: Prentice-Hall.

Leont'ev, A. N. (1981). *Problems of the development of mind.* Moscow: Progress Publishers.

Meshcheryakov, A. N. (1979). *Awakening to life: Forming behavior and the mind in deaf-blind children.* Moscow: Progress Publishers.

Minick, N. (1985). *L. S. Vygotsky and Soviety activity theory: New perspectives on the relationship between mind and society.* Unpublished doctoral dissertation, Northwestern University, Evanston, IL.

Minick, N. (in press). *The development of Vygotsky's thought. Introduction to L. S. Vygotsky, Collected works: Problems of general psychology* (Vol. 1). New York: Plenum.

Vygotsky, L. S. (in press). Thinking and speech. In V. V. Davydov (Ed.), *L. S. Vygotsky, Collected works: General Psychology Vol. 1* (N. Minick Trans.). New York: Plenum.

Wertsch, J. V. (Ed.). (1981). *The concept of activity in Soviet psychology.* New York: Sharpe.

Wertsch, J. V. (1985). *Vygotsky and the social formation of mind.* Cambridge, MA: Harvard University Press.

Zinchenko, V. P. (1985). Vygotsky's ideas about units for the analysis of mind. In J. V. Wertsch (Ed.), *Culture, communication, and cognition: Vygotskian perspectives* (pp. 94–118). New York: Cambridge University Press.

NORRIS MINICK
Center for Psychosocial Studies,
The Spencer Foundation,
Chicago, Illinois

VGOTSKY, L. S.
ZONE OF PROXIMAL DEVELOPMENT

THERAPEUTIC COMMUNITY

The therapeutic community as a model for psychosocial rehabilitation was developed following World War II by Maxwell Jones, a psychiatrist, in Great Britain. This approach developed out of Jones's experience in working with soldiers on a psychiatric unit who had suffered emotional trauma and with persons with personality problems. Jones's approach was a reaction to the traditional psychiatric hospital practice that produced dependent patients who needed resocialization in addition to treatment of their illness if they were to be discharged. He believed the hospital could be purposefully employed as a significant therapeutic milieu by facilitating full social participation by the patients (Main, 1946). Providing appropriately organized social environments, rather than just psychotherapeutic or medical approaches, was the method of effecting change in patients. Jones's work was significant for the development of social psychiatry, in which emphasis is placed on the environmental sources of stress that cause persons to learn maladaptive ways of coping rather than on illness or deviancy, the traditional psychiatric emphases.

Jones initially presented the principles and practices of the therapeutic community in *Social Psychiatry: A Study of Therapeutic Communities* (1952), but the book was limited in detail. A clearer explication of the underlying themes that guided and shaped the social interactions in the therapeutic community was provided by R. N. Rapoport, an anthropologist, in *Community as Doctor* (1960). Themes identified by Rapoport were those of (1) democratization—an equal sharing among community members of the power in decision making about community affairs; (2) permissiveness—the toleration of a wide degree of behavior from members of the community; (3) communalism—the free exchange of information and observations among all members of the community, including patients and staff; and (4) reality confrontation—the continuous presentation to the patients of interpretations of their behavior from the perspective of other members of the therapeutic community.

The principal social methods used in the therapeutic community were the discussion of events that occurred within the context of frequent community group meetings by all community members; the facilitation of exchange of information among members of the community; the development of relationships between staff and clients that emphasized their status as peers in learning through interacting with each other; the provision of frequent situations in which patients could learn more adaptive ways to cope with problematic situations by interacting with community members; and the continued examination by community members, especially staff members, of their roles to find more effective ways of functioning.

The ideology of the therapeutic community was never completely operationalized, and some found it extremely difficult to implement (Manning, 1975). Rapoport (1960) offered reasons for the difficulty in implementing Jones's ideology and explanations of why later therapeutic movements used many but not all of the principles. First, there were limits set by the local community on the extremes in democracy or permissiveness that would be tolerated; second, communalism encouraged communication in groups rather than between individuals; third, conflicts arose between ideological themes such as when excessively dominant behavior is permissively tolerated but might be antidemocratic; and fourth, there was an unresolved conflict between the rehabilitation goals that required the hospital to approximate the conditions of life outside the hospital and the treatment goals that required different conditions for the recovery of the patient than those in which the problems developed. About the same time that development of therapeutic communities was taking place, psychotropic medications were introduced into psychiatric practice. This resulted in the obscuring of the effects of the therapeutic community as psychotropic medications were often used with persons who were also in therapeutic communities. In addition, no satisfactory study of the efficacy of the therapeutic community as a treatment approach was ever conducted, though it had wide support among mental health clinicians.

The therapeutic community as developed by Jones declined from the period of the late 1950s (Manning, 1975). Other therapeutic community movements have developed that serve persons with drug, alcohol, and social adjustment problems, and persons in correctional settings. These movements have developed some distinctive characteristics in their approach to treatment but have been greatly influenced by the work of Jones.

REFERENCES

Jones, M. (1952). *Social psychiatry: A study of therapeutic communities.* London: Tavistock.

Main, T. F. (1946). The hospital as a therapeutic institution. *Bulletin of the Menniger Clinic, 10,* 66–70.

Manning, N. (1975). What happened to the therapeutic community. In K. Jones & S. Baldwin (Eds.), *The yearbook of social policy in Britain.* London: Routledge & Kegan Paul.

Rapoport, R. N. (1960). *Community as doctor.* London: Tavistock.

HAROLD HANSON
PAUL BATES
Southern Illinois University

COMMUNITY RESIDENTIAL PROGRAMS
PSYCHONEUROTIC DISORDERS
SOCIAL BEHAVIOR OF THE HANDICAPPED

THERAPEUTIC RECREATION

See RECREATION, THERAPEUTIC.

THINK ALOUD

Think Aloud is a cognitive behavior modification program designed to improve social and cognitive problem-solving skills in young children. Based on the pioneering work of Meichenbaum, Goodman, Shure, and Spevak, and tied to theory regarding development of self-control. Think Aloud was conceived as a training program to decrease impulsivity, encourage consideration of alternatives, and plan courses of action. It emphasizes the use of cognitive modeling as a teaching tool in which teachers model their own strategies for thinking through problems. Students are then encouraged to "think out loud" while systematically approaching each problem through asking and answering four basic questions: What is my problem? How can I solve it? Am I following my plan? How did I do?

The original small group (two to four students) program (Camp & Bash, 1985) was tested on 6- to 8-year-old boys identified as hyperaggressive by teachers. In the hands of trained teachers, improvement in cognitive impulsivity was demonstrated across several trials, as was improvement in prosocial classroom behavior. Although significant decreases in aggressive behavior were also observed, this was not significantly more than observed in attention-control groups. A refresher course 6 to 12 months after the original program supported previously developed skills and led to significant decreases in hyperactivity and increases in friendliness.

With some demonstrated success in altering thinking and behavior patterns in aggressive boys in the small group situation, the authors reasoned that a more "dilute" program such as found in a large classroom should benefit a broader range of children with mild to moderate deficits in social and cognitive problem skills. In addition, availability of a classroom version of the program would help regular classroom teachers to support skills learned in the small group program. Consequently, they began in 1976 to build Think Aloud Classroom Programs spanning grades 1 to 6 (Bash & Camp, 1985a, 1985b; Camp & Bash, 1985).

Development and study of these programs was supported in part by ESEA Title IV grants to the Denver public schools. Few of the classroom program studies could be conducted with random assignment to experimental or traditional teaching programs. However, within limitations imposed by a nonequivalent control group design, children in the Think Aloud classrooms improved on measures of both social and cognitive problem-solving skills more than children in nonprogram classrooms at all grade levels. Cognitive differences between children in the Think Aloud classroom programs and comparison children were most reliable for the program for grades 1 and 2 and the program for grades 5 and 6. Differences in social problem-solving skills were reliable at all grade levels. The classroom programs can easily be adapted for use in an individual or tutorial program to intensify and individualize the experience. The materials now provide challenge to children over a broad range of developmental levels, making them suitable for special education classrooms as well as regular classrooms, for some middle school children, and for children with special needs for social skills training or assistance in curbing impulsivity.

REFERENCES

Bash, M. A. S., & Camp, B. W. (1985a). *The Think Aloud Classroom Program for Grades 3 and 4*. Champaign, IL: Research.

Bash, M. A. S., & Camp, B. W. (1985b). *The Think Aloud Classroom Program for Grades 5 and 6*. Champaign, IL: Research.

Camp, B. W., & Bash, M. A. S. (1985). *The Think Aloud Classroom Program for Grades 1 and 2*. Champaign, IL: Research.

STAFF

CAMP, BONNIE
IMPULSE CONTROL

THINKING CENTERS

See CREATIVE STUDIES PROGRAM.

THIRD WORLD, SPECIAL EDUCATION IN THE

See MIDDLE EAST, SPECIAL EDUCATION IN THE.

THORAZINE

Thorazine is the trade name for the generic antipsychotic agent chlorpromazine. Though Thorazine was among the first synthesized drugs that were found effective in the control of behavioral symptoms associated with psychotic disorders, it is no longer as widely prescribed as it was 20 years ago. However, Thorazine is still used as a benchmark against which new antipsychotic agents are compared in terms of frequency of side effects and efficacy. Thorazine is of the drug class phenothiazine and tends to produce the classic panorama of side effects associated with the phenothiazine group.

In addition to use as a major tranquilizer with psychotic individuals, Thorazine also is used in emergency situations to limit the effects of LSD and to control prolonged behavioral reactions after intoxication with other hallucinogens. One of the major criticisms of Thorazine as a therapeutic agent has been its reported abuse as a chemical restraint (Leavitt, 1982).

In use with chidren, several cautions must be considered: children are more likely to show side effects; dose-related attentional problems can develop and thus create interference in learning (Seiden & Dykstra, 1977); and seizures may be potentiated in children with a preexisting seizure disorder (Bassuk & Schoonover, 1977).

REFERENCES

Bassuk, E. L., & Schoonover, S. C. (1977). *The practitioner's guide to psychoactive drugs*. New York: Plenum Medical.

Leavitt, F. (1982). *Drugs and behavior*. New York: Wiley.

Seiden, L. S., & Dykstra, L. A. (1977). *Psychopharmocology: A biochemical and behavioral approach*. New York: Van Nostrand Reinhold.

ROBERT F. SAWICKI
*Lake Erie Institute of
Rehabilitation, Lake Erie,
Pennsylvania*

STELAZINE

THORNDIKE, EDWARD L. (1847–1949)

E. L. Thorndike was an early theorist and writer who applied psychology to education. He was educated at Wesleyan, Harvard, and Columbia universities, with most of his professional career spent at Teachers' College, Columbia University. He is best known for his contributions to learning theory (Thorndike, 1905, 1931, 1932, 1935, 1949) and intellectual assessment (Thorndike, 1901, 1926, 1941).

Thorndike's major contribution to learning theory, termed the Law of Effect, is well known as a basic behavioral principle. The Law of Effect states; "any act which in a given situation produces satisfaction becomes associated with that situation, so that when the situation occurs, the act is more likely to recur also" (Thorndike, 1905, p. 203). His theory of connectionism was cognitively oriented, and viewed both physical and mental acts as involving the establishment of neural pathways. Learning was viewed as taking place when pathways were established through repetition.

Thorndike's measurement interests were diverse, as reflected by his famous dictum, "If anything exists, it exists in some amount. If it exists in some amount, it can be measured" (Thorndike, 1926, p. 38). His multifactored approach to measurement viewed intelligence as comprising abstract, mechanical, and social abilities. Intellectual assessment to Thorndike also involved the dimensions of attitude, breadth, and speed (i.e., level of difficulty, number of tasks, and rate of completion, respectively). This multifactored approach was in contrast to the approach of others of his time, who viewed intelligence as a general or unitary factor. Thorndike developed many tests, especially college entrance and achievement tests.

REFERENCES

Thorndike, E. L. (1901). *Notes on child study*. New York: Macmillan.

Thorndike, E. L. (1905). *The elements of psychology*. New York: Seiler.

Thorndike, E. L. (1926). *The measurement of intelligence*. New York: Teacher's College, Columbia University.

Thorndike, E. L. (1931). *Human learning*. New York: Century.

Thorndike, E. L. (1932). *Fundamentals of learning*. New York: Columbia University.

Thorndike, E. L. (1935). *The psychology of wants, interests and attitudes*. New York: Appleton-Century.

Thorndike, E. L. (1940). *Human nature and social order*. New York: Macmillan.

Thorndike, E. L. (1941). Mental abilities. *American Philosophical Society, 84*, 503–513.

Thorndike, E. L. (1949). *Selected writings from a connectionist's psychology*. New York: Appleton-Century-Crofts.

Thorndike, E. L., Bregman, E. O., Cobb, M. V., & Woodyard, E. (1925). *The measurement of intelligence*. New York: Columbia University.

Thorndike, E. L., & Lorge, I. (1944). *The teacher's wordbook of 30,000 words*. New York: Teacher's College, Columbia University.

JOSEPH D. PERRY
Kent State University

MEASUREMENT

THOUGHT DISORDERS

In the diagnosis of a psychiatric illness, it is common to evaluate disturbances in the following areas: consciousness, emotion, motor behavior, perception, memory, intelligence, and thinking (Ginsberg, 1985). Disorders in thinking, although most commonly associated with schizophrenia, may also occur in paranoid disorders, affective disorders, organic mental disorders, or organic delusional syndromes such as those owed to amphetamine or phencyclide abuse (*Diagnostic and Statistical Manual of Mental Disorders* [DSM III], 1980). Schizophrenic patients, however, tend to show more severe and specific forms of thought disorders, and may continue to show some degree of idiosyncratic thinking when not in the acute phases of the disease (Ginsberg, 1985). According to DSM III (1980), "at some phase of the illness, schizophrenia always involves delusions, hallucinations, or certain disturbances in the form of thought" (p. 181). A thought disorder is but one of the criteria needed for a diagnosis of schizophrenia; the illness is also characterized by disorganization in perceptions, communication, emotions, and motor activity. The term thought disorder encompasses a large array of dysfunctions, including disturbances in the form of thought, structure of associations, progression of thought, and content of thought.

Disturbances in Form of Thought. Thinking in a healthy individual occurs in a rational, orderly way. A thought might be stimulated by unconscious or conscious impulses, affective cues, or biological drives, yet the thinking process itself is directed by reason and results in a reality-oriented conclusion. As characterized by Ginsberg (1985), disturbances in the form of thought result in sequences that are no longer logical. In formal thought disorders, thinking is characterized by loosened associations, neologisms, and illogical constructs. In illogical thinking, thinking contains erroneous conclusions or internal contradictions. In dereism, there is mental activity not concordant with logic or experience. In autistic thinking, thinking gratifies unfilled desires but has no regard for reality (p. 500).

Disturbances in Structure and Progression of Associations. In DSM III, these disturbances are included under the Form of Thought category. However, as described by both Ginsberg (1985) and Kolb (1968), a division of this category is warranted. In a healthy individual, each separate idea is logically linked with ideas both preceding and following that idea. This progression occurs in a coherent fashion and at a relatively steady, moderate rate of speech. In severe cases of disorder, however, speech becomes so disjointed as to be incomprehensible. It then includes

1. Flight of ideas—an extremely rapid progression of ideas with a shifting from one topic to another so that a coherent whole is not maintained and considerable digression occurs from the beginning to the ending of the story. There is generally some association between thoughts; e.g., a single word in one sentence will lead to a following sentence. Flight of ideas is associated with a lack of goal-directed activity and with heightened distractibility and an accelerated inner drive. A patient might respond to the question, "What is your name?" with, "My name is David. David was in the *Bible* which is a religious document written many years ago. I feel that religion leads to persecution for many important citizens as a result of their beliefs which have been well thought out; however, thought is a very abstract concept as might be noted of music and art."

2. Clang associations—similar to flight of ideas. With clang associations, the stimulus that prompts a new thought is a word similar in sound, but not in meaning, to a new word.

3. Retardation—speech becomes slow and labored; often a lowered tone of voice is used. The patient may relate that his or her thoughts come slowly or that it is very difficult to concentrate or think about a topic.

4. Blocking—an unconscious interruption in the train of thought to such an extent that progression of thought comes to a complete halt. This is usually temporary, with thought processes resuming after a short time.

5. Pressure of speech—an excessive flow of words to such an extent that it becomes difficult to interrupt the speaker.

6. Perseveration—an occurrence in which the patient uses the same word, thought, or idea repeatedly, often in response to several different questions. One patient, when being diagnosed with the Rorschach Inkblot Test, responded to all 10 separate cards, "That looks like a man's genitals. Why are you showing me all these pictures of the same thing?"

7. Circumstantiality—the patient is eventually able to relate a given thought or story, but only after numerous digressions and unnecessary trivial details. This occurs largely in persons who are not able to distinguish essential from nonessential details. It is often observed in persons of low intelligence, in epileptics, and in cases of advanced senile mental disorder.

8. Neologism—when entirely new words are created by the patient.

9. Word salad—an incoherent mixture of words and phrases.

10. Incoherence—similar to word salad, the difference being that incoherence is generally marked by illogically connected phrases or ideas. Word salad generally consists of illogically connected single words or short phrases. A patient speaking incoherently may state, "Yes, this is the great reason for truth and validity as you must know and we all must know in times of need all great men who have an interest in greatness, perhaps, yes, cold is a very nice color, but, not inconsequentially as we have every reason to believe that our President is for better or worse, no, yesterday."

11. Irrelevant answer—an answer that has no direct relevance to the question asked.

12. Derailment—gradual or sudden deviation in one's train of thought without blocking.

Disturbances in Content of Thought. The most common disturbance in the content of thought involves a delusion, which is an idea or system of beliefs that is irrational, illogical, and with little or no basis in fact. In normal, healthy individuals, fantasy, daydreaming, rationalization, or projection can be used as effective ways to handle stress. Delusions appear to be an exaggerated form of this type of thinking. Delusions, however, are indicative of severe psychopathology in that they are patently absurd, and the patient cannot be argued out of his or her beliefs despite overwhelming evidence refuting the delusions. There are several different types of delusions, based on the specific thought content:

1. Delusions of grandeur—belief that an individual is special, important, or in some way superior to others. In many instances the patient may actually believe that he or she is someone else, e.g., God.

2. Delusions of reference—belief that innocent remarks or actions of someone else are directed exclusively at the patient. One hospitalized patient explained that whenever carrots were served at dinner, it meant that she was to take two baths that night; whenever ham was served, it meant that she was to avoid speaking to anyone until the following day.

3. Delusions of persecution—the belief that others are spying on, plotting against, or in some way planning to harm the patient.

4. Delusions of being controlled—the belief that one's thoughts and actions are imposed by someone else. Similar to this are thought broadcasting (the belief that one's ideas are broadcast to others); thought insertion (the belief that ideas are being inserted into one's head); and thought withdrawal (the belief that ideas are being removed from one's head).

Other less common delusions include self-accusation, sin, guilt, somatic illness, nihilism, religiosity, infidelity, and poverty (DSM III, 1980; Ginsberg, 1985; Kolb, 1968; MacKinnon & Michels, 1971).

Several theories have been advanced to account for the existence of thought disorders. The more psychogenic of these theories point to inadequate ego functioning, such that the patient creates his or her own reality to cope with overwhelming stress and anxiety. Biological theories view thought disorders as being genetically transmitted. Research in this area has focused on chemical neurotransmitters such as dopamine; it found differing levels of such chemicals in disturbed and healthy individuals. The effectiveness of drug therapy in treating thought disorders lends credence to biological theories. Other theories such as learning, cognitive, and family approaches are more environmentally based, and hold that persons with thought disorders may learn maladaptive ways of thinking or acting in response to live circumstances or unhealthy family situations (Worchel & Shebilske, 1983).

REFERENCES

American Psychiatric Association. (1980). *Diagnostic and statistical manual of mental disorders* (3rd ed.). Washington, DC: Author.

Ginsberg, G. (1985). The psychiatric interview. In H. Kaplan & B. Sadock (Eds.), *Comprehensive textbook of psychiatry/IV* (Vol. 1, pp. 500–501). Baltimore, MD: Williams & Wilkins.

Kolb, L. (1968). *Noye's modern clinical psychiatry* (7th ed.). Philadelphia: Saunders.

MacKinnon, R., & Michels, R. (1971). *The psychiatric interview.* Philadelphia: Saunders.

Worchel, S., & Shebilske, W. (1983). *Psychology: Principles and applications.* Englewood Cliffs, NJ: Prentice-Hall.

FRANCES F. WORCHEL
Texas A&M University

DIAGNOSTIC AND STATISTICAL MANUAL OF MENTAL DISORDERS (DSM III)
EMOTIONAL DISORDERS

TICS

Tics are recurrent, rapid, abrupt movements and vocalizations that represent the contraction of small muscle groups in one or more parts of the body. Motor tics may include eye blinking, shoulder shrugging, neck twisting, head shaking, or arm jerking. Vocal tics frequently take the form of grunting, throat clearing, sniffing, snorting, or squealing. These abnormal movements and sounds occur from once very few seconds to several times a day, with varying degrees of intensity. Although tics are involuntary, they often can be controlled briefly. However, temporary suppression results in a feeling of tension that can be relieved only when the tics are allowed to appear. Tics increase with anxiety and stress and diminish with intense concentration (Shapiro & Shapiro, 1981). The prevalence for tic disorders is 1.6% or about 3.5 million individuals in the United States. Boys are affected more frequently than girls (Baron, Shapiro, Shapiro, & Ranier, 1981).

The *Diagnostic and Statistical Manual of Mental Disorders*, third edition, delineates three major tic disorders that are based on age of onset, types of symptoms, and duration of the condition: transient tic disorder, chronic motor tic disorder, and Tourette syndrome (American Psychiatric Association, 1980). Familial studies suggest that these classifications may not represent distinct disorders but, rather, reflect a continuum of severity of the same disorder (Golden, 1981). The transient tic disorder or "habit spasm" is the mildest and most common of the disorders. Symptoms develop during childhood or adolescence and usually are observed in the face, head, or shoulders. Vocal tics are uncommon. Tic frequency, as well as intensity, generally fluctuates during the course of the disorder. Such childhood tics are transient and benign, disappearing after several months to 1 year.

Symptoms of the chronic motor tic disorder, which appear either in childhood or after the age of 40, are similar to those associated with the transient tic disorder. Vocalizations develop infrequently. When they are present, they tend to be grunts or other noises caused by contractions of the abdomen or diaphragm. The severity, intensity, and type of involuntary movement persist unchanged for years.

Tourette syndrome, the most severe condition, is differentiated from the other tic disorders by the presence of both motor and vocal tics and a pattern of symptoms that waxes and wanes as the tics slowly move from one part of the body to another. Complex movements such as jumping and dancing are often exhibited. Not always present, but confirmatory of Tourette syndrome, are echolalia (repetition of words or phrases spoken by others), palilalia (repetition of one's own words), coprolalia (involuntary swearing), echopraxia (imitation of the movement of others), and copropraxia (obscene gesturing). Although the nature and severity of these symptoms vary over time, the disorder rarely remits spontaneously and usually remains throughout life (Shapiro, Shapiro, Bruun, & Sweet, 1978).

REFERENCES

American Psychiatric Association. (1980). *Diagnostic and statistical manual of mental disorders* (3rd ed.). Washington, DC: Author.

Baron, M., Shapiro, A. K., Shapiro, E. S., & Rainer, T. D. (1981). Genetic analysis of Tourette syndrome suggesting major gene effect. *American Journal of Human Genetics, 33,* 767–775.

Golden, G. S. (1981). Gilles de la Tourette's syndrome. *Texas Medicine, 77,* 6–7.

Shapiro, A. K., & Shapiro, E. S. (1981). The treatment and etiology of tics and Tourette syndrome. *Comprehensive Psychiatry, 22,* 193–205.

Shapiro, A. K., Shapiro, E. S., Bruun, R. D., & Sweet, R. D. (1978). *Gilles de la Tourette's syndrome.* New York: Raven.

MARILYN P. DORNBUSH
Atlanta, Georgia

**ECHOLALIA
ECHOPRAXIA
TOURETTE'S SYNDROME**

TIME ON TASK

The amount of time that students spend on task has been an issue that concerns teachers in all fields, not just those involved with special education. Squires, Huitt, and Segars (1981) have identified three measures of student involvement that may be used to determine time on task. The first, allocated time, is simply the amount of time that is planned for instruction. Obviously, students will probably not be on task for the entire time that has been allocated. The second measure, which addresses this observation, is known as engagement rate. It is defined as the percent of allocated time that students actually attend to the tasks they are assigned. The third measure, engaged time, is the number of minutes per day students spend working on specific academic or related tasks; it is an integration of allocated time and engagement rate. Stallings and Kaskowitz (1974) found that, given certain maximum time limits based on a child's age and the subject matter at hand, engaged time is the most important variable that is related to student achievement. Given this finding, many researchers have focused on increasing time on task.

As an example, Bryant and Budd (1982) used self-instruction training with three young children who had difficulties in attending to task in kindergarten or preschool. The researchers trained the children to verbalize five separate types of self-instruction: (1) stop and look; (2) ask questions about the task; (3) find the answers to the questions posed in (2); (4) give instructions that provide guidance; and (5) give self-reinforcement for accomplished tasks. The results indicated an increase in on-task behavior for two of the children and, when used in combination with an unintrusive classroom intervention of reminders and stickers, all three of the children exhibited marked increases in their engaged time.

A somewhat different approach to the study of on-task behaviors was undertaken by Whalen et al. (1979), who examined the effects of medication (Ritalin) on the on- and off-task behaviors of children identified as hyperactive. They found clear differences in a maladaptive direction in the behaviors of their subjects who had been diagnosed as hyperactive under placebo conditions when compared with peers who had no diagnoses of hyperactivity. However, while the authors acknowledged that the medication did result in more on-task and prosocial behaviors in many of their subjects, they cautioned against a wholesale reliance on medications since many long-term effects had not yet been studied. Rather, the researchers felt that careful study of all variables in individual situations (e.g., teacher tolerance, cost effectiveness, environmental adaptations) must be undertaken when making treatment decisions.

REFERENCES

Bryant, L. E., & Budd, K. S. (1982). Self-instruction training to increase independent work performance in preschoolers. *Journal of Applied Behavior Analysis, 15,* 259–271.

Squires, D., Huitt, W., & Segars, J. (1981). Improving classrooms and schools: What's important. *Educational Leadership, 39,* 174–179.

Stallings, J. A., & Kaskowitz, D. (1974). *Follow through classroom observation evaluation, 1972–1973.* Menlo Park, CA: Stanford Research Institute.

Whalen, C. K., Henker, B., Collins, B., Finck, D., & Dotemoto, S. (1979). A social ecology of hyperactive boys: Medication effects in structured classroom environments. *Journal of Applied Behavior Analysis, 12,* 65–81.

ANDREW R. BRULLE
Eastern Illinois University

**ATTENTION DEFICIT DISORDER
ATTENTION SPAN
HYPERACTIVITY**

TIME-OUT

Time-out is an individual behavior management technique typically used to reduce or eliminate inappropriate attention-getting behaviors of children and sometimes adults (institutionalized disturbed). Time-out occurs when access to reinforcement is removed contingent on the emission of a response (Sulzer-Azaroff & Mayer, 1986).

The reductive effect is best demonstrated when time-out is implemented as follows:

Total removal of opportunities for reinforcement (e.g., removal from the reinforcing environment and placement in a nonstimulating environment).

Time-out durations of short to medium length (e.g., 3 to 10 minutes following the cessation of the inappropriate behavior).

Clear communication of conditions to the subject prior to use of time-out (e.g., the inappropriate behavior that will occasion time-out).

Consistent use of time-out after each occurrence of the inappropriate behavior until reduction has been maintained.

Reinforcement of desirable alternative behaviors to the inappropriate behavior to occur in conjunction with the use of time-out once the subject has returned to the natural environment.

In addition to its reductive effect on inappropriate behaviors, time-out allows for management of behaviors without the application of aversive stimuli. However, the incorrect use of time-out (e.g., extended durations of isolation) may prove ineffective as well as unethical (Hall & Hall, 1980). Sulzer-Azaroff and Mayer (1986) and Walker and Shea (1984) provide a more detailed description of time-out.

REFERENCES

Hall, R. V., & Hall, M. C. (1980). *How to use time-out*. Lawrence, KA: H & H Enterprises.

Sulzer-Azaroff, B., & Mayer, G. R. (1986). *Achieving educational excellence using behavioral strategies*. New York: Holt, Rinehart, & Winston.

Walker, J. E., & Shea, T. M. (1984). *Behavior management: A practical approach for educators* (3rd ed.). St. Louis: Mosby.

MARGARET LYONS
LOUIS J. LANUNZIATA
University of North Carolina,
Wilmington

AVERSIVE STIMULUS
BEHAVIOR MODIFICATION
PUNISHMENT

TIME SAMPLING

Time sampling is an intermittent means of recording behavior by observing the subject at certain prespecified times and recording his or her behavior in a manner prescribed by the time sampling method in use. According to Arrington (1943), the major impetus to developing various time sampling procedures was provided by the National Research Council between 1920 and 1935. The council, which controlled many research fund allocations, had become concerned because the diary records typically used in research on the behavior of children were neither comparable nor exact. This group began to encourage research that used quantifiable and replicable methods of data collection. One of the first researchers to accept the challenge was F. L. Goodenough (1928), whose technique involved dividing an observation session into a series of short intervals and recording whether or not the target behavior occurred during each of those intervals. Other researchers in child development and psychology (e.g., Arrington, 1932; Bindra & Blond, 1958; Olson, 1929; Parten, 1932) adopted and refined these procedures.

In more recent times, a common terminology has developed that defines the various types of time sampling methods. In a landmark study, Powell, et al. (1977) discussed three different types of time sampling procedures: (1) whole interval recording, (2) partial interval recording, and (3) momentary time sampling. In all of these procedures, the observation session is divided into a series of intervals. When the intervals are equal, the procedure is known as fixed interval (e.g., every 30 seconds). When the interval lengths are assigned at random but still average to the desired length (e.g., on the average, every 30 seconds), the procedure is known as variable interval.

In whole interval time sampling, the behavior is scored as having occurred only if it has endured for the entire interval; in partial interval time sampling the behavior is recorded as having occurred if it occurs at all (even for an instant) during the interval. In the technique known as momentary time sampling (MTS), the data collector records what behavior is occurring exactly at the end of each interval.

Repp et al. (1976) demonstrated conclusively that partial interval time sampling was not an accurate means of recording behaviors when frequency was the dimension of interest. Powell et al. (1977) conducted a study on the accuracy of all of these procedures and concluded that, when used to estimate the duration of a behavior, whole interval time sampling generally provided an underestimate while partial interval recording provided an overestimate. Momentary time sampling procedures both over- and underestimated the true duration of the behavior but, when averaged, provided the most accurate measure. The researchers felt that MTS interval lengths as long as 60 seconds could be used to collect accurate data. In an extension of this study, Brulle and Repp (1984) demonstrated that MTS procedures provide an accurate estimate of the duration of the behavior when averaged, but that each data entry, even when intervals are as short as 30 seconds, is subject to considerable error. They recommended that only very short intervals be used if averages are not acceptable.

REFERENCES

Arrington, R. E. (1932). Interrelations in the behavior of young children. *Child Development Monographs*, No. 8.

Arrington, R. E. (1943). Time sampling in studies of social behavior: A critical review of techniques and results with research suggestions. *Psychological Bulletin, 40*, 81–124.

Bindra, D., & Blond, J. (1958). A time-sample method for measuring general activity and its components. *Canadian Journal of Psychology, 12*, 74–76.

Brulle, A. R., & Repp, A. C. (1984). An investigation of the accuracy of momentary time sampling procedures with time series data. *British Journal of Psychology, 75*, 481–488.

Goodenough, F. L. (1928). Measuring behavior traits by means of repeated short samples. *Journal of Juvenile Research, 12*, 230–235.

Olson, W. C. (1929). A study of classroom behavior. *Journal of Educational Psychology, 22,* 449–454.

Parten, M. B. (1932). Social participation among preschool children. *Journal of Abnormal Social Psychology, 57,* 243–269.

Powell, J., Martindale, B., Kulp, S., Martindale, A., & Bauman, R. (1977). Taking a closer look: Time sampling and measurement error. *Journal of Applied Behavior Analysis, 10,* 325–332.

Repp, A. C., Roberts, D. M., Slack, D. J., Repp, C. F., & Berkler, M. S. (1976). A comparison of frequency, interval, and time-sampling methods of data collection. *Journal of Applied Behavior Analysis, 9,* 501–508.

ANDREW R. BRULLE
Eastern Illinois University

BEHAVIORAL CHARTING
BEHAVIOR ASSESSMENT
BEHAVIOR MODIFICATION

TOFRANIL

Tofranil is the proprietary name for the drug Imipramine, which primarily is used in the treatment of major depression and nocturnal enuresis. It has been suggested that Tofranil may be useful in the treatment of school phobia (Hersov, 1985).

Though Tofranil has proved to be an effective treatment for major depression in adults (AMA Drug Evaluations, 1983), its use with children is questionable. Shaffer (1985) reports that there have been few well-designed studies of the effectiveness of Tofranil and childhood depression. In one reported study in which Tofranil was compared double blind with a placebo, a 60% response rate was reported in both groups. In adults, Tofranil has a mild sedative effect that serves to lessen anxiety, though it is not intended to be used for this symptom. It has been suggested that it is this anxiety effect that may be helpful in a multidisciplinary approach toward school refusal (Hersov, 1985).

In children, Tofranil is most frequently used to ameliorate nocturnal enuresis. Numerous studies have demonstrated Tofranil's effectiveness in decreasing nighttime enuresis in most children (Shaffer, Costello, & Hill, 1968). The effect is seen rapidly, and almost always within the first week of treatment (Williams & Johnston, 1982). Unfortunately, research also has suggested that once the medication is withdrawn, many of these children begin wetting again. The effects of long-term treatment have not been studied (Shaffer, 1985). The relapse rate following cessation of the drug compares unfavorably with the withdrawal of the pad and bell procedure. The mode of action of Tofranil in decreasing nocturnal enuresis is not understood. An adverse side effect of Tofranil may be increased restlessness, agitation, and confusion.

REFERENCES

AMA Drug Evaluations (5th ed.). (1983). Philadelphia: Saunders.

Hersov, L. (1985). School refusal. In M. Rutter & L. Hersov (Eds.). *Child and adolescent psychiatry: Modern approaches* (2nd ed., pp. 382–399). St. Louis: Blackwell Scientific.

Shaffer D. (1985). Enuresis. In M. Rutter & L. Hersov (Eds.), *Child and adolescent psychiatry: Modern approaches* (2nd ed., pp. 465–481). St. Louis: Blackwell Scientific.

Shaffer, D., Costello, A. J., & Hill, I. D. (1968). Control of Enuresis with Imipramine *Archives of diseases in childhood, 43,* 665–671.

Williams, D. I., & Johnston, J. H. (1982). *Pediatric urology* (2nd ed.). London: Butterworth Scientific.

GRETA N. WILKENING
Children's Hospital, Denver, Colorado

DEPRESSION
ENURESIS

TOKEN ECONOMICS

A token economy is basically a miniature monetary system in which clients work for generalized, secondary reinforcers that are exchangeable for a variety of backup reinforcers. The token economy was first described in detail in the late 1960s (Ayllon & Azrin, 1965, 1968); it has since become one of the most popular means of providing reinforcers in special education settings. Successful token economies have been documented with such diverse populations as psychiatric patients (Ayllon & Azrin, 1965), sheltered workshop clients (Welch & Gist, 1974), and students in special education classes (Heward & Eachus, 1979).

When developing a token economy, the service provider needs to consider a number of different points. First, the token itself must be established. Just about anything can be used, however, some of the most popular items are plastic chips, check marks, and points. What is important in deciding what to use for tokens is that the tokens be easily administered and not easily counterfeited. A second consideration is the choice of backup reinforcers and their token prices. These reinforcers must be desirable for the clients and reasonably priced. A wide choice and constant variation of backup reinforcers will make the system appealing. A third consideration is access to the purchase of backup reinforcers. Regular times that provide access to the reinforcers on at least a weekly schedule are desirable. A fourth consideration is the record-keeping system devised by the service provider. Both clients and teachers should be aware of storage options or means of recording tokens earned. Finally, as with any behavioral procedure, the service provider must ensure that tokens are administered consistently. The clients and teachers must be clearly aware of what behaviors can earn tokens and what behaviors can result in fines, and these rules must be strictly enforced.

Kazdin (1982) and Kazdin and Bootzin (1972) have provided reviews of token economy systems. Most recently, Kazdin (1982) has commented on the progress within the profession on four critical issues (enhancing effects of token economies, staff training, client resistance to the program, and long-term effects) and has identified three emergent areas of concern (integrity of treatment, administrative and organizational issues, and dissemination of the token economy). In the first area of progress, enhancing effects, Kazdin (1982) notes that varying the strength of the reinforcers, emphasizing the economic aspects of the token system, and involving peers have all been helpful in improving the efficiency of token systems. Second, Kazdin (1982) points out that a number of studies have focused on effective means of training staff to administer token programs. Generally, training that includes several facets (e.g., modeling and informative feedback) has been most effective. When clients resist the program, Kazdin (1982) feels that providing opportunities that are not usually available (e.g., negotiating reinforcers) might help to reduce negative behaviors. As the final point of progress, Kazdin (1982) stresses that many descriptions of token programs are now providing follow-up data on their clients and that these data are necessary parts of the reporting process.

The emerging issues discussed by Kazdin (1982) are generally administrative in nature and focus on (a) whether or not the program was conducted as intended, (b) how various organizational variables (e.g., authority to make decisions) affect the token program, and (c) how well program methodologies and results are shared with others. Kazdin (1982) feels that currently, methodology for token economies has been well established, and that "the next step for research is to explore and evaluate procedures to integrate token economies routinely into settings where programs are likely to be of use" (p. 441–442).

For further information on the development of a token system, please consult Alberto and Troutman (1982) and for an in-depth review of the issues, Kazdin (1982) is an excellent source.

REFERENCES

Alberto, P. A., & Troutman, A. C. (1982). *Applied behavior analysis for teachers.* Columbus, OH: Merrill.

Ayllon, T., & Azrin, N. H. (1965). The measurement and reinforcement of behavior of psychotics. *Journal of the Experimental Analysis of Behavior, 8,* 356–383.

Ayllon, T., & Azrin, N. H. (1968). *The token economy: A motivational system for therapy and rehabilitation.* New York: Appleton-Century-Crofts.

Heward, W. L., & Eachus, H. T. (1979). Acquisition of adjectives and adverbs in sentences written by hearing impaired and aphasic children. *Journal of Applied Behavior Analysis, 12,* 391–400.

Kazdin, A. E. (1982). The token economy: A decade later. *Journal of Applied Behavior Analysis, 15,* 431–445.

Kazdin, A. E., & Bootzin, R. R. (1972). The token economy: An evaluative review. *Journal of Applied Behavior Analysis, 5,* 343–372.

Welch, M. W., & Gist, J. W. (1974). *The open token economy system: A handbook for a behavioral approach to rehabilitation.* Springfield, IL: Thomas.

ANDREW R. BRULLE
Eastern Illinois University

APPLIED BEHAVIOR ANALYSIS
BEHAVIORAL CHARTING
BEHAVIOR MODIFICATION

TONI

See TEST OF NON-VERBAL INTELLIGENCE.

TONIC NECK REFLEX, ASYMMETRICAL

See ASYMMETRICAL TONIC NECK REFLEX.

TOPICS IN LANGUAGE DISORDERS

Topics in Language Disorders, an interdisciplinary journal that is published quarterly, addresses topics within the general fields of language acquisition, language development, and language disorders. Contributors include speech and language pathologists, psycholinguists, pediatricians, neurologists, and special educators, especially remedial reading and learning disabilities teachers. This journal originated in 1980 to meet the need for published interactions across professional boundries on specific topics.

As the title implies, each journal presents a variety of issues surrounding one topic. A guest editor is responsible for soliciting manuscripts; in doing so, he or she seeks equality among disciplines as well as several views. Both clinical and educational application are sought with balance between theory and practice.

Members of the American Speech and Hearing Association may earn continuing education credits by reading each volume and responding to the questions at the end of the volume. Responses are then submitted to the address included in the journal. This service began with Volume 4.

ANNE CAMPBELL
Purdue University

TORCH COMPLEX

TORCH complex is a phrase used by some authors (e.g., Nahmias & Tomeh, 1977; Thompson & O'Quinn, 1979) to group a set of maternal infections whose clinical manifestations in children are so similar that differentiation among them on the basis of those symptoms alone may not be possible. TORCH stands for *TO*xoplasmosis, *Ru*bella, *C*ytomegalovirus, and *H*erpes. Generally speaking, with the exception of herpes, the infections have only mild and transitory effects on the mother, but through pre- or perinatal transmission, they may produce severe and irreversible damage to offspring. The major manifestations are visual and auditory defects and brain damage, which may result in mental retardation. The infections generally destroy already formed tissue rather than interfering with development; infants are frequently born asymptomatic, but gradually develop symptoms in the early years of life.

Although the major symptoms of the members of the TORCH complex are similar, the detailed symptoms, mechanisms of action, and times of major action differ.

REFERENCES

Nahmias, A. J., & Tomeh, M. O. (1977). Herpes simplex virus infections. In A. M. Rudolph (Ed.), *Pediatrics* (16th ed.). Englewood Cliffs, NJ: Prentice-Hall.

Thompson, R. J., & O'Quinn, A. N. (1979). *Developmental disabilities.* New York: Oxford University Press.

ROBERT T. BROWN
*University of North Carolina,
Wilmington*

**CYTOMEGALOVIRUS
HERPES SIMPLEX I AND II
RUBELLA
TOXOPLASMOSIS**

TORRANCE, ELLIS PAUL (1915–)

Ellis Paul Torrance earned his AA at Georgia Military College (1936), his BA at Mercer University (1940), his MA at the University of Minnesota (1944), and his PhD at the University of Michigan (1951). Since 1966 he has

Ellis Paul Torrance

served as professor of educational psychology and as department chairman at the University of Georgia. Although formally retired in 1984, Torrance continues to be active through the Torrance Studies for Gifted, Creative, and Future Behaviors.

Torrance is widely recognized for his voluminous contributions to the field of creative, gifted, and future education. At the heart of his philosophy is the impetus to change the goals, needs, and concepts in education. Future educational institutions will need to cultivate not only learning, but thinking. As a means of teaching versatility in thinking, Torrance reconceptualized and refined sociodrama as a group creative problem-solving technique. In addition, his efforts to identify gifted people from different cultures and all ages produced the Torrance Tests of Creative Thinking (TTCT). On the whole, Torrance has centered his distinguished career on helping society recognize the individual's creative potential and importance in forming visions of the future.

Torrance has contributed over 1100 publications and 27 books, including *Guiding Creative Talent, Education and the Creative Potential, Creative Learning and Teaching,* and *The Search for Satori and Creativity.* He has directed 118 doctoral dissertations, and 39 masters theses.

Torrance and his wife Pansy are the founders of the Future Problem Solving Program (1974), which teaches problem-solving skills to thousands of children in America and abroad. He is also the founder of the International Network of Gifted Students and Their Teachers/Sponsors. His many honors and awards include being appointed Alumni Foundation Distinguished Professor in 1973 and being awarded a grant by the Japan Society for the Promotion of Science to study creativity and creative instruction within Japanese educational institutions.

REFERENCES

Torrance, E. P. (1962). *Guiding creative talent.* Englewood Cliffs, NJ: Prentice-Hall.

Torrance, E. P. (1963). *Education and the creative potential.* Minneapolis: University of Minnesota Press.

Torrance, E. P. (1979). *The search for satori and creativity.* Buffalo, NY: Bearly.

MARY LEON PEERY
Texas A&M University

CREATIVITY TESTS
TORRANCE CENTER FOR CREATIVE STUDIES

TORRANCE CENTER FOR CREATIVE STUDIES

The Torrance Center for Creative Studies is a research center dedicated to investigations of the development of creative potential. Its research and development program honors and builds on the legacy of Ellis Paul Torrance, a native Georgian and a University of Georgia Alumni Foundation distinguished professor emeritus. This legacy is best reflected in the following statement:

> In almost every field of human achievement, creativity is usually the distinguishing characteristic of the truly eminent. The possession of high intelligence, special talent, and high technical skills is not enough to produce outstanding achievement. . . . It is tremendously important to society that our creative talent be identified, developed, and utilized. The future of our civilization—our very survival—depends upon the quality of the creative imagination of our next generation. (Torrance, 1959, p. 1)

Torrance, a pioneer in research on the identification and development of creative potential, is best known for his work in the development and refinement of the Torrance Tests of Creative Thinking (TTCT), the most widely used tests of creativity in the world.

The goals of the research and instructional program of the Torrance Center are to investigate and evaluate techniques and procedures for assessing creative potential and growth; to develop, apply, and evaluate strategies that enhance creative thinking; and to facilitate national and international systems that support creative development.

Four components—assessment, development, education, and evaluation—provide the organizational structure for the research and instructional programs of the center. Each component has been designed to contribute research that verifies and expands our understanding of creativity as a major ingredient in the development of human ability and that carries out the further development of instructional and evaluation technology to enhance the development of that ability.

Research on instruments and procedures to assess creative potential and to evaluate creative growth form the basis of the assessment component. Research on tests developed by Torrance, including validity studies, refinement of administration and scoring procedures, and interpretation of test results, and on the effects of strategies to develop creative ability, are coordinated through the center in conjunction with Scholastic Testing Service, the publishers of the Torrance tests and the Georgia Studies of Creative Behavior.

Two programs to investigate and evaluate techniques that facilitate or inhibit creative thinking and to determine the nature of systems and activities that support and encourage creative growth form the basis of the development component. The Future Problem Solving Program (FPS), founded in 1974 by E. Paul and J. Pansy Torrance, involves a deliberately interdisciplinary approach to studying and solving problems. It was motivated by a belief that we have reached a point in civilization at which education must devote a considerable part of the curriculum to helping students enlarge, enrich, and make more accurate their images of the future (Torrance, 1980). The FPS program is now international. Its headquarters are at St. Andrews College, Laurinburg, North Carolina. Anne Crabbe is the director. The Georgia FPS program is coordinated through the Torrance Center.

A major program initiative of the Torrance Center is the Torrance Creative Scholars Program. This program provides educational services to those individuals who score in the top $1\frac{1}{2}\%$ of the national population on the TTCT, verbal and/or figural. The program is consistent with Torrance's assertions (1984) that

> a common characteristic of people who have made outstanding social, scientific, and artistic contributions has been their creativity. Since we are living in an age of increasing rates of change, depleted natural resources, interdependence, and destandardization, there are stronger reasons than ever for creatively gifted children and adults to have a fair chance to grow. We must find these "world treasures" and give them support so that they can give society those things it so desperately needs.

A unique aspect of the Torrance Creative Scholars Program is its use of a mentoring component. This component provides a year-round mentoring network for the creative scholars. Individuals selected by Torrance are designated Torrance creative scholar-mentors; they provide mentoring services to the scholars in a variety of ways. These mentors are also eligible to become Torrance creative scholars and to receive the services of the program.

Scoring and validation of scores on the TTCT for the Torrance Creative Scholars Program are coordinated through Scholastic Testing Service. Programs and services are developed and implemented through the Torrance Center.

The third component, education, provides training for educators interested in creativity. This component operates in conjunction with the degree programs (master's, sixth year, and doctoral) offered through the department of educational psychology at the University of Georgia. Training programs offered through the center include the Torrance Center Summer Creativity Institute, the Challenge Program for preschool through fifth graders, and the Visiting Scholars Program for national and international scholars. In addition, there is the annual E. Paul Torrance Lecture and the library and archives donated to the university by Torrance. A future goal of the Torrance Center is to endow an E. Paul Torrance Research Professor Chair. The final component, evaluation, focuses on quantitative and qualitative evaluations of assessment techniques, educational strategies, and support systems for the various programs of the center.

The Torrance Center for Creative Studies was formally established at the University of Georgia in the spring of 1984 by Mary M. Frasier. It is located in the department of educational psychology, College of Education, 422 Aderhold Hall, University of Georgia, Athens, GA 30602.

REFERENCES

Torrance, E. P. (1959). *Understanding creativity in talented students*. Paper prepared at the Summer Guidance Institute Lecture Series on Understanding the Talented Student, University of Minnesota.

Torrance, E. P. (1980). Creativity and futurism in education: Retooling. *Education, 100*, 298–311.

Torrance, E. P. (1984). *The search for a nation's treasure* (Keynote address). St. Louis: National Association for Gifted Children.

MARY F. FRASIER
University of Georgia

CREATIVITY
CREATIVITY TEST
TORRANCE, ELLIS PAUL

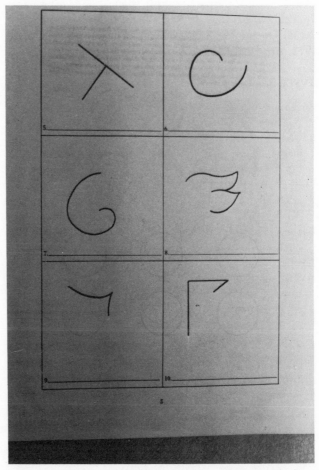

A sample page of items from the Torrance Tests of Creative Thinking, figural form, used to assess nonverbal creativity. The individual must complete each drawing and give it a name.

TORRANCE TESTS OF CREATIVE THINKING

E. Paul Torrance is an international leader in the field of creativity. He defines creativity as a process of becoming sensitive to problems, deficiencies, gaps in knowledge, or missing elements. Creativity also involves identifying a difficulty, searching for a solution, making guesses or formulating hypotheses (possibly modifying and retesting them), and communicating the results (1962).

Torrance has designed and published three major tests of creative thinking. Each test consists of a battery of subtests constructed to sample a variety of the more important kinds of creative thinking abilities (see Figure). The Torrance Test of Creative Thinking (figural form) can be used from kindergarten to graduate school. Thinking Creatively with Words is useful from fourth grade to graduate school. Thinking Creatively in Action and Movement is designed for 3 to 8 year olds. The tests can be administered by special trained personnel or teachers, and they can be purchased from Scholastic Testing Service.

The Torrance Test of Creative Thinking (figural forms

A and B) use tasks that require drawing. They report scores in terms of fluency—the ability to think of many ideas for a given topic; originality—the ability to think of new and unusual ideas; abstractness of titles—the ability to sense the essence of a problem and know what is essential; elaboration—the ability to add details to a basic idea; and resistance to premature closure—the ability to "keep open" in processing information and to consider a wide variety of information.

The Torrance Test of Creative Thinking (verbal forms A and B) require written responses and report scores in terms of fluency, originality, and flexibility (the ability to shift thinking and produce ideas in different categories).

Thinking Creatively in Action and Movement uses action, movement, and verbal responses to test creative thinking ability. It measures this in terms of fluency, originality, and imagination.

Test results indicate an individual's creative thinking ability as compared with other adults or children in the same grade. In addition, test results may be used to give additional insight into a student's style of thinking, learning, and creating. Several studies indicate that the Torrance Tests of Creative Thinking (figural and verbal) and Thinking Creatively in Action and Movement show no sexual, racial, or socioeconomic bias (Torrance, 1962, 1971, 1972, 1973, 1974).

REFERENCES

Torrance, E. P. (1962). *Guiding creative talent*. Englewood Cliffs, NJ: Prentice-Hall.

Torrance, E. P. (1971). Are the Torrance tests of creative thinking biased against or in favor of disadvantaged groups? *Gifted Child Quarterly, 15*, 75–80.

Torrance, E. P. (1972). Predictive validity of the Torrance tests of creative thinking. *Journal of Creative Behaviors, 6*, 236–252.

Torrance, E. P. (1973). Assessment of disadvantaged minority group children. *School Psychology Digest. 4*, 3–10.

Torrance, E. P. (1974). *Norms-technical manual: The Torrance Test of Creative Thinking*. Lexington, MA: Personnel Press/ Ginn.

JUNE SCOBEE
University of Houston, Clear Lake

GIFTED AND TALENTED CHILDREN
INSIGHT
TORRANCE, ELLIS PAUL

TORSIONAL DYSTONIA

The term "dystonia" was first used by H. Oppenheim in 1911 to denote the coexistence of muscular hypotonia and hypertonia. Since that time, the term has been used to describe a symptom of abnormal muscle contraction, a syndrome of abnormal involuntary movements, and a disease that has either a genetic or ideopathic origin. Torsional dystonia is commonly referred to as a progressive disorder characterized by slow, twisting movements that ultimately may result in bizarre, twisting postures of the extremities or trunk. Some causes of torsional dystonia are identifiable while other causes remain unknown, making classification of the condition difficult.

The disorder has a gradual onset, beginning between the ages of 5 and 15, and commonly involves the foot or leg. Torsional dystonia may spread to several parts or all of the body, but the condition is not present during sleep. Contractures or permanent muscle shortening and joint deformity ultimately occur. Hereditary forms of torsional dystonia are more common than ideopathic forms; one hereditary form is found most often in Ashkenazic Jews. The diagnosis of dystonia is based on clinical signs because diagnostic laboratory or biopsy findings are not known. The symptoms suggest dysfunction in the extrapyramidal system, since temporary drug-induced symptoms have oc-

curred from medications that have a known effect on the basal ganglia of the extrapyramidal system.

Treatment of torsional dystonia generally has been disappointing. Medications such as diazepam (Valium), carbamazepine (Tegretol), haloperidol, and, in some cases, levodapa or anticholinergic drugs have been helpful in reducing the severity of the symptoms; but none of these medications has been consistently effective. Various neurosurgical or biofeedback procedures have resulted in isolated improvement but consistent benefits have not been achieved through these approaches.

REFERENCES

Berkow, R. (Ed.). (1982). *The Merck Manual* (14th ed., p. 1363). Rahway, NJ: Merck, Sharp, & Dohme.

Fahn, S. (1985). The extrapyramidal disorders. In J. Wyngaarden & L. Smith, Jr. (Eds.), *Cecil textbook of medicine* (17th ed., pp. 2077–2078). Philadelphia: Saunders.

Fahn, S., & Roswell E. (1976). Definition of dystonia and classification of the dystonic states. In R. Eldridge & S. Fahn (Eds.), *Advances in neurology* (Vol. 14, pp. 1–5). New York: Raven.

Magalini, S., & Scarascia, E. (1981). *Dictionary of medical syndromes* (2nd ed.). Philadelphia: Lippincott.

Marsden, C. D. (1976). Dystonia: The spectrum of the disease. In M. D. Yahr (Ed.), *Basil ganglia* (pp. 351–365). New York: Raven.

Marsden, C. D., Harrison, M. J. G., & Bundey, S. (1976). Natural history of idiopathic torsion dystonia. In R. Eldrige & S. Fahn (Eds.), *Advances in neurology* (Vol. 14, pp. 177–187). New York: Raven.

Zeman, W. (1976). Dystonia: An overview. In R. Eldrige & S. Fahn (Eds.), *Advances in neurology* (Vol. 14, pp. 91–101). New York: Raven.

DANIEL D. LIPKA
Lincoln Way Special Education Regional Resource Center, Louisville, Ohio

PHYSICAL ANOMALIES
PHYSICAL HANDICAPS

TOTAL COMMUNICATION

The expression total communication can be used in the general sense of communication through all possible channels, not only vocal (including verbal) communication, but also communication provided by such other means as mimicry, gestures, etc. Recently, total communication has been used mainly in a more restricted field, namely the education of deaf children. It presents itself not as a method, but as "a philosophy incorporating the appropriate aural, manual, and oral methods of communication in order to ensure effective communication with and among hearing impaired persons" (Garretson, 1976, p. 300). It advocates the use of various modes of communication, such as speech (which should not be neglected, as the deaf live among a majority of hearing people), written language (reading and writing), sign language, finger spelling, pantomime, etc.

In recent years, methods of teaching deaf children applying this philosophy have been used in a steadily increasing number of schools in the United States and in Europe. These schools gave up the oral method that had prevailed since the end of the nineteenth century, mainly in Europe, where the resolutions of the International Congress held in Milan in 1880 were accepted and recommended almost unanimously (Lane, 1980).

According to the defenders of total communication, the oral approach, including lip reading, gives unsatisfactory results as far as linguistic and cognitive development are concerned (Conrad, 1979). It is argued that even if the hearing loss is discovered early, poor parent-infant communication delays the acquisition of language considerably and irretrievably, except with children whose residual hearing is sufficient to make communication possible. Ensuing education in specialized institutions is slower and less differentiated than with hearing children and, instead of reducing the gap, increases the retardation of the deaf children.

Total communication advocates the use of signing as the most appropriate mode of early communication between parents and hearing-impaired children. The double exposure to sign and speech (about 9 out of 10 deaf children have hearing parents) should allow partially hearing children equipped with appropriate audiological aids to be educated together with their hearing peers; children whose residual hearing is insufficient should be educated through a wide network of activities, of which "spoken language, finger spelling, signing, and written language constitute the linguistic core. Being capable of consistent transmission and internal symbolization of linguistic signals, these are the media of special relevance to linguistic and cognitive growth" (Evans, 1982, p. 91).

Evans (1982) shows three problematic issues for total communication: (1) the way the linguistic competence in sign language, with its own lexical, morphological, and syntactic characteristics, is to be transferred to linguistic competence in the spoken language of the community in which the deaf person is living; (2) the necessity for a specific training or recycling of teachers in total communication; and (3) the role of the (hearing) parents, who being confronted suddenly with the deafness of their baby, are obliged to learn the sign language in which they are going to communicate with the child in a very short time.

The philosophy of total communication remains unaltered in a variant in which the exposure to speech and sign is replaced by cued speech. The deaf child is taught to perceive the spoken language through a combination of residual hearing, lip reading, and a limited number of disambiguating signs near the speaker's face (Cornett, 1967).

Opponents of total communication think that signing may prove harmful and impede the acquisition of a spoken language and that too much time spent on teaching signs (finger spelling, etc.) could be used more appropriately to teach the spoken language. They stress the fact that some deaf children, albeit a minority, educated through the oral method succeed in obtaining a satisfactory level in spoken language perception and production.

REFERENCES

Conrad, R. (1979). *The deaf schoolchild: Language and cognitive functioning.* London: Harper & Row.

Cornett, O. (1967). Cued speech. *American Annals of the Deaf 112*, 3–13.

Evans, L. (1982). *Total communication: Structure and strategy.* Washington, DC: Gallaudet College Press.

Garretson, M. D. (1976). Total communication. In R. Frisina (Ed.), A bicentennial monograph on hearing impairment: Trends in the U.S.A. *Volta Review, 78.*

Lane, H. (1980). A chronology of the oppression of sign language in France and the United States. In H. Lane & F. Grosjean (Eds.), *Recent perspectives on american sign language.* Hillsdale, NJ: Erlbaum.

S. De Vriendt
*Vrije Universiteit Brussel,
Belgium*

AMERICAN SIGN LANGUAGE
DEAF EDUCATION

TOURETTE SYNDROME

Tourette syndrome is a tic disorder characterized by the appearance between the ages of 2 and 15 of involuntary muscular movements. A single, simple tic is generally the initial symptom and takes the form of an eye blink, head shake, or nose twitch. However, the symptoms gradually change over time, becoming more complex and involving other body parts. Complicated movements of the entire body are often observed, including kicking, jumping, and turning in circles. Vocalizations such as throat clearing, coughing, grunting, or barking are present. Later these noises may change into words and phrases. Echolalia (repetition of phrases made by others), palilalia (repetition of one's own words), coprolalia (utterance of obscene words), echopraxia (imitation of the movement of others), and copropraxia (obscene gesturing) frequently accompany the disorder.

While the frequency and severity of the symptoms fluctuate over time, the disorder is chronic and rarely remits spontaneously (Shapiro, Shapiro, Bruun, & Sweet, 1978). Associated features often include an attention deficit disorder with hyperactivity, school-related problems, and an increased incidence of learning disabilities (Jagger et al.,

1982). The etiology of Tourette syndrome remains unknown. However, the discovery of the efficacy of haloperidol in the treatment of the disorder has led researchers to postulate that Tourette syndrome may result from a biochemical imbalance in the nervous system (Snyder, Taylor, Coyle, & Meyerhoff, 1970). This hypothesis is further substantiated by the tendency of families of individuals with the disorder to have a positive history of Tourette syndrome or simple motor and vocal tics (Shapiro & Shapiro, 1982).

REFERENCES

Jagger, J., Prusoff, B. A., Cohen, D. J., Kidd, K. K., Carbonari, C. M., & John, K. (1982). The epidemiology of Tourette syndrome: A pilot study. *Schizophrenia Bulletin, 8,* 267–278.

Shapiro, A. K., & Shapiro, E. S. (1982). Tourette syndrome: Clinical aspects, treatment, and etiology. *Seminars in Neurology, 2,* 373–385.

Shapiro, A. K., Shapiro, E. S., Bruun, R. D., & Sweet, R. D. (1978). *Gilles de la Tourette's syndrome.* New York: Raven.

Snyder, S. H., Taylor, K. H., Coyle, J. T., & Meyerhoff, J. L. (1970). The role of brain dopamine in behavioral regulation and the action of psychotropic drugs. *American Journal of Psychiatry, 127,* 199–207.

MARILYN P. DORNBUSH
Atlanta, Georgia

ECHOLALIA
ECHOPRAXIA
TICS
TOURETTE SYNDROME ASSOCIATION

TOURETTE SYNDROME ASSOCIATION

The Tourette Syndrome Association, a voluntary nonprofit organization, was founded for the purpose of assisting individuals with Tourette syndrome, their families, friends, and concerned professionals. The primary objectives of the association include disseminating information regarding symptomatology and treatment of Tourette syndrome and raising funds to encourage and support scientific research into the nature and causes of the disorder.

In an effort to promote understanding of Tourette syndrome, the organization publishes quarterly newsletters, pamphlets, medical reprints, and films, and publicizes the disorder in newspapers, magazines, radio, and television. It provides support groups at a regional level for sharing current information about research, treatment, and management of Tourette syndrome. Information may be obtained from the Tourette Syndrome Association, Bell Plaza Building, 42-40 Bell Boulevard, Bayside, NY, 11361.

MARILYN P. DORNBUSH
Atlanta, Georgia

TICS
TOURETTE'S SYNDROME

TOXOPLASMOSIS

Toxoplasmosis is caused by an intracellular protozoan, Toxoplasma gondii, which is transmitted via the blood to the prenatal fetus. This congenital infection causes mild to severe mental and motor retardation. The largest number of newborns will be asymptomatic in the neonatal period so they must be observed for ocular and central nervous system disability. The newborn with symptomatic toxoplasmosis will present at birth with one or more of the following: head abnormalities (large or small), cerebral calcifications, brain damage, muscle spasticity, convulsions and seizures, visual and hearing impairments, and eye infections. An enlarged liver and spleen, which cause an extended abdomen, are often present. Rashes and jaundiced skin may be seen in infants. Motor impairment as a result of brain damage may be seen. Prognosis is poor; death occurs in 10 to 15% but a high percentage of children have neuromotor defects, seizure disorders, mental retardation, and damaged vision (Behrman, 1977; Carter, 1978).

Many children with toxoplasmosis may need to be placed in a fairly restrictive setting because of mental retardation and visual, hearing, and motor impairments. Children often need self-help skills training (including feeding and toileting) from an early age. Related services may be required for speech, vision, and hearing deficits. Physical and occupational therapy may also be needed. Since a variety of health problems may be present, a medical consultation will probably be needed. Team placement and management will be necessary for adequate educational programming.

REFERENCES

Behrman, R. (Ed.). (1977). *Neo-natal-perinatal diseases of the fetus and infant* (2nd ed.). St. Louis: Mosby.

Carter, C. (Ed.). (1978). *Medical aspects of mental retardation.* (2nd ed.). Springfield, IL: Thomas.

Hunt, M., & Gibby, R. (1979). *The mentally retarded child: Development, training and education* (4th ed.). Boston: Allyn & Bacon.

SALLY L. FLAGLER
University of Oklahoma

FUNCTIONAL SKILLS
MENTAL RETARDATION

TOY LENDING LIBRARIES

Toy libraries are lending libraries with a broad range of toys, learning materials, and equipment appropriate for young children. Many traditional public libraries offer a toy section that includes puzzles, games, stuffed animals, blocks, etc., that can be checked out and taken home by children and adults. However, the real growth in toy lending libraries is as a part of the increasing need for child care outside the traditional home setting. Toy lending libraries and resource centers are becoming more common across the country as child-care needs and services grow and as people become more interested and involved in meeting the needs of children and those who care for them. Such libraries allow the various child-care programs in a specific geographic area to pool their resources and share equipment, as well as to exchange ideas and information. These libraries are particularly useful to people in isolated areas or those who work alone. When these libraries limit their use to certified daycare providers, they may also serve as a motivating force that results in a greater pool of licensed and certified daycare providers.

Types of equipment typically found in such libraries include recreational equipment, sand and water play sets, transportation equipment, farm and animal sets, blocks and other manipulatives, housekeeping materials, make believe materials, infant toys, puzzles, perception, alphabet, and math materials, and large and small motor toys. Funding for toy lending libraries comes from a number of sources. The most common would be government (national, state, or local) grants, foundation awards, local United Ways, and dues from members. Special groups such as state (Councils for Exceptional Children) have also been known to provide start-up funds for such libraries.

DENISE M. SEDLAK
United Way of Dunn County,
Menomonie, Wisconsin

DAY-CARE CENTERS
PLAY

TRACE MINERALS

Trace minerals are minerals found in very small quantities in the human body but having significant relationships to certain metabolic events necessary for normal function. Severe deficiencies of trace minerals can result in a variety of handicaps, including orthopedic and learning disabilities. Some minerals and their relative levels in the body affect memory and attention as well. An overabundance or improper metabolism of some minerals also may produce problems. Depending on the particular mineral and the chronicity of the deficiency (or oversupply), mineral-related handicaps may or may not be reversible, though all are treatable to a large extent.

STAFF

ETIOLOGY
NUTRITIONAL DISORDERS

TRAINABLE MENTALLY RETARDED

Trainable mentally retarded is a category within a classification scheme used in many U.S. school systems to differentiate levels of educability of mentally retarded individuals. This classification system is based on intelligence quotients (IQ) and relates, but does not conform precisely, to the scheme advocated by the American Association of Mental Deficiency (Grossman, 1973, 1983).

This traditional organizational classification of special education (Robinson & Robinson, 1976) advances the distinction between educable mentally retarded (EMR) individuals with IQs between approximately 50 and 75, and trainable mentally retarded (TMR) students, with IQs between 25 and 55 (Robinson & Robinson, 1976). Typically, EMR persons are expected to achieve academic work at least to the third-grade level and occasionally to the grade 6 level by the time they leave school. By contrast, TMR individuals are not expected to achieve functionally useful academic skills. Rather, curricular goals include cleanliness, health, good eating behavior, communication skills, good work habits, social skills, and leisure behavior.

The TMR group of pupils has been relatively small over the years; Robinson and Robinson (1976) estimate that approximately 1 in 500 children fall in this range. Historically, this group has been excluded from school or placed in residential facilities because of their inability to profit from traditional school curricula and because of their frequent physical problems, including seizures, cerebral palsy, and toileting difficulties. However, with PL 94-142 and the establishment of the right to a free and appropriate public education for each child, along with an increase in facilities that support parents maintaining their retarded children at home, educational services within public school settings have increased dramatically. Concurrently, the technology of educating TMR individuals with respect to functional goals has improved considerably (Snell, 1983).

Additional developments that occurred in the same approximate time frame with PL 94-142 have operated to produce shifts in the types of students classified in the TMR category. First, the Grossman American Association of Mental Deficiency scheme for classifying mentally retarded individuals was modified (Grossman, 1973, 1983). The newer definition includes poor adaptive behavior as a requisite for categorization and lowers the cutoff for categorization from one to two standard deviations below the mean, changing the ceiling IQ score from 75 to 70. Second, litigation (*Diana* v. *State Board of Education*, 1970, and *Larry P.* v. *Riles*, 1972) called into question the placement of minority group children in classes for the mentally retarded. The basic assumptions in these cases were that the placement of these children in such classes was based on discriminatory procedures and that the outcomes of such placements for the pupils' educational progress were essentially negative (Reschly, 1982). Third, early intervention efforts with poor and handicapped children increased dramatically, reducing the psychosocial forces for mental retardation and improving the functioning of retarded individuals (Rynders, Spiker, & Horrobin, 1978).

These factors have converged to produce decreases in the numbers of children identified as retarded and to effect dramatic shifts in the mentally retarded population from TMR to EMR (Polloway & Smith, 1983). Review of federal demographic data indicates that between 1976–1977 and 1980–1981, all but eight states and territories demonstrated a decrease in the number of children served as retarded, with an average percentage decrease of 12.9 (Polloway & Smith, 1983). Concurrently, students moved from TMR to EMR classes, with both groups more disabled than previously (MacMillan & Borthwick, 1980).

REFERENCES

Grossman, H. J. (1973). *Manual on terminology and classification in mental retardation* (Special Publication No. 2). Washington, DC: American Association on Mental Deficiency.

Grossman, H. J. (1983). *Classification in mental retardation.* Washington, DC: American Association on Mental Deficiency.

MacMillan, D. L., & Borthwick, S. (1980). The new educable mentally retarded population: Can they be mainstreamed? *Mental Retardation, 14,* 3–10.

Polloway, E. A., & Smith, J. D. (1983). Changes in mild mental retardation: Population, programs, and perspectives. *Exceptional Children, 50,* 149–159.

Reschly, D. J. (1982). Assessing mild retardation: The influence of adaptive behavior, sociocultural status, and prospects for non-biased assessment. In C. R. Reynolds & T. B. Gutkin (Eds.), *A handbook for school psychology.* New York: Wiley.

Robinson, N. M., & Robinson, H. B. (1976). *The mentally retarded child: A psychosocial approach* (2nd ed.). New York: McGraw-Hill.

Rynders, J. E., Spiker, D., & Horrobin, J. M. (1978). Underestimating the educability of Down's syndrome children: Examination of methodological problems in recent literature. *American Journal of Mental Deficiency, 82,* 440–558.

Snell, M. E. (Ed.). (1983). *Systematic instruction of the moderately and severely handicapped* (2nd ed.). Columbus, OH: Merrill.

LYNN S. FUCHS
Peabody College, Vanderbilt University

AAMD
EDUCABLE MENTALLY RETARDED
MENTAL RETARDATION

TRAINING FOR EMPLOYMENT IN TRADITIONAL SETTINGS

Mildly and moderately handicapped students can be educated or trained to succeed as adult workers in many vocations. The vocational program that prepares handicapped students will be similar to regular vocational education; however, unique components should be evidenced.

All vocational preparation programs should begin with an assessment phase. Students' job interests, abilities, and readiness will be evaluated. For many special education students, this assessment procedure will be their first directed opportunity to examine their own capabilities and limitations as they relate to employment (Weisgerber, 1978).

The assessment phase should be comprehensive in order to provide information that will help the instructors and students to set appropriate vocational goals. Also, adequate assessment data will ensure that the subsequent training program will be effective. Specific job skills capabilities should be identified, as well as appropriate interpersonal relationship skills. More handicapped workers are dismissed from their employment because of lack of social skills than lack of job skills (Weisgerber, Dahl, & Appleby, 1981).

The primary goal of the training phase of a vocational program for handicapped students will be to prepare them for successful employment. To accomplish this goal, several components must be integrated into the total program (Weisgerber, Dahl, & Appleby, 1981).

The faculty responsible for these programs must continually be aware of the limitations and capabilities of the students and the employment community. Job analyses that include data concerning vocational opportunities, employers attitudes toward the handicapped, and the community's receptivity to accommodating the handicapped should be conducted periodically.

An amicable relationship among special education teachers, vocational education faculty, and community employers will facilitate successful employment of handicapped graduates. Teachers who are knowledgeable about their students' work abilities can be effective advocates for these students when they are seeking employment.

Vocational training programs should use technology to assist their students in increasing their abilities and reducing the effects of their handicapping conditions. Familiarity with new devices will enable the faculty to share this knowledge with prospective employers to promote employment of the handicapped in traditional settings.

Securing realistic work sites either at school or in businesses and factories will increase the effectiveness of a special education vocational program. By practicing specific job skills that will be used in a vocation, students will not have to be retrained when they become employed, saving the employers time and money.

Teachers who advocate employment of handicapped students should have expertise in the area of adaptations for job sites. Alteration of the work place and occasionally the work routine may enable the handicapped worker to become more productive. In these instances, it is the environment that is handicapping rather than the physical or mental limitations of the worker (Wade & Gold, 1978).

REFERENCES

Wade, M. G., & Gold, M. W. (1978). Removing some of the limitations of mentally retarded workers by improving job design. *Human Factors, 20,* 339–348.

Weisgerber, R. A. (Ed.). (1978). *Vocational education: Teaching the handicapped in regular classes.* Reston, VA: Council for Exceptional Children.

Weisgerber, R. A., Dahl, P. R., & Appleby, J. A. (1981). *Training the handicapped for productive employment.* Rockville, MD: Aspen.

JONI J. GLEASON
University of West Florida

COMMUNITY PLACEMENT
HABILITATION
PROFOUNDLY HANDICAPPED, COMPETENCIES OF
    TEACHERS OF
REHABILITATION
VOCATIONAL TRAINING

TRAINING IN THE HOME

Literature relating to child development frequently states that parents and other family members are the primary teachers of infants and young children. A great deal of the teaching and learning of young children in the home occurs during everyday activities such as watching TV and completing daily chores. As a result of the parent's role in teaching and socializing young children, it is essential to include the family and the home environment in any intervention plan for young children at risk (Fallen &

Umansky, 1985). According to Cartwright, Cartwright, and Ward (1984) many handicapped children tend to have problems generalizing from the specific teaching setting to other settings. Therefore, an advantage of home-based training is that many opportunities are available for the parents to apply learning to life activities.

One home-based approach to early education is the Portage project. This project was designed to meet the needs of young children in rural Wisconsin. Emphasis was placed on the skills of parents in teaching their handicapped children. A teacher would visit the home and provide the parents with the necessary materials, written instructions, and forms for record keeping. Some of the basic assumptions that this project was developed around are that parents are concerned about their children and want them to develop to their maximum potential; that parents can, with assistance, learn to be effective teachers; that the socioeconomic and educational levels of the parents are no indication of the willingness to help or the amount of gains the children will achieve; and that precision teaching maximizes the chances of success for children and parents. Research has shown that when parents are involved in their children's treatment and education, children do better. The family is considered the most effective system for fostering the development of the child (Shearer, 1974).

On the other hand, there are some educators who strongly suggest that parents should leave teaching of academics to the schools. Lerner (1981) states that when learning-disabled children are tutored by their parents, it makes the children feel stressed. This is because there is a good chance that the children will feel like failures in front of the most important people in their lives. This stress tends to have a negative effect on the parent-child relationship. Lerner emphasized that parents should concentrate on teaching children domestic tasks and helping them develop a good self-image. Barsch (1969) feels that parents do not have the patience to teach their children. He lists several reasons why parents should not teach academics. They include the following:

1. Parents lack essential teaching skills.

2. The parent-child instructional session often results in frustration and tension for both members.

3. Most parents and children wish that academics could be accomplished during the school day.

4. Most teachers do not have the time to guide the parent.

5. When both the home and school stress academics, the child finds little rest.

6. Parents differ greatly in their competence as teachers.

7. Parents may feel guilty if they do not find the time to tutor their child regularly.

It has been established that some parents can successfully tutor their children. Therefore, the parents' decision to tutor or not should be made on an individual basis. According to Kronick (1977), a major question that should be addressed in terms of whether to tutor or not is whether tutoring can be accomplished without depriving any family member of resources that assist in maintaining a well-balanced life. If the parents decide to teach their children at home, Lovitt (1977) has suggested four guidelines for parents. They should establish a specific time each day for the tutoring sessions; keep sessions short; keep responses to the child; and keep a record.

REFERENCES

Barsch, R. H. (1969). *The parent teacher partnership*. Reston, VA: Council for Exceptional Children.

Cartwright, G. P., Cartwright, C. A., & Ward, M. E. (1984). *Educating special needs learners* (2nd ed.). Belmont, CA: Wadsworth.

Fallen, N. H., & Umansky, W. (1985). *Children with special needs* (2nd ed.). Columbus, OH: Merrill.

Kronick, D. (1977). A parent's thoughts for parents and teachers. In N. G. Haring & B. Bateman (Eds.), *Teaching the learning disabled child*. Englewood Cliffs, NJ: Prentice-Hall.

Lerner, J. W. (1981). *Learning disabilities: Theories, diagnosis and teaching strategies* (3rd ed.). Boston: Houghton Mifflin.

Lovitt, T. C. (1977). *In spite of my resistance . . . I've learned from children*. Columbus, OH: Merrill.

Shearer, M. S. (1974). A home based parent training model. In J. Grim (Ed.), *First chance for children: Training parents to teach: Four models* (Vol.3, pp. 49–62). Chapel Hill: Technical Assistance Development System, North Carolina University.

JANICE HARPER
*North Carolina Central
University*

**FAMILY RESPONSE TO A HANDICAPPED CHILD
HOMEBOUND INSTRUCTION
HOMEWORK
TUTORING**

TRAINING SCHOOLS

Training schools were an intricate part of the larger multipurpose residential facilities known as the "colony plan" that were established in the late 1800s. These schools served children and adolescents who were not considered eligible for public school education because of their unique educational needs.

The evolvement of the training school concept was based on earlier work by Samuel Gridley Howe (1801–1876). Howe's Perkin School for the Deaf (1848) led to the development of other self-contained schools (e.g., Massachusetts School for Idiots and Feeble-Minded Youth, 1855). Although Howe's 10-bed unit was the first residential facility established, it was not until 1848 that the first large facility, the Syracuse Institution of the Feeble-Minded was developed. Harvey B. Wilbur (1820–1883), a physician, became the first superintendent of this facility. Like Howe, Wilbur was very much influenced by the philosophy and principles of Edward Seguin; he placed a great deal of emphasis on education.

Although institutions for exceptional individuals were initially viewed as beneficial by many throughout history, their purpose, programs, and administration changed drastically. The small homelike educational establishment was replaced by the larger, overcrowded, and underfinanced multipurpose facility that would typify institutions for generations to come.

Initially, training schools in institutions were intended to serve school-aged exceptional needs children and adolescents. As years passed, it became increasingly clear that individuals who reached the age limit for school programming had few choices for continued educational services. Typically, these adults were sent to almshouses or other similar institutions.

Though educational programs continued in institutions, there was a growing emphasis on vocational training. Most of the basic operations in running these large facilities were the sole responsibility of the individuals who resided at the facility. Therefore, skills that were taught to the residents had a direct application toward the continued function of the institution.

By 1890 the school facilities of the 1850s evolved into larger facilities intended to serve four distinct groups of residents. The colony plan was developed to serve (1) the teachable portion of a school-attending group, (2) the helpless, deformed, epileptic, and unteachable, (3) the male adults who had reached school age but were unable to become self-supportive, and (4) the female adults who at that time needed close supervision. The colony plan included training schools as well as an industrial, custodial, and farm department.

As early as the 1860s, however, advocacy of education in public schools was being heard. Although it is difficult to determine precisely when the first public school special education program was initiated, credit is usually given to the public school system of Providence, Rhode Island. An auxiliary school for 15 mentally retarded students opened in December 1896 (Woodhill, 1920). By 1898 the city of Providence established three more auxiliary schools and one special education classroom in a public school.

Other cities soon followed Providence's example. By the turn of the century, special education provisions for the mentally retarded shifted from total residential training schools to generally accepted, though not always implemented, education in public school systems.

REFERENCES

Kanner, L. (1964). *A history of case and study of the mentally retarded.* Springfield, IL: Thomas.

Scheerenberger, R. C. (1983). *The history of mental retardation.* Baltimore, MD: Brookes.

Woodhill, E. (1920). Public school clinics in connection with a state school for the feeble-minded. *Journal of Psycho Asthenics, 25,* 14–103.

MICHAEL G. BROWN
Central Wisconsin Center for the Developmentally Disabled, Madison, Wisconsin

HISTORY OF SPECIAL EDUCATION
HUMANISTIC SPECIAL EDUCATION

TRANQUILIZERS

The term tranquilizer is a superordinate that may be applied to two general classes of psychoactive drugs: antipsychotic agents (major tranquilizers) and antianxiety agents (minor tranquilizers). Both major and minor tranquilizers produce sedative effects, though to different degrees. Minor tranquilizers tend to produce fewer neurotoxic side effects, but appear to be more likely candidates for abuse (Blum, 1984). The following table summarizes the two groups of tranquilizers.

The major tranquilizers were developed in an attempt to humanize the treatment of psychotic individuals, who were being given long-term treatment in psychiatric hospitals. The drugs were developed based on observations of related agents that produced calming effects on wild animals. Like the minor tranquilizers, the major tranquilizers have not been found to be physically addictive. Abrupt withdrawal, however, has been reported to induce insomnia, anxiety, and gastrointestinal symptoms (Brooks, 1959). (see Table).

In terms of the general public, the minor tranquilizers are more familiar and also show more pervasive, popular use. The benzodiazapines are often used to reduce the effects of chronic stress, tension, and emotional discomfort. Valium has been described as the most prescribed drug in

Tranquilizers

Major	Minor
Phenothiazines	*Benzodiazapines*
Thorazine (Chlorpromazine)	Valium (Diazepam)
Stelazine (Trifluoperazine)	Librium (Chlordiazepoxide)
Mellaril (Thioridazine)	Dalmane (Flurazepam)
Prolixin (Fluphenazine)	Tranxene (Chlorazepate)
Thioxanthenes	*Meprobamate*
Navane (Thiothixene)	
Butyrophenones	
Haldol (Haloperidol)	

the United States, with 75% of the prescriptions being issued by nonpsychiatrists (Blum, 1984). Blum also reports that annual revenue of the antianxiety drug market in the United States is approximately $500 million. When added together, the prescriptions for Librium and Valium would account for approximately one out of five American adults (Blum, 1984).

In addition to more general stress-reducing effects, Valium is also a drug of abuse. Dosages of 100 to 500 mg produce intoxication (Patch, 1974). Valium also is used by substance abusers to deal with the frightening effects of a "bad trip" after hallucinogen (e.g., LSD) ingestion or to diminish the hangover effects after amphetamine intoxication (Blum, 1984). Therapeutically, Valium has been found to produce symptomatic relief for tension and anxiety states, free-floating agitation, mild depressive symptoms, fatigue, and short-term treatments of insomnia (Katzung, 1982). In addition, benzodiazapines have been used as adjuncts in the treatment of seizure disorders, since administration tends to raise the seizure threshold (Katzung, 1982). Valium also has been used to relieve skeletal muscle spasms, whether induced by local reactions or trauma, and spasticity secondary to upper motor neuron disorders (Blum, 1984).

Effects commonly reported owing to drug sensitivity or to intoxication include anticholinergic effects. In addition, lethargy, headache, slurred speech, tremor, and dizziness also have been reported (Blum, 1984). Paradoxical reactions including acute periods of increased excitability, increased anxiety, hallucinations, insomnia, rage, and increased muscle spasticity also have appeared in the literature (Blum, 1984). Though severe overdose of Valium is uncommon, symptoms include somnolence, confusion, coma, and blunted reflexes (Blum, 1984). The minor tranquilizers have not been found to be physically addictive; however, habituation (psychosocial accommodation to the effects of the drugs) has been reported frequently.

REFERENCES

Blum, K. B. (1984). *Handbook of abusable drugs.* New York: Gardner.

Brooks, G. W. (1959). Withdrawal from neuroleptic drugs. *American Journal of Psychiatry, 115,* 931.

Katzung, B. G. (1982). *Basic and clinical pharmocology.* Los Altos, CA: Lange Medical.

Patch, V. D. (1974). The dangers of diazepam: A street drug. *New England Journal of Medicine, 190,* 807.

ROBERT F. SAWICKI
Lake Erie Institute of Rehabilitation, Lake Erie, Pennsylvania

MELLARIL
STELAZINE
THORAZINE

TRANSDISCIPLINARY MODEL

Originally conceived by Hutchison (1974), the transdisciplinary model is one of several team approaches for the delivery of educational and related services to handicapped students. The other team models are the multidisciplinary model and the interdisciplinary model. In a multidisciplinary model, team members maintain their respective discipline boundaries with only minimal, if any, coordination, collaboration, or communication (McCormick, 1984). The interdisciplinary model differs from the multidisciplinary model in that there is some discussion among the involved professionals after their individual assessments have been completed and at least an attempt to develop a coordinated service delivery plan. However, the programming recommendations are often not realistic. The teacher may not have the skills to implement the recommendations or the authority to arrange for their provision (Hart, 1977). Another problem is the lack of provision for follow-up and feedback in the interdisciplinary model.

The transdisciplinary model is the only one of the three models to adequately address the issue of coordinated service delivery. This model suggests specific procedures for sharing information and skills among professionals and across discipline boundaries. It is differentiated from the other models by its emphasis on coordination, collaboration, and communication among the involved discipline representatives and its advocacy of integrated services.

The transdisciplinary model assumes the following: (1) joint functioning (team members performing assessment, planning, and service delivery functions together; (2) continuous staff development (commitment to expansion of each team member's competencies); and (3) role release (sharing functions across discipline boundaries; (Lyon & Lyon, 1980). The professional makeup of a transdisciplinary team varies depending on the needs of the student. It may include few or many professionals, but whenever possible they coordinate their assessment procedures and plan as a group for the student's daily programming.

Transdisciplinary team members are accountable for seeing that the best practices of their respective disciplines are implemented (McCormick & Goldman, 1979). However, their responsibility does not stop there. They are also responsible for monitoring program implementation, training others if necessary, and revising programs when evaluation data indicate that the procedures are not working. The teacher is usually coordinator and manager of team processes so that there is no duplication of efforts or splintering of services.

REFERENCES

Hart, V. (1977). The use of many disciplines with the severely and profoundly handicapped. In E. Sontag, J. Smith, & N. Certo (Eds.), *Educational programming for the severely and profoundly handicapped*. Reston, VA: Council for Exceptional Children, Division of Mental Retardation.

Hutchison, D. (1974). *A model for transcisciplinary staff development* (United Cerebral Palsy: Technical Report No. 8).

Lyon, S., & Lyon, G. (1980). Team functioning and staff development: A role release approach to providing integrated educational services for severely handicapped students. *Journal of the Association for Severely Handicapped, 5*(3), 250–263.

McCormick, L. (1984). Extracurricular roles and relationships. In L. McCormick & R. Schiefelbusch (Eds.), *Early language intervention*. Columbus, OH: Merrill.

McCormick, L., & Goldman, R. (1979). The transdisciplinary model: Implications for service delivery and personnel preparation for the severely handicapped. *AAESPH Review, 4*(2), 152–161.

LINDA MCCORMICK
University of Hawaii

ITINERANT SERVICES
MULTIDISCIPLINARY TEAM

TRANSFER OF LEARNING

Transfer of learning, also called concomitant or concurrent behavior change, occurs when modifications that take place in one behavior result in changes in other similar behaviors. A generalization issue that is closely related to transfer of learning is response maintenance, which refers to the persistence or durability of a behavior following the withdrawal of programmed contingencies. These two related issues each emphasize the response facet of the $S > R > C$ paradigm. Transfer of learning focuses on the generalized effect of newly acquired responses on other behaviors, while response maintenance addresses the degree to which the response persists over time or across environments.

Basic to the idea of transfer of learning is the concept of response classes. Examples of behaviors that are members of the same response class might include adding and subtracting, assembling items, and walking and sitting posture. As members of a response class become more similar, transfer of learning is enhanced. This generalization of learning can be reflected in quantitative or qualitative transfer to similar behaviors. Accordingly, when a teacher has reinforced the rate of completion or accuracy of one subcontracted assembly task and observes a concurrent rate or accuracy increase in a separate assembly task, transfer of learning is inferred.

Maintenance of learned behavior also plays an important role in education. The key consideration with this type of response generality is what happens to a behavior when the teaching contingencies have been removed. Specifically, if the behavior continues to occur as time passes, or occurs in other nontrained settings, the behavior has been maintained.

One cannot overemphasize the importance of transfer of learning and response maintenance with regard to the education of exceptional needs students. Public Law 94-142 mandates that educational services provided for such students must take place in the least restrictive setting appropriate. As a result of this law, many exceptional needs students spend all or part of their school day in varied settings that often have different behavioral requirements. Therefore, teachers must develop and implement programs that efficiently promote transfer of learning to the varied response requirements that may be placed on the student. These programs must also be planned such that the newly acquired behavior has the greatest likelihood of being maintained.

Aside from specific legal considerations, which provide a rationale for systematic training of transfer of learning and response maintenance, further justification for such efforts relates to the learning characteristics of exceptional needs students. Skill deficits, learning problems, and a host of other potentially limiting variables suggest that in educating such students, systematic interventions in these areas may directly predict teaching and learning effectiveness.

Two effective methods for encouraging transfer of learning have been the training of sufficient response examples and the allowance for differing acceptable responses during training (Stokes & Baer, 1977). The first technique involves the specific training of generalized responses. Thus the student is rewarded for acceptable generalizations of a response (e.g., rate increase on task one and rate increase on task two). The latter approach suggests reinforcement of varied, but similar, responses (e.g., "hi" or "hello") by the student to develop more effective learning transfer.

Techniques used to promote the maintenance of learned behaviors have included (1) the use of natural reinforcement contingencies, (2) changing of the natural environment, (3) the use of indiscriminable reinforcement schedules, and (4) the giving of "control" to the individual. The first technique makes use of the reinforcement that naturally might occur for the behavior. If necessary, the second technique changes the environmental requirements to maintain behavior. An alternative to either of these techniques might be the varying of reinforcement following a behavior to increase its durability. Another option mentioned by Stokes and Baer (1977) is the teaching of self-reinforcement or self-management skills so that the student relies on himself or herself for behavioral maintenance.

Each of the techniques mentioned requires planning as well as consistency in implementation. Systematic use of these techniques has been effective in promoting transfer of learning and response maintenance with exceptional needs learners. For a more detailed discussion of transfer of learning and response maintenance, as well as related teaching considerations, the reader is referred to texts by Sulzer-Azaroff and Mayer (1977) and Alberto and Troutman (1977).

REFERENCES

Alberto, P. A., & Troutman, A. C. (1977). *Applied behavior analysis for teachers: Influencing student performance.* Columbus, OH: Merrill.

Stokes, T. F., & Baer, D. M. (1977). An implicit technology of generalization. *Journal of Applied Behavior Analysis, 10,* 349–367.

Sulzer-Azaroff, B., & Mayer, G. R. (1977). *Applying behavior-analysis procedures with children and youth.* New York: Holt, Rinehart, & Winston.

J. Todd Stephens
*University of Wisconsin,
Madison*

APPLIED BEHAVIOR ANALYSIS
TRANSFER OF LEARNING

TRANSFER OF TRAINING

Transfer of training, also referred to as stimulus generalization or generalization, takes place when a behavior that has been reinforced in the presence of one stimulus event occurs in the presence of different but similar stimuli. Using the behavior analytic $S > R > C$ paradigm, the emphasis of this learning construct is on (1) the characteristics of the events that precede a behavior, and (2) the relationship of these characteristics to the occurrence of the behavior under similar stimulus conditions.

From this viewpoint, increasing similarities in events that precede a behavior result in an increased likelihood of stimulus generalization. Conversely, there is a decreased likelihood of the trained behavior occurring as these preceding events become more dissimilar. Applied to educational programming, the influence of these similarities might be beneficial or problematic. Thus a student may be trained to respond to questions asked by an adult male teacher by raising his or her hand. If this student responds likewise in other classroom settings to questions asked by female adults, a beneficial transfer of training has occurred. However, if the student responds to his father's inquiry, "Why are you late?" by raising his or her hand, the transfer of training that has taken place might be viewed as potentially problematic.

This example highlights some of the problems that relate to transfer of training and also touches on the fundamental role of this learning explanation in the educational process. Almost without exception, students are exposed to information and material with specific stimulus characteristics or in specific stimulus settings. Traditionally, this stimulus-specific training is assumed to automatically transfer to similar stimulus events. The accuracy of this assumption is highly questionable when teaching the learner with exceptional needs. As the severity of an individual's learning problems increase, so does the need for implementation of more specific interventions that are geared toward systematically promoting transfer of training.

A variety of approaches and procedures have been applied in order to increase the positive transfer of training. These attempts have been effective to varying degrees in achieving this purpose. Specific recommendations for achieving transfer of training have been offered by Martin and Pear (1983) and Stokes and Baer (1977). These recommendations include (1) training the skills in the situation where the behavior is to occur, (2) presenting a variety of stimulus events, (3) programming common stimulus characteristics across settings, and (4) training with sufficient examples.

Training the skill in the situation where it is expected to occur addresses the relationship between the training efforts extended to develop a student's skills in one setting and the implicit desire to have that student perform those skills in another setting. The use of this tactic requires the development of as many similarities as possible between the two settings, or actual skill training in the targeted situation. Therefore, if a student is being taught to locate the correct restroom using international door symbols, as much of the training as possible should take place in similar (analogue) or actual (in vivo) settings.

Another technique for promoting transfer of training is the presentation of a variety of stimulus events. Also referred to as training loosely, this tactic involves providing the student with a wide variety of stimuli to allow practicing of the response under different but similar conditions. Accordingly, training situations might involve different trainers, differing verbal requests, etc., each serving as a stimulus event for the same desired student response.

Programming of common stimuli is another tactic used to promote transfer of training. Alternatively referred to as the "don't teach basketball with a football" technique, this procedure focuses on the establishment of stimulus bridges between the training setting and the goal environment. Thus students are taught to respond to the materials, statements, or other stimulus events that will actually be present in the goal environment.

The final tactic suggested by these authors involves the presentation of representative stimulus events during training. In contrast to teaching a student to respond by presenting all possible stimulus options (e.g., every possible configuration of the word poison), the emphasis of "training sufficient examples" is on the use of stimulus events that encourage responses to example stimuli. Application of this technique in teaching a student to respond

to teacher greetings might involve training the student to say "hi" to one teacher and priming generalization of the response by rewarding the student's response to another teacher.

The effectiveness of education to a large extent relates to the amount of training that is transferred from one stimulus event to another similar events or settings. With the exceptional learner, this transfer must often be directly encouraged. For a comprehensive explanation of transfer of training and related teaching considerations, the reader is referred to texts by Sulzer-Azaroff and Mayer (1977) and Alberto and Troutman (1977).

REFERENCES

Alberto, P. A., & Troutman, A. C. (1977). *Applied behavior analysis for teachers: Influencing student performance.* Columbus, OH: Merrill.

Stokes, T. F., & Baer, D. M. (1977). An implicit technology of generalization. *Journal of Applied Behavior Analysis, 10,* 349–367.

Sulzer-Azaroff, B., & Mayer, G. R. (1977). *Applying behavior-analysis procedures with children and youth.* New York: Holt, Rinehart, & Winston.

J. Todd Stephens
*University of Wisconsin,
Madison*

GENERALIZATION
TRANSFER OF LEARNING

TRANSFORMATIONAL GENERATIVE GRAMMAR

In 1957 Noam Chomsky revolutionized the field of English grammar and research with the publication of the book *Syntactic Structures*. Chomsky, considered the father of the theory of transformational grammar, proposed a finite set of operations (called transformations) that produce (or generate) sentences of infinite number and variety without producing nonsentences. These operations are acquired during the first few years of life through exposure to conversation rather than through formal study. They are internalized by the speaker without his or her being aware of or able to state them.

Chomsky's theory describes the language people do use rather than the language they ought to use (Cattell, 1978). It focuses on competence, the ideal speaker-listener's complete command of language, as opposed to performance, the actual use of language in concrete situations as affected by imperfection and inconsistency. Unlike the traditional grammarian who deals with sentence form, or surface structure, Chomsky distinguishes between surface structure and its underlying meaning or deep structure.

This is the level at which grammatical relationships are preserved. By way of example, Quigley, Russell, and Power (1977) present the sentences "John is easy to please" and "John is eager to please." These two sentences are identical to one another in surface structure but completely different in deep structure. Muma (1978) elaborates by pointing out that the sentence "I bes here" (nonstandard dialect) is not inferior to the sentence "I am here" (standard dialect), as both are identical at the deep structure level.

Deep structures are turned into surface structures through transformations that expand, delete, and reorder sentence constituents, or component parts. These operations may be applied to all sentences without changing their meanings. Examples of transformations applied to the sentence "boys like girls" would include question (do boys like girls?), negation (boys don't like girls), and passive voice (girls are liked by boys) (Quigley, Russell, & Power, 1977).

Transformational grammarians view the sentence as a hierarchical organization of constituents. By applying a series of rewriting rules of increasing specificity, it is possible to analyze sentence structure, working backward through the derivation of a sentence to discover the initial transformational rule by which it was generated. These rewriting rules enable linguists to describe sentences pictorially using tree diagrams. Crystal, Fletcher, and Gorman (1977) point out that the easiest and best known of these rules is represented by the formula $S \rightarrow NP + VP$, or rewrite the sentence as a noun phrase and a verb phrase.

Transformational generative grammar has been applied successfully to research into language function (Dever, 1971), language development and delay, dialectic differences, and ESL studies (Quigley, Russell, & Power, 1977). Its detractors have noted that the distinction between language competence and performance is minimal at best when dealing with individuals with language disorders (Crystal, Fletcher, & Gorman, 1977). Akmajian, Demers, and Harnish (1980) note that Chomsky's model has been challenged at every level, resulting in numerous changes since the mid-1960s.

REFERENCES

Akmajian, A., Demers, R. A., & Harnish, R. M. (1980). *Linguistics: An introduction to language and communication.* Cambridge, MA: MIT Press.

Cattell, N. R. (1978). *The new English grammar.* Cambridge, MA: MIT Press.

Chomsky, N. (1957). *Syntactic structures.* The Hague: Mouton.

Chomsky, N. (1965). *Aspects of the theory of syntax.* Cambridge, MA: MIT Press.

Crystal, D., Fletcher, P., & Gorman, M. (1977). *The grammatical analysis of language disability: A procedure for assessment and remediation.* London: Arnold.

Dever, R. B. (1971). The case for data gathering. *Journal of Special Education, 5,* 119–126.

Muma, J. R. (1978). *Language handbook: Concepts, assessment, intervention.* Englewood Cliffs, NJ: Prentice-Hall.

Quigley, S. P., Russell, W. K., & Power, D. J. (1977). *Linguistics and deaf children.* Washington DC: A. G. Bell Association.

SUSAN SHANDELMIER
*Eastern Pennsylvania Special
Education Regional
Resources Center, King of
Prussia, Pennsylvania*

CHOMSKY, A. N.
LANGUAGE DEFICIENCIES AND DEFICITS
LINGUISTIC DEVIANCE

TRANSITION

Transition is the process of changing from one condition or place to another; it is common to individuals at various times throughout their lives. Transition from preschool to school environments as well as transition from school to postschool environments present problems for the young child and the adolescent. For individuals with special needs who are graduating or leaving school, this process is frequently more difficult than for others. The entitlement to a free appropriate public education may not necessarily culminate in opportunities for employment, integration into the community, or adult services. In recognition of the concerns of parents, educators, and service providers regarding the futures of handicapped students leaving publicly supported education programs, a national priority on transition from school to work for all individuals with disabilities was announced by the Office of Special Education and Rehabilitation Services (OSERS) in 1983. The need for transitional services and the provision of some degree of financial support for these activities are addressed in PL 98-199, the Education for All Handicapped Children Amendments.

Will (1984) has defined transition from school to work as "an outcome-oriented process encompassing a broad array of services and experiences that lead to employment" (p. 2). Transition refers to the period between school and work, and transitional services encompass both ends of a continuum between educational and adult services. The transition period includes the high school years, postsecondary services, and the first few years of employment. The goal of transition is meaningful paid employment and successful community functioning for individuals with disabilities. To obtain this goal, a restructuring and rethinking of the roles and responsibilities of various agencies at the federal, state, and local levels is necessary so as to ensure appropriate, nonduplicated services delivery (Vocational Transition, 1986).

The transition from school to work and adult life requires careful, systematic preparation and planning in the secondary school; cooperative support of interagency teams on graduation; and awareness and support of multiple employment options and services as needed by the community and professionals.

Generally, the difficulty in transition to postsecondary environments increases with the severity of the disability. Wilcox and Bellamy (1982) include the prevention of institutionalization in their definition of transition. They have suggested guidelines for effective transition of the more severely handicapped; these include using a case management approach to develop a comprehensive transition plan that is individualized, starts in the last years of school, has links with adult services, is locally designed, and ensures continuity of services without interruption. Preparation for the next environment should be stressed, as well as advocacy and family preparation.

Transition services may be grouped into three classes that reflect the nature of the public services used to provide support as the passage is completed: (1) transition with no special services—vocational technical schools and work experience; (2) transition with time-limited services—vocational rehabilitation, Job Training Partnership Act; and (3) transition with ongoing services—supported work environments for individuals with severe disabilities (Will, 1984).

Finally, one of the major issues surrounding transition is the lack of information about the status of special education graduates. Hasazi et al. (1985) cited the need to develop a body of data regarding the employment status of these individuals for use as a basis for future planning regarding transition activities.

REFERENCES

Hasazi, S. B., Gordon, L. R., & Roe, C. A. (1985). Factors associated with the emmployment status of handicapped youth exiting high school from 1979 to 1983. *Exceptional Children, 51*, 455–469.

Vocational transition: A priority for the '80s. (1986). *Project-Tie, 1*(1).

Wilcox, B., & Bellamy, G. T. (1982). *Design of high school programs for severely handicapped students.* Baltimore, MD: Brookes.

Will, M. (1984). *OSERS programming for the transition of youth with disabilities: Bridges from school to working life.* Washington, DC: Office of Special Education and Rehabilitative Services.

Eileen F. McCarthy
*University of Wisconsin,
Madison*

VOCATIONAL REHABILITATION
VOCATIONAL TRAINING OF HANDICAPPED

TRANSPORTATION OF HANDICAPPED STUDENTS

Transportation of handicapped students is usually viewed as an administrative requirement to ensure access to public education. It is seldom viewed as an opportunity to teach students community mobility skills. However, community mobility is the dynamic concept within the issue of transportation of handicapped students. The ability of an individual to participate independently or semiindependently in all aspects of community life (e.g., domestic, recreational, and vocational) is dependent on community mobility (Wehman, Renzaglia, & Bates, 1985). Community mobility refers to movement from one place to another within a particular setting and travel between two community locations. The concept of community mobility was originally developed in program practice and literature related to working with visually handicapped individuals. In this literature, community mobility is referred to as orientation and mobility training.

For visually impaired individuals, orientation and mobility training has long been a well-respected component of the curriculum. As the rights of all citizens to participate in the least restrictive environment have been acknowledged, the concept of community mobility has been broadened to include the physically handicapped, mentally retarded, emotionally disturbed, and other special education consumers. Assurances for meeting the basic transportation needs to and from school have been established within PL 94-142 for all special education students. However, the transportation needs of handicapped students are complex.

The ability of a person to be independently mobile is dependent on several factors. One of the primary factors that influences the degree of mobility attained by handicapped individuals is the opportunity for travel from one place to another. Opportunity for mobility can be restricted by both physical and attitudinal barriers. In many communities, extensive physical modifications have been made, including construction of ramps, widening of doorways, installment of elevators, cutting out of curbs, and purchase of lift buses. Although these modifications have removed many barriers to independent mobility, obstacles still exist in all communities. Realistically, many of these obstacles are not going to be eliminated. Some of these obstacles are outside of the control of engineers and educators (e.g., weather conditions, natural terrain). Since mobility obstacles are likely to remain in every community, efforts must be directed toward teaching individuals to overcome these problems. By combining environmental changes with specific instruction programs, handicapped citizens are provided easier access as well as more skills for traveling independently within their communities. Community mobility training programs should reflect this dual concern for improving physical accessibility and training skills that compensate for various environmental barriers.

Attitudinal barriers can severely restrict a person's chances for learning independent mobility skills in an even more devastating way than physical obstacles. These barriers result from a combination of overprotectiveness and lowered expectations. Parents and profesionals have contributed to this problem. According to Perske (1972), "such overprotection endangers the client's human dignity, and tends to keep him from experiencing the risk taking of ordinary life which is necessary for normal growth and development" (p. 29).

Overprotectiveness and lowered expectations can combine to present attitudinal barriers that severely limit a person's opportunity to acquire independent living skills. However, the development of responsible and effective community mobility training programs can alleviate fears and concerns regarding safety and consequently raise the expectations of parents and professionals for independent living by handicapped individuals. The development of such programs will significantly increase the opportunity an individual will have to acquire independent living skills.

Recently, more community mobility training programs have begun to emphasize the functional relationship between public transportation and access to community services. For example, Sowers, Rusch, and Hudson (1979) used systematic training procedures to teach a severely retarded adult to complete the following 10-behavior sequence to ride the city bus to and from work: (1) cross controlled intersections, (2) cross unmarked intersections, (3) use bus tickets, (4) walk to bus, (5) identify the correct bus, (6) board, (7) ride, (8) depart, (9) transfer, and (10) walk to work. Further, Marholin, O'Toole, Touchette, Berger, and Doyle (1979) taught four moderately and severely retarded adults to use public bus transportation to travel between a public institution and various community locations for shopping and eating in a restaurant.

The responsibility of public schools for transporting handicapped students to and from school programs must be expanded to include greater sensitivity to the unique community mobility needs of individual students. In meeting these responsibilities, educators should promote the development of a normalized repertoire of transportation skills. At a basic level, this could involve assistance that enables handicapped students to use the same transportation system in association with their nonhandicapped peers. At a more complex level, this would require a commitment to teaching a variety of mobility skills that would enhance a person's ability to access community activities throughout his or her lifetime.

REFERENCES

Marholin, D., Touchette, P., Berger, P., & Doyle, D. (1979). I'll have a Big Mac, Large Fries, Large Coke, and Apple Pie—of teaching adaptive community skills. *Behavior Therapy, 10,* 236–248.

Perske, R. (1972). The dignity of risk. In W. Wolfensberger (Ed.), *The principle of normalization in human services.* Toronto, Ontario: National Institute on Mental Retardation.

Sowers, J., Rusch, F. R., & Hudson, C. (1979). Training a severely retarded young adult to ride the city bus to and from work. *AAESPH Review, 4,* 15–22.

Wehman, P., Renzaglia, A., & Bates, P. (1985). *Functional living skills for the moderately and severely handicapped.* Austin, TX: Pro-Ed.

PAUL BATES
Southern Illinois University

ELECTRONIC TRAVEL AIDS
MOBILITY TRAINING
TRAVEL AIDS FOR HANDICAPPED

TRAVEL AIDS, ELECTRONIC

See ELECTRONIC TRAVEL AIDS.

TRAVEL AIDS FOR HANDICAPPED

Persons with disabilities may choose to travel by car, train, bus, plane, or ship, with or without a companion. Medical statements are generally required for commercial travel for medical reasons (e.g., the need for oxygen) rather than mobility or sensory limitations. Today there are a number of state laws that deal with access to public facilities. The American Hotel and Motel Association is implementing a plan to increase access to hotels and motels (Rosenburg, 1985). Many businesses are providing staff training to address the needs of disabled travelers. Holiday Inn is installing signal devices for the deaf for smoke alarms, door knockers, and phones (Rosenburg, 1985).

Many persons travel by personal or rented car. A number of adaptive devices are available: hand controls, spinner knobs, guard grips, toggle switches, mirrors, zero-based steering, raised seats, pedal extenders, car-top carriers, ramps, and lifts. Hertz, Avis, and National have specially equipped cars available with advance notice. Chambers of commerce and tourism departments can often provide local accessibility manuals. Large oil companies, the Automobile Association of America, and the President's Committee on Employment of the Handicapped can provide information on accessible routes, rest areas, and national parks. Special visitor parking permits are sometimes available in states where out-of-state disabled plates are not honored. Local lift-equipped transportation can sometimes be obtained with prior authorization.

Persons traveling by bus must consider the access of all stops, as well as narrow aisles and small rest rooms. Assistance and access may vary at each station. Persons with a doctor's statement to the effect that they are unable to travel alone may have a companion travel free on Greyhound and Trailways. Dog guides travel free and special discounts may be available to blind persons with coupons from the American Foundation for the Blind. Folding, non-motorized wheelchairs, crutches, canes, and walkers may be stored as baggage.

Train travel has varying degrees of access, and contact should be made with the local carrier to determine the access of all stations on the route. Access from the street, within the station, to the platform, on the train, and within the train must be considered. Aisles are narrow and bathrooms are small. Amtrak has a limited number of special cars with accessible seating, wheelchair storage behind the seating, and access to rest rooms and restaurant. Their staff is trained to deal with mobility- and sensory-impaired persons. Guide dogs travel free and blind persons may receive special rates. Meals can be served in the seat and special diets are available with advanced notice. Telephone typewriters may be available and the conductor will inform the hearing-impaired person of stops if the person identifies himself or herself. Amtrak will locate attendants at no charge, but services and fares are the customer's responsibility.

Persons traveling by plane must consider access in the terminal and on the plane. A travel agent may be able to arrange escort services, wheelchairs, aisle chairs, electric carts, special seating, special diets, and connections to other flights. Nonstop or direct flights are preferable. If there are plane changes, needed equipment should not be checked to the final destination and the flight attendant should be reminded before landing that the equipment needs to be at the plane door. Wheelchairs and motorized vehicles will be stored in the hold. There may be restrictions on wet-cell batteries and terminals must be taped. Crutches, canes, and walkers may be stored on board. Boarding may be by jetway, mobile lounge, fork lift, elevator, or aisle chair. Seating may be restricted to nonexit aisle seats. A blanket will be placed in the seat of mobility-impaired persons for emergency purposes. A limited number of airlines now have aisle seats for use in flight and removable armrests (Rosenburg, 1985). Flight attendants provide briefings to preboarded disabled passengers and blind persons are given a tour of the plane. Some airlines now have braille information and captioned cassettes.

Persons traveling by ship need to check the access to the pier, all areas of the ship, whether the ship anchors or docks at ports, cabin and bathroom sizes, tub or shower availability, door widths and risers between areas, and slope of boarding ramps. Some lines require a waiver of liability or a traveling companion. Use of the ship's wheelchair and storage of personal chairs may be required. Motorized chairs may not be permitted at some ports. Persons using crutches, walkers, or canes may find the use of a wheelchair more convenient. Rooms close to elevators serving main areas of activity should be requested. A dining table near the accessible restaurant entrance should be requested for dining. Any medical conditions should be indicated so the ship's hospital can be prepared for special needs. Adapters may be needed for persons using oxygen. Persons who can use commodes may be able to use rooms that do not have accessible rest rooms (Reamy, 1978).

Resource organizations for the traveling handicapped person include:

Access Amtrack
400 N. Capital Street, NW
Washington, DC 20001

American Foundation for the Blind
Travel Concessions for Blind Persons
15 W. 16th Street
New York, NY 10011

Centers for the Handicapped, Inc.
10501 New Hampshire Avenue
Silver Springs, MD 20903 (301-445-3350)

Diabetes Travel Service
349 E. 52nd Street
New York, NY 10022

INTERMEDIC
777 Third Avenue
New York, NY 10007

International Association for Medical Assistance for Travelers
350 5th Avenue, Suite 5620
New York, NY 10001

National Easter Seals Society
Information Center
2023 W. Ogden, Avenue
Chicago, IL 60612

Society for the Advancement of Travel for the Handicapped (SATH)
"The United States Welcomes Handicapped Visitors"
(cassette or braille available)
5014 42nd Street, NW
Washington, DC 20016 (202-966-3900)

Travel Tips for the Handicapped
U.S. Travel Service
Department of Commerce
Washington, DC 20230

Wheelchair Wagon Tours
P.O. Box 1270
Kissimmee, FL 32741 (305-846-7175)

Whole Person Tours
137 W. 32nd Street
Bayonne, New Jersey 07002 (201-858-3400)

REFERENCES

Reamy, L. (1978). *Travel ability*. New York: Macmillan.

Rosenburg, M. (1985, August 25). *Aid for handicapped traveler grows. Minneapolis Star and Tribune.*

SUE A. SCHMITT
University of Wisconsin, Stout

ELECTRONIC TRAVEL AIDS
TRANSPORTATION OF HANDICAPPED STUDENTS

TREATMENT ACCEPTABILITY

Treatment acceptability is a form of social validation that asks consumers how they feel about treatment methods prior to treatment. "Judgments of acceptability are likely to embrace evaluation of whether treatment is appropriate for the problem, whether treatment is fair, reasonable, and intrusive, and whether treatment meets with conventional notions about what treatment should be" (Kazdin, 1980, p. 259). The most basic assumption of the acceptability hypothesis is that the acceptability of a treatment method will influence the overall efficacy of the treatment. Methods that consumers feel are the most acceptable will be more effective than methods that are judged to be unacceptable. As Wolf (1978) stated, "If the participants don't like the treatment then they may avoid it, or run away, or complain loudly. And thus, society will be less likely to use our technology, no matter how potentially effective and efficient it might be" (p. 206).

Research efforts in treatment acceptability have followed the same general procedures. Subjects receive written, audio, oral, or audiovisual descriptions of problem behaviors and procedures for treating the problem behaviors. Then the subjects answer a number of questions designed to assess how acceptable the treatment is for improving the problem behavior. A number of scales of similar format have been developed for assessing treatment acceptability in different target populations. The Treatment Evaluation Inventory (TEI; Kazdin, 1980) has 15 questions scored on a seven-point Likert scale used with children and adults. The TEI requires subjects to make judgments about how acceptable an intervention is, how suitable the intervention is, how much the intervention is liked, and so on. The Intervention Rating Profile (IRP; Witt & Martens, 1983) has 20 questions scored on a six-point Likert scale; the questions were specifically written to assess teachers' acceptability judgments of interventions in classroom situations. The IRP has been used to delineate a number of treatment variables that effect teachers' acceptability ratings (Turco, Witt, & Elliott, in press; Witt, Elliott, & Martens, 1984). The Children's Intervention Rating Profile (CIRP; Elliott et al., 1986) has seven questions scored on a six-point Likert scale. The CIRP has been used by a number of researchers (Elliott et al., 1986; Turco & Elliott, 1986; Turco, Elliott, & Witt, in press) to assess children's treatment acceptability.

REFERENCES

Elliott, S. N. (1986). Children's ratings of the acceptability of classroom interventions for misbehavior: Findings and methodological considerations. *Journal of School Psychology, 24,* 23–35.

Elliott, S. N., Witt, J. C., Galvin, G. A., & Moe, G. L. (1986). Children's involvement in intervention selection: Acceptability of interventions for misbehaving peers. *Professional Psychology: Research and Practice, 17,* 235–241.

Kazdin, A. E. (1980). Acceptability of alternative treatments for deviant child behavior. *Journal of Applied Behavior Analysis, 13,* 259–273.

Turco, T. L., & Elliott, S. N. (1986). Assessment of students' acceptability of teacher-initiated interventions for classroom misbehaviors. *Journal of School Psychology, 24,* 277–283.

Turco, T. L., Elliott, S. N., & Witt, J. C. (in press). Children's involvement in treatment selection: A review of theory and analogue research on treatment acceptability. *Monograph on Secondary Behavioral Disorders.* Reston, VA: Council for Exceptional Children.

Turco, T. L., Witt, J. C., & Elliott, S. N. (in press). Factors influencing teachers' acceptability of classroom interventions for deviant student behavior. *Monograph on Secondary Behavioral Disorders.* Reston, VA: Council for Exceptional Children.

Witt, J. C., Elliott, S. N., & Martens, B. K. (1984). Factors affecting teachers' judgments of the acceptability of behavioral interventions: Time involvement, behavior problem severity, and type of intervention. *Behavior Therapy, 15,* 204–209.

Witt, J. C., & Martens, B. K. (1983). Assessing the acceptability of behavioral interventions. *Psychology in the Schools, 20,* 570–577.

Wolf, M. M. (1978). Social validity: The case for subjective measurement or how applied behavior analysis is finding its heart. *Journal of Applied Behavior Analysis, 11,* 203–214.

TIMOTHY L. TURCO
STEPHEN N. ELLIOTT
Louisiana State University

TEACHER EFFECTIVENESS
TEACHER EXPECTANCIES

TRICHOTILLOMANIA

Trichotillomania is a low-incidence disorder (occurring in less than 1% of pediatric referrals) of self-injurious behavior that consists of pulling out one's hair; it is often accompanied by trichophagia, subsequent eating of the hair. The etiology of trichotillomania is unknown, but it has long been held to be of a psychoanalytic or Freudian nature. It occurs most often in conjunction with a major psychological or psychiatric disorder, particularly schizophrenia and lower levels of mental retardation, though it also occurs with narcissistic personality disorders. In special education programs, it is most often encountered among mentally retarded populations. Incidences of trichotillomania have also been reported in conjunction with episodes of child abuse. Incidence is generally greater in females than males.

A variety of treatment approaches have been attempted with this unusual disorder, including psychoanalysis, traditional psychotherapies, hypnotherapy, and a variety of operant and other behavior modification techniques. Generally, the earlier the age of onset, the greater the likelihood of successful treatment (Sorosky & Sticker, 1980). Behavioral techniques appear to be the most successful methods of treating trichotillomania and trichophagia, particularly when competing responses can be developed, although success has been reported with a variety of techniques and the role of spontaneous remission is not known. Sources of treatment information include Azrin and Nunn (1973), Bayer (1972), and Mannino and Delgado (1969).

Some recent animal research suggests that a variety of self-injurious behaviors, including trichotillomania and trichophagia, may, in some cases, be of neurological origin. Relationships to damage of cells around the substantia nigra have been suggested.

REFERENCES

Azrin, N. H., & Nunn, R. G. (1973) Habit reversal: A method of eliminating nervous habits. *Behavior Research & Therapy, 11,* 619–628.

Bayer, C. A. (1972). Self-monitoring and mild aversion treatment of trichotillomania. *Journal of Behavior Therapy & Experimental Psychiatry, 3,* 139–141.

Mannino, F. C., & Delgado, R. A. (1969). Trichotillomania in children: A review. *American Journal of Psychiatry, 4,* 229–246.

Sorosky, A. D., & Sticker, M. B., (1980). Trichotillomania in adolescence. *Adolescent Psychiatry, 8* 437–454.

CECIL R. REYNOLDS
Texas A&M University

SELF-INJURIOUS BEHAVIOR

TRISOMY 18

As indicated by its name, trisomy 18 is a congenital disease owed to the presence of three chromosomes 18 instead of two. Trisomy 18 symptomatology was first described by Edwards et al. (1960); therefore, the term Edwards syndrome is sometimes used instead of trisomy 18. As in many autosomal trisomies, severe polymalformations are observed. Moreover, affected patients show many common features, so that trained physicians are able to diagnose the syndrome on clinical inspection. Generally, trisomy 18 newborns are postmature (42 weeks of pregnancy), but nevertheless show a birth weight below 2500 g (Hamerton, 1971); hydramnios (too much amniotic fluid) is the rule. An elongated skull with prominent occiput is noted, together with microcephaly. Micrognatia (small mandible), low-set ears, short neck, short sternum, prominent abdomen with umbilical hernia, and narrow hips are usual findings. The extremities are also characteristic: fingers are in forced flexion, very difficult to unfold, and deviated so that the third one is recovered by the second and the fourth. Arches are present in most, if not all, fingers. These dermatoglyphic configurations are rare in normal people or in those with other chromosome diseases. Clubfoot is frequent, and the big toe is in dorsiflexion. Internal malformations include severe congenital heart anomalies in more than 95% of all cases, either intraventricular, septal defects or patent ductus arteriosus. Indeed, premature death can be related to these heart defects. Failure to thrive is the rule and, despite palliative treatment, death occurs in a mean time of 70 days (Hamerton, 1971). Developmental retardation is always observed, but accurate testing is difficult.

From a cytogenetic point of view, standard trisomy 18 concerns more than 80% of all cases. Mosaicism trisomy 18/normal cell line occurs in less than 10% of patients; survival may be longer and symptomatology less severe. Trisomy 18 from a transmitted translocation by one of the parents is rare. Incidence is situated around 1 in 10,000 births (Hook & Hamerton, 1977). This is much less than in trisomy 21; the symptoms are more severe, and many affected embryos are spontaneously aborted early in pregnancy. Interestingly, 80% of all newborn cases are female, suggesting a strong lethality in the male. Some authors (Conen & Erkman, 1966) have also reported on a different survival rate depending on whether the baby is a girl (294 days) or a boy (96 days). Maternal age is above average (32 years), but the relationship is not as clear, as in trisomy 21. In the presence of a small fetus showing few movements and severe hydramnios, it may be profitable to have a late prenatal diagnosis, during the seventh or eighth month of pregnancy. This may avoid a caesarean section for the mother.

REFERENCES

Conen, P. E., & Erkman, B. (1966). Frequency and occurrence of chromosomal syndromes. II. E-trisomy. *American Journal of Human Genetics, 18,* 387–398.

Edwards, J. H., Harnden, D. G., Cameron, A. H., Crosse, V. M., & Wolff, O. H. (1960). A new trisomic syndrome. *Lancet, 1,* 787–790.

Hamerton, J. L. (1971). *Human cytogenetics* (Vol. 2). New York: Academic.

Hook, E. B., & Hamerton, J. L. (1977). The frequency of chromosome abnormalities detected in consecutive newborn studies—Differences between studies—Results by sex and by severity of phenotypic involvement. In E. B. Hook & I. A. Porter (Eds.), *Population cytogenetics—Studies in Human*. New York: Academic.

L. KOULISCHER
Institut de Morphologie
Pathologique, Belgium

CHROMOSOMAL ABNORMALITIES
GENETIC COUNSELING

TRISOMY 21

It is most likely that Langdon Down, in 1865, was the first to use the term mongolian idiocy to name a particular form of mental retardation, now referred to as mongolism or Down's syndrome. Affected patients show particular face features (Penrose & Smith, 1966): palpebral fissures that are oblique and narrow laterally, speckled iris, flatness of the nose bridge, enlarged tongue (protruding outside the mouth) with papillary hypertrophy, small ears, and short and broad neck. (See the following Figure.) Other common anomalies are brachycephaly, with flattening of the occiput, broad hands with the little finger curved in (clinodactyly) and a single palmar crease, short broad feet with a wide space between the first and second toes and a plantar furrow coming from the cleft between the first and second toes, pelvic anomalies, and congenital heart anomalies in almost 25% of patients (often associated with death during the first year of life).

Intellectual development is impaired. Many IQ figures have been proposed, most between 25 and 69 (Penrose & Smith, 1966). Indeed, figures seem to depend on the mode of education, the highest ones being observed in children

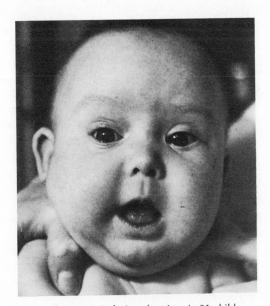

Characteristic facies of a trisomic 21 child.

Association Between Maternal Age and Trisomy 21

Maternal age	<20	20–24	25–29	30–34	35–39	40+
Down syndrome incidence per 1000	0.46	0.65	0.88	1.26	3.92	17.60

Down's syndrome incidence per thousand births in relation to mother's age (5-year intervals). A more detailed analysis, per single year maternal age, shows that incidence becomes higher than .5% over 37 (personal data).

raised at home and attending special schools. Whatever the IQ value, it seems safe to say that trisomic 21 patients will not be able to enjoy an independent life, even if some of them reach borderline intelligence.

Mongolism or Down's syndrome is due to the presence of three chromosomes 21 instead of two (trisomy 21). Three main cytogenetic forms are known: with 47 chromosomes and a standard trisomy 21 (95% of all cases); with normal mosaics, with 46 chromosomes/trisomy 21 with 47 chromosomes (2 to 3%), and with translocations (2 to 3%). Although it is still not known what the causes are, a close association between maternal age and trisomy 21 has been repeatedly demonstrated (Penrose & Smith, 1966; see Table).

Incidence is situated around 1 in 1000 (Mikkelsen, 1981); incidence at conception is higher and estimations show that 80% of all trisomic 21 embryos fail to survive (Boué et al., 1981). Until 15 years ago, more than 50% of affected babies were born to mothers over 35. However, in the early 1970s, it was pointed out that new demographic trends were changing the accepted concepts about trisomy 21, at least in developed countries (Stein et al., 1973). Two facts were responsible for the new situation: the decrease in the general population of older mothers among women of childbearing age and the general decline of the birthrate.

Today, prenatal diagnosis, applied to pregnant women over 35, as a means of prevention of the birth of trisomic 21 children, will have only a small impact on the reduction of the number of affected children. Moreover, the life span of trisomic 21 individuals has increased because of generally higher medical standards (surgical correction of birth defects, medical treatment of respiratory tract infections, etc.). Therefore, the prevalence of trisomy 21 (the number of affected persons in the population at a given time) tends to remain stable, if not to increase.

REFERENCES

Boué, J., Deluchat, C., Nicolas, H., Boué, A. (1981). Prenatal losses of trisomy 21. In G. R. Burgio, M. Fraccaro, L. Tiepolo, & U. Wolf (Eds.), *Trisomy 21*, Berlin: Springer-Verlag.

Mikkelsen, M. (1981). Epidemiology of trisomy 21: Population, peri- and antenatal data. In G. R. Burgio, M. Fraccaro, L. Tiepolo, & U. Wolf (Eds.), *Trisomy 21*, Berlin: Springer-Verlag.

Penrose, L. S., & Smith, G. F. (1966). *Down's anomaly* (Vol. 1). London: J. & A. Churchill.

Stein, Z., Susser, M., & Guterman, A. V. (1973). Screening program for the prevention of Down's syndrome. *Lancet, 1,* 305–309.

L. Koulischer
Institut de Morphologie
Pathologique, Belgium

CHROMOSOMAL ABNORMALITIES
DOWN'S SYNDROME
GENETIC COUNSELING

TUBERCULOSIS

See CHRONIC ILLNESS IN CHILDREN.

TUBEROUS SCLEROSIS

Tuberous sclerosis is an inherited disorder transmitted as an autosomal dominant trait with variable penetrance affecting the skin, brain, retina, heart, kidneys, and lungs. It belongs to the group of diseases called phakomatoses, characterized by malformations, the presence of birthmarks, and the tendency to tumor formation in the central nervous system, skin, and viscera. The estimated frequency of occurrence is 1 per 30,000 live births (Berg, 1982). About 25% of the patients are sporadic owing to new mutations.

Tuberous sclerosis is a protean disorder chiefly manifested by epilepsy, mental deficiency, and cutaneous lesions. Convulsions are the most frequent initial symptom (up to 88%), presenting often in early life as infantile spasms (about 70%), usually between the fourth and sixth months of life. The convulsions later become generalized grand mal epilepsy and focal or akinetic seizures (Gomez, 1979; Hunt, 1983; Jeavons & Bower, 1964; Pampiglione & Moynahan, 1976). Mental retardation, when present, is usually severe; one-third of the patients may have normal intelligence (Gomez, 1979). Only 12 to 15% of affected subjects are free of epilepsy and mental retardation. The cutaneous lesions are multiple. Adenoma sebaceum is the characteristic sign of the disease. It appears in the face between 1 and 5 years of age (usually after 4 years), starting as a macular rash over the cheeks in a butterfly appearance, then increasing in size and covering the nose, lips, and chin with a granular aspect. Those adenoma named Pringle's are seldom absent but they may grow very slowly. Hypopigmented leaf-shaped spots called white or achromatic spots or depigmented nevi are the most frequent sign in up to 95% of cases (Hunt, 1983); they are disseminated over the trunk and the limbs and are present at birth (Gold & Freeman, 1965), but they increase in number during the first 2 years of life. They appear more numerous under Wood's light and may be demonstrable in clinically asymptomatic parents. Shagreen patches are thickenings of skin best seen in the lumbosacral region. Periungueal fibroma (Koenen tumors) are more often present on the toes than on the fingers and appear after the first decade and in adults; they may be the only sign in parents of an affected child.

The pathology in the nervous system shows the presence of cortical malformations, variable in size (called tubers), that contain neurons, astrocytic nuclei, and giant cells. The tubers also can be located in the subependymal area and contain calcium deposits that can be identified on X-rays or CAT scans. They may grow into the ventricles, interfering with cerebral spinal fluid circulation, blocking the foramen of Monro or the aqueduct of Sylvius, and producing hydrocephalus and signs of raised intracranial pressure. Tumors can also be present in the heart, the lungs, and the kidneys, but they can be discovered easily by ultrasound examination showing angiomyolipoma or even cystic tumors (Avni et al., 1984). The examination of the ocular fundus may reveal tumoral lesions at the nerve head or about the disk, even in the absence of vision complaints.

Diagnosis of the disease is based on the association of epilepsy, mental retardation, and skin lesions. It can be made very early in life on the presence of infantile spasms and achromatic spots in correlation with the cerebral calcifications seen on CAT scans of the brain (Lee & Gawler, 1978).

REFERENCES

Avni, E. F., Szliwowski, H., Spehl, M., Lelong, B., Baudain, P., & Struyven, J. (1984). Renal involvement in tuberous sclerosis. *Annales de Radiologie, 27,* 2–3, 207–214.

Berg, B. O. (1982). Neurocutaneous syndromes. In K. F. Swaiman, & F. S. Wright (Eds.), *The practice of pediatric neurology.* New York: Mosby.

Gold, A. P., & Freeman, J. M. (1965). Depigmented nevi: The earliest sign of tuberose sclerosis. *Pediatrics, 35,* 1003–1005.

Gomez, M. R. (1979). Clinical experience at the Mayo Clinic. In M. R. Gomez (Ed.), *Tuberous sclerosis* pp. 16–20. New York: Raven.

Hunt, A. (1983). Tuberous sclerosis: A survey of 97 cases. *Developmental Medicine and Child Neurology, 25,* 346–357.

Jeavons, P. M., & Bower, B. D. (1969). Infantile spasms. *Clinics Developmental Medicine, 15,* London: Sime/Heinemann.

Lee, B. C., & Gawler, J. (1978). Tuberous sclerosis. Comparison of computed tomography and conventional neuroradiology. *Radiology, 127*(2), 403–407.

Pampiglione, G., & Moynahan, E. I. (1976). The tuberous sclerosis:

Clinical and EEG studies in 100 children. *Journal Neurology Neurosurgery & Psychiattry, 39,* 666–673.

HENRI B. SZLIWOWSKI
*Université Libre de Bruxelles
Hôpital Erasme, Brussels,
Belgium*

TURNBULL, ANN P. (1947–   )

An Alabama native, Ann P. Turnbull received her BSEd from the University of Georgia (1968), her MEd from Auburn University (1971), and her EdD from the University of Alabama (1972). Her formal education emphasized special education of children with mental retardation. Her early practical experience was as a teacher of children with mild mental retardation in the La Grange, Georgia, city schools (1968–1970).

For the past 10 years, Turnbull's work has focused on research and programmatic implementation of policy requirements associated with PL 94-142. Her most recent work concerns parental involvement in educational decision making and the development of a conceptual framework for family research and intervention based on family systems theory. She has written eight books (three of which are currently in second edition) and over 60 articles and chapters. As evidence of her strong commitment to a junior colleague model, approximately 65% of these publications are coauthored with students. Two of her recent works are *Families, Professionals and Exceptionality: A Special Partnership* and *Parents Speak Out: Then and Now.*

Turnbull's future goals are to pursue her research and intervention interests, focusing on strengthening family adjustment through the development of coping and problem-solving skills at various life-cycle stages and transitions; and to pursue preservice and in-service education related to constructive family-professional partnerships. Her policy interests include exploring government-pro-

vided services for enhancing the ability of families to provide care for their members with disabilities.

REFERENCES

Schulz, J. B., & Turnbull, A. P. (1984). *Mainstreaming handicapped students: A guide for the classroom teacher* (2nd ed.). Newton, MA: Allyn & Bacon.

Turnbull, A. P., & Turnbull, H. R. (1982). Parent involvement in the education of handicapped children: A critique. *Mental Retardation, 20*(3), 115–122.

Turnbull, A. P., Turnbull, H. R., Summers, J. A., Brotherson, M. J., & Benson, H. A. (1986). *Families, professionals, and exceptionality: A special partnership.* Columbus, OH: Merrill.

Turnbull, H. R., & Turnbull, A. P. (1985). *Parents speak out: Then and now.* (2nd ed.). Columbus, OH: Merrill.

E. VALERIE HEWITT
Texas A&M University

TURNBULL, H. R. (1937–   )

H. R. Turnbull received his BA in political science from Johns Hopkins University in 1959 and his LLB/JD from the University of Maryland Law School in 1964. He later attended Harvard Law School and received his LLM in 1969 in the urban studies program. Since 1974, Turnbull has specialized in law and public policy affecting persons with mental and developmental disabilities. He was a professor of public law and government at the Institute of Government, and a faculty member of the Bush Institute on Child and Family Policy at the University of North Carolina at Chapel Hill. He is currently professor of special education and law at the University of Kansas.

Turnbull's initial work in the areas of special education law and rights of institutionalized persons led him to concentrate on issues that define and redefine the concepts of consent, least restriction, and parent participation in the education of children with disabilities. He also works with

Ann P. Turnbull

H. R. Turnbull

policymakers and professional caregivers concerning the treatment of infants with disabilities and the restructuring of Medicaid financing of residential and other services for people who are mentally retarded.

Turnbull has served on several U.S. Department of Education policy task forces, has been a special consultant to the U.S. Department of Education assistant secretary, and a member of the American Bar Association Task Force on Mental Health-Criminal Justice Standards. Turnbull has been a senior officer (1980 to the present) and president (1985–1986) of the American Association on Mental Deficiency. He received the 1982 Educator of the Year Award from the Association for Retarded Citizens of the United States, which he served as national secretary from 1981 to 1983.

STAFF

TURNER'S SYNDROME

Turner's syndrome is a sex chromosome abnormality characterized by the absence of all or part of one X chromosome in females (Reed, 1975). That is, rather than having the two sex chromosomes of the normal female (XX), about 80% of females with Turner's syndrome have only one X chromosome, symbolized as XO. The remainder have a variety of mosaic patterns involving variability in cells with chromosome deletions or translocations (Bender, Puck, Salbenblatt, & Robinson, 1984). Physical and developmental stigmata are less pronounced for some of the mosaic types (Bender et al., 1984). Only a small percentage of fetuses with abnormal sex chromosomes result in live births and the estimated incidence of all types of Turner's syndrome is 1 out of 2500 female live births (Reed, 1975). Physical sequelae often associated with this syndrome are short stature, webbing of the neck, deformity of the elbow (i.e., cubitus valgus), sexual immaturity, and congenital heart defects (Park, Bailey, & Cowell, 1983). Medical treatment primarily involves estrogen replacement during adolescence.

Learning disorders have been consistently associated with Turner's syndrome. While earlier studies reported a greater risk for mental retardation (Haddad & Wilkins, 1959), several recent studies have replicated a finding that only visual-motor abilities rather than verbal and global cognitive skills are decreased (Bender et al., 1984). Children and adolescent girls have been found to have lower performance than verbal IQs on the Wechsler Intelligence Scale for Children Revised. Neuropsychological studies have reported reduced capabilities in the right cerebral hemisphere and particularly the right parietal lobe (Money, 1973). Hence girls with Turner's syndrome appear to have a particular risk for the neuropsychological

learning disorder type of visual-spatial dyslexia. There has been no particular vulnerability to general behavioral problems or psychopathology other than attention deficit disorder with hyperactivity (Hier, Atkins, & Perlo, 1980).

The primary implication for special education practitioners is that girls with Turner's syndrome should receive a comprehensive psychoeducational and perhaps neuropsychological evaluation to detect possible learning disorders. Behavioral practitioners also could provide anticipatory guidance to the child and family regarding such issues as sterility.

REFERENCES

Bender, B., Puck, M., Salbenblatt, J., & Roninson, A. (1984). Cognitive development of unselected girls with complete or partial X monosomy. *Pediatrics, 73,* 175–182.

Haddad, H. M., & Wilkins, L. (1959). Congenital anomalies associated with gonadal aplasia: Review of 55 cases. *Pediatrics, 23,* 885–902.

Hier, D., Atkins, L., & Perlo, V. (1980). Learning disorders and sex chromosome aberrations. *Journal of Mental Deficiency Research, 24,* 17–26.

Money, J. (1973). Turner's syndrome and parietal lobe functions. *Cortex, 9,* 385–393.

Park, E., Bailey, J. D., & Cowell, C. A. (1983). Growth maturation of patients with Turner's syndrome. *Pediatric Research, 17,* 1–7.

Reed, E. W. (1975). Genetic abnormalities in development. In F. D. Horowitz (Ed.), *Review of child development research* (Vol. 4, pp. 283–318). Chicago: University of Chicago Press.

JOSEPH D. PERRY
Kent State University

GENETIC VARIATIONS
KLEINFELTER'S SYNDROME
MOSAICISM

TUTORING

Tutoring is a method of instruction in which one or a small group of students (tutees) receive personalized and individualized education from a tutor. Tutoring is widely used with students of all ages and all levels of ability. However, in elementary and secondary schools, it is most often used as an adjunct to traditional classroom instruction: (1) to provide remedial or supplementary instruction to students who have difficulty learning by conventional methods, including mainstreamed, handicapped children; (2) to provide students with increased opportunities to actively participate in the learning process and receive immediate feedback; and (3) to help relieve the classroom teacher of instructional and noninstructional duties.

In most cases, tutoring is provided to students by someone other than the regular teacher. This may be an adult who volunteers or is paid, a college student, a programmed machine or computer, or, in many cases, another student. The term peer tutoring is used when children serve as tutors to others close to their age who are functioning at a lower level. The term cross-age tutoring is used when older children or adolescents work with tutees who are several years younger than themselves.

The practices of peer and cross-age tutoring were recorded as early as the first century AD by Quintilian in the *Institutio Oratoria*. However, the practice was not formalized and instituted on a widespread basis until the late eighteenth century by Andrew Bell in India and later by William Lancaster in England. Tutoring was standard practice in the one-room schoolhouses of America until graded classes helped reduce the heterogeneity of student ability. Renewed interest in children teaching children began in the early 1960s because of shortages in professional teachers. Educators argued that disadvantaged children might learn more from a peer than from an adult. Several large-scale tutoring programs in New York City, Washington, DC, Chicago, Michigan, and California were successful (Allen, 1976).

Since 1970, numerous research studies and anecdotal reports have documented the benefits of tutoring for both the tutee and the tutor. Both have been found to benefit in terms of increases in achievement, school attitudes, peer acceptance, and self-image (Devin-Sheehan, Feldman, & Allen, 1976). Successful outcomes of tutoring have been reported for nonhandicapped tutees, tutees in special education including the moderately retarded, and those with aggressive behavior disorders (Maher, 1982).

Research further indicates that the effectiveness of tutoring depends greatly on how it is organized and structured and the nature of the relationship between the tutor and tutee. Some guidelines for developing a successful tutoring program follow.

Tutors must be carefully selected, trained, and supervised. Prospective tutor recruits must be dependable, responsible, and knowledgeable in the skill to be taught. They must be trained in tutoring skills (e.g., praising, task analysis, direct instruction, communication) and be provided with specific materials. A designated tutor supervisor must be available. Tutors and tutees should be matched carefully so that they have good rapport and work together conscientiously. Contracts are helpful in spelling out the responsibilities of each. If possible, tutoring should be held twice weekly for at least 30 minutes each session over a minimum of 10 weeks. The program should be continually monitored to determine its effectiveness. Meetings should be scheduled separately with the tutors and tutees to discuss any problems.

Extensive descriptions of tutorial procedures can be found in Allen (1976) and Ehly and Larsen (1980). The use of handicapped students as tutors for the nonhandicapped has been discussed by Osguthorpe (1984).

REFERENCES

Allen, V. L. (1976). *Children as teachers: Theory and research on tutoring*. New York: Academic.

Devin-Sheehan, L., Feldman, R. S., & Allen, V. L. (1976). Research on children tutoring children: A critical review. *Review of Educational Research, 46,* 355–385.

Ehly, S. W., & Larsen, S. C. (1980). *Peer tutoring for individualized instruction*. Boston: Allyn & Bacon.

Maher, C. A. (1982). Behavioral effects of using conduct problem adolescents as cross-age tutors. *Psychology in the Schools, 10,* 360–364.

Osguthorpe, R. T. (1984). Handicapped students as tutors for nonhandicapped peers. *Academic Therapy, 19,* 473–483.

FREDERIC J. MEDWAY
University of South Carolina

TEACHING STRATEGIES

TWINS

Twins may pose a number of educational problems because of their close relationship and their strong attachment to one another. For instance, they often show language delay. Because they are content with each other's company and consequently socialize less with other children and adults than singletons, they tend to be less influenced by the linguistic environment (Luchsinger, 1961). Indeed, they may develop a jargon that enables them to communicate with one another but that is incomprehensible to others. This private idiom is called cryptophasia. Cryptophasia is not a language sui generis (as some have thought it was), but a sort of pidgin based on the language of the adults (Lebrun, 1982). Despite reduced vocabulary and absence of grammar, it makes communication possible between the twins; they have so many affinities that they can understand one another with just a few words. To improve the twins' language command, speech therapy may be necessary. Moreover, it may be desirable to separate them part of the day so that they can learn to socialize.

REFERENCES

Lebrun, Y., (1982). Cryptophasie et retard de langage chez les jumeaux. *Enfance* (3), 101–108.

Luchsinger, R. (1961). Die Sprachentwicklung von ein- und zwei-eiïgen Zwillingen und die Vererbung von Sprachstörungen in den ersten drie Lebensjahren. *Folia Phoniatrica* (13), 66–76.

YVAN LEBRUN
School of Medicine, V.U.B.,
Brussels, Belgium

TYPOLOGY OF BEHAVIOR PROBLEMS

Behavior rating scales and observation schedules have reached new popularity in recent years. Foremost examples are the Bristol Social Adjustment Guides (BSAG; Stott, 1985), the Child Behavior Checklist (CBCL; Achenbach & Edelbrock, 1981), the Conners Teacher Rating Scale–Trites Revision (CTRS; Trites, Blouin, & Laprade, 1982), and the Revised Behavior Problem Checklist (RBPC; Quay & Peterson, 1983). Advances in theoretical validity and measurement quality for such scales have encouraged their use in the formal diagnosis of emotional disturbance and social maladjustment. Today, special educators and psychologists are less inclined to have diagnoses rest on information drawn from projective personality tests, children's responses to paper-and-pencil personality inventories, or isolated clinical judgments by psychologists or psychiatrists. Consistent with this trend are growing numbers of state education departments that are requiring that social and emotional maladjustment be defined behaviorally (Miller & Epstein, 1979); e.g., the state of South Carolina now requires that behavior rating information be obtained from two independent sources as grounds for classifying childhood maladjustment.

Several factors explain rating scale popularity. These are given detailed analysis elsewhere (McDermott, 1986), but are summarized briefly here. Better rating scales are composed of phenomenological item content; i.e., the distinct behavioral nature of items reduces or eliminates the necessity for the observing teacher or parent to speculate about obscure motivations for behavior such as internal emotional states or neurological processes. The focus is on "what" rather than "why" behavior exists. Also, rating scales are completed by those most familiar with and natural to the specific social environs; namely, teachers in the school and parents in the home. Such evaluations are far less obtrusive and more natural than those gathered through isolated clinical examination sessions—sessions that themselves may evoke unnatural and irrelevant behaviors. When rating scales are employed by teachers, information is especially valuable because teachers, inasmuch as they work with different children over time, have a better comparative framework for evaluating child adjustment (also note that the classification of certain psychiatric disorders now prefers teacher observations; American Psychiatric Association, 1980).

In addition to these more intuitive and practical advantages of behavior rating scales, fundamental measurement characteristics also recommend their use. Basically, the items constituting such scales are designed to measure specific manifestations of problem behavior and are calibrated so that, when a group of related items is assembled, it reliably measures a particular syndrome or dimension of disturbance. For example, by grouping together those items reflecting acting-out, irascible, and hostile behavior, and then summing a teacher's responses

for those items, a single score for an aggressiveness dimension is produced. Moreover, as a child's score on that dimension increases, one can observe increasing severity of aggressiveness in a particular social context. This dimensional approach to the study of problem behavior is characteristic of most major behavior rating devices, including the BSAG, CBCL, CTRS, and RBPC cited previously.

However, as McDermott (1980) has demonstrated, most children deemed maladjusted are not distinguished by a high score on a single dimension; rather, over half of such children are found to have elevated scores on two or more dimensions. A conduct-disordered child, for instance, may be "aggressive" toward other children, "hyperactive" in class and recreation, and "withdrawn" in relationships with adult authorities—all of this represented by score elevations on respective dimensions of "aggressiveness," "hyperactivity," and "withdrawal." Consequently, a more accurate and comprehensive system of describing problem behavior should be multidimensional. One can think in terms of a profile of scores for a given child, with the profile composed of scores across several behavioral dimensions. Indeed, within the general population of children, including both adjusted and maladjusted children, unique multidimensional profiles are discovered. Each type of profile represents a different type of adjustment or maladjustment; some types adjusted, some showing mild disturbance in a solitary area, and others showing disturbance in several areas, often severe. Considered in this way, manifestations of problem behavior can be separated into distinct multidimensional profile types, with the general result being an objective typology of problem behavior.

Any of the rating scales earlier noted could be applied in such fashion. However, development of a meaningful typology requires certain measurement and statistical procedures beyond the scope of this discussion. Suffice it to say that if the developers of a particular behavior rating scale follow appropriate procedures, a useful typology can emerge. For present purposes, we shall demonstrate the use of a typology with one of the internationally popular rating scales, the BSAG.

The BSAG contains approximately 150 items describing behaviors that teachers rate as present or absent in a child's day-to-day behavior. Of these, 110 items are indicative of problem behavior. By various statistical processes, the 110 problem behavior items are separated into six syndromes of maladjustment. These are (1) unforthcomingness—a collection of unassertive, timid, and socially ineffective behaviors; (2) withdrawal—connoting social detachment, isolationism, and loss of affiliative needs; (3) depression—pointing to motivational deficits and failure to seek out or respond to environmental stimuli; (4) inconsequence—a complex of behaviors that indicate distractability, attention seeking, and impulsivity; (5) hostility—behaviors directed to test the limits of authority and to sever unrewarding relationships with others, particularly adults; and (6) peer maladaptiveness—domineering, intrusive, and aggressive reactions toward peers. After a teacher completes the BSAG scale for a given child, a score is obtained for each syndrome; the higher the score, the more problems observed for that area. Scores are converted to standardized T scores (mean = 50, standard deviation = 10), so that scores across the six syndromes are comparable and thus constitute a profile.

Using the entire BSAG standardization sample of 2527 5- to 15-year-old children, McDermott (1980, 1983) took each child's profile across the six syndromes and clustered the profiles into types by level and pattern of syndrome scores. Sixteen profile types resulted, representing children who were very well adjusted to those showing appreciable maladjustment in several syndrome areas. Each profile type was described in terms of its prevalence (i.e., rarity) in the child population and in terms of the relative proportion of boys versus girls constituting the type, trend in age levels, and nature of the disturbance as indicated by profile level and pattern and supportive research on the BSAG (McDermott, 1986).

The advantages of such a typology become obvious when it is applied for diagnosis with a particular child. Essentially, one compares the child's profile of syndrome

---

SOCIAL-EMOTIONAL ADJUSTMENT DIMENSION

BRISTOL SOCIAL ADJUSTMENT GUIDES (BSAG)

ANALYSIS BY SYNDROMIC PROFILE METHOD:

SYNDROMIC PROFILE GROUP	GROUP MEMBERSHIP INDEX
TP 1. GOOD ADJUSTMENT	3.6
TP 2. ADEQUATE ADJUSTMENT WITH IMPULSIVITY	5
TP 3. ADEQUATE ADJUSTMENT WITH PEER CONFLICT	6.5
TP 4. ADEQUATE ADJUSTMENT WITH EMANCIPATORY TRAITS	7.5
TP 5. ADEQUATE ADJUSTMENT WITH DISTURBANCE OF CONDUCT	16
TP 6. ADEQUATE ADJUSTMENT WITH MOTIVATIONAL DEFICITS	6.9
TP 7. ADEQUATE ADJUSTMENT WITH WITHDRAWAL	6.6
TP 8. ADEQUATE ADJUSTMENT WITH DEPRESSED MOOD	8.2
TP 9. ATTENTION DEFICIT DISORDER WITH HYPERACTIVITY	11.1
TP 10. CONDUCT DISORDER (SOCIALIZED AGGRESSIVE)	17.6
TP 11. CONDUCT DISORDER WITH ATTENTION DEFICITS	18.3
TP 12. CONDUCT DISORDER (UNDERSOCIALIZED AGGRESSIVE)	16.4
TP 13. ANXIETY-WITHDRAWAL DISORDER (AVOIDANT)	5.5
TP 14. ANXIETY-WITHDRAWAL DISORDER (OPPOSITIONAL)	11.5
TP 15. ANXIETY-WITHDRAWAL DISORDER (SCHIZOID)	8.2
TP 16. ANXIETY-WITHDRAWAL DISORDER (DYSTHYMIC)	7.9

ACCORDING TO THE OVERALL CONFIGURATION OF OBSERVED STYLES OF BEHAVIOR, THE CHILD'S SOCIAL AND EMOTIONAL REACTIONS ARE CONSIDERED MODERATELY MALADJUSTED AT THIS TIME.

THE PATTERN AND LEVELS OF SYNDROME ELEVATIONS MOST CLOSELY RESEMBLE THE TYPICAL PROFILE FOR TP 11, CONDUCT DISORDER WITH ATTENTION DEFICITS AND HYPERACTIVITY.

A GENERAL SYNOPSIS OF BEHAVIORAL CHARACTERISTICS AND POPULATION PREVALENCE FOR THIS PROFILE TYPE IS AS FOLLOWS:

TP 11. A CLASS OF SERIOUS GENERAL OVERREACTIVE BEHAVIOR MARKED BY THOUGHTLESS AGGRESSIVENESS AND INTRUSIONS UPON OTHERS' RIGHTS; A VICIOUS CYCLE MAY BE EVIDENT, INVOLVING THE CHILD'S INITIAL LACK OF FORETHOUGHT, IMPULSIVE INTERFERENCE WITH OTHERS, CONSEQUENT REJECTION BY PEERS AND ADULTS AND, IN TURN, INDUCED HOSTILITY ON THE CHILD'S PART; DELINQUENT-LIKE BEHAVIOR, AT LEAST PARTIALLY REACTIVE; SEEN IN BOYS VS. GIRLS THREE-FOURTHS OF THE TIME; THE SPECIFIC SUBTYPE OF DISORDER MAY BE CONSIDERED UNDER-SOCIALIZED, AGGRESSIVE.

ESTIMATED POPULATION PREVALENCE = 1%

THIS ASSESSMENT IS BASED ON SUMMATIVE EVALUATIONS FOLLOWING OBSERVATION OF THE CHILD OVER TIME IN CERTAIN NATURAL SOCIAL SETTINGS. HOWEVER, THE GENERALITY OF THE OBSERVED BEHAVIOR STYLES CANNOT BE ASSUMED AUTOMATICALLY ACROSS ALL IMPORTANT AREAS OF THE CHILD'S SOCIAL AND EMOTIONAL FUNCTIONING. VERIFICATION SHOULD PROCEED THROUGH ADDITIONAL OBSERVATION AND INQUIRY.

Problem behavior typing as generated by *McDermott Multidimensional Assessment of Children* (reproduced with permission. Copyright 1985 by The Psychological Corporation. All rights reserved)

scores with that for each of the 16 profile types. Classification is made to that profile type that the child's profile best matches. Ordinarily, the matching process is a straightforward matter requiring "eyeball" comparison of profiles. Occasionally, the task is difficult because a child's profile seems similar to aspects of two or more profile types. To remedy this situation and to provide other interpretive aids, a microcomputer system was developed. The McDermott Multidimensional Assessment of Children (McDermott & Watkins, 1985), known as M.MAC, automatically converts BSAG scores to T scores, performs all of the profile comparisons, shows the similarity of the child's profile to all 16 profile types, describes the profile type to which the child's is most similar, and reports the overall severity of detected maladjustment (i.e., mild, moderate, severe, or extreme). M.MAC also enables users to enter, compare, and combine behavior ratings made by two independent observers.

To illustrate, we shall consider the case of Tim, an 8 year old who was viewed as a "disturbing influence" in school. Tim's teacher completed the BSAG and syndrome scores were submitted to the M.MAC microcomputer system. The Figure presents a portion of the M.MAC printed record for this case.

The name of each of the 16 profile types is presented first. To the right is a column headed Group Membership Index. Such an index can range in value from 20.0 (indicating that the child's profile is a perfect match for that particular profile type), to 10.0 (indicating a match no better than chance; hence, a relative mismatch), to 0.0 (indicating a complete absence of similarity). Note that the highest index value for Tim is that for profile type 11, Conduct Disorder with Attention Deficits; this is reported in the narrative section further down the record. Also note that the narrative indicates a moderate level of disturbance. The record continues with a detailed description of the nature of the problem behavior associated with profile type 11 and indicates that such a disturbance is found in about 1% of the child population.

Other information can be obtained by closer inspection of the Group Membership Indexes on the record. Notice that after type 11, the next highest index is that for type 10, Conduct Disorder (Socialized Aggressive). This suggests that the child's adjustment pattern is somewhat similar to that of children constituting that type; namely, children whose aggressiveness (being more socialized) is not ordinarily directed toward classmates and peers, but primarily toward adult authority. Tim's secondary similarity to this group may provide valuable leads for remedial treatment, for it may suggest that, as a first step, it would be easier to modify Tim's behavior so that it falls in closer harmony with value systems recognized by the child's peers. Moreover, by repeating assessments over time, it is possible to substantiate improvements or other changes in adjustment by observing changes in a child's membership across the typology of problem behavior.

REFERENCES

Achenbach, T. M., & Edelbrock, C. S. (1981). Behavioral problems and correlates reported by parents of normal and disturbed children aged four through sixteen. *Monographs of the Society for Research in Child Development, 46*(1, Serial No. 188).

American Psychiatric Association. (1980). *Diagnostic and statistical manual of mental disorders* (3rd ed.). Washington, DC: Author.

McDermott, P. A. (1980). Prevalence and constituency of behavioral disturbance taxonomies in the regular school population. *Journal of Abnormal Child Psychology, 8*, 523–536.

McDermott, P. A. (1983). A syndromic typology for analyzing school children's disturbed social behavior. *School Psychology Review, 12*, 250–259.

McDermott, P. A. (1986). The observation and classification of exceptional child behavior. In R. T. Brown & C. R. Reynolds (Eds.), *Psychological perspectives on childhood exceptionality: A handbook* (pp. 136–180). New York: Wiley-Interscience.

McDermott, P. A., & Watkins, M. W. (1985). *Microcomputer systems manual for McDermott Multidimensional Assessment of Children*. New York: Psychological Corporation.

Miller, T. L., & Epstein, M. H. (1979). State terminology of behavioral disorders. *Psychology in the Schools, 16*, 224–229.

Quay, H. C., & Peterson, D. R. (1983). *Interim manual for the Revised Behavior Problem Checklist*. Coral Gables, FL: Authors.

Stott, D. H. (1985). *Manual to the Bristol Social Adjustment Guides*. San Diego: Educational & Industrial Testing.

Trites, R. L., Blouin, A. G., & Laprade, K. (1982). Factor analysis of the Conners Teacher Rating Scale based on a large normative sample. *Journal of Consulting and Clinical Psychology, 50*, 615–623.

PAUL A. McDERMOTT
University of Pennsylvania

U

ULCERS AND HANDICAPPED CHILDREN

While little empirical evidence exists to substantiate the relationship between ulcers and handicapped conditions, it appears that handicapped children may be more predisposed to ulceration than their nonhandicapped peers. Kim, Learman, Nada, & Thompson (1981) found that 5.4% of the residents in a large institution for mentally retarded children had peptic ulcers.

Other factors often associated with handicapping conditions also appear to lead to ulceration. For example, ulcers are more likely to occur in children with lower IQs (Christodoulou, Garigoulos, Poploukas, & Marinopoulou, 1977; Kim et al., 1981). Additionally, ulcers occur more often in children who are withdrawn and less likely to express their feelings or frustrations (Chapman & Loeb, 1967; Christodoulou et al., 1977), similar to some emotionally handicapped children. Finally, children who come from extended family situations (e.g., divorced or separated parents) are more likely to have ulcers, a factor that has been shown to be more likely to occur in handicapped children than in their nonhandicapped peers (Beattie & Maniscalco, 1985).

REFERENCES

Ackerman, S. H., Manaker, S., & Cohen, M. I. (1981). Recent separation and the onset of peptic ulcer disease in older children and adolescents. *Psychosomatic Medicine, 43,* 305–310.

Beattie, J., & Maniscalco, G. (1985). Special education and divorce: Is there a link. *Techniques, 1,* 342–345.

Chapman, A. H., & Loeb, D. G. (1967). Psychosomatic gastrointestinal problems. In I. Frank & M. Powell (Eds.), *Psychosomatic ailments in childhood and adolescence.* Springfield, IL: Thomas.

Christodoulou, G. N., Gargoulas, A., Poploukas, A., & Marinopoulou, A. (1977). Primary peptic ulcers in childhood: Psychosocial, psychological and psychiatric aspects. *Acta Psychiatrica Scandinavica, 56,* 215–222.

Kim, M., Learman, L., Nada, N., & Thompson, K. (1981). The prevalence of peptic ulcer in an institution for the mentally retarded. *Journal of Mental Deficiency Research, 25,* 105–111.

Mylander, M. (1982). *The great American stomach book.* New Haven, CT: Tichnor & Fields.

JOHN R. BEATTIE
University of North Carolina,
Charlotte

ANTISOCIAL BEHAVIOR
DIVORCE AND SPECIAL EDUCATION
EMOTIONAL DISORDERS

ULTIMATE INSTRUCTION FOR THE SEVERE AND PROFOUNDLY RETARDED

The criterion of ultimate functioning (Brown, Nietupski, & Hamre-Nietupski, 1976) refers to a method of prioritization that may be used in developing programs for the severely or profoundly handicapped learner. Although the type of handicapping condition may vary, this program development philosophy has most often been applied to individuals who have been classified as mentally retarded.

Use of this type of rationale to develop curricula for such persons extends from three major assumptions (Brown et al., 1976). First, the exceptional needs learner should be taught skills that increase the student's independence in and access to less restrictive environments. Second, transfer of training, response generalization, and response maintenance cannot be assumed to occur with such learners. Third, programming efforts with the severely or profoundly handicapped learner should address the wide variety of individual learning characteristics of this group. Thus application of the criterion of ultimate functioning in developing curricula for these students requires that the skills and behaviors taught to such individuals should relate directly to the behaviors that will be expected of them in nonschool environments.

Brown et al. (1976) developed the concept of the criterion of ultimate functioning in response to inadequacies of educational programs that had been generated based on alternative curriculum philosophies. With the severely or profoundly handicapped learner, these philosophies have often been either developmental or nontheoretical in nature (Haring & Bricker, 1976).

The developmental approach to curriculum delineation reflects adherence to a stage or hierarchical explanation of learning. From this perspective, the skills that are taught the severely or profoundly handicapped learner are dictated by the normal pattern of development that often takes place with the nonhandicapped child. Moving from the simple to the complex, the skills that are taught in developmentally oriented curricula might include teaching a student to vocalize before teaching words or teaching visual orientation before teaching word recognition. Proponents of a developmental approach to education feel that the simpler tasks must be mastered before the more complex skills are taught. Actual applications of a developmental orientation to the education of the severely or profoundly handicapped learner have often been criticized because of their inflexibility (e.g., "John is stabilized at the preoperational level") and lack of direct relationship to the teaching of immediately relevant skills (e.g., teaching object use through picture matching).

An alternative approach that has been used to develop curricula for the severely or profoundly handicapped learner has been referred to as nontheoretical (Haring & Bricker, 1976). This orientation develops curriculum content based on teacher-specified individual needs of the student. The emphasis of these types of programs has been on the use of specific methodologies that effectively teach the student new and increasingly complex skills. These skills do not reflect a particular developmental progression but instead are those skills that are relevant for the student as decided by the teacher. Although the emphasis on methodological consistency apparent in curricula of this type has often led to impressive skill acquisition, these skills have, at times, reflected teacher priorities that are not necessarily consistent with the best interests of the student (e.g., sitting quietly but not necessarily completing a task).

In response to the potential limitations of these curriculum development approaches, the criterion of ultimate functioning (Brown, et al., 1976) suggests teaching skills that are (1) relevant to student needs in light of individual learning characteristics; (2) immediately useful in terms of the environment(s) in which the student functions; and (3) able to increase the independence and ability of the student to attain access to more normative social environments. The teaching methods that are used from this perspective are based on specific analysis of the skills of the student and the requirements of the environment. Differences between these two assessment areas become the teaching objectives.

The criterion of ultimate functioning, used as a rationale for curriculum development with the severely or profoundly handicapped learner, breaks with the traditional developmental curriculum orientation. The skills that are taught are directly relevant in terms of the environments in which the student does, or is expected to, function. Building on techniques that emphasize specific analysis of student behaviors and environmental requirements, this approach systematically teaches the exceptional needs student skills that increase independence in and access to less restrictive settings. In contrast with the nontheoretical approach mentioned previously, this focus on independence and normative (chronologically age-appropriate) environments reflects a view of the student as an integral part of society. Theoretically, the degree to which the student might access social environments is a direct function of teaching the skills necessary for effective adaptation to those environments. Accordingly, the skills that are taught address not only the immediate relevance of learning experiences but also the long-term relevance of such skills.

REFERENCES

Brown, L., Nietupski, J., & Hamre-Nietupski, S. (1976). The criterion of ultimate functioning. In M. A. Thomas (Ed.), *Hey! Don't forget about me.* Reston, VA: Council for Exceptional Children.

Haring, H., & Bricker, D. (1976). *Overview of comprehensive services for the severely/profoundly handicapped.* New York: Grune & Stratton.

J. Todd Stephens
*University of Wisconsin,
Madison*

CURRICULUM FOR THE SEVERLY HANDICAPPED PROFOUNDLY RETARDTED

UNEMPLOYMENT OF THE HANDICAPPED

It is impossible to say with any degree of certainty how many Americans have a disability today. Gorski (1984) reports that some sources have placed the number as high as 50 million, while others such as the U.S. Commission on Civil Rights have been more conservative in their estimates, placing the number between 20 and 31 million. Bowe (1984) in his *U.S. Census and Disabled Adults* states, "the true figure, including children and senior citizens, probably was at least 21 million; however, we have no way of knowing."

A more accurate accounting system exists for those disabled persons of working age (16 to 64 years old), but there is considerable variation in the estimates. The 1978 Social Security Administration survey reported 9.6 million more disabled adults than did the 1980 U.S. census. Regarding the sizable discrepancy in these two government reports, McNeil (1983) suggests that past survey results indicate that responses to questions about work disability status are sensitive to differences in question wording and survey design. In order to standardize survey procedures and provide more consistency in the annual estimates, the U.S. Bureau of the Census began in 1981 to include questions about disabilities in the Current Population Surveys (CPS).

The most widely accepted statistics on the work status of disabled adults are those of the 1980 census and the 1981 and 1982 CPSs:

Total U.S. Population (1980 census)   226.5 million

Noninstitutional persons 16 to 64 years of age (1982 CPS) 147.3 million

With a work disability (1982 CPS)   13.1 million

In the labor force (1982 CPS)   3.6 million
(employed and unemployed seeking work)

The following generalizations were derived from these three sources:

1. Approximately 1 in every 11 adult (age 16 to 64) Americans has a work disability. This disability rate increases dramatically with age. Only 3.3% of those between ages 16 and 24 have a work disability, while 24% of those between ages 55 and 64 have a work disability.

2. The unemployment rate is directly related to the likelihood of having a work disability. The March 1982 unemployment rate for disabled males was 17% as compared to 10% for nondisabled males. The unemployment rate for disabled females was 18% as compared to a 9% rate for nondisabled females.

3. There is a substantial negative relationship between the presence of a work disability and being in the labor force or being employed. Of disabled males 65% and of disabled females 81% are either not in the labor force or are unemployed, whereas only 20% of the nondisabled males and 41% of the nondisabled females are either not in the labor force or are unemployed.

4. There is a substantial negative relationship between a person's educational level and the likelihood of having a work disability. Of those with less than an eighth grade education 31% had a work disability whereas, of college graduates, only 5% had a work disability. The explanation of this relationship between educational attainment and disability is not well understood.

5. There is a substantial negative relationship between income level and the likelihood of having a work disability. In 1981 the average earning for a disabled male as $13,863, compared with $17,481 for a nondisabled male. The average earning for a work disabled female was $5,835, compared with $8,470 for a nondisabled female. These differences in earnings were largely attributable to the less regular employment and fewer hours worked by disabled persons. When the comparison is between disabled and nondisabled persons working full-time, then the difference in the earnings gap diminishes considerably. In 1981 approximately 26% of the disabled adults were living in poverty, whereas the poverty rate for nondisabled adults was only 10%.

6. Occupational patterns are affected by disability. Disabled males are less likely to be employed in professional and technical positions than are nondisabled males. Disabled females are less likely to be employed as professional, technical, or clerical workers and more likely to be employed as professional, technical, or clerical workers and more likely to be employed as service workers than are nondisabled females.

7. Regions of the country differ substantially both in terms of the percentage of the population that is disabled, and in terms of the proportion of the disabled who participate in the labor force. At the time of the 1980 census, 8.5% was the national average of noninstitutionalized adults (ages 16 to 64) with a disability. Individual states ranged from a high of 12.7% in Arkansas to a low of 5.4% in Alaska.

In 1980 the percentage of disabled persons participating in the labor force varied from a high of 52.8% in Wyoming to a low of 26.5% in West Virginia, with the national average being 38.1%. Bowe (1984) reported that there seems to be a strong inverse relationship between the proportion of disabled persons in a state and the proportion of that state's disabled citizens who are in the labor force. For example, while West Virginia had the second highest percentage (12.3%) of disabled adults in its population, it had the lowest percentage (26.5%) of disabled adults participating in its labor force.

REFERENCES

Bowe, F. (1983). *Demography and disability: A chartbook for rehabilitation.* Fayetteville: Arkansas Rehabilitation Research and Training Center, University of Arkansas.

Bowe, F. (1984). *U.S. Census and disabled Adults: The 50 states and the District of Columbia.* Fayetteville: Arkansas Rehabilitation Research and Training Center, University of Arkansas.

Gorski, R. (1984). How many are we? Some statistical light on disability, *Disabled USA, 3,* 8–11.

McNeil, J. M. (1983). *Labor force status and other characteristics of persons with a work disability: 1982.* Washington, DC: U.S. Bureau of the Census, Current Population Reports, U.S. Government Printing Office.

JOHN D. SEE
University of Wisconsin, Stout

ADULT BASIC EDUCATION
SHELTERED WORKSHOPS

UNION OF SOVIET SOCIALIST REPUBLICS

See SOVIET UNION AND EASTERN EUROPE, SPECIAL EDUCATION IN THE.

UNITED CEREBRAL PALSY (UCP)

United Cerebral Palsy (UCP) is a national voluntary association comprised of state and local affiliates and the national organization, United Cerebral Palsy Associations

(UCPA), which is headquartered in New York City. A governmental affairs office is located in Washington, DC. Local affiliates provide direct services to individuals with cerebral palsy and their families, including special education, transitional services, and community living facilities. State affiliates coordinate the programs of local affiliates, provide services to areas not covered by locals, and work with agencies at the state level to further UCP goals. United Cerebal Palsy Associations assists state and local affiliates by formulating national policies on which affiliates are organized, managed, and supported. It also represents the UCP on a national level.

There are five district offices: UCP of Northeast in New York City; UCP of Midwest in Des Plaines, Illinois; UCP of southwest in Dallas, Texas; UCP of Western in Burlingame, California; and UCP of Southeast in East Point, Georgia. United Cerebral Palsy Associations' district offices were established to bring national services closer to affiliates and to transmit affiliate needs quickly to the national organization.

The UCP began as a parent group organized to improve services and educational programming for children with cerebral palsy. One of the first formal units was the Association for Cerebral Palsy, established in 1942 in California. In 1946, a parent group formed the New York State Association for Cerebral Palsy. These groups, along with others like them, evolved into a national agency that provides advocacy for legislative efforts, research and training, and direct services to clients. On August 12, 1948, the national organization was established as the National Foundation for Cerebral Palsy, a nonprofit membership corporation located in New York City. On August 12, 1949, the corporate name was changed to United Cerebral Palsy Associations, Inc. By 1952, more than 100 affiliates were linked with the national organization. As of September 1983, there were 228 local affiliates and 46 state affiliates.

UCPA works in many ways to generate new programs and services. In representing UCP in national affairs, UCPA cooperates with federal government agencies that administer programs that affect individuals with cerebral palsy. In addition, UCPA articulates UCP's positions on national issues such as national health services and transportation for people with disabilities. The UCPA develops model services for people with disabilities that are designed to be replicated in local communities (Cohen & Warren, 1985). The UCPA also suports national standards for the conduct of community programs. Through the UCP Research and Educational Foundation, UCPA promotes research into the causes of cerebral palsy, means of prevention, training of medical and allied personnel, and biomedical technology to improve mobility and communication. In addition, UCPA supports professional education by granting clinical fellowships and student traineeships and by running conferences and institutes. The UCPA uses national communications media to educate the public about cerebral palsy and to raise funds (e.g., public service messages are contributed to UCPA by television networks, radio and press syndicates, and national magazines). Public education and information materials are available from UCPA.

REFERENCES

Cohen, S., & Warren, R. (1985). *Respite care: Principles, programs, and policies.* Austin, TX: Pro-Ed.

Nielsen, C. (1978). *The cerebral palsy movement and the founding of UCPA, Inc.* Unpublished manuscript.

United Cerebral Palsy Associations. (1983). *Annual report 1983.* New York: Author.

United Cerebral Palsy Association. (undated) *Meet your national organization.* New York: Author.

CAROLE REITER GOTHELF
*Hunter College, City University
of New York*

ADVOCACY FOR THE HANDICAPPED
CEREBRAL PALSY

UNITED KINGDOM, SPECIAL EDUCATION IN THE

To suggest that special education is undergoing change in the United Kingdom is an understatement. The rethinking of policies and practices in dealing with children with problems since the publication of the Warnock report in 1978 has produced massive changes, both tangible and attitudinal. Policy has altered from one of removal from normal schooling to one that attempts to integrate. A new set of procedures designed to keep children within the mainstream of society has been developed.

The United Kingdom has had special schools for over 200 years and legislation for special education since 1893. The principles of this education provision have been sound in their concern for children and their potential. Educational provision has been based on an extension of a medical model in which assessment allows diagnosis, which in turn leads to treatment. Following the medical model, it is the individual who is treated. For children in the United Kingdom, this has meant screening, diagnosis, and classification into groups such as deaf, blind, educationally subnormal, maladjusted, delicate, physically handicapped, autistic, and so on. In turn, the classification has led to segregation, partly to regularize ordinary schools and partly to provide special treatment in institutions. It is only since 1971 that all children have been included within the education system. Prior to that date, there was a further classification of ineducable. Severely mentally handicapped children were kept at home, in hospitals, or in junior training centers.

By the mid-1970s, the climate of opinion had changed sufficiently for there to be a major rethinking of this approach (Brennan, 1981, Fish, 1985). Pressures from parents, the mainstreaming lobby, sociological theorists, and the report of the Warnock Committee (1978) produced a new Education Act in 1981 that rejected the previous classifications in favor of "children with special educational needs":

> A child has 'special educational needs' if he has a learning difficulty which calls for special education provision to be made for him. . . . A child has a 'learning difficulty' if: (a) he has a significantly greater difficulty in learning than the majority of children of his age; or (b) he has a disability which either prevents or hinders him from making use of educational facilities of a kind generally provided in schools within the area of the local authority concerned, for children of his age. (1981 Education Act)

By the time this Education Act came into force, provision was being made for 156,384 children in the United Kingdom (Fish, 1985). Of these, 45% were children with moderate learning difficulties, 20% had severe learning difficulties, 14% were maladjusted, 9% were physically handicapped, 5% were partially hearing or deaf, and 2% were partially sighted or blind. Following 1981 legislation, these categories were no longer used except where they would aid in the specification of need.

The Education Act requires local education authorities to be responsible for educational provision from birth if the parents request it and for the discovery of special educational needs from the age of 2. In addition, the procedures require parents to be active participants in every aspect of their child's assessment and placement. Within the school, procedures may be implemented differently from area to area but they must largely observe the following pattern:

1. The teacher concerned with pupil progress or behavior implements a program to assess and then develop those areas where problems arise.
2. Where change does not occur, alternative possibilities for the child are discussed at school meetings.
3. The parents are involved in these discussions.
4. Continuing difficulty leads, with the parents' permission, to outside professional involvement.
5. No progress leads to a full statement prepared on the child.
6. The local education authority acts on the basis of the statement in conjunction with the parents to place the child in a setting where special educational needs, as specified, can be met.
7. Reviews occur at least annually.

The central feature is the statement. This is the official document containing the local education authority's proposed placement of the child. In theory, the statement enforces multidisciplinary assessment of the child and allows the parents to offer evidence as well as their own opinions. In an ideal setting, the parents have considerable power in this process, as they must be consulted at every stage. The proposals for placement of the child and the statement of special education needs will be couched in positive terms to allow parents and education authorities to monitor progress and determine whether the child's needs are being met. Often, however, parents' involvement is small despite receiving written details on their rights. The proportion of parents offering evidence on their child is still very low. In effect, parents may not feel any more involved than before.

While a brief description of current practice is appropriate, it is also important to consider the main issues in special education in the United Kingdom today.

Not surprisingly, the first major issue is integration or mainstreaming. The Warnock report (1978) was widely taken as a charter for integration of the handicapped even though legislation had existed for this since 1976 and even though the report itself dealt warily with the issue. In essence, the report suggested that mainstreaming was less of an issue than might be imagined. This argument was based on simple arithmetic: around 16% of children have special educational needs at any one time in the United Kingdom; only 3% are receiving special educational provision (both integrated and segregated); therefore, the majority of children with needs are already in mainstream education. Nevertheless, better assessment is required to identify the missing 13% and better resources are required to provide for their special educational needs. Booth and Potts (1983) draw together many of the major themes: the need for a comprehensive schooling environment, reallocation of resources, clear policy and curriculum, support from the community, and, perhaps the most essential, a sense of group responsibility for all children.

There has been limited research on the effects of integration (Cave & Maddison, 1978) and it is likely that more integration could be taking place (Hegarty & Pocklington, 1982). There appears to have been an increase in segregated education in the last 15 years in the United Kingdom (Booth, 1981). The most common way to discuss integration has been as a managerial and administrative problem (Fish, 1985) rather than as an issue in the broader educational sense. It is relatively easy to highlight the different possible patterns of integration, from total integration with limited teacher support through partial integration (on-site units and specialist teacher support) to minimal integration (special schools). To implement provision on a regional basis requires consideration of factors that concern the location of resources and the allocation of funds. However, integration issues tend to have been submerged under the weight of the administrative load, with mainstreaming decisions made according to existing resources rather than with any dynamic concept of special needs. The result has been a lack of change in curriculum everywhere except in special schools. Swann (1983) has shown how the curriculum itself must change to meet the goals of integration, not just in title but in delivery to students. This is happening only to a limited extent. In practice, children with special needs are being required to adapt to normal curricula. When this is difficult and the children fail, they are shifted into low-ability groups or manual- or craft-oriented areas of the curriculum.

However, alteration of curriculum requires an alteration of attitude. Potts (1983) comments, "Facilitating integration involves a reassessment of the dominant values of selection, competition, specialization." It requires a different view about children and their active contribution in education; it requires an examination of teacher-pupil relations that in the past have been simply the transfer of knowledge from one to the other. In a fully integrated system, children need to contribute to their own learning and the responsibility for learning must be shared. This dissolves competitiveness in the acquisition of knowledge and allows for the fact that people learn differently, according to their needs and according to their capabilities.

Perhaps the most powerful criticism of special education in recent times has been from the discipline of sociology. Tomlinson (1982) is one of the severest critics:

> But it is important to recognize that the recognition, classification, provision for, or treatment of children who have been at various times defined as defective, handicapped, or as having special needs may very well be enlightened and advanced but it is also a social categorization of weaker social groups. (p. 5)

The whole process whereby professionals assess and deliver special education has been questioned. In effect, it has been proposed that those involved have had a vested interest in maintaining levels of provision that highlight their own roles. As a result, what is determined as need is what can be catered to by that group of professionals. This criticism strikes a chord with the increasingly heard views of people who have come through the system. Campling (1981), using self-assessment by disabled people, shows the strength of group identity. Thomas (1982), in examining how the experience of disability affects a person's ability to contribute to society, indicates how a special education system maintains the lower social status of disabled people. There is no simple response to criticism in this area since it is an attack on the most fundamental aspects of special education itself. It does require a response, however, and as yet there has been none that would lead to more positive integration and a more sensitive education system.

The special education of minority groups has become a much wider issue in education as a result of the Swann report (1985) on multicultural education. We know that the underachievement of children in some minority groups pushes them toward the special educational needs area. However, even if we were in an equitable system where all minorities were proportionally represented, we would still face major problems for remediation. In a multicultural system, the values of the minority are respected and their cultural norms recognized in the education system. When special educational needs are specified, the question must be, "To which cultural norms should the child be directed?" For example, if a child has a speech or literacy problem, should speech therapy or remedial reading be directed at the Gujerati spoken at home or the English valued in school? Do teachers understand adequately the requirements of a child with special educational needs when they do not understand the culture and cannot communicate with the parents? As one might expect, the response has been to call for more training or for a statement requiring English monocultural curricular values to be maintained. The solution is not yet in sight.

There has already been radical reorganization of services throughout the United Kingdom in the wake of the 1981 Education Act. It is not surprising that the discussion of special educational provision has meant a clarification of the respective roles of different agencies. In the preschool years, which for children with severe problems means only up to age 3, there has been greater cooperation between educational and medical professions. Legally, education can begin at birth if the parents or health services request it. This requires increased contact between health personnel and education services and should provide a much higher level of response to children and their families. In the school years, the peripatetic teams support not only the child, but also the teacher. In fact, the job of educating the classroom teacher about disability has largely fallen on the support teaching service.

In the postschool period, there has been greater attention to the child's transition to membership in adult society and continuing education for special needs. The former has meant the development of new curricula for young adults that are more relevant to society's demands. The latter has simply extended all special education issues into the areas of further education and adult education. The questions of integration and minority provision are no more easily answered in a college of further education than in an ordinary school.

While the 1981 act did not discuss teacher training in special education, at the center of all these issues are the teachers themselves. The structure of special education training is now undergoing marked change, with an increase in control from government. All initial teacher training programs throughout the United Kingdom now include a special education component. To teach as a specialist in special education now requires additional second-tier training in special education. Training for work with special handicaps such as teaching the deaf or blind may ultimately become a third tier rather than the second tier it is at present. The picture is one of more extensive and more thorough training for all teachers at both the initial and in-service stages, but these changes will take many years to affect the system.

The Warnock Committee (1978) viewed its task as a long-term one. It is unlikely that a further report will be made in the twentieth century. The debate begun by the Warnock report and the educational changes involved so far are widespread. The effects will be seen in the 1990s.

REFERENCES

Booth, T. (1981). Demystifying integration. In W. Swann (Ed.), *The practice of special education*. Oxford, England: Blackwell.

Booth, T., & Potts, P. (1983). *Integrating special education*. Oxford, England: Blackwell.

Brennan, W. (1981). *Changing special education*. Milton-Keynes, England: Open University Press.

Campling, J. (1981). *Images of ourselves*. London: Routledge & Kegan Paul.

Cave, C., & Maddison, P. (1978). *Research on special education* slough, England: National Foundation for Educational Research.

Fish, J. (1985). *Special education: The way ahead*. Milton Keynes, England: Open University Press.

Hegarty, S., & Pocklington, K. (1982). *Integration in action*. Slough, England: National Foundation for Educational Research-Nelson.

Potts, P. (1983). Summary and prospect. In T. Booth & P. Potts (Eds.), *Integrating special education*. Oxford, England: Blackwell.

Swann, W. (1983). Curriculum principles for integration. In T. Booth & P. Potts (Eds.), *Integration in action*. Oxford, England: Blackwell.

Thomas, D. (1982). *The experience of handicap*. London: Methuen.

Tomlinson, S. (1982). *A sociology of special education*. London: Routledge & Kegan Paul.

BENCIE WOLL
University of Bristol

FRANCE, SPECIAL EDUCATION IN
WESTERN EUROPE, SPECIAL EDUCATION IN

UNITED STATES OFFICE OF EDUCATION

The United States Office of Education, a precursor to the current federal Department of Education, was created by an act of Congress in 1867. Its original mission was to collect and disseminate information on the condition of education in the states and U.S. territories. According to Campbell et al. (1975), the Office of Education was responsible for establishing a system to identify and advance promising educational practices in school districts throughout the country.

During the nineteenth and early twentieth centuries, the Office of Education was located within the U.S. Department of the Interior. In 1939 the office was transferred to the jurisdiction of the Federal Security Agency. Its final home prior to achieving Cabinet level (departmental) status was with the U.S. Department of Health, Education, and Welfare (1953–1980).

Public Law 96-88, passed by Congress and signed by President Carter in 1979, created the U.S. Department of Education. The new department assumed all of the functions previously assigned to the Office of Education, and also included education-related programs and functions previously administered by other entities within HEW such as rehabilitation. Soll (1984) suggests that the rapid proliferation of social programs and the political mobilization of various educational constituencies combined to stimulate the creation of a Cabinet-level Department of Education.

Although exercising a modest role in American education during its first century of existence, the federal-level education agency has assumed an increasingly important role in administering national education initiatives. Recently (since the mid-1960s), the federal Office (now Department) of Education has been charged with (1) the collection and dissemination of educationally relevant national data; (2) the support of educational research; and (3) the financial and technical support of programs in compensatory education, special education, rehabilitation, higher education, vocational and adult education, and student financial assistance. The 1986 budget for all activities administered by the U.S. Department of Education was approximately $19 billion.

REFERENCES

Campbell, R. F., Cunningham, L. L., Nystrand, R. O., & Usdan M. D. (1975). *The organization and control of American schools*. Columbus, OH: Merrill.

Soll, C. D. (1984). The creation of the Department of Education. In R. J. Stillman (Ed.), *Public administration: Concepts and cases (3rd ed.)* (pp. 370–377). Boston: Houghton Mifflin.

GEORGE JAMES HAGERTY
Stonehill College

POLITICS AND SPECIAL EDUCATION

UNIVERSITY AFFILIATED FACILITIES (UAF)

Today's network of university affiliated facilities (UAFs) grew out of the recommendations of the 1962 President's Panel on Mental Retardation, which stressed the need for a "continuum of care" for mentally retarded persons, parents, and volunteers. In the following year, federal funds for construction of facilities to house services affiliated with universities or hospitals were authorized in PL 88-164. Maternal and Child Health, now the Division of Maternal and Child Health (DMCH), was the first agency to provide program support. In keeping with the mandate of this agency, funding was limited to support for faculty positions and trainees within the traditional maternal and child health disciplines that focused on children's services. The UAFs were the first major federally backed initiative to provide interdisciplinary training and diverse health care for persons with mental retardation.

The developmental disabilities legislation in 1979 expanded the scope of concern to include other disabilities, and the Developmental Disabilities Act (administered by what is now the ADD [the Administration on Developmental Disabilities]) provided core support for administrative costs of UAFs. Today, 19 programs receive DMCH funding for training and ADD core support goes to 36 UAFs and 7 satellite programs. Additional support is generated in each UAF from a variety of federal, state, and local sources. In addition to the DMCH and ADD-funded UAFs, 5 programs have elected to become members of the national association of UAFs, so that the present network of UAFs includes 55 programs in 38 states and the District of Columbia.

The mission of the UAFs includes four major elements: interdisciplinary training, exemplary services, applied research, and technical consultation/dissemination. The UAFs reduce both the incidence and the impact of mental retardation and developmental disabilities through a range of activities designed to prevent these disabilities or to enable persons who have these conditions to achieve their fullest potential. The latter is accomplished through early diagnosis, treatment, training in self-help and employment-related skills, and education tailored to specific needs and capabilities. These goals are pursued through four distinct programmatic activities that are the components of the mission: (1) interdisciplinary training for professional, administrative, technical, direct-care, and other specialized personnel to work with children and adults who are mentally retarded or developmentally disabled or at risk for developing such conditions; (2) a continuum of a full range of services; (3) technical assistance and dissemination of information to state, regional, and community-service programs through in-service training, continuing education, publications, development and dissemination of training materials, and conferences; and (4) applied research into related disorders and the efficiency of prevention, treatment, and remedial strategies.

JAMES BUTTON
United States Department of Education

MENTAL RETARDATION

V

VAKT

VAKT is a multisensory method of instruction that uses visual, auditory, kinesthetic, and tactile senses to reinforce learning (Richek, List, & Lerner, 1983). Unlike most other teaching strategies, the VAKT method emphasizes the kinesthetic sensory input provided by tracing and the tactile sensory input provided through varying textures of stimuli. The VAKT method is based on the principle that some children learn best when redundant cues are provided through many sensory channels (Mercer & Mercer, 1985). During instruction, the student sees the stimulus, listens to the teacher pronounce the stimulus, and then traces the stimulus over some textured material (e.g., sandpaper, corduroy, Jello). Thorpe and Sommer-Border (1985) contend that the kinesthetic-tactile component increases students' attention to the task. Under VAKT instruction conditions, students are more likely to attend selectively to distinctive features of the target letters and words. In addition, they tend to persevere or stay on task for longer periods of time at higher rates of engagement.

Many variations in the types of sensory activities have been devised. Depending on the style of learning of individual students, emphasis may be on one sensory channel over another. Some students may need more involved sensory experiences. More potent stimulation may be provided by such activities as tracing stimuli in sand trays, cornmeal, or Jello. Other activities include tracing in air, tracing in air while blindfolded, and tracing over raised stimuli of varying textures. Since the activities used with the VAKT method are time-consuming, it has been recommended they be used particularly in cases of severe learning deficits (Richek et al., 1983). However, VAKT activities can be used with milder deficits or even everyday learning.

Two instuctional systems used for teaching word recognition that highlight the VAKT methodology are the Fernald method (Fernald, 1943) and the Gillingham method (Gillingham & Stillman, 1968). The Fernald method combines the VAKT methods with a whole-word, language experience approach; the Gillingham method combines VAKT with a synthetic phonics approach.

The Fernald method consists of four learning stages through which students must pass. Each stage has specific procedures for teaching word recognition. As the student passes through the sequential stages, instruction entails less use of the kinesthetic and tactile senses. Words are chosen by the student for study based on stories generated by the student and written down by the teacher. This language experience approach is used to maintain student interest. Stage one emphasizes tracing and writing from memory individual words selected by the student. The teacher writes down a selected word on a large card and pronounces it while writing. Next, the student traces over the word with one or two fingers while saying the word. Word tracing is repeated until the student believes that the word can be written accurately from memory. The student now writes the word without looking at it and pronounces it while writing. If the word is written correctly from memory, it is stored in a word bank. If the student cannot write the word, the tracing procedure is repeated (Richek et al., 1983).

Stage two learning is initiated when the teacher believes that the student no longer needs to trace words for learning. Instruction differs from stage one in two ways: the words are presented on smaller cards and tracing is eliminated. As in stage one, words are selected from student-generated stories. A selected word is printed on a card; the student looks at it and says the word. The student then attempts to write the word from memory (Richek et al., 1983).

During stage three, the student begins to read from textbooks. Students can read from any material that they desire. Words are selected from the text, but are no longer written on cards. Instead, the student looks at the word in the text, says the word, then writes it down from memory (Richek et al., 1983).

Stage four is characterized by the student being able to read a word in context, say it, and remember it without having to write it. The student is taught to decode unknown words by associating them with known words or by using contextual cues. The student writes down for further review, the words that he or she cannot figure out using these means (Richek et al., 1983).

The Gillingham method is a highly structured phonics approach that uses the VAKT methods to enhance learning. The method is based on the work of Orton (1937) dealing with the relationship between cerebral dominance and reading and language disorders. A series of associative processes are used to link the names and sounds of phonemes with their written symbols. Six fundamental associations are used in instruction: (1) visual-auditory (V-A), (2) auditory-visual (A-V), (3) auditory-kinesthetic (A-K), (4) kinesthetic-auditory (K-A), (5) visual-kinesthetic, and (6) kinesthetic-visual (K-V) (Mercer & Mercer, 1985).

Instruction begins with the student learning letters and their sounds. Letter names are taught by the teacher showing the student a letter and saying the name (V-A). The student then repeats the letter name (A-K). The sounds of letters are taught next using the same procedures. The teacher prints the letter and explains its formation. The student then traces over the letter, copies the letter, and writes the letter from memory (A-K; K-A). The next stage involves reading words. The first set of words contains the vowels (V) a and i and consonants (C) b, g, h, j, k, n, p, and t. Sound blending is taught using letter patterns such as CVC, CVCe, etc. After a basic set of words is learned, words are combined into simple sentences and stories from which the student reads. Instruction proceeds with extensive use of spelling and dictation exercises (Mercer & Mercer, 1985; Richek et al., 1983).

REFERENCES

Fernald, G. M. (1943). *Remedial techniques in basic school subjects.* New York: McGraw-Hill.

Gillingham, A., & Stillman, B. (1968). *Remedial teaching for children with specific disability in reading, spelling, and penmanship.* Cambridge, MA: Educator's.

Mercer, C. D., & Mercer, A. R. (1985). *Teaching students with learning problems* (2nd ed.). Columbus, OH: Merrill.

Orton, S. T. (1937). *Reading, writing, and speech problems in children.* New York: Norton.

Richek, M. A., List, L. K., & Lerner, J. W. (1983). *Reading problems: Diagnosis and remediation.* Englewood Cliffs, NJ: Prentice-Hall.

Thorpe, H. W., & Sommer-Border, K. (1985). The effect of multisensory instruction upon the on task behavior and word reading accuracy of learning disabled children. *Journal of Learning Disabilities, 18,* 279–286.

LAWRENCE J. O'SHEA
University of Florida

FERNALD METHOD
GILLINGHAM-STILLMAN APPROACH
MULTISENSORY INSTRUCTION

VALETT DEVELOPMENTAL SURVEY OF BASIC LEARNING ABILITIES

The Valett Developmental Survey of Basic Learning Abilities was developed in 1966 by Robert E. Valett. The survey is designed to emphasize the use of psychoeducational diagnosis and evaluation to ascertain specific learning and behavioral problems in children ages 2 to 7 (Valett, 1967).

A total of 53 learning behaviors that may appear in a deficit form have been grouped under seven major areas of learning as follows: motor integration and physical development (e.g., "Throw me the ball"); tactile discrimination (e.g., "Put your hand in the bag and find the spoon"); auditory discrimination (e.g., "Say, we are going to buy some candy for mother"); visual motor coordination (e.g., "Draw me a picture like this"); visual discrimination (e.g., "Show me one like this"); language development and verbal fluency (e.g., "What burns?"); and conceptual development (e.g., "Give me two pennies"). A graded range of one to four items for a particular age level constitutes a 233-task survey. Each of the seven major areas is operationally defined and arranged developmentally in ascending order of difficulty (Southworth, Burr, & Cox, 1980; Valett, 1967; Mann, 1972; Roger, 1972). The instrument, educational rationale for remedial programming, and remedial materials are presented in a loose-leaf workbook format that are number-keyed to the major areas and subtasks (Mann, 1972; Valett, 1966). Scoring is based on correct, incorrect, or partial development. The range of developmental levels and strengths and weaknesses are noted for the purpose of planning remedial programming (Southworth, Burr, & Cox, 1980). Program suggestions that relate directly to the 53 learning behaviors are provided by Valett's (1968) *Psychological Resource Program.*

REFERENCES

Buros, O. K. (1972). *The seventh mental measurements yearbook.* Highland Park, NJ: Gryphon.

Johnson, S. K., & Marasky, R. L. (1980). *Learning disabilities* (2nd ed.). Boston: Allyn & Bacon.

Mann, L. (1972). Review of the Valett Developmental Survey of Basic Learning Abilities. In O. Buros (Ed.), *The seventh mental measurements yearbook.* Highland Park, NJ: Gryphon.

Mitchell, J. V. (1983). *Tests in print III: An index to tests, test reviews and the literature on specific tests.* Lincoln: University of Nebraska Press.

Roger, R. A. (1972). Review of the Valett Developmental Survey of Basic Learning Abilities. In O. Buros (Ed.), *The seventh mental measurements yearbook.* Highland Park, NJ: Gryphon.

Southworth, L. E., Burr, R. L., & Cox, A. E. (1980). *Screening and evaluation in the young child: A handbook of instruments to use from infancy to six years.* Springfield, IL: Thomas.

Valett, R. E. (1966). The Valett Developmental Survey of Basic Learning Abilities. Palo Alto, CA. Consulting Psychologist Press.

Valett, R. E. (1966). A psychoeducational profile of basic learning abilities. *Journal of School Psychology, 4,* 9–24.

Valett, R. E. (1967). A developmental task approach to early childhood education. *Journal of School Psychology, 2,* 136–147.

Valett, R. E. (1968). *Psychological resource program.* Belmont, CA: Fearson.

FRANCES HARRINGTON
Radford University

**PSYCHOEDUCATIONAL METHODS
REMEDIAL INSTRUCTION**

VALIUM

Valium (diazepam) may be used for the management of anxiety disorders or for the short-term relief of the symptoms of anxiety. It also is used for the relief of skeletal muscle spasms or for spasticity caused by upper motor neuron disorders such as cerebral palsy; thus, it may be used for some children in special education classes. In some cases, it also may be used as an adjunct in status epilepticus and severe recurrent epileptic seizures. It has a central nervous system depressant effect, and is thought to act on parts of the limbic system, the thalamus, and hypothalamus. Side effects may include drowsiness and fatigue, with less frequent reactions of confusion, depression, headache, hypoactivity, and slurred speech. Overdosage may product somnolence, confusion, or coma, and withdrawal symptoms such as convulsions, cramps, and tremor may occur following abrupt discontinuance.

A brand name of Hoffman-LaRoche, Inc., it is available in tablets of 2, 5, and 10 mg and in 2 ml ampuls for injection. Recommended dosages for children over 6 months of age is 1 to $2\frac{1}{2}$ mg three to four times daily, with gradual increase of dosage as needed and tolerated; in the injectable form, dosages of up to 5 mg for children under 5 years of age and up to 10 mg for children over 5 years of age.

REFERENCES

Physicians' desk reference. (1984). (pp. 1671–1674). Oradell, NJ: Medical Economics.

LAWRENCE C. HARTLAGE
Evans, Georgia

**ANTICONVULSANTS
DRUG THERAPY**

VALPROIC ACID

Valproic acid is the recommended nonproprietary name for dipropylacetic acid. The common (proprietary) name for this drug is Depakene. In the United States and Europe, the sodium salt of dipropylacetic acid is used. In South America, the magnesium salt of dipropylacetic acid also is marketed.

Valproic acid is effective in the treatment of absence seizures. It is considered of some use in the treatment of myoclonic seizures, and in tonic-clonic seizures (Dreiffus, 1983). The major side effects that are reported are drowsiness, gastrointestinal discomfort, and changes in appetite. The Committee on Drugs of the American Academy of Pediatrics lists valproic acid as having minimal adverse effects on cognitive functioning (Pruitt et al., 1985). The most significant and rare side effect of valproic acid is hepatic failure.

REFERENCES

Dreifuss, F. E. (1983). How to use valproate. In P. L. Morselli, C. E. Pippenger, & J. K. Penry (Eds.), *Antiepileptic drug therapy in pediatrics* (pp. 219–227). New York: Raven.

Pruitt, A. W., Kauffman, R. E., Mofenson, H. C., Roberts, R. J., Rumack, B. H., Singer, H. S., & Speilberg, S. S. (1985). Behavioral and cognitive effects of anticonvulsant therapy. *Pediatrics, 76*, 644–646.

Simon, S., & Penry, J. K. (1975). Sodium di-N-propylacetate (DPA) in the treatment of epilepsy. *Epilepsia, 16*, 549–573.

GRETA N. WILKENING
*Children's Hospital, Denver,
Colorado*

DEPAKANE

VALUES CLARIFICATION

Values clarification, an approach to moral instruction used with both handicapped and nonhandicapped pupils, stems from the humanistic education movement of the 1960s. Students trained in values clarification are taught to investigate the facts pertinent to a moral issue and to examine their feelings in a systematic manner. Values clarification teaches students the process of obtaining values and encourages them to explore personally held values and examine how they affect their decision-making processes (Casteel & Stahl, 1975). Rather than defining values in terms of good or bad, students learn to see values as guiding principles that affect choices. Critics of this approach have argued that values cannot be taught from a relativist position, and have questioned the appropriateness of using schools as settings for the teaching of values. As a result, values clarification started to lose its popularity as an educational force by the late 1970s (Brummer, 1984).

Raths, Harmin, and Simon (1978) outlined a seven-step process common to many values clarification curricula: (1) students are helped to examine and choose from alternative opinions; (2) they are assisted in weighing these alternatives in a thoughtful manner; (3) students are helped to see the value of making a free choice; (4) students are encouraged to prize their choices; (5) they are provided with an opportunity to publicly acclaim their chosen values; (6) students are encouraged to act on their choices; and (7) they are helped to establish behavior patterns that are consistent with their chosen values.

Students who are exposed to values clarification training become better consumers of information by learning to ask appropriate questions. Junell (1979) states that students' involvement and identification are heightened when values are taught in the context of an emotionally charged environment. As they develop their ability to integrate factual content with emotional responses, the trained students come to understand how they assign meaning and values to problems.

Values clarification activities might include rank ordering of preferential activities, sensitivity training, and listening skills development. Simulations are commonly employed to provide students with practice in values application. Social or philosophical dilemmas, based on real or hypothetical issues, are often presented as problems to be solved. Lockwood (1976) discusses the efficacy of using examples from other cultures when devising materials. The issues may be discussed in large or small groups, and students are encouraged to invoke their social decision-making skills in developing possible solutions.

Special education students are often faced with value decisions relating to their handicaps. For example, vocational programs for special education students may rule out certain academic options. The handicapped adolescent, limited in career opportunity, needs to explore the implications of vocational choices. Values clarification can help these youngsters to pick appropriate career directions and to learn decision-making principles necessary for adequate socialization at the work place (Miller & Schloss, 1982).

Some emotionally disturbed and learning-disabled children have been found to act without carefully considering the implications of their behaviors (Miller & Schloss, 1982). Values clarification provides a structure within which behaviorally disturbed children may find consistency. Thompson and Hudson (1982) found values clarification effective in reducing the maladaptive behavior of emotionally disturbed children. These children were also reported to be happier and less anxious.

Values clarification has also been used to help regular education students accept mainstreamed handicapped pupils. Simpson (1980) trained students to examine the effects of social influence and group affinity, and found that it eased the mainstreaming transition for both regular and handicapped students. Future research might focus on the long-range effects of values education on the attitudes of the general population toward handicapped individuals.

REFERENCES

Brummer, J. J. (1984). Moralizing and value education. *Educational Forum, 48*(3), 263–276.

Casteel, J. D., & Stahl, R. J. (1975). *Value clarification in the classroom: A primer.* Santa Monica, CA: Goodyear.

Junell, J. S. (1979). *Matters of feeling: Values education reconsidered.* Phi Delta Kappa Foundation.

Lockwood, A. L. (1976). *Values education and the study of other cultures.* Washington DC: National Educational Association.

Miller, S. R., & Schloss, P. J. (1982). *Career-vocational education for handicapped youths.* Rockville, MD: Aspen Systems.

Raths, L. E., Harmin, M., & Simon, S. B. (1978). *Values and teaching.* Columbus, OH: Merrill.

Simpson, R. L. (1980). Modifying the attitudes of regular class students toward the handicapped. *Focus on Exceptional Children, 13*(3), 1–11.

Thompson, D. G., & Hudson, G. R. (1982). Value clarification and behavioral group counseling with ninth grade boys in a residential school. *Journal of Counseling Psychology, 29,* 394–399.

GARY BERKOWITZ
Temple University

CONSCIENCE, LACK OF IN HANDICAPPED

MORAL REASONING

VAN DIJK, JAN (1937–   )

Jan van Dijk is world known for his work with rubella deaf-blind children. In 1958 he became a teacher of normal prelingual profoundly deaf children at the Institute for the Deaf, St. Michielsgestel, the Netherlands. His interest in the deaf-blind department led him to study at the Perkins Institute for the Blind, Watertown, Massachusetts, where he received the Inis Hall Award for his thesis. He continued his studies in education and special education at the Catholic University of Nijmegen and completed his doctoral program with the publication of *Rubella Handicapped Children* (1982), an extensive study of rubella children in Australia. Van Dijk continues his work at the institute as the director of the Deaf-Blind School and the Dyspraxic Deaf School. For his important contributions to the education of deaf-blind children, he received the Ann Sullivan Award in 1974. Since 1976 van Dijk has been affiliated with Florida State University. On a scheduled basis he has offered summer short courses and symposiums dealing primarily with the assessment of severely and multihandicapped children.

Educational programming begins with a differential diagnosis for each child, not only for appropriate placement within the nine schools at the institute, but also to determine the child's learning style. This diagnosis is accomplished through the clinical use of such instruments as the Test of Development of Eupraxia in Hands and Fingers in Young Children, Test for Finger Eupraxia for Intransitive Movements, Bergs-Lezine Test for Imitation of Simple Gestures, Rhythm Test of Hand and Mouth for Prelingually Deaf Preschool Children, Finger Block Test, Hiskey Nebraska Test for Learning Aptitude, Reynell-Zinkin Scales, Denver Developmental Screening Test, and an adaptation of the Rimland Diagnostic Checklist for Behavioral Disturbed Children (van Dijk, 1982).

The guiding principle of the method is that the child is in the central position. The teacher "follows" the child and "seizes," in a natural way, what the child is trying to express. In order to do this, a close attachment or bond must be developed between child and teacher so that the teacher can be sensitive to the slightest nuance of the child's expression. This guiding principle precludes the use of a teacher-developed curriculum. Rather, the curriculum develops from the child's interests and desires. As the environment responds, the child feels the sense of mastery or competency necessary to reach out into the world.

Because the deaf-blind child is deprived of the organizing senses of vision and hearing, the world appears chaotic and meaningless. Meaning is developed by ordering and structuring the child's day in place and time, and with people. At first, the activities are similar to those of normal mother-child activities. The teacher creates enjoyable situations that encourage the child to initiate activities. The child learns it is nice to do something together with someone else. Initially, he or she may need to be taken through the activities passively (resonance). Then the child begins to move together with the adult (coactive movement) until the activity is done successively rather than together (imitation).

As the child's day becomes ordered around activities of interest, ideas are formed. The child anticipates events and may express this anticipation through "signal behavior" or body language. As the teacher responds, the child realizes that these signals produce a positive reaction. They then form the child's idiosyncratic lexicon known and responded to by all adults associated with the child. Drawings and objects are also used to represent, or signal, activities (objects of reference). Gradually the drawings and objects become more and more abstract until the child is ready to use formal symbolic language systems.

The special quality of the van Dijk method is that language is not taught as a labeling process, but as a social interaction between two people having a conversation about objects, activities, and emotions of mutual interest. Results with this method may not be as immediate as with a stimulus-response program, for example. It may be several years before the child develops signal behavior. However, there is a possibility of reaching high levels of language performance. Although this method has been developed primarily for deaf children who have language potential based on a differential diagnosis, professionals working with the severely and profoundly handicapped are seeing value in it for their populations as well (Sternberg, Battle, & Hill, 1980).

REFERENCES

Hammer, E. (1982). The development of language in the deaf-blind multihandicapped child: Progression of instructional methods. In D. Tweedie & E. Shroyer (Eds.), *The multihandicapped hearing impaired: Identification and instruction*. Washington DC: Gallaudet College Press.

Sternberg, L., Battle, C., & Hill, J. (1980). Prelanguage communication programming for the severely and profoundly handicapped. *Teacher Education & Special Education, 3*, 224–233.

van Dijk, J. (1982). *Rubella handicapped children*. Lisse, the Netherlands: Swets & Zeitlinger.

van Dijk, J. (1986). An educational curriculum for deaf-blind multihandicapped persons. In D. Ellis (Ed.), *Sensory impairments in mentally handicapped people*. San Diego, CA: College Hill.

van Uden, A. (1977). *A world of language for deaf children. Part I: Basic principles*. Lisse, the Netherlands: Swets & Zeitlinger.

Visser, T. (1985). A development program for deaf-blind children. *Talking Sense, 31*(3), 6–7.

PEARL E. TAIT
Florida State University

RUBELLA
THEORY OF ACTIVITY

VAN RIPER, CHARLES (1905–   )

A native of Champion, Michigan, Charles Van Riper received both his BA (1926) and MA (1930) from the University of Michigan, and his PhD (1934) from the University of Iowa. His degrees are in speech pathology and psychology. He is a professor in the department of speech pathology and audiology of Western Michigan University. He also has been the director of the Speech and Hearing Clinic at that University since 1936.

One of the premier authorities in the field of speech correction, Van Riper has contributed to the theory and correction of stuttering and has developed methods for understanding, evaluating, and altering speech behavior. In 1978 the sixth edition of his textbook, *Speech Correction: Principles and Methods*, was published.

Van Riper has been concerned with involving the family in the therapy of any child with a speech problem. He believes that parents who know what they are doing are frequently better speech therapists than formally trained therapists. He began his book *Your Child's Speech Problems* (1961) with the statement that "once parents understand what the speech problem (of their child) is and what should be done, they can do great deeds" (p. xi).

A member of Phi Beta Kappa, Van Riper received the honors of the Association of the American Speech and Hearing Association. He has been included in *Leaders in Education, Who's Who in the South and Southwest*, and *American Men and Women of Science*.

REFERENCES

Van Riper, C. (1978). *Speech correction: Principles and methods* (6th ed.). Englewood Cliffs, NJ: Prentice-Hall.

Van Riper, C. (1961). *Your child's speech problems.* New York: Harper & Row.

E. VALERIE HEWITT
Texas A&M University

SPEECH AND LANGUAGE HANDICAPS
SPEECH DISORDERS

VERBAL DEFICIENCY

Verbal deficiency is a term with multifaceted meaning in the field of special education. It refers to the use and understanding of language and indicates abilities that are either deficient in terms of an individual's overall level of functioning or clearly below the norm for individuals of a certain age. Frequently, verbal deficiency is diagnosed when a child's verbal IQ on an individually administered intelligence measure such as the Wechsler Intelligence Scale for Children-Revised, is significantly lower than performance IQ (Kaufman, 1979b). Verbal deficiency is also inferred from a child's relative difficulty on those portions of group-administered standardized achievement tests that rely heavily on verbal skills. Parents and educators often note that a child's verbal skills are not age appropriate. A child may exhibit difficulty in following directions given orally or comprehending information presented orally. The child also may have difficulty with verbal expression. Language arts skills such as reading, composition, and spelling may be impaired. Speech pathologists working with children may use the term verbal deficiency when referring to subnormal development of language structures, verbal fluency, and knowledge of vocabulary.

A verbal deficiency may have roots and causes that are primarily medical. Hearing impairment, especially if mild, can be an undetected cause of verbal deficiency. A history of chronic otitis media (middle ear inflammation) and resulting intermittent hearing loss can be a factor as well. Neurological impairment can result in deficiencies in verbal skills while leaving other areas of functioning relatively intact. Although mentally retarded children often show depressed functioning in all areas, this possible cause must be considered when a child presents with verbal deficiency.

It is sometimes possible to infer through evaluation and testing specific developmental difficulties that lead to verbal deficiency. These include expressive or receptive language deficiencies or a central auditory processing disorder. A learning disability (as defined by failure to learn at a normal rate despite average intellectual ability) in the language arts area also can be associated with a verbal deficiency.

Emotional factors also must be considered in under-standing the concept of verbal deficiency in children. Physical or emotional abuse in the home as well as specific emotional disorders can affect the development of verbal skills. Sociocultural factors, some more readily apparent than others, may also play a role in the development of verbal deficiency. Manni, Winikur, and Keller (1984) provide discussion on this topic. English may not be the child's native language and may not be spoken in the home at all. Different dialects of the English language may be spoken at home. Educational level of the adult in the home, as well as the amount of time spent with the child on verbal tasks, may affect verbal development. Chronic school absenteeism, for medical or other reasons, can result in verbal deficiency.

Sattler (1982) and Kaufman (1979a) provide a more detailed discussion of the nature and causes of verbal deficiency. A single or combination of causes may be present with a child presents with verbal deficiency. Causes not described here may exist as well in individual cases.

REFERENCES

Kaufman, A. S. (1979a). *Intelligent testing with the WISC-R.* New York: Wiley.

Kaufman, A. S. (1979b). WISC-R research: Implications for interpretation. *School Psychology Digest, 8,* 5–27.

Manni, J. L., Winikur, D. W., & Keller, M. R. (1984). *Intelligence, mental retardation, and the culturally different child.* Springfield, IL: Thomas.

Sattler, J. M. (1982). *Assessment of children's intelligence and special abilities* (2nd ed.). Boston: Allyn & Bacon.

MELISSA M. GEORGE
*Montgomery County
Intermediate Unit,
Norristown, Pennsylvania*

EXPRESSIVE LANGUAGE DISORDERS
RECEPTIVE LANGUAGE DISORDERS

VERBALISMS

Verbalisms is a term coined by Cutsforth (1932) to describe the use of words by the blind that represent terms or concepts with which the blind could not have had first-hand experience. Color words are one example. Blind children learn quickly that sighted individuals refer to green grass, blue sky, and a bright orange sun and use such terms freely in their own language although they never experience these colors. The development of verbalisms is important to the mastery of language and communication by the blind; however, the blind should also be encouraged not to rely exclusively on verbal learning.

REFERENCE

Cutsforth, T. D. (1932). The unreality of words to the blind. *Teachers Forum, 4,* 86–89.

CECIL R. REYNOLDS
Texas A&M University

BLIND

VERBAL-PERFORMANCE IQ DISCREPANCIES

When interpreting the results of any of the three Wechsler scales, WAIS-R, WISC-R, or WPPSI, particular attention is focused on whether or not a discrepancy exists between the verbal (V) and performance (P) composite IQs. Other intelligence tests (e.g., McCarthy Scales of Children's Abilities) yield similar verbal and performance IQs. Tests assessing only verbal or nonverbal (performance) intelligence are also available. Although this discussion will focus on interpreting V and P discrepancies of the commonly used Wechsler scales, much of content is also applicable to these other intelligence tests.

The interpretation of IQ test data often focuses initially on the V-P discrepancy because it possesses particular diagnostic and/or prognostic value. The value lies in indicating particular strengths and weaknesses of the examinee as they apply to present or future educational or vocational pursuits (Kaufman, 1979; Sattler, 1982).

When considering a V-P IQ discrepancy, the test user must determine whether the observed discrepancy reflects a real difference rather than one that could be attributed to chance error. Sattler (1982) and the individual test manuals of many of the intelligence tests provide useful tables to allow the examiner to associate critical magnitudes of V-P IQ discrepancies with their levels of statistical significance. For the purpose of interpretation and planning appropriate remediation programs, the 95% (.05) level of confidence is recommended to determine whether a V-P IQ difference is real or should be attributed to chance (e.g., error measurement; Kaufman, 1979).

In addition to the determination of the statistical significance of an observed V-P IQ discrepancy, the clinical or practical importance of such information must also be assessed. A method to evaluate the value of a particular V-P IQ discrepancy involves determining how common or rare the discrepancy is for normal individuals. This is accomplished by calculating how often V-P IQ discrepancies of a given magnitude occurred in the test's standardization sample comprised of normal individuals. By inference, this information provides data or base rates as to how often particular discrepancies occur in the general population.

For example, Kaufman (1976) reported that as many as 50% of normal children in the WISC-R standardization sample had V-P IQ discrepancies of 9 points or greater and 34% of the sample obtained V-P IQ discrepancies of 12 points or greater. One out of every four children in the standardization sample earned V-P discrepancies of one standard deviation (15 points) or greater. Matarazzo & Herman (1984) presented similar base rates for the WAIS-R standardization sample. These statistics suggest that although statistically significant, discrepancies of these magnitudes are relatively common. Kaufman (1979) provides the following implications for interpreting both statistical and meaningful (i.e., base rate) significance that can be applied to all Wechsler scales:

> When a verbal-performance difference is significant, examiners have a basis for making remedial suggestions; when it is both significant and abnormal (i.e., occurring infrequently in the normal population), they also may have a basis for interpreting the test information in the context of other test scores and clinical evidence to reach a diagnostic hypothesis. (p. 52)

Based on analyses of the various standardization samples for the different Wechsler scales, equal percentages of subjects earn V greater (>) than P IQ discrepancies and P > V differences. Further, no pattern of V-P discrepancies were observed based on age, race, or sex. However, V-P IQ differences were related to overall IQ level (full-scale IQ) and background characteristics including parental occupation and socioeconomic status (SES). More V > P discrepancies were found at the higher IQ levels (average and above average) and for those from advantaged backgrounds, including individuals from professional families. Based also on standardization sample data, P > V discrepancies were more frequent in the lower IQ ranges (below average) and for those from lower SES backgrounds, including children of unskilled workers. These findings suggest that an examinee's background experiences help to influence the development of verbal and performance (nonverbal) cognitive skills. Also related to interpretation, the statistics suggest that a P > V discrepancy is particularly noteworthy for an individual from a professional, high SES background and a V > P difference is unusual for an examinee from a low-SES environment.

Extensive research has been conducted on the psychological significance of V-P discrepancies. Studies have reported a P > V discrepancy pattern for samples of delinquents and criminals, sociopaths, the poorly educated, disabled and underachieving readers, newly diagnosed pediatric cancer patients, the mentally retarded with familial and undifferentiated etiologies, and various racial/ethnic groups, including Chicanos and Native Americans Indians. The V > P IQ discrepancies have been found among the mentally retarded with known organic etiologies and other brain-injured examinees, including children with minimal brain dysfunction, and various groups with personality and psychiatric disorders such as schizophrenics and those with depression. Although the results of a number of research studies support the use of V-P IQ discrepancies as useful diagnostic indicators, generally the findings are contradictory and point to an inability to reliably identify V-P discrepancy patterns for various groups. Currently, psychologists do not possess the ability to reliably differentially diagnose various handicapping conditions based on V-P IQ discrepancy data (House & Lewis, 1985; Kaufman, 1979; LaGreca & Stringer, 1985; Sattler, 1982).

The primary use of investigating V-P IQ discrepancies lies in the ability of the test user to generate various hypotheses or explanations for the observed V-P IQ discrepancy. These hypotheses are then confirmed or refuted through examiner observations while assessing such activities as the subject's work habits and response style (e.g., lengthy explanations of verbal items). Additional diagnostic testing and testing of the limits (e.g., readministering timed items without a time limit) also contribute to selecting the most reasonable explanation for an observed V-P discrepancy. An examinee's age, overall ability level, and relevant background characteristics such as SES and other case history information, must be considered when choosing among various alternative explanations. A discussion of a number of alternative hypotheses or explanations follow and are based on the work of Kaufman (1979), Lutey (1977), and LaGreca and Stringer (1985).

Most individual IQ tests assessing verbal intelligence are comprised of items administered orally (auditorily) with the subject responding vocally. Performance IQ tests typically emphasize visual-motor channels, with most items visually presented and the subject performing a motor response. Undetected vision or hearing loss could represent a significant contributing factor to an observed V-P IQ discrepancy and should be ruled out prior to considering any alternative explanations.

A V-P IQ discrepancy may suggest an important intraindividual difference in style of thinking and learning. This explanation suggests that the V-P difference could reflect a meaningful difference in an individual's ability to express intelligence vocally in response to verbal stimuli; in the ability to think with words compared with expressing intelligence through manipulating visual concrete stimuli; or in the ability to think with symbols. Kaufman (1979) reviews the research speculating that this learning style difference can be traced to brain functioning with the left hemisphere being specialized in processing language/linguistic stimuli and the right hemisphere designed to handle visual-spatial stimuli. According to this explanation, a V-P IQ discrepancy suggests that one hemisphere is better developed than another.

Crystallized and fluid ability (Cattell, 1971) is yet another possible explanation for an observed V-P IQ discrepancy. Crystallized ability refers to those cognitive skills that are greatly influenced by specific training, education, and acculturation experiences. Often referred to as scholastic or academic ability, these verbal cognitive skills or crystallized abilities have a strong association with achievement. Crystallized ability is further characterized by more retrieval and application of general knowledge and is most strongly associated with verbal IQ scales. Fluid ability is related to the cognitive skills required in adaptation to new situations and solving novel problems that typically involve spatial, figural, or other nonverbal stimuli. Greater adaptiveness and flexibility in problem solving and a strong association with performance IQ scales also characterize fluid ability. Dependent on the particular direction of a V-P IQ discrepancy, a strength of weakness in either crystallized or fluid ability could be indicated.

A V-P IQ discrepancy can also reflect a psycholinguistic deficiency (Kirk & Kirk, 1971). The verbal scale emphasizes the auditory-vocal channel of communication while the performance scale involves the visual-motor modality such as visual reception.

Research also has been directed at the effects of bilingualism on observed V-P IQ discrepancies. Examinees who are bilingual and adept at speaking English frequently exhibit a significant $P > V$ IQ discrepancy. It remains unclear whether the verbal IQ deficit associated with bilingualism is related to the language ability, cultural, or cognitive structure characteristics of individual subjects (LaGreca & Stringer, 1985). Also related to language, a $V > P$ IQ discrepancy pattern characteristic of many black subjects has been hypothesized to be associated with their unique language development. This language development is reflected in the unique pronunciations, grammatical structures, and vocabulary that characterize black English. Jensen (1980) argues against black children possessing a language different from standard English that would contribute to a V-P IQ discrepancy. Jensen presents evidence that black youngsters do not perform at a higher level on nonverbal/performance tests. Despite these conflicting arguments, the language ability of black subjects exhibiting significant V-P IQ discrepancies must be considered (Kaufman, 1979).

Many performance IQ tests consist of items that demand responses involving some degree of fine motor coordination. For example, WISC-R subtests require the examinee to manipulate plastic blocks and jigsaw-type puzzle pieces and to copy geometric forms with a pencil. A $V > P$ IQ discrepancy may reflect a deficit in fine motor coordination and should be confirmed through careful observation of the examinee's pencil grip, motor movements, and pattern of scores on performance scale subtests. As an example of a pattern of scores on the WISC-R, the amount of fine motor coordination required is approximately inversely proportional to the order of administration of the performance scale subtests.

Many performance IQ test items are timed and often include the awarding of bonus points for quick performance. An examinee's negative reaction to working under time pressure is another possible explanation for an observed V-P IQ discrepancy. Additional evidence related to this hypothesis can be obtained by observing the subject's performance on the same items with and without time limits. Further, a particular V-P IQ discrepancy may be explained by an examinee's immaturity or lack of appreciation of the implications of observing the examiner using a stopwatch. The subjects may also be overly slow and deliberate, impulsive or reflective, anxious, or compulsive in their work approach. Compulsiveness in responding to verbal items can also contribute to V > P IQ score discrepancies as extra points can often be earned on verbal test items for elaborate verbal responses (LaGreca & Stringer, 1985).

Field independence/dependence (Witkin et al., 1974) represents another alternative explanation for an observed V-P IQ discrepancy. Field independence is associated with a P > V score discrepancy and field dependence is related to higher scores on the verbal scale. Guilford's (1967) operation of evaluation refers to the ability to make judgments related to a known standard and is required for successful completion of many performance scale items. A more complete discussion of the relationships between field independence/dependence and Guilford's operation of evaluation and V-P IQ discrepancies can be found in Kaufman (1979).

Further research is necessary to generate additional and refine existing hypotheses or explanations for observed V-P IQ discrepancies. However, it rests with the competent test user to combine observed V-P IQ discrepancy data with additional relevant assessment information to gain a further understanding of a particular client's unique abilities and limitations. This information can represent a significant contribution to more efficient present and future educational and/or vocational planning for children and adults.

REFERENCES

Cattell, R. B. (1971) *Abilities: Their structure, growth, and action.* Boston: Houghton Mifflin.

Guilford, J. P. (1967) *The nature of human intelligence.* New York: McGraw-Hill.

House, A. E., & Lewis, M. L. (1985). Wechsler Adult Intelligence Scale-Revised. In C. C. Newmark (Ed.), *Major psychological assessment instruments* (pp. 323–379). Boston: Allyn & Bacon.

Jensen, A. (1980). *Bias in mental testing.* New York: Free Press.

Kaufman, A. S. (1976). Verbal-Performance IQ discrepancies on the WISC-R. *Journal of Consulting & Clinical Psychology, 44,* 739–744.

Kaufman, A. S. (1979). *Intelligent testing with the WISC-R.* New York: Wiley.

Kirk, S. A., & Kirk, W. D. (1971) *Psycholinguistic learning disabilities.* Urbana: Illinois University Press.

LaGreca, A. M., & Stringer, S. A. (1985). The Wechsler Intelligence Scale for Children-Revised. In C. S. Newmark (Ed.), *Major psychological assessment instruments* (pp. 277–321). Boston: Allyn & Bacon.

Lutey, C. (1977) *Individual intelligence testing: A manual and source book.* (2nd ed.). Greeley, CO: Author.

Matarazzo, S. D., & Herman, D. O. (1984). Clinical uses of the WAIS-R: Base rates of differences between VIQ and PIQ in the WAIS-R standardization sample. In B. B. Wolman (Ed.), *Handbook of intelligence: Theories, measurements, and applications.* New York: Wiley.

Sattler, J. M. (1982). *Assessment of children's intelligence and special abilities* (2nd ed.). Boston: Allyn & Bacon.

Witkin, H. A., Faterson, H., Goodenough, D. R., & Karp, S. A. (1974). *Psychological differentiation.* Potomac, MD: Erlbaum.

MARK E. SWERDLIK
Illinois State University

INFORMATION PROCESSING
INTELLIGENCE TESTING
RIGHT BRAIN, LEFT BRAIN
WECHSLER SCALES

VERBAL SCALE IQ

The verbal scale IQ is a standard score (with mean of 100 and a standard deviation of 15) derived from a combination of five of the six subtests that comprise the verbal scale of the Wechsler Intelligence Scales. Every subtest on the verbal scale requires that the examinee listen to an auditorily presented verbal stimulus and respond verbally. The abilities measured include vocabulary, general information, verbal reasoning, and auditory-verbal memory. The verbal scale IQ is interpreted as a good indicator of verbal comprehension and expressive language skills. It is also considered to be an indicator of "crystallized" ability or intellectual functioning on tasks calling on previous training, education, and acculturation. Auditory attention is also reflected in the score.

Because of the verbal orientation of most American schools, the verbal scale IQ is by far the best predictor of academic achievement for students. Persons for whom English is a second language, or those from a low socioeconomic background or minority culture often earn a verbal scale IQ that is lower than their actual intellectual ability. Significant differences between verbal scale IQs and performance scale IQs are often used to document the presence of a learning or language disability.

REFERENCES

Kaufman, A. S. (1979). *Intelligent testing with the WISC-R.* New York: Wiley.

Sattler, J. M. (1982). *Assessment of children's intelligence and special abilities.* Boston: Allyn & Bacon.

Wechsler, D. (1967). *Manual for the Wechsler Preschool and Primary Scale of Intelligence.* New York: Psychological Corporation.

Wechsler, D. (1974). *Manual for the Wechsler Intelligence Scale for Children—Revised.* New York: Psychological Corporation.

Wechsler, D. (1981). *Manual for the Wechsler Adult Intelligence Scale—Revised.* New York, Psychological Corporation.

LIZANNE DESTEFANO
*University of Illinois,
Urbana-Champaign*

VERBAL-PERFORMANCE IQ DISCREPANCIES WECHSLER SCALES

VERBO-TONAL METHOD (VTM)

The verbo-tonal method (VTM) is primarily an auditory method for the education of deaf children. It was developed by Petar Guberina in Zagreb, Yugoslavia (Guberina, Skaric, & Zaga, 1972) and reformulated by Asp and Guberina (1981). The term verbo-tonal was first coined to characterize an original audiometric technique that measured the perception of speech segments called logatomes (hence the term *verbo*) of variable main frequency spectrum (hence the word *tonal*) from the low, such as *bru-bru*, to the high such as *si-si*.

Guberina insists on the importance of the suprasegmental, or prosodic, features of spoken language: rhythm, pitch variations, and stress. He considers that all deaf children and adults have some hearing capacities, not only inferior but also different from those of the normally hearing. Those whose cochlear function is completely lost can still perceive speech sounds through their vibro-tactile sensitivity. For every deaf individual, therefore, it is possible to determine an optimal field (OF) for speech reception, characterized by those frequencies of the speech spectrum in which residual hearing, and/or vibro-tactile perception, are most efficient. The OF can be limited to the low frequencies (including impulses of infrasound frequency perceptible by tactile sensation) or to the high frequencies. It also can be discontinuous, consisting of two restricted frequency bands, one low, one high. Having observed that better speech perception could be achieved by amplifying only the OF frequencies and eliminating the others, Guberina devised special apparatus capable of selecting distinct frequency bands.

Besides the technical equipment, specific training procedures characterize the VTM. Individual work consists of auditory and speech training. For speech correction, particular attention is given to the analysis of faults. Following this, the therapist modifies his or her own speech to counteract the erroneous perception that has led to faulty production. Several modifications of pitch, tension, duration, phonetic context, and even phonetic structure are used. The visual channel of speech reception, lip reading, is not trained specifically.

Body rhythm is based on the concept that speech is a function of the whole body, and that appropriate macromotricity movements involving the body will facilitate the finer micromotricity movements of speech organs. Specific movements based on the phonetic features of the various speech sounds are executed simultaneously with their utterance. The deaf child, equipped with appropriate amplification, first watches and listens to the therapist, then is asked to reproduce the associated speech and body movements with the control of the residual hearing.

Musical rhythm aims at sensitizing the deaf child to the rhythm and changing intonation pattern of normal speech, while simultaneously training him or her to perceive and reproduce every phoneme in its different positions: initial, intermediate, or terminal. This is accomplished by presenting to the child a series of comptines, each constructed with a limited number of repetitive nonsense syllables, allowing for easy identification and reproduction.

Phonetic graphism, a later adjunct to the verbo-tonal method was developed by Gladic (1982). This technique is based on coordination between the fine hand movements of painting and writing and the subtle vocal tract motricity of the speech act.

Although devised for the education of the deaf, VTM has been adapted to the rehabilitation of children with a wide variety of language and personality disorders (Asp & Guberina, 1981). First developed in Zagreb in the 1950s, VTM was shortly thereafter introduced in France. In the beginning of the 1960s, it was demonstrated in several other western European countries, the United States, Canada, and some Latin American countries. It has since developed worldwide, gaining variable degrees of acceptance among oralist-oriented educators and parents of deaf children.

REFERENCES

Asp, C., & Guberina, P. (1981). *The verbo-tonal method.* New York: World Rehabilitation Fund Monographs.

Gladic, V. A. (1982). *Le graphisme phonétique.* Brussels, Belgium: Labor.

Guberina, P., Skaric, I., & Zaga, B. (1972). *Case studies in the use of restricted bands of frequencies in auditory rehabilitation of the deaf.* Zagreb, Yugoslavia: Institute of Phonetics, Faculty of Arts.

OLIVIER PÉRIER
*Université Libre de Bruxelles
Centre Comprendre et
Parler, Belgium*

DEAF
DEAF EDUCATION

VERSABRAILLE

Versabraille, a device for the blind, is a microcomputer with a braille keyboard. In lieu of a screen, there are 20 electronic braille cells, each containing the usual six dots that can be selectively raised to form braille characters. After a period of machine familiarization, reading speed on the 20-cell display is comparable to paper braille reading rates.

One of the main advantages of this system is that it can store much braille information on small floppy disks. Furthermore, it does not necessitate any printing on paper, and makes word processing and the production of tables and charts possible.

MICHEL BOURDOT
*Centre d'Etude et de
Reclassement, Brussels,
Belgium*

BLIND
BRAILLE

VIDEOTAPING IN SPECIAL EDUCATION

Videotaping is a feedback technique that has been derived from the field of interaction analysis (Amidon & Hough, 1967; Flanders, 1970; Webb, 1981). In special education, it is often used as a training system that permits special education teachers to monitor and modify their own teaching behavior (Shea, 1974). A student teacher teaches a lesson, is critiqued, shown a videotape, and reteaches the lesson (Koetting, 1985). The interaction analysis technique allows the teacher to employ various schemes for identifying units of behavior and mapping the relationships of the behaviors in time and space.

Procedurally, an observer (special education teacher, student teacher, supervisor, or principal) sits in a classroom and views a videotape. As the observer follows the flow of events, he or she identifies specific units of behavior and makes notations of their occurrences. Identification of each unit is based on a set of descriptive categories; the resultant series of notations provides the "map," which is subject to interpretation and analysis.

The use of videotaping has improved many observation problems inherent in evaluating complex interactions of the teaching-learning process. In classrooms for the emotionally handicapped, videotaping provides a method of permanently recording and stimulating teacher-pupil interactions for professional preparation. It also provides the opportunity for immediate feedback, immediate and repetitive replay, accurate recording, and availability for analysis (Fargo, Fuchigami, & Cagauan, 1968; Haring & Fargo, 1969).

Birch (1969) demonstrated that categorizing and recording the frequency of one's own verbal behaviors may be a powerful training procedure leading to changes in recorded preservice teacher behaviors. Thomas's (1972) research supported Birch's findings that the self-monitoring procedure, viewing videotapes of one's own teaching and categorizing the behaviors observed, can have an effect on the behavior of teachers who are already teaching and who have had as many as 15 years of teaching experience.

Research also indicates that 4-minute videotape segments may provide the best, most practical diagnostic tool available to supervisors in both preservice and in-service programs (Hosford & Neuenfeldt, 1979).

Videotaping for improving target behaviors with various special education populations is reported throughout the literature. Bricker, Morgan, and Grabowski (1972) used taped recordings of cottage attendant behavior to increase the time and quality of interactions with developmentally delayed children on a ward in a residential facility. The use of commercial trading stamps as token reinforcers in combination with an on-ward training program was used. The results demonstrated increases in interaction time associated with a progressive increase in the suitability of tasks selected by the attendants across four intervention phases if training was paired with viewing the videotapes and the delivery of trading stamps.

Gilbert et al. (1982) studied the effects of a peer modeling film on anxiety reduction and skill acquisition with children with health-related disabilities who were learning to self-inject insulin. The modeling film had no effect on reducing anxiety but the girls viewing the peer modeling film showed greater skill in self-injection.

Performance training methods such as live modeling, videotaped modeling, and individual video feedback has been proven effective in altering parent-child behaviors and attitudes (O'Dell, Mahoney, Horton & Turner, 1979; Webster-Stratton, 1981). However, these studies addressed only the short-term effectiveness of videotape training methods. Webster-Stratton (1982) studied whether changes brought about by videotape modeling are maintained over longer periods of time with 35 mothers and their 3- to 5-year-old children who exhibited inappropriate behaviors. The results of this study indicated that most of the behavioral changes noted during the short evaluation were maintained. At 1-year follow-up, mother-child interactions were significantly more positive and significantly less negative, nonaccepting, and domineering than at baseline assessment. A significant reduction in behavior problems at 1-year follow-up compared with baseline also was noted. There was a notable drop, however, in mother-child positive affect behaviors (showing lack of confidence and inability to manage problem behaviors).

The positive effects of using videotaping as a training tool for special education personnel, teachers in training, and special learners and their parents is clearly supported in the literature. The opportunity to emit behaviors and obtain feedback on performance are crucial variables of the technique.

REFERENCES

Amidon, E. J., & Hough, J. B. (Eds.). (1967). *Interaction analysis: Theory, research and application*. Reading, MA: Addison-Wesley.

Birch, D. R. (1969). *Guided self-analysis and teacher education*. Unpublished doctoral dissertation, University of California, Berkeley.

Bricker, W. A., Morgan, D. G., & Grabowski, J. G. (1972). Development and maintenance of a behavior modification repertoire of cottage attendants through tv feedback. *American Journal of Mental Deficiency, 77*, 128–136.

Fargo, C., Fuchigami, R., & Cagauan, C. A. (1968). An investigation of selected variables in the teaching of specified objectives to mentally retarded students. *Education & Training of the Mentally Retarded, 3*, 202–208.

Flanders, N. A. (1970). *Analyzing teaching behavior*. Reading, MA: Addison-Wesley.

Gilbert, B. O., Johnson, S. B., McCallum, M., Silverstein, J. H., & Rosenbloom, A. (1982). The effects of a peer-modeling film on children learning to self-inject insulin. *Behavior Therapy, 13*, 186–193.

Haring, N. G., & Fargo, G. A. (1969). Evaluating programs for preparing teachers of emotionally disturbed children. *Exceptional Children, 36*, 157–162.

Hosford, P., & Neuenfeldt, J. (1979). Teacher evaluation via videotape: Hope or heresy? *Educational Leadership, 36*, 418–422.

Koetting, J. R. (1985). *Video as a means for analyzing teaching: A process of self-reflection and critique*. Paper presented at the annual convention of the Association for Educational Communications and Technology, Anaheim, CA.

O'Dell, S. L., Mahoney, N. D., Horton, N. G., & Turner, P. E. (1979). Media assisted parent training: Alternative models. *Behavior Therapy, 10*, 103–110.

Shea, T. M. (1974). *Special education microteaching clinic: Final report* (Report No. 020533). Edwardsville: Southern Illinois University, Special Education Microteaching Clinic. (ERIC Document Reproduction Service No. ED 126 665)

Thomas, D. R. (1972). *Self-monitoring as a technique for modifying teaching behaviors*. Unpublished doctoral dissertation, University of Illinois, Urbana-Champaign.

Webb, G. (1981). An evaluation of techniques for analyzing small group work. *Programmed Learning and Educational Technology, 18*, 64–66.

Webster-Stratton, C. (1981). Videotape modeling: A method of parent education. *Journal of Clinical Child Psychology, 10*, 93–98.

Webster-Stratton, C. (1982). The long-term effects of a videotape modeling parent training program: Comparison of immediate and 1-year follow-up results. *Behavior Therapy, 13*, 702–714.

DEBORAH A. SHANLEY
*Medgar Evers College, City
University of New York*

**SUPERVISION IN SPECIAL EDUCATION
TEACHER EFFECTIVENESS
TEACHER TRAINING**

VINELAND ADAPTIVE BEHAVIOR SCALES

The Vineland Adaptive Behavior Scales, a revision of the Vineland Social Maturity Scale, measure daily activities required for personal and social sufficiency. Three versions of the scales are available. Two interview editions, the survey form, and the expanded form (Sparrow, Balla, & Cicchetti, 1984a, 1984b) measure the adaptive behavior of children from birth through 18 years of age and low-functioning adults. Both are administered to parents or caregivers during a semistructured interview. The survey form provides a norm-referenced assessment of adaptive behavior while the expanded form indicates program planning information. The classroom edition (Harrison, 1985), for children ages 3 through 12 years, provides a norm-referenced measure of classroom adaptive behavior and consists of a questionnaire completed by teachers.

All three versions of the Vineland measure adaptive behavior in four domains: communication, daily living skills, socialization, and motor skills. The two interview editions also include the maladaptive behavior domain. The adaptive behavior composite provides an indication of overall adaptive behavior. Scores include standard scores, percentile ranks, age equivalents, and supplementary norms for handicapped individuals.

Norms for the Vineland are based on national samples of 3000 individuals (interview edition) and 2984 individuals (classroom edition) selected to match 1980 United States Census figures. Manuals for the three versions report the results of several reliability and validity studies.

REFERENCES

Harrison, P. L. (1985). *Vineland Adaptive Behavior Scales: Classroom edition manual*. Circle Pines, MN: American Guidance Service.

Sparrow, S. S., Balla, D. A., & Cicchetti, D. V. (1984a). *Vineland Adaptive Behavior Scales: Interview edition, survey form manual*. Circle Pines, MN: American Guidance Service.

Sparrow, S. S., Balla, D. A., & Cicchetti, D. V. (1984b). *Vineland*

Adaptive Behavior Scales: Interview edition, expanded form manual. Circle Pines, MN: American Guidance Service.

PATTI L. HARRISON
University of Alabama

ADAPTIVE BEHAVIOR
MENTAL RETARDATION
VINELAND SOCIAL MATURITY SCALE

VINELAND SOCIAL MATURITY SCALE

The Vineland Social Maturity Scale (Doll, 1935, 1965) measures the capacity of individuals for looking after themselves and engaging in activities leading to adult independence. The scale is administered to parents or caregivers of individuals from birth to adulthood. A semistructured interview technique is used during administration. Eight areas of competence are assessed: general self-help, self-help eating, self-help dressing, self-direction, occupation, communication, locomotion, and socialization.

The scale yields a social age that can be transformed into a social quotient by dividing the individual's social age by his or her chronological age and multiplying by 100. Norms are based on the performance of 620 people living in Vineland, New Jersey, in the 1930s. Doll (1953) reports the overall philosophy of the scale and details about development, administration, standardization, reliability, and validity.

REFERENCES

Doll, E. A. (1935). A genetic scale of social maturity. *American Journal of Orthopsychiatry, 5,* 180–188.

Doll, E. A. (1953). *Measurement of social competence.* Circle Pines, MN: American Guidance Service.

Doll, E. A. (1965). *Vineland Social Maturity Scale: Condensed manual of directions.* Circle Pines, MN: American Guidance Service.

PATTI L. HARRISON
University of Alabama

ADAPTIVE BEHAVIOR
VINELAND ADAPTIVE BEHAVIOR SCALES

VINELAND TRAINING SCHOOL

The Training School at Vineland, New Jersey, has had a long and influential role in the history of mental retardation in the United States. Originally founded in 1888 by Olin S. Garrison as a private school and institution for the "feebleminded," the Training School maintained a reputation for high standards of care and for pioneering experimental and research work. Rather than being a medical setting, it was designed to provide care and research within a psychological-educational context.

In 1901 Edward R. Johnstone became director of the Training School, a position he held until 1943. The genesis of many of the institution's later activities was the establishment in 1902 of the Feebleminded Club by a group of interested professionals and financial backers (Doll, 1972). In 1904 Johnstone started the summer school, one of the first programs designed to provide training for teachers of the mentally retarded. This program subsequently established university affiliations, and many leaders in the field were graduates of the program. In 1913 the Department of Extension was founded to publicize findings in the field. This led in 1914 to the Committee on Provisions for the Feebleminded, which undertook the first organized efforts of national scope to promote better state laws and increased institutional care for the retarded.

In 1906 the first psychological laboratory for the study of mental retardation was established at the Training School and Henry H. Goddard was appointed director of research. It was here that Goddard did his most famous work, translating and adapting the Binet intelligence scales, helping develop World War I army tests, and conducting extensive research on mental retardation. Goddard's (1912) study of the family history of Deborah Kallikak, a resident of the institution, became one of the most widely read research projects of the day; it gave impetus to the eugenics movement.

The laboratory Goddard directed continued to be considered a center for research on mental retardation for decades after his resignation in 1918. As director of research from 1925 to 1949, Edgar A. Doll made several important contributions, the most well known of his efforts being the establishment of criteria of social functioning. In the early 1960s the Training School changed its name to the American Institute for Mental Studies and in 1981 the Elwyn Institute assumed management responsibility for the facility.

REFERENCES

Doll, E. E. (1972). A historical survey of research and management of mental retardation in the United States. In E. P. Trapp & P. Himelstein (Eds.), *Readings on the exceptional child: Research and theory* (2nd ed., pp. 47–97). New York: Appleton-Century-Crofts.

Goddard, H. H. (1912). *The Kallikak family.* New York: Macmillan.

TIMOTHY D. LACKAYE
*Hunter College City University
of New York*

HISTORY OF SPECIAL EDUCATION
MENTAL RETARDATION

VISION TRAINING

Optometric visual training (vision therapy) is the art and science of developing visual abilities to achieve optimal vision performance and comfort. Training techniques are used in the prevention of the development of vision problems, the enhancement of visual efficiency, and the remediation and correction of existing visual problems.

Visual training encompasses orthoptics, which is a non-surgical method of treating disorders of binocular vision. Orthoptic techniques were used as early as the seventh century by a Greek physician, Paulus Aeginaeta, who used a mask with small perforations to correct strabismus. The mask was still in use in 1583 by George Bartisch, the founder of German ophthalmology.

In the early eighteenth century, Buffon advocated occlusion of the good eye to improve vision in the poorer eye. This was followed by Wheatstone's mirror invention of the stereoscope, which was employed to correct postoperative divergence of the eyes. Brewster modified the stereoscope, which is still in use in visual training programs today, with lenses.

In 1864 Javal founded orthoptics and demonstrated that binocular vision could be recovered with the use of a stereoscope. Orthoptics took a step forward in 1903 when Worth established a fusion theory, classified binocular vision into three grades, developed the amblyoscope, and devised the four-dot test to detect suppression. Worth, who headed up the English orthoptic school, which stressed fusional capacity, stated that the essential cause of squint is a defect of the fusional faculty. Worth believed that the weak fusion could be reeducated.

Optometric vision training techniques were developed by Arneson, who used the principle of peripheral stimulation with a circular disk of 30 inches in diameter. Patients were asked to fixate a rotating jewel on the Arneson rotator "to aid central fixation and fusion through motion." This was the first of many techniques that were developed by optometrists to modify visual behavior by changing the accommodative convergence relationship. In 1932 two optometrists, Crow and Fuog, published a series of visual training papers that introduced the concept of visual skills.

In addition, lens application, especially at the near point to enhance visual comfort, began to play an important role in the 1930s when Skeffington developed the analytical examination with a group of optometrists from the optometric extension program. Harmon further demonstrated that "appropriate lens for near point would reduce physiological stress." A plus lens is therefore prescribed as a single vision or bifocal during or after a program of optometric vision training.

The need for visual training is established with the objective and subjective findings of the visual analysis and an evaluation of the ocular motility, accommodative facility, eye teaming ability, and visual perception. The visual analysis includes a detailed ocular, medical, and genetic history followed by distance and near visual acuity determination, external evaluation of the eyes, and cover test to determine eye position. Pupillary reflexes, keratometry, objective and subjective refraction, distance and near acuity, horizontal and vertical ductions, fusional amplitudes, and accommodative tests precede any visual training therapy. Additional testing procedures evaluate suppressions, stereopsis, eye preference, macular integrity, and foveal fixation.

Visual symptoms indicating the possible need for visual training include crossed eyes, headaches, head tilt, short attention span, rubbing and constant blinking of the eyes, poor hand-eye coordination, blurring of vision, holding of books close to the eyes, double vision, word and letter reversals, covering an eye, losing the place when reading, or the avoidance of near work.

Many of the current visual training techniques developed by Brock, Nichols, Getman, MacDonald, Schrock, Kraskin, and Greenstein emphasize development of smooth eye movement skills (fixation ability). These include pursuit, the ability of the eyes to smoothly and accurately track a moving object or read a line of print, and saccadic movement, the ability to move the eyes from one object or word accurately.

Additional skills emphasized in visual training are eye-focusing skills, eye-aiming skills, eye-teaming skills (binocular fusion), eye-hand coordination, visualization, visual memory, visual imagery, and visual form perception. These techniques have been found to be effective in eliminating or reducing visual symptoms even when the visual acuity is 20/20 at distance and near on the Snellen acuity charts.

Techniques employing lenses, prisms, the steroscope, and rotator are used to align the eyes and maximize optimal visual efficiency. Visual training procedures also are used when there are overt eye turns such as those encountered in constant, intermittent, or alternating strabismus (esotropia or exotropia). Prism therapy is often used in conjunction with lens therapy in the correction of horizontal and vertical deviations of the eye.

Visual training techniques also have been used in the treatment of amblyopia, learning-related problems, and juvenile delinquency; in sports training programs; and with older adults and workers having visual difficulties on the job.

The optometrist often works on a multidisciplinary team that includes the educator, psychologist, social worker, rehabilitation specialist, orientation and mobility instructor, and child development specialist who specializes in the remediation of the child, teen, or adult with a learning or visual disability.

REFERENCES

American Optometric Association. (1985). *Vision therapy news backgrounder*. St. Louis: Author.

Borish, I. (1970). *Clinical refraction* (3rd ed.). Chicago; Professional.

Griffin, J. R. (1982). *Binocular anomalies procedures for vision therapy* (2nd ed.). Chicago: Professional.

Harmon, D. B. (1945). *Lighting and child development*. Philadelphia: Illuminating Engineering.

Hurtt, R. N., Rasicovici, A., & Windsor, C. (1952). *Comprehensive review of orthoptics and ocular motility*. St. Louis: Mosby.

McDonald, L. W. (1970). *Optometric visual training—Its history and development*. St. Louis: American Optometric Association.

Richman, J. E., Cron, M., & Cohen, E. (1983). *Basic vision therapy, A clinical handbook*. Ferris, MI:

Skeffington, A. M. (1946). *Visual rehabilitation, analytical optometry*. Duncan, OK: Occupational Education Programs.

Skeffington, A. M. (1959). *The role of a convex lens*. St. Louis: American Optometric Association.

Von Norden, G., & Maumenee, A. E. (1967). *Atlas of strabismus*. St. Louis: Mosby.

BRUCE P. ROSENTHAL
State University of New York

DEVELOPMENTAL OPTOMETRY
OPTOMETRISTS
VISUAL ACUITY
VISUALLY IMPAIRED

VISUAL ACUITY

Visual acuity refers to the degree to which the human eye can distinguish fine detail at varying distances. It is dependent on the eye's ability to bend light rays and focus them on the retina (Cartwright, Cartwright, & Ward, 1981). Tests of visual acuity provide measures of the smallest retinal formed images distinguishable by someone's eyes. The results of such tests are influenced by such factors as the area of retina stimulated, the intensity and distribution of illumination, the amount of time of exposure, the effects of movement, and whether the visual acuity test is conducted with each of the eyes separately or both together (Duke-Elder, 1968).

Distance visual acuity is usually measured with a Snellen chart (first published in 1862) and according to Snellen's formula (based on use with this chart). In this formula, $V = d/D$, with V standing for visual acuity; d representing the distance at which test types are read on the chart; and D representing the distance at which the letters subtend an overall angle of 5 minutes on the Snellen chart (Jan, Freeman, & Scott, 1977). Thus, if at a distance (d) of 20 feet a child can identify letters on the 20 line (D) of a Snellen chart, his or her visual acuity (V) is 20/20, which is considered to be normal vision.

If a child's visual acuity is assessed as 20/200 in the better eye without correction, the child is only able to see images at a distance of 20 feet that a person with normal vision can see at 200 feet. Such a child would be classified as legally blind. Some low-vision children are able to see images at distances no farther than a few feet. If a child has a visual acuity measurement of 5/40, it means that he or she can see the 40 line (D) on the Snellen chart from a distance of 5 feet (d). Since such a rating is an equivalent of 20/160, it would also classify such a child as legally blind (Jan et al., 1977). Below measurements of 20/400, visual acuity is usually assessed by having the subject count fingers seen at short distances. LP noted for an eye examination means that the child can only perceive light.

When assessing children's visual acuity, particularly those with low vision, it is important to use visual displays with high-contrast letters and to avoid glare and visual distractions. In instances where a child has difficulty in localizing the symbols to be discriminated, e.g., when testing a child with cognitive difficulties, it may be necessary to occlude parts of the chart (Jose, 1983).

When assessing young children, those who are learning disabled, or those who have multiple handicaps that limit their ability to identify the letters on the Snellen chart, it may be necessary to use alternate methods to assess visual acuity. One of these methods, the Snellen E, requires the student to indicate the position of the E symbol (whether left, right, up, or down). Caution must be used in administering this test since a grasp of directionality and some eye-hand coordination is required to succeed; some training of the child may facilitate the application.

Other methods of approximating visual acuity include the use of an optokinetic drum, Sheridan's Stycar miniature toys, the Rosenbaum Dot Test, and the New York Lighthouse Symbol Flashcards. The last test employs three symbols, a house, an umbrella, and an apple, that conform to the sizes of the Snellen letters. The child can identify the symbols on the chart by naming them in any understandable way or by pointing to a symbol placed in front of the table where the child is seated (Faye, Padula, Gurland, Greenberg, & Hood, 1984).

In addition to testing for distance visual acuity, it is important to assess a child's near distance acuity because so many school and work-related tasks are performed at close distances. Near tasks, required in much of school learning, are usually performed from a distance of 14 to 16 inches. A major problem confronting the assessment of near vision is the lack of standardization in the types of chart systems that are currently used for this purpose. The Snellen near-point card uses the metric system to indicate close distance visual acuity. The Jaeger consists of 20 different type sizes in increasing graduations; it indicates the type sizes that the student is able to identify. The Point system uses type sizes in which one point equals ¹⁄₇₂ of an inch. Thus a student who can read newspaper print has a near point Snellen equivalent of 20/40, a Jaeger recording of J4-5, and a Point recording of 8; a student who can only read newspaper headlines has a Snellen rating of 20/100, a Jaeger recording of J17, and a Point recording of 18 (Jose, 1983). A lay person may find it difficult to reconcile such diverse findings. For them to be understood by teachers and parents, the visual examiner should explain their nature and implications. Information respecting the visual acuity, both far and near, of all children, but particularly the handicapped, is an essential guide for children's instruction.

REFERENCES

Cartwright, G. P., Cartwright, C. A., & Ward, M. J. (1981). *Educating exceptional learners*. Belmont, CA: Wadsworth.

Duke-Elder, S. A. (1968). *Systems of opthalmology*. St. Louis: Mosby.

Faye, E. E., Padula, W. V., Padula, J. B., Gurland, J. E., Greenberg, M. L., & Hood, C. M. (1984). The low vision child. In E. E. Faye (Ed.), *Clinical low vision* (pp. 437–475). Boston: Little, Brown.

Jan, J. E., Freeman, R. D., & Scott, ER.P (1977). *Visual impairment in children & adolescents*. New York: Grune & Stratton.

Jose, R. T. (1983). *Understanding low vision*. New York: American Foundation for the Blind.

EMILY WAHLEN
*Hunter College, City University
of New York*

VISUALLY IMPAIRED
VISUAL-MOTOR AND VISUAL-PERCEPTUAL PROBLEMS
VISUAL TRAINING

VISUAL EFFICIENCY

Visual efficiency, as defined by Barraga (1970, 1976, 1980, 1983), relates to a variety of visual skills including eye movements, adapting to the physical environment, attending to visual stimuli, and processing information with speed and effectiveness.

In keeping with this definition is Barraga's (1983) definition of the visually handicapped child as a child whose visual impairments limit his or her learning and achievement unless there are adaptations made in the way that learning experiences are presented to the child and effective learning materials are provided in appropriate learning environments.

The basic idea behind the notion of visual efficiency is that children learn to see best by actively using their visual abilities. As applied to the visually handicapped (i.e.,

low-vision children), this means that they should be provided with such opportunities for learning and should be taught in such ways that they learn effectively to use their residual vision. Low-vision children, without proper opportunities and training, may not be able to extract much useful information from their visual environments simply by being provided with appropriate visual environments, but they can learn to use their visual information with proper opportunities and training so that they eventually can make sense out of what were previously indistinct, uncertain visual impressions. Barraga's program to develop efficiency in visual functioning, intended for the training of low-vision children (1983), is one that emphasizes structured training for visual efficiency.

Associated with the idea of visual efficiency is the concept of functional vision. This concept is concerned with the ways that children use their vision rather than with their physical visual limitations.

REFERENCES

Barraga, N. C. (1970). *Teacher's guide for development of visual learning abilities and utilization of low vision*. Louisville, KY: American Printing House for the Blind.

Barraga, N. C. (1976). *Visual handicaps and learning: A developmental approach*. Belmont CA: Wadsworth.

Barraga, N. C. (1980). *Source book on low vision*. Louisville, KY: American Printing House for the Blind.

Barraga, N. C. (1983). *Visual handicaps and learning*. Austin, TX: Exceptional Resources.

Heward, W. L., & Orlansky, M. D. (1984). *Exceptional children: An introductory survey of special education*. Columbus, OH: Merrill.

JANET S. BRAND
*Hunter College, City University
of New York*

FUNCTIONAL VISION

VISUAL IMPAIRMENT

Godfrey Stevens, in his study on *Taxonomy in Special Education for Children with Body Disorders* (1963), used the term impairment to mean any deviation from the normal. Thus impairment was interpreted by many to mean a disorder at the tissue level. Visual impairment, therefore, would mean the medical cause of the handicap. For example, cataract would be the impairment; diminished eyesight would be the disability or handicap. It would, therefore, be correct to refer to individuals with visual impairments.

In recent years, however, the term visual impairment has taken on a broader meaning. In many cases it denotes visual loss other than total blindness, such as the "blind" *and* the visually impaired, thereby separating the functionally blind from those who have some remaining vision. It is common also for experts in the field to refer to an individual with a visual impairment as anyone with a measured loss of any of the visual functions such as acuity, fields, color vision, or binocular vision (Barraga, 1983). Used in this context, visual impairment almost becomes synonymous with visual disability or visual handicap.

REFERENCES

Barraga, N. C. (1983). *Visual handicaps and learning* (rev. ed.). Austin, TX: Exceptional Resources.

Stevens, G. D. (1962). *Taxonomy in special education for children with body disorders*. Pittsburgh: Department of Special Education & Rehabilitation.

GIDEON JONES
Florida State University

VISUAL PERCEPTION AND DISCRIMINATION
VISUAL TRAINING

VISUALLY IMPAIRED

See VISUAL IMPAIRMENT.

VISUAL-MOTOR AND VISUAL-PERCEPTUAL PROBLEMS

Many researchers have emphasized the importance of perceptual-motor skills to the development of children. Piaget and Inhelder (1956) stated that early sensory-motor experiences are basic to more advanced mental development, and Sherrington (1948) proposed that the motor system is the first neurological system to develop and the foundation for later perceptual growth. The concern for perceptual-motor development is a recurring theme in many areas of the history of special education (Lerner, 1976). While this perceptual-motor framework can be used to discuss all areas of perception that relate to motor responses—auditory, visual, haptic, olfactory, etc.—the relationships between visual-motor perception and discrimination and learning problems have received the greatest attention. The interest in visual motor perceptual problems in the United States can be traced back to the early research of Werner and Strauss (1939) and Strauss and Lehtinen (1947) with brain-damaged children. They noted that disturbances in visual perception and visual motor perceptual functioning often accompany central nervous system damage. Their work also fostered the rapid growth and development of several visual motor training programs by theorists such as Barsch, Frostig, Getman, and Kephart.

Although early researchers reported that visual-perceptual and visual-motor problems were evident in individuals with brain damage, a distinction between these two types of disturbances was not always made. While Goldstein and Scheerer (1959) considered visual-motor and visual-perceptual deficits as separate entities, Bartley (1958) viewed perception as being either experiental or motor. Some of the assessment instruments used to measure visual perception are actually visual-motor copying tasks; for example, the Bender Gestalt Test, the coding subtest of the Wechsler scales of intelligence, and the developmental test of visual motor integration, all require motor responses.

The failure to differentiate between visual-perceptual and visual-motor tasks may have far-reaching consequences. Perception is most directly tested when objects or pictures of various shapes, positions, or sizes are matched, or in some other way differentiated; it is then a task of interpreting what is seen. When the difficulty is demonstrated in a task that requires reproducing designs or spatial relationships, it is described as a visual-motor difficulty; i.e., the acts of perceiving and reproducing an object are combined. It may be possible that the child who displays a visual-motor difficulty also has a perceptual problem, although that inference cannot be made on the basis of a reproduction task. In normal development, visual perception of form precedes the visual motor reproduction of the form (Piaget & Inhelder, 1956), and copying requires skills of an order different from perceiving (Abercrombie, 1964).

Children who have visual-motor problems have difficulty coordinating their movements with what they see. Kirk and Chalfant (1984) reported that breakdowns in three areas may occur when a child displays problems in visual-motor perception and discrimination. First, a child may have problems with laterality, or lateral dominance. This type of problem becomes apparent when both sides of the body perform the same act at the same time when that is not part of the task, or when a child uses only one side of his or her body when two sides are called for. Second, a child may have a directional disability. Directional disabilities manifest themselves when the child fails to develop an awareness of basic directions such as right from left, up from down, and front from back. Very young children will have problems in directionality; this is normal during the early stages of development, but as the child matures, this problem usually corrects itself. If these difficulties continue, the child may have problems in learning. Finally, a child is said to have a breakdown in visual-motor perception when the child's development is limited to the stage where the hand leads the eye. As visual-motor perception is refined, the eye should lead the hand.

Problems in visual-motor perception and discrimination can be seen in both academic and nonacademic tasks. In particular, visual-motor difficulties are most evident when children are involved in pencil and paper activities, play with or manipulate toys and objects, or catch or throw a ball, or when they are involved in any tasks that require good eye-hand coordination.

Many educators and psychologists have believed for years that adequate visual-motor development is directly related to academic achievement. As a result of this belief, a number of standardized tests were developed to assess children's visual-motor performance. Unfortunately, the use of these tests has not been supported by the literature. Visual-motor tests have been shown to be unreliable and theoretically or psychometrically unsound (Salvia & Ysseldyke, 1985). These inadequacies raise the question as to their usefulness, and whether or not they should be used in planning educational programs for children.

Despite the inadequacies of visual-motor tests, they are still being used in the schools. Advocates of visual-motor testing use these assessment instruments to diagnose brain injury, to identify children with visual-motor problems so that training programs can be established to remediate learning disabilities, and to determine the degree to which visual-motor perception and discrimination problems may be interfering with academic achievement. Some of the most common assessment devices used to measure visual-motor skills include the Bender-Gestalt Test, the Developmental Test of Visual Motor Integration, and the Purdue Perceptual Motor Survey.

The methods used in visual-motor training programs are generally developmental and emphasize the importance of early motor learning and visual-spatial development in children. While many of the advocates of visual-motor training programs have slightly different rationales for their programs, the basic perceptual-motor orientation and the recommended training activities are very similar. Barsch, Getman, Frostig, and Kephart all propose techniques for working with children with learning problems (Myers, & Hammill, 1969).

One of the areas of controversy that surrounds the use of these training programs is the emphasis on training visual-motor perception processes to improve a child's skills in academic areas such as reading. Hammill and Larsen (1974) have argued that there is no evidence to support the assumption that academic learning is dependent on these types of psychological processes. However, unfortunately, both the critics and advocates of these training programs have based their arguments on highly questionable research reports (Hallahan & Kauffman, 1976). It is crucial that sound research be conducted to demonstrate the efficacy of any method used with children. This has not been done in the area of visual-motor perception and discrimination.

REFERENCES

Abercrombie, M. (1964). *Perceptual and visuo-motor disorders in cerebral palsy.* London: Heinemann.

Bartley, S. (1958). *Principles of perception.* New York: American Orthopsychiatric Association.

Goldstein, K., & Scheerer, M. (1959). Abstract and concrete behavior: An experimental study with special tests. *Psychological Monographs, 83.*

Hallahan, D., & Kauffman, J. (1976). *Introduction to learning disabilities.* Englewood Cliffs, NJ: Prentice-Hall.

Hammill, D., & Larsen, S. (1974). The relationship of selected auditory perceptual skills and reading ability. *Journal of Learning Disabilities, 7,* 429–436.

Kirk, S., & Chalfant, J. (1984). *Academic and developmental learning disabilities.* Denver: Love.

Myers, P., & Hammill, D. (1969). *Methods for learning disorders.* New York: Wiley.

Piaget, J., & Inhelder, B. (1956). *The child's concept of space.* London: Routledge & Kegan Paul.

Salvia, J., & Ysseldyke, J. (1985). *Assessment in special and remedial education* (3rd ed.). Boston: Houghton Mifflin.

Sherrington, C. (1948). *The integrative action of the nervous system.* New Haven, CT: Yale University Press.

Strauss, A., & Lehtinen, L. (1947). *Psychopathology and education of the brain injured child.* New York: Grune & Stratton.

Werner, H., & Strauss, A. (1939). Types of visuo-motor activity and their relation to low and high performance ages. *Proceedings of the American Association of Mental Deficiency, 44,* 163–168.

DEBORAH C. MAY
State University of New York, Albany

DONALD S. MAROZAS
State University of New York, Geneseo

PERCEPTION
PERCEPTUAL MOTOR DIFFICULTIES
PERCEPTUAL REMEDIATION
VISUAL-MOTOR INTEGRATION

VISUAL-MOTOR INTEGRATION

Visual-motor integration, also referred to as visual-motor association, denotes the ability to relate visual stimuli to motor responses in an accurate, appropriate manner. Historically, visual-motor problems have been associated with learning disabilities and, within a diagnostic-remedial intervention model, visual-motor skills have been taught to learning-disabled pupils as a prerequisite to academic skills (Lerner, 1985). This interest in visual-motor development within the learning disabilities field can be traced to the early work of Strauss and Werner (1941), who studied the visual-motor problems of mentally retarded students and believed that faulty visual-motor coordination was a behavioral symptom of brain damage.

Werner and Strauss popularized the notion that adequate conceptual development is dependent on perceptual and motor development.

A prominent proponent of the importance of visual-motor integration to academic success is Getman. His visuomotor theory (Getman, 1965; Getman, Kane, & McKee, 1968) outlines the successive stages of visual-motor integration, including innate response, general motor systems, special motor systems, ocular motor systems, speech motor systems, visualization systems, vision or perception, and cognition. Each of these levels is conceptualized as more precise and exacting than the preceding one, with complete mastery at each stage required before completion of subsequent systems can be achieved. Therefore, within this model, academic learning must be preceded by extensive and successful motor learning. The implication is that learning-disabled children need exercise in the base levels of motor and visual-motor development before academics can be addressed.

Another proponent of the relation between learning disabilities and visual-motor integration is Kephart (1960, 1971), who theorized that breakdowns may occur at three key points in the development of visual-motor coordination. A child may fail to develop (1) an internal awareness of laterality of the left and right sides of the body and their differences; (2) left-right awareness within the body, which could lead to directionality problems; and (3) visual-motor coordination at the stage when the hand leads the eye. As Getman, Kephart believes that the education of the perceptually motor-disabled child must address motoric and visual development before conceptual skills.

Several teaching programs based on visual-motor integration theory have been designed, including Getman's Developing Learning Readiness: A Visual-Motor Tactile Skills Program. This program comprises activities in six areas: general coordination, balance, eye-hand coordination, eye movement, form recognition, and visual memory. Additionally, tests addressing visual-motor integration have been developed. One widely used measure, Beery and Buktenica's Developmental Test of Visual Motor Integration (1967), which requires examinees to reproduce geometric forms, is a norm-referenced test of the degree to which visual perception and motor behavior are integrated in young children.

Visual-motor integration assessment and remediation have been the focus of research. Results indicate the inability of visual-motor assessment to elucidate etiology of or instructional procedures for learning disabilities. Additionally, research has failed to support the effectiveness of visual-motor training for improving academic learning (Mann, 1979).

REFERENCES

Beery, K. D., & Buktenica, N. A. (1967). *Developmental Test of Visual-Motor Integration Student Test Booklet.* Chicago: Follett.

Getman, G. N. (1965). The visuomotor complex in the acquisition of learning skills. In J. Hellmuth (Ed.), *Learning disorders* (Vol. 1). Seattle, WA: Special Child.

Getman, G. N., Kane, E. R., & McKee, G. W. (1968). *Developing learning readiness: A visual-motor tactile skills program.* Manchester Webster Division, McGraw-Hill.

Kephart, N. C. (1960). *The slow learner in the classroom.* Columbus, OH: Merrill.

Kephart, N. C. (1971). *The slow learner in the classroom* (2nd ed.). Columbus, OH: Merrill.

Lerner, J. W. (1985). *Learning disabilities: Theories, diagnosis, and teaching strategies* (4th ed.). Boston: Houghton Mifflin.

Mann, L. (1979). *On the trail of process.* New York: Grune & Stratton.

Strauss, A. A., & Werner, H. (1941). The mental organization of the brain injured mentally defective child. *American Journal of Psychiatry, 97,* 1194–1202.

LYNN S. FUCHS
DOUGLAS FUCHS
Peabody College, Vanderbilt University

DIAGNOSTIC PRESCRIPTIVE TEACHING
DYSLEXIA
VISUAL-MOTOR AND VISUAL-PERCEPTUAL PROBLEMS

VISUAL PERCEPTION AND DISCRIMINATION

Visual perception is a difficult concept to define and measure because it involves complex interactions between the individual and the environment. Basically, visual perception and discrimination is the ability to interpret what is seen. Frostig and Horne (1973) describe it as the ability to recognize stimuli and to differentiate among them.

Visual-perceptual problems are concerned with disabilities that occur despite the fact that a child has physiologically healthy eyes. A child may have 20/20 visual acuity and adequate eye muscle control, and still have visual perceptual problems. These disabilities may include problems in form perception: discriminating the shapes of letters, numbers, pictures, or objects; position in space: discriminating the spatial orientation—left/right, top/bottom, etc.—of letters or words; visual closure: discriminating pictures or words with parts missing; and figure-ground discrimination: the ability to perceive a figure as distinct from the background (Hallahan, Kauffman, & Lloyd, 1985). A child who has problems with visual perception and discrimination may have difficulty in school because most academic activities require good visual-perceptual skills. In particular, the areas of math and reading will be difficult for the child who cannot distinguish between a multiplication and an addition sign, or who has difficulty discriminating pictures, letters, numbers, or words. During the early stages of a child's development, these problems are normal, but as a child matures, parents and teachers should become concerned if these difficulties persist.

The measurement of visual perception is complicated since many of the instruments used require a copying or drawing response. Tests such as the Bender-Gestalt Test, the coding subtest of the Wechsler Scales of Intelligence, and the Developmental Test of Visual-Motor Integration all require motor responses and are based on the assumption that the reproduced form is indicative of the individual's visual perception of the shape. However, Goldstein and Scheerer (1959) consider visual-perceptual and visual-motor deficits as separate entities. According to this perspective, if a child copies a figure incorrectly, a teacher cannot assume that the child has a visual-perceptual problem; additional information is needed. When a child copies a figure incorrectly, but can correctly select a picture of the figure from a group of choices, then there is an indication that the problem may be a visual-motor one. However, if the child selects an incorrect choice, then there is evidence that there may be a visual-perceptual difficulty (Hallahan et al., 1985). Some tests that measure visual perception and discrimination without requiring a drawing response include the Motor-Free Visual Perceptual Test, the Visual Reception and Visual Closure subtests of the Illinois Test of Psycholinguistic Abilities, the discrimination of forms and mutilated pictures subtests of the Stanford-Binet, and the Position in Space subtest of the Frostig Developmental Test of Visual Perception.

REFERENCES

Frostig, M., & Horne, D. (1973). *Frostig program for the development of visual perception.* Chicago: Follett.

Goldstein, K., & Scheerer, M. (1959). Abstract and concrete behavior: An experimental study with special tests. *Psychological Monographs, 83.*

Hallahan, D., Kauffman, J., & Lloyd, J. (1985). *Introduction to learning disabilities* (2nd ed.). Englewood Cliffs, NJ: Prentice-Hall.

DEBORAH C. MAY
*State University of New York,
Albany*

DONALD S. MAROZAS
*State University of New York,
Geneseo*

BENDER-GESTALT TEST
ILLINOIS TEST OF PSYCHOLINGUISTIC ABILITIES
VISUAL-MOTOR PERCEPTION AND DISCRIMINATION

VISUAL TRAINING

See VISION TRAINING.

VISUOMOTOR COMPLEX

Visuomotor complex is a term used by Getman (1965) to describe his model of the development of the visuomotor system and its relationship to the acquisition of learning skills. This model reflects Getman's training as an optometrist by emphasizing the visual aspects of perception. It illustrates the developmental sequences that a child progresses through while acquiring visual-perceptual and motor skills, and emphasizes that each successive stage is dependent on earlier stages of development.

The six systems of learning levels in this model are (from the lowest to the highest) the innate response system, the general motor system, the special motor system, the ocular motor system, the speech-motor system, and the visualization system. These systems all contribute to vision or the perceptual event that results in cognition when many perceptions are integrated (Lerner, 1971).

This visuomotor complex requires solid learning at each level before proceeding to the next level. Getman believes that children will not succeed in educational programs if they do not have adequate experiences in the lower systems of development. A teaching program, Developing Learning Readiness: A Visual-Motor Tactile Skills Program (Getman, Kane, & McKee, 1968), is based on this model.

This visuomotor model has been criticized for simplifying learning, overemphasizing the role of vision, neglecting the role of language, speech, and feedback, and not providing empirical evidence for the theory (Lerner, 1971; Myers & Hammill, 1969).

REFERENCES

Getman, G. (1965). The visuomotor complex in the acquisition of learning skills. In J. Hellmuth (Ed.), *Learning disorders* (Vol. 1, pp. 49–76). Seattle, WA: Special Child.

Getman, G., Kane, E., & McKee, G. (1968). *Developing learning readiness: A visual-motor tactile skills program.* Manchester, MO: Webster Division, McGraw-Hill.

Lerner, J. (1971). *Children with learning disabilities.* Boston: Houghton Mifflin.

Myers, P., & Hammill, D. (1969). *Methods for learning disorders.* New York: Wiley.

DEBORAH C. MAY
*State University of New York,
Albany*

VISUAL PERCEPTION AND DISCRIMINATION
VISUAL TRAINING

VOCABULARY DEVELOPMENT

The knowledge of vocabulary, that is, the ability to recognize words and understand their meanings, is recognized as possibly the most important factor in being able to use and understand spoken and written language. Vocabulary knowledge is very closely associated with the ability to comprehend what is heard or read, and may be related to general intelligence and reasoning ability.

According to Harris (1970), children develop a variety of types of vocabulary knowledge in a developmental sequence. First they develop a hearing vocabulary, or the ability to respond to spoken words even before they themselves are able to use speech. For a number of years children are able to respond to more words that they hear than words that they are able to use themselves. Following the appropriate development of a hearing vocabulary, children begin to acquire emerging reading skills and a reading vocabulary—words that they are able to recognize in print and know the meanings of in context. Gradually, the developing reader is able to recognize more words in print and is able to use more words than in the speaking and writing vocabulary. Harris has explained that a child's total vocabulary involves all of the words that he or she can eventually understand and use in all the communications skills, including listening, speaking, reading, and writing.

The significance of a varied and well-developed vocabulary cannot be overemphasized, according to Johnson and Pearson (1984). They have identified and explained the reading process as a communication between an author and a reader. That communication is successful only when the reader is able to understand the author's original intent by recognizing and understanding the vocabulary that the author uses. It follows, then, that in order to be a fluent, proficient, and successful reader, it is necessary to possess a rich and varied vocabulary and word knowledge background.

General vocabulary development, and the ability to recognize words either in isolation or in context, have a common link in the diversity of words that the reader can both understand and use. Many of the words that the developing learner and reader uses and understands have been with him or her from early years; other words are learned and developed as they are used in the context of school-related activities. Therefore, while a rich experiential background during the preschool years is certainly a requisite for later vocabulary learning, much of the vocabulary development that the child experiences is accomplished in school. According to Smith and Johnson (1980), Stauffer (1969), and Johnson and Pearson (1984), a meaningful vocabulary is developed through reading- and writing-related activities in a variety of ways. These include the development of a basic sight vocabulary, various word identification strategies, including phonics, structural analysis, context clues, and instruction in understanding the deeper meanings of words. Through the activities outlined in basal reading programs, and occasionally through the use of content area materials, students are taught to use and understand synonyms, antonyms, homophones, and multiple meaning words. They also are taught to use the various resources such as dictionaries and thesauruses for determining word meaning.

One of the best ways to learn new words and what they mean is to become involved with reading and listening. Moffett and Wagner (1983) have stated that children need to become habitual readers. They must immerse themselves in a variety of reading and listening activities that will enable them to experience words in a variety of contexts and allow them to make generalizations about the meanings of words and how they may be used. Particularly during the elementary years, they argue, much of schooling must be involved with providing children with a variety of language-related situations that require them to be actively engaged in the production and reception of language in both oral and written forms. As the child becomes more engaged in reading and writing activities, preferably related to different content areas, not only is general vocabulary knowledge increased, but reasoning ability and conceptual development are enhanced.

The essence of reading and writing is communication, and the crucial variable in communication seems to be vocabulary knowledge. What distinguishes the fluent, successful reader from the poor reader seems to be a knowledge of words and what they mean. A successful and appropriate program of vocabulary development in the school, coupled with the child's preschool experiential background, may provide that key ingredient to becoming a successful language user. Johnson and Pearson (1984) give a complete and detailed account of how to provide an appropriate program of vocabulary development in school.

REFERENCES

Harris, A. J. (1970). *How to increase reading ability* (5th ed.). New York: McKay.

Johnson, D. D., & Pearson, P. D. (1984). *Teaching reading vocabulary* (2nd ed.). New York: Holt, Rinehart, & Winston.

Moffett, J., & Wagner, B. J. (1983). *Student centered language arts and reading, K–13: A handbook for teachers* (3rd ed.). Boston: Houghton Mifflin.

Smith, R. J., & Johnson, D. D. (1980). *Teaching children to read* (2nd ed.). Reading, MA: Addison-Wesley.

Stauffer, R. G. (1969). *Directing reading maturity as a cognitive process*. New York: Harper & Row.

JOHN M. EELLS
*Souderton Area School District,
Souderton, Pennsylvania*

INTELLIGENCE
READING
READING REMEDIATION

VOCATIONAL EDUCATION

The goal of vocational education programs is to prepare students to enter the world of work. Astuto (1982) described vocational programs as focusing on the development of basic academic skills, good work habits, personally meaningful work values, self-understanding and identification of preferences, skills and aptitudes, occupational opportunities, the ability to plan and make career decisions, and the locating and securing of employment.

The basic program components for vocational education are recognized as remedial basic skills, specific job training, personal and social adjustment skills, career information, modified content in subject areas, and on-the-job training. Further, Ondell and Hardin (1981) delineated four types of occupational activities that would be part of a vocational program: paid work experience during the day, paid work experience after school hours, unpaid work observation, and in-school vocational laboratory.

From a historical perspective, the first piece of legislation to address the vocational educational needs of the handicapped was the Vocational Education Act of 1963 (PL 88-210). The Educational Amendments of 1976 (PL 94-482) strengthened provisions for handicapped youths in vocational education.

According to Ondell and Hardin (1981), legislation promoting vocational education and the rights of the handicapped has included the Smith-Hughes Act of 1917, which provided funds for vocational education in public schools; the Civilian Rehabilitation Act of 1920, which assigned responsibility for the administration of vocational rehabilitation to state boards of vocational education; the Vocational Rehabilitation Amendments of 1943, which expanded the 1920 act to include mentally and emotionally handicapped persons; the Vocational Education Act of 1963, which provided occupational training for persons with special needs and allowed some of a state's allotment to be used in funding these programs; the Vocational Amendments of 1965, which removed the responsibility for administration of these programs from state boards; and the Vocational Amendments of 1968, which included more specific terminology and specified that 10% of the monies received by the state be set aside for the vocational education of the handicapped. With these monies many specifically designed programs for the handicapped were started, thus expanding the area of vocational education to encompass special groups (pp. 2–3).

The Vocational Education Act, as amended in 1976 (PL 94-482, Title II), designated vocational education for handicapped persons as a national priority. This mandated that 10% of federal monies be used, in part, to pay up to 50% of the cost of additional services handicapped students need to succeed in vocational education.

Public Law 94-142 has unequivocally established that every handicapped youth be given the opportunity to participate in free and appropriate vocational education programs. According to Greenan (1982), the law states that

Vocational education means organized education programs which are directly related to the preparation of individuals for paid or unpaid employment, or for additional preparation for a career requiring other than a baccalaureate or advanced degree. (121a.14(b)(3))

And in addition

vocational education is "included as special education" if it consists of specially designed instruction, at no cost to the parents, to meet the unique needs of a handicapped child. [121.14(a)(3)]

Most recently, on October 19, 1984, the Carl D. Perkins Vocational Education Act, PL 98-524, was signed; it replaced the Vocational Education Act of 1963. The new act ordered federal involvement in vocational education around two broad themes. First, equal access to vocational education must be provided to handicapped persons. Second, the quality of vocational education must be improved. The act specifies that 10% of its funds must be allocated for vocational education services and activities designed to meet the special needs of, and enhance the participation of, handicapped individuals. This is accomplished through allotments to local school districts on a formula basis. Each local school district has to comply with five prescriptive requirements. The first of these is to provide information to handicapped students and parents concerning opportunities available in vocational education at least 1 year before the student enters the grade in which vocational education programs are first generally available, but in no event later than the beginning of ninth grade. Each handicapped student who enrolls in a vocational education program shall receive an assessment of his or her interests, abilities, and special needs; special services, including adaptation of curriculum; guidance, counseling, and career development activities conducted by professionally trained counselors; and counseling services designed to facilitate the transition from school to postsecondary environments.

Vocational education for students with disabilities generally entails at least two different approaches, depending on the severity of the disability. According to the U.S. Department of Education (1985), a major thrust at the state level has been to provide the necessary supportive services to handicapped persons enrolled in regular vocational education programs.

As of the last year for which data are available (1981–1982), approximately 78% of students with disabilities enrolled in vocational education are mainstreamed and may receive special or additional services. The remaining 22% of students may be considered as having more moderate to severe disabilities. Vocational education for these students is distinguished by strategies developed by Brown et al. (1983).

A leading example of a vocational education framework for youngsters with severe disabilities can be found in the Madison Metropolitan School District. Since 1976 severely handicapped students have been provided with systematic vocational training in nonsheltered community sites. There are two principles on which this framework was developed: that vocational training should occur in nonsheltered, nonschool environments and that all students must be taught to engage in meaningful work (Sweet et al., 1982).

In summary, Astuto (1982) discussed six aspects that defined excellence in vocational education programs: career exploration; vocational assessment/evaluation; training; work experience; follow-up with on-the-job placement; and advocacy. Also of importance were partnerships between vocational and special education as well as interagency agreement.

REFERENCES

Astuto, T. A. (1982). *Vocational education programs and services for high school handicapped students*. Bloomington: Council of Administrators of Special Education, Indiana University.

Brown, L., Shirago, B., Ford, A., Van Deventer, P., Nisbet, S., Loomis, R., & Sweet, M. (1983). Teaching severely handicapped students to perform meaningful work in nonsheltered vocational environments. In L. Brown, A. Ford, S. Nisbet, M. Sweet, B. Shiraga, & R. Loomis (Eds.), *Educational programs for severely handicapped students* (Vol. 13, pp. 1–100). Madison, WI: Madison Metropolitan School District.

Greenan, J. P. (1982). State planning for vocational/special education personnel development. *Teacher Education & Special Education, 5*(4), 69–76.

Ondell, J. T., & Hardin, L. (1981). *Vocational education programming for the handicapped*. Bloomington: Council of Administrators of Special Education, Indiana University.

Sweet, M., Shiraga, B., Fred, A., Nisbet, J., Graff, S., & Loomis, R. (1982). Are ecological strategies applicable for severely multihandicapped students? In L. Brown, J. Nisbet, A. Ford, M. Sweet, B. Shiraga, & L. Gruenewald (Eds.), *Educational programs for severely handicapped students* (Vol. 12, pp. 99–130). Madison, WI: Madison Metropolitan School District.

U.S. Department of Education. (1985). *Seventh annual report to Congress on the implementation of the Education of the Handicapped Act*. Washington, DC: U.S. Office of Special Education and Rehabilitative Services, Division of Educational Services.

EILEEN McCARTHY
*University of Wisconsin,
Madison*

**REHABILITATION
VOCATIONAL EVALUATION
VOCATIONAL TRAINING OF THE HANDICAPPED**

VOCATIONAL EDUCATION ACT OF 1963

Public Law 88-210, the Vocational Education Act of 1963, provided priority allotments of state funds for vocational education programs for the handicapped. Under 20 USCS, Section 2310, for each fiscal year, at least 10% of each state's allotments under Section 103 (20 USCS Section 2303) from appropriations made under Section 102(a) (20 USCS, Section 2303(a)) shall be used to pay up to 50% of the cost of programs, services, and activities under Subpart 2 (20 USCS, Section 2330 et seq.) and of program improvement and support services under Subpart 3 (20 USCS, Section 2350 et seq.) for handicapped persons.

DANIEL R. PAULSON
University of Wisconsin, Stout

**REHABILITATION
VOCATIONAL TRAINING OF THE HANDICAPPED**

VOCATIONAL EVALUATION

Vocational evaluation is a term that encompasses the processes undertaken in determining eligibility and appropriate program plans for students entering vocational education. Specific components and processes used in vocational evaluation include assessment of skills, aptitude, interests, work behaviors, social skills, and physical capabilities (Leconte, 1985; Levinson & Capps, 1985; Peterson, 1985; Rosenberg & Tesolowski, 1982). The area of vocational assessment is affected by the Carl Perkins Vocational Education Act of 1984, which mandates that schools provide each handicapped or disadvantaged student who enrolls in a vocational education program an assessment of the individual's interests, abilities, and special needs with respect to the successful completion of the vocational education program (Cobb and Larkin, 1985).

The terms vocational evaluation and vocational assessment are often used interchangeably. Although Leconte (1985) indicated that the Division on Career Development (DCD) of the Council for Exceptional Children (CEC) does not discriminate between vocational evaluation and vocational assessment, he differentiated between the two terms as follows: vocational assessment is an ongoing process carried out by professionals from many different disciplines, and information from vocational assessment is incorporated into a student's total educational program; vocational evaluation is an in-depth process conducted by a trained vocational evaluator, usually in a vocational evaluation center.

School personnel have not been able to agree on a term or title to represent the realm of student assessment in vocational education. When first introduced into school settings, programs were called vocational evaluation based on the service's origin in vocational rehabilitation. After PL 94-142, the service was aligned with services for special education and different forms of evaluation were frequently referred to as vocational assessment. In essence, vocational evaluation has been delineated as a more intensive, time-limited service than vocational assessment. Although the term vocational evaluation represents the broad umbrella under which vocational assessment is subsumed, for our purposes the terms will be referred to as vocational evaluation/assessment.

The purposes and goals are well defined and agreed on throughout the literature. Vocational assessment is a process that

Measures skills, attitudes, interests, and physical abilities

Predicts success in occupational placements

Prescribes the necessary program plan needed to reach the objectives

Explores interests and matches them with abilities

Observes behavioral changes

Levinson and Capps (1985) discussed vocational assessment as a process that yields critical information with which vocational programming decisions may be made. They include the identification of appropriate goals and instructional methods in the process.

Peterson (1985) suggested six guidelines for effective vocational assessment: (1) use trained personnel; (2) develop and use locally developed work samples; (3) obtain access to a vocational evaluation center; (4) plan to develop and expand vocational assessment in phases with a team; (5) ascertain that vocational assessment is instructionally relevant and useful; and (6) ensure that the vocational assessment is used for vocational guidance and the identification of appropriate career and vocational service.

Peterson (1985) stated that vocational assessment can be "a powerful tool in the education of special students" since it can provide a link between special education or Chapter 1 services and vocational education. The challenge to fully operationalize these services with respect to students with disabilities remains.

REFERENCES

Cobb, R. B., & Larkin, D. (1985). Assessment and placement of handicapped pupils into secondary vocational education programs. *Focus on Exceptional Children, 17*(7), 1–14.

Leconte, P. (1985, December). *Vocational assessment of the special needs learner: A vocational education perspective.* Paper presented at the meeting of the American Vocational Association Convention, Atlanta, GA.

Levinson, E. M., & Capps, C. F. (1985). Vocational assessment and special education triennial reevaluations at the secondary school level. *Psychology in the Schools, 22*, 283–292.

Peterson, M. (1985, December). *Vocational assessment of special students: A comprehensive developmental approach.* Paper presented at the meeting of the American Vocational Association Convention, Atlanta, GA.

Rosenberg, H., & Tesolowski, D. G. (1982). Assessment of critical

vocational behaviors. *Career Development for Exceptional Individuals, 5*, 25–37.

EILEEN F. McCARTHY
*University of Wisconsin,
Madison*

**VOCATIONAL REHABILITATION
VOCATIONAL REHABILITATION COUNSELOR
VOCATIONAL TRAINING OF THE HANDICAPPED**

VOCATIONAL REHABILITATION ACT OF 1973

Section 504 of what is commonly called the Rehabilitation Act is frequently cited as an important precursor to the passage of PL 94-142 two years later (Bersoff, 1982). Section 504, among other things, protects the rights of handicapped children and precludes discrimination in employment and education. The stipulations of the Rehabilitation Act apply to the programs receiving federal financial assistance.

The Rehabilitation Act was cited in the noted *Larry P.* v. *Riles* decision by Judge Peckham in 1979. This decision cited the state as being in noncompliance with Section 504 in its use of intelligence tests for making placement decisions in special education. Certainly, the Rehabilitation Act of 1973 has had an important impact on special education practice by encouraging more sophisticated and humane treatment of handicapped children.

REFERENCE

Bersoff, D. N. (1982). The legal regulation of school psychology. In C. R. Reynolds & T. B. Gutkin (Eds.), *The handbook of school psychology.* New York: Wiley.

RANDY W. KAMPHAUS
Eastern Kentucky University

**EDUCATION FOR ALL HANDICAPPED CHILDREN ACT OF 1975
LARRY P.**

VOCATIONAL REHABILITATION COUNSELING

According to the 1984–1985 edition of the *Occupational Outlook Handbook,* "Rehabilitation counselors assist physically, mentally, emotionally, or socially handicapped individuals to become self-sufficient and productive citizens." While this general definition is correct, the actual activities engaged in by rehabilitation counselors and the resources available to them vary considerably depending on their work setting.

Today there are approximately 19,000 rehabilitation counselors in the United States, over half of whom work in agencies supported by federal and state funds (Wright, 1980). The prototypical rehabilitation counselor works for one of the state Department of Vocational Rehabilitation (DVR) agencies and places primary emphasis on the vocational adjustment of disabled clients who are adjudged to have the potential for gainful employment. Rehabilitation counselors also work in a wide variety of allied settings such as sheltered workshops, centers for the developmentally disabled, rehabilitation centers, Veterans' Administration programs, employment services, alcohol and drug abuse programs, halfway houses, insurance companies, and private for-profit organizations that specialize in the rehabilitation of industrially injured clients. New developments in the rehabilitation counselor's role are seen in recent movements to provide independent living skills to the severely disabled and assistance to disabled youths as they make the transition from school to the world of work.

The profession of rehabilitation counseling emerged with the passage of PL 236 (Smith-Fess Act) in 1920, which established the civilian vocational rehabilitation program in the United States. However, it was not until the passage of PL 565 in 1954 that federal funds were available to encourage formal academic training for rehabilitation personnel. There are now approximately 90 master's degree programs in rehabilitation counseling offered by universities and colleges throughout the country (Rubin & Roessler, 1983). There are also numerous bachelor's and doctoral programs available in rehabilitation. Today the professional identity of the rehabilitation counselor is well established and there is consensus regarding an appropriate educational curriculum. The knowledge base and competencies for this profession are reflected in the following core subjects that are taught in most rehabilitation counselor training programs: history and philosophy of rehabilitation, vocational and personal counseling, physical disabilities, mental retardation, mental illness, psychosocial implications of disability, psychological testing, vocational evaluation, occupational information and employment trends, community resources, job placement, and supervised internships.

The most prominent professional organizations for rehabilitation counselors are the National Rehabilitation Association, the National Rehabilitation Counseling Association, and the American Rehabilitation Counseling Association. Within the past decade, certification procedures for rehabilitation counselors have been established through the efforts of various professional organizations. Certification is based on a combination of education, experience, and the successful completion of a national examination. While certification procedures do guarantee minimum standards of competency, they may be criticized for restricting entrance into the profession by those who are otherwise qualified but lack formal credentials. Many rehabilitation employers expect applicants to be certified, but this is by no means universal and the eventual status of certification is unclear at present.

The high social validity of rehabilitation counseling is indicated by the continuing bipartisan congressional support that rehabilitation legislation has enjoyed for over 65 years. Studies estimate that once disabled persons return to work they earn, and pay taxes on, between 8 and 33 times the amount of money that was spent on their rehabilitation (Bitter, 1979). Additional economic benefits accrue to society from the reductions in welfare, disability, and medical assistance payments after the disabled person enters the work force. In human terms, state DVR agencies rehabilitate between 200,000 and 300,000 handicapped persons per year. The dignity and self-esteem these individuals feel when they become contributing members of society cannot be measured in dollars.

REFERENCES

Bitter, J. A. (1979). *Introduction to rehabilitation.* St. Louis: Mosby.

Bureau of Labor Statistics. (1984). *Occupational outlook handbook: 1984–1985 edition (Bulletin 2205).* Washington, DC: U.S. Department of Labor.

Rubin, S. E. & Roessler, R. T. (1983). *Foundations of the vocational rehabilitation process* (2nd ed.). Austin, TX: Pro-Ed.

Wright, G. N. (1980). *Total rehabilitation.* Boston: Little, Brown.

JOHN D. SEE
University of Wisconsin, Stout

VOCATIONAL EVALUATION
VOCATIONAL TRAINING OF HANDICAPPED

VOCATIONAL TRAINING OF HANDICAPPED

See VOCATIONAL EDUCATION.

VOCATIONAL VILLAGE

A vocational village is a cloistered community in which handicapped and nonhandicapped persons live and work. It is often referred to as a sheltered village. There is a strong work ethic in the community. The setting is not usually designed for transition but rather as a permanent living/working arrangement for the handicapped. There is usually a deep religious undertone in such villages and a majority of the time they are church sponsored. The non-handicapped residents of the village are often volunteer workers who have made a long-term commitment to the village. There are also some nonhandicapped workers who are students working in practium arrangements or in work-study activities. Baker, Seltzer, and Seltzer (1977) explain that

> common to all sheltered villages is the segregation of the retarded person from the outside community and the implicit view that the retarded adult is better off in an environment that shelters him/her from many of the potential failures and frustrations of life in the outside community. (p. 109)

It is a delivery model that espouses the principle of separate but equal.

REFERENCES

Baker, B. L., Seltzer, G. B., & Seltzer, M. M. (1977). *As close as possible: Community residences for retarded adults.* Boston: Little, Brown.

ROBERT A. SEDLAK
University of Wisconsin, Stout

COMMUNITY PLACEMENT
COMMUNITY RESIDENTIAL PROGRAMS
SHELTERED WORKSHOPS

VOICE DISORDERS

Various voice disorders can occur in childhood. Some of them are similar to those observed in adults. Others are typical of children. For instance, mutational falsetto is a condition that appears only in male adolescents, since it is a failure to change from the high-pitched voice of preadolescence to the low-pitched voice of adolescence and adulthood. Another disorder, screamer's nodules, though not unknown in adults, is more frequent in children. Vocal nodules are small protuberances that appear on the free margin of the vocal folds as a result of vocal abuse. They are not infrequent in cheerleaders (Boone, 1971).

Psychogenic aphonia may also be observed in children. As a result of psychological stress, the child loses the ability to produce voice, although the larynx is intact. Psychogenic aphonia, also called hysterical aphonia, is a psychosomatic disorder (Aronson, 1985).

On the other hand, children may present with a number of laryngeal anomalies or lesions that result in dysphonia, i.e., breathy or harsh voice quality. For instance, children who become comatose and have to be ventilated after severe head trauma may have a hoarse voice as a consequence of damage caused to their laryngeal cartilages by the tube used to assist their respiration.

Voice disorders in children deserve the full attention of parents, educators, and physicians. Irreversible damage to the larynx may occur if voice problems are not dealt with promptly and by competent clinicians.

REFERENCES

Aronson, A. (1985), *Clinical voice disorders.* New York: Thieme.
Boone, D. (1971). *The voice and voice therapy.* Englewood Cliffs, NJ: Prentice-Hall.

YVAN LEBRUN
School of Medicine, V.U.B.,
Brussels, Belgium

SPEECH

VOLTA REVIEW

The Volta Review was founded in 1898. It is published seven times a year, with a monograph issue in September. This publication is a product of the Alexander Graham Bell Association for the Deaf, which was founded by Alexander Graham Bell in 1890. Bell believed that people with hearing losses could be taught to speak and through lip reading could learn to understand others. The Alexander Graham Bell Association is a nonprofit organization that serves as an information center for the hearing impaired.

Only articles devoted to the education, rehabilitation, and communicative development of hearing-impaired people are published by *The Volta Review*. The target audience includes teachers of the hearing impaired; professionals in the fields of education, speech, audiology, language, otology, and psychology; parents of the hearing impaired; and hearing-impaired adults. The articles are reviewed by a panel for possible publication. *The Volta Review* is 64 pages in length and includes advertisements and illustrations. Topics of articles include issues relating to hearing impairment such as language development, parental concerns, medical/technical and psychosocial issues, teaching, and computers.

REBECCA BAILEY
Texas A&M University

DEAF
DEAF EDUCATION

VOLUNTARY AGENCIES

Voluntary agencies are those agencies that use volunteers to deliver services or to serve on decision-making boards. Volunteers are those members of the community who give their time on a nonpay basis to agencies that serve particular groups in an area. Approximately 84 million Americans serve as volunteers in such agencies each year (Shtulman, 1985). Women have provided a large portion of volunteer service but the entry of large numbers of women into the work force has limited their availability for volunteer service. However, an increasingly active senior citizen population is providing a pool of dependable, dedicated volunteers. Another developing source is through the work place. Some firms make it possible for their employees to have released time for community service; these firms say that this "loaned executive" program contributes to a better work force through the opportunity for workers to apply or develop skills, a lower rate of absenteeism, and increased productivity (United Way, 1985).

Volunteers on agency governing boards make decisions on the purchase of property and capital equipment, organizational policy, specific human services that will be available in the community, allocation of funds to other agencies (United Way, foundations, etc.) or within their own agency, and fund-raising.

REFERENCES

Shtulman, J. (1985). *A question-and-answer session on voluntarism*. Holyoke, MA: Transcript-Telegram.

United Way. (1985). *Volunteer notes*. Alexandria, VA: United Way of America

DENISE M. SEDLAK
United Way of Dunn County,
Menomonie, Wisconsin

ADVOCACY FOR HANDICAPPED CHILDREN
LIBRARY SERVICES FOR THE HANDICAPPED

VON RECKLINGHAUSEN, FRIEDRICH (1833–1910)

Friedrich von Recklinghausen, a German pathologist, was a major contributor to the development of pathological anatomy as a branch of medicine. He is best known for his description, in 1863, of neurofibromatosis, or von Recklinghausen's disease, characterized by multiple small tumors affecting the subcutaneous nerves. The disease is hereditary and is associated with mental retardation.

REFERENCES

Talbott, J. H. (1970). *A biographical history of medicine*. Orlando, FL: Grune & Stratton.

von Recklinghausen, F. (1962). Multiple fibromas of the skin and multiple neuromas. In E. R. Long (Trans.), *Selected readings in pathology* (2nd ed.). Springfield, IL: Thomas.

PAUL IRVINE
Katonah, New York

NEUROFIBRAMATOSIS
MENTAL RETARDATION

VYGOTSKY, LEV S. (1896–1934)

Lev S. Vygotsky was a Soviet psychologist and semiotician. His work had a tremendous impact on the development of psychology in the Soviet Union and is currently attracting a great deal of interest outside the Soviet Union as well (Wertsch, 1985a, 1985b).

In the West, Vygotsky is known primarily for his work on the relationship between the development of thinking and speech in ontogenesis (Vygotsky, 1962, 1978, in press a). In Vygotsky's view, the more complex forms of human thinking, memory, and attention depend on the individual's mastery of historically and culturally developed means of organizing and mediating mental activity. Vygotsky argued that words and speech are first used in social interaction to organize and mediate the mental activity of several individuals working cooperatively on a task, and that these same linguistic means are later appropriated by the individual and internalized to be used in organizing and mediating his or her mental activity when working alone on similar tasks. In this sense, Vygotsky felt that certain kinds of social interaction between children and adults (or more competent peers) can create a "zone of proximal development" that raises the level of the child's cognitive functioning in the context of social interaction and helps move the child toward the next or proximal stage of independent functioning.

For Vygotsky, however, this work was only part of a much broader program of theory and research that was concerned with the relationships between historically developed modes of social behavior and the psychological development of the individual in all its aspects (Minick, in press). In the decade following his death, the efforts of his colleagues and students to develop this broader theoretical framework led to the emergence of what is known as the theory of activity, a theoretical and research paradigm that illuminates the work of many contemporary Soviet psychologists.

Vygotsky had a lifelong interest in developing theory, research, and practical intervention techniques relevant to abnormal psychological functioning and development in both children and adults. He wrote extensively on these topics (Vygotsky, in press b) and founded several institutes that continue to play an important role in Soviet work in this area. Through this work and that of colleagues and students such as A. R. Luria (Luria, 1979), Vygotsky played a central role in the development of Soviet work in this domain.

REFERENCES

Luria, A. R. (1979). *The making of mind: A personal account of Soviet psychology*. Cambridge, MA: Harvard University Press.

Minick, N. (in press). The development of Vygotsky's thought. *Introduction to L. S. Vygotsky, Collected works: Problems of general psychology* (Vol. 2) (N. Minick, Trans.). New York: Plenum.

Vygotsky, L. S. (1962). *Thought and language* (E. Hanfmann & G. Vakar, Eds. and Trans). Cambridge, MA: MIT Press. (Original work published 1934).

Vygotsky, L. S. (1978). *Mind in society* (M. Cole, V. John-Steiner, S. Scribner, & E. Souberman, Eds.). Cambridge, MA: Harvard University Press.

Vygotsky, L. S. (in press a). Thinking and speech. In V. V. Davydov (Ed.), *L. S. Vygotsky, Collected works: General Psychology* (Vol. 2) (N. Minick, Trans.). New York: Plenum. (Original work published 1934)

Vygotsky, L. S. (1978). (in press b). In A. V. Zaporozhets (Ed.), *L. S. Vygotsky, Collected works: The foundations of defectology* (Vol. 5) (J. Knox, Trans.). New York: Plenum.

Wertsch, J. V. (1985a). *Vygotsky and the social formation of mind.* Cambridge, MA: Harvard University Press.

Wertsch, J. V. (Ed.). (1985b). *Culture, communication, and cognition: Vygotskian perspectives.* New York: Cambridge University Press.

NORRIS MINICK
Center for Psychosocial Studies,
The Spencer Foundation,
Chicago, Illinois

THEORY OF ACTIVITY
ZONE OF PROXIMAL DEVELOPMENT

W

WAIS/WAIS-R

See WECHSLER ADULT INTELLIGENCE SCALE.

WALKER PROBLEM BEHAVIOR IDENTIFICATION CHECKLIST (WBPIC)

The lastest version of the Walker Problem Behavior Identification Checklist (WBPIC) was published in 1983 (Walker, 1983). The most recent edition consists of a teacher problem behavior rating scale for preschool through grade 6. The 50-item checklist contains six scales: acting-out, withdrawal, distractibility, disturbed peer relations, immaturity, and total. Separate forms are provided for boys and girls. The checklist is to be completed by a teacher who has known the child for at least a 2-month period. Raw scores on each scale are converted to T-scores for interpretation. The latest version was standardized on a sample of 1855 children from sites in Oregon and Washington. Norms are presented separately for males and females. The demographic characteristics of the norm group (e.g., socioeconomic status) are not specified in the manual.

Test-retest reliability coefficients for the six scales ranged from .43 to .88. No evidence of interrater agreement is reported. Validity data on the WBPIC are meager, although some discussion of content validity, the degree to which the items are of import to teachers, is presented. Mace (1985), in a review of the WBPIC, cites numerous shortcomings of the psychometric properties of the scales but concludes that it "may be useful for screening and target behavior selection."

REFERENCES

Mace, F. C. (1985). Review of the Walker Problem Behavior Identification Checklist. In J. W. Mitchell (Ed.), *The ninth mental measurements yearbook*. Lincoln: University of Nebraska Press.

Walker, H. M. (1983). *Walker Problem Behavior Identification Checklist*. Los Angeles: Western Psychological Services.

RANDY W. KAMPHAUS
Eastern Kentucky University

ASSESSMENT
BEHAVIORAL ASSESSMENT

WALLIN, JOHN EDWARD WALLACE (1876–1969)

John Edward Wallace Wallin was born on a farm in Page County, Iowa, on January 21, 1876. He received his BA from Augustana College in 1897, his MA from Yale University in 1899, and his PhD from Yale in 1901.

Trained as a clinical psychologist, Wallin developed an interest in the mentally retarded early in his career. Following several academic appointments in psychology and education, he spent a year at the Vineland Training School in New Jersey and, in 1912, established a psychoeducational clinic for the St. Louis public schools. Wallin was a leading proponent of the use of clinical psychology in education, especially as it relates to identification, diagnosis, and prescription for handicapped children.

He went on to serve as director of special education for the Baltimore public schools and as director of special education and mental hygiene in the Delaware Department of Public Instruction. In these administrative positions,

John Edward Wallace Wallin

Wallin worked to establish the principle that the public schools should provide programs for all handicapped children who can be maintained in the community, regardless of degree of handicap. Consistent with this principle, he was a leader in the development of public school programs for the trainable mentally retarded.

During an exceptionally long and productive career, Wallin was affiliated with more than 25 colleges and universities, was director of 8 psychoeducational clinics, and contributed to the literature of psychology and education in over 30 books and 350 articles. Critical, argumentative, and controversial, Wallin was a major force in the development of special education services in the United States. He died on August 5, 1969.

John B. Watson

REFERENCES

Blatte, B. (Ed.). (1968). Markings in the pioneer career of J. E. Wallace Wallin. *Journal of Education, 151,* 3–111.

Jacob, W. (1956). Dr. J. E. Wallace Wallin. *Training School Bulletin, 52,* 250–251.

Wallin, J. E. W. (1955). *Education of mentally handicapped children.* New York: Harper.

Wallin, J. E. W. (1955). *The odyssey of a psychologist: Pioneering experiences in special education, clinical psychology, and mental hygiene.* Wilmington, DE: Author.

PAUL IRVINE
Katonah, New York

VINELAND TRAINING SCHOOL

tional approaches. Watson eventually left the academic world, completing his career as an executive in the field of advertising.

REFERENCES

Skinner, B. F. (1959). John Broadus Watson, behaviorist. *Science, 129,* 197–198.

Watson, J. B. (1919). *Psychology from the standpoint of a behaviorist.* Philadelphia: Lippincott.

PAUL IRVINE
Katonah, New York

BEHAVIOR MODIFICATION
CONDITIONING

WATSON, JOHN B. (1878–1958)

John B. Watson developed and publicized the basic concepts of behaviorism, which in the 1920s became one of the major schools of psychological thought. Watson obtained his PhD at the University of Chicago and continued there as an instructor until 1908, when he accepted a professorship at Johns Hopkins University. Watson's behaviorism explained human behavior in terms of physiological responses to environmental stimuli and psychology as the study of the relationship between the two. Watson sought to make psychology "a purely objective experimental branch of natural science," with conditioning as one of its chief methods.

Watson's zealous environmentalism led him into some extreme positions, such as his assertion that he could train any healthy infant, regardless of its heredity, to become any type of person he might designate: "doctor, lawyer, artist, merchant-chief, and . . . even beggar-man and thief." Hyperbole aside, Watson's behaviorism was a dominant force in American psychology for decades and underlies many of today's behaviorally oriented instruc-

WECHSLER, DAVID (1896–1981)

Known primarily as the author of intelligence scales that played, and continue to play, a critical role in the lives of millions of individuals throughout the world, David Wechsler had a humanistic philosophy about testing as a part of assessment. His professional writing includes more than 60 articles and books that emphasize the importance of motivation, personality, drive, cultural opportunity, and other variables in determining an individual's functional level.

Born in Rumania, Wechsler moved with his family of nine to New York City at age 6. At 20 he completed a BA degree at City College (1916) and an MA the following year at Columbia University under Robert S. Woodworth. The next few years were spent with the armed forces, where Wechsler helped evaluate thousands of recruits, many of whom could not read English and who had little formal schooling. Near the end of his Army tour he studied with Charles Spearman and Karl Pearson in London and then, on a fellowship, with Henri Pieron and Louis Lapique in Paris. These studies provided the foundation for his continuous enthusiasm for the "nonintellective" components of intelligence.

While completing his PhD at Columbia (1925), Wechsler worked as a psychologist in New York City's newly created Bureau of Child Study. After serving as secretary for the Psychological Corporation (1925–1927) and in private clinical practice (1927–1932), Wechsler became chief psychologist at New York's Bellevue Hospital, a post he held for 35 years. In that position he developed the tests that carried both his and the hospital's name in the early editions: the Wechsler-Bellevue Intelligence Scale I (1939) and Scale II (1942), the Wechsler Intelligence Scale for Children (1949), the Wechsler Adult Intelligence Scale (1955), and the Wechsler Preschool and Primary Scale of Intelligence (1967). He continued to help with the revision of his scales in retirement. The utility of the scales has warranted periodic updating by the publisher.

Wechsler believed his most important work to be his article "The Range of Human Capacities" (1930), the seminal work for his book by the same name that was published in 1935 and revised in 1971. A more popular contribution is the concept of a deviation quotient used for reporting adult intelligence test scores in place of mental age and ratio IQ used with the Binet tests for children and youths. Today nearly all cognitive ability tests use standard scores patterned after the deviation IQ.

The many honors Wechsler received from professional groups and universities around the world include the Distinguished Professional Contribution Award from the American Psychological Association (APA) (1973), similar awards from APA's Division of Clinical Psychology (1960) and Division of School Psychology (1973), and an honorary doctorate from the Hebrew University in Jerusalem.

JOSEPH L. FRENCH
Pennsylvania State University

ASSESSMENT
INTELLIGENCE TESTING

WECHSLER ADULT INTELLIGENCE SCALE (WAIS)/WECHSLER ADULT INTELLIGENCE SCALE REVISED (WAIS-R)

The Wechsler Adult Intelligence Scale-Revised (WAIS–R; Wechsler, 1981) extends the line of test development that began with the publication of the Wechsler-Bellevue Intelligence Scale in 1939 and continued with its revision, the Wechsler Adult Intelligence Scale (WAIS), published in 1955 (Wechsler, 1939, 1955). The WAIS–R, like the Wechsler-Bellevue and WAIS before it, is an individually administered test of the intelligence of adolescents and

adults that is commonly used for clinical and neuropsychological assessment. These scales define levels of intelligence by comparing the performance of any individual of any age with the average scores obtained by members of that age group (Wechsler, 1981). The WAIS-R was normed on adults in the 16 to 74-year range.

Wechsler (1981) indicated:

> The WAIS-R, like its predecessor, is composed of 11 tests, verbal and nonverbal. The verbal and nonverbal groups may be administered separately or together to yield, respectively, a verbal, performance, and full-scale IQ. This feature permits one to use the performance section of the scale alone with subjects who are unable to comprehend or manage language, or the verbal section alone with subjects who are visually or motorically handicapped. But more importantly, the use of both verbal and performance tests together affords those examined additional ways to demonstrate their capabilities, and their examiners a greater opportunity to assess the abilities which the tests are designed to appraise. (pp. 9–10).

The sums of WAIS-R scaled scores are converted to verbal, performance, and full-scale IQs for each group. These deviation IQs have the same average of 100 and standard deviation of 15 for every age group. This permits direct comparison of a person's scores with the scores of others with a comparable amount of life experience. Each subtest has a mean of 10 and a standard deviation of 3. However, a reference group of adults ages 10 to 34 was used to determine subtest scaled scores for all adults in the 16 to 74 age range. Consequently, the average scaled score is closer to 9 for several age groups, making profile interpretation unnecessarily difficult (Kaufman, 1985).

The battery of tests included in the original Wechsler-Bellevue Scale and maintained in the WAIS and the present WAIS revision consist of the following subtests: (1) an information test, (2) a general comprehension test, (3) a memory span test (digits forward and backward), (4) an arithmetic reasoning test, (5) a similarities test, (6) a vocabulary test, (7) a picture arrangement test, (8) a picture completion test, (9) a block design test, (10) an object assembly test, and (11) a digit symbol test.

Matarazzo (1972), espousing Wechsler's philosophy, indicated that:

> The grouping of the subtests into verbal (1 to 6) and performance (7 to 11), while intending to emphasize a dichotomy as regards possible types of ability called for by the individual tests, does not imply that these are the only abilities involved in the tests. Nor does it presume that there are different kinds of intelligence, e.g., verbal, manipulative, etc. It merely implies that these are different ways in which intelligence may manifest itself. The subtests are different measures of intelligence, and the dichotomy into verbal and performance areas is only one of several ways in which the tests could be grouped. (p. 196)

A brief description of each of the subtests follows; these descriptions are modifications of those presented by Robb, Bernardoni, and Johnson (1972).

Verbal Scale. A measure of verbal comprehension and expression.

Information. This subtest consists of oral questions that cover a broad range of general information.

Comprehension. This subtest requires individuals to respond to socially relevant questions and to explain proverbs.

Arithmetic. All but the earliest items require the individual to use numerical reasoning to solve oral arithmetic problems without benefit of paper and pencil.

Similarities. Each item contains pairs of words. The examinee is required to indicate how the two things in each pair are alike.

Digit Span. The subject is required to listen to a series of digits given orally by the examiner and then repeat the digits without error. Series of digits are repeated forward in the first portion of the test and backward in the second.

Vocabulary. A list of words ordered in increasing difficulty is used in this test. The examinee is required to provide the meaning of each word as he or she views it on a word list.

Performance Scale is a measure of nonverbal reasoning and visual-motor coordination.

Digit Symbol. In this subtest the examinee is required to rapidly copy symbols that are paired with digits within a 90-second time limit.

Picture Completion. Cards, each having a drawing with an important part missing, are presented. The subject is asked to indicate the missing part.

Block Design. Individuals use nine blocks with red, white, and red-white sides to reproduce abstract designs of increasing difficulty.

Picture Arrangement. Sets of cards, each with a picture on it, are presented in incorrect sequence. The examinee is required to order them in correct sequence so that they tell a story.

Object Assembly. Four cut-up objects are presented to the subject, one at a time, in a disarranged pattern. The subject is required to arrange the pieces to form the whole object.

Wechsler (1981) indicated that most of the content of the WAIS was retained in the revised test. Some items that appeared dated were revised or deleted while some new ones were added. Changes in item difficulties were reflected in the order of administration of retained items in the new scale. About 80% of the WAIS-R items were retained from the 1955 WAIS, either intact or with slight modifications; many of these items were also included on the original 1939 Wechsler-Bellevue, Form I.

On the WAIS, all of the verbal tests are administered, followed by administration of the performance tests. On the WAIS-R, the administration of verbal tests is systematically alternated with the administration of performance tests. Wechsler (1981) indicated: "Experience has shown that varying the tests in this way often helps maintain the subjects' interest" (p. 12).

The WAIS-R manual (Wechsler, 1981) reports that the norms for this test were based on groups considered representative of the U.S. population. A stratified sample was drawn that included representative proportions of various classes of adults. Reports of the 1970 U.S. Census and more recent population reports provided the basis for stratification along the variables of age, sex, race (white-nonwhite), geographic region, occupation, education, and urban-rural residence. Matarazzo (1985) praised the WAIS-R as "probably the best standardized test designed for individual administration which the science and profession of psychology has produced to date" (p. 1703).

Anastasi (1982) noted that the first form of the Wechsler scales, the Wechsler-Bellevue Intelligence Scale, had as a primary objective in its preparation the provision of an intelligence test suitable for adults. In presenting this scale, Wechsler indicated that previously available intelligence tests had been designed primarily for schoolchildren and had been adapted for adult use by adding more difficult items of the same kinds. Therefore, the content of these tests was often of little interest to adults, lacked face validity, and hindered the development of rapport with examinees. Wechsler also noted that overemphasis on speed in most tests handicapped the older person. The undue weight on relatively routine manipulation of words, as well as the inapplicability of mental age norms to adults and the inclusion of few adults in the standardization for individual intelligence tests, were noted as objections to these tests. To overcome these objections, the Wechsler-Bellevue was developed. This scale closely resembled the WAIS and the WAIS-R in form and content.

The WAIS-R has attained a unique status within the field of adult assessment. It is *the* measure of intelligence for adults, appearing in a huge proportion of clinical and neuropsychological assessment batteries. It has a rich clinical history; furthermore, the WAIS-R, WAIS, and Wechsler-Bellevue have been the subjects of thousands of research investigations.

Kaufman (1985) criticized the WAIS-R manual for following "a time-worn mold with limited awareness of clinicians' practical needs or of pertinent psychological research" (p. 1700). Matarazzo (1985) similarly noted that "discussions of a number of . . . psychometric issues which are critical for the evaluation of a test consist of only a paragraph of two for each topic," and that the "discussion of the validity of the WAIS-R fared little better" (pp. 1704–1705). Nevertheless, Kaufman (1985) stressed that the

WAIS-R "embodies the genius of David Wechsler, has impressive ancestors in the WAIS and Wechsler-Bellevue, and was constructed with excellence and considerable psychometric expertise" (p. 1703). Matarazzo (1985) stated, "No other test currently extant, or which is likely to be published in the foreseeable future, is as reliable, valid, or clinically useful for assessing the measurable aspects of adult intelligence" (p. 1703).

REFERENCES

Anastasi, A. (1982). *Psychological testing* (5th ed.). New York: Macmillan.

Cronbach, L. J. (1970). *Essentials of psychological testing* (3rd ed.). New York: Harper & Row.

Kaufman, A. S. (1985). Review of the Wechsler Adult Intelligence Scale—Revised. In J. V. Mitchell (Ed.), *The ninth mental measurements yearbook* (pp. 1699–1703). Lincoln: University of Nebraska Press.

Matarazzo, J. D. (1972). *Wechsler's measurement and appraisal of adult intelligence* (5th ed.). Baltimore, MD: Williams & Wilkins.

Matarazzo, J. D. (1985). Review of Wechsler Adult Intelligence Scale—Revised. In J. V. Mitchell (Ed.), *The ninth mental measurements yearbook* (pp. 1703–1705). Lincoln: University of Nebraska Press.

Robb, G. P., Bernardoni, L. C., & Johnson, R. W. (1972). *Assessment of individual mental ability*. New York: Harper & Row.

Wechsler, D. (1939). *Wechsler-Bellevue Scale of Intelligence*. New York: Psychological Corporation.

Wechsler, D. (1955). *Manual for the Wechsler Adult Intelligence Scale*. New York: Psychological Corporation.

Wechsler, D. (1981). *Wechsler Adult Intelligence Scale—Revised manual*. New York: Harcourt Brace Jovanovich.

ALAN S. KAUFMAN
ANNA H. AVANT
University of Alabama

INTELLIGENCE TESTS
STANFORD BINET
WISC/WISC-R
WPPSI

WECHSLER INTELLIGENCE SCALE FOR CHILDREN (WISC)/WECHSLER INTELLIGENCE SCALE FOR CHILDREN— REVISED (WISC-R)

The Wechsler Intelligence Scale for Children (WISC; Wechsler, 1949) and its successor, the WISC–Revised (WISC–R; Wechsler, 1974) are individually administered intelligence tests for children and adolescents, given by psychologists or other highly trained professionals as part of clinical, psychoeducational, or neuropsychological test batteries. The WISC was first prepared as a downward extension of the original Wechsler-Bellevue Intelligence Scale (Wechsler, 1939), an adult intelligence test (Anastasi, 1982). Many items were taken directly from Form II of the adult scale (Wechsler, 1946).

In the WISC–R, attempts were made to replace or modify adult-oriented WISC items in order to make their content more relevant to childhood experiences; easier items were added to the low end of each subtest. An effort was made to delete items that were possibly differentially familiar to particular groups of children and more females and blacks were included in the various subtests' pictures. Several subtests were lengthened to increase their reliability. The administration and scoring procedures were improved and, unlike the WISC, black children were included in the standardization sample. The WISC–R covers an age range from 6-0 to 16-11; in contrast, the WISC covered the 5 to 15-year age range. A total of 72% of the WISC items were retained in the WISC–R, and many of the original Wechsler-Bellevue II items still survive in the present-day battery.

The WISC–R is presently one of the most widely used of all intelligence tests. It is one of three current Wechsler scales, the others being the Wechsler Preschool and Primary Scale of Intelligence (WPPSI; Wechsler, 1967), and the Wechsler Adult Intelligence Scale—Revised (WAIS–R; Wechsler, 1981). The WISC–R is comprised of 12 subtests. Six of these subtests are contained in the verbal scale, which measures verbal comprehension and expression, and six are included in the performance scale, which assesses nonverbal reasoning and visual-motor coordination. Those subtests that comprise the verbal portion of the test include information, similarities, arithmetic, vocabulary, comprehension, and digit span (optional). Performance subtests consist of picture completion, picture arrangement, block design, object assembly, coding, and mazes (optional).

Wechsler's quest for subtests was governed by his emphasis on the global nature of intelligence. He considered intelligence to be a part of the larger whole of personality itself. Therefore, the Wechsler scales were designed to provide for factors contributing to the total effective intelligence of the individual. The overall IQ derived from the scale denotes an index of general mental ability (Sattler, 1982). Wechsler's verbal-performance dichotomy reflects his recognition of two principal modes of expression of human capabilities. Wechsler (1958) defined intelligence as "the aggregate or global capacity of the individual to act purposefully, to think rationally, and to deal effectively with his environment" (p. 7). Sattler (1982) pointed out that Wechsler's (1958) definition implied that intelligence is comprised of qualitatively different abilities.

The verbal and performance subtests of which the WISC and its revision, the WISC–R, are composed are described in the following list. The abilities that each subtest is listed as measuring are illustrative, not exhaustive.

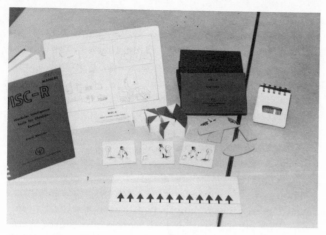

Sample testing materials from the Wechsler Intelligence Scale for Children-Revised.

Verbal Subtests

Information. This subtest is comprised of factual questions to which the child responds verbally. It is a measure of verbal comprehension, acquired knowledge, and long-term memory.

Similarities. Pairs of words are orally presented by the examiner, requiring the child to express verbally the similarity between the two words in each pair. This subtest measures verbal reasoning and concept formation.

Arithmetic. This subtest requires the child to count or perform a mental computation after an item is orally presented by the examiner. The task is a measure of verbal comprehension, acquired knowledge, long-term memory, and numerical reasoning; performance on the arithmetic subtest is affected greatly by distractibility, attention span, and anxiety.

Vocabulary. Words ordered by their level of difficulty are presented orally by the examiner and are defined by the child. Abilities measured by this subtest include verbal comprehension and expression, long-term memory, abstract thinking, and acquired knowledge.

Comprehension. The examiner asks questions of social or moral relevance that the child responds to; several questions require two different reasons or explanations for full credit. This subtest measures verbal comprehension and expression, reasoning, common sense, and social judgment.

Digit span (optional). The child is required to repeat a series of digits after the examiner orally presents them. The task has two portions: repeating the digits in the same order as given by the examiner and repeating the digits in reverse order. Abilities measured include sequential processing and short-term auditory memory; like arith-

metic, digit span performance is subject to the influence of distractibility, attention span, and anxiety.

Performance Subtests

Picture Completion. The child is presented an incomplete picture and indicates the missing part. This subtest measures perceptual organization, spatial ability, and visual organization of meaningful stimuli.

Picture Arrangement. The examiner presents a series of incorrectly arranged pictures and asks the child to rearrange them in correct sequence so that they tell a story. Abilities measured include perceptual organization, nonverbal reasoning, social judgment, and planning ability.

Block Design. The examiner presents models of abstract designs, some three-dimensional but most two-dimensional, that the child tries to copy using red and white blocks. This test measures perceptual organization, spatial ability, and visual perception of abstract stimuli.

Object Assembly. The child assembles a puzzle from parts laid out in a standardized manner. Abilities measured include perceptual organization, holistic processing, synthesis, and visual-motor coordination.

Coding. A paper-and-pencil task, this subtest requires the child to rapidly copy symbols that are paired with digits (ages 8 and above) or with other symbols (ages 6 and 7). Sequencing, visual-motor coordination, and psychomotor speed are measured by this subtest. As was true for arithmetic and digit span, distractibility, attention span, and anxiety affect test performance on coding.

Mazes. With a pencil, the child draws a path through a printed maze after receiving oral instructions. This subtest measures perceptual organization, spatial ability, planning ability, and reasoning.

Each subtest yields a raw score that is converted to a standard score with a mean of 10 and a standard deviation of 3. The WISC–R yields a verbal and performance IQ, as well as a full-scale IQ, all of which are derived from the subtest scores. Wechsler delineated his notion of IQ in 1949 in the manual accompanying the WISC. Still appropriate for the WISC–R, Wechsler (1974) reiterated:

Each person tested is assigned an IQ which, at his age, represents his relative intelligence rating. This IQ, and all others similarly obtained, are deviation IQs since they indicate the amount by which a subject deviated above or below the average performance of individuals of his own age group. The IQ of 100 on the WISC is set equal to the mean total score for each age and the standard deviation is set equal to 15 IQ points. In terms of percentile limits, the highest 1% will have IQs of 135 and above, and the lowest 1% IQs of 65 and below. The middle 50% of children at each age will have IQs from 90 to 110. (p. 4)

Factor-analytic studies have provided empirical support for the verbal-performance dichotomy conceptualized by Wechsler. Kaufman's (1975) factor analysis yielded three factors: verbal comprehension (information, similarities, vocabulary, and comprehension subtests), perceptual organization (picture completion, picture arrangement, block design, object assembly, and mazes), and freedom from distractibility (arithmetic, digit span, and coding). These factors have gained wide acceptance and have been confirmed through a number of subsequent investigations with a plethora of normal and exceptional samples. Although the subtest composition of the first two factors does not correspond perfectly to Wechsler's dichotomy, the congruence is sufficient to regard the verbal and performance IQs as analogous to the first two factors when interpreting test results. A thorough examination of the child's verbal, performance and full-scale IQs, the V-P IQ discrepancy, the distractibility factor, and the profile of subtest scores, should be conducted in order to provide a detailed understanding of the child's strengths and weaknesses and current level of intellectual functioning (Kaufman, 1979). The WISC-R is commonly used for learning disabilities (LD) assessment and neuropsychological evaluation. Research has not supported its use for LD diagnosis (Kaufman, 1981), and the WISC-R's use as a neuropsychological tool has been challenged (Witt & Gresham, 1985).

REFERENCES

Anastasi, A. (1982). *Psychological testing* (5th ed.). New York: Macmillan.

Kaufman, A. S. (1975). Factor analysis of the WISC-R at eleven age levels between 6½ and 16½ years. *Journal of Consulting & Clinical Psychology, 43*, 135–147.

Kaufman, A. S. (1979). *Intelligent testing with the WISC-R*. New York: Wiley-Interscience.

Kaufman, A. S. (1981). The WISC-R and learning disabilities assessment: State of the art. *Journal of Learning Disabilities, 14*, 520–526.

Sattler, J. M. (1982). *Assessment of children's intelligence and special abilities* (2nd ed.). Boston: Allyn & Bacon.

Wechsler, D. (1939). *Wechsler-Bellevue Scale of Intelligence*. New York: Psychological Corporation.

Wechsler, D. (1946). *Wechsler-Bellevue Intelligence Scale, Form II*. New York: Psychological Corporation.

Wechsler, D. (1949). *The Wechsler Intelligence Scale for Children*. New York: Psychological Corporation.

Wechsler, D. (1958). *The measurement and appraisal of adult intelligence*. Balt; MD: Williams & Wilkins.

Wechsler, D. (1967). *Manual for the Wechsler Preschool and Primary Scale of Intelligence (WPPSI)*. New York: Psychological Corporation.

Wechsler, D. (1974). *Manual for the Wechsler Intelligence Scale for Children—Revised*. New York: Psychological Corporation.

Wechsler, D. (1981). *Manual for the Wechsler Adult Intelligence Scale—Revised (WAIS-R)*. New York: Psychological Corporation.

Witt, J. C., & Gresham, F. M. (1985). Review of Wechsler Intelligence Scale for Children—Revised. In J. V. Mitchell (Ed.), *The ninth mental measurements yearbook* (pp. 1716–1719). Lincoln: University of Nebraska Press.

ALAN S. KAUFMAN
ANNA H. AVANT
University of Alabama

ASSESSMENT
INTELLIGENCE TESTING
WAIS—WAIS-R

WECHSLER PRESCHOOL AND PRIMARY SCALE OF INTELLIGENCE (WPPSI)

Designed for use with children 4 to 6½ years old, the Wechsler Preschool and Primary Scale of Intelligence (WPPSI; Wechsler, 1967), is a downward extension of the 1949 Wechsler Intelligence Scale for Children (WISC). It consists of 11 subtests, six verbal (information, vocabulary, arithmetic, similarities, comprehension, and sentences, a supplementary subtest) and five performance (animal house, picture completion, mazes, geometric design, and block design). Three deviation IQs (verbal, performance, and full scale) are derived from the battery of subtests. The full-scale IQ is a composite of the verbal and performance IQs and is viewed as "a measure of overall or global intellectual capacity" (p. 2). With a mean of 100 and a standard deviation of 15, the three IQs express various aspects of a child's mental endowment as compared with that of others of the same age.

The WPPSI was standardized on a sample of 1200 children. Each age group, ranging by half years from 4 through 6½, was represented by 100 girls and 100 boys. Data from the 1960 U.S. Census was used to stratify the sample on several different variables—age, sex, geographical region, urban-rural residence, white-nonwhite race, and father's occupation.

Sattler (1982) cites several studies that show that the WPPSI has excellent reliability, yielding values in the mid-90s for the three IQs for a variety of populations. Average reliability coefficients for the individual subtests are also impressive.

The WPPSI manual (Wechsler, 1967) provides information on the relationship between the WPPSI and three other individual ability tests: Stanford-Binet, Peabody Picture Vocabulary Test, and Pictorial Test of Intelligence. Correlation coefficients between the full-scale IQ and global scores on the aforementioned instruments ranged from .58 to .75. These results are typical of correlations between the WPPSI and other tests, as reported in the literature. One study of the WPPSI and the Wechsler Intelligence Scale for Children—Revised (WISC–R) (Reynolds, Wright, & Dappen, 1981) found the two tests to be equivalent predictors of academic achievement.

Factor-analytic studies of the WPPSI (Carlson & Reynolds, 1981; Hollenbeck & Kaufman, 1973) have strongly supported Wechsler's verbal-performance dichotomy, indicating a two-factor solution as most meaningful across all age groups. Further, the subtest placements have corresponded closely to the a priori groupings made by Wechsler; one notable exception is the arithmetic subtest, which tends to load heavily on both the verbal and performance factors.

Though the psychometric quality and diagnostic usefulness of the WPPSI is generally good, the instrument can be faulted for its directions that assume a child being tested understands a considerable number of basic concepts, e.g., "after," "next," "side," "other," and "skipping" (Kaufman, 1978). Other limitations of the WPPSI, according to Sattler (1982), include long administration time, limited floor and ceiling, and difficulty in scoring some responses.

Clinical interpretation of the WPPSI should take into consideration pertinent research comparing group differences on a number of variables. One such investigation examined the differences between scores of boys and girls at three age levels, 4 to 4½, 5 to 5½, and 6 to 6½ years (Kaufman, Daramola, & DiCuio, 1977). No important sex differences were found regarding the interpretation of the separate subtests. Comparisons of matched groups of blacks and whites at the same three age levels (Kaufman, 1973a) show a difference of approximately 10 points in favor of whites. Although verbal IQ differences were significant at each age level, performance IQ differences were only significant at ages 4 to 4½, with the gap between black and white scores growing smaller as children began school. In another study, the relationship of the WPPSI to socioeconomic status (SES) and other background variables was examined (Kaufman, 1973b). No difference was found between urban and rural residence, when other variables (e.g., SES) were held constant; there were significant geographic differences, with the West scoring significantly higher than other regions; SES was shown to be the most significant determinant of all. The top category (professional and technical) averaged about 18 IQ points higher than the lowest category (unskilled).

An analysis of WPPSI subtest scatter (Reynolds & Gutkin, 1981) has important implications for test interpretation. Contrary to a popular belief held for years, normal scoring patterns are not necessarily "flat." (Also see Kaufman, 1976.) The WPPSI study found that about one-third of the standardization sample had significant Verbal-Performance differences of 11 or more points and that the sample of normal children showed considerable variability in subtest scores. These rather large differences may give valuable information to the clinician in the assessment of intraindividual strengths and weaknesses, but they are not definitive indicators of particular exceptionalities such as learning disabilities or emotional disturbance.

REFERENCES

Carlson, L., & Reynolds, C. R. (1981). Factor structure and specific variance of the WPPSI subtests at six age levels. *Psychology in the Schools*, 18(1), 48–54.

Hollenbeck, G. P., & Kaufman, A. S. (1973). Factor analysis of the Wechsler Preschool and Primary Scale of Intelligence (WPPSI). *Journal of Clinical Psychology*, 29(1), 41–45.

Kaufman, A. S. (1973a). Comparison of the performance of matched groups of black children and white children on the Wechsler Preschool and Primary Scale of Intelligence. *Journal of Consulting & Clinical Psychology*, 41(2), 186–191.

Kaufman, A. S. (1973b). The relationship of WPPSI IQs to SES and other background variables. *Journal of Clinical Psychology*, 29(3), 354–357.

Kaufman, A. S. (1976). A new approach to the interpretation of test scatter on the WISC-R. *Journal of Learning Disabilities*, 9(3), 160–168.

Kaufman, A. S. (1978). The importance of basic concepts in the individual assessment of preschool children. *Journal of School Psychology*, 16(3), 207–211.

Kaufman, A. S., Daramola, S. F., & CiCuio, R. F. (1977). Interpretation of the separate WPPSI tests for boys and girls at three age levels. *Contemporary Educational Psychology*, 2, 232–238.

Reynolds, C. R., & Gutkin, T. B. (1981). Test scatter on the WPPSI: Normative analyses of the standardization sample. *Journal of Learning Disabilities*, 14(8), 460–464.

Reynolds, C. R., Wright, D., & Dappen, L. (1981). A comparison of the criterion-related validity (academic achievement) of the WPPSI and the WISC-R. *Psychology in the Schools*, 18(1), 20–23.

Sattler, J. M. (1982). *Assessment of children's intelligence and special abilities* (2nd ed.). Boston: Allyn & Bacon.

Wechsler, D. (1967). *Manual for the Wechsler Preschool and Primary Scale of Intelligence*. New York: Psychological Corporation.

ALAN S. KAUFMAN
MARY E. STINSON
University of Alabama

ASSESSMENT
INTELLIGENCE
INTELLIGENCE TESTS
KAUFMAN ASSESSMENT BATTERY FOR CHILDREN
STANFORD-BINET INTELLIGENCE TESTS
WISC—WISC-R

WELSH FIGURE PREFERENCE TEST

The Welsh Figure Preference Test (FPT) was developed by George Welsh in 1949, for his doctoral thesis, as a pro-

Examples of "like" and "don't like" items from the Welsh Figure.

REFERENCES

Welsh, G. S. (1949). *A projective figure-preference test for diagnosis of psychopathology: I, A preliminary investigation.* Doctoral thesis, University of Minnesota, Minneapolis.

Welsh, G. S. (1959). *Welsh figure preference test.* Palo Alto, CA: Consulting Psychologists.

Welsh, G. S. (1980). *Welsh Figure Preference Test, revised edition.* Palo Alto, CA: Consulting Psychologists.

Welsh, G. S. (1986). Positive exceptionality: The academically gifted and the creative. In R. T. Brown & C. R. Reynolds (Eds.), *Psychological perspectives on childhood exceptionality: A handbook.* New York: Wiley-Interscience.

CECIL R. REYNOLDS
Texas A&M University

CREATIVITY

jective assessment of psychopathology. More recently, it has been used as a measure of creativity more than as a diagnostic tool for the evaluation of psychopathology.

The Welsh FPT (Welsh, 1959) consists of a booklet containing 400 black and white line drawings. Examples of items from the Welsh FPT are shown in the Figure. The scale was revised by Welsh in 1980. It is designed for use with individuals aged 6 years and up. It requires nearly an hour to complete and, despite being intended as a projective, provides objective scoring. Instructions to the test taker are simple. Individuals are asked to view each drawing and indicate on an answer sheet whether they like or dislike the drawing. The intent was to provide nonlanguage stimulus materials suitable for a wide range of individuals who could not be assessed with language-laden measures such as the MMPI, or projective measures such as the TAT, requiring extensive verbal expression.

The Welsh FPT can separate artists from nonartists, as can many other tests; it can also separate clinical from nonclinical populations. However, it has not been extensively researched considering its publication date. Welsh (1986) contends that the Welsh FPT is useful as a measure of creativity; it has been used in creativity research since at least 1965. Its uses in creativity research seem well established at this time, but its validity as a measure of psychopathology is questionable.

WEPMAN AUDITORY DISCRIMINATION TEST

The Auditory Discrimination Test (ADT; Wepman, 1973) was designed to assess an individual's ability to discern the similarity or dissimilarity of spoken pairs of phonemes. The test consists of 40 pairs of phonemes, 10 of which are identical words (e.g., ball–ball). The remaining 30 dissimilar word pairs differ in initial consonant sounds (13 items), and medial vowel sounds (4 items).

The test is individually administered to children 5 to 8 years of age and takes approximately 10 minutes to give. The examiner, after presenting brief directions, merely reads the designated word pairs and the examinee indicates "yes" for identical sounds or "no" for words in the pair that differ in sound.

The ADT consists of two "equated forms," although neither the means of equating the forms nor the standardization sample are described. The ADT manual provides brief evidence of validity and reliability, though neither are detailed adequately. Item development is described in the manual, and care appears to have been taken to ensure that the items reflect the skills being assessed (auditory discrimination) rather than extraneous variables. For example, the test is purely auditory and contains no visual stimuli. Thus there is no cross-model confusion or interference.

REFERENCES

Wepman, J. M. (1973). *Auditory Discrimination Test.* Chicago: Language Research Associates.

BRUCE A. BRACKEN
LINDSAY S. GROSS
University of Wisconsin,
Milwaukee

AUDITORY DISCRIMINATION
GOLDMAN, FRISTOE, WOODCOCK TEST OF AUDITORY
    DISCRIMINATION

WERNER, HEINZ (1890–1964)

Heinz Werner received his PhD from Vienna University in 1914 with highest honors. Perhaps the beginning of his scholarly career began when he read about the evolution of animals, man, and the cosmos. He became increasingly interested in philosophy and psychology while at the University of Vienna. His work in the field of psychological phenomena is relevant to psychologists, educators, anthropologists, students of animal behavior, and scholars investigating aesthetic phenomena.

His contributions to the field have been many. He has published over 15 books and monographs and more than 150 articles within a 50-year period. His principal publications include *Comparative Psychology of Mental Development* and *Developmental Processess: Heinz Werner's Selected Writings*. His selected writings include his general theory and perceptual experiences in Volume I; Volume II focuses on cognition, language, and symbolization.

Werner was a great teacher and researcher, and he inspired others to follow his example in the search for understanding of psychological phenomena. His theory was interdisciplinary because all of his developmental principles apply to all the life sciences. He founded an Institute for Human Development at Clark University in 1958. This institute made Clark an "international center directed toward the developmental analysis of phenomena in all the life sciences" (Werner, 1978). Werner's contributions to the field of developmental psychology are steadily gaining recognition.

REFERENCES

Werner, H. (1940). *Comparative psychology of mental development*. New York: Harper & Brothers.

Werner, H. (1978). *Developmental processes: Heinz Werner's selected writings*. New York: International Universities Press.

REBECCA BAILEY
Texas A&M University

WERNICKE'S APHASIA

Wernicke's aphasia is one of several major aphasic syndromes observed in adults. This fluent type of aphasia was first described by the German neurologist C. Wernicke in 1874. It is characterized by ample production of speech in which words are used incorrectly and meaning is compromised. Understanding of language spoken by another is impaired, as is comprehension of written language. Wernicke's aphasics also exhibit difficulty on repetition tasks (Geschwind, 1979; Hecaen, 1979). This aphasic syndrome is known as sensory aphasia, receptive aphasia, syntactic aphasia, and acoustic aphasia in other classification systems (Hecaen, 1979).

The speech of Wernicke's aphasics has been described as fluent and even hyperfluent, with an increased rate of speech and a tendency to persist in stringing together words, phrases, and sentences (Hecaen, 1979). Paraphasias, errors in the use or construction of single words, are evident. Literal or phonemic paraphasias occur when the aphasic individual substitutes an incorrect letter in a word (e.g., substitutes "bed" for "ben"). Incorrect usages of words are called verbal paraphasias; these may be related (e.g., penny is called nickel) or unrelated (e.g., chair is called box). Wernicke's aphasics may invent new words, called neologisms, resulting in nonsensical speech (Geschwind, 1979; Kaufman, 1981). Circumlocutions (speech characterized by indirect, tangential content) and nonspecific phrases (employing words such as "stuff" or "thing") occur frequently (Kaufman, 1981).

Wernicke's aphasia is associated with lesions in the posterior first temporal gyrus of the dominant (left) hemisphere (Geschwind, 1979). Common causes include cerebral infarctions or tumors, although symptoms of Wernicke's aphasia may be evident in patients with degenerative conditions such as Alzheimer's and Creutzfeldt-Jakob's diseases (Kaufman, 1981). Neurologic examination may be normal, although visual disturbances such as right hemianopsia or right superior quadrantanopsia may be present (Hecaen, 1979; Kaufman, 1981). Other conditions such as schizophrenia or dementia may be confused with Wernicke's aphasia, since individuals with these disorders also may exhibit disturbances of the language system. Kaufman (1981) suggests history and clinical findings are important in distinguishing among these conditions, since Wernicke's aphasia generally is characterized by an acute onset in previously healthy middle-aged individuals.

Direct application of adult aphasic classification systems to children is not appropriate. Results of investigations of communication disorders in children suggest symptoms of Wernicke's aphasia in pediatric populations are rare (Geschwind, 1979). Hecaen (1979) reported his studies of children with acquired aphasia revealed increased frequency of mutism and absence of paraphasias, a profile in stark contrast to the classic Wernicke's aphasia. Similarly, in their description of developmental language disorders in children, Rapin and Allen (1983) do not include a type consistent with the features of Wernicke's. Symptoms of Wernicke's aphasia may occur more frequently in older adolescents whose neurologic development more closely resembles that of adults.

REFERENCES

Geschwind, N. (1979). Focal disturbances of higher nervous function. In P. B. Beeson, W. McDermott, & J. B. Wyngaarden (Eds.), *Cecil textbook of medicine* (pp. 656–659). Philadelphia: Saunders.

Hecaen, H. (1979). Aphasias. In M. S. Gazzaniga (Ed.), *Handbook of behavioral neurobiology: Vol. 2. Neuropsychology* (pp. 239–292). New York: Plenum.

Kaufman, D. M. (1981). *Clinical neurology for psychiatrists.* New York: Grune & Stratton.

Rapin, I., & Allen, D. A. (1983). Developmental language disorders: Nosologic considerations. In U. Kirk (Ed.), *Neuropsychology of language, reading, and spelling* (pp. 155–184). New York: Academic.

CATHY F. TELZROW
*Cuyahoga Special Education
Service Center, Maple
Heights, Ohio*

APHASIA
DYSPHASIA
LANGUAGE DISORDERS

WESTERN EUROPE, SPECIAL EDUCATION IN

Current special education practices in Europe differ from country to country and from region to region in any particular country. These practices have been strongly influenced by the affluence of particular European nations and their social welfare outlook. While Spain and Portugal are concerned about their handicapped children and youth, the funds and services available to them are far less than in Scandinavia.

The nature of special education funding and services also varies from country to country, depending on political structures and traditions. The degree of political-educational centralization plays an important role. In France, national authority is likely to be more strongly felt in the education of the handicapped than in West Germany, where the federal government has little or no authority in public schools, and where financial support and the provision of services for special education are likely to vary from one region to another. Generally, the most comprehensive financial support for services to the handicapped, at all ages, has been in Scandinavia.

Curriculum

Special education curriculum in Western Europe has not been as narrowly academic as in the United States. Traditionally, Western European special education has been more responsive to the extra-academic aspects of special education. The graphic arts, music, and social and vocational experiences are more often woven into the handicapped child's daily activities. Thus, music therapy for handicapped students has received widespread support (Pratt, 1983), and the educational usefulness of toy libraries has been widely recognized (deVincentis, 1984). Theater programs for children with mental retardation, motor disabilities, and cerebral palsy have received acclaim (Cohen, 1985). Excursions and travel are considered important educational experiences. The quality of relationships between teachers and pupils is strongly emphasized.

Europeans may be becoming more Americanized in their special education outlooks in that a more instructionally directed focus appears to be emerging. American influences are also revealed in European movements toward noncategorical types of special education, often in the face of previously accepted, and often complicated, categorical models (as in the Netherlands). European attention to integration of special education with general education has also been influenced by American practices, albeit in European terms (Organization for Economic Cooperation and Development, 1985a, 1985b). Even though Europeans have led the way in assisting the transition of handicapped youths into the world of work, American efforts in this area have influenced their practices considerably.

Early Intervention

The most pervasive effective interventions with Western European handicapped children, prior to their enrollment in formal educational programs, are medically related. Most European nations provide mandatory health screening and reporting for young children, as well as free medical services. In Austria, a multidisciplinary team headed by a social pediatrician steps in as soon as a child has a problem. Indeed, as soon as a child is officially identified as being handicapped, the child' parents begin receiving a disability pension. In France, early intervention begins with the compulsory screening of all infants at birth and again at 2 years. Interdisciplinary teams operate out of "early medico-social activity centers to provide therapies, education, and support in home and natural environments" (Zucman, 1985). However, day care of a more educational nature also can be observed. In Switzerland, a handicapped child's involvement with itinerant educational services begins at an early age (even at birth) and continues, when needed, until the child's integration into school (Pahud & Besson, 1985).

Preschool

Preschool special education had its beginnings in Germany, where Froebel was the first educator to formalize it on a public basis. Current preschool special education in Western Europe varies from nation to nation. For example, different nations have different beginning ages for compulsory education, so that even the definition of preschool education varies. Also, the Europeans have traditionally favored parents as the main educators of their children, particularly when young. The social welfare underpinnings of such states as Sweden have been very supportive of parents who remain at home with their young, offering them paid leave from employment. Countries such as Italy have made remarkable advances in integrating preschoolers into regular education programs.

Least Restrictive Environment and Mainstreaming

Modern-day principles of least restrictive environment and mainstreaming originated with the Bill of Rights for the mentally retarded and the principle of normalization in Scandinavia. Both concepts strongly influenced much of Western Europe. Thus the notion of integrating handicapped students into the main body of education was well on its way, even without American influences. Indeed, reforms in this respect were begun in Norway in 1920 (Booth, 1982). Nevertheless, the United States can take credit for institutionalizing the ideas of least restrictive environment and mainstreaming, and for offering models for the Europeans to adopt. The degree to which the principles of least restrictive environment have prevailed has differed from country to country.

In Denmark, special education is an integral part of regular education within a sophisticated range of educational services. In fact, administrative integration of services for the handicapped with those for the nonhandicapped was passed into law on January 1, 1979, on the premise that handicapped individuals should receive services in the same way as the nonhandicapped (Juul, 1980). Italy's Law 517/1977 has gone far beyond general recommendations for implementation of least restrictive environments to providing procedural plans for implementing the education of handicapped students within regular classrooms (Strain, 1985). On the other hand, in West Germany, where responsibility for the education of the handicapped was traditionally assumed by religious and voluntary organizations, terminology for such education was originally couched in the language of segregation. Public school teachers were unfamiliar with the education of children with special needs, and it was difficult for the teachers to prepare to work with the handicapped. This meant some hesitancy in certain European nations with respect to mainstreaming; however, mainstreaming has moved forward at an steady pace overall.

Transition

European efforts in transition education have been in the vanguard in many respects (Booth, 1982; Organization for Economic Cooperation Development, 1981, 1985a, 1985b), with significant efforts being made to help handicapped youths and young adults to move into the world of work. The Netherlands has been noteworthy for providing sheltered workshops for more involved handicapped youths and adults while supervising more able ones who are actively employed in the open market. Again, the social welfare outlook in nations such as the Netherlands, which

even purchases paintings from artists unable to sell their works, conditions Western European attitudes toward the handicapped. In France, the Union Nationale des Association de Parents d'Enfants Inadaptes, which operates hundreds of schools for moderately to severely handicapped children and youths, has a strong vocational emphasis in its curriculum. It also has operated the Centres d'Aide pour Travail to aid in the employment of the handicapped. In Austria an organization called Jugend am Werk (Youth at Work), which originated with the idea of providing shelter and work to disadvantaged youths, went on to provide vocational training centers, sheltered workshops, and residential centers for the handicapped. Unfortunately, the employment picture in most European countries has been dismal over the past decade, with high unemployment rates for nonhandicapped workers. Opportunities for the handicapped to work in the normal marketplace have been significantly reduced as a consequence.

The Educateur Movement

Educateurs are special types of teacher/child-care workers who are competent to work with maladapted young people, including handicapped youths. They are trained in nonacademic subjects such as sports, acting, arts and crafts, and other leisure-time activities. They teach vocational subjects, supervise vocational placements, work with families, schools, and communities, and act as advocates for their student clients. The educateur profession is well established in France, with numerous colleges providing rigorous training. The educateur movement has spread across much of Western Europe. It has also influenced Canadian services. In the United States, Project Re-Ed was a variant of the educateur model. In European nations, there have been adaptations according to national and local needs. Similar professions have emerged under different names with somewhat different identities and functions. In West Germany the educateurs are called erziehers; in the Netherlands they are identified as orthopedagogues; and in Scandinavia they are milieu therapists.

Therapeutic Communities

The Europeans have also been noted for their creation of therapeutic communities. Professionals and lay people critical of traditional government and professional roles in serving the handicapped and the ill have been instrumental in fostering these.

In Great Britain, psychiatrists Laing and Cooper created a therapeutic home at Kingsley Hall, London. They viewed mentally ill individuals as victims of home and society, and saw hospitals as degrading and dehumanizing them (1971). Laing's views of the causes of mental illness have altered over the years. His perceptions that mental hospitals dehumanize and often harm their residents, and that relationships between professionals and their clients on a day-to-day personal basis may be the best way to help the latter, have been increasingly shared by others.

In France the movement toward therapeutic communities following World War II began in earnest with the work of Jean Vanier (Wolfensberger, 1973) in the movement called l'Arche (place of refuge). Vanier built a small community in Trosly-Breuil, France, where mentally handicapped and nonhandicapped adults could live and work together as families. Vanier's work has inspired the creation of other similar facilities across France and elsewhere.

Most important in the therapeutic community movement has been the anthroposophic movement. This was inaugurated at the turn of the twentieth century by Rudolf Steiner, an Austrian philosopher and educator. The inspirations of the anthroposophic movement led to the creation of the Waldorf method and Waldorf schools. The Waldorf method, while originally intended for normal children, was found also to be applicable to handicapped children. Anthroposophic education is developmental in orientation, and multifaceted. It emphasizes art, bodily movement, music, community involvement, and work. Anthroposophic schools have sought to integrate therapy with education and to engage in therapies that find their expression in art, drama, role playing, etc. Anthroposophic schools serving the handicapped are now numerous in Great Britain and on the continent. Originally oriented toward the mentally retarded and multiply handicapped, they have recently expanded to serve the emotionally disturbed as well.

Particularly noteworthy within the anthroposophic movement has been the Camphill movement. This was begun in the early 1940s by Karl Konig, an Austrian psychiatrist who came to Scotland to escape Nazi persecution. Inspired by anthroposophic philosophy, which views an individual's inner personality as remaining whole and intact despite the nature and degree of that individual's handicaps, Konig created a special village in the vicinity of Aberdeen, Scotland, in which mentally retarded villagers and normal coworkers could live and worked together. The original Camphill movement has spread considerably since that time, both in Europe and the United States. Some settlements serve children, while others serve adults. The orientation of the Camphill settlements, which are self-contained communities, is contrary to modern-day notions of least restrictive environment. Nevertheless, they offer a remarkable combination of care and opportunity for self-fulfillment to many handicapped individuals.

Minority Handicapped

Changed immigration policies and intensive industrialization during the postwar period saw an influx of millions of immigrants or "guest workers" from Africa, Asia, and less affluent European nations into Western Europe. Today, there are second and third generations of these minorities in most Western European nations. With some exceptions, there has been difficulty in integrating them. Decreases in employment opportunities in Western Europe have meant increased hardships and alienation for many; e.g., Turks in Germany, Arabs in France, Indians and Pakistanis in Great Britain. The children of such families constitute a large proportion of underprivileged and disadvantaged students in Western Europe. Elevated levels of handicaps and school failure are the consequence. At the same time, such students, because of their alienated status, are less likely to benefit from benign European attitudes toward the handicapped. It should be observed that the Dutch have been particularly accepting of such minority populations.

Professional Preparation

There is considerable variation in the professional preparation of special education teachers in Europe. In some countries, there appear to be few special requirements. In others, licensure or certification requirements are demanding. In certain countries, there are likely to be differences from one region to another. Germany has traditionally been interested in experimenting with different training models. In England and Wales, more systematic training was instituted as a consequence of the Warnock Report. Switzerland has a number of different teacher institutes, each of which has a special orientation to the cantons that they serve. The Institut des Science de l'Education, at Geneva, associated with the name of Piaget, has been known for its research into the cognitive processes of handicapped students; it is a national training resource. Switzerland's Zentralstelle fur Heilpadagogik coordinates the efforts of its various teacher training centers in respect to special education. In several countries, specialization in special education is entirely on the graduate level. Some countries, e.g., Scotland, require that candidates for special education training have at least one year of teaching in regular education. In France, theoretical studies and practicum requirements are distinguished from each other.

Voluntary Agencies

As in the United States, voluntary organizations have a significant place with respect to assisting handicapped students. They run preschool centers, schools, sheltered workshops, group homes, and hospitals. They even provide professional training. In West Germany the largest of these is the Catholic Caritas. There is also Lebenshilfe, the National Association of Parents and Friends of the Mentally Handicapped, which operates day school nurseries, sheltered workshops, and hostels. In Switzerland, an umbrella organization called Pro Infirmis coordinates the work of other organizations serving the handicapped.

It provides a comprehensive educational program as well, publishes books and brochures, and offers consultations for children and adults. In Austria, the Save the Children Society assists children with special needs in homes and rehabilitation centers. It also offers help in times of crisis. In Great Britain, voluntary agencies work closely with public authorities. In Scandinavia, the Norwegian Red Cross has created special schools and vocational rehabilitation centers; after making them viable, it turns them over to the government.

Auxiliary Services

Widespread, comprehensive, and effective support services for handicapped students are likely to be obtained in most of the nations of Western Europe. For one thing, these nations have broad-based national health insurance systems combining private and public institutions into an easily accessible network of services (Massie, 1985). Many of the medical and ancillary medical services that handicapped children require are obtainable through such government-supported services.

REFERENCES

Booth, T. (1982). *Special need in education.* Stratford, England: Open University Educational Enterprises.

Cohen, H. U. (1985). "Var Teater": A Swedish model of children's theatre for participants with disabilities. *Children's Theatre Review, 34,*

deVincentis, S. (1984, April). *Swedish play intervention for handicapped children.* Paper presented at the annual convention of the Council for Exceptional Children. Washington, DC.

Juul, K. D. (1979). European approaches and innovations in serving the handicapped. *Exceptional Children, 44,* 322–330.

Juul, K. D. (1980). Special education in Western Europe and Scandinavia. In L. Mann & D. A. Sabatino (Eds.), *The fourth review of special education.* New York: Grune & Stratton.

Juul, K. D. (1984, April). *Toy libraries for the handicapped.* Paper presented at the annual convention of the Council for Exceptional Children, Washington, DC.

Juul, K. D., & Linton, T. E. (1978). European approaches to the treatment of behavior disordered children. *Behavior Disorders, 3,* 232–249.

Kugel, F. B., & Wolfensberger, W. (Eds.), (1968). *Changing patterns of residential services for the mentally retarded.* Washington, DC: President's Committee on Mental Retardation.

Linton, T. E. (1971). The educateur model: A theoretical monograph. *Journal of Special Education, 5,* 155–190.

Massie, R. K. (1985). The constant shadow: Reflections on the life of a chronically ill child. In N. Hobbes & J. M. Perrin (Eds.), *Issues in the care of children with chronic illness.* San Francisco: Jossey-Bass.

Organization for Economic Cooperation and Development. (1981). *Integration in the school.* Washington, DC: Author.

Organization for Economic Cooperation and Development. (1985a). *Integration of the handicapped in secondary schools: Five case studies. The Education of the handicapped adolescent: II.* Washington, DC: Author.

Organization for Economic Cooperation and Development. (1985b). *Handicapped youth at work: Personal experiences of school-leavers: The education of the handicapped adolescent: III.* Paris: Centre for Educational Research and Innovation.

Oyer, H. J. (1976). *Communication for the hearing handicapped. An international perspective.* Baltimore, MD: University Park Press.

Pahud, D., & Besson, F. (1985, Summer). Special education in Switzerland: Historical reflections and current applications. *Journal of the Division of Early Childhood, 9,* 222–29.

Pratt, R. R. (Ed.). (1983). *The International Symposium on Music in Medicine, Education, and Therapy for the Handicapped.* Lanham, MD: University Press of America.

Strain, P. (1985). A response to preschool handicapped in Italy: A research based developmental model. *Journal of the Division for Early Childhood. 29,* 269–271.

Tarnapol, L., & Tarnapol, M. (1976). *Reading disabilities: An international perspective.* Baltimore, MD: University Park Press.

Taylor, E. J. (1980). *Rehabilitation and world peace.* New York: International Society for Rehabilitation of the Disabled.

Taylor, W. W., & Taylor, I. W. (1960). *Special education of physically handicapped children in Western Europe.* New York: International Society for the Welfare of Cripples.

Wolfensberger, W. (1964). General observations on European countries. *Mental Retardation, 2,* 331–337.

Wolfensberger, W. (1973). *A selective overview of the work of Jean Vanier and the movement of L'Arche.* Toronto, Canada: National Institute of Mental Retardation.

Zucman, E. (1985). Early childhood programs for the handicapped in France. *Journal of the Division for Early Childhood, 9,* 237–245.

DON BRASWELL
Research Foundation,
City University of New York

EASTERN EUROPE, SPECIAL EDUCATION IN
FRANCE, SPECIAL EDUCATION IN
UNITED KINGDOM, SPECIAL EDUCATION IN

WHELAN, RICHARD J. (1931–   )

Born in Emmett, Kansas, Richard J. Whelan received his BA from Washburn University in 1955 with majors in history and political science and minors in psychology and education. In 1966 he received his EdD from the University of Kansas, with a major in special education and minors in educational research, measurement, and educational psychology.

Whelan's earliest professional experiences were as a child-care worker at the Southard School of the Menninger Clinic. The experiences at Southard convinced him that effective therapeutic treatment must concern itself with the time between psychotherapy sessions. Whelan advocates an emphasis on applied behavior analysis with its precise measurement techniques.

Whelan has explained the elements he deems necessary in all learning environments in his article "What's in a Label? A Hell of a Lot!" (1972). Publications concerning his theories of educational methodology include *Effective Teaching of Children with Behavior Disorders* (1972) and *Strategies for Teaching Exceptional Children* (1972). Whelan currently directs the Division of Training Programs, Bureau of Education for the Handicapped of the U.S. Office of Education in Washington, DC.

REFERENCES

Meyen, E., Vergason, G., & Whelan, R. J. (Eds.). (1972). *Strategies for teaching exceptional children*. Denver: Love.

Whelan, R. J. (1972). What's in a label? A hell of a lot! In R. Harth, E. Meyen, & G. Nelson (Eds.), *The legal and educational consequences of the intelligence testing movement: Handicapped children and minority-group children*. Columbia: University of Missouri Press.

Whelan, R. J., & Gallagher, P. A. (1972). Effective teaching of children with behavior disorders. In N. G. Haring & A. H. Hayden (Eds.), *The improvement of instruction* (pp. 183–218). Seattle, WA: Special Child.

E. VALERIE HEWITT
Texas A&M University

OFFICE OF SPECIAL EDUCATION

WHOLE WORD TEACHING

The term whole word teaching has been used as the label for two different approaches to beginning reading instruction. Mathews (1966) in *Teaching to Read: Historically Considered* describes the first approach as a "words-to-letters" method that was introduced into reading instruction in Germany in the eighteenth century and later brought to the United States.

The development of the words-to-letters method was motivated by dissatisfaction with the ABC method, the prevailing method of reading instruction since the invention of the Greek alphabet. Critics of the ABC method did not disagree with its underlying philosophy that mastery of the alphabet and syllables (combinations of vowels and consonants such as *ba, bē, bu*) were prerequisite skills for learning to read. However, they took issue with the procedures used to teach those skills, namely, years of drill, which they described as senseless, tortuous, desperately dull work. The method that eventually evolved presented beginning readers with whole words in their total form followed by an analysis of the sounds and letters. This was an analytic approach to teaching the alphabet, whereas the ABC method was a synthetic approach under which students were taught to combine syllables into words only after having mastered their pronunciation as isolated units.

Mathews (1966) refers to the second approach that has been called whole word teaching as a "words-to-reading" method. This method, commonly called the "look-and-say" method, also had its roots in Germany and may have been used by some teachers in the United States as early as the 1830s. Horace Mann, a strong advocate of the method is often credited with having brought about its widespread use (Betts, 1946). However, according to Mathews (1966), it was Francis Parker, the first widely known practitioner of the look-and-say method, who played a far more significant role in its initiation. Under his leadership as superintendent of schools in Quincy, Massachusetts (1875–1878), and later as principal of Cooke County Normal School, Illinois (1883–1899), students were taught to read 150 to 200 words in the context of sentences and stories before being introduced to the sounds of letters. The teaching of names of letters was delayed for at least 2 years so that they would not be confused with the sounds of letters. While Parker's schools were widely acclaimed, it is doubtful that the look-and-say method would have gained the foothold it did had he not become closely associated with John Dewey, head of the departments of philosophy, psychology, and pedagogy at the University of Chicago.

When Parker was appointed director of the School of Education at the university in 1900, the two joined forces. Although Dewey was not interested in developing a methodology for teaching children to read, he thoroughly agreed with Parker's educational philosophy and adopted the look-and-say method strongly advocated by Parker. In this way, the look-and-say method came to occupy a prominent place in a new system of education (advocated by Dewey) to which the adjective progressive was applied (Mathews, 1966). As the influence of the progressive education movement grew, so did the use of the look-and-say approach to reading. During the first two decades of the twentieth century, it became firmly entrenched in elementary reading programs and remained so until the mid-1950s, when Rudolf Flesch (1955) captured the growing public alarm over what was happening in the nation's elementary schools in his book *Why Johnny Can't Read*. Flesch challenged the prevailing practice in beginning reading instruction that emphasized a look-and-say approach. He advocated a return to a phonic approach using existing research as support for his position.

Flesch's book led to a great deal of public debate, which in turn spawned numerous research efforts to identify the best method(s) for beginning reading instruction. Among these were 27 U.S. Office of Education grade 1 studies and a study funded by the Carnegie Corporation of New York (Chall, 1967).

REFERENCES

Betts, E. A. (1946). *Foundations of reading instruction*. New York: American Book.

Chall, J. (1967). *Learning to read: The great debate*. New York: McGraw-Hill.

Flesch, R. (1955). *Why Johnny can't read and what you can do about it*. New York: Harper & Brothers.

Mathews, M. M. (1966). *Teaching to read: Historically considered*. Chicago: University of Chicago Press.

MARIANNE PRICE
*Montgomery County
Intermediate Unit,
Norristown, Pennsylvania*

**PHONOLOGY
READING DISORDERS
READING REMEDIATION**

WIDE RANGE ACHIEVEMENT TEST—REVISED (WRAT–R)

The Wide Range Achievement Test (WRAT) and Wide Range Achievement Test-Revised (WRAT-R) are both individually administered, pencil-and-paper screening tests designed to assess limited samples of behavior from the basic skills domains of spelling, arithmetic, and reading. Both the WRAT and WRAT–R are comprised of two tests: a Level I test used with children younger than age 12 and a Level II test used with persons age 12 or older. Each level test is divided into three subtests: spelling, which includes tasks assessing the ability to copy symbols from a code key, print or write one's name, and write dictated words; arithmetic, which includes tasks assessing counting, number recognition, the solution of orally presented addition and subtraction problems, and the solution of written computation problems; and reading, which includes tasks such as letter recognition, letter naming, and the pronunciation of isolated words. Administration time for each of the three subtest-level tests is approximately 30 minutes.

The WRAT and WRAT-R both yield subtest raw scores that can be converted to norm-referenced standard scores, percentile ranks, or grade equivalents. The item content of the WRAT–R is identical to that of the WRAT, with the following minor exceptions: the Level I arithmetic subtest of the WRAT–R includes one additional computation problem, and the Level II arithmetic subtest of the WRAT–R includes 10 additional computation problems. These items were added to the WRAT-R to improve the arithmetic subtests' abilities to make finer distinctions among students at the lower end of the computation skills continuum.

Test reviewers have consistently criticized the presentation and quality of reliability and validity information provided in the WRAT test manuals and the lack of nationally representative norms (Merwin, 1978; Salvia & Ysseldyke, 1985; Sattler, 1982; Thorndike, 1978). The WRAT-R may represent an improvement over the WRAT in terms of test standardization (Reinehr, 1985); the au-

thors report using sex, age, race, geographic region, and metropolitan/nonmetropolitan residence as stratification variables for sampling, but fail to report tables showing how the standardization sample compared with the targeted population proportions (Jastak & Wilkinson, 1984).

The most desirable feature of the WRAT and WRAT-R is that both tests can be administered and scored easily by teachers and psychologists to obtain an estimate of basic academic skill functioning. The WRAT has been, and remains, one of the most widely used individually administered screening devices despite reviewer criticisms and the apparent psychometric limitations of the test. Reynolds (in press) has noted numerous serious technical deficiencies in the WRAT-R and recommends, strongly against its, use in placement, planning, or diagnosis.

REFERENCES

Jastak, S., & Wilkinson, G. S. (1984). *Wide Range Achievement Test—Revised administration manual*. Wilmington, DE: Jastak.

Merwin, J. (1978). Review of the Wide Range Achievement Test. In O. K. Buros (Ed.), *The seventh mental measurements yearbook* (pp. 66–67). Highland Park, NJ: Gryphon.

Reinehr, R. C. (1985). Review of the Wide Range Achievement Test-Revised. In D. J. Keyser & R. C. Sweetland (Eds.), *Test critiques* (Vol. 1, pp. 758–761). Kansas City, MO: Test Corporation of America.

Reynolds, C. R. (in press). Review of the Wide Range Achievement Test-Revised. *Journal of Counseling and Development*.

Salvia, J., & Ysseldyke, J. E. (1985). *Assessment in special and remedial education* (3rd ed.). Boston, MA: Houghton Mifflin.

Sattler, J. M. (1982). *Assessment of children's intelligence and special abilities* (2nd ed.). Boston, MA: Allyn & Bacon.

Thorndike, R. L. (1978). Review of the Wide Range Achievement Test. In O. K. Buros (Ed.). *The seventh mental measurements yearbook* (pp. 67–68). Highland Park, NJ: Gryphon.

GEORGE MCCLOSKEY
*American Guidance Service,
Circle Pines, Minnesota*

ACHIEVEMENTS TESTS

WILBUR, HERVEY BACKUS (1820–1883)

Hervey Backus Wilbur, physician and educator, established the first school for mentally retarded children in the United States when he took a group of retarded children into his home in Barre, Massachusetts, in 1848. With the published accounts of the educational work of Edouard Seguin to guide him, Wilbur fashioned out of his own experience a system of teaching that was successful to a degree not previously thought possible.

In 1851, the New York State legislature established an

Hervey Backus Wilbur

experimental residential school for mentally retarded children, the second state school for the mentally retarded in the United States, with Wilbur as superintendent. Residential schools were opened in a number of other states during the next few years, many of them patterned after the New York School. This school, over which Wilbur presided until his death, is today the Syracuse Developmental Center.

Wilbur was a founder and the first vice president (with Edouard Seguin as president) of the Association of Medical Officers of American Institutions for Idiotic and Feeble-Minded Persons, now the American Association on Mental Deficiency. He produced numerous pamphlets and articles dealing with the care and treatment of mentally retarded persons.

REFERENCES

Godding, W. W. (1883). In memoriam: Hervey Backus Wilbur. *Journal of Nervous & Mental Diseases, 10,* 658–662.

Scheerenberger, R. D. (1983). *A history of mental retardation.* Baltimore, MD: Brookes.

PAUL IRVINE
Katonah, New York

AAMD ADAPTIVE BEHAVIOR SCALES

WILD BOY OF AVEYRON

The Wild Boy of Aveyron—or Victor, as he later came to be known—first was noticed by a group of peasants who witnessed him fleeing through the woods of south central France. He was spotted on subsequent occasions digging up turnips and potatoes or seeking acorns. He was captured in the forest of Aveyron, France, by three hunters in July 1799. It was determined that the boy was about 11 or 12 years of age, was unable to speak, and had been living a wild existence. He was taken to the Institution of Deaf Mutes in Paris and was assigned to the care of Jean Itard.

Itard, a young French physician, believed that this wild creature was physiologically normal and that his intellectual deficiencies were due to a lack of "appropriate sensory experiences in a socialized environment" (Scheerenberger, 1983). Itard was convinced that with an adequate training program, Victor would show great intellectual development and could be transformed from a savage to a civilized being. Because Victor's intellectual deficiencies were not seen as physiologically based, but were attributed to isolation and social and educational neglect, this was viewed as an opportunity to substantiate the effectiveness of educational methods being developed at the time (Maloney & Ward, 1979).

Over the next 5 years, Itard worked intensively with Victor and established a sequence of educational activities designed to teach him speech, self-care, and manners, and to develop his intellectual functions and emotional faculties. Itard employed socialization techniques and sensory training methods much like those he had used with deaf children (Robinson & Robinson, 1965).

Victor's progress was sometimes frustratingly slow, despite Itard's affection, effort, and ingenuity. Still, the doctor made tremendous gains in his 5 years of work with the boy, later documenting this in great detail (Kirk & Gallagher, 1979). Victor accomplished a great deal: he was able to recognize objects, identify letters of the alphabet, and comprehend the meaning of many words (Maloney & Ward, 1979). However, he never learned to speak, and Itard felt his program of instruction had failed. The physician decided to terminate the program after 5 years of intensive work with Victor.

Itard's experiences with the Wild Boy of Aveyron are particularly notable since his work was the first documented, systematic attempt to teach a handicapped person. Although his attempts to make the boy "normal" failed, Itard did make significant gains, and showed that even a severely handicapped individual could make great improvements with training.

REFERENCES

Kirk, S. A., & Gallagher, J. J. (1979). *Educating exceptional children* (3rd ed.). Boston: Houghton Mifflin.

Maloney, M. P., & Ward, M. P. (1979). *Mental retardation and modern society* New York: Oxford University Press.

Robinson, H. B., & Robinson, N. M. (1965). *The mentally retarded child.* New York: McGraw-Hill.

Scheerenberger, R. C. (1983). *A history of mental retardation.* Baltimore, MD: Brookes.

KATHLEEN RODDEN-NORD
GERALD TINDAL
University of Oregon

HISTORY OF SPECIAL EDUCATION
ITARD, JEAN MARC

WILL, MADELEINE C. (1945–   )

As assistant secretary for special education and rehabilitative services, Madeleine Will holds the nation's highest ranking federal position for the advocacy of disabled individuals. She is responsible for the programs in the department's Office of Special Education, the Rehabilitation Services Administration, and the National Institute for Handicapped Research—the three units that comprise the Office of Special Education and Rehabilitative Services. With a $2.6 billion budget, she supervises Education Department programs that serve 4.5 million disabled children and 936,000 adults with disabilities. Committed to the belief that federal programs must not be administered on the basis of concepts that underestimate the potential contribution of disabled citizens, Will was responsible for the initiation of transition and supported work models that strive to direct those with disabilities toward independent living and meaningful employment.

Madeleine C. Will

Prior to her federal role, Will received her BA from Smith College and MA from the University of Toronto. She also served in volunteer capacities for organizations advocating the rights of disabled citizens. In 1981 she served as a member of the Governmental Affairs Committee for the National Association of Retarded Citizens and chaired the Governmental Affairs Committee for the association's Maryland chapter. From 1974 to 1976, Will helped to develop and operate a program that integrated handicapped preschoolers into two nursery schools in Montgomery County, Maryland.

STAFF

OFFICE OF SPECIAL EDUCATION
NATIONAL ASSOCIATION OF RETARDED CITIZENS

WILLIAM'S SYNDROME

See INFANTILE HYPERCALCEMIA.

WILLOWBROOK CASE

The Willowbrook case, or *New York State Association for Retarded Children* v. *Carey*, was litigation tried by Judge Orrin Judd in which the conditions in the Willowbrook State School in New York State were challenged. Specific charges included widespread physical abuse, overcrowded conditions and understaffing, inhumane and destructive conditions, extended solitary confinement, and lack of therapeutic care. Brought on behalf of more than 5000 residents of the Willowbrook State School, this class-action suit is recognized as a landmark in protection from harm litigation.

During a series of Willowbrook trials, witnesses appeared and provided court testimony documenting the inhumane conditions and the physical, mental, and emotional deterioration of residents. On April 21, 1975, the New York Civil Liberties Union, the Legal Aid Society, the Mental Health Law Project, and the U.S. Department of Justice announced that the parties to the Willowbrook litigation had agreed on a consent judgment that would resolve the suit. This consent decree, which was approved on May 5, 1975, established standards in 23 areas to secure the constitutional rights of the Willowbrook residents to protection from harm.

This consent decree, which was to be implemented within 13 months or less, identified duty ratios of direct-care staff to residents of one to four during waking hours for most residents, and required an overall ratio of one clinical staff member for every three residents. The decree prohibited seclusion, corporal punishment, degradation, medical experimentation, and routine use of restraints. It established the primary goal of Willowbrook as the preparation of residents for development and life in the community, and it mandated individual plans for the residents' education, therapy, care, and development.

Additionally, the decree required (1) 6 hours of programmed activity each weekday; (2) nutritionally adequate diets; (3) dental services; (4) 2 hours of daily recreational activities; (5) adaptive equipment as needed; (6) adequate clothing; (7) continually available physicians; (8) contracted services with an accredited hospital; (9) an immunization program; (10) compensation for voluntary labor in accordance with minimum wage laws; and (11) correction of health and safety hazards.

Another set of requirements to be implemented, but not subject to the 13-month timetable, included reduction in the number of Willowbrook beds, establishment of 200 new community placements, increased funding to Willowbrook, creation of a review panel to oversee implementation of standards of the consent decree, initiation of a consumer advisory board composed of parents and relatives of residents, community leaders, residents, and former residents, and creation of a professional advisory board.

This Willowbrook case promoted improvements in the lives of the Willowbrook residents, focused public attention on the conditions of institutionalized individuals, and, as with other landmark cases, affected many similar cases.

DOUGLAS FUCHS
LYNN S. FUCHS
*Peabody College, Vanderbilt
University*

DEINSTITUTIONALIZATION
HUMANISTIC SPECIAL EDUCATION
MENTAL RETARDATION

WISC/WISC-R

See WECHSLER INTELLIGENCE SCALE FOR CHILDREN.

Lightner Witmer

the diagnostic method in teaching, Witmer developed an interdisciplinary approach to education; his clinic provided training for psychologists, teachers, social workers, and physicians. He formed special classes that served as training grounds for teachers from across the nation and as models for many of the special classes that were established in the early part of the twentieth century. Anticipating special education's strong influence on mainstream education, Witmer suggested that learning-disabled children would show the way for the education of all children.

REFERENCES

Watson, R. I. (1956). Lightner Witmer: 1867–1956. *American Journal of Psychology, 69,* 680.

Witmer, L. (1911). *The special class for backward children.* Philadelphia: Psychological Clinic.

PAUL IRVINE
Katonah, New York

WITMER, LIGHTNER (1867–1956)

Lightner Witmer established the world's first psychological clinic, at the University of Pennsylvania in 1896, an event that marked the beginning not only of clinical psychology but also of the diagnostic approach to teaching. Previously director of the psychological laboratory at the University of Pennsylvania, where he succeeded James McKeen Cattell, Witmer moved psychology from the theoretical concerns of the laboratory to the study of learning and behavior problems of children in the classroom. Proposing a merging of the clinical method in psychology and

WOLFENSBERGER, WOLF P. J. (1934–)

Born and reared in Germany in the period just before and during World War II, Wolf P. J. Wolfensberger studied in the United States. He earned a BA in philosophy from the now defunct Siena College of Memphis, Tennessee. He subsequently pursued graduate training in psychology and education at St. Louis University, during which time he became a naturalized U.S. citizen (1956), culminating with the awarding of the MA in psychology in 1957. Wolfensberger continued his studies of psychology and special education, earning the PhD in these fields in 1962 from

George Peabody College for Teachers (now Peabody College, Vanderbilt University).

Wolfensberger was mentored by two widely known psychologists while an intern: Walter Klopfer, the famous personality psychologist, at the Norfolk (Nebraska) State Hospital, and Jack Tizard, while Wolfensberger was a postdoctoral research fellow in mental retardation at Maudsley Hospital (the University of London teaching hospital) in England. Following the latter experience, Wolfensberger became a mental retardation research scientist at the Nebraska Psychiatric Institute (1964–1971), where he eventually rose to the rank of associate professor of medical psychology in the departments of psychiatry and pediatrics. For 2 years (1971–1973) he was a visiting scholar at the Canadian National Institute on Mental Retardation, with a joint faculty appointment at York University. Since 1973, Wolfensberger has served as a professor in the department of special education and rehabilitation at Syracuse University and as director of the Training Institute for Human Service Planning, Leadership, and Change Agentry.

A prolific writer and researcher, Wolfensberger has devoted nearly his entire career to social advocacy for the handicapped and to fostering the implementation of his principle of normalization for the handicapped. He has been one of the major (arguably *the* major) proponent of normalization. He formulated and elaborated the citizen advocacy scheme to promote social consciousness, high ideals, and social advocacy for the handicapped. His work on normalization has been recognized at many levels (Kugel & Wolfensberger, 1968; Wolfensberger, 1972, 1980; Wolfensberger & Zauha, 1973). Currently, Wolfensberger has turned his attention to in-service training workshops for human service personnel. More than 15,000 human service workers have now participated in Wolfensberger's workshops.

REFERENCES

Kugel, R., & Wolfensberger, W. (Eds). (1968). *Changing patterns in residential services for the mentally retarded*. Washington, DC: President's Committee on Mental Retardation.

Wolfensberger, W. (1972). *The principle of normalization in human services*. Toronto, Canada: National Institute on Mental Retardation.

Wolfensberger, W. (1980). Research, empiricism, and the principle of normalization. In R. J. Flynn & K. E. Witsch (Eds.), *Normalization, social integration, and commity services*, Baltimore, MD: University Park Press.

Wolfensberger, W., & Zauha, H. (Eds.). (1973). *Citizen advocacy and protective services for the impaired and handicapped*. Toronto, Canada: National Institute on Mental Retardation.

Cecil R. Reynolds
Texas A&M University

NORMALIZATION

WOOD, M. MARGARET (1931-   )

M. Margaret (Peggy) Wood began in special education as an NDEA fellow at the University of Georgia where, following the awarding of her BA in elementary education in 1953 from Goucher College, she earned her MEd (special education) in 1960. Wood immediately followed the MEd with an EdD, awarded with distinction in 1963 from the University of Georgia with a major in special education and a minor in psychology. Wood then did postdoctoral study at the Hillcrest Residential Treatment Center in Washington, DC. From 1964 to 1969, Wood was director of the teacher preparation program for teachers of emotionally disturbed students in the division for exceptional children at the University of Georgia. It was during this time that her view of therapeutic approaches to children in the schools matured and she began to work in earnest toward developing a psychoeducational approach to these children's problems. This approach has become known widely as developmental therapy.

In 1970 Wood received funding for the establishment of the Rutland Center for Severely Emotionally Disturbed Children; she directed the center until 1974. Developmental therapy, as practiced at the Rutland Center under Wood's direction, became a model approach to the provision of special education services to emotionally disturbed children in the public schools. More than 250 developmental therapy centers have been established in schools worldwide, though nearly all are in North and South America. Wood has continued her active interest in developmental therapy but has focused on research and dissemination activities since 1974, when she became project director of a federally sponsored model in-service training program. Wood was promoted to the rank of professor in the division for exceptional children at the University of Georgia in 1977, a position she still holds.

Wood has more than 50 scholarly publications to her credit, most dealing with some aspect of developmental therapy, and has authored or edited six books (Wood, 1975, 1982; Williams & Wood, 1977). Wood is best known as the

M. Margaret Wood

originator of developmental therapy, a major innovation in public school delivery of special education services to severely emotionally disturbed children. Wood has a significant reputation as a mentor and many well-known professionals have studied with her and practiced developmental therapy at the Rutland Center.

REFERENCES

Williams, G. H., & Wood, M. M. (1977). *Developmental art therapy.* Baltimore, MD: University Park Press.

Wood, M. M. (Ed.). (1975). *Developmental therapy.* Baltimore, MD: University Park Press.

Wood, M. M. (1982). Developmental therapy: A model for therapeutic intervention in the schools. In C. R. Reynolds & T. B. Gutkin (Eds.), *The handbook of school psychology.* New York: Wiley.

CECIL R. REYNOLDS
Texas A&M University

DEVELOPMENTAL THERAPY

WOODCOCK-JOHNSON PSYCH-EDUCATIONAL BATTERY

The Woodcock-Johnson Psych-Educational Battery (Woodcock & Johnson, 1977) is composed of three major sections: Part I, Tests of Cognitive Ability; Part Two, Tests of Achievement; and Part Three, Tests of Interest Level. Four cluster scores are generated within the cognitive section: verbal ability, reasoning, perceptual speed, and memory. A composite or global score is formed by a weighted combination of subtest scores. Subsequent to the publication of the battery, Woodcock revised the method for calculating the verbal ability and reasoning clusters to remove the influence of suppressor variables. The two modified clusters are termed oral language and broad reasoning.

The second major section of the battery focuses on academic achievement. Within this section there are four clusters: reading, written language, mathematics, and knowledge. Four scholastic aptitude clusters provide a means for determining whether a student is working up to his or her expected level of academic achievement. Various combinations of the cognitive subtests are used to predict achievement in academic domains. For instance, the reading aptitude cluster consists of four subtests from Part I: visual-auditory learning, blending, antonyms-synonyms, and analogies. These are combined to form an expected reading score. When this score and an individual's actual reading achievement score from Part II are compared, a relative performance index (RPI) is yielded. The RPI may be calculated for each of the four adaptive clusters.

The administration of the Woodcock-Johnson is relatively straightforward owing to the easel format of the tests, the concise directions at the beginning of each subtest, and the uniformity of the basal and ceiling rules. Consonant with the administration procedures is the care that went into the development of the scoring standards. Exemplars of correct and incorrect responses are located next to the examiner's questions; this facilitates immediate and accurate scoring of responses. Both Buros reviewers (Cummings, 1985; Kaufman, 1985) note that it is cumbersome and time-consuming to arrive at derived scores from raw scores. There are multiple score transformations and tables that must be consulted. In fact, there are 41 separate tables just for Part I. Both Cummings (1985) and Kaufman (1985) observed that the potential for clerical errors is high. The problems of potential clerical errors and excessive time in the mechanical scoring phase to find derived scores are overcome when one uses the Compuscore computer scoring program, available from DLM Teaching Resources.

Another aspect of administration that Cummings (1985) commented on was the lack of manipulative tasks for preschool and primary-aged children. Although the easel format facilitates the examiner's administration, it reduces the opportunities for the children to physically interact with the testing materials. As such, the easel format makes it more difficult to maintain the younger child's interest and keep him or her on task.

The technical manual of the Woodcock-Johnson (Woodcock, 1978) contains ample information on the technical properties of the battery. The number of individuals and their geographic representations puts the Woodcock-Johnson in the same genre (normatively) as the Wechsler Intelligence Scale for Children-Revised (WISC-R; Wechsler, 1974) and the Stanford-Binet (Terman & Merrill, 1973). A three-stage procedure was used in selecting schools representing various geographic regions of the United States and different degrees of urbanization and levels of socioeconomic status. The normative sample included 3935 children in grades kindergarten through 12, 555 preschoolers in the 3 to 5 age range, 503 individuals from the 18 to 64 age range, and 97 who were 65 or above. The standardization sample, in general, corresponded with the U.S. Census data. The exceptions were nonurban persons living in the Northeast and South, who were underrepresented. To correct for the underrepresentation, a weighting procedure was used. An important asset of the Woodcock-Johnson is that all parts of the battery, that is, both cognitive and achievement sections, were standardized on the same normative sample.

The reliability data presented in the manual are adequate or better for the vast majority of subtests and cluster scores. Even at the preschool level, most cluster scores are .90 and above. The only cluster with suspect reliability is perceptual speed. In this case $r = .70$; thus, caution must be exercised when interpreting this cluster.

The validity data included in the technical manual are voluminous. Criterion-related validation studies of normal children and adults and handicapped populations (mentally retarded, learning disabled, and emotionally disturbed) are reported in Woodcock's well written technical supplement. Concurrent validity was established with time-proven anchor measures. The Woodcock-Johnson Tests of Cognitive Ability were validated with the Wechsler Intelligence Scale for Children-Revised and the Stanford-Binet. The Peabody Individual Achievement Test and the Wide Range Achievement Test served as anchor tests for the Woodcock-Johnson Tests of Achievement.

The most controversial aspect of the Woodcock-Johnson Psych-Educational Battery has been Part I. The controversy began with two investigations (Reeve, Hall, & Zakreski, 1979; Ysseldyke, Shinn, & Epps, 1981) that reported mean score discrepancies between the Woodcock-Johnson Tests of Cognitive Ability and the WISC-R. The samples for both studies were learning-disabled students. The finding in both cases was that the Woodcock-Johnson Broad Cognitive score was significantly lower than that obtained for the WISC-R. The practical implication of this finding was that, on the average, a given child's estimated intelligence would be different depending on which test was selected. One hypothesis offered was that the Woodcock-Johnson Tests of Cognitive Ability are more achievement-oriented than traditional measures of intelligence. This was reasoned because, by definition, the learning-disabled students would be expected to have relatively lower scores in the area of academic achievement. Shinn, Algozzine, Marston, and Ysseldyke (1982) analyzed the Woodcock-Johnson Psych-Educational Battery from Cattell's perspective of fluid and crystallized intelligence. They provided some confirmation for the hypothesis that Part I of the Woodcock-Johnson was achievement-oriented or assessing product-dominant skills. They concluded this by examining the slopes calculated by the regression line between W-scores at ages 14 and 30.

However, a caveat in Shinn et al.'s reasoning was the achievement subtest used to define product-dominant slopes, i.e., word attack. Since word attack skills are developed in elementary school and not for the most part after age 14, the word attack slope should not have been used as the dividing line for fluid versus crystallized subtests. Woodcock (1984a, 1984b) has responded effectively to these criticisms. He cited serious methodological errors in the two initial studies and analyzed subsequent investigations in terms of the adequacy of their research design. Further background on the nature of the constructs underlying Part I of the Woodcock-Johnson is provided by Cummings and Moscato (1984a) and Estabrook (1984).

Evidence for the concurrent validity of Part II, the tests of achievement, is provided in the technical manual and by independent investigations. The correlation with an-

chor measures falls in the range from $r = .70$ to .90. As noted by Kaufman (1985), concurrent validity data are not presented for Part III, the tests of interest level.

REFERENCES

Breen, M. J. (1983). Comparing the Woodcock-Johnson Achievement cluster scores and Wide Range Achievement Test in a learning disabled and regular education population. *Journal of Clinical Psychology, 39*, 86–90.

Breen, M. J., & Lehman, J. (1982). Concurrent validity of the Woodcock-Johnson mathematics and reading subtests with a middle school learning disabled population. *Educational & Psychological Research, 2*, 173–179.

Cummings, J. A. (1985). Review of the Woodcock-Johnson Psych-Educational Battery. In J. F. Mitchell (Ed.), *The ninth mental measurements yearbook*. Lincoln: University of Nebraska Press.

Cummings, J. A., & Moscato, E. M. (1984a). Research on the Woodcock-Johnson Psych-Educational Battery: Implications for practice and future investigations. *School Psychology Review, 13*, 33–40.

Cummings, J. A., & Moscato, E. M. (1984b). Reply to Thompson and Brassard. *School Psychology Review, 13*, 45–48.

Estabrook, G. E. (1984). A canonical analysis of the Wechsler Intelligence Scale for Children-Revised and the Woodcock-Johnson Tests of Cognitive Ability in a sample referred for suspected learning disabilities. *Journal of Educational Psychology, 76*, 1170–1177.

Kaufman, A. S. (1985). Review of the Woodcock-Johnson Psych-Educational Battery. In J. F. Mitchell (Ed.), *The ninth mental measurements yearbook*. Lincoln: University of Nebraska Press.

Reeve, R. E., Hall, R. J., & Zakreski, R. S. (1979). The Woodcock-Johnson Tests of Cognitive Ability: Concurrent validity with the WISC-R. *Learning Disability Quarterly, 2*, 63–69.

Shinn, M., Algozzine, B., Marston, D., & Ysseldyke, J. A. (1982). Theoretical analysis of the performance of learning disabled students on the Woodcock-Johnson Psych-Educational Battery. *Journal of Learning Disabilities, 15*, 221–226.

Terman, L., & Merrill, M. (1973). *Stanford-Binet Intelligence Scale, 1972 norms edition*. Boston: Houghton Mifflin.

Wechsler, D. (1974). *Wechsler Intelligence Scale for Children—Revised*. New York: Psychological Corporation.

Woodcock, R. W. (1978). *Development and standardization of the Woodcock-Johnson Psych-Educational Battery*. Hingham, MA: Teaching Resources.

Woodcock, R. W. (1984a). A response to some questions raised about the Woodcock-Johnson I: The mean score discrepancy issue. *School Psychology Review, 13*, 342–354.

Woodcock, R. W. (1984b). A response to some questions raised about the Woodcock-Johnson II: Efficacy of aptitude clusters. *School Psychology Review, 13*, 355–362.

Woodcock, R. W., & Johnson, M. B. (1977). *Woodcock-Johnson Psych-Educational Battery*. Hingham, MA: Teaching Resources.

Ysseldyke, J., Shinn, M., & Epps, S. (1981). A comparison of the

WISC-R and Woodcock-Johnson Tests of Cognitive Ability. *Psychology in the Schools, 18*, 15–19.

JACK A. CUMMINGS
Indiana University

ACHIEVEMENT TESTS
CRITERION REFERENCED TESTS

WOODCOCK LANGUAGE PROFICIENCY BATTERY (WLPB)

The Woodcock Language Proficiency Battery (WLPB) was published in 1980–1981. It consists of a subset of eight subtests taken from the Woodcock-Johnson Psychoeducational Test Battery (WJPTB). The three oral language subtests include picture vocabulary, antonyms-synonyms, and analogies. Reading subtests include letter-word identification, word attack, and passage comprehension. The two written language subtests are diction and proofing. The test comes in English and Spanish forms.

The psychometric properties of the WLPB are essentially those of the WJPTB. The norms for the English form are based on the WJPTB on the 4732 case standardization sample. General Spanish norms for the Spanish form were collected in a separate standardization program in the urban areas of Costa Rica, Mexico, Peru, Puerto Rico, and Spain. The sample consisted of 802 subjects tested in grades 1, 3, 5, 8, and 11. These norms are intended for use in counties or other regions of the Spanish speaking world. It is noteworthy that by using the regular U.S. WJPTB norms, the English form of the WLPB has norms that date back to 1976 and 1977.

Scores yielded by the WLPB include part scores, cluster scores, grade equivalents, age equivalents, instructional ranges, cluster difference scores, relative performance indexes, percentile ranks, standard scores, and normal curve equivalents. The method for computing these scores on the record form is virtually identical to that for the WJPTB.

Accompanying the WLPB Spanish form is a potentially confusing errata sheet. The manual for this test indicates that while some of the interim scores (e.g., cluster scores) are computed using the Spanish norms, the scores with the most meaning (e.g., standard scores and percentiles) are to be obtained based on equated U.S. norms. Essentially, the WJPTB norms were equated to the general Spanish norms for the subtests included in the WLPB. This allows, for example, the examiner to determine the English grade equivalent. In other words, the equated U.S. norms allow examiners to make a statement such as, "His Spanish grade equivalent of 5.2 corresponds to an English-speaking child's grade equivalent of 5.2." The value of the equated U.S. norms is not clear at this time, nor is their value explicitly stated in the manual. In addition, the errata sheet explains that the equated U.S. norms should not be used until they are revised by the publisher. Customers are being asked to return a form to ensure that they receive these revised norms.

The reliability and validity evidence for the WLPB is taken from the WJPTB. The Spanish WLPB was published with no evidence of reliability and validity for Spanish populations. This is clearly not in compliance with the Standards for Educational and Psychological Testing (Committee to Revise the Standards, 1984).

Two recent reviews of the WLPB were favorable (Noyce, 1985; Quinn, 1985). These reviews, however, focused more on test content and practicality than on psychometric adequacy.

REFERENCES

Committee to Revise the Standards. (1984). *Standards for educational and psychological testing*. Washington, DC: American Psychological Association.

Noyce, R. (1985). Review of the Woodcock Language Proficiency Battery. In J. V. Mitchell (Ed.), *Ninth mental measurements yearbook*. Lincoln: University of Nebraska Press.

Quinn, M. (1985). Review of the Woodcock Language Proficiency Battery. In J. V. Mitchell (Ed.), *Ninth mental measurements yearbook*. Lincoln: University of Nebraska Press.

RANDY W. KAMPHAUS
Eastern Kentucky University

NONDISCRIMINATORY ASSESSMENT
WOODCOCK JOHNSON PSYCHOEDUCATIONAL TEST BATTERY

WOODCOCK READING MASTERY TESTS

The Woodcock Reading Mastery Tests can be used to measure reading growth, detect reading problems, group students for instruction, and evaluate curriculum and programs. Norms are provided for pupils in kindergarten through grade 12. It may also be administered to postsecondary students or adults for diagnostic purposes.

The tests are individually administered. Two equivalent forms of the tests are available. Test materials contain response forms that are completed by the examiner during testing and an examiner's manual that explains the test and includes the norms and scoring instructions. Each of the tests contains five subtests: letter identification measures the ability to name the letters of the English alphabet; word identification requires the naming of sight words; word attack measures the ability to pronounce words through phonic and structural analysis; word comprehension is for vocabulary; and passage comprehension is for understanding of extended text.

Test directions are clear and easy to follow. Supplementary directions are included in the manual. Several scores may be derived from the test: raw; mastery; grade; relational mastery; mastery at G (grade); achievement index; relative mastery at G; and percentile ranks. From these scores a mastery profile is developed for each student. The Woodcock tests are a widely used series that do not require special training or courses to administer.

REFERENCES

Manual: Woodcock reading mastery tests. (1973). Circle Pines, MN: American Guidance Service.

Woodcock reading mastery tests. (1978). In O. K. Buros (Ed.), *The eighth mental measurement yearbook* (Vol. 2, pp. 1303–1311). Highland Park, NJ: Gryphon.

RONALD V. SCHMELZER
Eastern Kentucky University

WOODCOCK-JOHNSON PSYCHOEDUCATIONAL BATTERY

WOODS SCHOOLS

The Woods Schools, located in Langhorne, Pennsylvania, was established in 1913 to provide educational and training programs for students with development delays, retardation, brain damage, and learning disabilities. The school is primarily a residential facility that features group home life in small cottages with an intensive staff ratio that provides for direct care and services to meet the individual needs of students. The school provides for day and residential students on a coed basis.

The school programs offer a wide range of educational experiences to students who are severely handicapped and who require therapeutic services. Vocational training is provided. Students are trained in a wide range of vocational exploration experiences that establish appropriate work habits, basic working skills, and prevocational experiences that lead to job training. Remedial services, tutorial instruction, and therapeutic services are designed to meet the individual needs of students as they progress through the programs.

REFERENCE

Sargent, J. K. (1982). *The directory for exceptional children* (9th ed.). Boston: Porter Sargent.

PAUL C. RICHARDSON
*Elwyn Institutes,
Elwyn, Pennsylvania*

VOCATIONAL TRAINING

WORD BLINDNESS

Congenital word blindness, word blindness, dyslexia, developmental dyslexia, specific dyslexia, developmental alexia, visual aphasia, and strephosymbolia are all terms that have on some occasions been used interchangeably in the special education literature (Evans, 1982; Orton, 1937; Wallin, 1968) to indicate a child's inability to learn to read. Developmental dyslexia was defined by Critchley (1964) as a specific difficulty in learning to read, often of genetic origin, which existed in spite of good general intelligence, and without emotional problems, brain damage, or impairments of vision or hearing. Ford (1973) defined congenital word blindness or dyslexia as the inability of a child to learn the meaning of graphic symbols.

Although literature is available from as early as the 1800s (Kussmaul, 1877), there is no clear agreed on cause for this problem. Causes that have been hypothesized ranged from maternal and natal factors, ophthalmological factors, cerebral dominance issues, and minor neurological impairments, to genetic issues (Critchley, 1964). Clemesha (1915) attributed word blindness to a congenital defect or deficiency in the brain or to some pathological process. Heitmuller (1918) felt that developmental alexia or word blindness was a developmental defect of the visual memory center for the graphic symbols of language. Orton (1937) postulated that dyslexic symptoms were the result of mixed dominance, which he called motor integrating abilities. His theory attributed reading reversals to the possibility that the mirrored counterparts of words located in the dominant hemisphere were stored in the subdominant hemisphere; therefore, children without a clearly established dominant hemisphere would have confusion with learning to read words. He also believed that this difficulty in establishing dominance was inherited. DeHirsch (Hallahan & Cruickshank, 1973) postulated a central nervous system dysfunction or developmental lag as the cause of word blindness. She believed "that both delayed cerebral dominance and language disorders may reflect a maturational dysfunction" (p. 106).

Although there continues to be a lack of consensus on which terminology to use, as well as on the meaning of the terms chosen, the literature is clearly divided between the medical (those professionals who are looking for a cause) and the educational (those professionals who are more interested in determining a means to remediate the problem). The medically oriented group is more likely to see word blindness or dyslexia as an inability to learn to read owing to a central nervous system dysfunction or brain damage, while the educationally oriented group is more likely to describe this group as children who are having trouble learning to read. There are other distinctions between the medical and educational professions. Educators are more concerned with the developmental sequence of reading skills; the medical community is concerned with disabilities in language and speech, motor development, and perception. Educators differentiate between reading problems of children and adults, and make a distinction between maturational lag and a central nervous system dysfunction. Educators do not see one easy way of remediating but base remediation on intensive diagnostic information related to the specific skills that individual children are missing, the child's best modality for learning, the appropriate materials, etc. Educators are less likely to recommend individual treatment, but work within the entire school population to improve reading instruction for all children (Lerner, 1971). One final distinction between the two groups of professionals is that the medically oriented research has been conducted most often by physicians in Europe, while the educational research has been done by educators, psychologists, and reading specialists in the United States. DeHirsch, a language pathology theorist and psychiatrist (Hallahan & Cruickshank, 1973), has done extensive research in the area of dyslexia and has been greatly responsible for the integration of research from both of these groups.

Specific behavioral characteristics that may be present in children who have been diagnosed as word blind include a general clumsiness or spatial disorientation, minor sensory disorders, difficulty in eye control, defects in body image, confusion of right and left, faulty estimates of spatial and temporal categories, difficulty in interpreting the meaning of facial expressions, difficulty in arithmetic skills, difficulty with processing of complex linguistic verbalizations, difficulty with formulation, a tendency for cluttering, disorganized verbal output, hyperactivity, and difficulty with figure-group concepts (Critchley, in Franklin, 1962; DeHirsch, 1952).

Heller (1963) described screening criteria for detecting word blindness in school-aged children. These criteria include normal intelligence, normal vision and hearing, marked reduction in reading and spelling ability, descrepancy between reading and other abilities, inability to read by the sight method, ability to learn to read by auditory repetition, and evidence of dissociation of visual word-image from acoustic word-image. Remediation techniques traditionally have emphasized the phonetic approach (Hinshelwood, 1917; Holt, 1962; Miles, 1962; Orton, 1937), with training occurring in individualized sessions. A more individualized eclectic approach was hypothesized by Naidoo (1972) and DeHirsch (Hallahan & Cruickshank, 1973), with emphasis on evaluating each student's strengths and weaknesses and devising an individualized program based on the results. Specific remediation techniques have been well developed by Wagner (1976).

The Word Blind Centre for Dyslexic Children was established in 1962 in London, England, by the Invalid Children's Aid Association (ICAA; Naidoo, 1972). It was in operation from 1962 to 1970; its goals were both research and the treatment of dyslexic children. The ICAA has been responsible, since 1963, for the publication of the *Word Blind Bulletin*. In the United States, the National Advisory Committee on Dyslexia and Related Reading Disorders was created by the Secretary of Health, Education and Welfare (HEW) in 1968. Its purpose was to investigate, clarify, and resolve the controversial issues surrounding dyslexia. The committee determined that the term dyslexia served no useful educational purpose. It recommended the creation of an Office of Reading Disorders within HEW to improve reading instruction for all children who were experiencing difficulty in reading (*Report to the Secretary of the Department of Health, Education and Welfare*, 1969).

REFERENCES

Clemesha, J. C. (1915). Congenital word blindness or inability to learn to read. *Journal of Ophthalmology Oto-Laryngoloy, 9*(1), 1–6.

Critchley, M. (1962). In A. W. Franklin (Ed.), *Word-blindness or specific developmental dyslexia*. Proceedings of a conference called by the Invalid Children's Aid Association. London: Pitman.

Critchley, M. (1964). *Developmental dyslexia*, London: Heinemann Medical.

DeHirsch, K. (1952). Specific dyslexia or strephosymbolia. *Folia Phoniatrica, 4*, 231–248.

DeHirsch, K. (1973). In D. P. Hallahan, & W. M. Cruickshank (Eds.), *Psychoeducational foundations of learning disabilities*. Englewood Cliffs, NJ: Prentice-Hall.

Evans, M. M. (1982). *Dyslexia: An annotated bibliography. Contemporary problems of childhood #5*. Westport, CT: Greenwood.

Fisher, J. H. (1905). Case of congenital word-blindness (inability to learn to read). *Ophthalmic Review, 20*, 315–318.

Ford, F. R. (1973). Developmental word blindness and mirror writing. In *Diseases of the nervous system in infancy, childhood, and adolescence* (6th ed.). Springfield, IL: Thomas.

Franklin, A. W. (Ed.) (1962). *Word-blindness or specific developmental dyslexia*. Proceedings of a conference called by the Invalid Children's Aid Association. London: Pitman.

Hallahan, D. P., & Cruickshank, W. M. (1973). *Psychoeducational foundations of learning disabilities*. Englewood Cliffs, NJ: Prentice-Hall.

Heitmuller, G. H. (1918). Cases of developmental alexia or congenital word blindness. *Washington Medical Annual, 17*, 124–129.

Heller, T. M. (1963). Word-blindness—A survey of the literature and a report of twenty-eight cases. *Pediatrics, 31*(4), 669–691.

Hinshelwood, J. (1917). *Congenital word-blindness*. London: H. K. Lewis.

Holt, L. M. (1962). In A. W. Franklin (Ed.), *Word-blindness or specific developmental dyslexia*. Proceedings of a conference called by the Invalid Children's Aid Association. London: Pitman.

Kussmaul, A. (1877). Word-deafness—Word blindness. In A. H. Buck & H. von Ziemssen (Eds.), *Diseases of the nervous system, and disturbances of speech.* Vol. 14 of *Cyclopaedia of the Practice of Medicine*. New York: Wood.

Lerner, J. W. (1971). *Children with learning disabilities* (2nd ed.). Boston: Houghton Mifflin.

Miles, T. R. (1962). In A. W. Franklin (Ed.), *Word-blindness or specific developmental dyslexia*. Proceedings of a conference called by the Invalid Children's Aid Association. London: Pitman.

Naidoo, S. (1972). *Specific dyslexia: The research report of the ICAA Word Blind Centre of Dyslexic Children*. London: Pitman.

Orton, S. T. (1937). *Reading, writing, and speech problems in children*. New York: Norton.

Orton, S. T. (1966). *Word-blindness in school children and other papers on strephosymbolia (specific language disability—dyslexia) 1925–1946*. Pomfret, CT: Orton Society.

Report to the Secretary of the Department of Health, Education, and Welfare (1969, Aug.). Washington, DC: National Advisory Committee on Dyslexia and Related Disorders.

Wagner, R. F. (1976). *Helping the word blind: effective intervention techniques for overcoming reading problems in older students*. West Hyzck, NY: Center for Applied Research in Education.

Wallin, J. E. W. (1968). Congenital word blindness (dyslexia) in children. *Journal of Education. 151*(1), 36–51.

SUSANNE BLOUGH ABBOTT
Stanford, Connecticut

DSYLEXIA
READING DISORDERS
READING REMEDIATION

WORD BLINDNESS

See CONGENTIAL WORD BLINDNESS, HISTORY OF.

WORD PROCESSING FOR THE HANDICAPPED

A word processor or text editor enters text into the short-term memory of a computer as the composer types onto the keyboard and views the text on the monitor. The word processor also provides procedures for manipulating text, whereby the writer, through simple commands, can (1) revise, delete, insert, and move text; (2) format text in alternative ways; (3) store text for future editing sessions; and (4) print text onto paper. The word processor is viewed as a tool with which individuals can overcome several physical and psychological constraints to writing; therefore, it has been seen as a potentially useful tool for assisting handicapped persons in the written expression process.

With respect to physical constraints, researchers have speculated that the word processor addresses the arduous task of recopying text that has been revised. Without a word processor, a writer may be reluctant to add or change words because the resulting product may look messy and because a good deal of time and labor is required to recopy text (Daiute, 1983). Daiute (1983) has speculated that, with the physical ease of revising with a word processor, and with the capacity of the text editor to produce instant electronic copies so that the writer can test various alternative versions, a writer is encouraged to experiment and to view writing as a dynamic process.

For certain disabled populations, where physical constraints are handicapping, the relative ease of editing, saving, and printing text has the potential to increase individuals' quality and quantity of written output. For example, word processing programs may be effective for the mildly cerebral palsied, the learning disabled, and the behavior disordered, for whom the task of revising and recopying may be especially arduous or frustrating (Kerchner & Kistinger, 1984). Additionally, for certain sensory impairments, word processing tools that are adapted to address specific disabilities can alleviate difficulties in writing. For example, placing braille characters onto a keyboard can increase the written expression capabilities of visually impaired individuals (Ashcroft & Young, 1981).

In terms of psychological constraints on writers, Bereiter and Scardamalia (1979) have documented that writing skills lag developmentally behind speaking abilities, perhaps because writing, unlike speaking, requires an internal dialogue between the writer as composer and the writer as editor. Immature writers may experience difficulty in supplying the interactive and contextual supports for themselves that are natural in conversational situations. For example, writers must include the referents to pronouns because the written page is blank, whereas speakers can clarify by pointing to an object while saying "that."

Additionally, written expression requires evaluative objectivity and related metacognitive skills that young writers frequently lack. It also demands relatively sophisticated short-term memory capacities. Psycholinguistic research suggests that syntactic errors are related to short-term memory deficits: as the writer plans and produces multiclause sentences, the exact wording of initial clauses fades from short-term memory. Because of short-term memory limitations, composers may have difficulty in carrying out all steps in the writing process simultaneously.

The word processor potentially can assist writers in overcoming these psychological constraints. The computer can temporarily relieve some burdens on short-term memory: typing may be faster than written production and many word processing programs require writers to focus on separate dimensions of the writing process sequentially rather than simultaneously. For example, by avoiding the task of recopying, there is less pressure for writers to perfect first drafts. Word processing thereby facilitates revising as a second-order, rather than a simultaneous, task to initial drafting (Daiute, 1983).

Daiute (1983) has speculated that the text editor is subtly interactive as it carries out commands provided by the user, responds by calling the user's attention to tasks it has completed, and waits for subsequent commands. The computer also demands more precision than handwritten products, by rejecting extra spaces and commas, ungrammatical constructions, and misspelled words in word processing checking programs. This form of monitoring may improve eventually the self-monitoring behavior of immature writers (Daiute, 1983).

Given these ways in which word processing programs may enhance the written products of immature writers, it stands to reason that certain cognitively handicapped populations may benefit from instruction with word processors. Recently, research concerning the use of word processors and their effects on the quality and quantity of written output, on written expression achievement, and on the process of revising has been conducted with learning-disabled students; results appear promising (Kerchner & Kistinger, 1984; MacArthur & Graham, 1986).

Despite these recent investigations concerning learning-disabled samples, relatively little research is available concerning the use of word processing programs among handicapped groups. Calls for systematic programmatic research with microcomputers, including word processing applications, have been issued (Stowitschek & Stowitschek, 1984). These calls must be heeded before widespread adoption of word processing programs for the handicapped become appropriate.

REFERENCES

Ashcroft, S. C., & Young, M. (1981). Microcomputers for visually-impaired and multihandicapped persons. *Journal of Special Education Technology, 4*, 24–27.

Bereiter, C., & Scardamalia, M. (1979). From conversation to composition: The role of instruction in the developmental process. In R. Glaser (Ed.), *Advances in instructional psychology* (Vol. 2). Hillsdale, NJ: Erlbaum.

Daiute, C. (1981). *Child-appropriate text editing*. Paper presented at the Child-Appropriate Computing Conference, New York.

Daiute, C. (1983). The computer as stylus and audience. *College Composition & Communication, 34*, 134–145.

Kerchner, L. B., & Kistinger, B. J. (1984). Language processing/word processing: Written expression, computers and learning disabled students. *Learning Disability Quarterly, 7*, 329–335.

MacArthur, C. A., & Graham, S. (1986). *Learning disabled students' composing with three methods: Handwriting, dictation, and word processing*. Paper presented at the annual meeting of the American Educational Research Association, San Francisco.

Stowitschek, J. J., & Stowitschek, C. E. (1984). Once more with

feeling: The absence of research on teacher use of microcomputers. *Exceptional Education Quarterly, 4*(4), 23–39.

LYNN S. FUCHS
Peabody College, Vanderbilt University

COMPUTER USE WITH HANDICAPPED
WRITING REMEDIATION
WRITTEN LANGUAGE OF HANDICAPPED

WORDS IN COLOR

Words in Color is a one-to-one sound-symbol approach to teaching reading that was devised in 1957 by Caleb Gattegno. Gattegno, a scientist, approached the problems of reading as he did the problems of mathematics and physics. He introduced the concept of temporal sequence into reading methodology (Gattegno, 1970) and proposed that our language is coded into a series of sounds that, when uttered in sequence, produce wholes that we call words. The timing of the sounds in sequence is essential learning for correct pronunciation (Aukerman, 1971). Words in Color is based on the premise that reading is a process of decoding printed symbols and translating them into sounds and words. Color is used in the initial stage of reading to help the learner make an association between the symbol and the sound.

In the Words in Color program, there are 21 charts of letter sounds, letters in combination, and word families. Included on these charts are the 47 distinct sounds of American English in 280 different instances of letters and letter combinations. In beginning reading instruction, the child looks at the colored charts of words, then writes the same letters or words in black and white and reads what he or she has written. The names of the letters are not used, only the sounds and colors. In Words in Color the vowels are taught as sound-symbol shapes. The learner's attention is focused on the shape of the letter and how it relates in shape to the other vowels.

Gattegno introduced his Words in Color program as a novel approach to teaching reading. He asserted that, "illiteracy can be wiped out at a far smaller cost than any wild dreamer has ever dreamed. [He is] prepared to do the computation if asked" (Gattegno, 1970). Results of research studies on the Words in Color program are mixed (Aukeman, 1971). Some studies have shown positive results (DeLacy, 1973) but Gattegno is far from reaching his goal of wiping out illiteracy with the Words in Color program.

REFERENCES

Aukerman, R. C. (1971). *Approaches to beginning reading*. New York: Wiley.

DeLacy, E. (1973). Clinical reading cases—Some speculations concerning sequence in colour and look-and-say. *Slow Learning Child, 20*(3), 160–163.

Gattegno, C. (1969). *Towards a visual culture*. New York: Outerbridge Dienstfrey.

Gattegno, C. (1970). The problem of reading is solved. *Harvard Educational Review, 40*(2), 283–286.

NANCY J. KAUFMAN
University of Wisconsin, Stevens Point

READING DISORDERS
READING REMEDIATION

WORKFARE

Workfare is a term that was coined in the 1980s to describe welfare reform efforts that require able-bodied AFDC parents to work in public service projects in exchange for monthly benefits. These unpaid jobs were typically at the city or county level and involved entry-level positions in clerical, human services, or park maintenance work. The majority of the participants were single females with children over the age of 6.

In 1981 the Reagan administration proposed a mandatory national workfare program, but Congress, reluctant to endorse such sweeping legislation in the absence of empirical evidence, instead passed the 1981 Omnibus Budget Reconciliation Act. This 1981 legislation encouraged, but did not require, the states to implement workfare programs as part of their welfare reform initiatives. By 1985, 37 states were experimenting with some type of workfare (*Wall Street Journal*, August, 5, 1985). In most cases, workfare was but one small component in a broader employment effort that might include career planning, vocational training, high school equivalency courses, job placement services, child-care vouchers, transportation assistance, and on-the-job training with subsidies to employers. The states were allowed to use Federal Work Incentive Program funds in these reform initiatives.

As the states began to generate their own welfare reform models compatible with local philosophies and resources, it became clear that there were widely different approaches being tried across the country. This diversity provided social researchers with an unprecedented natural laboratory in which to study different systems. The most thorough research on workfare was conducted by the Manpower Demonstration Research Corporation (MDRC) of New York City. In 1982, with financial help from the Ford Foundation, this nonprofit research group began a 4-year comparative study of welfare reform in 11 different states. The following generalizations and quotations were taken from MDRC's report on the first three study sites

(February, 1986): San Diego, California; Baltimore, Maryland; and two counties in Arkansas:

1. The studied states are increasing the employment of welfare recipients and, in some cases, reducing the costs of welfare. "Moreover, for the first time, there is reliable evidence that several different approaches—including a form of workfare—are cost-effective to operate."

2. The states place more emphasis on job search activities than on workfare activities and workfare "has not turned out to be either as punitive as its critics feared or as praiseworthy as its advocates claimed."

3. The findings indicate that the public service jobs are generally valued by both the participants and their supervisors, and are not considered "make work" activities.

4. In most cases, the participants already possess the necessary entry-level skills before they begin their jobs, so the workfare experience does not contribute to new vocational skills development.

5. Supervisors report that participants' productivity and attendance are as good as that of most other paid employees.

6. The majority of the participants agree that the work requirement is fair. Many feel positive about the work they do, and feel that they are making a contribution.

Undoubtedly, the most widely reported success story in work welfare reform comes from the state of Massachusetts, where 20,000 welfare recipients were placed in jobs in the past 2 years (*U.S. News & World Report*, October 28, 1985). This program, which was voluntary and did not have the punitive quality often associated with workfare, reported that 86% of its first-year beneficiaries were still off welfare after 12 months. This represented savings to the state of over $60 million. This was not a controlled experiment so it is not clear how much of Massachusetts' success was due to other variables such as general economic recovery.

In California another approach, which has the overwhelming support of both conservatives and liberals, is being tried. This approach will make participation mandatory with "strict provisions for cutting off payments to those who do not participate, and a large-scale effort to make sure that those who do will get adequate training and job-placement services" (*Time*, October 7, 1985).

In conclusion, workfare is being tried in numerous settings and has wide emotional appeal because of its logical connection with such concerns as the federal deficit and the poverty cycle of AFDC families. However, a final accounting of workfare and related strategies will not be available for a number of years so it would seem prudent for policy makers to heed the advice of Manpower Demonstration Research Corporation (1986) when it says, "no one model—including workfare—is at this point recommended for national replication. It will be important to continue studying the emerging state results and for the states to carry out further experimentation."

REFERENCES

Gueron, J. (1986). *Work initiatives for welfare recipients: Lessons from a multi-state experiment*. New York: Manpower Demonstration Research.

States refocus welfare, with eye on "real" jobs. (1985, October 28). *U.S. News & World Report*.

Work for welfare. (1985, October 7). *Time*.

Work-not-welfare effort encounters the deficit. (1985, July 19). *Wall Street Journal*.

JOHN D. SEE
University of Wisconsin, Stout

REHABILITATION
SOCIOECONOMIC STATUS

WORLD FEDERATION OF THE DEAF (WFD)

The World Federation of the Deaf (WFD) was founded in 1951. It consists of 83 members representing the languages of English, French, and Italian. Its central office is in Rome, Italy. The WFD is a collection of associations of the deaf from various countries. These national or international organizations encompass societies and bodies acting for the deaf, health, social, and educational groups related to the aims of the federation, professionals involved with deafness or performing special assignments for the federation, and parents and friends of the deaf. Through social rehabilitation of deaf individuals, the WFD is a leader in the fight against deafness.

Among its services, the federation makes available social legislation concerning the deaf as well as statistical data. It also serves as consultant to the World Health Organization and UNESCO. The WFD sustains a library and bestows awards for merit and special achievement in education and social rehabilitation of the deaf. The federation holds commissions in the areas of communication, arts and culture, pedagogy, psychology, medicine, audiology, social and vocational rehabilitation, and spiritual care. The federation publishes a journal triannually entitled *Voices of Silence*, in addition to the *Proceedings of International Congresses and Meetings* and a dictionary.

MARY LEON PEERY
Texas A&M University

WORLD HEALTH ORGANIZATION

WORLD HEALTH ORGANIZATION (WHO)

The World Health Organization (WHO) is a specialized agency of the United Nations with primary responsibility for international health matters and public health. Created in 1948, it comprises of delegates representing member states and is attended by representatives of intergovernmental organizations and nongovernmental organizations in official relationships with WHO. Assemblies are held annually, usually in Geneva.

The official functions of WHO are varied; they include (1) directing and coordinating authority on international health work; (2) assisting governments in strengthening health services; (3) furnishing technical assistance and emergency aid; (4) stimulating and advancing work to eradicate or control epidemic, endemic, and other diseases; (5) promoting improved nutrition, housing, sanitation, recreation, economic and working conditions, and other aspects of environmental hygiene; (6) encouraging cooperation among scientific and professional groups that contribute to the advancement of health; (7) promoting material and child health and welfare, and fostering the ability to live harmoniously in a changing total environment; (8) fostering activities in the field of mental health; (9) working for improved standards of teaching and training in health, medical, and related professions; (10) studying and reporting on administrative and social techniques affecting public health and medical care from preventive and curative perspectives; and (11) assisting in developing informed public opinion on health matters.

Several WHO activities relate directly to diagnostic and classificatory issues in special education. First, WHO produces key writings concerning the use of health statistics and undertakes psychiatric epidemiology devoted to comparative research on mental disorders. Second, WHO compiles the International Classification of Diseases (ICD), a statistical classification of diseases; complications of pregnancy, childbirth, and the puerperium; congenital abnormalities; accidents, poisonings, and violence; and symptoms and ill-defined conditions. The ICD has been adapted for use as a nomenclature of diseases, with mental disorders constituting one major category. Subsumed in this category are classifications along with operational definitions of handicapping conditions.

Several other systems are tied to the ICD, including the *Diagnostic and Statistical Manual (DSM)* as well as the *Grossman Manuals on Terminology and Classification* of the American Association on Mental Deficiency. Third, the Mental Health Unit of WHO has implemented an intensive program to acquire systematic data on variables in diagnostic practice and use of diagnostic mental disorder terms. This has resulted in a multiaxial scheme for the classification of childhood mental disorders, with three main axes: clinical psychiatric syndromes, individual intellectual levels of functioning regardless of etiology, and associated physical, organic, and psychosocial factors in etiology.

Douglas Fuchs
Lynn S. Fuchs
Peabody College, Vanderbilt University

WORLD FEDERATION OF THE DEAF

WORLD REHABILITATION FUND

The World Rehabilitation Fund, also known as the International Exchange of Experts and Information in Rehabilitation (IEEIR), seeks to identify, "import," disseminate, and promote the use of innovative rehabilitation and special education knowledge from other countries. Information about unique programs, practices, and research, as well as the policies of other nations, is sought for dissemination to professionals in the United States.

The IEEIR program is substantially supported by the Office of Special Education and Rehabilitation Services (OSERS) of the U.S. Department of Education. It is an outgrowth of the National Institute of Handicapped Research (NIHR, an OSERS division) mandate to facilitate the use of selected ideas and practices generated in other countries. Selection of knowledge or problem areas to guide the program staff are set jointly by OSERS, NIHR, and IEEIR staffs.

The IEEIR engages in the awarding of fellowships, the publication of monographs, and the dissemination of information. The fellowship program enables qualified U.S. experts to study and report on either special education or rehabilitation developments in other lands. This group includes rehabilitation and special education faculty, researchers, and administrators. Other specialists such as rehabilitation engineers, physicians, psychologists, independent living leaders, and consumer advocates also participate.

Overseas experts with substantial qualifications germane to the priorities set for the United States are identified and commissioned to prepare monographs for publication by the IEEIR program. Five monographs a year are commissioned.

To facilitate dissemination efforts, fellows commit themselves to reporting their observations and recommendations to their peers in relevant journals and at professional meetings. Since one of the criteria for selecting fellows is the degree to which they are centers of influence within their fields, IEEIR expects that they will influence not only students and researchers, but also practitioners and administrators. The communication skills and past record of a fellow are key considerations in awarding fellowships.

In addition to the reports they submit, fellows are expected to report their experiences and observations to professional meetings and other interested groups. Publication in professional journals is also encouraged. Both U.S. fellows and foreign monograph authors may be invited to present their findings at conferences designed for U.S. specialists to keep them abreast of innovations and new ideas.

The World Rehabilitation Fund headquarters is located at 400 East 34th Street, New York, NY 10016. Information on specific programs and monographs available may be requested from this office.

Diane E. Woods
*World Rehabilitation Fund,
New York, New York*

WORLD HEALTH ORGANIZATION

WPPSI

See WECHSLER PRESCHOOL AND PRIMARY SCALE OF INTELLIGENCE.

WRAT/WRAT-R

See WIDE-RANGE ACHIEVEMENT TEST-REVISED.

WRITING AS EXPRESSIVE LANGUAGE

Since written expression is the most complex and the last form of language to be achieved, it can best be explained from a perspective that considers the influence of linguistic and cognitive abilities as well as the uniqueness of this expressive mode. The interrelatedness of language skills has been conceptualized by Myklebust (1965) in terms of a hierarchical construct that suggests that listening, speaking, reading, and writing develop in a progression that is ascendable and reciprocal. Implicit to this theory is the premise that competency at each rung of the language ladder is prerequisite to success at the next. Credibility for this paradigm has been provided by many researchers, including Loban (1976), who longitudinally followed a group of students from kindergarten through twelfth grade and found a positive relationship of achievement among the language arts. Children who were judged to be good listeners and speakers in kindergarten were the same students who later excelled in reading and writing, retaining their status as superior language users throughout their school careers. Conversely, children who did not begin their schooling with oral language competence continued to be evaluated as below average in all language skills.

The concept that achievement in written forms is influenced by development in preceding forms has been easier to verify than the nature of the reciprocity that occurs among the linguistic functions. Wolf and Dickinson (1985) described the development of oral and written language systems as being profoundly interactive in that growth in each mode results in cognitive processing changes that exert influence in a cyclical manner. For example, these researchers noted that early phonological and metalinguistic development in oral language affects the acquisition of reading skills; in turn, achievement in the reading form influences perspectives of listening, speaking, and writing. Wolf and Dickinson further explained that written expression with its emphasis on refining alters one's cognitive orientation to speaking and reading. Thus it appears that written expression can be thought of as a shaper or enhancer of other linguistic forms.

Another complicating factor to understanding the relationship among language processes concerns the consideration that changes occur as development unfolds. Kroll (1981) has proposed a developmental model for examining the relationship between speaking and writing. This model describes four principal associations between these two expressive forms: the first phase is termed separate and involves the preparation for writing (the learning of technical skills required to produce the written symbols for speech); the second phrase involves consolidation of oral and written language (the understanding that writing is similar to talk written down); the third phase focuses on differentiation of oral and written language (awareness that talking is more casually conversational than the formality of writing); and the fourth stage addresses the systematic integration of speaking and writing (the knowledge that a wide range of different forms can be used in both speaking and writing depending on the context, audience, and purpose of the communication). Although Kroll admitted that this model presents an oversimplification of the interaction that occurs, it is nonetheless helpful for explaining broad outlines of development.

For the handicapped population, the acquisition of written expression is typically problematic. Difficulties that inhibit achievement in this skill can occur in each or all of the preceding forms; a child who has oral language deficits and/or reading problems will, in all likelihood, have deficiencies in written expression also. However, instruction in writing should not be postponed until competency in the other modes has been achieved. It is much more viable to simultaneously teach all language skills in a holistic manner that will encourage growth through reciprocity.

Phelps-Gunn and Phelps-Terasaki (1982) have described written expression from a multidimensional framework that considers the dynamics involved in effective writing. They have developed a Total Writing Process Model for identifying and remediating deficits. This model addresses problems with form, content, and structure; pragmatic abilities for audience and mode; and proofreading. This instructional plan appears to be extremely comprehensive and may prove to be an effective method for remediating writing deficits.

REFERENCES

Kroll, B. M. (1981). Developmental relationships between speaking and writing. In B. M. Kroll & R. J. Vann (Eds.), *Exploring speaking-writing relationships: Connections and contrasts* (pp. 32–54). Urbana, IL: National Counsel of Teachers of English.

Loban, W. (1976). *Language development: Kindergarten through grade twelve.* Urbana, IL: National Counsel of Teachers of English.

Myklebust, H. R. (1965). *Development and disorders of written language* (Vol. 1). New York: Grune & Stratton.

Phelps-Gunn, T., & Phelps-Terasaki, D. (1982). *Written language instruction.* Rockville, MD: Aspen.

Wolf, M., & Dickinson, D. (1985). From oral to written language: Transition in school years. In J. B. Gleason (Ed.), *The development of language* (pp. 227–276). Columbus, OH: Merrill.

PEGGY L. ANDERSON
University of New Orleans

WRITING ASSESSMENT
WRITTEN LANGUAGE OF THE HANDICAPPED
WRITING REMEDIATION

WRITING ASSESSMENT

Competence in writing requires the mastery and automation of a vast array of skills. To ensure that these skills develop in an efficient and efficacious manner, it is generally believed that assessment should be included as an integral part of handicapped students' writing programs. This belief is primarily based on the assumption that information from the assessment process should make it possible for teachers to more readily determine a student's writing strengths and weaknesses, individualize instruction, monitor writing performance, and evaluate the effectiveness of the composition program.

The assessment of handicapped students' writing

should focus on both the written product and the process of writing (Graham, 1982). There are a host of procedures for evaluating the various attributes embodied in the written product; the most popular of these will be reviewed at length. Relatively few techniques, however, are available for examining the process by which students compose. The most common procedures include: (1) observing and, in some instances, timing the various activities and behaviors that the student engages in during the act of writing; (2) interviewing students about their approach to writing and questioning them about their reasons for particular composing behaviors; and (3) asking students to verbally report what they are thinking while they write. Regrettably, the reliability and validity of these procedures have not been adequately established and the results from such assessments may, as many critics have suggested, yield a distorted picture of the writing process (Humes, 1983).

Both formal and informal assessment procedures have been used to examine the relative merits and/or shortcomings of handicapped students' writing. The most frequently used standardized test is the Test of Written Language (TOWL). According to the authors (Hammill & Larsen, 1983), this instrument "can be used to ascertain the general adequacy of a product written by a student and to determine specific proficiency in word usage, punctuation and capitalization (style), spelling, handwriting, vocabulary, and sentence production" (p. 5). The TOWL consists of six subtests. Scores for three of these subtests (vocabulary, thematic maturity, and handwriting) are derived from a spontaneous sample of writing. The remaining word usage, spelling, and style subtests employ a contrived format; e.g., a student's proficiency in word usage is determined by a sentence completion activity. Although the TOWL appears to have a sound theoretical basis and to be reasonably valid and reliable, there is some question as to the value of the vocabulary and thematic maturity scores (Williams, 1985).

A second standardized test that has been used with handicapped students is the Picture Story Language Test (PSLT) (Myklebust, 1965). The PSLT has been used as a writing achievement test, a diagnostic instrument, and a research tool for studying the development and disorders of written language. In using this test, a student writes a story in response to a picture and the resulting composition is scored in terms of productivity (number of words, sentences, and words per sentence), correctness (word usage, word endings, and punctuation), and meaning (actual content conveyed). Although the PSLT has been widely used with handicapped students, serious questions regarding the validity and reliability of the instrument have been raised (Anastasiow, 1972).

Informal assessment procedures have been used to assess a variety of factors ranging from story quality to writing mechanics. Not surprisingly, the quality of students' writing has proven to be the most difficult factor to define and measure. Probably the oldest measure of writing qual-

ity is the holistic method. With this method, an examiner makes a single overall judgment on the quality of a student's writing (Mishler & Hogan, 1982). Each paper is read at a fairly rapid pace and the examiner attempts to weigh the various factors (e.g., content, organization, grammar, etc.) in roughly equal proportions. The examiner's overall impression is quantified on a Likert-type scale, ranging from poor to high quality. To increase accuracy and reliability, most holistic scoring systems include representative examples of specific scores.

A more complex procedure for determining the quality of a student's writing is the analytic method. With this method, the student's paper is analyzed and scored on the basis of several different factors such as ideation, grammar, and spelling (Moran, 1982). The scores for each of these factors are then averaged to produce a single grand score. Although the analytic method may provide more useful information for instructional purposes, it is much more time-consuming than the holistic method.

A relatively recent development in the measurement of writing quality is the primary trait scoring method. With this procedure, different scoring systems are developed for different writing tasks. For a task such as writing a short story, the examiner would decide ahead of time what traits should be evaluated and what type of responses will be considered appropriate and inappropriate for each trait. For example, for a short story one of the primary traits might be the introduction and development of the protagonist (Graham & Harris, 1986). Consequently, stories that adequately present and develop the leading character would receive credit for this trait.

It must be pointed out that measures of writing quality can be influenced by a variety of factors (Graham, 1982). One prominent source of variability involves the writer. Students often evidence considerable variation in their writing quality from one assignment to the next. Writing performance also can be influenced by the popularity of the proctor, the intended audience, teacher directions, and so on. An additional source of variability resides in the examiner. There is considerable evidence that grades assigned to student's papers tend to be unreliable. Fortunately, the consistency with which examiners score writing quality can be improved if the following guidelines and recommendations are followed: (1) examiners should receive considerable practice and training in using the intended scoring procedure; (2) the writing task should be highly structured and the assigned topic should be interesting; (3) identifying factors such as name, grade, and date should be removed from each paper; and (4) papers should not be graded for lengthy periods of time or in noisy or distracting environments.

A number of procedures have been used to evaluate the various elements embodied in the written products. Writing fluency has typically been assessed by examining total number of words written, average sentence length, and number of words written per minute. Vocabulary diversity has been measured by counting the occurrence of particular vocabulary items such as adjectives or adverbs and by computing the corrected type/token ratio (number of different words divided by the square root of twice the number of words in the sample) or the index of diversification (average number of words that appear between each occurrence of the most frequently used word in a composition). Proficiency with the mechanics of writing is generally determined by tabulating the occurrence of a particular behavior (e.g., spelling errors), while syntactic maturity is often defined in terms of the average length of T-units (main clause plus any attached or embedded subordinate clauses).

It is important to note that students' knowledge of their writing performance can be a powerful motivator and have a potent effect on learning. Nevertheless, the value of circling every misspelled word, writing "AWK" above every clumsy wording, or red-marking each deviation from standard English is questionable. Intensive evaluation may have little or no effect on writing improvement and may, in fact, make students more aware of their limitations and less willing to write (Burton & Arnold, 1963). Feedback on the positive aspects of a student's composition, in contrast, can have a facilitative effect on writing performance (Beaven, 1977). It also is desirable to dramatize a student's success through the use of charts, graphs, verbal praise, and so on.

REFERENCES

Anastasiow, N. (1972). Review of the Picture Story Language Test. In O. K. Buros (Ed.), *Seventh mental measurement yearbook*. Highland Park, NJ: Gryphon.

Beaven, M. (1977). Individualized goal setting, self-evaluation, and peer evaluation. In C. Cooper & L. Odell (Eds.), *Evaluating writing: Describing, measuring, judging*. Urbana, IL: National Council of Teachers of English.

Burton, D., Arnold, L. (1963). *The effects of frequency of writing and intensity of teacher evaluation upon high school students' performance in written composition*. (Research Report No. 1523). Tallahassee, FL: USOE Cooperative.

Graham, S. (1982). Composition research and practice: A unified approach. *Focus on Exceptional Children, 14*, 1–16.

Graham, S., & Harris, K. (1986). *Improving learning disabled students' compositions via story grammars: A component analysis of self-control strategy training*. Paper presented at the American Educational Research Association, San Francisco.

Hammill, D., & Larsen, S. (1983). *Test of written language*. Austin, TX: Pro-Ed.

Humes, A. (1983). Research on the composing process. *Review of Educational Research, 53*, 201–216.

Mishler, C., & Hogan, T. (1982). Holistic scoring of essays: Remedy for evaluating the third R. *Diagnostique, 8*, 4–16.

Moran, M. (1982). Analytic evaluation of formal written language skills as a diagnostic procedure. *Diagnostique, 8*, 17–31.

Myklebust, H. (1965). *Development and disorders of written language*. New York: Grune & Stratton.

Williams, R. (1985). Review of test of written language. In J. V. Mitchell (Ed.), *Ninth mental measurement yearbook*. Lincoln: University of Nebraska Press.

STEVE GRAHAM
University of Maryland

WRITTEN LANGUAGE OF THE HANDICAPPED
WRITING REMEDIATION

WRITING DISORDERS

While research on writing disorders in context is limited, the sources of difficulty emerge when they are considered within a framework or model of writing. Writing is a complex cognitive activity (Hayes & Flower 1980) that requires writers to coordinate and regulate the use of task-specific strategies during three overlapping and recursive writing stages (i.e., prewriting, drafting, and revising). During prewriting, task-specific strategies focus on planning and organizing. Writers generate and select writing topics, decide on a purpose for writing, identify the audience, generate and gather ideas about the topic, and organize the ideas into a network or structural plan (e.g., text structure such as story narrative, compare/contrast, sequence). During drafting, task-specific strategies involve the activation of the structural plan, translation of ideas into printed sentences, fleshing out of placeholders in the plan with details, and signaling of relationships among the elements of the plan. During monitoring and revising, task-specific strategies pertain to evaluation and analysis. The writer reads the draft to see whether the objectives concerning audience, topic, purpose, and structure have been achieved, and applies correction strategies to portions of the text that fail to meet expectations.

Though these task-specific strategies are necessary, they are not sufficient for skilled writing. A second domain involves the execution of these strategies. Metacognitive knowledge is the executive or self-control mechanism that helps writers activate and orchestrate activities in each of the writing stages. Metacognitive knowledge includes the ability to self-instruct or direct oneself in the writing stages, to monitor strategy use, and to modify or correct strategy use on the basis of outcomes. Without metacognitive knowledge, writers fail to access writing strategies and monitor their use even when the strategies are in their behavioral repertoire.

A third domain includes the mechanical skills that make writing a fluent process. This domain involves writers' knowledge of rules related to spelling (orthographic knowledge), writing conventions (punctuation, capitalization), and language (syntactic knowledge). These skills are of primary importance to writers in the stage of final revision in light of the importance of legibility to the audience. In addition, for the successful strategic employment of these skills, writers must not only acquire mechanical skills, they must acquire the task-specific strategies and metacognitive knowledge governing their use. For example, writers who lack task-specific strategies may not know how to rehearse or study spelling words to improve recall, whereas writers who lack metacognitive knowledge may learn to accurately spell words for the weekly spelling test, but fail to accurately spell or monitor their spelling of the same words in written compositions. Skillful writers not only acquire the mechanical means to produce text, they acquire the cognitive tools that help them know when and how to use those means, how to monitor their use, and how to correct errors when they occur.

According to this model of writing, writing disorders may result from one of several causes (Walmsley, 1983). First, writing disorders may emanate from a lack of understanding of task-specific strategies. For example, disabled writers with task-specific strategy deficits in the use of specific organizational structures may have trouble employing a relevant text structure that can guide them in planning, organizing, drafting, and monitoring their ideas. Second, writing disabilities may result from deficiencies in metacognitive knowledge. Such writers may have learned strategies but fail to activate them in the appropriate situations. Third, impairments in related cognitive processes may affect writing performance. Specifically, inadequate or delayed development in listening, speaking, or reading may affect writing performance since these processes share a common language base and rely on similar strategic processes involving the communication and comprehension of ideas. Finally, the failure to acquire specific rule-governed principles in spelling, grammar, and writing conventions can detrimentally affect the mechanics of writing, writing fluency, and overall comprehensibility.

More is known about the specific disabilities of students in the domain of writing mechanics than is known about disabilities in the use of task-specific strategies or metacognitive knowledge. Several studies confirm that disabled learners commit more punctuation and capitalization errors than nondisabled learners (Myklebust, 1973; Poplin et al., 1980; Poteet, 1978). These deficiencies have been observed in terms of students' ability to rewrite sentences containing punctuation and capitalization errors and to generate error-free compositions. Even greater performance differences between disabled and nondisabled students have been found on measures of spelling accuracy (Myklebust, 1973; Poplin et al., 1980; Poteet, 1978). Furthermore, disabled learners have deficiencies in their ability to apply task-specific strategies involving the study of spelling words (Foster & Torgesen, 1983) and in their application of metacognitive knowledge to detect and correct spelling errors (Deshler, 1978; Gerber & Hall, in press). However, several studies suggest that strategy and metacognitive deficits may be ameliorated with training. For

example, research suggests that spelling deficits can be partly overcome by the teaching of task-specific strategies involving procedures for studying spelling words (Graham & Freeman, 1985; Nulman & Gerber, 1984), and for spelling novel words by analogy to known words (Englert, Hiebert, & Stewart, 1985). Likewise, metacognitive deficiencies involving the monitoring, detection, and correction of spelling errors or mechanical errors may be remediated with self-instructional training that directs students to reread and correct errors (Gerber & Hall, in press; Schumaker et al., 1982).

Mechanical aspects involving syntactic skills also have been studied, but the results are more equivocal. On tasks that require students to produce the correct syntactic form (e.g., subject-verb agreement, plurals) in incomplete sentences, disabled writers perform significantly lower than nondisabled writers (Poplin et al., 1980). On the other hand, on measures of syntactic complexity based on the average length of sentences and clauses produced by students, several studies have reported no qualitative differences in the presence of certain syntactic structures or the complexity of sentences (Moran, 1981; Nodine, Barenbaum, & Newcomer, 1985; Poteet, 1978). At the same time, several studies have found quantitative differences in students' written productions: disabled writers produced significantly fewer sentences and fewer total words (Myklebust, 1973; Nodine et al., 1985; Poteet, 1978). Thus performance seems to be delimited less by students' syntactic inadequacies than by difficulties in knowing how to generate ideas and how to sustain thoughts about a topic.

Though mechanical skills are important, they are not the barrier to proficient writing once thought (Walmsley, 1983). The teaching of mechanical skills does not necessarily improve the quality of compositions, and young writers do not need to master the mechanics of writing before being introduced to writing. Instead, writers' knowledge of task-specific strategies in the actual composing process may be a more critical determinant of writing success. Of particular importance in the domain of composing strategies is students' awareness of text structures. Text structures are specific organizational schemes internalized by writers that describe the elements that should be included and how they should be ordered. There are different text structures for different writing purposes. For example, stories usually consist of five major elements: a setting (i.e., main character, time, place), a problem confronting the main character, the main character's response to the problem, the outcome of the response, and the story's conclusion. Similarly, expository materials contain structures such as compare/contrast, problem/solution, and chronological sequence. Knowledge of these structures influences the ability of writers to successfully plan, generate, organize, compose, and monitor their ideas.

Nodine et al. (1985) conducted one of the few studies examining children's use of a story structure in written compositions. A group of learning-disabled, reading-disabled, and normally achieving students were asked to write a story about three related pictures. The results suggested that learning-disabled (LD) students differed from both reading-disabled and normally achieving students in their ability to produce a tale that was storylike. Almost half of the LD students failed to generate a story that met story structure expectations. Furthermore, LD students were less aware of potential confusions caused by unrelated or inexplicable events in their compositions. Similar deficits in structural awareness have been reported in studies examining students' knowledge of expository text structures (Englert & Thomas, in press; Wong & Wilson, 1984). Englert and Thomas (in press) found that LD students differed from low-achieving students in the extent to which knowledge of text structures created expectancies that helped students identify and write relevant details. Since LD students' writing was legible and interpretable, proficiency was not so much delimited by poor writing mechanics as by their insensitivity to higher-order units corresponding to text structure.

The domain important to both the successful use of task-specific strategies and mechanical skills in composing is metacognitive knowledge. Metacognitive knowledge includes the abilities to self-instruct, self-monitor, self-correct, and self-regulate the writing process. Several studies suggest that disabled learners have serious deficiencies in their ability to activate previously learned strategies and to self-instruct or self-monitor during text production and comprehension (Bos & Filip, 1984; Wong, 1985). That these problems are attributable to metacognitive knowledge is suggested by two studies that indicate that the training of self-control processes improves composing and organizational abilities. Wong and Sawatsky (1984), for example, taught learning-disabled students to elaborate on or finish an initial sentence stem (e.g., The tall man helped the woman) by employing a five-step self-control procedure that helped students determine the writing purpose, draft a response, and monitor their writing. Following training, the sentence elaborations of students significantly improved. Similarly, Wong and Wilson (1984) trained learning-disabled students to organize scrambled passages by applying a five-step self-instructional procedure. The ease with which students were trained suggested that the learning-disabled children may have had some rudimentary idea about passage organization, but it was either incompletely developed or not spontaneously activated by the students. Since students readily benefited from self-control training, the results suggested that metacognitive strategies were similarly inactive or incomplete.

In summary, the literature suggests that several deficiencies may impede students' writing performance. Deficiencies in spelling, grammar, and writing conventions have been reported—though these may not be the barriers to writing succcess as much as students' lack of task-specific strategies and metacognitive knowledge. Research is still needed to determine the impact of other elements of the writing process (e.g., audience, prior knowledge) on performance in each of the writing stages. However, it is certain that writing competence will be associated not only with the acquisition of efficient strategies pertaining to the use of each element, but with the metacognitive knowledge that helps the writer know when and how to use the element in planning, drafting, monitoring, and revising compositions.

REFERENCES

Bos, C. S., & Filip, D. (1984). Comprehension monitoring in learning disabled and average students. *Journal of Learning Disabilities, 17*, 229–233.

Deshler, D. D. (1978). *Psychoeducational aspects of learning-disabled adolescents.* In L. M. Mann, L. Goodman, & T. L. Wiederholt (Eds.), *Teaching the learning-disabled adolescent.* Boston: Houghton Mifflin.

Englert, C. S., Hiebert, E. H., & Stewart, S. R. (1985). Spelling unfamiliar words by an analogy strategy. *Journal of Special Education, 19*, 291–306.

Englert, C. S., & Thomas, C. C. (in press). Sensitivity to text structure in reading and writing: A comparison of learning disabled and nonhandicapped students. *Learning Disability Quarterly.*

Hayes, J. R., & Flower, L. S. (1980). Writing as problem solving. *Visible Language, 14*, 388–399.

Foster, K., & Torgesen, J. K. (1983). The effects of directed study on the spelling performance of two subgroups of learning disabled students. *Learning Disability Quarterly, 6*, 252–257.

Gerber, M. M., & Hall, R. J. (in press). Development of orthographic problem-solving in learning disabled and normally achieving children. *Monograph for the Society for Learning Disabilities & Remedial Education.*

Graham, S., & Freeman, S. (1985). Strategy training and teacher- vs. student-controlled study conditions: Effects on LD students' spelling performance. *Learning Disability Quarterly, 8*, 267–274.

Moran, M. R. (1981). Performance of learning disabled and low achieving secondary students on formal features of a paragraph-writing task. *Learning Disability Quarterly, 4*, 271–280.

Myklebust, H. R. (1973). *Development and disorders of written language. Vol. 2. Studies of normal and exceptional children.* NY: Grune & Stratton.

Nodine, B. F., Barenbaum, E., & Newcomer, P. (1985). Story composition by learning disabled, reading disabled, and normal children. *Learning Disability Quarterly, 8*, 167–179.

Nulman, J. A. H., & Gerber, M. M. (1984). Improving spelling performance by imitating a child's errors. *Journal of Learning Disabilities, 17*, 328–333.

Poplin, M. S., Gray, R., Larsen, S., Banikoski, A., & Mehring, T. (1980). A comparison of components of written expression abilities in learning disabled and non-learning disabled students at three grade levels. *Learning Disability Quarterly, 3*, 46–53.

Poteet, J. A. (1978). *Characteristics of written expression of learning disabled and non-learning disabled elementary school stu-*

dents. Muncie, IN: Ball State University. (ERIC Document Reproduction Service No. ED 1590830).

Schumaker, J. B., Deshler, D. D., Alley, G. R., Warner, M. M., Clark, F. L., & Nolan, S. (1982). Error monitoring: A learning strategy for improving adolescent academic performance. In M. W. Cruickshank & J. W. Lerner (Eds.), *Coming of age: Vol. 3. The best of ACLD*. Syracuse, NY: Syracuse University Press.

Walmsley, S. A. (1983). Writing disability. In P. Mosenthal, L. Tamor, & S. A. Walmsley (Eds.), *Research on writing: Principles and methods*. New York: Longman.

Wong, B. Y. L. (1985). Metacognition and learning disabilities. In D. L. Forrest-Pressley, G. E. MacKinnon, & T. G. Waller (Eds.), *Metacognition, cognition and human performance: Vol. 2. Instructional Practices* (pp. 137–180). New York: Academic.

Wong, B. Y. L., & Sawatsky, D. (1984). Sentence elaboration and retention of good, average and poor readers. *Learning Disability Quarterly, 7*, 229–236.

Wong, B. Y. L., & Wilson, (1984). Investigating awareness of and teaching passage organization in learning disabled children. *Journal of Learning Disabilities, 17*, 477–482.

Carol Sue Englert
Michigan State University

WRITING ASSESSMENT
WRITING REMEDIATION
WRITTEN LANGUAGE OF THE HANDICAPPED

WRITING REMEDIATION

The writing difficulties exhibited by many handicapped students necessitate the development and use of instructional procedures aimed at improving writing competence, particularly in terms of handicapped students' functional writing skills. The remediation of handicapped students' writing difficulties, however, has not received much attention in either the research literature or in school settings. Leinhardt, Zigmond, and Cooley (1980) found, for example, that handicapped students may spend less than 10 minutes a day generating written language. Although there are many possible reasons why writing remediation appears to receive a limited amount of time and emphasis in handicapped students' instructional programs, teacher attitudes and backgrounds may be the key factors in determining the quantity and quality of writing instruction for these students. According to Graham (1982), many teachers do not enjoy writing and are not prepared to teach composition. Furthermore, many special education teachers may feel that writing is not a critical skill for their students and may choose to spend their instructional time teaching what they consider to be more important skills (e.g., reading and arithmetic).

For the most part, writing instruction for handicapped students has drawn heavily on techniques used with normally achieving youngsters. One commonly recommended instructional procedure has been to use a phase approach.

This approach emphasizes the various stages of the composition process (prewriting, writing, and revising) and is designed to develop security in the use of these stages. In a phase approach described by Silverman et al. (1981), the teacher first structures the writing process with prewriting activities that involve thinking, experiencing, discussing, and interacting. The student and the teacher then develop a series of questions that are used to guide the writing process. During the revising stage, the teacher critiques the student's writing and they jointly revise the student's paper. Although empirical support for this particular model or other phase approaches is limited, this writing procedure does stress the development of two important skills: thinking as a preliminary facet of composing and revision of the initial draft of the written product. In addition, a phase approach to writing may be especially suitable for handicapped students since it helps reduce cognitive strain by taking a large complex problem such as writing and breaking it down into smaller subproblems.

Another traditional approach that has been used to teach specific writing skills to handicapped students is modeling. With this approach, students may be asked to imitate a specific type of sentence pattern, a well-known style of writing, a certain type of paragraph, and so on. There are two basic approaches to modeling. One approach stresses strategy explanation and model illustration; the other emphasizes problem solving. With the former, a student may be asked to mimic a specific type of paragraph (e.g., topic sentence located at the start of the paragraph) following an examination and analysis of several examples that are representative of the style to be emulated. The latter can be illustrated by examining a procedure developed by Schiff (1978). With this procedure, examples of a particular type of paragraph are selected. Sentences for each paragraph are then written on a separate strip of paper and their order randomized. Students rearrange the sentences in each paragraph and compare their arrangements with the original model. At present, it is impossible to draw any definitive conclusions on the relative effectiveness of these procedures, as there is virtually no research that examines them.

A greal deal of attention has been directed at teaching handicapped students information about language and writing with the aim of promoting the correct use of structure, form, and language. One of the most consistently held beliefs in the history of writing instruction is that the teaching of grammar and usage is critical to the development of writing competence. Formal grammar, however, is difficult to master and knowledge of grammatical concepts does not appear to be necessary for the skillful use of written language (Blount, 1973). This is not meant to imply that teachers should not attend to handicapped students' use of structure or form in their writing or that these skills cannot be improved. Rather, improvement of usage and form "may be more effectively achieved through direct practice of desirable forms when the need arises" (Graham, 1982, p. 6).

An interesting alternative to traditional writing approaches is the use of procedures that seek to minimize or circumvent handicapped students' poor writing skills. The most commonly used alternative is dictation. Traditionally, dictation has involved having a student furnish the content or ideas orally while the teacher or a peer structures the form the material takes on paper. The conventional dictation process can be adapted by using a tape recorder as an aid to organizing content; i.e., ideas are taped and later written and edited by the student. In some instances, dictation is employed as a temporary aid and its use diminishes as the student becomes more adept at the mechanics of writing. Dictation may represent a viable alternative for students with adequate oral language skills who have been unable, after years of intensive instruction, to automate and integrate basic writing skills.

A recent alternative to traditional writing instruction approaches is the cognitive-behavior modification (CBM) procedure. Typically CBM training involves teaching students to regulate task-specific and metacognitive strategies through processes such as self-instruction, self-assessment, and self-reinforcement (Harris, 1982). For example, Harris and Graham (1985) reported a CBM composition training procedure that significantly increased learning-disabled students' use of verbs, adverbs, and adjectives and resulted in higher story quality ratings. Further, generalization and maintenance probes taken up to 14 weeks after training yielded positive results. The CBM training regimen in this study included skills training (instruction on specific task-appropriate strategies), metacognitive training (instruction in the self-regulation of those strategies), and instruction concerning the significance of such activities. In a second study, Graham and Harris (1986) found that CBM procedures also could be used to improve the overall structure of learning-disabled students' compositions through the use of a story grammar strategy. Training procedures were similar to those in the first study; however, strategy training consisted of instruction in story grammar elements: setting, goal(s), action(s), emotional responses, and ending.

Educators also have attempted to improve handicapped students' writing skills by further refining or developing their reading, oral language, and thinking skills. Since reading, writing, thinking, and language skills are interrelated, it is assumed that intensive and generalized instruction in an area such as oral language, for example, will have an indirect and positive effect on a student's writing ability (Groff, 1978). Although these skills may be interrelated, they do not necessarily function in an interactive and supportive way. Generalized instruction in an area such as reading or oral language appears to be of limited value in the immediate improvement of a student's writing (Graham, 1982).

A recent development in the teaching of writing to the handicapped has been the advent of the computer, particularly the word processor. The word processor, with its various capabilities for storing and editing texts, has the potential to both strengthen and significantly change the nature of writing instruction. The word processor and other technological advances should not, however, be viewed as a cure-all for handicapped students' writing problems. MacArthur and Graham (1986), for instance, found no major differences between handwritten stories and those composed on a word processor, even though the learning-disabled students in their study had considerable experience using the computer.

Additional instructional recommendations for teaching writing to the handicapped have been summarized by Graham (1982). These include (1) providing students with plenty of opportunities to write and exposing them to a variety of practical and imaginative assignments; (2) having writing assignments, whenever possible, serve a real purpose and be directed at an authentic audience; (3) having a pleasant and encouraging composition program; and (4) deemphasizing writing errors.

REFERENCES

Blount, N. (1973). Research on teaching literature, language, and composition. In R. Travers (Ed.), *Second handbook of research on teaching*. Chicago; Rand McNally.

Graham, S. (1982). Composition research and practice: A unified approach. *Focus on Exceptional Children, 14*, 1–16.

Graham, S., & Harris, K. (1986). *Improving learning disabled students' compositions via story grammars: A component analysis of self-control strategy training.* Paper presented at the American Educational Research Association, San Francisco.

Groff, P. (1978). Children's oral language and their written composition. *Elementary School Journal, 78*, 181–191.

Harris, K. (1982). Cognitive behavior modification: Application with exceptional students. *Focus on Exceptional Children, 15*, 1–16.

Harris, K., & Graham, S. (1985). Improving learning disabled students' composition skills: Self-control strategy training. *Learning Disability Quarterly, 8*, 27–36.

Leinhardt, G., Zigmond, N., & Cooley, W. (1980). *Reading instruction and its effects.* Paper presented at the American Educational Research Association, Boston.

MacArthur, C., & Graham, S. (1986). *LD students' writing under three conditions: Word processing, dictation, and handwriting.* Paper presented at the American Educational Research Association, San Francisco.

Schiff, P. (1978). Problem solving and the composition model: Reorganization, manipulation, analysis. *Research in the Teaching of English, 12*, 203–210.

Silverman, R., Zigmond, N., Zimmerman, J., & Vallecorsa, A. (1981). Improving written expression in learning disabled students. *Topics in Language Disorders, 1*, 91–99.

STEVE GRAHAM
KAREN R. HARRIS
University of Maryland

WRITTEN COMPOSITION DISABILITIES

Research in the field of learning disabilities has recently expanded to include the area of written composition. Investigation of writing skills includes both a process and product approach. In a process approach, expert and novice writers are compared to identify methods of composing that differentiate the two. The population of learning disabilities has not been directly addressed in this research, but information regarding novice writers offers insight into the difficulties of disabled writers. In general, process research indicates that novice writers often become entangled in lower level subprocesses at the sentence and word levels of syntax and grammar (Hayes & Flower, 1983). Experts, however, have the ability to stratify their writing processes. They deal first with higher level rhetorical concerns such as form, meaning, and context, then move down through a continuum to lower level lexical concerns (Sommers, 1982).

Results of product research in which disabled writers and nondisabled writers are compared have fit well with results of process research. Product research has shown that disabled writers make more errors than nondisabled writers, and that these errors are at a lower level of concern, including word order, word usage, word endings, and punctuation (Myklebust, 1973; Poplin et al., 1980). Product research also has found the writing abilities of disabled students to be commensurate with the abilities of nondisabled students at the same reading level (Moran, 1981; Weiner, 1980). These studies indicate that writing and reading may be manifestations of a more general language deficit.

Instructional strategies for disabled writers have included sentence combining, peer and self-evaluation, reinforcement (Hallahan, Kauffman, & Lloyd, 1985), use of microcomputers (Lees, 1985), and use of auditory feedback for revision (Espin & Sindelar, 1986).

REFERENCES

Espin, C. A., & Sindelar, P. T. (1986). *The effects of auditory feedback on the written revisions of learning disabled and nondisabled students.* Unpublished master's thesis, Pennsylvania State University, State College, PA.

Hayes, J. R., & Flower, S. (1983). *A cognitive model of the writing process in adults. Final report.* Pittsburgh, PA; Carnegie-Mellon University. (ERIC Document Reproduction Service No. Ed 240 608)

Hallahan, D. P., Kauffman, J. M., & Lloyd, J. W. (1985). *Introduction to learning disabilities* (2nd ed.). Englewood Cliffs, NJ: Prentice-Hall.

Lees, E. O. (1985). Proofreading with ears: A case study of text-to-voice performance of a student's writing. *College Microcomputer, 3,* 339–343.

Moran, M. R. (1981). Performance of learning and low achieving secondary students on formal features of a paragraph writing task. *Learning Disability Quarterly, 4*(3), 271–279.

Myklebust, H. R. (1973). *Development and disorders of written language. Vol. 2: Studies of normal and exceptional children.* New York: Grune & Stratton.

Poplin, M. S., Gray, R., Larsen, S., Banikowski, A., & Mehring, T. (1980). A comparison of components of written expression abilities in learning disabled and non-learning disabled students at three grade levels. *Learning Disability Quarterly, 3*(4), 46–53.

Sommers, N. (1982). *Revision strategies of student writers and experienced adult writers.* Washington, DC: National Institution of Education. (ERIC Document Reproduction Service No. Ed 220 839)

Weiner, E. S. (1980). The diagnostic evaluation of writing skills (DEWS): Application of DEWS criteria to writing samples. *Learning Disability Quarterly, 3*(2), 54–59.

CHRISTINE A. ESPIN
University of Minnesota

WRITTEN LANGUAGE OF HANDICAPPED

In addition to other academic problems, it is generally agreed that handicapped students have difficulty using the medium of written language to express their ideas and thoughts (Graham, 1982). It would be difficult at present, however, to substantiate this belief since the written language problems of the handicapped have received little attention from either researchers or the educational community in general. While there are many possible reasons why there has been a notable lack of interest in this important language skill, two factors merit special attention. First, it is likely that handicapped students' writing problems have not received much emphasis because most special educators lack specific training in this particular area and feel that writing is not a critical skill for their students. Second, the difficulties inherent in measuring written language have proven to be formidable obstacles to researchers interested in describing the writing characteristics of the handicapped. Adequate procedures for measuring a complex phenomena such as composition quality, for instance, do not exist.

The information that is available on the written language of the handicapped has primarily centered on two disabilities: learning disabilities and hearing impairments. Even though some students with visual impairments and/or physical disabilities may require special writing programs and technological adaptations (Napier, 1973), no information is available on the writing characteristics of these students. Furthermore, the definitive source on the writing problems of students with emotional/ behavioral difficulties, mental retardation, and speech and language disorders is a single large-scale study conducted by Myklebust (1973).

Even in areas where a more solid research base exists, knowledge of students' writing characteristics is extremely limited. For example, considerable information has been gathered on the length, syntactic complexity, vocabulary diversity, etc., of learning-disabled students' compositions. Most of our knowledge concerning these factors, however, is restricted to elementary-age students and a fairly narrow range of writing tasks (primarily creative writing assignments). Our understanding of how handicapped students' writing skills develop is, at best, spotty. Virtually no attention has been directed at determining how they plan and revise their compositions, and the effects of different audiences on their writing performance is unknown.

Although it is generally agreed that written language development may be influenced by a variety of factors (Bereiter, 1980), surprisingly little research has been conducted with handicapped students to determine the relationship between their writing performance and various genetic and environmental variables. If research conducted with normal students can be used as a benchmark, then handicapped students' writing performance may be related to and, in some instances, influenced by the following: general language development, intelligence, maturity, reading achievement, sex, socioeconomic status, personality characteristics, school locale, and specific cognitive abilities such as short- and long-term memory (Graham, 1982).

It is also important to point out that although some similarities may exist, students with different disabilities often have different writing characteristics and ultimately different instructional needs. As a result, the remainder of this article will provide a brief survey of the writing characteristics of each disability area in which empirical evidence is available.

An examination of the available literature reveals that students who are labeled mentally retarded have severe writing difficulties that tend to persist over time. From elementary to high school, they score significantly lower than normal students on a variety of written language tasks. Retarded students make consistently more grammatical and spelling errors and their written compositions evidence less vocabulary diversity (Sedlack & Cartwright, 1972). If a study by Myklebust (1973) is representative, it also appears that creative stories composed by mentally retarded students are written on a more concrete level than those written by their normal counterparts. The severity of retarded students' writing difficulties is further reflected in the finding that these students have more

problems with writing than they do with speaking, listening, or reading (Durrell & Sullivan, 1958). Unfortunately, most retarded students evidence only modest growth in writing skills, which may reach its peak at the time of adolescence (Myklebust, 1973).

It is difficult to draw any definitive conclusions on the writing characteristics of students with emotional/behavioral problems because only one study was located that examined this question. Myklebust (1973) investigated the story writing characteristics of school-identified emotionally disturbed children and youths. In comparison with normal peers, these students scored lower on written measures of fluency, correctness, and meaning. Their greatest proficiency was in the area of syntax. It is interesting to note that they made impressive gains in several skill areas over time. Not surprisingly, the writing of the emotionally disturbed was superior to that of the mentally retarded, but inferior to the writing of students with reading disabilities.

Myklebust (1973) also examined the writing performance of students with articulation disorders. These students wrote extremely short stories comprised of only two to six sentences. While their stories tended to be less abstract than those written by normal students, the written syntax of the older students with articulation disorders was within the normal range. In comparison with other handicapped students, their writing performance was superior to that of students classified as emotionally disturbed and mentally retarded.

Studies examining the writing performance of students with hearing impairments have primarily been restricted to examining sentence structure, vocabulary diversity, spelling and grammatical errors, and productivity. In comparison with normal students, sentences composed by the hearing impaired tend to be less complex, with more errors and less diversity in vocabulary usage (Powers & Wilgus, 1983; Yoshinaga-Itano & Snyder, 1985). Wilbur and Nolen (in press) have indicated that stories written by the deaf often lack creativity, cohesiveness, and complexity in terms of temporal sequence. They further point out that the material written by these students is generally stilted and vocabulary choice is restricted to a small number of words. Although hearing-impaired students' poor performance on measures of written language is, in part, due to their hearing loss and resulting language deficits, instructional variables also appear to be a contributing factor.

Learning-disabled students typically have a great deal of difficulty expressing themselves in writing. In terms of overall quality and content, their writing has consistently been found to be inferior to that of average students. Graham and Harris (1986), for example, compared the stories of sixth-grade learning-disabled and average students using holistic ratings of quality. With the holistic method, raters make a single overall judgment about the quality of the writing sample based on a variety of factors, including content, imagination, structure, word choice, and writing conventions. Mean scores for the learning-disabled and average groups, on a scale ranging from 1 to 8, were 2.2 and 4.5, respectively.

In addition, Poplin et al. (1980) compared learning-disabled and normal students in grades three through eight on the thematic maturity subtest of the Test of Written Language. This subtest reportedly measures whether the student's story has been written in a logical manner that efficiently conveys meaning. The differences between the learning-disabled and normal students on the thematic maturity subtest increased with age. There were no significant differences between third to fourth graders, but at fifth through eighth grades, average students outperformed the learning disabled.

Other investigators have studied the structure and completeness of stories written by the learning disabled. MacArthur and Graham (1986) used an analytical scale based on the common elements contained in most short stories. Most of the stories written by learning-disabled students included main and supporting characters, action, and an ending, but few included explicit goals, starter events, or emotional reactions. Nodine, Barenbaum, and Newcomer (1985), on the other hand, had 11-year-old learning-disabled, reading-disabled, and normal students write narratives in response to a sequence of pictures. The students' compositions were classified as stories, storylike, descriptive, or expressive. To be judged as a story, a composition had to include a setting, conflict, and resolution. Complete stories were written by 71% of the normal students, 47% of the reading disabled, and only 30% of the learning disabled. Nearly half of the learning-disabled students (48%) wrote compositions with no story line.

Research has also shown that learning-disabled students write stories and essays that are shorter than those of their normally achieving peers. For instance, Nodine et al. (1985) reported that learning-disabled students' stories were on the average 54 words in length, while normal children wrote stories with approximately 104 words. Limited fluency may be related to lower overall quality and content. MacArthur and Graham (1986) found significant correlations between length and story structure and a measure of overall quality.

An additional difficulty exhibited by most learning-disabled students involves the mechanics of writing. On both standardized tests and informal measures of contextual writing, these students demonstrate considerable difficulty in spelling words correctly or using proper punctuation and capitalization (Moran, 1981). Spelling problems appear to be particularly pronounced among learning-disabled students.

Although it is generally assumed that learning-disabled students have difficulty with written grammar and vocabulary, research has yielded conflicting results concerning this issue. Morris and Crump (1982), for example, reported that learning-disabled students' written vocabulary is less varied than that of normal students. In contrast, Deno, Marston, & Mirkin (1982) found no differences between normal students and the learning disabled on several vocabulary measures. In terms of grammatical or syntactical difficulties, several studies have found no differences in the syntactical maturity of learning-disabled and normal students' compositions (Nodine et al., 1985). Learning-disabled students, however, tend to make more grammatical errors than their normal peers (Moran, 1981).

Finally, only one study was located that examined both the product and process of writing. MacArthur and Graham (1986) videotaped learning-disabled students as they composed stories using three different methods: handwriting, dictation, and word processing. Results from the study revealed that dictated stories were over three times as long as stories produced under the other conditions and that they were rated significantly higher on overall quality. Regardless of the mode of writing, students engaged in almost no planning prior to writing their stories. Furthermore, students made a few revisions (on average, about 24 per 100 words), but most revisions (57%) involved surface changes such as changing the spelling of a word. Only 10% of all revisions affected the meaning of what the student wrote. Further research on the writing process of learning-disabled and other handicapped students is needed to understand how these students write so that teachers can help them learn to write more effectively.

REFERENCES

Bereiter, C. (1980). Development in writing. In L. Gregg & E. Steinberg (Eds.), *Cognitive processes in writing*. Hillsdale, NJ: Erlbaum.

Deno, S., Marston, D., & Mirkin, P. (1982). Valid measurement procedures for continuous evaluation of written expression. *Exceptional Children, 48*, 368–371.

Durrell, D., & Sullivan, H. (1958). *Language achievement of mentally retarded children* (USOE Cooperative Research Report No. 014). Boston: Boston University.

Graham, S. (1982). Composition research and practice: A unified approach. *Focus on Exceptional Children, 14*, 1–16.

Graham, S., & Harris, K. (1986). *Improving learning disabled students' compositions via story grammars: A component analysis of self-control strategy training*. Paper presented at the American Educational Research Association, San Francisco.

MacArthur, C., & Graham, S. (1986). *LD students' writing under three conditions: Word processing, dictation, and handwriting*. Paper presented at the American Educational Research Association, San Francisco.

Moran, M. (1981). Performance of learning disabled and low achieving secondary students on formal features of a paragraph-writing task. *Learning Disability Quarterly, 4*, 271–280.

Morris, N., & Crump, D. (1982). Syntactic and vocabulary development in the written language of learning disabled and non-learning disabled students at four age levels. *Learning Disability Quarterly, 5*, 163–172.

Myklebust, H. (1973). *Development and disorders of written language: Studies of normal and exceptional children*. New York: Grune & Stratton.

Napier, G. (1973). A writing study relative to braille contractions to be mastered by primary level children. *Education of the Visually Handicapped, 5*, 74–78.

Nodine, B., Barenbaum, E., & Newcomer, P. (1985). Story composition by learning disabled, reading disabled, and normal children. *Learning Disability Quarterly, 8*, 167–179.

Poplin, M., Gray, R., Larsen, S., Banikowski, A., & Mehring, T. (1980). A comparison of components of written expression abilities in learning disabled and non-learning disabled students at three grade levels. *Learning Disability Quarterly, 3*, 46–53.

Powers, A., & Wilgus, S. (1983). Linguistic complexity of the written language of hearing-impaired children. *Volta Review, 85*, 201–210.

Sedlack, R., & Cartwright, G. (1972). Written language abilities of EMR and nonretarded children with the same mental age. *American Journal of Mental Deficiency, 77*, 95–99.

Wilbur, S., & Nolen, S. (in press). Reading and writing. In *Gallaudet encyclopedia of deaf people and deafness*. New York: McGraw-Hill.

Yoshinaga-Itano, C., & Snyder, L. (1985). Form and meaning in the written language of hearing-impaired children. *Volta Review, 87*, 75–90.

STEVE GRAHAM
CHARLES A. MACARTHUR
University of Maryland

DYSGRAPHIA
HANDWRITING
WRITING DISORDERS

WYATT v. STICKNEY

The case of *Wyatt* v. *Stickney* established constitutionally minimum standards of care and treatment for involuntarily committed patients in Alabama's state institutions for the mentally ill and mentally retarded. This landmark federal judicial intervention in the mental institutions of a sovereign state signaled dozens of *Wyatt*-type "right to treatment" lawsuits in nearly every part of the country. As a result of the unrefuted "atrocities" documented in *Wyatt* (1972), the "shocking" and "inhumane" conditions in New York's Willowbrook State School for the Mentally Retarded (1973), and 25 other suits involving the U.S. Justice Department (1979), congressional legislation for financial assistance and a "Bill of Rights" for institutionalized persons were enacted.

Only six decisions based on the Wyatt case have ever been published in the law reports (1971–1981), although it is cited in over 200 judicial decisions and is the subject of numerous law reviews and other professional journal articles.

Ricky Wyatt was one of about 5000 mental patients at Bryce State Hospital, Tuscaloosa, the same hospital established in 1861 through the urging of the advocate Dorothea Dix. Stonewall B. Stickney was a psychiatrist and the chief administrative officer of Alabama's Mental Health Board. The cases was filed initially by 99 of 100 dismissed staff members plus Ricky Wyatt's aunt and other guardians on October 23, 1970. The plaintiff employees alleged that this reduction in staff would deprive patients at Bryce of necessary treatment and sued for reinstatement. Stickney had released over 100 of the 1600 employees at Bryce owing to reduced state cigarette tax revenues allocated to the department, while redirecting the limited funds to community mental health services. Stickney believed in preventing institutionalization.

The employee plaintiffs withdrew their reinstatement claim prior to Judge Frank M. Johnson's initial reported decision on March 12, 1971. The court found that more than 1500 geriatric patients and about 1000 mentally retarded patients were involuntarily committed at Bryce for reasons other than being mentally ill, and were receiving custodial care but not treatment.

Judge Johnson ordered the development and implementation of adequate treatment standards and a report within 6 months; he requested the U.S. departments of Justice and Health, Education, and Welfare, as "friends of the court," to assist in evaluating the treatment programs and standards. On August 12, 1971, the court allowed the request. All involuntary patients from Partlow State School and Hospital in Tuscaloosa, housing nearly 2500 mental retardates with segregated facilities for blacks, and Searcy Hospital in Mount Vernon, a formerly all-black hospital for the mentally ill, were to be included in the class suit. Defendants filed the court-directed report on September 23, 1971, and Judge Johnson ruled on December 10, 1971, allowing the state 6 months to correct three basic deficiencies. He called for "a humane psychological and physical environment, . . . qualified staff in numbers sufficient to administer adequate treatment, and . . . individualized treatment plans." Following additional testimony, briefs, and standards proposed by "the foremost authorities on mental health in the United States," the parties agreed to standards that mandated a "constitutionally acceptable minimum treatment program" for the mentally ill at Bryce and Searcy as ordered by the court on April 13, 1972.

Judge Johnson also ruled, in a supplemental order issued the same day, that unrebutted evidence of the "hazardous and deplorable inadequacies in the institution's operations at Partlow was more shocking than at Bryce or Searcy." He said that "The result of almost 50 years of legislative neglect has been catastrophic; atrocities occur daily"; Judge Johnson published these findings (1972):

A few of the atrocious incidents cited at the hearing in this case include the following: (a) a resident was scalded to death by hydrant water; (b) a resident was restrained in a strait jacket for 9 years in order to prevent hand and finger sucking; (c) a resident was inappropriately confined in seclusion for a period of years, and (d) a resident died from the insertion by another resident of a running water hose into his rectum. Each of these incidents could have been avoided had adequate staff and facilities been available.

Judge Johnson ordered the defendants to (1) implement the standards for adequate habilitation for the retarded at Partlow; (2) establish a human rights committee; (3) employ a new administrator; (4) submit a progress report to the court within 6 months; and (5) pay attorneys' fees and costs to the plaintiffs.

The defendants appealed both decisions to the Fifth Circuit Court of Appeals in May 1972. The review court, on November 8, 1974, upheld the constitutional right to treatment concept and ruled that the federal judicially determined standards did not violate the state's legislative rights.

Although subsequent implementation and compliance with the court's orders continue to produce controversies, numerous motions, briefs, hearings, and additional opinions have been issued. However, no legal changes have occurred in *Wyatt* as of the last published order of the court on March 25, 1981.

REFERENCE

Civil rights of the institutionalized. Report of the Committee on Judiciary United States Senate on S.10 together with minority and additional views (1979). Washington, DC: U.S. Government Printing Office.

Louis Schwartz
Florida State University

HISTORY OF SPECIAL EDUCATION
LEGAL REGULATIONS OF SPECIAL EDUCATION
PHILOSOPHY OF EDUCATION FOR THE HANDICAPPED

X-LINKED DOMINANT INHERITANCE

The consequences of the presence of a recessive gene on one X chromosome are well known. X-linked dominant inheritance, however, follows a different pattern. First, males and females can show the trait equally, and, if a pathologic gene is concerned, patients of both sexes are affected. Second, if a male carrier of the dominant trait "A" marries an homozygous recessive female "aa," all his daughters will exhibit the trait "A" (they are heterozygous "Aa," having received one X from the "aa" mother and the paternal X with "A"), and all his sons will show the trait "a" (they have received the X chromosome from their mothers and the recessive "a" behaves like a dominant). This mode of transmission, from father to daughter, is in fact so characteristic that, when it is observed, the presence of an X-dominant gene is almost demonstrated. Only a few rare diseases are known to be X-linked dominants. X-linked dominant inherited diseases, though rare, result in a variety of handicapping conditions. Not all genetic disorders need result in handicaps, however. Proper care during pregnancy and throughout life can avoid many natural consequences of genetic disorders.

L. KOULISCHER
Institut de Morphologie
Pathologique, Belgium

ETIOLOGY
X-LINKED RECESSIVE INHERITANCE

X-LINKED RECESSIVE INHERITANCE

It is well known that the same gene may present different forms, called alleles. All alleles are located at a fixed place of a chromosome, the locus. In any person, only two alleles are present, one at each locus of the same chromosome pair. One of the two alleles originates from the father, the other from the mother. Alleles can be either dominant (usually represented by a capital letter: "A"), or recessive (represented by a small letter: "a"). As indicated by its name, the dominant form prevails over the recessive one. This means that the carrier of "Aa" (heterozygote) will show the character "A," the recessive "a" being masked.

To express itself, "a" must be in the homozygote state "aa." This happens when two "Aa" heterozygotes marry: 25% of all their children will be "aa."

This general rule does not apply to the sex chromosomes. In the XX female, only one X is active in any cell, the other one being inactivated (Lyon, 1961). In a heterozygote female "Aa," the gene "A" will express itself in half of the cells, and "a" in the other half. Most often, the fact that the normal allele is active in half of the cells is enough to determine normal characteristics. For instance, if a woman is a carrier of the recessive mutation responsible for blindness for the red color (daltonism), half of the cells of her retina will be blind for red, but the others not and this will be sufficient to give almost normal color vision. The male has an XY sex chromosome set: only one X, transmitted by the mother, is present. The Y chromosome is very small and has only a few genes.

Any boy has a 50% chance to inherit one of the two maternal Xs. If he receives the X with a normal dominant allele, there will be no problem. If he receives an X with a recessive abnormal allele from an heterozygous mother, all his cells (not half of them, as in his mother) will be affected. The gene "a" alone, although recessive, behaves like a dominant (e.g., in the case of daltonism, he will be blind to the red). In short, an X-linked recessive gene is transmitted by the mother to half of her sons. If the gene determines a disease, half of the male progeny will be affected, the mother herself being apparently normal. Moreover, half of her daughters will be "normal carriers" and thus will be at risk of having half of their sons affected. When an affected male marries, all his children will be normal. The boys receive their X chromosome from the normal mother and the girls are heterozygous (the problem concerns their future children). Only the exceptional and seldom reported marriage of a heterozygous woman "Aa" with an affected man "a" can produce affected "aa" homozygous females.

The striking fact in this sort of X-linked recessive pedigree is that only males are affected (black squares). Inversely, when a family is found with only males presenting a disease, the transmission of an X-linked recessive gene is likely. According to McKusick (1983), there are at present 115 confirmed and 128 possible X-linked genes. It is not possible to cite them all in this entry. The most commonly known recessives are those associated with hemophilia, agammaglobulenemia and other immunological diseases, eye diseases including colorblindness, ocular albinism, and some forms of cataract, a few deafness syndromes, Lesch-Nyhan syndrome (mental retardation, spastic cerebral palsy, choreoathetosis, uric acid urinary stones, and self-destructive biting of fingers and lips), muscular dystrophy, myopathy, and testicular feminization.

Mental deficiency and X-linked recessive genes deserve special comment. It is well known that more boys than girls show mental retardation. This suggests an excess of X-linked recessive diseases. Often, mental retardation is associated with other symptoms to form a syndrome (e.g., Lesch-Nyhan syndrome). A newly discovered disease is mental retardation, macroorchidism, and elongated face associated with the presence of a fragile site on the X-chromosome, known as the Xq28 fragile site, observed in 1 out of 2000 male births. Fryns (1984) has published a review of 83 families ascertained through 83 index patients. He summarizes the problems raised by this particular chromosome anomaly: in one-third of the families, pedigree data were consistent with X-linked recessive inheritance in the other two-thirds, the presenting symptom was familial mental retardation with a mentally retarded mother, or mental subnormality with hyperkinetic behavior. Even the transmission through a normal asymptomatic X-fragile male carrier seemed likely in four families. Although more data are still necessary, at present the fragile Xq28 syndrome appears to be an important cause of X-linked mental retardation, with the advantage that carriers can be detected by means of relatively simply cytogenetic techniques.

From a preventive point of view, it is important first to diagnose correctly any X-linked disease with mental retardation, and to detect the normal heterozygote mothers at risk. This is not always possible, but it is a new area of research and it is hoped, with the help of biochemistry and molecular DNA analysis, to prevent in the near future the birth of affected males.

REFERENCES

Fryns, J-P. (1984). The fragile X syndrome. A study of 83 families. *Clin. Genet. 26,* 497–528.

Lyon, M-F. (1961). Gene action in the X-chromosome of the mouse. (Mus musculus). *Nature, 190,* 372–373.

L. KOULISCHER
Institut de Morphologie
Pathologique, Belgium

CONGENITAL DISORDERS
GENETIC COUNSELING

X-RAYS AND HANDICAPPING CONDITIONS

Irradiation of the developing fetus during the early stages of development as a consequence of maternal X-rays is now clearly recognized as a potential cause of later physical and cognitive abnormalities. There may be dramatic effects associated with irradiation that are clearly recognized at birth. There may be other, more subtle effects appearing at later ages such as reduced head size. Pioneer studies on the subject were done by Zappert (1926), Murphy (1929), and Goldstein (1930; Berg, 1968).

Clinical X-rays are a major source of the radiation absorbed by the human body during any particular year. It has been estimated that people on the average absorb less than 4 rads a year and that half of this is from medical X-rays, e.g., upper gastrointestinal series, abdominal X-rays, and dental and chest X-rays. This does not include treatment for cancer during which ranges somewhere between 30–250 rads have been observed (Batshaw & Perrett, 1981).

Though the potential dangers to the fetus from X-ray radiation were recognized before World War II, the dangers of radiation were most dramatically brought into focus by the events of that war. It was found that there was a direct relationship between the distance of a pregnant woman from the point of impact of the atomic bombs at Hiroshima and Nagasaki and the degree of damage suffered by her unborn child. Women who survived the bomb explosion but were within a half-mile of it were found to have miscarriages, while there was an extremely high incidence of microcephalic children born to those who were $1\frac{1}{4}$ miles away (Wood, Johnson, & Omiri, 1967). Still farther away, there was no clear evidence of cognitive or physical damage to the children that were later born, but some 20 years later, as adults, they had a high incidence of leukemia (Miller, 1968).

One major study of pregnant women who were receiving cobalt treatments for cancer discovered that 20 out of 75 of the infants born to them had definitive central nervous system abnormalities. Sixteen of these were microcephalic (Cooper & Cooper, 1966). The corroboration of these findings in later studies has resulted in caution and forbearance on the part of physicians with respect to the use of X-rays with pregnant women. Normally, women should not have abdominal X-rays more than 2 weeks after the last period. X-rays during the first trimester are discouraged on any but the most necessary grounds. X-rays as diagnostic tests, such as those once carried out to establish fetal size, have been replaced with less invasive procedures like ultrasound. Indeed, there has been recent evidence suggesting that some of the more subtle kinds of handicaps, e.g., those associated with learning disabilities, may be the consequence of X-ray use.

On the positive side it should be observed that X-rays have played a role in assisting in the assessment of handicapped individuals. Thus X-rays of the bone structures of hands and wrists have provided estimates of carpal ossification in cases where delayed maturation has been suspected. X-rays also are essential for the diagnosis of various physical problems and deformities, e.g., dislocations, fractures, internal injuries, and congenital defects. Recently, computerized axial tomography (CAT) has revolutionized medical diagnosis. While X-rays by themselves can show only the length and width of a bodily organ, the CAT scan can also reveal depth. Significant contributions to our understanding of learning disorders have been made by CAT scans (Mann & Sabatino, 1985).

REFERENCES

Batshaw, M. L., & Perrett, Y. M. (1981). *Children with handicaps.* Baltimore, MD: Brookes.

Berg, J. M. (1968). Aetiological aspects of mental subnormality: Pathological factors. In A. M. Clarke & A. D. B. Clarke (Eds.), *Mental deficiency.* New York: Free Press.

Cooper, G., & Cooper, J. B. (1966). Radiation hazards to mother and fetus. *Clinical Obstetrics & Gynecology, 9,* 11.

Mann, L., & Sabatino, D. A. (1985). *Foundations of cognitive processes in remedial and special education.* Rockville, MD: Aspen.

Miller, R. W. (1968). Effects of ionizing radiation from the atomic bomb on Japanese children. *Pediatrics, 72,* 1483.

Wood, J. W., Johnson, K. G., & Omiri, Y. (1973). In utero exposure to the Hiroshima atomic bomb. An evaluation of head size and mental retardation: Twenty years after. *Pediatrics, 39,* 385.

LESTER MANN
*Hunter College, City University
of New York*

CAT SCAN
NEURAL EFFICIENCY ANALYZER

X-RAY SCANNING TECHNIQUES

The history of X-ray scanning techniques of the brain is eloquently outlined in the text by Oldendorf (1980). Up until the advent of CAT (computed axial tomography) scanning in 1973, the image of the brain could only be grossly inferred by either bony abnormalities of the skull as seen on routine skull X-rays or by a technique (pneumoencephalography) in which air was introduced into the brain ventricles (either directly or via spinal puncture). The resultant shadowy contrast between ventricle, brain, and bone would permit some visualization of major cerebral landmarks sufficient to detect some types of gross structural pathology (e.g., hydrocephalus, tumor). However, the technique of pneumoencephalography had significant morbidity risks and was invasive. The pneumoencephalogram has been replaced by CAT scanning.

An historical predecessor of CAT scanning was the radioactive isotope scan (based on differences in rate of absorption of radioactive particles in normal and abnormal brain tissue), which began clinical use in 1947 and continued until the advent and clinical implementation of CAT scanning. The CAT and other neuroimaging techniques have essentially replaced the radioactive isotope

scan. This is also the case with routine cerebral arteriography, which used to be the only way to visualize blood vessels of the neck and head; it has been replaced in large part by digital subtraction angiography (DSA). The DSA is an X-ray scanning technique that uses a computer program to "subtract" background tissue in the X-ray image that is not of the same density as blood vessels. Comparisons of these techniques, sample figures, and a more complete discussion of their diagnostic usefulness are presented in Bigler (1984).

Positron emission tomography (PET) is a new technique that permits the mapping of brain metabolism by using radioactive-labeled glucose or oxygen. Based on different metabolic rates, an image of the major cerebral structures can be obtained with specific indication of which brain areas were using the most glucose or oxygen (e.g., the brain area most involved in a particular task while PET scanning was being done).

REFERENCES

Bigler, E. D. (1984). *Diagnostic clinical neuropsychology.* Austin: University of Texas Press.

Oldendorf, W. H. (1980). *The quest for an image of brain.* New York: Raven.

ERIN D. BIGLER
*Austin Neurological Clinic
University of Texas, Austin*

CAT SCAN
NUCLEAR MAGNETIC RESONANCE
X-RAY, ASSOCIATED WITH LEARNING DISORDERS

XYY SYNDROME

Polysomy Y or XYY syndrome is a sex chromosome variation characterized by an extra Y chromosome in males. That is, rather than having two sex chromosomes of the normal male (46, XY), those with the XYY genotype have an extra male sex chromosome (47, XYY). There are no dysmorphic factors associated with this syndrome other than most males with it are tall (i.e., height is typically above the ninetieth percentile by age six and older). There are also no chronic health disorders associated with the syndrome, but XYY males were found to have a higher rate of broken bones and infections than normal peers (Stewart, 1982). Fertility appears to be normal (Cohen & Durnham, 1985). The incidence of XYY syndrome is 1 in 700 to 1 in 1000 live male births (Cohen & Durnham, 1985). Many XYY males are never identified because they are generally indistinguishable from the general male population.

There have been misconceptions in the past regarding the behavioral and developmental sequelae of XYY syndrome. Research with biased samples indicated that XYY males were typically violent criminals and mentally retarded (e.g., Jacobs et al., 1965). More recent and well-controlled studies have indicated that only 1 of every 950 is institutionalized. While this is higher than the general population, it is much less than suggested earlier (Jarvik, Klodin, & Matsuyama, 1973).

Research has identified the following developmental and behavioral problems when comparing school-age XYY males with normal peers and siblings: (1) IQ scores are slightly lower than normal but there is no increased risk for mental retardation; (2) fine-motor coordination and language development tend to be mildly decreased; (3) reading difficulties and a wide spectrum of learning disorders are more often present; (4) aggressive behavior does not have a higher frequency of occurrence rate; (5) behavioral problems related to general immaturity, impulsivity, and low frustration tolerance are more often present (Robinson, Lubs, & Bergsma, 1985; Stewart, 1982).

Cohen and Durnham (1985) have provided a comprehensive review of school management of children with XYY syndrome as well as other sex chromosome variations. It is suggested that children with suspected XYY syndrome be referred to school health personnel. Once identified, psychoeducational assessment is typically needed to identify possible learning and behavioral disorders. Anticipatory guidance concerning the risks of XYY syndrome is especially needed in view of the typical misconceptions cited earlier. Cohen and Durnham have listed the following resources for school personnel and parents for gaining further information about sex chromosome variations:

March of Dimes Birth Defects Foundation
1275 Mamaroneck Avenue
White Plains, NY 10605

Metropolitan Turner's Syndrome Association
P.O. Box 407C
Convent Station, NH 07961

National Center for Education in Maternal and Child
  Health
3520 Prospect Street NW
Washington, DC 20027

National Health Information Clearing House
Box 1133
Washington, DC 20013

National Information Center for Handicapped Children
1201 16th Street, NW
Washington, DC 20036

REFERENCES

Cohen, F. L., & Durnham, J. D. (1985). Sex chromosome variations in school-aged children. *Journal of School Health, 55,* 99–102.

Jacobs, P. A., Brunton, M., Mellville, M. M., Brittain, R. P., & McClemont, W. F. (1965). Aggressive behavior, mental subnormality, and the XYY male. *Nature, 208,* 1351–1352.

Jarvik, L. F., Klodin, V., & Matsuyama, S. S. (1973). Human aggression and the extra Y chromosome. *American Psychologist, 28,* 674–682.

Robinson, A., Lubs, H. A., Bergsma, D. (1985). *Sex chromosome aneuploidy: Prospective studies on children.* New York: Liss.

Stewart, D. A. (1982). *Children with sex chromosome aneuploidy: Follow-up studies.* New York: Liss.

JOSEPH D. PERRY
Kent State University

CHROMOSOMAL ABNORMALITIES
GENETIC COUNSELING

Y

YALE, CAROLINE A. (1848–1933)

Caroline A. Yale, teacher and principal at Clarke School for the Deaf in Northampton, Massachusetts, from 1870 to 1922, was a leading figure in the development of educational services for the deaf in the United States. She developed a system for teaching speech to the deaf and was a founder, with Alexander Graham Bell and others, of the American Association to Promote the Teaching of Speech to the Deaf. At Clarke School, she organized a teacher-education department that was responsible for the training of large numbers of student teachers. Through her teacher-training activities and numerous publications, Yale was a major contributor to the acceptance of instruction in speech as an essential element in the education of deaf children.

REFERENCES

Taylor, H. (1933). Caroline Ardelia Yale. *The Volta Review, 35,* 415–417.

Yale, C. A. (1931). *Years of building.* New York: Longmans, Green.

PAUL IRVINE
Katonah, New York

DEAF EDUCATION

YEAR-ROUND SCHOOLS

The concept and use of year-round schools for special and general education has developed, in part, as a result of changing expectations and roles of public education in the community (Hanna, 1972). The traditional answer to the question of school responsibility was simple: transmit the heritage, or at least that part of it considered to be important to the educated person. The traditional school said, in effect, fit children and youths into the fixed curriculum of academic subjects. If they do not care, or in the case of many exceptional students, cannot cope with it, that is unfortunate. In the cases of many exceptional students, traditional education models forced them out or openly expelled them if attendance laws permitted. In other cases,

students were tracked into vocational education or home economics. More progressive educators organized schools around a child-centered orientation in order to more effectively stimulate student interest, provide for the exploration and expression of those interests, and, therefore, assist in desirable personality growth (Olsen & Clark, 1977).

A system embracing year-round schooling is able to affirm the central values of the earlier concepts while providing programming in light of the school's basic responsibility to help improve the quality of living in the local community or region. The traditional school curriculum is still almost standard practice (Ysseldyke & Algozzine, 1983). The approach involved in year-round schools, however, provides curriculum flexibly structured about the enduring life concerns of humans everywhere. These concerns, with their attendant problems, are those of earning a living, communicating ideas and feelings, enjoying recreation, and finding some measure of self-identity.

REFERENCES

Hanna, P. (1972, May). What thwarts the community education curriculum? *Community Education Journal,* pp. 27–30.

Olsen, E. G., & Clark, P. A (1977). *Life-centering education.* Midland, MI: Pendell.

Ysseldyke, J., & Algozzine, B. (1983). *Introduction to special education.* Boston: Houghton Mifflin.

CRAIG D. SMITH
Georgia College

LICENSING AND CERTIFICATION OF SCHOOLS
SUMMER SCHOOL FOR HANDICAPPED

YPSILANTI PERRY PRESCHOOL PROJECT

The Perry Preschool Project, which operated from 1962 to 1967, was a program to help poor black children in Ypsilanti, Michigan, overcome the apparent effects of their disadvantaged environment. The project evolved from the recognition that a disproportionate number of low-income or minority children with no specific organic etiology were labeled mentally retarded. David Weikart and his associates who initiated the project sought to provide an equal educational opportunity at the preschool level for underprivileged children. Schweinhart and Weikart (1986) believe that effective programs for preschool children can compensate for socioeconomic factors that correlate with school performance. By providing preschool programs, Weikart's goal was to increase the probability of children succeeding in elementary and secondary school as well as the probability of their gaining employment.

Enrolled in the project for 2 years were 3- and 4- year old children (except for four-year-olds enrolled during the project's first year). The school year lasted for 7½ months; classes ran for 2½ hours each morning, 5 days a week. Teachers also made home visits once a week for 1½ hours to work with each parent and child. The preschool was staffed with four classroom teachers with graduate degrees and extensive in-service training at a ratio of five students for every teacher (Schweinhart & Weikart, 1986; Thurman & Widerstrom, 1985).

The Perry Preschool Project used a Piagetian-based curriculum consisting of a set of cognitive/developmental objectives (Thurman & Widerstrom, 1985; Weikart, 1974). Emphasis in the curriculum was on children developing the ability to reason and to understand their relation to the environment. Activities were designed so that learning to think and to solve problems took place through direct experiences. Development of cognitive abilities was viewed as more important and useful at the preschool level than direct instruction of academic skills. Consequently, preacademic and academic skills (i.e., reading and math concepts) were not emphasized in the curriculum. Rote memory and drill activities typically used in academic skills instruction were not part of the instructional format. Instead, an open format of instruction was used to allow teachers to devise activities that they believed would help individual children through the stages of cognitive development. Ispa and Matz (1978) contend that "because each child works at activities that are developmentally appropriate, he or she has the opportunity to grow and experience success without infringing on the needs of other children for a faster (or slower) pace or for an activity that is more personnally interesting" (p. 171).

Activities were both teacher and child initiated. Children enrolled in the project were able to select and engage in their own acitivites (Thurman & Widerstrom, 1985). Planning time was provided to children to devise their activities for the work time period. During work time, they executed their activities with the assistance of their teachers and peers. Snack time and small group activity time followed the work period. Outdoor activities emphasizing gross motor skills were also provided.

Extensive longitudinal research on the effects of early intervention has been generated from the Perry Preschool Project. Researchers from the project monitored five sets or "waves" of children from the time of enrollment until age 19. In the south side of Ypsilanti, where the preschool was located, project staff surveyed neighborhoods to identify preschool-aged children. A variety of socioeconomic and ability measures were taken on the children and their families, including parents' education, level of employment of the head of household, ratio of rooms in the home to persons in the household, and IQ levels of the preschool-aged children (Schweinhart, Berrueta-Clement, Barnett, Epstein & Weikart, 1985). Neighborhood 3 and 4 year olds were then randomly assigned to the preschool group and the nonpreschool group.

The outcome variables measured in the longitudinal study were divided into three domains: scholastic success, socioeconomic success, and social responsibility (Schweinhart et al., 1985). In terms of scholastic success, at age 19 individuals enrolled in the preschool were more likely to have graduated from high school, receive college or vocational training, and perform better on measures of functional competence. In addition, fewer of them were subsequently labeled mentally retarded and they spent a lower percentage of their school years in special education programs. On measures of social responsibility, fewer of the preschool group were ever arrested or detained by police and fewer of the females had teenage pregnancies. In terms of economic success, nearly twice as many individuals from the preschool group were employed and half as many were receiving welfare (Schweinhart et al., 1985).

A benefit-cost analysis of the project indicated that the Perry Preschool Project paid dividends in the long run. The return on investment was estimated to be three and a half times greater than the cost of the 2 years of preschool. The results of the analysis showed that the benefit of the project was in the areas of increased earnings and reduced educational costs for those who had been enrolled in the program (Schweinhart et al., 1985).

REFERENCES

Ipsa, J., & Matz, R. D. (1978). Integrating handicapped preschool children within a cognitively oriented program. In M. J. Guralnick (Ed.), *Early intervention and the integration of handicapped and nonhandicapped children*. Baltimore, MD: University Park Press.

Schweinhart, L. J., Berrueta-Clement, J. R., Barnett, W. S., Epstein, A. S., & Weikart, D. P. (1985). The promise of early childhood education. *Phi Delta Kappan, 67*, 548–553.

Schweinhart, L. J., and Weikart, D. P. (1986). What do we know so far? A review of the Head Start Synthesis Project. *Young Children, 41*, 50–55.

Thurman, K. S., & Widerstrom, A. E. (1985). *Young children with special needs: A developmental and ecological approach*. Boston: Allyn & Bacon.

Weikart, D. P. (1974). Curriculum for early childhood special education. *Focus on Exceptional Children, 6*, 1–8.

LAWRENCE J. O'SHEA
University of Florida

EARLY IDENTIFICATION OF HANDICAPPED CHILDREN
SOCIOECONOMIC IMPACT OF DISABILITIES
SOCIOECONOMIC STATUS

YSSELDYKE, JAMES EDWARD (1944–   )

Born in Grand Rapids, Michigan, James Edward Ysseldyke received his BA (1966) in psychology and biology from Western Michigan University. He received his MA (1968) and PhD (1971) in school psychology from the University of Illinois, where he studied with T. Ernest Newland. Currently, he is professor of educational psychology at the University of Minnesota, where he teaches principally in school psychology but also in special education. He is former director of the University of Minnesota Institute for Research in Learning Disabilities and is now editor of *Exceptional Children*, the primary journal of the Council for Exceptional Children.

Much of Ysseldyke's work has been in the area of special education assessment. Poland, Thurlow, Ysseldyke, and Mirkin (1982), for example, studied how validity, reliability, and other psychometric characteristics of tests relate to the decision-making process in multidisciplinary team meetings. They discovered that decisions on eligibility for special education and the most appropriate programming are often made prior to the official meeting of the assessment team and that test data may have little impact on the process. Similarly, Ysseldyke learned that there is little, if any, correlation between the results of standardized tests given to a child and the child's subsequent classroom placement (Ysseldyke, Algozzine, Richey, & Graden, 1982). These findings are controversial but they have led to more detailed research in the area.

At present, Ysseldyke is directing two major research projects, one on improving asssessment of preschool children and the other on the effectiveness of alternative strategies for increasing academically engaged time for mildly handicapped students. Ysseldyke is perhaps best known to students of special education for his highly successful text written with John Salvia (Salvia & Ysseldyke, 1985).

James Edward Ysseldyke

REFERENCES

Poland, S. F., Thurlow, M. L., Ysseldyke, J. E., & Mirkin, P. K. (1982). Current psychoeducational assessment and decision-making practices as reported by directors of special education. *Journal of School Psychology, 20,* 171–179.

Salvia, J., & Ysseldyke, J. E. (1985). *Assessment in special remedial education.* Boston: Houghton Mifflin.

Ysseldyke, J. E., Algozzine, B., Richey, L., & Graden, J. (1982). Declaring students eligible for learning disability services: Why bother with the data? *Learning Disability Quarterly, 5,* 37–44.

E. Valerie Hewitt
Texas A&M University

COUNCIL FOR EXCEPTIONAL CHILDREN
INSTITUTES FOR RESEARCH IN LEARNING DISABILITIES

Z

ZEAMAN, DAVID (1921–1984)

After receiving his PhD from Columbia University in experimental psychology in 1948, David Zeaman embarked on a lifelong career developing and elaborating on an attention theory of retardate discriminative learning. In the early 1950s, he conducted pilot studies specializing in animal learning with his wife, Betty House, at the Mansfield State Training School in Connecticut. They thought that the techniques developed for studying animal behavior could be adapted for retarded children with low ability to speak or understand language. That early work proved promising, leading to funding by the National Institute of Mental Health for a project that lasted 20 years. The Mansfield State School administrative provided space for a permanent laboratory that is still in existence.

The initial target behavior for Zeaman and House's research was a discriminative learning task disguised as a candy-finding game. Early results convinced them that the deficiency they observed in retarded subjects was due to attentional deficits rather than slow learning. They developed a mathematical attention model with the basic assumption that discriminative learning requires a learning chain of two responses: attending to the relevant dimension and approaching the correct cue of that dimension.

Their approach to retardation was to look for changes in parameter values of the model related to intelligence. The parameter that was most affected by level of intelligence turned out to be the initial probability of attending to the colors and forms that were the relevant dimensions of the tasks. Later work related this finding to three factors: (1) breadth and adjustability of breadth of attention—subjects of higher intelligence can attend to more dimensions at once and can narrow attention when necessary; (2) dimensionality of the stimulus—subjects of low intelligence are likely to attend to stimuli holistically rather than analytically; and (3) fixed as well as variable components of attention such that strong dimensional preferences interfere with learning—salience of position cues in retardates slows learning about colors, forms, sizes, and other aspects of stimuli. A history of research and theory development from the first publication of the model in 1963 to 1979 can be found in Ellis's *Handbook of Mental Deficiency* (1963).

Zeaman served as editor of the *Psychological Bulletin* and as associate editor of *Intelligence*. He received many awards and honors from organizations such as the American Psychological Association and the National Institute of Mental Health.

REFERENCE

Zeaman, D., & House, B. J. (1963). The role of attention in retardate discrimination learning. In N. R. Ellis (Ed.), *Handbook of mental deficiency: Psychological theory and research.* New York: McGraw-Hill.

STAFF

HOUSE, BETTY
ZEAMAN HOUSE RESEARCH

ZEAMAN-HOUSE RESEARCH

David Zeaman and Betty House, along with other researchers located primarily at the University of Connecticut and the Mansfield Training School, have contributed substantial research on attention theory to the literature on mental retardation. Though more than 100 years of psychological and educational research on attention has concluded that the process is multifactorial (Alabiso, 1972), the Zeaman-House, and later Fisher-Zeaman, focus on selective attention has provided several learning theories useful in understanding and teaching mentally retarded persons.

Using a series of simple visual discrimination tasks, Zeaman and House found that plotting of individual, rather than averaged, group responses produced learning curves that differed significantly from traditional learning curves. The former curves stayed around the chance (50%) correct level, then jumped quickly to 100% accuracy. Prior to plotting individual data with backward learning curves, the expectation would have been for a gradual, incremental curve from chance to the 100% correct level. This discontinuity caused these researchers to postulate two processes, one controlling the length of the first part of the curve, and one determining the rapid jump to correct problem solution. Mentally retarded learners in the 2- to 4-year mental age range performed more poorly on these tasks than children of normal intelligence at comparable mental ages. Also, Zeaman and House determined that, among mentally retarded subjects, IQ was a more accurate predictor of better discrimination, independent of mental age (Robinson & Robinson, 1976).

The two-stage or two-phase discrimination learning process proposed by Zeaman and House (1963) suggests an early attention phase during which the plotted learning curve is essentially horizontal, indicating chance-level responses. During this phase, the subject has not discovered the relevant stimuli of an object and is randomly attending to various stimulus dimensions. The second phase of the discrimination process involves attention to relevant stimulus dimensions, leading to rapid improvement in learning (Mercer & Snell, 1977).

Because mentally retarded subjects produced chance-level curves of longer initial duration (yet also demonstrated steeply sloped curves comparable to subjects with higher mental ages), Zeaman and House argued that the inefficient learning of mentally retarded persons was, at its core, a function of their attention. This finding was important because it suggested that the actual learning potential of mentally retarded persons was not defective, and that interventions could be devised to improve attention and discrimination. The differences observed between slower learning mentally retarded persons and faster or normal learners were based more on the time it took to learn to attend to relevant stimuli than to select the relevant cue itself (Zeaman & House, 1963). The work by Zeaman and House in the area of attention and discrimination learning led to studies of other relevant variables such as transfer of training, stimulus factors (e.g., size, position, color, shape), novelty and oddity learning, and the effects of reward characteristics.

Later, their attention theory was expanded to include examinations of the relationship of retention to attention and learning. Ten years after publication of the earlier work, Fisher and Zeaman (1973) noted that although the attention deficits that affect learning in mentally retarded persons are amenable to manipulation and improvement, the retention limitations attributable to the reduced cognitive capacity of such subjects may not be so flexible. Both the earlier and more recent work by Zeaman, House, and their colleagues have generated considerable productive research by others. These latter focuses, many of which suggest implications for education and training of mentally retarded learners, include work on the number of stimulus dimensions employed, reward and incentive conditions, and transfer and oddity learning.

REFERENCES

Alabiso, F. (1972). Inhibitory functions of attention in reducing hyperactive behavior. *American Journal of Mental Deficiency,* 77, 259–282.

Fisher, M. A., & Zeaman, D. (1973). An attention-retention theory of retardate discrimination learning. In N. R. Ellis (Ed.), *The international review of research in mental retardation* (Vol. 6). New York: Academic.

Mercer, C. D., & Snell, M. E. (1977). *Learning theory research in mental retardation: Implications for teaching.* Columbus, OH: Merrill.

Robinson, N. M., & Robinson, H. B. (1976). *The mentally retarded child: A psychological approach.* New York: McGraw-Hill.

Zeaman, D., & House, B. J. (1963). The role of attention in retardate discrimination learning. In N. R. Ellis (Ed.), *Handbook of mental deficiency.* New York: McGraw-Hill.

JOHN D. WILSON
Elwyn Institutes,
Elwyn, Pennsylvania

HOUSE, BETTY
ZEAMAN, DAVID

ZERO INFERENCE

Zero inference is a term that refers to the instructional needs of individuals with severe handicaps (Brown, Nietupski, & Hamre-Nietupski, 1976). Typically, teachers of nonhandicapped students teach a series of core skills using a variety of materials (e.g., counting using wooden cubes). It is assumed that these students will then learn strategies, roles, and concepts necessary to the use of such core skills in other natural settings. It cannot be inferred that severely handicapped students can be taught critical skills in an artificial (i.e., nonnatural) setting using artificial materials and be expected to perform the same skills in more natural settings.

Because of the nature of their mental, physical, or emotional problems, severely handicapped students often need educational, social, psychological, or medical services that are beyond those offered in classes for nonhandicapped students. Educational needs are notable in that some students with severe handicaps may have severe language or perceptual-cognitive deficits. They may fail to attend to even pronounced social stimuli and may lack even the most rudimentary forms of verbal control (U.S. Office of Education, 1975). Severely handicapped students may have the need for intensive instruction in areas including social behavior, communication skills, personal care, mobility and ambulation skills, academic and cognitive behaviors, and vocational skills (Wehman, Renzaglia, & Bates, 1985). Many of the skills required for adaptive performance in postschool environments will need to be taught to severely handicapped students because of the nature of their performance and cognitive deficits. Such instruction is referred to as the zero-degree inference strategy.

Characteristics of the zero-degree inference strategy of instruction include the belief that no inferences can be made about training a student to perform at a skill level that he or she will be able to use in postschool settings. In order for severely handicapped students to generalize skills taught in more natural (i.e., nonschool) settings, strategies must be used to ensure that generalization will occur (Stokes & Baer, 1977). Training across multiple settings, materials, and trainers may be included in instruction of students with severe handicaps. General case programming (Horner, Sprague, & Wilcox, 1982), in which common characteristics of several materials or settings are assessed in an effort to teach students a strategy that can be used in a variety of postschool settings, may be used. Additionally, techniques of systematic instruction, including data-based instruction and assessment of student progress, are necessary to ensure the acquisition of usable skills on the part of severely handicapped learners (Lynch, McGuigan, & Shoemaker, 1977).

Employing training techniques including generalization or general case strategies and systematic instruction will ensure the acquisition of skills that can be used by severely handicapped students in all necessary environments. Teachers who make zero inferences regarding student performance will be more likely to see success in student performance across situations requiring similar skills.

REFERENCES

Brown, L., Nietupski, J., & Hamre-Nietupski, S. (1976). Criterion of ultimate functioning. In M. A. Thomas (Ed.), *Hey, don't forget about me!* Reston, VA: Council for Exceptional Children.

Horner, R. H., Sprague, J., & Wilcox, B. (1982). General case programming for community activities. In B. Wilcox & G. T. Bellamy (Eds.), *Design for high school programs for severely handicapped students* (pp. 61–68). Baltimore, MD: Brookes.

Lynch, V., McGuigan, C., & Shoemaker, S. (1977). Systematic instruction: Defining the good teacher. In N. Haring (Ed.), *An inservice program for personnel serving the severely handicapped*. Seattle: Experimental Education Unit, University of Washington.

Stokes, T. F., & Baer, D. M. (1977). An implicit technology of generalization. *Journal of Applied Behavior Analysis, 10,* 349–367.

U.S. Office of Education. (1975). *Estimated number of handicapped children in the United States, 1974–75*. Washington, DC: Bureau of Education for the Handicapped.

Wehman, P., Renzaglia, A., & Bates, P. (1985). *Functional living skills for moderately and severely handicapped individuals*. Austin, TX: Pro-Ed.

CORNELIA LIVELY
*University of Illinois,
Urbana-Champaign*

SELF-CONTAINED CLASS
SELF-HELP TRAINING
TRANSFER OF LEARNING
TRANSFER OF TRAINING

ZERO-REJECT

The term *zero-reject* identifies a policy of providing to all children with handicapping conditions a free, appropriate, and publicly supported education. The constitutional foundation of zero-reject is the Fourteenth Amendment, which guarantees that no state may deny any person within its "jurisdiction the equal protection of the laws." The courts have interpreted this to mean that no government may deny public services to a person because of his or her unalterable characteristics (e.g., sex, race, age, or handicap). Advocates of children with handicaps have claimed that these children have the same rights to education as children who are not handicapped. If a state treats children with handicaps differently (e.g., by denying them the opportunity to attend school or by inappropriately assigning them to a special education program), then it is denying them "equal protection of the laws" on the basis of their unalterable characteristics.

In 1975 Congress passed PL 94-142, the Education of All Handicapped Children Act, which specifies that no child with a handicapping condition (aged 3 to 21) can be excluded from school by recipients of federal funds for the education of children with handicaps. Zero-reject, the mandate to include all children in public schools and to provide an appropriate education for them, represents a new responsibility for public school systems.

The successful implementation of the zero-reject policy is facilitated by the specific legislative requirements of PL 94-142. Both state and local education agencies (SEA, LEA) must adopt a policy of zero-reject and formulate a plan for achieving this goal. To be eligible for federal funds, each SEA and LEA must conduct an annual child census. Its purpose is to identify, locate, and evaluate all children with handicaps within their jurisdiction. Previously, many children excluded were those with the most severe handicaps. Zero-reject addresses this by setting up priority groups to receive services. First priority goes to children who are currently receiving no education, then to children with the most severe handicaps within each category of disability.

Zero-reject is further implemented by the prevention of functional exclusion. The law states that each child will receive an appropriate education. Each child must have an individualized education plan (IEP) based on a nondiscriminatory evaluation. Parents or guardians must be involved in the process of the development of a child's IEP. A due-process hearing can be convened if the appropriateness of the child's education is in question. Additionally, any related services that the child might need must be provided at public expense and in conformity with the child's IEP.

Public Law 94-142 has promoted the zero-reject policy by requiring the schools to provide an education that would be meaningful to the child when he or she leaves school. The policy of zero-reject addresses the need for a meaningful education that promotes qualified individuals with handicaps into mainstream employment. Additionally, SEAs and LEAs must take affirmative action in hiring workers with handicaps.

To prevent the shuffling of responsibility, Congress made the SEA singularly responsible for assuring that the policy of zero-reject is operational. The LEA is under the guidance of the SEA; the SEA has the power to preempt LEA programs if necessary. In addition, individuals with handicaps are guaranteed the right to sue to enforce their claim to a free appropriate education after all administrative remedies have been exhausted.

On September 23, 1973, Congress passed section 504 of the Vocational Rehabilitation Act of 1973 (PL 93-112). It states that no qualified individual with a handicap can be excluded from participation in any program that receives federal financial assistance. Section 504 extends the zero-reject policy to providers of education (including postsecondary schools and adult education) as well as to providers of health, welfare, and social services and potential employers who are the recipients of federal funds. The joint enforcement of PL 94-142 and section 504, form the basic elements of the zero-reject policy.

REFERENCES

Ballard, J., Ramirez, B. A., & Weintraub, F. J. (Eds.). (1982). *Special education in America: Its legal and governmental foundations*. Reston, VA: Council for Exceptional Children.

Turnbull, H. R., & Turnbull, A. (1978). *Free appropriate public education, law and implementation*. Denver: Love.

Weintraub, F. J., Abeson, A., Ballard, J., & Lavor, M. L. (1976). *Public policy and the education of exceptional children*. Reston, VA: Council for Exceptional Children.

CAROLE REITER GOTHELF
*Hunter College, City University
of New York*

PUBLIC SCHOOL'S ROLE IN SPECIAL EDUCATION EDUACTION FOR ALL HANDICAPPED CHILDREN ACT OF 1975

ZIGLER, EDWARD (1930–)

Edward Zigler received his BA in history from the University of Missouri at Kansas City in 1954 and his PhD in psychology from the University of Texas, Austin in 1958. He is currently Sterling Professor of Psychology at Yale University, Director of the Bush Center in Child Development and Social Policy, and head of the psychology section of the Child Study Center.

Named by President Carter to chair the fifteenth anniversary Head Start Committee in 1980, Zigler was a member of the National Planning and Steering Committee for Head Start and was appointed to Head Start's first

National Research Council. He was also the first director of the Office of Child Development and Chief of the U.S. Children's Bureau.

The essence of Zigler's work has been the systemic evaluation of experiential, motivational, personality factors in the behavior of mentally retarded persons, and the demonstration of how these factors (delineated by experimental results) affect retarded children's performance. He also proposed a classification system for mental retardation along two axes: one, individuals would be ordered by IQ and on the other, by organic, familial, and/or undifferentiated etiologies. Zigler believes that beyond any doubt, many of the reported differences between retarded and non-retarded persons of the same MA are a result of motivational and emotional differences that reflect variations in experiential histories (Blatt & Morris 1984).

Zigler has authored and co-authored over 300 publications in the field including: *Familial Mental Retardation: A continuing dilemma* (1967), and, with D. Balla, *The Social Policy Implications of a Research Program on the Effects of Institutionalization on Retarded Persons* (1977).

Recipient of many awards and honors, Zigler's current research interests are cognitive and social-emotional development in children (particularly those with mental retardation), motivational determinants of children's performance, and the applicability of developmental theory to the area of psychopathology.

REFERENCES

Blatt, B., Morris, R.J. (1984). Perspectives in Special Education Personal Orientations, Glenview, Illinois: Scott, Foresman.

Zigler, E. (1967). Familiar mental retardation: A continuing dilemma. *Science, 155*, 292–298.

Zigler, E., & Balla, D. (1977). The social policy implications of a research program on the effects of institutionalization on retarded persons. In P. Mittler (Ed.). *Research to practice in mental retardation*. (vol. 1) Baltimore: University Park Press, pp. 267–281.

ELAINE FLETCHER-JANZEN
Texas A&M University

HEAD START

ZONE OF PROXIMAL DEVELOPMENT

The concept of the zone of proximal development was outlined by the Soviet psychologist L. S. Vygotsky in several papers published in the years immediately preceding his death in 1934. This concept was a critical component of Vygotsky's more developed perspectives on the role of social interaction in cognitive development and offered the theoretical foundations for alternative approaches to the assessment of cognitive development. As part of Vygotsky's general theoretical framework, the concept has influenced the development of important traditions of theory, research, and practice within the Soviet Union, in particular, the theory of "activity" as it has been developed by Vygotsky's students and colleagues. In the past decade, as the work of Vygotsky et al. has become more widely known and more fully understood in the West, the concept of the zone of proximal development has stimulated theory and research on cognitive development (Rogoff & Wertsch, 1984; Wertsch, 1985a, 1985b) and its assessment (Brown & French, 1979; Lidz, in press; Minick, in press).

Four postulates were central to Vygotsky's theory and research:

1. The agent of complex cognitive processes such as thinking or remembering is not always an individual. It is often a dyad or larger group whose common activity is organized and mediated by speech. According to Vygotsky, cognitive functions are often intermental rather than intramental.

2. The development of certain cognitive processes in the individual is the product of his or her mastery and internalization of means of organizing and mediating cognitive activities that are first encountered in social interaction or intermental functioning.

3. These means of organizing and mediating complex cognitive activities represent one aspect of the historical development of human social and cultural systems.

4. These socially and historically developed means of mediating cognitive activity are transferred from one generation to the next through the child's interaction with adults and more capable peers in cooperative activity.

The concept of the zone of proximal development is a natural extension of these postulates. Vygotsky argued that two different measures of the individual's cognitive development are possible at any point in ontogenesis. First, focusing on the individual's activity when he or she is working alone, one can assess what Vygotsky called mature cognitive processes. In his view, these processes reflect the individual's mastery of modes of organizing and mediating cognitive activity that are first encountered in social interaction. It is this aspect of the individual's cognitive development that is tapped by traditional methodologies of experimentation and assessment. Second, Vygotsky argued that by analyzing the activity of the individual when assistance is provided by someone more skilled in a particular task or by someone at a more advanced level of cognitive development, it is possible to assess cognitive processes that are maturing. By focusing on the level at which the individual performs when acting in

collaboration, one can gain insight into the individual's current development state and the next or proximal stage that will emerge in his or her development given adequate experience with appropriate social interaction or collaboration.

Vygotsky defined the zone of proximal development as the difference between the child's actual level of development as defined by his or her independent activity and the level of performance that he or she achieves in collaboration with an adult or more competent peer (Vygotsky, 1978, pp. 85–86; in press a). Strictly speaking, the upper range of the zone of proximal development is not a characteristic of the child. It is created in the interaction between the child and those who provide the child with assistance. The level at which the child is able to participate in cooperative cognitive activity is determined simultaneously by the adult's interest and skills in facilitating the child's participation and by the knowledge, skills, and interests that allow the child to participate in intermental activity and benefit from this experience.

Reflecting his lifelong interest in developmental disabilities and delays, Vygotsky felt (in press b) that one important application of the concept of the zone of proximal development would be in assessing cognitive development in abnormal populations and designing techniques to facilitate that development. In his view, the application of the concept in assessment practice would permit a qualitative assessment of the child's strengths and weaknesses and help identify the kinds of assistance needed to move the child to more advanced levels of cognitive functioning (Minick, in press). These ideas are currently being developed and applied in the West by Brown and Campione (Brown & French, 1979; Campione, Brown, Ferrara, & Bryant, 1984) and are compatible with work being done by Feuerstein and others in developing dynamic assessment techniques (Feuerstein, 1979; Lidz, in press).

REFERENCES

Brown, A. L., & French, L. A. (1979). The zone of potential development: Implications for intelligence testing in the year 2000. *Intelligence, 3*, 255–273.

Campione, J. C., Brown, A. L., Ferrara, R. A., & Bryant, N. R. (1984). The zone of proximal development: implications for individual differences and learning. In B. Rogoff & J. V. Wertsch (Eds.), *Children's learning in the "zone of proximal development"* (pp. 77–92). San Francisco: Jossey-Bass.

Feuerstein, R. (1979). *The dynamic assessment of retarded performers: The learning potential assessment device, theory, instruments, and techniques.* Baltimore, MD: University Park Press.

Leont'ev, A. N. (1978). *Activity, consciousness, and personality* (M. J. Hall, Trans.). Englewood Cliffs, NJ: Prentice-Hall. (Original work published 1975).

Lidz, C. S. (Ed.). (in press). *Foundations of dynamic assessment.* New York: Guilford.

Minick, N. (in press). The zone of proximal development and dynamic assessment. In C. S. Lidz (Ed.), *Foundations of dynamic assessment.* New York: Guilford.

Rogoff, B., & Wertsch, J. V. (Eds.). (1984): *Children's learning in the "zone of proximal development."* San Francisco: Jossey-Bass.

Vygotsky, L. S. (1978). *Mind in society.* Cambridge, MA: Harvard University Press.

Vygotsky, L. S. (in press a). *Thinking and speech.* In *L. S. Vygotsky, collected works: General psychology* (Vol. 2) (N. Minick, Trans.). New York: Plenum. (Original work published 1934)

Vygotsky, L. S. (in press b). *L. S. Vygotsky, collected works: The foundations of defectology* (Vol. 5) (J. Knox, Trans.). New York: Plenum. (Original work published 1983)

Wertsch, J. V. (1985a). *Vygotsky and the social formation of mind.* Cambridge, MA: Harvard University Press.

Wertsch, J. V. (Ed.). (1985b). *Culture, communication, and cognition: Vygotskian perspectives.* New York: Cambridge University Press.

NORRIS MINICK
*Center for Psychosocial Studies,
The Spencer Foundation,
Chicago, Illinois*

ACTIVITY, THEORY OF VYGOTSKY, L. S.

ZONING: FAMILY CARE HOME

A family care home, sometimes referred to as a community residential facility, is a home intentionally located in residential neighborhoods and designed for handicapped adults as a permanent residence or a transitional training residence.

General zoning guidelines have been established by each state in conjunction with federal guidelines; however, specific procedures are developed by the individual municipality. The general statutes of North Carolina (1982) state:

A family care home shall be deemed a residential use of property for zoning purposes and shall be a permissible use in all residential districts of all political subdivisions. No political subdivision may require that a family care home, its owner, or operator obtain, because of the use, a conditional use permit, special use permit, special exception or variance from any such zoning ordinance or plan; provided, however, that a political subdivision may prohibit a family care home from being located within a one-half mile radius of an existing family care home. (Article 3, 168-22, p. 178)

An example of specific procedures developed for family care homes is given for Durham City, North Carolina. In this city, family care homes are permitted in all residential and residential apartment districts but are subject to certain limitations. These limitations include: (1) no more

than five persons served residing in such a home; (2) no more than one employee other than the primary family residing in and operating the home shall be employed on the premises; (3) a minimum of 100 square feet shall be provided in the way of bedroom area for each person served, except where two or more occupy a given bedroom, a minimum of 80 square feet shall be provided for each person; (4) all such homes shall be licensed by the state of North Carolina Department of Human Resources, and no person failing to secure such a license or allowing such a license to lapse shall operate a home; (5) a family care home shall be operated in a manner compatible with the surrounding residential land use and shall not create a public nuisance; (6) no traffic shall be generated by such a home in greater volumes than would normally be expected in a residential neighborhood, and any need for parking generated by the conduct of such a home, over and above that normally generated by a residential use in the neighborhood, shall be met off the street and other than in a required front yard; and (7) any house and lot on which such a family care home is hereafter initiated shall be in compliance with the housing code, the building code, and the zoning ordinance of Durham.

CECELIA STEPPE-JONES
*North Carolina Central
University*

COMMUNITY PLACEMENT
COMMUNITY RESIDENTIAL PROGRAMS
DEINSTITUTIONALIZATION

Z SCORES, IN DETERMINATION OF DISCREPANCIES

Since the passage of PL 94-142 (Education for all Handicapped Children Act of 1975) several measurement discrepancy models have been recommended in the measurement and special education literature for defining a child as learning disabled (Berk, 1984; Boodoo, 1985; Reynolds et al., 1984; Willson & Reynolds, 1985). These models are all used to estimate the difference between a child's aptitude and achievement, and to determine whether such a difference constitutes a severe discrepancy. The models recommended for use involve the use of standard scores. Under each model, a true discrepancy between a subject's aptitude and achievement is estimated using the subject's standard score on the respective aptitude and achievement test. Many of the standardized aptitude and achievement measures used for individualized testing are normed using the standard score scale with a mean ($\overline{X}$) of 100 and a standard deviation (S) of 15.

An alternative scale that simplifies the statistical formulas used in the discrepancy models for assessing a severe discrepancy is the Z score scale (Hopkins & Stanley, 1981). This scale has a mean of 0 and a standard deviation of 1 and has the advantage of representing the scores directly in standard deviation units. The following illustrates its use with the Simple Difference Model. Under this model, a difference is defined as [Aptitude (X)–Achievement (Y)] with the standard deviation of this difference, S_D, given by

$$S_D = (S_X{}^2 + S_Y{}^2 - 2r_{XY}S_XS_Y)^{1/2}$$

where r_{XY} is the correlation between X and Y. The standard error of estimate of a difference, SE, is given by

$$SE = [S_X{}^2(1 - r_{XX'}) + S_Y{}^2(1 - r_{YY'})]^{1/2}$$

where $r_{XX'}$, $r_{YY'}$, are the reliabilities of X and Y respectively.

Using the Z score scale, each of the aptitude and achievement scores is converted to the corresponding Z score using

$$Z_X = \frac{X - \overline{X}}{S_X}$$

and

$$Z_Y = \frac{Y - \overline{Y}}{S_Y}$$

Then, a simple difference is $(Z_X - Z_Y)$. The standard deviation of this difference is

$$S_D = (2 - 2r_{XY})^{1/2}$$

where r_{XY} is the correlation between X and Y, and the standard error of estimate is given by

$$SE = (2 - r_{XX'} - r_{YY'})^{1/2}$$

REFERENCES

Berk, R. A. (1984). *Screening and diagnosis of children with learning disabilities.* Springfield, IL: Thomas.

Boodoo, G. M. (1985). A multivariate perspective for aptitude-achievement discrepancy in learning disability assessment. *Journal of Special Education, 18,* 489–449.

Hopkins, K. D., & Stanley, J. C. (1981). *Educational and psychological measurement and evaluation* (6th ed.). Englewood Cliffs, NJ: Prentice-Hall.

Reynolds, C. R., Berk, R. A., Boodoo, G. M., Cox, J., Gutkin, T. B., Mann, L., Page, E. B., & Willson, V. L. (1984). *Critical measurement issues in learning disabilities.* Report of the USDE, SEP Work Group on Measurement Issues in the Assessment of Learning Disabilities.

Willson, V. L., & Reynolds, C. R. (1985). Another look at evaluating aptitude-achievement discrepancies in the diagnosis of learning disabilities. *Journal of Special Education, 18,* 477–488.

GWYNETH M. BOODOO
Texas A&M University

LEARNING DISABILITIES, SEVERE DISCREPANCY ANALYSIS IN
See **DISCREPANCY FROM GRADE**
SEVERE DISCREPANCY ANALYSIS

ZYGOSITY

Zygosity is twinning that may result in monozygotic (MZ) or identical twins and dizygotic (DZ) or fraternal twins. The cause of MZ twinning remains unknown while the cause of DZ twinning is largely the result of multiple ovulation (Groothuis, 1985). Placentation helps to explain zygosity of twins, where dichorionic placentas take place in all DZ pairs and in about 30% of MZ twins. Monochorionic placentas occur only with MZ twins (Siegel & Siegel, 1982). A twin birth occurs in approximately 1 in 80 pregnancies. For women who already have given birth to twins, the incidence of having a second set rises to 1 in 20. The incidence of MZ twins is 3.5 per 1000 live births independent of race and maternal age. With maternal age DZ twinning increases. It is slightly more frequent in blacks and most unusual in Orientals (Groothuis, 1985; Siegel & Siegel, 1982).

Twinning is of relevance to special education personnel because there are increased risks for medical, psychological, developmental, and educational problems. Twin pregnancies have been associated with higher rates of such symptoms as nausea and vomiting. The greatly increased mortality of twins at birth (i.e., 15%) has been attributed to the high prematurity rate (i.e., 60%) in terms of both gestation time and birth weight. Twins also experience a higher rate of such perinatal problems as entangling of cords, prolapsed cords, hypoxia anemia, respiratory distress syndrome, and jaundice. These risks are generally higher for MZ twins and the second born of both MZ and DZ twins (Young et al., 1985). Twins also experience congenital anomalies such as heart disease, cleft lip, and cleft palate about twice as frequently as children of single births.

There is a general consensus that twins experience higher rates of developmental and behavioral problems than the general population. Like the medical difficulties, these risks are generally more severe for MZ and second-born twins. During the preschool years, problems are focused in such areas as verbal and motor development, discipline, sharing, toilet training, separation, and individual needs. Many of the problems continue for school-aged twins with classroom assignments, school avoidance, peer relations, and academic performance as special concerns.

During adolescence, the identity crisis could be exacerbated for twins who have not resolved separation and individuation issues earlier. Regarding school-related abilities, the degree of impairment has been found to be dependent on birth problems and illness as antecedents (Matheny, Dolan, & Wilson, 1976). Moreover, Matheny et al. reported that twins in comparison with the general population have higher rates of learning disabilities and social immaturity. Siegel and Siegel (1982) point out that IQ deficits are questionable, especially when antecedent and environmental factors are controlled.

Typical recommendations for management and guidance follow: (1) encourage parents to avoid emphasizing similarities; (2) separate twins at school as soon as possible but delay if problems are encountered; (3) establish individual expectations for school performance; (4) give psychoeducation assessment to twins with early medical problems. Parents are referred to the National Mother of Twins Club for information and resources.

REFERENCES

Groothuis, J. R. (1985). Twins and twin families. A practical guide to outpatient management. *Clinics in Perinatology, 12,* 459–474.

Matheny, A. P., Dolan, A. B., & Wilson, R. S. (1976). Twins with academic learning problems: Antecedent characteristics. *American Journal of Orthopsychiatry, 46,* 464–469.

Siegel, S. J., & Siegel, M. M. (1982). Practical aspects of pediatric management of families with twins. *Pediatrics in Review, 4,* 8–12.

Young, B. K., Suidan, J., Antoine, C., Silverman, F., Lustig, I., & Wasserman, J. (1985). Differences in twins: The importance of birth order. *American Journal of Obstetrics and Gynecology, 151,* 915–921.

JOSEPH D. PERRY
Kent State University

SIBLINGS
TWINS

APPENDIX
PUBLIC LAW 94-142

94TH CONGRESS, S.6
NOVEMBER 29, 1975

TO AMEND THE EDUCATION OF THE HANDICAPPED ACT TO PROVIDE EDUCATIONAL ASSISTANCE TO ALL HANDICAPPED CHILDREN, AND FOR OTHER PURPOSES.

Be it enacted by the Senate and House of Representatives of the United States of America in Congress assembled, That this Act may be cited as the "Education for All Handicapped Children Act of 1975".

Education for All Handicapped Children Act of 1975.

EXTENSION OF EXISTING LAW

20 USC 1401 note.

SEC. 2. (a)(1)(A) Section 611(b)(2) of the Education of the Handicapped Act (20 U.S.C. 1411(b)(2)) (hereinafter in this Act referred to as the "Act"), as in effect during the fiscal years 1976 and 1977, is amended by striking out "the Commonwealth of Puerto Rico.".

(B) Section 611(c)(1) of the Act (20 U.S.C. 1411(c)(1), as in effect during the fiscal years 1976 and 1977, is amended by striking out "the Commonwealth of Puerto Rico,".

(2) Section 611(c)(2) of the Act (20 U.S.C. 1411(c)(2)), as in effect during the fiscal years 1976 and 1977, is amended by striking out "year ending June 30, 1975" and inserting in lieu thereof the following: "years ending June 30, 1975, and 1976, and for the fiscal year ending September 30, 1977", and by striking out "2 per centum" each place it appears therein and inserting in lieu thereof "1 per centum".

(3) Section 611(d) of the Act (20 U.S.C. 1411(d)), as in effect during the fiscal years 1976 and 1977, is amended by striking out "year ending June 30, 1975" and inserting in lieu thereof the following: "years ending June 30, 1975, and 1976, and for the fiscal year ending September 30, 1977".

(4) Section 612(a) of the Act (20 U.S.C. 1412(a)), as in effect during the fiscal years 1976 and 1977, is amended—

(A) by striking out "year ending June 30, 1975" and inserting in lieu thereof "years ending June 30, 1975, and 1976, for the period beginning July 1, 1976, and ending September 30, 1976, and for the fiscal year ending September 30, 1977"; and

(B) by striking out "fiscal year 1974" and inserting in lieu thereof "preceding fiscal year".

(b)(1) Section 614(a) of the Education Amendments of 1974 (Public Law 93–380; 88 Stat. 580) is amended by striking out "fiscal year 1975" and inserting in lieu thereof the following: "the fiscal years ending June 30, 1975, and 1976, for the period beginning July 1, 1976, and ending September 30, 1976, and for the fiscal year ending September 30, 1977,".

20 USC 1411 note.

(2) Section 614(b) of the Education Amendments of 1974 (Public Law 93–380; 88 Stat. 580) is amended by striking out "fiscal year 1974" and inserting in lieu thereof

20 USC 1411 note.

the following: "the fiscal years ending June 30, 1975, and 1976, for the period beginning July 1, 1976, and ending September 30, 1976, and for the fiscal year ending September 30, 1977,".

(3) Section 614(c) of the Education Amendments of 1974 (Public Law 93–380; 88 Stat. 580) is amended by striking out "fiscal year 1974" and inserting in lieu thereof the following: "the fiscal years ending June 30, 1975, and 1976, for the period beginning July 1, 1976, and ending September 30, 1976, and for the fiscal year ending September 30, 1977,".

20 USC 1413 note.

(c) Section 612(a) of the Act, as in effect during the fiscal years 1976 and 1977, and as amended by subsection (a)(4), is amended by inserting immediately before the period at the end thereof the following: ", or $300,000, whichever is greater".

Ante, p. 773.

(d) Section 612 of the Act (20 U.S.C. 1411), as in effect during the fiscal years 1976 and 1977, is amended by adding at the end thereof the following new subsection:

20 USC 1412.

"(d) The Commissioner shall, no later than one hundred twenty days after the date of the enactment of the Education for All Handicapped Children Act of 1975, prescribe and publish in the Federal Register such rules as he considers necessary to carry out the provisions of this section and section 611.".

Publication in Federal Register.

(e) Notwithstanding the provisions of section 611 of the Act, as in effect during the fiscal years 1976 and 1977, there are authorized to be appropriated $100,000,000 for the fiscal year 1976, such sums as may be necessary for the period beginning July 1, 1976, and ending September 30, 1976, and $200,000,000 for the fiscal year 1977, to carry out the provisions of part B of the Act, as in effect during such fiscal years.

Ante, p. 773. 20 USC 1411 note.

STATEMENT OF FINDINGS AND PURPOSE

SEC. 3. (a) Section 601 of the Act (20 U.S.C. 1401) is amended by inserting "(a)" immediately before "This title" and by adding at the end thereof the following new subsections:

20 USC 1401 note.

"(b) The Congress finds that—

"(1) there are more than eight million handicapped children in the United States today;

"(2) the special educational needs of such children are not being fully met;

"(3) more than half of the handicapped children in the United States do not receive appropriate educational services which would enable them to have full equality of opportunity;

"(4) one million of the handicapped children in the United States are excluded entirely from the public school system and will not go through the educational process with their peers;

"(5) there are many handicapped children throughout the United States participating in regular school programs whose handicaps prevent them from having a successful educational experience because their handicaps are undetected;

"(6) because of the lack of adequate services within the public school system, families are often forced to find services outside the public school system, often at great distance from their residence and at their own expense;

"(7) developments in the training of teachers and in diagnostic and instructional procedures and methods have advanced to the point that, given appropriate funding, State and local educational agencies can and will provide effective special education and related services to meet the needs of handicapped children;

"(8) State and local educational agencies have a responsibility to provide education for all handicapped children, but present financial resources are inadequate to meet the special educational needs of handicapped children; and

"(9) it is in the national interest that the Federal Government assist State and local efforts to provide programs to meet the educational needs of handicapped children in order to assure equal protection of the law.

"(c) It is the purpose of this Act to assure that all handicapped children have available to them, within the time periods specified in section 612(2)(B), a free appropriate public education which emphasizes special education and related services designed to meet their unique needs, to assure that the rights of handicapped children and their parents or guardians are protected, to assist States and localities to provide for the education of all handicapped children, and to assess and assure the effectiveness of efforts to educate handicapped children.".

Ante, p. 773.

(b) The heading for section 601 of the Act (20 U.S.C. 1401) is amended to read as follows:

"SHORT TITLE; STATEMENT OF FINDINGS AND PURPOSE".

DEFINITIONS

SEC. 4. (a) Section 602 of the Act (20 U.S.C. 1402) is amended—   20 USC 1401.
    (1) in paragraph (1) thereof, by striking out "crippled" and inserting in lieu thereof "orthopedically impaired", and by inserting immediately after "impaired children" the following: ", or children with specific learning disabilities,";
    (2) in paragraph (5) thereof, by inserting immediately after "instructional materials," the following: "telecommunications, sensory, and other technological aids and devices,";
    (3) in the last sentence of paragraph (15) thereof, by inserting immediately after "environmental" the following: ", cultural, or economic"; and
    (4) by adding at the end thereof the following new paragraphs:

"(16) The term 'special education' means specially designed instruction, at no cost to parents or guardians, to meet the unique needs of a handicapped child, including classroom instruction, instruction in physical education, home instruction, and instruction in hospitals and institutions.

"(17) The term 'related services' means transportation, and such developmental, corrective, and other supportive services (including speech pathology and audiology, psychological services, physical and occupational therapy, recreation, and medical and counseling services, except that such medical services shall be for diagnostic and evaluation purposes only) as may be required to assist a handicapped child to benefit from special education, and includes the early identification and assessment of handicapping conditions in children.

"(18) The term 'free appropriate public education' means special education and related services which (A) have been provided at public expense, under public supervision and direction, and without charge, (B) meet the standards of the State educational agency, (C) include an appropriate preschool, elementary, or secondary school education in the State involved, and (D) are provided in conformity with the individualized education program required under section 614(a)(5).

"(19) The term 'individualized education program' means a written statement for each handicapped child developed in any meeting by a representative of the local educational agency or an intermediate educational unit who shall be qualified to provide, or supervise the provision of, specially designed instruction to meet the unique needs of handicapped children, the teacher, the parents or guardian of such child, and, whenever appropriate, such child, which statement shall include (A) a statement of the present levels of educational performance of such child, (B) a statement of annual goals, including short-term instructional objectives, (C) a statement of the specific educational services to be provided to such child, and the extent to which such child will be able to participate in regular educational programs, (D) the projected date for initiation and anticipated duration of such services, and (E) appropriate objective criteria and evaluation procedures and schedules for determining, on at least an annual basis, whether instructional objectives are being achieved.

"(20) The term 'excess costs' means those costs which are in excess of the average annual per student expenditure in a local educational agency during the preceding school year for an elementary or secondary school student, as may be appropriate, and which shall be computed after deducting (A) amounts received under this part or under title I or title VII of the Elementary and Secondary Education Act of 1965, and (B) any   20 USC 241a note, 881. State or local funds expended for programs which would qualify for assistance under this part or under such titles.

"(21) The term 'native language' has the meaning given that term by section 703(a)(2) of the Bilingual Education Act (20 U.S.C. 880b–1(a)(2)).

"(22) The term 'intermediate educational unit' means any public authority, other than a local educational agency, which is under the general supervision of a State educational agency, which is established by State law for the purpose of providing free public education on a regional basis, and which provides special education and related services to handicapped children within that State.".

(b) The heading for section 602 of the Act (20 U.S.C. 1402) is amended to read as follows:

"DEFINITIONS".

ASSISTANCE FOR EDUCATION OF ALL HANDICAPPED CHILDREN

SEC. 5. (a) Part B of the Act (20 U.S.C. 1411 et seq.) is amended to read as follows:

"PART B—ASSISTANCE FOR EDUCATION OF ALL HANDICAPPED CHILDREN

"ENTITLEMENTS AND ALLOCATIONS

"SEC. 611. (a)(1) Except as provided in paragraph (3) and in section 619, the maximum amount of the grant to which a State is entitled under this part for any fiscal year shall be equal to— 20 USC 1411. <u>Post</u>, p. 793.

"(A) the number of handicapped children aged three to twenty-one, inclusive, in such State who are receiving special education and related services; multiplied by—

"(B)(i) 5 per centum, for the fiscal year ending September 30, 1978, of the average per pupil expenditure in public elementary and secondary schools in the United States;

"(ii) 10 per centum, for the fiscal year ending September 30, 1979, of the average per pupil expenditure in public elementary and secondary schools in the United States;

"(iii) 20 per centum, for the fiscal year ending September 30, 1980, of the average per pupil expenditure in public elementary and secondary schools in the United States;

"(iv) 30 per centum, for the fiscal year ending September 30, 1981, of the average per pupil expenditure in public elementary and secondary schools in the United States; and

"(v) 40 per centum, for the fiscal year ending September 30, 1982, and for each fiscal year thereafter, of the average per pupil expenditure in public elementary and secondary schools in the United States;

except that no State shall receive an amount which is less than the amount which such State received under this part for the fiscal year ending September 30, 1977.

"(2) For the purpose of this subsection and subsection (b) through subsection (e), the term 'State' does not include Guam, American Samoa, the Virgin Islands, and the Trust Territory of the Pacific Islands. "State."

"(3) The number of handicapped children receiving special education and related services in any fiscal year shall be equal to the average of the number of such children receiving special education and related services on October 1 and February 1 of the fiscal year preceding the fiscal year for which the determination is made.

"(4) For purposes of paragraph (1)(B), the term 'average per pupil expenditure', in the United States, means the aggregate current expenditures, during the second fiscal year preceding the fiscal year for which the computation is made (or, if satisfactory data for such year are not available at the time of computation, then during the most recent preceding fiscal year for which satisfactory data are available) of all local educational agencies in the United States (which, for purposes of this subsection, means the fifty States and the District of Columbia), as the case may be, plus any direct expenditures by the State for operation of such agencies (without regard to the source of funds from which either of such expenditures are made), divided by the aggregate number of children in average daily attendance to whom such agencies provided free public education during such preceding year. "Average per pupil expenditure."

"(5)(A) In determining the allotment of each State under paragraph (1), the Commissioner may not count—

"(i) handicapped children in such State under paragraph (1)(A) to the extent the number of such children is greater than 12 per centum of the number of all children aged five to seventeen, inclusive, in such State;

"(ii) as part of such percentage, children with specific learning disabilities to the extent the number of such children is greater than one-sixth of such percentage; and "(iii) handicapped children who are counted under section 121 of the Elementary 20 USC 241c–1. and Secondary Education Act of 1965.

"(B) For purposes of subparagraph (A), the number of children aged five to seventeen, inclusive, in any State shall be determined by the Commissioner on the basis of the most recent satisfactory data available to him.

"(b)(1) Of the funds received under subsection (a) by any State for the fiscal year ending September 30, 1978—

"(A) 50 per centum of such funds may be used by such State in accordance with the provisions of paragraph (2); and

"(B) 50 per centum of such funds shall be distributed by such State pursuant to subsection (d) to local educational agencies and intermediate educational units in such State, for use in accordance with the priorities established under section 612(3).

"(2) Of the funds which any State may use under paragraph (1)(A)—

"(A) an amount which is equal to the greater of—

"(i) 5 per centum of the total amount of funds received under this part by such State; or

"(ii) $200,000;

may be used by such State for administrative costs related to carrying out sections 612 and 613;

"(B) the remainder shall be used by such State to provide support services and direct services, in accordance with the priorities established under section 612(3).

"(c)(1) Of the funds received under subsection (a) by any State for the fiscal year ending September 30, 1979, and for each fiscal year thereafter—

"(A) 25 per centum of such funds may be used by such State in accordance with the provisions of paragraph (2); and

"(B) except as provided in paragraph (3), 75 per centum of such funds shall be distributed by such State pursuant to subsection (d) to local educational agencies and intermediate educational units in such State, for use in accordance with priorities established under section 612(3).

"(2)(A) Subject to the provisions of subparagraph (B), of the funds which any State may use under paragraph (1)(A)—

"(i) an amount which is equal to the greater of—

"(I) 5 per centum of the total amount of funds received under this part by such State; or

"(II) $200,000;

may be used by such State for administrative costs related to carrying out the provisions of sections 612 and 613; and

"(ii) the remainder shall be used by such State to provide support services and direct services, in accordance with the priorities established under section 612(3).

"(B) The amount expended by any State from the funds available to such State under paragraph (1)(A) in any fiscal year for the provision of support services or for the provision of direct services shall be matched on a program basis by such State, from funds other than Federal funds, for the provision of support services or for the provision of direct services for the fiscal year involved.

"(3) The provisions of section 613(a)(9) shall not apply with respect to amounts available for use by any State under paragraph (2).

"(4)(A) No funds shall be distributed by any State under this subsection in any fiscal year to any local educational agency or intermediate educational unit in such State if—

"(i) such local educational agency or intermediate educational unit is entitled, under subsection (d), to less than $7,500 for such fiscal year; or

"(ii) such local educational agency or intermediate educational unit has not submitted an application for such funds which meets the requirements of section 614.

"(B) Whenever the provisions of subparagraph (A) apply, the State involved shall use such funds to assure the provision of a free appropriate education to handicapped children residing in the area served by such local educational agency or such intermediate educational unit. The provisions of paragraph (2)(B) shall not apply to the use of such funds.

"(d) From the total amount of funds available to local educational agencies and intermediate educational units in any State under subsection (b)(1)(B) or subsection (c)(1)(B), as the case may be, each local educational agency or intermediate educational unit shall be entitled to an amount which bears the same ratio to the total amount available under subsection (b)(1)(B) or subsection (c)(1)(B), as the case may be, as the number of handicapped children aged three to twenty-one, inclusive, receiving special education and related services in such local educational agency or intermediate educational unit bears to the aggregate number of handicapped children aged three to twenty-one, inclusive, receiving special education and related services in all local educational agencies and intermediate educational units which apply to the State educational agency involved for funds under this part.

"(e)(1) The jurisdictions to which this subsection applies are Guam, American Samoa, the Virgin Islands, and the Trust Territory of the Pacific Islands.

"(2) Each jurisdiction to which this subsection applies shall be entitled to a grant for the purposes set forth in section 601(c) in an amount equal to an amount determined by the Commissioner in accordance with criteria based on respective needs, except that the aggregate of the amount to which such jurisdictions are so entitled for any fiscal year shall not exceed an amount equal to 1 per centum of the aggregate of the amounts available to all States under this part for that fiscal year. If the aggregate of the amounts, determined by the Commissioner pursuant to the preceding sentence, to be so needed for any fiscal year exceeds an amount equal to such 1 per centum limitation, the entitlement of each such jurisdiction shall be reduced proportionately until such aggregate does not exceed such 1 per centum limitation. Ante, p. 774.

"(3) The amount expended for administration by each jurisdiction under this subsection shall not exceed 5 per centum of the amount allotted to such jurisdiction for any fiscal year, or $35,000, whichever is greater.

"(f)(1) The Commissioner is authorized to make payments to the Secretary of the Interior according to the need for such assistance for the education of handicapped children on reservations serviced by elementary and secondary schools operated for Indian children by the Department of the Interior. The amount of such payment for any fiscal year shall not exceed 1 per centum of the aggregate amounts available to all States under this part for that fiscal year.

"(2) The Secretary of the Interior may receive an allotment under this subsection only after submitting to the Commissioner an application which meets the applicable requirements of section 614(a) and which is approved by the Commissioner. The provisions of section 616 shall apply to any such application.

"(g)(1) If the sums appropriated for any fiscal year for making payments to States under this part are not sufficient to pay in full the total amounts which all States are entitled to receive under this part for such fiscal year, the maximum amounts which all States are entitled to receive under this part for such fiscal year shall be ratably reduced. In case additional funds become available for making such payments for any fiscal year during which the preceding sentence is applicable, such reduced amounts shall be increased on the same basis as they were reduced.

"(2) In the case of any fiscal year in which the maximum amounts for which States are eligible have been reduced under the first sentence of paragraph (1), and in which additional funds have not been made available to pay in full the total of such maximum amounts under the last sentence of such paragraph, the State educational agency shall fix dates before which each local educational agency or intermediate educational unit shall report to the State educational agency on the amount of funds available to the local educational agency or intermediate educational unit, under the provisions of subsection (d), which it estimates that it will expend in accordance with the provisions of this part. The amounts so available to any local educational agency or intermediate educational unit, or any amount which would be available to any other local educational agency or intermediate educational unit if it were to submit a program meeting the requirements of this part, which the State educational agency determines will not be used for the period of its availability, shall be available for allocation to those local educational agencies or intermediate educational units, in the manner provided by this section, which the State educational agency determines will need and be able to use additional funds to carry out approved programs.

"ELIGIBILITY

"SEC. 612. In order to qualify for assistance under this part in any fiscal year, a State shall demonstrate to the Commissioner that the following conditions are met: 20 USC 1412.

"(1) The State has in effect a policy that assures all handicapped children the right to a free appropriate public education.

"(2) The State has developed a plan pursuant to section 613(b) in effect prior to the date of the enactment of the Education for All Handicapped Children Act of 1975 and submitted not later than August 21, 1975, which will be amended so as to comply with the provisions of this paragraph. Each such amended plan shall set forth in detail the policies and procedures which the State will undertake or has undertaken in order to assure that—

"(A) there is established (i) a goal of providing full educational opportunity to all handicapped children, (ii) a detailed timetable for accomplishing such a goal, and (iii) a description of the kind and number of facilities, personnel, and services necessary throughout the State to meet such a goal;

"(B) a free appropriate public education will be available for all handicapped children between the ages of three and eighteen within the State not later than September 1, 1978, and for all handicapped children between the ages of three and twenty-one within the State not later than September 1, 1980, except that, with respect to handicapped children aged three to five and aged eighteen to twenty-one, inclusive, the requirements of this clause shall not be applied in any State if the application of such requirements would be inconsistent with State law or practice, or the order of any court, respecting public education within such age groups in the State;

"(C) all children residing in the State who are handicapped, regardless of the severity of their handicap, and who are in need of special education and related services are identified, located, and evaluated, and that a practical method is developed and implemented to determine which children are currently receiving needed special education and related services and which children are not currently receiving needed special education and related services;

"(D) policies and procedures are established in accordance with detailed criteria prescribed under section 617(c); and

"(E) the amendment to the plan submitted by the State required by this section shall be available to parents, guardians, and other members of the general public at least thirty days prior to the date of submission of the amendment to the Commissioner.

"(3) The State has established priorities for providing a free appropriate public education to all handicapped children, which priorities shall meet the timetables set forth in clause (B) of paragraph (2) of this section, first with respect to handicapped children who are not receiving an education, and second with respect to handicapped children, within each disability, with the most severe handicaps who are receiving an inadequate education, and has made adequate progress in meeting the timetables set forth in clause (B) of paragraph (2) of this section.

"(4) Each local educational agency in the State will maintain records of the individualized education program for each handicapped child, and such program shall be established, reviewed, and revised as provided in section 614(a)(5).

"(5) The State has established (A) procedural safeguards as required by section 615, (B) procedures to assure that, to the maximum extent appropriate, handicapped children, including children in public or private institutions or other care facilities, are educated with children who are not handicapped, and that special classes, separate schooling, or other removal of handicapped children from the regular educational environment occurs only when the nature or severity of the handicap is such that education in regular classes with the use of supplementary aids and services cannot be achieved satisfactorily, and (C) procedures to assure that testing and evaluation materials and procedures utilized for the purposes of evaluation and placement of handicapped children will be selected and administered so as not to be racially or culturally discriminatory. Such materials or procedures shall be provided and administered in the child's native language or mode of communication, unless it clearly is not feasible to do so, and no single procedure shall be the sole criterion for determining an appropriate educational program for a child.

"(6) The State educational agency shall be responsible for assuring that the requirements of this part are carried out and that all educational programs for handicapped children within the State, including all such programs administered by any other State or local agency, will be under the general supervision of the persons responsible for

Administration.

educational programs for handicapped children in the State educational agency and shall meet education standards of the State educational agency.

"(7) The State shall assure that (A) in carrying out the requirements of this section procedures are established for consultation with individuals involved in or concerned with the education of handicapped children, including handicapped individuals and parents or guardians of handicapped children, and (B) there are public hearings, adequate notice of such hearings, and an opportunity for comment available to the general public prior to adoption of the policies, programs, and procedures required pursuant to the provisions of this section and section 613.

Notice, hearings.

"STATE PLANS

"SEC. 613. (a) Any State meeting the eligibility requirements set forth in section 612 and desiring to participate in the program under this part shall submit to the Commissioner, through its State educational agency, a State plan at such time, in such manner, and containing or accompanied by such information, as he deems necessary. Each such plan shall—

20 USC 1413.

"(1) set forth policies and procedures designed to assure that funds paid to the State under this part will be expended in accordance with the provisions of this part, with particular attention given to the provisions of sections 611(b), 611(c), 611(d), 612(2), and 612(3);

"(2) provide that programs and procedures will be established to assure that funds received by the State or any of its political subdivisions under any other Federal program, including section 121 of the Elementary and Secondary Education Act of 1965 (20 U.S.C. 241c-2), section 305(b)(8) of such Act (20 U.S.C. 844a(b)(8)) or its successor authority, and section 122(a)(4)(B) of the Vocational Education Act of 1963 (20 U.S.C. 1262(a)(4)(B)), under which there is specific authority for the provision of assistance for the education of handicapped children, will be utilized by the State, or any of its political subdivisions, only in a manner consistent with the goal of providing a free appropriate public education for all handicapped children, except that nothing in this clause shall be construed to limit the specific requirements of the laws governing such Federal programs;

20 USC 241c-1.

"(3) set forth, consistent with the purposes of this Act, a description of programs and procedures for (A) the development and implementation of a comprehensive system of personnel development which shall include the inservice training of general and special educational instructional and support personnel, detailed procedures to assure that all personnel necessary to carry out the purposes of this Act are appropriately and adequately prepared and trained, and effective procedures for acquiring and disseminating to teachers and administrators of programs for handicapped children significant information derived from educational research, demonstration, and similar projects, and (B) adopting, where appropriate, promising educational practices and materials development through such projects;

"(4) set forth policies and procedures to assure—

"(A) that, to the extent consistent with the number and location of handicapped children in the State who are enrolled in private elementary and secondary schools, provision is made for the participation of such children in the program assisted or carried out under this part by providing for such children special education and related services; and

"(B) that (i) handicapped children in private schools and facilities will be provided special education and related services (in conformance with an individualized educational program as required by this part) at no cost to their parents or guardian, if such children are placed in or referred to such schools or facilities by the State or appropriate local educational agency as the means of carrying out the requirements of this part or any other applicable law requiring the provision of special education and related services to all handicapped children within such State, and (ii) in all such instances the State educational agency shall determine whether such schools and facilities meet standards that apply to State and local educational agencies and that children so served have all the rights they would have if served by such agencies;

"(5) set forth policies and procedures which assure that the State shall seek to recover any funds made available under this part for services to any child who is determined to be erroneously classified as eligible to be counted under section 611(a) or section 611(d);

"(6) provide satisfactory assurance that the control of funds provided under this part, and title to property derived therefrom, shall be in a public agency for the uses and purposes provided in this part, and that a public agency will administer such funds and property;

"(7) provide for (A) making such reports in such form and containing such in-   Reports and records. formation as the Commissioner may require to carry out his functions under this part, and (B) keeping such records and affording such access thereto as the Commissioner may find necessary to assure the correctness and verification of such reports and proper disbursement of Federal funds under this part;

"(8) provide procedures to assure that final action with respect to any application   Notice, hearings. submitted by a local educational agency or an intermediate educational unit shall not be taken without first affording the local educational agency or intermediate educational unit involved reasonable notice and opportunity for a hearing;

"(9) provide satisfactory assurance that Federal funds made available under this part (A) will not be commingled with State funds, and (B) will be so used as to supplement and increase the level of State and local funds expended for the education of handicapped children and in no case to supplant such State and local funds, except that, where the State provides clear and convincing evidence that all handicapped children have available to them a free appropriate public education, the Commissioner may waive in part the requirement of this clause if he concurs with the evidence provided by the State;

"(10) provide, consistent with procedures prescribed pursuant to section 617(a)(2), satisfactory assurance that such fiscal control and fund accounting procedures will be adopted as may be necessary to assure proper disbursement of, and accounting for, Federal funds paid under this part to the State, including any such funds paid by the State to local educational agencies and intermediate educational units;

"(11) provide for procedures for evaluation at least annually of the effectiveness   Evaluation. of programs in meeting the educational needs of handicapped children (including evaluation of individualized education programs), in accordance with such criteria that the Commissioner shall prescribe pursuant to section 617; and

"(12) provide that the State has an advisory panel, appointed by the Governor   State advisory panel. or any other official authorized under State law to make such appointments, composed of individuals involved in or concerned with the education of handicapped children, including handicapped individuals, teachers, parents or guardians of handicapped children. State and local education officials, and administrators of programs for handicapped children, which (A) advises the State educational agency of unmet needs within the State in the education of handicapped children, (B) comments publicly on any rules or regulations proposed for issuance by the State regarding the education of handicapped children and the procedures for distribution of funds under this part, and (C) assists the State in developing and reporting such data and evaluations as may assist the Commissioner in the performance of his responsibilities under section 618.

"(b) Whenever a State educational agency provides free appropriate public education for handicapped children, or provides direct services to such children, such State educational agency shall include, as part of the State plan required by subsection (a) of this section, such additional assurances not specified in such subsection (a) as are contained in section 614(a), except that funds available for the provision of such education or services may be expended without regard to the provisions relating to excess costs in section 614(a).

"(c) The Commissioner shall approve any State plan and any modification thereof which—

"(1) is submitted by a State eligible in accordance with section 612; and

"(2) meets the requirements of subsection (a) and subsection (b).

The Commissioner shall disapprove any State plan which does not meet the require-   Notice, hearings. ments of the preceding sentence, but shall not finally disapprove a State plan except after reasonable notice and opportunity for a hearing to the State.

"SEC. 614. (a) A local educational agency or an intermediate educational unit which desires to receive payments under section 611(d) for any fiscal year shall submit an application to the appropriate State educational agency. Such application shall—   20 USC 1414.

"(1) provide satisfactory assurance that payments under this part will be used for excess costs directly attributable to programs which—

"(A) provide that all children residing within the jurisdiction of the local educational agency or the intermediate educational unit who are handicapped, regardless of the severity of their handicap, and are in need of special education and related services will be identified, located, and evaluated, and provide for the inclusion of a practical method of determining which children are currently receiving needed special education and related services and which children are not currently receiving such education and services;

"(B) establish policies and procedures in accordance with detailed criteria prescribed under section 617(c);

"(C) establish a goal of providing full educational opportunities to all handicapped children, including—

"(i) procedures for the implementation and use of the comprehensive system of personnel development established by the State educational agency under section 613(a)(3);

"(ii) the provision of, and the establishment of priorities for providing, a free appropriate public education to all handicapped children, first with respect to handicapped children who are not receiving an education, and second with respect to handicapped children, within each disability, with the most severe handicaps who are receiving an inadequate education;

"(iii) the participation and consultation of the parents or guardian of such children; and

"(iv) to the maximum extent practicable and consistent with the provisions of section 612(5)(B), the provision of special services to enable such children to participate in regular educational programs;

"(D) establish a detailed timetable for accomplishing the goal described in subclause (C); and

"(E) provide a description of the kind and number of facilities, personnel, and services necessary to meet the goal described in subclause (C);

"(2) provide satisfactory assurance that (A) the control of funds provided under this part, and title to property derived from such funds, shall be in a public agency for the uses and purposes provided in this part, and that a public agency will administer such funds and property, (B) Federal funds expended by local educational agencies and intermediate educational units for programs under this part (i) shall be used to pay only the excess costs directly attributable to the education of handicapped children, and (ii) shall be used to supplement and, to the extent practicable, increase the level of State and local funds expended for the education of handicapped chidren, and in no case to supplant such State and local funds, and (C) State and local funds will be used in the jurisdiction of the local educational agency or intermediate educational unit to provide services in program areas which, taken as a whole, are at least comparable to services being provided in areas of such jurisdiction which are not receiving funds under this part;

"(3)(A) provide for furnishing such information (which, in the case of reports relating to performance, is in accordance with specific performance criteria related to program objectives), as may be necessary to enable the State educational agency to perform its duties under this part, including information relating to the educational achievement of handicapped children participating in programs carried out under this part; and

"(B) provide for keeping such records, and provide for affording such access to   Recordkeeping.
such records, as the State educational agency may find necessary to assure the correctness and verification of such information furnished under subclause (A);

"(4) provide for making the application and all pertinent documents related to   Public information, availability.
such application available to parents, guardians, and other members of the general public, and provide that all evaluations and reports required under clause (3) shall be public information;

"(5) provide assurances that the local educational agency or intermediate educational unit will establish, or revise, whichever is apropriate, an individualized education program for each handicapped child at the beginning of each school year and will then review and, if appropriate revise, its provisions periodically, but not less than annually;

"(6) provide satisfactory assurance that policies and programs established and administered by the local educational agency or intermediate educational unit shall be consistent with the provisions of paragraph (1) through paragraph (7) of section 612 and section 613(a); and

"(7) provide satisfactory assurance that the local educational agency or intermediate educational unit will establish and maintain procedural safeguards in accordance with the provisions of sections 612(5)(B), 612(5)(C), and 615.

"(b)(1) A State educational agency shall approve any application submitted by a local educational agency or an intermediate educational unit under subsection (a) if the State educational agency determines that such application meets the requirements of subsection (a), except that no such application may be approved until the State plan submitted by such State educational agency under subsection (a) is approved by the Commissioner under section 613(c). A State educational agency shall disapprove any application submitted by a local educational agency or an intermediate educational unit under subsection (a) if the State educational agency determines that such application does not meet the requirements of subsection (a).

Application approval.

"(2)(A) Whenever a State educational agency, after reasonable notice and opportunity for a hearing, finds that a local educational agency or an intermediate educational unit, in the administration of an application approved by the State educational agency under paragraph (1), has failed to comply with any requirement set forth in such application, the State educational agency, after giving appropriate notice to the local educational agency or the intermediate educational unit, shall—

Notice, hearing.

"(i) make no further payments to such local educational agency or such intermediate educational unit under section 620 until the State educational agency is satisfied that there is no longer any failure to comply with the requirement involved; or

"(ii) take such finding into account in its review of any application made by such local educational agency or such intermediate educational unit under subsection (a).

"(B) The provisions of the last sentence of section 616(a) shall apply to any local educational agency or any intermediate educational unit receiving any notification from a State educational agency under this paragraph.

"(3) In carrying out its functions under paragraph (1), each State educational agency shall consider any decision made pursuant to a hearing held under section 615 which is adverse to the local educational agency or intermediate educational unit involved in such decision.

"(c)(1) A State educational agency may, for purposes of the consideration and approval of applications under this section, require local educational agencies to submit a consolidated application for payments if such State educational agency determines that any individual application submitted by any such local educational agency will be disapproved because such local educational agency is ineligible to receive payments because of the application of section 611(c)(4)(A)(i) or such local educational agency would be unable to establish and maintain programs of sufficient size and scope to effectively meet the educational needs of handicapped children.

"(2)(A) In any case in which a consolidated application of local educational agencies is approved by a State educational agency under paragraph (1), the payments which such local educational agencies may receive shall be equal to the sum of payments to which each such local educational agency would be entitled under section 611(d) if an individual application of any such local educational agency had been approved.

"(B) The State educational agency shall prescribe rules and regulations with respect to consolidated applications submitted under this subsection which are consistent with the provisions of paragraph (1) through paragraph (7) of section 612 and section 613(a) and which provide participating local educational agencies with joint responsibilities for implementing programs receiving payments under this part.

Rules and regulations.

"(C) In any case in which an intermediate educational unit is required pursuant to State law to carry out the provisions of this part, the joint responsibilities given to local educational agencies under subparagraph (B) shall not apply to the administration and disbursement of any payments received by such intermediate educational unit. Such responsibilities shall be carried out exclusively by such intermediate educational unit.

"(d) Whenever a State educational agency determines that a local educational agency—

"(1) is unable or unwilling to establish and maintain programs of free appropriate public education which meet the requirements established in subsection (a);

"(2) is unable or unwilling to be consolidated with other local educational agencies in order to establish and maintain such programs; or

"(3) has one or more handicapped children who can best be served by a regional or State center designed to meet the needs of such children;

the State educational agency shall use the payments which would have been available to such local educational agency to provide special education and related services directly to handicapped children residing in the area served by such local educational agency. The State educational agency may provide such education and services in such manner, and at such locations (including regional or State centers), as it considers appropriate, except that the manner in which such education and services are provided shall be consistent with the requirements of this part.

"(e) Whenever a State educational agency determines that a local educational agency is adequately providing a free appropriate public education to all handicapped children residing in the area served by such agency with State and local funds otherwise available to such agency, the State educational agency may reallocate funds (or such portion of those funds as may not be required to provide such education and services) made available to such agency, pursuant to section 611(d), to such other local educational agencies within the State as are not adequately providing special education and related services to all handicapped children residing in the areas served by such other local educational agencies.

Funds, reallocation.

"(f) Notwithstanding the provisions of subsection (a)(2)(B)(ii), any local educational agency which is required to carry out any program for the education of handicapped children pursuant to a State law shall be entitled to receive payments under section 611(d) for use in carrying out such program, except that such payments may not be used to reduce the level of expenditures for such program made by such local educational agency from State or local funds below the level of such expenditures for the fiscal year prior to the fiscal year for which such local educational agency seeks such payments.

"PROCEDURAL SAFEGUARDS

"Sec. 615. (a) Any State educational agency, any local educational agency, and any intermediate educational unit which receives assistance under this part shall establish and maintain procedures in accordance with subsection (b) through subsection (e) of this section to assure that handicapped children and their parents or guardians are guaranteed procedural safeguards with respect to the provision of free appropriate public education by such agencies and units.

20 USC 1415.

"(b)(1) The procedures required by this section shall include, but shall not be limited to—

"(A) an opportunity for the parents or guardian of a handicapped child to examine all relevant records with respect to the identification, evaluation, and educational placement of the child, and the provision of a free appropriate public education to such child, and to obtain an independent educational evaluation of the child;

"(B) procedures to protect the rights of the child whenever the parents or guardian of the child are not known, unavailable, or the child is a ward of the State, including the assignment of an individual (who shall not be an employee of the State educational agency, local educational agency, or intermediate educational unit involved in the education or care of the child) to act as a surrogate for the parents or guardian;

"(C) written prior notice to the parents or guardian of the child whenever such agency or unit—

"(i) proposes to initiate or change, or

"(ii) refuses to initiate or change,

the identification, evaluation, or educational placement of the child or the provision of a free appropriate public education to the child;

"(D) procedures designed to assure that the notice required by clause (C) fully inform the parents or guardian, in the parents' or guardian's native language, unless it clearly is not feasible to do so, of all procedures available pursuant to this section; and

"(E) an opportunity to present complaints with respect to any matter relating to the identification, evaluation, or educational placement of the child, or the provision of a free appropriate public education to such child.

"(2) Whenever a complaint has been received under paragraph (1) of this subsection, the parents or guardian shall have an opportunity for an impartial due process hearing which shall be conducted by the State educational agency or by the local educational agency or intermediate educational unit, as determined by State law or by the State educational agency. No hearing conducted pursuant to the requirements of this paragraph shall be conducted by an employee of such agency or unit involved in the education or care of the child.

Hearing.

"(c) If the hearing required in paragraph (2) of subsection (b) of this section is conducted by a local educational agency or an intermediate educational unit, any party aggrieved by the findings and decision rendered in such a hearing may appeal to the State educational agency which shall conduct an impartial review of such hearing. The officer conducting such review shall make an independent decision upon completion of such review.

"(d) Any party to any hearing conducted pursuant to subsections (b) and (c) shall be accorded (1) the right to be accompanied and advised by counsel and by individuals with special knowledge or training with respect to the problems of handicapped children, (2) the right to present evidence and confront, cross-examine, and compel the attendance of witnesses, (3) the right to a written or electronic verbatim record of such hearing, and (4) the right to written findings of fact and decisions (which findings and decisions shall also be transmitted to the advisory panel established pursuant to section 613(a)(12)).

"(e)(1) A decision made in a hearing conducted pursuant to paragraph (2) of subsection (b) shall be final, except that any party involved in such hearing may appeal such decision under the provisions of subsection (c) and paragraph (2) of this subsection. A decision made under subsection (c) shall be final, except that any party may bring an action under paragraph (2) of this subsection.

"(2) Any party aggrieved by the findings and decision made under subsection (b) who does not have the right to an appeal under subsection (c), and any party aggrieved by the findings and decision under subsection (c), shall have the right to bring a civil action with respect to the complaint presented pursuant to this section, which action may be brought in any State court of competent jurisdiction or in a district court of the United States without regard to the amount in controversy. In any action brought under this paragraph the court shall receive the records of the administrative proceedings, shall hear additional evidence at the request of a party, and, basing its decision on the preponderance of the evidence, shall grant such relief as the court determines is appropriate.

Civil action.

"(3) During the pendency of any proceedings conducted pursuant to this section, unless the State or local educational agency and the parents or guardian otherwise agree, the child shall remain in the then current educational placement of such child, or, if applying for initial admission to a public school, shall, with the consent of the parents or guardian, be placed in the public school program until all such proceedings have been completed.

"(4) The district courts of the United States shall have jurisdiction of actions brought under this subsection without regard to the amount in controversy.

District courts jurisdiction.

"WITHHOLDING AND JUDICIAL REVIEW

"SEC. 616. (a) Whenever the Commissioner, after reasonable notice and opportunity for hearing to the State educational agency involved (and to any local educational agency or intermediate educational unit affected by any failure described in clause (2)), finds—

Notice, hearing. 20 USC 1416.

"(1) that there has been a failure to comply substantially with any provision of section 612 or section 613, or

"(2) that in the administration of the State plan there is a failure to comply with any provision of this part or with any requirements set forth in the application of a local educational agency or intermediate educational unit approved by the State educational agency pursuant to the State plan,

the Commissioner (A) shall, after notifying the State educational agency, withhold any further payments to the State under this part, and (B) may, after notifying the State educational agency, withhold further payments to the State under the Federal programs specified in section 613(a)(2) within his jurisdiction, to the extent that funds under such programs are available for the provision of assistance for the education of handicapped children. If the Commissioner withholds further payments under clause (A) or clause (B) he may determine that such withholding will be limited to programs or projects under the State plan, or portions thereof, affected by the failure, or that the State educational agency shall not make further payments under this part to specified local educational agencies or intermediate educational units affected by the failure. Until the Commissioner is satisfied that there is no longer any failure to comply with the provisions of this part, as specified in clause (1) or clause (2), no further payments shall be made to the State under this part or under the Federal programs specified in section 613(a)(2) within his jurisdiction to the extent that funds under such programs are available for the provision of assistance for the education of handicapped children, or payments by the State educational agency under this part shall be limited to local educational agencies and intermediate educational units whose actions did not cause or were not involved in the failure, as the case may be. Any State educational agency, local educational agency, or intermediate educational unit in receipt of a notice pursuant to the first sentence of this subsection shall, by means of a public notice, take such measures as may be necessary to bring the pendency of an action pursuant to this subsection to the attention of the public within the jurisdiction of such agency or unit.

"(b)(1) If any State is dissatisfied with the Commissioner's final action with respect to its State plan submitted under section 613, such State may, within sixty days after notice of such action, file with the United States court of appeals for the circuit in which such State is located a petition for review of that action. A copy of the petition shall be forthwith transmitted by the clerk of the court to the Commissioner. The Commissioner thereupon shall file in the court the record of the proceedings on which he based his action, as provided in section 2112 of title 28, United States Code.   *[margin: Petition for review.]*

"(2) The findings of fact by the Commissioner, if supported by substantial evidence, shall be conclusive; but the court, for good cause shown, may remand the case to the Commissioner to take further evidence, and the Commissioner may thereupon make new or modified findings of fact and may modify his previous action, and shall file in the court the record of the further proceedings. Such new or modified findings of fact shall likewise be conclusive if supported by substantial evidence.

"(3) Upon the filing of such petition, the court shall have jurisdiction to affirm the action of the Commissioner or to set it aside, in whole or in part. The judgment of the court shall be subject to review by the Supreme Court of the United States upon certiorari or certification as provided in section 1254 of title 28, United States Code.

"ADMINISTRATION

"SEC. 617. (a)(1) In carrying out his duties under this part, the Commissioner shall—   *[margin: 20 USC 1417.]*

"(A) cooperate with, and furnish all technical assistance necessary, directly or by grant or contract, to the States in matters relating to the education of handicapped children and the execution of the provisions of this part;

"(B) provide such short-term training programs and institutes as are necessary;

"(C) disseminate information, and otherwise promote the education of all handicapped children within the States; and

"(D) assure that each State shall, within one year after the date of the enactment of the Education for All Handicapped Children Act of 1975, provide certification of the actual number of handicapped children receiving special education and related services in such State.

"(2) As soon as practicable after the date of the enactment of the Education for All Handicapped Children Act of 1975, the Commissioner shall, by regulation, prescribe   *[margin: Regulations.]*

a uniform financial report to be utilized by State educational agencies in submitting State plans under this part in order to assure equity among the States.

"(b) In carrying out the provisions of this part, the Commissioner (and the Secretary, in carrying out the provisions of subsection (c)) shall issue, not later than January 1, 1977, amend, and revoke such rules and regulations as may be necessary. No other less formal method of implementing such provisions is authorized.

"(c) The Secretary shall take appropriate action, in accordance with the provisions of section 438 of the General Education Provisions Act, to assure the protection of the confidentiality of any personally identifiable data, information, and records collected or maintained by the Commissioner and by State and local educational agencies pursuant to the provisions of this part.

20 USC 1232g.

"(d) The Commissioner is authorized to hire qualified personnel necessary to conduct data collection and evaluation activities required by subsections (b), (c) and (d) of section 618 and to carry out his duties under subsection (a)(1) of this subsection without regard to the provisions of title 5, United States Code, relating to appointments in the competitive service and without regard to chapter 51 and subchapter III of chapter 53 of such title relating to classification and general schedule pay rates except that no more than twenty such personnel shall be employed at any time.

5 USC 5101, 5331.

"EVALUATION

"SEC. 618. (a) The Commissioner shall measure and evaluate the impact of the program authorized under this part and the effectiveness of State efforts to assure the free appropriate public education of all handicapped children.

20 USC 1418.

"(b) The Commissioner shall conduct, directly or by grant or contract, such studies, investigations, and evaluations as are necessary to assure effective implementation of this part. In carrying out his responsibilities under this section, the Commissioner shall—

"(1) through the National Center for Education Statistics, provide to the appropriate committees of each House of the Congress and to the general public at least annually, and shall update at least annually, programmatic information concerning programs and projects assisted under this part and other Federal programs supporting the education of handicapped children, and such information from State and local educational agencies and other appropriate sources necessary for the implementation of this part, including—

"(A) the number of handicapped children in each State, within each disability, who require special education and related services;

"(B) the number of handicapped children in each State, within each disability, receiving a free appropriate public education and the number of handicapped children who need and are not receiving a free appropriate public education in each such State;

"(C) the number of handicapped children in each State, within each disability, who are participating in regular educational programs, consistent with the requirements of section 612(5)(B) and section 614(a)(1)(C)(iv), and the number of handicapped children who have been placed in separate classes or separate school facilities, or who have been otherwise removed from the regular education environment;

"(D) the number of handicapped children who are enrolled in public or private institutions in each State and who are receiving a free appropriate public education, and the number of handicapped children who are in such institutions and who are not receiving a free appropriate public education;

"(E) the amount of Federal, State, and local expenditures in each State specifically available for special education and related services; and

"(F) the number of personnel, by disability category, employed in the education of handicapped children, and the estimated number of additional personnel needed to adequately carry out the policy established by this Act; and

"(2) provide for the evaluation of programs and projects assisted under this part through—

"(A) the development of effective methods and procedures for evaluation;

"(B) the testing and validation of such evaluation methods and procedures; and

"(C) conducting actual evaluation studies designed to test the effectiveness of such programs and projects.

"(c) In developing and furnishing information under subclause (E) of clause (1) of subsection (b), the Commissioner may base such information upon a sampling of data available from State agencies, including the State educational agencies, and local educational agencies.

"(d)(1) Not later than one hundred twenty days after the close of each fiscal year, the Commissioner shall transmit to the appropriate committees of each House of the Congress a report on the progress being made toward the provision of free appropriate public education to all handicapped children, including a detailed description of all evaluation activities conducted under subsection (b). *Report, transmittal to congressional committees.*

"(2) The Commissioner shall include in each such report— *Contents.*

"(A) an analysis and evaluation of the effectiveness of procedures undertaken by each State educational agency, local educational agency, and intermediate educational unit to assure that handicapped children receive special education and related services in the least restrictive environment commensurate with their needs and to improve programs of instruction for handicapped children in day or residential facilities;

"(B) any recommendations for change in the provisions of this part, or any other Federal law providing support for the education of handicapped children; and

"(C) an evaluation of the effectiveness of the procedures undertaken by each such agency or unit to prevent erroneous classification of children as eligible to be counted under section 611, including actions undertaken by the Commissioner to carry out provisions of this Act relating to such erroneous classification.

In order to carry out such analyses and evaluations, the Commissioner shall conduct a statistically valid survey for assessing the effectiveness of individualized educational programs.

"(e) There are authorized to be appropriated for each fiscal year such sums as may be necessary to carry out the provisions of this section. *Appropriation authorization.*

"INCENTIVE GRANTS

"SEC. 619. (a) The Commissioner shall make a grant to any State which— 20 USC 1419.

"(1) has met the eligibility requirements of section 612;

"(2) has a State plan approved under section 613; and

"(3) provides special education and related services to handicapped children aged three to five, inclusive, who are counted for the purposes of section 611(a)(1)(A).

The maximum amount of the grant for each fiscal year which a State may receive under this section shall be $300 for each such child in that State.

"(b) Each State which—

"(1) has met the eligibility requirements of section 612,

"(2) has a State plan approved under section 613, and

"(3) desires to receive a grant under this section,

shall make an application to the Commissioner at such time, in such manner, and containing or accompanied by such information, as the Commissioner may reasonably require.

"(c) The Commissioner shall pay to each State having an application approved under subsection (b) of this section the amount to which the State is entitled under this section, which amount shall be used for the purpose of providing the services specified in clause (3) of subsection (a) of this section.

"(d) If the sums appropriated for any fiscal year for making payments to States under this section are not sufficient to pay in full the maximum amounts which all States may receive under this part for such fiscal year, the maximum amounts which all States may receive under this part for such fiscal year shall be ratably reduced. In case additional funds become available for making such payments for any fiscal year during which the preceding sentence is applicable, such reduced amounts shall be increased on the same basis as they were reduced.

"(e) In addition to the sums necessary to pay the entitlements under section 611, there are authorized to be appropriated for each fiscal year such sums as may be necessary to carry out the provisions of this section. *Appropriation authorization.*

"PAYMENTS

"Sec. 620. (a) The Commissioner shall make payments to each State in amounts which the State educational agency of such State is eligible to receive under this part. Any State educational agency receiving payments under this subsection shall distribute payments to the local educational agencies and intermediate educational units of such State in amounts which such agencies and units are eligible to receive under this part after the State educational agency has approved applications of such agencies or units for payments in accordance with section 614(b).   20 USC 1420.

"(b) Payments under this part may be made in advance or by way of reimbursement and in such installments as the Commissioner may determine necessary.".

(b)(1) The Commissioner of Education shall, no later than one year after the effective date of this subsection, prescribe—   Regulations.
                                                                                   20 USC 1411 note.

(A) regulations which establish specific criteria for determining whether a particular disorder or condition may be considered a specific learning disability for purposes of designating children with specific learning disabilities;

(B) regulations which establish and describe diagnostic procedures which shall be used in determining whether a particular child has a disorder or condition which places such child in the category of children with specific learning disabilities; and

(C) regulations which establish monitoring procedures which will be used to determine if State educational agencies, local educational agencies, and intermediate educational units are complying with the criteria established under clause (A) and clause (B).

(2) The Commissioner shall submit any proposed regulation written under paragraph (1) to the Committee on Education and Labor of the House of Representatives and the Committee on Labor and Public Welfare of the Senate, for review and comment by each such committee, at least fifteen days before such regulation is published in the Federal Register.   Proposed regulation, submittal to congressional committees. Publication in Federal Register.

(3) If the Commissioner determines, as a result of the promulgation of regulations under paragraph (1), that changes are necessary in the definition of the term "children with specific learning disabilities", as such term is defined by section 602(15) of the Act, he shall submit recommendations for legislation with respect to such changes to each House of the Congress.   20 USC 402.

(4) For purposes of this subsection: Definitions.

(A) The term "children with specific learning disabilities" means those children who have a disorder in one or more of the basic psychological processes involved in understanding or in using language, spoken or written, which disorder may manifest itself in imperfect ability to listen, think, speak, read, write, spell, or do mathematical calculations. Such disorders include such conditions as perceptual handicaps, brain injury, minimal brain dysfunction, dyslexia, and developmental aphasia. Such term does not include children who have learning problems which are primarily the result of visual, hearing, or motor handicaps, of mental retardation, of emotional disturbance, or environmental, cultural, or economic disadvantage.

(B) The term "Commissioner" means the Commissioner of Education.

(c) Effective on the date upon which final regulations prescribed by the Commissioner of Education under subsection (b) take effect, the amendment made by subsection (a) is amended, in subparagraph (A) of section 611(a)(5) (as such subparagraph would take effect on the effective date of subsection (a)), by adding "and" at the end of clause (i), by striking out clause (ii), and by redesignating clause (iii) as clause (ii).   20 USC 1411.

AMENDMENTS WITH RESPECT TO EMPLOYMENT OF HANDICAPPED INDIVIDUALS, REMOVAL OF ARCHITECTURAL BARRIERS, AND MEDIA CENTERS

Sec. 6. (a) Part A of the Act is amended by inserting after section 605 thereof the following new sections: 20 USC 1404.

"EMPLOYMENT OF HANDICAPPED INDIVIDUALS

"Sec. 606. The Secretary shall assure that each recipient of assistance under this Act shall make positive efforts to employ and advance in employment qualified handicapped individuals in programs assisted under this Act.   20 USC 1405.

"GRANTS FOR THE REMOVAL OF ARCHITECTURAL BARRIERS

"SEC. 607. (a) Upon application by any State or local educational agency or intermediate educational unit the Commissioner is authorized to make grants to pay part or all of the cost of altering existing builldings and equipment in the same manner and to the same extent as authorized by the Act approved August 12, 1968 (Public Law 90–480), relating to architectural barriers.   20 USC 1406.

"(b) For the purpose of carrying out the provisions of this section, there are authorized to be appropriated such sums as may be necessary."   Appropriation authorization.

(b) Section 653 of the Act (20 U.S.C. 1453) is amended to read as follows:

"CENTERS ON EDUCATIONAL MEDIA AND MATERIALS FOR THE HANDICAPPED

"SEC. 653. (a) The Secretary is authorized to enter into agreements with institutions of higher education, State and local educational agencies, or other appropriate nonprofit agencies, for the establishment and operation of centers on educational media and materials for the handicapped, which together will provide a comprehensive program of activities to facilitate the use of new educational technology in education programs for handicapped persons, including designing, developing, and adapting instructional materials, and such other activities consistent with the purposes of this part as the Secretary may prescribe in such agreements. Any such agreement shall—

"(1) provide that Federal funds paid to a center will be used solely for such purposes as are set forth in the agreement; and

"(2) authorize the center involved, subject to prior approval by the Secretary, to contract with public and private agencies and organizations for demonstration projects.

"(b) In considering proposals to enter into agreements under this section, the Secretary shall give preference to institutions and agencies—

"(1) which have demonstrated the capabilities necessary for the development and evaluation of educational media for the handicapped; and

"(2) which can serve the educational technology needs of the Model High School for the Deaf (established under Public Law 89–694).   80 Stat. 1027.

"(c) The Secretary shall make an annual report on activities carried out under this section which shall be transmitted to the Congress.".   Report to Congress.

CONGRESSIONAL DISAPPROVAL OF REGULATIONS

SEC. 7. (a)(1) Section 431(d)(1) of the General Education Provisions Act (20 U.S.C. 1232(d)(1)) is amended by inserting "final" immediately before "standard" each place it appears therein.

(2) The third sentence of section 431(d)(2) of such Act (20 U.S.C. 1232(d)(2)) is amended by striking out "proposed" and inserting in lieu thereof "final".

(3) The fourth and last sentences of section 431(d)(2) of such Act (20 U.S.C. 1232(d)(2)) each are amended by inserting "final" immediately before "standard".

(b) Section 431(d)(1) of the General Education Provisions Act (20 U.S.C. 1232(d)(1)) is amended by adding at the end thereof the following new sentence: "Failure of the Congress to adopt such a concurrent resolution with respect to any such final standard, rule, regulation, or requirement prescribed under any such Act, shall not represent, with respect to such final standard, rule, regulation, or requirement, an approval or finding of consistency with the Act from which it derives its authority for any purpose, nor shall such failure to adopt a concurrent resolution be construed as evidence of an approval or finding of consistency necessary to establish a prima facie case, or an inference or presumption, in any judicial proceeding.".

EFFECTIVE DATES

SEC. 8. (a) Notwithstanding any other provision of law, the amendments made by sections 2(a), 2(b), and 2(c) shall take effect on July 1, 1975.   20 USC 1411 note.

(b) The amendments made by sections 2(d), 2(e), 3, 6, and 7 shall take effect on the date of the enactment of this Act.

(c) The amendments made by sections 4 and 5(a) shall take effect on October 1, 1977, except that the provisions of clauses (A), (C), (D), and (E) of paragraph (2) of section 612 of the Act, as amended by this Act, section 617(a)(1)(D) of the Act, as amended by this Act, section 617(b) of the Act, as amended by this Act, and section 618(a) of the Act, as amended by this Act, shall take effect on the datel of the enactment of this Act.

(d) The provisions of section 5(b) shall take effect on the date of the enactment of this Act.

Approved November 29, 1975.

LEGISLATIVE HISTORY:
HOUSE REPORTS: No. 94–332 accompanying H.R. 7217 (Comm. on Education and Labor) and 94–664 (Comm. of Conference).
SENATE REPORTS: No. 94–168 (Comm. on Labor and Public Welfare) and No. 94–455 (Comm. of Conference).
CONGRESSIONAL RECORD, Vol. 121 (1975):
    June 18, considered and passed Senate.
    July 21, 29, considered and passed House, amended, in lieu of H.R. 7217.
    Nov. 18, House agreed to conference report.
    Nov. 19, Senate agreed to conference report.
WEEKLY COMPILATION OF PRESIDENTIAL DOCUMENTS, Vol. 11, No. 49:
    Dec. 2, Presidential statement.

NAME INDEX

Page numbers in *italics* indicate biographical entries.

Cantrell, R. P., *268–269*
Cantwell, D., 163, 1506
Cantwell, D. P., 508, 806
Caperaa, P., 1550
Capildeo, R., 1145
Caplan, F., 1216
Caplan, G., 186, 406, 427
Caplan, P., 1423
Caplan, P. J., 1428
Caplan, T., 1216
Capouillez, J. M., 462
Capps, C. F., 1635
Capute, A., 1473
Capute, A. J., 294, 295
Caputo, J., 1538
Caramazza, A., 964
Caramazzo, A., 771
Carbino, R., 674
Carbo, M., 943
Carbonari, C. M., 1581
Carey, G., 1312
Carey, J. T., 556
Carey, R. G., 1224
Carey, W. B., 341, 342, 1234, 1552
Carey, W. H., 1548, 1549, 1550
Carlberg, C., 409, 741
Carlson, B., 697
Carlson, C., 1392
Carlson, C. F., 479
Carlson, C. S., 1554
Carlson, F., 36
Carlson, G., 1506
Carlson, J. R., 1012
Carlson, L., 682, 1648
Carlson, S. A., 512
Carlton, P. L., 746
Carman, R. A., 1040
Carmel, S. J., 669
Carnine, D., 518, 519, 520, 995, 1267
Carnine, D. W., *272–273*, 519, 1358
Carnine, L., 781
Carpenter, B., 284
Carpenter, D. G., 1246
Carpenter, J., 503
Carpenter, L. J., 211, 212
Carpenter, M., 379
Carpenter, M. B., 1288
Carpenter, T. P., 23
Carpignano, J., 1134
Carr, C. J., 278
Carr, E., 1403, 1404
Carr, E. G., 1348, 1410
Carr, R. A., 93
Carr, T., 1533
Carri, L., 1039
Carrison, M. P., 979
Carroll, D. W., 1192
Carroll, J. B., 848
Carroll-Johnson, R. M., 270
Carrow, E., 273, 1559
Carrow-Woolfolk, E., 1125, 1559

Carson, G., 516
Carson, R. C., 448, 556
Carstens, A. A., 733
Carter, C., 65, 434, 749, 802, 1501, 1582
Carter, C. H., 426, 1127
Carter, C. O., 12, 395, 396
Carter, K. R., 1200, 1207, 1208
Carter, L., 380
Carterette, E. C., 1174
Cartwright, C. A., 274, 651, 690, 774, 781, 782, 794, 796, 825, 973, 1061, 1123, 1237, 1419, 1446, 1585, 1627
Cartwright, G. P., 44, 227, *273–274*, 322, 385, 651, 690, 774, 781, 782, 794, 796, 825, 973, 1061, 1123, 1419, 1446, 1585, 1627
Casale, J., 376
Case, R., 446
Case, R. S., 358
Casey, A., 1234, 1235
Casey, P. H., 554
Cassidy, J., 1524
Cassidy, S. B., 1228, 1229
Castaneda, A., 321
Casteel, J. D., 1615
Castellucci, V. F., 745
Casterline, D. C., 84, 986
Castle, T. C., 728, 729, 1163, 1164, 1222
Cataldo, M. F., 481
Cattell, J. K., *280*
Cattell, N. R., 1590
Cattell, R. B., 117, 435, 439, 646, 941, 1183, 1620
Catterson, J. H., 548
Cavalier, A. R., 1144
Cavalli-Sforza, L. L., 775
Cavanaugh, J. C., 363
Cavdar, A. O., 660
Cave, C., 1609
Cavenar, J. D., 1100
Cavenart, J. D., 361
Cavenaugh, P. J., 390
Caveness, W. F., 763
Cawley, J., 511, 995
Cawley, J. F., 127, 281, 511, 690, 994, 995, 996, 1336, 1444
Ceci, S. J., 167, 1358
Cegelka, P. T., 343, 425, 1039, 1048, 1350, 1351
Cegelka, W. G., 740
Celaya, C. Y., 1183
Center for Field Research and School Services, 965
Centers for Disease Control, 541, 543
Cerletti, U., 598, 599
Cermak, L. A., 293
Cermak, L. S., 1018

Cerreto, M. C., 774
Certo, N., 58, 374, 444, 447, 460, 702, 846, 1048, 1148, 1254, 1399, 1534, 1588
Cervantes, H. T., 614
Cervenka, R., 749
Chace, M., 1059, 1060
Chadwick, O., 619, 762, 763, 770
Chaffin, J. D., 1352
Chai, H., 71
Chaing, B., 1167
Chalfant, J., 434, 998, 1056, 1387, 1629
Chalfant, J. C., 285, 286, *297*, 660, 922, 926, 927, 928, 929, 930, 998, 1005, 1253, 1387, 1561
Chalkley, T., 1124
Chall, J., 965, 966, 1655
Chall, J. S., 244, *297–298*, 967
Chamberlain, H. D., 946
Chan, K. S., 1061
Chandler, H. N., 604, 1039, 1043
Chandler, M. J., 220, 563, 632, 633, 1207
Chao, D., 1271, 1272
Chapin, M., 151
Chaplin, S., 97
Chapman, A. H., 1605
Chapman, C. A., 279
Chard, R. L., 268, 953, 954
Charles, B., 914, 915
Charles, C., 98
Charles, C. M., 345, 346
Charlier, B., 464
Charlier, M., 906
Charney, D. S., 218
Chase, C., 698
Chase, J., 1010
Chase, J. A., 86
Chase, T., 803
Chasen, B., 1129
Chatelanat, G., 941
Chatman, S. P., 1562
Chaudhry, M. R., 97
Cheek, E. H., 1313
Cheek, M. C., 1313
Chelune, G. J., 239
Cherkes-Julkowski, M., 511, 995
Cherniss, C., 800
Chernoff, G. F., 663
Chernyhiv, 1470
Cherrington, C., 73, 1046, 1193
Chess, S., *302*, 605, 633, 1213, 1395, 1548, 1549, 1550
Chethik, M., 229, 1075
Chevalier, R. L., 1222
Chi, M. T. H., 17
Chien, L. T., 240
Children's Book Council, 1311
Children's Defense Fund, 321
Chilsom, J. J., Jr., 917

SUBJECT INDEX